COLLINS

FR

TRAVEL DICTIONARY

HarperCollins*Publishers*

first published in this edition 1996

©HarperCollins Publishers 1996

ISBN 0 00 471015-0

Typeset by Morton Word Processing Ltd, Scarborough
Printed and bound in Great Britain by
Caledonian International Book Manufacturing Ltd, Glasgow, G64

Contents

Note on trademarks

Words which we have reason to believe constitute trademarks have been designated as such. However, neither the presence nor the absence of such designation should be regarded as affecting the legal status of any trademark.

Introduction

We are delighted you have decided to buy the **Collins French Travel Dictionary** and hope you will benefit from using it whether you are travelling abroad for pleasure or on business.

This dictionary provides up-to-date coverage of all the French you will need, in a clear and user-friendly layout. The emphasis is on contemporary language, with numerous examples of idiomatic usage which will enable you not only to understand but also to communicate with confidence.

A special feature of the dictionary is the KEYWORD entries which highlight the most frequently-used words in both languages and treat them in depth. In addition, pronunciation is shown throughout in the International Phonetic Alphabet to help you with unfamiliar words.

We hope that you enjoy using the dictionary and that you find it an ideal travelling companion.

Using the Dictionary

The various typefaces, type sizes, symbols, abbreviations and brackets used throughout this dictionary all convey useful information. Take time to establish what they indicate and this will help you get the most out of your dictionary.

Finding the word you want

The information above the line at the top of each page helps you to locate, quickly and easily, the entry you want to consult. At the outside margin, the first and last entries on that page are shown, separated by an arrow. Information about which side of the dictionary you are using is shown at the inside margin.

above → acknowledge   ENGLISH-FRENCH   220

Headwords

The words you look up in a dictionary are called headwords and are printed in **bold** type. The phonetic spelling is given in square brackets immediately after the headword. An explanation of these symbols is given on pages x-xi. Information about the usage or form of certain headwords is given in brackets after the phonetic spelling. This usually appears in abbreviated form and in italics eg (*fam*), (COMM). Explanations of these are given on pages viii-ix.

Where appropriate, words related to headwords are grouped in the same entry in a slightly smaller type than the headword.

> **passion** [...] *nf* passion; **pas-sionant, e** *adj* fascinating; ...

> **explosion** [...] *n* explosion *f*; **explosive** [...] *adj* explosif (ive) ...

Common expressions in which the headword appears are shown in a smaller bold type.

> **autre** [...] *adj* **1** (*différent*) other, different; **je préférerais un ~ verre** I'd prefer another *ou* a different glass

Translation

Headword translations are given in ordinary type and, where more than one meaning or usage exists, these are separated by a semicolon. You will often find bracketed words in italics appearing before the translations. These are called "indicators" and they offer suggested contexts in which the headword might appear or provide synonyms for the headword to guide you to the most appropriate translation.

> **opposer** [...] *vt* (*personnes, armées, équipes*) to oppose; (*couleurs, termes, tons*) to contrast; ...

> **relation** [...] *n* (*person*) parent (e); (*link*) rapport *m*, lien *m*; ...

> **superposer** [...] *vi* (*faire chevaucher*) to superimpose; ...

> **retire** [...] *vi* (*give up work*) prendre sa retraite; ...

Key words

Special status is given to certain French and English words which are considered "key" words in each language. These words occur very frequently in French or English, or have several types of usage (eg **vouloir, plus; get, that**). A combination of lozenges and numbers helps you to distinguish different parts of speech and meanings.

Grammatical information

Parts of speech are given in abbreviated form in italics after the phonetic spellings of headwords (eg *vt, adv, conj*). A lozenge indicates a change in part of speech and different meanings are split into separate categories and numbered accordingly. Genders of French nouns are indicated as follows: *nm* for a masculine and *nf* for a feminine noun. Feminine and irregular plural forms of nouns and adjectives, along with any change in pronunciation, are also shown.

> **directeur, trice** [...] *nm/f* (*d'entreprise*) director; ....

> **cheval, aux** [...] *nm* horse; ...

Abbreviations

adjectif, locution adjective	*adj*	adjective, adjectival phrase
abréviation	*ab(b)r*	abbreviation
adverbe, locution adverbiale	*adv*	adverb, adverbial phrase
administration	*ADMIN*	administration
agriculture	*AGR*	agriculture
anatomie	*ANAT*	anatomy
architecture	*ARCHIT*	architecture
article défini	*art déf*	definite article
article indéfini	*art indéf*	indefinite article
l'automobile	*AUT(O)*	the motor car and motoring
auxiliaire	*aux*	auxiliary
aviation, voyages aériens	*AVIAT*	flying, air travel
biologie	*BIO(L)*	biology
botanique	*BOT*	botany
anglais de Grande-Bretagne	*BRIT*	British English
commerce, finance, banque	*COMM*	commerce, finance, banking
comparatif	*compar*	comparative
informatique	*COMPUT*	computing
chimie	*CHEM*	chemistry
conjonction	*conj*	conjunction
construction	*CONSTR*	building
nom utilisé comme adjectif, ne peut s'employer ni comme attribut, ni après le nom qualifié	*cpd*	compound element: noun used as an adjective and which cannot follow the noun it qualifies
cuisine, art culinaire	*CULIN*	cookery
article défini	*def art*	definite article
diminutif	*dimin*	diminutive
économie	*ECON*	economics
électricité, électronique	*ELEC*	electricity, electronics
exclamation, interjection	*excl*	exclamation, interjection
féminin	*f*	feminine
langue familière (! emploi vulgaire)	*fam (!)*	colloquial usage (! particularly offensive)
emploi figuré	*fig*	figurative use
(verbe anglais) dont la particule est inséparable du verbe	*fus*	(phrasal verb) where the particle cannot be separated from main verb
dans la plupart des sens; généralement	*gén, gen*	in most or all senses; generally
géographie, géologie	*GEO*	geography, geology
géométrie	*GEOM*	geometry
impersonnel	*impers*	impersonal
article indéfini	*indef art*	indefinite article
langue familière (! emploi vulgaire)	*inf(!)*	colloquial usage (! particularly offensive)
infinitif	*infin*	infinitive
informatique	*INFORM*	computing
invariable	*inv*	invariable

irrégulier	*irreg*	irregular
domaine juridique	*JUR*	law
grammaire, linguistique	*LING*	grammar, linguistics
masculin	*m*	masculine
mathématiques, algèbre	*MATH*	mathematics, calculus
médecine	*MÉD, MED*	medical term, medicine
masculin ou féminin, suivant le sexe	*m/f*	either masculine or feminine depending on sex
domaine militaire, armée	*MIL*	military matters
musique	*MUS*	music
nom	*n*	noun
navigation, nautisme	*NAVIG, NAUT*	sailing, navigation
adjectif ou nom numérique	*num*	numeral adjective or noun
	o.s.	oneself
péjoratif	*péj, pej*	derogatory, pejorative
photographie	*PHOT(O)*	photography
physiologie	*PHYSIOL*	physiology
pluriel	*pl*	plural
politique	*POL*	politics
participe passé	*pp*	past participle
préposition	*prép, prep*	preposition
pronom	*pron*	pronoun
psychologie, psychiatrie	*PSYCH*	psychology, psychiatry
temps du passé	*pt*	past tense
quelque chose	*qch*	
quelqu'un	*qn*	
religions, domaine ecclésiastique	*REL*	religions, church service
	sb	somebody
enseignement, système scolaire et universitaire	*SCOL*	schooling, schools and universities
singulier	*sg*	singular
	sth	something
subjonctif	*sub*	subjunctive
sujet (grammatical)	*su(b)j*	(grammatical) subject
superlatif	*superl*	superlative
techniques, technologie	*TECH*	technical term, technology
télécommunications	*TEL*	telecommunications
télévision	*TV*	television
typographie	*TYP(O)*	typography, printing
anglais des USA	*US*	American English
verbe	*vb*	verb
verbe ou groupe verbal à fonction intransitive	*vi*	verb or phrasal verb used intransitively
verbe ou groupe verbal à fonction transitive	*vt*	verb or phrasal verb used transitively
zoologie	*ZOOL*	zoology
marque déposée	®	registered trademark
indique une équivalence culturelle	≈	introduces a cultural equivalent

Phonetic Transcription

Consonnes		***Consonants***

NB. **p, b, t, d, k, g** sont suivis d'une aspiration en anglais.

NB. **p, b, t, d, k, g** are not aspirated in French.

*p*ou*p*ée	p	*p*u*pp*y
*b*om*b*e	b	*b*a*b*y
*t*en*t*e *th*ermal	t	*t*en*t*
*d*in*d*e	d	*d*a*dd*y
*c*o*q* *qu*i *k*épi	k	*c*ork *k*iss *ch*ord
*g*a*g* ba*gu*e	g	*g*ag *gu*ess
*s*ale *ce* na*ti*on	s	*s*o ri*c*e ki*ss*
*z*éro ro*s*e	z	cou*s*in bu*zz*
ta*ch*e *ch*at	ʃ	*sh*eep *s*ugar
gi*l*et *j*uge	ʒ	plea*s*ure bei*g*e
	tʃ	*ch*ur*ch*
	dʒ	*j*udge general
*f*er *ph*are	f	*f*arm ra*ff*le
*v*al*v*e	v	*v*ery re*v*
	θ	*th*in ma*th*s
	ð	*th*at o*th*er
*l*ent sa*ll*e	l	*l*ittle ba*ll*
*r*are *r*ent*r*er	ʀ	
	r	*r*at ra*r*e
*m*a*m*an fe*mm*e	m	*m*u*mm*y co*m*b
*n*on *nonn*e	n	*n*o ra*n*
a*gn*eau vi*gn*e	ɲ	
	ŋ	si*ng*i*ng* ba*nk*
*h*op!	h	*h*at re*h*eat
*y*eux pa*ill*e p*i*ed	j	*y*et
n*ou*er *ou*i	w	*w*all be*w*ail
*hu*ile l*u*i	ɥ	
	x	lo*ch*

Divers		***Miscellaneous***

pour l'anglais: précède la syllabe accentuée	'	in French wordlist and transcription: no liaison
pour l'anglais: le r final se prononce en liaison devant une voyelle	*	

x

Phonetic Transcription

Voyelles

NB. La mise en équivalence de certains sons n'indique qu'une ressemblance approximative.

Vowels

NB. The pairing of some vowel sounds only indicates approximate equivalence.

ici vie lyre	i i:	heel bead
	ɪ	hit pity
jouer été	e	set tent
lait jouet merci	ɛ	
plat amour	a æ	bat apple
bas pâte	ɑ ɑ:	after car calm
	ʌ	fun cousin
le premier	ə	over above
beurre peur	œ	
peu deux	ø ə:	urn fern work
or homme	ɔ	wash pot
mot eau gauche	o ɔ:	born cork
genou roue	u ʊ	full soot
	u:	boon lewd
rue urne	y	

Diphtongues

Diphthongs

	ɪə	beer tier
	ɛə	tear fair there
	eɪ	date plaice day
	aɪ	life buy cry
	aʊ	owl foul now
	əʊ	low no
	ɔɪ	boil boy oily
	ʊə	poor tour

Nasales

Nasal Vowels

matin plein	ɛ̃
brun	œ̃
sang an dans	ɑ̃
non pont	õ

FRANÇAIS - ANGLAIS
FRENCH - ENGLISH

A a

A *abr* = **autoroute**
a *vb voir* **avoir**

— *MOT CLÉ*

à [a] (*à + le* = **au**, *à + les* = **aux**) *prép* **1** (*endroit, situation*) at, in; **être ~ Paris/au Portugal** to be in Paris/Portugal; **être ~ la maison/~ l'école** to be at home/at school; **~ la campagne** in the country; **c'est ~ 10 km/~ 20 minutes (d'ici)** it's 10 km/20 minutes away
2 (*direction*) to; **aller ~ Paris/au Portugal** to go to Paris/Portugal; **aller ~ la maison/~ l'école** to go home/to school; **~ la campagne** to the country
3 (*temps*): **~ 3 heures/minuit** at 3 o'clock/midnight; **au printemps/mois de juin** in the spring/the month of June
4 (*attribution, appartenance*) to; **le livre est ~ Paul/~ lui/~ nous** this book is Paul's/his/ours; **donner qch ~ qn** to give sth to sb
5 (*moyen*) with; **se chauffer au gaz** to have gas heating; **~ bicyclette** on a *ou* by bicycle; **~ la main/machine** by hand/machine
6 (*provenance*) from; **boire ~ la bouteille** to drink from the bottle
7 (*caractérisation, manière*): **l'homme aux yeux bleus** the man with the blue eyes; **~ la russe** the Russian way
8 (*but, destination*): **tasse ~ café** coffee cup; **maison ~ vendre** house for sale
9 (*rapport, évaluation, distribution*): **100 km/unités ~ l'heure** 100 km/units per *ou* an hour; **payé ~ l'heure** paid by the hour; **cinq ~ six** five to six

---

abaisser [abese] *vt* to lower, bring down; (*manette*) to pull down; (*fig*) to debase; to humiliate; **s'~** *vi* to go down; (*fig*) to demean o.s.

abandon [abɑ̃dɔ̃] *nm* abandoning; giving up; withdrawal; **être à l'~** to be in a state of neglect
abandonner [abɑ̃dɔne] *vt* (*personne*) to abandon; (*projet, activité*) to abandon, give up; (*SPORT*) to retire *ou* withdraw from; (*céder*) to surrender; **s'~** *vi* to let o.s. go; **s'~ à** (*paresse, plaisirs*) to give o.s. up to
abasourdir [abazurdiʀ] *vt* to stun, stagger
abat-jour [abaʒuʀ] *nm inv* lampshade
abats [aba] *nmpl* (*de bœuf, porc*) offal *sg*; (*de volaille*) giblets
abattement [abatmɑ̃] *nm* (*déduction*) reduction; **~ fiscal** ≈ tax allowance
abattoir [abatwaʀ] *nm* slaughterhouse
abattre [abatʀ(ə)] *vt* (*arbre*) to cut down, fell; (*mur, maison*) to pull down; (*avion, personne*) to shoot down; (*animal*) to shoot, kill; (*fig*) to wear out, tire out; to demoralize; **s'~** *vi* to crash down; **s'~ sur** to beat down on; to rain down on
abbaye [abei] *nf* abbey
abbé [abe] *nm* priest; (*d'une abbaye*) abbot
abcès [apsɛ] *nm* abscess
abdiquer [abdike] *vi* to abdicate ♦ *vt* to renounce, give up
abeille [abɛj] *nf* bee
aberrant, e [abɛʀɑ̃, -ɑ̃t] *adj* absurd
abêtir [abetiʀ] *vt* to make morons of (*ou* moron of)
abîme [abim] *nm* abyss, gulf
abîmer [abime] *vt* to spoil, damage; **s'~** *vi* to get spoilt *ou* damaged
ablation [ablasjɔ̃] *nf* removal
abois [abwa] *nmpl*: **aux ~** at bay
abolir [abɔliʀ] *vt* to abolish
abondance [abɔ̃dɑ̃s] *nf* abundance; (*richesse*) affluence
abondant, e [abɔ̃dɑ̃, -ɑ̃t] *adj* plentiful, abundant, copious
abonder [abɔ̃de] *vi* to abound, be plentiful; **~ dans le sens de qn** to concur with sb

abonné, e [abɔne] nm/f subscriber; season ticket holder

abonnement [abɔnmɑ̃] nm subscription; (transports, concerts) season ticket

abonner [abɔne] vt: **s'~ à** to subscribe to, take out a subscription to

abord [abɔʀ] nm: **être d'un ~ facile** to be approachable; **~s** nmpl (environs) surroundings; **au premier ~** at first sight, initially; **d'~** first

abordable [abɔʀdabl(ə)] adj approachable; reasonably priced

aborder [abɔʀde] vi to land ♦ vt (sujet, difficulté) to tackle; (personne) to approach; (rivage etc) to reach; (NAVIG: attaquer) to board

aboutir [abutiʀ] vi (négociations etc) to succeed; **~ à/dans/sur** to end up at/in/on

aboyer [abwaje] vi to bark

abrégé [abʀeʒe] nm summary

abréger [abʀeʒe] vt to shorten

abreuver [abʀœve] vt (fig): **~ qn de** to shower ou swamp sb with; **s'~** vi to drink; **abreuvoir** nm watering place

abréviation [abʀevjasjɔ̃] nf abbreviation

abri [abʀi] nm shelter; **à l'~** under cover; **à l'~ de** sheltered from; (fig) safe from

abricot [abʀiko] nm apricot

abriter [abʀite] vt to shelter; (loger) to accommodate; **s'~** vt to shelter, take cover

abroger [abʀɔʒe] vt to repeal

abrupt, e [abʀypt] adj sheer, steep; (ton) abrupt

abrutir [abʀytiʀ] vt to daze; to exhaust; to stupefy

absence [apsɑ̃s] nf absence; (MÉD) blackout; mental blank

absent, e [apsɑ̃, -ɑ̃t] adj absent; (distrait: air) vacant, faraway ♦ nm/f absentee; **s'~er** vi to take time off work; (sortir) to leave, go out

absolu, e [apsɔly] adj absolute; (caractère) rigid, uncompromising; **absolument** adv absolutely

absorber [apsɔʀbe] vt to absorb; (gén MÉD: manger, boire) to take

absoudre [apsudʀ(ə)] vt to absolve

abstenir [apstəniʀ] : **s'~** vi (POL) to abstain; **s'~ de qch/de faire** to refrain from sth/from doing

abstraction [apstʀaksjɔ̃] nf abstraction; **faire ~ de** to set ou leave aside

abstrait, e [apstʀɛ, -ɛt] adj abstract

absurde [apsyʀd(ə)] adj absurd

abus [aby] nm abuse; **~ de confiance** breach of trust

abuser [abyze] vi to go too far, overstep the mark ♦ vt to deceive, mislead; **s'~** vi to be mistaken; **~ de** to misuse; (violer, duper) to take advantage of; **abusif, ive** adj exorbitant; excessive; improper

acabit [akabi] nm: **de cet ~** of that type

académie [akademi] nf academy; (ART: nu) nude; (SCOL: circonscription) ≈ regional education authority

acajou [akaʒu] nm mahogany

acariâtre [akaʀjɑtʀ(ə)] adj cantankerous

accablant, e [akablɑ̃, -ɑ̃t] adj (témoignage, preuve) overwhelming

accablement [akabləmɑ̃] nm despondency

accabler [akable] vt to overwhelm, overcome; (suj: témoignage) to condemn, damn; **~ qn d'injures** to heap ou shower abuse on sb

accalmie [akalmi] nf lull

accaparer [akapaʀe] vt to monopolize; (suj: travail etc) to take up (all) the time ou attention of

accéder [aksede]: **~ à** vt (lieu) to reach; (fig) to accede to, attain; (accorder: requête) to grant, accede to

accélérateur [akseleʀatœʀ] nm accelerator

accélération [akseleʀasjɔ̃] nf acceleration

accélérer [akseleʀe] vt to speed up ♦ vi to accelerate

accent [aksɑ̃] nm accent; (inflexions expressives) tone (of voice); (PHONÉTIQUE, fig) stress; **mettre l'~ sur** (fig) to stress; **~ aigu/grave** acute/grave accent

accentuer [aksɑ̃tɥe] vt (LING) to accent; (fig) to accentuate, emphasize; **s'~** vi to become more marked ou pronounced

acceptation [akseptasjɔ̃] nf acceptance

accepter [aksepte] vt to accept; (tolérer): **~ que qn fasse** to agree to sb doing; **~ de faire** to agree to do

accès [aksɛ] nm (à un lieu) access; (MÉD) attack; fit, bout; outbreak ♦ nmpl (routes etc) means of access, approaches; **d'~ facile** easily accessible; **~ de colère** fit of anger

accessible [aksesibl(ə)] adj accessible; (livre, sujet): **à qn** within the reach of sb; (sensible): **~ à** open to

accessoire [akseswaʀ] adj secondary; incidental ♦ nm accessory; (THÉÂTRE) prop

accident [aksidɑ̃] nm accident; **par ~** by chance; **~ de la route** road accident; **~ du travail** industrial injury ou accident; **~é, e** adj damaged; injured; (relief, terrain) uneven; hilly

acclamer [aklame] vt to cheer, acclaim

accolade [akɔlad] nf (amicale) embrace; (signe) brace

accommodant, e [akɔmɔdɑ̃, -ɑ̃t] adj accommodating; easy-going

accommoder [akɔmɔde] vt (CULIN) to prepare; (points de vue) to reconcile; **s'~ de** vt to put up with; to make do with

accompagnateur, trice [akɔ̃paɲatœʀ, -tʀis] nm/f (MUS) accompanist; (de voyage: guide) guide; (: d'enfants) accompanying adult; (de voyage organisé) courier

accompagner [akɔ̃paɲe] vt to accompany,

be *ou* go *ou* come with; (*MUS*) to accompany

accompli, e [akɔ̃pli] *adj* accomplished

accomplir [akɔ̃pliʀ] *vt* (*tâche, projet*) to carry out; (*souhait*) to fulfil; **s'~** *vi* to be fulfilled

accord [akɔʀ] *nm* agreement; (*entre des styles, tons etc*) harmony; (*MUS*) chord; **d'~!** OK!; **se mettre d'~** to come to an agreement; **être d'~** to agree

accordéon [akɔʀdeɔ̃] *nm* (*MUS*) accordion

accorder [akɔʀde] *vt* (*faveur, délai*) to grant; (*harmoniser*) to match; (*MUS*) to tune; **s'~** *vt* to get on together; to agree

accoster [akɔste] *vt* (*NAVIG*) to draw alongside ♦ *vi* to berth

accotement [akɔtmɑ̃] *nm* verge (*BRIT*), shoulder

accouchement [akuʃmɑ̃] *nm* delivery, (child)birth; labour

accoucher [akuʃe] *vi* to give birth, have a baby; (*être en travail*) to be in labour ♦ *vt* to deliver; **~ d'un garçon** to give birth to a boy

accouder [akude]: **s'~** *vi* to rest one's elbows on/against; **accoudoir** *nm* armrest

accoupler [akuple] *vt* to couple; (*pour la reproduction*) to mate; **s'~** *vt* to mate

accourir [akuʀiʀ] *vi* to rush *ou* run up

accoutrement [akutʀəmɑ̃] (*péj*) *nm* (*tenue*) outfit

accoutumance [akutymɑ̃s] *nf* (*gén*) adaptation; (*MÉD*) addiction

accoutumé, e [akutyme] *adj* (*habituel*) customary, usual

accoutumer [akutyme] *vt*: **s'~ à** to get accustomed *ou* used to

accréditer [akʀedite] *vt* (*nouvelle*) to substantiate

accroc [akʀo] *nm* (*déchirure*) tear; (*fig*) hitch, snag

accrochage [akʀɔʃaʒ] *nm* (*AUTO*) collision

accrocher [akʀɔʃe] *vt* (*suspendre*): **~ qch à** to hang sth (up) on; (*attacher: remorque*): **~ qch à** to hitch sth (up) to; (*heurter*) to catch; to catch on; to hit; (*déchirer*): **~ qch (à)** to catch sth (on); (*MIL*) to engage; (*fig*) to catch, attract; **s'~** (*se disputer*) to have a clash *ou* brush; **s'~ à** (*rester pris à*) to catch on; (*agripper, fig*) to hang on *ou* cling to

accroître [akʀwatʀ(ə)] *vt* to increase; **s'~** *vi* to increase

accroupir [akʀupiʀ]: **s'~** *vi* to squat, crouch (down)

accru, e [akʀy] *pp de* **accroître**

accueil [akœj] *nm* welcome; **comité d'~** reception committee

accueillir [akœjiʀ] *vt* to welcome; (*loger*) to accommodate

acculer [akyle] *vt*: **~ qn à** *ou* **contre** to drive sb back against

accumuler [akymyle] *vt* to accumulate, amass; **s'~** *vi* to accumulate; to pile up

accusation [akyzɑsjɔ̃] *nf* (*gén*) accusation; (*JUR*) charge; (*partie*) **l'~** the prosecution; **mettre en ~** to indict

accusé, e [akyze] *nm/f* accused; defendant; **~ de réception** acknowledgement of receipt

accuser [akyze] *vt* to accuse; (*fig*) to emphasize, bring out; to show; **~ qn de** to accuse sb of; (*JUR*) to charge sb with; **~ qch de** (*rendre responsable*) to blame sth for; **~ réception de** to acknowledge receipt of

acerbe [asɛʀb(ə)] *adj* caustic, acid

acéré, e [aseʀe] *adj* sharp

achalandé, e [aʃalɑ̃de] *adj*: **bien ~** well-stocked; well-patronized

acharné, e [aʃaʀne] *adj* (*lutte, adversaire*) fierce, bitter; (*travail*) relentless, unremitting

acharner [aʃaʀne]: **s'~** *vi* to go at fiercely; **s'~ contre** to set o.s. against; to dog; **s'~ à faire** to try doggedly to do; to persist in doing

achat [aʃa] *nm* buying *no pl*; purchase; **faire des ~s** to do some shopping

acheminer [aʃmine] *vt* (*courrier*) to forward, dispatch; (*troupes*) to convey, transport; (*train*) to route; **s'~ vers** to head for

acheter [aʃte] *vt* to buy, purchase; (*soudoyer*) to buy; **~ qch à** (*marchand*) to buy *ou* purchase sth from; (*ami etc: offrir*) to buy sth for; **acheteur, euse** *nm/f* buyer; shopper; (*COMM*) buyer

achever [aʃve] *vt* to complete, finish; (*blessé*) to finish off; **s'~** *vi* to end

acide [asid] *adj* sour, sharp; (*CHIMIE*) acid(ic) ♦ *nm* acid

acier [asje] *nm* steel; **aciérie** *nf* steelworks *sg*

acné [akne] *nf* acne

acolyte [akɔlit] (*péj*) *nm* associate

acompte [akɔ̃t] *nm* deposit; (*versement régulier*) instalment; (*sur somme due*) payment on account

à-côté [akote] *nm* side-issue; (*argent*) extra

à-coup [aku] *nm* (*du moteur*) (hic)cough; (*fig*) jolt; **par ~s** by fits and starts

acoustique [akustik] *nf* (*d'une salle*) acoustics *pl*

acquéreur [akeʀœʀ] *nm* buyer, purchaser

acquérir [akeʀiʀ] *vt* to acquire

acquis, e [aki, -iz] *pp de* **acquérir** ♦ *nm* (accumulated) experience; **être ~ à** (*plan, idée*) to fully agree with; **son aide nous est ~e** we can count on her help

acquit [aki] *vb voir* **acquérir** ♦ *nm* (*quittance*) receipt; **par ~ de conscience** to set one's mind at rest

acquitter [akite] *vt* (*JUR*) to acquit; (*facture*) to pay, settle; **s'~ de** *vt* to discharge, fulfil

âcre [akʀ(ə)] *adj* acrid, pungent

acrobate [akʀɔbat] *nm/f* acrobat

acte [akt(ə)] *nm* act, action; (*THÉÂTRE*) act; **~s** *nmpl* (*compte-rendu*) proceedings; **prendre ~ de** to note, take note of; **faire ~ de candidature** to apply; **faire ~ de présence** to put in an appearance; **~ de naissance** birth certificate

acteur [aktœʀ] *nm* actor

actif, ive [aktif, -iv] *adj* active ♦ *nm* (*COMM*) assets *pl*; (*fig*): **avoir à son ~** to have to one's credit; **population active** working population

action [aksjɔ̃] *nf* (*gén*) action; (*COMM*) share; **une bonne ~** a good deed; **~naire** *nm/f* shareholder; **~ner** *vt* to work; to activate; to operate

activer [aktive] *vt* to speed up; **s'~** *vi* to bustle about; to hurry up

activité [aktivite] *nf* activity

actrice [aktʀis] *nf* actress

actualiser [aktɥalize] *vt* to actualize; to bring up to date

actualité [aktɥalite] *nf* (*d'un problème*) topicality; (*événements*): **l'~** current events; **les ~s** *nfpl* (*CINÉMA, TV*) the news

actuel, le [aktɥɛl] *adj* (*présent*) present; (*d'actualité*) topical; **actuellement** *adv* at present; at the present time

acuité [akɥite] *nf* acuteness

adaptateur [adaptatœʀ] *nm* (*ÉLEC*) adapter

adapter [adapte] *vt* to adapt; **s'~ (à)** (*suj: personne*) to adapt (to); **~ qch à** (*approprier*) to adapt sth to (fit); **~ qch sur/ dans/à** (*fixer*) to fit sth on/into/to

additif [aditif] *nm* additive

addition [adisjɔ̃] *nf* addition; (*au café*) bill; **~ner** [adisjɔne] *vt* to add (up)

adepte [adɛpt(ə)] *nm/f* follower

adéquat, e [adekwa, -at] *adj* appropriate, suitable

adhérent, e [adeʀɑ̃, -ɑ̃t] *nm/f* (*de club*) member

adhérer [adeʀe]: **~ à** *vi* (*coller*) to adhere *ou* stick to; (*se rallier à*) to join; to support; **adhésif, ive** *adj* adhesive, sticky ♦ *nm* adhesive; **adhésion** *nf* joining; membership; support

adieu, x [adjø] *excl* goodbye ♦ *nm* farewell; **dire ~ à qn** to say goodbye *ou* farewell to sb

adjectif [adʒɛktif] *nm* adjective

adjoindre [adʒwɛ̃dʀ(ə)] *vt*: **~ qch à** to attach sth to; to add sth to; **s'~** *vt* (*collaborateur etc*) to take on, appoint; **adjoint, e** *nm/f* assistant; **adjoint au maire** deputy mayor; **directeur adjoint** assistant manager

adjudant [adʒydɑ̃] *nm* (*MIL*) warrant officer

adjudication [adʒydikɑsjɔ̃] *nf* sale by auction; (*pour travaux*) invitation to tender (*BRIT*) *ou* bid (*US*)

adjuger [adʒyʒe] *vt* (*prix, récompense*) to award; (*lors d'une vente*) to auction (off); **s'~** *vt* to take for o.s.

adjurer [adʒyʀe] *vt*: **~ qn de faire** to implore *ou* beg sb to do

admettre [admɛtʀ(ə)] *vt* (*laisser entrer*) to admit; (*candidat: SCOL*) to pass; (*tolérer*) to allow, accept; (*reconnaître*) to admit, acknowledge

administrateur, trice [administʀatœʀ, -tʀis] *nm/f* (*COMM*) director; (*ADMIN*) administrator; **~ judiciaire** receiver

administration [administʀɑsjɔ̃] *nf* administration; **l'A~** ≈ the Civil Service

administrer [administʀe] *vt* (*firme*) to manage, run; (*biens, remède, sacrement etc*) to administer

admirable [admiʀabl(ə)] *adj* admirable, wonderful

admirateur, trice [admiʀatœʀ, -tʀis] *nm/f* admirer

admiration [admiʀɑsjɔ̃] *nf* admiration

admirer [admiʀe] *vt* to admire

admis, e *pp de* **admettre**

admissible [admisibl(ə)] *adj* (*candidat*) eligible; (*comportement*) admissible, acceptable

admission [admisjɔ̃] *nf* admission; acknowledgement; **demande d'~** application for membership

adolescence [adɔlesɑ̃s] *nf* adolescence

adolescent, e [adɔlesɑ̃, -ɑ̃t] *nm/f* adolescent, teenager

adonner [adɔne]: **s'~ à** *vt* (*sport*) to devote o.s. to; (*boisson*) to give o.s. over to

adopter [adɔpte] *vt* to adopt; (*projet de loi etc*) to pass; **adoptif, ive** *adj* (*parents*) adoptive; (*fils, patrie*) adopted

adorer [adɔʀe] *vt* to adore; (*REL*) to worship

adosser [adose] *vt*: **~ qch à** *ou* **contre** to stand sth against; **~ à** *ou* **contre** to lean with one's back against

adoucir [adusiʀ] *vt* (*goût, température*) to make milder; (*avec du sucre*) to sweeten; (*peau, voix*) to soften; (*caractère*) to mellow

adresse [adʀɛs] *nf* (*voir adroit*) skill, dexterity; (*domicile*) address; **à l'~ de** (*pour*) for the benefit of

adresser [adʀese] *vt* (*lettre: expédier*) to send; (: *écrire l'adresse sur*) to address; (*injure, compliments*) to address; **s'~ à** (*parler à*) to speak to, address; (*s'informer auprès de*) to go and see; (: *bureau*) to enquire at; (*suj: livre, conseil*) to be aimed at; **~ la parole à** to speak to, address

adroit, e [adʀwa, -wat] *adj* skilful, skilled

adulte [adylt(ə)] *nm/f* adult, grown-up ♦ *adj* (*chien, arbre*) fully-grown, mature; (*attitude*) adult, grown-up

adultère [adyltɛʀ] *nm* (*acte*) adultery

advenir [advəniʀ] *vi* to happen

adverbe [advɛʀb(ə)] *nm* adverb

adversaire [advɛʀsɛʀ] nm/f (SPORT, gén) opponent, adversary; (MIL) adversary, enemy

adverse [advɛʀs(ə)] adj opposing

aération [aeʀɑsjɔ̃] nf airing; ventilation

aérer [aeʀe] vt to air; (fig) to lighten

aérien, ne [aeʀjɛ̃, -jɛn] adj (AVIAT) air cpd, aerial; (câble, métro) overhead; (fig) light

aéro... [aeʀɔ] préfixe: ~**bic** nm aerobics sg; ~**gare** nf airport (buildings); (en ville) air terminal; ~**glisseur** nm hovercraft; ~**naval, e** adj air and sea cpd; ~**phagie** [aeʀɔfaʒi] nf (MÉD) wind, aerophagia (TECH); ~**port** nm airport; ~**porté, e** adj airborne, airlifted; ~**sol** nm aerosol

affable [afabl(ə)] adj affable

affaiblir [afeblіʀ] vt to weaken; **s'~** vi to weaken

affaire [afɛʀ] nf (problème, question) matter; (criminelle, judiciaire) case; (scandaleuse etc) affair; (entreprise) business; (marché, transaction) deal; business no pl; (occasion intéressante) bargain; ~**s** nfpl (intérêts publics et privés) affairs; (activité commerciale) business sg; (effets personnels) things, belongings; **ce sont mes ~s** (cela me concerne) that's my business; **ceci fera l'~** this will do (nicely); **avoir ~ à** to be faced with; to be dealing with; **les A~s étrangères** Foreign Affairs; **affairer: s'affairer** vi to busy o.s., bustle about

affaisser [afese]: **s'~** vi (terrain, immeuble) to subside, sink; (personne) to collapse

affaler [afale]: **s'~** vi: **s'~ dans/sur** to collapse ou slump into/onto

affamé, e [afame] adj starving

affecter [afɛkte] vt to affect; (telle ou telle forme etc) to take on; ~ **qch à** to allocate ou allot sth to; ~ **qn à** to appoint sb to; (diplomate) to post sb to

affectif, ive [afɛktif, -iv] adj emotional

affection [afɛksjɔ̃] nf affection; (mal) ailment; ~**ner** vt to be fond of

affectueux, euse [afɛktɥø, -øz] adj affectionate

afférent, e [afeʀɑ̃, -ɑ̃t] adj: ~ **à** pertaining ou relating to

affermir [afɛʀmiʀ] vt to consolidate, strengthen

affichage [afiʃaʒ] nm billposting; (électronique) display

affiche [afiʃ] nf poster; (officielle) notice; (THÉÂTRE) bill; **tenir l'~** to run

afficher [afiʃe] vt (affiche) to put up; (réunion) to put up a notice about; (électroniquement) to display; (fig) to exhibit, display

affilée [afile]: **d'~** adv at a stretch

affiler [afile] vt to sharpen

affilier [afilje]: **s'~ à** vt (club, société) to join

affiner [afine] vt to refine

affirmatif, ive [afiʀmatif, -iv] adj affirmative

affirmation [afiʀmɑsjɔ̃] nf assertion

affirmer [afiʀme] vt (prétendre) to maintain, assert; (autorité etc) to assert

affligé, e [afliʒe] adj distressed, grieved; ~ **de** (maladie, tare) afflicted with

affliger [afliʒe] vt (peiner) to distress, grieve

affluence [aflyɑ̃s] nf crowds pl; **heures d'~** rush hours; **jours d'~** busiest days

affluent [aflyɑ̃] nm tributary

affluer [aflye] vi (secours, biens) to flood in, pour in; (sang) to rush, flow

affolement [afɔlmɑ̃] nm panic

affoler [afɔle] vt to throw into a panic; **s'~** vi to panic

affranchir [afʀɑ̃ʃiʀ] vt to put a stamp ou stamps on; (à la machine) to frank (BRIT), meter (US); (fig) to free, liberate; **affranchissement** nm postage

affréter [afʀete] vt to charter

affreux, euse [afʀø, -øz] adj dreadful, awful

affront [afʀɔ̃] nm affront

affrontement [afʀɔ̃tmɑ̃] nm clash, confrontation

affronter [afʀɔ̃te] vt to confront, face

affubler [afyble] (péj) vt: ~ **qn de** to rig ou deck sb out in; (surnom) to attach to sb

affût [afy] nm: **à l'~ (de)** (gibier) lying in wait (for); (fig) on the look-out (for)

affûter [afyte] vt to sharpen, grind

afin [afɛ̃]: ~ **que** conj so that, in order that; ~ **de faire** in order to do, so as to do

africain, e [afʀikɛ̃, -ɛn] adj, nm/f African

Afrique [afʀik] nf: **l'~** Africa; **l'~ du Sud** South Africa

agacer [agase] vt to pester, tease; (involontairement) to irritate

âge [ɑʒ] nm age; **quel ~ as-tu?** how old are you?; **prendre de l'~** to be getting on (in years); **l'~ ingrat** the awkward age; **l'~ mûr** maturity; **âgé, e** adj old, elderly; **âgé de 10 ans** 10 years old

agence [aʒɑ̃s] nf agency, office; (succursale) branch; ~ **de voyages** travel agency; ~ **immobilière** estate (BRIT) ou real estate (US) agent's (office); ~ **matrimoniale** marriage bureau

agencer [aʒɑ̃se] vt to put together; to arrange, lay out

agenda [aʒɛ̃da] nm diary

agenouiller [aʒnuje]: **s'~** vi to kneel (down)

agent [aʒɑ̃] nm (aussi: ~ **de police**) policeman; (ADMIN) official, officer; (fig: élément, facteur) agent; ~ **d'assurances** insurance broker; ~ **de change** stockbroker

agglomération [aglɔmeʀɑsjɔ̃] nf town; built-up area; **l'~ parisienne** the urban area of Paris

aggloméré [aglɔmeʀe] nm (bois) chipboard; (pierre) conglomerate

agglomérer [aglɔmeʀe] *vt* to pile up; (*TECH*: *bois, pierre*) to compress

aggraver [agʀave] *vt* to worsen, aggravate; (*JUR*: *peine*) to increase; **s'~** *vi* to worsen

agile [aʒil] *adj* agile, nimble

agir [aʒiʀ] *vi* to act; **il s'agit de** it's a matter *ou* question of; it is about; (*il importe que*): **il s'agit de faire** we (*ou* you *etc*) must do

agitation [aʒitɑsjɔ̃] *nf* (hustle and) bustle; agitation, excitement; (*politique*) unrest, agitation

agité, e [aʒite] *adj* fidgety, restless; agitated, perturbed; (*mer*) rough

agiter [aʒite] *vt* (*bouteille, chiffon*) to shake; (*bras, mains*) to wave; (*préoccuper, exciter*) to perturb

agneau, x [aɲo] *nm* lamb

agonie [agɔni] *nf* mortal agony, death pangs *pl*; (*fig*) death throes *pl*

agrafe [agʀaf] *nf* (*de vêtement*) hook, fastener; (*de bureau*) staple; **agrafer** *vt* to fasten; to staple; **agrafeuse** *nf* stapler

agraire [agʀɛʀ] *adj* land *cpd*

agrandir [agʀɑ̃diʀ] *vt* to enlarge; (*magasin, domaine*) to extend, enlarge; **s'~** *vi* to be extended; to be enlarged; **agrandissement** *nm* (*PHOTO*) enlargement

agréable [agʀeabl(ə)] *adj* pleasant, nice

agréé, e [agʀee] *adj*: **concessionnaire ~** registered dealer

agréer [agʀee] *vt* (*requête*) to accept; **~ à** to please, suit; **veuillez ~ ...** (*formule épistolaire*) yours faithfully

agrégation [agʀegɑsjɔ̃] *nf* highest teaching diploma in France; **agrégé, e** *nm/f* holder of the *agrégation*

agrément [agʀemɑ̃] *nm* (*accord*) consent, approval; (*attraits*) charm, attractiveness; (*plaisir*) pleasure

agrémenter [agʀemɑ̃te] *vt* to embellish, adorn

agresser [agʀese] *vt* to attack

agresseur [agʀesœʀ] *nm* aggressor, attacker; (*POL, MIL*) aggressor

agressif, ive [agʀesif, -iv] *adj* aggressive

agricole [agʀikɔl] *adj* agricultural

agriculteur [agʀikyltœʀ] *nm* farmer

agriculture [agʀikyltyʀ] *nf* agriculture; farming

agripper [agʀipe] *vt* to grab, clutch; (*pour arracher*) to snatch, grab; **s'~ à** to cling (on) to, clutch, grip

agrumes [agʀym] *nmpl* citrus fruit(s)

aguerrir [ageʀiʀ] *vt* to harden

aguets [agɛ] *nmpl*: **être aux ~** to be on the look out

aguicher [agiʃe] *vt* to entice

ahuri, e [ayʀi] *adj* (*stupéfait*) flabbergasted; (*idiot*) dim-witted

ai *vb voir* **avoir**

aide [ɛd] *nm/f* assistant; carer ♦ *nf* assistance, help; (*secours financier*) aid; **à l'~ de** (*avec*) with the help *ou* aid of; **appeler (qn) à l'~** to call for help (from sb); **~ judiciaire** *nf* legal aid; **~ sociale** *nf* (*assistance*) state aid; **~-mémoire** *nm inv* memoranda pages *pl*; (*key facts*) handbook; **~-soignant, e** *nm/f* auxiliary nurse

aider [ede] *vt* to help; **s'~ de** (*se servir de*) to use, make use of; **~ à qch** (*faciliter*) to help (towards) sth

aie *etc vb voir* **avoir**

aïe [aj] *excl* ouch

aïeul, e [ajœl] *nm/f* grandparent, grandfather(mother); forebear

aïeux [ajø] *nmpl* grandparents; forebears, forefathers

aigle [ɛgl(ə)] *nm* eagle

aigre [ɛgʀ(ə)] *adj* sour, sharp; (*fig*) sharp, cutting; **aigreur** *nf* sourness; sharpness; **aigreurs d'estomac** heartburn *sg*; **aigrir** *vt* (*personne*) to embitter; (*caractère*) to sour

aigu, ë [egy] *adj* (*objet, arête, douleur, intelligence*) sharp; (*son, voix*) high-pitched, shrill; (*note*) high (-pitched)

aiguille [eguij] *nf* needle; (*de montre*) hand; **~ à tricoter** knitting needle

aiguiller [eguije] *vt* (*orienter*) to direct

aiguilleur du ciel [eguijœʀ] *nm* air-traffic controller

aiguillon [eguijɔ̃] *nm* (*d'abeille*) sting; **~ner** *vt* to spur *ou* goad on

aiguiser [egize] *vt* to sharpen; (*fig*) to stimulate; to excite

ail [aj] *nm* garlic

aile [ɛl] *nf* wing; **aileron** *nm* (*de requin*) fin; **ailier** *nm* winger

aille *etc vb voir* **aller**

ailleurs [ajœʀ] *adv* elsewhere, somewhere else; **partout/nulle part ~** everywhere/nowhere else; **d'~** (*du reste*) moreover, besides; **par ~** (*d'autre part*) moreover, furthermore

aimable [ɛmabl(ə)] *adj* kind, nice

aimant [ɛmɑ̃] *nm* magnet

aimer [eme] *vt* to love; (*d'amitié, affection, par goût*) to like; (*souhait*): **j'~ais ...** I would like ...; **bien ~ qn/qch** to like sb/sth; **j'aime mieux ou autant vous dire que** I may as well tell you that; **j'~ais autant y aller maintenant** I'd rather go now; **j'~ais mieux faire** I'd much rather do

aine [ɛn] *nf* groin

aîné, e [ene] *adj* elder, older; (*le plus âgé*) eldest, oldest ♦ *nm/f* oldest child *ou* one, oldest boy *ou* son/girl *ou* daughter; **aînesse** *nf*: **droit d'aînesse** birthright

ainsi [ɛ̃si] *adv* (*de cette façon*) like this, in this way, thus; (*ce faisant*) thus ♦ *conj* thus, so; **~ que** (*comme*) (just) as; (*et aussi*) as well as; **pour ~ dire** so to speak; **et ~ de suite** and so on

air [ɛʀ] *nm* air; (*mélodie*) tune; (*expression*) look, air; **prendre l'~** to get some (fresh) air; (*avion*) to take off; **avoir l'~** (*sembler*) to look, appear; **avoir l'~ de** to look like; **avoir l'~ de faire** to look as though one is doing, appear to be doing

aire [ɛʀ] *nf* (*zone, fig, MATH*) area

aisance [ɛzɑ̃s] *nf* ease; (*richesse*) affluence

aise [ɛz] *nf* comfort ♦ *adj*: **être bien ~ que** to be delighted that; **être à l'~ ou à son ~** to be comfortable; (*pas embarrassé*) to be at ease; (*financièrement*) to be comfortably off; **se mettre à l'~** to make o.s. comfortable; **être mal à l'~ ou à son ~** to be uncomfortable; to be ill at ease; **en faire à son ~** to do as one likes; **aisé, e** *adj* easy; (*assez riche*) well-to-do, well-off

aisselle [ɛsɛl] *nf* armpit

ait *vb voir* **avoir**

ajonc [aʒɔ̃] *nm* gorse *no pl*

ajourner [aʒuʀne] *vt* (*réunion*) to adjourn; (*décision*) to defer, postpone

ajouter [aʒute] *vt* to add; **~ foi à** to lend *ou* give credence to

ajusté, e [aʒyste] *adj*: **bien ~** (*robe etc*) close-fitting

ajuster [aʒyste] *vt* (*régler*) to adjust; (*vêtement*) to alter; (*coup de fusil*) to aim; (*cible*) to aim at; (*TECH, gén: adapter*): **~ qch à** to fit sth to

alarme [alaʀm(ə)] *nf* alarm; **donner l'~** to give *ou* raise the alarm; **alarmer** *vt* to alarm; **s'~r** *vi* to become alarmed

album [albɔm] *nm* album

albumine [albymin] *nf* albumin; **avoir** *ou* **faire de l'~** to suffer from albuminuria

alcool [alkɔl] *nm*: **l'~** alcohol; **un ~** a spirit, a brandy; **~ à brûler** methylated spirits (*BRIT*), wood alcohol (*US*); **~ à 90°** surgical spirit; **~ique** *adj, nm/f* alcoholic; **~isé, e** *adj* alcoholic; **~isme** *nm* alcoholism

alco(o)test (®) [alkɔtɛst] *nm* Breathalyser (®); (*test*) breath-test

aléas [alea] *nmpl* hazards; **aléatoire** *adj* uncertain; (*INFORM*) random

alentour [alɑ̃tuʀ] *adv* around (about); **~s** *nmpl* (*environs*) surroundings; **aux ~s de** in the vicinity *ou* neighbourhood of, around about; (*temps*) around about

alerte [alɛʀt(ə)] *adj* agile, nimble; brisk, lively ♦ *nf* alert; warning; **alerter** *vt* to alert

algèbre [alʒɛbʀ(ə)] *nf* algebra

Alger [alʒe] *n* Algiers

Algérie [alʒeʀi] *nf*: **l'~** Algeria; **algérien, ne** *adj, nm/f* Algerian

algue [alg(ə)] *nf* (*gén*) seaweed *no pl*; (*BOT*) alga

alibi [alibi] *nm* alibi

aliéné, e [aljene] *nm/f* insane person, lunatic (*péj*)

aligner [aliɲe] *vt* to align, line up; (*idées, chiffres*) to string together; (*adapter*): **~ qch sur** to bring sth into alignment with; **s'~** (*soldats etc*) to line up; **s'~ sur** (*POL*) to

align o.s. on

aliment [alimɑ̃] *nm* food

alimentation [alimɑ̃tasjɔ̃] *nf* feeding; supplying; (*commerce*) food trade; (*produits*) groceries *pl*; (*régime*) diet; (*INFORM*) feed

alimenter [alimɑ̃te] *vt* to feed; (*TECH*): **~ (en)** to supply (with); to feed (with); (*fig*) to sustain, keep going

alinéa [alinea] *nm* paragraph

aliter [alite] *vt*: **s'~** *vi* to take to one's bed

allaiter [alete] *vt* to (breast-)feed, nurse; (*suj: animal*) to suckle

allant [alɑ̃] *nm* drive, go

allécher [aleʃe] *vt*: **~ qn** to make sb's mouth water; to tempt *ou* entice sb

allée [ale] *nf* (*de jardin*) path; (*en ville*) avenue, drive; **~s et venues** comings and goings

alléger [aleʒe] *vt* (*voiture*) to make lighter; (*chargement*) to lighten; (*souffrance*) to alleviate, soothe

allègre [alɛgʀ(ə)] *adj* lively, cheerful

alléguer [alege] *vt* to put forward (as proof *ou* an excuse)

Allemagne [aləmaɲ] *nf*: **l'~** Germany; **allemand, e** *adj, nm/f* German ♦ *nm* (*LING*) German

aller [ale] *nm* (*trajet*) outward journey; (*billet: aussi*: **~ simple**) single (*BRIT*) *ou* oneway (*US*) ticket ♦ *vi* (*gén*) to go; **~ à** (*convenir*) to suit; (*suj: forme, pointure etc*) to fit; **~ avec** (*couleurs, style etc*) to go (well) with; **je vais y ~/me fâcher** I'm going to go/to get angry; **~ voir** to go and see, go to see; **allez!** come on!; **allons!** come now!; **comment allez-vous?** how are you?; **comment ça va?** how are you?; (*affaires etc*) how are things?; **ça va bien/mal** he's well/not well, he's fine/ill; **ça va bien/mal** (*affaires etc*) it's going well/not going well; **~ mieux** to be better; **cela va sans dire** that goes without saying; **il y va de leur vie** their lives are at stake; **s'en ~** (*partir*) to be off, go, leave; (*disparaître*) to go away; **~ (et) retour** return journey (*BRIT*), round trip; (*billet*) return (ticket) (*BRIT*), round trip ticket (*US*)

allergique [alɛʀʒik] *adj*: **~ à** allergic to

alliage [aljaʒ] *nm* alloy

alliance [aljɑ̃s] *nf* (*MIL, POL*) alliance; (*mariage*) marriage; (*bague*) wedding ring

allier [alje] *vt* (*métaux*) to alloy; (*POL, gén*) to ally; (*fig*) to combine; **s'~** to become allies; to combine

allô [alo] *excl* hullo, hallo

allocation [alɔkasjɔ̃] *nf* allowance; **~ (de) chômage** unemployment benefit; **~ (de) logement** rent allowance; **~s familiales** ≈ child benefit

allocution [alɔkysjɔ̃] *nf* short speech

allonger [alɔ̃ʒe] *vt* to lengthen, make longer; (*étendre: bras, jambe*) to stretch (out);

s'~ *vi* to get longer; (*se coucher*) to lie down, stretch out; **~ le pas** to hasten one's step(s)

allouer [alwe] *vt* to allocate, allot

allumage [alymaʒ] *nm* (*AUTO*) ignition

allume-cigare [alymsigaʀ] *nm inv* cigar lighter

allumer [alyme] *vt* (*lampe, phare, radio*) to put *ou* switch on; (*pièce*) to put *ou* switch the light(s) on in; (*feu*) to light; **s'~** *vi* (*lumière, lampe*) to come *ou* go on

allumette [alymɛt] *nf* match

allure [alyʀ] *nf* (*vitesse*) speed, pace; (*démarche*) walk; (*maintien*) bearing; (*aspect, air*) look; **avoir de l'~** to have style; **à toute ~** at top speed

allusion [alyzjɔ̃] *nf* allusion; (*sous-entendu*) hint; **faire ~ à** to allude *ou* refer to; to hint at

aloi [alwa] *nm*: **de bon ~** of genuine worth *ou* quality

───────── *MOT CLÉ* ─────────

alors [alɔʀ] *adv* **1** (*à ce moment-là*) then, at that time; **il habitait ~ à Paris** he lived in Paris at that time

2 (*par conséquent*) then; **tu as fini? ~ je m'en vais** have you finished? I'm going then; **et ~? so what?**

~ que *conj* **1** (*au moment où*) when, as; **il est arrivé alors que je partais** he arrived as I was leaving

2 (*pendant que*) while, when; **~ qu'il était à Paris, il a visité ...** while *ou* when he was in Paris, he visited ...

3 (*tandis que*) whereas, while; **~ que son frère travaillait dur, lui se reposait** while his brother was working hard, HE would rest

─────────────────────────────

alouette [alwɛt] *nf* (sky)lark

alourdir [aluʀdiʀ] *vt* to weigh down, make heavy

alpage [alpaʒ] *nm* pasture

Alpes [alp(ə)] *nfpl*: **les ~** the Alps

alphabet [alfabɛ] *nm* alphabet; (*livre*) ABC (book); **alphabétiser** *vt* to teach to read and write; to eliminate illiteracy in

alpinisme [alpinism(ə)] *nm* mountaineering, climbing; **alpiniste** *nm/f* mountaineer, climber

Alsace [alzas] *nf* Alsace; **alsacien, ne** *adj, nm/f* Alsatian

altercation [altɛʀkasjɔ̃] *nf* altercation

altérer [alteʀe] *vt* to falsify; to distort; to debase; to impair

alternateur [altɛʀnatœʀ] *nm* alternator

alternatif, ive [altɛʀnatif, -iv] *adj* alternating; **alternative** *nf* (*choix*) alternative; **alternativement** *adv* alternately

Altesse [altɛs] *nf* Highness

altitude [altityd] *nf* altitude, height

alto [alto] *nm* (*instrument*) viola

altruisme [altʀɥism(ə)] *nm* altruism

aluminium [alyminjɔm] *nm* aluminium (*BRIT*), aluminum (*US*)

amabilité [amabilite] *nf* kindness, amiability

amadouer [amadwe] *vt* to coax, cajole; to mollify, soothe

amaigrir [amegʀiʀ] *vt* to make thin(ner)

amalgame [amalgam] *nm* (*alliage pour les dents*) amalgam

amande [amɑ̃d] *nf* (*de l'amandier*) almond; (*de noyau de fruit*) kernel; **amandier** *nm* almond (tree)

amant [amɑ̃] *nm* lover

amarrer [amaʀe] *vt* (*NAVIG*) to moor; (*gén*) to make fast

amas [amɑ] *nm* heap, pile

amasser [amɑse] *vt* to amass

amateur [amatœʀ] *nm* amateur; **en ~** (*péj*) amateurishly; **~ de musique/sport** *etc* music/sport *etc* lover

amazone [amazon] *nf*: **en ~** sidesaddle

ambages [ɑ̃baʒ]: **sans ~** *adv* plainly

ambassade [ɑ̃basad] *nf* embassy; (*mission*): **en ~** on a mission; **ambassadeur, drice** *nm/f* ambassador(dress)

ambiance [ɑ̃bjɑ̃s] *nf* atmosphere

ambiant, e [ɑ̃bjɑ̃, -ɑ̃t] *adj* (*air, milieu*) surrounding; (*température*) ambient

ambigu, ë [ɑ̃bigy] *adj* ambiguous

ambitieux, euse [ɑ̃bisjø, -øz] *adj* ambitious

ambition [ɑ̃bisjɔ̃] *nf* ambition

ambulance [ɑ̃bylɑ̃s] *nf* ambulance; **ambulancier, ière** *nm/f* ambulance man(woman) (*BRIT*), paramedic (*US*)

ambulant, e [ɑ̃bylɑ̃, -ɑ̃t] *adj* travelling, itinerant

âme [ɑm] *nf* soul

améliorer [ameljɔʀe] *vt* to improve; **s'~** *vi* to improve, get better

aménagements [amenaʒmɑ̃] *nmpl* developments; **~ fiscaux** tax adjustments

aménager [amenaʒe] *vt* (*agencer, transformer*) to fit out; to lay out; (*: quartier, territoire*) to develop; (*installer*) to fix up, put in; **ferme aménagée** converted farmhouse

amende [amɑ̃d] *nf* fine; **mettre à l'~** to penalize; **faire ~ honorable** to make amends

amender [amɑ̃de] *vt* (*loi*) to amend; **s'~** *vi* to mend one's ways

amener [amne] *vt* to bring; (*causer*) to bring about; (*baisser: drapeau, voiles*) to strike; **s'~** *vi* to show up (*fam*), turn up

amenuiser [amənɥize]: **s'~** *vi* to grow slimmer, lessen; to dwindle

amer, amère [amɛʀ] *adj* bitter

américain, e [ameʀikɛ̃, -ɛn] *adj, nm/f* American

Amérique [ameʀik] *nf* America; **l'~**

centrale/latine Central/Latin America; **l'~ du Nord/du Sud** North/South America

amerrir [amerir] vi to land (on the sea)

amertume [amertym] nf bitterness

ameublement [amœbləmã] nm furnishing; (meubles) furniture

ameuter [amøte] vt (badauds) to draw a crowd of; (peuple) to rouse

ami, e [ami] nm/f friend; (amant/maîtresse) boyfriend/girlfriend ♦ adj: **pays/groupe ~** friendly country/group; **être ~ de l'ordre** to be a lover of order; **un ~ des arts** a patron of the arts

amiable [amjabl(ə)]: **à l'~** adv (JUR) out of court; (gén) amicably

amiante [amjãt] nm asbestos

amical, e, aux [amikal, -o] adj friendly; **amicale** nf (club) association; **amicalement** adv in a friendly way; (formule épistolaire) regards

amidon [amidɔ̃] nm starch

amincir [amɛ̃sir] vt (objet) to thin (down); **s'~** vi to get thinner ou slimmer; **~ qn** to make sb thinner ou slimmer

amincissant, e adj: régime ~ (slimming) diet; **crème ~e** slenderizing cream

amiral, aux [amiral, -o] nm admiral

amitié [amitje] nf friendship; **prendre en ~** to befriend; **faire ou présenter ses ~s à qn** to send sb one's best wishes

ammoniac [amɔnjak] nm: **(gaz) ~** ammonia

ammoniaque [amɔnjak] nf ammonia (water)

amoindrir [amwɛ̃drir] vt to reduce

amollir [amɔlir] vt to soften

amonceler [amɔ̃sle] vt to pile ou heap up; **s'~** vi to pile ou heap up; (fig) to accumulate

amont [amɔ̃]: **en ~** adv upstream; (sur une pente) uphill

amorce [amɔrs(ə)] nf (sur un hameçon) bait; (explosif) cap; primer; priming; (fig: début) beginning(s), start

amorphe [amɔrf(ə)] adj passive, lifeless

amortir [amɔrtir] vt (atténuer: choc) to absorb, cushion; (bruit, douleur) to deaden; (COMM: dette) to pay off; (: mise de fonds, matériel) to write off; **~ un abonnement** to make a season ticket pay (for itself); **amortisseur** nm shock absorber

amour [amur] nm love; (liaison) love affair, love; **faire l'~** to make love; **amouracher: s'amouracher de** (péj) vt to become infatuated with; **amoureux, euse** adj (regard, tempérament) amorous; (vie, problèmes) love cpd; (personne): **amoureux (de qn)** in love (with sb) ♦ nmpl courting couple(s); **amour-propre** nm self-esteem, pride

amovible [amɔvibl(ə)] adj removable, detachable

ampère [ãper] nm amp(ere)

amphithéâtre [ãfiteatr(ə)] nm amphitheatre; (d'université) lecture hall ou theatre

ample [ãpl(ə)] adj (vêtement) roomy, ample; (gestes, mouvement) broad; (ressources) ample; **ampleur** nf (importance) scale, size; extent

amplificateur [ãplifikatœr] nm amplifier

amplifier [ãplifje] vt (son, oscillation) to amplify; (fig) to expand, increase

ampoule [ãpul] nf (électrique) bulb; (de médicament) phial; (aux mains, pieds) blister

ampoulé, e [ãpule] (péj) adj pompous, bombastic

amputer [ãpyte] vt (MÉD) to amputate; (fig) to cut ou reduce drastically

amusant, e [amyzã, -ãt] adj (divertissant, spirituel) entertaining, amusing; (comique) funny, amusing

amuse-gueule [amyzgœl] nm inv appetizer, snack

amusement [amyzmã] nm amusement; (jeu etc) pastime, diversion

amuser [amyze] vt (divertir) to entertain, amuse; (égayer, faire rire) to amuse; (détourner l'attention de) to distract; **s'~** vi (jouer) to amuse o.s., play; (se divertir) to enjoy o.s., have fun; (fig) to mess around

amygdale [amidal] nf tonsil

an [ã] nm year; **le jour de l'~, le premier de l'~, le nouvel ~** New Year's Day

analogique [analɔʒik] adj analogical; (IN-FORM, montre) analog

analogue [analɔg] adj: **~ (à)** analogous (to), similar (to)

analphabète [analfabɛt] nm/f illiterate

analyse [analiz] nf analysis; (MÉD) test; **analyser** vt to analyse; to test

ananas [anana] nm pineapple

anarchie [anarʃi] nf anarchy

anathème [anatɛm] nm: **jeter l'~ sur** to curse

anatomie [anatɔmi] nf anatomy

ancêtre [ãsɛtr(ə)] nm/f ancestor

anchois [ãʃwa] nm anchovy

ancien, ne [ãsjɛ̃, -jɛn] adj old; (de jadis, de l'antiquité) ancient; (précédent, ex-) former, old ♦ nm/f (dans une tribu) elder; **ancienneté** adv formerly; **ancienneté** nf oldness; antiquity; (ADMIN) (length of) service; seniority

ancre [ãkr(ə)] nf anchor; **jeter/lever l'~** to cast/weigh anchor; **à l'~** at anchor; **ancrer** [ãkre] vt (CONSTR: câble etc) to anchor; (fig) to fix firmly; **s'~r** vi (NAVIG) to (cast) anchor

Andorre [ãdɔr] nf Andorra

andouille [ãduj] nf (CULIN) sausage made of chitterlings; (fam) clot, nit

âne [ɑn] nm donkey, ass; (péj) dunce

anéantir [aneãtir] vt to annihilate, wipe

out; (fig) to obliterate, destroy; to overwhelm

anémie [anemi] nf anaemia; **anémique** adj anaemic

ânerie [ɑnʀi] nf stupidity; stupid ou idiotic comment etc

anesthésie [anɛstezi] nf anaesthesia; **faire une ~ locale/générale à qn** to give sb a local/general anaesthetic

ange [ɑ̃ʒ] nm angel; **être aux ~s** to be over the moon

angélus [ɑ̃ʒelys] nm angelus; evening bells pl

angine [ɑ̃ʒin] nf throat infection; **~ de poitrine** angina

anglais, e [ɑ̃glɛ, -ɛz] adj English ♦ nm/f: **A~, e** Englishman(woman) ♦ nm (LING) English; **les A~** the English; **filer à l'~e** to take French leave

angle [ɑ̃gl(ə)] nm angle; (coin) corner; **~ droit** right angle

Angleterre [ɑ̃glətɛʀ] nf: **l'~** England

anglo... [ɑ̃glo] préfixe Anglo-, anglo (-); **~phone** adj English-speaking

angoissé, e [ɑ̃gwase] adj (personne) full of anxieties ou hang-ups (inf)

angoisser [ɑ̃gwase] vt to harrow, cause anguish to ♦ vi to worry, fret

anguille [ɑ̃gij] nf eel

anicroche [anikʀɔʃ] nf hitch, snag

animal, e, aux [animal, -o] adj, nm animal

animateur, trice [animatœʀ, -tʀis] nm/f (de télévision) host; (de groupe) leader, organizer

animation [animɑsjɔ̃] nf (voir animé) busyness; liveliness; (CINÉMA: technique) animation

animé, e [anime] adj (lieu) busy, lively; (conversation, réunion) lively, animated; (opposé à in~) animate

animer [anime] vt (ville, soirée) to liven up; (mettre en mouvement) to drive

anis [ani] nm (CULIN) aniseed; (BOT) anise

ankyloser [ɑ̃kiloze]: **s'~** vi to get stiff

anneau, x [ano] nm (de rideau, bague) ring; (de chaîne) link

année [ane] nf year

annexe [anɛks(ə)] adj (problème) related; (document) appended; (salle) adjoining ♦ nf (bâtiment) annex(e); (de document, ouvrage) annex, appendix; (jointe à une lettre) enclosure

anniversaire [anivɛʀsɛʀ] nm birthday; (d'un événement, bâtiment) anniversary

annonce [anɔ̃s] nf announcement; (signe, indice) sign; (aussi: ~ publicitaire) advertisement; **les petites ~s** the classified advertisements, the small ads

annoncer [anɔ̃se] vt to announce; (être le signe de) to herald; **s'~ bien/difficile** to look promising/difficult; **annonceur, euse** nm/f (TV, RADIO: speaker) announcer;

(publicitaire) advertiser

annuaire [anɥɛʀ] nm yearbook, annual; **~ téléphonique** (telephone) directory, phone book

annuel, le [anɥɛl] adj annual, yearly

annuité [anɥite] nf annual instalment

annuler [anɥle] vt (rendez-vous, voyage) to cancel, call off; (mariage) to annul; (jugement) to quash (BRIT), repeal (US); (résultats) to declare void; (MATH, PHYSIQUE) to cancel out

anodin, e [anɔdɛ̃, -in] adj harmless; insignificant, trivial

anonyme [anɔnim] adj anonymous; (fig) impersonal

ANPE sigle f (= Agence nationale pour l'emploi) national employment agency

anse [ɑ̃s] nf (de panier, tasse) handle; (GÉO) cove

antan [ɑ̃tɑ̃]: **d'~** adj of long ago

antarctique [ɑ̃taʀktik] adj Antarctic ♦ nm: **l'A~** the Antarctic

antécédents [ɑ̃tesedɑ̃] nmpl (MÉD etc) past history sg

antenne [ɑ̃tɛn] nf (de radio) aerial; (d'insecte) antenna, feeler; (poste avancé) outpost; (petite succursale) sub-branch; **passer à l'~** to go on the air; **prendre l'~** to tune in; **2 heures d'~** 2 hours' broadcasting time

antérieur, e [ɑ̃teʀjœʀ] adj (d'avant) previous, earlier; (de devant) front

anti... [ɑ̃ti] préfixe anti...; **~alcoolique** adj anti-alcohol; **~atomique** adj: **abri ~atomique** fallout shelter; **~biotique** nm antibiotic; **~brouillard** adj: **phare ~brouillard** fog lamp (BRIT) ou light (US)

anticipation [ɑ̃tisipɑsjɔ̃] nf: **livre/film d'~** science fiction book/film

anticipé, e [ɑ̃tisipe] adj: **avec mes remerciements ~s** thanking you in advance ou anticipation

anticiper [ɑ̃tisipe] vt (événement, coup) to anticipate, foresee

anti: **~conceptionnel, le** adj contraceptive; **~corps** nm antibody; **~dote** nm antidote

antigel [ɑ̃tiʒɛl] nm antifreeze

antihistaminique [ɑ̃tiistaminik] nm antihistamine

Antilles [ɑ̃tij] nfpl: **les ~** the West Indies

antilope [ɑ̃tilɔp] nf antelope

anti: **~mite(s)** adj, nm: (produit) **~mite(s)** mothproofer; moth repellent; **~parasite** adj (RADIO, TV): **dispositif ~parasite** suppressor; **~pathique** adj unpleasant, disagreeable; **~pelliculaire** adj anti-dandruff

antipodes [ɑ̃tipɔd] nmpl (GÉO): **les ~** the antipodes; (fig): **être aux ~ de** to be the opposite extreme of

antiquaire [ɑ̃tikɛʀ] nm/f antique dealer

antique [ɑ̃tik] adj antique; (très vieux) ancient, antiquated

antiquité [ɑ̃tikite] *nf* (*objet*) antique; **l'A~** Antiquity; **magasin d'~s** antique shop

anti: ~rabique *adj* rabies *cpd*; **~rouille** *adj inv* anti-rust *cpd*; **traitement ~rouille** rustproofing; **~sémite** *adj* anti-Semitic; **~septique** *adj*, *nm* antiseptic; **~vol** *adj*, *nm*: (**dispositif**) **~vol** anti-theft device

antre [ɑ̃tʀ(ə)] *nm* den, lair

anxieux, euse [ɑ̃ksjø, -øz] *adj* anxious, worried

AOC *sigle f* (= *appellation d'origine contrôlée*) *label guaranteeing the quality of wine*

août [u] *nm* August

apaiser [apeze] *vt* (*colère, douleur*) to soothe; (*faim*) to appease; (*personne*) to calm (down), pacify; **s'~** *vi* (*tempête, bruit*) to die down, subside

apanage [apanaʒ] *nm*: **être l'~ de** to be the privilege *ou* prerogative of

aparté [apaʀte] *nm* (*THÉÂTRE*) aside; (*entretien*) private conversation

apathique [apatik] *adj* apathetic

apatride [apatʀid] *nm/f* stateless person

apercevoir [apɛʀsəvwaʀ] *vt* to see; **s'~ de** *vt* to notice; **s'~ que** to notice that

aperçu [apɛʀsy] *nm* (*vue d'ensemble*) general survey; (*intuition*) insight

apéritif [apeʀitif] *nm* (*boisson*) aperitif; (*réunion*) drinks *pl*

à-peu-près [apøpʀɛ] (*péj*) *nm inv* vague approximation

apeuré, e [apœʀe] *adj* frightened, scared

aphone [afɔn] *adj* voiceless

aphte [aft(ə)] *nm* mouth ulcer

apiculture [apikyltyʀ] *nf* beekeeping, apiculture

apitoyer [apitwaje] *vt* to move to pity; **s'~ (sur)** to feel pity (for)

aplanir [aplaniʀ] *vt* to level; (*fig*) to smooth away, iron out

aplatir [aplatiʀ] *vt* to flatten; **s'~** *vi* to become flatter; to be flattened; (*fig*) to lie flat on the ground

aplomb [aplɔ̃] *nm* (*équilibre*) balance, equilibrium; (*fig*) self-assurance; nerve; **d'~** steady; (*CONSTR*) plumb

apogée [apɔʒe] *nm* (*fig*) peak, apogee

apologie [apɔlɔʒi] *nf* vindication, praise

apostrophe [apɔstʀɔf] *nf* (*signe*) apostrophe

apostropher [apɔstʀɔfe] *vt* (*interpeller*) to shout at, address sharply

apothéose [apɔteoz] *nf* pinnacle (of achievement); (*MUS*) grand finale

apôtre [apotʀ(ə)] *nm* apostle

apparaître [apaʀɛtʀ(ə)] *vi* to appear

apparat [apaʀa] *nm*: **tenue/dîner d'~** ceremonial dress/dinner

appareil [apaʀɛj] *nm* (*outil, machine*) piece of apparatus, device; appliance; (*politique, syndical*) machinery; (*avion*) (aero)plane,

aircraft *inv*; (*téléphonique*) phone; (*dentier*) brace (*BRIT*), braces (*US*); **"qui est à l'~?"** "who's speaking?''; **dans le plus simple ~** in one's birthday suit; **~ler** [apaʀeje] *vi* (*NAVIG*) to cast off, get under way ♦ *vt* (*assortir*) to match up; **~(-photo)** [apaʀej(fɔtɔ)] *nm* camera

apparemment [apaʀamɑ̃] *adv* apparently

apparence [apaʀɑ̃s] *nf* appearance

apparent, e [apaʀɑ̃, -ɑ̃t] *adj* visible; obvious; (*superficiel*) apparent

apparenté, e [apaʀɑ̃te] *adj*: **~ à** related to; (*fig*) similar to

apparition [apaʀisjɔ̃] *nf* appearance; (*surnaturelle*) apparition

appartement [apaʀtəmɑ̃] *nm* flat (*BRIT*), apartment (*US*)

appartenir [apaʀtəniʀ]: **~ à** *vt* to belong to; **il lui appartient de** it is up to him to, it is his duty to

apparu, e *pp* de **apparaître**

appât [apɑ] *nm* (*PÊCHE*) bait; (*fig*) lure, bait

appauvrir [apovʀiʀ] *vt* to impoverish

appel [apɛl] *nm* call; (*nominal*) roll call; (: *SCOL*) register; (*MIL: recrutement*) call-up; **faire ~** (*invoquer*) to appeal to; (*avoir recours à*) to call on; (*nécessiter*) to call for, require; **faire ~** (*JUR*) to appeal; **faire l'~** to call the roll; to call the register; **sans ~** (*fig*) final, irrevocable; **~ d'offres** (*COMM*) invitation to tender; **faire un ~ de phares** to flash one's headlights; **~ (téléphonique)** (tele)phone call

appelé [aple] *nm* (*MIL*) conscript

appeler [aple] *vt* to call; (*faire venir: médecin etc*) to call, send for; (*fig: nécessiter*) to call for, demand; **s'~: elle s'appelle Gabrielle** her name is Gabrielle, she's called Gabrielle; **comment ça s'appelle?** what is it called?; **être appelé à** (*fig*) to be destined to; **~ qn à comparaître** (*JUR*) to summon sb to appear; **en ~ à** to appeal to

appendice [apɛ̃dis] *nm* appendix; **appendicite** *nf* appendicitis

appentis [apɑ̃ti] *nm* lean-to

appesantir [apzɑ̃tiʀ]: **s'~** *vi* to grow heavier; **s'~ sur** (*fig*) to dwell on

appétissant, e [apetisɑ̃, -ɑ̃t] *adj* appetizing, mouth-watering

appétit [apeti] *nm* appetite; **bon ~!** enjoy your meal!

applaudir [aplodiʀ] *vt* to applaud ♦ *vi* to applaud, clap; **applaudissements** *nmpl* applause *sg*, clapping *sg*

application [aplikɑsjɔ̃] *nf* application

applique [aplik] *nf* wall lamp

appliquer [aplike] *vt* to apply; (*loi*) to enforce; **s'~** *vi* (*élève etc*) to apply o.s.

appoint [apwɛ̃] *nm* (extra) contribution *ou* help; **avoir/faire l'~** (*en payant*) to have/ give the right change *ou* money; **chauffage d'~** extra heating

appointements [apwɛtmɑ̃] *nmpl* salary *sg*
appontement [apɔ̃tmɑ̃] *nm* landing stage,
wharf
apport [apɔR] *nm* supply; contribution
apporter [apɔRte] *vt* to bring
apposer [apoze] *vt* to append; to affix
appréciable [apResjabl(ə)] *adj* appreciable
apprécier [apResje] *vt* to appreciate; (*évaluer*) to estimate, assess
appréhender [apReɑ̃de] *vt* (*craindre*) to
dread; (*arrêter*) to apprehend
apprendre [apRɑ̃dR(ə)] *vt* to learn; (*événement, résultats*) to learn of, hear of; ~ **qch
à qn** (*informer*) to tell sb (of) sth; (*enseigner*) to teach sb sth; ~ **à faire qch** to
learn to do sth; ~ **à qn à faire qch** to
teach sb to do sth; **apprenti, e** *nm/f* apprentice; (*fig*) novice, beginner; **apprentissage** *nm* learning; (*COMM, SCOL: période*)
apprenticeship
apprêté, e [apRete] *adj* (*fig*) affected
apprêter [apRete] *vt* to dress, finish
appris, e *pp de* **apprendre**
apprivoiser [apRivwaze] *vt* to tame
approbation [apRɔbasjɔ̃] *nf* approval
approche [apRɔʃ] *nf* approaching; approach
approcher [apRɔʃe] *vi* to approach, come
near ♦ *vt* to approach; (*rapprocher*): ~ **qch
(de qch)** to bring *ou* put sth near (to sth);
s'~ de to approach, go *ou* come near to; ~
de to draw near to; (*quantité, moment*) to
approach
approfondir [apRɔfɔ̃diR] *vt* to deepen;
(*question*) to go further into
approprié, e [apRɔpRije] *adj*: ~ (**à**) appropriate (to), suited to
approprier [apRɔpRije]: **s'~** *vt* to appropriate, take over
approuver [apRuve] *vt* to agree with; (*autoriser: loi, projet*) to approve, pass; (*trouver
louable*) to approve of
approvisionner [apRɔvizjɔne] *vt* to supply;
(*compte bancaire*) to pay funds into; **s'~ en**
to stock up with
approximatif, ive [apRɔksimatif, -iv] *adj*
approximate, rough; vague
appui [apɥi] *nm* support; prendre ~ **sur** to
lean on; to rest on; **l'~ de la fenêtre** the
windowsill, the window ledge; **appui(e)-
tête** *nm inv* headrest
appuyer [apɥije] *vt* (*poser*): ~ **qch sur/
contre** to lean *ou* rest sth on/against; (*soutenir: personne, demande*) to support, back
(up) ♦ *vi*: ~ **sur** (*bouton, frein*) to press,
push; (*mot, détail*) to stress, emphasize;
(*suj: chose: peser sur*) to rest (heavily) on,
press against; **s'~ sur** to lean on; to rely
on; ~ **à droite** to bear (to the right)
âpre [ɑpR(ə)] *adj* acrid, pungent; (*fig*) harsh;
bitter; ~ **au gain** grasping
après [apRe] *prép* after ♦ *adv* afterwards; **2**

heures ~ 2 hours later; ~ **qu'il est parti**
after he left; ~ **avoir fait** after having done;
d'~ (*selon*) according to; ~ **coup** after the
event, afterwards; ~ **tout** (*au fond*) after
all; **et (puis)** ~? so what?; **après-demain**
adv the day after tomorrow; **après-guerre**
nm post-war years *pl*; **après-midi** *nm ou nf*
(*inv*) afternoon
à-propos [apRɔpo] *nm* (*d'une remarque*)
aptness; **faire preuve d'~** to show presence
of mind
apte [apt(ə)] *adj* capable; (*MIL*) fit
aquarelle [akwaRɛl] *nf* (*tableau*) waterco-
lour; (*genre*) watercolours *pl*
aquarium [akwaRjɔm] *nm* aquarium
arabe [aRab] *adj* Arabic; (*désert, cheval*)
Arabian; (*nation, peuple*) Arab ♦ *nm/f*: **A~**
Arab ♦ *nm* (*LING*) Arabic
Arabie [aRabi] *nf*: **l'~ (Saoudite)** Saudi
Arabia
arachide [aRaʃid] *nf* (*plante*) groundnut
(plant); (*graine*) peanut, groundnut
araignée [aRɛɲe] *nf* spider
arbitraire [aRbitRɛR] *adj* arbitrary
arbitre [aRbitR(ə)] *nm* (*SPORT*) referee; (:
TENNIS, CRICKET) umpire; (*fig*) arbiter,
judge; (*JUR*) arbitrator; **arbitrer** *vt* to referee; to umpire; to arbitrate
arborer [aRbɔRe] *vt* to bear, display
arbre [aRbR(ə)] *nm* tree; (*TECH*) shaft; ~ **de
transmission** (*AUTO*) driveshaft; ~ **généa-
logique** family tree
arbuste [aRbyst(ə)] *nm* small shrub
arc [aRk] *nm* (*arme*) bow; (*GÉOM*) arc; (*AR-
CHIT*) arch; **en** ~ **de cercle** semi-circular
arcade [aRkad] *nf* arch(way); ~**s** *nfpl* (*série*)
arcade *sg*, arches
arcanes [aRkan] *nmpl* mysteries
arc-boutant [aRkbutɑ̃] *nm* flying buttress
arceau, x [aRso] *nm* (*métallique etc*) hoop
arc-en-ciel [aRkɑ̃sjɛl] *nm* rainbow
arche [aRʃ(ə)] *nf* arch; ~ **de Noé** Noah's
Ark
archéologie [aRkeɔlɔʒi] *nf* archeology; **archéologue** *nm/f* arch(a)eologist
archet [aRʃe] *nm* bow
archevêque [aRʃəvɛk] *nm* archbishop
archipel [aRʃipɛl] *nm* archipelago
architecte [aRʃitɛkt(ə)] *nm* architect
architecture [aRʃitɛktyR] *nf* architecture
archive [aRʃiv] *nf* file; ~**s** *nfpl* (*collection*)
archives
arctique [aRktik] *adj* Arctic ♦ *nm*: **l'A~** the
Arctic
ardemment [aRdamɑ̃] *adv* ardently, ferv-
ently
ardent, e [aRdɑ̃, -ɑ̃t] *adj* (*soleil*) blazing;
(*fièvre*) raging; (*amour*) ardent, passionate;
(*prière*) fervent
ardoise [aRdwaz] *nf* slate
ardt *abr* = **arrondissement**
ardu, e [aRdy] *adj* (*travail*) arduous; (*pro-

blème) difficult; (pente) steep
arène [aʀɛn] nf arena; ~s nfpl (amphithéâtre) bull-ring sg
arête [aʀɛt] nf (de poisson) bone; (d'une montagne) ridge; (GÉOM etc) edge
argent [aʀʒɑ̃] nm (métal) silver; (monnaie) money; ~ **de poche** pocket money; ~ **liquide** ready money, (ready) cash; **argenterie** nf silverware; silver plate
argentin, e [aʀʒɑ̃tɛ̃, -in] adj (son) silvery; (d'Argentine) Argentinian, Argentine
Argentine [aʀʒɑ̃tin] nf: l'~ Argentina, the Argentine
argile [aʀʒil] nf clay
argot [aʀgo] nm slang; **argotique** adj slang cpd; slangy
arguer [aʀgɥe]: ~ **de** vt to put forward as a pretext ou reason
argument [aʀgymɑ̃] nm argument
argumentaire [aʀgymɑ̃tɛʀ] nm sales leaflet
argumenter [aʀgymɑ̃te] vi to argue
argus [aʀgys] nm guide to second-hand car etc prices
aristocratique [aʀistɔkʀatik] adj aristocratic
arithmétique [aʀitmetik] adj arithmetic(al) ♦ nf arithmetic
armateur [aʀmatœʀ] nm shipowner
armature [aʀmatyʀ] nf framework; (de tente etc) frame
arme [aʀm(ə)] nf weapon; (section de l'armée) arm; ~s nfpl (armement) weapons, arms; (blason) (coat of) arms; ~ **à feu** firearm
armée [aʀme] nf army; ~ **de l'air** Air Force; ~ **de terre** Army
armement [aʀməmɑ̃] nm (matériel) arms pl, weapons pl; (: d'un pays) arms pl, armament
armer [aʀme] vt to arm; (arme à feu) to cock; (appareil-photo) to wind on; ~ **qch de** to fit sth with; to reinforce sth with
armistice [aʀmistis] nm armistice; l'A~ ≈ Remembrance (BRIT) ou Veterans (US) Day
armoire [aʀmwaʀ] nf (tall) cupboard; (penderie) wardrobe (BRIT), closet (US)
armoiries [aʀmwaʀi] nfpl coat sg of arms
armure [aʀmyʀ] nf armour no pl, suit of armour; **armurier** [aʀmyʀje] nm gunsmith; armourer
arnaquer [aʀnake] vt to swindle
aromates [aʀɔmat] nmpl seasoning sg, herbs (and spices)
aromatisé, e [aʀɔmatize] adj flavoured
arôme [aʀom] nm aroma; fragrance
arpenter [aʀpɑ̃te] vt (salle, couloir) to pace up and down
arpenteur [aʀpɑ̃tœʀ] nm surveyor
arqué, e [aʀke] adj bandy
arrache-pied [aʀaʃpje]: d'~ adv relentlessly
arracher [aʀaʃe] vt to pull out; (page etc)

to tear off, tear out; (légumes, herbe) to pull up; (bras etc) to tear off; s'~ vt (article recherché) to fight over; ~ **qch à qn** to snatch sth from sb; (fig) to wring sth out of sb
arraisonner [aʀezɔne] vt (bateau) to board and search
arrangeant, e [aʀɑ̃ʒɑ̃, -ɑ̃t] adj accommodating, obliging
arrangement [aʀɑ̃ʒmɑ̃] nm agreement, arrangement
arranger [aʀɑ̃ʒe] vt (gén) to arrange; (réparer) to fix, put right; (régler) to settle, sort out; (convenir à) to suit, be convenient for; s'~ vi (se mettre d'accord) to come to an agreement; **je vais m'~** I'll manage; **ça va s'~** it'll sort itself out
arrestation [aʀestasjɔ̃] nf arrest
arrêt [aʀɛ] nm stopping; (de bus etc) stop; (JUR) judgment, decision; **rester** ou **tomber en** ~ **devant** to stop short in front of; **sans** ~ non-stop; continually; ~ **de mort** capital sentence; ~ **de travail** stoppage (of work)
arrêté [aʀete] nm order, decree
arrêter [aʀete] vt to stop; (chauffage etc) to turn off, switch off; (fixer: date etc) to appoint, decide on; (criminel, suspect) to arrest; s'~ vi to stop; ~ **de faire** to stop doing
arrhes [aʀ] nfpl deposit sg
arrière [aʀjɛʀ] nm back; (SPORT) fullback ♦ adj inv: **siège/roue** ~ back ou rear seat/wheel; à l'~ behind, at the back; **en** ~ behind; (regarder) back, behind; (tomber, aller) backwards; à l'~ (péj) back-ward ♦ nm (d'argent) arrears pl; ~-**goût** nm aftertaste; ~-**grand-mère** nf great-grandmother; ~-**grand-père** nm great-grandfather; ~-**pays** nm inv hinterland; ~-**pensée** nf ulterior motive; mental reservation; ~-**plan** nm background; ~-**saison** nf late autumn; ~-**train** nm hindquarters pl
arrimer [aʀime] vt to stow; to secure
arrivage [aʀivaʒ] nm arrival
arrivée [aʀive] nf arrival; (ligne d'~) finish; ~ **d'air** air inlet
arriver [aʀive] vi to arrive; (survenir) to happen, occur; **il arrive à Paris à 8h** he gets to ou arrives in Paris at 8; ~ **à** (atteindre) to reach; ~ **à faire qch** to succeed in doing sth; **il arrive que** it happens that; **il lui arrive de faire** he sometimes does; **arriviste** nm/f go-getter
arrogant, e [aʀɔgɑ̃, -ɑ̃t] adj arrogant
arroger [aʀɔʒe]: s'~ vt to assume (without right)
arrondir [aʀɔ̃diʀ] vt (forme, objet) to round; (somme) to round off; s'~ vi to become round(ed)
arrondissement [aʀɔ̃dismɑ̃] nm (ADMIN) ≈ district
arroser [aʀoze] vt to water; (victoire) to ce-

lebrate (over a drink); (*CULIN*) to baste; **arrosoir** *nm* watering can

arsenal, aux [arsənal, -o] *nm* (*NAVIG*) naval dockyard; (*MIL*) arsenal; (*fig*) gear, paraphernalia

art [ar] *nm* art; **~s ménagers** home economics *sg*

artère [arter] *nf* (*ANAT*) artery; (*rue*) main road

arthrite [artrit] *nf* arthritis

artichaut [artiʃo] *nm* artichoke

article [artikl(ə)] *nm* article; (*COMM*) item, article; **à l'~ de la mort** at the point of death; **~ de fond** (*PRESSE*) feature article

articulation [artikylɑsjɔ̃] *nf* articulation; (*ANAT*) joint

articuler [artikyle] *vt* to articulate

artifice [artifis] *nm* device, trick

artificiel, le [artifisjɛl] *adj* artificial

artificieux, euse [artifisjø, -øz] *adj* guileful, deceitful

artisan [artizɑ̃] *nm* artisan, (self-employed) craftsman; **artisanal, e, aux** *adj* of *ou* made by craftsmen; (*péj*) cottage industry *cpd*, unsophisticated; **artisanat** *nm* arts and crafts *pl*

artiste [artist(ə)] *nm/f* artist; (*de variétés*) entertainer; performer; **artistique** *adj* artistic

as[1] [a] *vb voir* **avoir**

as[2] [as] *nm* ace

ascendance [asɑ̃dɑ̃s] *nf* (*origine*) ancestry

ascendant, e [asɑ̃dɑ̃, -ɑ̃t] *adj* upward ♦ *nm* influence

ascenseur [asɑ̃sœr] *nm* lift (*BRIT*), elevator (*US*)

ascension [asɑ̃sjɔ̃] *nf* ascent; climb; **l'A~** (*REL*) the Ascension

aseptiser [asɛptize] *vt* to sterilize; to disinfect

asiatique [azjatik] *adj, nm/f* Asiatic, Asian **Asie** [azi] *nf*: **l'~** Asia

asile [azil] *nm* (*refuge*) refuge, sanctuary; (*POL*): **droit d'~** (political) asylum; (*pour malades etc*) home

aspect [aspɛ] *nm* appearance, look; (*fig*) aspect, side; **à l'~ de** at the sight of

asperge [aspɛrʒ(ə)] *nf* asparagus *no pl*

asperger [aspɛrʒe] *vt* to spray, sprinkle

aspérité [asperite] *nf* excrescence, protruding bit (of rock *etc*)

asphalte [asfalt(ə)] *nm* asphalt

asphyxier [asfiksje] *vt* to suffocate, asphyxiate; (*fig*) to stifle

aspirateur [aspiratœr] *nm* vacuum cleaner

aspirer [aspire] *vt* (*air*) to inhale; (*liquide*) to suck (up); (*suj: appareil*) to suck up; **~ à** to aspire to

aspirine [aspirin] *nf* aspirin

assagir [asaʒir] *vt* to quieten down; **s'~** *vi* to quieten down, sober down

assaillir [asajir] *vt* to assail, attack

assainir [asenir] *vt* to clean up; to purify

assaisonner [asɛzɔne] *vt* to season

assassin [asasɛ̃] *nm* murderer; assassin; **~er** [asasine] *vt* to murder; (*esp POL*) to assassinate

assaut [aso] *nm* assault, attack; **prendre d'~** to storm, assault; **donner l'~** to attack; **faire ~ de** (*rivaliser*) to vie with each other in

assécher [aseʃe] *vt* to drain

assemblée [asɑ̃ble] *nf* (*réunion*) meeting; (*public, assistance*) gathering; assembled people; (*POL*) assembly

assembler [asɑ̃ble] *vt* (*joindre, monter*) to assemble, put together; (*amasser*) to gather (together), collect (together); **s'~** *vi* to gather

assener [asene] *vt*: **~ un coup à qn** to deal sb a blow

asséner [asene] *vt* = **assener**

assentiment [asɑ̃timɑ̃] *nm* assent, consent; approval

asseoir [aswar] *vt* (*malade, bébé*) to sit up; to sit down; (*autorité, réputation*) to establish; **s'~** *vi* to sit (o.s.) down

assermenté, e [asɛrmɑ̃te] *adj* sworn, on oath

asservir [asɛrvir] *vt* to subjugate, enslave

assez [ase] *adv* (*suffisamment*) enough, sufficiently; (*passablement*) rather, quite, fairly; **~ de pain/livres** enough *ou* sufficient bread/books; **vous en avez ~?** have you got enough?

assidu, e [asidy] *adj* assiduous, painstaking; regular; **assiduités** *nfpl* assiduous attentions

assied *etc vb voir* **asseoir**

assiéger [asjeʒe] *vt* to besiege

assiérai *etc vb voir* **asseoir**

assiette [asjɛt] *nf* plate; (*contenu*) plate(ful); **~ à dessert** dessert plate; **~ anglaise** assorted cold meats; **~ creuse** (soup) dish, soup plate; **~ de l'impôt** basis of (tax) assessment; **~ plate** (dinner) plate

assigner [asiɲe] *vt*: **~ qch à** (*poste, part, travail*) to assign sth to; (*limites*) to set sth to; (*cause, effet*) to ascribe sth to; **~ qn à** to assign sb to

assimiler [asimile] *vt* to assimilate, absorb; (*comparer*): **~ qch/qn à** to liken *ou* compare sth/sb to; **s'~** *vi* (*s'intégrer*) to be assimilated *ou* absorbed

assis, e [asi, -iz] *pp de* **asseoir** ♦ *adj* sitting (down), seated; **assise** *nf* (*fig*) basis, foundation; **~es** *nfpl* (*JUR*) assizes; (*congrès*) (annual) conference

assistance [asistɑ̃s] *nf* (*public*) audience; (*aide*) assistance

assistant, e [asistɑ̃, -ɑ̃t] *nm/f* assistant; (*d'université*) probationary lecturer; **~e sociale** social worker

assisté, e [asiste] *adj* (*AUTO*) power assisted

assister [asiste] vt to assist; ~ **à** (scène, événement) to witness; (conférence, séminaire) to attend, be at; (spectacle, match) to be at, see

association [asɔsjɑsjɔ̃] nf association

associé, e [asɔsje] nm/f associate; partner

associer [asɔsje] vt to associate; **s'~** vi to join together ♦ vt (collaborateur) to take on (as a partner); **s'~ à qn pour faire** to join (forces) with sb to do; **s'~ à** to be combined with; (opinions, joie de qn) to share in; ~ **qn à** (profits) to give sb a share of; (affaire) to make sb a partner in; (joie, triomphe) to include sb in; ~ **qch à** (joindre, allier) to combine sth with

assoiffé, e [aswafe] adj thirsty

assombrir [asɔ̃bRiR] vt to darken; (fig) to fill with gloom

assommer [asɔme] vt to batter to death; (étourdir, abrutir) to knock out; to stun

Assomption [asɔ̃psjɔ̃] nf: **l'~** the Assumption

assorti, e [asɔRti] adj matched, matching; (varié) assorted; ~ **à** matching

assortiment [asɔRtimɑ̃] nm assortment, selection

assortir [asɔRtiR] vt to match; **s'~ de** to be accompanied by; ~ **qch à** to match sth with; ~ **qch de** to accompany sth with

assoupi, e [asupi] adj dozing, sleeping; (fig) (be)numbed; dulled; stilled

assouplir [asupliR] vt to make supple; (fig) to relax

assourdir [asuRdiR] vt (bruit) to deaden, muffle; (suj: bruit) to deafen

assouvir [asuviR] vt to satisfy, appease

assujettir [asyʒetiR] vt to subject

assumer [asyme] vt (fonction, emploi) to assume, take on

assurance [asyRɑ̃s] nf (certitude) assurance; (confiance en soi) (self-) confidence; (contrat) insurance (policy); (secteur commercial) insurance; ~ **maladie** health insurance; ~ **tous risques** (AUTO) comprehensive insurance; ~**s sociales** ≈ National Insurance (BRIT), ≈ Social Security (US); ~**vie** nf life assurance ou insurance

assuré, e [asyRe] adj (certain): ~ **de** confident of ♦ nm/f insured (person); **assurément** adv assuredly, most certainly

assurer [asyRe] vt to insure; (stabiliser) to steady; to stabilize; (victoire etc) to ensure; (frontières, pouvoir) to make secure; (service, garde) to provide; to operate; **s'~ (contre)** (COMM) to insure o.s. (against); **s'~ de/que** (vérifier) to make sure of/that; **s'~ (de)** (aide de qn) to secure; ~ **qch à qn** (garantir) to secure sth for sb; (certifier) to assure sb of sth; ~ **à qn que** to assure sb that; ~ **qn de** to assure sb of

asthme [asm(ə)] nm asthma

asticot [astiko] nm maggot

astiquer [astike] vt to polish, shine

astre [astR(ə)] nm star

astreignant, e [astRɛɲɑ̃, -ɑ̃t] adj demanding

astreindre [astRɛ̃dR(ə)] vt: ~ **qn à qch** to force sth upon sb; ~ **qn à faire** to compel ou force sb to do

astrologie [astRɔlɔʒi] nf astrology

astronaute [astRɔnot] nm/f astronaut

astronomie [astRɔnɔmi] nf astronomy

astuce [astys] nf shrewdness, astuteness; (truc) trick, clever way; (plaisanterie) wisecrack; **astucieux, euse** adj clever

atelier [atəlje] nm workshop; (de peintre) studio

athée [ate] adj atheistic ♦ nm/f atheist

Athènes [atɛn] n Athens

athlète [atlet] nm/f (SPORT) athlete; **athlétisme** nm athletics sg

atlantique [atlɑ̃tik] adj Atlantic ♦ nm: **l'(océan) A~** the Atlantic (Ocean)

atlas [atlɑs] nm atlas

atmosphère [atmɔsfɛR] nf atmosphere

atome [atom] nm atom; **atomique** adj atomic, nuclear; (nombre, masse) atomic

atomiseur [atɔmizœR] nm atomizer

atone [aton] adj lifeless

atours [atuR] nmpl attire sg, finery sg

atout [atu] nm trump; (fig) asset; trump card

âtre [ɑtR(ə)] nm hearth

atroce [atRɔs] adj atrocious

attabler [atable]: **s'~** vi to sit down at (the) table

attachant, e [ataʃɑ̃, -ɑ̃t] adj engaging, lovable, likeable

attache [ataʃ] nf clip, fastener; (fig) tie

attacher [ataʃe] vt to tie up; (étiquette) to attach, tie on; (souliers) to do up ♦ vi (poêle, riz) to stick; **s'~ à** (par affection) to become attached to; **s'~ à faire** to endeavour to do; ~ **qch à** to tie ou attach sth to

attaque [atak] nf attack; (cérébrale) stroke; (d'épilepsie) fit

attaquer [atake] vt to attack; (en justice) to bring an action against, sue; (travail) to tackle, set about ♦ vi to attack

attardé, e [atarde] adj (passants) late; (enfant) backward; (conceptions) old-fashioned

attarder [atarde]: **s'~** vi to linger; to stay on

atteindre [atɛ̃dR(ə)] vt to reach; (blesser) to hit; (émouvoir) to affect

atteint, e [atɛ̃, -ɛ̃t] adj (MÉD): **être ~ de** to be suffering from; **atteinte** nf attack; **hors d'atteinte** out of reach; **porter atteinte à** to strike a blow at; to undermine

atteler [atle] vt (cheval, bœufs) to hitch up; (wagons) to couple; **s'~ à** (travail) to buckle down to

attelle [atɛl] nf splint

attenant, e [atnã, -ãt] adj: ~ **(à)** adjoining
attendant [atãdã] adv: **en** ~ meanwhile, in the meantime
attendre [atãdʀ(ə)] vt (gén) to wait for; (être destiné ou réservé à) to await, be in store for ♦ vi to wait; **s'~ à (ce que)** to expect (that); ~ **un enfant** to be expecting a baby; ~ **de faire/d'être** to wait until one does/is; ~ **que** to wait until; ~ **qch de** to expect sth of; **en attendant** meanwhile, in the meantime; be that as it may
attendrir [atãdʀiʀ] vt to move (to pity); (viande) to tenderize
attendu, e [atãdy] adj (visiteur) expected; ~ **que** considering that, since
attentat [atãta] nm assassination attempt; ~ **à la bombe** bomb attack; ~ **à la pudeur** indecent exposure no pl; indecent assault no pl
attente [atãt] nf wait; (espérance) expectation
attenter [atãte]: ~ **à** vt (liberté) to violate; ~ **à la vie de qn** to make an attempt on sb's life
attentif, ive [atãtif, -iv] adj (auditeur) attentive; (travail) scrupulous; careful; ~ **à** mindful of; careful to
attention [atãsjɔ̃] nf attention; (prévenance) attention, thoughtfulness no pl; **à l'~ de** for the attention of; **faire** ~ **(à)** to be careful (of); **faire** ~ **(à ce) que** to be ou make sure that; ~**!** careful!, watch out!; **attentionné, e** adj thoughtful, considerate
atténuer [atenɥe] vt to alleviate, ease; to lessen
atterrer [ateʀe] vt to dismay, appal
atterrir [ateʀiʀ] vi to land; **atterrissage** nm landing
attestation [atɛstasjɔ̃] nf certificate
attester [atɛste] vt to testify to
attirail [atiʀaj] nm gear; (péj) paraphernalia
attirant, e [atiʀã, -ãt] adj attractive, appealing
attirer [atiʀe] vt to attract; (appâter) to lure, entice; ~ **qn dans un coin/vers soi** to draw sb into a corner/towards one; ~ **l'attention de qn (sur)** to attract sb's attention (to); to draw sb's attention (to); **s'~ des ennuis** to bring trouble upon o.s., get into trouble
attiser [atize] vt (feu) to poke (up)
attitré, e [atitʀe] adj qualified; accredited; appointed
attitude [atityd] nf attitude; (position du corps) bearing
attouchements [atuʃmã] nmpl touching sg; (sexuels) fondling sg
attraction [atʀaksjɔ̃] nf (gén) attraction; (de cabaret, cirque) number
attrait [atʀɛ] nm appeal, attraction; lure
attrape-nigaud [atʀapnigo] nm con
attraper [atʀape] vt (gén) to catch; (habi-

tude, amende) to get, pick up; (fam: duper) to con
attrayant, e [atʀɛjã, -ãt] adj attractive
attribuer [atʀibɥe] vt (prix) to award; (rôle, tâche) to allocate, assign; (imputer): ~ **qch à** to attribute sth to; **s'~** vt (s'approprier) to claim for o.s.
attribut [atʀiby] nm attribute; (LING) complement
attrister [atʀiste] vt to sadden
attroupement [atʀupmã] nm crowd, mob
attrouper [atʀupe]: **s'~** vi to gather
au [o] prép +dét = **à** +**le**
aubade [obad] nf dawn serenade
aubaine [obɛn] nf godsend; (financière) windfall
aube [ob] nf dawn, daybreak; **à l'~** at dawn ou daybreak
aubépine [obepin] nf hawthorn
auberge [obɛʀʒ(ə)] nf inn; ~ **de jeunesse** youth hostel
aubergine [obɛʀʒin] nf aubergine
aubergiste [obɛʀʒist(ə)] nm/f inn-keeper, hotel-keeper
aucun, e [okœ̃, -yn] dét no, tournure négative +any; (positif) any ♦ pron none, tournure négative +any; any(one); **sans** ~ **doute** without any doubt; **plus qu'~ autre** more than any other; ~ **des deux** neither of the two; ~ **d'entre eux** none of them; **d'~s** (certains) some; **aucunement** adv in no way, not in the least
audace [odas] nf daring, boldness; (péj) audacity; **audacieux, euse** adj daring, bold
au-delà [odla] adv beyond ♦ nm: **l'~** the hereafter; ~ **de** beyond
au-dessous [odsu] adv underneath; below; ~ **de** under(neath), below; (limite, somme etc) below, under; (dignité, condition) below
au-dessus [odsy] adv above; ~ **de** above
au-devant [odvã] : ~ **de** prép: **aller** ~ **de** (personne, danger) to go (out) and meet; (souhaits de qn) to anticipate
audience [odjãs] nf audience; (JUR: séance) hearing
audio-visuel, le [odjɔvizɥɛl] adj audio-visual
auditeur, trice [oditœʀ, -tʀis] nm/f listener
audition [odisjɔ̃] nf (ouïe, écoute) hearing; (JUR: de témoins) examination; (MUS, THÉÂTRE: épreuve) audition
auditoire [oditwaʀ] nm audience
auge [oʒ] nf trough
augmentation [ɔgmãtasjɔ̃] nf: ~ **(de salaire)** rise (in salary) (BRIT), (pay) raise (US)
augmenter [ɔgmãte] vt (gén) to increase; (salaire, prix) to increase, raise, put up; (employé) to increase the salary of ♦ vi to increase
augure [ɔgyʀ] nm soothsayer, oracle; **de bon/mauvais** ~ of good/ill omen; ~**r** [ɔgyʀe] vt: ~**r bien de** to augur well for

aujourd'hui [oʒuʀdɥi] *adv* today
aumône [omon] *nf inv* alms *sg*; **faire l'~** (**à qn**) to give alms (to sb)
aumônier [omonje] *nm* chaplain
auparavant [opaʀavã] *adv* before(hand)
auprès [opʀɛ]: ~ **de** *prép* next to, close to; (*recourir, s'adresser*) to; (*en comparaison de*) compared with
auquel [okɛl] *prép* +*pron* = **à** +**lequel**
aurai *etc vb voir* **avoir**
auréole [oʀeɔl] *nf* halo; (*tache*) ring
auriculaire [oʀikylɛʀ] *nm* little finger
aurons *etc vb voir* **avoir**
aurore [oʀoʀ] *nf* dawn, daybreak
ausculter [oskylte] *vt* to sound
aussi [osi] *adv* (*également*) also, too; (*de comparaison*) as ♦ *conj* therefore, consequently; ~ **fort que** as strong as; **moi** ~ me too; ~ **bien que** (*de même que*) as well as
aussitôt [osito] *adv* straight away, immediately; ~ **que** as soon as
austère [ostɛʀ] *adj* austere; stern
austral, e [ostʀal] *adj* southern
Australie [ostʀali] *nf*: **l'~** Australia; **australien, ne** *adj, nm/f* Australian
autant [otã] *adv* so much; (*comparatif*): ~ (**que**) as much (as); (*nombre*) as many (as); ~ (**de**) so much (*ou* many); as much (*ou* many); ~ **partir** we (*ou* you *etc*) may as well leave; ~ **dire que ...** one might as well say that ...; **pour** ~ for all that; **pour** ~ **que** assuming, as long as; **d'~ plus/mieux** (**que**) all the more/the better (since)
autel [otɛl] *nm* altar
auteur [otœʀ] *nm* author
authentique [otãtik] *adj* authentic, genuine
auto [oto] *nf* car
auto: ~**biographie** *nf* autobiography; ~**bus** *nm* bus; ~**car** *nm* coach
autochtone [otoktɔn] *nm/f* native
auto: ~**collant, e** *adj* self-adhesive; (*enveloppe*) self-seal ♦ *nm* sticker; ~**couchettes** *adj*: **train** ~**couchettes** car sleeper train; ~**cuiseur** *nm* pressure cooker; ~**défense** *nf* self-defence; **groupe d'~défense** vigilante committee; ~**didacte** *nm/f* self-taught person; ~**école** *nf* driving school; ~**gestion** *nf* self-management; ~**graphe** *nm* autograph
automate [otomat] *nm* (*machine*) (automatic) machine
automatique [otomatik] *adj* automatic ♦ *nm*: **l'~** direct dialling; **automatiser** *vt* to automate
automne [otɔn] *nm* autumn (*BRIT*), fall (*US*)
automobile [otomobil] *adj* motor *cpd* ♦ *nf* (motor) car; **l'~** motoring; the car industry; **automobiliste** *nm/f* motorist
autonome [otonɔm] *adj* autonomous; **autonomie** *nf* autonomy; (*POL*) self-government, autonomy
autopsie [otopsi] *nf* post-mortem (examination), autopsy
autoradio [otoʀadjo] *nm* car radio
autorisation [otoʀizasjɔ̃] *nf* permission, authorization; (*papiers*) permit
autorisé, e [otoʀize] *adj* (*opinion, sources*) authoritative
autoriser [otoʀize] *vt* to give permission for, authorize; (*fig*) to allow (of), sanction
autoritaire [otoʀitɛʀ] *adj* authoritarian
autorité [otoʀite] *nf* authority; **faire** ~ to be authoritative
autoroute [otoʀut] *nf* motorway (*BRIT*), highway (*US*)
auto-stop [otostɔp] *nm*: **faire de l'~** to hitch-hike; **auto-stoppeur, euse** *nm/f* hitch-hiker
autour [otuʀ] *adv* around; ~ **de** around; **tout** ~ all around

────────────────── **MOT CLÉ**

autre [otʀ(ə)] *adj* **1** (*différent*) other, different; **je préférerais un** ~ **verre** I'd prefer another *ou* a different glass
2 (*supplémentaire*) other; **je voudrais un** ~ **verre d'eau** I'd like another glass of water
3; ~ **chose** something else; ~ **part** somewhere else; **d'~ part** on the other hand
♦ *pron*: **un** ~ another (one); **nous/vous** ~**s** us/you; **d'~s** others; **l'~** the other (one); **les** ~**s** the others; (*autrui*) others; **l'un et l'~** both of them; **se détester l'un l'~/les uns les** ~**s** to hate each other *ou* one another; **d'une semaine à l'~** from one week to the next; (*incessamment*) any week now; **entre** ~**s** among other things

──────────────────────────────

autrefois [otʀəfwa] *adv* in the past
autrement [otʀəmã] *adv* differently; in another way; (*sinon*) otherwise; ~ **dit** in other words
Autriche [otʀiʃ] *nf*: **l'~** Austria; **autrichien, ne** *adj, nm/f* Austrian
autruche [otʀyʃ] *nf* ostrich
autrui [otʀɥi] *pron* others
auvent [ovã] *nm* canopy
aux [o] *prép* +*dét* = **à** +**les**
auxiliaire [oksiljɛʀ] *adj, nm/f* auxiliary
auxquelles [okɛl] *prép* +*pron* = **à** +**lesquelles**
auxquels [okɛl] *prép* +*pron* = **à** +**lesquels**
avachi, e [avaʃi] *adj* limp, flabby
aval [aval] *nm* (*accord*) endorsement, backing; (*GÉO*): **en** ~ downstream, downriver; (*sur une pente*) downhill
avalanche [avalãʃ] *nf* avalanche
avaler [avale] *vt* to swallow
avance [avãs] *nf* (*de troupes etc*) advance; progress; (*d'argent*) advance; (*opposé à retard*) lead; being ahead of schedule; ~**s** *nfpl* (*ouvertures*) overtures; (*amoureuses*) ad-

vances; **(être) en ~** (to be) early; (*sur un programme*) (to be) ahead of schedule; **à l'~, d'~** in advance

avancé, e [avɑ̃se] *adj* advanced; well on, well under way

avancement [avɑ̃smɑ̃] *nm* (*professionnel*) promotion

avancer [avɑ̃se] *vi* to move forward, advance; (*projet, travail*) to make progress; (*être en saillie*) to overhang; to jut out; (*montre, réveil*) to be fast; to gain ♦ *vt* to move forward, advance; (*argent*) to advance; (*montre, pendule*) to put forward; **s'~** *vi* to move forward, advance; (*fig*) to commit o.s.; to overhang; to jut out

avant [avɑ̃] *prép* before ♦ *adv*: **trop/plus ~** too far/further forward ♦ *adj inv*: **siège/roue ~** front seat/wheel ♦ *nm* (*d'un véhicule, bâtiment*) front; (*SPORT: joueur*) forward; **~ qu'il parte/de faire** before he leaves/doing; **~ tout** (*surtout*) above all; **à l'~** (*dans un véhicule*) in (the) front; **en ~** forward(s); **en ~ de** in front of

avantage [avɑ̃taʒ] *nm* advantage; **~s sociaux** fringe benefits; **avantager** *vt* (*favoriser*) to favour; (*embellir*) to flatter; **avantageux, euse** *adj* attractive; attractively priced

avant-: **~-bras** *nm inv* forearm; **~coureur** *adj inv*: **signe ~coureur** advance indication *ou* sign; **~-dernier, ière** *adj, nm/f* next to last, last but one; **~-goût** *nm* foretaste; **~-hier** *adv* the day before yesterday; **~-première** *nf* (*de film*) preview; **~-projet** *nm* (preliminary) draft; **~-propos** *nm* foreword; **~-veille** *nf*: **l'~** two days before

avare [avaʀ] *adj* miserly, avaricious ♦ *nm/f* miser; **~ de** (*compliments etc*) sparing of

avarié, e [avaʀje] *adj* rotting

avaries [avaʀi] *nfpl* (*NAVIG*) damage *sg*

avec [avɛk] *prép* with; (*à l'égard de*) to(wards), with

avenant, e [avnɑ̃, -ɑ̃t] *adj* pleasant; **à l'~** in keeping

avènement [avɛnmɑ̃] *nm* (*d'un roi*) accession, succession; (*d'un changement*) advent, coming

avenir [avniʀ] *nm* future; **à l'~** in future; **politicien d'~** politician with prospects *ou* a future

Avent [avɑ̃] *nm*: **l'~** Advent

aventure [avɑ̃tyʀ] *nf* adventure; (*amoureuse*) affair; **aventurer**: **s'aventurer** *vi* to venture; **aventureux, euse** *adj* adventurous, venturesome; (*projet*) risky, chancy

avenue [avny] *nf* avenue

avérer [aveʀe]: **s'~** *vb +attrib* to prove (to be)

averse [avɛʀs(ə)] *nf* shower

averti, e [avɛʀti] *adj* (well-)informed

avertir [avɛʀtiʀ] *vt*: **~ qn (de qch/que)** to warn sb (of sth/that); (*renseigner*) to in-

form sb (of sth/that); **avertissement** *nm* warning; **avertisseur** *nm* horn, siren

aveu, x [avø] *nm* confession

aveugle [avœgl(ə)] *adj* blind; **aveuglément** *adv* blindly; **~r** *vt* to blind

aviateur, trice [avjatœr, -tʀis] *nm/f* aviator, pilot

aviation [avjasjɔ̃] *nf* aviation; (*sport*) flying; (*MIL*) air force

avide [avid] *adj* eager; (*péj*) greedy, grasping

avilir [aviliʀ] *vt* to debase

avion [avjɔ̃] *nm* (aero)plane (*BRIT*), (air)plane (*US*); **aller (quelque part) en ~** to go (somewhere) by plane, fly (somewhere); **par ~** by airmail; **~ à réaction** jet (plane)

aviron [aviʀɔ̃] *nm* oar; (*sport*): **l'~** rowing

avis [avi] *nm* opinion; (*notification*) notice; **changer d'~** to change one's mind; **jusqu'à nouvel ~** until further notice

avisé, e [avize] *adj* sensible, wise

aviser [avize] *vt* (*voir*) to notice, catch sight of; (*informer*): **~ qn de/que** to advise *ou* inform sb of/that ♦ *vi* to think about things, assess the situation; **s'~ de qch/que** to become suddenly aware of sth/that; **s'~ de faire** to take it into one's head to do

avocat, e [avɔka, -at] *nm/f* (*JUR*) barrister (*BRIT*), lawyer ♦ *nm* (*CULIN*) avocado (pear); **~ général** assistant public prosecutor

avoine [avwan] *nf* oats *pl*

───── **MOT CLÉ**

avoir [avwaʀ] *nm* assets *pl*, resources *pl*; (*COMM*) credit

♦ *vt* **1** (*posséder*) to have; **elle a 2 enfants/une belle maison** she has (got) 2 children/a lovely house; **il a les yeux bleus** he has (got) blue eyes

2 (*âge, dimensions*) to be; **il a 3 ans** he is 3 (years old); **le mur a 3 mètres de haut** the wall is 3 metres high; *voir aussi* **faim**; **peur** *etc*

3 (*fam: duper*) to do, have; **on vous a eu!** you've been done *ou* had!

4: **en ~ contre qn** to have a grudge against sb; **en ~ assez** to be fed up; **j'en ai pour une demi-heure** it'll take me half an hour

♦ *vb aux* **1** to have; **~ mangé/dormi** to have eaten/slept

2 (*avoir +à +infinitif*): **~ à faire qch** to have to do sth; **vous n'avez qu'à lui demander** you only have to ask him

♦ *vb impers* **1**: **il y a** (+ *singulier*) there is; (+ *pluriel*) there are; **qu'y-a-t-il?**, **qu'est-ce qu'il y a?** what's the matter?, what is it?; **il doit y avoir une explication** there must be an explanation; **il n'y a qu'à ...** we (*ou* you *etc*) will just have to ...

2 (*temporel*): **il y a 10 ans** 10 years ago; **il**

y a 10 ans/longtemps que je le sais I've known it for 10 years/a long time; **il y a 10 ans qu'il est arrivé** it's 10 years since he arrived

avoisiner [avwazine] *vt* to be near *ou* close to; *(fig)* to border *ou* verge on

avortement [avɔʀtəmɑ̃] *nm* abortion

avorter [avɔʀte] *vi (MÉD)* to have an abortion; *(fig)* to fail

avoué, e [avwe] *adj* avowed ♦ *nm (JUR)* ≈ solicitor

avouer [avwe] *vt (crime, défaut)* to confess (to); ~ **avoir fait/que** to admit *ou* confess to having done/that

avril [avʀil] *nm* April

axe [aks(ə)] *nm* axis; *(de roue etc)* axle; *(fig)* main line; ~ **routier** main road, trunk road; **axer** *vt*: **axer qch sur** to centre sth on

ayons *etc vb voir* **avoir**

azote [azɔt] *nm* nitrogen

B b

babines [babin] *nfpl* chops

babiole [babjɔl] *nf (bibelot)* trinket; *(vétille)* trifle

bâbord [bɑbɔʀ] *nm*: **à** *ou* **par** ~ to port, on the port side

baby-foot [babifut] *nm* table football

bac [bak] *abr m* = **baccalauréat**; ♦ *nm (bateau)* ferry; *(récipient)* tub; tray; tank

baccalauréat [bakalɔʀea] *nm* high school diploma

bachelier, ière [baʃəlje, -jɛʀ] *nm/f holder of the baccalauréat*

bachoter [baʃɔte] *(fam) vi* to cram (for an exam)

bâcler [bɑkle] *vt* to botch (up)

badaud, e [bado, -od] *nm/f* idle onlooker, stroller

badigeonner [badiʒɔne] *vt* to distemper; to colourwash; *(barbouiller)* to daub

badin, e [badɛ̃, -in] *adj* playful

badiner [badine] *vi*: ~ **avec qch** to treat sth lightly

baffe [baf] *(fam) nf* slap, clout

bafouer [bafwe] *vt* to deride, ridicule

bafouiller [bafuje] *vi, vt* to stammer

bagage [bagaʒ] *nm*: ~s luggage *sg*; ~**s à main** hand-luggage

bagarre [bagaʀ] *nf* fight, brawl; **bagarrer:**

se bagarrer *vi* to have a fight *ou* scuffle, fight

bagatelle [bagatɛl] *nf* trifle

bagne [baɲ] *nm* penal colony

bagnole [baɲɔl] *(fam) nf* car

bagout [bagu] *nm*: **avoir du** ~ to have the gift of the gab

bague [bag] *nf* ring; ~ **de fiançailles** engagement ring; ~ **de serrage** clip

baguette [bagɛt] *nf* stick; *(cuisine chinoise)* chopstick; *(de chef d'orchestre)* baton; *(pain)* stick of (French) bread; ~ **magique** magic wand

baie [bɛ] *nf (GÉO)* bay; *(fruit)* berry; ~ **(vitrée)** picture window

baignade [bɛɲad] *nf* bathing

baigner [beɲe] *vt (bébé)* to bath; **se** ~ *vi* to have a swim, go swimming *ou* bathing; **baignoire** *nf* bath(tub)

bail [baj] *(pl* **baux)** *nm* lease

bâiller [bɑje] *vi* to yawn; *(être ouvert)* to gape

bâillon [bɑjɔ̃] *nm* gag; **bâillonner** *vt* to gag

bain [bɛ̃] *nm* bath; **prendre un** ~ to have a bath; **se mettre dans le** ~ *(fig)* to get into it *ou* things; ~ **de foule** walkabout; ~ **de soleil: prendre un** ~ **de soleil** to sunbathe; ~**s de mer** sea bathing *sg*; **bain-marie** *nm*: **faire chauffer au bain-marie** *(boîte etc)* to immerse in boiling water

baiser [beze] *nm* kiss ♦ *vt (main, front)* to kiss; *(fam!)* to screw *(!)*

baisse [bɛs] *nf* fall, drop; "~ **sur la viande"** "meat prices down"

baisser [bese] *vt* lower; *(radio, chauffage)* to turn down; *(AUTO: phares)* to dip *(BRIT)*, lower *(US)* ♦ *vi* to fall, drop, go down; **se** ~ *vi* to bend down

bal [bal] *nm* dance; *(grande soirée)* ball; ~ **costumé** fancy-dress ball

balader [balade] *vt (traîner)* to trail round; **se** ~ *vi* to go for a walk *ou* stroll; to go for a drive

baladeur [baladœʀ] *nm* personal stereo, Walkman (®)

balafre [balafʀ(ə)] *nf* gash, slash; *(cicatrice)* scar

balai [balɛ] *nm* broom, brush; **balai-brosse** *nm* (long-handled) scrubbing brush

balance [balɑ̃s] *nf* scales *pl*; *(de précision)* balance; *(signe)*: **la B**~ Libra

balancer [balɑ̃se] *vt* to swing; *(lancer)* to fling, chuck; *(renvoyer, jeter)* to chuck out ♦ *vi* to swing; **se** ~ *vi* to swing; to rock; to sway; **se** ~ **de** *(fam)* not to care about; **balancier** *nm (de pendule)* pendulum; *(perche)* (balancing) pole; **balançoire** *nf* swing; *(sur pivot)* seesaw

balayer [baleje] *vt (feuilles etc)* to sweep up, brush up; *(pièce)* to sweep; *(chasser)* to sweep away; to sweep aside; *(suj: radar)* to scan; **balayeur, euse** *nm/f* roadsweeper;

balayeuse [balɛjøz] *nf* (*machine*) roadsweeper

balbutier [balbysje] *vi, vt* to stammer

balcon [balkɔ̃] *nm* balcony; (*THÉÂTRE*) dress circle

baleine [balɛn] *nf* whale; (*de parapluie, corset*) rib; **baleinière** *nf* whaleboat

balise [baliz] *nf* (*NAVIG*) beacon; (*marker*) buoy; (*AVIAT*) runway light, beacon; (*AUTO, SKI*) sign, marker; **baliser** *vt* to mark out (with lights *etc*)

balivernes [balivɛrn(ə)] *nfpl* nonsense *sg*

ballant, e [balɑ̃, -ɑ̃t] *adj* dangling

balle [bal] *nf* (*de fusil*) bullet; (*de sport*) ball; (*paquet*) bale; (*fam: franc*) franc; ~ **perdue** stray bullet

ballerine [balrin] *nf* ballet dancer

ballet [balɛ] *nm* ballet

ballon [balɔ̃] *nm* (*de sport*) ball; (*jouet, AVIAT*) balloon; (*de vin*) glass; ~ **de football** football

ballot [balo] *nm* bundle; (*péj*) nitwit

ballottage [balɔtaʒ] *nm* (*POL*) second ballot

ballotter [balɔte] *vi* to roll around; to toss ♦ *vt* to shake about; to toss

balnéaire [balneɛr] *adj* seaside *cpd*

balourd, e [balur, -urd(ə)] *adj* clumsy ♦ *nm/f* clodhopper

balustrade [balystrad] *nf* railings *pl*, handrail

bambin [bɑ̃bɛ̃] *nm* little child

ban [bɑ̃] *nm* cheer; ~**s** *nmpl* (*de mariage*) banns; **mettre au** ~ **de** to outlaw from

banal, e [banal] *adj* banal, commonplace; (*péj*) trite

banane [banan] *nf* banana

banc [bɑ̃] *nm* seat, bench; (*de poissons*) shoal; ~ **d'essai** (*fig*) testing ground; ~ **de sable** sandbank

bancaire [bɑ̃kɛr] *adj* banking, bank *cpd*

bancal, e [bɑ̃kal] *adj* wobbly; bow-legged

bandage [bɑ̃daʒ] *nm* bandage

bande [bɑ̃d] *nf* (*de tissu etc*) strip; (*MÉD*) bandage; (*motif*) stripe; (*magnétique etc*) tape; (*groupe*) band; (: *péj*) bunch; **par la** ~ in a roundabout way; **faire** ~ **à part** to keep to o.s.; ~ **dessinée** comic strip; ~ **sonore** sound track

bandeau, x [bɑ̃do] *nm* headband; (*sur les yeux*) blindfold; (*MÉD*) head bandage

bander [bɑ̃de] *vt* (*blessure*) to bandage; (*muscle*) to tense; ~ **les yeux à qn** to blindfold sb

banderole [bɑ̃drɔl] *nf* banner, streamer

bandit [bɑ̃di] *nm* bandit; **banditisme** *nm* violent crime, armed robberies *pl*

bandoulière [bɑ̃duljɛr] *nf:* **en** ~ (slung *ou* worn) across the shoulder

banlieue [bɑ̃ljø] *nf* suburbs *pl*; **lignes/quartiers de** ~ suburban lines/areas; **trains de** ~ commuter trains

bannière [banjɛr] *nf* banner

bannir [banir] *vt* to banish

banque [bɑ̃k] *nf* bank; (*activités*) banking; ~ **d'affaires** merchant bank; ~**route** [bɑ̃krut] *nf* bankruptcy

banquet [bɑ̃kɛ] *nm* dinner; (*d'apparat*) banquet

banquette [bɑ̃kɛt] *nf* seat

banquier [bɑ̃kje] *nm* banker

banquise [bɑ̃kiz] *nf* ice field

baptême [batɛm] *nm* christening; baptism; ~ **de l'air** first flight

baquet [bakɛ] *nm* tub, bucket

bar [bar] *nm* bar

baraque [barak] *nf* shed; (*fam*) house; ~ **foraine** fairground stand

baraqué, e [barake] *adj* well-built, hefty

baraquements [barakmɑ̃] *nmpl* (*pour réfugiés, ouvriers*) huts

baratin [baratɛ̃] (*fam*) *nm* smooth talk, patter; **baratiner** *vt* to chat up

barbare [barbar] *adj* barbaric

barbe [barb(ə)] *nf* beard; **quelle** ~! (*fam*) what a drag *ou* bore!; **à la** ~ **de qn** under sb's nose; ~ **à papa** candy-floss (*BRIT*), cotton candy (*US*)

barbelé [barbəle] *nm* barbed wire *no pl*

barboter [barbɔte] *vi* to paddle, dabble; **barboteuse** [barbɔtøz] *nf* rompers *pl*

barbouiller [barbuje] *vt* to daub; **avoir l'estomac barbouillé** to feel queasy

barbu, e [barby] *adj* bearded

barda [barda] (*fam*) *nm* kit, gear

barder [barde] (*fam*) *vi:* **ça va** ~ sparks will fly, things are going to get hot

barème [barɛm] *nm* scale; table

baril [baril] *nm* barrel; keg

bariolé, e [barjɔle] *adj* gaudily-coloured

baromètre [barɔmɛtr(ə)] *nm* barometer

baron [barɔ̃] *nm* baron; **baronne** *nf* baroness

baroque [barɔk] *adj* (*ART*) baroque; (*fig*) weird

barque [bark(ə)] *nf* small boat

barquette [barkɛt] *nf* (*pour repas*) tray; (*pour fruits*) punnet

barrage [baraʒ] *nm* dam; (*sur route*) roadblock, barricade

barre [bar] *nf* bar; (*NAVIG*) helm; (*écrite*) line, stroke

barreau, x [baro] *nm* bar; (*JUR*): **le** ~ the Bar

barrer [bare] *vt* (*route etc*) to block; (*mot*) to cross out; (*chèque*) to cross (*BRIT*); (*NAVIG*) to steer; **se** ~ *vi* (*fam*) to clear off

barrette [barɛt] *nf* (*pour cheveux*) (hair) slide (*BRIT*) *ou* clip (*US*)

barricader [barikade] *vt* to barricade

barrière [barjɛr] *nf* fence; (*obstacle*) barrier; (*porte*) gate

barrique [barik] *nf* barrel, cask

bas, basse [ba, bas] *adj* low ♦ *nm* bottom, lower part; (*vêtement*) stocking ♦ *adv* low;

(parler) softly; **au ~ mot** at the lowest estimate; **en ~** down below; **at** *(ou* to) the bottom; *(dans une maison)* downstairs; **en ~ de** at the bottom of; **mettre ~** to give birth; **à ~ ...!** down with ...!; **~ morceaux** *nmpl (viande)* cheap cuts

basané, e [bazane] *adj* tanned, bronzed

bas-côté [bakote] *nm (de route)* verge *(BRIT)*, shoulder *(US)*

bascule [baskyl] *nf:* **(jeu de) ~** seesaw; **(balance à) ~** scales *pl;* **fauteuil à ~** rocking chair

basculer [baskyle] *vi* to fall over, topple (over); *(benne)* to tip up ♦ *vt* to topple over; to tip out, tip up

base [bɑz] *nf* base; *(POL)* rank and file; *(fondement, principe)* basis; **de ~** basic; **à ~ de café** *etc* coffee *etc* -based; **~ de données** database; **baser** *vt* to base; **se ~r sur** *vt (preuves)* to base one's argument on

bas-fond [bafɔ̃] *nm (NAVIG)* shallow; **~s** *nmpl (fig)* dregs

basilic [bazilik] *nm (CULIN)* basil

basket [baskɛt] *nm* trainer *(BRIT)*, sneaker *(US); (aussi: ~-ball)* basketball

basque [bask(ə)] *adj, nm/f* Basque

basse [bɑs] *adj voir* **bas** ♦ *nf (MUS)* bass; **~-cour** *nf* farmyard

bassin [basɛ̃] *nm (cuvette)* bowl; *(pièce d'eau)* pond, pool; *(de fontaine, GÉO)* basin; *(ANAT)* pelvis; *(portuaire)* dock

bassine [basin] *nf (ustensile)* basin; *(contenu)* bowl(ful)

basson [basɔ̃] *nm* bassoon

bas-ventre [bavɑ̃tR(ə)] *nm* (lower part of the) stomach

bat *vb voir* **battre**

bât [bɑ] *nm* packsaddle

bataille [batɑj] *nf* battle; fight

bâtard, e [bataR, -aRd(ə)] *nm/f* illegitimate child, bastard *(pej)*

bateau, x [bato] *nm* boat, ship; **bateau-mouche** *nm* passenger pleasure boat *(on the Seine)*

batelier, ière [batəlje, -jɛR] *nm/f (de bac)* ferryman(woman)

bâti, e [bati] *adj:* **bien ~** well-built

batifoler [batifɔle] *vi* to frolic about

bâtiment [batimɑ̃] *nm* building; *(NAVIG)* ship, vessel; *(industrie)* building trade

bâtir [batiR] *vt* to build

bâtisse [batis] *nf* building

bâton [batɔ̃] *nm* stick; **à ~s rompus** informally

bats *vb voir* **battre**

battage [bataʒ] *nm (publicité)* (hard) plugging

battant [batɑ̃] *nm (de cloche)* clapper; *(de volets)* shutter, flap; *(de porte)* side; *(fig: personne)* fighter; **porte à double ~** double door

battement [batmɑ̃] *nm (de cœur)* beat; *(intervalle)* interval *(between classes, trains)*; **10 minutes de ~** 10 minutes to spare; **~ de paupières** blinking *no pl (of eyelids)*

batterie [batRi] *nf (MIL, ÉLEC)* battery; *(MUS)* drums *pl,* drum kit; **~ de cuisine** pots and pans *pl;* kitchen utensils *pl*

batteur [batœR] *nm (MUS)* drummer; *(appareil)* whisk

battre [batR(ə)] *vt* to beat; *(suj: pluie, vagues)* to beat *ou* lash against; *(blé)* to thresh; *(passer au peigne fin)* to scour ♦ *vi (cœur)* to beat; *(volets etc)* to bang, rattle; **se ~** *vi* to fight; **~ la mesure** to beat time; **~ en brèche** to demolish; **~ son plein** to be at its height, be going full swing; **~ des mains** to clap one's hands

battue [baty] *nf (chasse)* beat; *(policière etc)* search, hunt

baume [bom] *nm* balm

baux [bo] *nmpl de* **bail**

bavard, e [bavaR, -aRd(ə)] *adj* (very) talkative; gossipy; **bavarder** *vi* to chatter; *(indiscrètement)* to gossip; to blab

bave [bav] *nf* dribble; *(de chien etc)* slobber; *(d'escargot)* slime; **~r** *vi* to dribble; to slobber; **en ~r** *(fam)* to have a hard time (of it); **~tte** *nf* bib; **baveux, euse** *adj (omelette)* runny

bavure [bavyR] *nf* smudge; *(fig)* hitch; blunder

bayer [baje] *vi:* **~ aux corneilles** to stand gaping

bazar [bazaR] *nm* general store; *(fam)* jumble; **~der** *(fam) vt* to chuck out

B.C.B.G. *sigle adj (= bon chic bon genre)* preppy, smart and trendy

B.C.G. *sigle m (= bacille Calmette-Guérin)* BCG

bd. *abr =* **boulevard**

B.D. *sigle f =* **bande dessinée**

béant, e [beɑ̃, -ɑ̃t] *adj* gaping

béat, e [bea, -at] *adj* showing open-eyed wonder; blissful; **béatitude** *nf* bliss

beau(bel), belle [bo, bɛl] *(mpl* **~x)** *adj* beautiful, lovely; *(homme)* handsome ♦ *adv:* **il fait ~** the weather's fine; **un ~ jour** one (fine) day; **de plus belle** more than ever, even more; **on a ~ essayer** however hard we try; **bel et bien** well and truly; **faire le ~** *(chien)* to sit up and beg

---

MOT CLÉ

beaucoup [boku] *adv* **1** a lot; **il boit ~** he drinks a lot; **il ne boit pas ~** he doesn't drink much *ou* a lot

2 *(suivi de plus, trop etc)* much, a lot, far; **il est ~ plus grand** he is much *ou* a lot *ou* far taller

3. **~ de** *(nombre)* many, a lot of; *(quantité)* a lot of; **~ d'étudiants/de touristes** a lot of *ou* many students/tourists; **~ de courage** a lot of courage; **il n'a pas ~ d'argent**

he hasn't got much *ou* at lot of money
4: de ~ by far

beau: ~-fils *nm* son-in-law; *(remariage)*
stepson; **~-frère** *nm* brother-in-law; **~-père** *nm* father-in-law; *(remariage)* step-
father

beauté [bote] *nf* beauty; **de toute ~** beautiful; **en ~** brilliantly

beaux-arts [bozaR] *nmpl* fine arts

beaux-parents [boparū] *nmpl* wife's *(ou*
husband's) family, in-laws

bébé [bebe] *nm* baby

bec [bɛk] *nm* beak, bill; *(de récipient)* spout;
lip; *(fam)* mouth; **~ de gaz** (street) gas-
lamp; **~ verseur** pouring lip

bécane [bekan] *(fam)* nf bike

bec-de-lièvre [bɛkdəljɛvR(ə)] *nm* harelip

bêche [bɛʃ] *nf* spade; **bêcher** *vt* to dig

bécoter [bekɔte]: **se ~** *vi* to smooch

becqueter [bɛkte] *(fam)* vt to eat

bedaine [bədɛn] *nf* paunch

bedonnant, e [bədɔnā, -āt] *adj* potbellied

bée [be] *adj:* **bouche ~** gaping

beffroi [befRwa] *nm* belfry

bégayer [begeje] *vt, vi* to stammer

bègue [bɛg] *nm/f:* **être ~** to have a stammer

béguin [begɛ̃] *nm:* **avoir le ~ de** *ou* **pour**
to have a crush on

beige [bɛʒ] *adj* beige

beignet [bɛɲɛ] *nm* fritter

bel [bɛl] *adj voir* beau

bêler [bele] *vi* to bleat

belette [bəlɛt] *nf* weasel

belge [bɛlʒ(ə)] *adj, nm/f* Belgian

Belgique [bɛlʒik] *nf:* **la ~** Belgium

bélier [belje] *nm* ram; *(signe):* **le B~** Aries

belle [bɛl] *adj voir* beau **♦** *nf* (SPORT) de-
cider; **~-fille** *nf* daughter-in-law; *(remariage)* stepdaughter; **~-mère** *nf* mother-in-
law; stepmother; **~-sœur** *nf* sister-in-law

belliqueux, euse [belikø, -øz] *adj* aggressive, warlike

belvédère [belvedeR] *nm* panoramic viewpoint *(or small building there)*

bémol [bemɔl] *nm* (MUS) flat

bénédiction [benediksjɔ̃] *nf* blessing

bénéfice [benefis] *nm* (COMM) profit;
(avantage) benefit; **bénéficier de** *vt* to enjoy; to benefit by *ou* from; to get, be given;
bénéfique *adj* beneficial

benêt [bənɛ] *nm* simpleton

bénévole [benevɔl] *adj* voluntary, unpaid

bénin, igne [benɛ̃, -iɲ] *adj* minor, mild;
(tumeur) benign

bénir [beniR] *vt* to bless; **bénit, e** *adj* con-
secrated; **eau bénite** holy water

benjamin, e [bɛ̃ʒamɛ̃, -in] *nm/f* youngest
child

benne [bɛn] *nf* skip; *(de téléphérique)*
(cable) car; **~ basculante** tipper *(BRIT)*,

dump truck *(US)*

B.E.P.C. *sigle m* = **brevet d'études du premier cycle**

béquille [bekij] *nf* crutch; *(de bicyclette)*
stand

berceau, x [bɛRso] *nm* cradle, crib

bercer [bɛRse] *vt* to rock, cradle; *(suj: musique etc)* to lull; **~ qn de** *(promesses etc)* to
delude sb with; **berceuse** *nf* lullaby

béret (basque) [beRɛ(bask(ə))] *nm* beret

berge [bɛRʒ(ə)] *nf* bank

berger, ère [bɛRʒe, -ɛR] *nm/f* shep-
herd(ess)

berlingot [bɛRlɛ̃go] *nm:* *(emballage)* carton
(pyramid shaped)

berlue [bɛRly] *nf:* **j'ai la ~** I must be seeing
things

berner [bɛRne] *vt* to fool

besogne [bəzɔɲ] *nf* work *no pl,* job

besoin [bəzwɛ̃] *nm* need; *(pauvreté):* **le ~**
need, want; **faire ses ~s** to relieve o.s.;
avoir ~ de qch/faire qch to need sth/to
do sth; **au ~** if need be

bestiaux [bɛstjo] *nmpl* cattle

bestiole [bɛstjɔl] *nf* (tiny) creature

bétail [betaj] *nm* livestock, cattle *pl*

bête [bɛt] *nf* animal; *(bestiole)* insect, creature **♦** *adj* stupid, silly; **il cherche la petite
~** he's being pernickety *ou* overfussy; **~
noire** pet hate

bêtise [betiz] *nf* stupidity; stupid thing (to
say *ou* do)

béton [betɔ̃] *nm* concrete; **(en) ~** *(alibi, argument)* cast iron; **~ armé** reinforced concrete; **bétonnière** *nf* cement mixer

betterave [bɛtRav] *nf* beetroot *(BRIT)*, beet
(US); **~ sucrière** sugar beet

beugler [bøgle] *vi* to low; *(radio etc)* to
blare **♦** *vt* *(chanson)* to bawl out

Beur [bœR] *nm/f* person of North African origin living in France

beurre [bœR] *nm* butter; **beurrer** *vt* to butter; **beurrier** [bœRje] *nm* butter dish

beuverie [bœvRi] *nf* drinking session

bévue [bevy] *nf* blunder

Beyrouth [beRut] *n* Beirut

bi... [bi] *préfixe* bi..., two-

biais [bjɛ] *nm* *(moyen)* device, expedient;
(aspect) angle; **en ~, de ~** *(obliquement)* at
an angle; *(fig)* indirectly; **biaiser** *vi* (fig) to
sidestep the issue

bibelot [biblo] *nm* trinket, curio

biberon [bibRɔ̃] *nm* (feeding) bottle; **nourrir
au ~** to bottle-feed

bible [bibl(ə)] *nf* bible

biblio... *préfixe:* **~bus** *nm* mobile library
van; **~phile** *nm/f* booklover; **~thécaire**
nm/f librarian; **~thèque** *nf* library; *(meuble)* bookcase

bicarbonate [bikaRbɔnat] *nm:* **~ (de soude)** bicarbonate of soda

biceps [bisɛps] *nm* biceps

biche [biʃ] nf doe
bichonner [biʃɔne] vt to groom
bicolore [bikɔlɔʀ] adj two-coloured
bicoque [bikɔk] (péj) nf shack
bicyclette [bisiklɛt] nf bicycle
bide [bid] nm (fam: ventre) belly; (THÉÂTRE) flop
bidet [bidɛ] nm bidet
bidon [bidɔ̃] nm can ♦ adj inv (fam) phoney
bidonville [bidɔ̃vil] nm shanty town
bidule [bidyl] (fam) nm thingumajig
bielle [bjɛl] nf connecting rod

MOT CLÉ

bien [bjɛ̃] nm **1** (avantage, profit): **faire du ~ à qn** to do sb good; **dire du ~ de** to speak well of; **c'est pour son ~** it's for his own good
2 (possession, patrimoine) possession, property; **son ~ le plus précieux** his most treasured possession; **avoir du ~** to have property; **~s (de consommation etc)** (consumer etc) goods
3 (moral): **le ~** good; **distinguer le ~ du mal** to tell good from evil
♦ adv **1** (de façon satisfaisante) well; **elle travaille/mange ~** she works/eats well; **croyant ~ faire, je/il ...** thinking I/he was doing the right thing, I/he ...; **c'est ~ fait!** it serves him (ou her etc) right!
2 (valeur intensive) quite; **~ jeune** quite young; **~ assez** quite enough; **~ mieux** (very) much better; **j'espère ~ y aller** I do hope to go; **je veux ~ le faire** (concession) I'm quite willing to do it; **il faut ~ le faire** it has to be done
3: **~ du temps/des gens** quite a time/a number of people
♦ adj inv **1** (en bonne forme, à l'aise): **je me sens ~** I feel fine; **je ne me sens pas ~** I don't feel well; **on est ~ dans ce fauteuil** this chair is very comfortable
2 (joli, beau) good-looking; **tu es ~ dans cette robe** you look good in that dress
3 (satisfaisant) good; **elle est ~, cette maison/secrétaire** it's a good house/she's a good secretary
4 (moralement) right; (: personne) good, nice; (respectable) respectable; **ce n'est pas ~ de ...** it's not right to ...; **elle est ~, cette femme** she's a nice woman, she's a good sort; **des gens ~s** respectable people
5 (en bons termes): **être ~ avec qn** to be on good terms with sb
♦ préfixe: **~-aimé** adj, nm/f beloved; **~-être** nm well-being; **~faisance** nf charity; **~faisant, e** adj (chose) beneficial; **~fait** nm act of generosity, benefaction; (de la science etc) benefit; **~faiteur, trice** nm/f benefactor/benefactress; **~-fondé** nm soundness; **~-fonds** nm property; **~heureux, euse** adj happy; (REL) blessed, blest;

~ que conj (al)though; **~ sûr** adv certainly

bienséant, e [bjɛ̃seã, -ãt] adj seemly
bientôt [bjɛ̃to] adv soon; **à ~** see you soon
bienveillant, e [bjɛ̃vɛjã, -ãt] adj kindly
bienvenu, e [bjɛ̃vny] adj welcome; **bienvenue** nf: **souhaiter la ~e à** to welcome; **~e à** welcome to
bière [bjɛʀ] nf (boisson) beer; (cercueil) bier; **~ (à la) pression** draught beer; **~ blonde** lager; **~ brune** brown ale
biffer [bife] vt to cross out
bifteck [biftɛk] nm steak
bifurquer [bifyʀke] vi (route) to fork; (véhicule) to turn off
bigarré, e [bigaʀe] adj multicoloured; (disparate) motley
bigorneau, x [bigɔʀno] nm winkle
bigot, e [bigo, -ɔt] (péj) adj bigoted
bigoudi [bigudi] nm curler
bijou, x [biʒu] nm jewel; **bijouterie** nf jeweller's (shop); jewellery; **bijoutier, ière** nm/f jeweller
bilan [bilã] nm (COMM) balance sheet(s); end of year statement; (fig) (net) outcome; (: de victimes) toll; **faire le ~ de** to assess; to review; **déposer son ~** to file a bankruptcy statement
bile [bil] nf bile; **se faire de la ~** (fam) to worry o.s. sick
bilieux, euse [biljø, -jøz] adj bilious; (fig: colérique) testy
bilingue [bilɛ̃g] adj bilingual
billard [bijaʀ] nm billiards sg; billiard table; **c'est du ~** (fam) it's a cinch
bille [bij] nf (gén) ball; (du jeu de billes) marble; (de bois) log
billet [bijɛ] nm (aussi: ~ de banque) (bank)note; (de cinéma, de bus etc) ticket; (courte lettre) note; **~ circulaire** round-trip ticket
billetterie [bijɛtʀi] nf ticket office; (distributeur) ticket machine; (BANQUE) cash dispenser
billion [biljɔ̃] nm billion (BRIT), trillion (US)
billot [bijo] nm block
bimensuel, le [bimãsɥɛl] adj bimonthly
binette [binɛt] nf hoe
binocle [binɔkl(ə)] nm pince-nez
bio... préfixe bio...; **~graphie** nf biography; **~logie** nf biology; **~logique** adj biological
Birmanie [biʀmani] nf Burma
bis¹, e [bi, biz] adj (couleur) greyish brown
bis² [bis] adv: **12 bis** 12a ou A ♦ excl, nm encore
bisannuel, le [bizanɥɛl] adj biennial
biscornu, e [biskɔʀny] adj twisted
biscotte [biskɔt] nf (breakfast) rusk
biscuit [biskɥi] nm biscuit; sponge cake
bise [biz] nf (baiser) kiss; (vent) North wind
bissextile [bisɛkstil] adj: **année ~** leap year

bistouri [bisturi] *nm* lancet

bistro(t) [bistro] *nm* bistro, café

bitume [bitym] *nm* asphalt

bizarre [bizar] *adj* strange, odd

blafard, e [blafar, -ard(ə)] *adj* wan

blague [blag] *nf* (*propos*) joke; (*farce*) trick; **sans ~!** no kidding!; **~ à tabac** tobacco pouch

blaguer [blage] *vi* to joke ♦ *vt* to tease

blaireau, x [blɛro] *nm* (*ZOOL*) badger; (*brosse*) shaving brush

blairer [blɛre] (*fam*) *vt*: **je ne peux pas le ~** I can't bear *ou* stand him

blâme [blam] *nm* blame; (*sanction*) reprimand

blâmer [blame] *vt* to blame

blanc, blanche [blɑ̃, blɑ̃ʃ] *adj* white; (*non imprimé*) blank; (*innocent*) pure ♦ *nm/f* white, white man(woman) ♦ *nm* (*couleur*) white; (*espace non écrit*) blank; (*aussi*: **~ d'œuf**) (egg-)white; (: **~ de poulet**) breast, white meat; (: *vin* **~**) white wine; **~ cassé** off-white; **chèque en ~** blank cheque; **à ~** (*chauffer*) white-hot; (*tirer, charger*) with blanks; **~-bec** *nm* greenhorn; **blanche** *nf* (*MUS*) minim (*BRIT*), half-note (*US*); **blancheur** *nf* whiteness

blanchir [blɑ̃ʃir] *vt* (*gén*) to whiten; (*linge*) to launder; (*CULIN*) to blanch; (*fig*: *disculper*) to clear ♦ *vi* to grow white; (*cheveux*) to go white

blanchisserie *nf* laundry

blason [blazɔ̃] *nm* coat of arms

blazer [blazɛr] *nm* blazer

blé [ble] *nm* wheat; **~ noir** (*nm*) buckwheat

bled [blɛd] (*péj*) *nm* hole

blême [blɛm] *adj* pale

blessé, e [blese] *adj* injured ♦ *nm/f* injured person; casualty

blesser [blese] *vt* to injure; (*délibérément*: *MIL etc*) to wound; (*suj*: *souliers etc, offenser*) to hurt; **se ~** to injure o.s.; **se ~ au pied etc** to injure one's foot *etc*

blessure [blesyr] *nf* injury; wound

bleu, e [blø] *adj* blue; (*bifteck*) very rare ♦ *nm* (*couleur*) blue; (*novice*) greenhorn; (*contusion*) bruise; (*vêtement*: *aussi*: **~s**) overalls *pl*; **~ marine** navy blue

bleuet [bløɛ] *nm* cornflower

bleuté, e [bløte] *adj* blue-shaded

blinder [blɛ̃de] *vt* to armour; (*fig*) to harden

bloc [blɔk] *nm* (*de pierre etc*) block; (*de papier à lettres*) pad; (*ensemble*) group, block; **serré à ~** tightened right down; **en ~** as a whole; wholesale; **~ opératoire** operating *ou* theatre block; **~ sanitaire** toilet block; **~age** [blɔkaʒ] *nm* blocking; jamming; freezing; (*PSYCH*) hang-up

bloc-notes [blɔknɔt] *nm* note pad

blocus [blɔkys] *nm* blockade

blond, e [blɔ̃, -ɔ̃d] *adj* fair; blond; (*sable, blés*) golden; **~ cendré** ash blond

bloquer [blɔke] *vt* (*passage*) to block; (*pièce mobile*) to jam; (*crédits, compte*) to freeze

blottir [blɔtir]: **se ~** *vi* to huddle up

blouse [bluz] *nf* overall

blouson [bluzɔ̃] *nm* blouson jacket; **~ noir** (*fig*) ≈ rocker

bluff [blœf] *nm* bluff

bluffer [blœfe] *vi* to bluff

bobard [bɔbar] (*fam*) *nm* tall story

bobine [bɔbin] *nf* reel; (*ÉLEC*) coil

bocal, aux [bɔkal, -o] *nm* jar

bock [bɔk] *nm* glass of beer

bœuf [bœf, *pl* bø] *nm* ox, steer; (*CULIN*) beef

bof! [bɔf] (*fam*) *excl* don't care!; (*pas terrible*) nothing special

bohème [bɔɛm] *adj* happy-go-lucky, unconventional; **bohémien, ne** [bɔemjɛ̃, -jɛn] *nm/f* gipsy

boire [bwar] *vt* to drink; (*s'imprégner de*) to soak up; **~ un coup** to have a drink

bois [bwa] *nm* wood; **de ~, en ~** wooden

boisé, e [bwaze] *adj* woody, wooded

boisson [bwasɔ̃] *nf* drink; **pris de ~** drunk, intoxicated

boîte [bwat] *nf* box; (*entreprise*) place, firm; **aliments en ~** canned *ou* tinned (*BRIT*) foods; **~ à gants** glove compartment; **~ aux lettres** letter box; **~ d'allumettes** box of matches; (*vide*) matchbox; **~ (de conserve)** can *ou* tin (*BRIT*) (of food); **~ de nuit** night club; **~ de vitesses** gear box; **~ postale** PO Box

boiter [bwate] *vi* to limp; (*fig*) to wobble; to be shaky

boîtier [bwatje] *nm* case

boive *etc vb voir* **boire**

bol [bɔl] *nm* bowl; **un ~ d'air** a breath of fresh air; **j'en ai ras le ~** (*fam*) I'm fed up with this

bolide [bɔlid] *nm* racing car; **comme un ~** at top speed, like a rocket

bombance [bɔ̃bɑ̃s] *nf*: **faire ~** to have a feast, revel

bombarder [bɔ̃barde] *vt* to bomb; **~ qn de** (*cailloux, lettres*) to bombard sb with; **bombardier** *nm* bomber

bombe [bɔ̃b] *nf* bomb; (*atomiseur*) (aerosol) spray

bomber [bɔ̃be] *vi* to bulge; to camber ♦ *vt*: **~ le torse** to swell out one's chest

─── *MOT CLÉ*

bon, bonne [bɔ̃, bɔn] *adj* **1** (*agréable, satisfaisant*) good; **un ~ repas/restaurant** a good meal/restaurant; **être ~ en maths** to be good at maths

2 (*charitable*): **être ~ (envers)** to be good (to)

3 (*correct*) right; **le ~ numéro/moment** the

right number/moment
4 (souhaits): ~ **anniversaire** happy birthday; ~ **voyage** have a good trip; **bonne chance** good luck; **bonne année** happy New Year; **bonne nuit** good night
5 (approprié): ~ **à/pour** fit to/for
6: ~ **enfant** adj inv accommodating, easygoing; **bonne femme** (péj) woman; **de bonne heure** early; ~ **marché** adj inv cheap ♦ adv cheap; ~ **mot** witticism; ~ **sens** common sense; ~ **vivant** jovial chap; **bonnes œuvres** charitable works, charities ♦ nm **1** (billet) voucher; (aussi: ~ **cadeau**) gift voucher; ~ **d'essence** petrol coupon; ~ **du Trésor** Treasury bond
2: **avoir du** ~ to have its good points; **pour de** ~ for good
♦ adv: **il fait** ~ it's ou the weather is fine; **sentir** ~ to smell good; **tenir** ~ to stand firm
♦ excl good!; **ah ~?** really?; voir aussi **bonne**

bonbon [bɔ̃bɔ̃] nm (boiled) sweet
bonbonne [bɔ̃bɔn] nf demijohn
bond [bɔ̃] nm leap; **faire un** ~ to leap in the air
bonde [bɔ̃d] nf bunghole
bondé, e [bɔ̃de] adj packed (full)
bondir [bɔ̃dir] vi to leap
bonheur [bɔnœr] nm happiness; **porter** ~ (**à qn**) to bring (sb) luck; **au petit** ~ haphazardly; **par** ~ fortunately
bonhomie [bɔnɔmi] nf goodnaturedness
bonhomme [bɔnɔm] (pl **bonshommes**) nm fellow; ~ **de neige** snowman
bonification [bɔnifikasjɔ̃] nf bonus
bonifier [bɔnifje] vt to improve
boniment [bɔnimɑ̃] nm patter no pl
bonjour [bɔ̃ʒur] excl, nm hello; good morning (ou afternoon)
bonne [bɔn] adj voir **bon** ♦ nf (domestique) maid; ~ **à tout faire** general help; ~ **d'enfant** nanny; **~ment** adv: **tout ~ment** quite simply
bonnet [bɔnɛ] nm bonnet, hat; (de soutien-gorge) cup; ~ **d'âne** dunce's cap; ~ **de bain** bathing cap
bonneterie [bɔnɛtri] nf hosiery
bonshommes [bɔ̃zɔm] nmpl de **bonhomme**
bonsoir [bɔ̃swar] excl good evening
bonté [bɔ̃te] nf kindness no pl
bonus [bɔnys] nm no-claims bonus
bord [bɔr] nm (de table, verre, falaise) edge; (de rivière, lac) bank; (de route) side; (monter) **à** ~ (to go) on board; **jeter par-dessus** ~ to throw overboard; **le commandant de ~/les hommes du** ~ the ship's master/crew; **au** ~ **de la mer** at the seaside; **être au** ~ **des larmes** to be on the verge of tears
bordeaux [bɔrdo] nm Bordeaux (wine) ♦

adj inv maroon
bordel [bɔrdɛl] nm brothel; (fam!) bloody mess (!)
border [bɔrde] vt (être le long de) to border; to line; (garnir): ~ **qch de** to line sth with; to trim sth with; (qn dans son lit) to tuck up
bordereau, x [bɔrdəro] nm slip; statement
bordure [bɔrdyr] nf border; **en** ~ **de** on the edge of
borgne [bɔrɲ(ə)] adj one-eyed
borne [bɔrn(ə)] nf boundary stone; (aussi: ~ **kilométrique**) kilometre-marker, ≈ milestone; **~s** nfpl (fig) limits; **dépasser les ~s** to go too far
borné, e [bɔrne] adj narrow; narrow-minded
borner [bɔrne] vt to limit; to confine; **se** ~ **à faire** to content o.s. with doing; to limit o.s. to doing
Bosnie-Herzégovine [bɔzni-ɛrtzegɔvin] nf Bosnia (and) Herzegovina
bosquet [bɔskɛ] nm grove
bosse [bɔs] nf (de terrain etc) bump; (enflure) lump; (du bossu, du chameau) hump; **avoir la** ~ **des maths** etc to have a gift for maths etc; **il a roulé sa** ~ he's been around
bosser [bɔse] (fam) vi to work; to slave (away)
bossu, e [bɔsy] nm/f hunchback
bot [bo] adj m: **pied** ~ club foot
botanique [bɔtanik] nf botany ♦ adj botanic(al)
botte [bɔt] nf (soulier) (high) boot; (gerbe): ~ **de paille** bundle of straw; ~ **de radis** bunch of radishes; **~s de caoutchouc** wellington boots; **~r** [bɔte] vt to put boots on; to kick; (fam)!: **ça me botte** ! fancy that
bottin [bɔtɛ̃] nm directory
bottine [bɔtin] nf ankle boot
bouc [buk] nm goat; (barbe) goatee; ~ **émissaire** scapegoat
boucan [bukɑ̃] nm din, racket
bouche [buʃ] nf mouth; **le** ~ **à** ~ the kiss of life; ~ **d'égout** manhole; ~ **d'incendie** fire hydrant; ~ **de métro** métro entrance
bouché, e [buʃe] adj (temps, ciel) overcast; (péj: personne) thick
bouchée [buʃe] nf mouthful; **~s à la reine** chicken vol-au-vents
boucher, ère [buʃe, -ɛr] nm/f butcher ♦ vt (pour colmater) to stop up; to fill up; (obstruer) to block (up); **se** ~ vi (tuyau etc) to block up, get blocked up; **se** ~ **le nez** to hold one's nose; **~rie** [buʃri] nf butcher's (shop); (fig) slaughter
bouche-trou [buʃtru] nm (fig) stop-gap
bouchon [buʃɔ̃] nm stopper; (en liège) cork; (fig: embouteillage) holdup; (PÊCHE) float; ~ **doseur** measuring cap
boucle [bukl(ə)] nf (forme, figure) loop;

(*objet*) buckle; ~ (**de cheveux**) curl; ~
d'oreilles earring
bouclé, e [bukle] *adj* curly
boucler [bukle] *vt* (*fermer: ceinture etc*) to
fasten; (: *magasin*) to shut; (*terminer*) to
finish off; (: *budget*) to balance; (*enfermer*)
to shut away; (: *quartier*) to seal off ♦ *vi* to
curl
bouclier [buklije] *nm* shield
bouddhiste [budist(ə)] *nm/f* Buddhist
bouder [bude] *vi* to sulk ♦ *vt* to turn one's
nose up at; to refuse to have anything to
do with
boudin [budɛ̃] *nm* (*CULIN*) black pudding
boue [bu] *nf* mud
bouée [bwe] *nf* buoy; ~ (**de sauvetage**)
lifebuoy
boueux, euse [bwø, -øz] *adj* muddy ♦ *nm*
refuse collector
bouffe [buf] *nf* (*fam*) grub (*fam*), food
bouffée [bufe] *nf* puff; ~ **de flèvre/de hon-**
te flush of fever/shame
bouffer [bufe] (*fam*) *vi* to eat
bouffi, e [bufi] *adj* swollen
bouge [buʒ] *nm* (low) dive; hovel
bougeoir [buʒwar] *nm* candlestick
bougeotte [buʒɔt] *nf*: **avoir la** ~ to have
the fidgets
bouger [buʒe] *vi* to move; (*dent etc*) to be
loose; (*changer*) to alter; (*agir*) to stir ♦ *vt*
to move
bougie [buʒi] *nf* candle; (*AUTO*) spark(ing)
plug
bougon, ne [bugɔ̃, -ɔn] *adj* grumpy
bougonner [bugɔne] *vi, vt* to grumble
bouillabaisse [bujabɛs] *nf* type of fish soup
bouillant, e [bujɑ̃, -ɑ̃t] *adj* (*qui bout*) boiling; (*très chaud*) boiling (hot)
bouillie [buji] *nf* gruel; (*de bébé*) cereal; **en**
~ (*fig*) crushed
bouillir [bujir] *vi, vt* to boil
bouilloire [bujwar] *nf* kettle
bouillon [bujɔ̃] *nm* (*CULIN*) stock *no pl*;
~**ner** [bujɔne] *vi* to bubble; (*fig*) to bubble
up; to foam
bouillotte [bujɔt] *nf* hot-water bottle
boulanger, ère [bulɑ̃ʒe, -ɛr] *nm/f* baker
boulangerie [bulɑ̃ʒri] *nf* bakery
boule [bul] *nf* (*gén*) ball; (*pour jouer*) bowl;
(*de machine à écrire*) golf-ball; **se mettre**
en ~ (*fig: fam*) to fly off the handle, to
blow one's top; ~ **de neige** snowball
bouleau, x [bulo] *nm* (silver) birch
boulet [bulɛ] *nm* (*aussi:* ~ **de canon**) can-
nonball
boulette [bulɛt] *nf* ball
boulevard [bulvar] *nm* boulevard
bouleversement [bulvɛrsəmɑ̃] *nm* upheaval
bouleverser [bulvɛrse] *vt* (*émouvoir*) to
overwhelm; (*causer du chagrin*) to distress;
(*pays, vie*) to disrupt; (*papiers, objets*) to

turn upside down
boulier [bulje] *nm* abacus
boulon [bulɔ̃] *nm* bolt
boulot, te [bulo, -ɔt] *adj* plump, tubby ♦
nm (*fam: travail*) work
boum [bum] *nm* bang ♦ *nf* (*fam*) party
bouquet [bukɛ] *nm* (*de fleurs*) bunch (of
flowers), bouquet; (*de persil etc*) bunch;
(*parfum*) bouquet
bouquin [bukɛ̃] (*fam*) *nm* book; **bouqui-**
ner (*fam*) *vi* to read; to browse around (in
a bookshop); **bouquiniste** *nm/f* bookseller
bourbeux, euse [burbø, -øz] *adj* muddy
bourbier [burbje] *nm* (quag)mire
bourde [burd(ə)] *nf* (*erreur*) howler; (*gaffe*)
blunder
bourdon [burdɔ̃] *nm* bumblebee
bourdonner [burdɔne] *vi* to buzz
bourg [bur] *nm* small market town
bourgeois, e [burʒwa, -waz] *adj* (*péj*) ≈
(upper) middle class; bourgeois; ~**ie**
[burʒwazi] *nf* ≈ upper middle classes *pl*;
bourgeoisie
bourgeon [burʒɔ̃] *nm* bud
Bourgogne [burgɔɲ] *nf*: **la** ~ Burgundy ♦
nm: **b~** burgundy (wine)
bourguignon, ne [burgiɲɔ̃, -ɔn] *adj* of *ou*
from Burgundy, Burgundian
bourlinguer [burlɛ̃ge] *vi* to knock about a
lot, get around a lot
bourrade [burad] *nf* shove, thump
bourrage [buraʒ] *nm*: ~ **de crâne** brainwashing; (*SCOL*) cramming
bourrasque [burask(ə)] *nf* squall
bourratif, ive [buratif] (*fam*) *adj* filling,
stodgy (*pej*)
bourré, e [bure] *adj* (*rempli*): ~ **de**
crammed full of; (*fam: ivre*) plastered,
tanked up (*BRIT*)
bourreau, x [buro] *nm* executioner; (*fig*)
torturer; ~ **de travail** workaholic
bourrelet [burlɛ] *nm* draught excluder; (*de*
peau) fold *ou* roll (of flesh)
bourrer [bure] *vt* (*pipe*) to fill; (*poêle*) to
pack; (*valise*) to cram (full)
bourrique [burik] *nf* (*âne*) ass
bourru, e [bury] *adj* surly, gruff
bourse [burs(ə)] *nf* (*subvention*) grant;
(*porte-monnaie*) purse; **la B~** the Stock Exchange
boursoufler [bursufle] *vt* to puff up, bloat
bous *vb voir* **bouillir**
bousculade [buskylad] *nf* rush; crush;
bousculer [buskyle] *vt* to knock over, to
knock into; (*fig*) to push, rush
bouse [buz] *nf* dung *no pl*
boussole [busɔl] *nf* compass
bout [bu] *vb voir* **bouillir** ♦ *nm* bit; (*d'un*
bâton etc) tip; (*d'une ficelle, table, rue, pé-*
riode) end; **au** ~ **de** at the end of, after;
pousser qn à ~ to push sb to the limit;
venir à ~ **de** to manage to finish; **à** ~ **por-**

tant at point-blank range; ~ **filtre** filter tip
boutade [butad] *nf* quip, sally
boute-en-train [butɑ̃trɛ̃] *nm inv* (*fig*) live wire
bouteille [butɛj] *nf* bottle; (*de gaz butane*) cylinder
boutique [butik] *nf* shop
bouton [butɔ̃] *nm* button; (*BOT*) bud; (*sur la peau*) spot; (*de porte*) knob; ~ **de manchette** cuff-link; ~ **d'or** buttercup; **boutonner** *vt* to button up; **boutonnière** *nf* buttonhole; **bouton-pression** *nm* press stud
bouture [butyʀ] *nf* cutting
bovins [bɔvɛ̃] *nmpl* cattle *pl*
bowling [bɔliŋ] *nm* (tenpin) bowling; (*salle*) bowling alley
box [bɔks] *nm* lock-up (garage); (*d'écurie*) loose-box
boxe [bɔks(ə)] *nf* boxing
boyau, x [bwajo] *nm* (*galerie*) passage(way); (narrow) gallery; ~**x** *nmpl* (*viscères*) entrails, guts
B.P. *abr* = **boîte postale**
bracelet [bʀaslɛ] *nm* bracelet; **bracelet-montre** *nm* wristwatch
braconnier [bʀakɔnje] *nm* poacher
brader [bʀade] *vt* to sell off; ~**ie** [bʀadʀi] *nf* cut-price shop *ou* stall
braguette [bʀagɛt] *nf* fly *ou* flies *pl* (*BRIT*), zipper (*US*)
brailler [bʀaje] *vi* to bawl, yell
braire [bʀɛʀ] *vi* to bray
braise [bʀɛz] *nf* embers *pl*
brancard [bʀɑ̃kaʀ] *nm* (*civière*) stretcher; **brancardier** *nm* stretcher-bearer
branchages [bʀɑ̃ʃaʒ] *nmpl* boughs
branche [bʀɑ̃ʃ] *nf* branch
branché, e [bʀɑ̃ʃe] (*fam*) *adj* trendy
brancher [bʀɑ̃ʃe] *vt* to connect (up); (*en mettant la prise*) to plug in
branle [bʀɑ̃l] *nm*: **donner le** ~ **à, mettre en** ~ to set in motion
branle-bas [bʀɑ̃lba] *nm inv* commotion
braquer [bʀake] *vi* (*AUTO*) to turn (the wheel) ♦ *vt* (*revolver etc*): ~ **qch sur** to aim sth at, point sth at; (*mettre en colère*): ~ **qn** to put sb's back up
bras [bʀa] *nm* arm ♦ *nmpl* (*fig: travailleurs*) labour *sg*, hands; **à** ~ **raccourcis** with fists flying; ~ **droit** (*fig*) right hand man
brasier [bʀazje] *nm* blaze, inferno
bras-le-corps [bʀalkɔʀ] : **à** ~ *adv* (a)round the waist
brassard [bʀasaʀ] *nm* armband
brasse [bʀas] *nf* (*nage*) breast-stroke; ~ **papillon** butterfly
brassée [bʀase] *nf* armful
brasser [bʀase] *vt* to mix; ~ **l'argent/les affaires** to handle a lot of money/business
brasserie [bʀasʀi] *nf* (*restaurant*) café-restaurant; (*usine*) brewery

brave [bʀav] *adj* (*courageux*) brave; (*bon, gentil*) good, kind
braver [bʀave] *vt* to defy
bravo [bʀavo] *excl* bravo ♦ *nm* cheer
bravoure [bʀavuʀ] *nf* bravery
break [bʀɛk] *nm* (*AUTO*) estate car
brebis [bʀəbi] *nf* ewe; ~ **galeuse** black sheep
brèche [bʀɛʃ] *nf* breach, gap; **être sur la** ~ (*fig*) to be on the go
bredouille [bʀəduj] *adj* empty-handed
bredouiller [bʀəduje] *vi, vt* to mumble, stammer
bref, brève [bʀɛf, bʀɛv] *adj* short, brief ♦ *adv* in short; **d'un ton** ~ sharply, curtly; **en** ~ in short, in brief
Brésil [bʀezil] *nm* Brazil
Bretagne [bʀətaɲ] *nf* Brittany
bretelle [bʀətɛl] *nf* (*de fusil etc*) sling; (*de vêtement*) strap; (*d'autoroute*) slip road (*BRIT*), entrance/exit ramp (*US*); ~**s** *nfpl* (*pour pantalon*) braces (*BRIT*), suspenders (*US*)
breton, ne [bʀətɔ̃, -ɔn] *adj, nm/f* Breton
breuvage [bʀœvaʒ] *nm* beverage, drink
brève [bʀɛv] *adj voir* **bref**
brevet [bʀəvɛ] *nm* diploma, certificate; ~ **d'études du premier cycle** *school certificate* (*taken at age 16*); ~ (**d'invention**) patent; **breveté, e** *adj* patented; (*diplômé*) qualified
bribes [bʀib] *nfpl* bits, scraps; snatches; **par** ~ piecemeal
bricolage [bʀikɔlaʒ] *nm*: **le** ~ do-it-yourself
bricole [bʀikɔl] *nf* trifle; small job
bricoler [bʀikɔle] *vi* to do DIY jobs; to potter about ♦ *vt* to fix up; to tinker with; **bricoleur, euse** *nm/f* handyman(woman), DIY enthusiast
bride [bʀid] *nf* bridle; (*d'un bonnet*) string, tie; **à** ~ **abattue** flat out, hell for leather; **laisser la** ~ **sur le cou à** to give free rein to
bridé, e [bʀide] *adj*: **yeux** ~**s** slit eyes
bridge [bʀidʒ(ə)] *nm* bridge
brièvement [bʀijɛvmɑ̃] *adv* briefly
brigade [bʀigad] *nf* (*POLICE*) squad; (*MIL*) brigade; (*gén*) team
brigadier [bʀigadje] *nm* sergeant
brigandage [bʀigɑ̃daʒ] *nm* robbery
briguer [bʀige] *vt* to aspire to
brillamment [bʀijamɑ̃] *adv* brilliantly
brillant, e [bʀijɑ̃, -ɑ̃t] *adj* brilliant; bright; (*luisant*) shiny, shining ♦ *nm* (*diamant*) brilliant
briller [bʀije] *vi* to shine
brimer [bʀime] *vt* to harass; to bully
brin [bʀɛ̃] *nm* (*de laine, ficelle etc*) strand; (*fig*): **un** ~ **de** a bit of; ~ **d'herbe** blade of grass; ~ **de muguet** sprig of lily of the valley
brindille [bʀɛ̃dij] *nf* twig

brio [bʀijo] *nm*: **avec ~** with panache
brioche [bʀijɔʃ] *nf* brioche (bun); (*fam*: *ventre*) paunch
brique [bʀik] *nf* brick ♦ *adj inv* brick red
briquer [bʀike] *vt* to polish up
briquet [bʀikɛ] *nm* (cigarette) lighter
brise [bʀiz] *nf* breeze
briser [bʀize] *vt* to break; **se ~** *vi* to break
britannique [bʀitanik] *adj* British ♦ *nm/f*: **B~** British person, Briton; **les B~s** the British
brocante [bʀɔkɑ̃t] *nf* junk, second-hand goods *pl*
brocanteur, euse [bʀɔkɑ̃tœʀ, -øz] *nm/f* junkshop owner; junk dealer
broche [bʀɔʃ] *nf* brooch; (*CULIN*) spit; (*MÉD*) pin; **à la ~** spit-roasted
broché, e [bʀɔʃe] *adj* (*livre*) paper-backed
brochet [bʀɔʃɛ] *nm* pike *inv*
brochette [bʀɔʃɛt] *nf* skewer
brochure [bʀɔʃyʀ] *nf* pamphlet, brochure, booklet
broder [bʀɔde] *vt* to embroider ♦ *vi* to embroider the facts; **broderie** *nf* embroidery
broncher [bʀɔ̃ʃe] *vi*: **sans ~** without flinching; without turning a hair
bronches [bʀɔ̃ʃ] *nfpl* bronchial tubes; **bronchite** *nf* bronchitis
bronze [bʀɔ̃z] *nm* bronze
bronzer [bʀɔ̃ze] *vt* to tan ♦ *vi* to get a tan; **se ~** to sunbathe
brosse [bʀɔs] *nf* brush; **coiffé en ~** with a crewcut; **~ à cheveux** hairbrush; **~ à dents** toothbrush; **~ à habits** clothesbrush; **brosser** *vt* (*nettoyer*) to brush; (*fig*: *tableau etc*) to paint; to draw; **se brosser les dents** to brush one's teeth
brouette [bʀuɛt] *nf* wheelbarrow
brouhaha [bʀuaa] *nm* hubbub
brouillard [bʀujaʀ] *nm* fog
brouille [bʀuj] *nf* quarrel
brouiller [bʀuje] *vt* to mix up; to confuse; (*rendre trouble*) to cloud; (*désunir*: *amis*) to set at odds; **se ~** *vi* (*vue*) to cloud over; (*détails*) to become confused; (*gens*) to fall out
brouillon, ne [bʀujɔ̃, -ɔn] *adj* disorganised; unmethodical ♦ *nm* draft
broussailles [bʀusaj] *nfpl* undergrowth *sg*; **broussailleux, euse** *adj* bushy
brousse [bʀus] *nf*: **la ~** the bush
brouter [bʀute] *vi* to graze
broutille [bʀutij] *nf* trifle
broyer [bʀwaje] *vt* to crush; **~ du noir** to be down in the dumps
bru [bʀy] *nf* daughter-in-law
brugnon [bʀyɲɔ̃] *nm* (*BOT*) nectarine
bruiner [bʀɥine] *vb impers*: **il bruine** it's drizzling, there's a drizzle
bruire [bʀɥiʀ] *vi* to murmur; to rustle
bruit [bʀɥi] *nm*: **un ~** a noise, a sound; (*fig*: *rumeur*) a rumour; **le ~** noise; **sans ~**

without a sound, noiselessly; **~ de fond** background noise
bruitage [bʀɥitaʒ] *nm* sound effects *pl*
brûlant, e [bʀylɑ̃, -ɑ̃t] *adj* burning; (*liquide*) boiling (hot); (*regard*) fiery
brûlé, e [bʀyle] *adj* (*fig*: *démasqué*) blown ♦ *nm*: **odeur de ~** smell of burning
brûle-pourpoint [bʀylpuʀpwɛ̃] : **à ~** *adv* point-blank
brûler [bʀyle] *vt* to burn; (*suj*: *eau bouillante*) to scald; (*consommer*: *électricité*, *essence*) to use; (*feu rouge*, *signal*) to go through ♦ *vi* to burn; (*jeu*) to be warm; **se ~** to burn o.s.; to scald o.s.; **se ~ la cervelle** to blow one's brains out
brûlure [bʀylyʀ] *nf* (*lésion*) burn; (*sensation*) burning (sensation); **~s d'estomac** heartburn *sg*
brume [bʀym] *nf* mist
brun, e [bʀɛ̃, -yn] *adj* brown; (*cheveux*, *personne*) dark; **brunir** *vi* to get a tan
brusque [bʀysk(ə)] *adj* abrupt; **brusquer** *vt* to rush
brut, e [bʀyt] *adj* raw, crude, rough; (*COMM*) gross; (*données*) raw; (*pétrole*) **~** crude (oil)
brutal, e, aux [bʀytal, -o] *adj* brutal; **brutaliser** *vt* to handle roughly, manhandle
Bruxelles [bʀysɛl] *n* Brussels
bruyamment [bʀɥijamɑ̃] *adv* noisily
bruyant, e [bʀɥijɑ̃, -ɑ̃t] *adj* noisy
bruyère [bʀɥijɛʀ] *nf* heather
bu, e *pp de* **boire**
buccal, e, aux [bykal, -o] *adj*: **par voie ~e** orally
bûche [byʃ] *nf* log; **prendre une ~** (*fig*) to come a cropper; **~ de Noël** Yule log; **~r** [byʃe] *nm* pyre; bonfire ♦ *vi* (*fam*) to swot (*BRIT*), slave (away) ♦ *vt* to swot up (*BRIT*), slave away at; **~ron** [byʃʀɔ̃] *nm* woodcutter
budget [bydʒɛ] *nm* budget
buée [bɥe] *nf* (*sur une vitre*) mist; (*de l'haleine*) steam
buffet [byfɛ] *nm* (*meuble*) sideboard; (*de réception*) buffet; **~ (de gare)** (station) buffet, snack bar
buffle [byfl(ə)] *nm* buffalo
buis [bɥi] *nm* box tree; (*bois*) box(wood)
buisson [bɥisɔ̃] *nm* bush
buissonnière [bɥisɔnjɛʀ] *adj*: **faire l'école ~** to skip school
bulbe [bylb(ə)] *nm* (*BOT*, *ANAT*) bulb; (*coupole*) onion-shaped dome
Bulgarie [bylgaʀi] *nf* Bulgaria
bulle [byl] *nf* bubble
bulletin [byltɛ̃] *nm* (*communiqué*, *journal*) bulletin; (*papier*) form; (*SCOL*) report; **~ d'informations** news bulletin; **~ de salaire** pay-slip; **~ (de vote)** ballot paper; **~ météorologique** weather report
bureau, x [byʀo] *nm* (*meuble*) desk; (*pièce*,

service) office; ~ **de change** (foreign) exchange office *ou* bureau; ~ **de location** box office; ~ **de poste** post office; ~ **de tabac** tobacconist's (shop); ~ **de vote** polling station; **bureaucratie** *nf* bureaucracy

bureautique [byʀɔtik] *nf* office automation

burin [byʀɛ̃] *nm* cold chisel; (*ART*) burin

burlesque [byʀlɛsk(ə)] *adj* ridiculous; (*LITTÉRATURE*) burlesque

bus¹ [by] *vb voir* **boire**; **bus²** [bys] *nm* bus

busqué, e [byske] *adj* (*nez*) hook(ed)

buste [byst(ə)] *nm* (*ANAT*) chest; bust

but [by] *vb voir* **boire** ♦ *nm* (*cible*) target; (*fig*) goal; aim; (*FOOTBALL etc*) goal; **de ~ en blanc** point-blank; **avoir pour ~ de faire** to aim to do; **dans le ~ de** with the intention of

butane [bytan] *nm* butane; Calor gas (®)

buté, e [byte] *adj* stubborn, obstinate

buter [byte] *vi*: ~ **contre/sur** to bump into; to stumble against ♦ *vt* to antagonize; **se ~** *vi* to get obstinate; to dig in one's heels

butin [bytɛ̃] *nm* booty, spoils *pl*; (*d'un vol*) loot

butte [byt] *nf* mound, hillock; **être en ~ à** to be exposed to

buvais *etc vb voir* **boire**

buvard [byvaʀ] *nm* blotter

buvette [byvɛt] *nf* bar

buveur, euse [byvœʀ, -øz] *nm/f* drinker

C c

c' [s] *dét voir* **ce**

ça [sa] *pron* (*pour désigner*) this; (: *plus loin*) that; (*comme sujet indéfini*) it; ~ **va?** how are you?; how are things?; (*d'accord?*) OK?, all right?; ~ **alors!** well really!; ~ **fait 10 ans (que)** it's 10 years (since); **c'est** ~ that's right

çà [sa] *adv*: ~ **et là** here and there

cabane [kaban] *nf* hut, cabin

cabaret [kabaʀɛ] *nm* night club

cabas [kaba] *nm* shopping bag

cabillaud [kabijo] *nm* cod *inv*

cabine [kabin] *nf* (*de bateau*) cabin; (*de plage*) (beach) hut; (*de piscine etc*) cubicle; (*de camion, train*) cab; (*d'avion*) cockpit; ~ **d'essayage** fitting room; ~ **spatiale** space capsule; ~ **(téléphonique)** call *ou* (tele)phone box

cabinet [kabinɛ] *nm* (*petite pièce*) closet;

(*de médecin*) surgery (*BRIT*), office (*US*); (*de notaire etc*) office; (: *clientèle*) practice; (*POL*) Cabinet; ~s *nmpl* (*w.-c.*) toilet *sg*; ~ **d'affaires** business consultants' (bureau), business partnership; ~ **de toilette** toilet; ~ **de travail** study

câble [kɑbl(ə)] *nm* cable

cabrer [kɑbʀe]: **se** ~ *vi* (*cheval*) to rear up; (*avion*) to nose up; (*fig*) to revolt, rebel

cabriole [kabʀijɔl] *nf* caper; somersault

cacahuète [kakaɥɛt] *nf* peanut

cacao [kakao] *nm* cocoa (powder); (*boisson*) cocoa

cache [kaʃ] *nm* mask, card (for masking) ♦ *nf* hiding place

cache-cache [kaʃkaʃ] *nm*: **jouer à** ~ to play hide-and-seek

cachemire [kaʃmiʀ] *nm* cashmere

cache-nez [kaʃne] *nm inv* scarf, muffler

cacher [kaʃe] *vt* to hide, conceal; **se** ~ *vi* to hide; to be hidden *ou* concealed; ~ **qch à qn** to hide *ou* conceal sth from sb; **il ne s'en cache pas** he makes no secret of it

cachet [kaʃɛ] *nm* (*comprimé*) tablet; (*sceau: du roi*) seal; (: *de la poste*) postmark; (*rétribution*) fee; (*fig*) style, character; **cacheter** *vt* to seal

cachette [kaʃɛt] *nf* hiding place; **en** ~ on the sly, secretly

cachot [kaʃo] *nm* dungeon

cachotterie [kaʃɔtʀi] *nf*: **faire des** ~s to be secretive

cactus [kaktys] *nm* cactus

cadavre [kadavʀ(ə)] *nm* corpse, (dead) body

caddie [kadi] *nm* (supermarket) trolley

caddy *nm* = **caddie**

cadeau, x [kado] *nm* present, gift; **faire un** ~ **à qn** to give sb a present *ou* gift; **faire ~ de qch à qn** to make a present of sth to sb, give sb sth as a present

cadenas [kadna] *nm* padlock

cadence [kadɑ̃s] *nf* (*MUS*) cadence; (: *tempo*) rhythm; (*de travail etc*) rate; **en** ~ rhythmically; in time

cadet, te [kadɛ, -ɛt] *adj* younger; (*le plus jeune*) youngest ♦ *nm/f* youngest child *ou* one, youngest boy *ou* son/girl *ou* daughter

cadran [kadʀɑ̃] *nm* dial; ~ **solaire** sundial

cadre [kadʀ(ə)] *nm* frame; (*environnement*) surroundings *pl*; (*limites*) scope ♦ *nm/f* (*ADMIN*) managerial employee, executive; **dans le** ~ **de** (*fig*) within the framework *ou* context of; **rayer qn des** ~s to dismiss sb

cadrer [kadʀe] *vi*: ~ **avec** to tally *ou* correspond with ♦ *vt* to centre

caduc, uque [kadyk] *adj* obsolete; (*BOT*) deciduous

cafard [kafaʀ] *nm* cockroach; **avoir le** ~ to be down in the dumps

café [kafe] *nm* coffee; (*bistro*) café ♦ *adj inv* coffee(-coloured); ~ **au lait** white coffee; ~

noir black coffee; ~ **tabac** tobacconist's or newsagent's serving coffee and spirits; **cafetière** nf (pot) coffee-pot

cafouillage [kafujaʒ] nm shambles sg

cage [kaʒ] nf cage; ~ **(des buts)** goal; ~ **d'escalier** (stair)well; ~ **thoracique** rib cage

cageot [kaʒo] nm crate

cagibi [kaʒibi] nm shed

cagneux, euse [kaɲø, -øz] adj knock-kneed

cagnotte [kaɲɔt] nf kitty

cagoule [kagul] nf cowl; hood; (SKI etc) cagoule

cahier [kaje] nm notebook; ~ **de brouillons** roughbook, jotter; ~ **d'exercices** exercise book

cahot [kao] nm jolt, bump

caïd [kaid] nm big chief, boss

caille [kaj] nf quail

cailler [kaje] vi (lait) to curdle; (sang) to clot

caillot [kajo] nm (blood) clot

caillou, x [kaju] nm (little) stone; **caillouteux, euse** adj stony; pebbly

Caire [kɛʀ] nm: le ~ Cairo

caisse [kɛs] nf box; (où l'on met la recette) cashbox; till; (où l'on paye) cash desk (BRIT), check-out; (de banque) cashier's desk; (TECH) case, casing; ~ **d'épargne** savings bank; ~ **de retraite** pension fund; ~ **enregistreuse** cash register; **caissier, ière** nm/f cashier

cajoler [kaʒɔle] vt to wheedle, coax; to surround with love

cake [kɛk] nm fruit cake

calandre [kalɑ̃dʀ(ə)] nf radiator grill

calanque [kalɑ̃k] nf rocky inlet

calcaire [kalkɛʀ] nm limestone ♦ adj (eau) hard; (GÉO) limestone cpd

calciné, e [kalsine] adj burnt to ashes

calcul [kalkyl] nm calculation; le ~ (SCOL) arithmetic; ~ **(biliaire)** (gall)stone; ~ **(rénal)** (kidney) stone; **calculateur** nm calculator; **calculatrice** nf calculator

calculer [kalkyle] vt to calculate, work out; (combiner) to calculate

calculette [kalkylɛt] nf pocket calculator

cale [kal] nf (de bateau) hold; (en bois) wedge; ~ **sèche** dry dock

calé, e [kale] (fam) adj clever, bright

caleçon [kalsɔ̃] nm pair of underpants, trunks pl

calembour [kalɑ̃buʀ] nm pun

calendes [kalɑ̃d] nfpl: **renvoyer aux ~ grecques** to postpone indefinitely

calendrier [kalɑ̃dʀije] nm calendar; (fig) timetable

calepin [kalpɛ̃] nm notebook

caler [kale] vt to wedge; ~ **(son moteur/véhicule)** to stall (one's engine/vehicle)

calfeutrer [kalføtʀe] vt to (make) draught-proof; **se** ~ vi to make o.s. snug and comfortable

calibre [kalibʀ(ə)] nm (d'un fruit) grade; (d'une arme) bore, calibre; (fig) calibre

califourchon [kalifuʀʃɔ̃]: **à** ~ adv astride

câlin, e [kɑlɛ̃, -in] adj cuddly, cuddlesome; tender

câliner [kɑline] vt to fondle, cuddle

calmant [kalmɑ̃] nm tranquillizer, sedative; (pour la douleur) painkiller

calme [kalm(ə)] adj calm, quiet ♦ nm calm(ness), quietness

calmer [kalme] vt to calm (down); (douleur, inquiétude) to ease, soothe; **se** ~ vi to calm down

calomnie [kalɔmni] nf slander; (écrite) libel; **calomnier** vt to slander; to libel

calorie [kalɔʀi] nf calorie

calorifuge [kalɔʀifyʒ] adj (heat-) insulating, heat-retaining

calotte [kalɔt] nf (coiffure) skullcap; (gifle) slap; **calotte glaciaire** nf (GÉO) icecap

calquer [kalke] vt to trace; (fig) to copy exactly

calvaire [kalvɛʀ] nm (croix) wayside cross, calvary; (souffrances) suffering

calvitie [kalvisi] nf baldness

camarade [kamaʀad] nm/f friend, pal; (POL) comrade; **camaraderie** nf friendship

cambouis [kɑ̃bwi] nm dirty oil ou grease

cambrer [kɑ̃bʀe] vt to arch

cambriolage [kɑ̃bʀijɔlaʒ] nm burglary; **cambrioler** [kɑ̃bʀijɔle] vt to burgle (BRIT), burglarize (US); **cambrioleur, euse** nm/f burglar

came [kam] nf: **arbre à** ~**s** camshaft

camelote [kamlɔt] nf rubbish, trash, junk

caméra [kameʀa] nf (CINÉMA, TV) camera; (d'amateur) cine-camera

caméscope nm camcorder

camion [kamjɔ̃] nm lorry (BRIT), truck; (plus petit, fermé) van; ~ **de dépannage** breakdown (BRIT) ou tow (US) truck; **camion-citerne** nm tanker; **camionnette** nf (small) van; **camionneur** nm (entrepreneur) haulage contractor (BRIT), trucker (US); (chauffeur) lorry (BRIT) ou truck driver; van driver

camisole [kamizɔl] nf: ~ **(de force)** straitjacket

camomille [kamɔmij] nf camomile; (boisson) camomile tea

camoufler [kamufle] vt to camouflage; (fig) to conceal, cover up

camp [kɑ̃] nm camp; (fig) side

campagnard, e [kɑ̃paɲaʀ, -aʀd(ə)] adj country cpd

campagne [kɑ̃paɲ] nf country, countryside; (MIL, POL, COMM) campaign; **à la** ~ in the country

camper [kɑ̃pe] vi to camp ♦ vt to sketch; **se** ~ **devant** to plant o.s. in front of; **cam-**

peur, euse nm/f camper
camphre [kɑ̃fʀ(ə)] nm camphor
camping [kɑ̃piŋ] nm camping; **(terrain de)** ~ campsite, camping site; **faire du** ~ to go camping
Canada [kanada] nm: **le** ~ Canada; **canadien, ne** adj, nm/f Canadian; **canadienne** nf (veste) fur-lined jacket
canaille [kanɑj] (péj) nf scoundrel
canal, aux [kanal, -o] nm canal; (naturel) channel; **canalisation** [kanalizɑsjɔ̃] nf (tuyau) pipe; **canaliser** [kanalize] vt to canalize; (fig) to channel
canapé [kanape] nm settee, sofa
canard [kanaʀ] nm duck
canari [kanaʀi] nm canary
cancans [kɑ̃kɑ̃] nmpl (malicious) gossip sg
cancer [kɑ̃sɛʀ] nm cancer; (signe): **le C**~ Cancer; ~ **de la peau** skin cancer
cancre [kɑ̃kʀ(ə)] nm dunce
candeur [kɑ̃dœʀ] nf ingenuousness, guilelessness
candidat, e [kɑ̃dida, -at] nm/f candidate; (à un poste) applicant, candidate; **candidature** nf candidature; application; **poser sa candidature** to submit an application, apply
candide [kɑ̃did] adj ingenuous, guileless
cane [kan] nf (female) duck
caneton [kantɔ̃] nm duckling
canette [kanɛt] nf (de bière) (flip-top) bottle
canevas [kanva] nm (COUTURE) canvas
caniche [kaniʃ] nm poodle
canicule [kanikyl] nf scorching heat
canif [kanif] nm penknife, pocket knife
canine [kanin] nf canine (tooth)
caniveau, x [kanivo] nm gutter
canne [kan] nf (walking) stick; ~ **à pêche** fishing rod; ~ **à sucre** sugar cane
cannelle [kanɛl] nf cinnamon
canoë [kanɔe] nm canoe; (sport) canoeing
canon [kanɔ̃] nm (arme) gun; (HISTOIRE) cannon; (d'une arme: tube) barrel; (fig) model; (MUS) canon; ~ **rayé** rifled barrel
canot [kano] nm ding(h)y; ~ **de sauvetage** lifeboat; ~ **pneumatique** inflatable ding(h)y; ~**age** nm rowing; ~**ier** [kanɔtje] nm boater
cantatrice [kɑ̃tatʀis] nf (opera) singer
cantine [kɑ̃tin] nf canteen
cantique [kɑ̃tik] nm hymn
canton [kɑ̃tɔ̃] nm district consisting of several communes; (en Suisse) canton
cantonade [kɑ̃tɔnad] : **à la** ~ adv to everyone in general; from the rooftops
cantonner [kɑ̃tɔne] vt (MIL) to quarter, station; **se** ~ **dans** to confine o.s. to
cantonnier [kɑ̃tɔnje] nm roadmender
canular [kanylaʀ] nm hoax
caoutchouc [kautʃu] nm rubber; ~ **mousse** foam rubber

cap [kap] nm (GÉO) cape; headland; (fig) hurdle; watershed; (NAVIG): **changer de** ~ to change course; **mettre le** ~ **sur** to head ou steer for
C.A.P. sigle m (= Certificat d'aptitude professionnelle) vocational training certificate taken at secondary school
capable [kapabl(ə)] adj able, capable; ~ **de qch/faire** capable of sth/doing
capacité [kapasite] nf (compétence) ability; (JUR, contenance) capacity; ~ **(en droit)** basic legal qualification
cape [kap] nf cape, cloak; **rire sous** ~ to laugh up one's sleeve
C.A.P.E.S. [kapɛs] sigle m (= Certificat d'aptitude pédagogique à l'enseignement secondaire) teaching diploma
capillaire [kapilɛʀ] adj (soins, lotion) hair cpd; (vaisseau etc) capillary
capitaine [kapitɛn] nm captain
capital, e, aux [kapital, -o] adj major; of paramount importance; fundamental ♦ nm capital; (fig) stock; asset; voir aussi **capitaux**; ~ **(social)** authorized capital; ~**e** nf (ville) capital; (lettre) capital (letter); ~**iser** vt to amass, build up; ~**isme** nm capitalism; ~**iste** adj, nm/f capitalist; **capitaux** [kapito] nmpl (fonds) capital sg
capitonné, e [kapitɔne] adj padded
caporal, aux [kapɔʀal, -o] nm lance corporal
capot [kapo] nm (AUTO) bonnet (BRIT), hood (US)
capote [kapɔt] nf (de voiture) hood (BRIT), top (US); (fam) condom
capoter [kapɔte] vi to overturn
câpre [kɑpʀ(ə)] nf caper
caprice [kapʀis] nm whim, caprice; passing fancy; **capricieux, euse** adj capricious; whimsical; temperamental
Capricorne [kapʀikɔʀn] nm: **le** ~ Capricorn
capsule [kapsyl] nf (de bouteille) cap; (BOT etc, spatiale) capsule
capter [kapte] vt (ondes radio) to pick up; (eau) to harness; (fig) to win, capture
captivant, e [kaptivɑ̃, ɑ̃t] adj captivating; fascinating
captivité [kaptivite] nf captivity
capturer [kaptyʀe] vt to capture
capuche [kapyʃ] nf hood
capuchon [kapyʃɔ̃] nm hood; (de stylo) cap, top
caquet [kakɛ] nm: **rabattre le** ~ **à qn** to bring sb down a peg or two
caqueter [kakte] vi to cackle
car [kaʀ] nm coach ♦ conj because, for
carabine [kaʀabin] nf carbine, rifle
caractère [kaʀaktɛʀ] nm (gén) character; **avoir bon/mauvais** ~ to be good-/ill-natured; **en** ~**s gras** in bold type; **en petits** ~**s** in small print; ~**s d'imprimerie**

(block) capitals; **caractériel, le** *adj* (of) character ♦ *nm/f* emotionally disturbed child

caractérisé, e [kaʀakteʀize] *adj*: **c'est une grippe ~e** it is a clear (-cut) case of flu

caractéristique [kaʀakteʀistik] *adj, nf* characteristic

carafe [kaʀaf] *nf* decanter; carafe

caraïbe [kaʀaib] *adj* Caribbean ♦ *n*: **les C~s** the Caribbean (Islands); **la mer des C~s** the Caribbean Sea

carambolage [kaʀɑ̃bɔlaʒ] *nm* multiple crash, pileup

caramel [kaʀamɛl] *nm* (*bonbon*) caramel, toffee; (*substance*) caramel

carapace [kaʀapas] *nf* shell

caravane [kaʀavan] *nf* caravan; **caravaning** *nm* caravanning; (*emplacement*) caravan site

carbone [kaʀbɔn] *nm* carbon; (*feuille*) carbon, sheet of carbon paper; (*double*) carbon (copy); **carbonique** [kaʀbɔnik] *adj*: **neige carbonique** dry ice; **carbonisé, e** [kaʀbɔnize] *adj* charred

carburant [kaʀbyʀɑ̃] *nm* (motor) fuel

carburateur [kaʀbyʀatœʀ] *nm* carburettor

carcan [kaʀkɑ̃] *nm* (*fig*) yoke, shackles *pl*

carcasse [kaʀkas] *nf* carcass; (*de véhicule etc*) shell

cardiaque [kaʀdjak] *adj* cardiac, heart *cpd* ♦ *nm/f* heart patient

cardigan [kaʀdigɑ̃] *nm* cardigan

cardiologue [kaʀdjɔlɔg] *nm/f* cardiologist, heart specialist

carême [kaʀɛm] *nm*: **le C~** Lent

carence [kaʀɑ̃s] *nf* incompetence, inadequacy; (*manque*) deficiency

caresse [kaʀɛs] *nf* caress

caresser [kaʀese] *vt* to caress, fondle; (*fig: projet*) to toy with

cargaison [kaʀgɛzɔ̃] *nf* cargo, freight

cargo [kaʀgo] *nm* cargo boat, freighter

carie [kaʀi] *nf*: **la ~ (dentaire)** tooth decay; **une ~** a bad tooth

carillon [kaʀijɔ̃] *nm* (*d'église*) bells *pl*; (*de pendule*) chimes *pl*; (*de porte*) door chime *ou* bell

carlingue [kaʀlɛ̃g] *nf* cabin

carnassier, ière [kaʀnasje, -jɛʀ] *adj* carnivorous

carnaval [kaʀnaval] *nm* carnival

carnet [kaʀnɛ] *nm* (*calepin*) notebook; (*de tickets, timbres etc*) book; (*d'école*) school report; (*journal intime*) diary; **~ de chèques** cheque book

carotte [kaʀɔt] *nf* carrot

carpette [kaʀpɛt] *nf* rug

carré, e [kaʀe] *adj* square; (*fig: franc*) straightforward ♦ *nm* (*de terrain, jardin*) patch, plot; (*MATH*) square; **mètre/kilomètre ~** square metre/kilometre

carreau, x [kaʀo] *nm* (*en faïence etc*)

(floor) tile; (wall) tile; (*de fenêtre*) (window) pane; (*motif*) check, square; (*CARTES: couleur*) diamonds *pl*; (: *carte*) diamond; **tissu à ~x** checked fabric

carrefour [kaʀfuʀ] *nm* crossroads *sg*

carrelage [kaʀlaʒ] *nm* tiling; (tiled) floor

carrelet [kaʀlɛ] *nm* (*poisson*) plaice

carrément [kaʀemɑ̃] *adv* straight out, bluntly; completely, altogether

carrière [kaʀjɛʀ] *nf* (*de roches*) quarry; (*métier*) career; **militaire de ~** professional soldier

carriole [kaʀjɔl] (*péj*) *nf* old cart

carrossable [kaʀɔsabl(ə)] *adj* suitable for (motor) vehicles

carrosse [kaʀɔs] *nm* (horse-drawn) coach

carrosserie [kaʀɔsʀi] *nf* body, coachwork *no pl*; (*activité, commerce*) coachbuilding

carrure [kaʀyʀ] *nf* build; (*fig*) stature, calibre

cartable [kaʀtabl(ə)] *nm* (*d'écolier*) satchel, (school)bag

carte [kaʀt(ə)] *nf* (*de géographie*) map; (*marine, du ciel*) chart; (*de fichier, d'abonnement etc, à jouer*) card; (*au restaurant*) menu; (*aussi*: **~ postale**) (post)card; (: **~ de visite**) (visiting) card; **à la ~** (*au restaurant*) à la carte; **~ bancaire** cash card; **~ de crédit** credit card; **~ d'identité** identity card; **~ de séjour** residence permit; **~ grise** (*AUTO*) ≈ (car) registration book, logbook; **~ routière** road map; **~ téléphonique** phonecard

carter [kaʀtɛʀ] *nm* sump

carton [kaʀtɔ̃] *nm* (*matériau*) cardboard; (*boîte*) (cardboard) box; (*d'invitation*) invitation card; **faire un ~** (*au tir*) to have a go at the rifle range; to score a hit; (**à dessin**) portfolio; **cartonné, e** *adj* (*livre*) hardback, cased; **carton-pâte** *nm* pasteboard

cartouche [kaʀtuʃ] *nf* cartridge; (*de cigarettes*) carton

cas [kɑ] *nm* case; **faire peu de ~/grand ~ de** to attach little/great importance to; **en aucun ~** on no account; **au ~ où** in case; **en ~ de** in case of, in the event of; **en ~ de besoin** if need be; **en tout ~** in any case, at any rate; **~ de conscience** matter of conscience

casanier, ière [kazanje, -jɛʀ] *adj* stay-at-home

cascade [kaskad] *nf* waterfall, cascade; (*fig*) stream, torrent

cascadeur, euse [kaskadœʀ, -øz] *nm/f* stuntman(girl)

case [kɑz] *nf* (*hutte*) hut; (*compartiment*) compartment; (*pour le courrier*) pigeonhole; (*sur un formulaire, de mots croisés etc*) box

caser [kɑze] *vt* (*trouver de la place pour*) to put (away); to put up; (*fig*) to find a job for; to marry off

caserne [kazɛʀn(ə)] *nf* barracks *pl*

cash [kaʃ] *adv*: **payer** ~ to pay cash down
casier [kazje] *nm* (*à journaux etc*) rack; (*de bureau*) filing cabinet; (: *à cases*) set of pigeonholes; (*case*) compartment; pigeonhole; (: *à clef*) locker; ~ **judiciaire** police record
casino [kazino] *nm* casino
casque [kask(ə)] *nm* helmet; (*chez le coiffeur*) (hair-)drier; (*pour audition*) (head-)phones *pl*, headset
casquette [kaskɛt] *nf* cap
cassant, e [kasɑ̃, -ɑ̃t] *adj* brittle; (*fig*) brusque, abrupt
cassation [kasɑsjɔ̃] *nf*: **cour de** ~ final court of appeal
casse [kas] *nf* (*pour voitures*) **mettre à la** ~ to scrap; (*dégâts*): **il y a eu de la** ~ there were a lot of breakages; ~-**cou** *adj inv* daredevil, reckless; ~-**croûte** *nm inv* snack; ~-**noisette(s)** *nm inv* nutcrackers *pl*; ~-**noix** *nm inv* nutcrackers *pl*; ~-**pieds** (*fam*) *adj inv*: **il est** ~-**pieds** he's a pain in the neck
casser [kɑse] *vt* to break; (*ADMIN*: *gradé*) to demote; (*JUR*) to quash; **se** ~ *vi* to break
casserole [kasʀɔl] *nf* saucepan
casse-tête [kɑstɛt] *nm inv* (*jeu*) brain teaser; (*difficultés*) headache (*fig*)
cassette [kasɛt] *nf* (*bande magnétique*) cassette; (*coffret*) casket
casseur [kɑsœʀ] *nm* hooligan
cassis [kasis] *nm* blackcurrant
cassoulet [kasulɛ] *nm* bean and sausage hot-pot
cassure [kɑsyʀ] *nf* break, crack
castor [kastɔʀ] *nm* beaver
castrer [kastʀe] *vt* (*mâle*) to castrate; (: *cheval*) to geld; (*femelle*) to spay
catalogue [katalɔg] *nm* catalogue
cataloguer [katalɔge] *vt* to catalogue, to list; (*péj*) to put a label on
catalyseur *nm* catalytic convertor
catalyseur [katalizœʀ] *nm* catalyst
cataplasme [kataplasm(ə)] *nm* poultice
cataracte [kataʀakt(ə)] *nf* cataract
catastrophe [katastʀɔf] *nf* catastrophe, disaster; **catastrophé, e** [katastʀɔfe] (*fam*) *adj* deeply saddened
catch [katʃ] *nm* (all-in) wrestling; **catcheur, euse** *nm/f* (all-in) wrestler
catéchisme [kateʃism(ə)] *nm* catechism
catégorie [kategɔʀi] *nf* category
catégorique [kategɔʀik] *adj* categorical
cathédrale [katedʀal] *nf* cathedral
catholique [katɔlik] *adj*, *nm/f* (Roman) Catholic; **pas très** ~ a bit shady *ou* fishy
catimini [katimini] : **en** ~ *adv* on the sly
cauchemar [kɔʃmaʀ] *nm* nightmare
cause [koz] *nf* cause; (*JUR*) lawsuit, case; **à** ~ **de** because of, owing to; **pour** ~ **de** on account of; owing to; (**et**) **pour** ~ and for (a very) good reason; **être en** ~ to be at

stake; to be involved; to be in question; **mettre en** ~ to implicate; to call into question; **remettre en** ~ to challenge; ~**r** [koze] *vt* to cause ♦ *vi* to chat, talk; ~**rie** [kozʀi] *nf* talk
caution [kosjɔ̃] *nf* guarantee, security; deposit; (*JUR*) bail (bond); (*fig*) backing, support; **payer la** ~ **de qn** to stand bail for sb; **libéré sous** ~ released on bail; ~**ner** [kosjɔne] *vt* to guarantee; (*soutenir*) to support
cavalcade [kavalkad] *nf* (*fig*) stampede
cavalier, ière [kavalje, -jɛʀ] *adj* (*désinvolte*) offhand ♦ *nm/f* rider; (*au bal*) partner ♦ *nm*, (*ÉCHECS*) knight; **faire** ~ **seul** to go it alone
cave [kav] *nf* cellar ♦ *adj*: **yeux** ~**s** sunken eyes
caveau, x [kavo] *nm* vault
caverne [kavɛʀn(ə)] *nf* cave
C.C.P. *sigle m* = **compte chèques postaux**
CD *sigle m* (= *compact disc*) CD
CD-ROM *sigle m* CD-ROM
CE *n abr* (= *Communauté Européenne*) EC

───────── *MOT CLÉ* ─────────

ce, cette [sə, sɛt] (*devant nm* **cet** + *voyelle ou h aspiré*; *pl* **ces**) *dét* (*proximité*) this; these *pl*; (*non-proximité*) that; those *pl*; **cette maison-ci/là** this/that house; **cette nuit** (*qui vient*) tonight; (*passée*) last night
♦ *pron* **1**: **c'est** it's *ou* it is; **c'est un peintre** he's *ou* he is a painter; **ce sont des peintres** they're *ou* they are painters; **c'est le facteur etc** (*à la porte*) it's the postman; **qui est-ce?** who is it?; (*en désignant*) who is he/she?; **qu'est-ce?** what is it?
2: ~ **qui**, ~ **que** what; (*chose qui*): **il est bête**, ~ **qui me chagrine** he's stupid, which saddens me; **tout** ~ **qui bouge** everything that *ou* which moves; **tout** ~ **que je sais** all I know; ~ **dont j'ai parlé** what I talked about; ~ **que c'est grand!** it's so big!; *voir aussi* -**ci**; **est-ce que**; **n'est-ce pas**; **c'est-à-dire**

─────────────────────────────

ceci [səsi] *pron* this
cécité [sesite] *nf* blindness
céder [sede] *vt* to give up ♦ *vi* (*pont, barrage*) to give way; (*personne*) to give in; ~ **à** to yield to, give in to
CEDEX [sedɛks] *sigle m* (= *courrier d'entreprise à distribution exceptionnelle*) postal service for bulk users
cédille [sedij] *nf* cedilla
cèdre [sɛdʀ(ə)] *nm* cedar
CEI *abr m* (= *Communauté des États Indépendants*) CIS
ceinture [sɛ̃tyʀ] *nf* belt; (*taille*) waist; (*fig*) ring; belt; circle; ~ **de sécurité** safety *ou* seat belt; ~**r** *vt* (*saisir*) to grasp (round the waist)

cela [səla] *pron* that; (*comme sujet indéfini*) it; **quand/où ~?** when/where (was that)?
célèbre [selɛbʀ(ə)] *adj* famous
célébrer [selebʀe] *vt* to celebrate; (*louer*) to extol
céleri [sɛlʀi] *nm*: **~(-rave)** celeriac; **~ (en branche)** celery
célérité [seleʀite] *nf* speed, swiftness
célibat [seliba] *nm* celibacy; bachelorhood; spinsterhood; **célibataire** [selibatɛʀ] *adj* single, unmarried
celle(s) [sɛl] *pron voir* **celui**
cellier [selje] *nm* storeroom
cellulaire [selylɛʀ] *adj*: **voiture** *ou* **fourgon ~** prison *ou* police van
cellule [selyl] *nf* (*gén*) cell
cellulite [selylit] *nf* excess fat, cellulite

--- MOT CLÉ ---

celui, celle [səlɥi, sɛl] (*mpl* **ceux,** *fpl* **celles**) *pron* **1:** **~-ci/là, celle-ci/là** this one/that one; **ceux-ci, celles-ci** these (ones); **ceux-là, celles-là** those (ones); **~ de mon frère** my brother's; **~ du salon/du dessous** the one in (*ou* from) the lounge/below
2: **~ qui bouge** the one which *ou* that moves; (*personne*) the one who moves; **~ que je vois** the one (which *ou* that) I see; the one (whom) I see; **~ dont je parle** the one I'm talking about
3 (*valeur indéfinie*): **~ qui veut** whoever wants

cendre [sɑ̃dʀ(ə)] *nf* ash; **~s** *nfpl* (*d'un foyer*) ash(es), cinders; (*volcaniques*) ash *sg*; (*d'un défunt*) ashes; **sous la ~** (*CULIN*) in (the) embers; **cendrier** *nm* ashtray
cène [sɛn] *nf*: **la ~** (Holy) Communion
censé, e [sɑ̃se] *adj*: **être ~ faire** to be supposed to do
censeur [sɑ̃sœʀ] *nm* (*SCOL*) deputy-head (*BRIT*), vice-principal (*US*); (*CINÉMA, POL*) censor
censure [sɑ̃syʀ] *nf* censorship; **~r** [sɑ̃syʀe] *vt* (*CINÉMA, PRESSE*) to censor; (*POL*) to censure
cent [sɑ̃] *num* a hundred, one hundred; **centaine** *nf*: **une centaine (de)** about a hundred, a hundred or so; **plusieurs centaines (de)** several hundred; **des centaines (de)** hundreds (of); **centenaire** *adj* hundred-year-old ♦ *nm* (*anniversaire*) centenary; **centième** *num* hundredth; **centigrade** *nm* centigrade; **centilitre** *nm* centilitre; **centime** *nm* centime; **centimètre** *nm* centimetre; (*ruban*) tape measure, measuring tape
central, e, aux [sɑ̃tʀal, -o] *adj* central ♦ *nm*: **~ (téléphonique)** (telephone) exchange; **centrale** *nf* power station
centre [sɑ̃tʀ(ə)] *nm* centre; **~ commercial**

shopping centre; **~ d'apprentissage** training college; **centre-ville** *nm* town centre, downtown (area) (*US*)
centuple [sɑ̃typl(ə)] *nm*: **le ~ de qch** a hundred times sth; **au ~** a hundredfold
cep [sɛp] *nm* (vine) stock
cèpe [sɛp] *nm* (edible) boletus
cependant [səpɑ̃dɑ̃] *adv* however
céramique [seʀamik] *nf* ceramics *sg*
cercle [sɛʀkl(ə)] *nm* circle; (*objet*) band, hoop; **~ vicieux** vicious circle
cercueil [sɛʀkœj] *nm* coffin
céréale [seʀeal] *nf* cereal
cérémonie [seʀemɔni] *nf* ceremony; **~s** *nfpl* (*péj*) fuss *sg*, to-do *sg*
cerf [sɛʀ] *nm* stag
cerfeuil [sɛʀfœj] *nm* chervil
cerf-volant [sɛʀvɔlɑ̃] *nm* kite
cerise [səʀiz] *nf* cherry; **cerisier** *nm* cherry (tree)
cerné, e [sɛʀne] *adj*: **les yeux ~s** with dark rings *ou* shadows under the eyes
cerner [sɛʀne] *vt* (*MIL etc*) to surround; (*fig: problème*) to delimit, define
certain, e [sɛʀtɛ̃, -ɛn] *adj* certain ♦ *dét* certain; **d'un ~ âge** past one's prime, not so young; **un ~ temps** (quite) some time; **~s** some; **certainement** *adv* (*probablement*) most probably *ou* likely; (*bien sûr*) certainly, of course
certes [sɛʀt(ə)] *adv* admittedly; of course; indeed (yes)
certificat [sɛʀtifika] *nm* certificate
certitude [sɛʀtityd] *nf* certainty
cerveau, x [sɛʀvo] *nm* brain
cervelas [sɛʀvəla] *nm* saveloy
cervelle [sɛʀvɛl] *nf* (*ANAT*) brain
ces [se] *dét voir* **ce**
C.E.S. *sigle m* (= *Collège d'enseignement secondaire*) ≈ (junior) secondary school (*BRIT*)
cesse [sɛs]: **sans ~** *adv* continually, constantly; continuously; **il n'avait de ~ que** he would not rest until
cesser [sese] *vt* to stop ♦ *vi* to stop, cease; **~ de faire** to stop doing
cessez-le-feu *nm inv* ceasefire
c'est-à-dire [sɛtadiʀ] *adv* that is (to say)
cet, cette [sɛt] *dét voir* **ce**
ceux [sø] *pron voir* **celui**
CFC *abr* (= *chlorofluorocarbon*) CFC
C.F.D.T. *sigle f* = **Confédération française démocratique du travail**
C.G.T. *sigle f* = **Confédération générale du travail**
chacun, e [ʃakœ̃, -yn] *pron* each; (*indéfini*) everyone, everybody
chagrin [ʃagʀɛ̃] *nm* grief, sorrow; **chagriner** *vt* to grieve; to bother
chahut [ʃay] *nm* uproar; **chahuter** *vt* to rag, bait ♦ *vi* to make an uproar
chaîne [ʃɛn] *nf* chain; (*RADIO, TV: stations*)

channel; **travail à la** ~ production line work; ~ **(de montage** ou **de fabrication)** production ou assembly line; ~ **(de montagnes)** (mountain) range; ~ **(haute-fidélité** ou **hi-fi)** hi-fi system; ~ **(stéréo)** stereo (system)

chair [ʃɛʀ] *nf* flesh ♦ *adj*: **(couleur)** ~ flesh-coloured; **avoir la** ~ **de poule** to have goosepimples ou gooseflesh; **bien en** ~ plump, well-padded; **en** ~ **et en os** in the flesh

chaire [ʃɛʀ] *nf* (d'église) pulpit; (d'université) chair

chaise [ʃɛz] *nf* chair; ~ **longue** deckchair

châle [ʃɑl] *nm* shawl

chaleur [ʃalœʀ] *nf* heat; (fig) warmth; fire, fervour; heat

chaleureux, euse [ʃalœʀø, -øz] *adj* warm

chaloupe [ʃalup] *nf* launch; (de sauvetage) lifeboat

chalumeau, x [ʃalymo] *nm* blowlamp, blowtorch

chalutier [ʃalytje] *nm* trawler

chamailler [ʃamaje]: **se** ~ *vi* to squabble, bicker

chambouler [ʃɑbule] *vt* to disrupt, turn upside down

chambre [ʃɑbʀ(ə)] *nf* bedroom; (TECH) chamber; (POL) chamber, house; (JUR) court; (COMM) chamber; federation; **faire** ~ **à part** to sleep in separate rooms; ~ **à air** (de pneu) (inner) tube; ~ **à coucher** bedroom; ~ **à un lit/deux lits** (à l'hôtel) single-/twin-bedded room; ~ **d'amis** spare ou guest room; ~ **noire** (PHOTO) dark room

chambrer [ʃɑbʀe] *vt* (vin) to bring to room temperature

chameau, x [ʃamo] *nm* camel

champ [ʃɑ] *nm* field; **prendre du** ~ to draw back; ~ **de bataille** battlefield; ~ **de courses** racecourse; ~ **de tir** rifle range

champagne [ʃɑpaɲ] *nm* champagne

champêtre [ʃɑpɛtʀ(ə)] *adj* country *cpd*, rural

champignon [ʃɑpiɲɔ̃] *nm* mushroom; (terme générique) fungus; ~ **de Paris** button mushroom

champion, ne [ʃɑpjɔ̃, -jɔn] *adj, nm/f* champion; **championnat** *nm* championship

chance [ʃɑs] *nf*: **la** ~ luck; ~s *nfpl* (probabilités) chances; **une** ~ a stroke ou piece of luck ou good fortune; (occasion) a lucky break; **avoir de la** ~ to be lucky

chanceler [ʃɑsle] *vi* to totter

chancelier [ʃɑsəlje] *nm* (allemand) chancellor

chanceux, euse [ʃɑsø, -øz] *adj* lucky

chandail [ʃɑdaj] *nm* (thick) sweater

chandelier [ʃɑdəlje] *nm* candlestick

chandelle [ʃɑdɛl] *nf* (tallow) candle; **dîner**

aux ~**s** candlelight dinner

change [ʃɑʒ] *nm* (COMM) exchange

changement [ʃɑʒmɑ] *nm* change; ~ **de vitesses** gears *pl*; gear change

changer [ʃɑʒe] *vt* (modifier) to change, alter; (remplacer, COMM, rhabiller) to change ♦ *vi* to change, alter; **se** ~ *vi* to change (o.s.); ~ **de** (remplacer: adresse, nom, voiture etc) to change one's; (échanger, alterner: côté, place, train etc) to change +*npl*; ~ **de couleur/direction** to change colour/direction; ~ **d'idée** to change one's mind; ~ **de vitesse** to change gear

chanson [ʃɑsɔ̃] *nf* song

chant [ʃɑ] *nm* song; (art vocal) singing; (d'église) hymn; ~**age** [ʃɑtaʒ] *nm* blackmail; **faire du** ~ to use blackmail; ~**er** [ʃɑte] *vt, vi* to sing; **si cela lui chante** (fam) if he feels like it; ~**eur, euse** [ʃɑtœr, -øz] *nm/f* singer

chantier [ʃɑtje] *nm* (building) site; (sur une route) roadworks *pl*; **mettre en** ~ to put in hand; ~ **naval** shipyard

chantilly [ʃɑtiji] *nf* voir **crème**

chantonner [ʃɑtɔne] *vi, vt* to sing to oneself, hum

chanvre [ʃɑvʀ(ə)] *nm* hemp

chaparder [ʃapaʀde] *vt* to pinch

chapeau, x [ʃapo] *nm* hat; ~ **mou** trilby

chapelet [ʃaplɛ] *nm* (REL) rosary

chapelle [ʃapɛl] *nf* chapel; ~ **ardente** chapel of rest

chapelure [ʃaplyʀ] *nf* (dried) bread-crumbs *pl*

chapiteau, x [ʃapito] *nm* (de cirque) marquee, big top

chapitre [ʃapitʀ(ə)] *nm* chapter; (fig) subject, matter

chaque [ʃak] *dét* each, every; (indéfini) every

char [ʃaʀ] *nm* (à foin etc) cart, waggon; (de carnaval) float; ~ **(d'assaut)** tank

charabia [ʃaʀabja] (péj) *nm* gibberish

charade [ʃaʀad] *nf* riddle; (mimée) charade

charbon [ʃaʀbɔ̃] *nm* coal; ~ **de bois** charcoal

charcuterie [ʃaʀkytʀi] *nf* (magasin) pork butcher's shop and delicatessen; (produits) cooked pork meats *pl*; **charcutier, ière** *nm/f* pork butcher

chardon [ʃaʀdɔ̃] *nm* thistle

charge [ʃaʀʒ(ə)] *nf* (fardeau) load, burden; (explosif, ÉLEC, MIL, JUR) charge; (rôle, mission) responsibility; ~**s** *nfpl* (du loyer) service charges; **à la** ~ **de** (dépendant de) dependent upon; (aux frais de) chargeable to; **j'accepte, à** ~ **de revanche** I accept, provided I can do the same for you one day; **prendre en** ~ to take charge of; (suj: véhicule) to take on; (dépenses) to take care of; ~**s sociales** social security contributions; ~**ment** [ʃaʀʒɔmɑ] *nm* (objets)

load
charger [ʃaʀʒe] vt (*voiture, fusil, caméra*) to load; (*batterie*) to charge ♦ vi (*MIL etc*) to charge; **se ~ de** vt to see to; **~ qn de (faire) qch** to put sb in charge of (doing) sth
chariot [ʃaʀjo] nm trolley; (*charrette*) waggon; (*de machine à écrire*) carriage
charité [ʃaʀite] nf charity; **faire la ~ à** to give (something) to
charmant, e [ʃaʀmɑ̃, -ɑ̃t] adj charming
charme [ʃaʀm(ə)] nm charm; **charmer** vt to charm
charnel, le [ʃaʀnɛl] adj carnal
charnière [ʃaʀnjɛʀ] nf hinge; (*fig*) turning-point
charnu, e [ʃaʀny] adj fleshy
charpente [ʃaʀpɑ̃t] nf frame(work); **charpentier** nm carpenter
charpie [ʃaʀpi] nf: **en ~** (*fig*) in shreds *ou* ribbons
charrette [ʃaʀɛt] nf cart
charrier [ʃaʀje] vt to carry (along); to cart, carry
charrue [ʃaʀy] nf plough (*BRIT*), plow (*US*)
chasse [ʃas] nf hunting; (*au fusil*) shooting; (*poursuite*) chase; (*aussi:* **~ d'eau**) flush; **la ~ est ouverte** the hunting season is open; **~ gardée** private hunting grounds *pl*; **prendre en ~** to give chase to; **tirer la ~ (d'eau)** to flush the toilet, pull the chain; **~ à courre** hunting
chassé-croisé [ʃasekʀwaze] nm (*fig*) mix-up where people miss each other in turn
chasse-neige [ʃasnɛʒ] nm inv snowplough (*BRIT*), snowplow (*US*)
chasser [ʃase] vt to hunt; (*expulser*) to chase away *ou* out, drive away *ou* out; **chasseur, euse** nm/f hunter ♦ nm (*avion*) fighter; **chasseur de têtes** nm (*fig*) head-hunter
châssis [ʃasi] nm (*AUTO*) chassis; (*cadre*) frame; (*de jardin*) cold frame
chat [ʃa] nm cat
châtaigne [ʃatɛɲ] nf chestnut; **châtaignier** nm chestnut (tree)
châtain [ʃatɛ̃] adj inv chestnut (brown); chestnut-haired
château, x [ʃɑto] nm castle; **~ d'eau** water tower; **~ fort** stronghold, fortified castle
châtier [ʃɑtje] vt to punish; (*fig: style*) to polish; **châtiment** nm punishment
chaton [ʃatɔ̃] nm (*ZOOL*) kitten
chatouiller [ʃatuje] vt to tickle; (*l'odorat, le palais*) to titillate; **chatouilleux, euse** adj ticklish; (*fig*) touchy, over-sensitive
chatoyer [ʃatwaje] vi to shimmer
châtrer [ʃɑtʀe] vt (*mâle*) to castrate; (: *cheval*) to geld; (*femelle*) to spay
chatte [ʃat] nf (she-)cat
chaud, e [ʃo, -od] adj (*gén*) warm; (*très chaud*) hot; (*fig*) hearty; heated; **il fait ~** it's warm; it's hot; **avoir ~** to be warm; to

be hot; **ça me tient ~** it keeps me warm; **rester au ~** to stay in the warm
chaudière [ʃodjɛʀ] nf boiler
chaudron [ʃodʀɔ̃] nm cauldron
chauffage [ʃofaʒ] nm heating; **~ central** central heating
chauffard [ʃofaʀ] nm (*péj*) reckless driver; hit-and-run driver
chauffe-eau [ʃofo] nm inv water-heater
chauffer [ʃofe] vt to heat ♦ vi to heat up, warm up; (*trop* ~: *moteur*) to overheat; **se ~** vi (*se mettre en train*) to warm up; (*au soleil*) to warm o.s.
chauffeur [ʃofœʀ] nm driver; (*privé*) chauffeur
chaume [ʃom] nm (*du toit*) thatch
chaumière [ʃomjɛʀ] nf (thatched) cottage
chaussée [ʃose] nf road(way)
chausse-pied [ʃospje] nm shoe-horn
chausser [ʃose] vt (*bottes, skis*) to put on; (*enfant*) to put shoes on; **~ du 38/42** to take size 38/42
chaussette [ʃosɛt] nf sock
chausson [ʃosɔ̃] nm slipper; (*de bébé*) bootee; **~ (aux pommes)** (apple) turnover
chaussure [ʃosyʀ] nf shoe; **~s basses** flat shoes; **~s de ski** ski boots
chauve [ʃov] adj bald
chauve-souris [ʃovsuʀi] nf bat
chauvin, e [ʃovɛ̃, -in] adj chauvinistic
chaux [ʃo] nf lime; **blanchi à la ~** whitewashed
chavirer [ʃaviʀe] vi to capsize
chef [ʃɛf] nm head, leader; (*de cuisine*) chef; **en ~** (*MIL etc*) in chief; **~ d'accusation** charge; **~ d'entreprise** company head; **~ d'état** head of state; **~ de file** (*de parti etc*) leader; **~ de gare** station master; **~ d'orchestre** conductor (*BRIT*), director (*US*); **~-d'œuvre** [ʃedœvʀ(ə)] nm masterpiece; **~-lieu** [ʃefljø] nm county town
chemin [ʃəmɛ̃] nm path; (*itinéraire, direction, trajet*) way; **en ~** on the way; **~ de fer** railway (*BRIT*), railroad (*US*); **par chemin de fer** by rail
cheminée [ʃəmine] nf chimney; (*à l'intérieur*) chimney piece, fireplace; (*de bateau*) funnel
cheminement [ʃəminmɑ̃] nm progress; course
cheminot [ʃəmino] nm railwayman
chemise [ʃəmiz] nf shirt; (*dossier*) folder; **~ de nuit** nightdress
chemisier [ʃəmizje] nm blouse
chenal, aux [ʃənal, -o] nm channel
chêne [ʃɛn] nm oak (tree); (*bois*) oak
chenil [ʃənil] nm kennels *pl*
chenille [ʃənij] nf (*ZOOL*) caterpillar; (*AUTO*) caterpillar track
chèque [ʃɛk] nm cheque (*BRIT*), check (*US*); **~ sans provision** bad cheque; **~ de voyage** traveller's cheque; **chéquier** nm

cheque book

cher, ère [ʃɛʀ] *adj* (*aimé*) dear; (*coûteux*) expensive, dear ♦ *adv*: **cela coûte ~** it's expensive

chercher [ʃɛʀʃe] *vt* to look for; (*gloire etc*) to seek; **aller ~** to go for, go and fetch; **~ à faire** to try to do; **chercheur, euse** [ʃɛʀʃœʀ, -øz] *nm/f* researcher, research worker

chère [ʃɛʀ] *adj voir* **cher** ♦ *nf*: **la bonne ~** good food

chéri, e [ʃeʀi] *adj* beloved, dear; (**mon**) **~** darling

chérir [ʃeʀiʀ] *vt* to cherish

oherté [ʃɛʀte] *nf*: **la ~ de la vie** the high cost of living

chétif, ive [ʃetif, -iv] *adj* puny, stunted

cheval, aux [ʃəval, -o] *nm* horse; (*AUTO*): **~ (vapeur)** horsepower *no pl*; **faire du ~** to ride; **à ~** on horseback; **à ~ sur** astride; (*fig*) overlapping; **~ de course** racehorse

chevalet [ʃəvalɛ] *nm* easel

chevalier [ʃəvalje] *nm* knight

chevalière [ʃəvaljɛʀ] *nf* signet ring

chevalin, e [ʃəvalɛ̃, -in] *adj*: **boucherie ~e** horse-meat butcher's

chevaucher [ʃəvoʃe] *vi* (*aussi*: **se ~**) to overlap (each other) ♦ *vt* to be astride, straddle

chevaux [ʃəvo] *nmpl de* **cheval**

chevelu, e [ʃəvly] *adj* with a good head of hair, hairy (*péj*)

chevelure [ʃəvlyʀ] *nf* hair *no pl*

chevet [ʃəvɛ] *nm*: **au ~ de qn** at sb's bedside; **lampe de ~** bedside lamp

cheveu, x [ʃəvø] *nm* hair; **~x** *nmpl* (*chevelure*) hair *sg*; **avoir les ~x courts** to have short hair

cheville [ʃəvij] *nf* (*ANAT*) ankle; (*de bois*) peg; (*pour une vis*) plug

chèvre [ʃɛvʀ(ə)] *nf* (she-)goat

chevreau, x [ʃəvʀo] *nm* kid

chèvrefeuille [ʃɛvʀəfœj] *nm* honeysuckle

chevreuil [ʃəvʀœj] *nm* roe deer *inv*; (*CULIN*) venison

chevronné, e [ʃəvʀɔne] *adj* seasoned

MOT CLÉ
---

chez [ʃe] *prép* **1** (*à la demeure de*) at; (: *direction*) to; **~ qn** at/to sb's house *ou* place; **~ moi** at home; (*direction*) home
2 (+*profession*) at; (: *direction*) to; **~ le boulanger/dentiste** at *or* to the baker's/dentist's
3 (*dans le caractère, l'œuvre de*) in; **~ les renards/Racine** in foxes/Racine

---

chez-soi [ʃeswa] *nm inv* home

chic [ʃik] *adj inv* chic, smart; (*généreux*) nice, decent ♦ *nm* stylishness; **~!** great!; **avoir le ~ de** to have the knack of

chicane [ʃikan] *nf* (*querelle*) squabble

chicaner [ʃikane] *vi* (*ergoter*): **~ sur** to quibble about

chiche [ʃiʃ] *adj* niggardly, mean ♦ *excl* (*à un défi*) you're on!

chichi [ʃiʃi] (*fam*) *nm* fuss

chicorée [ʃikɔʀe] *nf* (*café*) chicory; (*salade*) endive

chien [ʃjɛ̃] *nm* dog; **en ~ de fusil** curled up; **~ de garde** guard dog

chiendent [ʃjɛ̃dɑ̃] *nm* couch grass

chienne [ʃjɛn] *nf* dog, bitch

chier [ʃje] (*fam!*) *vi* to crap (*!*)

chiffon [ʃifɔ̃] *nm* (piece of) rag; **~ner** [ʃifɔne] *vt* to crumple; (*tracasser*) to concern; **~nier** [ʃifɔnje] *nm* rag-and-bone man

chiffre [ʃifʀ(ə)] *nm* (*représentant un nombre*) figure; numeral; (*montant, total*) total, sum; **en ~s ronds** in round figures; **~ d'affaires** turnover; **chiffrer** *vt* (*dépense*) to put a figure to, assess; (*message*) to (en)code, cipher

chignon [ʃiɲɔ̃] *nm* chignon, bun

Chili [ʃili] *nm*: **le ~** Chile

chimie [ʃimi] *nf* chemistry; **chimique** *adj* chemical; **produits chimiques** chemicals

Chine [ʃin] *nf*: **la ~** China

chinois, e [ʃinwa, -waz] *adj, nm/f* Chinese ♦ *nm* (*LING*) Chinese

chiot [ʃjo] *nm* pup(py)

chips [ʃips] *nfpl* crisps (*BRIT*), (potato) chips (*US*)

chiquenaude [ʃiknod] *nf* flick, flip

chirurgical, e, aux [ʃiʀyʀʒikal, -o] *adj* surgical

chirurgie [ʃiʀyʀʒi] *nf* surgery; **~ esthétique** plastic surgery; **chirurgien, ne** *nm/f* surgeon

choc [ʃɔk] *nm* impact; shock; crash; (*moral*) shock; (*affrontement*) clash

chocolat [ʃɔkɔla] *nm* chocolate; (*boisson*) (hot) chocolate; **~ au lait** milk chocolate

chœur [kœʀ] *nm* (*chorale*) choir; (*OPÉRA, THÉÂTRE*) chorus; **en ~** in chorus

choisir [ʃwaziʀ] *vt* to choose, select

choix [ʃwa] *nm* choice, selection; **avoir le ~** to have the choice; **premier ~** (*COMM*) class one; **de ~** choice, selected; **au ~** as you wish

chômage [ʃomaʒ] *nm* unemployment; **mettre au ~** to make redundant, put out of work; **être au ~** to be unemployed *ou* out of work; **chômeur, euse** *nm/f* unemployed person

chope [ʃɔp] *nf* tankard

choquer [ʃɔke] *vt* (*offenser*) to shock; (*commotionner*) to shake (up)

choriste [kɔʀist(ə)] *nm/f* choir member; (*OPÉRA*) chorus member

chorus [kɔʀys] *nm*: **faire ~ (avec)** to voice one's agreement (with)

chose [ʃoz] *nf* thing; **c'est peu de ~** it's nothing (really); it's not much

chou, x [ʃu] *nm* cabbage; **mon petit ~** (my) sweetheart; **~ à la crème** cream bun (*made of choux pastry*)

chouchou, te [ʃuʃu, -ut] *nm/f* (*SCOL*) teacher's pet

choucroute [ʃukʀut] *nf* sauerkraut

chouette [ʃwɛt] *nf* owl ♦ *adj* (*fam*) great, smashing

chou-fleur [ʃuflœʀ] *nm* cauliflower

choyer [ʃwaje] *vt* to cherish; to pamper

chrétien, ne [kʀetjɛ̃, -ɛn] *adj, nm/f* Christian

Christ [kʀist] *nm*: **le ~** Christ; **christianisme** *nm* Christianity

chrome [kʀom] *nm* chromium; **chromé, e** *adj* chromium-plated

chronique [kʀɔnik] *adj* chronic ♦ *nf* (*de journal*) column, page; (*historique*) chronicle; (*RADIO, TV*): **la ~ sportive/théâtrale** the sports/theatre review; **la ~ locale** local news and gossip

chronologique [kʀɔnɔlɔʒik] *adj* chronological

chronomètre [kʀɔnɔmetʀ(ə)] *nm* stopwatch; **chronométrer** *vt* to time

chrysanthème [kʀizɑ̃tɛm] *nm* chrysanthemum

C.H.U. *sigle m* (= *centre hospitalier universitaire*) ≈ (teaching) hospital

chuchoter [ʃyʃɔte] *vt, vi* to whisper

chuinter [ʃɥɛ̃te] *vi* to hiss

chut [ʃyt] *excl* sh!

chute [ʃyt] *nf* fall; (*de bois, papier: déchet*) scrap; **faire une ~ (de 10 m)** to fall (10 m); **~ (d'eau)** waterfall; **la ~ des cheveux** hair loss; **~ libre** free fall; **~s de pluie/neige** rain/snowfalls

Chypre [ʃipʀ] *nm/f* Cyprus

-ci [si] *adv voir* **par** ♦ *dét*: **ce garçon-ci/-là** this/that boy; **ces femmes-ci/-là** these/those women

ci-après [siapʀɛ] *adv* hereafter

cible [sibl(ə)] *nf* target

ciboulette [sibulɛt] *nf* (small) chive

cicatrice [sikatʀis] *nf* scar

cicatriser [sikatʀize] *vt* to heal

ci-contre [sikɔ̃tʀ(ə)] *adv* opposite

ci-dessous [sidəsu] *adv* below

ci-dessus [sidəsy] *adv* above

cidre [sidʀ(ə)] *nm* cider

Cie *abr* (= *compagnie*) Co.

ciel [sjɛl] *nm* sky; (*REL*) heaven; **cieux** *nmpl* (*littéraire*) sky *sg*, skies; **à ~ ouvert** open-air; (*mine*) opencast

cierge [sjɛʀʒ(ə)] *nm* candle

cieux [sjø] *nmpl* *de* **ciel**

cigale [sigal] *nf* cicada

cigare [sigaʀ] *nm* cigar

cigarette [sigaʀɛt] *nf* cigarette

ci-gît [siʒi] *adv +vb* here lies

cigogne [sigɔɲ] *nf* stork

ci-inclus, e [siɛ̃kly, -yz] *adj, adv* enclosed

ci-joint, e [siʒwɛ̃, -ɛt] *adj, adv* enclosed

cil [sil] *nm* (eye)lash

cime [sim] *nf* top; (*montagne*) peak

ciment [simɑ̃] *nm* cement; **~ armé** reinforced concrete

cimetière [simtjɛʀ] *nm* cemetery; (*d'église*) churchyard

cinéaste [sineast(ə)] *nm/f* film-maker

cinéma [sinema] *nm* cinema; **~tographique** *adj* film *cpd*, cinema *cpd*

cinéphile [sinefil] *nm/f* cinema-goer

cinglant, e [sɛ̃glɑ̃, -ɑ̃t] *adj* (*échec*) crushing

cinglé, e [sɛ̃gle] (*fam*) *adj* crazy

cingler [sɛ̃gle] *vt* to lash; (*fig*) to sting

cinq [sɛ̃k] *num* five

cinquantaine [sɛ̃kɑ̃tɛn] *nf*: **une ~ (de)** about fifty; **avoir la ~ (âge)** to be around fifty

cinquante [sɛ̃kɑ̃t] *num* fifty; **cinquantenaire** *adj, nm/f* fifty-year-old

cinquième [sɛ̃kjɛm] *num* fifth

cintre [sɛ̃tʀ(ə)] *nm* coat-hanger

cintré, e [sɛ̃tʀe] *adj* (*chemise*) fitted

cirage [siʀaʒ] *nm* (shoe) polish

circonflexe [siʀkɔ̃flɛks(ə)] *adj*: **accent ~** circumflex accent

circonscription [siʀkɔ̃skʀipsjɔ̃] *nf* district; **~ électorale** (*d'un député*) constituency

circonscrire [siʀkɔ̃skʀiʀ] *vt* to define, delimit; (*incendie*) to contain

circonstance [siʀkɔ̃stɑ̃s] *nf* circumstance; (*occasion*) occasion

circonvenir [siʀkɔ̃vniʀ] *vt* to circumvent

circuit [siʀkɥi] *nm* (*trajet*) tour, (round) trip; (*ÉLEC, TECH*) circuit

circulaire [siʀkyleʀ] *adj, nf* circular

circulation [siʀkylasjɔ̃] *nf* circulation; (*AUTO*): **la ~** (the) traffic

circuler [siʀkyle] *vi* to drive (along); to walk along; (*train etc*) to run; (*sang, devises*) to circulate; **faire ~** (*nouvelle*) to spread (about), circulate; (*badauds*) to move on

cire [siʀ] *nf* wax; **ciré** [siʀe] *nm* oilskin; **cirer** [siʀe] *vt* to wax, polish

cirque [siʀk(ə)] *nm* circus; (*GÉO*) cirque; (*fig*) chaos, bedlam; carry-on

cisaille(s) [sizaj] *nf(pl)* (gardening) shears *pl*

ciseau, x [sizo] *nm*: **~ (à bois)** chisel; **~x** *nmpl* (*paire de* **~x**) (pair of) scissors

ciseler [sizle] *vt* to chisel, carve

citadin, e [sitadɛ̃, -in] *nm/f* city dweller

citation [sitasjɔ̃] *nf* (*d'auteur*) quotation; (*JUR*) summons *sg*

cité [site] *nf* town; (*plus grande*) city; **~ universitaire** students' residences *pl*

citer [site] *vt* (*un auteur*) to quote (from); (*nommer*) to name; (*JUR*) to summon

citerne [sitɛʀn(ə)] *nf* tank

citoyen, ne [sitwajɛ̃, -ɛn] *nm/f* citizen

citron [sitʀɔ̃] *nm* lemon; **~ vert** lime; **citronnade** *nf* lemonade; **citronnier** *nm*

lemon tree
citrouille [sitʀuj] nf pumpkin
civet [sivɛ] nm stew
civière [sivjɛʀ] nf stretcher
civil, e [sivil] adj (JUR, ADMIN, poli) civil; (non militaire) civilian; **en ~** in civilian clothes; **dans le ~** in civilian life
civilisation [sivilizɑsjɔ̃] nf civilization
civisme [sivism(ə)] nm public-spiritedness
clair, e [klɛʀ] adj light; (chambre) light, bright; (eau, son, fig) clear ♦ adv: **voir ~** to see clearly; **tirer qch au ~** to clear sth up, clarify sth; **mettre au ~** (notes etc) to tidy up; **le plus ~ de son temps** the better part of his time; **~ de lune** nm moonlight; **clairement** adv clearly
clairière [klɛʀjɛʀ] nf clearing
clairon [klɛʀɔ̃] nm bugle
claironner [klɛʀɔne] vt (fig) to trumpet, shout from the rooftops
clairsemé, e [klɛʀsəme] adj sparse
clairvoyant, e [klɛʀvwajɑ̃, -ɑ̃t] adj perceptive, clear-sighted
clandestin, e [klɑ̃dɛstɛ̃, -in] adj clandestine, covert; **passager ~** stowaway
clapier [klapje] nm (rabbit) hutch
clapoter [klapɔte] vi to lap
claque [klak] nf (gifle) slap
claquer [klake] vi (drapeau) to flap; (porte) to bang, slam; (coup de feu) to ring out ♦ vt (porte) to slam, bang; (doigts) to snap; **se ~ un muscle** to pull ou strain a muscle
claquettes [klakɛt] nfpl tap-dancing sg
clarinette [klaʀinɛt] nf clarinet
clarté [klaʀte] nf lightness; brightness; (d'un son, de l'eau) clearness; (d'une explication) clarity
classe [klɑs] nf class; (SCOL: local) class(room); (: leçon, élèves) class; **faire la ~** to be a ou the teacher; to teach; **~ment** [klɑsmɑ̃] nm (rang: SCOL) place; (: SPORT) placing; (liste: SCOL) class list (in order of merit); (: SPORT) placings pl; **~r** [klɑse] vt (idées, livres) to classify; (papiers) to file; (candidat, concurrent) to grade; (JUR: affaire) to close; **se ~r premier/dernier** to come first/last; (SPORT) to finish first/last
classeur [klɑsœʀ] nm (cahier) file; (meuble) filing cabinet
classique [klasik] adj classical; (sobre: coupe etc) classic(al); (habituel) standard, classic
clause [kloz] nf clause
claustrer [klostʀe] vt to confine
clavecin [klavsɛ̃] nm harpsichord
clavicule [klavikyl] nf collarbone
clavier [klavje] nm keyboard
clé [kle] nf key; (MUS) clef; (de mécanicien) spanner (BRIT), wrench (US); **~s en main** (d'une voiture) on-the-road price; **~ anglaise** (monkey) wrench; **~ de contact** ignition key

clef [kle] nf = **clé**
clément, e [klemɑ̃, -ɑ̃t] adj (temps) mild; (indulgent) lenient
clerc [klɛʀ] nm: **~ de notaire** solicitor's clerk
clergé [klɛʀʒe] nm clergy
cliché [klife] nm (PHOTO) negative; print; (LING) cliché
client, e [klijɑ̃, -ɑ̃t] nm/f (acheteur) customer, client; (d'hôtel) guest, patron; (du docteur) patient; (de l'avocat) client; **clientèle** nf (du magasin) customers pl, clientèle; (du docteur, de l'avocat) practice
cligner [kliɲe] vi: **~ des yeux** to blink (one's eyes); **~ de l'œil** to wink
clignotant [kliɲɔtɑ̃] nm (AUTO) indicator
clignoter [kliɲɔte] vi (étoiles etc) to twinkle; (lumière) to flash; (: vaciller) to flicker
climat [klima] nm climate
climatisation [klimatizɑsjɔ̃] nf air conditioning; **climatisé, e** adj air-conditioned
clin d'œil [klɛ̃dœj] nm wink; **en un ~** in a flash
clinique [klinik] nf nursing home
clinquant, e [klɛ̃kɑ̃, -ɑ̃t] adj flashy
cliqueter [klikte] vi to clash; to jangle, jingle; to chink
clochard, e [klɔʃaʀ, -aʀd(ə)] nm/f tramp
cloche [klɔʃ] nf (d'église) bell; (fam) clot; **~ à fromage** cheese-cover
cloche-pied [klɔʃpje]: **à ~** adv on one leg, hopping (along)
clocher [klɔʃe] nm church tower; (en pointe) steeple ♦ vi (fam) to be ou go wrong; **de ~** (péj) parochial
cloison [klwazɔ̃] nf partition (wall)
cloître [klwatʀ(ə)] nm cloister
cloîtrer [klwatʀe] vt: **se ~** to shut o.s. up ou away
cloque [klɔk] nf blister
clore [klɔʀ] vt to close; **clos, e** adj voir **maison**; **huis** ♦ nm (enclosed) field
clôture [klotyʀ] nf closure; (barrière) enclosure; **clôturer** vt (terrain) to enclose; (débats) to close
clou [klu] nm nail; (MÉD) boil; **~s** nmpl (passage clouté) pedestrian crossing; **pneus à ~s** studded tyres; **le ~ du spectacle** the highlight of the show; **~ de girofle** clove; **clouer** vt to nail down ou up
clown [klun] nm clown
club [klœb] nm club
C.N.R.S. sigle m = **Centre nationale de la recherche scientifique**
coasser [kɔase] vi to croak
cobaye [kɔbaj] nm guinea-pig
coca [kɔka] nm Coke (®)
cocaïne [kɔkain] nf cocaine
cocasse [kɔkas] adj comical, funny
coccinelle [kɔksinɛl] nf ladybird (BRIT), ladybug (US)
cocher [kɔʃe] nm coachman ♦ vt to tick

off; (*entailler*) to notch

cochère [kɔʃɛʀ] *adj f*: **porte ~** carriage entrance

cochon, ne [kɔʃɔ̃, -ɔn] *nm* pig ♦ *adj* (*fam*) dirty, smutty; **cochonnerie** (*fam*) *nf* filth; rubbish, trash

cocktail [kɔktɛl] *nm* cocktail; (*réception*) cocktail party

coco [koko] *nm voir* **noix**; (*fam*) bloke

cocorico [kokɔriko] *excl, nm* cock-a-doodle-do

cocotier [kokɔtje] *nm* coconut palm

cocotte [kokɔt] *nf* (*en fonte*) casserole; **~ (minute)** pressure cooker; **ma ~** (*fam*) sweetie (*pie*)

cocu [kɔky] *nm* cuckold

code [kɔd] *nm* code ♦ *adj*: **phares ~s** dipped lights; **se mettre en ~(s)** to dip one's (head)lights; **~ à barres** bar code; **~ civil** Common Law; **~ de la route** highway code; **~ pénal** penal code; **~ postal** (*numéro*) post (*BRIT*) *ou* zip (*US*) code

cœur [kœʀ] *nm* heart; (*CARTES: couleur*) hearts *pl*; (: *carte*) heart; **avoir bon ~** to be kind-hearted; **avoir mal au ~** to feel sick; **en avoir le ~ net** to be clear in one's own mind (about it); **par ~** by heart; **de bon ~** willingly; **cela lui tient à ~** that's (very) close to his heart

coffre [kɔfʀ(ə)] *nm* (*meuble*) chest; (*d'auto*) boot (*BRIT*), trunk (*US*); **coffre(-fort)** *nm* safe

coffret [kɔfʀɛ] *nm* casket

cognac [kɔɲak] *nm* brandy, cognac

cogner [kɔɲe] *vi* to knock

cohérent, e [kɔeʀɑ̃, -ɑ̃t] *adj* coherent, consistent

cohorte [kɔɔʀt(ə)] *nf* troop

cohue [kɔy] *nf* crowd

coi, coite [kwa, kwat] *adj*: **rester ~** to remain silent

coiffe [kwaf] *nf* headdress

coiffé, e [kwafe] *adj*: **bien/mal ~** with tidy/untidy hair; **~ en arrière** with one's hair brushed *ou* combed back

coiffer [kwafe] *vt* (*fig*) to cover, top; **se ~** *vi* to do one's hair; to put on one's hat; **~ qn** to do sb's hair

coiffeur, euse [kwafœʀ, -øz] *nm/f* hairdresser; **coiffeuse** *nf* (*table*) dressing table

coiffure [kwafyʀ] *nf* (*cheveux*) hairstyle, hairdo; (*chapeau*) hat, headgear *no pl*; (*art*): **la ~** hairdressing

coin [kwɛ̃] *nm* corner; (*pour coincer*) wedge; **l'épicerie du ~** the local grocer; **dans le ~** (*aux alentours*) in the area, around about; locally; **au ~ du feu** by the fireside; **regard en ~** sideways glance

coincé, e [kwɛ̃se] *adj* stuck, jammed; (*fig: inhibé*) inhibited, hung up (*fam*)

coincer [kwɛ̃se] *vt* to jam

coïncidence [kɔɛ̃sidɑ̃s] *nf* coincidence

coïncider [kɔɛ̃side] *vi* to coincide

col [kɔl] *nm* (*de chemise*) collar; (*encolure, cou*) neck; (*de montagne*) pass; **~ de l'utérus** cervix; **~ roulé** polo-neck

colère [kɔlɛʀ] *nf* anger; **une ~** a fit of anger; **(se mettre) en ~** (to get) angry; **coléreux, euse** *adj*; **colérique** *adj* quick-tempered, irascible

colifichet [kɔlifiʃɛ] *nm* trinket

colimaçon [kɔlimasɔ̃] *nm*: **escalier en ~** spiral staircase

colin [kɔlɛ̃] *nm* hake

colique [kɔlik] *nf* diarrhoea; colic (*pains*)

colis [kɔli] *nm* parcel

collaborateur, trice [kɔlabɔʀatœʀ, -tʀis] *nm/f* (*aussi POL*) collaborator; (*d'une revue*) contributor

collaborer [kɔlabɔʀe] *vi* to collaborate; **~ à** to collaborate on; (*revue*) to contribute to

collant, e [kɔlɑ̃, -ɑ̃t] *adj* sticky; (*robe etc*) clinging, skintight; (*péj*) clinging ♦ *nm* (*bas*) tights *pl*

collation [kɔlasjɔ̃] *nf* light meal

colle [kɔl] *nf* glue; (*à papiers peints*) (wallpaper) paste; (*devinette*) teaser, riddle; (*SCOL: fam*) detention

collecte [kɔlɛkt(ə)] *nf* collection

collectif, ive [kɔlɛktif, -iv] *adj* collective; (*visite, billet*) group *cpd*

collection [kɔlɛksjɔ̃] *nf* collection; (*ÉDITION*) series; **collectionner** *vt* (*tableaux, timbres*) to collect; **collectionneur, euse** *nm/f* collector

collectivité [kɔlɛktivite] *nf* group; **~s locales** (*ADMIN*) local authorities

collège [kɔlɛʒ] *nm* (*école*) (secondary) school; (*assemblée*) body; **collégien** *nm* schoolboy; **collégienne** *nf* schoolgirl

collègue [kɔlɛg] *nm/f* colleague

coller [kɔle] *vt* (*papier, timbre*) to stick (on); (*affiche*) to stick up; (*enveloppe*) to stick down; (*morceaux*) to stick *ou* glue together; (*fam: mettre, fourrer*) to stick, shove; (*SCOL: fam*) to keep in ♦ *vi* (*être collant*) to be sticky; (*adhérer*) to stick; **~ à** to stick to

collet [kɔlɛ] *nm* (*piège*) snare, noose; (*cou*): **prendre qn au ~** to grab sb by the throat; **~ monté** *adj inv* straight-laced

collier [kɔlje] *nm* (*bijou*) necklace; (*de chien, TECH*) collar; **~ (de barbe)** narrow beard along the line of the jaw

collimateur [kɔlimatœʀ] *nm*: **avoir qn/qch dans le ~** (*fig*) to have sb/sth in one's sights

colline [kɔlin] *nf* hill

collision [kɔlizjɔ̃] *nf* collision, crash; **entrer en ~ (avec)** to collide (with)

colmater [kɔlmate] *vt* (*fuite*) to seal off; (*brèche*) to plug, fill in

colombe [kɔlɔ̃b] *nf* dove

colon [kɔlɔ̃] *nm* settler

colonel [kɔlɔnɛl] *nm* colonel

colonie [kɔlɔni] *nf* colony; ~ **(de vacances)** holiday camp *(for children)*

colonne [kɔlɔn] *nf* column; **se mettre en** ~ **par deux** to get into twos; ~ **(vertébrale)** spine, spinal column

colorant [kɔlɔrɑ̃] *nm* colouring

colorer [kɔlɔre] *vt* to colour

colorier [kɔlɔrje] *vt* to colour (in)

coloris [kɔlɔri] *nm* colour, shade

colporter [kɔlpɔrte] *vt* to hawk, peddle

colza [kɔlza] *nm* rape (seed)

coma [kɔma] *nm* coma

combat [kɔ̃ba] *nm* fight; fighting *no pl*; ~ **de boxe** boxing match

combattant [kɔ̃batɑ̃] *nm*: **ancien** ~ war veteran

combattre [kɔ̃batʀ(ə)] *vt* to fight; *(épidémie, ignorance)* to combat, fight against

combien [kɔ̃bjɛ̃] *adv (quantité)* how much; *(nombre)* how many; *(exclamatif)* how; ~ **de** how much; how many; ~ **de temps** how long; ~ **coûte/pèse ceci?** how much does this cost/weigh?

combinaison [kɔ̃binɛzɔ̃] *nf* combination; *(astuce)* device, scheme; *(de femme)* slip; *(d'aviateur)* flying suit; *(d'homme-grenouille)* wetsuit; *(bleu de travail)* boiler suit *(BRIT)*, coveralls *pl (US)*

combine [kɔ̃bin] *nf* trick; *(péj)* scheme, fiddle *(BRIT)*

combiné [kɔ̃bine] *nm (aussi: ~ téléphonique)* receiver

combiner [kɔ̃bine] *vt* to combine; *(plan, horaire)* to work out, devise

comble [kɔ̃bl(ə)] *adj (salle)* packed (full) ♦ *nm (du bonheur, plaisir)* height; ~**s** *nmpl (CONSTR)* attic *sg*, loft *sg*; **c'est le** ~! that beats everything!

combler [kɔ̃ble] *vt (trou)* to fill in; *(besoin, lacune)* to fill; *(déficit)* to make good; *(satisfaire)* to fulfil

combustible [kɔ̃bystibl(ə)] *nm* fuel

comédie [kɔmedi] *nf* comedy; *(fig)* play-acting *no pl*; ~ **musicale** musical; **comédien, ne** *nm/f* actor(tress)

comestible [kɔmɛstibl(ə)] *adj* edible

comique [kɔmik] *adj (drôle)* comical; *(THÉÂTRE)* comic ♦ *nm (artiste)* comic, comedian

comité [kɔmite] *nm* committee; ~ **d'entreprise** works council

commandant [kɔmɑ̃dɑ̃] *nm (gén)* commander, commandant; *(NAVIG, AVIAT)* captain

commande [kɔmɑ̃d] *nf (COMM)* order; ~**s** *nfpl (AVIAT etc)* controls; **sur** ~ to order; ~ **à distance** remote control

commandement [kɔmɑ̃dmɑ̃] *nm* command; *(REL)* commandment

commander [kɔmɑ̃de] *vt (COMM)* to order; *(diriger, ordonner)* to command; ~ **à qn de faire** to command *ou* order sb to do

commando [kɔmɑ̃do] *nm* commando (squad)

MOT CLÉ

comme [kɔm] *prép* **1** *(comparaison)* like; **tout** ~ **son père** just like his father; **fort** ~ **un boeuf** as strong as an ox; **joli** ~ **tout** ever so pretty

2 *(manière)* like; **faites-le** ~ **ça** do it like this, do it this way; ~ **ci,** ~ **ça** so-so, middling

3 *(en tant que)* as a; **donner** ~ **prix** to give as a prize; **travailler** ~ **secrétaire** to work as a secretary

♦ *conj* **1** *(ainsi que)* as; **elle écrit** ~ **elle parle** she writes as she talks; ~ **si** as if

2 *(au moment où, alors que)* as; **il est parti** ~ **j'arrivais** he left as I arrived

3 *(parce que, puisque)* as; ~ **il était en retard, il ...** as he was late, he ...

♦ *adv*: ~ **il est fort/c'est bon!** he's so strong/it's so good!

---

commémorer [kɔmemɔre] *vt* to commemorate

commencement [kɔmɑ̃smɑ̃] *nm* beginning, start, commencement

commencer [kɔmɑ̃se] *vt, vi* to begin, start, commence; ~ **à** *ou* **de faire** to begin *ou* start doing

comment [kɔmɑ̃] *adv* how ♦ *nm*: **le** ~ **et le pourquoi** the whys and wherefores; ~? *(que dites-vous)* pardon?

commentaire [kɔmɑ̃tɛʀ] *nm* comment; remark

commenter [kɔmɑ̃te] *vt (jugement, événement)* to comment (up)on; *(RADIO, TV: match, manifestation)* to cover

commérages [kɔmeʀaʒ] *nmpl* gossip *sg*

commerçant, e [kɔmɛʀsɑ̃, -ɑ̃t] *nm/f* shopkeeper, trader

commerce [kɔmɛʀs(ə)] *nm (activité)* trade, commerce; *(boutique)* business; **vendu dans le** ~ sold in the shops; **commercial, e, aux** *adj* commercial, trading; *(péj)* commercial; **commercialiser** *vt* to market

commère [kɔmɛʀ] *nf* gossip

commettre [kɔmɛtʀ(ə)] *vt* to commit

commis [kɔmi] *nm (de magasin)* (shop) assistant; *(de banque)* clerk; ~ **voyageur** commercial traveller

commissaire [kɔmisɛʀ] *nm (de police)* ≈ (police) superintendent; ~**-priseur** *nm* auctioneer

commissariat [kɔmisaʀja] *nm* police station

commission [kɔmisjɔ̃] *nf (comité, pourcentage)* commission; *(message)* message; *(course)* errand; ~**s** *nfpl (achats)* shopping *sg*

commode [kɔmɔd] *adj (pratique)* convenient, handy; *(facile)* easy; *(air, personne)* easy-going; (*personne*): **pas** ~ awkward (to deal with) ♦ *nf* chest of drawers; **commodité** *nf* convenience

commotion [kɔmosjɔ̃] *nf*: ~ **(cérébrale)** concussion; **commotionné, e** *adj* shocked, shaken

commun, e [kɔmœ̃, -yn] *adj* common; (*pièce*) communal, shared; (*réunion, effort*) joint; **cela sort du** ~ it's out of the ordinary; **le** ~ **des mortels** the common run of people; **en** ~ (*faire*) jointly; **mettre en** ~ to pool, share; *voir aussi* **communs**

communauté [kɔmynote] *nf* community; (*JUR*): **régime de la** ~ communal estate settlement

commune [kɔmyn] *nf* (*ADMIN*) commune, ≈ district; (: *urbaine*) ≈ borough

communication [kɔmynikasjɔ̃] *nf* communication; ~ **(téléphonique)** (telephone) call

communier [kɔmynje] *vi* (*REL*) to receive communion; (*fig*) to be united; **communion** [kɔmynjɔ̃] *nf* communion

communiquer [kɔmynike] *vt* (*nouvelle, dossier*) to pass on, convey; (*maladie*) to pass on; (*peur etc*) to communicate; (*chaleur, mouvement*) to transmit ♦ *vi* to communicate; **se** ~ **à** (*se propager*) to spread to

communisme [kɔmynism(ə)] *nm* communism; **communiste** *adj, nm/f* communist

communs [kɔmœ̃] *nmpl* (*bâtiments*) outbuildings

commutateur [kɔmytatœr] *nm* (*ÉLEC*) (change-over) switch, commutator

compact, e [kɔ̃pakt] *adj* dense; compact

compagne [kɔ̃paɲ] *nf* companion

compagnie [kɔ̃paɲi] *nf* (*firme, MIL*) company; (*groupe*) gathering; **tenir** ~ **à qn** to keep sb company; **fausser** ~ **à qn** to give sb the slip, slip *ou* sneak away from sb; ~ **aérienne** airline (company)

compagnon [kɔ̃paɲɔ̃] *nm* companion

comparable [kɔ̃parabl(ə)] *adj*: ~ **(à)** comparable (to)

comparaison [kɔ̃parɛzɔ̃] *nf* comparison

comparaître [kɔ̃parɛtr(ə)] *vi*: ~ **(devant)** to appear (before)

comparer [kɔ̃pare] *vt* to compare; ~ **qch/ qn à** *ou* **et** (*pour choisir*) to compare sth/sb with *ou* and; (*pour établir une similitude*) to compare sth/sb to

comparse [kɔ̃pars(ə)] (*péj*) *nm/f* associate, stooge

compartiment [kɔ̃partimɑ̃] *nm* compartment

comparution [kɔ̃parysjɔ̃] *nf* appearance

compas [kɔ̃pa] *nm* (*GÉOM*) (pair of) compasses *pl*; (*NAVIG*) compass

compatible [kɔ̃patibl(ə)] *adj* compatible

compatir [kɔ̃patir] *vi*: ~ **(à)** to sympathize (with)

compatriote [kɔ̃patrijɔt] *nm/f* compatriot

compenser [kɔ̃pɑ̃se] *vt* to compensate for, make up for

compère [kɔ̃pɛr] *nm* accomplice

compétence [kɔ̃petɑ̃s] *nf* competence

compétent, e [kɔ̃petɑ̃, -ɑ̃t] *adj* (*apte*) competent, capable

compétition [kɔ̃petisjɔ̃] *nf* (*gén*) competition; (*SPORT*: *épreuve*) event; **la** ~ competitive sport; **la** ~ **automobile** motor racing

complainte [kɔ̃plɛ̃t] *nf* lament

complaire [kɔ̃plɛr] : **se** ~ *vi*: **se** ~ **dans/ parmi** to take pleasure in/in being among

complaisance [kɔ̃plɛzɑ̃s] *nf* kindness; **pavillon de** ~ flag of convenience; **complaisant, e** [kɔ̃plɛzɑ̃, -ɑ̃t] *adj* (*aimable*) kind, obliging

complément [kɔ̃plemɑ̃] *nm* complement; remainder; ~ **d'information** (*ADMIN*) supplementary *ou* further information; **complémentaire** *adj* complementary; (*additionnel*) supplementary

complet, ète [kɔ̃plɛ, -ɛt] *adj* complete; (*plein*: *hôtel etc*) full ♦ *nm* (*aussi*: ~-*veston*) suit; **complètement** *adv* completely; **compléter** *vt* (*porter à la quantité voulue*) to complete; (*augmenter*) to complement, supplement; to add to

complexe [kɔ̃plɛks(ə)] *adj, nm* complex; **complexé, e** *adj* mixed-up, hung-up

complication [kɔ̃plikasjɔ̃] *nf* complexity, intricacy; (*difficulté, ennui*) complication

complice [kɔ̃plis] *nm* accomplice

compliment [kɔ̃plimɑ̃] *nm* (*louange*) compliment; ~**s** *nmpl* (*félicitations*) congratulations

compliqué, e [kɔ̃plike] *adj* complicated, complex; (*personne*) complicated

complot [kɔ̃plo] *nm* plot

comportement [kɔ̃pɔrtəmɑ̃] *nm* behaviour

comporter [kɔ̃pɔrte] *vt* to consist of, comprise; (*être équipé de*) to have; (*impliquer*) to entail; **se** ~ *vi* to behave

composant [kɔ̃pozɑ̃] *nm* component

composante [kɔ̃pozɑ̃t] *nf* component

composé [kɔ̃poze] *nm* compound

composer [kɔ̃poze] *vt* (*musique, texte*) to compose; (*mélange, équipe*) to make up; (*faire partie de*) to make up, form ♦ *vi* (*transiger*) to come to terms; **se** ~ **de** to be composed of, be made up of; ~ **un numéro** to dial a number

compositeur, trice [kɔ̃pozitœr, -tris] *nm/f* (*MUS*) composer

composition [kɔ̃pozisjɔ̃] *nf* composition; (*SCOL*) test; **de bonne** ~ (*accommodant*) easy to deal with

composter [kɔ̃pɔste] *vt* to date-stamp; to punch

compote [kɔ̃pɔt] *nf* stewed fruit *no pl*; ~ **de pommes** stewed apples; **compotier** *nm* fruit dish *ou* bowl

compréhensible [kɔ̃pʀeɑ̃sibl(ə)] *adj* comprehensible; (*attitude*) understandable
compréhensif, ive [kɔ̃pʀeɑ̃sif, -iv] *adj* understanding
comprendre [kɔ̃pʀɑ̃dʀ(ə)] *vt* to understand; (*se composer de*) to comprise, consist of
compresse [kɔ̃pʀɛs] *nf* compress
compression [kɔ̃pʀɛsjɔ̃] *nf* compression; reduction
comprimé [kɔ̃pʀime] *nm* tablet
comprimer [kɔ̃pʀime] *vt* to compress; (*fig: crédit etc*) to reduce, cut down
compris, e [kɔ̃pʀi, -iz] *pp de* **comprendre** ♦ *adj* (*inclus*) included; ~ **entre** (*situé*) contained between; **la maison ~e/non ~e, y/non ~ la maison** including/excluding the house; **100 F tout ~** 100 F all inclusive *ou* all-in
compromettre [kɔ̃pʀɔmɛtʀ(ə)] *vt* to compromise
compromis [kɔ̃pʀɔmi] *nm* compromise
comptabilité [kɔ̃tabilite] *nf* (*activité, technique*) accounting, accountancy; (*d'une société: comptes*) accounts *pl*, books *pl*; (: *service*) accounts office
comptable [kɔ̃tabl(ə)] *nm/f* accountant
comptant [kɔ̃tɑ̃] *adv*: **payer ~** to pay cash; **acheter ~** to buy for cash
compte [kɔ̃t] *nm* count, counting; (*total, montant*) count, (*right*) number; (*bancaire, facture*) account; ~ **nmpl** (*FINANCE*) accounts, books; (*fig*) explanation *sg*; **en fin de ~** all things considered; **à bon ~** at a favourable price; (*fig*) lightly; **avoir son ~** (: *fam*) to have had it; **pour le ~ de** on behalf of; **pour son propre ~** for one's own benefit; **tenir ~ de** to take account of; **travailler à son ~** to work for oneself; **rendre ~ (à qn) de qch** to give (sb) an account of sth; *voir aussi* **rendre**; ~ **à rebours** countdown; ~ **chèques postaux** Post Office account; ~ **courant** current account
compte-gouttes [kɔ̃tgut] *nm inv* dropper
compter [kɔ̃te] *vt* to count; (*facturer*) to charge for; (*avoir à son actif, comporter*) to have; (*prévoir*) to allow, reckon; (*penser, espérer*): ~ **réussir** to expect to succeed ♦ *vi* to count; (*être économe*) to economize; (*figurer*): ~ **parmi** to be *ou* rank among; ~ **sur** to count (up)on; ~ **avec qch/qn** to reckon with *ou* take account of sth/sb; **sans ~ que** besides which
compte rendu [kɔ̃tʀɑ̃dy] *nm* account, report; (*de film, livre*) review
compte-tours [kɔ̃ttuʀ] *nm inv* rev(olution) counter
compteur [kɔ̃tœʀ] *nm* meter; ~ **de vitesse** speedometer
comptine [kɔ̃tin] *nf* nursery rhyme
comptoir [kɔ̃twaʀ] *nm* (*de magasin*) counter

compulser [kɔ̃pylse] *vt* to consult
comte [kɔ̃t] *nm* count
comtesse [kɔ̃tɛs] *nf* countess
con, ne [kɔ̃, kɔn] (*fam!*) *adj* damned *ou* bloody (*BRIT*) stupid (*!*)
concéder [kɔ̃sede] *vt* to grant; (*défaite, point*) to concede
concentrer [kɔ̃sɑ̃tʀe] *vt* to concentrate; **se ~** *vi* to concentrate
concept [kɔ̃sɛpt] *nm* concept
conception [kɔ̃sɛpsjɔ̃] *nf* conception; (*d'une machine etc*) design
concerner [kɔ̃sɛʀne] *vt* to concern; **en ce qui me concerne** as far as I am concerned
concert [kɔ̃sɛʀ] *nm* concert; **de ~** in unison; together
concerter [kɔ̃sɛʀte] *vt* to devise; **se ~** *vi* (*collaborateurs etc*) to put our (*ou* their *etc*) heads together
concessionnaire [kɔ̃sesjɔnɛʀ] *nm/f* agent, dealer
concevoir [kɔ̃svwaʀ] *vt* (*idée, projet*) to conceive (of); (*méthode, plan d'appartement, décoration*) to plan, design; (*enfant*) to conceive; **bien/mal conçu** well-/badly-designed
concierge [kɔ̃sjɛʀʒ(ə)] *nm/f* caretaker; (*d'hôtel*) head porter
concile [kɔ̃sil] *nm* council
conciliabules [kɔ̃siljabyl] *nmpl* (private) discussions, confabulations
concilier [kɔ̃silje] *vt* to reconcile; **se ~** *vt* to win over
concitoyen, ne [kɔ̃sitwajɛ̃, -jɛn] *nm/f* fellow citizen
concluant, e [kɔ̃klyɑ̃, -ɑ̃t] *adj* conclusive
conclure [kɔ̃klyʀ] *vt* to conclude
conclusion [kɔ̃klyzjɔ̃] *nf* conclusion
conçois *etc vb voir* **concevoir**
concombre [kɔ̃kɔ̃bʀ(ə)] *nm* cucumber
concorder [kɔ̃kɔʀde] *vi* to tally, agree
concourir [kɔ̃kuʀiʀ] *vi* (*SPORT*) to compete; ~ **à** (*effet etc*) to work towards
concours [kɔ̃kuʀ] *nm* competition; (*SCOL*) competitive examination; (*assistance*) aid, help; ~ **de circonstances** combination of circumstances; ~ **hippique** horse show
concret, ète [kɔ̃kʀɛ, -ɛt] *adj* concrete
concrétiser [kɔ̃kʀetize] *vt* (*plan, projet*) to put in concrete form; **se ~** *vi* to materialize
conçu, e [kɔ̃sy] *pp de* **concevoir**
concubinage [kɔ̃kybinaʒ] *nm* (*JUR*) cohabitation
concurrence [kɔ̃kyʀɑ̃s] *nf* competition; **jusqu'à ~ de** up to
concurrent, e [kɔ̃kyʀɑ̃, -ɑ̃t] *nm/f* (*SPORT, ÉCON etc*) competitor; (*SCOL*) candidate
condamner [kɔ̃dɑne] *vt* (*blâmer*) to condemn; (*JUR*) to sentence; (*porte, ouverture*) to fill in, block up; (*malade*) to give up (hope for); ~ **qn à 2 ans de prison** to sentence sb to 2 years' imprisonment
condensation [kɔ̃dɑ̃sasjɔ̃] *nf* condensation

condenser [kɔ̃dɑ̃se] vt to condense; **se ~** vi to condense

condisciple [kɔ̃disipl(ə)] nm/f school fellow, fellow student

condition [kɔ̃disjɔ̃] nf condition; **~s** nfpl (tarif, prix) terms; (circonstances) conditions; **sans ~** unconditional ♦ adv unconditionally; **à ~ de ou que** provided that; **conditionnel, le** adj conditional ♦ nm conditional (tense)

conditionnement [kɔ̃disjɔnmɑ̃] nm (emballage) packaging

conditionner [kɔ̃disjɔne] vt (déterminer) to determine; (COMM: produit) to package; (fig: personne) to condition; **air conditionné** air conditioning

condoléances [kɔ̃dɔleɑ̃s] nfpl condolences

conducteur, trice [kɔ̃dyktœr, -tris] nm/f driver ♦ nm (ÉLEC etc) conductor

conduire [kɔ̃dɥir] vt to drive; (délégation, troupeau) to lead; **se ~** vi to behave; **~ vers/à** to lead towards/to; **~ qn quelque part** to take sb somewhere; to drive sb somewhere

conduite [kɔ̃dɥit] nf (comportement) behaviour; (d'eau, de gaz) pipe; **sous la ~ de** led by; **~ à gauche** left-hand drive; **~ intérieure** saloon (car)

cône [kon] nm cone

confection [kɔ̃fɛksjɔ̃] nf (fabrication) making; (COUTURE): **la ~** the clothing industry; **vêtement de ~** ready-to-wear ou off-the-peg garment

confectionner [kɔ̃fɛksjɔne] vt to make

conférence [kɔ̃ferɑ̃s] nf (exposé) lecture; (pourparlers) conference; **~ de presse** press conference

confesser [kɔ̃fese] vt to confess; **se ~** vi (REL) to go to confession

confession [kɔ̃fesjɔ̃] nf confession; (culte: catholique etc) denomination

confiance [kɔ̃fjɑ̃s] nf confidence, trust; faith; **avoir ~ en** to have confidence ou faith in, trust; **mettre qn en ~** to win sb's trust; **~ en soi** self-confidence

confiant, e [kɔ̃fjɑ̃, -ɑ̃t] adj confident; trusting

confidence [kɔ̃fidɑ̃s] nf confidence

confidentiel, le [kɔ̃fidɑ̃sjɛl] adj confidential

confier [kɔ̃fje] vt: **~ à qn** (objet en dépôt, travail etc) to entrust to sb; (secret, pensée) to confide to sb; **se ~ à qn** to confide in sb

confiné, e [kɔ̃fine] adj enclosed; stale

confins [kɔ̃fɛ̃] nmpl: **aux ~ de** on the borders of

confirmation [kɔ̃firmasjɔ̃] nf confirmation

confirmer [kɔ̃firme] vt to confirm

confiserie [kɔ̃fizri] nf (magasin) confectioner's ou sweet shop; **~s** nfpl (bonbons) confectionery sg; **confiseur, euse** nm/f

confectioner

confisquer [kɔ̃fiske] vt to confiscate

confit, e [kɔ̃fi, -it] adj: **fruits ~s** crystallized fruits ♦ nm: **~ d'oie** conserve of goose

confiture [kɔ̃fityr] nf jam; **~ d'oranges** (orange) marmalade

conflit [kɔ̃fli] nm conflict

confondre [kɔ̃fɔ̃dr(ə)] vt (jumeaux, faits) to confuse, mix up; (témoin, menteur) to confound; **se ~** vi to merge; **se ~ en excuses** to apologize profusely; **confondu, e** [kɔ̃fɔ̃dy] adj (stupéfait) speechless, overcome

conforme [kɔ̃fɔrm(ə)] adj: **~ à** in accordance with; in keeping with; true to

conformément [kɔ̃fɔrmemɑ̃] adv: **~ à** in accordance with

conformer [kɔ̃fɔrme] vt: **se ~ à** to conform to

conformité [kɔ̃fɔrmite] nf: **en ~ avec** in accordance with, in keeping with

confort [kɔ̃fɔr] nm comfort; **tout ~** (COMM) with all modern conveniences; **confortable** adj comfortable

confrère [kɔ̃frɛr] nm colleague; fellow member; **confrérie** nf brotherhood

confronter [kɔ̃frɔ̃te] vt to confront; (textes) to compare, collate

confus, e [kɔ̃fy, -yz] adj (vague) confused; (embarrassé) embarrassed

confusion [kɔ̃fyzjɔ̃] nf (voir confus) confusion; embarrassment; (voir confondre) confusion, mixing up

congé [kɔ̃ʒe] nm (vacances) holiday; **en ~** on holiday; off (work); **semaine de ~** week off; **prendre ~ de qn** to take one's leave of sb; **donner son ~ à** to give in one's notice to; **~ de maladie** sick leave; **~s payés** paid holiday

congédier [kɔ̃ʒedje] vt to dismiss

congélateur [kɔ̃ʒelatœr] nm freezer, deep freeze

congeler [kɔ̃ʒle] vt to freeze

congestion [kɔ̃ʒɛstjɔ̃] nf congestion; **~ cérébrale** stroke

congestionner [kɔ̃ʒɛstjɔne] vt to congest; (MÉD) to flush

congrès [kɔ̃grɛ] nm congress

congru, e [kɔ̃gry] adj: **la portion ~e** the smallest ou meanest share

conifère [kɔnifɛr] nm conifer

conjecture [kɔ̃ʒɛktyr] nf conjecture

conjoint, e [kɔ̃ʒwɛ̃, -wɛ̃t] adj joint ♦ nm/f spouse

conjonction [kɔ̃ʒɔ̃ksjɔ̃] nf (LING) conjunction

conjonctivite [kɔ̃ʒɔ̃ktivit] nf conjunctivitis

conjoncture [kɔ̃ʒɔ̃ktyr] nf circumstances pl; climate

conjugaison [kɔ̃ʒygɛzɔ̃] nf (LING) conjugation

conjuguer [kɔ̃ʒyge] vt (LING) to conjugate;

(efforts etc) to combine

conjuration [kɔ̃ʒyʀɑsjɔ̃] nf conspiracy

conjurer [kɔ̃ʒyʀe] vt (sort, maladie) to avert; (implorer) to beseech, entreat

connaissance [kɔnɛsɑ̃s] nf (savoir) knowledge no pl; (personne connue) acquaintance; **être sans** ~ to be unconscious; **perdre/reprendre** ~ to lose/regain consciousness; **à ma/sa** ~ to (the best of) my/his knowledge; **avoir** ~ **de** to be aware of; **prendre** ~ **de** (document etc) to peruse; **en** ~ **de cause** with full knowledge of the facts

connaître [kɔnɛtʀ(ə)] vt to know; (éprouver) to experience; (avoir) to have; to enjoy; ~ **de nom/vue** to know by name/sight; **ils se sont connus à Genève** they (first) met in Geneva

connecté, e [kɔnɛkte] adj on line

connecter [kɔnɛkte] vt to connect

connerie [kɔnʀi] (fam!) nf stupid thing (to do ou say)

connu, e [kɔny] adj (célèbre) well-known

conquérir [kɔ̃keʀiʀ] vt to conquer, win; **conquête** nf conquest

consacrer [kɔ̃sakʀe] vt (REL) to consecrate; (fig: usage etc) to sanction, establish; (employer) to devote, dedicate

conscience [kɔ̃sjɑ̃s] nf conscience; **avoir/prendre** ~ **de** to be/become aware of; **perdre** ~ to lose consciousness; **avoir bonne/mauvaise** ~ to have a clear/guilty conscience; **consciencieux, euse** adj conscientious; **conscient, e** adj conscious

conscrit [kɔ̃skʀi] nm conscript

consécutif, ive [kɔ̃sekytif, -iv] adj consecutive; ~ **à** following upon

conseil [kɔ̃sɛj] nm (avis) piece of advice, advice no pl; (assemblée) council; **prendre** ~ **(auprès de qn)** to take advice (from sb); ~ **d'administration** board (of directors); **le** ~ **des ministres** ≈ the Cabinet

conseiller, ère [kɔ̃seje, kɔ̃sɛjɛʀ] nm/f adviser ♦ vt (personne) to advise; (méthode, action) to recommend, advise; ~ **à qn de** to advise sb to

consentement [kɔ̃sɑ̃tmɑ̃] nm consent

consentir [kɔ̃sɑ̃tiʀ] vt to agree, consent

conséquence [kɔ̃sekɑ̃s] nf consequence; **en** ~ (donc) consequently; (de façon appropriée) accordingly; **ne pas tirer à** ~ to be unlikely to have any repercussions

conséquent, e [kɔ̃sekɑ̃, -ɑ̃t] adj logical, rational; (fam: important) substantial; **par** ~ consequently

conservateur, trice [kɔ̃sɛʀvatœʀ, -tʀis] nm/f (POL) conservative; (de musée) curator

conservatoire [kɔ̃sɛʀvatwaʀ] nm academy; (ÉCOLOGIE) conservation area

conserve [kɔ̃sɛʀv(ə)] nf (gén pl) canned ou tinned (BRIT) food; **en** ~ canned, tinned (BRIT)

conserver [kɔ̃sɛʀve] vt (faculté) to retain, keep; (amis, livres) to keep; (préserver, aussi CULIN) to preserve

considérable [kɔ̃sideʀabl(ə)] adj considerable, significant, extensive

considération [kɔ̃sideʀɑsjɔ̃] nf consideration; (estime) esteem

considérer [kɔ̃sideʀe] vt to consider; ~ **qch comme** to regard sth as

consigne [kɔ̃siɲ] nf (de gare) left luggage (office) (BRIT), checkroom (US); (ordre, instruction) instructions pl; ~ **(automatique)** left-luggage locker; ~**r** [kɔ̃siɲe] vt (note, pensée) to record; (punir) to confine to barracks; to put in detention; (COMM) to put a deposit on

consistant, e [kɔ̃sistɑ̃, -ɑ̃t] adj thick; solid

consister [kɔ̃siste] vi: ~ **en/dans/à faire** to consist of/in/in doing

consœur [kɔ̃sœʀ] nf (lady) colleague; fellow member

consoler [kɔ̃sɔle] vt to console

consolider [kɔ̃sɔlide] vt to strengthen; (fig) to consolidate

consommateur, trice [kɔ̃sɔmatœʀ, -tʀis] nm/f (ÉCON) consumer; (dans un café) customer

consommation [kɔ̃sɔmɑsjɔ̃] nf (boisson) drink; ~ **aux 100 km** (AUTO) (fuel) consumption per 100 km

consommer [kɔ̃sɔme] vt (suj: personne) to eat ou drink, consume; (: voiture, usine, poêle) to use, consume ♦ vi (dans un café) to (have a) drink

consonne [kɔ̃sɔn] nf consonant

conspirer [kɔ̃spiʀe] vi to conspire

constamment [kɔ̃stamɑ̃] adv constantly

constant, e [kɔ̃stɑ̃, -ɑ̃t] adj constant; (personne) steadfast

constat [kɔ̃sta] nm (d'huissier) certified report; (de police) report; (affirmation) statement

constatation [kɔ̃statɑsjɔ̃] nf (observation) (observed) fact, observation; (affirmation) statement

constater [kɔ̃state] vt (remarquer) to note; (ADMIN, JUR: attester) to certify; (dire) to state

consterner [kɔ̃stɛʀne] vt to dismay

constipé, e [kɔ̃stipe] adj constipated

constitué, e [kɔ̃stitɥe] adj: ~ **de** made up ou composed of

constituer [kɔ̃stitɥe] vt (comité, équipe) to set up; (dossier, collection) to put together; (suj: éléments: composer) to make up, constitute; (représenter, être) to constitute; **se** ~ **prisonnier** to give o.s. up

constitution [kɔ̃stitysjɔ̃] nf (composition) composition, make-up; (santé, POL) constitution

constructeur [kɔ̃stʀyktœʀ] nm manufacturer, builder

construction [kɔ̃stryksjɔ̃] *nf* construction, building

construire [kɔ̃strɥiʀ] *vt* to build, construct

consul [kɔ̃syl] *nm* consul; **consulat** *nm* consulate

consultation [kɔ̃syltɑsjɔ̃] *nf* consultation; **~s** *nfpl* (*POL*) talks; **heures de ~** (*MÉD*) surgery (*BRIT*) ou office (*US*) hours

consulter [kɔ̃sylte] *vt* to consult ♦ *vi* (*médecin*) to hold surgery (*BRIT*), be in (the office) (*US*)

consumer [kɔ̃syme] *vt* to consume; **se ~** *vi* to burn

contact [kɔ̃takt] *nm* contact; **au ~ de** (*air, peau*) on contact with; (*gens*) through contact with; **mettre/couper le ~** (*AUTO*) to switch on/off the ignition; **entrer en** ou **prendre ~ avec** to get in touch ou contact with; **contacter** *vt* to contact, get in touch with

contagieux, euse [kɔ̃taʒjø, -øz] *adj* contagious; infectious

contaminer [kɔ̃tamine] *vt* to contaminate

conte [kɔ̃t] *nm* tale; **~ de fées** fairy tale

contempler [kɔ̃tɑ̃ple] *vt* to contemplate, gaze at

contemporain, e [kɔ̃tɑ̃pɔʀɛ̃, -ɛn] *adj, nm/f* contemporary

contenance [kɔ̃tnɑ̃s] *nf* (*d'un récipient*) capacity; (*attitude*) bearing, attitude; **perdre ~** to lose one's composure

conteneur [kɔ̃tnœʀ] *nm* container

contenir [kɔ̃tniʀ] *vt* to contain; (*avoir une capacité de*) to hold

content, e [kɔ̃tɑ̃, -ɑ̃t] *adj* pleased, glad; **~ de** pleased with; **contenter** *vt* to satisfy, please; **se ~er de** to content o.s. with

contentieux [kɔ̃tɑ̃sjø] *nm* (*COMM*) litigation; litigation department

contenu [kɔ̃tny] *nm* (*d'un bol*) contents *pl*; (*d'un texte*) content

conter [kɔ̃te] *vt* to recount, relate

contestable [kɔ̃tɛstabl(ə)] *adj* questionable

contestation [kɔ̃tɛstɑsjɔ̃] *nf* (*POL*) protest

conteste [kɔ̃tɛst(ə)] : **sans ~** *adv* unquestionably, indisputably

contester [kɔ̃tɛste] *vt* to question, contest ♦ *vi* (*POL, gén*) to protest, rebel (against established authority)

contexte [kɔ̃tɛkst(ə)] *nm* context

contigu, ë [kɔ̃tigy] *adj*: **~ (à)** adjacent (to)

continent [kɔ̃tinɑ̃] *nm* continent

continu, e [kɔ̃tiny] *adj* continuous; (**courant**) **~** direct current, DC

continuel, le [kɔ̃tinɥɛl] *adj* (*qui se répète*) constant, continual; (*continu*) continuous

continuer [kɔ̃tinɥe] *vt* (*travail, voyage etc*) to continue (with), carry on (with), go on (with); (*prolonger: alignement, rue*) to continue ♦ *vi* (*pluie, vie, bruit*) to continue, go on; (*voyageur*) to go on; **~ à** ou **de faire** to go on ou continue doing

contorsionner [kɔ̃tɔʀsjɔne]: **se ~** *vi* to contort o.s., writhe about

contour [kɔ̃tuʀ] *nm* outline, contour

contourner [kɔ̃tuʀne] *vt* to go round

contraceptif, ive [kɔ̃tʀasɛptif, -iv] *adj, nm* contraceptive; **contraception** [kɔ̃tʀasɛpsjɔ̃] *nf* contraception

contracté, e [kɔ̃tʀakte] *adj* tense

contracter [kɔ̃tʀakte] *vt* (*muscle etc*) to tense, contract; (*maladie, dette, obligation*) to contract; (*assurance*) to take out; **se ~** *vi* (*métal, muscles*) to contract

contractuel, le [kɔ̃tʀaktɥɛl] *nm/f* (*agent*) traffic warden

contradiction [kɔ̃tʀadiksjɔ̃] *nf* contradiction; **contradictoire** *adj* contradictory, conflicting

contraignant, e [kɔ̃tʀɛɲɑ̃, -ɑ̃t] *adj* restricting

contraindre *vt*: **~ qn à faire** to compel sb to do; **contraint, e** [kɔ̃tʀɛ̃, -ɛ̃t] *adj* (*mine, air*) constrained, forced; **contrainte** *nf* constraint

contraire [kɔ̃tʀɛʀ] *adj, nm* opposite; **~ à** contrary to; **au ~** on the contrary

contrarier [kɔ̃tʀaʀje] *vt* (*personne*) to annoy, bother; (*fig*) to impede; to thwart, frustrate; **contrariété** [kɔ̃tʀaʀjete] *nf* annoyance

contraste [kɔ̃tʀast(ə)] *nm* contrast

contrat [kɔ̃tʀa] *nm* contract; **~ de travail** employment contract

contravention [kɔ̃tʀavɑ̃sjɔ̃] *nf* (*amende*) fine; (*P.V. pour stationnement interdit*) parking ticket

contre [kɔ̃tʀ(ə)] *prép* against; (*en échange*) (in exchange) for; **par ~** on the other hand

contrebande [kɔ̃tʀəbɑ̃d] *nf* (*trafic*) contraband, smuggling; (*marchandise*) contraband, smuggled goods *pl*; **faire la ~ de** to smuggle

contrebas [kɔ̃tʀəbɑ] : **en ~** *adv* (down) below

contrebasse [kɔ̃tʀəbɑs] *nf* (double) bass

contre: **~carrer** *vt* to thwart; **~cœur**: **à ~cœur** *adv* (be)grudgingly, reluctantly; **~coup** *nm* repercussions *pl*; **par ~coup** as an indirect consequence; **~dire** *vt* (*personne*) to contradict; (*témoignage, assertion, faits*) to refute

contrée [kɔ̃tʀe] *nf* region; land

contrefaçon [kɔ̃tʀəfasɔ̃] *nf* forgery

contrefaire [kɔ̃tʀəfɛʀ] *vt* (*document, signature*) to forge, counterfeit; (*personne, démarche*) to mimic; (*dénaturer: sa voix etc*) to disguise

contre-indication (*pl* **contre-indications**) *nf* (*MÉD*) contra-indication

contre-jour [kɔ̃tʀəʒuʀ]: **à ~** *adv* against the sunlight

contremaître [kɔ̃tʀəmɛtʀ(ə)] *nm* foreman

contrepartie [kɔ̃tʀəparti] *nf* compensation;

en ~ in return

contre-pied [kɔ̃trəpje] nm: **prendre le ~ de** to take the opposing view of; to take the opposite course to

contre-plaqué [kɔ̃trəplake] nm plywood

contrepoids [kɔ̃trəpwa] nm counterweight, counterbalance

contrer [kɔ̃tre] vt to counter

contresens [kɔ̃trəsɑ̃s] nm misinterpretation; mistranslation; nonsense no pl; **à ~** the wrong way

contretemps [kɔ̃trətɑ̃] nm hitch; **à ~** (MUS) out of time; (fig) at an inopportune moment

contrevenir [kɔ̃trəvnir]: **~ à** vt to contravene

contribuable [kɔ̃tribɥabl(ə)] nm/f taxpayer

contribuer [kɔ̃tribɥe]: **~ à** vt to contribute towards; **contribution** nf contribution; **contributions directes/indirectes** direct/indirect taxation; **mettre à contribution** to call upon

contrôle [kɔ̃trol] nm checking no pl, check; supervision; monitoring; (test) test, examination; **perdre le ~ de** (véhicule) to lose control of; **~ continu** (SCOL) continuous assessment; **~ d'identité** identity check; **~ des naissances** birth control

contrôler [kɔ̃trole] vt (vérifier) to check; (surveiller) to supervise; to monitor, control; (maîtriser, COMM: firme) to control; **contrôleur, euse** nm/f (de train) (ticket) inspector; (de bus) (bus) conductor(tress)

contrordre [kɔ̃trɔrdr(ə)] nm: **sauf ~** unless otherwise directed

controversé, e [kɔ̃trɔvɛrse] adj (personnage, question) controversial

contusion [kɔ̃tyzjɔ̃] nf bruise, contusion

convaincre [kɔ̃vɛ̃kr(ə)] vt: **~ qn (de qch)** to convince sb (of sth); **~ qn (de faire)** to persuade sb (to do); **~ qn de** (JUR: délit) to convict sb of

convalescence [kɔ̃valesɑ̃s] nf convalescence

convenable [kɔ̃vnabl(ə)] adj suitable; (assez bon, respectable) decent

convenance [kɔ̃vnɑ̃s] nf: **à ma/votre ~** to my/your liking; **~s** nfpl (normes sociales) proprieties

convenir [kɔ̃vnir] vi to be suitable; **~ à** to suit; **il convient de** it is advisable to; (bienséant) it is right ou proper to; **~ de** (bienfondé de qch) to admit (to), acknowledge; (date, somme etc) to agree upon; **~ que** (admettre) to admit that; **~ de faire** to agree to do

convention [kɔ̃vɑ̃sjɔ̃] nf convention; **~s** nfpl (convenances) convention sg; **~ collective** (ÉCON) collective agreement; **conventionné, e** adj (ADMIN) applying charges laid down by the state

convenu, e [kɔ̃vny] pp de **convenir** ♦ adj

agreed

conversation [kɔ̃vɛrsasjɔ̃] nf conversation

convertir [kɔ̃vɛrtir] vt: **~ qn (à)** to convert sb (to); **se ~ (à)** to be converted (to); **~ qch en** to convert sth into

conviction [kɔ̃viksjɔ̃] nf conviction

convienne etc vb voir **convenir**

convier [kɔ̃vje] vt: **~ qn à** (dîner etc) to (cordially) invite sb to

convive [kɔ̃viv] nm/f guest (at table)

convivial, e [kɔ̃vivjal] adj (INFORM) user-friendly

convocation [kɔ̃vɔkasjɔ̃] nf (document) notification to attend; summons sg

convoi [kɔ̃vwa] nm (de voitures, prisonniers) convoy; (train) train

convoiter [kɔ̃vwate] vt to covet

convoquer [kɔ̃vɔke] vt (assemblée) to convene; (subordonné) to summon; (candidat) to ask to attend; **~ qn (à)** (réunion) to invite sb (to attend)

convoyeur [kɔ̃vwajœr] nm (NAVIG) escort ship; **~ de fonds** security guard

coopération [kɔɔperasjɔ̃] nf co-operation; (ADMIN): **la C~** ≈ Voluntary Service Overseas (BRIT), ≈ Peace Corps (US)

coopérer [kɔɔpere] vi: **~ (à)** to co-operate (in)

coordonner [kɔɔrdɔne] vt to coordinate

copain [kɔpɛ̃] nm mate, pal

copeau, x [kɔpo] nm shaving

copie [kɔpi] nf copy; (SCOL) script, paper; exercise

copier [kɔpje] vt, vi to copy; **~ sur** to copy from

copieur [kɔpjœr] nm (photo)copier

copieux, euse [kɔpjø, -øz] adj copious

copine [kɔpin] nf = **copain**

copropriété [kɔprɔprijete] nf coownership, joint ownership

coq [kɔk] nm cock, rooster; **~-à-l'âne** [kɔkalɑn] nm inv abrupt change of subject

coque [kɔk] nf (de noix, mollusque) shell; (de bateau) hull; **à la ~** (CULIN) (soft-)boiled

coquelicot [kɔkliko] nm poppy

coqueluche [kɔklyʃ] nf whooping-cough

coquet, te [kɔkɛ, -ɛt] adj flirtatious; appearance-conscious; pretty

coquetier [kɔktje] nm egg-cup

coquillage [kɔkijaʒ] nm (mollusque) shellfish inv; (coquille) shell

coquille [kɔkij] nf shell; (TYPO) misprint; **~ St Jacques** scallop

coquin, e [kɔkɛ̃, -in] adj mischievous, roguish; (polisson) naughty

cor [kɔr] nm (MUS) horn; (MÉD): **~ (au pied)** corn; **réclamer à ~ et à cri** to clamour for

corail, aux [kɔraj, -o] nm coral no pl

Coran [kɔrɑ̃] nm: **le ~** the Koran

corbeau, x [kɔrbo] nm crow

corbeille [kɔʀbɛj] *nf* basket; ~ **à papier** waste paper basket *ou* bin

corbillard [kɔʀbijaʀ] *nm* hearse

corde [kɔʀd(ə)] *nf* rope; (*de violon, raquette, d'arc*) string; (*ATHLÉTISME, AUTO*): **la ~** the rails *pl*; **usé jusqu'à la ~** threadbare; **à linge** washing *ou* clothes line; **~ à sauter** skipping rope; **~s vocales** vocal cords; **cordée** [kɔʀde] *nf* (*d'alpinistes*) rope, roped party

cordialement [kɔʀdjalmã] *adv* (*formule épistolaire*) (kind) regards

cordon [kɔʀdɔ̃] *nm* cord, string; ~ **ombilical** umbilical cord; ~ **sanitaire/de police** sanitary/police cordon

cordonnerie [kɔʀdɔnʀi] *nf* shoe repairer's (shop); **cordonnier** [kɔʀdɔnje] *nm* shoe repairer

Corée [kɔʀe] *nf*: **la ~ du Sud/du Nord** South/North Korea

coriace [kɔʀjas] *adj* tough

corne [kɔʀn(ə)] *nf* horn; (*de cerf*) antler

corneille [kɔʀnɛj] *nf* crow

cornemuse [kɔʀnəmyz] *nf* bagpipes *pl*

cornet [kɔʀnɛ] *nm* (paper) cone; (*de glace*) cornet, cone

corniche [kɔʀniʃ] *nf* (*de meuble, neigeuse*) cornice; (*route*) coast road

cornichon [kɔʀniʃɔ̃] *nm* gherkin

Cornouailles [kɔʀnwaj] *nf* Cornwall

corporation [kɔʀpɔʀasjɔ̃] *nf* corporate body

corporel, le [kɔʀpɔʀɛl] *adj* bodily; (*punition*) corporal

corps [kɔʀ] *nm* body; **à son ~ défendant** against one's will; **à ~ perdu** headlong; **perdu ~ et biens** lost with all hands; **prendre ~** to take shape; **~ à ~** *adv* hand-to-hand ♦ *nm* clinch; ~ **de garde** guardroom; **le ~ électoral** the electorate; **le ~ enseignant** the teaching profession

corpulent, e [kɔʀpylã, -ãt] *adj* stout

correct, e [kɔʀɛkt] *adj* correct; (*passable*) adequate

correction [kɔʀɛksjɔ̃] *nf* (*voir corriger*) correction; (*voir correct*) correctness; (*rature, surcharge*) correction, emendation; (*coups*) thrashing

correctionnel, le [kɔʀɛksjɔnɛl] *adj* (*JUR*): **tribunal ~** ≈ criminal court

correspondance [kɔʀɛspɔ̃dãs] *nf* correspondence; (*de train, d'avion*) connection; **cours par ~** correspondence course; **vente par ~** mail-order business

correspondant, e [kɔʀɛspɔ̃dã, -ãt] *nm/f* correspondent; (*TÉL*) person phoning (*ou* being phoned)

correspondre [kɔʀɛspɔ̃dʀ(ə)] *vi* to correspond, tally; ~ **à** to correspond to; ~ **avec qn** to correspond with sb

corrida [kɔʀida] *nf* bullfight

corridor [kɔʀidɔʀ] *nm* corridor

corriger [kɔʀiʒe] *vt* (*devoir*) to correct; (*punir*) to thrash; ~ **qn de** (*défaut*) to cure sb of

corrompre [kɔʀɔ̃pʀ(ə)] *vt* to corrupt; (*acheter: témoin etc*) to bribe

corruption [kɔʀypsjɔ̃] *nf* corruption; bribery

corsage [kɔʀsaʒ] *nm* bodice; blouse

corse [kɔʀs(ə)] *adj, nm/f* Corsican ♦ *nf*: **la C~** Corsica

corsé, e [kɔʀse] *adj* vigorous; (*vin, goût*) full-flavoured; (*fig*) spicy; tricky

corset [kɔʀsɛ] *nm* corset; bodice

cortège [kɔʀtɛʒ] *nm* procession

corvée [kɔʀve] *nf* chore, drudgery *no pl*

cosmétique [kɔsmetik] *nm* beauty care product

cossu, e [kɔsy] *adj* well-to-do

costaud, e [kɔsto, -od] *adj* strong, sturdy

costume [kɔstym] *nm* (*d'homme*) suit; (*de théâtre*) costume; **costumé, e** *adj* dressed up

cote [kɔt] *nf* (*en Bourse etc*) quotation; quoted value; (*d'un cheval*): **la ~ de** the odds *pl* on; (*d'un candidat etc*) rating; (*sur un croquis*) dimension; ~ **d'alerte** danger *ou* flood level

côte [kot] *nf* (*rivage*) coast(line); (*pente*) slope; (: *sur une route*) hill; (*ANAT*) rib; (*d'un tricot, tissu*) rib, ribbing *no pl*; ~ **à ~** side by side; **la C~ (d'Azur)** the (French) Riviera

côté [kote] *nm* (*gén*) side; (*direction*) way, direction; **de chaque ~ (de)** on each side (of); **de tous les ~s** from all directions; **de quel ~ est-il parti?** which way did he go?; **de ce/de l'autre ~** this/the other way; **du ~ de** (*provenance*) from; (*direction*) towards; (*proximité*) near; **de ~** sideways; on one side; to one side; aside; **laisser/mettre de ~** to leave/put to one side; **à ~** (right) nearby; beside; next door; (*d'autre part*) besides; **à ~ de** beside; next to; (*comparé à*) compared to; **être aux ~s de** to be by the side of

coteau, x [kɔto] *nm* hill

côtelette [kotlɛt] *nf* chop

coter [kɔte] *vt* (*en Bourse*) to quote

côtier, ière [kotje, -jɛʀ] *adj* coastal

cotisation [kɔtizasjɔ̃] *nf* subscription, dues *pl*; (*pour une pension*) contributions *pl*

cotiser [kɔtize] *vi*: ~ **(à)** to pay contributions (to); **se ~** *vi* to club together

coton [kɔtɔ̃] *nm* cotton; ~ **hydrophile** cotton wool (*BRIT*), absorbent cotton (*US*)

côtoyer [kotwaje] *vt* to be close to; to rub shoulders with; to run alongside

cou [ku] *nm* neck

couchant [kuʃã] *adj*: **soleil ~** setting sun

couche [kuʃ] *nf* (*strate: gén, GÉO*) layer; (*de peinture, vernis*) coat; (*de bébé*) nappy (*BRIT*), diaper (*US*); **~s** *nfpl* (*MÉD*) confinement *sg*; ~ **d'ozone** ozone layer; **~s socia-**

les social levels *ou* strata

couché, e [kuʃe] *adj* lying down; (*au lit*) in bed

couche-culotte [kuʃkylɔt] *nf* disposable nappy (*BRIT*) *ou* diaper (*US*) and waterproof pants in one

coucher [kuʃe] *nm* (*du soleil*) setting ♦ *vt* (*personne*) to put to bed; (: *loger*) to put up; (*objet*) to lay on its side ♦ *vi* to sleep; **se ~** *vi* (*pour dormir*) to go to bed; (*pour se reposer*) to lie down; (*soleil*) to set; **~ de soleil** sunset

couchette [kuʃɛt] *nf* couchette; (*de marin*) bunk

coucou [kuku] *nm* cuckoo

coude [kud] *nm* (*ANAT*) elbow; (*de tuyau, de la route*) bend; **~ à ~** shoulder to shoulder, side by side

coudre [kudʀ(ə)] *vt* (*bouton*) to sew on; (*robe*) to sew (up) ♦ *vi* to sew

couenne [kwan] *nf* (*de lard*) rind

couette [kwɛt] *nf* duvet, quilt; **~s** *nfpl* (*cheveux*) bunches

couffin [kufɛ̃] *nm* Moses basket

couler [kule] *vi* to flow, run; (*fuir: stylo, récipient*) to leak; (*sombrer: bateau*) to sink ♦ *vt* (*cloche, sculpture*) to cast; (*bateau*) to sink; (*fig*) to ruin, bring down

couleur [kulœʀ] *nf* colour (*BRIT*), color (*US*), (*CARTES*) suit; **film/télévision en ~s** colo(u)r film/television

couleuvre [kulœvʀ(ə)] *nf* grass snake

coulisse [kulis] *nf*: **~s** *nfpl* (*THÉÂTRE*) wings; (*fig*): **dans les ~s** behind the scenes; **coulisser** *vi* to slide, run

couloir [kulwaʀ] *nm* corridor, passage; (*de bus*) gangway; (*d'avion*) aisle; (*sur la route*) bus lane; (*SPORT: de piste*) lane; (*GÉO*) gully; **~ aérien/de navigation** air/shipping lane

coup [ku] *nm* (*heurt, choc*) knock; (*affectif*) blow, shock; (*agressif*) blow; (*avec arme à feu*) shot; (*de l'horloge*) chime; stroke; (*SPORT*) stroke; shot; blow; (*fam: fois*) time; **~ de coude** nudge (with the elbow); **~ de tonnerre** clap of thunder; **~ de sonnette** ring of the bell; **~ de crayon** stroke of the pencil; **donner un ~ de balai** to give the floor a sweep; **avoir le ~** (*fig*) to have the knack; **boire un ~** to have a drink; **être dans le ~** to be in on it; **du ~ ...** so (you see) ...; **d'un seul ~** (*subitement*) suddenly; (*à la fois*) at one go; in one blow; **du premier ~** first time; **du même ~** at the same time; **à ~ sûr** definitely, without fail; **~ sur ~** in quick succession; **sur le ~** outright; **sous le ~ de** (*surprise etc*) under the influence of; **~ de chance** stroke of luck; **~ de couteau** stab (of a knife); **~ d'envoi** kick-off; **~ d'essai** first attempt; **~ de feu** shot; **~ de filet** (*POLICE*) haul; **~ de frein** (sharp) braking *no pl*; **~ de main**:

donner un ~ de main à qn to give sb a (helping) hand; **~ d'œil** glance; **~ de pied** kick; **~ de poing** punch; **~ de soleil** sunburn *no pl*; **~ de téléphone** phone call; **~ de tête** (*fig*) (sudden) impulse; **~ de théâtre** (*fig*) dramatic turn of events; **~ de vent** gust of wind; **en coup de vent** in a tearing hurry; **~ franc** free kick

coupable [kupabl(ə)] *adj* guilty ♦ *nm/f* (*gén*) culprit; (*JUR*) guilty party

coupe [kup] *nf* (*verre*) goblet; (*à fruits*) dish; (*SPORT*) cup; (*de cheveux, de vêtement*) cut; (*graphique, plan*) (cross) section; **être sous la ~ de** to be under the control of

coupe-papier [kuppapje] *nm inv* paper knife

couper [kupe] *vt* to cut; (*retrancher*) to cut (out); (*route, courant*) to cut off; (*appétit*) to take away; (*vin, cidre*) to blend; (: *à table*) to dilute ♦ *vi* to cut; (*prendre un raccourci*) to take a short-cut; **se ~** *vi* (*se blesser*) to cut o.s.; **~ la parole à qn** to cut sb short

couple [kupl(ə)] *nm* couple

couplet [kuplɛ] *nm* verse

coupole [kupɔl] *nf* dome; cupola

coupon [kupɔ̃] *nm* (*ticket*) coupon; (*de tissu*) remnant; roll; **~-réponse** *nm* reply coupon

coupure [kupyʀ] *nf* cut; (*billet de banque*) note; (*de journal*) cutting; **~ de courant** power cut

cour [kuʀ] *nf* (*de ferme, jardin*) (court)yard; (*d'immeuble*) back yard; (*JUR, royale*) court; **faire la ~ à qn** to court sb; **~ d'assises** court of assizes; **~ martiale** court-martial

courage [kuʀaʒ] *nm* courage, bravery; **courageux, euse** *adj* brave, courageous

couramment [kuʀamɑ̃] *adv* commonly; (*parler*) fluently

courant, e [kuʀɑ̃, -ɑ̃t] *adj* (*fréquent*) common; (*COMM, gén: normal*) standard; (*en cours*) current ♦ *nm* current; (*fig*) movement; trend; **être au ~ (de)** (*fait, nouvelle*) to know (about); **mettre qn au ~ (de)** to tell sb (about); (*nouveau travail etc*) to teach sb the basics (of); **se tenir au ~ (de)** (*techniques etc*) to keep o.s. up-to-date (on); **dans le ~ de** (*pendant*) in the course of; **le 10 ~** (*COMM*) the 10th inst.; **~ d'air** draught; **~ électrique** (electric) current, power

courbature [kuʀbatyʀ] *nf* ache

courbe [kuʀb(ə)] *adj* curved ♦ *nf* curve; **~r** [kuʀbe] *vt* to bend

coureur, euse [kuʀœʀ, -øz] *nm/f* (*SPORT*) runner (*ou* driver); (*péj*) womanizer; manhunter; **~ automobile** racing driver

courge [kuʀʒ(ə)] *nf* (*CULIN*) marrow; **courgette** [kuʀʒɛt] *nf* courgette (*BRIT*), zucchini (*US*)

courir [kuʀiʀ] *vi* to run ♦ *vt* (*SPORT: épreuve*) to compete in; (*risque*) to run;

(*danger*) to face; ~ **les magasins** to go round the shops; **le bruit court que** the rumour is going round that

couronne [kuʀɔn] *nf* crown; (*de fleurs*) wreath, circlet

courons *etc vb voir* **courir**

courrier [kuʀje] *nm* mail, post; (*lettres à écrire*) letters *pl*; **avion long/moyen** ~ long-/medium-haul plane

courroie [kuʀwa] *nf* strap; (*TECH*) belt

courrons *etc vb voir* **courir**

cours [kuʀ] *nm* (*leçon*) lesson; class; (*série de leçons, cheminement*) course; (*écoulement*) flow; (*COMM*) rate; price; **donner libre** ~ **à** to give free expression to; **avoir** ~ (*monnaie*) to be legal tender; (*fig*) to be current; (*SCOL*) to have a class *ou* lecture; **en** ~ (*année*) current; (*travaux*) in progress; **en** ~ **de route** on the way; **au** ~ **de** in the course of, during; ~ **d'eau** waterway; ~ **du soir** night school

course [kuʀs(ə)] *nf* running; (*SPORT*: *épreuve*) race; (*d'un taxi, autocar*) journey, trip; (*petite mission*) errand; ~**s** *nfpl* (*achats*) shopping *sg*; **faire des** ~**s** to do some shopping

court, e [kuʀ, kuʀt(ə)] *adj* short ♦ *adv* short ♦ *nm*: ~ (**de tennis**) (tennis) court; **tourner** ~ to come to a sudden end; **ça fait** ~ that's not very long; **à** ~ **de** short of; **prendre qn de** ~ to catch sb unawares; **tirer à la** ~**e paille** to draw lots; ~**-circuit** *nm* short-circuit

courtier, ère [kuʀtje, -jɛʀ] *nm/f* broker

courtiser [kuʀtize] *vt* to court, woo

courtois, e [kuʀtwa, -waz] *adj* courteous

couru, e [kuʀy] *pp de* **courir** ♦ *adj*: **c'est** ~ it's a safe bet

cousais *etc vb voir* **coudre**

couscous [kuskus] *nm* couscous

cousin, e [kuzɛ̃, -in] *nm/f* cousin

coussin [kusɛ̃] *nm* cushion

cousu, e [kuzy] *pp de* **coudre**

coût [ku] *nm* cost; **le** ~ **de la vie** the cost of living

coûtant [kutɑ̃] *adj m*: **au prix** ~ at cost price

couteau, x [kuto] *nm* knife; ~ **à cran d'arrêt** flick-knife

coûter [kute] *vt, vi* to cost; **combien ça coûte?** how much is it?, what does it cost?; **coûte que coûte** at all costs; **coûteux, euse** *adj* costly, expensive

coutume [kutym] *nf* custom

couture [kutyʀ] *nf* sewing; dress-making; (*points*) seam; **couturier** [kutyʀje] *nm* fashion designer; **couturière** [kutyʀjɛʀ] *nf* dressmaker

couvée [kuve] *nf* brood, clutch

couvent [kuvɑ̃] *nm* (*de sœurs*) convent; (*de frères*) monastery

couver [kuve] *vt* to hatch; (*maladie*) to be

sickening for ♦ *vi* (*feu*) to smoulder; (*révolte*) to be brewing

couvercle [kuvɛʀkl(ə)] *nm* lid; (*de bombe aérosol etc, qui se visse*) cap, top

couvert, e [kuvɛʀ, -ɛʀt(ə)] *pp de* **couvrir** ♦ *adj* (*ciel*) overcast ♦ *nm* place setting; (*place à table*) place; (*au restaurant*) cover charge; ~**s** *nmpl* (*ustensiles*) cutlery *sg*; ~ **de** covered with *ou* in; **mettre le** ~ to lay the table

couverture [kuvɛʀtyʀ] *nf* blanket; (*de bâtiment*) roofing; (*de livre, assurance, fig*) cover; (*presse*) coverage; ~ **chauffante** electric blanket

couveuse [kuvøz] *nf* (*de maternité*) incubator

couvre-feu *nm* curfew

couvre-lit *nm* bedspread

couvrir [kuvʀiʀ] *vt* to cover; **se** ~ *vi* (*ciel*) to cloud over; (*s'habiller*) to cover up; (*se coiffer*) to put on one's hat

crabe [kʀab] *nm* crab

cracher [kʀaʃe] *vi, vt* to spit

crachin [kʀaʃɛ̃] *nm* drizzle

craie [kʀɛ] *nf* chalk

craindre [kʀɛ̃dʀ(ə)] *vt* to fear, be afraid of; (*être sensible à: chaleur, froid*) to be easily damaged by

crainte [kʀɛ̃t] *nf* fear; **de** ~ **de/que** for fear of/that; **craintif, ive** *adj* timid

cramoisi, e [kʀamwazi] *adj* crimson

crampe [kʀɑ̃p] *nf* cramp

cramponner [kʀɑ̃pɔne] : **se** ~ *vi*: **se** ~ (**à**) to hang *ou* cling on (to)

cran [kʀɑ̃] *nm* (*entaille*) notch; (*de courroie*) hole; (*courage*) guts *pl*; ~ **d'arrêt** safety catch

crâne [kʀɑn] *nm* skull

crâner [kʀɑne] (*fam*) *vi* to show off

crapaud [kʀapo] *nm* toad

crapule [kʀapyl] *nf* villain

craquement [kʀakmɑ̃] *nm* crack, snap; (*du plancher*) creak, creaking *no pl*

craquer [kʀake] *vi* (*bois, plancher*) to creak; (*fil, branche*) to snap; (*couture*) to come apart; (*fig*) to break down ♦ *vt* (*allumette*) to strike

crasse [kʀas] *nf* grime, filth

cravache [kʀavaʃ] *nf* (*riding*) crop

cravate [kʀavat] *nf* tie

crawl [kʀol] *nm* crawl; **dos** ~**é** backstroke

crayeux, euse [kʀɛjø, -øz] *adj* chalky

crayon [kʀɛjɔ̃] *nm* pencil; ~ **à bille** ballpoint pen; ~ **de couleur** crayon, colouring pencil; ~ **optique** light pen; **crayon-feutre** [kʀɛjɔ̃føtʀ(ə)] (*pl* **crayons-feutres**) *nm* felt(-tip) pen

créancier, ière [kʀeɑ̃sje, -jɛʀ] *nm/f* creditor

création [kʀeasjɔ̃] *nf* creation

créature [kʀeatyʀ] *nf* creature

crèche [kʀɛʃ] *nf* (*de Noël*) crib; (*garderie*)

crèche, day nursery

crédit [kʀedi] *nm* (*gén*) credit; ~**s** *nmpl* (*fonds*) funds; **payer/acheter à** ~ to pay/ buy on credit *ou* on easy terms; **faire** ~ **à qn** to give sb credit; **créditer** *vt*: **créditer un compte (de)** to credit an account (with)

crédule [kʀedyl] *adj* credulous, gullible

créer [kʀee] *vt* to create; (*THÉÂTRE*) to pro- duce (for the first time)

crémaillère [kʀemajɛʀ] *nf* (*RAIL*) rack; **pendre la** ~ to have a house-warming par- ty

crématoire [kʀematwaʀ] *adj*: **four** ~ cre- matorium

crème [kʀɛm] *nf* cream; (*entremets*) cream dessert ♦ *adj inv* cream (-coloured); **un (ca- fé)** ~ ≈ a white coffee; ~ **à raser** shaving cream; ~ **chantilly** whipped cream; ~ **fouettée = crème chantilly; crémerie** *nf* dairy; **crémeux, euse** *adj* creamy

créneau, x [kʀeno] *nm* (*de fortification*) crenel(le); (*fig*) gap, slot; (*AUTO*): **faire un** ~ to reverse into a parking space (*along- side the kerb*)

crêpe [kʀɛp] *nf* (*galette*) pancake ♦ *nm* (*tis- su*) crêpe; **crêpé, e** *adj* (*cheveux*) back- combed; **crêperie** *nf* pancake shop *ou* rest- aurant

crépir [kʀepiʀ] *vt* to roughcast

crépiter [kʀepite] *vi* to sputter, splutter; to crackle

crépu, e [kʀepy] *adj* frizzy, fuzzy

crépuscule [kʀepyskyl] *nm* twilight, dusk

cresson [kʀesɔ̃] *nm* watercress

crête [kʀɛt] *nf* (*de coq*) comb; (*de vague, montagne*) crest

creuser [kʀøze] *vt* (*trou, tunnel*) to dig; (*sol*) to dig a hole in; (*bois*) to hollow out; (*fig*) to go (deeply) into; **ça creuse** that gives you a real appetite; **se** ~ **(la cervelle)** to rack one's brains

creux, euse [kʀø, -øz] *adj* hollow ♦ *nm* hollow; (*fig: sur graphique etc*) trough; **heu- res creuses** slack periods; off-peak periods

crevaison [kʀəvɛzɔ̃] *nf* puncture

crevasse [kʀəvas] *nf* (*dans le sol*) crack, fissure; (*de glacier*) crevasse

crevé, e [kʀəve] *adj* (*fatigué*) all in, ex- hausted

crever [kʀəve] *vt* (*papier*) to tear, break; (*tambour, ballon*) to burst ♦ *vi* (*pneu*) to burst; (*automobiliste*) to have a puncture (*BRIT*) *ou* a flat (tire) (*US*); (*fam*) to die; **cela lui a crevé un œil** it blinded him in one eye

crevette [kʀəvɛt] *nf*: ~ **(rose)** prawn; ~ **grise** shrimp

cri [kʀi] *nm* cry, shout; (*d'animal: spécifique*) cry, call; **c'est le dernier** ~ (*fig*) it's the lat- est fashion

criant, e [kʀijɑ̃, -ɑ̃t] *adj* (*injustice*) glaring

criard, e [kʀijaʀ, -aʀd(ə)] *adj* (*couleur*) gar-

ish, loud; (*voix*) yelling

crible [kʀibl(ə)] *nm* riddle; **passer qch au** ~ (*fig*) to go over sth with a fine-tooth comb

criblé, e [kʀible] *adj*: ~ **de** riddled with; (*de dettes*) crippled with

cric [kʀik] *nm* (*AUTO*) jack

crier [kʀije] *vi* (*pour appeler*) to shout, cry (out); (*de peur, de douleur etc*) to scream, yell ♦ *vt* (*ordre, injure*) to shout (out), yell (out)

crime [kʀim] *nm* crime; (*meurtre*) murder; **criminel, le** *nm/f* criminal; murderer

crin [kʀɛ̃] *nm* hair *no pl*; (*fibre*) horsehair; ~**ière** [kʀinjɛʀ] *nf* mane

crique [kʀik] *nf* creek, inlet

criquet [kʀike] *nm* locust; grasshopper

crise [kʀiz] *nf* crisis; (*MÉD*) attack; fit; ~ **cardiaque** heart attack; ~ **de foie** bilious attack; ~ **de nerfs** attack of nerves

crisper [kʀispe] *vt* to tense; (*poings*) to clench; **se** ~ *vi* to tense; to clench; (*per- sonne*) to get tense

crisser [kʀise] *vi* (*neige*) to crunch; (*pneu*) to screech

cristal, aux [kʀistal, -o] *nm* crystal; ~**lin, e** *adj* crystal-clear

critère [kʀitɛʀ] *nm* criterion

critiquable [kʀitikabl(ə)] *adj* open to criti- cism

critique [kʀitik] *adj* critical ♦ *nm/f* (*de théâtre, musique*) critic ♦ *nf* criticism; (*THÉÂTRE etc: article*) review; ~**r** [kʀitike] *vt* (*dénigrer*) to criticize; (*évaluer, juger*) to assess, examine (critically)

croasser [kʀoase] *vi* to caw

Croatie [kʀoasi] *nf* Croatia

croc [kʀo] *nm* (*dent*) fang; (*de boucher*) hook

croc-en-jambe [kʀɔkɑ̃ʒɑ̃b] *nm*: **faire un** ~ **à qn** to trip sb up

croche [kʀɔʃ] *nf* (*MUS*) quaver (*BRIT*), eighth note (*US*); ~**-pied** [kʀɔʃpje] *nm* = **croc-en-jambe**

crochet [kʀɔʃe] *nm* hook; (*détour*) detour; (*TRICOT: aiguille*) crochet hook; (: *techni- que*) crochet; **vivre aux** ~**s de qn** to live *ou* sponge off sb; **crocheter** *vt* (*serrure*) to pick

crochu, e [kʀɔʃy] *adj* hooked; claw-like

crocodile [kʀɔkɔdil] *nm* crocodile

crocus [kʀɔkys] *nm* crocus

croire [kʀwaʀ] *vt* to believe; **se** ~ **fort** to think one is strong; ~ **que** to believe *ou* think that; ~ **à**, ~ **en** to believe in

crois *vb voir* **croître**

croisade [kʀwazad] *nf* crusade

croisé, e [kʀwaze] *adj* (*veston*) double- breasted

croisement [kʀwazmɑ̃] *nm* (*carrefour*) crossroads *sg*; (*BIO*) crossing; crossbreed

croiser [kʀwaze] *vt* (*personne, voiture*) to

pass; (*route*) to cross, cut across; (*BIO*) to cross ♦ *vi* (*NAVIG*) to cruise; **se ~** *vi* (*personnes, véhicules*) to pass each other; (*routes, lettres*) to cross; (*regards*) to meet; **~ les jambes/bras** to cross one's legs/fold one's arms

croiseur [kʀwazœʀ] *nm* cruiser (*warship*)

croisière [kʀwazjɛʀ] *nf* cruise; **vitesse de ~** (*AUTO etc*) cruising speed

croissance [kʀwasɑ̃s] *nf* growth

croissant [kʀwasɑ̃] *nm* (*à manger*) croissant; (*motif*) crescent

croître [kʀwatʀ(ə)] *vi* to grow

croix [kʀwa] *nf* cross; **en ~** in the form of a cross; **la C~ Rouge** the Red Cross

croque-monsieur [kʀɔkmɔsjø] *nm inv* toasted ham and cheese sandwich

croquer [kʀɔke] *vt* (*manger*) to crunch; to munch; (*dessiner*) to sketch ♦ *vi* to be crisp *ou* crunchy; **chocolat à ~** plain dessert chocolate

croquis [kʀɔki] *nm* sketch

crosse [kʀɔs] *nf* (*de fusil*) butt; (*de revolver*) grip

crotte [kʀɔt] *nf* droppings *pl*

crotté, e [kʀɔte] *adj* muddy, mucky

crottin [kʀɔtɛ̃] *nm* dung, manure

crouler [kʀule] *vi* (*s'effondrer*) to collapse; (*être délabré*) to be crumbling

croupe [kʀup] *nf* rump; **en ~** pillion

croupir [kʀupiʀ] *vi* to stagnate

croustillant, e [kʀustijɑ̃, -ɑ̃t] *adj* crisp; (*fig*) spicy

croûte [kʀut] *nf* crust; (*du fromage*) rind; (*MÉD*) scab; **en ~** in pastry

croûton [kʀutɔ̃] *nm* (*CULIN*) crouton; (*bout du pain*) crust, heel

croyable [kʀwajabl(ə)] *adj* credible

croyant, e [kʀwajɑ̃, -ɑ̃t] *nm/f* believer

C.R.S. *sigle fpl* (= *Compagnies républicaines de sécurité*) state security police force ♦ *sigle m* member of the C.R.S.

cru, e [kʀy] *pp de* **croire** ♦ *adj* (*non cuit*) raw; (*lumière, couleur*) harsh; (*paroles, description*) crude ♦ *nm* (*vignoble*) vineyard; (*vin*) wine

crû *pp de* **croître**

cruauté [kʀyote] *nf* cruelty

cruche [kʀyʃ] *nf* pitcher, jug

crucifix [kʀysifi] *nm* crucifix

crucifixion [kʀysifiksjɔ̃] *nf* crucifixion

crudités [kʀydite] *nfpl* (*CULIN*) salads

cruel, le [kʀyɛl] *adj* cruel

crus *etc vb voir* **croire; croître**

crûs *etc vb voir* **croître**

crustacés [kʀystase] *nmpl* shellfish

Cuba [kyba] *nf* Cuba

cube [kyb] *nm* cube; (*jouet*) brick; **mètre ~** cubic metre; **2 au ~** 2 cubed

cueillette [kœjɛt] *nf* picking; (*quantité*) crop, harvest

cueillir [kœjiʀ] *vt* (*fruits, fleurs*) to pick,

gather; (*fig*) to catch

cuiller [kɥijɛʀ] *nf* spoon; **~ à café** coffee spoon; (*CULIN*) ≈ teaspoonful; **~ à soupe** soup-spoon; (*CULIN*) ≈ tablespoonful

cuillère [kɥijɛʀ] *nf* = **cuiller**

cuillerée [kɥijʀe] *nf* spoonful

cuir [kɥiʀ] *nm* leather; **~ chevelu** scalp

cuire [kɥiʀ] *vt* (*aliments*) to cook; (*au four*) to bake; (*poterie*) to fire ♦ *vi* to cook; **bien cuit** (*viande*) well done; **trop cuit** overdone

cuisant, e [kɥizɑ̃, -ɑ̃t] *adj* (*douleur*) stinging; (*fig: souvenir, échec*) bitter

cuisine [kɥizin] *nf* (*pièce*) kitchen; (*art culinaire*) cookery, cooking; (*nourriture*) cooking, food; **faire la ~** to cook

cuisiné, e [kɥizine] *adj*: **plat ~** ready-made meal *ou* dish; **cuisiner** *vt* to cook; (*fam*) to grill ♦ *vi* to cook; **cuisinier, ière** *nm/f* cook; **cuisinière** *nf* (*poêle*) cooker

cuisse [kɥis] *nf* thigh; (*CULIN*) leg

cuisson [kɥisɔ̃] *nf* cooking; firing

cuit, e *pp de* **cuire**

cuivre [kɥivʀ(ə)] *nm* copper; **les ~s** (*MUS*) the brass

cul [ky] (*fam!*) *nm* arse (*!*)

culasse [kylas] *nf* (*AUTO*) cylinder-head; (*de fusil*) breech

culbute [kylbyt] *nf* somersault; (*accidentelle*) tumble, fall

culminant, e [kylminɑ̃, -ɑ̃t] *adj*: **point ~** highest point

culminer [kylmine] *vi* to reach its highest point; to tower

culot [kylo] *nm* (*effronterie*) cheek

culotte [kylɔt] *nf* (*de femme*) knickers *pl* (*BRIT*), panties *pl*; **~ de cheval** riding breeches *pl*

culpabilité [kylpabilite] *nf* guilt

culte [kylt(ə)] *nm* (*religion*) religion; (*hommage, vénération*) worship; (*protestant*) service

cultivateur, trice [kyltivatœʀ, -tʀis] *nm/f* farmer

cultivé, e [kyltive] *adj* (*personne*) cultured, cultivated

cultiver [kyltive] *vt* to cultivate; (*légumes*) to grow, cultivate

culture [kyltyʀ] *nf* cultivation; growing; (*connaissances etc*) culture; **~ physique** physical training; **culturisme** *nm* body-building

cumin [kymɛ̃] *nm* cumin; (*carvi*) caraway seeds *pl*

cumuler [kymyle] *vt* (*emplois, honneurs*) to hold concurrently; (*salaires*) to draw concurrently; (*JUR: droits*) to accumulate

cupide [kypid] *adj* greedy, grasping

cure [kyʀ] *nf* (*MÉD*) course of treatment; **n'avoir ~ de** to pay no attention to

curé [kyʀe] *nm* parish priest

cure-dent [kyʀdɑ̃] *nm* toothpick

cure-pipe [kyʀpip] *nm* pipe cleaner

curer [kyʀe] *vt* to clean out
curieux, euse [kyʀjø, -øz] *adj* (*étrange*) strange, curious; (*indiscret*) curious, inquisitive ♦ *nmpl* (*badauds*) onlookers; **curiosité** *nf* curiosity; (*site*) unusual feature
curriculum vitae [kyʀikylɔmvite] *nm inv* curriculum vitae
curseur [kyʀsœʀ] *nm* (*INFORM*) cursor
cuti-réaction [kytiʀeaksjɔ̃] *nf* (*MÉD*) skin-test
cuve [kyv] *nf* vat; (*à mazout etc*) tank; **cuvée** [kyve] *nf* vintage
cuvette [kyvɛt] *nf* (*récipient*) bowl, basin; (*GÉO*) basin
C.V. *sigle m* (*AUTO*) = **cheval vapeur**; (*COMM*) = **curriculum vitae**
cyanure [sjanyʀ] *nm* cyanide
cyclable [siklabl(ə)] *adj*: **piste ~** cycle track
cycle [sikl(ə)] *nm* cycle
cyclisme [siklism(ə)] *nm* cycling
cycliste [siklist(ə)] *nm/f* cyclist ♦ *adj* cycle *cpd*; **coureur ~** racing cyclist
cyclomoteur [siklɔmɔtœʀ] *nm* moped
cyclone [siklon] *nm* hurricane
cygne [siɲ] *nm* swan
cylindre [silɛ̃dʀ(ə)] *nm* cylinder; **cylindrée** *nf* (*AUTO*) (cubic) capacity
cymbale [sɛ̃bal] *nf* cymbal
cynique [sinik] *adj* cynical
cystite [sistit] *nf* cystitis

D d

---

d' [d] *prép voir* **de**
dactylo [daktilo] *nf* (*aussi: ~graphe*) typist; (: *~graphie*) typing; **~graphier** *vt* to type (out)
dada [dada] *nm* hobby-horse
daigner [deɲe] *vt* to deign
daim [dɛ̃] *nm* (fallow) deer *inv*; (*peau*) buckskin; (*imitation*) suede
dalle [dal] *nf* paving stone; slab
daltonien, ne [daltɔnjɛ̃, -jɛn] *adj* colour-blind
dam [dam] *nm*: **au grand ~ de** much to the detriment (*ou* annoyance) of
dame [dam] *nf* lady; (*CARTES, ÉCHECS*) queen; **~s** *nfpl* (*jeu*) draughts *sg* (*BRIT*), checkers *sg* (*US*)
damner [dane] *vt* to damn
dancing [dɑ̃siŋ] *nm* dance hall
Danemark [danmaʀk] *nm* Denmark

danger [dɑ̃ʒe] *nm* danger; **dangereux, euse** [dɑ̃ʒʀø, -øz] *adj* dangerous
danois, e [danwa, -waz] *adj* Danish ♦ *nm/f*: **D~, e** Dane ♦ *nm* (*LING*) Danish

┌─────────────── MOT CLÉ

dans [dɑ̃] *prép* **1** (*position*) in; (*à l'intérieur de*) inside; **c'est ~ le tiroir/le salon** it's in the drawer/lounge; **~ la boîte** in *ou* inside the box; **marcher ~ la ville** to walk about the town
2 (*direction*) into; **elle a couru ~ le salon** she ran into the lounge
3 (*provenance*) out of, from; **je l'ai pris ~ le tiroir/salon** I took it out of *ou* from the drawer/lounge; **boire ~ un verre** to drink out of *ou* from a glass
4 (*temps*) in; **~ 2 mois** in 2 months, in 2 months' time
5 (*approximation*) about; **~ les 20F** about 20F

└────────────────────────

danse [dɑ̃s] *nf*: **la ~** dancing; **une ~** a dance; **danser** *vi, vt* to dance; **danseur, euse** *nm/f* ballet dancer; (*au bal etc*) dancer; partner
dard [daʀ] *nm* sting (*organ*)
date [dat] *nf* date; **de longue ~** longstanding; **~ de naissance** date of birth; **~ limite** deadline; **dater** *vt, vi* to date; **dater de** to date from; **à dater de** (as) from
datte [dat] *nf* date; **dattier** *nm* date palm
dauphin [dofɛ̃] *nm* (*ZOOL*) dolphin
davantage [davɑ̃taʒ] *adv* more; (*plus longtemps*) longer; **~ de** more

┌─────────────── MOT CLÉ

de(d') (*de +le = du, de +les = des*) *prép* **1** (*appartenance*) of; **le toit ~ la maison** the roof of the house; **la voiture d'Elisabeth/~ mes parents** Elizabeth's/my parents' car
2 (*provenance*) from; **il vient ~ Londres** he comes from London; **elle est sortie du cinéma** she came out of the cinema
3 (*caractérisation, mesure*): **un mur ~ brique/bureau d'acajou** a brick wall/mahogany desk; **un billet ~ 50F** a 50F note; **une pièce ~ 2m ~ large** *ou* **large ~ 2m** a room 2m wide, a 2m-wide room; **un bébé ~ 10 mois** a 10-month-old baby; **12 mois ~ crédit/travail** 12 months' credit/work; **augmenter ~ 10F** to increase by 10F; **~ 14 à 18** from 14 to 18
♦ *dét* **1** (*phrases affirmatives*) some (*souvent omis*); **du vin, ~ l'eau, des pommes** (some) wine, (some) water, (some) apples; **des enfants sont venus** some children came; **pendant des mois** for months
2 (*phrases interrogatives et négatives*) any; **a-t-il du vin?** has he got any wine?; **il n'a pas ~ pommes/d'enfants** he hasn't (got) any apples/children, he has no apples/

children

dé [de] *nm* (*à jouer*) die *ou* dice; (*aussi*: ~ *à coudre*) thimble

déambuler [deãbyle] *vi* to stroll about

débâcle [debɑkl(ə)] *nf* rout

déballer [debale] *vt* to unpack

débandade [debɑ̃dad] *nf* rout; scattering

débarbouiller [debaʀbuje] *vt* to wash; **se ~** *vi* to wash (one's face)

débarcadère [debaʀkadɛʀ] *nm* wharf

débardeur [debaʀdœʀ] *nm* (*maillot*) tank top

débarquer [debaʀke] *vt* to unload, land ♦ *vi* to disembark; (*fig*) to turn up

débarras [debaʀa] *nm* lumber room; junk cupboard; **bon ~!** good riddance!

débarrasser [debaʀase] *vt* to clear; **se ~ de** *vt* to get rid of; **~ qn de** (*vêtements, paquets*) to relieve sb of

débat [deba] *nm* discussion, debate

débattre [debatʀ(ə)] *vt* to discuss, debate; **se ~** *vi* to struggle

débaucher [deboʃe] *vt* (*licencier*) to lay off, dismiss; (*entraîner*) to lead astray, debauch

débile [debil] *adj* weak, feeble; (*fam*: *idiot*) dim-witted

débit [debi] *nm* (*d'un liquide, fleuve*) flow; (*d'un magasin*) turnover (of goods); (*élocution*) delivery; (*bancaire*) debit; **~ de boissons** drinking establishment; **~ de tabac** tobacconist's; **~er** *vt* (*compte*) to debit; (*liquide, gaz*) to give out; (*couper*: *bois, viande*) to cut up; (*péj*: *paroles etc*) to churn out; **~eur, trice** *nm/f* debtor ♦ *adj* in debit; (*compte*) debit *cpd*

déblayer [debleje] *vt* to clear

débloquer [debloke] *vt* (*frein*) to release; (*prix, crédits*) to free

déboires [debwaʀ] *nmpl* setbacks

déboiser [debwaze] *vt* to deforest

déboîter [debwate] *vt* (*AUTO*) to pull out; **se ~ le genou** *etc* to dislocate one's knee *etc*

débonnaire [debɔnɛʀ] *adj* easy-going, good-natured

débordé, e [debɔʀde] *adj*: **être ~ (de)** (*travail, demandes*) to be snowed under (with)

déborder [debɔʀde] *vi* to overflow; (*lait etc*) to boil over; **~ (de) qch** (*dépasser*) to extend beyond sth

débouché [debuʃe] *nm* (*pour vendre*) outlet; (*perspective d'emploi*) opening

déboucher [debuʃe] *vt* (*évier, tuyau etc*) to unblock; (*bouteille*) to uncork ♦ *vi*: **~ de** to emerge from; **~ sur** to come out onto; to open out onto

débourser [debuʀse] *vt* to pay out

debout [dəbu] *adv*: **être ~** (*personne*) to be standing, stand; (: *levé, éveillé*) to be up; (*chose*) to be upright; **être encore ~** (*fig*: *en état*) to be still going; **se mettre ~** to

stand up; **se tenir ~** to stand; **~!** stand up!; (*du lit*) get up!; **cette histoire ne tient pas ~** this story doesn't hold water

déboutonner [debutɔne] *vt* to undo, unbutton

débraillé, e [debʀaje] *adj* slovenly, untidy

débrancher [debʀɑ̃ʃe] *vt* to disconnect; (*appareil électrique*) to unplug

débrayage [debʀɛjaʒ] *nm* (*AUTO*) clutch; **débrayer** [debʀeje] *vi* (*AUTO*) to declutch; (*cesser le travail*) to stop work

débris [debʀi] *nm* (*fragment*) fragment ♦ *nmpl* rubbish *sg*; debris *sg*

débrouillard, e [debʀujaʀ, -aʀd(ə)] *adj* smart, resourceful

débrouiller [debʀuje] *vt* to disentangle, untangle; **se ~** *vi* to manage

débusquer [debyske] *vt* to drive out (from cover)

début [deby] *nm* beginning, start; **~s** *nmpl* (*dans la vie*) beginnings; (*de carrière*) début *sg*

débutant, e [debytɑ̃, -ɑ̃t] *nm/f* beginner, novice

débuter [debyte] *vi* to begin, start; (*faire ses débuts*) to start out

deçà [dəsa] : **en ~ de** *prép* this side of

décacheter [dekaʃte] *vt* to unseal

décadence [dekadɑ̃s] *nf* decadence; decline

décaféiné, e [dekafeine] *adj* decaffeinated

décalage [dekalaʒ] *nm* gap; discrepancy; **~ horaire** time difference (*between time zones*); time-lag

décaler [dekale] *vt* (*dans le temps*: *avancer*) to bring forward; (: *retarder*) to put back; (*changer de position*) to shift forward *ou* back

décalquer [dekalke] *vt* to trace; (*par pression*) to transfer

décamper [dekɑ̃pe] *vi* to clear out *ou* off

décaper [dekape] *vt* to strip; (*avec abrasif*) to scour; (*avec papier de verre*) to sand

décapiter [dekapite] *vt* to behead; (*par accident*) to decapitate

décapotable [dekapɔtabl(ə)] *adj* convertible

décapsuler [dekapsyle] *vt* to take the cap *ou* top off; **décapsuleur** *nm* bottle-opener

décédé, e [desede] *adj* deceased

décéder [desede] *vi* to die

déceler [desle] *vt* to discover, detect; to indicate, reveal

décembre [desɑ̃bʀ(ə)] *nm* December

décemment [desamɑ̃] *adv* decently

décennie [deseni] *nf* decade

décent, e [desɑ̃, -ɑ̃t] *adj* decent

déception [desɛpsjɔ̃] *nf* disappointment

décerner [desɛʀne] *vt* to award

décès [desɛ] *nm* death, decease

décevoir [desvwaʀ] *vt* to disappoint

déchaîner [deʃene] *vt* to unleash, arouse; **se ~** to be unleashed

déchanter [deʃɑ̃te] *vi* to become disillusioned

décharge [deʃaʀʒ(ə)] *nf* (*dépôt d'ordures*) rubbish tip *ou* dump; (*électrique*) electrical discharge; **à la ~ de** in defence of

décharger [deʃaʀʒe] *vt* (*marchandise, véhicule*) to unload; (*ÉLEC, faire feu*) to discharge; **~ qn de** (*responsabilité*) to release sb from

décharné, e [deʃaʀne] *adj* emaciated

déchausser [deʃose] *vt* (*skis*) to take off; **se ~** *vi* to take off one's shoes; (*dent*) to come *ou* work loose

déchéance [deʃeɑ̃s] *nf* degeneration; decay, decline; fall

déchet [deʃɛ] *nm* (*de bois, tissu etc*) scrap; (*perte: gén COMM*) wastage, waste; **~s** *nmpl* (*ordures*) refuse *sg*, rubbish *sg*

déchiffrer [deʃifʀe] *vt* to decipher

déchiqueter [deʃikte] *vt* to tear *ou* pull to pieces

déchirant, e [deʃiʀɑ̃, -ɑ̃t] *adj* heart-rending

déchirement [deʃiʀmɑ̃] *nm* (*chagrin*) wrench, heartbreak; (*gén pl: conflit*) rift, split

déchirer [deʃiʀe] *vt* to tear; (*en morceaux*) to tear up; (*pour ouvrir*) to tear off; (*arracher*) to tear out; (*fig*) to rack; to tear (apart); **se ~** *vi* to tear, rip; **se ~ un muscle** to tear a muscle

déchirure [deʃiʀyʀ] *nf* (*accroc*) tear, rip; **~ musculaire** torn muscle

déchoir [deʃwaʀ] *vi* (*personne*) to lower o.s., demean o.s.

déchu, e [deʃy] *adj* fallen; deposed

décidé, e [deside] *adj* (*personne, air*) determined; **c'est ~** it's decided

décidément [desidemɑ̃] *adv* undoubtedly; really

décider [deside] *vt*: **~ qch** to decide on sth; **se ~ (à faire)** to decide (to do), make up one's mind (to do); **se ~ pour** to decide on *ou* in favour of; **~ de faire/que** to decide to do/that; **~ qn (à faire qch)** to persuade sb (to do sth); **~ de qch** to decide upon sth; (*suj: chose*) to determine sth

décilitre [desilitʀ(ə)] *nm* decilitre

décimal, e, aux [desimal, -o] *adj* decimal; **décimale** *nf* decimal

décimètre [desimɛtʀ(ə)] *nm* decimetre; **double ~** (20 cm) ruler

décisif, ive [desizif, -iv] *adj* decisive

décision [desizjɔ̃] *nf* decision; (*fermeté*) decisiveness, decision

déclaration [deklaʀasjɔ̃] *nf* declaration; registration; (*discours: POL etc*) statement; **~ (d'impôts)** ≈ tax return; **~ (de sinistre)** (insurance) claim

déclarer [deklaʀe] *vt* to declare; (*décès, naissance*) to register; **se ~** *vi* (*feu, maladie*) to break out

déclasser [deklɑse] *vt* to relegate; to downgrade; to lower in status

déclencher [deklɑ̃ʃe] *vt* (*mécanisme etc*) to release; (*sonnerie*) to set off, activate; (*attaque, grève*) to launch; (*provoquer*) to trigger off; **se ~** *vi* to release itself; to go off

déclic [deklik] *nm* trigger mechanism; (*bruit*) click

décliner [dekline] *vi* to decline ♦ *vt* (*invitation*) to decline; (*responsabilité*) to refuse to accept; (*nom, adresse*) to state

déclivité [deklivite] *nf* slope, incline

décocher [dekɔʃe] *vt* to throw; to shoot

décoiffer [dekwafe] *vi*: **se ~** to take off one's hat

déçois *etc vb voir* **décevoir**

décollage [dekɔlaʒ] *nm* (*AVIAT*) takeoff

décoller [dekɔle] *vt* to unstick ♦ *vi* (*avion*) to take off; **se ~** *vi* to come unstuck

décolleté, e [dekɔlte] *adj* low-cut; wearing a low-cut dress ♦ *nm* low neck(line); (*bare*) neck and shoulders; (*plongeant*) cleavage

décolorer [dekɔlɔʀe] *vt* (*tissu*) to fade; (*cheveux*) to bleach, lighten; **se ~** *vi* to fade

décombres [dekɔ̃bʀ(ə)] *nmpl* rubble *sg*, debris *sg*

décommander [dekɔmɑ̃de] *vt* to cancel; (*invités*) to put off; **se ~** *vi* to cancel one's appointment *etc*, cry off

décomposé, e [dekɔ̃poze] *adj* (*pourri*) decomposed; (*visage*) haggard, distorted

décompte [dekɔ̃t] *nm* deduction; (*facture*) detailed account

déconcerter [dekɔ̃sɛʀte] *vt* to disconcert, confound

déconfit, e [dekɔ̃fi, -it] *adj* crestfallen; **~ure** [dekɔ̃fityʀ] *nf* failure, defeat; collapse, ruin

décongeler [dekɔ̃ʒle] *vt* to thaw

déconner [dekɔne] (*fam*) *vi* to talk rubbish

déconseiller [dekɔ̃seje] *vt*: **~ qch (à qn)** to advise (sb) against sth

déconsidérer [dekɔ̃sideʀe] *vt* to discredit

décontracté, e [dekɑ̃tʀakte] *adj* relaxed, laid-back (*fam*)

décontracter [dekɔ̃tʀakte] *vt* to relax; **se ~** *vi* to relax

déconvenue [dekɔ̃vny] *nf* disappointment

décor [dekɔʀ] *nm* décor; (*paysage*) scenery; **~s** *nmpl* (*THÉÂTRE*) scenery *sg*, décor *sg*; (*CINÉMA*) set *sg*; **~ateur** [dekɔʀatœʀ] *nm* (interior) decorator; (*CINÉMA*) set designer; **~ation** [dekɔʀasjɔ̃] *nf* decoration; **~er** [dekɔʀe] *vt* to decorate

décortiquer [dekɔʀtike] *vt* to shell; (*riz*) to hull; (*fig*) to dissect

découcher [dekuʃe] *vi* to spend the night away from home

découdre [dekudʀ(ə)] *vt* to unpick; **se ~** *vi* to come unstitched; **en ~** (*fig*) to fight, do battle

découler [dekule] *vi*: **~ de** to ensue *ou* follow from

découper [dekupe] *vt* (*papier, tissu etc*) to cut up; (*volaille, viande*) to carve; (*détacher: manche, article*) to cut out; **se ~ sur** (*ciel, fond*) to stand out against

décourager [dekuraʒe] *vt* to discourage; **se ~** *vi* to lose heart, become discouraged

décousu, e [dekuzy] *adj* unstitched; (*fig*) disjointed, disconnected

découvert, e [dekuvɛʀ, -ɛʀt(ə)] *adj* (*tête*) bare, uncovered; (*lieu*) open, exposed ♦ *nm* (*bancaire*) overdraft; **découverte** *nf* discovery

découvrir [dekuvʀiʀ] *vt* to discover; (*apercevoir*) to see; (*enlever ce qui couvre ou protège*) to uncover; (*montrer, dévoiler*) to reveal; **se ~** *vi* to take off one's hat; to take something off; (*au lit*) to uncover o.s.; (*ciel*) to clear

décret [dekʀɛ] *nm* decree; **décréter** *vt* to decree; to order; to declare

décrié, e [dekʀije] *adj* disparaged

décrire [dekʀiʀ] *vt* to describe

décrocher [dekʀɔʃe] *vt* (*dépendre*) to take down; (*téléphone*) to take off the hook; (: *pour répondre*): **~ (le téléphone)** to lift the receiver; (*fig: contrat etc*) to get, land ♦ *vi* to drop out; to switch off

décroître [dekʀwatʀ(ə)] *vi* to decrease, decline

décrypter [dekʀipte] *vt* to decipher

déçu, e [desy] *pp de* **décevoir**

décupler [dekyple] *vt, vi* to increase tenfold

dédaigner [dedeɲe] *vt* to despise, scorn; (*négliger*) to disregard, spurn

dédaigneux, euse [dedɛɲø, -øz] *adj* scornful, disdainful

dédain [dedɛ̃] *nm* scorn, disdain

dédale [dedal] *nm* maze

dedans [dədɑ̃] *adv* inside; (*pas en plein air*) indoors, inside ♦ *nm* inside; **au ~** on the inside; inside; **en ~** (*vers l'intérieur*) inwards; *voir aussi* **là**

dédicacer [dedikase] *vt*: **~ (à qn)** to sign (for sb), autograph (for sb)

dédier [dedje] *vt* to dedicate

dédire [dediʀ] : **se ~** *vi* to go back on one's word; to retract, recant

dédommager [dedɔmaʒe] *vt*: **~ qn (de)** to compensate sb (for); (*fig*) to repay sb (for)

dédouaner [dedwane] *vt* to clear through customs

dédoubler [deduble] *vt* (*classe, effectifs*) to split (into two); **~ les trains** to run additional trains

déduire [dedɥiʀ] *vt*: **~ qch (de)** (*ôter*) to deduct sth (from); (*conclure*) to deduce *ou* infer sth (from)

déesse [deɛs] *nf* goddess

défaillance [defajɑ̃s] *nf* (*syncope*) blackout; (*fatigue*) (sudden) weakness *no pl*; (*technique*) fault, failure; (*morale etc*) weakness; **~ cardiaque** heart failure

défaillir [defajiʀ] *vi* to faint; to feel faint; (*mémoire etc*) to fail

défaire [defɛʀ] *vt* (*installation*) to take down, dismantle; (*paquet etc, nœud, vêtement*) to undo; **se ~** *vi* to come undone; **se ~ de** (*se débarrasser de*) to get rid of; (*se séparer de*) to part with

défait, e [defɛ, -ɛt] *adj* (*visage*) haggard, ravaged; **défaite** *nf* defeat

défalquer [defalke] *vt* to deduct

défaut [defo] *nm* (*moral*) fault, failing, defect; (*d'étoffe, métal*) fault, flaw, defect; (*manque, carence*): **~ de** lack of; shortage of; **en ~** at fault; in the wrong; **faire ~** (*manquer*) to be lacking; **à ~** failing that; **à ~ de** for lack *ou* want of; **par ~** (*JUR*) in his (*ou* her *etc*) absence

défavorable [defavɔʀabl(ə)] *adj* (*avis, conditions, jury*) unfavourable (*BRIT*), unfavorable (*US*)

défavoriser [defavɔʀize] *vt* to put at a disadvantage

défection [defɛksjɔ̃] *nf* defection, failure to give support *ou* assistance; failure to appear; **faire ~** (*d'un parti etc*) to withdraw one's support, leave

défectueux, euse [defɛktɥø, -øz] *adj* faulty, defective

défendre [defɑ̃dʀ(ə)] *vt* to defend; (*interdire*) to forbid; **se ~** *vi* to defend o.s.; **~ à qn qch/de faire** to forbid sb sth/to do; **il se défend** (*fig*) he can hold his own; **se ~ de/contre** (*se protéger*) to protect o.s. from/against; **se ~ de** (*se garder de*) to refrain from; (*nier*): **se ~ de vouloir** to deny wanting

défense [defɑ̃s] *nf* defence; (*d'éléphant etc*) tusk; **"~ de fumer/cracher"** "no smoking/spitting"

déférer [defeʀe] *vt* (*JUR*) to refer; **~ à** (*requête, décision*) to defer to

déferler [defɛʀle] *vi* (*vagues*) to break; (*fig*) to surge

défi [defi] *nm* (*provocation*) challenge; (*bravade*) defiance

défiance [defjɑ̃s] *nf* mistrust, distrust

déficit [defisit] *nm* (*COMM*) deficit

défier [defje] *vt* (*provoquer*) to challenge; (*fig*) to defy, brave; **se ~ de** (*se méfier de*) to distrust

défigurer [defigyʀe] *vt* to disfigure

défilé [defile] *nm* (*GÉO*) (narrow) gorge *ou* pass; (*soldats*) parade; (*manifestants*) procession, march

défiler [defile] *vi* (*troupes*) to march past; (*sportifs*) to parade; (*manifestants*) to march; (*visiteurs*) to pour, stream; **se ~** *vi* (*se dérober*) to slip away, sneak off

définir [definiʀ] *vt* to define

définitif, ive [definitif, -iv] *adj* (*final*) final, definitive; (*pour longtemps*) permanent, definitive; (*sans appel*) final, definite; **définitive** *nf*: **en définitive** eventually; (*somme toute*) when all is said and done

définitivement [definitivmɑ̃] *adv* definitively; permanently; definitely

déflagration [deflagrɑsjɔ̃] *nf* explosion

défoncer [defɔ̃se] *vt* (*caisse*) to stave in; (*porte*) to smash in *ou* down; (*lit, fauteuil*) to burst (the springs of); (*terrain, route*) to rip *ou* plough up

déformation [defɔrmɑsjɔ̃] *nf*: **~ professionnelle** conditioning by one's job

déformer [defɔrme] *vt* to put out of shape; (*corps*) to deform; (*pensée, fait*) to distort; **se ~** *vi* to lose its shape

défouler [defule]: **se ~** *vi* to unwind, let off steam

défraîchir [defreʃir]: **se ~** *vi* to fade; to become worn

défrayer [defreje] *vt*: **~ qn** to pay sb's expenses; **~ la chronique** to be in the news

défricher [defriʃe] *vt* to clear (for cultivation)

défroquer [defrɔke] *vi* (*aussi: se ~*) to give up the cloth

défunt, e [defœ̃, -œ̃t] *adj*: **son ~ père** his late father ♦ *nm/f* deceased

dégagé, e [degaʒe] *adj* clear; (*ton, air*) casual, jaunty

dégagement [degaʒmɑ̃] *nm*: **voie de ~** slip road; **itinéraire de ~** alternative route (*to relieve congestion*)

dégager [degaʒe] *vt* (*exhaler*) to give off; (*délivrer*) to free, extricate; (*désencombrer*) to clear; (*isoler: idée, aspect*) to bring out; **se ~** *vi* (*odeur*) to be given off; (*passage, ciel*) to clear

dégarnir [degarnir] *vt* (*vider*) to empty, clear; **se ~** *vi* (*tempes, crâne*) to go bald

dégâts [degɑ] *nmpl* damage *sg*

dégel [deʒɛl] *nm* thaw

dégeler [deʒle] *vt* to thaw (out); (*fig*) to unfreeze ♦ *vi* to thaw (out)

dégénérer [deʒenere] *vi* to degenerate; (*empirer*) to go from bad to worse

dégingandé, e [deʒɛ̃gɑ̃de] *adj* gangling

dégivrer [deʒivre] *vt* (*frigo*) to defrost; (*vitres*) to de-ice

déglutir [deglytir] *vt, vi* to swallow

dégonflé, e [degɔ̃fle] *adj* (*pneu*) flat

dégonfler [degɔ̃fle] *vt* (*pneu, ballon*) to let down, deflate; **se ~** *vi* (*fam*) to chicken out

dégouliner [deguline] *vi* to trickle, drip

dégourdi, e [degurdi] *adj* smart, resourceful

dégourdir [degurdir] *vt*: **se ~ (les jambes)** to stretch one's legs (*fig*)

dégoût [degu] *nm* disgust, distaste

dégoûtant, e [degutɑ̃, -ɑ̃t] *adj* disgusting

dégoûté, e [degute] *adj* disgusted; **~ de** sick of

dégoûter [degute] *vt* to disgust; **~ qn de** qch to put sb off sth

dégoutter [degute] *vi* to drip

dégradé [degrade] *nm* (*PEINTURE*) gradation

dégrader [degrade] *vt* (*MIL: officier*) to degrade; (*abîmer*) to damage, deface; **se ~** *vi* (*relations, situation*) to deteriorate

dégrafer [degrafe] *vt* to unclip, unhook

degré [dəgre] *nm* degree; (*d'escalier*) step; **alcool à 90 ~s** surgical spirit

dégressif, ive [degresif, -iv] *adj* on a decreasing scale

dégrèvement [degrɛvmɑ̃] *nm* tax relief

dégringoler [degrɛ̃gɔle] *vi* to tumble (down)

dégrossir [degrosir] *vt* (*fig*) to work out roughly; to knock the rough edges off

déguenillé, e [degnije] *adj* ragged, tattered

déguerpir [degɛrpir] *vi* to clear off

dégueulasse [degølas] (*fam*) *adj* disgusting

déguisement [degizmɑ̃] *nm* disguise

déguiser [degize] *vt* to disguise; **se ~** *vi* (*se costumer*) to dress up; (*pour tromper*) to disguise o.s.

déguster [degyste] *vt* (*vins*) to taste; (*fromages etc*) to sample; (*savourer*) to enjoy, savour

dehors [dəɔr] *adv* outside; (*en plein air*) outdoors ♦ *nm* outside ♦ *nmpl* (*apparences*) appearances; **mettre** *ou* **jeter ~** (*expulser*) to throw out; **au ~** outside; outwardly; **au ~ de** outside; **en ~** (*vers l'extérieur*) outside; outwards; **en ~ de** (*hormis*) apart from

déjà [deʒa] *adv* already; (*auparavant*) before, already

déjeuner [deʒœne] *vi* to (have) lunch; (*le matin*) to have breakfast ♦ *nm* lunch; breakfast

déjouer [deʒwe] *vt* to elude; to foil

delà [dəla] *adv*: **par ~, en ~ (de), au ~ (de)** beyond

délabrer [delabre]: **se ~** *vi* to fall into decay, become dilapidated

délacer [delase] *vt* to unlace

délai [dele] *nm* (*attente*) waiting period; (*sursis*) extension (of time); (*temps accordé*) time limit; **à bref ~** shortly, very soon; at short notice; **dans les ~s** within the time limit

délaisser [delese] *vt* to abandon, desert

délasser [delase] *vt* (*reposer*) to relax; (*divertir*) to divert, entertain; **se ~** *vi* to relax

délateur, trice [delatœr, -tris] *nm/f* informer

délavé, e [delave] *adj* faded

délayer [deleje] *vt* (*CULIN*) to mix (with water *etc*); (*peinture*) to thin down

delco [dɛlko] *nm* (*AUTO*) distributor

délecter [delɛkte]: **se ~** *vi* to revel *ou* delight in

délégué, e [delege] *nm/f* delegate; representative

déléguer [delege] *vt* to delegate

délibéré, e [delibeʀe] *adj (conscient)* deliberate; *(déterminé)* determined

délibérer [delibeʀe] *vi* to deliberate

délicat, e [delika, -at] *adj* delicate; *(plein de tact)* tactful; *(attentionné)* thoughtful; *(exigeant)* fussy, particular; **procédés peu ~s** unscrupulous methods; **délicatement** *adv* delicately; *(avec douceur)* gently

délice [delis] *nm* delight

délicieux, euse [delisjø, -jøz] *adj (au goût)* delicious; *(sensation, impression)* delightful

délimiter [delimite] *vt* to delimit, demarcate; to determine; to define

délinquance [delɛ̃kɑ̃s] *nf* criminality; **délinquant, e** [delɛ̃kɑ̃, -ɑ̃t] *adj, nm/f* delinquent

délirer [deliʀe] *vi* to be delirious; *(fig)* to be raving, be going wild

délit [deli] *nm* (criminal) offence; **~ d'initié** *(BOURSE)* insider dealing *ou* trading

délivrer [delivʀe] *vt (prisonnier)* to (set) free, release; *(passeport, certificat)* to issue; **~ qn de** *(ennemis)* to deliver *ou* free sb from; *(fig)* to relieve sb of; to rid sb of

déloger [deloʒe] *vt (locataire)* to turn out; *(objet coincé, ennemi)* to dislodge

deltaplane [dɛltaplan] *nm* hang-glider

déluge [delyʒ] *nm (biblique)* Flood

déluré, e [delyʀe] *adj* smart, resourceful; *(péj)* forward, pert

demain [dəmɛ̃] *adv* tomorrow

demande [dəmɑ̃d] *nf (requête)* request; *(revendication)* demand; *(ADMIN, formulaire)* application; *(ÉCON):* **la ~** demand; **"~s d'emploi"** "situations wanted"; **~ de poste** job application

demandé, e [dəmɑ̃de] *adj (article etc):* **très ~** (very) much in demand

demander [dəmɑ̃de] *vt* to ask for; *(date, heure etc)* to ask; *(nécessiter)* to require, demand; **se ~** to wonder; *(sens purement réfléchi)* to ask o.s.; **~ qch à qn** to ask sb for sth; to ask sb sth; **~ à qn de faire** to ask sb to do; **on vous demande au téléphone** you're wanted on the phone

demandeur, euse [dəmɑ̃dœʀ, -øz] *nm/f:* **~ d'emploi** job-seeker; (job) applicant

démangeaison [demɑ̃ʒɛzɔ̃] *nf* itching

démanger [demɑ̃ʒe] *vi* to itch

démanteler [demɑ̃tle] *vt* to break up; to demolish

démaquillant [demakijɑ̃] *nm* make-up remover

démaquiller [demakije] *vt:* **se ~** to remove one's make-up

démarche [demaʀʃ(ə)] *nf (allure)* gait, walk; *(intervention)* step; approach; *(fig: intellectuelle)* thought processes *pl;* approach; **faire des ~s auprès de qn** to approach sb

démarcheur, euse [demaʀʃœʀ, -øz] *nm/f*

(COMM) door-to-door salesman(woman)

démarquer [demaʀke] *vt (prix)* to mark down; *(joueur)* to stop marking

démarrage [demaʀaʒ] *nm* start

démarrer [demaʀe] *vi (conducteur)* to start (up); *(véhicule)* to move off; *(travaux)* to get moving; **démarreur** *nm (AUTO)* starter

démêler [demele] *vt* to untangle

démêlés [demele] *nmpl* problems

déménagement [demenaʒmɑ̃] *nm* move, removal; **camion de ~** removal van

déménager [demenaʒe] *vt (meubles)* to (re)move ♦ *vi* to move (house); **déménageur** *nm* removal man; *(entrepreneur)* furniture remover

démener [demne] : **se ~** *vi* to thrash about; *(fig)* to exert o.s.

dément, e [demɑ̃, -ɑ̃t] *adj (fou)* mad, crazy; *(fam)* brilliant, fantastic

démentiel, le [demɑ̃sjɛl] *adj* insane

démentir [demɑ̃tiʀ] *vt* to refute; **~ que** to deny that

démerder [demɛʀde] *(fam) :* **se ~** *vi* to sort things out for o.s.

démesuré, e [deməzyʀe] *adj* immoderate

démettre [demɛtʀ(ə)] *vt:* **~ qn de** *(fonction, poste)* to dismiss sb from; **se ~ (de ses fonctions)** to resign (from) one's duties; **se ~ l'épaule** *etc* to dislocate one's shoulder *etc*

demeurant [dəmœʀɑ̃] : **au ~** *adv* for all that

demeure [dəmœʀ] *nf* residence; **mettre qn en ~ de faire** to enjoin *ou* order sb to do; **à ~** permanently

demeurer [dəmœʀe] *vi (habiter)* to live; *(séjourner)* to stay; *(rester)* to remain

demi, e [dəmi] *adj* half ♦ *nm (bière)* ≈ half-pint *(0,25 litres)* ♦ *préfixe:* **~...** half-, semi-..., demi-; **trois heures/bouteilles et ~es** three and a half hours/bottles, three hours/bottles and a half; **il est 2 heures/midi et ~e** it's half past 2/12; **à ~** half-; **à la ~e** *(heure)* on the half-hour; **~-cercle** *nm* semicircle; **en ~-cercle** *adj* semicircular ♦ *adv* in a half circle; **~-douzaine** *nf* half-dozen, half a dozen; **~-finale** *nf* semifinal; **~-frère** *nm* half-brother; **~-heure** *nf* half-hour, half an hour; **~-journée** *nf* half-day, half a day; **~-litre** *nm* half-litre, half a litre; **~-livre** *nf* half-pound, half a pound; **~-mot** *adv:* **à ~-mot** without having to spell things out; **~-pension** *nf (à l'hôtel)* half-board; **~-place** *nf* half-fare

démis, e [demi, -iz] *adj (épaule etc)* dislocated

demi: **~-saison** *nf:* **vêtements de ~-saison** spring *ou* autumn clothing; **~-sel** *adj inv (beurre, fromage)* slightly salted; **~-sœur** *nf* half-sister

démission [demisjɔ̃] *nf* resignation; **donner sa ~** to give *ou* hand in one's notice; **dé-**

missionner vi (de son poste) to resign

demi-tarif [dəmitaʀif] nm half-price; (TRANSPORTS) half-fare

demi-tour [dəmituʀ] nm about-turn; faire ~ to turn (and go) back; (AUTO) to do a U-turn

démocratie [demɔkʀasi] nf democracy; **démocratique** [demɔkʀatik] adj democratic

démodé, e [demɔde] adj old-fashioned

démographique [demɔgʀafik] adj demographic, population cpd

demoiselle [dəmwazɛl] nf (jeune fille) young lady; (célibataire) single lady, maiden lady; ~ **d'honneur** bridesmaid

démolir [demɔliʀ] vt to demolish

démon [demɔ̃] nm (enfant turbulent) devil, demon; **le D~** the Devil

démonstration [demɔ̃stʀɑsjɔ̃] nf demonstration; (aérienne, navale) display

démonté, e [demɔ̃te] adj (fig) raging, wild

démonter [demɔ̃te] vt (machine etc) to take down, dismantle; **se ~** vi (personne) to lose countenance

démontrer [demɔ̃tʀe] vt to demonstrate

démordre [demɔʀdʀ(ə)] vi: **ne pas ~ de** to refuse to give up, stick to

démouler [demule] vt (gâteau) to turn out

démuni, e [demyni] adj (sans argent) impoverished

démunir [demyniʀ] vt: ~ **qn de** to deprive sb of; **se ~ de** to part with, give up

dénatalité [denatalite] nf fall in the birth rate

dénaturer [denatyʀe] vt (goût) to alter; (pensée, fait) to distort

déniaiser [denjeze] vt: ~ **qn** to teach sb about life

dénicher [deniʃe] vt to unearth; to track ou hunt down

dénier [denje] vt to deny

dénigrer [denigʀe] vt to denigrate, run down

dénivellation [denivelɑsjɔ̃] nf = **dénivellement**

dénivellement [denivɛlmɑ̃] nm ramp; dip; difference in level

dénombrer [denɔ̃bʀe] vt (compter) to count; (énumérer) to enumerate, list

dénomination [denɔminɑsjɔ̃] nf designation, appellation

dénommer [denɔme] vt to name

dénoncer [denɔ̃se] vt to denounce; **se ~** vi to give o.s. up, come forward

dénouement [denumɑ̃] nm outcome

dénouer [denwe] vt to unknot, undo

dénoyauter [denwajote] vt to stone

denrée [dɑ̃ʀe] nf: ~**s (alimentaires)** foodstuffs

dense [dɑ̃s] adj dense

densité [dɑ̃site] nf density

dent [dɑ̃] nf tooth; **en ~s de scie** serrated; jagged; ~ **de lait/sagesse** milk/wisdom

tooth; ~**aire** adj dental

dentelé, e [dɑ̃tle] adj jagged, indented

dentelle [dɑ̃tɛl] nf lace no pl

dentier [dɑ̃tje] nm denture

dentifrice [dɑ̃tifʀis] nm toothpaste

dentiste [dɑ̃tist(ə)] nm/f dentist

dénuder [denyde] vt to bare

dénué, e [denye] adj: ~ **de** devoid of; lacking in; **dénuement** [denymɑ̃] nm destitution

déodorant [deɔdɔʀɑ̃] nm deodorant

dépannage [depanaʒ] nm; **service de ~** (AUTO) breakdown service

dépanner [depane] vt (voiture, télévision) to fix, repair; (fig) to bail out, help out; **dépanneuse** nf breakdown lorry (BRIT), tow truck (US)

dépareillé, e [depaʀeje] adj (collection, service) incomplete; (objet) odd

déparer [depaʀe] vt to spoil, mar

départ [depaʀ] nm leaving no pl, departure; (SPORT) start; (sur un horaire) departure; **au ~** at the start; **à son ~** when he left

départager [depaʀtaʒe] vt to decide between

département [depaʀtəmɑ̃] nm department

départir [depaʀtiʀ]: **se ~ de** vt to abandon, depart from

dépassé, e [depase] adj superseded, outmoded; (affolé) panic-stricken

dépasser [depase] vt (véhicule, concurrent) to overtake; (endroit) to pass, go past; (somme, limite) to exceed; (fig: en beauté etc) to surpass, outshine; (être en saillie sur) to jut out above (ou in front of) ♦ vi (jupon) to show

dépaysé, e [depeize] adj disoriented

dépecer [depəse] vt to joint, cut up

dépêche [depɛʃ] nf dispatch

dépêcher [depeʃe] vt to dispatch; **se ~** vi to hurry

dépeindre [depɛ̃dʀ(ə)] vt to depict

dépendre [depɑ̃dʀ(ə)]: ~ **de** vt to depend on; (financièrement etc) to be dependent on

dépens [depɑ̃] nmpl: **aux ~ de** at the expense of

dépense [depɑ̃s] nf spending no pl, expense, expenditure no pl; (fig) consumption; expenditure

dépenser [depɑ̃se] vt to spend; (gaz, eau) to use; (fig) to expend, use up; **se ~** vi (se fatiguer) to exert o.s.

dépensier, ière [depɑ̃sje, -jɛʀ] adj: **il est ~** he's a spendthrift

déperdition [depɛʀdisjɔ̃] nf loss

dépérir [depeʀiʀ] vi to waste away; to wither

dépêtrer [depetʀe] vt: **se ~ de** to extricate o.s. from

dépeupler [depœple] vt to depopulate; **se ~** vi to be depopulated

dépilatoire [depilatwaʀ] adj depilatory,

hair-removing

dépister [depiste] *vt* to detect; (*voleur*) to track down; (*poursuivants*) to throw off the scent

dépit [depi] *nm* vexation, frustration; **en ~ de** in spite of; **en ~ du bon sens** contrary to all good sense; **dépité, e** *adj* vexed, frustrated

déplacé, e [deplase] *adj* (*propos*) out of place, uncalled-for

déplacement [deplasmɑ̃] *nm* (*voyage*) trip, travelling *no pl*

déplacer [deplase] *vt* (*table, voiture*) to move, shift; (*employé*) to transfer, move; (*os, vertèbre etc*) to displace; **se ~** *vi* to move; (*voyager*) to travel

déplaire [deplɛʀ] *vt*: **ceci me déplaît** I don't like this, I dislike this; **se ~** *vr*: **se quelque part** to be unhappy somewhere; **déplaisant, e** *adj* disagreeable

dépliant [deplijɑ̃] *nm* leaflet

déplier [deplije] *vt* to unfold

déplorer [deplɔʀe] *vt* (*regretter*) to deplore

déployer [deplwaje] *vt* to open out, spread; to deploy; to display, exhibit

déporter [depɔʀte] *vt* (*POL*) to deport; (*dévier*) to carry off course

déposer [depoze] *vt* (*gén: mettre, poser*) to lay *ou* put down; (*à la banque, à la consigne*) to deposit; (*passager*) to drop (off), set down; (*roi*) to depose; (*ADMIN: faire enregistrer*) to file; to register; (*JUR*): **(contre)** to testify *ou* give evidence (against); **se ~** *vi* to settle; **dépositaire** *nm/f* (*COMM*) agent

dépôt [depo] *nm* (*à la banque, sédiment*) deposit; (*entrepôt, réserve*) warehouse, store; (*gare*) depot; (*prison*) cells *pl*

dépotoir [depɔtwaʀ] *nm* dumping ground, rubbish dump

dépouille [depuj] *nf* (*d'animal*) skin, hide; (*humaine*): **~ (mortelle)** mortal remains *pl*

dépouillé, e [depuje] *adj* (*fig*) bare, bald

dépouiller [depuje] *vt* (*animal*) to skin; (*spolier*) to deprive of one's possessions; (*documents*) to go through, peruse; **~ qn/qch de** to strip sb/sth of; **~ le scrutin** to count the votes

dépourvu, e [depuʀvy] *adj*: **~ de** lacking in, without; **au ~** unprepared

déprécier [depʀesje] *vt* to depreciate; **se ~** *vi* to depreciate

dépression [depʀesjɔ̃] *nf* depression; **~ (nerveuse)** (nervous) breakdown

déprimer [depʀime] *vt* to depress

──────────── *MOT CLÉ*

depuis [dəpɥi] *prép* **1** (*point de départ dans le temps*) since; **il habite Paris ~ 1983/l'an dernier** he has been living in Paris since 1983/last year; **~ quand le connaissez-vous?** how long have you known him?

2 (*temps écoulé*) for; **il habite Paris ~ 5 ans** he has been living in Paris for 5 years; **je le connais ~ 3 ans** I've known him for 3 years

3 (*lieu*): **il a plu ~ Metz** it's been raining since Metz; **elle a téléphoné ~ Valence** she rang from Valence

4 (*quantité, rang*) from; **~ les plus petits jusqu'aux plus grands** from the youngest to the oldest

♦ *adv* (*temps*) since (then); **je ne lui ai pas parlé ~** I haven't spoken to him since (then); **~ que** *conj* (ever) since; **~ qu'il m'a dit ça** (ever) since he said that to me

député, e [depyte] *nm/f* (*POL*) ≈ Member of Parliament (*BRIT*), ≈ Member of Congress (*US*)

députer [depyte] *vt* to delegate

déraciner [deʀasine] *vt* to uproot

dérailler [deʀaje] *vi* (*train*) to be derailed; **faire ~** to derail

déraisonner [deʀezɔne] *vi* to talk nonsense, rave

dérangement [deʀɑ̃ʒmɑ̃] *nm* (*gêne*) trouble; (*gastrique etc*) disorder; (*mécanique*) breakdown; **en ~** (*téléphone*) out of order

déranger [deʀɑ̃ʒe] *vt* (*personne*) to trouble, bother; to disturb; (*projets*) to disrupt, upset; (*objets, vêtements*) to disarrange; **se ~** *vi* to put o.s. out; to (take the trouble to) come *ou* go out; **est-ce que cela vous dérange si ...?** do you mind if ...?

déraper [deʀape] *vi* (*voiture*) to skid; (*personne, semelles, couteau*) to slip

déréglé, e [deʀegle] *adj* (*mœurs*) dissolute

dérégler [deʀegle] *vt* (*mécanisme*) to put out of order; (*estomac*) to upset

dérider [deʀide] *vt* to brighten up; **se ~** *vi* to brighten up

dérision [deʀizjɔ̃] *nf*: **tourner en ~** to deride

dérivatif [deʀivatif] *nm* distraction

dérive [deʀiv] *nf* (*de dériveur*) centre-board; **aller à la ~** (*NAVIG, fig*) to drift

dérivé, e [deʀive] *nm* (*TECH*) by-product; **~e** *nf* (*MATH*) derivative

dériver [deʀive] *vt* (*MATH*) to derive; (*cours d'eau etc*) to divert ♦ *vi* (*bateau*) to drift; **~ de** to derive from

dermatologue [dɛʀmatɔlɔg] *nm/f* dermatologist

dernier, ière [dɛʀnje, -jɛʀ] *adj* last; (*le plus récent*) latest, last; **lundi/le mois ~** last Monday/month; **du ~ chic** extremely smart; **les ~s honneurs** the last tribute; **en ~** last; **ce ~** the latter; **dernièrement** *adv* recently

dérobé, e [deʀobe] *adj* (*porte*) secret, hidden; **à la ~e** surreptitiously

dérober [deʀobe] *vt* to steal; **se ~** *vi* (*s'esquiver*) to slip away; to shy away; **se ~**

sous (s'effondrer) to give way beneath; **se ~ à** (justice, regards) to hide from; (obligation) to shirk; **~ qch à (la vue de) qn** to conceal ou hide sth from sb('s view)

dérogation [derɔgasjɔ̃] nf (special) dispensation

déroger [derɔʒe] : **~ à** vt to go against, depart from

dérouiller [deruje] vt: **se ~ les jambes** to stretch one's legs (fig)

déroulement [derulmɑ̃] nm (d'une opération etc) progress

dérouler [derule] vt (ficelle) to unwind; (papier) to unroll; **se ~ vi** (avoir lieu) to take place; (se passer) to go on; to go (off); to unfold

déroute [derut] nf rout; total collapse; **~r** [derute] vt (avion, train) to reroute, divert; (étonner) to disconcert, throw (out)

derrière [derjɛr] adv, prép behind ♦ nm (d'une maison) back; (postérieur) behind, bottom; **les pattes de ~** the back ou hind legs; **par ~** from behind; (fig) behind one's back

des [de] dét voir **de** ♦ prép +dét = **de** +**les**

dès [de] prép from; **~ que** as soon as; **~ son retour** as soon as he was (ou is) back; **~ lors** from then on; **~ lors que** from the moment (that)

désabusé, e [dezabyze] adj disillusioned

désaccord [dezakɔr] nm disagreement; **~é, e** [dezakɔrde] adj (MUS) out of tune

désaffecté, e [dezafɛkte] adj disused

désagréable [dezagreable(ə)] adj unpleasant

désagréger [dezagreʒe] : **se ~ vi** to disintegrate, break up

désagrément [dezagremɑ̃] nm annoyance, trouble no pl

désaltérer [dezaltere] vt: **se ~** to quench one's thirst

désamorcer [dezamɔrse] vt to defuse; to forestall

désapprobateur, trice [dezaprɔbatœr, -tris] adj disapproving

désapprouver [dezapruve] vt to disapprove of

désarçonner [dezarsɔne] vt to unseat, throw; (fig) to throw, puzzle

désarmant, e [dezarmɑ̃, -ɑ̃t] adj disarming

désarroi [dezarwa] nm disarray

désarticulé, e [dezartikyle] adj (pantin, corps) dislocated

désastre [dezastr(ə)] nm disaster

désavantage [dezavɑ̃taʒ] nm disadvantage; (inconvénient) drawback, disadvantage; **désavantager** vt to put at a disadvantage

désavouer [dezavwe] vt to disown

désaxé, e [dezakse] adj (fig) unbalanced

descendre [desɑ̃dr(ə)] vt (escalier, montagne) to go (ou come) down; (valise, paquet) to take ou get down; (étagère etc) to

lower; (fam: abattre) to shoot down ♦ vi to go (ou come) down; (passager: s'arrêter) to get out, alight; **~ à pied/en voiture** to walk/drive down; **~ de** (famille) to be descended from; **~ du train** to get out of ou get off the train; **~ d'un arbre** to climb down from a tree; **~ de cheval** to dismount; **~ à l'hôtel** to stay at a hotel

descente [desɑ̃t] nf descent, going down; (chemin) way down; (SKI) downhill (race); **au milieu de la ~** halfway down; **~ de lit** bedside rug; **~ (de police)** (police) raid

description [dɛskripsjɔ̃] nf description

désemparé, e [dezɑ̃pare] adj bewildered, distraught

désemparer [dezɑ̃pare] vi: **sans ~** without stopping

désemplir [dezɑ̃plir] vi: **ne pas ~** to be always full

déséquilibre [dezekilibr(ə)] nm (position): **en ~** unsteady; (fig: des forces, du budget) imbalance; **déséquilibré, e** [dezekilibre] nm/f (PSYCH) unbalanced person; **déséquilibrer** [dezekilibre] vt to throw off balance

désert, e [dezɛr, -ɛrt(ə)] adj deserted ♦ nm desert

déserter [dezɛrte] vi, vt to desert

désertique [dezɛrtik] adj desert cpd; barren, empty

désespéré, e [dezɛspere] adj desperate

désespérer [dezɛspere] vt to drive to despair ♦ vi: **~ de** to despair of

désespoir [dezɛspwar] nm despair; **en ~ de cause** in desperation

déshabillé [dezabije] nm négligée

déshabiller [dezabije] vt to undress; **se ~ vi** to undress (o.s.)

désherbant [dezɛrbɑ̃] nm weed-killer

déshériter [dezerite] vt to disinherit

déshérités [dezerite] nmpl: **les ~** the underprivileged

déshonneur [dezɔnœr] nm dishonour

déshydraté, e [dezidrate] adj dehydrated

desiderata [deziderata] nmpl requirements

désigner [deziɲe] vt (montrer) to point out, indicate; (dénommer) to denote; (candidat etc) to name

désinfectant, e [dezɛ̃fɛktɑ̃, -ɑ̃t] adj, nm disinfectant; **désinfecter** [dezɛ̃fɛkte] vt to disinfect

désintégrer [dezɛ̃tegre] vt to disintegrate; **se ~ vi** to disintegrate

désintéressé, e [dezɛ̃terese] adj disinterested, unselfish

désintéresser [dezɛ̃terese] vt: **se ~ (de)** to lose interest (in)

désintoxication [dezɛ̃tɔksikasjɔ̃] nf: **faire une cure de ~** to undergo treatment for alcoholism (ou drug addiction)

désinvolte [dezɛ̃vɔlt(ə)] adj casual, offhand; **désinvolture** nf casualness

désir [deziʀ] *nm* wish; (*fort, sensuel*) desire
désirer [deziʀe] *vt* to want, wish for; (*sexuellement*) to desire; **je désire ...** (*formule de politesse*) I would like ...
désister [deziste]: **se ~** *vi* to stand down, withdraw
désobéir [dezɔbeiʀ] *vi*: **~ (à qn/qch)** to disobey (sb/sth); **désobéissant, e** *adj* disobedient
désobligeant, e [dezɔbliʒɑ̃, -ɑ̃t] *adj* disagreeable
désodorisant [dezɔdɔʀizɑ̃] *nm* air freshener, deodorizer
désœuvré, e [dezœvʀe] *adj* idle
désolé, e [dezɔle] *adj* (*paysage*) desolate; **je suis ~** I'm sorry
désoler [dezɔle] *vt* to distress, grieve
désolidariser [desɔlidaʀize] *vt*: **se ~ de** *ou* **d'avec** to dissociate o.s. from
désopilant, e [dezɔpilɑ̃, -ɑ̃t] *adj* hilarious
désordonné, e [dezɔʀdɔne] *adj* untidy
désordre [dezɔʀdʀ(ə)] *nm* disorder(liness), untidiness; (*anarchie*) disorder; **~s** *nmpl* (*POL*) disturbances, disorder *sg*; **en ~** in a mess, untidy
désorienté, e [dezɔʀjɑ̃te] *adj* disorientated
désormais [dezɔʀmɛ] *adv* from now on
désosser [dezɔse] *vt* to bone
desquelles [dekɛl] *prép +pron* = **de +lesquelles**
desquels [dekɛl] *prép +pron* = **de +lesquels**
dessaisir [deseziʀ]: **se ~ de** *vt* to give up, part with
dessaler [desale] *vt* (*eau de mer*) to desalinate; (*CULIN*) to soak
desséché, e [deseʃe] *adj* dried up
dessécher [deseʃe] *vt* to dry out, parch; **se ~** *vi* to dry out
dessein [desɛ̃] *nm* design; **à ~** intentionally, deliberately
desserrer [deseʀe] *vt* to loosen; (*frein*) to release
dessert [desɛʀ] *nm* dessert, pudding
desserte [desɛʀt(ə)] *nf* (*table*) side table; (*transport*): **la ~ du village est assurée par autocar** there is a coach service to the village
desservir [desɛʀviʀ] *vt* (*ville, quartier*) to serve; (*nuire à*) to go against, put at a disadvantage; (*débarrasser*): **~ (la table)** to clear the table
dessin [desɛ̃] *nm* (*œuvre, art*) drawing; (*motif*) pattern, design; (*contour*) (out)line; **~ animé** cartoon (film); **~ humoristique** cartoon
dessinateur, trice [desinatœʀ, -tʀis] *nm/f* drawer; (*de bandes dessinées*) cartoonist; (*industriel*) draughtsman(woman) (*BRIT*), draftsman(woman) (*US*)
dessiner [desine] *vt* to draw; (*concevoir*) to design

dessous [dəsu] *adv* underneath, beneath ♦ *nm* underside ♦ *nmpl* (*sous-vêtements*) underwear *sg*; **en ~, par ~** underneath; below; **au-dessous (de)** below; (*peu digne de*) beneath; **avoir le ~** to get the worst of it; **dessous-de-plat** *nm inv* tablemat
dessus [dəsy] *adv* on top; (*collé, écrit*) on it ♦ *nm* top; **en ~** above; **par ~** over it ♦ *prép* over; **au-dessus (de)** above; **avoir le ~** to get the upper hand; **dessus-de-lit** *nm inv* bedspread
destin [destɛ̃] *nm* fate; (*avenir*) destiny
destinataire [destinatɛʀ] *nm/f* (*POSTES*) addressee; (*d'un colis*) consignee
destination [destinɑsjɔ̃] *nf* (*lieu*) destination; (*usage*) purpose; **à ~ de** bound for, travelling to
destinée [destine] *nf* fate; (*existence, avenir*) destiny
destiner [destine] *vt*: **~ qn à** (*poste, sort*) to destine sb for; **~ qn/qch à** (*prédestiner*) to destine sb/sth to +*verbe*; **~ qch à qn** (*envisager de donner*) to intend sb to have sth; (*adresser*) to intend sth for sb; to aim sth at sb; **être destiné à** (*sort*) to be destined to +*verbe*; (*usage*) to be meant for; (*suj: sort*) to be in store for
destituer [destitɥe] *vt* to depose
désuet, ète [desɥɛ, -ɛt] *adj* outdated, outmoded; **désuétude** *nf*: **tomber en désuétude** to fall into disuse
détachant [detaʃɑ̃] *nm* stain remover
détachement [detaʃmɑ̃] *nm* detachment
détacher [detaʃe] *vt* (*enlever*) to detach, remove; (*délier*) to untie; (*ADMIN*): **~ qn (auprès de** *ou* **à)** to post sb (to); **se ~** *vi* (*tomber*) to come off; to come out; (*se défaire*) to come undone; **se ~ sur** to stand out against; **se ~ de** (*se désintéresser*) to grow away from
détail [detaj] *nm* detail; (*COMM*): **le ~** retail; **en ~** in detail; **au ~** (*COMM*) retail; separately
détaillant [detajɑ̃] *nm* retailer
détailler [detaje] *vt* (*expliquer*) to explain in detail; to detail; (*examiner*) to look over, examine
détartrant [detaʀtʀɑ̃] *nm* scale remover
détecter [detɛkte] *vt* to detect
détective [detɛktiv] *nm* detective; **~ (privé)** private detective
déteindre [detɛ̃dʀ(ə)] *vi* (*tissu*) to fade; (*fig*): **~ sur** to rub off on
dételer [detle] *vt* to unharness
détendre [detɑ̃dʀ(ə)] *vt*: **se ~** to lose its tension; to relax
détenir [detniʀ] *vt* (*fortune, objet, secret*) to be in possession of; (*prisonnier*) to detain, hold; (*record, pouvoir*) to hold
détente [detɑ̃t] *nf* relaxation; (*d'une arme*) trigger
détention [detɑ̃sjɔ̃] *nf* possession; deten-

tion; holding; ~ **préventive** (pre-trial) custody

détenu, e [detny] *nm/f* prisoner

détergent [deterʒã] *nm* detergent

détériorer [deterjɔʀe] *vt* to damage; **se ~** *vi* to deteriorate

déterminé, e [detɛʀmine] *adj* (*résolu*) determined; (*précis*) specific, definite

déterminer [detɛʀmine] *vt* (*fixer*) to determine; (*décider*): ~ **qn à faire** to decide sb to do

déterrer [detɛʀe] *vt* to dig up

détestable [detɛstabl(ə)] *adj* foul, ghastly; detestable, odious

détester [detɛste] *vt* to hate, detest

détonation [detɔnɑsjɔ̃] *nf* detonation, bang, report (of a gun)

détonner [detɔne] *vi* (*MUS*) to go out of tune; (*fig*) to clash

détour [detuʀ] *nm* detour; (*tournant*) bend, curve; **sans ~** (*fig*) plainly

détourné, e [detuʀne] *adj* (*moyen*) roundabout

détournement [detuʀnəmã] *nm*: ~ **d'avion** hijacking; ~ **de mineur** corruption of a minor

détourner [detuʀne] *vt* to divert; (*par la force*) to hijack; (*yeux, tête*) to turn away; (*de l'argent*) to embezzle; **se ~** *vi* to turn away

détracteur, trice [detʀaktœʀ, -tʀis] *nm/f* disparager, critic

détraquer [detʀake] *vt* to put out of order; (*estomac*) to upset; **se ~** *vi* to go wrong

détrempé, e [detʀãpe] *adj* (*sol*) sodden, waterlogged

détresse [detʀɛs] *nf* distress

détriment [detʀimã] *nm*: **au ~ de** to the detriment of

détritus [detʀitys] *nmpl* rubbish *sg*, refuse *sg*

détroit [detʀwa] *nm* strait

détromper [detʀɔ̃pe] *vt* to disabuse

détrôner [detʀone] *vt* to dethrone

détrousser [detʀuse] *vt* to rob

détruire [detʀɥiʀ] *vt* to destroy

dette [dɛt] *nf* debt

D.E.U.G. [døg] *sigle m* = **diplôme d'études universitaires générales**

deuil [dœj] *nm* (*perte*) bereavement; (*période*) mourning; (*chagrin*) grief; **être en ~** to be in mourning

deux [dø] *num* two; **les ~** both; **ses ~ mains** both his hands, his two hands; **deuxième** *num* second; **deuxièmement** *adv* secondly, in the second place; **deux-pièces** *nm inv* (*tailleur*) two-piece suit; (*de bain*) two-piece (swimsuit); (*appartement*) two-roomed flat (*BRIT*) *ou* apartment (*US*); **deux-roues** *nm inv* two-wheeled vehicle

deux points *nm inv* colon *sg*

devais *etc vb voir* **devoir**

dévaler [devale] *vt* to hurtle down

dévaliser [devalize] *vt* to rob, burgle

dévaloriser [devalɔʀize] *vt* to depreciate; **se ~** *vi* to depreciate

dévaluation [devalɥasjɔ̃] *nf* depreciation; (*ÉCON: mesure*) devaluation

devancer [dəvãse] *vt* to be ahead of; to get ahead of; to arrive before; (*prévenir*) to anticipate

devant [dəvã] *adv* in front; (*à distance: en avant*) ahead ♦ *prép* in front of; ahead of; (*avec mouvement: passer*) past; (*fig*) before, in front of; faced with; in view of ♦ *nm* front; **prendre les ~s** to make the first move; **les pattes de ~** the front legs, the forelegs; **par ~** (*boutonner*) at the front; (*entrer*) the front way; **aller au-devant de qn** to go out to meet sb; **aller au-devant de** (*désirs de qn*) to anticipate

devanture [dəvãtyʀ] *nf* (*façade*) (shop) front; (*étalage*) display; (shop) window

déveine [devɛn] *nf* rotten luck *no pl*

développement [devlɔpmã] *nm* development

développer [devlɔpe] *vt* to develop; **se ~** *vi* to develop

devenir [dəvniʀ] *vb +attrib* to become; ~ **instituteur** to become a teacher; **que sont-ils devenus?** what has become of them?

dévergondé, e [devɛʀgɔ̃de] *adj* wild, shameless

déverser [devɛʀse] *vt* (*liquide*) to pour (out); (*ordures*) to tip (out); **se ~ dans** (*fleuve, mer*) to flow into

dévêtir [devetiʀ] *vt* to undress; **se ~** *vi* to undress

devez *etc vb voir* **devoir**

déviation [devjɑsjɔ̃] *nf* deviation; (*AUTO*) diversion (*BRIT*), detour (*US*)

dévider [devide] *vt* to unwind

devienne *etc vb voir* **devenir**

dévier [devje] *vt* (*fleuve, circulation*) to divert; (*coup*) to deflect ♦ *vi* to veer (off course)

devin [dəvɛ̃] *nm* soothsayer, seer

deviner [dəvine] *vt* to guess; (*prévoir*) to foresee; (*apercevoir*) to distinguish; **devinette** [dəvinɛt] *nf* riddle

devins *etc vb voir* **devenir**

devis [dəvi] *nm* estimate, quotation

dévisager [devizaʒe] *vt* to stare at

devise [dəviz] *nf* (*formule*) motto, watchword; (*ÉCON: monnaie*) currency; **~s** *nfpl* (*argent*) currency *sg*

deviser [dəvize] *vi* to converse

dévisser [devise] *vt* to unscrew, undo; **se ~** *vi* to come unscrewed

dévoiler [devwale] *vt* to unveil

devoir [dəvwaʀ] *nm* duty; (*SCOL*) homework *no pl*; (: *en classe*) exercise ♦ *vt* (*argent, respect*): ~ **qch (à qn)** to owe (sb) sth; (*suivi de l'infinitif: obligation*): **il doit le faire** he has to do it, he must do it; (: *in-*

tention): **il doit partir demain** he is (due) to leave tomorrow; (: *probabilité*): **il doit être tard** it must be late

dévolu, e [devɔly] *adj:* ~ **à** allotted to ♦ *nm:* **jeter son** ~ **sur** to fix one's choice on

dévorer [devɔʀe] *vt* to devour; (*suj: feu, soucis*) to consume

dévot, e [devo, -ɔt] *adj* devout, pious

dévotion [devosjɔ̃] *nf* devoutness; **être à la** ~ **de qn** to be totally devoted to sb

dévoué, e [devwe] *adj* devoted

dévouer [devwe] : **se** ~ *vi* (*se sacrifier*): **se** ~ **(pour)** to sacrifice o.s. (for); (*se consacrer*): **se** ~ **à** to devote *ou* dedicate o.s. to

dévoyé, e [devwaje] *adj* delinquent

devrai *etc vb voir* **devoir**

diabète [djabɛt] *nm* diabetes *sg;* **diabétique** *nm/f* diabetic

diable [djɑbl(ə)] *nm* devil

diabolo [djabɔlo] *nm* (*boisson*) lemonade with fruit cordial

diacre [djakʀ(ə)] *nm* deacon

diagnostic [djagnɔstik] *nm* diagnosis *sg*

diagonal, e, aux [djagɔnal, -o] *adj* diagonal; **~e** *nf* diagonal; **en ~e** diagonally; **lire en ~e** to skim through

diagramme [djagʀam] *nm* chart, graph

dialecte [djalɛkt(ə)] *nm* dialect

dialogue [djalɔg] *nm* dialogue

diamant [djamɑ̃] *nm* diamond; **diamantaire** *nm* diamond dealer

diamètre [djamɛtʀ(ə)] *nm* diameter

diapason [djapazɔ̃] *nm* tuning fork

diaphragme [djafʀagm(ə)] *nm* diaphragm

diaporama [djapɔʀama] *nm* slide show

diapositive [djapozitiv] *nf* transparency, slide

diarrhée [djaʀe] *nf* diarrhoea

dictateur [diktatœʀ] *nm* dictator; **dictature** *nf* dictatorship

dictée [dikte] *nf* dictation

dicter [dikte] *vt* to dictate

dictionnaire [diksjɔnɛʀ] *nm* dictionary

dicton [diktɔ̃] *nm* saying, dictum

dièse [djɛz] *nm* sharp

diesel [djezɛl] *nm* diesel ♦ *adj inv* diesel

diète [djɛt] *nf* (*jeûne*) starvation diet; (*régime*) diet

diététique [djetetik] *adj:* **magasin** ~ health food shop

dieu, x [djø] *nm* god; **D~** God; **mon D~**! good heavens!

diffamation [difamɑsjɔ̃] *nf* slander; (*écrite*) libel

différé [difeʀe] *nm* (*TV*): **en** ~ (pre-)recorded

différence [difeʀɑ̃s] *nf* difference; **à la** ~ **de** unlike; **différencier** [difeʀɑ̃sje] *vt* to differentiate; **différend** [difeʀɑ̃] *nm* difference (of opinion), disagreement

différent, e [difeʀɑ̃, -ɑ̃t] *adj:* ~ **(de)** different (from); **~s objets** different *ou* various

objects

différer [difeʀe] *vt* to postpone, put off ♦ *vi:* ~ **(de)** to differ (from)

difficile [difisil] *adj* difficult; (*exigeant*) hard to please; **difficilement** *adv* with difficulty

difficulté [difikylte] *nf* difficulty; **en** ~ (*bateau, alpiniste*) in difficulties

difforme [difɔʀm(ə)] *adj* deformed, misshapen

diffuser [difyze] *vt* (*chaleur, bruit*) to diffuse; (*émission, musique*) to broadcast; (*nouvelle, idée*) to circulate; (*COMM*) to distribute

digérer [diʒeʀe] *vt* to digest; (*fig: accepter*) to stomach, put up with; **digestif** *nm* (after-dinner) liqueur

digne [diɲ] *adj* dignified; ~ **de** worthy of; ~ **de foi** trustworthy

dignité [diɲite] *nf* dignity

digression [digʀesjɔ̃] *nf* digression

digue [dig] *nf* dike, dyke

dilapider [dilapide] *vt* to squander

dilemme [dilɛm] *nm* dilemma

diligence [diliʒɑ̃s] *nf* stagecoach; (*empressement*) despatch

diluer [dilɥe] *vt* to dilute

diluvien, ne [dilyvjɛ̃, -jɛn] *adj:* **pluie ~ne** torrential rain

dimanche [dimɑ̃ʃ] *nm* Sunday

dimension [dimɑ̃sjɔ̃] *nf* (*grandeur*) size; (*cote, de l'espace*) dimension

diminuer [diminɥe] *vt* to reduce, decrease; (*ardeur etc*) to lessen; (*personne: physiquement*) to undermine; (*dénigrer*) to belittle ♦ *vi* to decrease, diminish; **diminutif** *nm* (*surnom*) pet name; **diminution** *nf* decreasing, diminishing

dinde [dɛ̃d] *nf* turkey

dindon [dɛ̃dɔ̃] *nm* turkey

dîner [dine] *nm* dinner ♦ *vi* to have dinner

dingue [dɛ̃g] (*fam*) *adj* crazy

diplomate [diplɔmat] *adj* diplomatic ♦ *nm* diplomat; (*fig*) diplomatist

diplomatie [diplɔmasi] *nf* diplomacy

diplôme [diplom] *nm* diploma; **diplômé, e** *adj* qualified

dire [diʀ] *nm:* **au** ~ **de** according to ♦ *vt* to say; (*secret, mensonge*) to tell; **leurs ~s** what they say; ~ **l'heure/la vérité** to tell the time/the truth; ~ **qch à qn** to tell sb sth; ~ **à qn qu'il fasse** *ou* **de faire** to tell sb to do; **on dit que** they say that; **ceci dit** that being said; (*à ces mots*) whereupon; **si cela lui dit** (*plaire*) if he fancies it; **que dites-vous de** (*penser*) what do you think of; **on dirait que** it looks (*ou* sounds *etc*) as if; **dis/dites (donc)** I say; (*à propos*) by the way

direct, e [diʀɛkt] *adj* direct ♦ *nm* (*TV*): **en** ~ live; **directement** *adv* directly

directeur, trice [diʀɛktœʀ, -tʀis] *nm/f* (*d'entreprise*) director; (*de service*) manager(eress); (d'école) head (teacher) (BRIT), principal (US)

direction [diʀɛksjɔ̃] nf management; conducting; supervision; (AUTO) steering; (sens) direction; **"toutes ~s"** "all routes"

dirent vb voir **dire**

dirigeant, e [diʀiʒɑ̃, -ɑ̃t] adj managerial; ruling ♦ nm/f (d'un parti etc) leader; (d'entreprise) manager

diriger [diʀiʒe] vt (entreprise) to manage, run; (véhicule) to steer; (orchestre) to conduct; (recherches, travaux) to supervise; (braquer: regard, arme): ~ **sur** to point ou level at; **se** ~ vi (s'orienter) to find one's way; **se** ~ **vers** ou **sur** to make ou head for

dirigisme [diʀiʒism(ə)] nm (ÉCON) state intervention, interventionism

dis etc vb voir **dire**

discernement [disɛʀnəmɑ̃] nm (bon sens) discernment, judgement

discerner [disɛʀne] vt to discern, make out

discipline [disiplin] nf discipline; **discipliner** vt to discipline; to control

discontinu, e [diskɔ̃tiny] adj intermittent

discontinuer [diskɔ̃tinɥe] vi: **sans** ~ without stopping, without a break

disconvenir [diskɔ̃vniʀ] vi: **ne pas** ~ **de** qch/que not to deny sth/that

discordant, e [diskɔʀdɑ̃, -ɑ̃t] adj discordant; conflicting

discothèque [diskɔtɛk] nf (disques) record collection; (: dans une bibliothèque) record library; (boîte de nuit) disco(thèque)

discourir [diskuʀiʀ] vi to discourse, hold forth

discours [diskuʀ] nm speech

discret, ète [diskʀɛ, -ɛt] adj discreet; (fig) unobtrusive; quiet

discrétion [diskʀesjɔ̃] nf discretion; **être à la** ~ **de** qn to be in sb's hands; **à** ~ unlimited; as much as one wants

discrimination [diskʀiminasjɔ̃] nf discrimination; **sans** ~ indiscriminately

disculper [diskylpe] vt to exonerate

discussion [diskysjɔ̃] nf discussion

discutable [diskytabl(ə)] adj debatable

discuté, e [diskyte] adj controversial

discuter [diskyte] vt (contester) to question, dispute; (débattre: prix) to discuss ♦ vi to talk; (ergoter) to argue; ~ **de** to discuss

dise etc vb voir **dire**

disette [dizɛt] nf food shortage

diseuse [dizøz] nf: ~ **de bonne aventure** fortuneteller

disgracieux, euse [disgʀasjø, -jøz] adj ungainly, awkward

disjoindre [disʒwɛ̃dʀ(ə)] vt to take apart; **se** ~ vi to come apart

disjoncteur [disʒɔ̃ktœʀ] nm (ÉLEC) circuit breaker

disloquer [dislɔke] vt (chaise) to dismantle;

se ~ vi (parti, empire) to break up; **se** ~ **l'épaule** to dislocate one's shoulder

disons vb voir **dire**

disparaître [dispaʀɛtʀ(ə)] vi to disappear; (à la vue) to vanish, disappear; to be hidden ou concealed; (se perdre: traditions etc) to die out; **faire** ~ to remove; to get rid of

disparition [dispaʀisjɔ̃] nf disappearance

disparu, e [dispaʀy] nm/f missing person; (défunt) dead person, departed (littér)

dispensaire [dispɑ̃sɛʀ] nm community clinic

dispenser [dispɑ̃se] vt (donner) to lavish, bestow; (exempter): ~ **qn de** to exempt sb from; **se** ~ **de** vt to avoid; to get out of

disperser [dispɛʀse] vt to scatter; (fig: son attention) to dissipate

disponibilité [dispɔnibilite] nf (ADMIN): **être en** ~ to be on leave of absence

disponible [dispɔnibl(ə)] adj available

dispos [dispo] adj m: **(frais et)** ~ fresh (as a daisy)

disposé, e [dispoze] adj: **bien/mal** ~ (humeur) in a good/bad mood; ~ **à** (prêt à) willing ou prepared to

disposer [dispoze] vt (arranger, placer) to arrange ♦ vi: **vous pouvez** ~ you may leave; ~ **de** to have (at one's disposal); to use; **se** ~ **à faire** to prepare to do, be about to do

dispositif [dispozitif] nm device; (fig) system, plan of action; set-up

disposition [dispozisjɔ̃] nf (arrangement) arrangement, layout; (humeur) mood; (tendance) tendency; ~**s** nfpl (mesures) steps, measures; (préparatifs) arrangements; (loi, testament) provisions; (aptitudes) bent sg, aptitude sg; **à la** ~ **de** qn at sb's disposal

disproportionné, e [dispʀɔpɔʀsjɔne] adj disproportionate, out of all proportion

dispute [dispyt] nf quarrel, argument

disputer [dispyte] vt (match) to play; (combat) to fight; (course) to run, fight; **se** ~ vi to quarrel; ~ **qch à** qn to fight with sb over sth

disquaire [diskɛʀ] nm/f record dealer

disqualifier [diskalifje] vt to disqualify

disque [disk(ə)] nm (MUS) record; (forme, pièce) disc; (SPORT) discus; ~ **compact** compact disc; ~ **d'embrayage** (AUTO) clutch plate

disquette [diskɛt] nf floppy disk, diskette

disséminer [disemine] vt to scatter

disséquer [diseke] vt to dissect

dissertation [disɛʀtasjɔ̃] nf (SCOL) essay

disserter [disɛʀte] vi: ~ **sur** to discourse upon

dissimuler [disimyle] vt to conceal

dissiper [disipe] vt to dissipate; (fortune) to squander; **se** ~ vi (brouillard) to clear, disperse; (doutes) to melt away; (élève) to become unruly

dissolu, e [disɔly] *adj* dissolute
dissolvant [disɔlvã] *nm* solvent; **~ (gras)** nail polish remover
dissonant, e [disɔnã, -ãt] *adj* discordant
dissoudre [disudʀ(ə)] *vt* to dissolve; **se ~** *vi* to dissolve
dissuader [disɥade] *vt*: **~ qn de faire/de qch** to dissuade sb from doing/from sth
dissuasion [disɥazjõ] *nf*: **force de ~** deterrent power
distance [distãs] *nf* distance; (*fig*: *écart*) gap; **à ~** at *ou* from a distance; **distancer** *vt* to outdistance
distant, e [distã, -ãt] *adj* (*réservé*) distant; **~ de** (*lieu*) far away from
distendre [distãdʀ(ə)] *vt* to distend; **se ~** *vi* to distend
distiller [distile] *vt* to distil; **distillerie** *nf* distillery
distinct, e [distɛ̃(kt), distɛ̃kt(ə)] *adj* distinct; **distinctif, ive** *adj* distinctive
distingué, e [distɛ̃ge] *adj* distinguished
distinguer [distɛ̃ge] *vt* to distinguish
distraction [distʀaksjõ] *nf* (*manque d'attention*) absent-mindedness; (*oubli*) lapse (in concentration); (*détente*) diversion, recreation; (*passe-temps*) distraction, entertainment
distraire [distʀɛʀ] *vt* (*déranger*) to distract; (*divertir*) to entertain, divert; **se ~** *vi* to amuse *ou* enjoy o.s.
distrait, e [distʀɛ, -ɛt] *adj* absent-minded
distribuer [distʀibɥe] *vt* to distribute; to hand out; (*CARTES*) to deal (out); (*courrier*) to deliver; **distributeur** *nm* (*COMM*) distributor; (*automatique*) (vending) machine; (: *de billets*) (cash) dispenser; **distribution** *nf* distribution; (*postale*) delivery; (*choix d'acteurs*) casting, cast
dit, e [di, dit] *pp de* dire ♦ *adj* (*fixé*): **le jour ~** the arranged day; (*surnommé*): **X, ~ Pierrot** X, known as Pierrot
dites *vb voir* dire
divaguer [divage] *vi* to ramble; to rave
divan [divã] *nm* divan
divers, e [divɛʀ, -ɛʀs(ə)] *adj* (*varié*) diverse, varied; (*différent*) different, various ♦ *dét* (*plusieurs*) various, several; **(frais) ~** sundries, miscellaneous (expenses)
divertir [divɛʀtiʀ] *vt* to amuse, entertain; **se ~** *vi* to amuse *ou* enjoy o.s.
divin, e [divɛ̃, -in] *adj* divine
diviser [divize] *vt* (*gén, MATH*) to divide; (*morceler, subdiviser*) to divide (up), split (up); **division** *nf* division
divorce [divɔʀs(ə)] *nm* divorce; **divorcé, e** *nm/f* divorcee; **divorcer** *vi* to get a divorce, get divorced; **divorcer de** *ou* **d'avec qn** to divorce sb
divulguer [divylge] *vt* to divulge, disclose
dix [dis] *num* ten; **dixième** *num* tenth
dizaine [dizɛn] *nf* (*10*) ten; (*environ 10*):

une ~ (de) about ten, ten or so
do [do] *nm* (*note*) C; (*en chantant la gamme*) do(h)
dock [dɔk] *nm* dock
docker [dɔkɛʀ] *nm* docker
docte [dɔkt(ə)] *adj* learned
docteur [dɔktœʀ] *nm* doctor
doctorat [dɔktɔʀa] *nm*: **~ (d'Université)** doctorate; **~ d'État** ≈ Ph.D.
doctrine [dɔktʀin] *nf* doctrine
document [dɔkymã] *nm* document
documentaire [dɔkymãtɛʀ] *adj, nm* documentary
documentaliste [dɔkymãtalist(ə)] *nm/f* archivist; researcher
documentation [dɔkymãtasjõ] *nf* documentation, literature; (*PRESSE, TV*: *service*) research
documenter [dɔkymãte] *vt*: **se ~ (sur)** to gather information (on)
dodeliner [dɔdline] *vi*: **~ de la tête** to nod one's head gently
dodo [dɔdo] *nm*: **aller faire ~** to go to beddy-byes
dodu, e [dɔdy] *adj* plump
dogue [dɔg] *nm* mastiff
doigt [dwa] *nm* finger; **à deux ~s de** within an inch of; **un ~ de lait** a drop of milk; **~ de pied** toe
doigté [dwate] *nm* (*MUS*) fingering; (*fig*: *habileté*) diplomacy, tact
doit *etc vb voir* devoir
doléances [dɔleãs] *nfpl* complaints; grievances
dollar [dɔlaʀ] *nm* dollar
D.O.M. [deɔɛm, dɔm] *sigle m* = **département d'outre-mer**
domaine [dɔmɛn] *nm* estate, property; (*fig*) domain, field
domestique [dɔmɛstik] *adj* domestic ♦ *nm/f* servant, domestic
domicile [dɔmisil] *nm* home, place of residence; **à ~** at home; **domicilié, e** *adj*: **être domicilié à** to have one's home in *ou* at
dominant, e [dɔminã, -ãt] *adj* dominant; predominant
dominateur, trice [dɔminatœʀ, -tʀis] *adj* dominating; domineering
dominer [dɔmine] *vt* to dominate; (*passions etc*) to control, master; (*surpasser*) to outclass, surpass ♦ *vi* to be in the dominant position; **se ~** *vi* to control o.s.
domino [dɔmino] *nm* domino
dommage [dɔmaʒ] *nm* (*préjudice*) harm, injury; (*dégâts, pertes*) damage *no pl*; **c'est ~ de faire/que** it's a shame *ou* pity to do/ that; **dommages-intérêts** *nmpl* damages
dompter [dõte] *vt* to tame; **dompteur, euse** *nm/f* trainer; liontamer
don [dõ] *nm* (*cadeau*) gift; (*charité*) donation; (*aptitude*) gift, talent; **avoir des ~s pour** to have a gift *ou* talent for

donc [dɔ̃k] conj therefore, so; (après une digression) so, then

donjon [dɔ̃ʒɔ̃] nm keep

donné, e [dɔne] adj (convenu) given; (pas cher): **c'est** ~ it's a gift; **étant** ~ ... given ...; **donnée** nf (MATH, gén) datum

donner [dɔne] vt to give; (vieux habits etc) to give away; (spectacle) to put on; (film) to show; ~ **qch à qn** to give sb sth, give sth to sb; ~ **sur** (suj: fenêtre, chambre) to look (out) onto; ~ **dans** (piège etc) to fall into; **se** ~ **à fond** to give one's all; **s'en** ~ **à cœur joie** (fam) to have a great time

---

MOT CLÉ

dont [dɔ̃] pron relatif **1** (appartenance: objets) whose, of which; (appartenance: êtres animés) whose; **la maison** ~ **le toit est rouge** the house the roof of which is red; the house whose roof is red; **l'homme** ~ **je connais la sœur** the man whose sister I know

2 (parmi lesquel(le)s): **2 livres,** ~ **l'un est ...** 2 books, one of which is ...; **il y avait plusieurs personnes,** ~ **Gabrielle** there were several people, among them Gabrielle; **10 blessés,** ~ **2 grièvement** 10 injured, 2 of them seriously

3 (complément d'adjectif, de verbe): **le fils** ~ **il est si fier** the son he's so proud of; **ce** ~ **je parle** what I'm talking about

---

doré, e [dɔʀe] adj golden; (avec dorure) gilt, gilded

dorénavant [dɔʀenavɑ̃] adv henceforth

dorer [dɔʀe] vt (cadre) to gild; (faire) ~ (CULIN) to brown

dorloter [dɔʀlɔte] vt to pamper

dormir [dɔʀmiʀ] vi to sleep; (être endormi) to be asleep

dortoir [dɔʀtwaʀ] nm dormitory

dorure [dɔʀyʀ] nf gilding

dos [do] nm back; (de livre) spine; **"voir au** ~**"** "see over"; **de** ~ from the back

dosage [dozaʒ] nm mixture

dose [doz] nf dose; ~**r** [doze] vt to measure out; to mix in the correct proportions; (fig) to expend in the right amounts; to strike a balance between

dossard [dosaʀ] nm number (worn by competitor)

dossier [dosje] nm (renseignements, fichier) file; (de chaise) back; (PRESSE) feature

dot [dɔt] nf dowry

doter [dɔte] vt to equip

douane [dwan] nf (poste, bureau) customs pl; (taxes) (customs) duty; **douanier, ière** adj customs cpd ♦ nm customs officer

double [dubl(ə)] adj, adv double ♦ nm (2 fois plus): **le** ~ **(de)** twice as much (ou many) (as); (autre exemplaire) duplicate, copy; (sosie) double; (TENNIS) doubles sg;

en ~ **(exemplaire)** in duplicate; **faire** ~ **emploi** to be redundant

doubler [duble] vt (multiplier par 2) to double; (vêtement) to line; (dépasser) to overtake, pass; (film) to dub; (acteur) to stand in for ♦ vi to double

doublure [dublyʀ] nf lining; (CINÉMA) stand-in

douce [dus] adj voir doux; **douceâtre** adj sickly sweet; **doucement** adv gently; slowly; **doucereux, euse** (péj) adj sugary; **douceur** nf softness; sweetness; mildness; gentleness; **douceurs** nfpl (friandises) sweets

douche [duʃ] nf shower; ~**s** nfpl (salle) shower room sg; **doucher: se doucher** vi to have ou take a shower

doudoune [dudun] nf padded jacket; boob (fam)

doué, e [dwe] adj gifted, talented; ~ **de** endowed with

douille [duj] nf (ÉLEC) socket; (de projectile) case

douillet, te [dujɛ, -ɛt] adj cosy; (péj) soft

douleur [dulœʀ] nf pain; (chagrin) grief, distress; **douloureux, euse** adj painful

doute [dut] nm doubt; **sans** ~ no doubt; (probablement) probably

douter [dute] vt to doubt; ~ **de** (allié) to doubt, have (one's) doubts about; (résultat) to be doubtful of; **se** ~ **de qch/que** to suspect sth/that; **je m'en doutais** I suspected as much

douteux, euse [dutø, -øz] adj (incertain) doubtful; (discutable) dubious, questionable; (péj) dubious-looking

Douvres [duvʀ(ə)] n Dover

doux, douce [du, dus] adj (gén) soft; (sucré, agréable) sweet; (peu fort: moutarde, clément: climat) mild; (pas brusque) gentle

douzaine [duzɛn] nf (12) dozen; (environ 12): **une** ~ **(de)** a dozen or so, twelve or so

douze [duz] num twelve; **douzième** num twelfth

doyen, ne [dwajɛ̃, -ɛn] nm/f (en âge, ancienneté) most senior member; (de faculté) dean

dragée [dʀaʒe] nf sugared almond; (MÉD) (sugar-coated) pill

dragon [dʀagɔ̃] nm dragon

draguer [dʀage] vt (rivière) to dredge; to drag; (fam) to try to pick up

dramatique [dʀamatik] adj dramatic; (tragique) tragic ♦ nf (TV) (television) drama

dramaturge [dʀamatyʀʒ(ə)] nm dramatist, playwright

drame [dʀam] nm (THÉÂTRE) drama

drap [dʀa] nm (de lit) sheet; (tissu) woollen fabric

drapeau, x [dʀapo] nm flag; **sous les** ~**x** with the colours, in the army

dresser [dʀese] vt (mettre vertical, monter)

to put up, erect; (*fig: liste, bilan, contrat*) to draw up; (*animal*) to train; **se ~** *vi* (*falaise, obstacle*) to stand; to tower (up); (*personne*) to draw o.s. up; **~ qn contre qn** to set sb against sb; **~ l'oreille** to prick up one's ears

drogue [dʀɔg] *nf* drug; **la ~** drugs *pl*; **drogué, e** [dʀɔge] *nm/f* drug addict

droguer [dʀɔge] *vt* (*victime*) to drug; (*malade*) to give drugs to; **se ~** *vi* (*aux stupéfiants*) to take drugs; (*péj: de médicaments*) to dose o.s. up

droguerie [dʀɔgʀi] *nf* hardware shop

droguiste [dʀɔgist(ə)] *nm* keeper (*ou* owner) of a hardware shop

droit, e [dʀwa, dʀwat] *adj* (*non courbe*) straight; (*vertical*) upright, straight; (*fig: loyal*) upright, straight(forward); (*opposé à gauche*) right, right-hand ♦ *adv* straight ♦ *nm* (*prérogative*) right; (*taxe*) duty, tax; (: *d'inscription*) fee; (*JUR*): **le ~** law; **avoir le ~ de** to be allowed to; **avoir ~ à** to be entitled to; **être en ~ de** to have a *ou* the right to; **être dans son ~** to be within one's rights; **à ~e** on the right; (*direction*) (to the) right; **~s d'auteur** royalties; **~s d'inscription** *nmpl* enrolment fee; (*competition*) entry fee; **droite** *nf* (*POL*): **la droite** the right (wing)

droitier, ière [dʀwatje, -jɛʀ] *nm/f* right-handed person

droits *nmpl voir* **droit**

droiture [dʀwatyʀ] *nf* uprightness, straightness

drôle [dʀol] *adj* funny; **une ~ d'idée** a funny idea; **drôlement** *adv* (*très*) terribly, awfully

dromadaire [dʀɔmadɛʀ] *nm* dromedary

dru, e [dʀy] *adj* (*cheveux*) thick, bushy; (*pluie*) heavy

du [dy] *dét voir de* ♦ *prép* +*dét* = **de** +**le**

dû, due [dy] *vb voir* **devoir** ♦ *adj* (*somme*) owing, owed; (: *venant à échéance*) due; (*causé par*): **~ à** due to ♦ *nm* due; (*somme*) dues *pl*

dubitatif, ive [dybitatif, -iv] *adj* doubtful, dubious

duc [dyk] *nm* duke; **duchesse** *nf* duchess

dûment [dymɑ̃] *adv* duly

Dunkerque [dœ̃kɛʀk] *n* Dunkirk

duo [dɥo] *nm* (*MUS*) duet

dupe [dyp] *nf* dupe ♦ *adj*: **(ne pas) être ~ de** (not) to be taken in by

duplex [dyplɛks] *nm* (*appartement*) split-level apartment, duplex

duplicata [dyplikata] *nm* duplicate

duquel [dykɛl] *prép* +*pron* = **de** +**lequel**

dur, e [dyʀ] *adj* (*pierre, siège, travail, problème*) hard; (*lumière, voix, climat*) harsh; (*sévère*) hard, harsh; (*cruel*) hard(-hearted); (*porte, col*) stiff; (*viande*) tough ♦ *adv* hard; **~ d'oreille** hard of hearing

durant [dyʀɑ̃] *prép* (*au cours de*) during; (*pendant*) for; **des mois ~** for months

durcir [dyʀsiʀ] *vt, vi* to harden; **se ~** *vi* to harden

durée [dyʀe] *nf* length; (*d'une pile etc*) life; (*déroulement: des opérations etc*) duration

durement [dyʀmɑ̃] *adv* harshly

durer [dyʀe] *vi* to last

dureté [dyʀte] *nf* hardness; harshness; stiffness; toughness

durit [dyʀit] (®) *nf* (car radiator) hose

dus *etc vb voir* **devoir**

duvet [dyvɛ] *nm* down; (*sac de couchage*) down-filled sleeping bag

dynamique [dinamik] *adj* dynamic

dynamite [dinamit] *nf* dynamite

dynamiter [dinamite] *vt* to (blow up with) dynamite

dynamo [dinamo] *nf* dynamo

dysenterie [disɑ̃tʀi] *nf* dysentery

dyslexie [dislɛksi] *nf* dyslexia, word-blindness

——————— *E e*

eau, x [o] *nf* water; **~x** *nfpl* (*MED*) waters; **prendre l'~** to leak, let in water; **tomber à l'~** (*fig*) to fall through; **~ courante** running water; **~ de Cologne** Eau de Cologne; **~ de Javel** bleach; **~ de toilette** toilet water; **~ douce** fresh water; **~ minérale** mineral water; **~ plate** still water; **~ salée** salt water; **eau-de-vie** *nf* brandy; **eau-forte** *nf* etching

ébahi, e [ebai] *adj* dumbfounded

ébattre [ebatʀ(ə)] : **s'~** *vi* to frolic

ébaucher [eboʃe] *vt* to sketch out, outline; **s'~** *vi* to take shape

ébène [ebɛn] *nf* ebony

ébéniste [ebenist(ə)] *nm* cabinetmaker

éberlué, e [ebɛʀlɥe] *adj* astounded

éblouir [ebluiʀ] *vt* to dazzle

éblouissement [ebluismɑ̃] *nm* (*faiblesse*) dizzy turn

éborgner [ebɔʀɲe] *vt*: **~ qn** to blind sb in one eye

éboueur [ebwœʀ] *nm* dustman (*BRIT*), garbageman (*US*)

ébouillanter [ebujɑ̃te] *vt* to scald; (*CULIN*) to blanch

éboulement [ebulmɑ̃] *nm* rock fall

ébouler [ebule] : **s'~** *vi* to crumble, collapse

éboulis [ebuli] *nmpl* fallen rocks

ébouriffé, e [eburife] *adj* tousled

ébranler [ebrɑ̃le] *vt* to shake; (*rendre instable*: *mur*) to weaken; **s'~** *vi* (*partir*) to move off

ébrécher [ebreʃe] *vt* to chip

ébriété [ebrijete] *nf*: **en état d'~** in a state of intoxication

ébrouer [ebrue]: **s'~** *vi* to shake o.s.; (*souffler*) to snort

ébruiter [ebrɥite] *vt* to spread, disclose

ébullition [ebylisjɔ̃] *nf* boiling point; **en ~** boiling; (*fig*) in an uproar

écaille [ekɑj] *nf* (*de poisson*) scale; (*de coquillage*) shell; (*matière*) tortoiseshell; **~r** [ekɑje] *vt* (*poisson*) to scale; (*huître*) to open; **s'~r** *vi* to flake *ou* peel (off)

écarlate [ekarlat] *adj* scarlet

écarquiller [ekarkije] *vt*: **~ les yeux** to stare wide-eyed

écart [ekar] *nm* gap; (*embardée*) swerve; sideways leap; (*fig*) departure, deviation; **à l'~** out of the way; **à l'~ de** away from

écarté, e [ekarte] *adj* (*lieu*) out-of-the-way, remote; (*ouvert*): **les jambes ~es** legs apart; **les bras ~s** arms outstretched

écarteler [ekartəle] *vt* to quarter; (*fig*) to tear

écarter [ekarte] *vt* (*séparer*) to move apart, separate; (*éloigner*) to push back, move away; (*ouvrir*: *bras, jambes*) to spread, open; (: *rideau*) to draw (back); (*éliminer*: *candidat, possibilité*) to dismiss; **s'~** *vi* to part; to move away; **s'~ de** to wander from

écervelé, e [esɛrvəle] *adj* scatterbrained, featherbrained

échafaud [eʃafo] *nm* scaffold

échafaudage [eʃafodaʒ] *nm* scaffolding

échafauder [eʃafode] *vt* (*plan*) to construct

échalote [eʃalɔt] *nf* shallot

échancrure [eʃɑ̃kryr] *nf* (*de robe*) scoop neckline; (*de côte, arête rocheuse*) indentation

échange [eʃɑ̃ʒ] *nm* exchange; **en ~ de** in exchange *ou* return for

échanger [eʃɑ̃ʒe] *vt*: **~ qch (contre)** to exchange sth (for); **échangeur** *nm* (*AUTO*) interchange

échantillon [eʃɑ̃tijɔ̃] *nm* sample

échappement [eʃapmɑ̃] *nm* (*AUTO*) exhaust

échapper [eʃape]: **~ à** *vt* (*gardien*) to escape (from); (*punition, péril*) to escape; **s'~** *vi* to escape; **~ à qn** (*détail, sens*) to escape sb; (*objet qu'on tient*) to slip out of sb's hands; **laisser ~** (*cri etc*) to let out; **l'~ belle** to have a narrow escape

écharde [eʃard(ə)] *nf* splinter (of wood)

écharpe [eʃarp(ə)] *nf* scarf; (*de maire*) sash; (*MÉD*) sling

échasse [eʃɑs] *nf* stilt

échauffer [eʃofe] *vt* (*métal, moteur*) to overheat; (*fig*: *exciter*) to fire, excite; **s'~** *vi* (*SPORT*) to warm up; (*dans la discussion*) to become heated

échéance [eʃeɑ̃s] *nf* (*d'un paiement*: *date*) settlement date; (: *somme due*) financial commitment(s); (*fig*) deadline; **à brève/longue ~** *adj* short-/long-term ♦ *adv* in the short/long run

échéant [eʃeɑ̃]: **le cas ~** *adv* if the case arises

échec [eʃɛk] *nm* failure; (*ÉCHECS*): **~ et mat/au roi** checkmate/check; **~s** *nmpl* (*jeu*) chess *sg*; **tenir en ~** to hold in check; **faire ~ à** to foil *ou* thwart

échelle [eʃɛl] *nf* ladder; (*fig, d'une carte*) scale

échelon [eʃlɔ̃] *nm* (*d'échelle*) rung; (*ADMIN*) grade

échelonner [eʃlɔne] *vt* to space out

échevelé, e [eʃəvle] *adj* tousled, dishevelled; wild, frenzied

échine [eʃin] *nf* backbone, spine

échiquier [eʃikje] *nm* chessboard

écho [eko] *nm* echo; **~s** *nmpl* (*potins*) gossip *sg*, rumours

échoir [eʃwar] *vi* (*dette*) to fall due; (*délais*) to expire; **~ à** to fall to

échouer [eʃwe] *vi* to fail; **s'~** *vi* to run aground

échu, e [eʃy] *pp de* **échoir**

éclabousser [eklabuse] *vt* to splash

éclair [eklɛr] *nm* (*d'orage*) flash of lightning, lightning *no pl*; (*gâteau*) éclair

éclairage [eklɛraʒ] *nm* lighting

éclaircie [eklɛrsi] *nf* bright interval

éclaircir [eklɛrsir] *vt* to lighten; (*fig*) to clear up; to clarify; (*CULIN*) to thin (down); **s'~** *vi* (*ciel*) to clear; **s'~ la voix** to clear one's throat; **éclaircissement** *nm* clearing up; clarification

éclairer [eklere] *vt* (*lieu*) to light (up); (*personne: avec une lampe etc*) to light the way for; (*fig*) to enlighten; to shed light on ♦ *vi*: **~ mal/bien** to give a poor/good light; **s'~ à l'électricité** to have electric lighting

éclaireur, euse [eklɛrœr, -øz] *nm/f* (*scout*) (boy) scout/(girl) guide ♦ *nm* (*MIL*) scout

éclat [ekla] *nm* (*de bombe, de verre*) fragment; (*du soleil, d'une couleur etc*) brightness, brilliance; (*d'une cérémonie*) splendour; (*scandale*): **faire un ~** to cause a commotion; **~s de voix** shouts; **~ de rire** *nm* roar of laughter

éclatant, e [eklatɑ̃, -ɑ̃t] *adj* brilliant

éclater [eklate] *vi* (*pneu*) to burst; (*bombe*) to explode; (*guerre, épidémie*) to break out; (*groupe, parti*) to break up; **~ en sanglots/de rire** to burst out sobbing/laughing

éclipser [eklipse]: **s'~** *vi* to slip away

éclopé, e [eklɔpe] *adj* lame

éclore [eklɔr] *vi* (*œuf*) to hatch; (*fleur*) to open (out)

écluse [eklyz] *nf* lock

écœurant, e [ekœrɑ̃, -ɑ̃t] *adj* (*gâteau etc*) sickly

écœurer [ekœre] *vt*: ~ **qn** to make sb feel sick

école [ekɔl] *nf* school; **aller à l'~** to go to school; ~ **normale** teachers' training college; ~ **publique** *nf* state school; **écolier, ière** *nm/f* schoolboy/girl

écologie [ekɔlɔʒi] *nf* ecology; environmental studies *pl*

écologique [ekɔlɔʒik] *adj* environment-friendly

éconduire [ekɔ̃dɥir] *vt* to dismiss

économe [ekɔnɔm] *adj* thrifty ♦ *nm/f* (*de lycée etc*) bursar (*BRIT*), treasurer (*US*)

économie [ekɔnɔmi] *nf* economy; (*gain: d'argent, de temps etc*) saving; (*science*) economics *sg*; ~**s** *nfpl* (*pécule*) savings; **économique** *adj* (*avantageux*) economical; (*ÉCON*) economic; **économiser** [ekɔnɔmize] *vt, vi* to save

écoper [ekɔpe] *vi* to bale out; (*fig*) to cop it; ~ **(de) qch** to get

écorce [ekɔrs(ə)] *nf* bark; (*de fruit*) peel

écorcher [ekɔrʃe] *vt* (*animal*) to skin; (*égratigner*) to graze; **écorchure** *nf* graze

écossais, e [ekɔse, -ɛz] *adj* Scottish ♦ *nm/ f*: **É~, e** Scot

Écosse [ekɔs] *nf*: **l'~** Scotland

écosser [ekɔse] *vt* to shell

écouler [ekule] *vt* to sell; to dispose of; **s'~** *vi* (*eau*) to flow (out); (*jours, temps*) to pass (by)

écourter [ekurte] *vt* to curtail, cut short

écoute [ekut] *nf* (*RADIO, TV*): **temps/heure d'~** listening (*ou* viewing) time/hour; **prendre l'~** to tune in; **rester à l'~ (de)** to stay tuned in (to)

écouter [ekute] *vt* to listen to; **écoutes téléphoniques** phone tapping *sg*; **écouteur** *nm* (*TÉL*) receiver; (*RADIO*) headphones *pl*, headset

écran [ekrɑ̃] *nm* screen

écrasant, e [ekrazɑ̃, -ɑ̃t] *adj* overwhelming

écraser [ekraze] *vt* to crush; (*piéton*) to run over; **s'~ (au sol)** to crash; **s'~ contre** to crash into

écrémer [ekreme] *vt* to skim

écrevisse [ekrəvis] *nf* crayfish *inv*

écrier [ekrije]: **s'~** *vi* to exclaim

écrin [ekrɛ̃] *nm* case, box

écrire [ekrir] *vt* to write; **s'~** to write to each other; **ça s'écrit comment?** how is it spelt?; **écrit** *nm* document; (*examen*) written paper; **par écrit** in writing

écriteau, x [ekrito] *nm* notice, sign

écriture [ekrityr] *nf* writing; (*COMM*) entry; ~**s** *nfpl* accounts, books; **l'É~, les É~s** the Scriptures

écrivain [ekrivɛ̃] *nm* writer

écrou [ekru] *nm* nut

écrouer [ekrue] *vt* to imprison; to remand in custody

écrouler [ekrule]: **s'~** *vi* to collapse

écru, e [ekry] *adj* (*toile*) raw, unbleached; (*couleur*) off-white, écru

ECU *sigle m* ECU

écueil [ekœj] *nm* reef; (*fig*) pitfall; stumbling block

écuelle [ekɥɛl] *nf* bowl

éculé, e [ekyle] *adj* (*chaussure*) down-at-heel; (*fig: péj*) hackneyed

écume [ekym] *nf* foam; (*CULIN*) scum; **écumer** *vt* (*CULIN*) to skim; (*fig*) to plunder

écureuil [ekyrœj] *nm* squirrel

écurie [ekyri] *nf* stable

écusson [ekysɔ̃] *nm* badge

écuyer, ère [ekɥije, -ɛr] *nm/f* rider

eczéma [ɛgzema] *nm* eczema

édenté, e [edɑ̃te] *adj* toothless

E.D.F. *sigle f* (= *Électricité de France*) national electricity company

édifice [edifis] *nm* edifice, building

édifier [edifje] *vt* to build, erect; (*fig*) to edify

édit [edi] *nm* edict

éditer [edite] *vt* (*publier*) to publish; (: *disque*) to produce; **éditeur, trice** *nm/f* editor; publisher; **édition** *nf* editing *no pl*; edition; (*industrie du livre*) publishing

édredon [edrədɔ̃] *nm* eiderdown, comforter (*US*)

éducateur, trice [edykatœr, -tris] *nm/f* teacher; (*in special school*) instructor

éducatif, ive [edykatif, -iv] *adj* educational

éducation [edykasjɔ̃] *nf* education; (*familiale*) upbringing; (*manières*) (good) manners *pl*; ~ **physique** physical education

édulcorer [edylkɔre] *vt* to sweeten; (*fig*) to tone down

éduquer [edyke] *vt* to educate; (*élever*) to bring up; (*faculté*) to train

effacé, e [efase] *adj* unassuming

effacer [efase] *vt* to erase, rub out; **s'~** *vi* (*inscription etc*) to wear off; (*pour laisser passer*) to step aside

effarant, e [efarɑ̃, -ɑ̃t] *adj* alarming

effarer [efare] *vt* to alarm

effaroucher [efaruʃe] *vt* to frighten *ou* scare away; to alarm

effectif, ive [efɛktif, -iv] *adj* real; effective ♦ *nm* (*MIL*) strength; (*SCOL*) (pupil) numbers *pl*; **effectivement** *adv* effectively; (*réellement*) actually, really; (*en effet*) indeed

effectuer [efɛktɥe] *vt* (*opération*) to carry out; (*déplacement, trajet*) to make; (*mouvement*) to execute

efféminé, e [efemine] *adj* effeminate

effervescent, e [efɛrvesɑ̃, -ɑ̃t] *adj* effervescent; (*fig*) agitated

effet [efɛ] *nm* (*résultat, artifice*) effect; (*impression*) impression; **~s** *nmpl* (*vêtements etc*) things; **faire de l'~** (*médicament, menace*) to have an effect; **en** ~ indeed; **~ de serre** greenhouse effect; **gaz à ~ de serre** greenhouse gas

efficace [efikas] *adj* (*personne*) efficient; (*action, médicament*) effective

effilé, e [efile] *adj* slender; sharp; streamlined

effiler [efile] *vt* (*tissu*) to fray

effilocher [efilɔʃe] : **s'~** *vi* to fray

efflanqué, e [eflɑ̃ke] *adj* emaciated

effleurer [eflœre] *vt* to brush (against); (*sujet*) to touch upon; (*suj: idée, pensée*): ~ **qn** to cross sb's mind

effluves [eflyv] *nmpl* exhalation(s)

effondrer [efɔ̃dre]: **s'~** *vi* to collapse

efforcer [efɔrse]: **s'~ de** *vt*: **s'~ de faire** to try hard to do, try hard to

effort [efɔr] *nm* effort

effraction [efraksjɔ̃] *nf*: **s'introduire par ~ dans** to break into

effrayant, e [efrejɑ̃, -ɑ̃t] *adj* frightening

effrayer [efreje] *vt* to frighten, scare

effréné, e [efrene] *adj* wild

effriter [efrite]: **s'~** *vi* to crumble

effroi [efrwa] *nm* terror, dread *no pl*

effronté, e [efrɔ̃te] *adj* insolent, brazen

effroyable [efrwajabl(ə)] *adj* horrifying, appalling

effusion [efyzjɔ̃] *nf* effusion; **sans ~ de sang** without bloodshed

égal, e, aux [egal, -o] *adj* equal; (*plan: surface*) even, level; (*constant: vitesse*) steady; (*équitable*) even ♦ *nm/f* equal; **être ~ à** (*prix, nombre*) to be equal to; **ça lui est ~** it's all the same to him; he doesn't mind; **sans ~** matchless, unequalled; **à l'~ de** (*comme*) just like; **d'~ à ~** as equals; **~ement** *adv* equally; evenly; steadily; (*aussi*) too, as well; **~er** *vt* to equal; **~iser** *vt* (*sol, salaires*) to level (out); (*chances*) to equalize ♦ *vi* (*SPORT*) to equalize; **~ité** *nf* equality; evenness; steadiness; (*MATH*) identity; **être à ~ (de points)** to be level

égard [egar] *nm*: **~s** *nmpl* consideration *sg*; **à cet ~** in this respect; **eu ~ à** in view of; **par ~ pour** out of consideration for; **sans ~ pour** without regard for; **à l'~ de** towards; concerning

égarement [egarmɑ̃] *nm* distraction; aberration

égarer [egare] *vt* to mislay; (*moralement*) to lead astray; **s'~** *vi* to get lost, lose one's way; (*objet*) to go astray; (*dans une discussion*) to wander

égayer [egeje] *vt* (*personne*) to amuse; to cheer up; (*récit, endroit*) to brighten up, liven up

églantine [eglɑ̃tin] *nf* wild *ou* dog rose

église [egliz] *nf* church; **aller à l'~** to go to church

égoïsme [egɔism(ə)] *nm* selfishness; **égoïste** *adj* selfish

égorger [egɔrʒe] *vt* to cut the throat of

égosiller [egozije]: **s'~** *vi* to shout o.s. hoarse

égout [egu] *nm* sewer

égoutter [egute] *vt* (*linge*) to wring out; (*vaisselle*) to drain ♦ *vi* to drip; **s'~** *vi* to drip; **égouttoir** *nm* draining board; (*mobile*) draining rack

égratigner [egratiɲe] *vt* to scratch; **égratignure** *nf* scratch

égrillard, e [egrijar, -ard(ə)] *adj* ribald

Égypte [eʒipt(ə)] *nf*: **l'~** Egypt; **égyptien, ne** *adj, nm/f* Egyptian

eh [e] *excl* hey!; **~ bien** well

éhonté, e [eɔ̃te] *adj* shameless, brazen

éjecter [eʒɛkte] *vt* (*TECH*) to eject; (*fam*) to kick *ou* chuck out

élaborer [elabɔre] *vt* to elaborate; (*projet, stratégie*) to work out; (*rapport*) to draft

élaguer [elage] *vt* to prune

élan [elɑ̃] *nm* (*ZOOL*) elk, moose; (*SPORT: avant le saut*) run up; (*d'objet en mouvement*) momentum; (*fig: de tendresse etc*) surge; **prendre de l'~** to gather speed

élancé, e [elɑ̃se] *adj* slender

élancement [elɑ̃smɑ̃] *nm* shooting pain

élancer [elɑ̃se]: **s'~** *vi* to dash, hurl o.s.; (*fig: arbre, clocher*) to soar (upwards)

élargir [elarʒir] *vt* to widen; (*vêtement*) to let out; (*JUR*) to release; **s'~** *vi* to widen; (*vêtement*) to stretch

élastique [elastik] *adj* elastic ♦ *nm* (*de bureau*) rubber band; (*pour la couture*) elastic *no pl*

électeur, trice [elɛktœr, -tris] *nm/f* elector, voter

élection [elɛksjɔ̃] *nf* election

électorat [elɛktɔra] *nm* electorate

électricien, ne [elɛktrisjɛ̃, -jɛn] *nm/f* electrician

électricité [elɛktrisite] *nf* electricity; **allumer/éteindre l'~** to put on/off the light

électrique [elɛktrik] *adj* electric(al)

électrochoc [elɛktrɔʃɔk] *nm* electric shock treatment

électroménager [elɛktrɔmenaʒe] *adj, nm*: **appareils ~s, l'~** domestic (electrical) appliances

électronique [elɛktrɔnik] *adj* electronic ♦ *nf* electronics *sg*

électrophone [elɛktrɔfɔn] *nm* record player

élégant, e [elegɑ̃, -ɑ̃t] *adj* elegant; (*solution*) neat, elegant; (*attitude, procédé*) courteous, civilized

élément [elemɑ̃] *nm* element; (*pièce*) component, part; **élémentaire** *adj* elementary

éléphant [elefɑ̃] *nm* elephant

élevage [ɛlvaʒ] *nm* breeding; *(de bovins)* cattle rearing

élévation [elevɑsjɔ̃] *nf (gén)* elevation; *(voir élever)* raising; *(voir s'élever)* rise

élevé, e [ɛlve] *adj (prix, sommet)* high; *(fig: noble)* elevated; **bien/mal ~** well-/ill-mannered

élève [ɛlɛv] *nm/f* pupil

élever [ɛlve] *vt (enfant)* to bring up, raise; *(bétail, volaille)* to breed; *(abeilles)* to keep; *(hausser: taux, niveau)* to raise; *(fig: âme, esprit)* to elevate; *(édifier: monument)* to put up, erect; **s'~** *vi (avion, alpiniste)* to go up; *(niveau, température, aussi: cri etc)* to rise; *(survenir: difficultés)* to arise; **s'~ à** *(suj: frais, dégâts)* to amount to, add up to; **s'~ contre qch** to rise up against sth; **~ la voix** to raise one's voice; **éleveur, euse** *nm/f* breeder

élimé, e [elime] *adj* threadbare

éliminatoire [eliminatwaʀ] *nf (SPORT)* heat

éliminer [elimine] *vt* to eliminate

élire [eliʀ] *vt* to elect

elle [ɛl] *pron (sujet)* she; (: *chose)* it; *(complément)* her; it; **~s** they; them; **~-même** herself; itself; **~s-mêmes** themselves; *voir aussi* **il**

élocution [elɔkysjɔ̃] *nf* delivery; **défaut d'~** speech impediment

éloge [elɔʒ] *nm (gén no pl)* praise; **élogieux, euse** *adj* laudatory, full of praise

éloigné, e [elwaɲe] *adj* distant, far-off; **éloignement** *nm* removal; putting off; estrangement; *(fig)* distance

éloigner [elwaɲe] *vt (objet)*: **~ qch (de)** to move *ou* take sth away (from); *(personne)*: **~ qn (de)** to take sb away *ou* remove sb (from); *(échéance)* to put off, postpone; *(soupçons, danger)* to ward off; **s'~ (de)** *(personne)* to go away (from); *(véhicule)* to move away (from); *(affectivement)* to become estranged (from)

élongation [elɔ̃gɑsjɔ̃] *nf* strained muscle

élu, e [ely] *pp de* **élire** ♦ *nm/f (POL)* elected representative

élucubrations [elykybʀɑsjɔ̃] *nfpl* wild imaginings

éluder [elyde] *vt* to evade

Élysée *nm*: **(le palais de) l'~** the Élysée Palace *(the French president's residence)*

émacié, e [emasje] *adj* emaciated

émail, aux [emaj, -o] *nm* enamel

émaillé, e [emaje] *adj (fig)*: **~ de** dotted with

émanciper [emɑ̃sipe] *vt* to emancipate; **s'~** *vi (fig)* to become emancipated *ou* liberated

émaner [emane]: **~ de** *vt* to come from; *(ADMIN)* to proceed from

emballage [ɑ̃balaʒ] *nm* wrapping; packaging

emballer [ɑ̃bale] *vt* to wrap (up); *(dans un*

carton) to pack (up); *(fig: fam)* to thrill (to bits); **s'~** *vi (moteur)* to race; *(cheval)* to bolt; *(fig: personne)* to get carried away

embarcadère [ɑ̃baʀkadɛʀ] *nm* wharf, pier

embarcation [ɑ̃baʀkɑsjɔ̃] *nf* (small) boat, (small) craft *inv*

embardée [ɑ̃baʀde] *nf*: **faire une ~** to swerve

embarquement [ɑ̃baʀkəmɑ̃] *nm* embarkation; loading; boarding

embarquer [ɑ̃baʀke] *vt (personne)* to embark; *(marchandise)* to load; *(fam)* to cart off; to nick ♦ *vi (passager)* to board; **s'~** *vi* to board; **s'~ dans** *(affaire, aventure)* to embark upon

embarras [ɑ̃baʀa] *nm (obstacle)* hindrance; *(confusion)* embarrassment

embarrassant, e [ɑ̃baʀasɑ̃, -ɑ̃t] *adj* embarrassing

embarrasser [ɑ̃baʀase] *vt (encombrer)* to clutter (up); *(gêner)* to hinder, hamper; *(fig)* to cause embarrassment to; to put in an awkward position

embauche [ɑ̃boʃ] *nf* hiring; **bureau d'~** labour office; **~r** [ɑ̃boʃe] *vt* to take on, hire

embaumer [ɑ̃bome] *vt* to embalm; to fill with its fragrance; **~ la lavande** to be fragrant with (the scent of) lavender

embellie [ɑ̃beli] *nf* brighter period

embellir [ɑ̃beliʀ] *vt* to make more attractive; *(une histoire)* to embellish ♦ *vi* to grow lovelier *ou* more attractive

embêtements [ɑ̃bɛtmɑ̃] *nmpl* trouble *sg*

embêter [ɑ̃bete] *vt* to bother; **s'~** *vi (s'ennuyer)* to be bored

emblée [ɑ̃ble]: **d'~** *adv* straightaway

emboîter [ɑ̃bwate] *vt* to fit together; **s'~ (dans)** to fit (into); **~ le pas à qn** to follow in sb's footsteps

embonpoint [ɑ̃bɔ̃pwɛ̃] *nm* stoutness

embouchure [ɑ̃buʃyʀ] *nf (GÉO)* mouth

embourber [ɑ̃buʀbe]: **s'~** *vi* to get stuck in the mud

embourgeoiser [ɑ̃buʀʒwaze]: **s'~** *vi* to adopt a middle-class outlook

embouteillage [ɑ̃butejaʒ] *nm* traffic jam

emboutir [ɑ̃butiʀ] *vt (heurter)* to crash into, ram

embranchement [ɑ̃bʀɑ̃ʃmɑ̃] *nm (routier)* junction; *(classification)* branch

embraser [ɑ̃bʀaze]: **s'~** *vi* to flare up

embrasser [ɑ̃bʀase] *vt* to kiss; *(sujet, période)* to embrace, encompass; *(carrière, métier)* to enter upon

embrasure [ɑ̃bʀazyʀ] *nf*: **dans l'~ de la porte** in the door(way)

embrayage [ɑ̃bʀejaʒ] *nm* clutch

embrayer [ɑ̃bʀeje] *vi (AUTO)* to let in the clutch

embrigader [ɑ̃bʀigade] *vt* to recruit

embrocher [ɑ̃bʀɔʃe] *vt* to put on a spit

embrouiller [ɑ̃bʀuje] *vt (fils)* to tangle

(up); (*fiches, idées, personne*) to muddle up; **s'~** *vi* (*personne*) to get in a muddle

embruns [ãbʀœ] *nmpl* sea spray *sg*

embûches [ãbyʃ] *nfpl* pitfalls, traps

embué, e [ãbɥe] *adj* misted up

embuscade [ãbyskad] *nf* ambush

éméché, e [emeʃe] *adj* tipsy, merry

émeraude [emʀod] *nf* emerald

émerger [emɛʀʒe] *vi* to emerge; (*faire saillie, aussi fig*) to stand out

émeri [ɛmʀi] *nm*: **toile** *ou* **papier ~** emery paper

émérite [emeʀit] *adj* highly skilled

émerveiller [emɛʀveje] *vt* to fill with wonder; **s'~ de** to marvel at

émetteur, trice [emɛtœʀ, -tʀis] *adj* transmitting; (**poste**) ~ transmitter

émettre [emɛtʀ(ə)] *vt* (*son, lumière*) to give out, emit; (*message etc*: RADIO) to transmit; (*billet, timbre, emprunt*) to issue; (*hypothèse, avis*) to voice, put forward ♦ *vi* to broadcast

émeus *etc vb voir* **émouvoir**

émeute [emøt] *nf* riot

émietter [emjete] *vt* to crumble

émigrer [emigʀe] *vi* to emigrate

éminence [eminãs] *nf* distinction; (*colline*) knoll, hill; **Son É~** His Eminence; **éminent, e** [eminã, -ãt] *adj* distinguished

émission [emisjɔ̃] *nf* emission; transmission; issue; (*RADIO, TV*) programme, broadcast; **~s** *fpl* emissions

emmagasiner [ãmagazine] *vt* to (put into) store; (*fig*) to store up

emmanchure [ãmãʃyʀ] *nf* armhole

emmêler [ãmele] *vt* to tangle (up); (*fig*) to muddle up; **s'~** *vi* to get into a tangle

emménager [ãmenaʒe] *vi* to move in; ~ **dans** to move into

emmener [ãmne] *vt* to take (with one); (*comme otage, capture*) to take away; ~ **qn au cinéma** to take sb to the cinema

emmerder [ãmɛʀde] (*fam!*) *vt* to bug, bother; **s'~** *vi* to be bored stiff

emmitoufler [ãmitufle] *vt* to wrap up (warmly)

émoi [emwa] *nm* commotion; (*trouble*) agitation

émonder [emɔ̃de] *vt* to prune

émotif, ive [emɔtif, -iv] *adj* emotional

émotion [emosjɔ̃] *nf* emotion

émousser [emuse] *vt* to blunt; (*fig*) to dull

émouvoir [emuvwaʀ] *vt* (*troubler*) to stir, affect; (*toucher, attendrir*) to move; (*indigner*) to rouse; **s'~** *vi* to be affected; to be moved; to be roused

empailler [ãpaje] *vt* to stuff

empaler [ãpale] *vt* to impale

emparer [ãpaʀe]: **s'~ de** *vt* (*objet*) to seize, grab; (*comme otage, MIL*) to seize; (*suj: peur etc*) to take hold of

empâter [ãpate]: **s'~** *vi* to thicken out

empêchement [ãpɛʃmã] *nm* (unexpected) obstacle, hitch

empêcher [ãpeʃe] *vt* to prevent; ~ **qn de faire** to prevent *ou* stop sb (from) doing; **il n'empêche que** nevertheless; **il n'a pas pu s'~ de rire** he couldn't help laughing

empereur [ãpʀœʀ] *nm* emperor

empeser [ãpəze] *vt* to starch

empester [ãpɛste] *vi* to stink, reek

empêtrer [ãpetʀe] *vt*: **s'~ dans** (*fils etc*) to get tangled up in

emphase [ãfɑz] *nf* pomposity, bombast

empiéter [ãpjete] *vi*: ~ **sur** to encroach upon

empiffrer [ãpifʀe]: **s'~** (*péj*) *vi* to stuff o.s.

empiler [ãpile] *vt* to pile (up)

empire [ãpiʀ] *nm* empire; (*fig*) influence

empirer [ãpiʀe] *vi* to worsen, deteriorate

emplacement [ãplasmã] *nm* site

emplettes [ãplɛt] *nfpl* shopping *sg*

emplir [ãpliʀ] *vt* to fill; **s'~ (de)** to fill (with)

emploi [ãplwa] *nm* use; (*COMM, ÉCON*) employment; (*poste*) job, situation; ~ **du temps** timetable, schedule

employé, e [ãplwaje] *nm/f* employee; ~ **de bureau** office employee *ou* clerk

employer [ãplwaje] *vt* (*outil, moyen, méthode, mot*) to use; (*ouvrier, main-d'œuvre*) to employ; **s'~ à faire** to apply *ou* devote o.s. to doing; **employeur, euse** *nm/f* employer

empocher [ãpɔʃe] *vt* to pocket

empoigner [ãpwaɲe] *vt* to grab

empoisonner [ãpwazɔne] *vt* to poison; (*empester: air, pièce*) to stink out; (*fam*): ~ **qn** to drive sb mad

emporté, e [ãpɔʀte] *adj* quick-tempered

emporter [ãpɔʀte] *vt* to take (with one); (*en dérobant ou enlevant, emmener: blessés, voyageurs*) to take away; (*entraîner*) to carry away; (*arracher*) to tear off; (*avantage, approbation*) to win; **s'~** *vi* (*de colère*) to lose one's temper; **l'~ (sur)** to get the upper hand (of); (*méthode etc*) to prevail (over); **boissons à ~** take-away drinks

empreint, e [ãpʀɛ̃, -ɛ̃t] *adj*: ~ **de** marked with; tinged with; **empreinte** *nf* (*de pied, main*) print; (*fig*) stamp, mark; **~e (digitale)** fingerprint

empressé, e [ãpʀese] *adj* attentive

empressement [ãpʀɛsmã] *nm* (*hâte*) eagerness

empresser [ãpʀese]: **s'~** *vi*: **s'~ auprès de qn** to surround sb with attentions; **s'~ de faire** (*se hâter*) to hasten to do

emprise [ãpʀiz] *nf* hold, ascendancy

emprisonner [ãpʀizɔne] *vt* to imprison

emprunt [ãpʀœ̃] *nm* borrowing *no pl*, loan

emprunté, e [ãpʀœ̃te] *adj* (*fig*) ill-at-ease, awkward

emprunter [ãpʀœ̃te] *vt* to borrow; (*itiné-*

raire) to take, follow; (*style, manière*) to adopt, assume

ému, e [emy] *pp de* **émouvoir** ♦ *adj* excited; touched; moved

émulsion [emylsjɔ̃] *nf* (*cosmétique*) (water-based) lotion

─────────── *MOT CLÉ*

en [ɑ̃] *prép* **1** (*endroit, pays*) in; (*direction*) to; **habiter ~ France/ville** to live in France/town; **aller ~ France/ville** to go to France/town

2 (*moment, temps*) in; **~ été/juin** in summer/June

3 (*moyen*) by; **~ avion/taxi** by plane/taxi

4 (*composition*) made of; **c'est ~ verre** it's (made of) glass; **un collier ~ argent** a silver necklace

5 (*description, état*): **une femme (habillée) ~ rouge** a woman (dressed) in red; **peindre qch ~ rouge** to paint sth red; **~ T/ étoile** T/star-shaped; **~ chemise/ chaussettes** in one's shirt sleeves/socks; **~ soldat** as a soldier; **cassé ~ plusieurs morceaux** broken into several pieces; **~ réparation** being repaired, under repair; **~ vacances** on holiday; **~ deuil** in mourning; **le même ~ plus grand** the same but *ou* only bigger

6 (*avec gérondif*) while; on; by; **~ dormant** while sleeping, as one sleeps; **~ sortant** on going out, as he *etc* went out; **sortir ~ courant** to run out

♦ *pron* **1** (*indéfini*): **j'~ ai/veux** I have/want some; **~ as-tu?** have you got any?; **je n'~ veux pas** I don't want any; **j'~ ai 2** I've got 2; **combien y ~ a-t-il?** how many (of them) are there?; **j'~ ai assez** I've got enough (of it *ou* them); (*j'en ai marre*) I've had enough

2 (*provenance*) from there; **j'~ viens** I've come from there

3 (*cause*): **il ~ est malade/perd le sommeil** he is ill/can't sleep because of it

4 (*complément de nom, d'adjectif, de verbe*): **j'~ connais les dangers** I know its *ou* the dangers; **j'~ suis fier/ai besoin** I am proud of it/need it

E.N.A. [ena] *sigle f* (= *École Nationale d'Administration*) one of the *Grandes Écoles*

encadrer [ɑ̃kadʀe] *vt* (*tableau, image*) to frame; (*fig: entourer*) to surround; (*personnel, soldats etc*) to train

encaissé, e [ɑ̃kese] *adj* steep-sided; with steep banks

encaisser [ɑ̃kese] *vt* (*chèque*) to cash; (*argent*) to collect; (*fig: coup, défaite*) to take

encart [ɑ̃kaʀ] *nm* insert

encastrer [ɑ̃kastʀe] *vt*: **~ qch dans** (*mur*) to embed sth in(to); (*boîtier*) to fit sth into

encaustique [ɑ̃kɔstik] *nf* polish, wax

enceinte [ɑ̃sɛ̃t] *adj f*: **~ (de 6 mois)** (6 months) pregnant ♦ *nf* (*mur*) wall; (*espace*) enclosure

encens [ɑ̃sɑ̃] *nm* incense

encercler [ɑ̃sɛʀkle] *vt* to surround

enchaîner [ɑ̃ʃene] *vt* to chain up; (*mouvements, séquences*) to link (together) ♦ *vi* to carry on

enchanté, e [ɑ̃ʃɑ̃te] *adj* delighted; enchanted; **~ (de faire votre connaissance)** pleased to meet you

enchantement [ɑ̃ʃɑ̃tmɑ̃] *nm* delight; (*magie*) enchantment

enchâsser [ɑ̃ʃase] *vt* to set

enchère [ɑ̃ʃɛʀ] *nf* bid; **mettre/vendre aux ~s** to put up for (sale by)/sell by auction

enchevêtrer [ɑ̃ʃvetʀe] *vt* to tangle (up)

enclencher [ɑ̃klɑ̃ʃe] *vt* (*mécanisme*) to engage; **s'~** *vi* to engage

enclin, e [ɑ̃klɛ̃, -in] *adj*: **~ à** inclined *ou* prone to

enclos [ɑ̃klo] *nm* enclosure

enclume [ɑ̃klym] *nf* anvil

encoche [ɑ̃kɔʃ] *nf* notch

encoignure [ɑ̃kɔɲyʀ] *nf* corner

encolure [ɑ̃kɔlyʀ] *nf* (*tour de cou*) collar size; (*col, cou*) neck

encombrant, e [ɑ̃kɔ̃bʀɑ̃, -ɑ̃t] *adj* cumbersome, bulky

encombre [ɑ̃kɔ̃bʀ(ə)]: **sans ~** *adv* without mishap *ou* incident

encombrer [ɑ̃kɔ̃bʀe] *vt* to clutter (up); (*gêner*) to hamper; **s'~ de** (*bagages etc*) to load *ou* burden o.s. with

encontre [ɑ̃kɔ̃tʀ(ə)]: **à l'~ de** *prép* against, counter to

─────────── *MOT CLÉ*

encore [ɑ̃kɔʀ] *adv* **1** (*continuation*) still; **il y travaille ~** he's still working on it; **pas ~** not yet

2 (*de nouveau*) again; **j'irai ~ demain** I'll go again tomorrow; **~ une fois** (once) again; **~ deux jours** two more days

3 (*intensif*) even, still; **~ plus fort/mieux** even louder/better, louder/better still

4 (*restriction*) even so *ou* then, only; **~ pourrais-je le faire si ...** even so, I might be able to do it if ...; **si ~** if only

encore que *conj* although

encourager [ɑ̃kuʀaʒe] *vt* to encourage

encourir [ɑ̃kuʀiʀ] *vt* to incur

encrasser [ɑ̃kʀase] *vt* to clog up; (*AUTO: bougies*) to soot up

encre [ɑ̃kʀ(ə)] *nf* ink; **~ de Chine** Indian ink; **encrier** *nm* inkwell

encroûter [ɑ̃kʀute]: **s'~** *vi* (*fig*) to get into a rut, get set in one's ways

encyclopédie [ɑ̃siklɔpedi] *nf* encyclopaedia

endetter [ɑ̃dete] *vt* to get into debt; **s'~** *vi* to get into debt

endiablé, e [ɑ̃djable] *adj* furious; boisterous

endiguer [ɑ̃dige] *vt* to dyke (up); (*fig*) to check, hold back

endimancher [ɑ̃dimɑ̃ʃe] *vt*: **s'~** to put on one's Sunday best

endive [ɑ̃div] *nf* chicory *no pl*

endoctriner [ɑ̃dɔktRine] *vt* to indoctrinate

endommager [ɑ̃dɔmaʒe] *vt* to damage

endormi, e [ɑ̃dɔrmi] *adj* asleep

endormir [ɑ̃dɔRmiR] *vt* to put to sleep; (*suj: chaleur etc*) to send to sleep; (*MÉD: dent, nerf*) to anaesthetize; (*fig: soupçons*) to allay; **s'~** *vi* to fall asleep, go to sleep

endosser [ɑ̃dose] *vt* (*responsabilité*) to take, shoulder; (*chèque*) to endorse; (*uniforme, tenue*) to put on, don

endroit [ɑ̃dRwa] *nm* place; (*opposé à l'envers*) right side; **à l'~** the right way out; the right way up; **à l'~ de** regarding

enduire [ɑ̃dɥiR] *vt* to coat

enduit [ɑ̃dɥi] *nm* coating

endurant, e [ɑ̃dyRɑ̃, -ɑ̃t] *adj* tough, hardy

endurcir [ɑ̃dyRsiR] *vt* (*physiquement*) to toughen; (*moralement*) to harden; **s'~** *vi* to become tough; to become hardened

endurer [ɑ̃dyRe] *vt* to endure, bear

énergie [enɛRʒi] *nf* (*PHYSIQUE*) energy; (*TECH*) power; (*morale*) vigour, spirit; **énergique** *adj* energetic; vigorous; (*mesures*) drastic, stringent

énergumène [enɛRgymɛn] *nm* rowdy character *ou* customer

énerver [enɛRve] *vt* to irritate, annoy; **s'~** *vi* to get excited, get worked up

enfance [ɑ̃fɑ̃s] *nf* (*âge*) childhood; (*fig*) infancy; (*enfants*) children *pl*

enfant [ɑ̃fɑ̃] *nm/f* child; **~ de chœur** *nm* (*REL*) altar boy; **~er** *vi* to give birth ♦ *vt* to give birth to; **~illage** (*péj*) *nm* childish behaviour *no pl*; **~in, e** *adj* childlike; child *cpd*

enfer [ɑ̃fɛR] *nm* hell

enfermer [ɑ̃fɛRme] *vt* to shut up; (*à clef, interner*) to lock up

enflévré, e [ɑ̃fjevRe] *adj* (*fig*) feverish

enfiler [ɑ̃file] *vt* (*vêtement*) to slip on, slip into; (*insérer*): **~ qch dans** to stick sth into; (*rue, couloir*) to take; (*perles*) to string; (*aiguille*) to thread

enfin [ɑ̃fɛ̃] *adv* at last; (*en énumérant*) lastly; (*de restriction, résignation*) still; well; (*pour conclure*) in a word

enflammer [ɑ̃flame] *vt* to set fire to; (*MÉD*) to inflame; **s'~** *vi* to catch fire; to become inflamed

enflé, e [ɑ̃fle] *adj* swollen

enfler [ɑ̃fle] *vi* to swell (up)

enfoncer [ɑ̃fɔ̃se] *vt* (*clou*) to drive in; (*faire pénétrer*): **~ qch dans** to push (*ou* drive) sth into; (*forcer: porte*) to break open; (: *plancher*) to cause to cave in ♦ *vi* (*dans la*

vase etc) to sink in; (*sol, surface*) to give way; **s'~** *vi* to sink; **s'~ dans** to sink into; (*forêt, ville*) to disappear into

enfouir [ɑ̃fwiR] *vt* (*dans le sol*) to bury; (*dans un tiroir etc*) to tuck away

enfourcher [ɑ̃fuRʃe] *vt* to mount

enfourner [ɑ̃fuRne] *vt* to put in the oven

enfreindre [ɑ̃fRɛ̃dR(ə)] *vt* to infringe, break

enfuir [ɑ̃fɥiR]: **s'~** *vi* to run away *ou* off

enfumer [ɑ̃fyme] *vt* to smoke out

engageant, e [ɑ̃gaʒɑ̃, -ɑ̃t] *adj* attractive, appealing

engagement [ɑ̃gaʒmɑ̃] *nm* (*promesse, contrat, POL*) commitment; (*MIL: combat*) engagement

engager [ɑ̃gaʒe] *vt* (*embaucher*) to take on, engage; (*commencer*) to start; (*lier*) to bind, commit; (*impliquer, entraîner*) to involve; (*investir*) to invest, lay out; (*faire intervenir*) to engage; (*inciter*) to urge; (*faire pénétrer*) to insert; **s'~** *vi* to hire o.s., get taken on; (*MIL*) to enlist; (*promettre, politiquement*) to commit o.s.; (*débuter*) to start; **s'~ à faire** to undertake to do; **s'~ dans** (*rue, passage*) to turn into; (*s'emboîter*) to engage into; (*fig: affaire, discussion*) to enter into, embark on

engelures [ɑ̃ʒlyR] *nfpl* chilblains

engendrer [ɑ̃ʒɑ̃dRe] *vt* to father

engin [ɑ̃ʒɛ̃] *nm* machine; instrument; vehicle; (*AVIAT*) aircraft *inv*; missile

englober [ɑ̃glɔbe] *vt* to include

engloutir [ɑ̃glutiR] *vt* to swallow up

engoncé, e [ɑ̃gɔ̃se] *adj*: **~ dans** cramped in

engorger [ɑ̃gɔRʒe] *vt* to obstruct, block

engouement [ɑ̃gumɑ̃] *nm* (sudden) passion

engouffrer [ɑ̃gufRe] *vt* to swallow up, devour; **s'~ dans** to rush into

engourdir [ɑ̃guRdiR] *vt* to numb; (*fig*) to dull, blunt; **s'~** *vi* to go numb

engrais [ɑ̃gRɛ] *nm* manure; **~ (chimique)** (chemical) fertilizer

engraisser [ɑ̃gRese] *vt* to fatten (up)

engrenage [ɑ̃gRənaʒ] *nm* gears *pl*, gearing; (*fig*) chain

engueuler [ɑ̃gœle] (*fam*) *vt* to bawl at

enhardir [ɑ̃aRdiR]: **s'~** *vi* to grow bolder

énigme [enigm(ə)] *nf* riddle

enivrer [ɑ̃nivRe] *vt*: **s'~** to get drunk; **s'~ de** (*fig*) to become intoxicated with

enjambée [ɑ̃ʒɑ̃be] *nf* stride

enjamber [ɑ̃ʒɑ̃be] *vt* to stride over; (*suj: pont etc*) to span, straddle

enjeu, x [ɑ̃ʒø] *nm* stakes *pl*

enjoindre [ɑ̃ʒwɛ̃dR(ə)] *vt* to enjoin, order

enjôler [ɑ̃ʒole] *vt* to coax, wheedle

enjoliver [ɑ̃ʒolive] *vt* to embellish; **enjoliveur** *nm* (*AUTO*) hub cap

enjoué, e [ɑ̃ʒwe] *adj* playful

enlacer [ɑ̃lase] *vt* (*étreindre*) to embrace,

hug

enlaidir [ɑ̃lediʀ] *vt* to make ugly ♦ *vi* to become ugly

enlèvement [ɑ̃lɛvmɑ̃] *nm (rapt)* abduction, kidnapping

enlever [ɑ̃lve] *vt (ôter: gén)* to remove; (: *vêtement, lunettes)* to take off; *(emporter: ordures etc)* to take away; *(prendre)*: ~ **qch à qn** to take sth (away) from sb; *(kidnapper)* to abduct, kidnap; *(obtenir: prix, contrat)* to win

enliser [ɑ̃lize]: **s'~** *vi* to sink, get stuck

enluminure [ɑ̃lyminyʀ] *nf* illumination

enneigé, e [ɑ̃neʒe] *adj* snowy; snowed-up

ennemi, e [ɛnmi] *adj* hostile; *(MIL)* enemy *cpd* ♦ *nm/f* enemy

ennui [ɑ̃nɥi] *nm (lassitude)* boredom; *(difficulté)* trouble *no pl;* **avoir des ~s** to have problems; **ennuyer** *vt* to bother; *(lasser)* to bore; **s'ennuyer** *vi* to be bored; **s'ennuyer de** *(regretter)* to miss; **ennuyeux, euse** *adj* boring, tedious; annoying

énoncé [enɔ̃se] *nm* terms *pl;* wording

énoncer [enɔ̃se] *vt* to say, express; *(conditions)* to set out, state

enorgueillir [ɑ̃nɔʀɡœjiʀ]: **s'~ de** *vt* to pride o.s. on; to boast

énorme [enɔʀm(ə)] *adj* enormous, huge; **énormément** *adv* enormously; **énormément de neige/gens** an enormous amount of snow/number of people

enquérir [ɑ̃keʀiʀ]: **s'~ de** *vt* to inquire about

enquête [ɑ̃kɛt] *nf (de journaliste, de police)* investigation; *(judiciaire, administrative)* inquiry; *(sondage d'opinion)* survey; **enquêter** *vi* to investigate; to hold an inquiry; to conduct a survey

enquiers *etc vb voir* **enquérir**

enraciné, e [ɑ̃ʀasine] *adj* deep-rooted

enragé, e [ɑ̃ʀaʒe] *adj (MÉD)* rabid, with rabies; *(fig)* fanatical

enrageant, e [ɑ̃ʀaʒɑ̃, -ɑ̃t] *adj* infuriating

enrager [ɑ̃ʀaʒe] *vi* to be in a rage

enrayer [ɑ̃ʀeje] *vt* to check, stop; **s'~** *vi (arme à feu)* to jam

enregistrement [ɑ̃ʀʒistʀəmɑ̃] *nm* recording; *(ADMIN)* registration; ~ **des bagages** *(à l'aéroport)* baggage check-in; **enregistrer** [ɑ̃ʀʒistʀe] *vt (MUS etc, remarquer, noter)* to record; *(fig: mémoriser)* to make a mental note of; *(ADMIN)* to register; *(bagages: par train)* to register; (: *à l'aéroport)* to check in

enrhumer [ɑ̃ʀyme]: **s'~** *vi* to catch a cold

enrichir [ɑ̃ʀiʃiʀ] *vt* to make rich(er); *(fig)* to enrich; **s'~** *vi* to get rich(er)

enrober [ɑ̃ʀɔbe] *vt*: ~ **qch de** to coat sth with; *(fig)* to wrap sth up in

enrôler [ɑ̃ʀole] *vt* to enlist; **s'~ (dans)** to enlist (in)

enrouer [ɑ̃ʀwe]: **s'~** *vi* to go hoarse

enrouler [ɑ̃ʀule] *vt (fil, corde)* to wind (up); **s'~** *vi* to coil up; to wind; ~ **qch autour de** to wind sth (a)round

ensanglanté, e [ɑ̃sɑ̃ɡlɑ̃te] *adj* covered with blood

enseignant, e [ɑ̃sɛɲɑ̃, -ɑ̃t] *nm/f* teacher

enseigne [ɑ̃sɛɲ] *nf* sign; **à telle ~ que** so much so that; **l'~ lumineuse** neon sign

enseignement [ɑ̃sɛɲmɑ̃] *nm* teaching; *(ADMIN)* education

enseigner [ɑ̃seɲe] *vt, vi* to teach; ~ **qch à qn/à qn que** to teach sb sth/sb that

ensemble [ɑ̃sɑ̃bl(ə)] *adv* together ♦ *nm (assemblage, MATH)* set; *(totalité)*: **l'~ de la** the whole *ou* entire; *(unité, harmonie)* unity; **impression/idée d'~** overall *ou* general impression/idea; **dans l'~** *(en gros)* on the whole

ensemencer [ɑ̃smɑ̃se] *vt* to sow

ensevelir [ɑ̃sevliʀ] *vt* to bury

ensoleillé, e [ɑ̃sɔleje] *adj* sunny

ensommeillé, e [ɑ̃sɔmeje] *adj* drowsy

ensorceler [ɑ̃sɔʀsəle] *vt* to enchant, bewitch

ensuite [ɑ̃sɥit] *adv* then, next; *(plus tard)* afterwards, later; ~ **de quoi** after which

ensuivre [ɑ̃sɥivʀ(ə)]: **s'~** *vi* to follow, ensue

entailler [ɑ̃tɑje] *vt* to notch; to cut

entamer [ɑ̃tame] *vt (pain, bouteille)* to start; *(hostilités, pourparlers)* to open; *(fig: altérer)* to make a dent in; to shake; to damage

entasser [ɑ̃tɑse] *vt (empiler)* to pile up, heap up; *(tenir à l'étroit)* to cram together; **s'~** *vi* to pile up; to cram

entendre [ɑ̃tɑ̃dʀ(ə)] *vt* to hear; *(comprendre)* to understand; *(vouloir dire)* to mean; *(vouloir)*: ~ **être obéi/que** to mean to be obeyed/that; **s'~** *vi (sympathiser)* to get on; *(se mettre d'accord)* to agree; **s'~ à qch/à faire** *(être compétent)* to be good at sth/doing; **j'ai entendu dire que** I've heard (it said) that

entendu, e [ɑ̃tɑ̃dy] *adj (réglé)* agreed; *(au courant: air)* knowing; **(c'est)** ~ all right, agreed; **c'est** ~ *(concession)* all right, granted; **bien** ~ of course

entente [ɑ̃tɑ̃t] *nf* understanding; *(accord, traité)* agreement; **à double** ~ *(sens)* with a double meaning

entériner [ɑ̃teʀine] *vt* to ratify, confirm

enterrement [ɑ̃tɛʀmɑ̃] *nm (cérémonie)* funeral, burial

enterrer [ɑ̃teʀe] *vt* to bury

entêtant, e [ɑ̃tɛtɑ̃, -ɑ̃t] *adj* heady

entêté, e [ɑ̃tete] *adj* stubborn

en-tête [ɑ̃tɛt] *nm* heading; **papier à** ~ headed notepaper

entêter [ɑ̃tete]: **s'~** *vi*: **s'~ (à faire)** to persist (in doing)

enthousiasme [ɑ̃tuzjasm(ə)] *nm* enthusiasm; **~r** vt to fill with enthusiasm; **s'~r (pour qch)** to get enthusiastic (about sth)

enticher [ɑ̃tiʃe]: **s'~ de** vt to become infatuated with

entier, ère [ɑ̃tje, -jɛR] adj (non entamé, en totalité) whole; (total, complet) complete; (fig: caractère) unbending ♦ nm (MATH) whole; **en ~** totally; in its entirety; **lait ~** full-cream milk; **entièrement** adv entirely, wholly

entonner [ɑ̃tɔne] vt (chanson) to strike up

entonnoir [ɑ̃tɔnwaR] nm funnel

entorse [ɑ̃tɔRs(ə)] nf (MÉD) sprain; (fig): **~ au règlement** infringement of the rule

entortiller [ɑ̃tɔRtije] vt (envelopper) to wrap; (enrouler) to twist, wind; (duper) to deceive

entourage [ɑ̃tuRaʒ] nm circle; family (circle); entourage; (ce qui enclôt) surround

entourer [ɑ̃tuRe] vt to surround; (apporter son soutien à) to rally round; **~ de** to surround with; (trait) to encircle with

entourloupettes [ɑ̃tuRlupɛt] nfpl mean tricks

entracte [ɑ̃tRakt(ə)] nm interval

entraide [ɑ̃tRɛd] nf mutual aid; **s'~r** vi to help each other

entrain [ɑ̃tRɛ̃] nm spirit; **avec/sans ~** spiritedly/half-heartedly

entraînement [ɑ̃tRɛnmɑ̃] nm training; (TECH) drive

entraîner [ɑ̃tRene] vt (tirer: wagons) to pull; (charrier) to carry ou drag along; (TECH) to drive; (emmener: personne) to take (off); (mener à l'assaut, influencer) to lead; (SPORT) to train; (impliquer) to entail; (causer) to lead to, bring about; **s'~** vi (SPORT) to train; **s'~ à qch/à faire** to train o.s. for sth/to do; **~ qn à faire** (inciter) to lead sb to do; **entraîneur, euse** nm/f (SPORT) coach, trainer ♦ nm (HIPPISME) trainer; **entraîneuse** nf (de bar) hostess

entraver [ɑ̃tRave] vt (circulation) to hold up; (action, progrès) to hinder

entre [ɑ̃tR(ə)] prép between; (parmi) among(st); **l'un d'~ eux/nous** one of them/us; **~ eux** among(st) themselves

entre: **~bâillé, e** adj half-open, ajar; **~choquer: s'~choquer** vi to knock ou bang together; **~côte** nf entrecôte ou rib steak; **~couper** vt: **~couper qch de** to intersperse sth with; **~croiser: s'~croiser** vi to intertwine

entrée [ɑ̃tRe] nf entrance; (accès: au cinéma etc) admission; (billet) (admission) ticket; (CULIN) first course; **d'~** from the outset; **~ en matière** introduction

entrefaites [ɑ̃tRəfɛt]: **sur ces ~** adv at this juncture

entrefilet [ɑ̃tRəfile] nm paragraph (short article)

entrejambes [ɑ̃tRəʒɑ̃b] nm crotch

entrelacer [ɑ̃tRəlase] vt to intertwine

entrelarder [ɑ̃tRəlaRde] vt to lard

entremêler [ɑ̃tRəmele] vt: **~ qch de** to (inter)mingle sth with

entremets [ɑ̃tRəmɛ] nm (cream) dessert

entremetteur, euse [ɑ̃tRəmɛtœR, -øz] nm/f go-between

entremise [ɑ̃tRəmiz] nf intervention; **par l'~ de** through

entreposer [ɑ̃tRəpoze] vt to store, put into storage

entrepôt [ɑ̃tRəpo] nm warehouse

entreprenant, e [ɑ̃tRəpRənɑ̃, -ɑ̃t] adj (actif) enterprising; (trop galant) forward

entreprendre [ɑ̃tRəpRɑ̃dR(ə)] vt (se lancer dans) to undertake; (commencer) to begin ou start (upon); (personne) to buttonhole; to tackle

entrepreneur [ɑ̃tRəpRənœR] nm: **~ (en bâtiment)** (building) contractor

entreprise [ɑ̃tRəpRiz] nf (société) firm, concern; (action) undertaking, venture

entrer [ɑ̃tRe] vi to go (ou come) in, enter ♦ vt (INFORM) to enter, input; **(faire) ~ qch dans** to get sth into; **~ dans** (gén) to enter; (pièce) to go (ou come) into, enter; (club) to join; (heurter) to run into; (être une composante de) to go into; to form part of; **~ à l'hôpital** to go into hospital; **faire ~** (visiteur) to show in

entresol [ɑ̃tRəsɔl] nm mezzanine

entre-temps [ɑ̃tRətɑ̃] adv meanwhile

entretenir [ɑ̃tRətniR] vt to maintain; (famille, maîtresse) to support, keep; **s'~ (de)** to converse (about); **~ qn (de)** to speak to sb (about)

entretien [ɑ̃tRətjɛ̃] nm maintenance; (discussion) discussion, talk; (audience) interview

entrevoir [ɑ̃tRəvwaR] vt (à peine) to make out; (brièvement) to catch a glimpse of

entrevue [ɑ̃tRəvy] nf meeting; (audience) interview

entrouvert, e [ɑ̃tRuvɛR, -ɛRt(ə)] adj half-open

énumérer [enymeRe] vt to list, enumerate

envahir [ɑ̃vaiR] vt to invade; (suj: inquiétude, peur) to come over; **envahissant, e** (péj) adj (personne) interfering, intrusive

enveloppe [ɑ̃vlɔp] nf (de lettre) envelope; (TECH) casing; outer layer

envelopper [ɑ̃vlɔpe] vt to wrap; (fig) to envelop, shroud

envenimer [ɑ̃vnime] vt to aggravate

envergure [ɑ̃vɛRgyR] nf (fig) scope; calibre

enverrai etc vb voir **envoyer**

envers [ɑ̃vɛR] prép towards, to ♦ nm other side; (d'une étoffe) wrong side; **à l'~** upside down; back to front; (vêtement) inside out

envie [ɑ̃vi] nf (sentiment) envy; (souhait) desire, wish; **avoir ~ de (faire)** to feel like (doing); (plus fort) to want (to do); **avoir ~**

que to wish that; **ça lui fait** ~ he would like that; **envier** *vt* to envy; **envieux, euse** *adj* envious

environ [ɑ̃viʀɔ̃] *adv*: ~ **3 h/2 km** (around) about 3 o'clock/2 km; *voir aussi* **environs**

environnement [ɑ̃viʀɔnmɑ̃] *nm* environment

environner [ɑ̃viʀɔne] *vt* to surround

environs [ɑ̃viʀɔ̃] *nmpl* surroundings

envisager [ɑ̃vizaʒe] *vt* (*examiner, considérer*) to view, contemplate; (*avoir en vue*) to envisage

envoi [ɑ̃vwa] *nm* (*paquet*) parcel, consignment

envoler [ɑ̃vɔle]: **s'**~ *vi* (*oiseau*) to fly away *ou* off; (*avion*) to take off; (*papier, feuille*) to blow away; (*fig*) to vanish (into thin air)

envoûter [ɑ̃vute] *vt* to bewitch

envoyé, e [ɑ̃vwaje] *nm/f* (*POL*) envoy; (*PRESSE*) correspondent

envoyer [ɑ̃vwaje] *vt* to send; (*lancer*) to hurl, throw; ~ **chercher** to send for

épagneul, e [epaɲœl] *nm/f* spaniel

épais, se [epɛ, -ɛs] *adj* thick; **épaisseur** *nf* thickness

épancher [epɑ̃ʃe]: **s'**~ *vi* to open one's heart

épanouir [epanwiʀ]: **s'**~ *vi* (*fleur*) to bloom, open out; (*visage*) to light up; (*fig*) to blossom; to open up

épargne [epaʀɲ(ə)] *nf* saving

épargner [epaʀɲe] *vt* to save; (*ne pas tuer ou endommager*) to spare ♦ *vi* to save; ~ **qch à qn** to spare sb sth

éparpiller [epaʀpije] *vt* to scatter; (*pour répartir*) to disperse; **s'**~ *vi* to scatter; (*fig*) to dissipate one's efforts

épars, e [epaʀ, -aʀs(ə)] *adj* scattered

épatant, e [epatɑ̃, -ɑ̃t] (*fam*) *adj* super

épater [epate] *vt* to amaze; to impress

épaule [epol] *nf* shoulder

épauler [epole] *vt* (*aider*) to back up, support; (*arme*) to raise (to one's shoulder) ♦ *vi* to (take) aim

épaulette [epolɛt] *nf* epaulette; (*rembourrage*) shoulder pad

épave [epav] *nf* wreck

épée [epe] *nf* sword

épeler [eple] *vt* to spell

éperdu, e [epɛʀdy] *adj* distraught, overcome; passionate; frantic

éperon [epʀɔ̃] *nm* spur

épi [epi] *nm* (*de blé, d'orge*) ear

épice [epis] *nf* spice

épicer [epise] *vt* to spice

épicerie [episʀi] *nf* grocer's shop; (*denrées*) groceries *pl*; ~ **fine** delicatessen; **épicier, ière** *nm/f* grocer

épidémie [epidemi] *nf* epidemic

épier [epje] *vt* to spy on, watch closely; (*occasion*) to look out for

épilepsie [epilɛpsi] *nf* epilepsy

épiler [epile] *vt* (*jambes*) to remove the hair from; (*sourcils*) to pluck

épilogue [epilɔg] *nm* (*fig*) conclusion, dénouement; ~**r** [epilɔge] *vi*: ~**r sur** to hold forth on

épinards [epinaʀ] *nmpl* spinach *sg*

épine [epin] *nf* thorn, prickle; (*d'oursin etc*) spine; ~ **dorsale** backbone

épingle [epɛ̃gl(ə)] *nf* pin; ~ **de nourrice** safety pin; ~ **de sûreté** *ou* **double** safety pin

épingler [epɛ̃gle] *vt* (*badge, décoration*): ~ **qch sur** to pin sth on(to); (*fam*) to catch, nick

épique [epik] *adj* epic

épisode [epizɔd] *nm* episode; **film/roman à** ~**s** serial; **épisodique** *adj* occasional

éploré, e [eplɔʀe] *adj* tearful

épluche-légumes [eplyʃlegym] *nm inv* (potato) peeler

éplucher [eplyʃe] *vt* (*fruit, légumes*) to peel; (*fig*) to go over with a fine-tooth comb; **épluchures** *nfpl* peelings

éponge [epɔ̃ʒ] *nf* sponge; ~**r** *vt* (*liquide*) to mop up; (*surface*) to sponge; (*fig: déficit*) to soak up; **s'**~**r le front** to mop one's brow

épopée [epɔpe] *nf* epic

époque [epɔk] *nf* (*de l'histoire*) age, era; (*de l'année, la vie*) time; **d'**~ (*meuble*) period *cpd*

époumoner [epumɔne]: **s'**~ *vi* to shout o.s. hoarse

épouse [epuz] *nf* wife

épouser [epuze] *vt* to marry; (*fig: idées*) to espouse; (*: forme*) to fit

épousseter [epuste] *vt* to dust

époustouflant, e [epustuflɑ̃, -ɑ̃t] *adj* staggering, mind-boggling

épouvantable [epuvɑ̃tabl(ə)] *adj* appalling, dreadful

épouvantail [epuvɑ̃taj] *nm* (*à oiseaux*) scarecrow

épouvante [epuvɑ̃t] *nf* terror; **film d'**~ horror film; **épouvanter** *vt* to terrify

époux [epu] *nm* husband ♦ *nmpl* (*married*) couple

éprendre [epʀɑ̃dʀ(ə)]: **s'**~ **de** *vt* to fall in love with

épreuve [epʀœv] *nf* (*d'examen*) test; (*malheur, difficulté*) trial, ordeal; (*PHOTO*) print; (*TYPO*) proof; (*SPORT*) event; **à l'**~ **des balles** bulletproof; **à toute** ~ unfailing; **mettre à l'**~ to put to the test

épris, e [epʀi, -iz] *pp de* **éprendre**

éprouver [epʀuve] *vt* (*tester*) to test; (*marquer, faire souffrir*) to afflict, distress; (*ressentir*) to experience

éprouvette [epʀuvɛt] *nf* test tube

épuisé, e [epɥize] *adj* exhausted; (*livre*) out of print; **épuisement** [epɥizmɑ̃] *nm* exhaustion

épuiser [epɥize] *vt* (*fatiguer*) to exhaust,

wear *ou* tire out; *(stock, sujet)* to exhaust; **s'~** *vi* to wear *ou* tire o.s. out, exhaust o.s.; *(stock)* to run out

épurer [epyʀe] *vt (liquide)* to purify; *(parti etc)* to purge; *(langue, texte)* to refine

équateur [ekwatœʀ] *nm* equator; **(la république de) l'É~** Ecuador

équation [ekwasjɔ̃] *nf* equation

équerre [ekɛʀ] *nf (à dessin)* (set) square; *(pour fixer)* brace; **en ~** at right angles; **à l'~, d'~** straight

équilibre [ekilibʀ(ə)] *nm* balance; *(d'une balance)* equilibrium; **garder/perdre l'~** to keep/lose one's balance; **être en ~** to be balanced; **équilibré, e** *adj (fig)* well-balanced, stable; **équilibrer** *vt* to balance; **s'~r** *vi (poids)* to balance; *(fig: défauts etc)* to balance each other out

équipage [ekipaʒ] *nm* crew

équipe [ekip] *nf* team; *(bande: parfois péj)* bunch

équipé, e [ekipe] *adj*: **bien/mal ~** well-/poorly-equipped

équipée [ekipe] *nf* escapade

équipement [ekipmɑ̃] *nm* equipment; **~s** *nmpl (installations)* amenities, facilities

équiper [ekipe] *vt* to equip; *(voiture, cuisine)* to equip, fit out; **~ qn/qch de** to equip sb/sth with

équipier, ière [ekipje, -jɛʀ] *nm/f* team member

équitable [ekitabl(ə)] *adj* fair

équitation [ekitasjɔ̃] *nf* (horse-) riding

équivalent, e [ekivalɑ̃, -ɑ̃t] *adj, nm* equivalent

équivaloir [ekivalwaʀ]: **~ à** *vt* to be equivalent to

équivoque [ekivɔk] *adj* equivocal, ambiguous; *(louche)* dubious

érable [eʀabl(ə)] *nm* maple

érafler [eʀafle] *vt* to scratch; **éraflure** *nf* scratch

éraillé, e [eʀaje] *adj (voix)* rasping

ère [ɛʀ] *nf* era; **en l'an 1050 de notre ~** in the year 1050 A.D.

érection [eʀɛksjɔ̃] *nf* erection

éreinter [eʀɛ̃te] *vt* to exhaust, wear out

ériger [eʀiʒe] *vt (monument)* to erect

ermite [ɛʀmit] *nm* hermit

éroder [eʀɔde] *vt* to erode

érotique [eʀɔtik] *adj* erotic

errer [eʀe] *vi* to wander

erreur [eʀœʀ] *nf* mistake, error; *(morale)* error; **faire ~** to be mistaken; **par ~** by mistake; **~ judiciaire** miscarriage of justice

érudit, e [eʀydi, -it] *nm/f* scholar

éruption [eʀypsjɔ̃] *nf* eruption; *(MÉD)* rash

es *vb voir* **être**

ès [ɛs] *prép*: **licencié ~ lettres/sciences** ≈ Bachelor of Arts/Science

escabeau, x [ɛskabo] *nm (tabouret)* stool; *(échelle)* stepladder

escadre [ɛskadʀ(ə)] *nf (NAVIG)* squadron; *(AVIAT)* wing

escadron [ɛskadʀɔ̃] *nm* squadron

escalade [ɛskalad] *nf* climbing *no pl*; *(POL etc)* escalation

escalader [ɛskalade] *vt* to climb

escale [ɛskal] *nf (NAVIG)* call; port of call; *(AVIAT)* stop(over); **faire ~ à** to put in at; to stop over at

escalier [ɛskalje] *nm* stairs *pl*; **dans l'~** *ou* **les ~s** on the stairs; **~ roulant** escalator

escamoter [ɛskamɔte] *vt (esquiver)* to get round, evade; *(faire disparaître)* to conjure away

escapade [ɛskapad] *nf*: **faire une ~** to go on a jaunt; to run away *ou* off

escargot [ɛskaʀgo] *nm* snail

escarmouche [ɛskaʀmuʃ] *nf* skirmish

escarpé, e [ɛskaʀpe] *adj* steep

escient [esjɑ̃] *nm*: **à bon ~** advisedly

esclaffer [ɛsklafe]: **s'~** *vi* to guffaw

esclandre [ɛsklɑ̃dʀ(ə)] *nm* scene, fracas

esclavage [ɛsklavaʒ] *nm* slavery

esclave [ɛsklav] *nm/f* slave

escompter [ɛskɔ̃te] *vt (COMM)* to discount; *(espérer)* to expect, reckon upon

escorte [ɛskɔʀt(ə)] *nf* escort

escrime [ɛskʀim] *nf* fencing

escrimer [ɛskʀime]: **s'~** *vi*: **s'~ à faire** to wear o.s. out doing

escroc [ɛskʀo] *nm* swindler, conman

escroquer [ɛskʀɔke] *vt*: **~ qn (de qch)/qch (à qn)** to swindle sb (out of sth)/sth (out of sb); **escroquerie** *nf* swindle

espace [ɛspas] *nm* space

espacer [ɛspase] *vt* to space out; **s'~** *vi (visites etc)* to become less frequent

espadon [ɛspadɔ̃] *nm* swordfish *inv*

espadrille [ɛspadʀij] *nf* rope soled sandal

Espagne [ɛspaɲ(ə)] *nf*: **l'~** Spain; **espagnol, e** *adj* Spanish ♦ *nm/f*: **Espagnol, e** Spaniard ♦ *nm (LING)* Spanish

espèce [ɛspɛs] *nf (BIO, BOT, ZOOL)* species *inv*; *(gén: sorte)* sort, kind, type; *(péj)*: **~ de maladroit!** you clumsy oaf!; **~s** *nfpl (COMM)* cash *sg*; **en ~** in cash; **en l'~** in the case in point

espérance [ɛspeʀɑ̃s] *nf* hope; **~ de vie** life expectancy

espérer [ɛspeʀe] *vt* to hope for; **j'espère (bien)** I hope so; **~ que/faire** to hope that/to do; **~ en** to trust in

espiègle [ɛspjɛgl(ə)] *adj* mischievous

espion, ne [ɛspjɔ̃, -ɔn] *nm/f* spy

espionnage [ɛspjɔnaʒ] *nm* espionage, spying

espionner [ɛspjɔne] *vt* to spy (up)on

esplanade [ɛsplanad] *nf* esplanade

espoir [ɛspwaʀ] *nm* hope

esprit [ɛspʀi] *nm (pensée, intellect)* mind; *(humour, ironie)* wit; *(mentalité, d'une loi etc, fantôme etc)* spirit; **faire de l'~** to try to be witty; **reprendre ses** ~**s** to come to; **perdre l'**~ to lose one's mind

esquimau, de, x [ɛskimo, -od] *adj, nm/f* Eskimo ♦ *nm* ice lolly (*BRIT*), popsicle (*US*)

esquinter [ɛskɛ̃te] (*fam*) *vt* to mess up

esquisse [ɛskis] *nf* sketch

esquisser [ɛskise] *vt* to sketch; **s'**~ *vi* (*amélioration*) to begin to be detectable; ~ **un sourire** to give a vague smile

esquiver [ɛskive] *vt* to dodge; **s'**~ *vi* to slip away

essai [esɛ] *nm* trying; testing; (*tentative*) attempt, try; (*RUGBY*) try; (*LITTÉRATURE*) essay; ~**s** *nmpl* (*AUTO*) trials; ~ **gratuit** (*COMM*) free trial; **à l'**~ on a trial basis

essaim [esɛ̃] *nm* swarm

essayer [eseje] *vt* (*gén*) to try; (*vêtement, chaussures*) to try (on); (*restaurant, méthode, voiture*) to try (out) ♦ *vi* to try; ~ **de faire** to try *ou* attempt to do

essence [esɑ̃s] *nf* (*de voiture*) petrol (*BRIT*), gas(oline) (*US*); (*extrait de plante, PHILOSOPHIE*) essence; (*espèce: d'arbre*) species

essentiel, le [esɑ̃sjɛl] *adj* essential; **c'est l'**~ (*ce qui importe*) that's the main thing; **l'**~ **de** the main part of

essieu, x [esjø] *nm* axle

essor [esɔʀ] *nm* (*de l'économie etc*) rapid expansion

essorer [esɔʀe] *vt* (*en tordant*) to wring (out); (*par la force centrifuge*) to spin-dry; **essoreuse** *nf* mangle, wringer; spin-dryer

essouffler [esufle] *vt* to make breathless; **s'**~ *vi* to get out of breath; (*fig*) to run out of steam

essuie-glace [esɥiglas] *nm inv* windscreen (*BRIT*) *ou* windshield (*US*) wiper

essuie-main [esɥimɛ̃] *nm* hand towel

essuyer [esɥije] *vt* to wipe; (*fig: subir*) to suffer; **s'**~ *vi* (*après le bain*) to dry o.s.; ~ **la vaisselle** to dry up

est¹ [ɛ] *vb voir* **être**

est² [ɛst] *nm* east ♦ *adj inv* east; (*région*) east(ern); **à l'est** in the east; (*direction*) to the east, east(wards); **à l'est de** (to the) east of

estampe [ɛstɑ̃p] *nf* print, engraving

est-ce que [ɛskə] *adv*: ~ **c'est cher/c'était bon?** is it expensive/was it good?; **quand est-ce qu'il part?** when does he leave?, when is he leaving?; *voir aussi* **que**

esthéticienne [ɛstetisjɛn] *nf* beautician

esthétique [ɛstetik] *adj* attractive; aesthetically pleasing

estimation [ɛstimasjɔ̃] *nf* valuation; assessment

estime [ɛstim] *nf* esteem, regard

estimer [ɛstime] *vt* (*respecter*) to esteem; (*expertiser*) to value; (*évaluer*) to assess, estimate; (*penser*): ~ **que/être** to consider that/o.s. to be

estival, e, aux [ɛstival, -o] *adj* summer *cpd*

estivant, e [ɛstivɑ̃, -ɑ̃t] *nm/f* (summer) holiday-maker

estomac [ɛstɔma] *nm* stomach

estomaqué, e [ɛstɔmake] *adj* flabbergasted

estomper [ɛstɔ̃pe] *vt* (*fig*) to blur, dim; **s'**~ *vi* to soften; to become blurred

estrade [ɛstʀad] *nf* platform, rostrum

estragon [ɛstʀagɔ̃] *nm* tarragon

estropier [ɛstʀɔpje] *vt* to cripple, maim; (*fig*) to twist, distort

et [e] *conj* and; ~ **lui?** what about him?; ~ **alors!** so what!

étable [etabl(ə)] *nf* cowshed

établi [etabli] *nm* (work)bench

établir [etabliʀ] *vt* (*papiers d'identité, facture*) to make out; (*liste, programme*) to draw up; (*entreprise, camp, gouvernement, artisan*) to set up; (*réputation, usage, fait, culpabilité*) to establish; **s'**~ *vi* (*se faire: entente etc*) to be established; **s'**~ (**à son compte**) to set up in business; **s'**~ **à/près de** to settle in/near

établissement [etablismɑ̃] *nm* making out; drawing up; setting up, establishing; (*entreprise, institution*) establishment; ~ **scolaire** school, educational establishment

étage [etaʒ] *nm* (*d'immeuble*) storey, floor; (*de fusée*) stage; (*GÉO: de culture, végétation*) level; **à l'**~ upstairs; **au 2ème** ~ on the 2nd (*BRIT*) *ou* 3rd (*US*) floor; **de bas** ~ low-born

étagère [etaʒɛʀ] *nf* (*rayon*) shelf; (*meuble*) shelves *pl*

étai [etɛ] *nm* stay, prop

étain [etɛ̃] *nm* tin; (*ORFÈVRERIE*) pewter *no pl*

étais *etc vb voir* **être**

étal [etal] *nm* stall

étalage [etalaʒ] *nm* display; display window; **faire** ~ **de** to show off, parade

étaler [etale] *vt* (*carte, nappe*) to spread (out); (*peinture, liquide*) to spread; (*échelonner: paiements, vacances*) to spread, stagger; (*marchandises*) to display; (*richesses, connaissances*) to parade; **s'**~ *vi* (*liquide*) to spread out; (*fam*) to fall flat on one's face; **s'**~ **sur** (*suj: paiements etc*) to be spread out over

étalon [etalɔ̃] *nm* (*mesure*) standard; (*cheval*) stallion

étamer [etame] *vt* (*casserole*) to tin(plate); (*glace*) to silver

étanche [etɑ̃ʃ] *adj* (*récipient*) watertight; (*montre, vêtement*) waterproof

étancher [etɑ̃ʃe] *vt*: ~ **sa soif** to quench one's thirst

étang [etɑ̃] *nm* pond

étant [etɑ̃] *vb voir* **être; donné**

étape [etap] *nf* stage; (*lieu d'arrivée*) stopping place; (: *CYCLISME*) staging point; **faire** ~ **à** to stop off at

état [eta] *nm* (*POL, condition*) state; (*liste*)

inventory, statement; **en mauvais ~** in poor condition; **en ~ (de marche)** in (working) order; **remettre en ~** to repair; **hors d'~** out of order; **être en ~/hors d'~ de faire** to be in a/in no fit state to do; **en tout ~ de cause** in any event; **être dans tous ses ~s** to be in a state; **faire ~ de** (*alléguer*) to put forward; **en ~ d'arrestation** under arrest; **~ civil** civil status; **~ des lieux** inventory of fixtures; **étatiser** *vt* to bring under state control

état-major [etamaʒɔʀ] *nm* (*MIL*) staff

États-Unis [etazyni] *nmpl*: **les ~** the United States

étau, x [eto] *nm* vice (*BRIT*), vise (*US*)

étayer [eteje] *vt* to prop *ou* shore up

etc. *adv etc*

et c(a)etera [ɛtseteʀa] *adv* et cetera, and so on

été [ete] *pp de* être ♦ *nm* summer

éteindre [etɛ̃dʀ(ə)] *vt* (*lampe, lumière, radio*) to turn *ou* switch off; (*cigarette, incendie, bougie*) to put out, extinguish; (*JUR: dette*) to extinguish; **s'~** *vi* to go out; to go off; (*mourir*) to pass away; **éteint, e** *adj* (*fig*) lacklustre, dull; (*volcan*) extinct

étendard [etɑ̃daʀ] *nm* standard

étendre [etɑ̃dʀ(ə)] *vt* (*pâte, liquide*) to spread; (*carte etc*) to spread out; (*linge*) to hang up; (*bras, jambes, par terre: blessé*) to stretch out; (*diluer*) to dilute, thin; (*fig: agrandir*) to extend; **s'~** *vi* (*augmenter, se propager*) to spread; (*terrain, forêt etc*) to stretch; (*s'allonger*) to stretch out; (*se coucher*) to lie down; (*fig: expliquer*) to elaborate

étendu, e [etɑ̃dy] *adj* extensive; **étendue** *nf* (*d'eau, de sable*) stretch, expanse; (*importance*) extent

éternel, le [etɛʀnɛl] *adj* eternal

éterniser [etɛʀnize]: **s'~** *vi* to last for ages; to stay for ages

éternité [etɛʀnite] *nf* eternity

éternuer [etɛʀnɥe] *vi* to sneeze

êtes *vb voir* être

éthique [etik] *adj* ethical

ethnie [ɛtni] *nf* ethnic group

éthylisme [etilism(ə)] *nm* alcoholism

étiez *vb voir* être

étinceler [etɛ̃sle] *vi* to sparkle

étincelle [etɛ̃sɛl] *nf* spark

étioler [etjɔle]: **s'~** *vi* to wilt

étiqueter [etikte] *vt* to label

étiquette [etikɛt] *nf* label; (*protocole*): **l'~** etiquette

étirer [etire] *vt* to stretch; **s'~** *vi* (*personne*) to stretch; (*convoi, route*): **s'~ sur** to stretch out over

étoffe [etɔf] *nf* material, fabric

étoffer [etɔfe] *vt* to fill out; **s'~** *vi* to fill out

étoile [etwal] *nf* star; **à la belle ~** in the open; **~ de mer** starfish; **~ filante** shooting star; **étoilé, e** *adj* starry

étole [etɔl] *nf* stole

étonnant, e [etɔnɑ̃, -ɑ̃t] *adj* amazing

étonner [etɔne] *vt* to surprise, amaze; **s'~ que/de** to be amazed that/at; **cela m'~ait (que)** (*j'en doute*) I'd be very surprised (if)

étouffée [etufe]: **à l'~** *adv* (*CULIN*) steamed; braised

étouffer [etufe] *vt* to suffocate; (*bruit*) to muffle; (*scandale*) to hush up ♦ *vi* to suffocate; **s'~** *vi* (*en mangeant etc*) to choke

étourderie [eturdəri] *nf* heedlessness *no pl*; thoughtless blunder

étourdi, e [eturdi] *adj* (*distrait*) scatterbrained, heedless

étourdir [eturdir] *vt* (*assommer*) to stun, daze; (*griser*) to make dizzy *ou* giddy; **étourdissement** *nm* dizzy spell

étourneau, x [eturno] *nm* starling

étrange [etrɑ̃ʒ] *adj* strange

étranger, ère [etrɑ̃ʒe, -ɛr] *adj* foreign; (*pas de la famille, non familier*) strange ♦ *nm/f* foreigner; stranger ♦ *nm*: **à l'~** abroad; **de l'~** from abroad; **~ à** (*fig*) unfamiliar to; irrelevant to

étranglement [etrɑ̃gləmɑ̃] *nm* (*d'une vallée etc*) constriction

étrangler [etrɑ̃gle] *vt* to strangle; **s'~** *vi* (*en mangeant etc*) to choke

étrave [etrav] *nf* stem

—————————— MOT CLÉ

être [ɛtr(ə)] *nm* being; **~ humain** human being

♦ *vb +attrib* **1** (*état, description*) to be; **il est instituteur** he is *ou* he's a teacher; **vous êtes grand/intelligent/fatigué** you are *ou* you're tall/clever/tired

2 (*+à: appartenir*) to be; **le livre est à Paul** the book is Paul's *ou* belongs to Paul; **c'est à moi/eux** it is *ou* it's mine/theirs

3 (*+de: provenance*): **il est de Paris** he is from Paris; (*: appartenance*): **il est des nôtres** he is one of us

4 (*date*): **nous sommes le 10 janvier** it's the 10th of January (today)

♦ *vi* to be; **je ne serai pas ici demain** I won't be here tomorrow

♦ *vb aux* **1** to have; to be; **~ arrivé/allé** to have arrived/gone; **il est parti** he has left, he has gone

2 (*forme passive*) to be; **~ fait par** to be made by; **il a été promu** he has been promoted

3 (*+à: obligation*): **c'est à réparer** it needs repairing; **c'est à essayer** it should be tried

♦ *vb impers* **1**: **il est +adjectif** it is +adjective; **il est impossible de le faire** it's impossible to do it

2 (*heure, date*): **il est 10 heures** it is *ou* it's 10 o'clock

3 (*emphatique*): **c'est moi** it's me; **c'est à lui de le faire** it's up to him to do it

étreindre [etʀɛ̃dʀ(ə)] *vt* to clutch, grip; (*amoureusement, amicalement*) to embrace; **s'~** *vi* to embrace

étrenner [etʀene] *vt* to use (*ou* wear) for the first time

étrennes [etʀɛn] *nfpl* Christmas box *sg*

étrier [etʀije] *nm* stirrup

étriller [etʀije] *vt* (*cheval*) to curry; (*fam: battre*) to slaughter (*fig*)

étriqué, e [etʀike] *adj* skimpy

étroit, e [etʀwa, -wat] *adj* narrow; (*vêtement*) tight; (*fig: serré*) close, tight; **à l'~** cramped; **~ d'esprit** narrow-minded

étude [etyd] *nf* studying; (*ouvrage, rapport*) study; (*de notaire: bureau*) office; (: *charge*) practice; (*SCOL: salle de travail*) study room; **~s** *nfpl* (*SCOL*) studies; **être à l'~** (*projet etc*) to be under consideration; **faire des ~s (de droit/médecine)** to study (law/medicine)

étudiant, e [etydjɑ̃, -ɑ̃t] *nm/f* student

étudié, e [etydje] *adj* (*démarche*) studied; (*système*) carefully designed; (*prix*) keen

étudier [etydje] *vt, vi* to study

étui [etɥi] *nm* case

étuve [etyv] *nf* steamroom

étuvée [etyve] : **à l'~** *adv* braised

eu, eue [y] *pp de* avoir

euh [ø] *excl* er

Europe [øʀɔp] *nf*: **l'~** Europe; **européen, ne** *adj, nm/f* European

eus *etc vb voir* avoir

eux [ø] *pron* (*sujet*) they; (*objet*) them

évacuer [evakɥe] *vt* to evacuate

évader [evade]: **s'~** *vi* to escape

évangile [evɑ̃ʒil] *nm* gospel

évanouir [evanwiʀ]: **s'~** *vi* to faint; (*disparaître*) to vanish, disappear

évanouissement [evanwismɑ̃] *nm* (*syncope*) fainting fit; (*dans un accident*) loss of consciousness

évaporer [evapɔʀe]: **s'~** *vi* to evaporate

évaser [evɑze] *vt* (*tuyau*) to widen, open out; (*jupe, pantalon*) to flare

évasif, ive [evazif, -iv] *adj* evasive

évasion [evazjɔ̃] *nf* escape

évêché [eveʃe] *nm* bishopric; bishop's palace

éveil [evɛj] *nm* awakening; **être en ~** to be alert

éveillé, e [eveje] *adj* awake; (*vif*) alert, sharp

éveiller [eveje] *vt* to (a)waken; **s'~** *vi* to (a)waken; (*fig*) to be aroused

événement [evɛnmɑ̃] *nm* event

éventail [evɑ̃taj] *nm* fan; (*choix*) range

éventaire [evɑ̃tɛʀ] *nm* stall, stand

éventer [evɑ̃te] *vt* (*secret*) to uncover; **s'~** *vi* (*parfum*) to go stale

éventrer [evɑ̃tʀe] *vt* to disembowel; (*fig*) to tear *ou* rip open

éventualité [evɑ̃tɥalite] *nf* eventuality; possibility; **dans l'~ de** in the event of

éventuel, le [evɑ̃tɥɛl] *adj* possible; **éventuellement** *adv* possibly

évêque [evɛk] *nm* bishop

évertuer [evɛʀtɥe]: **s'~ vi: s'~ à faire** to try very hard to do

éviction [eviksjɔ̃] *nf* ousting; (*de locataire*) eviction

évidemment [evidamɑ̃] *adv* obviously

évidence [evidɑ̃s] *nf* obviousness; obvious fact; **de toute ~** quite obviously *ou* evidently; **en ~** conspicuous; **mettre en ~** to highlight; to bring to the fore; **évident, e** [evidɑ̃, -ɑ̃t] *adj* obvious, evident

évider [evide] *vt* to scoop out

évier [evje] *nm* (kitchen) sink

évincer [evɛ̃se] *vt* to oust

éviter [evite] *vt* to avoid; **~ de faire/que qch ne se passe** to avoid doing/sth happening; **~ qch à qn** to spare sb sth

évolué, e [evɔlɥe] *adj* advanced

évoluer [evɔlɥe] *vi* (*enfant, maladie*) to develop; (*situation, moralement*) to evolve, develop; (*aller et venir: danseur etc*) to move about, circle; **évolution** *nf* development; evolution

évoquer [evɔke] *vt* to call to mind, evoke; (*mentionner*) to mention

ex... [ɛks] *préfixe* ex-

exact, e [ɛgzakt] *adj* (*précis*) exact, accurate, precise; (*correct*) correct; (*ponctuel*) punctual; **l'heure ~e** the right *ou* exact time; **exactement** *adv* exactly, accurately, precisely; correctly; (*c'est cela même*) exactly

ex aequo [ɛgzeko] *adj* equally placed

exagéré, e [ɛgzaʒeʀe] *adj* (*prix etc*) excessive

exagérer [ɛgzaʒeʀe] *vt* to exaggerate ♦ *vi* (*abuser*) to go too far; to overstep the mark; (*déformer les faits*) to exaggerate

exalter [ɛgzalte] *vt* (*enthousiasmer*) to excite, elate; (*glorifier*) to exalt

examen [ɛgzamɛ̃] *nm* examination; (*SCOL*) exam, examination; **à l'~** under consideration; (*COMM*) on approval

examiner [ɛgzamine] *vt* to examine

exaspérant, e [ɛgzaspeʀɑ̃, -ɑ̃t] *adj* exasperating

exaspérer [ɛgzaspeʀe] *vt* to exasperate; to exacerbate

exaucer [ɛgzose] *vt* (*vœu*) to grant

excédent [ɛksedɑ̃] *nm* surplus; **en ~** surplus; **~ de bagages** excess luggage

excéder [ɛksede] *vt* (*dépasser*) to exceed; (*agacer*) to exasperate

excellence [ɛkselɑ̃s] *nf* (*titre*) Excellency

excellent, e [ɛkselɑ̃, -ɑ̃t] *adj* excellent

excentrique [ɛksɑ̃tʀik] *adj* eccentric;

(quartier) outlying

excepté, e [ɛksɛpte] *adj*, *prép*: **les élèves ~s, ~ les élèves** except for the pupils; **~ si** except if

exception [ɛksɛpsjɔ̃] *nf* exception; **à l'~ de** except for, with the exception of; **d'~** *(mesure, loi)* special, exceptional; **exceptionnel, le** *adj* exceptional

excès [ɛksɛ] *nm* surplus ♦ *nmpl* excesses; **à l'~** to excess; **~ de vitesse** speeding *no pl*; **excessif, ive** *adj* excessive

excitant, e [ɛksitɑ̃, -ɑ̃t] *adj* exciting ♦ *nm* stimulant; **excitation** [ɛksitasjɔ̃] *nf (état)* excitement

exciter [ɛksite] *vt* to excite; *(suj: café etc)* to stimulate; **s'~** *vi* to get excited

exclamation [ɛksklamɑsjɔ̃] *nf* exclamation

exclamer [ɛksklame]: **s'~** *vi* to exclaim

exclure [ɛksklyʀ] *vt (faire sortir)* to expel; *(ne pas compter)* to exclude, leave out; *(rendre impossible)* to exclude, rule out; **il est exclu que** it's out of the question that ...; **il n'est pas exclu que** ..., it's not impossible that ...; **exclusif, ive** *adj* exclusive; **exclusion** *nf* expulsion; **à l'exclusion de** with the exclusion *ou* exception of; **exclusivité** *nf (COMM)* exclusive rights *pl*; **film passant en exclusivité à** film showing only at

excursion [ɛkskyʀsjɔ̃] *nf (en autocar)* excursion, trip; *(à pied)* walk, hike

excuse [ɛkskyz] *nf* excuse; **~s** *nfpl (regret)* apology *sg*, apologies

excuser [ɛkskyze] *vt* to excuse; **s'~ (de)** to apologize (for); **"excusez-moi"** "I'm sorry"; *(pour attirer l'attention)* "excuse me"

exécrable [ɛgzekʀabl(ə)] *adj* atrocious

exécrer [ɛgzekʀe] *vt* to loathe, abhor

exécuter [ɛgzekyte] *vt (prisonnier)* to execute; *(tâche etc)* to execute, carry out; *(MUS: jouer)* to perform, execute; *(INFORM)* to run; **s'~** *vi* to comply; **exécutif, ive** *adj*, *nm (POL)* executive; **exécution** *nf* execution; carrying out; **mettre à exécution** to carry out

exemplaire [ɛgzɑ̃plɛʀ] *nm* copy

exemple [ɛgzɑ̃pl(ə)] *nm* example; **par ~** for instance, for example; **donner l'~** to set an example; **prendre ~ sur** to take as a model; **à l'~ de** just like

exempt, e [ɛgzɑ̃, -ɑ̃t] *adj*: **~ de** *(dispensé de)* exempt from; *(sans)* free from

exercer [ɛgzɛʀse] *vt (pratiquer)* to exercise, practise; *(prérogative)* to exercise; *(influence, contrôle)* to exert; *(former)* to exercise, train; **s'~** *vi (sportif, musicien)* to practise; *(se faire sentir: pression etc)* to be exerted

exercice [ɛgzɛʀsis] *nm (tâche, travail)* exercise; **l'~** exercise; *(MIL)* drill; **en ~** *(juge)* in office; *(médecin)* practising

exhaustif, ive [ɛgzostif, -iv] *adj* exhaustive

exhiber [ɛgzibe] *vt (montrer: papiers, certifi-*

cat) to present, produce; *(péj)* to display, flaunt; **s'~** *vi* to parade; *(suj: exhibitionniste)* to expose o.s.

exhorter [ɛgzɔʀte] *vt* to urge

exigeant, e [ɛgziʒɑ̃, -ɑ̃t] *adj* demanding; *(péj)* hard to please

exigence [ɛgziʒɑ̃s] *nf* demand, requirement

exiger [ɛgziʒe] *vt* to demand, require

exigu, ë [ɛgzigy] *adj (lieu)* cramped, tiny

exil [ɛgzil] *nm* exile; **exiler** *vt* to exile; **s'~er** *vi* to go into exile

existence [ɛgzistɑ̃s] *nf* existence

exister [ɛgziste] *vi* to exist; **il existe un/des** there is a/are (some)

exonérer [ɛgzɔneʀe] *vt*: **~ de** to exempt from

exorbitant, e [ɛgzɔʀbitɑ̃, -ɑ̃t] *adj (somme, nombre)* exorbitant

exorbité, e [ɛgzɔʀbite] *adj*: **yeux ~s** bulging eyes

exotique [ɛgzɔtik] *adj* exotic

expatrier [ɛkspatʀije] *vt*: **s'~** to leave one's country

expectative [ɛkspɛktativ] *nf*: **être dans l'~** to be still waiting

expédient [ɛkspedjɑ̃] *(péj) nm* expedient; **vivre d'~s** to live by one's wits

expédier [ɛkspedje] *vt (lettre, paquet)* to send; *(troupes)* to dispatch; *(péj: travail etc)* to dispose of, dispatch; **expéditeur, trice** *nm/f* sender

expédition [ɛkspedisjɔ̃] *nf* sending; *(scientifique, sportive, MIL)* expedition

expérience [ɛkspeʀjɑ̃s] *nf (de la vie)* experience; *(scientifique)* experiment

expérimenté, e [ɛkspeʀimɑ̃te] *adj* experienced

expérimenter [ɛkspeʀimɑ̃te] *vt* to test out, experiment with

expert, e [ɛkspɛʀ, -ɛʀt(ə)] *adj*, *nm* expert; **~ en assurances** insurance valuer; **expert-comptable** *nm* ≈ chartered accountant *(BRIT)*, ≈ certified public accountant *(US)*

expertise [ɛkspɛʀtiz] *nf* valuation; assessment; valuer's *(ou* assessor's) report; *(JUR)* (forensic) examination

expertiser [ɛkspɛʀtize] *vt (objet de valeur)* to value; *(voiture accidentée etc)* to assess damage to

expier [ɛkspje] *vt* to expiate, atone for

expirer [ɛkspiʀe] *vi (prendre fin, mourir)* to expire; *(respirer)* to breathe out

explicatif, ive [ɛksplikatif, -iv] *adj* explanatory

explication [ɛksplikɑsjɔ̃] *nf* explanation; *(discussion)* discussion; argument; **~ de texte** *(SCOL)* critical analysis

explicite [ɛksplisit] *adj* explicit

expliquer [ɛksplike] *vt* to explain; **s'~** to explain (o.s.); *(discuter)* to discuss things; to have it out; **son erreur s'explique** one can understand his mistake

exploit [ɛksplwa] *nm* exploit, feat

exploitation [ɛksplwatɑsjɔ̃] *nf* exploitation; running; ~ **agricole** farming concern; **exploiter** [ɛksplwate] *vt* (*mine*) to exploit, work; (*entreprise, ferme*) to run, operate; (*clients, ouvriers, erreur, don*) to exploit

explorer [ɛksplɔʀe] *vt* to explore

exploser [ɛksploze] *vi* to explode, blow up; (*engin explosif*) to go off; (*fig: joie, colère*) to burst out, explode; **explosif, ive** *adj, nm* explosive; **explosion** *nf* explosion

exportateur, trice [ɛkspɔʀtatœʀ, -tʀis] *adj* export *cpd*, exporting ♦ *nm* exporter

exportation [ɛkspɔʀtɑsjɔ̃] *nf* exportation; export

exporter [ɛkspɔʀte] *vt* to export

exposant [ɛkspozɑ̃] *nm* exhibitor

exposé, e [ɛkspoze] *nm* talk ♦ *adj*: ~ **au sud** facing south; **bien** ~ well situated

exposer [ɛkspoze] *vt* (*marchandise*) to display; (*peinture*) to exhibit, show; (*parler de*) to explain, set out; (*mettre en danger, orienter, PHOTO*) to expose; **exposition** *nf* (*manifestation*) exhibition; (*PHOTO*) exposure

exprès[1] [ɛkspʀɛ] *adv* (*délibérément*) on purpose; (*spécialement*) specially

exprès[2]**, esse** [ɛkspʀɛs] *adj* (*ordre, défense*) express, formal ♦ *adj inv* (*PTT*) express ♦ *adv* express

express [ɛkspʀɛs] *adj, nm*: (**café**) ~ espresso (coffee); (**train**) ~ fast train

expressément [ɛkspʀɛsemɑ̃] *adv* expressly; specifically

expression [ɛkspʀɛsjɔ̃] *nf* expression

exprimer [ɛkspʀime] *vt* (*sentiment, idée*) to express; (*jus, liquide*) to press out; **s'**~ *vi* (*personne*) to express o.s.

exproprier [ɛkspʀɔpʀije] *vt* to buy up by compulsory purchase, expropriate

expulser [ɛkspylse] *vt* to expel; (*locataire*) to evict; (*SPORT*) to send off

exquis, e [ɛkski, -iz] *adj* exquisite; delightful

exsangue [ɛksɑ̃g] *adj* bloodless, drained of blood

extase [ɛkstɑz] *nf* ecstasy; **extasier**: **s'extasier** *vi* to go into raptures over

extension [ɛkstɑ̃sjɔ̃] *nf* (*d'un muscle, ressort*) stretching; (*fig*) extension; expansion

exténuer [ɛkstenɥe] *vt* to exhaust

extérieur, e [ɛksteʀjœʀ] *adj* (*porte, mur etc*) outer, outside; (*au dehors: escalier, w.-c*) outside; (*commerce*) foreign; (*influences*) external; (*apparent: calme, gaieté etc*) surface *cpd* ♦ *nm* (*d'une maison, d'un récipient etc*) outside, exterior; (*apparence*) exterior; (*d'un groupe social*) **l'**~ the outside world; **à l'**~ outside; (*à l'étranger*) abroad; **extérieurement** *adv* on the outside; (*en apparence*) on the surface

exterminer [ɛkstɛʀmine] *vt* to exterminate, wipe out

externat [ɛkstɛʀna] *nm* day school

externe [ɛkstɛʀn(ə)] *adj* external, outer ♦ *nm/f* (*MÉD*) non-resident medical student (*BRIT*), extern (*US*); (*SCOL*) day pupil

extincteur [ɛkstɛ̃ktœʀ] *nm* (fire) extinguisher

extinction [ɛkstɛ̃ksjɔ̃] *nf*: ~ **de voix** loss of voice

extorquer [ɛkstɔʀke] *vt* to extort

extra [ɛkstʀa] *adj inv* first-rate; top-quality ♦ *nm inv* extra help

extrader [ɛkstʀade] *vt* to extradite

extraire [ɛkstʀɛʀ] *vt* to extract; **extrait** *nm* extract

extraordinaire [ɛkstʀaɔʀdinɛʀ] *adj* extraordinary; (*POL: mesures etc*) special

extravagant, e [ɛkstʀavagɑ̃, -ɑ̃t] *adj* extravagant; wild

extraverti, e [ɛkstʀavɛʀti] *adj* extrovert

extrême [ɛkstʀɛm] *adj, nm* extreme; **extrêmement** *adv* extremely; **extrême-onction** *nf* last rites *pl*; **Extrême-Orient** *nm* Far East

extrémité [ɛkstʀemite] *nf* end; (*situation*) straits *pl*, plight; (*geste désespéré*) extreme action; ~**s** *nfpl* (*pieds et mains*) extremities; **à la dernière** ~ on the point of death

exutoire [ɛgzytwaʀ] *nm* outlet, release

F f

F *abr* = **franc**

fa [fa] *nm inv* (*MUS*) F; (*en chantant la gamme*) fa

fable [fɑbl(ə)] *nf* fable

fabricant [fabʀikɑ̃] *nm* manufacturer

fabrication [fabʀikɑsjɔ̃] *nf* manufacture

fabrique [fabʀik] *nf* factory

fabriquer [fabʀike] *vt* to make; (*industriellement*) to manufacture; (*fig*): **qu'est-ce qu'il fabrique?** what is he doing?

fabulation [fabylɑsjɔ̃] *nf* fantasizing

fac [fak] (*fam*) *abr f* (*SCOL*) = **faculté**

façade [fasad] *nf* front, façade

face [fas] *nf* face; (*fig: aspect*) side ♦ *adj*: **le côté** ~ heads; **perdre la** ~ to lose face; **en** ~ **de** opposite; (*fig*) in front of; **de** ~ from the front; face on; ~ **à** facing; (*fig*) faced with, in the face of; **faire** ~ **à** to face; ~ **à** ~ *adv* facing each other ♦ *nm inv* encounter

facétieux, euse [fasesjø, -øz] *adj* mischievous

fâché, e [fɑʃe] *adj* angry; (*désolé*) sorry

fâcher [fɑʃe] *vt* to anger; **se ~** *vi* to get angry; **se ~ avec** (*se brouiller*) to fall out with

fâcheux, euse [fɑʃø, -øz] *adj* unfortunate, regrettable

facile [fasil] *adj* easy; (*accommodant*) easygoing; **~ment** *adv* easily; **facilité** *nf* easiness; (*disposition, don*) aptitude; **facilités** *nfpl* (*possibilités*) facilities; **facilités de paiement** easy terms; **faciliter** *vt* to make easier

façon [fasɔ̃] *nf* (*manière*) way; (*d'une robe etc*) making-up; cut; **~s** *nfpl* (*péj*) fuss *sg*; **de quelle ~?** (in) what way?; **de ~ à/à ce que** so as to/that; **de toute ~** anyway, in any case; **~ner** [fasɔne] *vt* (*fabriquer*) to manufacture; (*travailler: matière*) to shape, fashion; (*fig*) to mould, shape

facteur, trice [faktœʀ, -tʀis] *nm/f* postman(woman) (*BRIT*), mailman(woman) (*US*) *nm* (*MATH, fig: élément*) factor; **~ de pianos** piano maker

factice [faktis] *adj* artificial

faction [faksjɔ̃] *nf* faction; (*MIL*) guard *ou* sentry (duty); watch

facture [faktyʀ] *nf* (*à payer: gén*) bill; (*COMM*) invoice; (*d'un artisan, artiste*) technique, workmanship; **facturer** *vt* to invoice

facultatif, ive [fakyltatif, -iv] *adj* optional; (*arrêt de bus*) request *cpd*

faculté [fakylte] *nf* (*intellectuelle, d'université*) faculty; (*pouvoir, possibilité*) power

fade [fad] *adj* insipid

faible [fɛbl(ə)] *adj* weak; (*voix, lumière, vent*) faint; (*rendement, intensité, revenu etc*) low *nm* weak point; (*pour quelqu'un*) weakness, soft spot; **~ d'esprit** feebleminded; **faiblesse** *nf* weakness; **faiblir** *vi* to weaken; (*lumière*) to dim; (*vent*) to drop

faïence [fajɑ̃s] *nf* earthenware *no pl*; piece of earthenware

faignant, e [fɛɲɑ̃, -ɑ̃t] *nm/f* = **fainéant, e**

faille [faj] *vb voir* **falloir** *nf* (*GÉO*) fault; (*fig*) flaw, weakness

faillir [fajiʀ] *vi*: **j'ai failli tomber** I almost *ou* very nearly fell

faillite [fajit] *nf* bankruptcy

faim [fɛ̃] *nf* hunger; **avoir ~** to be hungry; **rester sur sa ~** (*aussi fig*) to be left wanting more

fainéant, e [fɛneɑ̃, -ɑ̃t] *nm/f* idler, loafer

──────── MOT CLÉ ────────

faire [fɛʀ] *vt* **1** (*fabriquer, être l'auteur de*) to make; **~ du vin/une offre/un film** to make wine/an offer/a film; **~ du bruit** to make a noise

2 (*effectuer: travail, opération*) to do; **que faites-vous?** (*quel métier etc*) what do you do?; (*quelle activité: au moment de la question*) what are you doing?; **~ la lessive** to do the washing

3 (*études*) to do; (*sport, musique*) to play; **~ du droit/du français** to do law/French; **~ du rugby/piano** to play rugby/the piano

4 (*simuler*): **~ le malade/l'ignorant** to act the invalid/the fool

5 (*transformer, avoir un effet sur*): **~ de qn un frustré/avocat** to make sb frustrated/a lawyer; **ça ne me fait rien** (*m'est égal*) I don't care *ou* mind; (*me laisse froid*) it has no effect on me; **ça ne fait rien** it doesn't matter; **~ que** (*impliquer*) to mean that

6 (*calculs, prix, mesures*): **2 et 2 font 4** 2 and 2 are *ou* make 4; **ça fait 10 m/15F** it's 10 m/15F; **je vous le fais 10F** I'll let you have it for 10F

7: **qu'a-t-il fait de sa valise?** what has he done with his case?

8: **ne ~ que**: **il ne fait que critiquer** (*sans cesse*) all he (ever) does is criticize; (*seulement*) he's only criticizing

9 (*dire*) to say; **vraiment? fit-il** really? he said

10 (*maladie*) to have; **~ du diabète** to have diabetes *sg*

vi **1** (*agir, s'y prendre*) to act, do; **il faut ~ vite** (*ou you etc*) must act quickly; **comment a-t-il fait pour?** how did he manage to?; **faites comme chez vous** make yourself at home

2 (*paraître*) to look; **~ vieux/démodé** to look old/old-fashioned; **ça fait bien** it looks good

vb substitut to do; **ne le casse pas comme je l'ai fait** don't break it as I did; **je peux le voir? - faites!** can I see it? - please do!

vb impers **1**: **il fait beau** *etc* the weather is fine *etc*; *voir aussi* **jour froid** *etc*

2 (*temps écoulé, durée*): **ça fait 2 ans qu'il est parti** it's 2 years since he left; **ça fait 2 ans qu'il y est** he's been there for 2 years

vb semi-aux **1**: **~ +infinitif** (*action directe*) to make; **~ tomber/bouger qch** to make sth fall/move; **~ démarrer un moteur/chauffer de l'eau** to start up an engine/heat some water; **cela fait dormir** it makes you sleep; **~ travailler les enfants** to make the children work *ou* get the children to work

2 (*indirectement, par un intermédiaire*): **~ réparer qch** to get *ou* have sth repaired; **~ punir les enfants** to have the children punished **se** *vi* **1** (*vin, fromage*) to mature

2: **cela se fait beaucoup/ne se fait pas** it's done a lot/not done

3: **se ~ +nom ou pron**: **se faire une jupe** to make o.s. a skirt; **se ~ des amis** to make friends; **se ~ du souci** to worry; **il**

ne s'en fait pas he doesn't worry
4: se ~ vieux (*devenir*): **se faire vieux** to be
getting old; (*délibérément*): **se ~ beau** to
do o.s. up
5: **se ~ à** (*s'habituer*) to get used to; **je
n'arrive pas à me ~ à la nourriture/au climat** I can't get used to the food/climate
6: **se ~ +***infinitif*: **se ~ examiner la vue/
opérer** to have one's eyes tested/have an
operation; **se ~ couper les cheveux** to get
one's hair cut; **il va se ~ tuer/punir** he's
going to get himself killed/get (himself) punished; **il s'est fait aider** he got somebody
to help him; **il s'est fait aider par Simon**
he got Simon to help him; **se ~ ~
un vêtement** to get a garment made for
o.s.
7 (*impersonnel*): **comment se fait-il/
faisait-il que?** how is it/was it that?

faire-part [fɛʀpaʀ] *nm inv* announcement
(*of birth, marriage etc*)
faisable [fəzabl(ə)] *adj* feasible
faisan, e [fəzɑ̃, -an] *nm/f* pheasant
faisandé, e [fəzɑ̃de] *adj* high (*bad*)
faisceau, x [fɛso] *nm* (*de lumière etc*)
beam; (*de branches etc*) bundle
faisons *vb voir* **faire**
fait, e [fɛ, fɛt] *adj* (*mûr: fromage, melon*)
ripe ♦ *nm* (*événement*) event, occurrence;
(*réalité, donnée*) fact; **c'en est ~ de** that's
the end of; **être le ~ de** (*causé par*) to be
the work of; **être au ~ (de)** to be informed
(of); **au ~** (*à propos*) by the way; **en venir
au ~** to get to the point; **de ~** *adj* (*opposé
à: de droit*) de facto ♦ *adv* in fact; **du ~ de
ceci/qu'il a menti** because of *ou* on account of this/his having lied; **de ce ~** for
this reason; **en ~** in fact; **en ~ de repas**
by way of a meal; **prendre ~ et cause
pour qn** to support sb, side with sb; **prendre qn sur le ~** to catch sb in the act; ~
divers news item; ~**s et gestes: les ~s et
gestes de qn** sb's actions *ou* doings
faîte [fɛt] *nm* top; (*fig*) pinnacle, height
faites *vb voir* **faire**
faitout [fɛtu] *nm* = **fait-tout**
fait-tout [fɛtu] *nm inv* stewpot
falaise [falɛz] *nf* cliff
fallacieux, euse [falasjø, -øz] *adj* falla-
cious; deceptive; illusory
falloir [falwaʀ] *vb impers*: **il va ~ 100 F**
we'll (*ou* I'll) need 100 F; **s'en ~: il s'en
est fallu de 100 F/5 minutes** we (*ou* they)
were 100 F short/5 minutes late (*ou* early);
il s'en faut de beaucoup qu'il soit he is
far from being; **il s'en est fallu de peu que
cela n'arrive** it very nearly happened; **ou
peu s'en faut** or as good as; **il doit ~ du
temps** that must take time; **il me faudrait
100 F** I would need 100 F; **il vous faut
tourner à gauche après l'église** you have

to turn left past the church; **nous avons ce
qu'il (nous) faut** we have what we need; **il
faut qu'il parte/a fallu qu'il parte** (*obligation*) he has to *ou* must leave/had to leave;
il a fallu le faire it had to be done
falsifier [falsifje] *vt* to falsify; to doctor
famé, e [fame] *adj*: **mal ~** disreputable, of
ill repute
famélique [famelik] *adj* half-starved
fameux, euse [famø, -øz] *adj* (*illustre*) famous; (*bon: repas, plat etc*) first-rate, first-
class; (*valeur intensive*) real, downright
familial, e, aux [familjal, -o] *adj* family
cpd; **familiale** *nf* (*AUTO*) estate car (*BRIT*),
station wagon (*US*)
familiarité [familjaʀite] *nf* informality; fa-
miliarity; ~**s** *nfpl* (*privautés*) familiarities
familier, ère [familje, -ɛʀ] *adj* (*connu, impertinent*) familiar; (*dénotant une certaine intimité*) informal, friendly; (*LING*) informal,
colloquial ♦ *nm* regular (*visitor*)
famille [famij] *nf* family; **il a de la ~ à Paris** he has relatives in Paris
famine [famin] *nf* famine
fanatique [fanatik] *adj* fanatical ♦ *nm/f* fanatic; **fanatisme** *nm* fanaticism
faner [fane]: **se ~** *vi* to fade
fanfare [fɑ̃faʀ] *nf* (*orchestre*) brass band;
(*musique*) fanfare
fanfaron, ne [fɑ̃faʀɔ̃, -ɔn] *nm/f* braggart
fanion [fanjɔ̃] *nm* pennant
fantaisie [fɑ̃tezi] *nf* (*spontanéité*) fancy,
imagination; (*caprice*) whim; extravagance ♦
adj: **bijou/pain (de) ~** costume jewellery/
fancy bread; **fantaisiste** *adj* (*péj*) unorthodox, eccentric ♦ *nm/f* (*de music-hall*) variety
artist *ou* entertainer
fantasme [fɑ̃tasm(ə)] *nm* fantasy
fantasque [fɑ̃task(ə)] *adj* whimsical, capricious; fantastic
fantastique [fɑ̃tastik] *adj* fantastic
fantôme [fɑ̃tom] *nm* ghost, phantom
faon [fɑ̃] *nm* fawn
farce [faʀs(ə)] *nf* (*viande*) stuffing; (*blague*)
(practical) joke; (*THÉÂTRE*) farce; **farcir** *vt*
(*viande*) to stuff
fard [faʀ] *nm* make-up
fardeau, x [faʀdo] *nm* burden
farder [faʀde] *vt* to make up
farfelu, e [faʀfəly] *adj* hare-brained
farine [faʀin] *nf* flour; **farineux, euse** *adj*
(*sauce, pomme*) floury ♦ *nmpl* (*aliments*)
starchy foods
farouche [faʀuʃ] *adj* shy, timid; savage,
wild; fierce
fart [faʀ(t)] *nm* (ski) wax
fascicule [fasikyl] *nm* volume
fasciner [fasine] *vt* to fascinate
fascisme [faʃism(ə)] *nm* fascism
fasse *etc vb voir* **faire**
faste [fast(ə)] *nm* splendour ♦ *adj*: **c'est un
jour ~** it's his (*ou* our *etc*) lucky day

fastidieux, euse [fastidjø, -øz] *adj* tedious, tiresome

fastueux, euse [fastɥø, -øz] *adj* sumptuous, luxurious

fatal, e [fatal] *adj* fatal; (*inévitable*) inevitable; **fatalité** *nf* fate; fateful coincidence; inevitability

fatidique [fatidik] *adj* fateful

fatigant, e [fatigɑ̃, -ɑ̃t] *adj* tiring; (*agaçant*) tiresome

fatigue [fatig] *nf* tiredness, fatigue

fatigué, e [fatige] *adj* tired

fatiguer [fatige] *vt* to tire, make tired; (*TECH*) to put a strain on, strain; (*fig: importuner*) to wear out ♦ *vi* (*moteur*) to labour, strain; **se ~** to get tired; to tire o.s. (out)

fatras [fatra] *nm* jumble, hotchpotch

fatuité [fatɥite] *nf* conceitedness, smugness

faubourg [fobur] *nm* suburb

fauché, e [foʃe] *adj* (*fam*) broke

faucher [foʃe] *vt* (*herbe*) to cut; (*champs, blés*) to reap; (*fig*) to cut down; to mow down

faucille [fosij] *nf* sickle

faucon [fokɔ̃] *nm* falcon, hawk

faudra *vb voir* **falloir**

faufiler [fofile] *vt* to tack, baste; **se ~** *vi*: **se ~ dans** to edge one's way into; **se ~ parmi/entre** to thread one's way among/between

faune [fon] *nf* (*ZOOL*) wildlife, fauna

faussaire [fosɛr] *nm* forger

fausse [fos] *adj voir* **faux**

faussement [fosmɑ̃] *adv* (*accuser*) wrongly, wrongfully; (*croire*) falsely

fausser [fose] *vt* (*objet*) to bend, buckle; (*fig*) to distort

fausseté [foste] *nf* wrongness; falseness

faut *vb voir* **falloir**

faute [fot] *nf* (*erreur*) mistake, error; (*péché, manquement*) misdemeanour; (*FOOTBALL etc*) offence; (*TENNIS*) fault; **c'est de sa/ma ~** it's his/my fault; **être en ~** to be in the wrong; **~ de** (*temps, argent*) for *ou* through lack of; **sans ~** without fail; **~ de frappe** typing error; **~ professionnelle** professional misconduct *no pl*

fauteuil [fotœj] *nm* armchair; **~ d'orchestre** seat in the front stalls; **~ roulant** wheelchair

fauteur [fotœr] *nm*: **~ de troubles** trouble-maker

fautif, ive [fotif, -iv] *adj* (*incorrect*) incorrect, inaccurate; (*responsable*) at fault, in the wrong; guilty

fauve [fov] *nm* wildcat ♦ *adj* (*couleur*) fawn

faux¹ [fo] *nf* scythe

faux², fausse [fo, fos] *adj* (*inexact*) wrong; (*piano, voix*) out of tune; (*falsifié*) fake; forged; (*sournois, postiche*) false ♦ *adv* (*MUS*) out of tune ♦ *nm* (*copie*) fake, forgery; (*opposé au vrai*): **le faux** falsehood; **faire faux bond à qn** to stand sb up; **fausse alerte** false alarm; **fausse couche** miscarriage; **faux frais** *nmpl* extras, incidental expenses; **faux pas** tripping *no pl*; (*fig*) faux pas; **faux témoignage** (*délit*) perjury; **faux-filet** *nm* sirloin; **faux-fuyant** *nm* equivocation; **faux-monnayeur** *nm* counterfeiter, forger

faveur [favœr] *nf* favour; **traitement de ~** preferential treatment; **à la ~ de** under cover of; thanks to; **en ~ de** in favour of

favorable [favɔrabl(ə)] *adj* favourable

favori, te [favɔri, -it] *adj, nm/f* favourite; **~s** *nmpl* (*barbe*) sideboards (*BRIT*), sideburns

favoriser [favɔrize] *vt* to favour

fax [faks] *nm* fax

fébrile [febril] *adj* feverish, febrile

fécond, e [fekɔ̃, -ɔ̃d] *adj* fertile; **~er** *vt* to fertilize; **~ité** *nf* fertility

fécule [fekyl] *nf* potato flour

féculent [fekylɑ̃] *nm* starchy food

fédéral, e, aux [federal, -o] *adj* federal

fée [fe] *nf* fairy; **~rie** *nf* enchantment; **~rique** *adj* magical, fairytale *cpd*

feignant, e [fɛɲɑ̃, -ɑ̃t] *nm/f* = **fainéant, e**

feindre [fɛ̃dr(ə)] *vt* to feign ♦ *vi* to dissemble; **~ de faire** to pretend to do

feinte [fɛ̃t] *nf* (*SPORT*) dummy

fêler [fele] *vt* to crack

félicitations [felisitasjɔ̃] *nfpl* congratulations

féliciter [felisite] *vt*: **~ qn (de)** to congratulate sb (on); **se ~ (de)** to congratulate o.s. (on)

félin, e [felɛ̃, -in] *adj* feline ♦ *nm* (big) cat

fêlure [felyr] *nf* crack

femelle [fəmɛl] *adj, nf* female

féminin, e [feminɛ̃, -in] *adj* feminine; (*sexe*) female; (*équipe, vêtements etc*) women's ♦ *nm* (*LING*) feminine; **féministe** *adj* feminist

femme [fam] *nf* woman; (*épouse*) wife; **~ au foyer** *nf* housewife; **~ de chambre** cleaning lady; **~ de ménage** = femme de chambre

fémur [femyr] *nm* femur, thighbone

fendre [fɑ̃dr(ə)] *vt* (*couper en deux*) to split; (*fissurer*) to crack; (*fig: traverser*) to cut through; to cleave through; **se ~** *vi* to cleave through; to crack

fenêtre [fənɛtr(ə)] *nf* window

fenouil [fənuj] *nm* fennel

fente [fɑ̃t] *nf* (*fissure*) crack; (*de boîte à lettres etc*) slit

féodal, e, aux [feɔdal, -o] *adj* feudal

fer [fɛr] *nm* iron; (*de cheval*) shoe; **~ à cheval** horseshoe; **~ (à repasser)** iron; **~ forgé** wrought iron

ferai *etc vb voir* **faire**

fer-blanc [fɛrblɑ̃] *nm* tin(plate)

férié, e [feʀje] *adj:* **jour** ~ public holiday
ferions *etc vb voir* **faire**
ferme [fɛʀm(ə)] *adj* firm ♦ *adv* (*travailler etc*) hard ♦ *nf* (*exploitation*) farm; (*maison*) farmhouse
fermé, e [fɛʀme] *adj* closed, shut; (*gaz, eau etc*) off; (*fig: personne*) uncommunicative; (: *milieu*) exclusive
fermenter [fɛʀmɑ̃te] *vi* to ferment
fermer [fɛʀme] *vt* to close, shut; (*cesser l'exploitation de*) to close down, shut down; (*eau, lumière, électricité, robinet*) to put off, turn off; (*aéroport, route*) to close ♦ *vi* to close, shut; to close down, shut down; **se** ~ *vi* (*yeux*) to close, shut; (*fleur, blessure*) to close up
fermeté [fɛʀməte] *nf* firmness
fermeture [fɛʀmətyʀ] *nf* closing; shutting; closing *ou* shutting down; putting *ou* turning off; (*dispositif*) catch; fastening, fastener; ~ **à glissière** = **fermeture éclair**; ~ **éclair**Ⓡ zip (fastener) (*BRIT*), zipper (*US*)
fermier [fɛʀmje] *nm* farmer; **fermière** *nf* woman farmer; farmer's wife
fermoir [fɛʀmwaʀ] *nm* clasp
féroce [feʀɔs] *adj* ferocious, fierce
ferons *vb voir* **faire**
ferraille [feʀɑj] *nf* scrap iron; **mettre à la** ~ to scrap
ferré, e [feʀe] *adj* hobnailed; steel-tipped; (*fam*): ~ **en** well up on, hot at; **ferrer** [feʀe] *vt* (*cheval*) to shoe
ferronnerie [feʀɔnʀi] *nf* ironwork
ferroviaire [feʀɔvjɛʀ] *adj* rail(way) *cpd* (*BRIT*), rail(road) *cpd* (*US*)
ferry(boat) [feʀe(bɔt)] *nm* ferry
fertile [fɛʀtil] *adj* fertile; ~ **en incidents** eventful, packed with incidents
féru, e [feʀy] *adj:* ~ **de** with a keen interest in
férule [feʀyl] *nf:* **être sous la** ~ **de qn** to be under sb's (iron) rule
fervent, e [fɛʀvɑ̃, -ɑ̃t] *adj* fervent
fesse [fɛs] *nf* buttock; **fessée** *nf* spanking
festin [fɛstɛ̃] *nm* feast
festival [fɛstival] *nm* festival
festoyer [fɛstwaje] *vi* to feast
fêtard [fɛtaʀ] (*péj*) *nm* high liver, merry-maker
fête [fɛt] *nf* (*religieuse*) feast; (*publique*) holiday; (*en famille etc*) celebration; (*kermesse*) fête, fair, festival; (*du nom*) feast day, name day; **faire la** ~ to live it up; **faire** ~ **à qn** to give sb a warm welcome; **les** ~**s** (**de fin d'année**) the festive season; **la salle/le comité des** ~**s** the village hall/festival committee; ~ **foraine** (fun)fair; **la F**~ **Nationale** the national holiday; **fêter** *vt* to celebrate; (*personne*) to have a celebration for
fétu [fety] *nm:* ~ **de paille** wisp of straw
feu, x [fø] *nm* (*gén*) fire; (*signal lumineux*) light; (*de cuisinière*) ring; (*sensation de brûlure*) burning (sensation) ♦ *adj inv:* ~ **son père** his late father; ~**x** *nmpl* (*éclat, lumière*) fire *sg*; (*AUTO*) (traffic) lights; **au** ~**!** (*incendie*) fire!; **à** ~ **doux/vif** over a slow/brisk heat; **à petit** ~ (*CULIN*) over a gentle heat; (*fig*) slowly; **faire** ~ to fire; **prendre** ~ to catch fire; **mettre le** ~ **à** to set fire to; **faire du** ~ to make a fire; **avez-vous du** ~**?** (*pour cigarette*) have you (got) a light?; ~ **arrière** rear light; ~ **d'artifice** firework; (*spectacle*) fireworks *pl*; ~ **de joie** bonfire; ~ **rouge/vert/orange** red/green/amber (*BRIT*) *ou* yellow (*US*) light; ~**x de brouillard** fog-lamps; ~**x de croisement** dipped (*BRIT*) *ou* dimmed (*US*) headlights; ~**x de position** sidelights; ~**x de route** headlights
feuillage [fœjaʒ] *nm* foliage, leaves *pl*
feuille [fœj] *nf* (*d'arbre*) leaf; (*de papier*) sheet; ~ **d'impôts** tax form; ~ **de maladie** medical expenses claim form; ~ **de paie** pay slip; ~ **de vigne** (*BOT*) vine leaf; (*sur statue*) fig leaf; ~ **volante** loose sheet
feuillet [fœjɛ] *nm* leaf
feuilleté, e [fœjte] *adj* (*CULIN*) flaky; (*verre*) laminated
feuilleter [fœjte] *vt* (*livre*) to leaf through
feuilleton [fœjtɔ̃] *nm* serial
feuillu, e [fœjy] *adj* leafy ♦ *nm* broad-leaved tree
feutre [føtʀ(ə)] *nm* felt; (*chapeau*) felt hat; (*aussi: stylo-*~) felt-tip pen; **feutré, e** *adj* feltlike; (*pas, voix*) muffled
fève [fɛv] *nf* broad bean
février [fevʀije] *nm* February
fi [fi] *excl:* **faire** ~ **de** to snap one's fingers at
fiable [fjabl(ə)] *adj* reliable
fiacre [fjakʀ(ə)] *nm* (hackney) cab *ou* carriage
fiançailles [fjɑ̃sɑj] *nfpl* engagement *sg*
fiancé, e [fjɑ̃se] *nm/f* fiancé(fiancée) ♦ *adj:* **être** ~ (**à**) to be engaged (to)
fiancer [fjɑ̃se]: **se** ~ *vi* to become engaged
fibre [fibʀ(ə)] *nf* fibre; ~ **de verre** fibreglass, glass fibre
ficeler [fisle] *vt* to tie up
ficelle [fisɛl] *nf* string *no pl*; piece *ou* length of string
fiche [fiʃ] *nf* (*pour fichier*) (index) card; (*formulaire*) form; (*ÉLEC*) plug
ficher [fiʃe] *vt* (*dans un fichier*) to file; (*POLICE*) to put on file; (*planter*) to stick, drive; (*fam*) to do; to give; to stick *ou* shove; **se** ~ **de** (*fam*) to make fun of; not to care about; **fiche-(moi) le camp** (*fam*) clear off; **fiche-moi la paix** leave me alone
fichier [fiʃje] *nm* file; card index
fichu, e [fiʃy] *pp de* **ficher** (*fam*) ♦ *adj* (*fam:* *fini, inutilisable*) bust, done for; (: *intensif*) wretched, darned ♦ *nm* (*foulard*)

(head)scarf; **mal** ~ *(fam)* feeling lousy; useless

fictif, ive [fiktif, -iv] *adj* fictitious

fiction [fiksjɔ̃] *nf* fiction; *(fait imaginé)* invention

fidèle [fidɛl] *adj* faithful ♦ *nm/f* (REL): **les** ~**s** the faithful *pl*; *(à l'église)* the congregation *sg*

fief [fjɛf] *nm* fief; *(fig)* preserve; stronghold

fier¹ [fje]: **se fier à** *vt* to trust

fier², fière [fjɛr] *adj* proud; **fierté** *nf* pride

fièvre [fjɛvʀ(ə)] *nf* fever; **avoir de la** ~**/39 de** ~ to have a high temperature/a temperature of 39°C; **fiévreux, euse** *adj* feverish

figer [fiʒe] *vt* to congeal; *(fig: personne)* to freeze, root to the spot; **se** ~ *vi* to congeal; to freeze; *(institutions etc)* to become set, stop evolving

figue [fig] *nf* fig; **figuier** *nm* fig tree

figurant, e [figyʀɑ̃, -ɑ̃t] *nm/f* (THÉÂTRE) walk-on; (CINÉMA) extra

figure [figyʀ] *nf* (*visage*) face; *(image, tracé, forme, personnage)* figure; *(illustration)* picture, diagram; **faire** ~ **de** to look like

figuré, e [figyʀe] *adj* (*sens*) figurative

figurer [figyʀe] *vi* to appear ♦ *vt* to represent; **se** ~ **que** to imagine that

fil [fil] *nm* (*brin, fig: d'une histoire*) thread; *(du téléphone)* cable, wire; *(textile de lin)* linen; *(d'un couteau)* edge; **au** ~ **des années** with the passing of the years; **au** ~ **de l'eau** with the stream *ou* current; **coup de** ~ phone call; ~ **à coudre** (sewing) thread; ~ **à pêche** fishing line; ~ **à plomb** plumbline; ~ **de fer** wire; ~ **de fer barbelé** barbed wire; ~ **électrique** electric wire

filament [filamɑ̃] *nm* (ÉLEC) filament; *(de liquide)* trickle, thread

filandreux, euse [filɑ̃dʀø, -øz] *adj* stringy

filasse [filas] *adj inv* white blond

filature [filatyʀ] *nf* (*fabrique*) mill; *(policière)* shadowing *no pl*, tailing *no pl*

file [fil] *nf* line; (AUTO) lane; **en** ~ **indienne** in single file; **à la** ~ *(d'affilée)* in succession; ~ **(d'attente)** queue (BRIT), line (US)

filer [file] *vt* (*tissu, toile*) to spin; *(prendre en filature)* to shadow, tail; *(fam: donner)*: ~ **qch à qn** to slip sb sth ♦ *vi* (*bas, liquide, pâte*) to run; *(aller vite)* to fly past; *(fam: partir)* to make off; ~ **doux** to toe the line

filet [filɛ] *nm* net; (CULIN) fillet; *(d'eau, de sang)* trickle; ~ **(à provisions)** string bag

filiale [filjal] *nf* (COMM) subsidiary

filière [filjɛʀ] *nf*: **passer par la** ~ to go through the (administrative) channels; **suivre la** ~ *(dans sa carrière)* to work one's way up (through the hierarchy)

filiforme [filifɔʀm(ə)] *adj* spindly; threadlike

filigrane [filigʀan] *nm* (*d'un billet, timbre*) watermark; **en** ~ *(fig)* showing just beneath the surface

fille [fij] *nf* girl; *(opposé à fils)* daughter; **vieille** ~ old maid; **fillette** *nf* (little) girl

filleul, e [fijœl] *nm/f* godchild, godson/daughter

film [film] *nm* *(pour photo)* (roll of) film; *(œuvre)* film, picture, movie; *(couche)* film; ~ **d'animation** animated film; ~ **policier** thriller

filon [filɔ̃] *nm* vein, lode; *(fig)* lucrative line, money spinner

fils [fis] *nm* son; ~ **à papa** daddy's boy

filtre [filtʀ(ə)] *nm* filter; ~ **à air** (AUTO) air filter; **filtrer** *vt* to filter; *(fig: candidats, visiteurs)* to screen ♦ *vi* to filter (through)

fin¹ [fɛ̃] *nf* end; **fins** *nfpl* (*but*) ends; **prendre fin** to come to an end; **mettre fin à** to put an end to; **à la fin** in the end, eventually; **sans fin** *adj* endless ♦ *adv* endlessly

fin², e [fɛ̃, fin] *adj* (*papier, couche, fil*) thin; *(cheveux, poudre, pointe, visage)* fine; *(taille)* neat, slim; *(esprit, remarque)* subtle; shrewd ♦ *adv* (*moudre, couper*) finely; **un fin tireur** a crack shot; **avoir la vue/l'ouïe fine** to have sharp *ou* keen eyes/ears; **vin fin** fine wine; **fin gourmet** gourmet; **fin prêt** quite ready; **fines herbes** mixed herbs

final, e [final] *adj* final ♦ *nm* (MUS) finale; **finale** *nf* final; **quarts de finale** quarter finals; **8èmes/16èmes de finale** 2nd/1st round *(in knock-out competition)*; **finalement** *adv* finally, in the end; *(après tout)* after all

finance [finɑ̃s] *nf* finance; ~**s** *nfpl* (*situation*) finances; *(activités)* finance *sg*; **moyennant** ~ for a fee; **financer** *vt* to finance; **financier, ière** *adj* financial

finaud, e [fino, -od] *adj* wily

fine [fin] *nf* *(alcool)* liqueur brandy

finesse [fines] *nf* thinness; fineness; neatness, slimness; subtlety; shrewdness

fini, e [fini] *adj* finished; (MATH) finite; *(intensif)*: **un menteur** ~ a liar through and through ♦ *nm* *(d'un objet manufacturé)* finish

finir [finir] *vt* to finish ♦ *vi* to finish, end; ~ **quelque part/par faire** to end up *ou* finish up somewhere/doing; ~ **de faire** to finish doing; *(cesser)* to stop doing; **il finit par m'agacer** he's beginning to get on my nerves; ~ **en pointe/tragédie** to end in a point/in tragedy; **en** ~ **avec** to be *ou* have done with; **il va mal** ~ he will come to a bad end

finition [finisjɔ̃] *nf* finishing; finish

finlandais, e [fɛ̃lɑ̃dɛ, -ɛz] *adj* Finnish ♦ *nm/f*: **F**~, **e** Finn

Finlande [fɛ̃lɑ̃d] *nf*: **la** ~ Finland

fiole [fjɔl] *nf* phial

fioriture [fjɔʀityʀ] *nf* embellishment, flourish

firme [fiʀm(ə)] *nf* firm

fis vb voir **faire**

fisc [fisk] nm tax authorities pl; ~**al, e, aux** adj tax cpd, fiscal; ~**alité** nf tax system; (charges) taxation

fissure [fisyʀ] nf crack; ~**r** [fisyʀe] vt to crack; **se** ~**r** vi to crack

fiston [fistɔ̃] (fam) nm son, lad

fit vb voir **faire**

fixation [fiksɑsjɔ̃] nf fixing; fastening; setting; (de ski) binding; (PSYCH) fixation

fixe [fiks(ə)] adj fixed; (emploi) steady, regular ♦ nm (salaire) basic salary; **à heure** ~ at a set time; **menu à prix** ~ set menu

fixé, e [fikse] adj: **être** ~ (**sur**) (savoir à quoi s'en tenir) to have made up one's mind (about); to know for certain (about)

fixer [fikse] vt (attacher): ~ **qch (à/sur)** to fix ou fasten sth (to/onto); (déterminer) to fix, set; (CHIMIE, PHOTO) to fix; (regarder) to stare at; **se** ~ vi (s'établir) to settle down; **se** ~ **sur** (suj: attention) to focus on

flacon [flakɔ̃] nm bottle

flageller [flaʒele] vt to flog, scourge

flageoler [flaʒɔle] vi (jambes) to sag

flageolet [flaʒɔlɛ] nm (MUS) flageolet; (CULIN) dwarf kidney bean

flagrant, e [flagʀɑ̃, -ɑ̃t] adj flagrant, blatant; **en** ~ **délit** in the act

flair [flɛʀ] nm sense of smell; (fig) intuition; **flairer** vt (humer) to sniff (at); (détecter) to scent

flamand, e [flamɑ̃, -ɑ̃d] adj Flemish ♦ nm (LING) Flemish ♦ nm/f: **F~, e** Fleming; **les F~s** the Flemish

flamant [flamɑ̃] nm flamingo

flambant [flɑ̃bɑ̃] adv: ~ **neuf** brand new

flambé, e [flɑ̃be] adj (CULIN) flambé

flambeau, x [flɑ̃bo] nm (flaming) torch

flambée [flɑ̃be] nf blaze; (fig) flaring-up, explosion

flamber [flɑ̃be] vi to blaze (up)

flamboyer [flɑ̃bwaje] vi to blaze (up); to flame

flamme [flam] nf flame; (fig) fire, fervour; **en** ~**s** on fire, ablaze

flan [flɑ̃] nm (CULIN) custard tart ou pie

flanc [flɑ̃] nm side; (MIL) flank; **prêter le** ~ **à** (fig) to lay o.s. open to

flancher [flɑ̃ʃe] vi to fail, pack up; to quit

flanelle [flanɛl] nf flannel

flâner [flɑne] vi to stroll; **flânerie** nf stroll

flanquer [flɑ̃ke] vt to flank; (fam: mettre) to chuck, shove; (: jeter): ~ **par terre/à la porte** to fling to the ground/chuck out

flaque [flak] nf (d'eau) puddle; (d'huile, de sang etc) pool

flash [flaʃ] (pl **flashes**) nm (PHOTO) flash; ~ (**d'information**) newsflash

flasque [flask(ə)] adj flabby

flatter [flate] vt to flatter; **se** ~ **de qch** to pride o.s. on sth; **flatterie** nf flattery no pl; **flatteur, euse** adj flattering ♦ nm/f flatterer

fléau, x [fleo] nm scourge

flèche [flɛʃ] nf arrow; (de clocher) spire; (de grue) jib; **monter en** ~ (fig) to soar, rocket; **partir en** ~ to be off like a shot; **fléchette** nf dart; **fléchettes** nfpl (jeu) darts sg

fléchir [fleʃiʀ] vt (corps, genou) to bend; (fig) to sway, weaken ♦ vi (poutre) to sag, bend; (fig) to weaken, flag; to yield

flemmard, e [flemaʀ, -aʀd(ə)] nm/f lazybones sg, loafer

flétrir [fletʀiʀ] vt to wither; **se** ~ vi to wither

fleur [flœʀ] nf flower; (d'un arbre) blossom; **en** ~ (arbre) in blossom; **à** ~ **de terre** just above the ground

fleurer [flœʀe] vt: ~ **la lavande** to have the scent of lavender

fleuri, e [flœʀi] adj in flower ou bloom; surrounded by flowers; (fig) flowery; florid

fleurir [flœʀiʀ] vi (rose) to flower; (arbre) to blossom; (fig) to flourish ♦ vt (tombe) to put flowers on; (chambre) to decorate with flowers

fleuriste [flœʀist(ə)] nm/f florist

fleuron [flœʀɔ̃] nm (fig) jewel

fleuve [flœv] nm river

flexible [flɛksibl(ə)] adj flexible

flexion [flɛksjɔ̃] nf flexing, bending

flic [flik] (fam: péj) nm cop

flipper [flipœʀ] nm pinball (machine)

flirter [flœʀte] vi to flirt

flocon [flɔkɔ̃] nm flake

floraison [flɔʀɛzɔ̃] nf flowering; blossoming; flourishing

flore [flɔʀ] nf flora

florissant [flɔʀisɑ̃] vb voir **fleurir**

flot [flo] nm flood, stream; ~**s** nmpl (de la mer) waves; **être à** ~ (NAVIG) to be afloat; (fig) to be on an even keel; **entrer à** ~**s** to stream ou pour in

flotte [flɔt] nf (NAVIG) fleet; (fam) water; rain

flottement [flɔtmɑ̃] nm (fig) wavering, hesitation

flotter [flɔte] vi to float; (nuage, odeur) to drift; (drapeau) to fly; (vêtements) to hang loose; (monnaie) to float ♦ vt to float; **faire** ~ to float; **flotteur** nm float

flou, e [flu] adj fuzzy, blurred; (fig) woolly, vague

flouer [flue] vt to swindle

fluctuation [flyktɥasjɔ̃] nf fluctuation

fluet, te [flyɛ, -ɛt] adj thin, slight

fluide [flɥid] adj fluid; (circulation etc) flowing freely ♦ nm fluid; (force) (mysterious) power

fluor [flyɔʀ] nm fluorine

fluorescent, e [flyɔʀesɑ̃, -ɑ̃t] adj fluorescent

flûte [flyt] nf flute; (verre) flute glass; (pain) long loaf; ~**!** drat it!; ~ **à bec** recorder

flux [fly] *nm* incoming tide; (*écoulement*) flow; **le ~ et le reflux** the ebb and flow

FM *sigle f* (= *fréquence modulée*) FM

foc [fɔk] *nm* jib

foi [fwa] *nf* faith; **sous la ~ du serment** under *ou* on oath; **ajouter ~ à** to lend credence to; **digne de ~** reliable; **sur la ~ de** on the word *ou* strength of; **être de bonne/mauvaise ~** to be sincere/insincere; **ma ~ ... well ...**

foie [fwa] *nm* liver

foin [fwɛ̃] *nm* hay; **faire du ~** (*fig: fam*) to kick up a row

foire [fwaʀ] *nf* fair; (*fête foraine*) (fun) fair; **faire la ~** (*fig: fam*) to whoop it up; **~ (exposition)** trade fair

fois [fwa] *nf* time; **une/deux ~** once/twice; **2 ~ 2** times 2; **quatre ~ plus grand (que)** four times as big (as); **une ~ (passé)** once; (*futur*) sometime; **une ~ pour toutes** once and for all; **une ~ que** once; **des ~ (parfois)** sometimes; **à la ~ (ensemble)** at once

foison [fwazɔ̃] *nf*: **une ~ de** an abundance of; **à ~** in plenty

foisonner [fwazɔne] *vi* to abound

fol [fɔl] *adj voir* **fou**

folâtrer [fɔlɑtʀe] *vi* to frolic (about)

folie [fɔli] *nf* (*d'une décision, d'un acte*) madness, folly; (*état*) madness, insanity; (*acte*) folly; **la ~ des grandeurs** delusions of grandeur; **faire des ~s** (*en dépenses*) to be extravagant

folklorique [fɔlklɔʀik] *adj* folk *cpd*; (*fam*) weird

folle [fɔl] *adj, nf voir* **fou**; **follement** *adv* (*très*) madly, wildly

foncé, e [fɔ̃se] *adj* dark

foncer [fɔ̃se] *vi* to go darker; (*fam: aller vite*) to tear *ou* belt along; **~ sur** to charge at

foncier, ère [fɔ̃sje, -ɛʀ] *adj* (*honnêteté etc*) basic, fundamental; (*malhonnêteté*) deep-rooted; (*COMM*) real estate *cpd*

fonction [fɔ̃ksjɔ̃] *nf* (*rôle, MATH, LING*) function; (*emploi, poste*) post, position; **~s** *nfpl* (*professionnelles*) duties; **entrer en ~s** to take up one's post *ou* duties; to take up office; **voiture de ~** company car; **être ~ de** (*dépendre de*) to depend on; **en ~ de** (*par rapport à*) according to; **faire ~ de** to serve as; **la ~ publique** the state *ou* civil (*BRIT*) service; **fonctionnaire** [fɔ̃ksjɔnɛʀ] *nm/f* state employee, local authority employee; (*dans l'administration*) ≈ civil servant; **fonctionner** [fɔ̃ksjɔne] *vi* to work, function; (*entreprise*) to operate, function

fond [fɔ̃] *nm* (*d'un récipient, trou*) bottom; (*d'une salle, scène*) back; (*d'un tableau, décor*) background; (*opposé à la forme*) content; (*SPORT*): **le ~** long distance (running); **sans ~** bottomless; **au ~ de** at the bottom of; at the back of; **à ~** (*connaître, soutenir*) thoroughly; (*appuyer, visser*) right down *ou* home; **à ~ (de train)** (*fam*) full tilt; **dans le ~, au ~** (*en somme*) basically, really; **de ~ en comble** from top to bottom; *voir aussi* **fonds**; **~ de teint** (make-up) foundation; **~ sonore** background noise; background music

fondamental, e, aux [fɔ̃damɑ̃tal, -o] *adj* fundamental

fondant, e [fɔ̃dɑ̃, -ɑ̃t] *adj* (*neige*) melting; (*fruit*) that melts in the mouth

fondateur, trice [fɔ̃datœʀ, -tʀis] *nm/f* founder

fondation [fɔ̃dɑsjɔ̃] *nf* founding; (*établissement*) foundation; **~s** *nfpl* (*d'une maison*) foundations

fondé, e [fɔ̃de] *adj* (*accusation etc*) well-founded ♦ *nm*: **~ de pouvoir** authorized representative; **être ~ à** to have grounds for *ou* good reason to

fondement [fɔ̃dmɑ̃] *nm* (*derrière*) behind; **~s** *nmpl* (*base*) foundations; **sans ~** (*rumeur etc*) groundless, unfounded

fonder [fɔ̃de] *vt* to found; (*fig*) to base; **se ~ sur** (*suj: personne*) to base o.s. on

fonderie [fɔ̃dʀi] *nf* smelting works *sg*

fondre [fɔ̃dʀ(ə)] *vt* (*aussi: faire ~*) to melt; (*dans l'eau*) to dissolve; (*fig: mélanger*) to merge, blend ♦ *vi* to melt; to dissolve; (*fig*) to melt away; (*se précipiter*): **~ sur** to swoop down on; **~ en larmes** to burst into tears

fonds [fɔ̃] *nm* (*de bibliothèque*) collection; (*COMM*): **~ (de commerce)** business ♦ *nmpl* (*argent*) funds; **à ~ perdus** with little or no hope of getting the money back

fondu, e [fɔ̃dy] *adj* (*beurre, neige*) melted; (*métal*) molten; **fondue** *nf* (*CULIN*) fondue

font [fɔ̃] *vb voir* **faire**

fontaine [fɔ̃tɛn] *nf* fountain; (*source*) spring

fonte [fɔ̃t] *nf* melting; (*métal*) cast iron; **la ~ des neiges** the (spring) thaw

foot [fut] (*fam*) *nm* football

football [futbol] *nm* football, soccer; **footballeur** *nm* footballer

footing [futiŋ] *nm* jogging; **faire du ~** to go jogging

for [fɔʀ] *nm*: **dans son ~ intérieur** in one's heart of hearts

forain, e [fɔʀɛ̃, -ɛn] *adj* fairground *cpd* ♦ *nm* stallholder; fairground entertainer

forçat [fɔʀsa] *nm* convict

force [fɔʀs(ə)] *nf* strength; (*puissance: surnaturelle etc*) power; (*PHYSIQUE, MÉCANIQUE*) force; **~s** *nfpl* (*physiques*) strength *sg*; (*MIL*) forces; **à ~ d'insister** by dint of insisting; as he (*ou* I *etc*) kept on insisting; **de ~** forcibly, by force; **être de ~ à faire** to be up to doing; **de première ~** first class; **les ~s de l'ordre** the police

forcé, e [fɔʀse] *adj* forced; unintended; inevitable

forcément [fɔrsemɑ̃] *adv* necessarily; inevitably; *(bien sûr)* of course

forcené, e [fɔrsəne] *nm/f* maniac

forcer [fɔrse] *vt (porte, serrure, plante)* to force; *(moteur, voix)* to strain ♦ *vi (SPORT)* to overtax o.s.; ~ **la dose** to overdo it; ~ **l'allure** to increase the pace; **se ~ (pour faire)** to force o.s. (to do)

forcir [fɔrsir] *vi (grossir)* to broaden out; *(vent)* to freshen

forer [fɔre] *vt* to drill, bore

forestier, ère [fɔrɛstje, -ɛr] *adj* forest *cpd*

forêt [fɔrɛ] *nf* forest

forfait [fɔrfɛ] *nm (COMM)* fixed *ou* set price; all-in deal *ou* price; *(crime)* infamy; **déclarer** ~ to withdraw; **travailler à** ~ to work for a lump sum; ~**aire** *adj* inclusive; set

forge [fɔrʒ(ə)] *nf* forge, smithy

forger [fɔrʒe] *vt* to forge; *(fig: personnalité)* to form; (: *prétexte)* to contrive, make up

forgeron [fɔrʒərɔ̃] *nm* (black)smith

formaliser [fɔrmalize]: **se** ~ *vi*: **se** ~ **(de)** to take offence (at)

formalité [fɔrmalite] *nf (ADMIN, JUR)* formality; *(acte sans importance)*: **simple** ~ mere formality

format [fɔrma] *nm* size

formater [fɔrmate] *vt (disque)* to format

formation [fɔrmɑsjɔ̃] *nf* forming; training; *(MUS)* group; *(MIL, AVIAT, GÉO)* formation; ~ **permanente** continuing education; ~ **professionnelle** vocational training

forme [fɔrm(ə)] *nf (gén)* form; *(d'un objet)* shape, form; ~**s** *nfpl (bonnes manières)* proprieties; *(d'une femme)* figure *sg*; **en** ~ **de poire** pear-shaped; **être en** ~ *(SPORT etc)* to be on form; **en bonne et due** ~ in due form

formel, le [fɔrmɛl] *adj (preuve, décision)* definite, positive; *(logique)* formal; **formellement** *adv (absolument)* positively

former [fɔrme] *vt* to form; *(éduquer)* to train; **se** ~ *vi* to form

formidable [fɔrmidabl(ə)] *adj* tremendous

formulaire [fɔrmylɛr] *nm* form

formule [fɔrmyl] *nf (gén)* formula; *(formulaire)* form; ~ **de politesse** polite phrase; letter ending

formuler [fɔrmyle] *vt (émettre: réponse, vœux)* to formulate; *(expliciter: sa pensée)* to express

fort, e [fɔr, fɔrt(ə)] *adj* strong; *(intensité, rendement)* high, great; *(corpulent)* stout; *(doué)* good, able ♦ *adv (serrer, frapper)* hard; *(sonner)* loud(ly); *(beaucoup)* greatly, very much; *(très)* very ♦ *nm (édifice)* fort; *(point fort)* strong point, forte; **se faire** ~ **de ...** to claim one can ...; **au plus** ~ **de** *(au milieu de)* in the thick of; at the height of; ~**e tête** rebel

fortifiant [fɔrtifjɑ̃] *nm* tonic

fortifier [fɔrtifje] *vt* to strengthen, fortify; *(MIL)* to fortify

fortiori [fɔrtjɔri]: **à** ~ *adv* all the more so

fortuit, e [fɔrtɥi, -it] *adj* fortuitous, chance *cpd*

fortune [fɔrtyn] *nf* fortune; **faire** ~ to make one's fortune; **de** ~ makeshift; chance *cpd*

fortuné, e [fɔrtyne] *adj* wealthy

fosse [fos] *nf (grand trou)* pit; *(tombe)* grave; ~ **(d'orchestre)** (orchestra) pit

fossé [fose] *nm* ditch; *(fig)* gulf, gap

fossette [fosɛt] *nf* dimple

fossile [fosil] *nm* fossil

fossoyeur [foswajœr] *nm* gravedigger

fou(fol), folle [fu, fɔl] *adj* mad; *(déréglé etc)* wild, erratic; *(fam: extrême, très grand)* terrific, tremendous ♦ *nm/f* madman(woman) ♦ *nm (du roi)* jester; **être fou de** to be mad *ou* crazy about; **avoir le fou rire** to have the giggles; **faire le fou** to act the fool

foudre [fudr(ə)] *nf*: **la** ~ lightning

foudroyant, e [fudrwajɑ̃, -ɑ̃t] *adj* lightning *cpd*, stunning; *(maladie, poison)* violent

foudroyer [fudrwaje] *vt* to strike down; **être foudroyé** to be struck by lightning; ~ **qn du regard** to glare at sb

fouet [fwɛ] *nm* whip; *(CULIN)* whisk; **de plein** ~ *(se heurter)* head on; **fouetter** *vt* to whip; to whisk

fougère [fuʒɛr] *nf* fern

fougue [fug] *nf* ardour, spirit

fouille [fuj] *nf* search; ~**s** *nfpl (archéologiques)* excavations

fouiller [fuje] *vt* to search; *(creuser)* to dig ♦ *vi* to rummage

fouillis [fuji] *nm* jumble, muddle

fouiner [fwine] *(péj)* *vi*: ~ **dans** to nose around *ou* about in

foulard [fular] *nm* scarf

foule [ful] *nf* crowd; **les** ~**s** the masses; **la** ~ crowds *pl*; **une** ~ **de** masses of

foulée [fule] *nf* stride

fouler [fule] *vt* to press; *(sol)* to tread upon; **se** ~ *vi (fam)* to overexert o.s.; **se** ~ **la cheville** to sprain one's ankle; ~ **aux pieds** to trample underfoot; **foulure** [fulyr] *nf* sprain

four [fur] *nm* oven; *(de potier)* kiln; *(THÉÂTRE: échec)* flop

fourbe [furb(ə)] *adj* deceitful

fourbu, e [furby] *adj* exhausted

fourche [furʃ(ə)] *nf* pitchfork; *(de bicyclette)* fork

fourchette [furʃɛt] *nf* fork; *(STATISTIQUE)* bracket, margin

fourgon [furgɔ̃] *nm* van; *(RAIL)* wag(g)on

fourmi [furmi] *nf* ant; ~**s** *nfpl (fig)* pins and needles; **fourmilière** *nf* ant-hill

fourmiller [furmije] *vi* to swarm

fournaise [furnɛz] nf blaze; (fig) furnace, oven

fourneau, x [furno] nm stove

fournée [furne] nf batch

fourni, e [furni] adj (barbe, cheveux) thick; (magasin): **bien ~ (en)** well stocked (with)

fournir [furnir] vt to supply; (preuve, exemple) to provide, supply; (effort) to put in; **fournisseur, euse** nm/f supplier

fourniture [furnityr] nf supply(ing); **~s** nfpl (provisions) supplies

fourrage [furaʒ] nm fodder

fourrager[1], **ère** [furaʒe, -ɛr] adj fodder cpd

fourrager[2] vi: **fourrager dans/parmi** (fouiller) to rummage through /among

fourré, e [fure] adj (bonbon etc) filled; (manteau etc) fur-lined ♦ nm thicket

fourreau, x [furo] nm sheath

fourrer [fure] (fam) vt to stick, shove; **se ~ dans/sous** to get into/under

fourre-tout [furtu] nm inv (sac) holdall; (péj) junk room (ou cupboard); (fig) ragbag

fourrière [furjɛr] nf pound

fourrure [furyr] nf fur; (sur l'animal) coat

fourvoyer [furvwaje]: **se ~** vi to go astray, stray

foutre [futr(ə)] (fam!) vt = **ficher**; **foutu, e** (fam!) adj = **fichu, e**

foyer [fwaje] nm (de cheminée) hearth; (famille) family; (maison) home; (de jeunes etc) (social) club; hostel; (salon) foyer; (OPTIQUE, PHOTO) focus sg; **lunettes à double ~** bi-focal glasses

fracas [fraka] nm din; crash; roar

fracasser [frakase] vt to smash

fraction [fraksjɔ̃] nf fraction; **fractionner** vt to divide (up), split (up)

fracture [fraktyr] nf fracture; **~ du crâne** fractured skull; **~r** [fraktyre] vt (coffre, serrure) to break open; (os, membre) to fracture

fragile [fraʒil] adj fragile, delicate; (fig) frail; **fragilité** nf fragility

fragment [fragmã] nm (d'un objet) fragment, piece; (d'un texte) passage, extract

fraîche [frɛʃ] adj voir frais; **fraîcheur** nf coolness; freshness; **fraîchir** vi to get cooler; (vent) to freshen

frais, fraîche [frɛ, frɛʃ] adj fresh; (froid) cool ♦ adv (récemment) newly, fresh(ly) ♦ nm: **mettre au ~** to put in a cool place ♦ nmpl (débours) expenses; (COMM) costs; (facturés) charges; **il fait ~** it's cool; **servir ~** serve chilled; **prendre le ~** to take a breath of cool air; **faire des ~** to spend; to go to a lot of expense; **faire les ~ de** to bear the brunt of; **~ de scolarité** school fees (BRIT), tuition (US); **~ généraux** overheads

fraise [frɛz] nf strawberry; (TECH) countersink (bit); (de dentiste) drill; **~ des bois** wild strawberry

framboise [frãbwaz] nf raspberry

franc, franche [frã, frãʃ] adj (personne) frank, straightforward; (visage) open; (net: refus, couleur) clear; (: coupure) clean; (intensif) downright; (exempt): **~ de port** postage paid ♦ adv: **parler ~** to be frank ou candid ♦ nm franc

français, e [frãsɛ, -ɛz] adj French ♦ nm/f: **F~, e** Frenchman(woman) ♦ nm (LING) French; **les F~** the French

France [frãs] nf: **la ~** France

franche [frãʃ] adj voir franc; **franchement** adv frankly, clearly; (tout à fait) downright

franchir [frãʃir] vt (obstacle) to clear, get over; (seuil, ligne, rivière) to cross; (distance) to cover

franchise [frãʃiz] nf frankness; (douanière, d'impôt) exemption; (ASSURANCES) excess

franciser [frãsize] vt to gallicize, Frenchify

franc-maçon [frãmasɔ̃] nm freemason

franco [frãko] adv (COMM): **~ (de port)** postage paid

francophone [frãkɔfɔn] adj French-speaking; **francophonie** nf French-speaking communities

franc-parler [frãparle] nm inv outspokenness

franc-tireur [frãtirœr] nm (MIL) irregular; (fig) freelance

frange [frãʒ] nf fringe

frangipane [frãʒipan] nf almond paste

franquette [frãkɛt]: **à la bonne ~** adv without any fuss

frappe [frap] nf (de pianiste, machine à écrire) touch; (BOXE) punch

frappé, e [frape] adj iced

frapper [frape] vt to hit, strike; (étonner) to strike; (monnaie) to strike, stamp; **se ~** vi (s'inquiéter) to get worked up; **~ dans ses mains** to clap one's hands; **~ du poing sur** to bang one's fist on; **frappé de stupeur** dumbfounded

frasques [frask(ə)] nfpl escapades

fraternel, le [fratɛrnɛl] adj brotherly, fraternal

fraternité [fratɛrnite] nf brotherhood

fraude [frod] nf fraud; (SCOL) cheating; **passer qch en ~** to smuggle sth in (ou out); **~ fiscale** tax evasion; **frauder** vi, vt to cheat; **frauduleux, euse** adj fraudulent

frayer [freje] vt to open up, clear ♦ vi to spawn; (fréquenter): **~ avec** to mix with

frayeur [frejœr] nf fright

fredonner [frədɔne] vt to hum

freezer [frizœr] nm freezing compartment

frein [frɛ̃] nm brake; **~ à main** handbrake; **~s à disques/tambour** disc/drum brakes

freiner [frene] vi to brake ♦ vt (progrès etc) to check

frelaté, e [frəlate] adj adulterated; (fig)

tainted

frêle [fʀɛl] *adj* frail, fragile

frelon [fʀɔlɔ̃] *nm* hornet

frémir [fʀemiʀ] *vi* to tremble, shudder; to shiver; to quiver

frêne [fʀɛn] *nm* ash

frénétique [fʀenetik] *adj* frenzied, frenetic

fréquemment [fʀekamã] *adv* frequently

fréquent, e [fʀekã, -ãt] *adj* frequent

fréquentation [fʀekãtɑsjɔ̃] *nf* frequenting; seeing; ~s *nfpl* (*relations*) company *sg*

fréquenté, e [fʀekãte] *adj*: **très** ~ (very) busy; **mal** ~ patronized by disreputable elements

fréquenter [fʀekãte] *vt* (*lieu*) to frequent; (*personne*) to see; **se** ~ to see each other

frère [fʀɛʀ] *nm* brother

fresque [fʀɛsk(ə)] *nf* (*ART*) fresco

fret [fʀɛ] *nm* freight

frétiller [fʀetije] *vi* to wriggle; to quiver; (*chien*) to wag its tail

fretin [fʀətɛ̃] *nm*: **menu** ~ small fry

friable [fʀijabl(ə)] *adj* crumbly

friand, e [fʀijã, -ãd] *adj*: ~ **de** very fond of

friandise [fʀijãdiz] *nf* sweet

fric [fʀik] (*fam*) *nm* cash, bread

friche [fʀiʃ] : **en** ~ *adj, adv* (lying) fallow

friction [fʀiksjɔ̃] *nf* (*massage*) rub, rub-down; (*TECH, fig*) friction; **frictionner** *vt* to rub (down); to massage

frigidaire [fʀiʒidɛʀ] (®) *nm* refrigerator

frigide [fʀiʒid] *adj* frigid

frigo [fʀigo] *nm* fridge

frigorifier [fʀigɔʀifje] *vt* to refrigerate; **frigorifique** *adj* refrigerating

frileux, euse [fʀilø, -øz] *adj* sensitive to (the) cold

frimer [fʀime] *vi* to put on an act

frimousse [fʀimus] *nf* (sweet) little face

fringale [fʀɛ̃gal] *nf*: **avoir la** ~ to be ravenous

fringant, e [fʀɛ̃gã, -ãt] *adj* dashing

fringues [fʀɛ̃g] (*fam*) *nfpl* clothes

fripé, e [fʀipe] *adj* crumpled

fripon, ne [fʀipɔ̃, -ɔn] *adj* roguish, mischievous ♦ *nm/f* rascal, rogue

fripouille [fʀipuj] *nf* scoundrel

frire [fʀiʀ] *vt, vi*: **faire** ~ to fry

frisé, e [fʀize] *adj* curly; curly-haired

frisson [fʀisɔ̃] *nm* shudder, shiver; quiver; **frissonner** *vi* to shudder, shiver; to quiver

frit, e [fʀi, fʀit] *pp de* **frire**; **frite** *nf*: (**pommes**) **frites** chips (*BRIT*), French fries; **friteuse** *nf* chip pan; **friture** *nf* (*huile*) (deep) fat; (*plat*): **friture (de poissons)** fried fish; (*RADIO*) crackle

frivole [fʀivɔl] *adj* frivolous

froid, e [fʀwa, fʀwad] *adj, nm* cold; **il fait** ~ it's cold; **avoir/prendre** ~ to be/catch cold; **être en** ~ **avec** to be on bad terms with; **~ement** *adv* (*accueillir*) coldly; (*décider*) coolly

froisser [fʀwase] *vt* to crumple (up), crease; (*fig*) to hurt, offend; **se** ~ *vi* to crumple, crease; to take offence; **se** ~ **un muscle** to strain a muscle

frôler [fʀole] *vt* to brush against; (*suj: projectile*) to skim past; (*fig*) to come very close to

fromage [fʀɔmaʒ] *nm* cheese; ~ **blanc** soft white cheese; **fromager, ère** *nm/f* cheese merchant

froment [fʀɔmã] *nm* wheat

froncer [fʀɔ̃se] *vt* to gather; ~ **les sourcils** to frown

frondaisons [fʀɔ̃dɛzɔ̃] *nfpl* foliage *sg*

fronde [fʀɔ̃d] *nf* sling; (*fig*) rebellion, rebelliousness

front [fʀɔ̃] *nm* forehead, brow; (*MIL*) front; **de** ~ (*se heurter*) head-on; (*rouler*) together (*i.e. 2 or 3 abreast*); (*simultanément*) at once; **faire** ~ **à** to face up to; ~ **de mer** (sea) front

frontalier, ère [fʀɔ̃talje, -ɛʀ] *adj* border *cpd*, frontier *cpd* ♦ *nm/f*: (**travailleurs**) ~s commuters from across the border

frontière [fʀɔ̃tjɛʀ] *nf* frontier, border; (*fig*) frontier, boundary

fronton [fʀɔ̃tɔ̃] *nm* pediment

frotter [fʀote] *vi* to rub, scrape ♦ *vt* to rub; (*pour nettoyer*) to rub (up); to scrub; ~ **une allumette** to strike a match

fructifier [fʀyktifje] *vi* to yield a profit; **faire** ~ to turn to good account

fructueux, euse [fʀyktɥø, -øz] *adj* fruitful; profitable

fruit [fʀɥi] *nm* fruit *gen no pl*; ~s **de mer** seafood(s); ~s **secs** dried fruit *sg*; ~é, e *adj* fruity; ~ier, ère *adj*: **arbre** ~ier fruit tree ♦ *nm/f* fruiterer (*BRIT*), fruit merchant (*US*)

fruste [fʀyst(ə)] *adj* unpolished, uncultivated

frustrer [fʀystʀe] *vt* to frustrate

fuel(-oil) [fjul(ɔjl)] *nm* fuel oil; heating oil

fugace [fygas] *adj* fleeting

fugitif, ive [fyʒitif, -iv] *adj* (*lueur, amour*) fleeting; (*prisonnier etc*) fugitive, runaway ♦ *nm/f* fugitive

fugue [fyg] *nf*: **faire une** ~ to run away, abscond

fuir [fɥiʀ] *vt* to flee from; (*éviter*) to shun ♦ *vi* to run away; (*gaz, robinet*) to leak

fuite [fɥit] *nf* flight; (*écoulement, divulgation*) leak; **être en** ~ to be on the run; **mettre en** ~ to put to flight

fulgurant, e [fylgyʀã, -ãt] *adj* lightning *cpd*, dazzling

fulminer [fylmine] *vi* to thunder forth

fumé, e [fyme] *adj* (*CULIN*) smoked; (*verre*) tinted

fume-cigarette [fymsigaʀɛt] *nm inv* cigarette holder

fumée [fyme] *nf* smoke

fumer [fyme] *vi* to smoke; (*soupe*) to steam
♦ *vt* to smoke; (*terre, champ*) to manure

fûmes *etc vb voir* **être**

fumet [fyme] *nm* aroma

fumeur, euse [fymœʀ, -øz] *nm/f* smoker

fumeux, euse [fymø, -øz] (*péj*) *adj* woolly,
hazy

fumier [fymje] *nm* manure

fumiste [fymist(ə)] *nm/f* (*péj: paresseux*)
shirker; (*charlatan*) phoney

fumisterie [fymistəʀi] (*péj*) *nf* fraud, con

funambule [fynɑ̃byl] *nm* tightrope walker

funèbre [fynebʀ(ə)] *adj* funeral *cpd*; (*fig*)
doleful; funereal

funérailles [fyneʀɑj] *nfpl* funeral *sg*

funeste [fynɛst(ə)] *adj* disastrous; deathly

fur [fyʀ]: **au ~ et à mesure** *adv* as one
goes along; **au ~ et à mesure que** as

furet [fyʀɛ] *nm* ferret

fureter [fyʀte] (*péj*) *vi* to nose about

fureur [fyʀœʀ] *nf* fury; (*passion*): ~ **de** passion for; **faire ~** to be all the rage

furibond, e [fyʀibɔ̃, -ɔ̃d] *adj* furious

furie [fyʀi] *nf* fury; (*femme*) shrew, vixen;
en ~ (*mer*) raging; **furieux, euse** *adj* furious

furoncle [fyʀɔ̃kl(ə)] *nm* boil

furtif, ive [fyʀtif, -iv] *adj* furtive

fus *vb voir* **être**

fusain [fyzɛ̃] *nm* (*ART*) charcoal

fuseau, x [fyzo] *nm* (*pour filer*) spindle;
(*pantalon*) (ski) pants; ~ **horaire** time zone

fusée [fyze] *nf* rocket; ~ **éclairante** flare

fuselé, e [fyzle] *adj* slender; tapering

fuser [fyze] *vi* (*rires etc*) to burst forth

fusible [fyzibl(ə)] *nm* (*ÉLEC: fil*) fuse wire; (*:
fiche*) fuse

fusil [fyzi] *nm* (*de guerre, à canon rayé*) rifle,
gun; (*de chasse, à canon lisse*) shotgun,
gun; **fusillade** *nf* gunfire *no pl*, shooting *no
pl*; shooting battle; **fusiller** *vt* to shoot;
fusil-mitrailleur *nm* machine gun

fusionner [fyzjɔne] *vi* to merge

fustiger [fystiʒe] *vt* to denounce

fut *vb voir* **être**

fût [fy] *vb voir* **être** ♦ *nm* (*tonneau*) barrel,
cask

futaie [fytɛ] *nf* forest, plantation

futé, e [fyte] *adj* crafty

futile [fytil] *adj* futile; frivolous

futur, e [fytyʀ] *adj, nm* future

fuyant, e [fɥijɑ̃, -ɑ̃t] *vb voir* **fuir** ♦ *adj* (*regard etc*) evasive; (*lignes etc*) receding; (*perspective*) vanishing

fuyard, e [fɥijaʀ, -aʀd(ə)] *nm/f* runaway

G g

gabarit [gabaʀi] *nm* (*fig*) size; calibre

gâcher [gɑʃe] *vt* (*gâter*) to spoil, ruin;
(*gaspiller*) to waste

gâchette [gɑʃɛt] *nf* trigger

gâchis [gɑʃi] *nm* waste *no pl*

gadoue [gadu] *nf* sludge

gaffe [gaf] *nf* (*instrument*) boat hook; (*erreur*) blunder; **faire ~** (*fam*) to be careful

gage [gaʒ] *nm* (*dans un jeu*) forfeit; (*fig: de
fidélité*) token; ~**s** *nmpl* (*salaire*) wages;
(*garantie*) guarantee *sg*; **mettre en ~** to
pawn

gager [gaʒe] *vt* to bet, wager

gageure [gaʒyʀ] *nf*: **c'est une ~** it's attempting the impossible

gagnant, e [gaɲɑ̃, -ɑ̃t] *nm/f* winner

gagne-pain [gaɲpɛ̃] *nm inv* job

gagner [gaɲe] *vt* to win; (*somme d'argent,
revenu*) to earn; (*aller vers, atteindre*) to
reach; (*envahir*) to overcome; to spread to
♦ *vi* to win; (*fig*) to gain; ~ **du temps/de
la place** to gain time/save space; ~ **sa vie**
to earn one's living

gai, e [ge] *adj* gay, cheerful; (*un peu ivre*)
merry

gaieté [gete] *nf* cheerfulness; **de ~ de
cœur** with a light heart

gaillard, e [gajaʀ, -aʀd(ə)] *adj* (*grivois*)
bawdy, ribald ♦ *nm* (strapping) fellow

gain [gɛ̃] *nm* (*revenu*) earnings *pl*; (*bénéfice*:
gén pl) profits *pl*; (*au jeu*) winnings *pl*; (*fig:
de temps, place*) saving; **avoir ~ de cause**
to win the case; (*fig*) to be proved right

gaine [gɛn] *nf* (*corset*) girdle; (*fourreau*)
sheath

galant, e [galɑ̃, -ɑ̃t] *adj* (*courtois*) courteous, gentlemanly; (*entreprenant*) flirtatious, gallant; (*aventure, poésie*) amorous

galère [galɛʀ] *nf* galley

galérer [galeʀe] (*fam*) *vi* to slog away, work
hard

galerie [galʀi] *nf* gallery; (*THÉÂTRE*) circle;
(*de voiture*) roof rack; (*fig: spectateurs*)
audience; ~ **de peinture** (private) art gallery; ~ **marchande** shopping arcade

galet [galɛ] *nm* pebble; (*TECH*) wheel

galette [galɛt] *nf* flat cake

Galles [gal] *nfpl*: **le pays de ~** Wales

gallois, e [galwa, -waz] *adj* Welsh ♦ *nm*
(*LING*) Welsh ♦ *nm/f*: **G~, e** Welsh-

man(woman)

galon [galɔ̃] *nm* (*MIL*) stripe; (*décoratif*) piece of braid

galop [galo] *nm* gallop

galoper [galɔpe] *vi* to gallop

galopin [galɔpɛ̃] *nm* urchin, ragamuffin

galvauder [galvode] *vt* to debase

gambader [gãbade] *vi* (*animal, enfant*) to leap about

gamelle [gamɛl] *nf* mess tin; billy can

gamin, e [gamɛ̃, -in] *nm/f* kid ♦ *adj* mischievous, playful

gamme [gam] *nf* (*MUS*) scale; (*fig*) range

gammé, e [game] *adj*: **croix** ~**e** swastika

gant [gã] *nm* glove; ~ **de toilette** face flannel (*BRIT*), face cloth

garage [gaɾaʒ] *nm* garage; **garagiste** *nm/f* garage owner; garage mechanic

garant, e [gaɾã, -ãt] *nm/f* guarantor ♦ *nm* guarantee; **se porter** ~ **de** to vouch for; to be answerable for

garantie [gaɾãti] *nf* guarantee; (*gage*) security, surety; **(bon de)** ~ guarantee *ou* warranty slip

garantir [gaɾãtiɾ] *vt* to guarantee; (*protéger*): ~ **de** to protect from

garçon [gaɾsɔ̃] *nm* boy; (*célibataire*) bachelor; (*serveur*): ~ **(de café)** waiter; ~ **de courses** messenger; **garçonnet** *nm* small boy; **garçonnière** *nf* bachelor flat

garde [gaɾd(ə)] *nm* (*de prisonnier*) guard; (*de domaine etc*) warden; (*soldat, sentinelle*) guardsman ♦ *nf* guarding; looking after; (*soldats, BOXE, ESCRIME*) guard; (*faction*) watch; (*TYPO*): **(page de)** ~ endpaper; flyleaf; **de** ~ on duty; **monter la** ~ to stand guard; **mettre en** ~ to warn; **prendre** ~ **(à)** to be careful (of); ~ **champêtre** rural policeman; ~ **du corps** *nm* bodyguard; ~ **des enfants** *nf* (*après divorce*) custody of the children; ~ **des Sceaux** *nm* ≈ Lord Chancellor (*BRIT*), ≈ Attorney General (*US*); ~ **à vue** *nf* (*JUR*) ≈ police custody; ~**-à-vous** *nm*: **être/se mettre au** ~**-à-vous** to be at/stand to attention; ~**-barrière** *nm/f* level-crossing keeper; ~**-boue** *nm inv* mudguard; ~**-chasse** *nm* gamekeeper; ~**-fou** *nm* railing, parapet; ~**-malade** *nf* home nurse; ~**-manger** *nm inv* meat safe; pantry, larder

garder [gaɾde] *vt* (*conserver*) to keep; (*surveiller: enfants*) to look after; (: *immeuble, lieu, prisonnier*) to guard; **se** ~ *vi* (*aliment: se conserver*) to keep; **se** ~ **de faire** to be careful not to do; ~ **le lit/la chambre** to stay in bed/indoors; **pêche/chasse gardée** private fishing/hunting (ground)

garderie [gaɾdəɾi] *nf* day nursery, crèche

garde-robe [gaɾdəɾɔb] *nf* wardrobe

gardien, ne [gaɾdjɛ̃, -jɛn] *nm/f* (*garde*) guard; (*de prison*) warder; (*de domaine, réserve*) warden; (*de musée etc*) attendant; (*de phare, cimetière*) keeper; (*d'immeuble*) caretaker; (*fig*) guardian; ~ **de but** goalkeeper; ~ **de la paix** policeman; ~ **de nuit** night watchman

gare [gaɾ] *nf* (*railway*) station, train station (*US*) ♦ *excl* watch out!; ~ **routière** bus station

garer [gaɾe] *vt* to park; **se** ~ *vi* to park; (*pour laisser passer*) to draw into the side

gargariser [gaɾgaɾize]: **se** ~ *vi* to gargle; **gargarisme** *nm* gargling *no pl*; gargle

gargote [gaɾgɔt] *nf* cheap restaurant

gargouille [gaɾguj] *nf* gargoyle

gargouiller [gaɾguje] *vi* to gurgle

garnement [gaɾnəmã] *nm* rascal, scallywag

garni, e [gaɾni] *adj* (*plat*) served with vegetables (*and chips or rice etc*) ♦ *nm* furnished accommodation *no pl*

garnir [gaɾniɾ] *vt* (*orner*) to decorate; to trim; (*approvisionner*) to fill, stock; (*protéger*) to fit

garnison [gaɾnizɔ̃] *nf* garrison

garniture [gaɾnityɾ] *nf* (*CULIN*) vegetables *pl*; filling; (*décoration*) trimming; (*protection*) fittings *pl*; ~ **de frein** brake lining

garrot [gaɾo] *nm* (*MÉD*) tourniquet

gars [gɑ] *nm* lad; guy

Gascogne [gaskɔɲ] *nf* Gascony; **le golfe de** ~ the Bay of Biscay

gas-oil [gazɔjl] *nm* diesel (oil)

gaspiller [gaspije] *vt* to waste

gastronomique [gastɾɔnɔmik] *adj* gastronomic

gâteau, x [gɑto] *nm* cake; ~ **sec** biscuit

gâter [gɑte] *vt* to spoil; **se** ~ *vi* (*dent, fruit*) to go bad; (*temps, situation*) to change for the worse

gâterie [gɑtɾi] *nf* little treat

gâteux, euse [gɑtø, -øz] *adj* senile

gauche [goʃ] *adj* left, left-hand; (*maladroit*) awkward, clumsy ♦ *nf* (*POL*) left (wing); **à** ~ on the left; (*direction*) (to the) left; **gaucher, ère** *adj* left-handed; **gauchiste** *nm/f* leftist

gaufre [gofɾ(ə)] *nf* waffle

gaufrette [gofɾɛt] *nf* wafer

gaulois, e [golwa, -waz] *adj* Gallic; (*grivois*) bawdy ♦ *nm/f*: **G**~, **e** Gaul

gausser [gose]: **se** ~ **de** *vt* to deride

gaver [gave] *vt* to force-feed; (*fig*): ~ **de** to cram with, fill up with

gaz [gaz] *nm inv* gas

gaze [gaz] *nf* gauze

gazéifié, e [gazeifje] *adj* aerated

gazette [gazɛt] *nf* news sheet

gazeux, euse [gazø, -øz] *adj* gaseous; (*boisson*) fizzy; (*eau*) sparkling

gazoduc [gazɔdyk] *nm* gas pipeline

gazon [gazɔ̃] *nm* (*herbe*) turf; grass; (*pelouse*) lawn

gazouiller [gazuje] *vi* to chirp; (*enfant*) to

babble
geai [ʒɛ] *nm* jay
géant, e [ʒeã, -ãt] *adj* gigantic, giant;
(*COMM*) giant-size ♦ *nm/f* giant
geindre [ʒɛ̃dʀ(ə)] *vi* to groan, moan
gel [ʒɛl] *nm* frost; freezing
gélatine [ʒelatin] *nf* gelatine
gelée [ʒəle] *nf* jelly; (*gel*) frost
geler [ʒəle] *vt, vi* to freeze; **il gèle** it's
freezing
gélule [ʒelyl] *nf* (*MÉD*) capsule
gelures [ʒəlyʀ] *nfpl* frostbite *sg*
Gémeaux [ʒemo] *nmpl*: **les ~** Gemini
gémir [ʒemiʀ] *vi* to groan, moan
gemme [ʒɛm] *nf* gem(stone)
gênant, e [ʒɛnã, -ãt] *adj* annoying; embarrassing
gencive [ʒãsiv] *nf* gum
gendarme [ʒãdaʀm(ə)] *nm* gendarme;
~rie *nf* military police force in countryside
and small towns; their police station or barracks
gendre [ʒãdʀ(ə)] *nm* son-in-law
gêne [ʒɛn] *nf* (*à respirer, bouger*) discomfort, difficulty; (*dérangement*) bother,
trouble; (*manque d'argent*) financial difficulties *pl ou* straits *pl*; (*confusion*) embarrassment
gêné, e [ʒɛne] *adj* embarrassed
gêner [ʒɛne] *vt* (*incommoder*) to bother;
(*encombrer*) to hamper; to be in the way;
(*embarrasser*): ~ **qn** to make sb feel ill-at-
ease; **se ~** *vi* to put o.s. out
général, e, aux [ʒeneʀal, -o] *adj, nm* general; **en ~** usually, in general; **~e** *nf*: (*répétition*) **~e** final dress rehearsal; **~ement**
adv generally
généraliser [ʒeneʀalize] *vt, vi* to generalize;
se ~ *vi* to become widespread
généraliste [ʒeneʀalist(ə)] *nm/f* general
practitioner, G.P.
générateur, trice [ʒeneʀatœʀ, -tʀis] *adj*:
~ **de** which causes
génération [ʒeneʀasjɔ̃] *nf* generation
généreux, euse [ʒeneʀø, -øz] *adj* generous
générique [ʒeneʀik] *nm* (*CINÉMA*) credits
pl, credit titles *pl*
générosité [ʒeneʀozite] *nf* generosity
genêt [ʒənɛ] *nm* broom *no pl* (*shrub*)
génétique [ʒenetik] *adj* genetic
Genève [ʒənɛv] *n* Geneva
génial, e, aux [ʒenjal, -o] *adj* of genius;
(*fam: formidable*) fantastic, brilliant
génie [ʒeni] *nm* genius; (*MIL*): **le ~** the En-
gineers *pl*; ~ **civil** civil engineering
genièvre [ʒənjɛvʀ(ə)] *nm* juniper
génisse [ʒenis] *nf* heifer
genou, x [ʒnu] *nm* knee; **à ~x** on one's
knees; **se mettre à ~x** to kneel down
genre [ʒãʀ] *nm* kind, type, sort; (*allure*)
manner; (*LING*) gender

gens [ʒã] *nmpl* (*f in some phrases*) people *pl*
gentil, le [ʒãti, -ij] *adj* kind; (*enfant: sage*)
good; (*endroit etc*) nice; **gentillesse** *nf*
kindness; **gentiment** *adv* kindly
géographie [ʒeɔgʀafi] *nf* geography
geôlier [ʒolje] *nm* jailer
géologie [ʒeɔlɔʒi] *nf* geology
géomètre [ʒeɔmɛtʀ(ə)] *nm*: (**arpenteur-**)~
(land) surveyor
géométrie [ʒeɔmetʀi] *nf* geometry; **géométrique** *adj* geometric
gérance [ʒeʀãs] *nf* management; **mettre en
~** to appoint a manager for
géranium [ʒeʀanjɔm] *nm* geranium
gérant, e [ʒeʀã, -ãt] *nm/f* manager(eress)
gerbe [ʒɛʀb(ə)] *nf* (*de fleurs*) spray; (*de blé*)
sheaf; (*fig*) shower, burst
gercé, e [ʒɛʀse] *adj* chapped
gerçure [ʒɛʀsyʀ] *nf* crack
gérer [ʒeʀe] *vt* to manage
germain, e [ʒɛʀmɛ̃, -ɛn] *adj*: **cousin ~** first
cousin
germe [ʒɛʀm(ə)] *nm* germ; **~r** [ʒɛʀme] *vi*
to sprout; to germinate
geste [ʒɛst(ə)] *nm* gesture; move; motion
gestion [ʒɛstjɔ̃] *nf* management
gibecière [ʒibsjɛʀ] *nf* gamebag
gibet [ʒibɛ] *nm* gallows *pl*
gibier [ʒibje] *nm* (*animaux*) game; (*fig*) prey
giboulée [ʒibule] *nf* sudden shower
gicler [ʒikle] *vi* to spurt, squirt
gifle [ʒifl(ə)] *nf* slap (in the face); **gifler** *vt*
to slap (in the face)
gigantesque [ʒigãtɛsk(ə)] *adj* gigantic
gigogne [ʒigɔɲ] *adj*: **lits ~s** truckle (*BRIT*)
ou trundle beds
gigot [ʒigo] *nm* leg (of mutton *ou* lamb)
gigoter [ʒigɔte] *vi* to wriggle (about)
gilet [ʒilɛ] *nm* waistcoat; (*pull*) cardigan;
(*de corps*) vest; ~ **de sauvetage** life jacket
gingembre [ʒɛ̃ʒãbʀ(ə)] *nm* ginger
girafe [ʒiʀaf] *nf* giraffe
giratoire [ʒiʀatwaʀ] *adj*: **sens ~** roundabout
girofle [ʒiʀɔfl(e)] *nf*: **clou de ~** clove
girouette [ʒiʀwɛt] *nf* weather vane *ou* cock
gisait *etc vb voir* **gésir**
gisement [ʒizmã] *nm* deposit
gît *vb voir* **gésir**
gitan, e [ʒitã, -an] *nm/f* gipsy
gîte [ʒit] *nm* home; shelter; ~ (**rural**) holiday cottage *ou* apartment
givre [ʒivʀ(ə)] *nm* (hoar) frost
glabre [glabʀ(ə)] *adj* hairless; clean-shaven
glace [glas] *nf* ice; (*crème glacée*) ice cream;
(*verre*) sheet of glass; (*miroir*) mirror; (*de
voiture*) window
glacé, e [glase] *adj* icy; (*boisson*) iced
glacer [glase] *vt* to freeze; (*boisson*) to chill,
ice; (*gâteau*) to ice; (*papier, tissu*) to glaze;
(*fig*): ~ **qn** to chill sb; to make sb's blood
run cold

glacial, e [glasjal] *adj* icy
glacier [glasje] *nm* (*GÉO*) glacier; (*marchand*) ice-cream maker
glacière [glasjɛʀ] *nf* icebox
glaçon [glasɔ̃] *nm* icicle; (*pour boisson*) ice cube
glaise [glɛz] *nf* clay
gland [glɑ̃] *nm* acorn; (*décoration*) tassel
glande [glɑ̃d] *nf* gland
glaner [glane] *vt, vi* to glean
glapir [glapiʀ] *vi* to yelp
glas [glɑ] *nm* knell, toll
glauque [glok] *adj* dull blue-green
glissant, e [glisɑ̃, -ɑ̃t] *adj* slippery
glissement [glismɑ̃] *nm*: ~ **de terrain** landslide
glisser [glise] *vi* (*avancer*) to glide *ou* slide along; (*coulisser, tomber*) to slide; (*déraper*) to slip; (*être glissant*) to be slippery ♦ *vt* to slip; **se** ~ **dans** to slip into
global, e, aux [glɔbal, -o] *adj* overall
globe [glɔb] *nm* globe
globule [glɔbyl] *nm* (*du sang*) corpuscle
globuleux, euse [glɔbylø, -øz] *adj*: **yeux** ~ protruding eyes
gloire [glwaʀ] *nf* glory; (*mérite*) distinction, credit; (*personne*) celebrity; **glorieux, euse** *adj* glorious
glousser [gluse] *vi* to cluck; (*rire*) to chuckle
glouton, ne [glutɔ̃, -ɔn] *adj* gluttonous
gluant, e [glyɑ̃, -ɑ̃t] *adj* sticky, gummy
glycine [glisin] *nf* wisteria
go [go] : **tout de** ~ *adv* straight out
G.O. *sigle* = **grandes ondes**
gobelet [gɔblɛ] *nm* tumbler; beaker; (*à dés*) cup
gober [gɔbe] *vt* to swallow
godasse [gɔdas] (*fam*) *nf* shoe
godet [gɔdɛ] *nm* pot
goéland [gɔelɑ̃] *nm* (sea)gull
goélette [gɔelɛt] *nf* schooner
goémon [gɔemɔ̃] *nm* wrack
gogo [gɔgo] : **à** ~ *adv* galore
goguenard, e [gɔgnaʀ, -aʀd(ə)] *adj* mocking
goinfre [gwɛ̃fʀ(ə)] *nm* glutton
golf [gɔlf] *nm* golf; golf course
golfe [gɔlf(ə)] *nm* gulf; bay
gomme [gɔm] *nf* (*à effacer*) rubber (*BRIT*), eraser; **gommer** *vt* to rub out (*BRIT*), erase
gond [gɔ̃] *nm* hinge; **sortir de ses** ~**s** (*fig*) to fly off the handle
gondoler [gɔ̃dɔle] : **se** ~ *vi* to warp; to buckle
gonflé, e [gɔ̃fle] *adj* swollen; bloated
gonfler [gɔ̃fle] *vt* (*pneu, ballon*) to inflate, blow up; (*nombre, importance*) to inflate ♦ *vi* to swell (up); (*CULIN: pâte*) to rise
gonzesse [gɔ̃zɛs] (*fam*) *nf* chick, bird (*BRIT*)
goret [gɔʀɛ] *nm* piglet

gorge [gɔʀʒ(ə)] *nf* (*ANAT*) throat; (*poitrine*) breast
gorgé, e [gɔʀʒe] *adj*: ~ **de** filled with; (*eau*) saturated with; **gorgée** *nf* mouthful; sip; gulp
gorille [gɔʀij] *nm* gorilla; (*fam*) bodyguard
gosier [gozje] *nm* throat
gosse [gɔs] *nm/f* kid
goudron [gudʀɔ̃] *nm* tar; **goudronner** *vt* to tar(mac) (*BRIT*), asphalt (*US*)
gouffre [gufʀ(ə)] *nm* abyss, gulf
goujat [guʒa] *nm* boor
goulot [gulo] *nm* neck; **boire au** ~ to drink from the bottle
goulu, e [guly] *adj* greedy
gourd, e [guʀ, guʀd(ə)] *adj* numb (with cold)
gourde [guʀd(ə)] *nf* (*récipient*) flask; (*fam*) (clumsy) clot *ou* oaf ♦ *adj* oafish
gourdin [guʀdɛ̃] *nm* club, bludgeon
gourmand, e [guʀmɑ̃, -ɑ̃d] *adj* greedy; **gourmandise** *nf* greed; (*bonbon*) sweet
gousse [gus] *nf*: ~ **d'ail** clove of garlic
goût [gu] *nm* taste; **de bon** ~ tasteful; **de mauvais** ~ tasteless; **prendre** ~ **à** to develop a taste *ou* a liking for
goûter [gute] *vt* (*essayer*) to taste; (*apprécier*) to enjoy ♦ *vi* to have (afternoon) tea ♦ *nm* (afternoon) tea
goutte [gut] *nf* drop; (*MÉD*) gout; (*alcool*) brandy
goutte-à-goutte [gutagut] *nm* (*MÉD*) drip; **tomber** ~ to drip
gouttière [gutjɛʀ] *nf* gutter
gouvernail [guvɛʀnaj] *nm* rudder; (*barre*) helm, tiller
gouvernante [guvɛʀnɑ̃t] *nf* governess
gouverne [guvɛʀn(ə)] *nf*: **pour sa** ~ for his guidance
gouvernement [guvɛʀnəmɑ̃] *nm* government; **gouvernemental, e, aux** *adj* government *cpd*; pro-government
gouverner [guvɛʀne] *vt* to govern
grabuge [gʀabyʒ] *nm* mayhem
grâce [gʀɑs] *nf* grace; favour; (*JUR*) pardon; ~**s** *nfpl* (*REL*) grace *sg*; **faire** ~ **à qn de qch** to spare sb sth; **rendre** ~(**s**) **à** to give thanks to; **demander** ~ to beg for mercy; ~ **à** thanks to; **gracier** *vt* to pardon; **gracieux, euse** *adj* graceful
grade [gʀad] *nm* rank; **monter en** ~ to be promoted
gradé [gʀade] *nm* officer
gradin [gʀadɛ̃] *nm* tier; step; ~**s** *nmpl* (*de stade*) terracing *sg*
graduel, le [gʀadyɛl] *adj* gradual; progressive
graduer [gʀadye] *vt* (*effort etc*) to increase gradually; (*règle, verre*) to graduate
grain [gʀɛ̃] *nm* (*gén*) grain; (*NAVIG*) squall; ~ **de beauté** beauty spot; ~ **de café** coffee bean; ~ **de poivre** peppercorn; ~ **de pous-**

sière speck of dust; ~ **de raisin** grape
graine [gʀɛn] nf seed
graissage [gʀɛsaʒ] nm lubrication, greasing
graisse [gʀɛs] nf fat; (lubrifiant) grease; **graisser** vt to lubricate, grease; (tacher) to make greasy
grammaire [gʀamɛʀ] nf grammar; **grammatical, e, aux** adj grammatical
gramme [gʀam] nm gramme
grand, e [gʀɑ̃, gʀɑ̃d] adj (haut) tall; (gros, vaste, large) big, large; (long) long; (sens abstraits) great ♦ adv: ~ **ouvert** wide open; **au ~ air** in the open (air); **les ~s blessés** the severely injured; ~ **ensemble** housing scheme; ~ **magasin** department store; ~**e personne** grown-up; ~**e surface** hypermarket; ~**es écoles** prestige schools of university level; ~**es lignes** (RAIL) main lines; ~**es vacances** summer holidays; **grand-chose** nm/f inv: **pas grand-chose** not much; **Grande-Bretagne** nf (Great) Britain; **grandeur** nf (dimension) size; magnitude; (fig) greatness; ~**eur nature** life-size; **grandir** vi to grow ♦ vt: **grandir qn** (suj: vêtement, chaussure) to make sb look taller; ~**-mère** nf grandmother; ~**-messe** nf high mass; ~**-peine** adv: **à ~-peine** with difficulty; ~**-père** nm grandfather; ~**-route** nf main road; ~**s-parents** nmpl grandparents
grange [gʀɑ̃ʒ] nf barn
granit(e) [gʀanit] nm granite
graphique [gʀafik] adj graphic ♦ nm graph
grappe [gʀap] nf cluster; ~ **de raisin** bunch of grapes
grappiller [gʀapije] vt to glean
grappin [gʀapɛ̃] nm grapnel; **mettre le ~ sur** (fig) to get one's claws on
gras, se [gʀɑ, gʀɑs] adj (viande, soupe) fatty; (personne) fat; (surface, main) greasy; (plaisanterie) coarse; (TYPO) bold ♦ nm (CULIN) fat; **faire la ~se matinée** to have a lie-in (BRIT), sleep late (US); **grassement** adv: **grassement payé** handsomely paid; **grassouillet, te** adj podgy, plump
gratifiant, e [gʀatifjɑ̃, -ɑ̃t] adj gratifying, rewarding
gratifier [gʀatifje] vt: ~ **qn de** to favour sb with; to reward sb with
gratiné, e [gʀatine] adj (CULIN) au gratin
gratis [gʀatis] adv free
gratitude [gʀatityd] nf gratitude
gratte-ciel [gʀatsjɛl] nm inv skyscraper
gratte-papier [gʀatpapje] (péj) nm inv pen-pusher
gratter [gʀate] vt (frotter) to scrape; (enlever) to scrape off; (bras, bouton) to scratch
gratuit, e [gʀatɥi, -ɥit] adj (entrée, billet) free; (fig) gratuitous
gravats [gʀava] nmpl rubble sg
grave [gʀav] adj (maladie, accident) serious, bad; (sujet, problème) serious, grave; (air)

grave, solemn; (voix, son) deep, low-pitched; **gravement** adv seriously; gravely
graver [gʀave] vt to engrave
gravier [gʀavje] nm gravel no pl; **gravillons** nmpl loose gravel sg
gravir [gʀaviʀ] vt to climb (up)
gravité [gʀavite] nf seriousness; gravity
graviter [gʀavite] vi to revolve
gravure [gʀavyʀ] nf engraving; (reproduction) print; plate
gré [gʀe] nm: **à son ~** to his liking; as he pleases; **au ~ de** according to, following; **contre le ~ de qn** against sb's will; **de son (plein) ~** of one's own free will; **bon ~ mal ~** like it or not; **de ~ ou de force** whether one likes it or not; **savoir ~ à qn de qch** to be grateful to sb for sth
grec, grecque [gʀɛk] adj Greek; (classique: vase etc) Grecian ♦ nm/f Greek
Grèce [gʀɛs] nf: **la ~** Greece
gréement [gʀemɑ̃] nm rigging
greffer [gʀefe] vt (BOT, MÉD: tissu) to graft; (MÉD: organe) to transplant
greffier [gʀefje] nm clerk of the court
grêle [gʀɛl] adj (very) thin ♦ nf hail
grêlé, e [gʀɛle] adj pockmarked
grêler [gʀɛle] vb impers: **il grêle** it's hailing; **grêlon** [gʀɛlɔ̃] nm hailstone
grelot [gʀəlo] nm little bell
grelotter [gʀələte] vi to shiver
grenade [gʀənad] nf (explosive) grenade; (BOT) pomegranate
grenat [gʀəna] adj inv dark red
grenier [gʀənje] nm attic; (de ferme) loft
grenouille [gʀənuj] nf frog
grès [gʀɛ] nm sandstone; (poterie) stoneware
grésiller [gʀezije] vi to sizzle; (RADIO) to crackle
grève [gʀɛv] nf (d'ouvriers) strike; (plage) shore; **se mettre en/faire ~** to go on/be on strike; ~ **de la faim** hunger strike; ~ **du zèle** work-to-rule (BRIT), slowdown (US)
grever [gʀəve] vt to put a strain on
gréviste [gʀevist(ə)] nm/f striker
gribouiller [gʀibuje] vt to scribble, scrawl
grief [gʀijɛf] nm grievance; **faire ~ à qn de** to reproach sb for
grièvement [gʀijɛvmɑ̃] adv seriously
griffe [gʀif] nf claw; (fig) signature
griffer [gʀife] vt to scratch
griffonner [gʀifɔne] vt to scribble
grignoter [gʀiɲɔte] vt to nibble ou gnaw at
gril [gʀil] nm steak ou grill pan
grillade [gʀijad] nf grill
grillage [gʀijaʒ] nm (treillis) wire netting; wire fencing
grille [gʀij] nf (clôture) railings pl; (portail) (metal) gate; (d'égout) (metal) grate; (fig) grid
grille-pain [gʀijpɛ̃] nm inv toaster

griller [gʀije] *vt* (*aussi: faire ~: pain*) to toast; (: *viande*) to grill; (*fig: ampoule etc*) to burn out, blow

grillon [gʀijɔ̃] *nm* cricket

grimace [gʀimas] *nf* grimace; (*pour faire rire*): **faire des ~s** to pull *ou* make faces

grimer [gʀime] *vt* to make up

grimper [gʀɛ̃pe] *vi, vt* to climb

grincer [gʀɛ̃se] *vi* (*porte, roue*) to grate; (*plancher*) to creak; **~ des dents** to grind one's teeth

grincheux, euse [gʀɛ̃ʃø, -øz] *adj* grumpy

grippe [gʀip] *nf* flu, influenza; **grippé, e** *adj*: **etre grippé** to have flu

gris, e [gʀi, gʀiz] *adj* grey; (*ivre*) tipsy; **faire ~e mine** to pull a miserable *ou* wry face

grisaille [gʀizaj] *nf* greyness, dullness

griser [gʀize] *vt* to intoxicate

grisonner [gʀizɔne] *vi* to be going grey

grisou [gʀizu] *nm* firedamp

grive [gʀiv] *nf* thrush

grivois, e [gʀivwa, -waz] *adj* saucy

Groenland [gʀɔɛnlɑ̃d] *nm* Greenland

grogner [gʀɔɲe] *vi* to growl; (*fig*) to grumble

groin [gʀwɛ̃] *nm* snout

grommeler [gʀɔmle] *vi* to mutter to o.s.

gronder [gʀɔ̃de] *vi* to rumble; (*fig: révolte*) to be brewing ♦ *vt* to scold

gros, se [gʀo, gʀos] *adj* big, large; (*obèse*) fat; (*travaux, dégâts*) extensive; (*large: trait, fil*) thick, heavy ♦ *adv*: **risquer/gagner ~** to risk/win a lot ♦ *nm* (*COMM*): **le ~** the wholesale business; **prix de ~** wholesale price; **par ~ temps/grosse mer** in rough weather/heavy seas; **le ~ de** the main body of; **the bulk of; en ~** roughly; (*COMM*) wholesale; **~ lot** jackpot; **~ mot** coarse word; **~ œuvre** *nm* (*CONSTR*) shell (of building); **~ plan** (*PHOTO*) close-up; **~ sel** cooking salt; **~se caisse** big drum

groseille [gʀozɛj] *nf*: **~ (rouge)/(blanche)** red/white currant; **~ à maquereau** gooseberry

grosse [gʀos] *adj voir* **gros**

grossesse [gʀoses] *nf* pregnancy

grosseur [gʀosœʀ] *nf* size; fatness; (*tumeur*) lump

grossier, ière [gʀosje, -ɛʀ] *adj* coarse; (*travail*) rough; crude; (*évident: erreur*) gross

grossir [gʀosiʀ] *vi* (*personne*) to put on weight; (*fig*) to grow, get bigger; (*rivière*) to swell ♦ *vt* to increase; to exaggerate; (*au microscope*) to magnify; (*suj: vêtement*): **~ qn** to make sb look fatter

grossiste [gʀosist(ə)] *nm/f* wholesaler

grosso modo [gʀosomodo] *adv* roughly

grotte [gʀot] *nf* cave

grouiller [gʀuje] *vi* to mill about; to swarm about; **~ de** to be swarming with

groupe [gʀup] *nm* group; **le ~ des 7** Group of 7; **~ sanguin** *nm* blood group; **~ment** [gʀupmɑ̃] *nm* grouping; group

grouper [gʀupe] *vt* to group; **se ~** *vi* to get together

grue [gʀy] *nf* crane

grumeaux [gʀymo] *nmpl* lumps

gué [ge] *nm* ford; **passer à ~** to ford

guenilles [gənij] *nfpl* rags

guenon [gənɔ̃] *nf* female monkey

guépard [gepaʀ] *nm* cheetah

guêpe [gɛp] *nf* wasp

guêpier [gepje] *nm* (*fig*) trap

guère [gɛʀ] *adv* (*avec adjectif, adverbe*): **ne ... ~** hardly; (*avec verbe*): **ne ... ~** *tournure négative* +much; hardly ever; *tournure négative* +(very) long; **il n'y a ~ que/de** there's hardly anybody (*ou* anything) but/hardly any

guéridon [geʀidɔ̃] *nm* pedestal table

guérilla [geʀija] *nf* guerrilla warfare

guérir [geʀiʀ] *vt* (*personne, maladie*) to cure; (*membre, plaie*) to heal ♦ *vi* to recover; be cured; to heal; **guérison** *nf* curing; healing; recovery

guérite [geʀit] *nf* sentry box

guerre [gɛʀ] *nf* war; (*méthode*): **~ atomique** atomic warfare *no pl*; **en ~** at war; **faire la ~ à** to wage war against; **de ~ lasse** finally; **~ d'usure** war of attrition; **guerrier, ière** *adj* warlike ♦ *nm/f* warrior

guet [gɛ] *nm*: **faire le ~** to be on the watch *ou* look-out

guet-apens [gɛtapɑ̃] *nm* ambush

guetter [gete] *vt* (*épier*) to watch (intently); (*attendre*) to watch (out) for; to be lying in wait for

gueule [gœl] *nf* mouth; (*fam*) face; mouth; **ta ~!** (*fam*) shut up!; **~ de bois** (*fam*) hangover

gueuler [gœle] (*fam*) *vi* to bawl

gui [gi] *nm* mistletoe

guichet [giʃɛ] *nm* (*de bureau, banque*) counter, window; (*d'une porte*) wicket, hatch; **les ~s** (*à la gare, au théâtre*) the ticket office *sg*

guide [gid] *nm* guide

guider [gide] *vt* to guide

guidon [gidɔ̃] *nm* handlebars *pl*

guignol [giɲɔl] *nm* ≈ Punch and Judy show; (*fig*) clown

guillemets [gijmɛ] *nmpl*: **entre ~** in inverted commas

guillotiner [gijotine] *vt* to guillotine

guindé, e [gɛ̃de] *adj* stiff, starchy

guirlande [giʀlɑ̃d] *nf* garland; (*de papier*) paper chain

guise [giz] *nf*: **à votre ~** as you wish *ou* please; **en ~ de** by way of

guitare [gitaʀ] *nf* guitar

gymnase [ʒimnɑz] *nm* gym(nasium)

gymnastique [ʒimnastik] *nf* gymnastics *sg*; (*au réveil etc*) keep-fit exercises *pl*

gynécologie [ʒinekɔlɔʒi] *nf* gynaecology; **gynécologue** *nm/f* gynaecologist

H h

habile [abil] *adj* skillful; (*malin*) clever; **habileté** *nf* skill, skilfulness; cleverness

habilité, e [abilite] *adj*: **~ à faire** entitled to do, empowered to do

habillé, e [abije] *adj* dressed; (*chic*) dressy; (*TECH*): **~ de** covered with; encased in

habillement [abijmɑ̃] *nm* clothes *pl*

habiller [abije] *vt* to dress; (*fournir en vêtements*) to clothe; **s'~** *vi* to dress (o.s.); (*se déguiser, mettre des vêtements chic*) to dress up

habit [abi] *nm* outfit; **~s** *nmpl* (*vêtements*) clothes; **~ (de soirée)** tails *pl*; evening dress

habitant, e [abitɑ̃, -ɑ̃t] *nm/f* inhabitant; (*d'une maison*) occupant

habitation [abitusjɔ̃] *nf* living; residence; home; house; **~s à loyer modéré** low-rent housing *sg*

habiter [abite] *vt* to live in; (*suj: sentiment*) to dwell in ♦ *vi*: **~ à/dans** to live in *ou* at/in

habitude [abityd] *nf* habit; **avoir l'~ de faire** to be in the habit of doing; (*expérience*) to be used to doing; **d'~** usually; **comme d'~** as usual

habitué, e [abitye] *nm/f* regular visitor; regular (customer)

habituel, le [abituɛl] *adj* usual

habituer [abitye] *vt*: **~ qn à** to get sb used to; **s'~ à** to get used to

'hache [aʃ] *nf* axe

'hacher [aʃe] *vt* (*viande*) to mince; (*persil*) to chop

'hachis [aʃi] *nm* mince *no pl*

'hachoir [aʃwaʀ] *nm* chopper; (*meat*) mincer; chopping board

'hagard, e [agaʀ, -aʀd(ə)] *adj* wild, distraught

'haie [ɛ] *nf* hedge; (*SPORT*) hurdle; (*fig: rang*) line, row

'haillons [ujɔ̃] *nmpl* rags

'haine [ɛn] *nf* hatred

'haïr [aiʀ] *vt* to detest, hate

'hâlé, e [ɑle] *adj* (sun)tanned, sunburnt

haleine [alɛn] *nf* breath; **hors d'~** out of breath; **tenir en ~** to hold spellbound; to keep in suspense; **de longue ~** long-term

'haler [ale] *vt* to haul in; to tow

'haleter [alte] *vt* to pant

'hall [ol] *nm* hall

'halle [al] *nf* (covered) market; **~s** *nfpl* (*d'une grande ville*) central food market *sg*

hallucinant, e [alysinɑ̃, -ɑ̃t] *adj* staggering

hallucination [alysinasjɔ̃] *nf* hallucination

'halte [alt(ə)] *nf* stop, break; stopping place; (*RAIL*) halt ♦ *excl* stop!; **faire ~** to stop

haltère [altɛʀ] *nm* dumbbell, barbell; **~s** *nmpl*: **(poids et) ~s** (*activité*) weight lifting *sg*

'hamac [amak] *nm* hammock

'hameau, x [amo] *nm* hamlet

hameçon [amsɔ̃] *nm* (fish) hook

'hanche [ɑ̃ʃ] *nf* hip

'handicapé, e [ɑ̃dikape] *nm/f* physically (*ou mentally*) handicapped person; **~ moteur** spastic

'hangar [ɑ̃gaʀ] *nm* shed; (*AVIAT*) hangar

'hanneton [antɔ̃] *nm* cockchafer

'hanter [ɑ̃te] *vt* to haunt

'hantise [ɑ̃tiz] *nf* obsessive fear

'happer [ape] *vt* to snatch; (*suj: train etc*) to hit

'haras [aʀɑ] *nm* stud farm

'harassant, e [aʀasɑ̃, -ɑ̃t] *adj* exhausting

'harceler [aʀsəle] *vt* (*MIL, CHASSE*) to harass, harry; (*importuner*) to plague

'hardi, e [aʀdi] *adj* bold, daring

'hareng [aʀɑ̃] *nm* herring

'hargne [aʀɲ(ə)] *nf* aggressiveness

'haricot [aʀikɔ] *nm* bean; **haricot blanc** haricot bean; **haricot vert** green bean

harmonica [aʀmɔnika] *nm* mouth organ

harmonie [aʀmɔni] *nf* harmony

'harnacher [aʀnaʃe] *vt* to harness

'harnais [aʀnɛ] *nm* harness

'harpe [aʀp(ə)] *nf* harp

'harponner [aʀpɔne] *vt* to harpoon; (*fam*) to collar

'hasard [azaʀ] *nm*: **le ~** chance, fate; **un ~** a coincidence; a stroke of luck; **au ~** aimlessly; at random; haphazardly; **par ~** by chance; **à tout ~** just in case; on the off chance (*BRIT*); **'hasarder** [azaʀde] *vt* (*mot*) to venture; (*fortune*) to risk

'hâte [ɑt] *nf* haste; **à la ~** hurriedly, hastily; **en ~** posthaste, with all possible speed; **avoir ~ de** to be eager *ou* anxious to; **~r** *vt* to hasten; **se ~r** *vi* to hurry

'hâtif, ive [ɑtif, -iv] *adj* hurried; hasty; (*légume*) early

'hausse [os] *nf* rise, increase

'hausser [ose] *vt* to raise; **~ les épaules** to shrug (one's shoulders)

'haut, e [o, ot] *adj* high; (*grand*) tall; (*son, voix*) high(-pitched) ♦ *adv* high ♦ *nm* top (part); **de 3 m ~** 3 m high, 3 m in height; **des ~s et des bas** ups and downs; **en ~ lieu** in high places; **à ~e voix, (tout) ~** aloud, out loud; **du ~ de** from the top of; **de ~ en bas** from top to bottom;

downwards; **plus** ~ higher up, further up; (*dans un texte*) above; (*parler*) louder; **en** ~ up above; at (*ou* to) the top; (*dans une maison*) upstairs; **en** ~ **de** at the top of
'hautain, e ['otɛ̃, -ɛn] *adj* haughty
'hautbois ['obwa] *nm* oboe
'haut-de-forme ['odfɔʀm(ə)] *nm* top hat
'hauteur ['otœʀ] *nf* height; (*fig*) loftiness; haughtiness; **à la** ~ **de** (*sur la même ligne*) level with; by; (*fig*) equal to; **à la** ~ up to it
'haut-fond ['ofɔ̃] *nm* shallow, shoal
'haut-fourneau ['ofuʀno] *nm* blast *ou* smelting furnace
'haut-le-cœur ['olkœʀ] *nm inv* retch, heave
'haut-parleur ['opaʀlœʀ] *nm* (loud) speaker
'havre ['ɑvʀ(ə)] *nm* haven
'Haye ['ɛ] *n*: **la Haye** the Hague
hebdo [ɛbdɔ] (*fam*) *nm* weekly
hebdomadaire [ɛbdɔmadɛʀ] *adj, nm* weekly
héberger [ebɛʀʒe] *vt* to accommodate, lodge; (*réfugiés*) to take in
hébété, e [ebete] *adj* dazed
hébreu, x [ebʀø] *adj m, nm* Hebrew
hécatombe [ekatɔ̃b] *nf* slaughter
hectare [ɛktaʀ] *nm* hectare
'hein ['ɛ̃] *excl* eh?
'hélas ['elɑs] *excl* alas! ♦ *adv* unfortunately
'héler ['ele] *vt* to hail
hélice [elis] *nf* propeller
hélicoptère [elikɔptɛʀ] *nm* helicopter
helvétique [ɛlvetik] *adj* Swiss
hémicycle [emisikl(ə)] *nm* semicircle; (*POL*): **l'**~ ≈ the benches (of the Commons) (*BRIT*), ≈ the floor (of the House of Representatives) (*US*)
hémorragie [emɔʀaʒi] *nf* bleeding *no pl*, haemorrhage
hémorroïdes [emɔʀɔid] *nfpl* piles, haemorrhoids
'hennir ['eniʀ] *vi* to neigh, whinny
herbe [ɛʀb(ə)] *nf* grass; (*CULIN, MÉD*) herb; **en** ~ unripe; (*fig*) budding; **herbicide** *nm* weed-killer; **herboriste** *nm/f* herbalist
'hère ['ɛʀ] *nm*: **pauvre hère** poor wretch
héréditaire [eʀeditɛʀ] *adj* hereditary
'hérisser ['eʀise] *vt*: ~ **qn** (*fig*) to ruffle sb; **se** ~ *vi* to bristle, bristle up
'hérisson ['eʀisɔ̃] *nm* hedgehog
héritage [eʀitaʒ] *nm* inheritance; (*fig*) heritage; legacy
hériter [eʀite] *vi*: ~ **de qch (de qn)** to inherit sth (from sb); **héritier, ière** *nm/f* heir(ess)
hermétique [ɛʀmetik] *adj* airtight; watertight; (*fig*) abstruse; impenetrable
hermine [ɛʀmin] *nf* ermine
'hernie ['ɛʀni] *nf* hernia
héroïne [eʀɔin] *nf* heroine; (*drogue*) heroin

'héron ['eʀɔ̃] *nm* heron
'héros ['eʀo] *nm* hero
hésitation [ezitasjɔ̃] *nf* hesitation
hésiter [ezite] *vi*: ~ **(à faire)** to hesitate (to do)
hétéroclite [eteʀɔklit] *adj* heterogeneous; (*objets*) sundry
'hêtre ['ɛtʀ(ə)] *nm* beech
heure [œʀ] *nf* hour; (*SCOL*) period; (*moment*) time; **c'est l'**~ it's time; **quelle** ~ **est-il?** what time is it?; **2** ~**s (du matin)** 2 o'clock (in the morning); **être à l'**~ to be on time; (*montre*) to be right; **mettre à l'**~ to set right; **à toute** ~ at any time; **24** ~**s sur 24** round the clock, 24 hours a day; **à l'**~ **qu'il est** at this time (of day); by now; **sur l'**~ at once; ~ **de pointe** *nf* rush hour; ~**s supplémentaires** overtime *sg*
heureusement [œʀøzmɑ̃] *adv* (*par bonheur*) fortunately, luckily
heureux, euse [œʀø, -øz] *adj* happy; (*chanceux*) lucky, fortunate; (*judicieux*) felicitous, fortunate
heurt ['œʀ] *nm* (*choc*) collision; ~**s** *nmpl* (*fig*) clashes
'heurter ['œʀte] *vt* (*mur*) to strike, hit; (*personne*) to collide with; (*fig*) to go against, upset; **se** ~ **à** *vt* to come up against; **'heurtoir** *nm* door knocker
hexagone [ɛgzagɔn] *nm* hexagon; (*la France*) France (*because of its shape*)
hiberner [ibɛʀne] *vi* to hibernate
'hibou, x ['ibu] *nm* owl
'hideux, euse ['idø, -øz] *adj* hideous
hier [jɛʀ] *adv* yesterday; **toute la journée d'**~ all day yesterday; **toute la matinée d'**~ all yesterday morning
'hiérarchie ['jeʀaʀʃi] *nf* hierarchy
hilare [ilaʀ] *adj* mirthful
hippique [ipik] *adj* equestrian, horse *cpd*
hippodrome [ipodʀom] *nm* racecourse
hippopotame [ipopɔtam] *nm* hippopotamus
hirondelle [iʀɔ̃dɛl] *nf* swallow
hirsute [iʀsyt] *adj* hairy; shaggy; tousled
'hisser ['ise] *vt* to hoist, haul up
histoire [istwaʀ] *nf* (*science, événements*) history; (*anecdote, récit, mensonge*) story; (*affaire*) business *no pl*; ~**s** *nfpl* (*chichis*) fuss *no pl*; (*ennuis*) trouble *sg*; **historique** *adj* historic*al*; (*important*) historic
hiver [ivɛʀ] *nm* winter; **hivernal, e, aux** *adj* winter *cpd*; wintry; **hiverner** *vi* to winter
HLM *sigle m/f* = **habitation(s) à loyer modéré**
'hobby ['ɔbi] *nm* hobby
'hocher ['ɔʃe] *vt*: ~ **la tête** to nod; (*signe négatif ou dubitatif*) to shake one's head
'hochet ['ɔʃɛ] *nm* rattle
'hockey ['ɔkɛ] *nm*: ~ **(sur glace/gazon)** (ice/field) hockey

'**hold-up** ['ɔldœp] nm inv hold-up
'**hollandais, e** ['ɔlɑ̃dɛ, -ɛz] adj Dutch ♦ nm
(LING) Dutch ♦ nm/f: **Hollandais, e** Dutchman(woman); **les Hollandais** the Dutch
'**Hollande** ['ɔlɑ̃d] nf: **la ~** Holland
'**homard** ['ɔmar] nm lobster
homéopathique [ɔmeɔpatik] adj homoeopathic
homicide [ɔmisid] nm murder; **~ involontaire** manslaughter
hommage [ɔmaʒ] nm tribute; **~s** nmpl:
présenter ses ~s to pay one's respects;
rendre ~ à to pay tribute ou homage to
homme [ɔm] nm man; **~ d'affaires** businessman; **~ d'État** statesman; **~ de main**
hired man; **~ de paille** stooge; **~-grenouille** nm frogman
homo: **~gène** adj homogeneous; **~logue**
nm/f counterpart, opposite number; **~logué, e** adj (SPORT) officially recognized,
ratified; (tarif) authorized; **~nyme** nm
(LING) homonym; (d'une personne) namesake; **~sexuel, le** adj homosexual
'**Hongrie** ['ɔ̃gri] nf: **la Hongrie** Hungary;
'**hongrois, e** adj, nm/f Hungarian
honnête [ɔnɛt] adj (intègre) honest; (juste,
satisfaisant) fair; **~ment** adv honestly; **~té**
nf honesty
honneur [ɔnœr] nm honour; (mérite) credit; **en l'~ de** in honour of; (événement) on
the occasion of; **faire ~ à** (engagements) to
honour; (famille) to be a credit to; (fig: repas etc) to do justice to
honorable [ɔnɔrabl(ə)] adj worthy, honourable; (suffisant) decent
honoraire [ɔnɔrɛr] adj honorary; **professeur ~** professor emeritus; **honoraires**
nmpl fees pl
honorer [ɔnɔre] vt to honour; (estimer) to
hold in high regard; (faire honneur à) to do
credit to; **s'~ de** vt to pride o.s. upon; **honorifique** adj honorary
'**honte** ['ɔ̃t] nf shame; **avoir ~ de** to be
ashamed of; **faire ~ à qn** to make sb (feel)
ashamed; '**honteux, euse** adj ashamed;
(conduite, acte) shameful, disgraceful
hôpital, aux [ɔpital, -o] nm hospital ·
'**hoquet** ['ɔkɛ] nm: **avoir le hoquet** to have
(the) hiccoughs; '**hoqueter** vi to hiccough
horaire [ɔrɛr] adj hourly ♦ nm timetable,
schedule; **~s** nmpl (d'employé) hours; **~
souple** flexitime
horizon [ɔrizɔ̃] nm horizon; (paysage)
landscape, view
horizontal, e, aux [ɔrizɔ̃tal, -o] adj horizontal
horloge [ɔrlɔʒ] nf clock; **horloger, ère**
nm/f watchmaker; clockmaker; **horlogerie**
nf watch-making; watchmaker's (shop);
clockmaker's (shop)
'**hormis** ['ɔrmi] prép save
horoscope [ɔrɔskɔp] nm horoscope

horreur [ɔrœr] nf horror; **avoir ~ de** to
loathe ou detest; **horrible** adj horrible
horripiler [ɔripile] vt to exasperate
'**hors** ['ɔr] prép except (for); **~ de** out of;
~ pair outstanding; **~ de propos** inopportune; **être ~ de soi** to be beside o.s.; **~
d'usage** out of service; **~-bord** nm inv
speedboat (with outboard motor); **~-concours** adj ineligible to compete; **~-
d'œuvre** nm inv hors d'œuvre; **~-jeu** nm
inv offside; **~-la-loi** nm inv outlaw; **~-taxe**
adj (boutique, articles) duty-free
hospice [ɔspis] nm (de vieillards) home
hospitalier, ière [ɔspitalje, -jɛr] adj (accueillant) hospitable; (MÉD: service, centre)
hospital cpd
hospitalité [ɔspitalite] nf hospitality
hostie [ɔsti] nf host (REL)
hostile [ɔstil] adj hostile; **hostilité** nf hostility
hôte [ot] nm (maître de maison) host; (invité) guest
hôtel [otɛl] nm hotel; **aller à l'~** to stay in
a hotel; **~ de ville** town hall; **~ (particulier)** (private) mansion; **hôtelier, ière**
adj hotel cpd ♦ nm/f hotelier; **hôtellerie** nf
hotel business; (auberge) inn
hôtesse [otɛs] nf hostess; **~ de l'air** air
stewardess
'**hotte** ['ɔt] nf (panier) basket (carried on the
back); (de cheminée) hood; **hotte aspirante**
cooker hood
'**houblon** ['ublɔ̃] nm (BOT) hop; (pour la
bière) hops pl
'**houille** ['uj] nf coal; **houille blanche**
hydroelectric power
'**houle** ['ul] nf swell
'**houlette** ['ulɛt] nf: **sous la ~ de** under
the guidance of
'**houleux, euse** ['ulø, -øz] adj heavy,
swelling; (fig) stormy, turbulent
'**houspiller** ['uspije] vt to scold
'**housse** ['us] nf cover; dust cover; loose ou
stretch cover
'**houx** ['u] nm holly
'**hublot** ['yblo] nm porthole
'**huche** ['yʃ] nf: **~ à pain** bread bin
'**huer** ['ɥe] vt to boo
huile [ɥil] nf oil; **huiler** vt to oil; **huileux,
euse** adj oily
huis [ɥi] nm: **à ~ clos** in camera
huissier [ɥisje] nm usher; (JUR) ≈ bailiff
'**huit** ['ɥit] num eight; **samedi en huit** a
week on Saturday; '**huitaine** nf: **une huitaine (de jours)** a week or so; '**huitième**
num eighth
huître [ɥitr(ə)] nf oyster
humain, e [ymɛ̃, -ɛn] adj human; (compatissant) humane ♦ nm human (being); **humanité** nf humanity
humble [œ̃bl(ə)] adj humble
humecter [ymɛkte] vt to dampen

'humer ['yme] vt to smell; to inhale

humeur [ymœR] nf mood; (tempérament) temper; (irritation) bad temper; de bonne/mauvaise ~ in a good/bad mood

humide [ymid] adj damp; (main, yeux) moist; (climat, chaleur) humid; (saison, route) wet

humilier [ymilje] vt to humiliate

humilité [ymilite] nf humility, humbleness

humoristique [ymɔristik] adj humorous; humoristic

humour [ymuR] nm humour; avoir de l'~ to have a sense of humour; ~ noir sick humour

'hurlement ['yRləmɑ̃] nm howling no pl, howl, yelling no pl, yell

'hurler ['yRle] vi to howl, yell

hurluberlu [yRlybɛRly] (péj) nm crank

'hutte ['yt] nf hut

hydratant, e [idRatɑ̃, -ɑ̃t] adj (crème) moisturizing

hydrate [idRat] nm: ~s de carbone carbohydrates

hydraulique [idRolik] adj hydraulic

hydravion [idRavjɔ̃] nm seaplane

hydrogène [idRɔʒɛn] nm hydrogen

hydroglisseur [idRɔglisœR] nm hydroplane

hygiénique [iʒjenik] adj hygienic

hymne [imn(ə)] nm hymn; ~ national national anthem

hypermarché [ipɛRmaRʃe] nm hypermarket

hypermétrope [ipɛRmetRɔp] adj longsighted

hypnotiser [ipnɔtize] vt to hypnotize

hypocrite [ipɔkRit] adj hypocritical

hypothèque [ipɔtɛk] nf mortgage

hypothèse [ipɔtɛz] nf hypothesis

hystérique [isteRik] adj hysterical

_____ / i

iceberg [isbɛRg] nm iceberg

ici [isi] adv here; jusqu'~ as far as this; until now; d'~ là by then; in the meantime; d'~ peu before long

idéal, e, aux [ideal, -o] adj ideal ♦ nm ideal; ideals pl

idée [ide] nf idea; avoir dans l'~ que to have an idea that; ~s noires black ou dark thoughts

identifier [idɑ̃tifje] vt to identify; s'~ à (héros etc) to identify with

identique [idɑ̃tik] adj: ~ (à) identical (to)

identité [idɑ̃tite] nf identity

idiot, e [idjo, idjɔt] adj idiotic ♦ nm/f idiot

idole [idɔl] nf idol

if [if] nm yew

ignare [iɲaR] adj ignorant

ignoble [iɲɔbl(ə)] adj vile

ignorant, e [iɲɔRɑ̃, -ɑ̃t] adj ignorant

ignorer [iɲɔRe] vt (ne pas connaître) not to know, be unaware ou ignorant of; (être sans expérience de: plaisir, guerre etc) not to know about, have no experience of; (bouder: personne) to ignore

il [il] pron he; (animal, chose, en tournure impersonnelle) it; ~s they; voir aussi avoir

île [il] nf island; les ~s anglo-normandes the Channel Islands; les ~s Britanniques the British Isles

illégal, e, aux [ilegal, -o] adj illegal

illégitime [ileʒitim] adj illegitimate

illettré, e [iletRe] adj, nm/f illiterate

illimité, e [ilimite] adj unlimited

illisible [ilizibl(ə)] adj illegible; (roman) unreadable

illumination [ilyminasjɔ̃] nf illumination, floodlighting; (idée) flash of inspiration

illuminer [ilymine] vt to light up; (monument, rue: pour une fête) to illuminate, floodlight

illusion [ilyzjɔ̃] nf illusion; se faire des ~s to delude o.s.; faire ~ to delude ou fool people; illusionniste nm conjuror

illustration [ilystRasjɔ̃] nf illustration

illustre [ilystR(ə)] adj illustrious

illustré, e [ilystRe] adj illustrated ♦ nm illustrated magazine; comic

illustrer [ilystRe] vt to illustrate; s'~ to become famous, win fame

îlot [ilo] nm small island, islet; (de maisons) block

ils [il] pron voir il

image [imaʒ] nf (gén) picture; (comparaison, ressemblance, OPTIQUE) image; ~ de marque brand image; (fig) public image

imagination [imaʒinasjɔ̃] nf imagination; (chimère) fancy; avoir de l'~ to be imaginative

imaginer [imaʒine] vt to imagine; (inventer: expédient) to devise, think up; s'~ vt (se figurer: scène etc) to imagine, picture; s'~ que to imagine that

imbécile [ɛ̃besil] adj idiotic ♦ nm/f idiot

imberbe [ɛ̃bɛRb(ə)] adj beardless

imbiber [ɛ̃bibe] vt to moisten, wet; s'~ de to become saturated with

imbu, e [ɛ̃by] adj: ~ de full of

imitateur, trice [imitatœR, -tRis] nm/f (gén) imitator; (MUSIC-HALL) impersonator

imitation [imitasjɔ̃] nf imitation; (sketch) imitation, impression; impersonation

imiter [imite] vt to imitate; (contrefaire) to forge; (ressembler à) to look like

immaculé, e [imakyle] *adj* spotless; immaculate

immatriculation [imatʀikylɑsjɔ̃] *nf* registration

immatriculer [imatʀikyle] *vt* to register; **faire/se faire ~** to register

immédiat, e [imedja, -at] *adj* immediate ♦ *nm*: **dans l'~** for the time being; **~ement** *adv* immediately

immense [imɑ̃s] *adj* immense

immerger [imɛʀʒe] *vt* to immerse, submerge

immeuble [imœbl(ə)] *nm* building; **~ loca-tif** block of rented flats (*BRIT*), rental build-ing (*US*)

immigration [imigʀɑsjɔ̃] *nf* immigration

immigré, e [imigʀe] *nm/f* immigrant

imminent, e [iminɑ̃, -ɑ̃t] *adj* imminent

immiscer [imise]: **s'~** *vi* to interfere in *ou* with

immobile [imɔbil] *adj* still, motionless; (*fig*) unchanging

immobilier, ière [imɔbilje, -jɛʀ] *adj* property *cpd* ♦ *nm*: **l'~** the property business

immobiliser [imɔbilize] *vt* (*gén*) to immo-bilize; (*circulation, véhicule, affaires*) to bring to a standstill; **s'~** (*personne*) to stand still; (*machine, véhicule*) to come to a halt

immonde [imɔ̃d] *adj* foul

immondices [imɔ̃dis] *nmpl* refuse *sg*; filth *sg*

immoral, e, aux [imɔʀal, -o] *adj* immoral

immuable [imɥabl(ə)] *adj* immutable; un-changing

immunisé, e [imynize] *adj*: **~ contre** im-mune to

immunité [imynite] *nf* immunity

impact [ɛ̃pakt] *nm* impact

impair, e [ɛ̃pɛʀ] *adj* odd ♦ *nm* faux pas, blunder

impardonnable [ɛ̃paʀdɔnabl(ə)] *adj* unpar-donable, unforgivable

imparfait, e [ɛ̃paʀfɛ, -ɛt] *adj* imperfect

impartial, e, aux [ɛ̃paʀsjal, -o] *adj* impar-tial, unbiased

impartir [ɛ̃paʀtiʀ] *vt* to assign; to bestow

impasse [ɛ̃pɑs] *nf* dead-end, cul-de-sac; (*fig*) deadlock

impassible [ɛ̃pasibl(ə)] *adj* impassive

impatience [ɛ̃pasjɑ̃s] *nf* impatience

impatient, e [ɛ̃pasjɑ̃, -ɑ̃t] *adj* impatient

impayable [ɛ̃pejabl(ə)] *adj* (*drôle*) priceless

impeccable [ɛ̃pekabl(ə)] *adj* faultless, im-peccable; spotlessly clean; impeccably dressed; (*fam*) smashing

impensable [ɛ̃pɑ̃sabl(ə)] *adj* unthinkable; unbelievable

impératif, ive [ɛ̃peʀatif, -iv] *adj* imperative ♦ *nm* (*LING*) imperative; **~s** *nmpl* (*exi-gences*) requirements; demands

impératrice [ɛ̃peʀatʀis] *nf* empress

impérial, e, aux [ɛ̃peʀjal, -o] *adj* imperial; **impériale** *nf* top deck

impérieux, euse [ɛ̃peʀjø, -øz] *adj* (*carac-tère, ton*) imperious; (*obligation, besoin*) pressing, urgent

impérissable [ɛ̃peʀisabl(ə)] *adj* undying; imperishable

imperméable [ɛ̃pɛʀmeabl(ə)] *adj* water-proof; (*GÉO*) impermeable; (*fig*): **~ à** im-pervious to ♦ *nm* raincoat

impertinent, e [ɛ̃pɛʀtinɑ̃, -ɑ̃t] *adj* imperti-nent

impétueux, euse [ɛ̃petɥø, -øz] *adj* fiery

impie [ɛ̃pi] *adj* impious, ungodly

impitoyable [ɛ̃pitwajabl(ə)] *adj* pitiless, merciless

implanter [ɛ̃plɑ̃te] *vt* (*usine, industrie, usage*) to establish; (*colons etc*) to settle; (*idée, préjugé*) to implant

impliquer [ɛ̃plike] *vt* to imply; **~ qn (dans)** to implicate sb (in)

impoli, e [ɛ̃pɔli] *adj* impolite, rude

importance [ɛ̃pɔʀtɑ̃s] *nf* importance; **sans ~** unimportant

important, e [ɛ̃pɔʀtɑ̃, -ɑ̃t] *adj* important; (*en quantité*) considerable, sizeable; exten-sive; (*péj*: *airs, ton*) self-important ♦ *nm*: **l'~** the important thing

importateur, trice [ɛ̃pɔʀtatœʀ, -tʀis] *nm/f* importer

importation [ɛ̃pɔʀtɑsjɔ̃] *nf* importation; introduction; (*produit*) import

importer [ɛ̃pɔʀte] *vt* (*COMM*) to import; (*maladies, plantes*) to introduce ♦ *vi* (*être important*) to matter; **il importe qu'il fasse** it is important that he should do; **peu m'importe** I don't mind; I don't care; **peu importe (que)** it doesn't matter (if); *voir aussi* **n'importe**

importun, e [ɛ̃pɔʀtœ̃, -yn] *adj* irksome, im-portunate; (*arrivée, visite*) inopportune, ill-timed ♦ *nm* intruder; **importuner** *vt* to bother

imposable [ɛ̃pozabl(e)] *adj* taxable

imposant, e [ɛ̃pozɑ̃, -ɑ̃t] *adj* imposing

imposer [ɛ̃poze] *vt* (*taxer*) to tax; **s'~** (*être nécessaire*) to be imperative; (*montrer sa proéminence*) to stand out, emerge; (*artiste*: *se faire connaître*) to win recognition; **~ qch à qn** to impose sth on sb; **en ~ à** to impress; **imposition** [ɛ̃pozisjɔ̃] *nf* (*ADMIN*) taxation

impossible [ɛ̃pɔsibl(ə)] *adj* impossible; **il m'est ~ de le faire** it is impossible for me to do it, I can't possibly do it; **faire l'~** to do one's utmost

impôt [ɛ̃po] *nm* tax; (*taxes*) taxation; taxes *pl*; **~s** *nmpl* (*contributions*) (income) tax *sg*; **payer 1000 F d'~s** to pay 1,000 F in tax; **~ foncier** land tax; **~ sur le chiffre d'affai-res** corporation tax; (*BRIT*) *ou* corporate (*US*) tax; **~ sur le revenu** income tax

impotent, e [ɛpɔtɑ̃, -ɑ̃t] *adj* disabled

impraticable [ɛpratikabl(ə)] *adj* (*projet*) impracticable, unworkable; (*piste*) impassable

imprécis, e [ɛpresi, -iz] *adj* imprecise

imprégner [ɛpreɲe] *vt* (*tissu, tampon*) to soak, impregnate; (*lieu, air*) to fill; **s'~ de** (*fig*) to absorb

imprenable [ɛprənabl(ə)] *adj* (*forteresse*) impregnable; **vue ~** unrestricted view

impression [ɛpresjɔ̃] *nf* impression; (*d'un ouvrage, tissu*) printing; **faire bonne ~** to make a good impression

impressionnant, e [ɛpresjɔnɑ̃, -ɑ̃t] *adj* impressive; upsetting

impressionner [ɛpresjɔne] *vt* (*frapper*) to impress; (*troubler*) to upset

imprévisible [ɛprevizibl(ə)] *adj* unforeseeable

imprévoyant, e [ɛprevwajɑ̃, -ɑ̃t] *adj* lacking in foresight; (*en matière d'argent*) improvident

imprévu, e [ɛprevy] *adj* unforeseen, unexpected ♦ *nm* unexpected incident; **en cas d'~** if anything unexpected happens

imprimante [ɛprimɑ̃t] *nf* printer; **~ matricielle** dot-matrix printer

imprimé [ɛprime] *nm* (*formulaire*) printed form; (*POSTES*) printed matter *no pl*

imprimer [ɛprime] *vt* to print; (*empreinte etc*) to imprint; (*publier*) to publish; (*communiquer: mouvement, impulsion*) to impart, transmit; **imprimerie** *nf* printing; (*établissement*) printing works *sg*; **imprimeur** *nm* printer

impromptu, e [ɛprɔ̃pty] *adj* impromptu; sudden

impropre [ɛprɔpr(ə)] *adj* inappropriate; **~ à** unsuitable for

improviser [ɛprɔvize] *vt, vi* to improvise

improviste [ɛprɔvist(ə)]: **à l'~** *adv* unexpectedly, without warning

imprudence [ɛprydɑ̃s] *nf* carelessness *no pl*; imprudence *no pl*

imprudent, e [ɛprydɑ̃, -ɑ̃t] *adj* (*conducteur, geste, action*) careless; (*remarque*) unwise, imprudent; (*projet*) foolhardy

impudent, e [ɛpydɑ̃, -ɑ̃t] *adj* impudent; brazen

impudique [ɛpydik] *adj* shameless

impuissant, e [ɛpɥisɑ̃, -ɑ̃t] *adj* helpless; (*sans effet*) ineffectual; (*sexuellement*) impotent; **~ à faire** powerless to do

impulsif, ive [ɛpylsif, -iv] *adj* impulsive

impulsion [ɛpylsjɔ̃] *nf* (*ÉLEC, instinct*) impulse; (*élan, influence*) impetus

impunément [ɛpynemɑ̃] *adv* with impunity

imputer [ɛpyte] *vt* (*attribuer*) to ascribe, impute; (*COMM*): **~ à** *ou* **sur** to charge to

inabordable [inabɔrdabl(ə)] *adj* (*cher*) prohibitive

inaccessible [inaksesibl(ə)] *adj* inaccessible; unattainable; (*insensible*): **~ à** impervious to

inachevé, e [inaʃve] *adj* unfinished

inadapté, e [inadapte] *adj* (*gén*): **~ à** not adapted to, unsuited to; (*PSYCH*) maladjusted

inadmissible [inadmisibl(ə)] *adj* inadmissible

inadvertance [inadvɛrtɑ̃s] : **par ~** *adv* inadvertently

inaltérable [inaltɛrabl(ə)] *adj* (*matière*) stable; (*fig*) unchanging; **~ à** unaffected by

inamovible [inamɔvibl(ə)] *adj* fixed; (*JUR*) irremovable

inanimé, e [inanime] *adj* (*matière*) inanimate; (*évanoui*) unconscious; (*sans vie*) lifeless

inanition [inanisjɔ̃] *nf*: **tomber d'~** to faint with hunger (and exhaustion)

inaperçu, e [inapɛrsy] *adj*: **passer ~** to go unnoticed

inappréciable [inapresjabl(ə)] *adj* (*service*) invaluable

inapte [inapt(ə)] *adj*: **~ à** incapable of; (*MIL*) unfit for

inattaquable [inatakabl(ə)] *adj* (*texte, preuve*) irrefutable

inattendu, e [inatɑ̃dy] *adj* unexpected

inattentif, ive [inatɑ̃tif, -iv] *adj* inattentive; **~ à** (*dangers, détails*) heedless of; **inattention** *nf*: **faute d'inattention** careless mistake

inaugurer [inɔgyre] *vt* (*monument*) to unveil; (*exposition, usine*) to open; (*fig*) to inaugurate

inavouable [inavwabl(ə)] *adj* shameful; undisclosable

inavoué, e [inavwe] *adj* unavowed

incandescence [ɛkɑ̃desɑ̃s] *nf*: **porter à ~** to heat white-hot

incapable [ɛkapabl(ə)] *adj* incapable; **~ de faire** incapable of doing; (*empêché*) unable to do

incapacité [ɛkapasite] *nf* incapability; (*JUR*) incapacity

incarcérer [ɛkarsere] *vt* to incarcerate, imprison

incarner [ɛkarne] *vt* to embody, personify; (*THÉÂTRE*) to play

incartade [ɛkartad] *nf* prank

incassable [ɛkasabl(ə)] *adj* unbreakable

incendiaire [ɛsɑ̃djɛr] *adj* incendiary; (*fig: discours*) inflammatory ♦ *nm/f* fire-raiser, arsonist

incendie [ɛsɑ̃di] *nm* fire; **~ criminel** arson *no pl*; **~ de forêt** forest fire; **~r** [ɛsɑ̃dje] *vt* (*mettre le feu à*) to set fire to, set alight; (*brûler complètement*) to burn down

incertain, e [ɛsɛrtɛ̃, -ɛn] *adj* uncertain; (*temps*) uncertain, unsettled; (*imprécis: contours*) indistinct, blurred; **incertitude** *nf* uncertainty

incessamment [ɛ̃sɛsamɑ̃] *adv* very shortly

incidemment [ɛ̃sidamɑ̃] *adv* in passing

incident [ɛ̃sidɑ̃] *nm* incident; ~ **de parcours** minor hitch *ou* setback; ~ **technique** technical difficulties *pl*

incinérer [ɛ̃sineʀe] *vt* (*ordures*) to incinerate; (*mort*) to cremate

incisive [ɛ̃siziv] *nf* incisor

inciter [ɛ̃site] *vt*: ~ **qn à (faire) qch** to encourage sb to do sth; (*à la révolte etc*) to incite sb to do sth

inclinable [ɛ̃klinabl(ə)] *adj*: **siège à dossier** ~ reclining seat

inclinaison [ɛ̃klinɛzɔ̃] *nf* (*déclivité: d'une route etc*) incline; (: *d'un toit*) slope; (*état penché*) tilt

inclination [ɛ̃klinasjɔ̃] *nf*: ~ **de (la) tête** nod (of the head); ~ **(de buste)** bow

incliner [ɛ̃kline] *vt* (*tête, bouteille*) to tilt ♦ *vi*: ~ **à qch/à faire** to incline towards sth/doing; **s'~ (devant)** to bow (before); (*céder*) to give in *ou* yield (to); ~ **la tête** *ou* **le front** to give a slight bow

inclure [ɛ̃klyʀ] *vt* to include; (*joindre à un envoi*) to enclose; **jusqu'au 10 mars inclus** until 10th March inclusive

incoercible [ɛ̃kɔɛʀsibl(ə)] *adj* uncontrollable

incohérent, e [ɛ̃kɔeʀɑ̃, -ɑ̃t] *adj* inconsistent; incoherent

incollable [ɛ̃kɔlabl(ə)] *adj*: **il est** ~ he's got all the answers

incolore [ɛ̃kɔlɔʀ] *adj* colourless

incomber [ɛ̃kɔ̃be] : ~ **à** *vt* (*suj: devoirs, responsabilité*) to rest upon; (: *frais, travail*) to be the responsibility of

incommensurable [ɛ̃kɔmɑ̃syʀabl(ə)] *adj* immeasurable

incommode [ɛ̃kɔmɔd] *adj* inconvenient; (*posture, siège*) uncomfortable

incommoder [ɛ̃kɔmɔde] *vt*: ~ **qn** to inconvenience sb; (*embarrasser*) to make sb feel uncomfortable

incompétent, e [ɛ̃kɔ̃petɑ̃, -ɑ̃t] *adj* incompetent

incompris, e [ɛ̃kɔ̃pʀi, -iz] *adj* misunderstood

inconcevable [ɛ̃kɔ̃svabl(ə)] *adj* incredible

inconciliable [ɛ̃kɔ̃siljabl(ə)] *adj* irreconcilable

inconditionnel, le [ɛ̃kɔ̃disjɔnɛl] *adj* unconditional; (*partisan*) unquestioning

incongru, e [ɛ̃kɔ̃gʀy] *adj* unseemly

inconnu, e [ɛ̃kɔny] *adj* unknown; new, strange ♦ *nm/f* stranger; unknown person (*ou* artist *etc*) ♦ *nm*: **l'**~ the unknown; ~**e** *nf* unknown

inconsciemment [ɛ̃kɔ̃sjamɑ̃] *adv* unconsciously

inconscient, e [ɛ̃kɔ̃sjɑ̃, -ɑ̃t] *adj* unconscious; (*irréfléchi*) thoughtless, reckless ♦

nm (*PSYCH*): **l'**~ the unconscious; ~ **de** unaware of

inconsidéré, e [ɛ̃kɔ̃sideʀe] *adj* ill-considered

inconsistant, e [ɛ̃kɔ̃sistɑ̃, -ɑ̃t] *adj* flimsy, weak; runny

incontestable [ɛ̃kɔ̃tɛstabl(ə)] *adj* indisputable

incontournable [ɛ̃kɔ̃tuʀnabl(ə)] *adj* unavoidable

inconvenant, e [ɛ̃kɔ̃vnɑ̃, -ɑ̃t] *adj* unseemly, improper

inconvénient [ɛ̃kɔ̃venjɑ̃] *nm* (*d'une situation, d'un projet*) disadvantage, drawback; (*d'un remède, changement etc*) inconvenience; **si vous n'y voyez pas d'**~ if you have no objections

incorporer [ɛ̃kɔʀpɔʀe] *vt*: ~ **(à)** to mix in (with); (*paragraphe etc*): ~ **(dans)** to incorporate (in); (*MIL: appeler*) to recruit, call up

incorrect, e [ɛ̃kɔʀɛkt] *adj* (*impropre, inconvenant*) improper; (*défectueux*) faulty; (*inexact*) incorrect; (*impoli*) impolite; (*déloyal*) underhand

incrédule [ɛ̃kʀedyl] *adj* incredulous; (*REL*) unbelieving

increvable [ɛ̃kʀəvabl(ə)] (*fam*) *adj* tireless

incriminer [ɛ̃kʀimine] *vt* (*personne*) to incriminate; (*action, conduite*) to bring under attack; (*bonne foi, honnêteté*) to call into question

incroyable [ɛ̃kʀwajabl(ə)] *adj* incredible; unbelievable

incruster [ɛ̃kʀyste] *vt* (*ART*) to inlay; **s'**~ *vi* (*invité*) to take root; (*radiateur etc*) to become coated with fur *ou* scale

inculpé, e [ɛ̃kylpe] *nm/f* accused

inculper [ɛ̃kylpe] *vt*: ~ **(de)** to charge (with)

inculquer [ɛ̃kylke] *vt*: ~ **qch à** to inculcate sth in *ou* instil sth into

inculte [ɛ̃kylt(ə)] *adj* uncultivated; (*esprit, peuple*) uncultured; (*barbe*) unkempt

Inde [ɛ̃d] *nf*: **l'**~ India

indécis, e [ɛ̃desi, -iz] *adj* indecisive; (*perplexe*) undecided

indéfendable [ɛ̃defɑ̃dabl(ə)] *adj* indefensible

indéfini, e [ɛ̃defini] *adj* (*imprécis, incertain*) undefined; (*illimité, LING*) indefinite; **indéfiniment** *adv* indefinitely; **indéfinissable** *adj* indefinable

indélébile [ɛ̃delebil] *adj* indelible

indélicat, e [ɛ̃delika, -at] *adj* tactless; dishonest

indemne [ɛ̃dɛmn(ə)] *adj* unharmed

indemniser [ɛ̃dɛmnize] *vt*: ~ **qn (de)** to compensate sb (for)

indemnité [ɛ̃dɛmnite] *nf* (*dédommagement*) compensation *no pl*; (*allocation*) allowance; ~ **de licenciement** redundancy payment

indépendamment [ɛ̃depɑ̃damɑ̃] *adv* independently; ~ **de** (*abstraction faite de*) irrespective of; (*en plus de*) over and above

indépendance [ɛ̃depɑ̃dɑ̃s] *nf* independence

indépendant, e [ɛ̃depɑ̃dɑ̃, -ɑ̃t] *adj* independent; ~ **de** independent of

indescriptible [ɛ̃dɛskriptibl(ə)] *adj* indescribable

indétermination [ɛ̃detɛrminɑsjɔ̃] *nf* indecision; indecisiveness

indéterminé, e [ɛ̃detɛrmine] *adj* unspecified; indeterminate

index [ɛ̃dɛks] *nm* (*doigt*) index finger; (*d'un livre etc*) index; **mettre à l'~** to blacklist

indexé, e [ɛ̃dɛkse] *adj* (*ÉCON*): ~ (**sur**) index-linked (to)

indicateur [ɛ̃dikatœr] *nm* (*POLICE*) informer; (*livre*) guide; directory; (*TECH*) gauge; indicator; ~ **des chemins de fer** railway timetable

indicatif, ive [ɛ̃dikatif, -iv] *adj*: **à titre** ~ for (your) information ♦ *nm* (*LING*) indicative; (*RADIO*) theme *ou* signature tune; (*TÉL*) dialling code

indication [ɛ̃dikɑsjɔ̃] *nf* indication; (*renseignement*) information *no pl*; ~**s** *nfpl* (*directives*) instructions

indice [ɛ̃dis] *nm* (*marque, signe*) indication, sign; (*POLICE: lors d'une enquête*) clue; (*JUR: présomption*) piece of evidence; (*SCIENCE, ÉCON, TECH*) index

indicible [ɛ̃disibl(ə)] *adj* inexpressible

indien, ne [ɛ̃djɛ̃, -jɛn] *adj, nm/f* Indian

indifféremment [ɛ̃diferamɑ̃] *adv* (*sans distinction*) equally (well); indiscriminately

indifférence [ɛ̃diferɑ̃s] *nf* indifference; **indifférent, e** [ɛ̃diferɑ̃, -ɑ̃t] *adj* (*peu intéressé*) indifferent

indigence [ɛ̃diʒɑ̃s] *nf* poverty

indigène [ɛ̃diʒɛn] *adj* native, indigenous; local ♦ *nm/f* native

indigeste [ɛ̃diʒɛst(ə)] *adj* indigestible

indigestion [ɛ̃diʒɛstjɔ̃] *nf* indigestion *no pl*

indigne [ɛ̃diɲ] *adj* unworthy

indigner [ɛ̃diɲe] *vt*: **s'~** (**de** *ou* **contre**) to be indignant (at)

indiqué, e [ɛ̃dike] *adj* (*date, lieu*) given; (*adéquat, conseillé*) suitable

indiquer [ɛ̃dike] *vt* (*désigner*): ~ **qch/qn à qn** to point sth/sb out to sb; (*suj: pendule, aiguille*) to show; (: *étiquette, plan*) to show, indicate; (*faire connaître: médecin, restaurant*): ~ **qch/qn à qn** to tell sb of sth/sb; (*renseigner sur*) to point out, tell; (*déterminer: date, lieu*) to give, state; (*dénoter*) to indicate, point to

indirect, e [ɛ̃dirɛkt] *adj* indirect

indiscipline [ɛ̃disiplin] *nf* lack of discipline; **indiscipliné, e** *adj* undisciplined; (*fig*) unmanageable

indiscret, ète [ɛ̃diskrɛ, -ɛt] *adj* indiscreet

indiscutable [ɛ̃diskytabl(ə)] *adj* indisputable

indispensable [ɛ̃dispɑ̃sabl(ə)] *adj* indispensable; essential

indisposé, e [ɛ̃dispoze] *adj* indisposed

indisposer [ɛ̃dispoze] *vt* (*incommoder*) to upset; (*déplaire à*) to antagonize

indistinct, e [ɛ̃distɛ̃, -ɛkt(ə)] *adj* indistinct; **indistinctement** *adv* (*voir, prononcer*) indistinctly; (*sans distinction*) indiscriminately

individu [ɛ̃dividy] *nm* individual

individuel, le [ɛ̃dividɥɛl] *adj* (*gén*) individual; (*opinion, livret, contrôle, avantages*) personal; **chambre** ~**le** single room; **maison** ~**le** detached house

indolore [ɛ̃dɔlɔr] *adj* painless

indomptable [ɛ̃dɔ̃tabl(ə)] *adj* untameable; (*fig*) invincible, indomitable

Indonésie [ɛ̃dɔnezi] *nf* Indonesia

indu, e [ɛ̃dy] *adj*: **à des heures** ~**es** at some ungodly hour

induire [ɛ̃dɥir] *vt*: ~ **qn en erreur** to lead sb astray, mislead sb

indulgent, e [ɛ̃dylʒɑ̃, -ɑ̃t] *adj* (*parent, regard*) indulgent; (*juge, examinateur*) lenient

indûment [ɛ̃dymɑ̃] *adv* wrongfully; without due cause

industrie [ɛ̃dystri] *nf* industry; **industriel, le** *adj* industrial ♦ *nm* industrialist; manufacturer

inébranlable [inebrɑ̃labl(ə)] *adj* (*masse, colonne*) solid; (*personne, certitude, foi*) steadfast, unwavering

inédit, e [inedi, -it] *adj* (*correspondance etc*) hitherto unpublished; (*spectacle, moyen*) novel, original

ineffaçable [inefasabl(ə)] *adj* indelible

inefficace [inefikas] *adj* (*remède, moyen*) ineffective; (*machine, employé*) inefficient

inégal, e, aux [inegal, -o] *adj* unequal; uneven; **inégalable** [inegalabl(e)] *adj* matchless; **inégalé, e** [inegale] *adj* unmatched, unequalled

inerte [inɛrt(ə)] *adj* lifeless; inert

inestimable [inɛstimabl(e)] *adj* priceless; (*fig: bienfait*) invaluable

inévitable [inevitabl(ə)] *adj* unavoidable; (*fatal, habituel*) inevitable

inexact, e [inɛgzakt] *adj* inaccurate, inexact; unpunctual

in extremis [inɛkstremis] *adv* at the last minute ♦ *adj* last-minute

infaillible [ɛ̃fajibl(ə)] *adj* infallible

infâme [ɛ̃fɑm] *adj* vile

infanticide [ɛ̃fɑ̃tisid] *nm/f* childmurderer(eress) ♦ *nm* (*meurtre*) infanticide

infarctus [ɛ̃farktys] *nm*: ~ (**du myocarde**) coronary (thrombosis)

infatigable [ɛ̃fatigabl(ə)] *adj* tireless

infect, e [ɛ̃fɛkt] *adj* vile; foul; (*repas, vin*) revolting

infecter [ɛ̃fɛkte] *vt* (*atmosphère, eau*) to contaminate; (*MÉD*) to infect; **s'~** to become infected *ou* septic; **infection** *nf* infection

inférieur, e [ɛ̃feʀjœʀ] *adj* lower; (*en qualité, intelligence*) inferior; ~ **à** (*somme, quantité*) less *ou* smaller than; (*moins bon que*) inferior to

infernal, e, aux [ɛ̃fɛʀnal, -o] *adj* (*chaleur, rythme*) infernal; (*méchanceté, complot*) diabolical

infidèle [ɛ̃fidɛl] *adj* unfaithful

infiltrer [ɛ̃filtʀe] : **s'~** *vi* to penetrate into; (*liquide*) to seep into; (*fig: noyauter*) to infiltrate

infime [ɛ̃fim] *adj* minute, tiny; (*inférieur*) lowly

infini, e [ɛ̃fini] *adj* infinite ♦ *nm* infinity; **à l'~** (*MATH*) to infinity; (*agrandir, varier*) infinitely; (*interminablement*) endlessly; **infinité** *nf*: **une infinité de** an infinite number of

infinitif [ɛ̃finitif] *nm* infinitive

infirme [ɛ̃fiʀm(ə)] *adj* disabled ♦ *nm/f* disabled person; ~ **de guerre** war cripple

infirmerie [ɛ̃fiʀməʀi] *nf* sick bay

infirmier, ière [ɛ̃fiʀmje, -jɛʀ] *nm/f* nurse; **infirmière chef** sister; **infirmière visiteuse** ≈ district nurse

infirmité [ɛ̃fiʀmite] *nf* disability

inflammable [ɛ̃flamabl(ə)] *adj* (in)flammable

inflation [ɛ̃flasjɔ̃] *nf* inflation

inflexion [ɛ̃flɛksjɔ̃] *nf* inflexion; ~ **de la tête** slight nod (of the head)

infliger [ɛ̃fliʒe] *vt*: ~ **qch (à qn)** to inflict sth (on sb); (*amende, sanction*) to impose sth (on sb)

influence [ɛ̃flyɑ̃s] *nf* influence; (*d'un médicament*) effect; **influencer** *vt* to influence; **influent, e** *adj* influential

influer [ɛ̃flye] : ~ **sur** *vt* to have an influence upon

Informaticien, ne [ɛ̃fɔʀmatisjɛ̃, -jɛn] *nm/f* computer scientist

information [ɛ̃fɔʀmasjɔ̃] *nf* (*renseignement*) piece of information; (*PRESSE, TV: nouvelle*) item of news; (*diffusion de renseignements, INFORM*) information; (*JUR*) inquiry, investigation; ~**s** *nfpl* (*TV*) news *sg*; **voyage d'~** fact-finding trip

informatique [ɛ̃fɔʀmatik] *nf* (*technique*) data processing; (*science*) computer science ♦ *adj* computer *cpd*; **informatiser** *vt* to computerize

informe [ɛ̃fɔʀm(ə)] *adj* shapeless

informer [ɛ̃fɔʀme] *vt*: ~ **qn (de)** to inform sb (of); **s'~ (de/si)** to inquire *ou* find out (about/whether *ou* if)

infortune [ɛ̃fɔʀtyn] *nf* misfortune

infraction [ɛ̃fʀaksjɔ̃] *nf* offence; ~ **à** violation *ou* breach of; **être en** ~ to be in breach of the law

infranchissable [ɛ̃fʀɑ̃ʃisabl(ə)] *adj* impassable; (*fig*) insuperable

infrastructure [ɛ̃fʀastʀyktyʀ] *nf* (*AVIAT, MIL*) ground installations *pl*; (*ÉCON: touristique etc*) infrastructure

infuser [ɛ̃fyze] *vt, vi* (*thé*) to brew; (*tisane*) to infuse; **infusion** *nf* (*tisane*) herb tea

ingénier [ɛ̃ʒenje] : **s'~** *vi* to strive to do

ingénierie [ɛ̃ʒenjəʀi] *nf* engineering; ~ **génétique** genetic engineering

ingénieur [ɛ̃ʒenjœʀ] *nm* engineer; ~ **du son** sound engineer

ingénieux, euse [ɛ̃ʒenjø, -øz] *adj* ingenious, clever

ingénu, e [ɛ̃ʒeny] *adj* ingenuous, artless

ingérer [ɛ̃ʒeʀe] : **s'~** *vi* to interfere in

ingrat, e [ɛ̃gʀa, -at] *adj* (*personne*) ungrateful; (*sol*) poor; (*travail, sujet*) thankless; (*visage*) unprepossessing

ingrédient [ɛ̃gʀedjɑ̃] *nm* ingredient

ingurgiter [ɛ̃gyʀʒite] *vt* to swallow

inhabitable [inabitabl(ə)] *adj* uninhabitable

inhabituel, le [inabituɛl] *adj* unusual

inhérent, e [ineʀɑ̃, -ɑ̃t] *adj*: ~ **à** inherent in

inhibition [inibisjɔ̃] *nf* inhibition

inhumain, e [inymɛ̃, -ɛn] *adj* inhuman

inhumer [inyme] *vt* to inter, bury

inimitié [inimitje] *nf* enmity

initial, e, aux [inisjal, -o] *adj* initial; **initiale** *nf* initial

initiateur, trice [inisjatœʀ, -tʀis] *nm/f* initiator; (*d'une mode, technique*) innovator, pioneer

initiative [inisjativ] *nf* initiative

initier [inisje] *vt*: ~ **qn à** to initiate sb into; (*faire découvrir: art, jeu*) to introduce sb to

injecté, e [ɛ̃ʒɛkte] *adj*: **yeux ~s de sang** bloodshot eyes

injecter [ɛ̃ʒɛkte] *vt* to inject; **injection** *nf* injection; **à injection** (*AUTO*) fuel injection *cpd*

injure [ɛ̃ʒyʀ] *nf* insult, abuse *no pl*

injurier [ɛ̃ʒyʀje] *vt* to insult, abuse; **injurieux, euse** *adj* abusive, insulting

injuste [ɛ̃ʒyst(ə)] *adj* unjust, unfair; **injustice** *nf* injustice

inlassable [ɛ̃lasabl(ə)] *adj* tireless

inné, e [ine] *adj* innate, inborn

innocent, e [inɔsɑ̃, -ɑ̃t] *adj* innocent; **innocenter** *vt* to clear, prove innocent

innombrable [inɔ̃bʀabl(ə)] *adj* innumerable

innommable [inɔmabl(ə)] *adj* unspeakable

innover [inɔve] *vi* to break new ground

inoccupé, e [inɔkype] *adj* unoccupied

inoculer [inɔkyle] *vt* (*volontairement*) to inoculate; (*accidentellement*) to infect

inodore [inɔdɔʀ] *adj* (*gaz*) odourless; (*fleur*) scentless

inoffensif, ive [inɔfɑ̃sif, -iv] *adj* harmless, innocuous

inondation [inɔ̃dasjɔ̃] *nf* flooding *no pl*;

flood; **inonder** [inɔ̃de] *vt* to flood; *(fig)* to inundate, overrun

inopérant, e [inɔpeʀɑ̃, -ɑ̃t] *adj* inoperative, ineffective

inopiné, e [inɔpine] *adj* unexpected, sudden

inopportun, e [inɔpɔʀtœ̃, -yn] *adj* ill-timed, untimely; inappropriate

inoubliable [inublijabl(ə)] *adj* unforgettable

inouï, e [inwi] *adj* unheard-of, extraordinary

inox(ydable) [inɔks(idabl(ə))] *adj* stainless

inqualifiable [ɛ̃kalifjabl(ə)] *adj* unspeakable

inquiet, ète [ɛ̃kjɛ, -ɛt] *adj* anxious

inquiétant, e [ɛ̃kjetɑ̃, -ɑ̃t] *adj* worrying, disturbing

inquiéter [ɛ̃kjete] *vt* to worry; *(harceler)* to harass; **s'~** to worry; **s'~ de** to worry about; *(s'enquérir de)* to inquire about

inquiétude [ɛ̃kjetyd] *nf* anxiety

insaisissable [ɛ̃sezisabl(ə)] *adj* elusive

insatisfait, e [ɛ̃satisfɛ, -ɛt] *adj* *(non comblé)* unsatisfied; unfulfilled; *(mécontent)* dissatisfied

inscription [ɛ̃skʀipsjɔ̃] *nf* inscription; *(voir s'inscrire)* enrolment; registration

inscrire [ɛ̃skʀiʀ] *vt* *(marquer: sur son calepin etc)* to note *ou* write down; *(: sur un mur, une affiche etc)* to write; *(: dans la pierre, le métal)* to inscribe; *(mettre: sur une liste, un budget etc)* to put down; **s'~** *(pour une excursion etc)* to put one's name down; **s'~ (à)** *(club, parti)* to join; *(université)* to register *ou* enrol (at); *(examen, concours)* to register (for); **s'~ en faux contre** to challenge; **~ qn à** *(club, parti)* to enrol sb at

insecte [ɛ̃sɛkt(ə)] *nm* insect; **insecticide** *nm* insecticide

insensé, e [ɛ̃sɑ̃se] *adj* mad

insensibiliser [ɛ̃sɑ̃sibilize] *vt* to anaesthetize

insensible [ɛ̃sɑ̃sibl(ə)] *adj* *(nerf, membre)* numb; *(dur, indifférent)* insensitive; *(imperceptible)* imperceptible

insérer [ɛ̃seʀe] *vt* to insert; **s'~ dans** to fit into; to come within

insigne [ɛ̃siɲ] *nm* *(d'un parti, club)* badge ♦ *adj* distinguished

insignifiant, e [ɛ̃siɲifjɑ̃, -ɑ̃t] *adj* insignificant; trivial

insinuer [ɛ̃sinɥe] *vt* to insinuate, imply; **s'~ dans** *(fig)* to creep into

insister [ɛ̃siste] *vi* to insist; *(s'obstiner)* to keep on; **~ sur** *(détail, note)* to stress

insolation [ɛ̃sɔlɑsjɔ̃] *nf* *(MÉD)* sunstroke *no pl*

insolent, e [ɛ̃sɔlɑ̃, -ɑ̃t] *adj* insolent

insolite [ɛ̃sɔlit] *adj* strange, unusual

insomnie [ɛ̃sɔmni] *nf* insomnia *no pl*, sleeplessness *no pl*

insondable [ɛ̃sɔ̃dabl(ə)] *adj* unfathomable

insonoriser [ɛ̃sɔnɔʀize] *vt* to soundproof

insouciant, e [ɛ̃susjɑ̃, -ɑ̃t] *adj* carefree; *(imprévoyant)* heedless

insoumis, e [ɛ̃sumi, -iz] *adj* *(caractère, enfant)* rebellious, refractory; *(contrée, tribu)* unsubdued

insoupçonnable [ɛ̃supsɔnabl(ə)] *adj* unsuspected; *(personne)* above suspicion

insoupçonné, e [ɛ̃supsɔne] *adj* unsuspected

insoutenable [ɛ̃sutnabl(ə)] *adj* *(argument)* untenable; *(chaleur)* unbearable

inspecter [ɛ̃spɛkte] *vt* to inspect

inspecteur, trice [ɛ̃spɛktœʀ, -tʀis] *nm/f* inspector; **~ d'Académie** (regional) director of education; **~ des finances** ≈ tax inspector *(BRIT)*, ≈ Internal Revenue Service agent *(US)*

inspection [ɛ̃spɛksjɔ̃] *nf* inspection

inspirer [ɛ̃spiʀe] *vt* *(gén)* to inspire ♦ *vi* *(aspirer)* to breathe in; **s'~ de** *(suj: artiste)* to draw one's inspiration from

instable [ɛ̃stabl(ə)] *adj* *(meuble, équilibre)* unsteady; *(population, temps)* unsettled; *(régime, caractère)* unstable

installation [ɛ̃stalɑsjɔ̃] *nf* putting in *ou* up; fitting out; settling in; *(appareils etc)* fittings *pl*, installations *pl*; **~s** *nfpl* *(appareils)* equipment; *(équipements)* facilities

installer [ɛ̃stale] *vt* *(loger)*: **~ qn** to get sb settled; *(placer)* to put, place; *(meuble, gaz, électricité)* to put in; *(rideau, étagère, tente)* to put up; *(appartement)* to fit out; **s'~** *(s'établir: artisan, dentiste etc)* to set o.s. up; *(se loger)* to settle (o.s.); *(emménager)* to settle in; *(sur un siège, à un emplacement)* to settle (down); *(fig: maladie, grève)* to take a firm hold

instamment [ɛ̃stamɑ̃] *adv* urgently

instance [ɛ̃stɑ̃s] *nf* *(ADMIN: autorité)* authority; **~s** *nfpl* *(prières)* entreaties; **affaire en ~** matter pending; **être en ~ de divorce** to be awaiting a divorce

instant [ɛ̃stɑ̃] *nm* moment, instant; **dans un ~** in a moment; **à l'~** this instant; **à tout** *ou* **chaque ~** at any moment; constantly; **pour l'~** for the moment, for the time being; **par ~s** at times; **de tous les ~s** perpetual

instantané, e [ɛ̃stɑ̃tane] *adj* *(lait, café)* instant; *(explosion, mort)* instantaneous ♦ *nm* snapshot

instar [ɛ̃staʀ]: **à l'~ de** *prép* following the example of, like

instaurer [ɛ̃stɔʀe] *vt* to institute

instinct [ɛ̃stɛ̃] *nm* instinct

instituer [ɛ̃stitɥe] *vt* to set up

institut [ɛ̃stity] *nm* institute; **~ de beauté** beauty salon; **I~ Universitaire de Technologie** ≈ polytechnic

instituteur, trice [ɛ̃stitytœʀ, -tʀis] *nm/f* (primary school) teacher

institution [ɛ̃stitysjɔ̃] nf institution; (collège) private school

instruction [ɛ̃stryksjɔ̃] nf (enseignement, savoir) education; (JUR) (preliminary) investigation and hearing; ~s nfpl (ordres, mode d'emploi) directions, instructions; ~ civique civics sg

instruire [ɛ̃strɥir] vt (élèves) to teach; (recrues) to train; (JUR: affaire) to conduct the investigation for; s'~ to educate o.s.; **instruit, e** adj educated

instrument [ɛ̃strymɑ̃] nm instrument; ~ à cordes/vent stringed/wind instrument; ~ de mesure measuring instrument; ~ de musique musical instrument; ~ de travail (working) tool

insu [ɛ̃sy] nm: à l'~ de qn without sb knowing (it)

insubmersible [ɛ̃sybmɛrsibl(ə)] adj unsinkable

insubordination [ɛ̃sybɔrdinasjɔ̃] nf rebelliousness; (MIL) insubordination

insuccès [ɛ̃syksɛ] nm failure

insuffisant, e [ɛ̃syfizɑ̃, -ɑ̃t] adj insufficient; (élève, travail) inadequate

insuffler [ɛ̃syfle] vt to blow; to inspire

insulaire [ɛ̃sylɛr] adj island cpd; (attitude) insular

insuline [ɛ̃sylin] nf insulin

insulte [ɛ̃sylt(ə)] nf insult; **insulter** vt to insult

insupportable [ɛ̃sypɔrtabl(ə)] adj unbearable

insurger [ɛ̃syrʒe]: s'~ (contre) vi to rise up ou rebel (against)

insurmontable [ɛ̃syrmɔ̃tabl(ə)] adj (difficulté) insuperable; (aversion) unconquerable

intact, e [ɛ̃takt] adj intact

intangible [ɛ̃tɑ̃ʒibl(ə)] adj intangible; (principe) inviolable

intarissable [ɛ̃tarisabl(ə)] adj inexhaustible

intégral, e, aux [ɛ̃tegral, -o] adj complete

intégrant, e [ɛ̃tegrɑ̃, -ɑ̃t] adj: faire partie ~e de to be an integral part of

intègre [ɛ̃tɛgr(ə)] adj upright

intégrer [ɛ̃tegre] vt to integrate; s'~ à ou dans to become integrated into

intégrisme [ɛ̃tegrism(e)] nm fundamentalism

intellectuel, le [ɛ̃telɛktɥɛl] adj intellectual ♦ nm/f intellectual; (péj) highbrow

intelligence [ɛ̃teliʒɑ̃s] nf intelligence; (compréhension): l'~ de the understanding of; (complicité): regard d'~ glance of complicity; (accord): vivre en bonne ~ avec qn to be on good terms with sb

intelligent, e [ɛ̃teliʒɑ̃, -ɑ̃t] adj intelligent

intempéries [ɛ̃tɑ̃peri] nfpl bad weather sg

intempestif, ive [ɛ̃tɑ̃pɛstif, -iv] adj untimely

intenable [ɛ̃tnabl(ə)] adj (chaleur) unbearable

intendant, e [ɛ̃tɑ̃dɑ̃, -ɑ̃t] nm/f (MIL) quartermaster; (SCOL) bursar; (d'une propriété) steward

intense [ɛ̃tɑ̃s] adj intense; **intensif, ive** adj intensive

intenter [ɛ̃tɑ̃te] vt: ~ un procès contre ou à to start proceedings against

intention [ɛ̃tɑ̃sjɔ̃] nf intention; (JUR) intent; avoir l'~ de faire to intend to do; à l'~ de for; (renseignement) for the benefit of; (film, ouvrage) aimed at; à cette ~ with this aim in view; **intentionné, e** adj: bien intentionné well-meaning ou -intentioned; mal intentionné ill-intentioned

interactif, ive [ɛ̃tɛraktif, -iv] adj (COMPUT) interactive

intercaler [ɛ̃tɛrkale] vt to insert

intercepter [ɛ̃tɛrsɛpte] vt to intercept; (lumière, chaleur) to cut off

interchangeable [ɛ̃tɛrʃɑ̃ʒabl(ə)] adj interchangeable

interclasse [ɛ̃tɛrklɑs] nm (SCOL) break (between classes)

interdiction [ɛ̃tɛrdiksjɔ̃] nf ban

interdire [ɛ̃tɛrdir] vt to forbid; (ADMIN) to ban, prohibit; (: journal, livre) to ban; ~ à qn de faire to forbid sb to do, prohibit sb from doing; (suj: empêchement) to prevent sb from doing

interdit, e [ɛ̃tɛrdi, -it] adj (stupéfait) taken aback ♦ nm prohibition

intéressant, e [ɛ̃teresɑ̃, -ɑ̃t] adj interesting

intéressé, e [ɛ̃terese] adj (parties) involved, concerned; (amitié, motifs) self-interested

intéresser [ɛ̃terese] vt (captiver) to interest; (toucher) to be of interest to; (ADMIN: concerner) to affect, concern; s'~ à to be interested in

intérêt [ɛ̃terɛ] nm (aussi COMM) interest; (égoïsme) self-interest; avoir ~ à faire to do well to do

intérieur, e [ɛ̃terjœr] adj (mur, escalier, poche) inside; (commerce, politique) domestic; (cour, calme, vie) inner; (navigation) inland ♦ nm (d'une maison, d'un récipient etc) inside; (d'un pays, aussi: décor, mobilier) interior; (POL): l'I~ the Interior; à l'~ (de) inside; (fig) within

intérim [ɛ̃terim] nm interim period; assurer l'~ (de) to deputize (for); par ~ interim

intérimaire [ɛ̃terimɛr] nm/f (secrétaire) temporary secretary, temp (BRIT); (suppléant) temporary replacement

intérioriser [ɛ̃terjɔrize] vt to internalize

interlocuteur, trice [ɛ̃tɛrlɔkytœr, -tris] nm/f speaker; **son** ~ the person he was speaking to

interloquer [ɛ̃tɛrlɔke] vt to take aback

intermède [ɛ̃tɛrmɛd] nm interlude

intermédiaire [ɛ̃tɛrmedjɛr] adj intermediate; middle; half-way ♦ *nm/f* intermediary; (*COMM*) middleman; **sans ~** directly; **par l'~ de** through

intermittence [ɛ̃tɛʀmitɑ̃s] *nf*: **par ~** sporadically, intermittently

internat [ɛ̃tɛʀna] *nm* (*SCOL*) boarding school

International, e, aux [ɛ̃tɛʀnasjɔnal, -o] *adj, nm/f* international

interne [ɛ̃tɛʀn(ə)] *adj* internal ♦ *nm/f* (*SCOL*) boarder; (*MÉD*) houseman; **~r** [ɛ̃tɛʀne] *vt* (*POL*) to intern; (*MÉD*) to confine to a mental institution

interpeller [ɛ̃tɛʀpəle] *vt* (*appeler*) to call out to; (*apostropher*) to shout at; (*POLICE*) to take in for questioning; (*POL*) to question

interphone [ɛ̃tɛʀfɔn] *nm* intercom

interposer [ɛ̃tɛʀpoze] *vt* to interpose; **s'~** *vi* to intervene; **par personnes interposées** through a third party

interprète [ɛ̃tɛʀpʀɛt] *nm/f* interpreter; (*porte-parole*) spokesperson

interpréter [ɛ̃tɛʀpʀete] *vt* to interpret

interrogateur, trice [ɛ̃teʀɔgatœʀ, -tʀis] *adj* questioning, inquiring

interrogatif, ive [ɛ̃teʀɔgatif, -iv] *adj* (*LING*) interrogative

interrogation [ɛ̃teʀɔgasjɔ̃] *nf* question; (*SCOL*) (written *ou* oral) test

interrogatoire [ɛ̃teʀɔgatwaʀ] *nm* (*POLICE*) questioning *no pl*; (*JUR*) cross-examination

interroger [ɛ̃teʀɔʒe] *vt* to question; (*IN-FORM*) to consult; (*SCOL*) to test

interrompre [ɛ̃teʀɔ̃pʀ(ə)] *vt* (*gén*) to interrupt; (*travail, voyage*) to break off, interrupt; **s'~** to break off

interrupteur [ɛ̃teʀyptœʀ] *nm* switch

interruption [ɛ̃teʀypsjɔ̃] *nf* interruption; (*pause*) break

interstice [ɛ̃teʀstis] *nm* crack; slit

interurbain [ɛ̃teʀyʀbɛ̃] *nm* (*TÉL*) long-distance call service ♦ *adj* long-distance

intervalle [ɛ̃teʀval] *nm* (*espace*) space; (*de temps*) interval; **dans l'~** in the meantime

intervenir [ɛ̃teʀvəniʀ] *vi* (*gén*) to intervene; (*survenir*) to take place; **~ auprès de qn** to intervene with sb

intervention [ɛ̃teʀvɑ̃sjɔ̃] *nf* intervention; (*discours*) paper; **~ chirurgicale** (surgical) operation

intervertir [ɛ̃teʀvɛʀtiʀ] *vt* to invert (the order of), reverse

interview [ɛ̃teʀvju] *nf* interview

intestin, e [ɛ̃tɛstɛ̃, -in] *adj* internal ♦ *nm* intestine

intime [ɛ̃tim] *adj* intimate; (*vie, journal*) private; (*conviction*) inmost; (*dîner, cérémonie*) quiet ♦ *nm/f* close friend

intimer [ɛ̃time] *vt* (*JUR*) to notify; **~ à qn l'ordre de faire** to order sb to do

intimider [ɛ̃timide] *vt* to intimidate

intimité [ɛ̃timite] *nf*: **dans l'~** in private; (*sans formalités*) with only a few friends, quietly

intitulé, e [ɛ̃tityle] *adj* entitled

intolérable [ɛ̃tɔleʀabl(ə)] *adj* intolerable

intoxication [ɛ̃tɔksikɑsjɔ̃] *nf*: **~ alimentaire** food poisoning

intoxiquer [ɛ̃tɔksike] *vt* to poison; (*fig*) to brainwash

intraduisible [ɛ̃tʀadɥizibl(ə)] *adj* untranslatable; (*fig*) inexpressible

intraitable [ɛ̃tʀɛtabl(ə)] *adj* inflexible, uncompromising

intransigeant, e [ɛ̃tʀɑ̃ziʒɑ̃, -ɑ̃t] *adj* intransigent; (*morale*) uncompromising

intransitif, ive [ɛ̃tʀɑ̃zitif, -iv] *adj* (*LING*) intransitive

intrépide [ɛ̃tʀepid] *adj* dauntless

intrigue [ɛ̃tʀig] *nf* (*scénario*) plot

intriguer [ɛ̃tʀige] *vi* to scheme ♦ *vt* to puzzle, intrigue

intrinsèque [ɛ̃tʀɛ̃sɛk] *adj* intrinsic

introduction [ɛ̃tʀɔdyksjɔ̃] *nf* introduction

introduire [ɛ̃tʀɔdɥiʀ] *vt* to introduce; (*visiteur*) to show in; (*aiguille, clef*): **~ qch dans** to insert *ou* introduce 'sth into; **s'~ dans** to gain entry into; to get o.s. accepted into; (*eau, fumée*) to get into

introuvable [ɛ̃tʀuvabl(ə)] *adj* which cannot be found; (*COMM*) unobtainable

introverti, e [ɛ̃tʀɔvɛʀti] *nm/f* introvert

intrus, e [ɛ̃tʀy, -yz] *nm/f* intruder

intrusion [ɛ̃tʀyzjɔ̃] *nf* intrusion; interference

intuition [ɛ̃tɥisjɔ̃] *nf* intuition

inusable [inyzabl(ə)] *adj* hard-wearing

inusité, e [inyzite] *adj* rarely used

inutile [inytil] *adj* useless; (*superflu*) unnecessary; **inutilisable** *adj* unusable

invalide [ɛ̃valid] *adj* disabled ♦ *nm*: **~ de guerre** disabled ex-serviceman

invasion [ɛ̃vazjɔ̃] *nf* invasion

invectiver [ɛ̃vɛktive] *vt* to hurl abuse at

invendable [ɛ̃vɑ̃dabl(ə)] *adj* unsaleable; unmarketable; **invendus** *nmpl* unsold goods

inventaire [ɛ̃vɑ̃tɛʀ] *nm* inventory; (*COMM: liste*) stocklist; (: *opération*) stocktaking *no pl*; (*fig*) survey

inventer [ɛ̃vɑ̃te] *vt* to invent; (*subterfuge*) to devise, invent; (*histoire, excuse*) to make up, invent; **inventeur** *nm* inventor; **inventif, ive** *adj* inventive; **invention** *nf* invention

inverse [ɛ̃vɛʀs(ə)] *adj* reverse; opposite; inverse ♦ *nm* inverse, reverse; **dans l'ordre ~** in the reverse order; **en sens ~** in (*ou* from) the opposite direction; **inversement** *adv* conversely; **inverser** *vt* to invert, reverse; (*ÉLEC*) to reverse

investir [ɛ̃vɛstiʀ] *vt* to invest; **investissement** *nm* investment; **investiture** *nf* investiture; (à une élection) nomination

invétéré, e [ɛ̃vetere] *adj* (habitude) ingrained; (bavard, buveur) inveterate

invisible [ɛ̃vizibl(ə)] *adj* invisible

invitation [ɛ̃vitasjɔ̃] *nf* invitation

invité, e [ɛ̃vite] *nm/f* guest

inviter [ɛ̃vite] *vt* to invite; ~ qn à faire (suj: chose) to induce ou tempt sb to do

involontaire [ɛ̃vɔlɔ̃tɛr] *adj* (mouvement) involuntary; (insulte) unintentional; (complice) unwitting

invoquer [ɛ̃vɔke] *vt* (Dieu, muse) to call upon, invoke; (prétexte) to put forward (as an excuse); (loi, texte) to refer to

invraisemblable [ɛ̃vrɛsɑ̃blabl(ə)] *adj* unlikely, improbable; incredible

iode [jɔd] *nm* iodine

irai *etc vb voir* **aller**

Irak [irak] *nm* Iraq

Iran [irɑ̃] *nm* Iran

irions *etc vb voir* **aller**

irlandais, e [irlɑ̃dɛ, -ɛz] *adj* Irish ♦ *nm/f:* I~, e Irishman(woman); les I~ the Irish

Irlande [irlɑ̃d] *nf* Ireland; ~ du Nord Northern Ireland

ironie [irɔni] *nf* irony; **ironique** *adj* ironical; **ironiser** *vi* to be ironical

irons *etc vb voir* **aller**

irradier [iradje] *vi* to radiate ♦ *vt* (aliment) to irradiate

irraisonné, e [irezɔne] *adj* irrational, unreasoned

irrationnel, le [irasjɔnɛl] *adj* irrational

irréalisable [irealizabl(ə)] *adj* unrealizable; impracticable

irrécupérable [irekyperabl(ə)] *adj* unreclaimable, beyond repair; (personne) beyond redemption

irrécusable [irekyzabl(ə)] *adj* unimpeachable; incontestable

irréductible [iredyktibl(ə)] *adj* indomitable, implacable

irréel, le [ireɛl] *adj* unreal

irréfléchi, e [irefleʃi] *adj* thoughtless

irrégularité [iregylarite] *nf* irregularity; unevenness *no pl*

irrégulier, ière [iregylje, -jɛr] *adj* irregular; uneven; (élève, athlète) erratic

irrémédiable [iremedjabl(ə)] *adj* irreparable

irréprochable [ireprɔʃabl(ə)] *adj* irreproachable, beyond reproach; (tenue) impeccable

irrésistible [irezistibl(ə)] *adj* irresistible; (preuve, logique) compelling

irrespectueux, euse [irɛspɛktɥø, -øz] *adj* disrespectful

irriguer [irige] *vt* to irrigate

irritable [iritabl(ə)] *adj* irritable

irriter [irite] *vt* to irritate

irruption [irypsjɔ̃] *nf* irruption *no pl;* **faire ~ dans** to burst into

islamique [islamik] *adj* Islamic

Islande [islɑ̃d] *nf* Iceland

isolant, e [izɔlɑ̃, -ɑ̃t] *adj* insulating; (insonorisant) soundproofing

isolation [izɔlasjɔ̃] *nf* insulation

isolé, e [izɔle] *adj* isolated; insulated

isoler [izɔle] *vt* to isolate; (prisonnier) to put in solitary confinement; (ville) to cut off, isolate; (ÉLEC) to insulate

isoloir *nm* polling booth

Israël [israɛl] *nm* Israel; **israélien, ne** *adj, nm/f* Israeli; **israélite** *adj* Jewish ♦ *nm/f* Jew(Jewess)

issu, e [isy] *adj:* ~ de descended from; (fig) stemming from; ~e *nf* (ouverture, sortie) exit; (solution) way out, solution; (dénouement) outcome; à l'~e de at the conclusion ou close of; rue sans ~e dead end

Italie [itali] *nf* Italy; **Italien, ne** *adj, nm/f* Italian ♦ *nm* (LING) Italian

italique [italik] *nm:* en ~ in italics

itinéraire [itinerɛr] *nm* itinerary, route

IUT *sigle m* = **Institut universitaire de technologie**

IVG *sigle f* (= interruption volontaire de grossesse) abortion

ivoire [ivwar] *nm* ivory

ivre [ivr(ə)] *adj* drunk; ~ de (colère, bonheur) wild with; **ivresse** *nf* drunkenness; **ivrogne** *nm/f* drunkard

J j

j' [ʒ] *pron* I

jachère [ʒaʃɛr] *nf:* (être) en ~ (to lie) fallow

jacinthe [ʒasɛ̃t] *nf* hyacinth

jack [ʒak] *nm* jack plug

jadis [ʒadis] *adv* in times past, formerly

jaillir [ʒajir] *vi* (liquide) to spurt out; (fig) to burst out; to flood out

jais [ʒɛ] *nm* jet; (d'un noir) de ~ jet-black

jalon [ʒalɔ̃] *nm* range pole; (fig) milestone; **jalonner** *vt* to mark out; (fig) to mark, punctuate

jalousie [ʒaluzi] *nf* jealousy; (store) (Venetian) blind

jaloux, ouse [ʒalu, -uz] *adj* jealous

jamais [ʒamɛ] *adv* never; (sans négation) ever; ne ... ~ never; à ~ for ever

jambe [ʒɑ̃b] *nf* leg

jambon [ʒɑ̃bɔ̃] *nm* ham

jambonneau, x [ʒɑ̃bɔno] *nm* knuckle of

ham

jante [ʒɑ̃t] *nf* (wheel) rim

janvier [ʒɑ̃vje] *nm* January

Japon [ʒapɔ̃] *nm* Japan; **japonais, e** *adj, nm/f* Japanese ♦ *nm* (*LING*) Japanese

japper [ʒape] *vi* to yap, yelp

jaquette [ʒakɛt] *nf* (*de cérémonie*) morning coat; (*de dame*) jacket

jardin [ʒaʀdɛ̃] *nm* garden; ~ **d'enfants** nursery school; **jardinage** *nm* gardening; **jardinier, ière** *nm/f* gardener; **jardinière** *nf* (*de fenêtre*) window box

jarre [ʒaʀ] *nf* (earthenware) jar

jarret [ʒaʀɛ] *nm* back of knee, ham; (*CULIN*) knuckle, shin

jarretelle [ʒaʀtɛl] *nf* suspender (*BRIT*), garter (*US*)

jarretière [ʒaʀtjɛʀ] *nf* garter

jaser [ʒaze] *vi* to chatter, prattle; (*indiscrètement*) to gossip

jatte [ʒat] *nf* basin, bowl

jauge [ʒoʒ] *nf* (*instrument*) gauge; **jauger** *vt* (*fig*) to size up

jaune [ʒon] *adj, nm* yellow ♦ *adv* (*fam*): **rire** ~ to laugh on the other side of one's face; ~ **d'œuf** (egg) yolk; **jaunir** *vi, vt* to turn yellow

jaunisse [ʒonis] *nf* jaundice

Javel [ʒavɛl] *nf voir* **eau**

javelot [ʒavlo] *nm* javelin

J.-C. *sigle* = **Jésus-Christ**

je(j') [ʒ(ə)] *pron* I

jean [dʒin] *nm* jeans *pl*

Jésus-Christ [ʒezykʀi(st)] *n* Jesus Christ; **600 avant/après** ~ *ou* **J.-C.** 600 B.C./A.D.

jet¹ [ʒɛ] *nm* (*lancer*) throwing *no pl*, throw; (*jaillissement*) jet; spurt; (*de tuyau*) nozzle; **du premier** ~ at the first attempt *or* shot; **jet d'eau** fountain; spray

jet² [dʒɛt] *nm* (*avion*) jet

jetable [ʒətabl(ə)] *adj* disposable

jetée [ʒəte] *nf* jetty; pier

jeter [ʒəte] *vt* (*gén*) to throw; (*se défaire de*) to throw away *ou* out; (*son, lueur etc*) to give out; **se** ~ **dans** to flow into; ~ **qch à qn** to throw sth to sb; (*de façon agressive*) to throw sth at sb; ~ **un coup d'œil (à)** to take a look (at); ~ **un sort à qn** to cast a spell on sb

jeton [ʒətɔ̃] *nm* (*au jeu*) counter; (*de téléphone*) token

jette etc vb *voir* **jeter**

jeu, x [ʒø] *nm* (*divertissement, TECH: d'une pièce*) play; (*TENNIS: partie, FOOTBALL etc: façon de jouer*) game; (*THÉÂTRE etc*) acting; (*au casino*): **le** ~ gambling; (*fonctionnement*) working, interplay; (*série d'objets, jouet*) set; (*CARTES*) hand; **en** ~ at stake; at work; **remettre en** ~ to throw in; **entrer/mettre en** ~ to come/bring into play; ~ **de cartes** pack of cards; ~ **d'échecs** chess set; ~ **de hasard** game of

chance; ~ **de mots** pun

jeudi [ʒødi] *nm* Thursday

jeun [ʒœ̃]: **à** ~ *adv* on an empty stomach

jeune [ʒœn] *adj* young; ~ **fille** girl; ~ **homme** young man

jeûne [ʒøn] *nm* fast

jeunesse [ʒœnɛs] *nf* youth; (*aspect*) youthfulness; youngness

joaillerie [ʒoajʀi] *nf* jewel trade; jewellery

joaillier, ière *nm/f* jeweller

joie [ʒwa] *nf* joy

joindre [ʒwɛ̃dʀ(ə)] *vt* to join; (*à une lettre*): ~ **qch à** to enclose sth with; (*contacter*) to contact, get in touch with; **se** ~ **à** to join; ~ **les mains** to put one's hands together

joint, e [ʒwɛ̃, ʒwɛ̃t] *adj*: **pièce** ~**e** enclosure ♦ *nm* joint; (*ligne*) join; ~ **de culasse** cylinder head gasket; ~ **de robinet** washer

joli, e [ʒɔli] *adj* pretty, attractive; **c'est du** ~**!** (*ironique*) that's very nice!; **c'est bien** ~, **mais ...** that's all very well but ...

jonc [ʒɔ̃] *nm* (bul)rush

joncher [ʒɔ̃ʃe] *vt* (*suj: choses*) to be strewed on

jonction [ʒɔ̃ksjɔ̃] *nf* joining; (**point de**) ~ junction

jongleur, euse [ʒɔ̃glœʀ, -øz] *nm/f* juggler

jonquille [ʒɔ̃kij] *nf* daffodil

Jordanie [ʒɔʀdani] *nf*: **la** ~ Jordan

joue [ʒu] *nf* cheek; **mettre en** ~ to take aim at

jouer [ʒwe] *vt* to play; (*somme d'argent, réputation*) to stake, wager; (*pièce, rôle*) to perform; (*film*) to show; (*simuler: sentiment*) to affect, feign ♦ *vi* to play; (*THÉÂTRE, CINÉMA*) to act, perform; (*bois, porte: se voiler*) to warp; (*clef, pièce: avoir du jeu*) to be loose; **se** ~ **de** (*difficultés*) to make light of; to deceive; ~ **sur** (*miser*) to gamble on; ~ **de** (*MUS*) to play; ~ **des coudes** to use one's elbows; ~ **à** (*jeu, sport, roulette*) to play; ~ **avec** (*risquer*) to gamble with; ~ **un tour à qn** to play a trick on sb; ~ **serré** to play a close game; ~ **de malchance** to be dogged with ill-luck

jouet [ʒwɛ] *nm* toy; **être le** ~ **de** (*illusion etc*) to be the victim of

joueur, euse [ʒwœʀ, -øz] *nm/f* player; **être beau** ~ to be a good loser

joufflu, e [ʒufly] *adj* chubby-cheeked

joug [ʒu] *nm* yoke

jouir [ʒwiʀ]: ~ **de** *vt* to enjoy; **jouissance** *nf* pleasure; (*JUR*) use

joujou [ʒuʒu] (*fam*) *nm* toy

jour [ʒuʀ] *nm* day; (*opposé à la nuit*) day, daytime; (*clarté*) daylight; (*fig: aspect*) light; (*ouverture*) opening; **au** ~ **le** ~ from day to day; **de nos** ~**s** these days; **il fait** ~ it's daylight; **au grand** ~ (*fig*) in the open; **mettre au** ~ to disclose; **mettre à** ~ to update; **donner le** ~ **à** to give birth to; **voir le** ~ to be born; ~ **férié** *nm* public holiday

journal, aux [ʒuʀnal, -o] *nm* (news)paper; (*personnel*) journal, diary; ~ **de bord** log; ~ **parlé/télévisé** radio/television news *sg*

journalier, ière [ʒuʀnalje, -jɛʀ] *adj* daily; (*banal*) everyday

journalisme [ʒuʀnalism(ə)] *nm* journalism; **journaliste** *nm/f* journalist

journée [ʒuʀne] *nf* day; **la ~ continue** the 9 to 5 working day

journellement [ʒuʀnɛlma] *adv* daily

joyau, x [ʒwajo] *nm* gem, jewel

joyeux, euse [ʒwajø, -øz] *adj* joyful, merry; ~ **Noël!** merry Christmas!; ~ **anniversaire!** happy birthday!

jubiler [ʒybile] *vi* to be jubilant, exult

jucher [ʒyʃe] *vt, vi* to perch

judas [ʒyda] *nm* (*trou*) spy-hole

judiciaire [ʒydisjɛʀ] *adj* judicial

judicieux, euse [ʒydisjø, -øz] *adj* judicious

judo [ʒydo] *nm* judo

juge [ʒyʒ] *nm* judge; ~ **d'instruction** examining (*BRIT*) *ou* committing (*US*) magistrate; ~ **de paix** justice of the peace

jugé [ʒyʒe] : **au ~** *adv* by guesswork

jugement [ʒyʒma] *nm* judgment; (*JUR*: *au pénal*) sentence; (: *au civil*) decision

juger [ʒyʒe] *vt* to judge; ~ **qn/qch satisfaisant** to consider sb/sth (to be) satisfactory; ~ **bon de faire** to see fit to do; ~ **de** to appreciate

juif, ive [ʒɥif, -iv] *adj* Jewish ♦ *nm/f* Jew(Jewess)

juillet [ʒɥije] *nm* July

juin [ʒɥɛ̃] *nm* June

jumeau, elle, x [ʒymo, -ɛl] *adj, nm/f* twin; *voir aussi* **jumelle**

jumeler [ʒymle] *vt* to twin

jumelle [ʒymɛl] *adj, nf voir* **jumeau**; ~**s** *nfpl* (*appareil*) binoculars

jument [ʒyma] *nf* mare

jungle [ʒɔ̃gl(ə)] *nf* jungle

jupe [ʒyp] *nf* skirt

jupon [ʒypɔ̃] *nm* waist slip

juré, e [ʒyʀe] *nm/f* juror

jurer [ʒyʀe] *vt* (*obéissance etc*) to swear, vow ♦ *vi* (*dire des jurons*) to swear, curse; (*dissoner*): ~ (**avec**) to clash (with); (*s'engager*): ~ **de faire/que** to swear *ou* vow to do/that; (*affirmer*): ~ **que** to swear *ou* vouch that; ~ **de qch** (*s'en porter garant*) to swear to sth

juridique [ʒyʀidik] *adj* legal

juron [ʒyʀɔ̃] *nm* curse, swearword

jury [ʒyʀi] *nm* jury; board

jus [ʒy] *nm* juice; (*de viande*) gravy, (meat) juice; ~ **de fruit** fruit juice

jusque [ʒysk(ə)] : **jusqu'à** *prép* (*endroit*) as far as, (up) to; (*moment*) until, till; (*limite*) up to; ~ **sur/dans** up to; (*y compris*) even on/in; **jusqu'à ce que** until; **jusqu'à présent** until now

juste [ʒyst(ə)] *adj* (*équitable*) just, fair; (*légi-*

time) just, justified; (*exact, vrai*) right; (*étroit, insuffisant*) tight ♦ *adv* right; tight; (*chanter*) in tune; (*seulement*) just; ~ **assez/au-dessus** just enough/above; **au** ~ exactly; **le** ~ **milieu** the happy medium; **justement** *adv* rightly, justly; (*précisément*) just, precisely; **justesse** *nf* (*précision*) accuracy; (*d'une remarque*) aptness; (*d'une opinion*) soundness; **de justesse** just

justice [ʒystis] *nf* (*équité*) fairness, justice; (*ADMIN*) justice; **rendre la** ~ to dispense justice; **rendre** ~ **à qn** to do sb justice; **justicier, ière** [ʒystisje, -jɛʀ] *nm/f* judge, righter of wrongs

justificatif, ive [ʒystifikatif, -iv] *adj* (*document*) supporting; **pièce justificative** written proof

justifier [ʒystifje] *vt* to justify; ~ **de** to prove

juteux, euse [ʒytø, -øz] *adj* juicy

juvénile [ʒyvenil] *adj* young, youthful

K k

K [ka] *nm* (*INFORM*) K

kaki [kaki] *adj inv* khaki

kangourou [kãguʀu] *nm* kangaroo

karaté [kaʀate] *nm* karate

karting [kaʀtiŋ] *nm* go-carting, karting

kermesse [kɛʀmɛs] *nf* bazaar, (charity) fête; village fair

kidnapper [kidnape] *vt* to kidnap

kilo [kilo] *nm* = **kilogramme**

kilo: ~**gramme** *nm* kilogramme; ~**métrage** *nm* number of kilometres travelled, ≈ mileage; ~**mètre** *nm* kilometre; ~**métrique** *adj* (*distance*) in kilometres

kinésithérapeute [kineziteʀapøt] *nm/f* physiotherapist

kiosque [kjɔsk(ə)] *nm* kiosk, stall

klaxon [klaksɔn] *nm* horn; **klaxonner** *vi, vt* to hoot (*BRIT*), honk (*US*)

km. *abr* = **kilomètre**; **km/h** (= *kilomètres/heure*) ≈ m.p.h.

Ko [kao] *abr* (*INFORM*: *kilooctet*) K

K.-O. [kao] *adj inv* (knocked) out

kyste [kist(ə)] *nm* cyst

L l

l' [l] dét voir **le**

la [la] dét voir **le** ♦ nm (MUS) A; (en chantant la gamme) la

là [la] adv there; (ici) here; (dans le temps) then; **elle n'est pas ~** she isn't here; **c'est ~ que** this is where; **~ où** where; **de ~** (fig) hence; **par ~** by that; **tout est ~** that's what it's all about; voir aussi **-ci; celui; là-bas** adv there

label [label] nm stamp, seal

labeur [labœʀ] nm toil no pl, toiling no pl

labo [labo] abr m (= laboratoire) lab

laboratoire [labɔʀatwaʀ] nm laboratory; **~ de langues** language laboratory

laborieux, euse [labɔʀjø, -øz] adj (tâche) laborious; **classes laborieuses** working classes

labour [labuʀ] nm ploughing no pl; **~s** nmpl (champs) ploughed fields; **cheval de ~** plough- ou cart-horse; **bœuf de ~** ox

labourer [labuʀe] vt to plough; (fig) to make deep gashes ou furrows in

labyrinthe [labiʀɛ̃t] nm labyrinth, maze

lac [lak] nm lake

lacer [lase] vt to lace ou do up

lacérer [laseʀe] vt to tear to shreds

lacet [lasɛ] nm (de chaussure) lace; (de route) sharp bend; (piège) snare

lâche [lɑʃ] adj (poltron) cowardly; (desserré) loose, slack ♦ nm/f coward

lâcher [lɑʃe] nm (de ballons, oiseaux) release ♦ vt to let go of; (ce qui tombe, abandonner) to drop; (oiseau, animal: libérer) to release, set free; (fig: mot, remarque) to let slip, come out with; (SPORT: distancer) to leave behind ♦ vi (fil, amarres) to break, give way; (freins) to fail; **~ les amarres** (NAVIG) to cast off (the moorings); **~ les chiens** to unleash the dogs; **~ prise** to let go

lâcheté [lɑʃte] nf cowardice; lowness

lacrymogène [lakʀimɔʒɛn] adj: **gaz ~** teargas

lacté, e [lakte] adj (produit, régime) milk cpd

lacune [lakyn] nf gap

là-dedans [ladədɑ̃] adv inside (there), in it; (fig) in that

là-dessous [ladsu] adv underneath, under there; (fig) behind that

là-dessus [ladsy] adv on there; (fig) at that point; about that

ladite [ladit] dét voir **ledit**

lagune [lagyn] nf lagoon

là-haut [la'o] adv up there

laïc [laik] adj, nm/f = **laïque**

laid, e [lɛ, lɛd] adj ugly; **laideur** nf ugliness no pl

lainage [lɛnaʒ] nm woollen garment; woollen material

laine [lɛn] nf wool

laïque [laik] adj lay, civil; (SCOL) state cpd ♦ nm/f layman(woman)

laisse [lɛs] nf (de chien) lead, leash; **tenir en ~** to keep on a lead ou leash

laisser [lese] vt to leave ♦ vb aux: **~ qn faire** to let sb do; **se ~ aller** to let o.s. go; **laisse-toi faire** let me (ou him etc) do it; **laisser-aller** nm carelessness, slovenliness; **laissez-passer** nm inv pass

lait [lɛ] nm milk; **frère/sœur de ~** foster brother/sister; **~ condensé/concentré** evaporated/condensed milk; **laiterie** nf dairy; **laitier, ière** adj dairy cpd ♦ nm/f milkman(dairywoman)

laiton [lɛtɔ̃] nm brass

laitue [lety] nf lettuce

laïus [lajys] (péj) nm spiel

lambeau, x [lɑ̃bo] nm scrap; **en ~x** in tatters, tattered

lambris [lɑ̃bʀi] nm panelling no pl

lame [lam] nf blade; (vague) wave; (lamelle) strip; **~ de fond** ground swell no pl; **~ de rasoir** razor blade

lamelle [lamɛl] nf thin strip ou blade

lamentable [lamɑ̃tabl(ə)] adj appalling; pitiful

lamenter [lamɑ̃te]: **se ~** vi to moan (over)

lampadaire [lɑ̃padɛʀ] nm (de salon) standard lamp; (dans la rue) street lamp

lampe [lɑ̃p(ə)] nf lamp; (TECH) valve; **~ à souder** blowlamp; **~ de poche** torch (BRIT), flashlight (US)

lampion [lɑ̃pjɔ̃] nm Chinese lantern

lance [lɑ̃s] nf spear; **~ d'incendie** fire hose

lancée [lɑ̃se] nf: **être/continuer sur sa ~** to be under way/keep going

lancement [lɑ̃smɑ̃] nm launching

lance-pierres [lɑ̃spjɛʀ] nm inv catapult

lancer [lɑ̃se] nm (SPORT) throwing no pl, throw ♦ vt to throw; (émettre, projeter) to throw out, send out; (produit, fusée, bateau, artiste) to launch; (injure) to hurl, fling; (proclamation, mandat d'arrêt) to issue; **se ~** vi (prendre de l'élan) to build up speed; (se précipiter): **se ~ sur** ou **contre** to rush at; **se ~ dans** (discussion) to launch into; (aventure) to embark on; **~ qch à qn** to throw sth to sb; (de façon agressive) to throw sth at sb; **~ du poids** nm putting the shot

lancinant, e [lɑ̃sinɑ̃, -ɑ̃t] adj (regrets etc)

haunting; (douleur) shooting
landau [lɑ̃do] nm pram (BRIT), baby carriage (US)
lande [lɑ̃d] nf moor
langage [lɑ̃gaʒ] nm language
langer [lɑ̃ʒe] vt to change (the nappy (BRIT) ou diaper (US) of)
langouste [lɑ̃gust(ə)] nf crayfish inv; **langoustine** nf Dublin Bay prawn
langue [lɑ̃g] nf (ANAT, CULIN) tongue; (LING) language; **tirer la ~ (à)** to stick out one's tongue (at); **de ~ française** French-speaking; **~ maternelle** native language, mother tongue; **~ verte** slang; **~ vivante** modern language
langueur [lɑ̃gœʀ] nf languidness
languir [lɑ̃giʀ] vi to languish; (conversation) to flag; **faire ~ qn** to keep sb waiting
lanière [lanjɛʀ] nf (de fouet) lash; (de valise, bretelle) strap
lanterne [lɑ̃tɛʀn(ə)] nf (portable) lantern; (électrique) light, lamp; (de voiture) (side)light
laper [lape] vt to lap up
lapidaire [lapidɛʀ] adj stone cpd; (fig) terse
lapin [lapɛ̃] nm rabbit; (peau) rabbitskin; (fourrure) cony
Laponie [laponi] nf Lapland
laps [laps] nm: **~ de temps** space of time, time no pl
laque [lak] nf lacquer; (brute) shellac; (pour cheveux) hair spray
laquelle [lakɛl] pron voir **lequel**
larcin [laʀsɛ̃] nm theft
lard [laʀ] nm (graisse) fat; (bacon) (streaky) bacon
lardon [laʀdɔ̃] nm: **~s** chopped bacon
large [laʀʒ(ə)] adj wide; broad; (fig) generous ♦ adv: **calculer/voir ~** to allow extra/think big ♦ nm (largeur): **5 m de ~** 5 m wide ou in width; (mer): **le ~** the open sea; **au ~ de** off; **~ d'esprit** broad-minded; **largement** adv widely; greatly; easily; generously; **largesse** nf generosity; **largesses** nfpl (dons) liberalities; **largeur** nf (qu'on mesure) width; (impression visuelle) wideness, width; breadth; broadness
larguer [laʀge] vt to drop; **~ les amarres** to cast off (the moorings)
larme [laʀm(ə)] nf tear; (fig) drop; **en ~s** in tears; **larmoyer** vi (yeux) to water; (se plaindre) to whimper
larvé, e [laʀve] adj (fig) latent
laryngite [laʀɛ̃ʒit] nf laryngitis
las, lasse [la, las] adj weary
laser [lazɛʀ] nm: (rayon) **~** laser (beam); **chaîne ~** compact disc (player); **disque ~** compact disc
lasse [las] adj voir **las**
lasser [lase] vt to weary, tire; **se ~ de** vt to grow weary ou tired of
latéral, e, aux [lateʀal, -o] adj side cpd;

lateral
latin, e [latɛ̃, -in] adj, nm/f Latin ♦ nm (LING) Latin
latitude [latityd] nf latitude
latte [lat] nf lath, slat; (de plancher) board
lauréat, e [lɔʀea, -at] nm/f winner
laurier [lɔʀje] nm (BOT) laurel; (CULIN) bay leaves pl; **~s** nmpl (fig) laurels
lavable [lavabl(ə)] adj washable
lavabo [lavabo] nm washbasin; **~s** nmpl (toilettes) toilet sg
lavage [lavaʒ] nm washing no pl, wash; **~ de cerveau** brainwashing no pl
lavande [lavɑ̃d] nf lavender
lave [lav] nf lava no pl
lave-glace [lavglas] nm windscreen (BRIT) ou windshield (US) washer
lave-linge [lavlɛ̃ʒ] nm inv washing machine
laver [lave] vt to wash; (tache) to wash off; **se ~** vi to have a wash, wash; **se ~ les mains/dents** to wash one's hands/clean one's teeth; **~ qn de** (accusation) to clear sb of; **laverie** nf: **laverie (automatique)** launderette; **lavette** nf dish cloth; (fam) drip; **laveur, euse** nm/f cleaner; **~-vaisselle** nm inv dishwasher; lavoir nm wash house
laxatif, ive [laksatif, -iv] adj, nm laxative

le(l'), la [l(ə)] (pl **les**) art déf **1** the; **~ livre/la pomme/l'arbre** the book/the apple/the tree; **les étudiants** the students
2 (noms abstraits): **~ courage/l'amour/la jeunesse** courage/love/youth
3 (indiquant la possession): **se casser la jambe** etc to break one's leg etc; **levez la main** put your hand up; **avoir les yeux gris/~ nez rouge** to have grey eyes/a red nose
4 (temps): **~ matin/soir** in the morning/evening; mornings/evenings; **~ jeudi** etc (d'habitude) on Thursdays etc; (ce jeudi-là etc) on (the) Thursday
5 (distribution, évaluation) a, an; **10F ~ mètre/kilo** 10F a ou per metre/kilo; **~ tiers/quart de** a third/quarter of
♦ pron **1** (personne: mâle) him; (: femelle) her; (: pluriel) them; **je ~/la/les vois** I can see him/her/them
2 (animal, chose: singulier) it; (: pluriel) them; **je ~ (ou la) vois** I can see it; **je les vois** I can see them
3 (remplaçant une phrase): **je ne ~ savais pas** I didn't know (about it); **il était riche et ne l'est plus** he was once rich but no longer is

lécher [leʃe] vt to lick; (laper: lait, eau) to lick ou lap up; **~ les vitrines** to go window-shopping
leçon [ləsɔ̃] nf lesson; **faire la ~ à** (fig) to

give a lecture to; **~s de conduite** driving lessons

lecteur, trice [lɛktœʀ, -tʀis] *nm/f* reader; (*d'université*) foreign language assistant ♦ *nm* (*TECH*): **~ de cassettes** cassette player; **~ de disque compact** compact disc player; **~ de disquette** disk drive

lecture [lɛktyʀ] *nf* reading

ledit, ladite [lədi] (*mpl* **lesdits**, *fpl* **lesdites**) *dét* the aforesaid

légal, e, aux [legal, -o] *adj* legal

légende [leʒɑ̃d] *nf* (*mythe*) legend; (*de carte, plan*) key; (*de dessin*) caption

léger, ère [leʒe, -ɛʀ] *adj* light; (*bruit, retard*) slight; (*superficiel*) thoughtless; (*volage*) free and easy; flighty; **à la légère** (*parler, agir*) rashly, thoughtlessly; **légèrement** *adv* lightly; thoughtlessly; slightly

législatif, ive [leʒislatif, -iv] *adj* legislative; **législatives** *nfpl* general election *sg*; **législature** [leʒislatyʀ] *nf* legislature; term (of office)

légitime [leʒitim] *adj* (*JUR*) lawful, legitimate; (*fig*) rightful, legitimate; **en état de ~ défense** in self-defence

legs [lɛg] *nm* legacy

léguer [lege] *vt*: **~ qch à qn** (*JUR*) to bequeath sth to sb; (*fig*) to hand sth down *ou* pass sth on to sb

légume [legym] *nm* vegetable

lendemain [lɑ̃dmɛ̃] *nm*: **le ~** the next *ou* following day; **le ~ matin/soir** the next *ou* following morning/evening; **le ~ de** the day after; **sans ~** short-lived

lent, e [lɑ̃, lɑ̃t] *adj* slow; **lentement** *adv* slowly; **lenteur** *nf* slowness *no pl*

lentille [lɑ̃tij] *nf* (*OPTIQUE*) lens *sg*; (*CULIN*) lentil

léopard [leɔpaʀ] *nm* leopard

lèpre [lɛpʀ(ə)] *nf* leprosy

─────────── MOT CLÉ ───────────

lequel, laquelle [ləkɛl, lakɛl] (*mpl* **lesquels**, *fpl* **lesquelles**; **à + lequel = auquel**, **de + lequel = duquel**) *pron* **1** (*interrogatif*) which, which one
2 (*relatif: personne: sujet*) who; (: *objet, après préposition*) whom; (: *chose*) which
♦ *adj*: **auquel cas** in which case

les [le] *dét voir* **le**

lesbienne [lɛsbjɛn] *nf* lesbian

lesdites [ledit] *dét pl voir* **ledit**

lesdits [ledi] *dét pl voir* **ledit**

léser [leze] *vt* to wrong

lésiner [lezine] *vi*: **~ (sur)** to skimp (on)

lésion [lezjɔ̃] *nf* lesion, damage *no pl*

lesquelles [lekɛl] *pron pl voir* **lequel**

lesquels [lekɛl] *pron pl voir* **lequel**

lessive [lesiv] *nf* (*poudre*) washing powder; (*linge*) washing *no pl*, wash

lessiver [lesive] *vt* to wash

lest [lɛst] *nm* ballast

leste [lɛst(ə)] *adj* sprightly, nimble

lettre [lɛtʀ(ə)] *nf* letter; **~s** *nfpl* (*littérature*) literature *sg*; (*SCOL*) arts (subjects); **à la ~** literally; **en toutes ~s** in full

lettré, e [letʀe] *adj* well-read

leucémie [løsemi] *nf* leukaemia

─────────── MOT CLÉ ───────────

leur [lœʀ] *adj possessif* their; **~ maison** their house; **~s amis** their friends
♦ *pron* **1** (*objet indirect*) (to) them; **je ~ ai dit la vérité** I told them the truth; **je le ~ ai donné** I gave it to them, I gave them it
2 (*possessif*): **le(la) ~, les ~s** theirs

leurre [lœʀ] *nm* (*appât*) lure; (*fig*) delusion; snare

leurrer [lœʀe] *vt* to delude, deceive

leurs [lœʀ] *dét voir* **leur**

levain [ləvɛ̃] *nm* leaven

levé, e [ləve] *adj*: **être ~** to be up

levée [ləve] *nf* (*POSTES*) collection; (*CARTES*) trick; **~ de boucliers** general outcry

lever [ləve] *vt* (*vitre, bras etc*) to raise; (*soulever de terre, supprimer: interdiction, siège*) to lift; (*séance*) to close; (*impôts, armée*) to levy ♦ *vi* to rise ♦ *nm*: **au ~** on getting up; **se ~** *vi* to get up; (*soleil*) to rise; (*jour*) to break; (*brouillard*) to lift; **~ de soleil** sunrise; **~ du jour** daybreak

levier [ləvje] *nm* lever

lèvre [lɛvʀ(ə)] *nf* lip

lévrier [levʀije] *nm* greyhound

levure [ləvyʀ] *nf* yeast; **~ chimique** baking powder

lexique [lɛksik] *nm* vocabulary; lexicon

lézard [lezaʀ] *nm* lizard

lézarde [lezaʀd(ə)] *nf* crack

liaison [ljɛzɔ̃] *nf* link; (*amoureuse*) affair; (*PHONÉTIQUE*) liaison; **entrer/être en ~ avec** to get/be in contact with

liane [ljan] *nf* creeper

liant, e [ljɑ̃, -ɑ̃t] *adj* sociable

liasse [ljas] *nf* wad, bundle

Liban [libɑ̃] *nm*: **le ~** (the) Lebanon; **libanais, e** *adj*, *nm/f* Lebanese

libeller [libele] *vt* (*chèque, mandat*): **~ (au nom de)** to make out (to); (*lettre*) to word

libellule [libelyl] *nf* dragonfly

libéral, e, aux [liberal, -o] *adj*, *nm/f* liberal

libérer [libere] *vt* (*délivrer*) to free, liberate; (: *moralement, PSYCH*) to liberate; (*relâcher, dégager: gaz*) to release; to discharge; **se ~** *vi* (*de rendez-vous*) to get out of previous engagements

liberté [libɛʀte] *nf* freedom; (*loisir*) free time; **~s** *nfpl* (*privautés*) liberties; **mettre/être en ~** to set/be free; **en ~ provisoire/surveillée/conditionnelle** on bail/

probation/parole; ~s **individuelles** personal freedom sg
libraire [libʀɛʀ] nm/f bookseller
librairie [libʀɛʀi] nf bookshop
libre [libʀ(ə)] adj free; (route) clear; (place etc) vacant; empty; not engaged; not taken; (SCOL) non-state; **de** ~ (place) free; ~ **de qch/de faire** free from sth/to do; ~ **arbitre** free will; ~-**échange** nm free trade; ~-**service** nm self-service store
Libye [libi] nf: **la** ~ Libya
licence [lisɑ̃s] nf (permis) permit; (diplôme) degree; (liberté) liberty; licence (BRIT), license (US); licentiousness; **e** nm/f (SCOL): **licencié ès lettres/en droit** ≈ Bachelor of Arts/Law; (SPORT) member of a sports federation
licencier [lisɑ̃sje] vt (renvoyer) to dismiss; (débaucher) to make redundant; to lay off
licite [lisit] adj lawful
lie [li] nf dregs pl, sediment
lié, e [lje] adj: **très** ~ **avec** very friendly with ou close to; ~ **par** (serment) bound by
liège [ljɛʒ] nm cork
lien [ljɛ̃] nm (corde, fig: affectif) bond; (rapport) link, connection; ~ **de parenté** family tie
lier [lje] vt (attacher) to tie up; (joindre) to link up; (fig: unir, engager) to bind; (CULIN) to thicken; **se** ~ **avec** to make friends with; ~ **qch à** to tie ou link sth to; ~ **conversation avec** to strike up a conversation with
lierre [ljɛʀ] nm ivy
liesse [ljɛs] nf: **être en** ~ to be celebrating ou jubilant
lieu, x [ljø] nm place; ~**x** nmpl (habitation) premises; (endroit: d'un accident etc) scene sg; **en** ~ **sûr** in a safe place; **en premier** ~ in the first place; **en dernier** ~ lastly; **avoir** ~ to take place; **avoir** ~ **de faire** to have grounds for doing; **tenir** ~ **de** to take the place of; to serve as; **donner** ~ **à** to give rise to; **au** ~ **de** instead of
lieu-dit [ljødi] (pl **lieux-dits**) nm locality
lieutenant [ljøtnɑ̃] nm lieutenant
lièvre [ljɛvʀ(ə)] nm hare
ligament [ligamɑ̃] nm ligament
ligne [liɲ] nf (gén) line; (TRANSPORTS: liaison) service; (: trajet) route; (silhouette) figure; **entrer en** ~ **de compte** to come into it
lignée [liɲe] nf line; lineage; descendants pl
ligoter [ligɔte] vt to tie up
ligue [lig] nf league; **liguer** vt: **se liguer contre** (fig) to combine against
lilas [lila] nm lilac
limace [limas] nf slug
limaille [limaj] nf: ~ **de fer** iron filings pl
limande [limɑ̃d] nf dab
lime [lim] nf file; ~ **à ongles** nail file; **li-**

mer vt to file
limier [limje] nm bloodhound; (détective) sleuth
limitation [limitɑsjɔ̃] nf: ~ **de vitesse** speed limit
limite [limit] nf (de terrain) boundary; (partie ou point extrême) limit; **vitesse/charge** ~ maximum speed/load; **cas** ~ borderline case; **date** ~ deadline
limiter [limite] vt (restreindre) to limit, restrict; (délimiter) to border
limitrophe [limitʀɔf] adj border cpd
limoger [limɔʒe] vt to dismiss
limon [limɔ̃] nm silt
limonade [limɔnad] nf lemonade (BRIT), (lemon) soda (US)
lin [lɛ̃] nm flax
linceul [lɛ̃sœl] nm shroud
linge [lɛ̃ʒ] nm (serviettes etc) linen; (pièce de tissu) cloth; (aussi: ~ **de corps**) underwear; (: ~ **de toilette**) towels pl; (lessive) washing
lingerie [lɛ̃ʒʀi] nf lingerie, underwear
lingot [lɛ̃go] nm ingot
linguistique [lɛ̃gɥistik] adj linguistic ♦ nf linguistics sg
lion, ne [ljɔ̃, ljɔn] nm/f lion(lioness); (signe): **le L~** Leo; **lionceau, x** nm lion cub
liqueur [likœʀ] nf liqueur
liquide [likid] adj liquid ♦ nm liquid; (COMM): **en** ~ in ready money ou cash; **liquider** [likide] vt (société, biens, témoin gênant) to liquidate; (compte, problème) to settle; (COMM: articles) to clear, sell off; **liquidités** [likidite] nfpl (COMM) liquid assets
lire [liʀ] nf (monnaie) lira ♦ vt, vi to read
lis [lis] nm = **lys**
lisible [lizibl(ə)] adj legible
lisière [lizjɛʀ] nf (de forêt) edge; (de tissu) selvage
lisons vb voir **lire**
lisse [lis] adj smooth
liste [list(ə)] nf list; **faire la** ~ **de** to list; ~ **électorale** electoral roll
listing [listiŋ] nm (INFORM) printout
lit [li] nm (gén) bed; **faire son** ~ to make one's bed; **aller/se mettre au** ~ to go to/get into bed; ~ **de camp** campbed; ~ **d'enfant** cot (BRIT), crib (US)
literie [litʀi] nf bedding, bedclothes pl
litière [litjɛʀ] nf litter
litige [litiʒ] nm dispute
litre [litʀ(ə)] nm litre; (récipient) litre measure
littéraire [liteʀɛʀ] adj literary
littéral, e, aux [liteʀal, -o] adj literal
littérature [liteʀatyʀ] nf literature
littoral, aux [litɔʀal, -o] nm coast
liturgie [lityʀʒi] nf liturgy
livide [livid] adj livid, pallid

livraison [livʀɛzɔ̃] nf delivery
livre [livʀ(ə)] nm book ♦ nf (poids, monnaie) pound; ~ **de bord** logbook; ~ **de poche** paperback (pocket size)
livré, e [livʀe] adj: ~ **à soi-même** left to o.s. ou one's own devices; **livrée** nf livery
livrer [livʀe] vt (COMM) to deliver; (otage, coupable) to hand over; (secret, information) to give away; **se** ~ **à** (se confier) to confide in; (se rendre, s'abandonner) to give o.s. up to; (faire: pratiques, actes) to indulge in; (: travail) to engage in; (: sport) to practise; (travail: enquête) to carry out
livret [livʀɛ] nm booklet; (d'opéra) libretto; ~ **de caisse d'épargne** (savings) bankbook; ~ **de famille** (official) family record book; ~ **scolaire** (school) report book
livreur, euse [livʀœʀ, -øz] nm/f delivery boy ou man/girl ou woman
local, e, aux [lɔkal, -o] adj local ♦ nm (salle) premises pl; voir aussi **locaux**
localiser [lɔkalize] vt (repérer) to locate, place; (limiter) to confine
localité [lɔkalite] nf locality
locataire [lɔkatɛʀ] nm/f tenant; (de chambre) lodger
location [lɔkasjɔ̃] nf (par le locataire, le loueur) renting; (par le propriétaire) renting out, letting; (THÉÂTRE) booking office; "~ **de voitures**" "car rental"
location-vente [lɔkasjɔ̃vɑ̃t] (pl ~s-~s) nf hire purchase (BRIT), instalment plan (US)
locaux [lɔko] nmpl premises
locomotive [lɔkɔmɔtiv] nf locomotive, engine; (fig) pacesetter, pacemaker
locution [lɔkysjɔ̃] nf phrase
loge [lɔʒ] nf (THÉÂTRE: d'artiste) dressing room; (: de spectateurs) box; (de concierge, franc-maçon) lodge
logement [lɔʒmɑ̃] nm accommodation no pl (BRIT), accommodations pl (US); flat (BRIT), apartment (US); housing no pl
loger [lɔʒe] vt to accommodate ♦ vi to live; **se** ~ **dans** (suj: balle, flèche) to lodge itself in; **trouver à se** ~ to find accommodation; **logeur, euse** nm/f landlord(lady)
logiciel [lɔʒisjɛl] nm software
logique [lɔʒik] adj logical ♦ nf logic
logis [lɔʒi] nm home; abode, dwelling
loi [lwa] nf law; **faire la** ~ to lay down the law
loin [lwɛ̃] adv far; (dans le temps) a long way off; a long time ago; **plus** ~ further; **de** ~ far from; **au** ~ far off; **de** ~ from a distance; (fig: de beaucoup) by far; **il vient de** ~ he's come a long way
lointain, e [lwɛ̃tɛ̃, -ɛn] adj faraway, distant; (dans le futur, passé) distant, far-off; (cause, parent) remote, distant ♦ nm: **dans le** ~ in the distance
loir [lwaʀ] nm dormouse
loisir [lwaziʀ] nm: **heures de** ~ spare time;

~s nmpl leisure sg; leisure activities; **avoir le** ~ **de faire** to have the time ou opportunity to do; **à** ~ at leisure; at one's pleasure
londonien, ne [lɔ̃dɔnjɛ̃, -jɛn] adj London cpd, of London ♦ nm/f: L~, **ne** Londoner
Londres [lɔ̃dʀ] n London
long, longue [lɔ̃, lɔ̃g] adj long ♦ adv: **en savoir** ~ to know a great deal ♦ nm: **de 3 m de** ~ 3 m long, 3 m in length; **ne pas faire** ~ **feu** not to last long; **(tout) le** ~ **de** (all) along; **tout au** ~ **de** (année, vie) throughout; **de** ~ **en large** (marcher) to and fro, up and down; voir aussi **longue**
longer [lɔ̃ʒe] vt to go (ou walk ou drive) along(side); (suj: mur, route) to border
longiligne [lɔ̃ʒiliɲ] adj long-limbed
longitude [lɔ̃ʒityd] nf longitude
longitudinal, e, aux [lɔ̃ʒitydinal, -o] adj (running) lengthways
longtemps [lɔ̃tɑ̃] adv (for) a long time, (for) long; **avant** ~ before long; **pour** ou **pendant** ~ for a long time; **mettre** ~ **à faire** to take a long time to do
longue [lɔ̃g] adj voir **long** ♦ nf: **à la** ~ in the end; **longuement** adv for a long time
longueur [lɔ̃gœʀ] nf length; ~s nfpl (fig: d'un film etc) tedious parts; **en** ~ lengthwise; **tirer en** ~ to drag on; **à** ~ **de journée** all day long; ~ **d'onde** wavelength
longue-vue [lɔ̃gvy] nf telescope
lopin [lɔpɛ̃] nm: ~ **de terre** patch of land
loque [lɔk] nf (personne) wreck; ~s nfpl (habits) rags
loquet [lɔkɛ] nm latch
lorgner [lɔʀɲe] vt to eye; (fig) to have one's eye on
lors [lɔʀ]: ~ **de** prép at the time of; during; ~ **même que** even though
lorsque [lɔʀsk(ə)] conj when, as
losange [lɔzɑ̃ʒ] nm diamond; (GÉOM) lozenge
lot [lo] nm (part) share; (de loterie) prize; (fig: destin) fate, lot; (COMM, INFORM) batch
loterie [lɔtʀi] nf lottery; raffle
loti, e [lɔti] adj: **bien/mal** ~ well-/badly off
lotion [lɔsjɔ̃] nf lotion
lotir [lɔtiʀ] vt (terrain) to divide into plots; to sell by lots; **lotissement** nm housing development; plot, lot
loto [lɔto] nm lotto; numerical lottery
louable [lwabl(ə)] adj commendable
louanges [lwɑ̃ʒ] nfpl praise sg
loubard [lubaʀ] (fam) nm lout
louche [luʃ] adj shady, fishy, dubious ♦ nf ladle
loucher [luʃe] vi to squint
louer [lwe] vt (maison: suj: propriétaire) to let, rent (out); (: locataire) to rent; (voiture etc: entreprise) to hire out (BRIT), rent (out); (: locataire) to hire, rent; (réserver) to

book; (faire l'éloge de) to praise; **"à ~"** "to let" (BRIT), "for rent" (US)
loup [lu] nm wolf
loupe [lup] nf magnifying glass
louper [lupe] vt (manquer) to miss
lourd, e [luʀ, luʀd(ə)] adj, adv heavy; ~ **de** (conséquences, menaces) charged with; **lourdaud, e** (péj) adj clumsy
loutre [lutʀ(ə)] nf otter
louveteau, x [luvto] nm wolf-cub; (scout) cub (scout)
louvoyer [luvwaje] vi (NAVIG) to tack; (fig) to hedge, evade the issue
lover [lɔve] : **se** ~ vi to coil up
loyal, e, aux [lwajal, -o] adj (fidèle) loyal, faithful; (fair-play) fair; **loyauté** nf loyalty, faithfulness; fairness
loyer [lwaje] nm rent
lu, e [ly] pp de lire
lubie [lybi] nf whim, craze
lubrifiant [lybʀifjɑ̃] nm lubricant
lubrifier [lybʀifje] vt to lubricate
lubrique [lybʀik] adj lecherous
lucarne [lykaʀn(ə)] nf skylight
lucratif, ive [lykʀatif, -iv] adj lucrative; profitable; **à but non** ~ non profit-making
lueur [lɥœʀ] nf (chatoyante) glimmer no pl; (métallique, mouillée) gleam no pl; (rougeoyante, chaude) glow no pl; (pâle) (faint) light; (fig) glimmer; gleam
luge [lyʒ] nf sledge (BRIT), sled (US)
lugubre [lygybʀ(ə)] adj gloomy; dismal

─────────── MOT CLÉ ───────────

lui [lɥi] pron **1** (objet indirect: mâle) (to) him; (: femelle) (to) her; (: chose, animal) (to) it; **je** ~ **ai parlé** I have spoken to him (ou to her); **il** ~ **a offert un cadeau** he gave him (ou her) a present
2 (après préposition, comparatif: personne) him; (: chose, animal) it; **elle est contente de** ~ she is pleased with him; **je la connais mieux que** ~ I know her better than he does; I know her better than him
3 (sujet, forme emphatique) he; ~, **il est à Paris** HE is in Paris
4: ~-**même** himself; itself

luire [lɥiʀ] vi to shine; to glow
lumière [lymjɛʀ] nf light; ~s nfpl (d'une personne) wisdom sg; **mettre en** ~ (fig) to highlight; ~ **du jour** daylight
luminaire [lyminɛʀ] nm lamp, light
lumineux, euse [lyminø, -øz] adj (émettant de la lumière) luminous; (éclairé) illuminated; (ciel, couleur) bright; (relatif à la lumière: rayon etc) of light, light cpd; (fig: regard) radiant
lunaire [lynɛʀ] adj lunar, moon cpd
lunatique [lynatik] adj whimsical, temperamental
lundi [lœ̃di] nm Monday; ~ **de Pâques** Easter Monday
lune [lyn] nf moon; ~ **de miel** honeymoon
lunette [lynɛt] nf: ~s nfpl glasses, spectacles; (protectrices) goggles; ~ **arrière** (AUTO) rear window; ~s **de soleil** sun glasses; ~s **noires** dark glasses
lus etc vb voir lire
lustre [lystʀ(ə)] nm (de plafond) chandelier; (fig: éclat) lustre
lustrer [lystʀe] vt to shine
lut vb voir lire
luth [lyt] nm lute
lutin [lytɛ̃] nm imp, goblin
lutte [lyt] nf (conflit) struggle; (sport) wrestling; **lutter** vi to fight, struggle
luxe [lyks(ə)] nm luxury; **de** ~ luxury cpd
Luxembourg [lyksɑ̃buʀ] nm: **le** ~ Luxembourg
luxer [lykse] vt: **se** ~ **l'épaule** to dislocate one's shoulder
luxueux, euse [lyksɥø, -øz] adj luxurious
luxure [lyksyʀ] nf lust
lycée [lise] .nm secondary school; **lycéen, ne** nm/f secondary school pupil
lyrique [liʀik] adj lyrical; (OPÉRA) lyric; **artiste** ~ opera singer
lys [lis] nm lily

M m

M abr = Monsieur
m' [m] pron voir me
ma [ma] dét voir mon
macaron [makaʀɔ̃] nm (gâteau) macaroon; (insigne) (round) badge
macaronis [makaʀɔni] nmpl macaroni sg
macédoine [masedwan] nf: ~ **de fruits** fruit salad; ~ **de légumes** nf mixed vegetables
macérer [masere] vi, vt to macerate; (dans du vinaigre) to pickle
mâcher [mɑʃe] vt to chew; **ne pas** ~ **ses mots** not to mince one's words
machin [maʃɛ̃] (fam) nm thing(umajig)
machinal, e, aux [maʃinal, -o] adj mechanical, automatic
machination [maʃinɑsjɔ̃] nf scheming, frame-up
machine [maʃin] nf machine; (locomotive) engine; (fig: rouages) machinery; ~ **à écrire** typewriter; ~ **à laver/coudre** washing/sewing machine; ~ **à sous** fruit machine; ~ **à vapeur** steam engine; **machinerie** nf

machinery, plant; (*d'un navire*) engine room; **machiniste** *nm* (*de bus, métro*) driver

mâchoire [mɑʃwaʀ] *nf* jaw; ~ **de frein** brake shoe

mâchonner [mɑʃɔne] *vt* to chew (at)

maçon [masɔ̃] *nm* bricklayer; builder; ~**nerie** [masɔnʀi] *nf* (*murs*) brickwork; masonry, stonework; (*activité*) bricklaying; building

maculer [makyle] *vt* to stain

Madame [madam] (*pl* **Mesdames**) *nf*: ~ X Mrs X; **occupez-vous de** ~/**Monsieur/Mademoiselle** please serve this lady/gentleman/(young) lady; **bonjour** ~/**Monsieur/Mademoiselle** good morning; (*ton déférent*) good morning Madam/Sir/Madam; (*le nom est connu*) good morning Mrs/Mr/Miss X; ~/**Monsieur/Mademoiselle!** (*pour appeler*) Madam/Sir/Miss!; ~/**Monsieur/Mademoiselle** (*sur lettre*) Dear Madam/Sir/Madam; **chère** ~/**cher Monsieur/chère Mademoiselle** Dear Mrs/Mr/Miss X; **Mesdames** Ladies

Mademoiselle [madmwazɛl] (*pl* **Mesdemoiselles**) *nf* Miss; *voir aussi* **Madame**

madère [madɛʀ] *nm* Madeira (wine)

magasin [magazɛ̃] *nm* (*boutique*) shop; (*entrepôt*) warehouse; (*d'une arme*) magazine; **en** ~ (*COMM*) in stock

magazine [magazin] *nm* magazine

magicien, ne [maʒisjɛ̃, -jɛn] *nm/f* magician

magie [maʒi] *nf* magic; **magique** *adj* magic; (*enchanteur*) magical

magistral, e, aux [maʒistʀal, -o] *adj* (*œuvre, adresse*) masterly; (*ton*) authoritative; (*ex cathedra*): **enseignement** ~ lecturing, lectures *pl*

magistrat [maʒistʀa] *nm* magistrate

magnétique [maɲetik] *adj* magnetic

magnétiser [maɲetize] *vt* to magnetize; (*fig*) to mesmerize, hypnotize

magnétophone [maɲetɔfɔn] *nm* tape recorder; ~ **à cassettes** cassette recorder

magnétoscope [maɲetɔskɔp] *nm* video-tape recorder

magnifique [maɲifik] *adj* magnificent

magot [mago] *nm* (*argent*) pile (of money); nest egg

magouille [maguj] *nf* scheming

mai [mɛ] *nm* May

maigre [mɛgʀ(ə)] *adj* (very) thin, skinny; (*viande*) lean; (*fromage*) low-fat; (*végétation*) thin, sparse; (*fig*) poor, meagre, skimpy ♦ *adv*: **faire** ~ not to eat meat; **jours** ~**s** days of abstinence, fish days; **maigreur** *nf* thinness; **maigrir** *vi* to get thinner, lose weight

maille [maj] *nf* stitch; **avoir** ~ **à partir avec qn** to have a brush with sb; ~ **à l'endroit/à l'envers** plain/purl stitch

maillet [majɛ] *nm* mallet

maillon [majɔ̃] *nm* link

maillot [majo] *nm* (*aussi*: ~ **de corps**) vest; (*de danseur*) leotard; (*de sportif*) jersey; ~ **de bain** swimsuit; (*d'homme*) bathing trunks *pl*

main [mɛ̃] *nf* hand; **à la** ~ in one's hand; **se donner la** ~ to hold hands; **donner** *ou* **tendre la** ~ **à qn** to hold out one's hand to sb; **se serrer la** ~ to shake hands; **serrer la** ~ **à qn** to shake hands with sb; **sous la** ~ *ou* **at hand**; **attaque à** ~ **armée** armed attack; **à** ~ **droite/gauche** to the right/left; **à remettre en** ~**s propres** to be delivered personally; **de première** ~ (*COMM: voiture etc*) second-hand with only one previous owner; **mettre la dernière** ~ **à** to put the finishing touches to; **se faire/perdre la** ~ to get one's hand in/lose one's touch; **avoir qch bien en** ~ to have (got) the hang of sth

main-d'œuvre [mɛ̃dœvʀ(ə)] *nf* manpower, labour

main-forte [mɛ̃fɔʀt(ə)] *nf*: **prêter** ~ **à qn** to come to sb's assistance

mainmise [mɛ̃miz] *nf* seizure; (*fig*): ~ **sur** complete hold on

maint, e [mɛ̃, mɛt] *adj* many a; ~**s** many; **à** ~**es reprises** time and (time) again

maintenant [mɛ̃tnɑ̃] *adv* now; (*actuellement*) nowadays

maintenir [mɛ̃tniʀ] *vt* (*retenir, soutenir*) to support; (*contenir: foule etc*) to hold back; (*conserver, affirmer*) to maintain; **se** ~ *vi* to hold; to keep steady; to persist

maintien [mɛ̃tjɛ̃] *nm* maintaining; (*attitude*) bearing

maire [mɛʀ] *nm* mayor

mairie [meʀi] *nf* (*bâtiment*) town hall; (*administration*) town council

mais [mɛ] *conj* but; ~ **non!** of course not!; ~ **enfin** but after all; (*indignation*) look here!; ~ **encore?** is that all?

maïs [mais] *nm* maize (*BRIT*), corn (*US*)

maison [mezɔ̃] *nf* house; (*chez-soi*) home; (*COMM*) firm ♦ *adj inv* (*CULIN*) home-made; made by the chef; (*fig*) in-house, own; **à la** ~ at home; (*direction*) home; ~ **close** *ou* **de passe** brothel; ~ **de correction** reformatory; ~ **de repos** convalescent home; ~ **de santé** mental home; ~ **des jeunes** youth club; ~ **mère** parent company; **maisonnée** *nf* household, family; **maisonnette** *nf* small house, cottage

maître, esse [mɛtʀ(ə), mɛtʀɛs] *nm/f* master(mistress); (*SCOL*) teacher, schoolmaster(mistress) ♦ *nm* (*peintre etc*) master; (*titre*): **M~** Maître, *term of address gen for a barrister* ♦ *adj* (*principal, essentiel*) main; **être** ~ **de** (*soi-même, situation*) to be in control of sth; **une** ~**sse femme** a managing woman; ~ **chanteur** blackmailer; ~/**maîtresse d'école** schoolmaster(mistress);

~ **d'hôtel** (*domestique*) butler; (*d'hôtel*) head waiter; ~ **nageur** lifeguard; **maîtresse** *nf* (*amante*) mistress; **maîtresse de maison** hostess; housewife

maîtrise [metʀiz] *nf* (*aussi:* ~ **de soi**) self-control, self-possession; (*habileté*) skill, mastery; (*suprématie*) mastery, command; (*diplôme*) ≈ master's degree

maîtriser [metʀize] *vt* (*cheval, incendie*) to (bring under) control; (*sujet*) to master; (*émotion*) to control, master; **se** ~ to control o.s.

majestueux, euse [maʒɛstɥø, -øz] *adj* majestic

majeur, e [maʒœʀ] *adj* (*important*) major; (*JUR*) of age; (*fig*) adult ♦ *nm* (*doigt*) middle finger; **en ~e partie** for the most part

majorer [maʒɔʀe] *vt* to increase

majoritaire [maʒɔʀitɛʀ] *adj* majority *cpd*

majorité [maʒɔʀite] *nf* (*gén*) majority; (*parti*) party in power; **en** ~ mainly

majuscule [maʒyskyl] *adj, nf*: **(lettre)** ~ capital (letter)

mal [mal, mo] (*pl* **maux**) *nm* (*opposé au bien*) evil; (*tort, dommage*) harm; (*douleur physique*) pain, ache; (*maladie*) illness, sickness *no pl* ♦ *adv* badly ♦ *adj* bad, wrong; **être** ~ to be uncomfortable; **être** ~ **avec qn** to be on bad terms with sb; **être au plus** ~ (*malade*) to be at death's door; (*brouillé*) to be at daggers drawn; **il a** ~ **compris** he misunderstood; **dire/penser du** ~ **de** to speak/think ill of; **ne voir aucun** ~ **à** to see no harm in, see nothing wrong in; **craignant** ~ **faire** fearing he was doing the wrong thing; **faire du** ~ **à qn** to hurt sb; to harm sb; **se faire** ~ to hurt o.s.; **se donner du** ~ **pour faire qch** to go to a lot of trouble to do sth; **ça fait** ~ it hurts; **j'ai** ~ **au dos** my back hurts; **avoir** ~ **à la tête/à la gorge/aux dents** to have a headache/a sore throat/toothache; **avoir le** ~ **du pays** to be homesick; **prendre** ~ to be taken ill, feel unwell; *voir aussi* **cœur**; **maux;** ~ **de mer** seasickness; ~ **en point** *adj inv* in a bad state

malade [malad] *adj* ill, sick; (*poitrine, jambe*) bad; (*plante*) diseased ♦ *nm/f* invalid, sick person; (*à l'hôpital etc*) patient; **tomber** ~ to fall ill; **être** ~ **du cœur** to have heart trouble *ou* a bad heart; ~ **mental** mentally sick *ou* ill person

maladie [maladi] *nf* (*spécifique*) disease, illness; (*mauvaise santé*) illness, sickness; ~ **d'Alzheimer** *nf* Alzheimer's (disease); **maladif, ive** *adj* sickly; (*curiosité, besoin*) pathological

maladresse [maladʀɛs] *nf* clumsiness *no pl*; (*gaffe*) blunder

maladroit, e [maladʀwa, -wat] *adj* clumsy

malaise [malɛz] *nm* (*MÉD*) feeling of faintness; feeling of discomfort; (*fig*) uneasiness, malaise

malaisé, e [maleze] *adj* difficult

malaria [malaʀja] *nf* malaria

malaxer [malakse] *vt* to knead; to mix

malchance [malʃɑ̃s] *nf* misfortune, ill luck *no pl*; **par** ~ unfortunately

mâle [mɑl] *adj* (*aussi* ÉLEC, TECH) male; (*viril: voix, traits*) manly ♦ *nm* male

malédiction [malediksjɔ̃] *nf* curse

mal: ~**encontreux, euse** *adj* unfortunate, untoward; ~**-en-point** *adj inv* in a sorry state; ~**entendu** *nm* misunderstanding; ~**façon** *nf* fault; ~**faisant, e** *adj* evil, harmful; ~**faiteur** *nm* lawbreaker, criminal; burglar, thief; ~**famé, e** *adj* disreputable

malgache [malgaʃ] *adj, nm/f* Màdàgascan, Malagasy ♦ *nm* (*LING*) Malagasy

malgré [malgʀe] *prép* in spite of, despite; ~ **tout** all the same

malheur [malœʀ] *nm* (*situation*) adversity, misfortune; (*événement*) misfortune; disaster, tragedy; **faire un** ~ to be a smash hit; **malheureusement** *adv* unfortunately; **malheureux, euse** *adj* (*triste*) unhappy, miserable; (*infortuné, regrettable*) unfortunate; (*malchanceux*) unlucky; (*insignifiant*) wretched ♦ *nm/f* poor soul; unfortunate creature; **les** ~**eux** the destitute

malhonnête [malɔnɛt] *adj* dishonest

malice [malis] *nf* mischievousness; (*méchanceté*): **par** ~ out of malice *ou* spite; **sans** ~ guileless; **malicieux, euse** *adj* mischievous

malin, igne [malɛ̃, -iɲ] *adj* (*futé: f gén: maline*) smart, shrewd; (*MÉD*) malignant

malingre [malɛ̃gʀ(ə)] *adj* puny

malle [mal] *nf* trunk

mallette [malɛt] *nf* (small) suitcase; overnight case; attaché case

malmener [malməne] *vt* to manhandle; (*fig*) to give a rough handling to

malodorant, e [malɔdɔʀɑ̃, -ɑ̃t] *adj* foul- *ou* ill-smelling

malotru [malɔtʀy] *nm* lout, boor

malpropre [malpʀɔpʀ(ə)] *adj* dirty

malsain, e [malsɛ̃, -ɛn] *adj* unhealthy

malt [malt] *nm* malt

Malte [malt(ə)] *nf* Malta

maltraiter [maltʀete] *vt* (*brutaliser*) to manhandle, ill-treat

malveillance [malvɛjɑ̃s] *nf* (*animosité*) ill will; (*intention de nuire*) malevolence; (*JUR*) malicious intent *no pl*

malversation [malvɛʀsasjɔ̃] *nf* embezzlement

maman [mamɑ̃] *nf* mum(my), mother

mamelle [mamɛl] *nf* teat

mamelon [mamlɔ̃] *nm* (*ANAT*) nipple; (*colline*) knoll, hillock

mamie [mami] (*fam*) *nf* granny

mammifère [mamifɛʀ] *nm* mammal

manche [mɑ̃ʃ] nf (de vêtement) sleeve; (d'un jeu, tournoi) round; (GÉO): **la M~** the Channel ♦ nm (d'outil, casserole) handle; (de pelle, pioche etc) shaft; **~ à balai** nm broomstick; (AVIAT, INFORM) joystick

manchette [mɑ̃ʃɛt] nf (de chemise) cuff; (coup) forearm blow; (titre) headline

manchon [mɑ̃ʃɔ̃] nm (de fourrure) muff

manchot [mɑ̃ʃo] nm one-armed man; armless man; (ZOOL) penguin

mandarine [mɑ̃daʀin] nf mandarin (orange), tangerine

mandat [mɑ̃da] nm (postal) postal ou money order; (d'un député etc) mandate; (procuration) power of attorney, proxy; (POLICE) warrant; **~ d'amener** summons sg; **~ d'arrêt** warrant for arrest; **mandataire** nm/f representative; proxy

manège [manɛʒ] nm riding school; (à la foire) roundabout, merry-go-round; (fig) game, ploy

manette [manɛt] nf lever, tap; **~ de jeu** joystick

mangeable [mɑ̃ʒabl(ə)] adj edible, eatable

mangeoire [mɑ̃ʒwaʀ] nf trough, manger

manger [mɑ̃ʒe] vt to eat; (ronger: suj: rouille etc) to eat into ou away ♦ vi to eat

mangue [mɑ̃g] nf mango

maniable [manjabl(ə)] adj (outil) handy; (voiture, voilier) easy to handle

maniaque [manjak] adj finicky, fussy; suffering from a mania ♦ nm/f maniac

manie [mani] nf mania; (tic) odd habit

manier [manje] vt to handle

manière [manjɛʀ] nf (façon) way, manner; **~s** nfpl (attitude) manners; (chichis) fuss sg; **de ~ à** so as to; **de telle ~ que** in such a way that; **de cette ~** in this way ou manner; **d'une certaine ~** in a way; **d'une ~ générale** generally speaking, as a general rule; **de toute ~** in any case

maniéré, e [manjeʀe] adj affected

manifestant, e [manifɛstɑ̃, -ɑ̃t] nm/f demonstrator

manifestation [manifɛstasjɔ̃] nf (de joie, mécontentement) expression, demonstration; (symptôme) outward sign; (fête etc) event; (POL) demonstration

manifeste [manifɛst(ə)] adj obvious, evident ♦ nm manifesto

manifester [manifɛste] vt (volonté, intentions) to show, indicate; (joie, peur) to express, show ♦ vi to demonstrate; **se ~** vi (émotion) to show ou express itself; (difficultés) to arise; (symptômes) to appear; (témoin etc) to come forward

manigance [manigɑ̃s] nf scheme

manigancer [manigɑ̃se] vt to plot

manipuler [manipyle] vt to handle; (fig) to manipulate

manivelle [manivɛl] nf crank

mannequin [mankɛ̃] nm (COUTURE) dummy; (MODE) model

manœuvre [manœvʀ(ə)] nf (gén) manœuvre (BRIT), maneuver (US) ♦ nm labourer; **~r** [manœvʀe] vt to manœuvre (BRIT), maneuver (US); (levier, machine) to operate ♦ vi to manœuvre

manoir [manwaʀ] nm manor ou country house

manque [mɑ̃k] nm (insuffisance): **~ de** lack of; (vide) emptiness, gap; (MÉD) withdrawal; **~s** nmpl (lacunes) faults, defects

manqué, e [mɑ̃ke] adj failed; **garçon ~** tomboy

manquer [mɑ̃ke] vi (faire défaut) to be lacking; (être absent) to be missing; (échouer) to fail ♦ vt to miss ♦ vb impers: **il (nous) manque encore 100 F** we are still 100 F short; **il manque des pages (au livre)** there are some pages missing (from the book); **il/cela me manque** I miss him/ this; **~ à** (règles etc) to be in breach of, fail to observe; **~ de** to lack; **il a manqué (de) se tuer** he very nearly got killed

mansarde [mɑ̃saʀd(ə)] nf attic

mansuétude [mɑ̃sɥetyd] nf leniency

manteau, x [mɑ̃to] nm coat

manucure [manykyʀ] nf manicurist

manuel, le [manɥɛl] adj manual ♦ nm (ouvrage) manual, handbook

manufacture [manyfaktyʀ] nf factory; **manufacturé, e** [manyfaktyʀe] adj manufactured

manuscrit, e [manyskʀi, -it] adj handwritten ♦ nm manuscript

manutention [manytɑ̃sjɔ̃] nf (COMM) handling; (local) storehouse

mappemonde [mapmɔ̃d] nf (plane) map of the world; (sphère) globe

maquereau, x [makʀo] nm (ZOOL) mackerel inv; (fam) pimp

maquette [makɛt] nf (d'un décor, bâtiment, véhicule) (scale) model; (d'une page illustrée) paste-up

maquillage [makijaʒ] nm making up; faking; (crème etc) make-up

maquiller [makije] vt (personne, visage) to make up; (truquer: passeport, statistique) to fake; (: voiture volée) to do over (respray etc); **se ~** vi to make up (one's face)

maquis [maki] nm (GÉO) scrub; (MIL) maquis, underground fighting no pl

maraîcher, ère [maʀeʃe, maʀeʃɛʀ] adj: **cultures maraîchères** market gardening sg ♦ nm/f market gardener; **jardin ~** market garden (BRIT), truck farm (US)

marais [maʀɛ] nm marsh, swamp

marasme [maʀasm(ə)] nm stagnation, slump

marathon [maʀatɔ̃] nm marathon

marâtre [maʀɑtʀ(ə)] nf cruel mother

maraudeur [maʀodœʀ] nm prowler

marbre [maʀbʀ(ə)] nm (pierre, statue) marble; *(d'une table, commode)* marble top; **marbrer** *vt* to mottle, blotch

marc [maʀ] *nm (de raisin, pommes)* marc; ~ **de café** coffee grounds *pl ou* dregs *pl*

marchand, e [maʀʃɑ̃, -ɑ̃d] *nm/f* shopkeeper, tradesman(woman); *(au marché)* stallholder ♦ *adj:* **prix/valeur** ~(e) market price/value; ~**/e de fruits** fruiterer *(BRIT)*, fruit seller *(US)*; ~**/e de journaux** newsagent *(BRIT)*, newsdealer *(US)*; ~**/e de légumes** greengrocer *(BRIT)*, produce dealer *(US)*; ~**/e de quatre saisons** costermonger *(BRIT)*, street vendor *(selling fresh fruit and vegetables) (US)*

marchander [maʀʃɑ̃de] *vi* to bargain, haggle

marchandise [maʀʃɑ̃diz] *nf* goods *pl*, merchandise *no pl*

marche [maʀʃ(ə)] *nf (d'escalier)* step; *(activité)* walking; *(promenade, trajet, allure)* walk; *(démarche)* walk, gait; *(MIL etc, MUS)* march; *(fonctionnement)* running; *(progression)* progress; course; **ouvrir/fermer la** ~ to lead the way/bring up the rear; **dans le sens de la** ~ *(RAIL)* facing the engine; **en** ~ *(monter etc)* while the vehicle is moving *ou* in motion; **mettre en** ~ to start; **se mettre en** ~ *(personne)* to get moving; *(machine)* to start; ~ **à suivre** *(correct)* procedure; *(sur notice)* (step by step) instructions *pl*; ~ **arrière** reverse (gear); **faire** ~ **arrière** to reverse; *(fig)* to backtrack, back-pedal

marché [maʀʃe] *nm (lieu, COMM, ÉCON)* market; *(ville)* trading centre; *(transaction)* bargain, deal; **faire du** ~ **noir** to buy and sell on the black market; ~ **aux puces** flea market; **M**~ **commun** Common Market

marchepied [maʀʃəpje] *nm (RAIL)* step; *(fig)* stepping stone

marcher [maʀʃe] *vi* to walk; *(MIL)* to march; *(aller: voiture, train, affaires)* to go; *(prospérer)* to go well; *(fonctionner)* to work, run; *(fam)* to go along, agree; to be taken in; ~ **sur** to walk on; *(mettre le pied sur)* to step on *ou* in; *(MIL)* to march upon; ~ **dans** *(herbe etc)* to walk in *ou* on; *(flaque)* to step in; **faire** ~ **qn** to pull sb's leg; to lead sb up the garden path; **marcheur, euse** *nm/f* walker

mardi [maʀdi] *nm* Tuesday; **M**~ **gras** Shrove Tuesday

mare [maʀ] *nf* pond

marécage [maʀekaʒ] *nm* marsh, swamp

maréchal, aux [maʀeʃal, -o] *nm* marshal

marée [maʀe] *nf (poissons)* fresh (sea) fish; ~ **haute/basse** high/low tide; ~ **montante/descendante** rising/ebb tide

marémotrice [maʀemɔtʀis] *adj f* tidal

margarine [maʀɡaʀin] *nf* margarine

marge [maʀʒ(ə)] *nf* margin; **en** ~ **de** *(fig)* on the fringe of; cut off from; ~ **bénéficiai-**

re profit margin

marguerite [maʀɡəʀit] *nf* marguerite, (oxeye) daisy; *(d'imprimante)* daisy-wheel

mari [maʀi] *nm* husband

mariage [maʀjaʒ] *nm (union, état, fig)* marriage; *(noce)* wedding; ~ **civil/religieux** registry office *(BRIT) ou* civil/church wedding

marié, e [maʀje] *adj* married ♦ *nm* (bride)groom; **les** ~**s** the bride and groom; **les (jeunes)** ~**s** the newly-weds; **mariée** *nf* bride

marier [maʀje] *vt* to marry; *(fig)* to blend; **se** ~ **(avec)** to marry

marin, e [maʀɛ̃, -in] *adj* sea *cpd*, marine ♦ *nm* sailor

marine [maʀin] *adj voir* **marin** ♦ *adj inv* navy (blue) ♦ *nm (MIL)* marine ♦ *nf* navy; ~ **de guerre** navy; ~ **marchande** merchant navy

marionnette [maʀjɔnɛt] *nf* puppet

maritime [maʀitim] *adj* sea *cpd*, maritime

mark [maʀk] *nm* mark

marmelade [maʀməlad] *nf* stewed fruit, compote; ~ **d'oranges** marmalade

marmite [maʀmit] *nf* (cooking-)pot

marmonner [maʀmɔne] *vt, vi* to mumble, mutter

marmotter [maʀmɔte] *vt* to mumble

Maroc [maʀɔk] *nm:* **le** ~ Morocco; **marocain, e** *adj, nm/f* Moroccan

maroquinerie [maʀɔkinʀi] *nf* leather craft; fine leather goods *pl*

marquant, e [maʀkɑ̃, -ɑ̃t] *adj* outstanding

marque [maʀk(ə)] *nf* mark; *(SPORT, JEU:* décompte des points) score; *(COMM: de produits)* brand; make; *(de disques)* label; **de** ~ *(COMM)* brand-name *cpd*; proprietary; *(fig)* high-class; distinguished; ~ **de fabrique** trademark; ~ **déposée** registered trademark

marquer [maʀke] *vt* to mark; *(inscrire)* to write down; *(bétail)* to brand; *(SPORT: but etc)* to score; (: *joueur)* to mark; *(accentuer: taille etc)* to emphasize; *(manifester: refus, intérêt)* to show ♦ *vi (événement, personnalité)* to stand out, be outstanding; *(SPORT)* to score; ~ **les points** *(tenir la marque)* to keep the score

marqueterie [maʀkətʀi] *nf* inlaid work, marquetry

marquis [maʀki] *nm* marquis *ou* marquess

marquise [maʀkiz] *nf* marchioness; *(auvent)* glass canopy *ou* awning

marraine [maʀɛn] *nf* godmother

marrant, e [maʀɑ̃, -ɑ̃t] *(fam) adj* funny

marre [maʀ] *(fam) adv:* **en avoir** ~ **de** to be fed up with

marrer [maʀe] : **se** ~ *(fam) vi* to have a (good) laugh

marron [maʀɔ̃] *nm (fruit)* chestnut ♦ *adj inv* brown; **marronnier** *nm* chestnut (tree)

mars [maʀs] *nm* March

marsouin [marswɛ̃] *nm* porpoise
marteau, x [marto] *nm* hammer; *(de porte)* knocker; **marteau-piqueur** *nm* pneumatic drill
marteler [martəle] *vt* to hammer
martien, ne [marsjɛ̃, -jɛn] *adj* Martian, of *ou* from Mars
martinet [martinɛ] *nm* *(fouet)* small whip; *(ZOOL)* swift
martyr, e [martir] *nm/f* martyr
martyre [martir] *nm* martyrdom; *(fig: sens affaibli)* agony, torture
martyriser [martirize] *vt* *(REL)* to martyr; *(fig)* to bully; *(enfant)* to batter, beat
marxiste [marksist(ə)] *adj, nm/f* Marxist
masculin, e [maskylɛ̃, -in] *adj* masculine; *(sexe, population)* male; *(équipe, vêtements)* men's; *(viril)* manly ♦ *nm* masculine
masque [mask(ə)] *nm* mask; ~**r** [maske] *vt* *(cacher: paysage, porte)* to hide, conceal; *(dissimuler: vérité, projet)* to mask, obscure
massacre [masakr(ə)] *nm* massacre, slaughter; ~**r** [masakre] *vt* to massacre, slaughter; *(fig: texte etc)* to murder
massage [masaʒ] *nm* massage
masse [mas] *nf* mass; *(péj):* **la** ~ the masses *pl*; *(ÉLEC)* earth; *(maillet)* sledgehammer; **une** ~ **de** *(fam)* masses *ou* loads of; **en** ~ *(en bloc)* in bulk; *(en foule)* en masse ♦ *adj* *(exécutions, production)* mass *cpd*
masser [mase] *vt* *(assembler)* to gather; *(pétrir)* to massage; **se** ~ *vi* to gather; **masseur, euse** *nm/f* masseur(euse)
massif, ive [masif, -iv] *adj* *(porte)* solid, massive; *(visage)* heavy, large; *(bois, or)* solid; *(dose)* massive; *(déportations etc)* mass *cpd* ♦ *nm* *(montagneux)* massif; *(de fleurs)* clump, bank
massue [masy] *nf* club, bludgeon
mastic [mastik] *nm* *(pour vitres)* putty; *(pour fentes)* filler
mastiquer [mastike] *vt* *(aliment)* to chew, masticate; *(fente)* to fill; *(vitre)* to putty
mat, e [mat] *adj* *(couleur, métal)* mat(t); *(bruit, son)* dull ♦ *adj inv* *(ÉCHECS):* **être** ~ to be checkmate
mât [mɑ] *nm* *(NAVIG)* mast; *(poteau)* pole, post
match [matʃ] *nm* match; **faire** ~ **nul** to draw; ~ **aller** first leg; ~ **retour** second leg, return match
matelas [matla] *nm* mattress; ~ **pneumatique** air bed *ou* mattress
matelassé, e [matlase] *adj* padded; quilted
matelot [matlo] *nm* sailor, seaman
mater [mate] *vt* *(personne)* to bring to heel, subdue; *(révolte)* to put down
matérialiste [materjalist(ə)] *adj* materialistic
matériaux [materjo] *nmpl* material(s)
matériel, le [materjɛl] *adj* material ♦ *nm* equipment *no pl*; *(de camping etc)* gear *no*

pl
maternel, le [matɛrnɛl] *adj* *(amour, geste)* motherly, maternal; *(grand-père, oncle)* maternal; **maternelle** *nf* *(aussi: école maternelle)* *(state)* nursery school
maternité [matɛrnite] *nf* *(établissement)* maternity hospital; *(état de mère)* motherhood, maternity; *(grossesse)* pregnancy
mathématique [matematik] *adj* mathematical; **mathématiques** *nfpl* *(science)* mathematics *sg*
matière [matjɛr] *nf* *(PHYSIQUE)* matter; *(COMM, TECH)* material, matter *no pl*; *(fig: d'un livre etc)* subject matter, material; *(SCOL)* subject; **en** ~ **de** as regards; ~**s grasses** fat content *sg*; ~**s premières** raw materials
matin [matɛ̃] *nm, adv* morning; **du** ~ **au soir** from morning till night; **de bon** *ou* **grand** ~ early in the morning; **matinal, e, aux** *adj* *(toilette, gymnastique)* morning *cpd*; *(de bonne heure)* early; **être matinal** *(personne)* to be up early; to be an early riser
matinée [matine] *nf* morning; *(spectacle)* matinée
matou [matu] *nm* tom(cat)
matraque [matrak] *nf* club; *(de policier)* truncheon *(BRIT)*, billy *(US)*
matricule [matrikyl] *nf* *(aussi: registre* ~*)* roll, register ♦ *nm* (: *numéro* ~: *MIL*) regimental number; (: *ADMIN*) reference number
matrimonial, e, aux [matrimɔnjal, -o] *adj* marital, marriage *cpd*
maudire [modir] *vt* to curse
maudit, e [modi, -it] *(fam) adj* *(satané)* blasted, confounded
maugréer [mogree] *vi* to grumble
maussade [mosad] *adj* sullen
mauvais, e [mɔvɛ, -ɛz] *adj* bad; *(faux):* **le** ~ **numéro/moment** the wrong number/moment; *(méchant, malveillant)* malicious, spiteful; **il fait** ~ the weather is bad; **la mer est** ~**e** the sea is rough; ~ **plaisant** hoaxer; ~**e herbe** weed; ~**e langue** gossip, scandalmonger *(BRIT)*; ~**e passe** difficult situation; bad patch; ~**e tête** rebellious *ou* headstrong customer
maux [mo] *nmpl de* **mal**; ~ **de ventre** stomachache *sg*
maximum [maksimɔm] *adj, nm* maximum; **au** ~ *(le plus possible)* to the full; as much as one can; *(tout au plus)* at the (very) most *ou* maximum
mayonnaise [majɔnɛz] *nf* mayonnaise
mazout [mazut] *nm* *(fuel)* oil
Me *abr* = **Maître**
me(m') [m(ə)] *pron* me; *(réfléchi)* myself
mec [mɛk] *(fam) nm* bloke, guy
mécanicien, ne [mekanisjɛ̃, -jɛn] *nm/f* mechanic; *(RAIL)* *(train ou engine)* driver
mécanique [mekanik] *adj* mechanical ♦ *nf*

(*science*) mechanics *sg*; (*technologie*) mechanical engineering; (*mécanisme*) mechanism; engineering; works *pl*; **ennui** ~ engine trouble *no pl*

mécanisme [mekanism(ə)] *nm* mechanism

méchamment [meʃamɑ̃] *adv* nastily, maliciously, spitefully

méchanceté [meʃɑ̃ste] *nf* nastiness, maliciousness; nasty *ou* spiteful *ou* malicious remark (*ou* action)

méchant, e [meʃɑ̃, -ɑ̃t] *adj* nasty, malicious, spiteful; (*enfant: pas sage*) naughty; (*animal*) vicious; (*avant le nom: valeur péjorative*) nasty; miserable; (: *intensive*) terrific

mèche [mɛʃ] *nf* (*de lampe, bougie*) wick; (*d'un explosif*) fuse; (*de vilebrequin, perceuse*) bit; (*de cheveux*) lock; **de** ~ **avec** in league with

mécompte [mekɔ̃t] *nm* miscalculation; (*déception*) disappointment

méconnaissable [mekɔnɛsabl(ə)] *adj* unrecognizable

méconnaître [mekɔnɛtʀ(ə)] *vt* (*ignorer*) to be unaware of; (*mésestimer*) to misjudge

mécontent, e [mekɔ̃tɑ̃, -ɑ̃t] *adj*: ~ (**de**) discontented *ou* dissatisfied *ou* displeased (with); (*contrarié*) annoyed (at); **mécontentement** *nm* dissatisfaction, discontent, displeasure; annoyance

médaille [medaj] *nf* medal

médaillon [medajɔ̃] *nm* (*portrait*) medallion; (*bijou*) locket

médecin [medsɛ̃] *nm* doctor; ~ **légiste** forensic surgeon

médecine [medsin] *nf* medicine; ~ **légale** forensic medicine

média [medja] *nmpl*: **les** ~ the media

médiatique [medjatik] *adj* media *cpd*

médical, e, aux [medikal, -o] *adj* medical

médicament [medikamɑ̃] *nm* medicine, drug

médiéval, e, aux [medjeval, -o] *adj* medieval

médiocre [medjɔkʀ(ə)] *adj* mediocre, poor

médire [mediʀ] *vi*: ~ **de** to speak ill of; **médisance** *nf* scandalmongering (*BRIT*); piece of scandal *ou* of malicious gossip

méditer [medite] *vt* (*approfondir*) to meditate on, ponder (over); (*combiner*) to meditate ♦ *vi* to meditate

Méditerranée [mediteʀane] *nf*: **la (mer)** ~ the Mediterranean (Sea); **méditerranéen, ne** *adj*, *nm/f* Mediterranean

méduse [medyz] *nf* jellyfish

meeting [mitiŋ] *nm* (*POL, SPORT*) rally

méfait [mefɛ] *nm* (*faute*) misdemeanour, wrongdoing; ~**s** *nmpl* (*ravages*) ravages, damage *sg*

méfiance [mefjɑ̃s] *nf* mistrust, distrust; **méfiant, e** [mefjɑ̃, -ɑ̃t] *adj* mistrustful, distrustful

méfier [mefje] : **se** ~ *vi* to be wary; to be careful; **se** ~ **de** to mistrust, distrust, be wary of; (*faire attention*) to be careful about

mégarde [megaʀd(ə)] *nf*: **par** ~ accidentally; by mistake

mégère [meʒɛʀ] *nf* shrew

mégot [mego] *nm* cigarette end

meilleur, e [mɛjœʀ] *adj*, *adv* better; (*valeur superlative*) best ♦ *nm*: **le** ~ (*celui qui ...*) the best (one); (*ce qui ...*) the best; **le** ~ **des deux** the better of the two; **de** ~**e heure** earlier; ~ **marché** cheaper; **meilleure** *nf*: **la meilleure** the best (one)

mélancolie [melɑ̃kɔli] *nf* melancholy, gloom; **mélancolique** *adj* melancholic, melancholy

mélange [melɑ̃ʒ] *nm* mixture

mélanger [melɑ̃ʒe] *vt* (*substances*) to mix; (*vins, couleurs*) to blend; (*mettre en désordre*) to mix up, muddle (up)

mélasse [melas] *nf* treacle, molasses *sg*

mêlée [mele] *nf* mêlée, scramble; (*RUGBY*) scrum(mage)

mêler [mele] *vt* (*substances, odeurs, races*) to mix; (*embrouiller*) to muddle (up), mix up; **se** ~ *vi* to mix; to mingle; **se** ~ **à** (*suj: personne*) to join; to mix with; (*suj: odeurs etc*) to mingle with; **se** ~ **de** (: *personne*) to meddle with, interfere in; ~ **qn à** (*affaire*) to get sb mixed up *ou* involved in

mélodie [melɔdi] *nf* melody

melon [məlɔ̃] *nm* (*BOT*) (honeydew) melon; (*aussi: chapeau* ~) bowler (hat)

membre [mɑ̃bʀ(ə)] *nm* (*ANAT*) limb; (*personne, pays, élément*) member ♦ *adj* member *cpd*

mémé [meme] (*fam*) *nf* granny

──────────── MOT CLÉ

même [mɛm] *adj* **1** (*avant le nom*) same; **en** ~ **temps** at the same time

2 (*après le nom: renforcement*): **il est la loyauté** ~ he is loyalty itself; **ce sont ses paroles/celles-là** ~ they are his very words/the very ones

♦ *pron*: **le(la)** ~ the same one

♦ *adv* **1** (*renforcement*): **il n'a** ~ **pas pleuré** he didn't even cry; ~ **lui l'a dit** even HE said it; **ici** ~ at this very place

2: **à** ~: **à** ~ **la bouteille** straight from the bottle; **à** ~ **la peau** next to the skin; **être à** ~ **de faire** to be in a position to do, be able to do

3: **de** ~ to do likewise; **lui de** ~ so does (*ou* did *ou* is) he; **de** ~ **que** just as; **il en va de** ~ **pour** the same goes for

──────────────

mémento [memɛ̃to] *nm* (*agenda*) appointments diary; (*ouvrage*) summary

mémoire [memwaʀ] *nf* memory ♦ *nm* (*ADMIN, JUR*) memorandum; (*SCOL*) dissertation, paper; ~**s** *nmpl* (*souvenirs*) memoirs;

à la ~ **de** to the *ou* in memory of; **pour** ~ for the record; **de** ~ from memory; ~ **morte/vive** (*INFORM*) ROM/RAM

menace [mənas] *nf* threat

menacer [mənase] *vt* to threaten

ménage [menaʒ] *nm* (*travail*) housekeeping, housework; (*couple*) (married) couple; (*famille, ADMIN*) household; **faire le** ~ to do the housework

ménagement [menaʒmã] *nm* care and attention; ~**s** *nmpl* (*égards*) consideration *sg*, attention *sg*

ménager, ère [menaʒe, -ɛʀ] *adj* household *cpd*, domestic ♦ *vt* (*traiter*) to handle with tact; to treat considerately; (*utiliser*) to use sparingly; to use with care; (*prendre soin de*) to take (great) care of, look after; (*organiser*) to arrange; (*installer*) to put in; to make; ~ **qch à qn** (*réserver*) to have sth in store for sb; **ménagère** *nf* housewife

mendiant, e [mãdjã, -ãt] *nm/f* beggar; **mendier** [mãdje] *vi* to beg ♦ *vt* to beg (for)

mener [məne] *vt* to lead; (*enquête*) to conduct; (*affaires*) to manage ♦ *vi*: **(à la marque)** to lead, be in the lead; ~ **à/dans** (*emmener*) to take to/into; ~ **qch à terme** *ou* **à bien** to see sth through (to a successful conclusion), complete sth successfully

meneur, euse [mənœʀ, -øz] *nm/f* leader; (*péj*) agitator; ~ **de jeu** host, quizmaster

méningite [menɛ̃ʒit] *nf* meningitis *no pl*

ménopause [menɔpoz] *nf* menopause

menottes [mənɔt] *nfpl* handcuffs

mensonge [mãsɔ̃ʒ] *nm* lie; lying *no pl*; **mensonger, ère** *adj* false

mensualité [mãsyalite] *nf* monthly payment; monthly salary

mensuel, le [mãsɥɛl] *adj* monthly

mensurations [mãsyʀasjɔ̃] *nfpl* measurements

mentalité [mãtalite] *nf* mentality

menteur, euse [mãtœʀ, -øz] *nm/f* liar

menthe [mãt] *nf* mint

mention [mãsjɔ̃] *nf* (*note*) note, comment; (*SCOL*): ~ **bien** *etc* ≈ grade B *etc* (*ou* upper 2nd class *etc*) pass (*BRIT*), ≈ pass with (high) honors (*US*); **mentionner** *vt* to mention

mentir [mãtiʀ] *vi* to lie; to be lying

menton [mãtɔ̃] *nm* chin

menu, e [məny] *adj* slim, slight; tiny; (*frais, difficulté*) minor ♦ *adv* (*couper, hacher*) very fine ♦ *nm* menu; **par le** ~ (*raconter*) in minute detail; ~ **e monnaie** small change

menuiserie [mənɥizʀi] *nf* (*travail*) joinery, carpentry; woodwork; (*local*) joiner's workshop; (*ouvrage*) woodwork *no pl*; **menuisier** [mənɥizje] *nm* joiner, carpenter

méprendre [mepʀãdʀ(ə)] : **se** ~ *vi* to be mistaken (about)

mépris [mepʀi] *nm* (*dédain*) contempt, scorn; (*indifférence*): **le** ~ **de** contempt *ou*

disregard for; **au** ~ **de** regardless of, in defiance of

méprisable [mepʀizabl(ə)] *adj* contemptible, despicable

méprise [mepʀiz] *nf* mistake, error; misunderstanding

mépriser [mepʀize] *vt* to scorn, despise; (*gloire, danger*) to scorn, spurn

mer [mɛʀ] *nf* sea; (*marée*) tide; **en** ~ at sea; **prendre la** ~ to put out to sea; **en haute** *ou* **pleine** ~ off shore, on the open sea; **la** ~ **du Nord/Rouge** the North/Red Sea

mercantile [mɛʀkãtil] (*péj*) *adj* mercenary

mercenaire [mɛʀsənɛʀ] *nm* mercenary, hired soldier

mercerie [mɛʀsəʀi] *nf* haberdashery (*BRIT*), notions (*US*); haberdasher's shop (*BRIT*), notions store (*US*)

merci [mɛʀsi] *excl* thank you ♦ *nf*: **à la** ~ **de qn/qch** at sb's mercy/the mercy of sth; ~ **de** thank you for; **sans** ~ merciless(ly)

mercredi [mɛʀkʀədi] *nm* Wednesday

mercure [mɛʀkyʀ] *nm* mercury

merde [mɛʀd(ə)] (*fam!*) *nf* shit (*!*) ♦ *excl* (bloody) hell (*!*)

mère [mɛʀ] *nf* mother; ~ **célibataire** unmarried mother

méridional, e, aux [meʀidjɔnal, -o] *adj* southern ♦ *nm/f* Southerner

meringue [məʀɛ̃g] *nf* meringue

mérite [meʀit] *nm* merit; **le** ~ **(de ceci) lui revient** the credit (for this) is his

mériter [meʀite] *vt* to deserve

merlan [mɛʀlã] *nm* whiting

merle [mɛʀl(ə)] *nm* blackbird

merveille [mɛʀvɛj] *nf* marvel, wonder; **faire** ~ to work wonders; **à** ~ perfectly, wonderfully

merveilleux, euse [mɛʀvejø, -øz] *adj* marvellous, wonderful

mes [me] *dét voir* **mon**

mésange [mezãʒ] *nf* tit(mouse)

mésaventure [mezavãtyʀ] *nf* misadventure, misfortune

Mesdames [medam] *nfpl de* **Madame**

Mesdemoiselles [medmwazɛl] *nfpl de* **Mademoiselle**

mésentente [mezãtãt] *nf* dissension, disagreement

mesquin, e [mɛskɛ̃, -in] *adj* mean, petty

message [mesaʒ] *nm* message; **messager, ère** *nm/f* messenger

messe [mɛs] *nf* mass; **aller à la** ~ to go to mass; ~ **de minuit** midnight mass

Messieurs [mesjø] *nmpl de* **Monsieur**

mesure [məzyʀ] *nf* (*évaluation, dimension*) measurement; (*étalon, récipient, contenu*) measure; (*MUS: cadence*) time, tempo; (: *division*) bar; (*retenue*) moderation; (*disposition*) measure, step; **sur** ~ (*costume*) made-to-measure; **à la** ~ **de** (*fig*) worthy of; on the same scale as; **dans la** ~ **où** insofar as, inasmuch as; **à ~ que** as; **être en ~ de** to be in a position to

mesurer [məzyʀe] *vt* to measure; (*juger*) to weigh up, assess; (*limiter*) to limit, ration; (*modérer*) to moderate; **se ~ avec** to have a confrontation with; to tackle; **il mesure 1 m 80** he's 1 m 80 tall

met *vb voir* **mettre**

métal, aux [metal, -o] *nm* metal; **métallique** *adj* metallic

météo [meteo] *nf* weather report; ≈ Met Office (*BRIT*), ≈ National Weather Service (*US*)

météorologie [meteɔʀɔlɔʒi] *nf* meteorology

méthode [metɔd] *nf* method; (*livre, ouvrage*) manual, tutor

métier [metje] *nm* (*profession: gén*) job; (: *manuel*) trade; (*artisanal*) craft; (*technique, expérience*) (acquired) skill *ou* technique; (*aussi: ~ à tisser*) (weaving) loom

métis, se [metis] *adj, nm/f* half-caste, half-breed

métisser [metise] *vt* to cross

métrage [metʀaʒ] *nm* (*de tissu*) length, ≈ yardage; (*CINÉMA*) footage, length; **long/moyen/court ~** full-length/medium-length/short film

mètre [mɛtʀ(ə)] *nm* metre; (*règle*) (metre) rule; (*ruban*) tape measure; **métrique** *adj* metric

métro [metʀo] *nm* underground (*BRIT*), subway

métropole [metʀɔpɔl] *nf* (*capitale*) metropolis; (*pays*) home country

mets [mɛ] *nm* dish

metteur [mɛtœʀ] *nm*: **~ en scène** (*THÉÂTRE*) producer; (*CINÉMA*) director; **~ en ondes** producer

─────────────── **MOT CLÉ** ───────────────

mettre [mɛtʀ(ə)] *vt* **1** (*placer*) to put; **~ en bouteille/en sac** to bottle/put in bags *ou* sacks

2 (*vêtements: revêtir*) to put on; (: *porter*) to wear; **mets ton gilet** put your cardigan on; **je ne mets plus mon manteau** I no longer wear my coat

3 (*faire fonctionner: chauffage, électricité*) to put on; (: *reveil, minuteur*) to set; (*installer: gaz, eau*) to put in, to lay on; **~ en marche** to start up

4 (*consacrer*): **~ du temps à faire qch** to take time to do sth *ou* over sth

5 (*noter, écrire*) to say, put (down); **qu'est-ce qu'il a mis sur la carte?** what did he say *ou* write on the card?; **mettez au pluriel ...** put ... into the plural

6 (*supposer*): **mettons que ...** let's suppose *ou* say that ...

7: **y ~ du sien** to pull one's weight

se ~ *vi* **1** (*se placer*): **vous pouvez vous ~**

là you can sit (*ou* stand) there; **où ça se met?** where does it go?; **se ~ au lit** to get into bed; **se ~ au piano** to sit down at the piano; **se ~ de l'encre sur les doigts** to get ink on one's fingers

2 (*s'habiller*): **se ~ en maillot de bain** to get into *ou* put on a swimsuit; **n'avoir rien à se ~** to have nothing to wear

3: **se ~ à** to begin, start; **se ~ à faire** to begin *ou* start doing *ou* to do; **se ~ au piano** to start learning the piano; **se ~ au travail/à l'étude** to get down to work/one's studies

────────────────────────────────

meuble [mœbl(ə)] *nm* piece of furniture; furniture *no pl* ♦ *adj* (*terre*) loose, friable; **meublé** *nm* furnished flatlet (*BRIT*) *ou* room; **meubler** *vt* to furnish; (*fig*) **meubler qch (de)** to fill sth (with)

meugler [møgle] *vi* to low, moo

meule [møl] *nf* (*à broyer*) millstone; (*à aiguiser*) grindstone; (*de foin, blé*) stack; (*de fromage*) round

meunier [mønje] *nm* miller; **meunière** *nf* miller's wife

meure *etc vb voir* **mourir**

meurtre [mœʀtʀ(ə)] *nm* murder; **meurtrier, ière** *adj* (*arme etc*) deadly; (*fureur, instincts*) murderous ♦ *nm/f* murderer (eress); **meurtrière** *nf* (*ouverture*) loophole

meurtrir [mœʀtʀiʀ] *vt* to bruise; (*fig*) to wound; **meurtrissure** *nf* bruise; (*fig*) scar

meus *etc vb voir* **mouvoir**

meute [møt] *nf* pack

Mexico [mɛksiko] *n* Mexico City

Mexique [mɛksik] *nm*: **le ~** Mexico

Mgr *abr* = **Monseigneur**

mi [mi] *nm* (*MUS*) E; (*en chantant la gamme*) mi ♦ *préfixe*: **~...** half(-); mid-; **à la ~-janvier** in mid-January; **à ~-jambes/-corps** (up *ou* down) to the knees/waist; **à ~-hauteur/-pente** halfway up *ou* down/up *ou* down the hill

miauler [mjole] *vi* to mew

miche [miʃ] *nf* round *ou* cob loaf

mi-chemin [miʃmɛ̃]: **à ~** *adv* halfway, midway

mi-clos, e [miklo, -kloz] *adj* half-closed

micro [mikʀo] *nm* mike, microphone; (*INFORM*) micro

microbe [mikʀɔb] *nm* germ, microbe

micro: **~-onde** *nf*: **four à ~s** microwave oven; **~-ordinateur** *nm* microcomputer; **~scope** *nm* microscope

midi [midi] *nm* midday, noon; (*moment du déjeuner*) lunchtime; (*sud*) south; **à ~** at 12 (o'clock) *ou* midday *ou* noon; **en plein ~** (right) in the middle of the day; facing south; **le M~** the South (of France), the Midi

mie [mi] *nf* crumb (of the loaf)

miel [mjɛl] *nm* honey

mien, ne [mjɛ̃, mjɛn] *pron*: **le(la) ~(ne), les ~(ne)s** mine; **les ~s** my family

miette [mjɛt] *nf* (*de pain, gâteau*) crumb; (*fig: de la conversation etc*) scrap; **en ~s** in pieces *ou* bits

--- MOT CLÉ ---

mieux [mjø] *adv* **1** (*d'une meilleure façon*): **~ (que)** better (than); **elle travaille/mange ~** she works/eats better; **elle va ~** she is better

2 (*de la meilleure façon*) best; **ce que je sais le ~** what I know best; **les livres les ~ faits** the best made books

3: **de ~ en ~** better and better

♦ *adj* **1** (*plus à l'aise, en meilleure forme*) better; **se sentir ~** to feel better

2 (*plus satisfaisant*) better; **c'est ~ ainsi** it's better like this; **c'est le ~ des deux** it's the better of the two; **le(la) ~, les ~** the best; **demandez-lui, c'est le ~** ask him, it's the best thing

3 (*plus joli*) better-looking

4: **au ~** at best; **au ~ avec** on the best of terms with; **pour le ~** for the best

♦ *nm* **1** (*progrès*) improvement

2: **de mon/ton ~** as best I/you can (*ou* could); **faire de son ~** to do one's best

mièvre [mjɛvʀ(ə)] *adj* mawkish (*BRIT*), sickly sentimental

mignon, ne [miɲɔ̃, -ɔn] *adj* sweet, cute

migraine [migʀɛn] *nf* headache; migraine

mijoter [miʒɔte] *vt* to simmer; (*préparer avec soin*) to cook lovingly; (*affaire, projet*) to plot, cook up ♦ *vi* to simmer

mil [mil] *num* = **mille**

milieu, x [miljø] *nm* (*centre*) middle; (*fig*) middle course *ou* way; happy medium; (*BIO, GÉO*) environment; (*entourage social*) milieu; background; circle; (*pègre*): **le ~** the underworld; **au ~ de** in the middle of; **au beau** *ou* **en plein ~ (de)** right in the middle (of)

militaire [militɛʀ] *adj* military, army *cpd* ♦ *nm* serviceman

militant, e [militɑ̃, -ɑ̃t] *adj, nm/f* militant

militer [milite] *vi* to be a militant; **~ pour/contre** (*suj: faits, raisons etc*) to militate in favour of/against

mille [mil] *num* a *ou* one thousand ♦ *nm* (*mesure*): **~ (marin)** nautical mile; **mettre dans le ~** to hit the bull's-eye; to be bang on target; **millefeuille** *nm* cream *ou* vanilla slice; **millénaire** *nm* millennium ♦ *adj* thousand-year-old; (*fig*) ancient; **mille-pattes** *nm inv* centipede

millésime [milezim] *nm* year; **millésimé, e** *adj* vintage *cpd*

millet [mijɛ] *nm* millet

milliard [miljaʀ] *nm* milliard, thousand million (*BRIT*), billion (*US*); **milliardaire** *nm/f*

multimillionaire (*BRIT*), billionaire (*US*)

millier [milje] *nm* thousand; **un ~ (de)** a thousand or so, about a thousand; **par ~s** in (their) thousands, by the thousand

milligramme [miligʀam] *nm* milligramme

millimètre [milimɛtʀ(ə)] *nm* millimetre

million [miljɔ̃] *nm* million; **deux ~s de** two million; **millionnaire** *nm/f* millionaire

mime [mim] *nm/f* (*acteur*) mime(r) ♦ *nm* (*art*) mime, miming

mimer [mime] *vt* to mime; (*singer*) to mimic, take off

mimique [mimik] *nf* (*funny*) face; (*signes*) gesticulations *pl*, sign language *no pl*

minable [minabl(ə)] *adj* shabby(-looking); pathetic

mince [mɛ̃s] *adj* thin; (*personne, taille*) slim, slender; (*fig: profit, connaissances*) slight, small, weak ♦ *excl*: **~ alors!** drat it!, darn it! (*US*); **minceur** *nf* thinness; slimness, slenderness

mine [min] *nf* (*physionomie*) expression, look; (*extérieur*) exterior, appearance; (*de crayon*) lead; (*gisement, exploitation, explosif, fig*) mine; **avoir bonne ~** (*personne*) to look well; (*ironique*) to look an utter idiot; **avoir mauvaise ~** to look unwell *ou* poorly; **faire ~ de faire** to make a pretence of doing; to make as if to do; **~ de rien** with a casual air; although you wouldn't think so

miner [mine] *vt* (*saper*) to undermine, erode; (*MIL*) to mine

minerai [minʀɛ] *nm* ore

minéral, e, aux [mineʀal, -o] *adj, nm* mineral

minéralogique [mineʀalɔʒik] *adj*: **numéro ~** registration number

minet, te [minɛ, -ɛt] *nm/f* (*chat*) pussy-cat; (*péj*) young trendy

mineur, e [minœʀ] *adj* minor ♦ *nm/f* (*JUR*) minor, person under age ♦ *nm* (*travailleur*) miner

miniature [minjatyʀ] *adj, nf* miniature

minibus [minibys] *nm* minibus

mini-cassette [minikasɛt] *nf* cassette (recorder)

minier, ière [minje, -jɛʀ] *adj* mining

mini-jupe [miniʒyp] *nf* mini-skirt

minime [minim] *adj* minor, minimal

minimiser [minimize] *vt* to minimize; (*fig*) to play down

minimum [minimɔm] *adj, nm* minimum; **au ~** (*au moins*) at the very least

ministère [ministɛʀ] *nm* (*aussi REL*) ministry; (*cabinet*) government; **~ public** (*JUR*) Prosecution, public prosecutor

ministre [ministʀ(ə)] *nm* (*aussi REL*) minister; **~ d'État** senior minister

Minitel [minitɛl] (®) *nm* videotext terminal and service

minorité [minɔʀite] *nf* minority; **être en ~**

to be in the *ou* a minority; **mettre en** ~ (*POL*) to defeat

minoterie [minɔtʀi] *nf* flour-mill

minuit [minɥi] *nm* midnight

minuscule [minyskyl] *adj* minute, tiny ♦ *nf*: **(lettre)** ~ small letter

minute [minyt] *nf* minute; (*JUR*: *original*) minute, draft; **à la** ~ (just) this instant; there and then; **minuter** *vt* to time; **minuterie** *nf* time switch

minutieux, euse [minysjø, -øz] *adj* meticulous; minutely detailed

mirabelle [miʀabɛl] *nf* (cherry) plum

miracle [miʀɑkl(ə)] *nm* miracle

mirage [miʀaʒ] *nm* mirage

mire [miʀ] *nf*: **point de** ~ target; (*fig*) focal point; **ligne de** ~ line of sight

miroir [miʀwaʀ] *nm* mirror

miroiter [miʀwate] *vi* to sparkle, shimmer; **faire** ~ **qch à qn** to paint sth in glowing colours for sb, dangle sth in front of sb's eyes

mis, e [mi, miz] *pp de* **mettre** ♦ *adj*: **bien** ~ well-dressed

mise [miz] *nf* (*argent: au jeu*) stake; (*tenue*) clothing; attire; **être de** ~ to be acceptable *ou* in season; ~ **à feu** blast-off; ~ **au point** (*fig*) clarification; ~ **de fonds** capital outlay; ~ **en plis** set; ~ **en scène** production

miser [mize] *vt* (*enjeu*) to stake, bet; ~ **sur** (*cheval, numéro*) to bet on; (*fig*) to bank *ou* count on

misérable [mizeʀabl(ə)] *adj* (*lamentable, malheureux*) pitiful, wretched; (*pauvre*) poverty-stricken; (*insignifiant, mesquin*) miserable ♦ *nm/f* wretch; (*miséreux*) poor wretch

misère [mizɛʀ] *nf* (*extreme*) poverty, destitution; ~**s** *nfpl* (*malheurs*) woes, miseries; (*ennuis*) little troubles; **salaire de** ~ starvation wage

miséricorde [mizeʀikɔʀd(ə)] *nf* mercy, forgiveness

missile [misil] *nm* missile

mission [misjɔ̃] *nf* mission; **partir en** ~ (*ADMIN, POL*) to go on an assignment; **missionnaire** *nm/f* missionary

mit *vb voir* **mettre**

mité, e [mite] *adj* moth-eaten

mi-temps [mitɑ̃] *nf inv* (*SPORT: période*) half; (: *pause*) half-time; **à** ~ part-time

mitigé, e [mitiʒe] *adj* lukewarm; mixed

mitonner [mitɔne] *vt* to cook with loving care; (*fig*) to cook up quietly

mitoyen, ne [mitwajɛ̃, -ɛn] *adj* common, party *cpd*

mitrailler [mitʀaje] *vt* to machine-gun; (*fig*) to pelt, bombard; (: *photographier*) to take shot after shot of; **mitraillette** *nf* submachine gun; **mitrailleuse** *nf* machine gun

mi-voix [mivwa]: **à** ~ *adv* in a low *ou* hushed voice

mixage [miksaʒ] *nm* (*CINÉMA*) (sound) mixing

mixer [miksœʀ] *nm* (food) mixer

mixte [mikst(ə)] *adj* (*gén*) mixed; (*SCOL*) mixed, coeducational; **à usage** ~ dual-purpose

mixture [mikstyʀ] *nf* mixture; (*fig*) concoction

MLF *sigle m* = Mouvement de Libération de la femme

Mlle (*pl* **Mlles**) *abr* = **Mademoiselle**

MM *abr* = **Messieurs**

Mme (*pl* **Mmes**) *abr* = **Madame**

Mo *abr* = **métro**

mobile [mɔbil] *adj* mobile; (*pièce de machine*) moving; (*élément de meuble etc*) movable ♦ *nm* (*motif*) motive; (*œuvre d'art*) mobile

mobilier, ière [mɔbilje, -jɛʀ] *adj* (*JUR*) personal ♦ *nm* furniture

mobiliser [mɔbilize] *vt* (*MIL, gén*) to mobilize

moche [mɔʃ] (*fam*) *adj* ugly; rotten

modalité [mɔdalite] *nf* form, mode; ~**s** *nfpl* (*d'un accord etc*) clauses, terms

mode [mɔd] *nf* fashion ♦ *nm* (*manière*) form, mode; **à la** ~ fashionable, in fashion; ~ **d'emploi** directions *pl* (for use)

modèle [mɔdɛl] *nm* model; (*qui pose: de peintre*) sitter; ~ **déposé** registered design; ~ **réduit** small-scale model; **modeler** [mɔdle] *vt* (*ART*) to model, mould; (*suj: vêtement, érosion*) to mould, shape

modem [mɔdɛm] *nm* modem

modéré, e [mɔdeʀe] *adj, nm/f* moderate

modérer [mɔdeʀe] *vt* to moderate; **se** ~ *vi* to restrain o.s.

moderne [mɔdɛʀn(ə)] *adj* modern ♦ *nm* modern style; modern furniture; **moderniser** *vt* to modernize

modeste [mɔdɛst(ə)] *adj* modest; **modestie** *nf* modesty

modifier [mɔdifje] *vt* to modify, alter; **se** ~ *vi* to alter

modique [mɔdik] *adj* modest

modiste [mɔdist(ə)] *nf* milliner

modulation [mɔdylɑsjɔ̃] *nf*: ~ **de fréquence** frequency modulation

module [mɔdyl] *nm* module

moelle [mwal] *nf* marrow

moelleux, euse [mwalø, -øz] *adj* soft; (*au goût, à l'ouïe*) mellow

moellon [mwalɔ̃] *nm* rubble stone

mœurs [mœʀ] *nfpl* (*conduite*) morals; (*manières*) manners; (*pratiques sociales, mode de vie*) habits

mohair [mɔɛʀ] *nm* mohair

moi [mwa] *pron* me; (*emphatique*): ~, **je** ... for my part, I ..., I myself ...

moignon [mwaɲɔ̃] *nm* stump

moi-même [mwamɛm] *pron* myself; (*emphatique*) I myself

moindre [mwɛ̃dʀ(ə)] *adj* lesser; lower; **le(la)** ~, **les** ~**s** the least, the slightest
moine [mwan] *nm* monk, friar
moineau, x [mwano] *nm* sparrow

--- MOT CLÉ ---

moins [mwɛ̃] *adv* **1** (*comparatif*): ~ **(que)** less (than); ~ **grand que** less tall·than, not as tall as; ~ **je travaille, mieux je me porte** the less I work, the better I feel
2 (*superlatif*). **le** ~ (the) least; **c'est ce que j'aime le** ~ it's what I like (the) least; **le(la)** ~ **doué(e)** the least gifted; **au** ~, **du** ~ at least; **pour le** ~ at the very least
3: ~ **de** (*quantité*) less (than); (*nombre*) fewer (than); ~ **de sable/d'eau** less sand/water; ~ **de livres/gens** fewer books/people; ~ **de 2 ans** less than 2 years; ~ **de midi** not yet midday
4: **de** ~, **en** ~: **100F/3 jours de** ~ 100F/3 days less; **3 livres en** ~ 3 books fewer; **3 books too few; **de l'argent en** ~ less money; **le soleil en** ~ but for the sun, minus the sun; **de** ~ **en** ~ less and less
5: **à** ~ **de, à** ~ **que** unless; **à** ~ **de faire** unless we do (*ou* he does *etc*); **à** ~ **que tu ne fasses** unless you do; **à** ~ **d'un accident** barring any accident
♦ *prép*: **4** ~ **2** 4 minus 2; **il est** ~ **5** it's 5 to; **il fait** ~ **5** it's 5 (degrees) below (freezing), it's minus 5

---

mois [mwa] *nm* month; ~ **double** (*COMM*) extra month's salary
moisi [mwazi] *nm* mould, mildew; **odeur de** ~ musty smell
moisir [mwaziʀ] *vi* to go mouldy; (*fig*) to rot; to hang about
moisissure [mwazisyʀ] *nf* mould *nopl*
moisson [mwasɔ̃] *nf* harvest; **moissonner** *vt* to harvest, reap; **moissonneuse** *nf* (*machine*) harvester
moite [mwat] *adj* sweaty, sticky
moitié [mwatje] *nf* half; **la** ~ half; **la** ~ **de** half (of); **la** ~ **du temps/des gens** half the time/the people; **à la** ~ **de** halfway through; **à** ~ (*avant le verbe*) half; (*avant l'adjectif*) half-; **de** ~ by half; ~ ~ half-and-half
mol [mɔl] *adj voir* **mou**
molaire [mɔlɛʀ] *nf* molar
molester [mɔlɛste] *vt* to manhandle, maul (about)
molle [mɔl] *adj voir* **mou**; **mollement** *adv* softly; (*péj*) sluggishly; (*protester*) feebly
mollet [mɔlɛ] *nm* calf ♦ *adj m*: **œuf** ~ soft-boiled egg
molletonné, e [mɔltɔne] *adj* fleece-lined
mollir [mɔliʀ] *vi* to give way; to relent; to go soft
môme [mom] (*fam*) *nm/f* (*enfant*) brat ♦ *nf* (*fille*) chick

moment [mɔmɑ̃] *nm* moment; **ce n'est pas le** ~ this is not the (right) time; **à un certain** ~ at some point; **à un** ~ **donné** at a certain point; **pour un bon** ~ for a good while; **pour le** ~ for the moment, for the time being; **au** ~ **de** at the time of; **au** ~ **où** as; at a time when; **à tout** ~ at any time *ou* moment; constantly, continually; **en ce** ~ at the moment; at present; **sur le** ~ at the time; **par** ~**s** now and then, at times; **du** ~ **où** *ou* **que** seeing that, since; **momentané, e** *adj* temporary, momentary
momie [mɔmi] *nf* mummy
mon, ma [mɔ̃, ma] (*pl* **mes**) *dét* my
Monaco [mɔnako] *nm*: **le** ~ Monaco
monarchie [mɔnaʀʃi] *nf* monarchy
monastère [mɔnastɛʀ] *nm* monastery
monceau, x [mɔ̃so] *nm* heap
mondain, e [mɔ̃dɛ̃, -ɛn] *adj* society *cpd*; social; fashionable; ~ *ou nf*: **la M**~**e, la police** ~**e** ≈ the vice squad
monde [mɔ̃d] *nm* world; (*haute société*): **le** ~ (high) society; (*milieu*): **être du même** ~ to move in the same circles; (*gens*): **il y a du** ~ (*beaucoup de gens*) there are a lot of people; (*quelques personnes*) there are some people; **beaucoup/peu de** ~ many/few people; **le meilleur** *etc* **du** ~ the best *etc* in the world *ou* on earth; **mettre au** ~ to bring into the world; **pas le moins du** ~ not in the least; **se faire un** ~ **de qch** to make a great deal of fuss about sth; **mondial, e, aux** *adj* (*population*) world *cpd*; (*influence*) world-wide; **mondialement** *adv* throughout the world
monégasque [mɔnegask(ə)] *adj* Monegasque, of *ou* from Monaco
monétaire [mɔnetɛʀ] *adj* monetary
moniteur, trice [mɔnitœʀ, -tʀis] *nm/f* (*SPORT*) instructor(tress); (*de colonie de vacances*) supervisor ♦ *nm* (*écran*) monitor
monnaie [mɔnɛ] *nf* (*pièce*) coin; (*ÉCON, gén*: *moyen d'échange*) currency; (*petites pièces*): **avoir de la** ~ to have (some) change; **faire de la** ~ to get (some) change; **avoir/faire la** ~ **de 20 F** to have change of/get change for 20 F; **rendre à qn la** ~ (**sur 20 F**) to give sb the change (out of *ou* from 20 F); **monnayer** *vt* to convert into cash; (*talent*) to capitalize on
monologue [mɔnɔlɔg] *nm* monologue, soliloquy; **monologuer** *vi* to soliloquize
monopole [mɔnɔpɔl] *nm* monopoly
monotone [mɔnɔtɔn] *adj* monotonous
monseigneur [mɔ̃sɛɲœʀ] *nm* (*archevêque, évêque*) Your (*ou* His) Grace; (*cardinal*) Your (*ou* His) Eminence
Monsieur [məsjø] (*pl* **Messieurs**) *titre* Mr ♦ *nm* (*homme quelconque*): **un/le m**~ a/the gentleman; *voir aussi* **Madame**
monstre [mɔ̃stʀ(ə)] *nm* monster ♦ *adj*: **un travail** ~ a fantastic amount of work; an

enormous job

mont [mɔ̃] *nm*: **par ~s et par vaux** up hill and down dale; **le M~ Blanc** Mont Blanc

montage [mɔ̃taʒ] *nm* putting up; mounting, setting; assembly; (*PHOTO*) photomontage; (*CINÉMA*) editing

montagnard, e [mɔ̃taɲaʀ, -aʀd(ə)] *adj* mountain *cpd* ♦ *nm/f* mountain-dweller

montagne [mɔ̃taɲ] *nf* (*cime*) mountain; (*région*): **la ~** the mountains *pl*; **~s russes** big dipper *sg*, switchback *sg*; **montagneux, euse** [mɔ̃taɲø, -øz] *adj* mountainous; hilly

montant, e [mɔ̃tɑ̃, -ɑ̃t] *adj* rising; (*robe, corsage*) high-necked ♦ *nm* (*somme, total*) (sum) total, (total) amount; (*de fenêtre*) upright; (*de lit*) post

monte-charge [mɔ̃tʃaʀʒ(ə)] *nm inv* goods lift, hoist

montée [mɔ̃te] *nf* rising, rise; ascent, climb; (*chemin*) way up; (*côte*) hill; **au milieu de la ~** halfway up

monter [mɔ̃te] *vt* (*escalier, côte*) to go (*ou* come) up; (*valise, paquet*) to take (*ou* bring) up; (*cheval*) to mount; (*étagère*) to raise; (*tente, échafaudage*) to put up; (*machine*) to assemble; (*bijou*) to mount, set; (*COUTURE*) to set in; to sew on; (*CINÉMA*) to edit; (*THÉÂTRE*) to put on, stage; (*société etc*) to set up ♦ *vi* to go (*ou* come) up; (*avion etc*) to climb, go up; (*chemin, niveau, température*) to go up, rise; (*passager*) to get on; (*à cheval*): **~ bien/mal** to ride well/badly; **se ~ à** (*frais etc*) to add up to, come to; **~ à pied** to walk up, go up on foot; **~ à bicyclette/en voiture** to cycle/drive up, go up by bicycle/by car; **~ dans le train/l'avion** to get into the train/plane, board the train/plane; **~ sur** to climb up onto; **~ à cheval** to get on *ou* mount a horse

monticule [mɔ̃tikyl] *nm* mound

montre [mɔ̃tʀ(ə)] *nf* watch; **faire ~ de** to show, display; **contre la ~** (*SPORT*) against the clock; **montre-bracelet** *nf* wristwatch

montrer [mɔ̃tʀe] *vt* to show; **~ qch à qn** to show sb sth

monture [mɔ̃tyʀ] *nf* (*bête*) mount; (*d'une bague*) setting; (*de lunettes*) frame

monument [mɔnymɑ̃] *nm* monument; **~ aux morts** war memorial

moquer [mɔke] : **se ~ de** *vt* to make fun of, laugh at; (*fam: se désintéresser de*) not to care about; (*tromper*): **se ~ de qn** to take sb for a ride

moquette [mɔkɛt] *nf* fitted carpet

moqueur, euse [mɔkœʀ, -øz] *adj* mocking

moral, e, aux [mɔʀal, -o] *adj* moral ♦ *nm* morale; **avoir le ~ à zéro** to be really down; **morale** *nf* (*conduite*) morals *pl*; (*règles*) moral code, ethic; (*valeurs*) moral standards *pl*, morality; (*science*) ethics *sg*,

moral philosophy; (*conclusion: d'une fable etc*) moral; **faire la morale à** to lecture, preach at; **moralité** *nf* morality; (*conduite*) morals *pl*; (*conclusion, enseignement*) moral

morceau, x [mɔʀso] *nm* piece, bit; (*d'une œuvre*) passage, extract; (*MUS*) piece; (*CULIN: de viande*) cut; **mettre en ~x** to pull to pieces *ou* bits

morceler [mɔʀsəle] *vt* to break up, divide up

mordant, e [mɔʀdɑ̃, -ɑ̃t] *adj* scathing, cutting; biting

mordiller [mɔʀdije] *vt* to nibble at, chew at

mordre [mɔʀdʀ(ə)] *vt* to bite; (*suj: lime, vis*) to bite into ♦ *vi* (*poisson*) to bite; **~ sur** (*fig*) to go over into, overlap into; **~ à l'hameçon** to bite, rise to the bait

mordu, e [mɔʀdy] *nm/f*: **un ~ du jazz** a jazz fanatic

morfondre [mɔʀfɔ̃dʀ(ə)] : **se ~** *vi* to mope

morgue [mɔʀg(ə)] *nf* (*arrogance*) haughtiness; (*lieu: de la police*) morgue; (: *à l'hôpital*) mortuary

morne [mɔʀn(ə)] *adj* dismal, dreary

mors [mɔʀ] *nm* bit

morse [mɔʀs(ə)] *nm* (*ZOOL*) walrus; (*TÉL*) Morse (code)

morsure [mɔʀsyʀ] *nf* bite

mort¹ [mɔʀ] *nf* death

mort², e [mɔʀ, mɔʀt(ə)] *pp de* **mourir** ♦ *adj* dead ♦ *nm/f* (*défunt*) dead man(woman); (*victime*): **il y a eu plusieurs ~s** several people were killed, there were several killed ♦ *nm* (*CARTES*) dummy; **~ ou vif** dead or alive; **~ de peur/fatigue** frightened to death/dead tired

mortalité [mɔʀtalite] *nf* mortality, death rate

mortel, le [mɔʀtɛl] *adj* (*poison etc*) deadly, lethal; (*accident, blessure*) fatal; (*REL*) mortal; (*fig*) deathly; deadly boring

mortier [mɔʀtje] *nm* (*gén*) mortar

mort-né, e [mɔʀne] *adj* (*enfant*) stillborn

mortuaire [mɔʀtɥɛʀ] *adj* funeral *cpd*

morue [mɔʀy] *nf* (*ZOOL*) cod *inv*

mosaïque [mɔzaik] *nf* (*ART*) mosaic; (*fig*) patchwork

Moscou [mɔsku] *n* Moscow

mosquée [mɔske] *nf* mosque

mot [mo] *nm* word; (*message*) line, note; (*bon mot etc*) saying; sally; **~ à ~** word for word; **~ d'ordre** watchword; **~ de passe** password; **~s croisés** crossword (puzzle) *sg*

motard [mɔtaʀ] *nm* biker; (*policier*) motorcycle cop

motel [mɔtɛl] *nm* motel

moteur, trice [mɔtœʀ, -tʀis] *adj* (*ANAT, PHYSIOL*) motor; (*TECH*) driving; (*AUTO*): **à 4 roues motrices** 4-wheel drive ♦ *nm* engine, motor; **à ~** power-driven, motor *cpd*

motif [mɔtif] *nm* (*cause*) motive; (*décoratif*)

design, pattern, motif; (*d'un tableau*) subject, motif; ~s nmpl (*JUR*) grounds pl; **sans ~** groundless

motiver [mɔtive] vt (*justifier*) to justify, account for; (*ADMIN, JUR, PSYCH*) to motivate

moto [mɔto] nf (motor)bike; **motocycliste** nm/f motorcyclist

motorisé, e [mɔtɔrize] adj (*troupe*) motorized; (*personne*) having transport *ou* a car

motrice [mɔtris] adj voir **moteur**

motte [mɔt] nf: ~ **de terre** lump of earth, clod (of earth); ~ **de beurre** lump of butter; ~ **de gazon** turf, sod

mou(mol), molle [mu, mɔl] adj soft; (*péj*) flabby; sluggish ♦ nm (*abats*) lights pl, lungs pl; (*de la corde*): **avoir du ~** to be slack

mouche [muʃ] nf fly

moucher [muʃe] vt (*enfant*) to blow the nose of; (*chandelle*) to snuff (out); **se ~** vi to blow one's nose

moucheron [muʃRɔ̃] nm midge

moucheté, e [muʃte] adj dappled; flecked

mouchoir [muʃwaR] nm handkerchief, hanky; ~ **en papier** tissue, paper hanky

moudre [mudʀ(ə)] vt to grind

moue [mu] nf pout; **faire la ~** to pout; (*fig*) to pull a face

mouette [mwɛt] nf (sea)gull

moufle [mufl(ə)] nf (*gant*) mitt(en)

mouillé, e [muje] adj wet

mouiller [muje] vt (*humecter*) to wet, moisten; (*tremper*): ~ **qn/qch** to make sb/ sth wet; (*couper, diluer*) to water down; (*mine etc*) to lay (*NAVIG*) to lie *ou* be at anchor; **se ~** to get wet; (*fam*) to commit o.s.; to get o.s. involved

moule [mul] nf mussel ♦ nm (*creux, CULIN*) mould; (*modèle plein*) cast; ~ **à gâteaux** nm cake tin (*BRIT*) ou pan (*US*)

moulent vb voir **moudre; mouler**

mouler [mule] vt (*suj: vêtement*) to hug, fit closely round; ~ **qch sur** (*fig*) to model sth on

moulin [mulɛ̃] nm mill; ~ **à café/à poivre** coffee/pepper mill; ~ **à légumes** (vegetable) shredder; ~ **à paroles** (*fig*) chatterbox; ~ **à vent** windmill

moulinet [mulinɛ] nm (*de treuil*) winch; (*de canne à pêche*) reel; (*mouvement*): **faire des ~s avec qch** to whirl sth around

moulinette [mulinɛt] nf (vegetable) shredder

moulu, e [muly] pp de **moudre**

moulure [mulyR] nf (*ornement*) moulding

mourant, e [muRɑ̃, -ɑ̃t] adj dying

mourir [muRiR] vi to die; (*civilisation*) to die out; ~ **de froid/faim** to die of exposure/ hunger; ~ **de faim/d'ennui** (*fig*) to be starving/be bored to death; ~ **d'envie de faire** to be dying to do

mousse [mus] nf (*BOT*) moss; (*écume: sur eau, bière*) froth, foam; (: *shampooing*) lather; (*CULIN*) mousse ♦ nm (*NAVIG*) ship's boy; **bas ~** stretch stockings; ~ **à raser** shaving foam; ~ **carbonique** (firefighting) foam

mousseline [muslin] nf muslin; chiffon

mousser [muse] vi to foam; to lather

mousseux, euse [musø, -øz] adj frothy ♦ nm: (**vin**) ~ sparkling wine

mousson [musɔ̃] nf monsoon

moustache [mustaʃ] nf moustache; ~s nfpl (*du chat*) whiskers pl

moustiquaire [mustikɛR] nf mosquito net (ou screen)

moustique [mustik] nm mosquito

moutarde [mutard(ə)] nf mustard

mouton [mutɔ̃] nm (*ZOOL, péj*) sheep inv; (*peau*) sheepskin; (*CULIN*) mutton

mouvant, e [muvɑ̃, -ɑ̃t] adj unsettled; changing; shifting

mouvement [muvmɑ̃] nm (*gén, aussi: mécanisme*) movement; (*fig*) activity; impulse; gesture; (*MUS: rythme*) tempo; **en ~** in motion; on the move; **mouvementé, e** adj (*vie, poursuite*) eventful; (*réunion*) turbulent

mouvoir [muvwaR] vt (*levier, membre*) to move; **se ~** vi to move

moyen, ne [mwajɛ̃, -ɛn] adj average; (*tailles, prix*) medium; (*de grandeur moyenne*) medium-sized ♦ nm (*façon*) means sg, way; ~s nmpl (*capacités*) means; **au ~ de** by means of; **par tous les ~s** by every possible means, every possible way; **par ses propres ~s** all by oneself; ~ **âge** Middle Ages; ~ **de transport** means of transport

moyennant [mwajɛnɑ̃] prép (*somme*) for; (*service, conditions*) in return for; (*travail, effort*) with

moyenne [mwajɛn] nf average; (*MATH*) mean; (*SCOL: à l'examen*) pass mark; (*AUTO*) average speed; **en ~** on (an) average; ~ **d'âge** average age

Moyen-Orient [mwajɛnɔRjɑ̃] nm: **le ~** the Middle East

moyeu, x [mwajø] nm hub

MST sigle f (= *maladie sexuellement transmissible*) STD

mû, mue [my] pp de **mouvoir**

muer [mɥe] vi (*oiseau, mammifère*) to moult; (*serpent*) to slough; (*jeune garçon*): **il mue** his voice is breaking; **se ~ en** to transform into

muet, te [mɥɛ, -ɛt] adj dumb; (*fig*): ~ **d'admiration** etc speechless with admiration etc; (*joie, douleur, CINÉMA*) silent; (*carte*) blank mute

mufle [myfl(ə)] nm muzzle; (*goujat*) boor

mugir [myʒiR] vi (*taureau*) to bellow; (*vache*) to low; (*fig*) to howl

muguet [mygɛ] nm lily of the valley

mule [myl] nf (*ZOOL*) (she-)mule

mulet [mylɛ] nm (ZOOL) (he-)mule
multiple [myltipl(ə)] adj multiple, numerous; (varié) many, manifold ♦ nm (MATH) multiple
multiplication [myltiplikɑsjɔ̃] nf multiplication
multiplier [myltiplije] vt to multiply; **se ~** vi to multiply; to increase in number
municipal, e, aux [mynisipal, -o] adj municipal; town cpd, ≈ borough cpd
municipalité [mynisipalite] nf (corps municipal) town council, corporation
munir [mynlʀ] vt: **~ qn/qch de** to equip sb/sth with
munitions [mynisjɔ̃] nfpl ammunition sg
mur [myʀ] nm wall; **~ du son** sound barrier
mûr, e [myʀ] adj ripe; (personne) mature
muraille [myʀɑj] nf (high) wall
mural, e, aux [myʀal, -o] adj wall cpd; mural
mûre [myʀ] nf blackberry; mulberry
murer [myʀe] vt (enclos) to wall (in); (porte, issue) to wall up; (personne) to wall up ou in
muret [myʀɛ] nm low wall
mûrir [myʀiʀ] vi (fruit, blé) to ripen; (abcès, furoncle) to come to a head; (fig: idée, personne) to mature ♦ vt to ripen; to (make) mature
murmure [myʀmyʀ] nm murmur; **~s** nmpl (plaintes) murmurings, mutterings; **murmurer** vi to murmur; (se plaindre) to mutter, grumble
muscade [myskad] nf (aussi: noix ~) nutmeg
muscat [myska] nm muscat grape; muscatel (wine)
muscle [myskl(ə)] nm muscle; **musclé, e** adj muscular, (fig) strong-arm
museau, x [myzo] nm muzzle
musée [myze] nm museum; art gallery
museler [myzle] vt to muzzle; **muselière** nf muzzle
musette [myzɛt] nf (sac) lunchbag ♦ adj inv (orchestre etc) accordion cpd
musical, e, aux [myzikal, -o] adj musical
music-hall [myzikol] nm variety theatre; (genre) variety
musicien, ne [myzisjɛ̃, -jɛn] adj musical ♦ nm/f musician
musique [myzik] nf music; (fanfare) band; **~ de chambre** chamber music
musulman, e [myzylmɑ̃, -an] adj, nm/f Moslem, Muslim
mutation [mytɑsjɔ̃] nf (ADMIN) transfer
mutilé, e [mytile] nm/f disabled person (through loss of limbs)
mutiler [mytile] vt to mutilate, maim
mutin, e [mytɛ̃, -in] adj (air, ton) mischievous, impish ♦ nm/f (MIL, NAVIG) mutineer
mutinerie [mytinʀi] nf mutiny

mutisme [mytism(ə)] nm silence
mutuel, le [mytɥɛl] adj mutual; **mutuelle** nf mutual benefit society
myope [mjɔp] adj short-sighted
myosotis [mjozɔtis] nm forget-me-not
myrtille [miʀtij] nf bilberry
mystère [mistɛʀ] nm mystery; **mystérieux, euse** adj mysterious
mystifier [mistifje] vt to fool; to mystify
mythe [mit] nm myth
mythologie [mitɔlɔʒi] nf mythology

N n

n' [n] adv voir **ne**
nacre [nakʀ(ə)] nf mother-of-pearl
nage [naʒ] nf swimming; style of swimming, stroke; **traverser/s'éloigner à la ~** to swim across/away; **en ~** bathed in perspiration
nageoire [naʒwaʀ] nf fin
nager [naʒe] vi to swim; **nageur, euse** nm/f swimmer
naguère [nagɛʀ] adv formerly
naïf, ïve [naif, naiv] adj naïve
nain, e [nɛ̃, nɛn] nm/f dwarf
naissance [nɛsɑ̃s] nf birth; **donner ~ à** to give birth to; (fig) to give rise to
naître [nɛtʀ(ə)] vi to be born; (fig): **~ de** to arise from, be born out of; **il est né en 1960** he was born in 1960; **faire ~** (fig) to give rise to, arouse
naïve [naiv] adj voir **naïf**
nana [nana] (fam) nf (fille) chick, bird (BRIT)
nantir [nɑ̃tiʀ] vt: **~ qn de** to provide sb with; **les nantis** (péj) the well-to-do
nappe [nap] nf tablecloth; (fig) sheet; layer; **napperon** nm table-mat
naquit etc vb voir **naître**
narguer [naʀge] vt to taunt
narine [naʀin] nf nostril
narquois, e [naʀkwa, -waz] adj derisive, mocking
naseau, x [nazo] nm nostril
natal, e [natal] adj native
natalité [natalite] nf birth rate
natation [natɑsjɔ̃] nf swimming
natif, ive [natif, -iv] adj native
nation [nɑsjɔ̃] nf nation
national, e, aux [nasjɔnal, -o] adj national; **nationale** nf: **(route) nationale** ≈ A road (BRIT), ≈ state highway (US); **nationaliser** vt to nationalize; **nationalité** nf

nationality

natte [nat] *nf (tapis)* mat; *(cheveux)* plait

naturaliser [natyʀalize] *vt* to naturalize

nature [natyʀ] *nf* nature ♦ *adj, adv (CULIN)* plain, without seasoning or sweetening; *(café, thé)* black, without sugar; **payer en ~** to pay in kind; **~ morte** still-life; **naturel, le** *adj (gén, aussi: enfant)* natural ♦ *nm* naturalness; disposition; nature; *(autochtone)* native; **naturellement** *adv* naturally; *(bien sûr)* of course

naufrage [nofʀaʒ] *nm* (ship)wreck; *(fig)* wreck; **faire ~** to be shipwrecked

nauséabond, e [nozeabɔ̃, -ɔ̃d] *adj* foul, nauseous

nausée [noze] *nf* nausea

nautique [notik] *adj* nautical, water *cpd*

nautisme [notism(ə)] *nm* water sports

navet [navɛ] *nm* turnip

navette [navɛt] *nf* shuttle; **faire la ~ (entre)** to go to and fro *ou* shuttle (between)

navigateur [navigatœʀ] *nm (NAVIG)* seafarer, sailor; *(AVIAT)* navigator

navigation [navigasjɔ̃] *nf* navigation, sailing; shipping

naviguer [navige] *vi* to navigate, sail

navire [naviʀ] *nm* ship

navrer [navʀe] *vt* to upset, distress; **je suis navré** I'm so sorry

ne(n') [n(ə)] *adv voir* **pas; plus; jamais** *etc;* *(explétif) non traduit*

né, e [ne] *pp (voir naître):* **~ en 1960** born in 1960; **~e Scott** née Scott

néanmoins [neɑ̃mwɛ̃] *adv* nevertheless

néant [neɑ̃] *nm* nothingness; **réduire à ~** to bring to nought; *(espoir)* to dash

nécessaire [nesesɛʀ] *adj* necessary ♦ *nm* necessary; *(sac)* kit; **~ de couture** sewing kit; **~ de toilette** toilet bag; **nécessité** *nf* necessity; **nécessiter** *vt* to require; **nécessiteux, euse** *adj* needy

nécrologique [nekʀɔlɔʒik] *adj:* **article ~** obituary; **rubrique ~** obituary column

nectar [nɛktaʀ] *nm (sucré)* nectar; *(boisson) sweetened, diluted fruit juice*

néerlandais, e [neɛʀlɑ̃dɛ, -ɛz] *adj* Dutch

nef [nɛf] *nf (d'église)* nave

néfaste [nefast(ə)] *adj* baneful; ill-fated

négatif, ive [negatif, -iv] *adj* negative ♦ *nm (PHOTO)* negative

négligé, e [negliʒe] *adj (en désordre)* slovenly ♦ *nm (tenue)* negligee

négligent, e [negliʒɑ̃, -ɑ̃t] *adj* careless; negligent

négliger [negliʒe] *vt (épouse, jardin)* to neglect; *(tenue)* to be careless about; *(avis, précautions)* to disregard; **~ de faire** to fail to do, not bother to do

négoce [negɔs] *nm* trade

négociant [negɔsjɑ̃] *nm* merchant

négociation [negɔsjasjɔ̃] *nf* negotiation

négocier [negɔsje] *vi, vt* to negotiate

nègre [nɛgʀ(ə)] *nm* Negro; ghost (writer)

négresse [negʀɛs] *nf* Negro woman

neige [nɛʒ] *nf* snow; **neiger** *vi* to snow

nénuphar [nenyfaʀ] *nm* water-lily

néon [neɔ̃] *nm* neon

néophyte [neɔfit] *nm/f* novice

néo-zélandais, e [neɔzelɑ̃dɛ, -ɛz] *adj* New Zealand *cpd* ♦ *nm/f:* **N~, e** New Zealander

nerf [nɛʀ] *nm* nerve; *(fig)* spirit; stamina; **nerveux, euse** *adj* nervous; *(voiture)* nippy, responsive; *(tendineux)* sinewy; **nervosité** *nf* excitability; state of agitation; nervousness

nervure [nɛʀvyʀ] *nf* vein

n'est-ce pas [nɛspa] *adv* isn't it?, won't you? *etc, selon le verbe qui précède*

net, nette [nɛt] *adj (sans équivoque, distinct)* clear; *(évident)* definite; *(propre)* neat, clean; *(COMM: prix, salaire)* net ♦ *adv (refuser)* flatly ♦ *nm:* **mettre au ~** to copy out; **s'arrêter ~** to stop dead; **nettement** *adv* clearly, distinctly; **netteté** *nf* clearness

nettoyage [nɛtwajaʒ] *nm* cleaning; **~ à sec** dry cleaning

nettoyer [nɛtwaje] *vt* to clean; *(fig)* to clean out

neuf[1] [nœf] *num* nine

neuf[2]**, neuve** [nœf, nœv] *adj* new ♦ *nm:* **repeindre à ~** to redecorate; **remettre à ~** to do up (as good as new), refurbish

neutre [nøtʀ(ə)] *adj* neutral; *(LING)* neuter ♦ *nm* neuter

neuve [nœv] *adj voir* **neuf**[2]

neuvième [nœvjɛm] *num* ninth

neveu, x [nəvø] *nm* nephew

névrosé, e [nevʀoze] *adj, nm/f* neurotic

nez [ne] *nm* nose; **~ à ~ avec** face to face with; **avoir du ~** to have flair

ni [ni] *conj:* **~ l'un ~ l'autre ne sont** neither one nor the other are; **il n'a rien dit ~ fait** he hasn't said or done anything

niais, e [njɛ, -ɛz] *adj* silly, thick

niche [niʃ] *nf (du chien)* kennel; *(de mur)* recess, niche

nicher [niʃe] *vi* to nest

nid [ni] *nm* nest; **~ de poule** pothole

nièce [njɛs] *nf* niece

nier [nje] *vt* to deny

nigaud, e [nigo, -od] *nm/f* booby, fool

Nil [nil] *nm:* **le ~** the Nile

n'importe [nɛ̃pɔʀt(ə)] *adv:* **~ qui/quoi/où** anybody/anything/anywhere; **~ quand** any time; **~ quel/quelle** any; **~ lequel/laquelle** any (one); **~ comment** *(sans soin)* carelessly

niveau, x [nivo] *nm* level; *(des élèves, études)* standard; **de ~ (avec)** level (with); **le ~ de la mer** sea level; **~ de vie** standard of living

niveler [nivle] *vt* to level

NN *abr (= nouvelle norme) revised standard of hotel classification*

noble [nɔbl(ə)] *adj* noble; **noblesse** *nf* nobility; (*d'une action etc*) nobleness

noce [nɔs] *nf* wedding; (*gens*) wedding party (*ou* guests *pl*); **faire la ~** (*fam*) to go on a binge; **~s d'or/d'argent** golden/silver wedding

nocif, ive [nɔsif, -iv] *adj* harmful, noxious

noctambule [nɔktɑ̃byl] *nm* night-bird

nocturne [nɔktyʀn(ə)] *adj* nocturnal ♦ *nf* late-night opening

Noël [nɔel] *nm* Christmas

nœud [nø] *nm* (*de corde, du bois, NAVIG*) knot; (*ruban*) bow; (*fig: liens*) bond, tie; **~ papillon** bow tie

noir, e [nwaʀ] *adj* black; (*obscur, sombre*) dark ♦ *nm/f* black man(woman), Negro ♦ *nm*: **dans le ~** in the dark; **travail au ~** moonlighting; **noirceur** *nf* blackness; darkness; **noircir** *vt, vi* to blacken; **noire** *nf* (*MUS*) crotchet (*BRIT*), quarter note (*US*)

noisette [nwazɛt] *nf* hazelnut

noix [nwa] *nf* walnut; (*CULIN*): **une ~ de beurre** a knob of butter; **~ de cajou** cashew nut; **~ de coco** coconut

nom [nɔ̃] *nm* name; (*LING*) noun; **~ d'emprunt** assumed name; **~ de famille** surname; **~ de jeune fille** maiden name; **~ déposé** *nm* trade name; **~ propre** *nm* proper noun

nombre [nɔ̃bʀ(ə)] *nm* number; **venir en ~** to come in large numbers; **depuis ~ d'années** for many years; **ils sont au ~ de 3** there are 3 of them; **au ~ de mes amis** among my friends

nombreux, euse [nɔ̃bʀø, -øz] *adj* many, numerous; (*avec nom sg: foule etc*) large; **peu ~** few; small

nombril [nɔ̃bʀi] *nm* navel

nommer [nɔme] *vt* (*baptiser, mentionner*) to name; (*qualifier*) to call; (*élire*) to appoint, nominate; **se ~: il se nomme Pascal** his name's Pascal, he's called Pascal

non [nɔ̃] *adv* (*réponse*) no; (*avec loin, sans, seulement*) not; **~ pas que = non que; ~ que** not that; **moi ~ plus** neither do I, I don't either

non: ~-alcoolisé, e *adj* non-alcoholic; **~-fumeur** *nm* non-smoker; **~-lieu** *nm*: **il y a eu ~-lieu** the case was dismissed; **~-sens** *nm* absurdity

nord [nɔʀ] *nm* North ♦ *adj* northern; north; **au ~** (*situation*) in the north; (*direction*) to the north; **au ~ de** (to the) north of; **nord-est** *nm* North-East; **nord-ouest** *nm* North-West

normal, e, aux [nɔʀmal, -o] *adj* normal; **normale** *nf*: **la normale** the norm, the average; **normalement** *adv* (*en général*) normally; **normaliser** *vt* (*COMM, TECH*) to standardize

normand, e [nɔʀmɑ̃, -ɑ̃d] *adj* of Normandy

Normandie [nɔʀmɑ̃di] *nf* Normandy

norme [nɔʀm(ə)] *nf* norm; (*TECH*) standard

Norvège [nɔʀvɛʒ] *nf* Norway; **norvégien, ne** *adj, nm/f* Norwegian ♦ *nm* (*LING*) Norwegian

nos [no] *dét voir* **notre**

nostalgie [nɔstalʒi] *nf* nostalgia

notable [nɔtabl(ə)] *adj* notable, noteworthy; (*marqué*) noticeable, marked ♦ *nm* prominent citizen

notaire [nɔtɛʀ] *nm* notary; solicitor

notamment [nɔtamɑ̃] *adv* in particular, among others

note [nɔt] *nf* (*écrite, MUS*) note; (*SCOL*) mark (*BRIT*), grade; (*facture*) bill; **~ de service** memorandum

noté, e [nɔte] *adj*: **être bien/mal ~** (*employé etc*) to have a good/bad record

noter [nɔte] *vt* (*écrire*) to write down; (*remarquer*) to note, notice

notice [nɔtis] *nf* summary, short article; (*brochure*) leaflet, instruction book

notifier [nɔtifje] *vt*: **~ qch à qn** to notify sb of sth, notify sth to sb

notion [nɔsjɔ̃] *nf* notion, idea

notoire [nɔtwaʀ] *adj* widely known; (*en mal*) notorious

notre [nɔtʀ(ə), no] (*pl* **nos**) *dét* our

nôtre [notʀ(ə)] *pron*: **le ~, la ~, les ~s** ours ♦ *adj* ours; **les ~s** ours; (*alliés etc*) our own people; **soyez des ~s** join us

nouer [nwe] *vt* to tie, knot; (*fig: alliance etc*) to strike up

noueux, euse [nwø, -øz] *adj* gnarled

nouilles [nuj] *nfpl* noodles; pasta *sg*

nourrice [nuʀis] *nf* wet-nurse

nourrir [nuʀiʀ] *vt* to feed; (*fig: espoir*) to harbour, nurse; **logé nourri** with board and lodging; **nourrissant, e** *adj* nourishing, nutritious

nourrisson [nuʀisɔ̃] *nm* (unweaned) infant

nourriture [nuʀityʀ] *nf* food

nous [nu] *pron* (*sujet*) we; (*objet*) us; **nous-mêmes** *pron* ourselves

nouveau(nouvel), elle, x [nuvo, -ɛl] *adj* new ♦ *nm/f* new pupil (*ou* employee); **de ~, à ~** again; **~ venu, nouvelle venue** newcomer; **~-né, e** *nm/f* newborn baby; **~té** *nf* novelty; (*COMM*) new film (*ou* book *ou* creation etc)

nouvel [nuvɛl] *adj voir* **nouveau; N~ An** New Year

nouvelle [nuvɛl] *adj voir* **nouveau** ♦ *nf* (piece of) news *sg*; (*LITTÉRATURE*) short story; **je suis sans ~s de lui** I haven't heard from him; **N~-Calédonie** *nf* New Caledonia; **N~-Zélande** *nf* New Zealand

novembre [nɔvɑ̃bʀ(ə)] *nm* November

novice [nɔvis] *adj* inexperienced

noyade [nwajad] *nf* drowning *no pl*

noyau, x [nwajo] *nm* (*de fruit*) stone; (*BIO, PHYSIQUE*) nucleus; (*ÉLEC, GÉO, fig: centre*) core; **noyauter** *vt* (*POL*) to infiltrate

noyer [nwaje] *nm* walnut (tree); (*bois*) walnut ♦ *vt* to drown; (*fig*) to flood; to submerge; **se ~** *vi* to be drowned, drown; (*suicide*) to drown o.s.

nu, e [ny] *adj* naked; (*membres*) naked, bare; (*chambre, fil, plaine*) bare ♦ *nm* (*ART*) nude; **se mettre ~** to strip; **mettre à ~** to bare

nuage [nɥaʒ] *nm* cloud; **nuageux, euse** *adj* cloudy

nuance [nɥɑ̃s] *nf* (*de couleur, sens*) shade; **il y a une ~ (entre)** there's a slight difference (between); **nuancer** *vt* (*opinion*) to bring some reservations *ou* qualifications to

nucléaire [nyklɛɛʀ] *adj* nuclear

nudiste [nydist(ə)] *nm/f* nudist

nuée [nɥe] *nf*: **une ~ de** a cloud *ou* host *ou* swarm of

nues [ny] *nfpl*: **tomber des ~** to be taken aback; **porter qn aux ~** to praise sb to the skies

nuire [nɥiʀ] *vi* to be harmful; **~ à** to harm, do damage to; **nuisible** *adj* harmful; **animal nuisible** pest

nuit [nɥi] *nf* night; **il fait ~** it's dark; **cette ~** last night; tonight; **~ blanche** sleepless night; **~ de noces** wedding night

nul, nulle [nyl] *adj* (*aucun*) no; (*minime*) nil, non-existent; (*non valable*) null; (*péj*) useless, hopeless ♦ *pron* none, no one; **match ~** draw; **résultat ~ =** match nul; **~le part** nowhere; **nullement** *adv* by no means

numérique [nymeʀik] *adj* numerical

numéro [nymeʀo] *nm* number; (*spectacle*) act, turn; **~ de téléphone** (tele)phone number; **~ vert** *nm* ≈ freefone (®) number (*BRIT*), ≈ toll-free number (*US*); **numéroter** *vt* to number

nu-pieds [nypje] *adj inv* barefoot

nuque [nyk] *nf* nape of the neck

nu-tête [nytɛt] *adj inv* bareheaded

nutritif, ive [nytʀitif, -iv] *adj* nutritional; (*aliment*) nutritious

nylon [nilɔ̃] *nm* nylon

--- ***O o*** ---

oasis [ɔazis] *nf* oasis

obéir [ɔbeiʀ] *vi* to obey; **~ à** to obey; (*suj: moteur, véhicule*) to respond to; **obéissant, e** *adj* obedient

objecter [ɔbʒɛkte] *vt* (*prétexter*) to plead,

put forward as an excuse; **~ (à qn) que** to object (to sb) that

objecteur [ɔbʒɛktœʀ] *nm*: **~ de conscience** conscientious objector

objectif, ive [ɔbʒɛktif, -iv] *adj* objective ♦ *nm* (*OPTIQUE, PHOTO*) lens *sg*, objective; (*MIL, fig*) objective; **~ à focale variable** zoom lens

objection [ɔbʒɛksjɔ̃] *nf* objection

objet [ɔbʒɛ] *nm* object; (*d'une discussion, recherche*) subject; **être *ou* faire l'~ de** (*discussion*) to be the subject of; (*soins*) to be given *ou* shown; **sans ~** purposeless; groundless; **~ d'art** objet d'art; **~s personnels** personal items; **~s trouvés** lost property *sg* (*BRIT*), lost-and-found *sg* (*US*)

obligation [ɔbligɑsjɔ̃] *nf* obligation; (*COMM*) bond, debenture; **obligatoire** *adj* compulsory, obligatory

obligé, e [ɔbliʒe] *adj* (*redevable*): **être très ~ à qn** to be most obliged to sb

obligeance [ɔbliʒɑ̃s] *nf*: **avoir l'~ de ...** to be kind *ou* good enough to ...; **obligeant, e** *adj* obliging; kind

obliger [ɔbliʒe] *vt* (*contraindre*): **~ qn à faire** to force *ou* oblige sb to do; (*JUR: engager*) to bind; (*rendre service à*) to oblige; **je suis bien obligé** I have to

oblique [ɔblik] *adj* oblique; **regard ~** sidelong glance; **en ~** diagonally; **obliquer** *vi*: **obliquer vers** to turn off towards

oblitérer [ɔblitere] *vt* (*timbre-poste*) to cancel

obscène [ɔpsɛn] *adj* obscene

obscur, e [ɔpskyʀ] *adj* dark; (*fig*) obscure; lowly; **~cir** *vt* to darken; (*fig*) to obscure; **s'~cir** *vi* to grow dark; **~ité** *nf* darkness; **dans l'~ité** in the dark, in darkness

obséder [ɔpsede] *vt* to obsess, haunt

obsèques [ɔpsɛk] *nfpl* funeral *sg*

observateur, trice [ɔpsɛʀvatœʀ, -tʀis] *adj* observant, perceptive ♦ *nm/f* observer

observation [ɔpsɛʀvɑsjɔ̃] *nf* observation; (*d'un règlement etc*) observance; (*reproche*) reproof

observatoire [ɔpsɛʀvatwaʀ] *nm* observatory; (*lieu élevé*) observation post, vantage point

observer [ɔpsɛʀve] *vt* (*regarder*) to observe, watch; (*examiner*) to examine; (*scientifiquement, aussi: règlement, jeûne etc*) to observe; (*surveiller*) to watch; (*remarquer*) to observe, notice; **faire ~ qch à qn** (*dire*) to point out sth to sb

obstacle [ɔpstakl(ə)] *nm* obstacle; (*ÉQUITATION*) jump, hurdle; **faire ~ à** (*lumière*) to block out; (*projet*) to hinder, put obstacles in the path of

obstiné, e [ɔpstine] *adj* obstinate

obstiner [ɔpstine]: **s'~** *vi* to insist, dig one's heels in; **s'~ à faire** to persist (obstinately) in doing; **s'~ sur qch** to keep working at sth, labour away at sth

obstruer [ɔpstʀye] *vt* to block, obstruct

obtempérer [ɔptɑ̃peʀe] *vi* to obey

obtenir [ɔptəniʀ] *vt* to obtain, get; *(total, résultat)* to arrive at, reach; to achieve, obtain; ~ **de pouvoir faire** to obtain permission to do; ~ **de qn qu'il fasse** to get sb to agree to do; **obtention** *nf* obtaining

obturateur [ɔptyʀatœʀ] *nm* (PHOTO) shutter

obturer [ɔptyʀe] *vt* to close (up); *(dent)* to fill

obus [ɔby] *nm* shell

occasion [ɔkazjɔ̃] *nf* *(aubaine, possibilité)* opportunity; *(circonstance)* occasion; *(COMM: article non neuf)* secondhand buy; *(: acquisition avantageuse)* bargain; **à plusieurs ~s** on several occasions; **être l'~ de** to occasion, give rise to; **à l'~** sometimes, on occasions; some time; **d'~** secondhand; **occasionnel, le** *adj* *(fortuit)* chance *cpd*; *(non régulier)* occasional; casual

occasionner [ɔkazjɔne] *vt* to cause, bring about; ~ **qch à qn** to cause sb sth

occident [ɔksidɑ̃] *nm:* **l'O~** the West; **occidental, e, aux** *adj* western; *(POL)* Western

occupation [ɔkypasjɔ̃] *nf* occupation

occupé, e [ɔkype] *adj* (MIL, POL) occupied; *(personne: affairé, pris)* busy; *(place, sièges)* taken; *(toilettes)* engaged; *(ligne)* engaged *(BRIT)*, busy *(US)*

occuper [ɔkype] *vt* to occupy; *(main-d'œuvre)* to employ; **s'~ de** *(être responsable de)* to be in charge of; *(se charger de: affaire)* to take charge of, deal with; *(: clients etc)* to attend to; *(s'intéresser à, pratiquer)* to be involved in; **s'~ (à qch)** to occupy o.s. *ou* keep o.s. busy (with sth); **ça occupe trop de place** it takes up too much room

occurrence [ɔkyʀɑ̃s] *nf:* **en l'~** in this case

océan [ɔseɑ̃] *nm* ocean; **l'~ Indien** the Indian Ocean

octet [ɔktɛt] *nm* byte

octobre [ɔktɔbʀ(ə)] *nm* October

octroyer [ɔktʀwaje] *vt:* ~ **qch à qn** to grant sth to sb, grant sb sth

oculiste [ɔkylist(ə)] *nm/f* eye specialist

odeur [ɔdœʀ] *nf* smell

odieux, euse [ɔdjø, -øz] *adj* hateful

odorant, e [ɔdɔʀɑ̃, -ɑ̃t] *adj* sweet-smelling, fragrant

odorat [ɔdɔʀa] *nm* (sense of) smell

œil [œj] *(pl* **yeux)** *nm* eye; **à l'~** *(fam)* for free; **à l'~ nu** with the naked eye; **tenir qn à l'~** to keep an eye *ou* a watch on sb; **avoir l'~ à** to keep an eye on; **fermer les yeux (sur)** *(fig)* to turn a blind eye (to)

œillade [œjad] *nf:* **lancer une ~ à qn** to wink at sb, give sb a wink; **faire des ~s à** to make eyes at

œillères [œjɛʀ] *nfpl* blinkers *(BRIT)*, blinders *(US)*

œillet [œjɛ] *nm* (BOT) carnation

œuf [œf, *pl* ø] *nm* egg; ~ **à la coque** *nm* boiled egg; ~ **au plat** fried egg; ~ **de Pâques** Easter egg; ~ **dur** hard-boiled egg; **~s brouillés** scrambled eggs

œuvre [œvʀ(ə)] *nf* *(tâche)* task, undertaking; *(ouvrage achevé, livre, tableau etc)* work; *(ensemble de la production artistique)* works *pl*; *(organisation charitable)* charity ♦ *nm* *(d'un artiste)* works *pl*; (CONSTR): **le gros** ~ the shell; **être à l'~** to be at work; **mettre en** ~ *(moyens)* to make use of; ~ **d'art** work of art

offense [ɔfɑ̃s] *nf* insult

offenser [ɔfɑ̃se] *vt* to offend, hurt; *(principes, Dieu)* to offend against; **s'~ de** to take offence at

offert, e [ɔfɛʀ, -ɛʀt(ə)] *pp de* **offrir**

office [ɔfis] *nm* *(charge)* office; *(agence)* bureau, agency; *(REL)* service ♦ *nm ou nf* *(pièce)* pantry; **faire** ~ **de** to act as; to do duty as; **d'~** automatically; ~ **du tourisme** tourist bureau

officiel, le [ɔfisjɛl] *adj, nm/f* official

officier [ɔfisje] *nm* officer ♦ *vi* to officiate; ~ **de l'état-civil** registrar

officieux, euse [ɔfisjø, -øz] *adj* unofficial

officinal, e, aux [ɔfisinal, -o] *adj:* **plantes ~es** medicinal plants

officine [ɔfisin] *nf* *(de pharmacie)* dispensary; *(bureau)* agency, office

offrande [ɔfʀɑ̃d] *nf* offering

offre [ɔfʀ(ə)] *nf* offer; *(aux enchères)* bid; *(ADMIN: soumission)* tender; *(ÉCON)* **l'~** supply; **"~s d'emploi"** "situations vacant"; ~ **d'emploi** job advertised; ~ **publique d'achat** takeover bid

offrir [ɔfʀiʀ] *vt:* ~ **(à qn)** to offer (to sb); *(faire cadeau de)* to give (to sb); **s'~** *vi (occasion, paysage)* to present itself ♦ *vt (vacances, voiture)* to treat o.s. to; ~ **(à qn) de faire qch** to offer to do sth (for sb); ~ **à boire à qn** to offer sb a drink; **s'~ comme guide/en otage** to offer one's services as (a) guide/offer o.s. as hostage

offusquer [ɔfyske] *vt* to offend

ogive [ɔʒiv] *nf:* ~ **nucléaire** nuclear warhead

oie [wa] *nf* (ZOOL) goose

oignon [ɔɲɔ̃] *nm* (BOT, CULIN) onion; *(de tulipe etc: bulbe)* bulb; (MÉD) bunion

oiseau, x [wazo] *nm* bird; ~ **de proie** bird of prey

oiseux, euse [wazø, -øz] *adj* pointless; trivial

oisif, ive [wazif, -iv] *adj* idle ♦ *nm/f (péj)* man(woman) of leisure

oléoduc [ɔleɔdyk] *nm* (oil) pipeline

olive [ɔliv] *nf* (BOT) olive; **olivier** *nm* olive (tree)

OLP *sigle f* = **Organisation de libération**

de la Palestine
olympique [ɔlɛ̃pik] *adj* Olympic
ombrage [ɔ̃braʒ] *nm* (*ombre*) (leafy) shade; **ombragé, e** *adj* shaded, shady; **ombrageux, euse** *adj* (*cheval*) skittish, nervous; (*personne*) touchy, easily offended
ombre [ɔ̃br(ə)] *nf* (*espace non ensoleillé*) shade; (~ *portée, tache*) shadow; **à l'~** in the shade; **tu me fais de l'~** you're in my light; **ça nous donne de l'~** it gives us (some) shade; **dans l'~** (*fig*) in obscurity; in the dark; **~ à paupières** eyeshadow; **ombrelle** [ɔ̃brɛl] *nf* parasol, sunshade
omelette [ɔmlɛt] *nf* omelette
omettre [ɔmɛtr(ə)] *vt* to omit, leave out
omnibus [ɔmnibys] *nm* slow *ou* stopping train
omoplate [ɔmɔplat] *nf* shoulder blade

MOT CLÉ
---

on [ɔ̃] *pron* **1** (*Indéterminé*) you, one; ~ **peut le faire ainsi** you *ou* one can do it like this, it can be done like this
2 (*quelqu'un*): ~ **les a attaqués** they were attacked; ~ **vous demande au téléphone** there's a phone call for you, you're wanted on the phone
3 (*nous*) we; ~ **va y aller demain** we're going tomorrow
4 (*les gens*) they; **autrefois,** ~ **croyait ...** they used to believe ...
5: ~ **ne peut plus** *adv*: ~ **ne peut plus stupide** as stupid as can be

oncle [ɔ̃kl(ə)] *nm* uncle
onctueux, euse [ɔ̃ktɥø, -øz] *adj* creamy, smooth; (*fig*) smooth, unctuous
onde [ɔ̃d] *nf* (*PHYSIQUE*) wave; **sur les ~s** on the radio; **mettre en ~s** to produce for the radio; **sur ~s courtes** on short wave *sg*; **moyennes/longues ~s** medium/long wave *sg*
ondée [ɔ̃de] *nf* shower
on-dit [ɔ̃di] *nm inv* rumour
ondoyer [ɔ̃dwaje] *vi* to ripple, wave
onduler [ɔ̃dyle] *vi* to undulate; (*cheveux*) to wave
onéreux, euse [ɔnerø, -øz] *adj* costly; **à titre** ~ in return for payment
ongle [ɔ̃gl(ə)] *nm* (*ANAT*) nail; **se faire les ~s** to do one's nails
onguent [ɔ̃gɑ̃] *nm* ointment
ont *vb voir* avoir
O.N.U. [ɔny] *sigle f* = Organisation des Nations Unies
onze [ɔ̃z] *num* eleven; **onzième** *num* eleventh
O.P.A. *sigle f* = offre publique d'achat
opaque [ɔpak] *adj* opaque
opéra [ɔpera] *nm* opera; (*édifice*) opera house
opérateur, trice [ɔperatœr, -tris] *nm/f*

operator; ~ **(de prise de vues)** cameraman
opération [ɔperɔsjɔ̃] *nf* operation; (*COMM*) dealing
opératoire [ɔperatwar] *adj* operating; (*choc etc*) post-operative
opérer [ɔpere] *vt* (*MÉD*) to operate on; (*faire, exécuter*) to carry out, make ♦ *vi* (*remède: faire effet*) to act, work; (*procéder*) to proceed; (*MÉD*) to operate; **s'~** *vi* (*avoir lieu*) to occur, take place; **se faire** ~ to have an operation
opiner [ɔpine] *vi*: ~ **de la tête** to nod assent
opinion [ɔpinjɔ̃] *nf* opinion; **l'~ (publique)** public opinion
opportun, e [ɔpɔrtœ̃, -yn] *adj* timely, opportune; **en temps** ~ at the appropriate time; **~iste** [ɔpɔrtynist(ə)] *nm/f* opportunist
opposant, e [ɔpozɑ̃, -ɑ̃t] *adj* opposing; **opposants** *nmpl* opponents
opposé, e [ɔpoze] *adj* (*direction, rive*) opposite; (*faction*) opposing; (*couleurs*) contrasting; (*opinions, intérêts*) conflicting; (*contre*): ~ **à** opposed to, against ♦ *nm*: **l'~** the other *ou* opposite side (*ou* direction); (*contraire*) the opposite; **à l'~** (*fig*) on the other hand; **à l'~ de** on the other *ou* opposite side from; (*fig*) contrary to, unlike
opposer [ɔpoze] *vt* (*personnes, armées, équipes*) to oppose; (*couleurs, termes, tons*) to contrast; **s'~** (*sens réciproque*) to conflict; to clash; to contrast; **s'~ à** (*interdire, empêcher*) to oppose; (*tenir tête à*) to rebel against; ~ **qch à** (*comme obstacle, défense*) to set sth against; (*comme objection*) to put sth forward against
opposition [ɔpozisjɔ̃] *nf* opposition; **par** ~ **à** as opposed to, in contrast with; **entrer en** ~ **avec** to come into conflict with; **être en** ~ **avec** (*idées, conduite*) to be at variance with; **faire** ~ **à un chèque** to stop a cheque
oppresser [ɔprese] *vt* to oppress; **oppression** *nf* oppression; (*malaise*) feeling of suffocation
opprimer [ɔprime] *vt* to oppress; (*liberté, opinion*) to suppress, stifle; (*suj: chaleur etc*) to suffocate, oppress
opter [ɔpte] *vi*: ~ **pour** to opt for; ~ **entre** to choose between
opticien, ne [ɔptisjɛ̃, -ɛn] *nm/f* optician
optimiste [ɔptimist(ə)] *nm/f* optimist ♦ *adj* optimistic
option [ɔpsjɔ̃] *nf* option; **matière à** ~ (*SCOL*) optional subject
optique [ɔptik] *adj* (*nerf*) optic; (*verres*) optical ♦ *nf* (*PHOTO*: *lentilles etc*) optics *pl*; (*science, industrie*) optics *sg*; (*fig: manière de voir*) perspective
opulent, e [ɔpylɑ̃, -ɑ̃t] *adj* wealthy, opulent; (*formes, poitrine*) ample, generous
or [ɔr] *nm* gold ♦ *conj* now, but; **en** ~ gold

cpd; (*fig*) golden, marvellous

orage [ɔʀaʒ] *nm* (thunder)storm; **orageux, euse** *adj* stormy

oraison [ɔʀɛzɔ̃] *nf* orison, prayer; ~ **funèbre** funeral oration

oral, e, aux [ɔʀal, -o] *adj, nm* oral

orange [ɔʀɑ̃ʒ] *nf* orange ♦ *adj inv* orange; **oranger** *nm* orange tree

orateur [ɔʀatœʀ] *nm* speaker; orator

orbite [ɔʀbit] *nf* (*ANAT*) (eye-) socket; (*PHYSIQUE*) orbit

orchestre [ɔʀkɛstʀ(ə)] *nm* orchestra; (*de jazz, danse*) band; (*places*) stalls *pl* (*BRIT*), orchestra (*US*); **orchestrer** *vt* (*MUS*) to orchestrate; (*fig*) to mount, stage-manage

orchidée [ɔʀkide] *nf* orchid

ordinaire [ɔʀdinɛʀ] *adj* ordinary; everyday; standard ♦ *nm* ordinary; (*menus*) everyday fare ♦ *nf* (*essence*) ≈ two-star (petrol) (*BRIT*), ≈ regular gas (*US*); **d'**~ usually, normally; **à l'**~ usually, ordinarily

ordinateur [ɔʀdinatœʀ] *nm* computer; ~ **domestique** home computer; ~ **individuel** personal computer

ordonnance [ɔʀdɔnɑ̃s] *nf* organization; layout; (*MÉD*) prescription; (*JUR*) order; (*MIL*) orderly, batman (*BRIT*)

ordonné, e [ɔʀdɔne] *adj* tidy, orderly; (*MATH*) ordered

ordonner [ɔʀdɔne] *vt* (*agencer*) to organize, arrange; (*donner un ordre*): ~ **à qn de faire** to order sb to do; (*REL*) to ordain; (*MÉD*) to prescribe

ordre [ɔʀdʀ(ə)] *nm* (*gén*) order; (*propreté et soin*) orderliness, tidiness; (*nature*): **d'**~ **pratique** of a practical nature; ~**s** *nmpl* (*REL*) holy orders; **mettre en** ~ to tidy (up), put in order; **à l'**~ **de qn** payable to sb; **être aux** ~**s de qn/sous les** ~**s de qn** to be at sb's disposal/under sb's command; **jusqu'à nouvel** ~ until further notice; **dans le même** ~ **d'idées** in this connection; **donnez-nous un** ~ **de grandeur** give us some idea as regards size (*ou* the amount); **de premier** ~ first-rate; ~ **du jour** (*d'une réunion*) agenda; (*MIL*) order of the day; **à l'**~ **du jour** (*fig*) topical

ordure [ɔʀdyʀ] *nf* filth *no pl*; ~**s** *nfpl* (*balayures, déchets*) rubbish *sg*, refuse *sg*; ~**s ménagères** household refuse

oreille [ɔʀɛj] *nf* (*ANAT*) ear; (*de marmite, tasse*) handle; **avoir de l'**~ to have a good ear (for music)

oreiller [ɔʀeje] *nm* pillow

oreillons [ɔʀɛjɔ̃] *nmpl* mumps *sg*

ores [ɔʀ] : **d'**~ **et déjà** *adv* already

orfèvrerie [ɔʀfɛvʀəʀi] *nf* goldsmith's (*ou* silversmith's) trade; (*ouvrage*) gold (*ou* silver) plate

organe [ɔʀgan] *nm* organ; (*porte-parole*) representative, mouthpiece

organigramme [ɔʀganigʀam] *nm* organization chart; flow chart

organique [ɔʀganik] *adj* organic

organisateur, trice [ɔʀganizatœʀ, -tʀis] *nm/f* organizer

organisation [ɔʀganizasjɔ̃] *nf* organization; **O**~ **des Nations Unies** United Nations (Organization); **O**~ **du traité de l'Atlantique Nord** North Atlantic Treaty Organization

organiser [ɔʀganize] *vt* to organize; (*mettre sur pied: service etc*) to set up; **s'**~ to get organized

organisme [ɔʀganism(ə)] *nm* (*BIO*) organism; (*corps, ADMIN*) body

organiste [ɔʀganist(ə)] *nm/f* organist

orgasme [ɔʀgasm(ə)] *nm* orgasm, climax

orge [ɔʀʒ(ə)] *nf* barley

orgie [ɔʀʒi] *nf* orgy

orgue [ɔʀg(ə)] *nm* organ; ~**s** *nfpl* (*MUS*) organ *sg*

orgueil [ɔʀgœj] *nm* pride; **orgueilleux, euse** *adj* proud

Orient [ɔʀjɑ̃] *nm*: **l'**~ the East, the Orient

oriental, e, aux [ɔʀjɑ̃tal, -o] *adj* oriental, eastern; (*frontière*) eastern

orientation [ɔʀjɑ̃tasjɔ̃] *nf* positioning; orientation; (*d'une maison etc*) aspect; (*d'un journal*) leanings *pl*; **avoir le sens de l'**~ to have a (good) sense of direction; ~ **professionnelle** careers advising; careers advisory service

orienté, e [ɔʀjɑ̃te] *adj* (*fig: article, journal*) slanted; **bien/mal** ~ (*appartement*) well/badly positioned; ~ **au sud** facing south, with a southern aspect

orienter [ɔʀjɑ̃te] *vt* (*placer, disposer: pièce mobile*) to adjust, position; (*tourner*) to direct, turn; (*voyageur, touriste, recherches*) to direct; (*fig: élève*) to orientate; **s'**~ (*se repérer*) to find one's bearings; **s'**~ **vers** (*fig*) to turn towards

origan [ɔʀigɑ̃] *nm* (*BOT*) oregano

originaire [ɔʀiʒinɛʀ] *adj*: **être** ~ **de** to be a native of

original, e, aux [ɔʀiʒinal, -o] *adj* original; (*bizarre*) eccentric ♦ *nm/f* eccentric ♦ *nm* (*document etc, ART*) original; (*dactylographie*) top copy

origine [ɔʀiʒin] *nf* origin; **dès l'**~ at *ou* from the outset; **à l'**~ originally; **originel, le** *adj* original

O.R.L. *sigle nm/f* = **oto-rhino-laryngologiste**

orme [ɔʀm(ə)] *nm* elm

ornement [ɔʀnəmɑ̃] *nm* ornament; (*fig*) embellishment, adornment

orner [ɔʀne] *vt* to decorate, adorn

ornière [ɔʀnjɛʀ] *nf* rut

orphelin, e [ɔʀfəlɛ̃, -in] *adj* orphan(ed) ♦ *nm/f* orphan; ~ **de père/mère** fatherless/motherless; **orphelinat** *nm* orphanage

orteil [ɔʀtɛj] *nm* toe; **gros** ~ big toe

orthographe [ɔʀtɔgʀaf] *nf* spelling; **ortho-graphier** *vt* to spell
orthopédiste [ɔʀtɔpedist(ə)] *nm/f* orthopaedic specialist
ortie [ɔʀti] *nf* (stinging) nettle
os [ɔs, *pl* o] *nm* bone
osciller [ɔsile] *vi* (*pendule*) to swing; (*au vent etc*) to rock; (*TECH*) to oscillate; (*fig*): ~ **entre** to waver *ou* fluctuate between
osé, e [oze] *adj* daring, bold
oseille [ozɛj] *nf* sorrel
oser [oze] *vi, vt* to dare; ~ **faire** to dare (to) do
osier [ozje] *nm* willow; **d'~** wicker(work); **en ~ = d'osier**
ossature [ɔsatyʀ] *nf* (*ANAT*) frame, skeletal structure; (*fig*) framework
osseux, euse [ɔsø, -øz] *adj* bony; (*tissu, maladie, greffe*) bone *cpd*
ostensible [ɔstɑ̃sibl(ə)] *adj* conspicuous
otage [ɔtaʒ] *nm* hostage; **prendre qn comme ~** to take sb hostage
O.T.A.N. [ɔtɑ̃] *sigle f* = **Organisation du traité de l'Atlantique Nord**
otarie [ɔtaʀi] *nf* sea-lion
ôter [ote] *vt* to remove; (*soustraire*) to take away; ~ **qch à qn** to take sth (away) from sb; ~ **qch de** to remove sth from
otite [ɔtit] *nf* ear infection
oto-rhino-(-laryngologiste) [ɔtɔʀino(la-ʀɛ̃gɔlɔʒist(ə))] *nm/f* ear nose and throat specialist
ou [u] *conj* or; ~ ... ~ either ... or; ~ **bien** or (else)

----------------- *MOT CLÉ* ------------------

où [u] *pron relatif* **1** (*position, situation*) where, that (*souvent omis*); **la chambre ~ il était** the room (that) he was in, the room where he was; **la ville ~ je l'ai rencontré** the town where I met him; **la pièce d'~ il est sorti** the room he came out of; **le village d'~ je viens** the village I come from; **les villes par ~ il est passé** the towns he went through
2 (*temps, état*) that (*souvent omis*); **le jour ~ il est parti** the day (that) he left; **au prix ~ c'est** at the price it is
♦ *adv* **1** (*interrogation*) where; ~ **est-il/va-t-il?** where is he/is he going?; **par ~?** which way?; **d'~ vient que ...?** how come ...?
2 (*position*) where; **je sais ~ il est** I know where he is; ~ **que l'on aille** wherever you go

----

ouate [wat] *nf* cotton wool (*BRIT*), cotton (*US*); (*bourre*) padding, wadding
oubli [ubli] *nm* (*acte*): **l'~ de** forgetting; (*étourderie*) forgetfulness *no pl*; (*négligence*) omission, oversight; (*absence de souvenirs*) oblivion

oublier [ublije] *vt* (*gén*) to forget; (*ne pas voir: erreurs etc*) to miss; (*ne pas mettre: virgule, nom*) to leave out; (*laisser quelque part: chapeau etc*) to leave behind; **s'~** to forget o.s.
oubliettes [ublijɛt] *nfpl* dungeon *sg*
ouest [wɛst] *nm* west ♦ *adj inv* west; (*région*) western; **à l'~** in the west; (*to the*) west, westwards; **à l'~ de** (*to the*) west of
ouf [uf] *excl* phew!
oui [wi] *adv* yes
ouï-dire [widiʀ]: **par ~** *adv* by hearsay
ouïe [wi] *nf* hearing; ~**s** *nfpl* (*de poisson*) gills
ouïr [wiʀ] *vt* to hear; **avoir ouï dire que** to have heard it said that
ouragan [uʀagɑ̃] *nm* hurricane
ourlet [uʀlɛ] *nm* hem
ours [uʀs] *nm* bear; ~ **brun/blanc** brown/polar bear; ~ **(en peluche)** teddy (bear)
oursin [uʀsɛ̃] *nm* sea urchin
ourson [uʀsɔ̃] *nm* (bear-)cub
ouste [ust(ə)] *excl* hop it!
outil [uti] *nm* tool
outiller [utije] *vt* (*ouvrier, usine*) to equip
outrage [utʀaʒ] *nm* insult; **faire subir les derniers ~s à** (*femme*) to ravish; ~ **à la pudeur** indecent conduct *no pl*; ~**r** [utʀaʒe] *vt* to offend gravely
outrance [utʀɑ̃s]: **à ~** *adv* excessively, to excess
outre [utʀ(ə)] *nf* goatskin, water skin ♦ *prép* besides ♦ *adv*: **passer ~ à** to disregard, take no notice of; **en ~** besides, moreover; ~ **que** apart from the fact that; ~ **mesure** immoderately; unduly; ~-**Atlantique** *adv* across the Atlantic; ~-**Manche** *adv* across the Channel; ~-**mer** *adj inv* ultramarine; ~-**mer** *adv* overseas; ~**passer** *vt* to go beyond, exceed
ouvert, e [uvɛʀ, -ɛʀt(ə)] *pp de* **ouvrir** ♦ *adj* open; (*robinet, gaz etc*) on; **ouvertement** *adv* openly
ouverture [uvɛʀtyʀ] *nf* opening; (*MUS*) overture; (*PHOTO*): ~ **(du diaphragme)** aperture; ~**s** *nfpl* (*propositions*) overtures; ~ **d'esprit** open-mindedness
ouvrable [uvʀabl(ə)] *adj*: **jour ~** working day, weekday
ouvrage [uvʀaʒ] *nm* (*tâche, de tricot etc, MIL*) work *no pl*; (*texte, livre*) work
ouvragé, e [uvʀaʒe] *adj* finely embroidered (*ou* worked *ou* carved)
ouvre-boîte(s) [uvʀəbwat] *nm inv* tin (*BRIT*) *ou* can opener
ouvre-bouteille(s) [uvʀəbutɛj] *nm inv* bottle-opener
ouvreuse [uvʀøz] *nf* usherette
ouvrier, ière [uvʀje, -jɛʀ] *nm/f* worker ♦ *adj* working-class; industrial; labour *cpd*; **classe ouvrière** working class
ouvrir [uvʀiʀ] *vt* (*gén*) to open; (*brèche,*

passage, MÉD: abcès) to open up; (*commencer l'exploitation de, créer*) to open (up); (*eau, électricité, chauffage, robinet*) to turn on ♦ *vi* to open; to open up; **s'~** *vi* to open; **s'~ à qn** to open one's heart to sb; **~ l'appétit à qn** to whet sb's appetite

ovaire [ɔvɛʀ] *nm* ovary

ovale [ɔval] *adj* oval

ovni [ɔvni] *sigle m* (= *objet volant non identifié*) UFO

oxyder [ɔkside]: **s'~** *vi* to become oxidized

oxygène [ɔksiʒɛn] *nm* oxygen; (*fig*): **cure d'~** fresh air cure

oxygéné, e [ɔksiʒene] *adj*: **eau ~e** hydrogen peroxide

P p

pacifique [pasifik] *adj* peaceful ♦ *nm*: **le P~, l'océan P~** the Pacific (Ocean)

pacte [pakt(ə)] *nm* pact, treaty

pactiser [paktize] *vi*: **~ avec** to come to terms with

pagaie [pagɛ] *nf* paddle

pagaille [pagaj] *nf* mess, shambles *sg*

page [paʒ] *nf* page ♦ *nm* page (boy); **à la ~** (*fig*) up-to-date

paiement [pemɑ̃] *nm* payment

païen, ne [pajɛ̃, -jɛn] *adj, nm/f* pagan, heathen

paillard, e [pajaʀ, -aʀd(ə)] *adj* bawdy

paillasson [pajasɔ̃] *nm* doormat

paille [pɑj] *nf* straw; (*défaut*) flaw

paillettes [pajɛt] *nfpl* (*décoratives*) sequins, spangles; **lessive en ~** soapflakes *pl*

pain [pɛ̃] *nm* (*substance*) bread; (*unité*) loaf (of bread); (*morceau*): **~ de cire** *etc* bar of wax *etc*; **~ bis/complet** brown/wholemeal (*BRIT*) *ou* wholewheat (*US*) bread; **~ d'épice** gingerbread; **~ de mie** sandwich loaf; **~ de sucre** sugar loaf; **~ grillé** toast

pair, e [pɛʀ] *adj* (*nombre*) even ♦ *nm* peer; **aller de ~** to go hand in hand *ou* together; **jeune fille au ~** *au* pair

paire [pɛʀ] *nf* pair

paisible [pezibl(ə)] *adj* peaceful, quiet

paître [pɛtʀ(ə)] *vi* to graze

paix [pɛ] *nf* peace; (*fig*) peacefulness, peace; **faire/avoir la ~** to make/have peace

Pakistan [pakistɑ̃] *nm*: **le ~** Pakistan

palace [palas] *nm* luxury hotel

palais [palɛ] *nm* palace; (*ANAT*) palate

pale [pal] *nf* (*d'hélice, de rame*) blade

pâle [pɑl] *adj* pale; **bleu ~** pale blue

Palestine [palɛstin] *nf*: **la ~** Palestine

palet [palɛ] *nm* disc; (*HOCKEY*) puck

palette [palɛt] *nf* (*de peintre*) palette; (*produits*) range

pâleur [palœʀ] *nf* paleness

palier [palje] *nm* (*d'escalier*) landing; (*fig*) level, plateau; (*TECH*) bearing; **par ~s** in stages

pâlir [paliʀ] *vi* to turn *ou* go pale; (*couleur*) to fade

palissade [palisad] *nf* fence

palliatif [paljatif] *nm* palliative; (*expédient*) stopgap measure

pallier [palje] : **~ à** *vt* to offset, make up for

palmarès [palmaʀɛs] *nm* record (of achievements); (*SCOL*) prize list; (*SPORT*) list of winners

palme [palm(ə)] *nf* (*symbole*) palm; (*de plongeur*) flipper; **palmé, e** *adj* (*pattes*) webbed

palmier [palmje] *nm* palm tree

palombe [palɔ̃b] *nf* woodpigeon

pâlot, te [palo, -ɔt] *adj* pale, peaky

palourde [paluʀd(ə)] *nf* clam

palper [palpe] *vt* to feel, finger

palpitant, e [palpitɑ̃, -ɑ̃t] *adj* thrilling

palpiter [palpite] *vi* (*cœur, pouls*) to beat; (: *plus fort*) to pound, throb

paludisme [palydism(ə)] *nm* malaria

pamphlet [pɑ̃flɛ] *nm* lampoon, satirical tract

pamplemousse [pɑ̃pləmus] *nm* grapefruit

pan [pɑ̃] *nm* section, piece ♦ *excl* bang!

panachage [panaʃaʒ] *nm* blend, mix

panache [panaʃ] *nm* plume; (*fig*) spirit, panache

panaché, e [panaʃe] *adj*: **glace ~e** mixed-flavour ice cream; **bière ~e** shandy

pancarte [pɑ̃kaʀt(ə)] *nf* sign, notice; (*dans un défilé*) placard

pancréas [pɑ̃kʀeas] *nm* pancreas

pané, e [pane] *adj* fried in breadcrumbs

panier [panje] *nm* basket; **mettre au ~** to chuck away; **~ à provisions** shopping basket

panique [panik] *nf, adj* panic; **paniquer** *vi* to panic

panne [pan] *nf* (*d'un mécanisme, moteur*) breakdown; **être/tomber en ~** to have broken down/break down; **être en ~ d'essence** *ou* **sèche** to have run out of petrol (*BRIT*) *ou* gas (*US*); **~ d'électricité** *ou* **de courant** power *ou* electrical failure

panneau, x [pano] *nm* (*écriteau*) sign, notice; (*de boiserie, de tapisserie etc*) panel; **~ d'affichage** notice board; **~ de signalisation** roadsign

panonceau, x [panɔ̃so] *nm* sign

panoplie [panɔpli] *nf* (*jouet*) outfit; (*d'armes*) display; (*fig*) array

panorama [panɔrama] *nm* panorama

panse [pɑ̃s] *nf* paunch

pansement [pɑ̃smɑ̃] *nm* dressing, bandage; ~ **adhésif** sticking plaster

panser [pɑ̃se] *vt* (*plaie*) to dress, bandage; (*bras*) to put a dressing on, bandage; (*cheval*) to groom

pantalon [pɑ̃talɔ̃] *nm* (*aussi*: ~s, *paire de* ~s) trousers *pl*, pair of trousers; ~ **de ski** ski pants *pl*

pantelant, e [pɑ̃tlɑ̃, -ɑ̃t] *adj* gasping for breath, panting

panthère [pɑ̃tɛr] *nf* panther

pantin [pɑ̃tɛ̃] *nm* jumping jack; (*péj*) puppet

pantois [pɑ̃twa] *adj m*: **rester** ~ to be flabbergasted

pantomime [pɑ̃tɔmim] *nf* mime; (*pièce*) mime show

pantoufle [pɑ̃tufl(ə)] *nf* slipper

paon [pɑ̃] *nm* peacock

papa [papa] *nm* dad(dy)

pape [pap] *nm* pope

paperasse [papras] (*péj*) *nf* bumf *no pl*, papers *pl*; **paperasserie** (*péj*) *nf* red tape *no pl*; paperwork *no pl*

papeterie [papetri] *nf* (*usine*) paper mill; (*magasin*) stationer's (shop)

papier [papje] *nm* paper; (*article*) article; ~**s** *nmpl* (*aussi*: ~s *d'identité*) (identity) papers; ~ **à lettres** writing paper, notepaper; ~ **buvard** blotting paper; ~ **carbone** carbon paper; ~ (**d'**)**aluminium** aluminium (*BRIT*) *ou* aluminum (*US*) foil, tinfoil; ~ **de verre** sandpaper; ~ **hygiénique** toilet paper; ~ **journal** newsprint; (*pour emballer*) newspaper; ~ **peint** wallpaper

papillon [papijɔ̃] *nm* butterfly; (*fam*: *contravention*) (parking) ticket; (*TECH*: *écrou*) wing nut; ~ **de nuit** moth

papilloter [papijɔte] *vi* to blink, flicker

paquebot [pakbo] *nm* liner

pâquerette [pɑkrɛt] *nf* daisy

Pâques [pɑk] *nm, nfpl* Easter

paquet [pakɛ] *nm* packet; (*colis*) parcel; (*fig*: *tas*): ~ **de pile** *ou* heap of; **paquet-cadeau** *nm* gift-wrapped parcel

par [par] *prép* by; **finir** *etc* ~ to end *etc* with; ~ **amour** out of love; **passer** ~ **Lyon/la côte** to go via *ou* through Lyons/ along by the coast; ~ **la fenêtre** (*jeter, regarder*) out of the window; **3** ~ **jour/ personne** 3 a *ou* per day/head; **2** ~ **2** two at a time; **in twos**; ~ **ici** this way; (*dans le coin*) round here; ~**-ci**, ~**-là** here and there

parabole [parabɔl] *nf* (*REL*) parable

parachever [paraʃve] *vt* to perfect

parachute [paraʃyt] *nm* parachute

parachutiste [paraʃytist(ə)] *nm/f* parachutist; (*MIL*) paratrooper

parade [parad] *nf* (*spectacle, défilé*) parade; (*ESCRIME, BOXE*) parry

paradis [paradi] *nm* heaven, paradise

paradoxe [paradɔks(ə)] *nm* paradox

paraffine [parafin] *nf* paraffin

parages [paraʒ] *nmpl*: **dans les** ~ (**de**) in the area *ou* vicinity (of)

paragraphe [paragraf] *nm* paragraph

paraître [parɛtr(ə)] *vb* +*attrib* to seem, look, appear ♦ *vi* to appear; (*être visible*) to show; (*PRESSE, ÉDITION*) to be published, come out, appear; (*briller*) to show off ♦ *vb impers*: **il paraît que** ... it seems *ou* appears that ..., they say that ...; **il me paraît que** ... it seems to me that ...

parallèle [paralɛl] *adj* parallel; (*police, marché*) unofficial ♦ *nm* (*comparaison*): **faire un** ~ **entre** to draw a parallel between; (*GÉO*) parallel ♦ *nf* parallel (line)

paralyser [paralize] *vt* to paralyse

paramédical, e, aux [paramedikal] *adj*: **personnel** ~ paramedics *pl*, paramedical workers *pl*

parapet [parapɛ] *nm* parapet

parapher [parafe] *vt* to initial; to sign

paraphrase [parafrɑz] *nf* paraphrase

parapluie [paraplɥi] *nm* umbrella

parasite [parazit] *nm* parasite; ~**s** *nmpl* (*TÉL*) interference *sg*

parasol [parasɔl] *nm* parasol, sunshade

paratonnerre [paratɔnɛr] *nm* lightning conductor

paravent [paravɑ̃] *nm* folding screen

parc [park] *nm* (*public*) park, gardens *pl*; (*de château etc*) grounds *pl*; (*pour le bétail*) pen, enclosure; (*d'enfant*) playpen; (*MIL*: *entrepôt*) depot; (*ensemble d'unités*) stock; (*de voitures etc*) fleet; ~ **automobile** (*d'un pays*) number of cars on the roads; ~ (**d'attractions**) **à thème** theme park; ~ **de stationnement** car park

parcelle [parsɛl] *nf* fragment, scrap; (*de terrain*) plot, parcel

parce que [parskə] *conj* because

parchemin [parʃəmɛ̃] *nm* parchment

parc(o)mètre [park(ɔ)mɛtr(ə)] *nm* parking meter

parcourir [parkurir] *vt* (*trajet, distance*) to cover; (*article, livre*) to skim *ou* glance through; (*lieu*) to go all over, travel up and down; (*suj*: *frisson, vibration*) to run through

parcours [parkur] *nm* (*trajet*) journey; (*itinéraire*) route; (*SPORT*: *terrain*) course; (: *tour*) round; run; lap

par-dessous [pardəsu] *prép, adv* under(neath)

pardessus [pardəsy] *nm* overcoat

par-dessus [pardəsy] *prép* over (the top of) ♦ *adv* over (the top); ~ **le marché** on top of all that

par-devant [pardəvɑ̃] *prép* in the presence of, before ♦ *adv* at the front; round the front

pardon [paʀdɔ̃] nm forgiveness no pl ♦ excl sorry!; (pour interpeller etc) excuse me!; **demander ~ à qn (de)** to apologize to sb (for); **je vous demande ~** I'm sorry; excuse me

pardonner [paʀdɔne] vt to forgive; **~ qch à qn** to forgive sb for sth

pare: **~-balles** adj inv bulletproof; **~-boue** nm inv mudguard; **~-brise** nm inv windscreen (BRIT), windshield (US); **~-chocs** nm inv bumper

pareil, le [paʀej] adj (identique) the same, alike; (similaire) similar; (tel): **un courage/livre ~** such courage/a book, courage/a book like this; **de ~s livres** such books; **ses ~s** one's fellow men; one's peers; **ne pas avoir son(sa) ~(le)** to be second to none; **~ à** the same as; similar to; **sans ~** unparalleled, unequalled

parent, e [paʀɑ̃, -ɑ̃t] nm/f: **un/une ~/e** a relative ou relation ♦ adj: **être ~ de** to be related to; **~s** nmpl (père et mère) parents; **parenté** nf (lien) relationship

parenthèse [paʀɑ̃tɛz] nf (ponctuation) bracket, parenthesis; (MATH) bracket; (digression) parenthesis, digression; **ouvrir/fermer la ~** to open/close the brackets; **entre ~s** in brackets; (fig) incidentally

parer [paʀe] vt to adorn; (CULIN) to dress, trim; (éviter) to ward off

paresse [paʀɛs] nf laziness; **paresseux, euse** adj lazy; (fig) slow, sluggish

parfaire [paʀfɛʀ] vt to perfect

parfait, e [paʀfɛ, -ɛt] adj perfect ♦ nm (LING) perfect (tense); **parfaitement** adv perfectly ♦ excl (most) certainly

parfois [paʀfwa] adv sometimes

parfum [paʀfœ̃] nm (produit) perfume, scent; (odeur: de fleur) scent, fragrance; (: de tabac, vin) aroma; (goût) flavour; **parfumé, e** adj (fleur, fruit) fragrant; (femme) perfumed; **parfumé au café** coffee-flavoured; **parfumer** vt (suj: odeur, bouquet) to perfume; (mouchoir) to put scent ou perfume on; (crème, gâteau) to flavour; **parfumerie** nf (commerce) perfumery; (produits) perfumes pl; (boutique) perfume shop

pari [paʀi] nm bet, wager; (SPORT) bet

paria [paʀja] nm outcast

parier [paʀje] vt to bet

Paris [paʀi] n Paris; **parisien, ne** adj Parisian; (GÉO, ADMIN) Paris cpd ♦ nm/f: **Parisien, ne** Parisian

paritaire [paʀitɛʀ] adj joint

parjure [paʀʒyʀ] nm perjury

parking [paʀkiŋ] nm (lieu) car park

parlant, e [paʀlɑ̃, -ɑ̃t] adj (fig) graphic, vivid; eloquent; (CINÉMA) talking

parlement [paʀləmɑ̃] nm parliament; **parlementaire** adj parliamentary ♦ nm/f member of parliament

parlementer [paʀləmɑ̃te] vi to negotiate, parley

parler [paʀle] vi to speak, talk; (avouer) to talk; **~ (à qn) de** to talk ou speak (to sb) about; **~ le/en français** to speak French/in French; **~ affaires** to talk business; **~ en dormant** to talk in one's sleep; **sans ~ de** (fig) not to mention, to say nothing of; **tu parles!** you must be joking!

parloir [paʀlwaʀ] nm (de prison, d'hôpital) visiting room; (REL) parlour

parmi [paʀmi] prép among(st)

paroi [paʀwa] nf wall; (cloison) partition; **~ rocheuse** rock face

paroisse [paʀwas] nf parish

parole [paʀɔl] nf (faculté): **la ~** speech; (mot, promesse) word; **~s** nfpl (MUS) words, lyrics; **tenir ~** to keep one's word; **prendre la ~** to speak; **demander la ~** to ask for permission to speak; **je le crois sur ~** I'll take his word for it

parquer [paʀke] vt (voiture, matériel) to park; (bestiaux) to pen (in ou up)

parquet [paʀke] nm (parquet) floor; (JUR): **le ~** the Public Prosecutor's department

parrain [paʀɛ̃] nm godfather; (d'un nouvel adhérent) sponsor, proposer

parrainer [paʀene] vt (suj: entreprise) to sponsor

pars vb voir **partir**

parsemer [paʀsəme] vt (suj: feuilles, papiers) to be scattered over; **~ qch de** to scatter sth with

part [paʀ] nf (qui revient à qn) share; (fraction, partie) part; (FINANCE) (non-voting) share; **prendre ~ à** (débat etc) to take part in; (soucis, douleur de qn) to share in; **faire ~ de qch à qn** to announce sth to sb, inform sb of sth; **pour ma ~** as for me, as far as I'm concerned; **à ~ entière** full; **de la ~ de** (au nom de) on behalf of; (donné par) from; **de toute(s) ~(s)** from all sides ou quarters; **de ~ et d'autre** on both sides, on either side; **de ~ en ~** right through; **d'une ~ ... d'autre ~** on the one hand ... on the other hand; **à ~** adv separately; (de côté) aside ♦ prép apart from, except for ♦ adj exceptional, special; **faire la ~ des choses** to make allowances

partage [paʀtaʒ] nm dividing up; sharing (out) no pl, share-out; sharing; **recevoir qch en ~** to receive sth as one's share (ou lot)

partager [paʀtaʒe] vt to share; (distribuer, répartir) to share (out); (morceler, diviser) to divide (up); **se ~** vt (héritage etc) to share between themselves (ou ourselves)

partance [paʀtɑ̃s]: **en ~** adv outbound, due to leave; **en ~ pour** (bound) for

partant [paʀtɑ̃] vb voir **partir** ♦ nm (SPORT) starter; (HIPPISME) runner

partenaire [paʀtənɛʀ] nm/f partner

parterre [paʀtɛʀ] *nm* (*de fleurs*) (flower) bed; (*THÉÂTRE*) stalls *pl*

parti [paʀti] *nm* (*POL*) party; (*décision*) course of action; (*personne à marier*) match; **tirer ~ de** to take advantage of, turn to good account; **prendre le ~ de qn** to stand up for sb, side with sb; **prendre ~ (pour/contre)** to take sides *ou* a stand (for/against); **prendre son ~ de** to come to terms with; **~ pris** bias

partial, e, aux [paʀsjal, -o] *adj* biased, partial

participant, e [paʀtisipɑ̃, -ɑ̃t] *nm/f* participant; (*à un concours*) entrant

participation [paʀtisipɑsjɔ̃] *nf* participation; sharing; (*COMM*) interest; **la ~ aux bénéfices** profit-sharing

participe [paʀtisip] *nm* participle

participer [paʀtisipe]: **~ à** *vt* (*course, réunion*) to take part in; (*profits etc*) to share in; (*frais etc*) to contribute to; (*chagrin, succès de qn*) to share (in)

particularité [paʀtikylaʀite] *nf* particularity; (*distinctive*) characteristic

particule [paʀtikyl] *nf* particle

particulier, ière [paʀtikylje, -jɛʀ] *adj* (*personnel, privé*) private; (*spécial*) special, particular; (*caractéristique*) characteristic, distinctive; (*spécifique*) particular ♦ *nm* (*individu: ADMIN*) private individual; **~ à** peculiar to; **en ~** (*surtout*) in particular, particularly; (*en privé*) in private; **particulièrement** *adv* particularly

partie [paʀti] *nf* (*gén*) part; (*profession, spécialité*) field, subject; (*JUR etc*: *protagonistes*) party; (*de cartes, tennis etc*) game; **une ~ de campagne/de pêche** an outing in the country/a fishing party *ou* trip; **en ~** partly, in part; **faire ~ de** to belong to; (*suj: chose*) to be part of; **prendre qn à ~** to take sb to task; (*malmener*) to set on sb; **en grande ~** largely, in the main; **~ civile** (*JUR*) party claiming damages in a criminal case

partiel, le [paʀsjɛl] *adj* partial ♦ *nm* (*SCOL*) class exam

partir [paʀtiʀ] *vi* (*gén*) to go; (*quitter*) to go, leave; (*s'éloigner*) to go (*ou* drive *etc*) away *ou* off; (*moteur*) to start; **~ de** (*lieu: quitter*) to leave; (: *commencer à*) to start from; (*date*) to run *ou* start from; **à ~ de** from

partisan, e [paʀtizɑ̃, -an] *nm/f* partisan ♦ *adj*: **être ~ de qch/de faire** to be in favour of sth/doing

partition [paʀtisjɔ̃] *nf* (*MUS*) score

partout [paʀtu] *adv* everywhere; **~ où il allait** everywhere *ou* wherever he went; **trente ~** (*TENNIS*) thirty all

paru *pp de* **paraître**

parure [paʀyʀ] *nf* (*bijoux etc*) finery *no pl*; jewellery *no pl*; (*assortiment*) set

parution [paʀysjɔ̃] *nf* publication, appear-ance

parvenir [paʀvəniʀ]: **~ à** *vt* (*atteindre*) to reach; (*réussir*): **~ à faire** to manage to do, succeed in doing; **faire ~ qch à qn** to have sth sent to sb

parvis [paʀvi] *nm* square (*in front of a church*)

pas¹ [pɑ] *nm* (*allure, mesure*) pace; (*démarche*) tread; (*enjambée, DANSE*) step; (*bruit*) (foot)step; (*trace*) footprint; (*TECH: de vis, d'écrou*) thread; **~ à ~** step by step; **au ~** at walking pace; **à ~ de loup** stealthily; **faire les cent ~** to pace up and down; **faire les premiers ~** to make the first move; **sur le ~ de la porte** on the doorstep

─────────── **MOT CLÉ** ───────────

pas² [pɑ] *adv* **1** (*en corrélation avec ne, non etc*) not; **il ne pleure ~** he does not *ou* doesn't cry; **he's not** *ou* isn't crying; **il n'a ~ pleuré/ne pleurera ~** he did not *ou* didn't/will not *ou* won't cry; **ils n'ont ~ de voiture/d'enfants** they haven't got a car/ any children, they have no car/children; **il m'a dit de ne ~ le faire** he told me not to do it; **non ~ que ...** not that ...

2 (*employé sans ne etc*): **~ moi** not me; not I, I don't (*ou* can't *etc*); **une pomme ~ mûre** an apple which isn't ripe; **~ plus tard qu'hier** only yesterday; **~ du tout** not at all

3: **~ mal** not bad; not badly; **~ mal de** quite a lot of

─────────────────────────────

passage [pɑsaʒ] *nm* (*fait de passer*) *voir* **passer**; (*lieu, prix de la traversée, extrait*) passage; (*chemin*) way; **de ~** (*touristes*) passing through; (*amants etc*) casual; **~ à niveau** level crossing; **~ clouté** pedestrian crossing; "**~ interdit**" "no entry"; "**~ protégé**" right of way over secondary road(s) *on your right*; **~ souterrain** subway (*BRIT*), underpass

passager, ère [pɑsaʒe, -ɛʀ] *adj* passing ♦ *nm/f* passenger; **~ clandestin** stowaway

passant, e [pɑsɑ̃, -ɑ̃t] *adj* (*rue, endroit*) busy ♦ *nm/f* passer-by; **en ~** in passing

passe [pɑs] *nf* (*SPORT, magnétique, NAVIG*) pass ♦ *nm* (*passe-partout*) master *ou* skeleton key; **être en ~ de faire** to be on the way to doing

passé, e [pɑse] *adj* (*événement, temps*) past; (*couleur, tapisserie*) faded ♦ *prép* after ♦ *nm* past; (*LING*) past (tense); **~ de mode** out of fashion; **~ composé** perfect (tense); **~ simple** past historic

passe-: **~-droit** *nm* special privilege; **~-montagne** *nm* balaclava; **~-partout** *nm inv* master *ou* skeleton key ♦ *adj inv* all-purpose; **~-~** *nm*: **tour de ~-~** trick, sleight of hand *no pl*

passeport [pɑspɔʀ] *nm* passport
passer [pɑse] *vi* (*se rendre, aller*) to go; (*voiture, piétons*: *défiler*) to pass (by), go by; (*faire une halte rapide: facteur, laitier etc*) to come, call; (: *pour rendre visite*) to call *ou* drop in; (*air, lumière*: franchir un obstacle *etc*) to get through; (*accusé, projet de loi*): ~ **devant** to come before; (*film, émission*) to be on; (*temps, jours*) to pass, go by; (*couleur, papier*) to fade; (*mode*) to die out; (*douleur*) to pass, go away; (*CARTES*) to pass; (*SCOL*) to go up (to the next class) ♦ *vt* (*frontière, rivière etc*) to cross; (*douane*) to go through; (*examen*) to sit, take; (*visite médicale etc*) to have; (*journée, temps*) to spend; (*donner*): ~ **qch à qn** to pass sth to sb; to give sb sth; (*transmettre*): ~ **qch à qn** to pass sth on to sb; (*enfiler: vêtement*) to slip on; (*faire entrer, mettre*): **(faire)** ~ **qch dans/par** to get sth into/through; (*café*) to pour the water on; (*thé, soupe*) to strain; (*film, pièce*) to show, put on; (*disque*) to play, put on; (*marché, accord*) to agree on; (*tolérer*): ~ **qch à qn** to let sb get away with sth; **se** ~ *vi* (*avoir lieu: scène, action*) to take place; (*se dérouler: entretien etc*) to go; (*s'écouler: semaine etc*) to pass, go by; (*arriver*): **que s'est-il passé?** what happened?; **se** ~ **de** to go *ou* do without; **se** ~ **les mains sous l'eau/de l'eau sur le visage** to put one's hands under the tap/ run water over one's face; ~ **par** to go through; ~ **sur** (*faute, détail inutile*) to pass over; ~ **avant qch/qn** (*fig*) to come before sth/sb; **laisser** ~ (*air, lumière, personne*) to let through; (*occasion*) to let slip, miss; (*erreur*) to overlook; ~ **à la radio/télévision** to be on the radio/on television; ~ **pour riche** to be taken for a rich man; ~ **en seconde**, ~ **la seconde** (*AUTO*) to change into second; ~ **le balai/l'aspirateur** to sweep up/hoover; **je vous passe M. X** (*je vous mets en communication avec lui*) I'm putting you through to Mr X; (*je lui passe l'appareil*) here is Mr X, I'll hand you over to Mr X
passerelle [pɑsʀɛl] *nf* footbridge; (*de navire, avion*) gangway
passe-temps [pɑstɑ̃] *nm inv* pastime
passeur, euse [pɑsœʀ, -øz] *nm/f* smuggler
passible [pasibl(ə)] *adj*: ~ **de** liable to
passif, ive [pasif, -iv] *adj* passive ♦ *nm* (*LING*) passive; (*COMM*) liabilities *pl*
passion [pɑsjɔ̃] *nf* passion; **passionnant, e** *adj* fascinating; **passionné, e** *adj* passionate; impassioned; **passionner** *vt* (*personne*) to fascinate, grip; **se passionner pour** to take an avid interest in; to have a passion for
passoire [pɑswaʀ] *nf* sieve; (*à légumes*) colander; (*à thé*) strainer
pastèque [pastɛk] *nf* watermelon

pasteur [pastœʀ] *nm* (*protestant*) minister, pastor
pastille [pastij] *nf* (*à sucer*) lozenge, pastille; (*de papier etc*) (small) disc
patate [patat] *nf*: ~ **douce** sweet potato
patauger [patoʒe] *vi* (*pour s'amuser*) to splash about; (*avec effort*) to wade about
pâte [pɑt] *nf* (*à tarte*) pastry; (*à pain*) dough; (*à frire*) batter; (*substance molle*) paste; cream; ~**s** *nfpl* (*macaroni etc*) pasta *sg*; ~ **à modeler** modelling clay, Plasticine (®: *BRIT*); ~ **brisée** shortcrust pastry; ~ **d'amandes** almond paste; ~ **de fruits** crystallized fruit *no pl*
pâté [pɑte] *nm* (*charcuterie*) pâté; (*tache*) ink blot; (*de sable*) sandpie; ~ **de maisons** block (of houses); ~ **en croûte** ≈ pork pie
pâtée [pɑte] *nf* mash, feed
patente [patɑ̃t] *nf* (*COMM*) trading licence
paternel, le [patɛʀnɛl] *adj* (*amour, soins*) fatherly; (*ligne, autorité*) paternal
pâteux, euse [pɑtø, -øz] *adj* thick; pasty
pathétique [patetik] *adj* moving
patience [pasjɑ̃s] *nf* patience
patient, e [pasjɑ̃, -ɑ̃t] *adj, nm/f* patient
patienter [pasjɑ̃te] *vi* to wait
patin [patɛ̃] *nm* skate; (*sport*) skating; ~**s (à glace)** (ice) skates; ~**s à roulettes** roller skates
patinage [patinaʒ] *nm* skating
patiner [patine] *vi* to skate; (*embrayage*) to slip; (*roue, voiture*) to spin; **se** ~ *vi* (*meuble, cuir*) to acquire a sheen; **patineur, euse** *nm/f* skater; **patinoire** *nf* skating rink, (ice) rink
pâtir [pɑtiʀ] : ~ **de** *vt* to suffer because of
pâtisserie [pɑtisʀi] *nf* (*boutique*) cake shop; (*métier*) confectionery; (*à la maison*) pastry- *ou* cake-making, baking; ~**s** *nfpl* (*gâteaux*) pastries, cakes; **pâtissier, ière** *nm/f* pastrycook; confectioner
patois [patwa] *nm* dialect, patois
patrie [patʀi] *nf* homeland
patrimoine [patʀimwan] *nm* inheritance, patrimony; (*culture*) heritage
patriotique [patʀijɔtik] *adj* patriotic
patron, ne [patʀɔ̃, -ɔn] *nm/f* boss; (*REL*) patron saint ♦ *nm* (*COUTURE*) pattern
patronat [patʀɔna] *nm* employers *pl*
patronner [patʀɔne] *vt* to sponsor, support
patrouille [patʀuj] *nf* patrol
patte [pat] *nf* (*jambe*) leg; (*pied: de chien, chat*) paw; (: *d'oiseau*) foot; (*languette*) strap
pâturage [pɑtyʀaʒ] *nm* pasture
pâture [pɑtyʀ] *nf* food
paume [pom] *nf* palm
paumé, e [pome] (*fam*) *nm/f* drop-out
paumer [pome] (*fam*) *vt* to lose
paupière [popjɛʀ] *nf* eyelid
pause [poz] *nf* (*arrêt*) break; (*en parlant, MUS*) pause

pauvre [povʀ(ə)] *adj* poor; **pauvreté** *nf* (*état*) poverty

pavaner [pavane]: **se ~** *vi* to strut about

pavé, e [pave] *adj* paved; cobbled ♦ *nm* (*bloc*) paving stone; cobblestone; (*pavage*) paving

pavillon [pavijɔ̃] *nm* (*de banlieue*) small (detached) house; (*kiosque*) lodge; pavilion; (*drapeau*) flag

pavoiser [pavwaze] *vi* to put out flags; (*fig*) to rejoice, exult

pavot [pavo] *nm* poppy

payant, e [pejɑ̃, -ɑ̃t] *adj* (*spectateurs etc*) paying; (*fig: entreprise*) profitable; **c'est ~** you have to pay, there is a charge

paye [pɛj] *nf* pay, wages *pl*

payer [peje] *vt* (*créancier, employé, loyer*) to pay; (*achat, réparations, fig: faute*) to pay for ♦ *vi* to pay; (*métier*) to be well-paid; (*tactique etc*) to pay off; **il me l'a fait ~ 10 F** he charged me 10 F for it; **~ qch à qn** to buy sth for sb, buy sb sth; **cela ne paie pas de mine** it doesn't look much

pays [pei] *nm* country; land; region; village; **du ~** local

paysage [peizaʒ] *nm* landscape

paysan, ne [peizɑ̃, -an] *nm/f* countryman(woman); farmer; (*péj*) peasant ♦ *adj* country *cpd*, farming; farmers'

Pays-Bas [peibɑ] *nmpl*: **les ~** the Netherlands

PC *nm* (*INFORM*) PC

PDG *sigle m* = **président directeur général**

péage [peaʒ] *nm* toll; (*endroit*) tollgate; **pont à ~** toll bridge

peau, x [po] *nf* skin; **gants de ~** fine leather gloves; **~ de chamois** (*chiffon*) chamois leather, shammy; **Peau-Rouge** *nm/f* Red Indian, redskin

péché [peʃe] *nm* sin

pêche [pɛʃ] *nf* (*sport, activité*) fishing; (*poissons pêchés*) catch; (*fruit*) peach; **~ à la ligne** (*en rivière*) angling

pécher [peʃe] *vi* (*REL*) to sin; (*fig: personne*) to err; (: *chose*) to be flawed

pêcher [peʃe] *nm* peach tree ♦ *vi* to go fishing ♦ *vt* to catch; to fish for

pécheur, eresse [peʃœʀ, peʃʀɛs] *nm/f* sinner

pêcheur [pɛʃœʀ] *nm* fisherman; angler

pécule [pekyl] *nm* savings *pl*, nest egg

pécuniaire [pekynjɛʀ] *adj* financial

pédagogie [pedagoʒi] *nf* educational methods *pl*, pedagogy; **pédagogique** *adj* educational

pédale [pedal] *nf* pedal

pédalo [pedalo] *nm* pedal-boat

pédant, e [pedɑ̃, -ɑ̃t] (*péj*) *adj* pedantic

pédestre [pedɛstʀ(ə)] *adj*: **tourisme ~** hiking

pédiatre [pedjatʀ(ə)] *nm/f* paediatrician, child specialist

pédicure [pedikyʀ] *nm/f* chiropodist

pègre [pɛgʀ(ə)] *nf* underworld

peignais *etc vb voir* **peindre; peigner**

peigne [pɛɲ] *nm* comb

peigner [peɲe] *vt* to comb (the hair of); **se ~** *vi* to comb one's hair

peignoir [peɲwaʀ] *nm* dressing gown; **~ de bain** bathrobe

peindre [pɛ̃dʀ(ə)] *vt* to paint; (*fig*) to portray, depict

peine [pɛn] *nf* (*affliction*) sorrow, sadness *no pl*; (*mal, effort*) trouble *no pl*, effort; (*difficulté*) difficulty; (*punition, châtiment*) punishment; (*JUR*) sentence; **faire de la ~ à qn** to distress *ou* upset sb; **prendre la ~ de faire** to go to the trouble of doing; **se donner de la ~** to make an effort; **ce n'est pas la ~ de faire** there's no point in doing, it's not worth doing; **à ~** scarcely, hardly, barely; **à ~ ... que** hardly ... than; **défense d'afficher sous ~ d'amende** billposters will be fined; **~ capitale** *ou* **de mort** capital punishment, death sentence; **peiner** *vi* to work hard; to struggle; (*moteur, voiture*) to labour ♦ *vt* to grieve, sadden

peintre [pɛ̃tʀ(ə)] *nm* painter; **~ en bâtiment** house painter

peinture [pɛ̃tyʀ] *nf* painting; (*couche de couleur, couleur*) paint; (*surfaces peintes: aussi: ~s*) paintwork; **"~ fraîche**" "wet paint"; **~ mate/brillante** matt/gloss paint

péjoratif, ive [peʒɔʀatif, -iv] *adj* pejorative, derogatory

pelage [pəlaʒ] *nm* coat, fur

pêle-mêle [pɛlmɛl] *adv* higgledy-piggledy

peler [pəle] *vt, vi* to peel

pèlerin [pɛlʀɛ̃] *nm* pilgrim

pelle [pɛl] *nf* shovel; (*d'enfant, de terrassier*) spade; **~ mécanique** mechanical digger

pellicule [pelikyl] *nf* film; **~s** *nfpl* (*MÉD*) dandruff *sg*

pelote [pəlɔt] *nf* (*de fil, laine*) ball; (*d'épingles*) pin cushion; **~ basque** pelota

peloton [pəlɔtɔ̃] *nm* group, squad; (*CYCLISME*) pack; **~ d'exécution** firing squad

pelotonner [pəlɔtɔne]: **se ~** *vi* to curl (o.s.) up

pelouse [pəluz] *nf* lawn

peluche [pəlyʃ] *nf*: **animal en ~** fluffy animal, soft toy

pelure [pəlyʀ] *nf* peeling, peel *no pl*

pénal, e, aux [penal, -o] *adj* penal

pénalité [penalite] *nf* penalty

penaud, e [pəno, -od] *adj* sheepish, contrite

penchant [pɑ̃ʃɑ̃] *nm* tendency, propensity; liking, fondness

pencher [pɑ̃ʃe] *vi* to tilt, lean over ♦ *vt* to tilt; **se ~** *vi* to lean over; (*se baisser*) to bend down; **se ~ sur** to bend over; (*fig: problème*) to look into; **se ~ au dehors** to lean out; **~ pour** to be inclined to favour

pendaison [pɑ̃dɛzɔ̃] *nf* hanging
pendant [pɑ̃dɑ̃] *nm*: **faire ~ à** to match; to be the counterpart of ♦ *prép* during; **~ que** while
pendentif [pɑ̃dɑ̃tif] *nm* pendant
penderie [pɑ̃dʀi] *nf* wardrobe
pendre [pɑ̃dʀ(ə)] *vt, vi* to hang; **se ~ (à)** (*se suicider*) to hang o.s. (on); **~ à** to hang (down) from; **~ qch à** to hang sth (up) on
pendule [pɑ̃dyl] *nf* clock ♦ *nm* pendulum
pénétrer [penetʀe] *vi, vt* to penetrate; **~ dans** to enter; (*suj: projectile*) to penetrate; (: *air, eau*) to come into, get into
pénible [penibl(ə)] *adj* (*astreignant*) hard; (*affligeant*) painful; (*personne, caractère*) tiresome; **~ment** *adv* with difficulty
péniche [peniʃ] *nf* barge
pénicilline [penisilin] *nf* penicillin
péninsule [penɛ̃syl] *nf* peninsula
pénis [penis] *nm* penis
pénitence [penitɑ̃s] *nf* (*repentir*) penitence; (*peine*) penance
pénitencier [penitɑ̃sje] *nm* penitentiary
pénombre [penɔ̃bʀ(ə)] *nf* half-light; darkness
pensée [pɑ̃se] *nf* thought; (*démarche, doctrine*) thinking *no pl*; (*BOT*) pansy; **en ~** in one's mind
penser [pɑ̃se] *vi* to think ♦ *vt* to think; (*concevoir: problème, machine*) to think out; **~ à** to think of; (*songer à: ami, vacances*) to think of ou about; (*réfléchir à: problème, offre*): **~ à qoh** to think about sth ou think sth over; **faire ~ à** to remind one of; **~ faire qch** to be thinking of doing sth, intend to do sth
pensif, ive [pɑ̃sif, -iv] *adj* pensive, thoughtful
pension [pɑ̃sjɔ̃] *nf* (*allocation*) pension; (*prix du logement*) board and lodgings, bed and board; (*maison particulière*) boarding house; (*hôtel*) guesthouse, hotel; (*école*) boarding school; **prendre qn en ~** to take sb (in) as a lodger; **mettre en ~** to send to boarding school; **~ alimentaire** (*d'étudiant*) living allowance; (*de divorcée*) maintenance allowance; alimony; **~ complète** full board; **~ de famille** boarding house, guesthouse; **pensionnaire** *nm/f* boarder; guest; **pensionnat** *nm* boarding school
pente [pɑ̃t] *nf* slope; **en ~** sloping
Pentecôte [pɑ̃tkot] *nf*: **la ~** Whitsun (*BRIT*), Pentecost
pénurie [penyʀi] *nf* shortage
pépé [pepe] (*fam*) *nm* grandad
pépin [pepɛ̃] *nm* (*BOT: graine*) pip; (*ennui*) snag, hitch
pépinière [pepinjɛʀ] *nf* nursery
perçant, e [pɛʀsɑ̃, -ɑ̃t] *adj* sharp, keen; piercing, shrill
percée [pɛʀse] *nf* (*trouée*) opening; (*MIL, technologique*) breakthrough; (*SPORT*)

break
perce-neige [pɛʀsənɛʒ] *nf inv* snowdrop
percepteur [pɛʀsɛptœʀ] *nm* tax collector
perception [pɛʀsɛpsjɔ̃] *nf* perception; (*d'impôts etc*) collection; (*bureau*) tax office
percer [pɛʀse] *vt* to pierce; (*ouverture etc*) to make; (*mystère, énigme*) to penetrate ♦ *vi* to come through; to break through; **~ une dent** to cut a tooth; **perceuse** *nf* drill
percevoir [pɛʀsəvwaʀ] *vt* (*distinguer*) to perceive, detect; (*taxe, impôt*) to collect; (*revenu, indemnité*) to receive
perche [pɛʀʃ(ə)] *nf* (*bâton*) pole
percher [pɛʀʃe] *vt, vi* to perch; **se ~** *vi* to perch; **perchoir** *nm* perch
perçois *etc vb voir* **percevoir**
percolateur [pɛʀkɔlatœʀ] *nm* percolator
perçu, e *pp de* **percevoir**
percussion [pɛʀkysjɔ̃] *nf* percussion
percuter [pɛʀkyte] *vt* to strike; (*suj: véhicule*) to crash into
perdant, e [pɛʀdɑ̃, -ɑ̃t] *nm/f* loser
perdition [pɛʀdisjɔ̃] *nf*: **en ~** (*NAVIG*) in distress; **lieu de ~** den of vice
perdre [pɛʀdʀ(ə)] *vt* to lose; (*gaspiller: temps, argent*) to waste; (*personne: moralement etc*) to ruin ♦ *vi* to lose; (*sur une vente etc*) to lose out; **se ~** *vi* (*s'égarer*) to get lost, lose one's way; (*fig*) to go to waste; to disappear, vanish
perdrix [pɛʀdʀi] *nf* partridge
perdu, e [pɛʀdy] *pp de* **perdre** ♦ *adj* (*isolé*) out-of-the-way; (*COMM: emballage*) non-returnable; (*malade*): **il est ~** there's no hope left for him; **à vos moments ~s** in your spare time
père [pɛʀ] *nm* father; **~s** *nmpl* (*ancêtres*) forefathers; **~ de famille** father; family man; **le ~ Noël** Father Christmas
perfectionné, e [pɛʀfɛksjɔne] *adj* sophisticated
perfectionner [pɛʀfɛksjɔne] *vt* to improve, perfect
perforatrice [pɛʀfɔʀatʀis] *nf* (*pour cartes*) card-punch; (*de bureau*) punch
perforer [pɛʀfɔʀe] *vt* to perforate; to punch a hole (*ou* holes) in; (*ticket, bande, carte*) to punch
performant, e [pɛʀfɔʀmɑ̃, -ɑ̃t] *adj*: **très ~** high-performance *cpd*
perfusion [pɛʀfyzjɔ̃] *nf*: **faire une ~ à qn** to put sb on a drip
péril [peʀil] *nm* peril
périmé, e [peʀime] *adj* (out)dated; (*ADMIN*) out-of-date, expired
périmètre [peʀimɛtʀ(ə)] *nm* perimeter
période [peʀjɔd] *nf* period; **périodique** *adj* (*phases*) periodic; (*publication*) periodical ♦ *nm* periodical
péripéties [peʀipesi] *nfpl* events, episodes
périphérique [peʀifeʀik] *adj* (*quartiers*) outlying; (*ANAT, TECH*) peripheral; (*station*

de radio) operating from outside France ♦ *nm* (*AUTO*) ring road; (*INFORM*) peripheral

périple [peʀipl(ə)] *nm* journey

périr [peʀiʀ] *vi* to die, perish

périssable [peʀisabl(ə)] *adj* perishable

perle [peʀl(ə)] *nf* pearl; (*de plastique, métal, sueur*) bead

perlé, e [peʀle] *adj*: **grève ~e** go-slow

perler [peʀle] *vi* to form in droplets

permanence [peʀmanɑ̃s] *nf* permanence; (*local*) (duty) office; emergency service; **assurer une ~** (*service public, bureaux*) to operate *ou* maintain a basic service; **être de ~** to be on call *ou* duty; **en ~** permanently; continuously

permanent, e [peʀmanɑ̃, -ɑ̃t] *adj* permanent; (*spectacle*) continuous; **permanente** *nf* perm

perméable [peʀmeabl(ə)] *adj* (*terrain*) permeable; **~ à** (*fig*) receptive *ou* open to

permettre [peʀmɛtʀ(ə)] *vt* to allow, permit; **~ à qn de faire/qch** to allow sb to do/sth; **se ~ de faire** to take the liberty of doing; **permettez!** excuse me!

permis [peʀmi] *nm* permit, licence; **~ de chasse** hunting permit; **~ (de conduire)** (driving) licence (*BRIT*), (driver's) license (*US*); **~ de construire** planning permission (*BRIT*), building permit (*US*); **~ de séjour** residence permit; **~ de travail** work permit

permission [peʀmisjɔ̃] *nf* permission; (*MIL*) leave; **avoir la ~ de faire** to have permission to do; **en ~** on leave

permuter [peʀmyte] *vt* to change around, permutate ♦ *vi* to change, swap

Pérou [peʀu] *nm* Peru

perpétuel, le [peʀpetɥɛl] *adj* perpetual; (*ADMIN etc*) permanent; for life

perpétuité [peʀpetɥite] *nf*: **à ~** *adj, adv* for life; **être condamné à ~** to receive a life sentence

perplexe [peʀplɛks(ə)] *adj* perplexed, puzzled

perquisitionner [peʀkizisjɔne] *vi* to carry out a search

perron [peʀɔ̃] *nm* steps *pl* (*in front of mansion etc*)

perroquet [peʀɔkɛ] *nm* parrot

perruche [peʀyʃ] *nf* budgerigar (*BRIT*), budgie (*BRIT*), parakeet (*US*)

perruque [peʀyk] *nf* wig

persan, e [peʀsɑ̃, -an] *adj* Persian

persécuter [peʀsekyte] *vt* to persecute

persévérer [peʀseveʀe] *vi* to persevere

persiennes [peʀsjɛn] *nfpl* (metal) shutters

persiflage [peʀsiflaʒ] *nm* mockery *no pl*

persil [peʀsi] *nm* parsley

Persique [peʀsik] *adj*: **le golfe ~** the (Persian) Gulf

persistant, e [peʀsistɑ̃, -ɑ̃t] *adj* persistent; (*feuilles*) evergreen

persister [peʀsiste] *vi* to persist; **~ à faire**

qch to persist in doing sth

personnage [peʀsɔnaʒ] *nm* (*notable*) personality; figure; (*individu*) character, individual; (*THÉÂTRE*) character; (*PEINTURE*) figure

personnalité [peʀsɔnalite] *nf* personality; (*personnage*) prominent figure

personne [peʀsɔn] *nf* person ♦ *pron* nobody, no one; (*quelqu'un*) anybody, anyone; **~s** *nfpl* (*gens*) people *pl*; **il n'y a ~** there's nobody there, there isn't anybody there; **~ âgée** elderly person; **personnel, le** *adj* personal ♦ *nm* staff, personnel; **personnellement** *adv* personally

perspective [peʀspɛktiv] *nf* (*ART*) perspective; (*vue, coup d'œil*) view; (*point de vue*) viewpoint, angle; (*chose escomptée, envisagée*) prospect; **en ~** in prospect

perspicace [peʀspikas] *adj* clear-sighted, gifted with (*ou* showing) insight

persuader [peʀsɥade] *vt*: **~ qn (de/de faire)** to persuade sb (of/to do)

perte [peʀt(ə)] *nf* loss; (*de temps*) waste; (*fig: morale*) ruin; **à ~** (*COMM*) at a loss; **à ~ de vue** as far as the eye can (*ou* could) see; **~ sèche** dead loss; **~s blanches** (vaginal) discharge *sg*

pertinemment [peʀtinamɑ̃] *adv* to the point; full well

pertinent, e [peʀtinɑ̃, -ɑ̃t] *adj* apt, relevant

perturbation [peʀtyʀbɑsjɔ̃] *nf* disruption; perturbation; **~ (atmosphérique)** atmospheric disturbance

perturber [peʀtyʀbe] *vt* to disrupt; (*PSYCH*) to perturb, disturb

pervers, e [peʀvɛʀ, -ɛʀs(ə)] *adj* perverted, depraved; perverse

pervertir [peʀvɛʀtiʀ] *vt* to pervert

pesant, e [pəzɑ̃, -ɑ̃t] *adj* heavy; (*fig*) burdensome

pesanteur [pəzɑ̃tœʀ] *nf* gravity

pèse-personne [pɛzpɛʀsɔn] *nm* (bathroom) scales *pl*

peser [pəze] *vt* to weigh ♦ *vi* to be heavy; (*fig*) to carry weight; **~ sur** (*fig*) to lie heavy on; to influence

pessimiste [pesimist(ə)] *adj* pessimistic ♦ *nm/f* pessimist

peste [pɛst(ə)] *nf* plague

pester [pɛste] *vi*: **~ contre** to curse

pétale [petal] *nm* petal

pétanque [petɑ̃k] *nf* type of bowls

pétarader [petaʀade] *vi* to backfire

pétard [petaʀ] *nm* banger (*BRIT*), firecracker

péter [pete] *vi* (*fam: casser, sauter*) to burst; to bust; (*fam!*) to fart (*!*)

pétillant, e [petijɑ̃, -ɑ̃t] *adj* (*eau etc*) sparkling

pétiller [petije] *vi* (*flamme, bois*) to crackle; (*mousse, champagne*) to bubble; (*yeux*) to sparkle

petit, e [pəti, -it] *adj* (*gén*) small; (*main, objet, colline, en âge: enfant*) small, little; (*voyage*) short, little; (*bruit etc*) faint, slight; (*mesquin*) mean; **~s** *nmpl* (*d'un animal*) young *pl*; **faire ~s** to have kittens (*ou* puppies *etc*); **les tout-petits** the little ones, the tiny tots; **~ à ~** bit by bit, gradually; **~(e) ami(e)** boyfriend/girlfriend; **~ déjeuner** breakfast; **~ pain** (bread) roll; **les ~es annonces** the small ads; **~s pois** garden peas; **~-bourgeois** (*f* **~-bourgeoise**: *péj*) *adj* middle-class; **~-fille** *nf* granddaughter; **~-fils** *nm* grandson

pétition [petisjɔ̃] *nf* petition

petits-enfants [pətizɑ̃fɑ̃] *nmpl* grandchildren

petit-suisse [pətisɥis] (*pl* **petits-suisses**) *nm* small individual pot of cream cheese

pétrin [petrɛ̃] *nm* kneading-trough; (*fig*): **dans le ~** in a jam *ou* fix

pétrir [petRiR] *vt* to knead

pétrole [petRɔl] *nm* oil; (*pour lampe, réchaud etc*) paraffin (oil); **pétrolier, ière** *adj* oil *cpd* ♦ *nm* oil tanker

──────────── *MOT CLÉ* ────────────

peu [pø] *adv* **1** (*modifiant verbe, adjectif, adverbe*): **il boit ~** he doesn't drink (very) much; **il est ~ bavard** he's not very talkative; **~ avant/après** shortly before/afterwards

2 (*modifiant nom*): **~ de: ~ de gens/d'arbres** few *ou* not (very) many people/trees; **il a ~ d'espoir** he hasn't (got) much hope, he has little hope; **pour ~ de temps** for (only) a short while

3: **~ à ~** little by little; **à ~ près** just about, more or less; **à ~ près 10 kg/10F** approximately 10 kg/10F

♦ *nm* **1**: **le ~ de gens qui** the few people who; **le ~ de sable qui** what little sand, the little sand which

2: **un ~** a little; **un petit ~** a little bit; **un ~ d'espoir** a little hope

♦ *pron*: **~ le savent** few know (it); **avant** *ou* **sous ~** shortly, before long; **de ~** (only) just

────────────────────────────────────

peuple [pœpl(ə)] *nm* people

peupler [pœple] *vt* (*pays, région*) to populate; (*étang*) to stock; (*suj: hommes, poissons*) to inhabit; (*fig: imagination, rêves*) to fill

peuplier [pøplije] *nm* poplar (tree)

peur [pœR] *nf* fear; **avoir ~ (de/de faire/que)** to be frightened *ou* afraid (of/of doing/that); **faire ~ à** to frighten; **de ~ de/que** for fear of/that; **peureux, euse** *adj* fearful, timorous

peut *vb voir* **pouvoir**

peut-être [pøtetR(ə)] *adv* perhaps, maybe; **~ que** perhaps, maybe; **~ bien qu'il fera/**

est he may well do/be

peux *etc vb voir* **pouvoir**

phare [faR] *nm* (*en mer*) lighthouse; (*de véhicule*) headlight; **mettre ses ~s** to put on one's headlights; **~s de recul** reversing lights

pharmacie [faRmasi] *nf* (*magasin*) chemist's (*BRIT*), pharmacy; (*officine*) pharmacy; (*de salle de bain*) medicine cabinet; **pharmacien, ne** *nm/f* pharmacist, chemist (*BRIT*)

phénomène [fenɔmɛn] *nm* phenomenon; (*monstre*) freak

philanthrope [filɑ̃tRɔp] *nm/f* philanthropist

philatélie [filateli] *nf* philately, stamp collecting

philosophe [filɔzɔf] *nm/f* philosopher ♦ *adj* philosophical

philosophie [filɔzɔfi] *nf* philosophy

phobie [fɔbi] *nf* phobia

phonétique [fɔnetik] *nf* phonetics *sg*

phoque [fɔk] *nm* seal; (*fourrure*) sealskin

phosphorescent, e [fɔsfɔResɑ̃, -ɑ̃t] *adj* luminous

photo [fɔto] *nf* photo(graph); **en ~** in *ou* on a photograph; **prendre en ~** to take a photo of; **aimer la/faire de la ~** to like taking/take photos; **~ d'identité** passport photograph; **~copie** *nf* photocopying; photocopy; **~copier** *vt* to photocopy; **~copieuse** [fɔtɔkɔpjøz] *nf* photocopier; **~graphe** *nm/f* photographer; **~graphie** *nf* (*procédé, technique*) photography; (*cliché*) photograph; **~graphier** *vt* to photograph

phrase [fRɑz] *nf* (*LING*) sentence; (*propos, MUS*) phrase

physicien, ne [fizisjɛ̃, -ɛn] *nm/f* physicist

physionomie [fizjɔnɔmi] *nf* face

physique [fizik] *adj* physical ♦ *nm* physique ♦ *nf* physics *sg*; **au ~** physically; **~ment** *adv* physically

piaffer [pjafe] *vi* to stamp

piailler [pjɑje] *vi* to squawk

pianiste [pjanist(ə)] *nm/f* pianist

piano [pjano] *nm* piano

pianoter [pjanɔte] *vi* to tinkle away (at the piano); (*tapoter*): **~ sur** to drum one's fingers on

pic [pik] *nm* (*instrument*) pick(axe); (*montagne*) peak; (*ZOOL*) woodpecker; **à ~** vertically; (*fig*) just at the right time

pichet [piʃɛ] *nm* jug

picorer [pikɔRe] *vt* to peck

picoter [pikɔte] *vt* (*suj: oiseau*) to peck ♦ *vi* (*irriter*) to smart, prickle

pie [pi] *nf* magpie; (*fig*) chatterbox

pièce [pjɛs] *nf* (*d'un logement*) room; (*THÉÂTRE*) play; (*de mécanisme, machine*) part; (*de monnaie*) coin; (*COUTURE*) patch; (*document*) document; (*de drap, fragment, de collection*) piece; **dix francs ~** ten francs each; **vendre à la ~** to sell separately; **travailler/payer à la ~** to do piecework/

pay piece rate; **un maillot une** ~ a one-piece swimsuit; **un deux-pièces cuisine** a two-room(ed) flat (*BRIT*) *ou* apartment (*US*) with kitchen; ~ **à conviction** exhibit; ~ **d'eau** ornamental lake *ou* pond; ~ **d'identité: avez-vous une** ~ **d'identité?** have you got any (means of) identification?; ~ **montée** tiered cake; **~s détachées** spares, (spare) parts; **~s justificatives** supporting documents

pied [pje] *nm* foot; (*de verre*) stem; (*de table*) leg; (*de lampe*) base; (*plante*) plant; **à** ~ on foot; **à** ~ **sec** without getting one's feet wet; **au** ~ **de la lettre** literally; **de** ~ **en cap** from head to foot; **en** ~ (*portrait*) full-length; **avoir** ~ to be able to touch the bottom, not to be out of one's depth; **avoir le** ~ **marin** to be a good sailor; **sur** ~ (*debout, rétabli*) up and about; **mettre sur** ~ (*entreprise*) to set up; **mettre à** ~ to dismiss; to lay off; ~ **de vigne** vine

piédestal, aux [pjedɛstal, -o] *nm* pedestal

pied-noir [pjenwaʀ] *nm* Algerian-born Frenchman

piège [pjɛʒ] *nm* trap; **prendre au** ~ to trap; **piéger** *vt* (*avec une bombe*) to booby-trap; **lettre/voiture piégée** letter-/car-bomb

pierraille [pjɛʀɑj] *nf* loose stones *pl*

pierre [pjɛʀ] *nf* stone; ~ **à briquet** flint; ~ **fine** semiprecious stone; ~ **tombale** tombstone; **pierreries** [pjɛʀʀi] *nfpl* gems, precious stones

piétiner [pjetine] *vi* (*trépigner*) to stamp (one's foot); (*marquer le pas*) to stand about; (*fig*) to be at a standstill ♦ *vt* to trample on

piéton, ne [pjetɔ̃, -ɔn] *nm/f* pedestrian; **piétonnier, ière** *adj*: **rue** *ou* **zone piétonnière** pedestrian precinct

pieu, x [pjø] *nm* post; (*pointu*) stake

pieuvre [pjœvʀ(ə)] *nf* octopus

pieux, euse [pjø, -øz] *adj* pious

piffer [pife] (*fam*) *vt*: **je ne peux pas le** ~ I can't stand him

pigeon [piʒɔ̃] *nm* pigeon

piger [piʒe] (*fam*) *vi, vt* to understand

pigiste [piʒist(ə)] *nm/f* freelance(r)

pignon [piɲɔ̃] *nm* (*de mur*) gable; (*d'engrenage*) cog(wheel), gearwheel

pile [pil] *nf* (*tas*) pile; (*ÉLEC*) battery ♦ *adv* (*s'arrêter etc*) dead; **à deux heures** ~ at two on the dot; **jouer à** ~ *ou* **face** to toss up (for it); ~ *ou* **face?** heads or tails?

piler [pile] *vt* to crush, pound

pileux, euse [pilø, -øz] *adj*: **système** ~ (body) hair

pilier [pilje] *nm* pillar

piller [pije] *vt* to pillage, plunder, loot

pilon [pilɔ̃] *nm* pestle

pilote [pilɔt] *nm* (*de char, voiture*) driver ♦ *adj* pilot *cpd*; ~ **de course** racing driver; ~ **de ligne/d'essai/de chasse** air-

line/test/fighter pilot; **~r** [pilɔte] *vt* to pilot, fly; to drive

pilule [pilyl] *nf* pill; **prendre la** ~ to be on the pill

piment [pimɑ̃] *nm* (*BOT*) pepper, capsicum; (*fig*) spice, piquancy

pimpant, e [pɛ̃pɑ̃, -ɑ̃t] *adj* spruce

pin [pɛ̃] *nm* pine (tree); (*bois*) pine(wood)

pinard [pinaʀ] (*fam*) *nm* (cheap) wine, plonk (*BRIT*)

pince [pɛ̃s] *nf* (*outil*) pliers *pl*; (*de homard, crabe*) pincer, claw; (*COUTURE: pli*) dart; ~ **à épiler** tweezers *pl*; ~ **à linge** clothes peg (*BRIT*) *ou* pin (*US*); ~ **à sucre** sugar tongs *pl*

pincé, e [pɛ̃se] *adj* (*air*) stiff

pinceau, x [pɛ̃so] *nm* (paint)brush

pincée [pɛ̃se] *nf*: **une** ~ **de** a pinch of

pincer [pɛ̃se] *vt* to pinch; (*MUS: cordes*) to pluck; (*fam*) to nab

pincettes [pɛ̃sɛt] *nfpl* (*pour le feu*) (fire) tongs

pinède [pinɛd] *nf* pinewood, pine forest

pingouin [pɛ̃gwɛ̃] *nm* penguin

ping-pong [piŋpɔ̃g] ® *nm* table tennis

pingre [pɛ̃gʀ(ə)] *adj* niggardly

pinson [pɛ̃sɔ̃] *nm* chaffinch

pintade [pɛ̃tad] *nf* guinea-fowl

pioche [pjɔʃ] *nf* pickaxe; **piocher** *vt* to dig up (with a pickaxe)

piolet [pjɔlɛ] *nm* ice axe

pion [pjɔ̃] *nm* (*ÉCHECS*) pawn; (*DAMES*) piece

pionnier [pjɔnje] *nm* pioneer

pipe [pip] *nf* pipe

pipeau, x [pipo] *nm* (reed-)pipe

piquant, e [pikɑ̃, -ɑ̃t] *adj* (*barbe, rosier etc*) prickly; (*saveur, sauce*) hot, pungent; (*fig*) racy; biting ♦ *nm* (*épine*) thorn, prickle; (*fig*) spiciness, spice

pique [pik] *nf* pike; (*fig*) cutting remark ♦ *nm* (*CARTES: couleur*) spades *pl*; (: *carte*) spade

pique-nique [piknik] *nm* picnic

piquer [pike] *vt* (*percer*) to prick; (*planter*): ~ **qch dans** to stick sth into; (*MÉD*) to give a jab to; (: *animal blessé etc*) to put to sleep; (*suj: insecte, fumée, ortie*) to sting; (: *poivre*) to burn; (: *froid*) to bite; (*COUTURE*) to machine (stitch); (*intérêt etc*) to arouse; (*fam*) to pick up; (: *voler*) to pinch; (: *arrêter*) to nab ♦ *vi* (*avion*) to go into a dive; **se** ~ **de faire** to pride o.s. on doing; ~ **un galop/un cent mètres** to break into a gallop/put on a sprint

piquet [pike] *nm* (*pieu*) post, stake; (*de tente*) peg; ~ **de grève** (strike-) picket; ~ **d'incendie** fire-fighting squad

piqûre [pikyʀ] *nf* (*d'épingle*) prick; (*d'ortie*) sting; (*de moustique*) bite; (*MÉD*) injection, shot (*US*); (*COUTURE*) (straight) stitch; straight stitching; **faire une** ~ **à qn** to give sb an injection

pirate [piʀat] *nm, adj* pirate; ~ **de l'air** hijacker

pire [piʀ] *adj* worse; *(superlatif)*: **le(la)** ~ ... the worst ... ♦ *nm*: **le** ~ **(de)** the worst (of)

pis [pi] *nm (de vache)* udder; *(pire)*: **le** ~ the worst ♦ *adj, adv* worse; ~-**aller** *nm inv* stopgap

piscine [pisin] *nf* (swimming) pool; ~ **couverte** indoor (swimming) pool

pissenlit [pisɑ̃li] *nm* dandelion

pistache [pistaʃ] *nf* pistachio (nut)

piste [pist(ə)] *nf (d'un animal, sentier)* track, trail; *(indice)* lead; *(de stade, de magnétophone)* track; *(de cirque)* ring; *(de danse)* floor; *(de patinage)* rink; *(de ski)* run; *(AVIAT)* runway; ~ **cyclable** cycle track

pistolet [pistɔlɛ] *nm (arme)* pistol, gun; *(à peinture)* spray gun; ~ **à air comprimé** airgun; ~-**mitrailleur** *nm* submachine gun

piston [pistɔ̃] *nm (TECH)* piston; **pistonner** *vt (candidat)* to pull strings for

piteux, euse [pitø, -øz] *adj* pitiful *(avant le nom)*, sorry *(avant le nom)*

pitié [pitje] *nf* pity; **faire** ~ to inspire pity; **avoir** ~ **de** *(compassion)* to pity, feel sorry for; *(merci)* to have pity *ou* mercy on

piton [pitɔ̃] *nm (clou)* peg; ~ **rocheux** rocky outcrop

pitoyable [pitwajabl(ə)] *adj* pitiful

pitre [pitʀ(ə)] *nm* clown; **pitrerie** *nf* tomfoolery *no pl*

pittoresque [pitɔʀɛsk(ə)] *adj* picturesque

pivot [pivo] *nm* pivot; **pivoter** *vi* to swivel; to revolve

P.J. *sigle f (= police judiciaire)* ≈ CID *(BRIT)*, ≈ FBI *(US)*

placard [plakaʀ] *nm (armoire)* cupboard; *(affiche)* poster, notice; ~**er** *vt (affiche)* to put up

place [plas] *nf (emplacement, situation, classement)* place; *(de ville, village)* square; *(espace libre)* room, space; *(de parking)* space; *(siège: de train, cinéma, voiture)* seat; *(emploi)* job; **en** ~ *(mettre)* in its place; **sur** ~ on the spot; **faire** ~ **à** to give way to; **faire de la** ~ **à** to make room for; **ça prend de la** ~ it takes up a lot of room *ou* space; **à la** ~ **de** in place of, instead of; **il y a 20** ~**s assises/debout** there are 20 seats/there is standing room for 20

placement [plasmɑ̃] *nm* placing; *(FINANCE)* investment; **bureau de** ~ employment agency

placer [plase] *vt* to place; *(convive, spectateur)* to seat; *(capital, argent)* to place, invest; *(dans la conversation)* to put *ou* get in; **se** ~ **au premier rang** to go and stand *(ou* sit) in the first row

plafond [plafɔ̃] *nm* ceiling

plafonner [plafɔne] *vi* to reach one's *(ou* a) ceiling

plage [plaʒ] *nf* beach; *(fig)* band, bracket; *(de disque)* track, band; ~ **arrière** *(AUTO)* parcel *ou* back shelf

plagiat [plaʒja] *nm* plagiarism

plaider [plede] *vi (avocat)* to plead; *(plaignant)* to go to court, litigate ♦ *vt* to plead; ~ **pour** *(fig)* to speak for; **plaidoyer** *nm* *(JUR)* speech for the defence; *(fig)* plea

plaie [plɛ] *nf* wound

plaignant, e [plɛɲɑ̃, -ɑ̃t] *nm/f* plaintiff

plaindre [plɛ̃dʀ(ə)] *vt* to pity, feel sorry for; **se** ~ *vi (gémir)* to moan; *(protester, rouspéter)*: **se** ~ **(à qn) (de)** to complain (to sb) (about); *(souffrir)*: **se** ~ **de** to complain of

plaine [plɛn] *nf* plain

plain-pied [plɛ̃pje] *adv*: **de** ~ **(avec)** on the same level (as)

plainte [plɛ̃t] *nf (gémissement)* moan, groan; *(doléance)* complaint; **porter** ~ to lodge a complaint

plaire [plɛʀ] *vi* to be a success, be successful; to please; ~ **à**: **cela me plaît** I like it; **se** ~ **quelque part** to like being somewhere *ou* like it somewhere; **s'il vous plaît** please

plaisance [plɛzɑ̃s] *nf (aussi: navigation de ~)* (pleasure) sailing, yachting

plaisant, e [plɛzɑ̃, -ɑ̃t] *adj* pleasant; *(histoire, anecdote)* amusing

plaisanter [plɛzɑ̃te] *vi* to joke; **plaisanterie** *nf* joke; joking *no pl*

plaise *etc vb voir* **plaire**

plaisir [plɛziʀ] *nm* pleasure; **faire** ~ **à qn** *(délibérément)* to be nice to sb, please sb; *(suj: cadeau, nouvelle etc)*: **ceci me fait** ~ I'm delighted *ou* very pleased with this; **pour le** *ou* **par** ~ for pleasure

plaît *vb voir* **plaire**

plan, e [plɑ̃, -an] *adj* flat ♦ *nm* plan; *(GÉOM)* plane; *(fig)* level, plane; *(CINEMA)* shot; **au premier/second** ~ in the foreground/middle distance; **à l'arrière** ~ in the background; ~ **d'eau** lake; pond

planche [plɑ̃ʃ] *nf (pièce de bois)* plank, (wooden) board; *(illustration)* plate; **les** ~**s** *nfpl (THÉÂTRE)* the stage *sg*, the boards; ~ **à repasser** ironing board; ~ **à roulettes** skateboard; ~ **de salut** *(fig)* sheet anchor

plancher [plɑ̃ʃe] *nm* floor; floorboards *pl*; *(fig)* minimum level ♦ *vi* to work hard

planer [plane] *vi* to glide; ~ **sur** *(fig)* to hang over; to hover above

planète [planɛt] *nf* planet

planeur [planœʀ] *nm* glider

planification [planifikasjɔ̃] *nf* (economic) planning

planifier [planifje] *vt* to plan

planning [planiŋ] *nm* programme, schedule; ~ **familial** family planning

planque [plɑ̃k] *(fam) nf (emploi peu fatigant)* cushy *(BRIT) ou* easy number; *(cachette)* hiding place

plant [plɑ̃] *nm* seedling, young plant

plante [plɑ̃t] *nf* plant; ~ **d'appartement** house *ou* pot plant; ~ **du pied** sole (of the foot)

planter [plɑ̃te] *vt* (*plante*) to plant; (*enfoncer*) to hammer *ou* drive in; (*tente*) to put up, pitch; (*fam*) to dump; to ditch; **se** ~ (*fam: se tromper*) to get it wrong

plantureux, euse [plɑ̃tyʀø, -øz] *adj* copious, lavish; (*femme*) buxom

plaque [plak] *nf* plate; (*de verglas, d'eczéma*) patch; (*avec inscription*) plaque; ~ **chauffante** hotplate; ~ **de chocolat** bar of chocolate; ~ (**minéralogique** *ou* **d'immatriculation**) number (*BRIT*) *ou* license (*US*) plate; ~ **tournante** (*fig*) centre

plaqué, e [plake] *adj:* ~ **or/argent** gold-/silver-plated; ~ **acajou** veneered in mahogany

plaquer [plake] *vt* (*aplatir*); ~ **qch sur** *ou* **contre** to make sth stick *ou* cling to; (*RUGBY*) to bring down; (*fam: laisser tomber*) to drop

plaquette [plakɛt] *nf* (*de chocolat*) bar; (*beurre*) pack(et)

plastic [plastik] *nm* plastic explosive

plastique [plastik] *adj, nm* plastic

plastiquer [plastike] *vt* to blow up (*with a plastic bomb*)

plat, e [pla, -at] *adj* flat; (*cheveux*) straight; (*personne, livre*) dull ♦ *nm* (*récipient, CULIN*) dish; (*d'un repas*): **le premier** ~ the first course; **à** ~ **ventre** face down; **à** ~ (*pneu, batterie*) flat; (*personne*) dead beat; ~ **cuisiné** pre-cooked meal; ~ **de résistance** main course; ~ **du jour** dish of the day

platane [platan] *nm* plane tree

plateau, x [plato] *nm* (*support*) tray; (*GÉO*) plateau; (*de tourne-disques*) turntable; (*CINÉMA*) set; ~ **à fromages** cheeseboard

plate-bande [platbɑ̃d] *nf* flower bed

plate-forme [platfɔʀm(ə)] *nf* platform; ~ **de forage/pétrolière** drilling/oil rig

platine [platin] *nm* platinum ♦ *nf* (*d'un tourne-disque*) turntable

plâtras [plɑtʀa] *nm* rubble *no pl*

plâtre [plɑtʀ(ə)] *nm* (*matériau*) plaster; (*statue*) plaster statue; (*MÉD*) (plaster) cast; **avoir un bras dans le** ~ to have an arm in plaster

plein, e [plɛ̃, -ɛn] *adj* full; (*porte, roue*) solid; (*chienne, jument*) big (with young) ♦ *nm*: **faire le** ~ (**d'essence**) to fill up (with petrol); **à** ~**es mains** (*ramasser*) in handfuls; (*empoigner*) firmly; **à** ~ **régime** at maximum revs; (*fig*) full steam; **à** ~ **temps** full-time; **en** ~ **air** in the open air; **en** ~ **soleil** in direct sunlight; **en** ~**e nuit/rue** in the middle of the night/street; **en** ~ **jour** in broad daylight; **en** ~ **sur** right on; **plein-emploi** *nm* full employment

plénitude [plenityd] *nf* fullness

pleurer [plœʀe] *vi* to cry; (*yeux*) to water ♦ *vt* to mourn (for); ~ **sur** to lament (over), to bemoan

pleurnicher [plœʀniʃe] *vi* to snivel, whine

pleurs [plœʀ] *nmpl*: **en** ~ in tears

pleut *vb voir* **pleuvoir**

pleuvoir [pløvwaʀ] *vb impers* to rain ♦ *vi* (*fig*): ~ (**sur**) to shower down (upon); to be showered upon; **il pleut** it's raining

pli [pli] *nm* fold; (*de jupe*) pleat; (*de pantalon*) crease; (*aussi: faux* ~) crease; (*enveloppe*) envelope; (*lettre*) letter; (*CARTES*) trick

pliant, e [plijɑ̃, -ɑ̃t] *adj* folding ♦ *nm* folding stool, campstool

plier [plije] *vt* to fold; (*pour ranger*) to fold up; (*table pliante*) to fold down; (*genou, bras*) to bend ♦ *vi* to bend; (*fig*) to yield; **se** ~ **à** to submit to

plinthe [plɛ̃t] *nf* skirting board

plisser [plise] *vt* (*rider, chiffonner*) to crease; (*jupe*) to put pleats in

plomb [plɔ̃] *nm* (*métal*) lead; (*d'une cartouche*) (lead) shot; (*PÊCHE*) sinker; (*sceau*) (lead) seal; (*ÉLEC*) fuse; **sans** ~ (*essence etc*) unleaded

plombage [plɔ̃baʒ] *nm* (*de dent*) filling

plomber [plɔ̃be] *vt* (*canne, ligne*) to weight (with lead); (*dent*) to fill

plomberie [plɔ̃bʀi] *nf* plumbing

plombier [plɔ̃bje] *nm* plumber

plongeant, e [plɔ̃ʒɑ̃, -ɑ̃t] *adj* (*vue*) from above; (*tir, décolleté*) plunging

plongée [plɔ̃ʒe] *nf* (*SPORT*) diving *no pl*; (: *sans scaphandre*) skin diving

plongeoir [plɔ̃ʒwaʀ] *nm* diving board

plongeon [plɔ̃ʒɔ̃] *nm* dive

plonger [plɔ̃ʒe] *vi* to dive ♦ *vt:* ~ **qch dans** to plunge sth into

ployer [plwaje] *vt* to bend ♦ *vi* to sag; to bend

plu *pp de* **plaire; pleuvoir**

pluie [plɥi] *nf* rain; (*fig*): ~ **de** shower of

plume [plym] *nf* feather; (*pour écrire*) (pen) nib; (*fig*) pen; ~**r** [plyme] *vt* to pluck; **plumier** [plymje] *nm* pencil box

plupart [plypaʀ]: **la** ~ *pron* the majority, most (of them); **la** ~ **des** most, the majority of; **la** ~ **du temps/d'entre nous** most of the time/of us; **pour la** ~ for the most part, mostly

pluriel [plyʀjɛl] *nm* plural

plus¹ [ply] *vb voir* **plaire**

─────────── *MOT CLÉ*

plus² [ply] *adv* **1** (*forme négative*): **ne ...** ~ no more, no longer; **je n'ai** ~ **d'argent** I've got no more money *ou* no money left; **il ne travaille** ~ he's no longer working, he doesn't work any more

2 [ply, plyz, + *voyelle*] (*comparatif*) more, ...+er; (*superlatif*): **le** ~ the most, the

...+est; ~ **grand/intelligent (que)** bigger/ more intelligent (than); **le ~ grand/ intelligent** the biggest/most intelligent; **tout au ~** at the very most
3 [plys] (*davantage*) more; **il travaille ~ (que)** he works more (than); **~ il travaille, ~ il est heureux** the more he works, the happier he is; **~ de** pain more bread; **~ de 10 personnes** more than 10 people, over 10 people; **3 heures de ~ que** 3 hours more than; **de ~** what's more, moreover; **3 kilos en ~** 3 kilos more; **en ~ de** in addition to; **de ~ en ~** more and more; **~ ou moins** more or less; **ni ~ ni moins** no more, no less

♦ *prép* [plys]: **4 ~ 2** 4 plus 2

plusieurs [plyzjœʀ] *dét, pron* several; **ils sont ~** there are several of them
plus-que-parfait [plyskəpaʀfɛ] *nm* pluperfect, past perfect
plus-value [plyvaly] *nf* appreciation; capital gain; surplus
plut *vb voir* **plaire**
plutôt [plyto] *adv* rather; **je ferais ~ ceci** I'd rather *ou* sooner do this; **fais ~ comme ça** try this way instead, you'd better try this way; **~ que (de) faire** rather than *ou* instead of doing
pluvieux, euse [plyvjø, -øz] *adj* rainy, wet
PMU *sigle m* (= *pari mutuel urbain*) system of betting on horses; (*café*) betting agency
pneu [pnø] *nm* tyre (*BRIT*), tire (*US*)
pneumatique [pnømatik] *nm* tyre (*BRIT*), tire (*US*)
pneumonie [pnømɔni] *nf* pneumonia
poche [pɔʃ] *nf* pocket; (*déformation*): **faire une** *ou* **des ~(s)** to bag; (*sous les yeux*) bag, pouch; **de ~** pocket *cpd*
pocher [pɔʃe] *vt* (*CULIN*) to poach
pochette [pɔʃɛt] *nf* (*de timbres*) wallet, envelope; (*d'aiguilles etc*) case; (*mouchoir*) breast pocket handkerchief; **~ de disque** record sleeve
poêle [pwal] *nm* stove ♦ *nf*: **~ (à frire)** frying pan
poêlon [pwalɔ̃] *nm* casserole
poème [pɔɛm] *nm* poem
poésie [pɔezi] *nf* (*poème*) poem; (*art*): **la ~** poetry
poète [pɔɛt] *nm* poet
poids [pwa] *nm* weight; (*SPORT*) shot; **vendre au ~** to sell by weight; **prendre du ~** to put on weight; **~ lourd** (*camion*) lorry (*BRIT*), truck (*US*)
poignard [pwaɲaʀ] *nm* dagger; **~er** *vt* to stab, knife
poigne [pwaɲ] *nf* grip; (*fig*): **à ~** firm-handed
poignée [pwaɲe] *nf* (*de sel etc, fig*) handful; (*de couvercle, porte*) handle; **~ de main** handshake

poignet [pwaɲɛ] *nm* (*ANAT*) wrist; (*de chemise*) cuff
poil [pwal] *nm* (*ANAT*) hair; (*de pinceau, brosse*) bristle; (*de tapis*) strand; (*pelage*) coat; **à ~** (*fam*) starkers; **au ~** (*fam*) hunky-dory; **poilu, e** *adj* hairy
poinçon [pwɛ̃sɔ̃] *nm* awl; bodkin; (*marque*) hallmark; **poinçonner** *vt* to stamp; to hallmark; (*billet*) to punch
poing [pwɛ̃] *nm* fist
point [pwɛ̃] *nm* (*marque, signe*) dot; (: *de ponctuation*) full stop, period (*US*); (*moment, de score etc, fig*: *question*) point; (*endroit*) spot; (*COUTURE, TRICOT*) stitch ♦ *adv* = **pas**; **faire le ~** (*NAVIG*) to take a bearing; (*fig*) to take stock (of the situation); **en tout ~** in every respect; **sur le ~ de faire** (just) about to do; **à tel ~ que** so much so that; **mettre au ~** (*mécanisme, procédé*) to develop; (*appareil-photo*) to focus; (*affaire*) to settle; **à ~** (*CULIN*) medium; just right; **à ~ (nommé)** just at the right time; **~ (de côté)** (*pain*); **~ d'eau** spring; water point; **~ d'exclamation** exclamation mark; **~ d'interrogation** question mark; **~ de repère** landmark; (*dans le temps*) point of reference; **~ de vente** retail outlet; **~ de vue** viewpoint; (*fig*: *opinion*) point of view; **~ faible** weak point; **~ final** full stop, period; **~ mort** (*AUTO*): **au ~ mort** in neutral; **~s de suspension** suspension points
pointe [pwɛ̃t] *nf* point; (*fig*): **une ~ de** a hint of; **être à la ~ de** (*fig*) to be in the forefront of; **sur la ~ des pieds** on tiptoe; **en ~** *adv* (*tailler*) into a point ♦ *adj* pointed, tapered; **de ~** (*technique etc*) leading; **heures/jours de ~** peak hours/days; **~ de vitesse** burst of speed
pointer [pwɛ̃te] *vt* (*cocher*) to tick off; (*employés etc*) to check in; (*diriger: canon, doigt*): **~ vers qch** to point at sth ♦ *vi* (*employé*) to clock in
pointillé [pwɛ̃tije] *nm* (*trait*) dotted line
pointilleux, euse [pwɛ̃tijø, -øz] *adj* particular, pernickety
pointu, e [pwɛ̃ty] *adj* pointed; (*clou*) sharp; (*voix*) shrill; (*analyse*) precise
pointure [pwɛ̃tyʀ] *nf* size
point-virgule [pwɛ̃viʀgyl] *nm* semi-colon
poire [pwaʀ] *nf* pear; (*fam: péj*) mug
poireau, x [pwaʀo] *nm* leek
poirier [pwaʀje] *nm* pear tree
pois [pwa] *nm* (*BOT*) pea; (*sur une étoffe*) dot, spot; **à ~** (*cravate etc*) spotted, polka-dot *cpd*
poison [pwazɔ̃] *nm* poison
poisse [pwas] *nf* rotten luck
poisseux, euse [pwaso, -øz] *adj* sticky
poisson [pwasɔ̃] *nm* fish *gén inv*; **les P~s** (*signe*) Pisces; **~ d'avril!** April fool!; **~ rouge** goldfish; **poissonnerie** *nf* fish-shop;

poissonnier, ière *nm/f* fishmonger (*BRIT*), fish merchant (*US*)

poitrine [pwatʀin] *nf* chest; (*seins*) bust, bosom; (*CULIN*) breast; ~ **de bœuf** brisket

poivre [pwavʀ(ə)] *nm* pepper; **poivrier** *nm* (*ustensile*) pepperpot

poivron [pwavʀɔ̃] *nm* pepper, capsicum

polar [pɔlaʀ] *nm* (*fam*) detective novel

pôle [pol] *nm* (*GÉO, ÉLEC*) pole

poli, e [pɔli] *adj* polite; (*lisse*) smooth; polished

police [pɔlis] *nf* police; **peine de simple ~** *sentence given by magistrates' or police court*; ~ **d'assurance** insurance policy; ~ **des mœurs** ≈ vice squad; ~ **judiciaire** ≈ Criminal Investigation Department (*BRIT*), ≈ Federal Bureau of Investigation (*US*); ~ **secours** ≈ emergency services *pl* (*BRIT*), ≈ paramedics *pl* (*US*)

policier, ière [pɔlisje, -jɛʀ] *adj* police *cpd* ♦ *nm* policeman; (*aussi: roman ~*) detective novel

polio [pɔljo] *nf* polio

polir [pɔliʀ] *vt* to polish

polisson, ne [pɔlisɔ̃, -ɔn] *adj* naughty

politesse [pɔlitɛs] *nf* politeness

politicien, ne [pɔlitisjɛ̃, -ɛn] *nm/f* politician

politique [pɔlitik] *adj* political ♦ *nf* (*science, pratique, activité*) politics *sg*; (*mesures, méthode*) policies *pl*; **politiser** *vt* to politicize

pollen [pɔlɛn] *nm* pollen

pollution [pɔlysjɔ̃] *nf* pollution

polo [pɔlo] *nm* polo shirt

Pologne [pɔlɔɲ] *nf*: **la ~** Poland; **polonais, e** *adj, nm* (*LING*) Polish; **Polonais, e** *nm/f* Pole

poltron, ne [pɔltʀɔ̃, -ɔn] *adj* cowardly

polycopier [pɔlikɔpje] *vt* to duplicate

Polynésie [pɔlinezi] *nf*: **la ~** Polynesia

polyvalent, e [pɔlivalɑ̃, -ɑ̃t] *adj* versatile; multi-purpose

pommade [pɔmad] *nf* ointment, cream

pomme [pɔm] *nf* (*BOT*) apple; **tomber dans les ~s** (*fam*) to pass out; ~ **d'Adam** Adam's apple; ~ **d'arrosoir** (sprinkler) rose; ~ **de pin** pine ou fir cone; ~ **de terre** potato

pommeau, x [pɔmo] *nm* (*boule*) knob; (*de selle*) pommel

pommette [pɔmɛt] *nf* cheekbone

pommier [pɔmje] *nm* apple tree

pompe [pɔ̃p] *nf* pump; (*faste*) pomp (and ceremony); ~ **à essence** petrol (*BRIT*) ou gas (*US*) pump; ~**s funèbres** funeral parlour *sg*, undertaker's *sg*

pomper [pɔ̃pe] *vt* to pump; (*évacuer*) to pump out; (*aspirer*) to pump up; (*absorber*) to soak up

pompeux, euse [pɔ̃pø, -øz] *adj* pompous

pompier [pɔ̃pje] *nm* fireman

pompiste [pɔ̃pist(ə)] *nm/f* petrol (*BRIT*) ou gas (*US*) pump attendant

poncer [pɔ̃se] *vt* to sand (down)

ponctuation [pɔ̃ktɥasjɔ̃] *nf* punctuation

ponctuel, le [pɔ̃ktɥɛl] *adj* (*à l'heure, aussi TECH*) punctual; (*fig: opération etc*) one-off, single; (*scrupuleux*) punctilious, meticulous

ponctuer [pɔ̃ktɥe] *vt* to punctuate

pondéré, e [pɔ̃deʀe] *adj* level-headed, composed

pondre [pɔ̃dʀ(ə)] *vt* to lay; (*fig*) to produce

poney [pɔnɛ] *nm* pony

pont [pɔ̃] *nm* bridge; (*AUTO*) axle; (*NAVIG*) deck; **faire le ~** to take the extra day off; ~ **de graissage** ramp (*in garage*); ~ **suspendu** suspension bridge; **P~s et Chaussées** highways department

pont-levis [pɔ̃lvi] *nm* drawbridge

pop [pɔp] *adj inv* pop

populace [pɔpylas] (*péj*) *nf* rabble

populaire [pɔpylɛʀ] *adj* popular; (*manifestation*) mass *cpd*; (*milieux, clientèle*) working-class

population [pɔpylasjɔ̃] *nf* population; ~ **active** *nf* working population

populeux, euse [pɔpylø, -øz] *adj* densely populated

porc [pɔʀ] *nm* (*ZOOL*) pig; (*CULIN*) pork; (*peau*) pigskin

porcelaine [pɔʀsəlɛn] *nf* porcelain, china; piece of china(ware)

porc-épic [pɔʀkepik] *nm* porcupine

porche [pɔʀʃ(ə)] *nm* porch

porcherie [pɔʀʃəʀi] *nf* pigsty

pore [pɔʀ] *nm* pore

porno [pɔʀno] *adj abr* pornographic, porno

port [pɔʀ] *nm* (*NAVIG*) harbour, port; (*ville*) port; (*de l'uniforme etc*) wearing; (*pour lettre*) postage; (*pour colis, aussi: posture*) carriage; ~ **d'arme** (*JUR*) carrying of a firearm

portable [pɔʀtabl(ə)] *nm* (*COMPUT*) laptop (computer)

portail [pɔʀtaj] *nm* gate; (*de cathédrale*) portal

portant, e [pɔʀtɑ̃, -ɑ̃t] *adj*: **bien/mal ~** in good/poor health

portatif, ive [pɔʀtatif, -iv] *adj* portable

porte [pɔʀt(ə)] *nf* door; (*de ville, forteresse, SKI*) gate; **mettre à la ~** to throw out; ~ **à ~** *nm* door-to-door selling; ~ **d'entrée** front door; ~**-à-faux** *nm*: **en ~-à-faux** cantilevered; (*fig*) in an awkward position; ~**-avions** *nm inv* aircraft carrier; ~**-bagages** *nm inv* luggage rack; ~**-clefs** *nm inv* key ring; ~**-documents** *nm inv* attaché ou document case

portée [pɔʀte] *nf* (*d'une arme*) range; (*fig*) impact, import; scope, capability; (*de chatte etc*) litter; (*MUS*) stave, staff; **à/hors de (de)** within/out of reach (of); **à ~ de (la) main** within (arm's) reach; **à ~ de voix**

within earshot; **à la ~ de qn** (*fig*) at sb's level, within sb's capabilities

porte: **~-fenêtre** *nf* French window; **~feuille** *nm* wallet; (*POL, BOURSE*) portfolio; **~-jarretelles** *nm inv* suspender belt; **~-manteau, x** *nm* coat hanger; coat rack; **~-mine** *nm* propelling (*BRIT*) *ou* mechanical (*US*) pencil; **~-monnaie** *nm inv* purse; **~-parole** *nm inv* spokesman

porter [pɔʀte] *vt* to carry; (*sur soi: vêtement, barbe, bague*) to wear; (*fig: responsabilité etc*) to bear, carry; (*inscription, marque, titre, patronyme: suj: arbre, fruits, fleurs*) to bear; (*apporter*): **~ qch quelque part/à** qn to take sth somewhere/to sb ♦ *vi* (*voix, regard, canon*) to carry; (*coup, argument*) to hit home; **~** ♦ *vi* (*se sentir*): **se ~ bien/mal** to be well/unwell; **~ sur** (*peser*) to rest on; (*accent*) to fall on; (*conférence etc*) to concern; (*heurter*) to strike; **être porté à faire** to be apt *ou* inclined to do; **se faire ~ malade** to report sick; **~ la main à son chapeau** to raise one's hand to one's hat; **~ son effort sur** to direct one's efforts towards; **~ à croire** to lead one to believe

porte-serviettes [pɔʀtsɛʀvjɛt] *nm inv* towel rail

porteur [pɔʀtœʀ] *nm* (*de bagages*) porter; (*de chèque*) bearer

porte-voix [pɔʀtəvwa] *nm inv* megaphone

portier [pɔʀtje] *nm* doorman

portière [pɔʀtjɛʀ] *nf* door

portillon [pɔʀtijɔ̃] *nm* gate

portion [pɔʀsjɔ̃] *nf* (*part*) portion, share; (*partie*) portion, section

portique [pɔʀtik] *nm* (*RAIL*) gantry

porto [pɔʀto] *nm* port (wine)

portrait [pɔʀtʀɛ] *nm* portrait; photograph; **portrait-robot** *nm* Identikit ® *ou* photofit ® picture

portuaire [pɔʀtɥɛʀ] *adj* port *cpd*, harbour *cpd*

portugals, e [pɔʀtygɛ, -ɛz] *adj, nm/f* Portuguese

Portugal [pɔʀtygal] *nm*: **le ~** Portugal

pose [poz] *nf* laying; hanging; (*attitude, d'un modèle*) pose; (*PHOTO*) exposure

posé, e [poze] *adj* serious

poser [poze] *vt* (*déposer*): **~ qch (sur)/qn à** to put sth down (on)/drop sb at; (*placer*): **~ qch sur/quelque part** to put sth on/somewhere; (*installer: moquette, carrelage*) to lay; (*rideaux, papier peint*) to hang; (*question*) to ask; (*principe, conditions*) to lay *ou* set down; (*problème*) to formulate; (*difficulté*) to pose ♦ *vi* (*modèle*) to pose; **se ~** *vi* (*oiseau, avion*) to land; (*question*) to arise

positif, ive [pozitif, -iv] *adj* positive

position [pozisjɔ̃] *nf* position; **prendre ~** (*fig*) to take a stand

posologie [pozɔlɔʒi] *nf* directions for use, dosage

posséder [pɔsede] *vt* to own, possess; (*qualité, talent*) to have, possess; (*bien connaître: métier, langue*) to have mastered, have a thorough knowledge of; (*sexuellement, aussi: suj: colère etc*) to possess; **possession** *nf* ownership *no pl*; possession

possibilité [pɔsibilite] *nf* possibility; **~s** *nfpl* (*moyens*) means; (*potentiel*) potential *sg*

possible [pɔsibl(ə)] *adj* possible; (*projet, entreprise*) feasible ♦ *nm*: **faire son ~** to do all one can, do one's utmost; **le plus/moins de livres** ~ as many/few books as possible; **le plus/moins d'eau** ~ as much/little water as possible; **dès que ~** as soon as possible

postal, e, aux [pɔstal, -o] *adj* postal

poste [pɔst(ə)] *nf* (*service*) post, postal service; (*administration, bureau*) post office ♦ *nm* (*fonction, MIL*) post; (*TÉL*) extension; (*de radio etc*) set; **mettre à la ~** to post; **P~s, Télécommunications et Télédiffusion** postal and telecommunications service; **~ d'essence** *nm* petrol *ou* filling station; **~ d'incendie** *nm* fire point; **~ de pilotage** *nm* cockpit; **~ (de police)** *nm* police station; **~ de secours** *nm* first-aid post; **~ de travail** *nm* work station; **poste restante** *nf* poste restante (*BRIT*), general delivery (*US*)

poster¹ [pɔste] *vt* to post

poster² [pɔstɛʀ] *nm* poster

postérieur, e [pɔsteʀjœʀ] *adj* (*date*) later; (*partie*) back ♦ *nm* (*fam*) behind

posthume [pɔstym] *adj* posthumous

postiche [pɔstiʃ] *nm* hairpiece

postuler [pɔstyle] *vt* (*emploi*) to apply for, put in for

posture [pɔstyʀ] *nf* posture; position

pot [po] *nm* jar, pot; (*en plastique, carton*) carton; (*en métal*) tin; **boire** *ou* **prendre un ~** (*fam*) to have a drink; **~ (de chambre)** (chamber)pot; **~ d'échappement** exhaust pipe; **~ de fleurs** plant pot, flowerpot; (*plante*) pot plant

potable [pɔtabl(ə)] *adj*: **eau (non)** ~ (non-)drinking water

potage [pɔtaʒ] *nm* soup; soup course

potager, ère [pɔtaʒe, -ɛʀ] *adj* (*plante*) edible, vegetable *cpd*; (*jardin*) **~** kitchen *ou* vegetable garden

pot-au-feu [pɔtofø] *nm inv* (beef) stew

pot-de-vin [podvɛ̃] *nm* bribe

pote [pɔt] (*fam*) *nm* pal

poteau, x [pɔto] *nm* post; **~ indicateur** signpost

potelé, e [pɔtle] *adj* plump, chubby

potence [pɔtɑ̃s] *nf* gallows *sg*

potentiel, le [pɔtɑ̃sjɛl] *adj, nm* potential

poterie [pɔtʀi] *nf* pottery; piece of pottery

potier [pɔtje] *nm* potter
potins [pɔtɛ̃] *nmpl* gossip *sg*
potiron [pɔtiʀɔ̃] *nm* pumpkin
pou, x [pu] *nm* louse
poubelle [pubɛl] *nf* (dust)bin
pouce [pus] *nm* thumb
poudre [pudʀ(ə)] *nf* powder; (*fard*) (face) powder; (*explosif*) gunpowder; **en ~: café en ~** instant coffee; **lait en ~** dried *ou* powdered milk; **poudrier** *nm* (powder) compact
pouffer [pufe] *vi*: **~ (de rire)** to snigger; to giggle
pouilleux, euse [pujø, -øz] *adj* flea-ridden; (*fig*) grubby; seedy
poulailler [pulaje] *nm* henhouse
poulain [pulɛ̃] *nm* foal; (*fig*) protégé
poule [pul] *nf* (*ZOOL*) hen; (*CULIN*) (boiling) fowl
poulet [pulɛ] *nm* chicken; (*fam*) cop
poulie [puli] *nf* pulley; block
pouls [pu] *nm* pulse; **prendre le ~ de qn** to feel sb's pulse
poumon [pumɔ̃] *nm* lung
poupe [pup] *nf* stern; **en ~** astern
poupée [pupe] *nf* doll
poupon [pupɔ̃] *nm* babe-in-arms; **pouponnière** *nf* crèche, day nursery
pour [puʀ] *prép* for ♦ *nm*: **le ~ et le contre** the pros and cons; **~ faire** (so as) to do, in order to do; **~ avoir fait** for having done; **~ que** so that, in order that; **~ 100 francs d'essence** 100 francs' worth of petrol; **~ cent** per cent; **~ ce qui est de** as for
pourboire [puʀbwaʀ] *nm* tip
pourcentage [puʀsɑ̃taʒ] *nm* percentage
pourchasser [puʀʃase] *vt* to pursue
pourparlers [puʀpaʀle] *nmpl* talks, negotiations
pourpre [puʀpʀ(ə)] *adj* crimson
pourquoi [puʀkwa] *adv, conj* why ♦ *nm inv*: **le ~ (de)** the reason (for)
pourrai *etc vb voir* **pouvoir**
pourri, e [puʀi] *adj* rotten
pourrir [puʀiʀ] *vi* to rot; (*fruit*) to go rotten *ou* bad ♦ *vt* to rot; (*fig*) to spoil thoroughly; **pourriture** *nf* rot
pourrons *etc vb voir* **pouvoir**
poursuite [puʀsɥit] *nf* pursuit, chase; **~s** *nfpl* (*JUR*) legal proceedings
poursuivre [puʀsɥivʀ(ə)] *vt* to pursue, chase (after); (*relancer*) to hound, harry; (*obséder*) to haunt; (*JUR*) to bring proceedings against, prosecute; (: *au civil*) to sue; (*but*) to strive towards; (*voyage, études*) to carry on with, continue ♦ *vi* to carry on, go on; **se ~** *vi* to go on, continue
pourtant [puʀtɑ̃] *adv* yet; **c'est ~ facile** (and) yet it's easy
pourtour [puʀtuʀ] *nm* perimeter
pourvoir [puʀvwaʀ] *vt*: **~ qch/qn de** to equip sth/sb with ♦ *vi*: **~ à** to provide for;

(*emploi*) to fill; **se ~** *vi* (*JUR*): **se ~ en cassation** to take one's case to the Court of Appeal
pourvoyeur [puʀvwajœʀ] *nm* supplier
pourvu, e [puʀvy] *adj*: **~ de** equipped with; **~ que** (*si*) provided that, so long as; (*espérons que*) let's hope (that)
pousse [pus] *nf* growth; (*bourgeon*) shoot
poussé, e [puse] *adj* exhaustive
poussée [puse] *nf* thrust; (*coup*) push; (*MÉD*) eruption; (*fig*) upsurge
pousser [puse] *vt* to push; (*inciter*): **~ qn à** to urge *ou* press sb to +*infin*; (*acculer*): **~ qn à** to drive sb to; (*émettre: cri etc*) to give; (*stimuler*) to urge on; to drive hard; (*poursuivre*) to carry on (further) ♦ *vi* to push; (*croître*) to grow; **se ~** *vi* to move over; **faire ~** (*plante*) to grow
poussette [pusɛt] *nf* (*voiture d'enfant*) push chair (*BRIT*), stroller (*US*)
poussière [pusjɛʀ] *nf* dust; (*grain*) speck of dust; **poussiéreux, euse** *adj* dusty
poussin [pusɛ̃] *nm* chick
poutre [putʀ(ə)] *nf* beam; (*en fer, ciment armé*) girder

MOT CLÉ

pouvoir [puvwaʀ] *nm* power; (*POL*: *dirigeants*): **le ~** those in power; **les ~s publics** the authorities; **~ d'achat** purchasing power

♦ *vb semi-aux* **1** (*être en état de*) can, be able to; **je ne peux pas le réparer** I can't *ou* I am not able to repair it; **déçu de ne pas ~ le faire** disappointed not to be able to do it

2 (*avoir la permission*) can, may, be allowed to; **vous pouvez aller au cinéma** you can *ou* may go to the pictures

3 (*probabilité, hypothèse*) may, might, could; **il a pu avoir un accident** he may *ou* might *ou* could have had an accident; **il aurait pu le dire!** he might *ou* could have said (so)!

♦ *vb impers* may, might, could; **il peut arriver que** it may *ou* might *ou* could happen that

♦ *vt* can, be able to; **j'ai fait tout ce que j'ai pu** I did all I could; **je n'en peux plus** (*épuisé*) I'm exhausted; (*à bout*) I can't take any more

se ~ *vi*: **il se peut que** it may *ou* might be that; **cela se pourrait** that's quite possible

---

prairie [pʀeʀi] *nf* meadow
praline [pʀalin] *nf* sugared almond
praticable [pʀatikabl(ə)] *adj* passable, practicable
praticien, ne [pʀatisjɛ̃, -jɛn] *nm/f* practitioner
pratique [pʀatik] *nf* practice ♦ *adj* practical
pratiquement [pʀatikmɑ̃] *adv* (*pour ainsi*

dire) practically, virtually

pratiquer [pʀatike] *vt* to practise; (*SPORT etc*) to go in for; to play; (*intervention, opération*) to carry out; (*ouverture, abri*) to make

pré [pʀe] *nm* meadow

préalable [pʀealabl(ə)] *adj* preliminary; **condition ~ (de)** precondition (for), prerequisite (for); **au ~** beforehand

préambule [pʀeãbyl] *nm* preamble; (*fig*) prelude; **sans ~** straight away

préavis [pʀeavi] *nm* notice; **communication avec ~** (*TÉL*) personal *ou* person to person call

précaution [pʀekosjɔ̃] *nf* precaution; **avec ~** cautiously; **par ~** as a precaution

précédemment [pʀesedamã] *adv* before, previously

précédent, e [pʀesedã, -ãt] *adj* previous ♦ *nm* precedent; **le jour ~** the day before, the previous day; **sans ~** unprecedented

précéder [pʀesede] *vt* to precede; (*marcher ou rouler devant*) to be in front of

précepteur, trice [pʀesɛptœʀ, -tʀis] *nm/f* (private) tutor

prêcher [pʀeʃe] *vt* to preach

précieux, euse [pʀesjø, -øz] *adj* precious; invaluable; (*style, écrivain*) précieux, precious

précipice [pʀesipis] *nm* drop, chasm; (*fig*) abyss

précipitamment [pʀesipitamã] *adv* hurriedly, hastily

précipitation [pʀesipitasjɔ̃] *nf* (*hâte*) haste; **~s** *nfpl* (*pluie*) rain *sg*

précipité, e [pʀesipite] *adj* hurried, hasty

précipiter [pʀesipite] *vt* (*faire tomber*): **~ qn/qch du haut de** to throw *ou* hurl sb/ sth off *ou* from; (*hâter: marche*) to quicken; (: *départ*) to hasten; **se ~** *vi* to speed up; **se ~ sur/vers** to rush at/towards

précis, e [pʀesi, -iz] *adj* precise; (*tir, mesures*) accurate, precise ♦ *nm* handbook; **précisément** *adv* precisely; **préciser** *vt* (*expliquer*) to be more specific about, clarify; (*spécifier*) to state, specify; **se ~er** *vi* to become clear(er); **précision** *nf* precision; accuracy; point *ou* detail (*being or to be clarified*)

précoce [pʀekɔs] *adj* early; (*enfant*) precocious; (*calvitie*) premature

préconiser [pʀekɔnize] *vt* to advocate

prédécesseur [pʀedesesœʀ] *nm* predecessor

prédilection [pʀedilɛksjɔ̃] *nf*: **avoir une ~ pour** to be partial to; **de ~** favourite

prédire [pʀediʀ] *vt* to predict

prédominer [pʀedɔmine] *vi* to predominate; (*avis*) to prevail

préface [pʀefas] *nf* preface

préfecture [pʀefɛktyʀ] *nf* prefecture; **~ de police** police headquarters *pl*

préférable [pʀefeʀabl(ə)] *adj* preferable

préféré, e [pʀefeʀe] *adj, nm/f* favourite

préférence [pʀefeʀãs] *nf* preference; **de ~** preferably

préférer [pʀefeʀe] *vt*: **~ qn/qch (à)** to prefer sb/sth (to), like sb/sth better (than); **~ faire** to prefer to do; **je ~ais du thé** I would rather have tea, I'd prefer tea

préfet [pʀefɛ] *nm* prefect

préfixe [pʀefiks(ə)] *nm* prefix

préhistorique [pʀeistɔʀik] *adj* prehistoric

préjudice [pʀeʒydis] *nm* (*matériel*) loss; (*moral*) harm *no pl*; **porter ~ à** to harm, be detrimental to; **au ~ de** at the expense of

préjugé [pʀeʒyʒe] *nm* prejudice; **avoir un ~ contre** to be prejudiced *ou* biased against

préjuger [pʀeʒyʒe]: **~ de** *vt* to prejudge

prélasser [pʀelase]: **se ~** *vi* to lounge

prélèvement [pʀelɛvmã] *nm*: **faire un ~ de sang** to take a blood sample

prélever [pʀelve] *vt* (*échantillon*) to take; (*argent*): **~ (sur)** to deduct (from); (: *sur son compte*) to withdraw (from)

prématuré, e [pʀematyʀe] *adj* premature; (*retraite*) early ♦ *nm* premature baby

premier, ière [pʀəmje, -jɛʀ] *adj* first; (*branche, marche*) bottom; (*fig*) basic; prime; initial; **le ~ venu** the first person to come along; **P~ Ministre** Prime Minister; **première** *nf* (*THÉÂTRE*) first night; (*AUTO*) first (gear); (*AVIAT, RAIL etc*) first class; (*CINÉMA*) première; (*exploit*) first; **premièrement** *adv* firstly

prémonition [pʀemɔnisjɔ̃] *nf* premonition

prémunir [pʀemyniʀ]: **se ~** *vi*: **se ~ contre** to guard against

prenant, e [pʀənã, -ãt] *adj* absorbing, engrossing

prénatal, e [pʀenatal] *adj* (*MÉD*) antenatal

prendre [pʀãdʀ(ə)] *vt* to take; (*ôter*): **~ qch à** to take sth from; (*aller chercher*) to get, fetch; (*se procurer*) to get; (*malfaiteur, poisson*) to catch; (*passager*) to pick up; (*personnel, aussi: couleur, goût*) to take on; (*locataire*) to take in; (*élève etc: traiter*) to handle; (*voix, ton*) to put on; (*coincer*): **se ~ les doigts dans** to get one's fingers caught in ♦ *vi* (*liquide, ciment*) to set; (*greffe, vaccin*) to take; (*feu: foyer*) to go; (: *incendie*) to start; (*allumette*) to light; (*se diriger*): **~ à gauche** to turn (to the) left; **à tout ~** on the whole, all in all; **se ~ pour** to think one is; **s'en ~ à** to attack; **se ~ d'amitié/d'affection pour** to befriend/ become fond of; **s'y ~** (*procéder*) to set about it

preneur [pʀənœʀ] *nm*: **être/trouver ~** to be willing to buy/find a buyer

preniez *vb voir* **prendre**

prenne *etc vb voir* **prendre**

prénom [pʀenɔ̃] *nm* first *ou* Christian

name

prénuptial, e, aux [pʀenypsjal, -o] *adj*
premarital

préoccupation [pʀeɔkypasjɔ̃] *nf* (*souci*)
concern; (*idée fixe*) preoccupation

préoccuper [pʀeɔkype] *vt* to concern; to
preoccupy

préparatifs [pʀeparatif] *nmpl* preparations

préparation [pʀeparasjɔ̃] *nf* preparation;
(*SCOL*) piece of homework

préparer [pʀepaʀe] *vt* to prepare; (*café*) to
make; (*examen*) to prepare for; (*voyage, entreprise*) to plan; **se ~** *vi* (*orage, tragédie*)
to brew, be in the air; **se ~ (à qch/faire)**
to prepare (o.s.) *ou* get ready (for sth/to
do); **~ qch à qn** (*surprise etc*) to have sth
in store for sb

prépondérant, e [pʀepɔ̃deʀɑ̃, -ɑ̃t] *adj* major, dominating

préposé, e [pʀepoze] *adj*: **~ à** in charge
of ♦ *nm/f* employee; official; attendant

préposition [pʀepozisjɔ̃] *nf* preposition

près [pʀɛ] *adv* near, close; **~ de** near (to),
close to; (*environ*) nearly, almost; **de ~**
closely; **à 5 kg ~** to within about 5 kg; **à
cela ~ que** apart from the fact that

présage [pʀezaʒ] *nm* omen

présager [pʀezaʒe] *vt* to foresee

presbyte [pʀɛsbit] *adj* long-sighted

presbytère [pʀɛsbiteʀ] *nm* presbytery

prescription [pʀɛskʀipsjɔ̃] *nf* (*instruction*)
order, instruction; (*MÉD, JUR*) prescription

prescrire [pʀɛskʀiʀ] *vt* to prescribe

préséance [pʀeseɑ̃s] *nf* precedence *no pl*

présence [pʀezɑ̃s] *nf* presence; (*au bureau
etc*) attendance; **~ d'esprit** presence of
mind

présent, e [pʀezɑ̃, -ɑ̃t] *adj, nm* present; **à
~ (que)** now (that)

présentation [pʀezɑ̃tasjɔ̃] *nf* introduction;
presentation; (*allure*) appearance

présenter [pʀezɑ̃te] *vt* to present; (*sympathie, condoléances*) to offer; (*soumettre*)
to submit; (*invité, conférencier*): **~ qn (à)** to
introduce sb (to) ♦ *vi*: **~ mal/bien** to have
an unattractive/a pleasing appearance; **se
~** *vi* (*sur convocation*) to report, come; (*à
une élection*) to stand; (*occasion*) to arise;
se ~ bien/mal to look good/not too good;
se ~ à (*examen*) to sit

préservatif [pʀezeʀvatif] *nm* sheath, condom

préserver [pʀezeʀve] *vt*: **~ de** to protect
from; to save from

président [pʀezidɑ̃] *nm* (*POL*) president;
(*d'une assemblée, COMM*) chairman; **~ directeur général** chairman and managing
director

présider [pʀezide] *vt* to preside over;
(*dîner*) to be the guest of honour at; **~ à** to
direct; to govern

présomptueux, euse [pʀezɔ̃ptɥø, -øz] *adj*

presumptuous

presque [pʀɛsk(ə)] *adv* almost, nearly; **~
rien** hardly anything; **~ pas** hardly (at all);
~ pas de hardly any

presqu'île [pʀɛskil] *nf* peninsula

pressant, e [pʀesɑ̃, -ɑ̃t] *adj* urgent; **se faire ~** to become insistent

presse [pʀɛs] *nf* press; (*affluence*): **heures
de ~** busy times

pressé, e [pʀese] *adj* in a hurry; (*air*) hurried; (*besogne*) urgent; **orange ~e** fresh orange juice

pressentiment [pʀesɑ̃timɑ̃] *nm* fore-
boding, premonition

pressentir [pʀesɑ̃tiʀ] *vt* to sense; (*prendre
contact avec*) to approach

presse-papiers [pʀɛspapje] *nm inv* paper-
weight

presser [pʀese] *vt* (*fruit, éponge*) to
squeeze; (*bouton*) to press; (*allure, affaire*)
to speed up; (*inciter*): **~ qn de faire** to urge
ou press sb to do ♦ *vi* to be urgent; **se ~** *vi*
(*se hâter*) to hurry (up); **se ~ contre qn** to
squeeze up against sb; **rien ne presse**
there's no hurry

pressing [pʀesiŋ] *nm* steam-pressing; (*magasin*) dry-cleaner's

pression [pʀesjɔ̃] *nf* pressure; **faire ~ sur**
to put pressure on; **~ artérielle** blood pressure

pressoir [pʀeswaʀ] *nm* (*wine ou oil etc*)
press

prestance [pʀɛstɑ̃s] *nf* presence, imposing
bearing

prestataire [pʀɛstateʀ] *nm/f* supplier

prestation [pʀɛstasjɔ̃] *nf* (*allocation*)
benefit; (*d'une entreprise*) service provided;
(*d'un artiste*) performance

prestidigitateur, trice [pʀɛstidiʒitatœʀ,
-tʀis] *nm/f* conjurer

prestigieux, euse [pʀɛstiʒjø, -øz] *adj* pres-
tigious

présumer [pʀezyme] *vt*: **~ que** to presume
ou assume that; **~ de** to overrate

présupposer [pʀesypoze] *vt* to presuppose

prêt, e [pʀɛ, pʀɛt] *adj* ready ♦ *nm* lending
no pl; loan; **prêt-à-porter** *nm* ready-to-
wear *ou* off-the-peg (*BRIT*) clothes *pl*

prétendant [pʀetɑ̃dɑ̃] *nm* pretender; (*d'une
femme*) suitor

prétendre [pʀetɑ̃dʀ(ə)] *vt* (*affirmer*): **~ que**
to claim that; (*avoir l'intention de*): **~ faire
qch** to mean *ou* intend to do sth; **~ à**
(*droit, titre*) to lay claim to; **prétendu, e**
adj (*supposé*) so-called

prête-nom [pʀɛtnɔ̃] (*péj*) *nm* figurehead

prétentieux, euse [pʀetɑ̃sjø, -øz] *adj* pre-
tentious

prétention [pʀetɑ̃sjɔ̃] *nf* claim; pretentious-
ness

prêter [pʀete] *vt* (*livres, argent*): **~ qch (à)**
to lend sth (to); (*supposer*): **~ à qn** (*carac-*

tère, propos) to attribute to sb ♦ *vi* (*aussi*: se ~: *tissu, cuir*) to give; **se ~ à** to lend o.s. (*ou* itself) to; (*manigances etc*) to go along with; **~ à** (*commentaires etc*) to be open to, give rise to; **~ assistance à** to give help to; **~ attention à** to pay attention to; **~ serment** to take the oath; **~ l'oreille** to listen

prétexte [pRetɛkst(ə)] *nm* pretext, excuse; **sous aucun ~** on no account; **prétexter** *vt* to give as a pretext *ou* an excuse

prêtre [pRɛtR(ə)] *nm* priest

preuve [pRœv] *nf* proof; (*indice*) proof, evidence *no pl*; **faire ~ de** to show; **faire ses ~s** to prove o.s. (*ou* itself)

prévaloir [pRevalwaR] *vi* to prevail; **se ~ de** *vt* to take advantage of; to pride o.s. on

prévenant, e [pRevnã, -ãt] *adj* thoughtful, kind

prévenir [pRevniR] *vt* (*avertir*): **~ qn (de)** to warn sb (about); (*informer*): **~ qn (de)** to tell *ou* inform sb (about); (*éviter*) to avoid, prevent; (*anticiper*) to forestall; to anticipate

prévention [pRevãsjɔ̃] *nf* prevention; **~ routière** road safety

prévenu, e [pRevny] *nm/f* (*JUR*) defendant, accused

prévision [pRevizjɔ̃] *nf*: **~s** predictions; forecast *sg*; **en ~ de** in anticipation of; **~s météorologiques** weather forecast *sg*

prévoir [pRevwaR] *vt* (*deviner*) to foresee; (*s'attendre à*) to expect, reckon on; (*prévenir*) to anticipate; (*organiser*) to plan; (*préparer, réserver*) to allow; **prévu pour 10h** scheduled for 10 o'clock

prévoyance [pRevwajãs] *nf*: **caisse de ~** contingency fund

prévoyant, e [pRevwajã, -ãt] *adj* gifted with (*ou* showing) foresight

prévu, e [pRevy] *pp de* **prévoir**

prier [pRije] *vi* to pray ♦ *vt* (*Dieu*) to pray to; (*implorer*) to beg; (*demander*): **~ qn de faire** to ask sb to do; **se faire ~** to need coaxing *ou* persuading; **je vous en prie** (*allez-y*) please do; (*de rien*) don't mention it

prière [pRijɛR] *nf* prayer; "**~ de faire ...**" "please do ..."

primaire [pRimɛR] *adj* primary; (*péj*) simple-minded; simplistic ♦ *nm* (*SCOL*) primary education

prime [pRim] *nf* (*bonification*) bonus; (*subside*) premium; allowance; (*COMM: cadeau*) free gift; (*ASSURANCES, BOURSE*) premium ♦ *adj*: **de ~ abord** at first glance

primer [pRime] *vt* (*l'emporter sur*) to prevail over; (*récompenser*) to award a prize to ♦ *vi* to dominate; to prevail

primeurs [pRimœR] *nfpl* early fruits and vegetables

primevère [pRimvɛR] *nf* primrose

primitif, ive [pRimitif, -iv] *adj* primitive; (*originel*) original

prince [pRɛ̃s] *nm* prince; **princesse** *nf* princess

principal, e, aux [pRɛ̃sipal, -o] *adj* principal, main ♦ *nm* (*SCOL*) principal, head(master); (*essentiel*) main thing

principe [pRɛ̃sip] *nm* principle; **pour le ~** on principle; **de ~** (*accord, hostilité*) automatic; **par ~** on principle; **en ~** (*habituellement*) as a rule; (*théoriquement*) in principle

printemps [pRɛ̃tã] *nm* spring

priorité [pRijoRite] *nf* (*AUTO*): **avoir la ~ (sur)** to have right of way (over); **~ à droite** right of way to vehicles coming from the right

pris, e [pRi, pRiz] *pp de* **prendre** ♦ *adj* (*place*) taken; (*journée, mains*) full; (*billets*) sold; (*personne*) busy; **avoir le nez/la gorge ~(e)** to have a stuffy nose/a hoarse throat; **être ~ de panique** to be panic-stricken

prise [pRiz] *nf* (*d'une ville*) capture; (*PÊCHE, CHASSE*) catch; (*point d'appui ou pour empoigner*) hold; (*ÉLEC: fiche*) plug; (: *femelle*) socket; **être aux ~s avec** to be grappling with; **~ de contact** *nf* (*rencontre*) initial meeting, first contact; **~ de courant** power point; **~ de sang** blood test; **~ de terre** earth; **~ de vue** (*photo*) shot; **~ multiple** adaptor

priser [pRize] *vt* (*tabac, héroïne*) to take; (*estimer*) to prize, value ♦ *vi* to take snuff

prison [pRizɔ̃] *nf* prison; **aller/être en ~** to go to/be in prison *ou* jail; **faire de la ~** to serve time; **prisonnier, ière** *nm/f* prisoner ♦ *adj* captive

prit *vb voir* **prendre**

privé, e [pRive] *adj* private; **en ~** in private

priver [pRive] *vt*: **~ qn de** to deprive sb of; **se ~ de** to go *ou* do without

privilège [pRivilɛʒ] *nm* privilege

prix [pRi] *nm* (*valeur*) price; (*récompense, SCOL*) prize; **hors de ~** exorbitantly priced; **à aucun ~** not at any price; **à tout ~** at all costs; **~ d'achat/de vente/de revient** purchasing/selling/cost price

probable [pRɔbabl(ə)] *adj* likely, probable; **~ment** *adv* probably

probant, e [pRɔbã, -ãt] *adj* convincing

problème [pRɔblɛm] *nm* problem

procédé [pRɔsede] *nm* (*méthode*) process; (*comportement*) behaviour *no pl*

procéder [pRɔsede] *vi* to proceed; to behave; **~ à** to carry out

procès [pRɔsɛ] *nm* trial; (*poursuites*) proceedings *pl*; **être en ~ avec** to be involved in a lawsuit with

processus [pRɔsesys] *nm* process

procès-verbal, aux [pRɔsɛvɛRbal, -o] *nm* (*constat*) statement; (*aussi*: *P.V.*): **avoir un ~** to get a parking ticket; to be booked; (*de réunion*) minutes *pl*

prochain, e [prɔʃɛ̃, -ɛn] adj next; (proche) impending; near ♦ nm fellow man; **la ~e fois/semaine** ~e next time/week; **prochainement** adv soon, shortly

proche [prɔʃ] adj nearby; (dans le temps) imminent; (parent, ami) close; **~s** nmpl (parents) close relatives; **être ~ (de)** to be near, be close (to); **de ~ en ~** gradually; **le P~ Orient** the Middle East

proclamer [prɔklame] vt to proclaim

procuration [prɔkyrasjɔ̃] nf proxy; power of attorney

procurer [prɔkyre] vt: **~ qch à qn** (fournir) to obtain sth for sb; (causer: plaisir etc) to bring sb sth; **se ~** vt to get

procureur [prɔkyrœr] nm public prosecutor

prodige [prɔdiʒ] nm marvel, wonder; (personne) prodigy

prodigue [prɔdig] adj generous; extravagant; **fils ~** prodigal son

prodiguer [prɔdige] vt (argent, biens) to be lavish with; (soins, attentions): **~ qch à qn** to give sb sth

producteur, trice [prɔdyktœr, -tris] nm/f producer

production [prɔdyksjɔ̃] nf (gén) production; (rendement) output

produire [prɔdɥir] vt to produce; **se ~** vi (acteur) to perform, appear; (événement) to happen, occur

produit [prɔdɥi] nm (gén) product; **~ d'entretien** cleaning product; **~ national brut** gross national product; **~s agricoles** farm produce sg; **~s alimentaires** nmpl foodstuffs

prof [prɔf] (fam) nm teacher

profane [prɔfan] adj (REL) secular ♦ nm/f layman(woman)

proférer [prɔfere] vt to utter

professeur [prɔfesœr] nm teacher; (titulaire d'une chaire) professor; **~ (de faculté)** (university) lecturer

profession [prɔfesjɔ̃] nf profession; **sans ~** unemployed; **professionnel, le** adj, nm/f professional

profil [prɔfil] nm profile; (d'une voiture) line, contour; **de ~** in profile; **profiler** vt to streamline

profit [prɔfi] nm (avantage) benefit, advantage; (COMM, FINANCE) profit; **au ~ de** in aid of; **tirer ~ de** to profit from

profitable [prɔfitabl(ə)] adj beneficial; profitable

profiter [prɔfite] vi: **~ de** to take advantage of; to make the most of; **~ à** to benefit; to be profitable to

profond, e [prɔfɔ̃, -ɔ̃d] adj deep; (méditation, mépris) profound; **profondeur** nf depth

progéniture [prɔʒenityr] nf offspring inv

programme [prɔgram] nm programme;

(TV, RADIO) programmes pl; (SCOL) syllabus, curriculum; (INFORM) program; **programmer** vt (TV, RADIO) to put on, show; (INFORM) to program; **programmeur, euse** nm/f programmer

progrès [prɔgrɛ] nm progress no pl; **faire des ~** to make progress

progresser [prɔgrese] vi to progress; (troupes etc) to make headway ou progress; **progressif, ive** adj progressive

prohiber [prɔibe] vt to prohibit, ban

proie [prwa] nf prey no pl

projecteur [prɔʒɛktœr] nm projector; (de théâtre, cirque) spotlight

projectile [prɔʒɛktil] nm missile

projection [prɔʒɛksjɔ̃] nf projection; showing; **conférence avec ~s** lecture with slides (ou a film)

projet [prɔʒɛ] nm plan; (ébauche) draft; **~ de loi** bill

projeter [prɔʒte] vt (envisager) to plan; (film, photos) to project; (passer) to show; (ombre, lueur) to throw, cast; (jeter) to throw up (ou off ou out)

prolixe [prɔliks(ə)] adj verbose

prolongement [prɔlɔ̃ʒmɑ̃] nm extension; **~s** nmpl (fig) repercussions, effects; **dans le ~ de** running on from

prolonger [prɔlɔ̃ʒe] vt (débat, séjour) to prolong; (délai, billet, rue) to extend; (suj: chose) to be a continuation ou an extension of; **se ~** vi to go on

promenade [prɔmnad] nf walk (ou drive ou ride); **faire une ~** to go for a walk; **une ~ en voiture/à vélo** a drive/(bicycle) ride

promener [prɔmne] vt (chien) to take out for a walk; (doigts, regard): **~ qch sur** to run sth over; **se ~** vi to go for (ou be out for) a walk

promesse [prɔmɛs] nf promise

promettre [prɔmɛtr(ə)] vt to promise ♦ vi to be ou look promising; **~ à qn de faire** to promise sb that one will do

promiscuité [prɔmiskɥite] nf crowding; lack of privacy

promontoire [prɔmɔ̃twar] nm headland

promoteur, trice [prɔmɔtœr, -tris] nm/f (instigateur) instigator, promoter; **~ (immobilier)** property developer (BRIT), real estate promoter (US)

promotion [prɔmɔsjɔ̃] nf promotion

promouvoir [prɔmuvwar] vt to promote

prompt, e [prɔ̃, prɔ̃t] adj swift, rapid

prôner [prone] vt to advocate

pronom [prɔnɔ̃] nm pronoun

prononcer [prɔnɔ̃se] vt (son, mot, jugement) to pronounce; (dire) to utter; (allocution) to deliver; **se ~** vi to reach a decision, give a verdict; **se ~ sur** to give an opinion on; **se ~ contre** to come down against; **prononciation** nf pronunciation

pronostic [prɔnɔstik] nm (MÉD) prognosis;

(*fig: aussi:* ~s) forecast

propagande [pʀɔpagɑ̃d] *nf* propaganda

propager [pʀɔpaʒe] *vt* to spread; **se** ~ *vi* to spread

prophète [pʀɔfɛt] *nm* prophet

prophétie [pʀɔfesi] *nf* prophecy

propice [pʀɔpis] *adj* favourable

proportion [pʀɔpɔʀsjɔ̃] *nf* proportion; **toute(s)** ~**(s) gardée(s)** making due allowance(s)

propos [pʀɔpo] *nm* (*paroles*) talk *no pl*, remark; (*intention*) intention, aim; (*sujet*): **à quel** ~? what about?; **à** ~ **de** about, regarding; **à tout** ~ for no reason at all; **à** ~ by the way; (*opportunément*) at the right moment

proposer [pʀɔpoze] *vt* (*suggérer*): ~ **qch (à qn)/de faire** to suggest sth (to sb)/doing, propose sth (to sb)/to do; (*offrir*): ~ **qch à qn/de faire** to offer sb sth/to do; (*candidat*) to put forward; (*loi, motion*) to propose; **se** ~ to offer one's services; **se** ~ **de faire** to intend *ou* propose to do; **proposition** *nf* suggestion; proposal; offer; (*LING*) clause

propre [pʀɔpʀ(ə)] *adj* clean; (*net*) neat, tidy; (*possessif*) own; (*sens*) literal; (*particulier*): ~ **à** peculiar to; (*approprié*): ~ **à** suitable for; (*de nature à*): ~ **à faire** likely to do ♦ *nm*: **recopier au** ~ to make a fair copy of; **proprement** *adv* cleanly; neatly, tidily; **le village proprement dit** the village itself; **à proprement parler** strictly speaking; **propreté** *nf* cleanliness; neatness; tidiness

propriétaire [pʀɔpʀijetɛʀ] *nm/f* owner; (*pour le locataire*) landlord(lady)

propriété [pʀɔpʀijete] *nf* (*gén*) property; (*droit*) ownership; (*objet, immeuble, terres*) property *gén no pl*

propulser [pʀɔpylse] *vt* (*missile*) to propel; (*projeter*) to hurl, fling

proroger [pʀɔʀɔʒe] *vt* to put back, defer; (*prolonger*) to extend

proscrire [pʀɔskʀiʀ] *vt* (*bannir*) to banish; (*interdire*) to ban, prohibit

prose [pʀoz] *nf* (*style*) prose

prospecter [pʀɔspɛkte] *vt* to prospect; (*COMM*) to canvass

prospectus [pʀɔspɛktys] *nm* leaflet

prospère [pʀɔspɛʀ] *adj* prosperous

prosterner [pʀɔstɛʀne] : **se** ~ *vi* to bow low, prostrate o.s.

prostituée [pʀɔstitɥe] *nf* prostitute

protecteur, trice [pʀɔtɛktœʀ, -tʀis] *adj* protective; (*air, ton: péj*) patronizing ♦ *nm/f* protector

protection [pʀɔtɛksjɔ̃] *nf* protection; (*d'un personnage influent: aide*) patronage

protéger [pʀɔteʒe] *vt* to protect; **se** ~ **de** *ou* **contre** to protect o.s. from

protéine [pʀɔtein] *nf* protein

protestant, e [pʀɔtɛstɑ̃, -ɑ̃t] *adj, nm/f* Protestant

protestation [pʀɔtɛstasjɔ̃] *nf* (*plainte*) protest

protester [pʀɔtɛste] *vi*: ~ **(contre)** to protest (against *ou* about); ~ **de** (*son innocence, sa loyauté*) to protest

prothèse [pʀɔtɛz] *nf* artificial limb, prosthesis; ~ **dentaire** denture

protocole [pʀɔtɔkɔl] *nm* (*fig*) etiquette

proue [pʀu] *nf* bow(s *pl*), prow

prouesse [pʀuɛs] *nf* feat

prouver [pʀuve] *vt* to prove

provenance [pʀɔvnɑ̃s] *nf* origin; (*de mot, coutume*) source; **avion en** ~ **de** plane (arriving) from

provenir [pʀɔvniʀ] : ~ **de** *vt* to come from; (*résulter de*) to be the result of

proverbe [pʀɔvɛʀb(ə)] *nm* proverb

province [pʀɔvɛ̃s] *nf* province

proviseur [pʀɔvizœʀ] *nm* ≈ head(teacher) (*BRIT*), ≈ principal (*US*)

provision [pʀɔvizjɔ̃] *nf* (*réserve*) stock, supply; (*avance: à un avocat, avoué*) retainer, retaining fee; (*COMM*) funds *pl* (in account); reserve; ~**s** *nfpl* (*vivres*) provisions, food *no pl*

provisoire [pʀɔvizwaʀ] *adj* temporary; (*JUR*) provisional

provoquer [pʀɔvɔke] *vt* (*inciter*): ~ **qn à** to incite sb to; (*défier*) to provoke; (*causer*) to cause, bring about

proxénète [pʀɔksenɛt] *nm* procurer

proximité [pʀɔksimite] *nf* nearness, closeness; (*dans le temps*) imminence, closeness; **à** ~ near *ou* close by; **à** ~ **de** near (to), close to

prude [pʀyd] *adj* prudish

prudemment [pʀydamɑ̃] *adv* carefully, cautiously; wisely, sensibly

prudence [pʀydɑ̃s] *nf* carefulness; caution; **avec** ~ carefully; cautiously; **par (mesure de)** ~ as a precaution

prudent, e [pʀydɑ̃, -ɑ̃t] *adj* (*pas téméraire*) careful, cautious; (: *en général*) safety-conscious; (*sage, conseillé*) wise, sensible; (*réservé*) cautious

prune [pʀyn] *nf* plum

pruneau, x [pʀyno] *nm* prune

prunelle [pʀynɛl] *nf* pupil; eye

prunier [pʀynje] *nm* plum tree

psaume [psom] *nm* psalm

pseudonyme [psødɔnim] *nm* (*gén*) fictitious name; (*d'écrivain*) pseudonym, pen name; (*de comédien*) stage name

psychiatre [psikjatʀ(ə)] *nm/f* psychiatrist

psychiatrique [psikjatʀik] *adj* psychiatric

psychique [psiʃik] *adj* psychological

psychologie [psikɔlɔʒi] *nf* psychology; **psychologique** *adj* psychological; **psychologue** *nm/f* psychologist

P.T.T. *sigle fpl* = Postes, Télécommunications et Télédiffusion

pu *pp de* **pouvoir**
puanteur [pɥɑ̃tœʀ] *nf* stink, stench
pub [pyb] *(fam) abr f (= publicité)*: **la ~** advertising
public, ique [pyblik] *adj* public; *(école, instruction)* state *cpd* ♦ *nm* public; *(assistance)* audience; **en ~** in public
publicitaire [pyblisitɛʀ] *adj* advertising *cpd*; *(film, voiture)* publicity *cpd*
publicité [pyblisite] *nf (méthode, profession)* advertising; *(annonce)* advertisement; *(révélations)* publicity
publier [pyblije] *vt* to publish
publique [pyblik] *adj voir* **public**
puce [pys] *nf* flea; *(INFORM)* chip; **~s** *nfpl (marché)* flea market *sg*
pudeur [pydœʀ] *nf* modesty
pudique [pydik] *adj (chaste)* modest; *(discret)* discreet
puer [pɥe] *(péj) vi* to stink
puéricultrice [pɥeʀikyltʀis] *nf* p(a)ediatric nurse
puériculture [pɥeʀikyltyʀ] *nf* p(a)ediatric nursing; infant care
puéril, e [pɥeʀil] *adj* childish
puis [pɥi] *vb voir* **pouvoir** ♦ *adv* then
puiser [pɥize] *vt*: **~ (dans)** to draw (from)
puisque [pɥisk(ə)] *conj* since
puissance [pɥisɑ̃s] *nf* power; **en ~** *adj* potential
puissant, e [pɥisɑ̃, -ɑ̃t] *adj* powerful
puisse *etc vb voir* **pouvoir**
puits [pɥi] *nm* well; **~ de mine** mine shaft
pull(-over) [pul(ɔvœʀ)] *nm* sweater
pulluler [pylyle] *vi* to swarm
pulpe [pylp(ə)] *nf* pulp
pulvérisateur [pylveʀizatœʀ] *nm* spray
pulvériser [pylveʀize] *vt* to pulverize; *(liquide)* to spray
punaise [pynɛz] *nf (ZOOL)* bug; *(clou)* drawing pin *(BRIT)*, thumbtack *(US)*
punch¹ [pɔ̃ʃ] *nm (boisson)* punch
punch² [pœnʃ] *nm (BOXE, fig)* punch
punir [pyniʀ] *vt* to punish; **punition** *nf* punishment
pupille [pypij] *nf (ANAT)* pupil ♦ *nm/f (enfant)* ward; **~ de l'État** child in care
pupitre [pypitʀ(ə)] *nm (SCOL)* desk; *(REL)* lectern; *(de chef d'orchestre)* rostrum
pur, e [pyʀ] *adj* pure; *(vin)* undiluted; *(whisky)* neat; **en ~e perte** to no avail
purée [pyʀe] *nf*: **~ (de pommes de terre)** mashed potatoes *pl*; **~ de marrons** chestnut purée
purger [pyʀʒe] *vt (radiateur)* to drain; *(circuit hydraulique)* to bleed; *(MÉD, POL)* to purge; *(JUR: peine)* to serve
purin [pyʀɛ̃] *nm* liquid manure
pur-sang [pyʀsɑ̃] *nm inv* thoroughbred
pusillanime [pyzilanim] *adj* fainthearted
putain [pytɛ̃] *(fam!) nf* whore *(!)*
puzzle [pœzl(ə)] *nm* jigsaw (puzzle)

P.V. *sigle m* = **procès-verbal**
pyjama [piʒama] *nm* pyjamas *pl (BRIT)*, pajamas *pl (US)*
pyramide [piʀamid] *nf* pyramid
Pyrénées [piʀene] *nfpl*: **lès ~** the Pyrenees

Q q

QG [kyʒe] *sigle m (= quartier général)* HQ
QI [kyi] *sigle m (= quotient intellectuel)* IQ
quadragénaire [kadʀaʒenɛʀ] *nm/f* man/woman in his/her forties
quadriller [kadʀije] *vt (papier)* to mark out in squares; *(POLICE)* to keep under tight control
quadruple [k(w)adʀypl(ə)] *nm*: **le ~ de** four times as much as; **quadruplés, ées** *nm/fpl* quadruplets, quads
quai [ke] *nm (de port)* quay; *(de gare)* platform; **être à ~** *(navire)* to be alongside; *(train)* to be in the station
qualifier [kalifje] *vt* to qualify; **se ~** *vi* to qualify; **~ qch/qn de** to describe sth/sb as
qualité [kalite] *nf* quality; *(titre, fonction)* position
quand [kɑ̃] *conj, adv* when; **~ je serai riche** when I'm rich; **~ même** all the same; really; **~ bien même** even though
quant [kɑ̃] : **~ à** *prép* as for, as to; regarding
quant-à-soi [kɑ̃taswa] *nm*: **rester sur son ~** to remain aloof
quantité [kɑ̃tite] *nf* quantity, amount; *(SCIENCE)* quantity; *(grand nombre)*: **une ou des ~(s) de** a great deal of
quarantaine [kaʀɑ̃tɛn] *nf (MÉD)* quarantine; **avoir la ~** *(âge)* to be around forty; **une ~ (de)** forty or so, about forty
quarante [kaʀɑ̃t] *num* forty
quart [kaʀ] *nm (fraction, partie)* quarter; *(surveillance)* watch; **un ~ de beurre** a quarter kilo of butter; **un ~ de vin** a quarter litre of wine; **une livre un ~** *ou* **et ~** one and a quarter pounds; **le ~ de** a quarter of; **d'heure** quarter of an hour
quartier [kaʀtje] *nm (de ville)* district, area; *(de bœuf)* quarter; *(de fruit, fromage)* piece; **~s** *nmpl (MIL, BLASON)* quarters; **cinéma de ~** local cinema; **avoir ~ libre** *(fig)* to be free; **~ général** headquarters *pl*
quartz [kwaʀts] *nm* quartz
quasi [kazi] *adv* almost, nearly; **quasiment** *adv* almost, nearly

quatorze [katɔʀz(ə)] *num* fourteen
quatre [katʀ(ə)] *num* four; **à ~ pattes** on all fours; **tiré à ~ épingles** dressed up to the nines; **faire les ~ cent coups** to get a bit wild; **se mettre en ~ pour qn** to go out of one's way for sb; **~ à ~** (*monter, descendre*) four at a time; **quatre-vingt-dix** *num* ninety; **quatre-vingts** *num* eighty; **quatrième** *num* fourth
quatuor [kwatyɔʀ] *nm* quartet(te)

─────── *MOT CLÉ* ───────

que [kə] *conj* **1** (*introduisant complétive*) that; **il sait ~ tu es là** he knows (that) you're here; **je veux ~ tu acceptes** I want you to accept; **il a dit ~ oui** he said he would (*ou it was etc*)
2 (*reprise d'autres conjonctions*): **quand il rentrera et qu'il aura mangé** when he gets back and (when) he has eaten; **si vous y allez ou ~ vous ...** if you go there or if you ...
3 (*en tête de phrase: hypothèse, souhait etc*): **qu'il le veuille ou non** whether he likes it or not; **qu'il fasse ce qu'il voudra!** let him do as he pleases!
4 (*après comparatif*) than; as; *voir aussi* **plus; aussi; autant** *etc*
5 (*seulement*): **ne ... ~** only; **il ne boit ~ de l'eau** he only drinks water
♦ *adv* (*exclamation*): **qu'il** *ou* **qu'est-ce qu'il est bête/court vite!** he's so silly!/he runs so fast!; **~ de livres!** what a lot of books!
♦ *pron* **1** (*relatif: personne*) whom; (: *chose*) that, which; **l'homme ~ je vois** the man (whom) I see; **le livre ~ tu vois** the book (that *ou* which) you see; **un jour ~ j'étais ...** a day when I was ...
2 (*interrogatif*) what; **~ fais-tu?, qu'est-ce ~ tu fais?** what are you doing?; **qu'est-ce ~ c'est?** what is it?, what's that?; **~ faire?** what can one do?

─────── *MOT CLÉ* ───────

quel, quelle [kɛl] *adj* **1** (*interrogatif: personne*) who; (: *chose*) what; which; **~ est cet homme?** who is this man?; **~ est ce livre?** what is this book?; **~ livre/homme?** what book/man?; (*parmi un certain choix*) which book/man?; **~s acteurs préférez-vous?** which actors do you prefer?; **dans ~s pays êtes-vous allé?** which *ou* what countries did you go to?
2 (*exclamatif*): **quelle surprise!** what a surprise!
3: **quel(le) que soit le coupable** whoever is guilty; **~ que soit votre avis** whatever your opinion

quelconque [kɛlkɔ̃k] *adj* (*médiocre*) indifferent, poor; (*sans attrait*) ordinary, plain;

(*indéfini*): **un ami ~** some friend or other

─────── *MOT CLÉ* ───────

quelque [kɛlkə] *adj* **1** some; a few; (*tournure interrogative*) any; **~ espoir** some hope; **il a ~s amis** he has a few *ou* some friends; **a-t-il ~s amis?** has he any friends?; **les ~s livres qui** the few books which; **20 kg et ~(s)** a bit over 20 kg
2: **~ ... que: quelque livre qu'il choisisse** whatever (*ou* whichever) book he chooses
3: **~ chose** something; (*tournure interrogative*) anything; **~ chose d'autre** something else; anything else; **~ part** somewhere; anywhere; **en ~ sorte** as it were
♦ *adv* **1** (*environ*): **~ 100 mètres** some 100 metres
2: **~ peu** rather, somewhat

quelquefois [kɛlkəfwa] *adv* sometimes
quelques-uns, -unes [kɛlkəzœ̃, -yn] *pron* a few, some
quelqu'un [kɛlkœ̃] *pron* someone, somebody; (+*tournure interrogative*) anyone *ou* anybody; **~ d'autre** someone *ou* somebody else; anybody else
quémander [kemɑ̃de] *vt* to beg for
qu'en dira-t-on [kɑ̃diʀatɔ̃] *nm inv*: **le ~** gossip, what people say
querelle [kəʀɛl] *nf* quarrel
quereller [kəʀele]: **se ~** *vi* to quarrel
qu'est-ce que [kɛskə] *voir* **que**
qu'est-ce qui [kɛski] *voir* **qui**
question [kɛstjɔ̃] *nf* (*gén*) question; (*fig*) matter; issue; **il a été ~ de** we (*ou* they) spoke about; **de quoi est-il ~?** what is it about?; **il n'en est pas ~** there's no question of it; **hors de ~** out of the question; **remettre en ~** to question; **~naire** [kɛstjɔnɛʀ] *nm* questionnaire; **~ner** [kɛstjɔne] *vt* to question
quête [kɛt] *nf* collection; (*recherche*) quest, search; **faire la ~** (*à l'église*) to take the collection; (*artiste*) to pass the hat round; **quêter** *vi* (*à l'église*) to take the collection
quetsche [kwɛtʃ(ə)] *nf* damson
queue [kø] *nf* tail; (*fig: du classement*) bottom; (: *de poêle*) handle; (: *de fruit, feuille*) stalk; (: *de train, colonne, file*) rear; **faire la ~** to queue (up) (*BRIT*), line up (*US*); **~ de cheval** ponytail; **queue-de-pie** *nf* (*habit*) tails *pl*, tail coat
qui [ki] *pron* (*personne*) who; (+*prép*) whom; (*chose, animal*) which, that; **qu'est-ce ~ est sur la table?** what is on the table?; **~ est-ce ~?** who?; **~ est-ce que?** who?; whom?; **à ~ est ce sac?** whose bag is this?; **à ~ parlais-tu?** who were you talking to?, to whom were you talking?; **amenez ~ vous voulez** bring who you like; **~ que ce soit** whoever it may be
quiconque [kikɔ̃k] *pron* (*celui qui*) who-

ever, anyone who; (*personne*) anyone, any-body

quiétude [kjetyd] *nf* (*d'un lieu*) quiet, tranquillity; **en toute ~** in complete peace

quille [kij] *nf*: **(jeu de) ~s** skittles *sg* (*BRIT*), bowling (*US*)

quincaillerie [kɛ̃kajʀi] *nf* (*ustensiles*) hardware; (*magasin*) hardware shop; **quincaillier, ière** *nm/f* hardware dealer

quinquagénaire [kɛ̃kaʒenɛʀ] *nm/f* man/woman in his/her fifties

quintal, aux [kɛ̃tal, -o] *nm* quintal (*100 kg*)

quinte [kɛ̃t] *nf*: **~ (de toux)** coughing fit

quintuple [kɛ̃typl(ə)] *nm*: **le ~ de** five times as much as; **quintuplés, ées** *nm/fpl* quintuplets, quins

quinzaine [kɛ̃zɛn] *nf*: **une ~ (de)** about fifteen, fifteen or so; **une ~ (de jours)** a fortnight (*BRIT*), two weeks

quinze [kɛ̃z] *num* fifteen; **demain en ~** a fortnight *ou* two weeks tomorrow; **dans ~ jours** in a fortnight('s time), in two weeks (' time)

quiproquo [kipʀɔko] *nm* misunderstanding

quittance [kitɑ̃s] *nf* (*reçu*) receipt; (*facture*) bill

quitte [kit] *adj*: **être ~ envers qn** to be no longer in sb's debt; (*fig*) to be quits with sb; **être ~ de** (*obligation*) to be clear of; **en être ~ à bon compte** to have got off lightly; **~ à faire** even if it means doing

quitter [kite] *vt* to leave; (*espoir, illusion*) to give up; (*vêtement*) to take off; **se ~** *vi* (*couples, interlocuteurs*) to part; **ne quittez pas** (*au téléphone*) hold the line

qui-vive [kiviv] *nm*: **être sur le ~** to be on the alert

quoi [kwa] *pron* (*interrogatif*) what; **~ de neuf?** what's the news?; **as-tu de ~ écrire?** have you anything to write with?; **il n'a pas de ~ se l'acheter** he can't afford it; **~ qu'il arrive** whatever happens; **~ qu'il en soit** be that as it may; **~ que ce soit** anything at all; **"il n'y a pas de ~"** "(please) don't mention it"; **à ~ bon?** what's the use?; **en ~ puis-je vous aider?** how can I help you?

quoique [kwak(ə)] *conj* (al)though

quolibet [kɔlibɛ] *nm* gibe, jeer

quote-part [kɔtpaʀ] *nf* share

quotidien, ne [kɔtidjɛ̃, -ɛn] *adj* daily; (*banal*) everyday ♦ *nm* (*journal*) daily (paper)

R r

r. *abr* = **route; rue**

rab [ʀab] (*fam*) *abr m* = **rabiot**

rabâcher [ʀabɑʃe] *vt* to keep on repeating

rabais [ʀabɛ] *nm* reduction, discount

rabaisser [ʀabese] *vt* (*rabattre*) to reduce; (*dénigrer*) to belittle

rabattre [ʀabatʀ(ə)] *vt* (*couvercle, siège*) to pull down; (*gibier*) to drive; **se ~** *vi* (*bords, couvercle*) to fall shut; (*véhicule, coureur*) to cut in; **se ~ sur** to fall back on

rabbin [ʀabɛ̃] *nm* rabbi

rabiot [ʀabjo] (*fam*) *nm* extra, more

râblé, e [ʀable] *adj* stocky

rabot [ʀabo] *nm* plane

rabougri, e [ʀabugʀi] *adj* stunted

rabrouer [ʀabʀue] *vt* to snub

racaille [ʀakaj] (*péj*) *nf* rabble, riffraff

raccommoder [ʀakɔmɔde] *vt* to mend, repair; (*chaussette etc*) to darn

raccompagner [ʀakɔ̃paɲe] *vt* to take *ou* see back

raccord [ʀakɔʀ] *nm* link

raccorder [ʀakɔʀde] *vt* to join (up), link up; (*suj: pont etc*) to connect, link

raccourci [ʀakuʀsi] *nm* short cut

raccourcir [ʀakuʀsiʀ] *vt* to shorten

raccrocher [ʀakʀɔʃe] *vt* (*tableau*) to hang back up; (*récepteur*) to put down ♦ *vi* (*TÉL*) to hang up, ring off; **se ~ à** *vt* to cling to, hang on to

race [ʀas] *nf* race; (*d'animaux, fig*) breed; (*ascendance*) stock, race; **de ~** purebred, pedigree

rachat [ʀaʃa] *nm* buying; buying back

racheter [ʀaʃte] *vt* (*article perdu*) to buy another; (*davantage*): **~ du lait/3 œufs** to buy more milk/another 3 eggs *ou* 3 more eggs; (*après avoir vendu*) to buy back; (*d'occasion*) to buy; (*COMM: part, firme*) to buy up; (: *pension, rente*) to redeem; **se ~** *vi* (*fig*) to make amends

racial, e, aux [ʀasjal, -o] *adj* racial

racine [ʀasin] *nf* root; **~ carrée/cubique** square/cube root

raciste [ʀasist(ə)] *adj, nm/f* raci(al)ist

racket [ʀakɛt] *nm* racketeering *no pl*

racler [ʀakle] *vt* (*surface*) to scrape; (*tache, boue*) to scrape off

racoler [ʀakɔle] *vt* (*attirer: suj: prostituée*) to solicit; (: *parti, marchand*) to tout for

racontars [ʀakɔ̃taʀ] *nmpl* gossip *sg*
raconter [ʀakɔ̃te] *vt*: ~ **(à qn)** *(décrire)* to relate (to sb), tell (sb) about; *(dire)* to tell (sb)
racorni, e [ʀakɔʀni] *adj* hard(ened)
radar [ʀadaʀ] *nm* radar
rade [ʀad] *nf* (natural) harbour; **rester en ~** *(fig)* to be left stranded
radeau, x [ʀado] *nm* raft
radiateur [ʀadjatœʀ] *nm* radiator, heater; *(AUTO)* radiator; ~ **électrique/à gaz** electric/gas heater *ou* fire
radiation [ʀadjasjɔ̃] *nf (voir radier)* striking off *no pl*; *(PHYSIQUE)* radiation
radical, e, aux [ʀadikal, -o] *adj* radical
radier [ʀadje] *vt* to strike off
radieux, euse [ʀadjø, -øz] *adj* radiant; brilliant, glorious
radin, e [ʀadɛ̃, -in] *(fam) adj* stingy
radio [ʀadjo] *nf* radio; *(MÉD)* X-ray ♦ *nm* radio operator; **à la ~** on the radio; **ra-dioactif, ive** *adj* radioactive; **radiodiffuser** *vt* to broadcast; **radiographie** *nf* radio-graphy; *(photo)* X-ray photograph; **radio-phonique** *adj* radio *cpd*; **radio-réveil** *(pl* **radios-réveils)** *nm* radio alarm clock; **ra-diotélévisé, e** *adj* broadcast on radio and television
radis [ʀadi] *nm* radish
radoter [ʀadɔte] *vi* to ramble on
radoucir [ʀadusiʀ]: **se ~** *vi (se réchauffer)* to become milder; *(se calmer)* to calm down; to soften
rafale [ʀafal] *nf (vent)* gust (of wind); *(tir)* burst of gunfire
raffermir [ʀafɛʀmiʀ] *vt* to firm up; *(fig)* to strengthen
raffiner [ʀafine] *vt* to refine; **raffinerie** *nf* refinery
raffoler [ʀafɔle]: ~ **de** *vt* to be very keen on
rafle [ʀafl(ə)] *nf (de police)* raid
rafler [ʀafle] *(fam) vt* to swipe, nick
rafraîchir [ʀafʀeʃiʀ] *vt (atmosphère, tem-pérature)* to cool (down); *(aussi: mettre à ~)* to chill; *(fig: rénover)* to brighten up; **se ~** *vi* to grow cooler; to freshen up; to re-fresh o.s.; **rafraîchissant, e** *adj* refreshing; **rafraîchissement** *nm* cooling; *(boisson)* cool drink; **rafraîchissements** *nmpl (bois-sons, fruits etc)* refreshments
rage [ʀaʒ] *nf (MÉD)*: **la ~** rabies; *(fureur)* rage, fury; **faire ~** to rage; ~ **de dents** (raging) toothache
ragot [ʀago] *(fam) nm* malicious gossip *no pl*
ragoût [ʀagu] *nm (plat)* stew
raide [ʀɛd] *adj (tendu)* taut, tight; *(escarpé)* steep; *(droit: cheveux)* straight; *(ankylosé, dur, guindé)* stiff; *(fam)* steep, stiff; flat broke ♦ *adv (en pente)* steeply; ~ **mort** stone dead; **raidir** *vt (muscles)* to stiffen;

(câble) to pull taut; **se raidir** *vi* to stiffen; to become taut; *(personne)* to tense up; to brace o.s.
raie [ʀɛ] *nf (ZOOL)* skate, ray; *(rayure)* stripe; *(des cheveux)* parting
raifort [ʀɛfɔʀ] *nm* horseradish
rail [ʀaj] *nm* rail; *(chemins de fer)* railways *pl*; **par ~** by rail
railler [ʀaje] *vt* to scoff at, jeer at
rainure [ʀenyʀ] *nf* groove; slot
raisin [ʀezɛ̃] *nm (aussi: ~s)* grapes *pl*; **~s secs** raisins
raison [ʀezɔ̃] *nf* reason; **avoir ~** to be right; **donner ~ à qn** to agree with sb; to prove sb right; **se faire une ~** to learn to live with it; **perdre la ~** to become insane; **to take leave of one's senses;** ~ **de plus** all the more reason; **à plus forte ~** all the more so; **en ~ de** because of; according to; in proportion to; **à ~ de** at the rate of; ~ **sociale** corporate name; **raisonnable** *adj* reasonable, sensible
raisonnement [ʀezɔnmɑ̃] *nm* reasoning; arguing; argument
raisonner [ʀezɔne] *vi (penser)* to reason; *(argumenter, discuter)* to argue ♦ *vt (per-sonne)* to reason with
rajeunir [ʀaʒœniʀ] *vt (suj: coiffure, robe)*: ~ **qn** to make sb look younger; *(: cure etc)* to rejuvenate; *(fig)* to give a new look to; to inject new blood into ♦ *vi* to become *(ou* look) younger
rajouter [ʀaʒute] *vt*: ~ **du sel/un œuf** to add some more salt/another egg
rajuster [ʀaʒyste] *vt (vêtement)* to straight-en, tidy; *(salaires)* to adjust; *(machine)* to readjust
ralenti [ʀalɑ̃ti] *nm*: **au ~** *(AUTO)*: **tourner au ~** to tick over *(AUTO)*, idle; **au ~** *(CINÉMA)* in slow motion; *(fig)* at a slower pace
ralentir [ʀalɑ̃tiʀ] *vt* to slow down
râler [ʀale] *vi* to groan; *(fam)* to grouse, moan (and groan)
rallier [ʀalje] *vt (rassembler)* to rally; *(re-joindre)* to rejoin; *(gagner à sa cause)* to win over; **se ~ à** *(avis)* to come over *ou* round to
rallonge [ʀalɔ̃ʒ] *nf (de table)* (extra) leaf; *(argent etc)* extra *no pl*
rallonger [ʀalɔ̃ʒe] *vt* to lengthen
rallye [ʀali] *nm* rally; *(POL)* march
ramassage [ʀamɑsaʒ] *nm*: ~ **scolaire** school bus service
ramassé, e [ʀamɑse] *adj (trapu)* squat
ramasser [ʀamɑse] *vt (objet tombé ou par terre, fam)* to pick up; *(recueillir)* to collect; *(récolter)* to gather; **se ~** *vi (sur soi-même)* to huddle up; to crouch; **ramassis** *(péj) nm* bunch; jumble
rambarde [ʀɑ̃baʀd(ə)] *nf* guardrail
rame [ʀam] *nf (aviron)* oar; *(de métro)*

train; (*de papier*) ream

rameau, x [ʀamo] *nm* (small) branch; **les R~x** (*REL*) Palm Sunday *sg*

ramener [ʀamne] *vt* to bring back; (*reconduire*) to take back; (*rabattre: couverture, visière*): ~ **qch sur** to pull sth back over; ~ **qch à** (*réduire à, aussi MATH*) to reduce sth to

ramer [ʀame] *vi* to row

ramollir [ʀamɔliʀ] *vt* to soften; **se ~** *vi* to go soft

ramoner [ʀamɔne] *vt* to sweep

rampe [ʀɑ̃p] *nf* (*d'escalier*) banister(s *pl*); (*dans un garage, d'un terrain*) ramp; (*THÉÂTRE*): **la ~** the footlights *pl*; ~ **de lancement** launching pad

ramper [ʀɑ̃pe] *vi* to crawl

rancard [ʀɑ̃kaʀ] (*fam*) *nm* date; tip

rancart [ʀɑ̃kaʀ] *nm*: **mettre au ~** to scrap

rance [ʀɑ̃s] *adj* rancid

rancœur [ʀɑ̃kœʀ] *nf* rancour

rançon [ʀɑ̃sɔ̃] *nf* ransom; (*fig*) price

rancune [ʀɑ̃kyn] *nf* grudge, rancour; **garder ~ à qn (de qch)** to bear sb a grudge (for sth); **sans ~!** no hard feelings!; **rancunier, ière** *adj* vindictive, spiteful

randonnée [ʀɑ̃dɔne] *nf* ride; (*à pied*) walk, ramble; hike, hiking *no pl*

rang [ʀɑ̃] *nm* (*rangée*) row; (*grade, classement*) rank; **~s** *nmpl* (*MIL*) ranks; **se mettre en ~s/sur un ~** to get into *ou* form rows/a line; **au premier ~** in the first row; (*fig*) ranking first

rangé, e [ʀɑ̃ʒe] *adj* (*sérieux*) orderly, steady

rangée [ʀɑ̃ʒe] *nf* row

ranger [ʀɑ̃ʒe] *vt* (*classer, grouper*) to order, arrange; (*mettre à sa place*) to put away; (*voiture dans la rue*) to park; (*mettre de l'ordre dans*) to tidy up; (*arranger*) to arrange; (*fig: classer*): ~ **qn/qch parmi** to rank sb/sth among; **se ~** *vi* (*véhicule, conducteur*) to pull over *ou* in; (*piéton*) to step aside; (*s'assagir*) to settle down; **se ~ à** (*avis*) to come round to

ranimer [ʀanime] *vt* (*personne*) to bring round; (*forces, courage*) to restore; (*troupes etc*) to kindle new life in; (*douleur, souvenir*) to revive; (*feu*) to rekindle

rap [ʀap] *nm* rap (music)

rapace [ʀapas] *nm* bird of prey

râpe [ʀɑp] *nf* (*CULIN*) grater

râpé, e [ʀɑpe] *adj* (*tissu*) threadbare

râper [ʀɑpe] *vt* (*CULIN*) to grate

rapetisser [ʀaptise] *vt* to shorten

rapide [ʀapid] *adj* fast; (*prompt*) quick ♦ *nm* express (train); (*de cours d'eau*) rapid; **rapidement** *adv* fast; quickly

rapiécer [ʀapjese] *vt* to patch

rappel [ʀapɛl] *nm* (*THÉÂTRE*) curtain call; (*MÉD: vaccination*) booster; (*ADMIN: de salaire*) back pay *no pl*; (*d'une aventure, d'un nom*) reminder

rappeler [ʀaple] *vt* to call back; (*ambassadeur, MIL*) to recall; (*faire se souvenir*): ~ **qch à qn** to remind sb of sth; **se ~** *vt* (*se souvenir de*) to remember, recall

rapport [ʀapɔʀ] *nm* (*compte rendu*) report; (*profit*) yield, return; revenue; (*lien, analogie*) relationship; (*MATH, TECH*) ratio; **~s** *nmpl* (*entre personnes, pays*) relations; **avoir ~ à** to have something to do with; **être en ~ avec** (*idée de corrélation*) to be related to; **être/se mettre en ~ avec qn** to be/get in touch with sb; **par ~ à** in relation to; ~ **qualité-prix** *nm* value (for money); **~s (sexuels)** (sexual) intercourse *sg*

rapporter [ʀapɔʀte] *vt* (*rendre, ramener*) to bring back; (*apporter davantage*) to bring more; (*suj: investissement*) to yield; (: *activité*) to bring in; (*relater*) to report ♦ *vi* (*investissement*) to give a good return *ou* yield; (: *activité*) to be very profitable; **se ~ à** (*correspondre à*) to relate to; **s'en ~ à** to rely on; ~ **qch à** (*fig: rattacher*) to relate sth to; **rapporteur, euse** *nm/f* (*de procès, commission*) reporter; (*péj*) telltale ♦ *nm* (*GÉOM*) protractor

rapprochement [ʀapʀɔʃmɑ̃] *nm* (*de nations, familles*) reconciliation; (*analogie, rapport*) parallel

rapprocher [ʀapʀɔʃe] *vt* (*chaise d'une table*): ~ **qch (de)** to bring sth closer (to); (*deux objets*) to bring closer together; (*réunir*) to bring together; (*comparer*) to establish a parallel between; **se ~** *vi* to draw closer *ou* nearer; **se ~ de** to come closer to; (*présenter une analogie avec*) to be close to

rapt [ʀapt] *nm* abduction

raquette [ʀakɛt] *nf* (*de tennis*) racket; (*de ping-pong*) bat; (*à neige*) snowshoe

rare [ʀaʀ] *adj* rare; (*main-d'œuvre, denrées*) scarce; (*cheveux, herbe*) sparse

rarement [ʀaʀmɑ̃] *adv* rarely, seldom

ras, e [ʀɑ, ʀɑz] *adj* (*tête, cheveux*) close-cropped; (*poil, herbe*) short ♦ *adv* short; **en ~e campagne** in open country; **à ~ bords** to the brim; **au ~ de** level with; **en avoir ~ le bol** (*fam*) to be fed up; ~ **du cou** *adj* (*pull, robe*) crew-neck

rasade [ʀazad] *nf* glassful

raser [ʀaze] *vt* (*barbe, cheveux*) to shave off; (*menton, personne*) to shave; (*fam: ennuyer*) to bore; (*démolir*) to raze (to the ground); (*frôler*) to graze, skim; **se ~** *vi* to shave; (*fam*) to be bored (to tears); **rasoir** *nm* razor

rassasier [ʀasazje] *vt* to satisfy

rassemblement [ʀasɑ̃bləmɑ̃] *nm* (*groupe*) gathering; (*POL*) union

rassembler [ʀasɑ̃ble] *vt* (*réunir*) to assemble, gather; (*regrouper, amasser*) to gather together, collect; **se ~** *vi* to gather

rassis, e [Rasi, -iz] *adj* (*pain*) stale
rassurer [RasyRe] *vt* to reassure; **se ~** *vi* to be reassured; **rassure-toi** don't worry
rat [Ra] *nm* rat
rate [Rat] *nf* spleen
raté, e [Rate] *adj* (*tentative*) unsuccessful, failed ♦ *nm/f* failure ♦ *nm* misfiring *no pl*
râteau, x [Rato] *nm* rake
râtelier [Ratəlje] *nm* rack; (*fam*) false teeth *pl*
rater [Rate] *vi* (*affaire, projet etc*) to go wrong, fail ♦ *vt* (*cible, train, occasion*) to miss; (*démonstration, plat*) to spoil; (*examen*) to fail
ration [Rasjɔ̃] *nf* ration; (*fig*) share
ratisser [Ratise] *vt* (*allée*) to rake; (*feuilles*) to rake up; (*suj: armée, police*) to comb
R.A.T.P. *sigle f* (= *Régie autonome des transports parisiens*) *Paris transport authority*
rattacher [Ratafe] *vt* (*animal, cheveux*) to tie up again; (*incorporer: ADMIN etc*): **~ qch à** to join sth to; (*fig: relier*): **~ qch à** to link sth with; (: *lier*): **~ qn à** to bind *ou* tie sb to
rattraper [RatRape] *vt* (*fugitif*) to recapture; (*empêcher de tomber*) to catch (hold of); (*atteindre, rejoindre*) to catch up with; (*réparer: imprudence, erreur*) to make up for; **se ~** *vi* to make good one's losses; to make up for it; **se ~ (à)** (*se raccrocher*) to stop o.s. falling (by catching hold of)
rature [RatyR] *nf* deletion, erasure
rauque [Rok] *adj* raucous; hoarse
ravages [Ravaʒ] *nmpl*: **faire des ~** to wreak havoc
ravaler [Ravale] *vt* (*mur, façade*) to restore; (*déprécier*) to lower
ravi, e [Ravi] *adj*: **être ~ de/que** to be delighted with/that
ravin [Ravɛ̃] *nm* gully, ravine
ravir [RaviR] *vt* (*enchanter*) to delight; (*enlever*): **~ qch à qn** to rob sb of sth; **à ~** beautifully
raviser [Ravize] : **se ~** *vi* to change one's mind
ravissant, e [Ravisɑ̃, -ɑ̃t] *adj* delightful
ravisseur, euse [RavisœR, -øz] *nm/f* abductor, kidnapper
ravitailler [Ravitaje] *vt* to resupply; (*véhicule*) to refuel; **se ~** *vi* to get fresh supplies
raviver [Ravive] *vt* (*feu, douleur*) to revive; (*couleurs*) to brighten up
rayé, e [Reje] *adj* (*à rayures*) striped
rayer [Reje] *vt* (*érafler*) to scratch; (*barrer*) to cross out; (*d'une liste*) to cross off
rayon [Rejɔ̃] *nm* (*de soleil etc*) ray; (*GÉOM*) radius; (*de roue*) spoke; (*étagère*) shelf; (*grand magasin*) department; **dans un ~ de** within a radius of; **~ d'action** range; **~ de soleil** sunbeam; **~s X** X-rays
rayonnement [Rejɔnmɑ̃] *nm* radiation; (*fig*) radiance; influence

rayonner [Rejɔne] *vi* (*chaleur, énergie*) to radiate; (*fig*) to shine forth; to be radiant; (*touriste*) to go touring (*from one base*)
rayure [RejyR] *nf* (*motif*) stripe; (*éraflure*) scratch; (*rainure, d'un fusil*) groove
raz-de-marée [Radmare] *nm inv* tidal wave
ré [Re] *nm* (*MUS*) D; (*en chantant la gamme*) re
réacteur [Reaktœr] *nm* jet engine
réaction [Reaksjɔ̃] *nf* reaction; **moteur à ~** jet engine
réadapter [Readapte] *vt* to readjust; (*MÉD*) to rehabilitate; **se ~ (à)** to readjust (to)
réagir [ReaʒiR] *vi* to react
réalisateur, trice [RealizatœR, -tRis] *nm/f* (*TV, CINÉMA*) director
réalisation [Realizasjɔ̃] *nf* carrying out; realization; fulfilment; achievement; production; (*œuvre*) production; creation; work
réaliser [Realize] *vt* (*projet, opération*) to carry out, realize; (*rêve, souhait*) to realize, fulfil; (*exploit*) to achieve; (*achat, vente*) to make; (*film*) to produce; (*se rendre compte de, COMM: bien, capital*) to realize; **se ~** *vi* to be realized
réaliste [Realist(ə)] *adj* realistic
réalité [Realite] *nf* reality; **en ~** in (actual) fact; **dans la ~** in reality; **~ virtuelle** (*COMPUT*) virtual reality
réanimation [Reanimasjɔ̃] *nf* resuscitation; **service de ~** intensive care unit
réarmer [ReaRme] *vt* (*arme*) to reload ♦ *vi* (*état*) to rearm
rébarbatif, ive [RebaRbatif, -iv] *adj* forbidding
rebattu, e [Rəbaty] *adj* hackneyed
rebelle [Rəbɛl] *nm/f* rebel ♦ *adj* (*troupes*) rebel; (*enfant*) rebellious; (*mèche etc*) unruly; **~ à** unamenable to
rebeller [Rəbele]: **se ~** *vi* to rebel
rebondi, e [Rəbɔ̃di] *adj* rounded; chubby
rebondir [RəbɔdiR] *vi* (*ballon: au sol*) to bounce; (: *contre un mur*) to rebound; (*fig*) to get moving again; **rebondissement** *nm* new development
rebord [RəbɔR] *nm* edge
rebours [RəbuR]: **à ~** *adv* the wrong way
rebrousse-poil [Rəbruspwal]: **à ~** *adv* the wrong way
rebrousser [Rəbruse] *vt*: **~ chemin** to turn back
rebut [Rəby] *nm*: **mettre au ~** to scrap; **~er** [Rəbyte] *vt* to put off
récalcitrant, e [Rekalsitrɑ̃, -ɑ̃t] *adj* refractory
recaler [Rəkale] *vt* (*SCOL*) to fail
récapituler [Rekapityle] *vt* to recapitulate; to sum up
receler [Rəsəle] *vt* (*produit d'un vol*) to receive; (*malfaiteur*) to harbour; (*fig*) to con-

ceal; **receleur, euse** *nm/f* receiver

récemment [resamã] *adv* recently

recenser [rəsãse] *vt* (*population*) to take a census of; (*inventorier*) to list

récent, e [resã, -ãt] *adj* recent

récépissé [resepise] *nm* receipt

récepteur [reseptœr] *nm* receiver; ~ **(de radio)** radio set *ou* receiver

réception [resepsjõ] *nf* receiving *no pl*; (*accueil*) reception, welcome; (*bureau*) reception desk; (*réunion mondaine*) reception, party; **réceptionniste** *nm/f* receptionist

recette [rəsɛt] *nf* (*CULIN*) recipe; (*fig*) formula, recipe; (*COMM*) takings *pl*; ~**s** *nfpl*: (*rentrées*) receipts

receveur, euse [rəsvœr, -øz] *nm/f* (*des contributions*) tax collector; (*des postes*) postmaster(mistress); (*d'autobus*) conductor(tress)

recevoir [rəsvwar] *vt* to receive; (*client, patient*) to see ♦ *vi* to receive visitors; to give parties; to see patients *etc*; **se** ~ *vi* (*athlète*) to land; **être reçu** (*à un examen*) to pass

rechange [rəʃãʒ]: **de** ~ *adj* (*pièces, roue*) spare; (*fig: solution*) alternative; **des vêtements de** ~ a change of clothes

rechaper [rəʃape] *vt* to remould, retread

réchapper [reʃape]: ~ **de** *ou* **à** *vt* (*accident, maladie*) to come through

recharge [rəʃarʒ(ə)] *nf* refill

recharger [rəʃarʒe] *vt* (*camion, fusil, appareil-photo*) to reload; (*briquet, stylo*) to refill; (*batterie*) to recharge

réchaud [reʃo] *nm* (*portable*) stove; platewarmer

réchauffer [reʃofe] *vt* (*plat*) to reheat; (*mains, personne*) to warm; **se** ~ *vi* (*température*) to get warmer

rêche [rɛʃ] *adj* rough

recherche [rəʃɛrʃ(ə)] *nf* (*action*): **la** ~ **de** the search for; (*raffinement*) affectedness, studied elegance; (*scientifique etc*): **la** ~ research; ~**s** *nfpl* (*de la police*) investigations; (*scientifiques*) research *sg*; **se mettre à la** ~ **de** to go in search of

recherché, e [rəʃɛrʃe] *adj* (*rare, demandé*) much sought-after; (*raffiné*) studied, affected

rechercher [rəʃɛrʃe] *vt* (*objet égaré, personne*) to look for; (*causes, nouveau procédé*) to try to find; (*bonheur, amitié*) to seek

rechute [rəʃyt] *nf* (*MÉD*) relapse

récidiver [residive] *vi* to commit a subsequent offence; (*fig*) to do it again

récif [resif] *nm* reef

récipient [resipjã] *nm* container

réciproque [resiprɔk] *adj* reciprocal

récit [resi] *nm* story

récital [resital] *nm* recital

réciter [resite] *vt* to recite

réclamation [reklamasjõ] *nf* complaint; ~**s**

nfpl (*bureau*) complaints department *sg*

réclame [reklam] *nf* ad, advert(isement); **article en** ~ special offer

réclamer [reklame] *vt* (*aide, nourriture etc*) to ask for; (*revendiquer*) to claim, demand; (*nécessiter*) to demand, require ♦ *vi* to complain

réclusion [reklyzjõ] *nf* imprisonment

recoin [rəkwɛ̃] *nm* nook, corner; (*fig*) hidden recess

reçois *etc vb voir* **recevoir**

récolte [rekɔlt(ə)] *nf* harvesting; gathering; (*produits*) harvest, crop; (*fig*) crop, collection

récolter [rekɔlte] *vt* to harvest, gather (in); (*fig*) to collect; to get

recommandé [rəkɔmãde] *nm* (*POSTES*): **en** ~ by registered mail

recommander [rəkɔmãde] *vt* to recommend; (*suj: qualités etc*) to commend; (*POSTES*) to register; **se** ~ **de qn** to give sb's name as a reference

recommencer [rəkɔmãse] *vt* (*reprendre: lutte, séance*) to resume, start again; (*refaire: travail, explications*) to start afresh, start (over) again; (*récidiver: erreur*) to make again ♦ *vi* to start again; (*récidiver*) to do it again

récompense [rekõpãs] *nf* reward; (*prix*) award; **récompenser** *vt*: **récompenser qn (de** *ou* **pour)** to reward sb (for)

réconcilier [rekõsilje] *vt* to reconcile; **se** ~ **(avec)** to be reconciled (with)

reconduire [rəkõdɥir] *vt* (*raccompagner*) to take *ou* see back; (*JUR, POL: renouveler*) to renew

réconfort [rekõfɔr] *nm* comfort

réconforter [rekõfɔrte] *vt* (*consoler*) to comfort; (*revigorer*) to fortify

reconnaissance [rəkɔnɛsãs] *nf* recognition; acknowledgement; (*gratitude*) gratitude, gratefulness; (*MIL*) reconnaissance, recce; **reconnaissant, e** [rəkɔnɛsã, -ãt] *adj* grateful

reconnaître [rəkɔnɛtr(ə)] *vt* to recognize; (*MIL: lieu*) to reconnoitre; (*JUR: enfant, dette, droit*) to acknowledge; ~ **que** to admit *ou* acknowledge that; ~ **qn/qch à** to recognize sb/sth by

reconnu, e [r(ə)kɔny] *adj* (*indiscuté, connu*) recognized

reconstituant, e [rəkõstitɥã, -ãt] *adj* (*aliment, régime*) strength-building

reconstituer [rəkõstitɥe] *vt* (*monument ancien*) to recreate; (*fresque, vase brisé*) to piece together, reconstitute; (*événement, accident*) to reconstruct; (*fortune, patrimoine*) to rebuild

reconstruire [rəkõstrɥir] *vt* to rebuild

reconvertir [rəkõvɛrtir]: **se** ~ *vr* (*un métier, une branche*) to go into

record [rəkɔr] *nm, adj* record

recoupement [ʀəkupmɑ̃] *nm*: **par ~** by cross-checking

recouper [ʀəkupe]: **se ~** *vi* (*témoignages*) to tie *ou* match up

recourbé, e [ʀəkuʀbe] *adj* curved; hooked; bent

recourir [ʀəkuʀiʀ]: **~ à** *vt* (*ami, agence*) to turn *ou* appeal to; (*force, ruse, emprunt*) to resort to

recours [ʀəkuʀ] *nm* (*JUR*) appeal; **avoir ~ à** = **recourir à**; **en dernier ~** as a last resort; **~ en grâce** plea for clemency

recouvrer [ʀəkuvʀe] *vt* (*vue, santé etc*) to recover, regain; (*impôts*) to collect; (*créance*) to recover

recouvrir [ʀəkuvʀiʀ] *vt* (*couvrir à nouveau*) to re-cover; (*couvrir entièrement, aussi fig*) to cover; (*cacher, masquer*) to conceal, hide; **se ~** *vi* (*se superposer*) to overlap

récréation [ʀekʀeɑsjɔ̃] *nf* recreation, entertainment; (*SCOL*) break

récrier [ʀekʀije]: **se ~** *vi* to exclaim

récriminations [ʀekʀiminɑsjɔ̃] *nfpl* remonstrations, complaints

recroqueviller [ʀəkʀɔkvije]: **se ~** *vi* (*feuilles*) to curl *ou* shrivel up; (*personne*) to huddle up

recrudescence [ʀəkʀydesɑ̃s] *nf* fresh outbreak

recrue [ʀəkʀy] *nf* recruit

recruter [ʀəkʀyte] *vt* to recruit

rectangle [ʀɛktɑ̃gl(ə)] *nm* rectangle; **rectangulaire** *adj* rectangular

recteur [ʀɛktœʀ] *nm* ≈ (regional) director of education (*BRIT*), ≈ state superintendent of education (*US*)

rectificatif, -iv [ʀɛktifikatif, -iv] *nm* correction

rectifier [ʀɛktifje] *vt* (*tracé, virage*) to straighten; (*calcul, adresse*) to correct; (*erreur, faute*) to rectify

rectiligne [ʀɛktiliɲ] *adj* straight; (*GÉOM*) rectilinear

reçu, e [ʀəsy] *pp de* **recevoir** ♦ *adj* (*admis, consacré*) accepted ♦ *nm* (*COMM*) receipt

recueil [ʀəkœj] *nm* collection

recueillir [ʀəkœjiʀ] *vt* to collect; (*voix, suffrages*) to win; (*accueillir: réfugiés, chat*) to take in; **se ~** *vi* to gather one's thoughts; to meditate

recul [ʀəkyl] *nm* retreat; recession; decline; (*d'arme à feu*) recoil, kick; **avoir un mouvement de ~** to recoil; **prendre du ~** to stand back

reculé, e [ʀəkyle] *adj* remote

reculer [ʀəkyle] *vi* to move back, back away; (*AUTO*) to reverse, back (up); (*fig*) to (be on the) decline; to be losing ground; (: *se dérober*) to shrink back ♦ *vt* to move back; to reverse, back (up); (*fig: possibilités, limites*) to extend; (: *date, décision*) to postpone

reculons [ʀəkylɔ̃]: **à ~** *adv* backwards

récupérer [ʀekypeʀe] *vt* to recover, get back; (*heures de travail*) to make up; (*déchets*) to salvage; (*délinquant etc*) to rehabilitate ♦ *vi* to recover

récurer [ʀekyʀe] *vt* to scour

récuser [ʀekyze] *vt* to challenge; **se ~** *vi* to decline to give an opinion

reçut *vb voir* **recevoir**

recycler [ʀəsikle] *vt* (*SCOL*) to reorientate; (*employés*) to retrain; (*TECH*) to recycle

rédacteur, trice [ʀedaktœʀ, -tʀis] *nm/f* (*journaliste*) writer; subeditor; (*d'ouvrage de référence*) editor, compiler; **~ en chef** chief editor; **~ publicitaire** copywriter

rédaction [ʀedaksjɔ̃] *nf* writing; (*rédacteurs*) editorial staff; (*bureau*) editorial office(s); (*SCOL: devoir*) essay, composition

reddition [ʀedisjɔ̃] *nf* surrender

redemander [ʀədmɑ̃de] *vt* to ask again for; to ask for more of

redescendre [ʀədesɑ̃dʀ(ə)] *vi* to go back down ♦ *vt* (*pente etc*) to go down

redevable [ʀədvabl(ə)] *adj*: **être ~ de qch à qn** (*somme*) to owe sb sth; (*fig*) to be indebted to sb for sth

redevance [ʀədvɑ̃s] *nf* (*TÉL*) rental charge; (*TV*) licence fee

rédiger [ʀediʒe] *vt* to write; (*contrat*) to draw up

redire [ʀədiʀ] *vt* to repeat; **trouver à ~ à** to find fault with

redoublé, e [ʀəduble] *adj*: **à coups ~s** even harder, twice as hard

redoubler [ʀəduble] *vi* (*tempête, violence*) to intensify; (*SCOL*) to repeat a year; **~ de** to be twice as +*adjectif*

redoutable [ʀədutabl(ə)] *adj* formidable, fearsome

redouter [ʀədute] *vt* to fear; (*appréhender*) to dread

redresser [ʀədʀese] *vt* (*arbre, mât*) to set upright; (*pièce tordue*) to straighten out; (*situation, économie*) to put right; **se ~** *vi* (*objet penché*) to right itself; (*personne*) to sit (*ou* stand up) (straight)

réduction [ʀedyksjɔ̃] *nf* reduction

réduire [ʀeduiʀ] *vt* to reduce; (*prix, dépenses*) to cut, reduce; (*MÉD: fracture*) to set; **se ~ à** (*revenir à*) to boil down to; **se ~ en** (*se transformer en*) to be reduced to

réduit [ʀedui] *nm* tiny room; recess

rééducation [ʀeedykɑsjɔ̃] *nf* (*d'un membre*) re-education; (*de délinquants, d'un blessé*) rehabilitation

réel, le [ʀeɛl] *adj* real

réellement [ʀeɛlmɑ̃] *adv* really

réévaluer [ʀeevalɥe] *vt* to revalue

réexpédier [ʀeɛkspedje] *vt* (*à l'envoyeur*) to return, send back; (*au destinataire*) to send on, forward

refaire [ʀəfɛʀ] *vt* (*faire de nouveau, recommencer*) to do again; (*réparer, restaurer*) to do up

réfection [ʀefɛksjɔ̃] *nf* repair

réfectoire [ʀefɛktwaʀ] *nm* refectory

référence [ʀefeʀɑ̃s] *nf* reference; ~s *nfpl* (*recommandations*) reference *sg*

référer [ʀefeʀe] : se ~ à *vt* to refer to; en ~ à qn to refer the matter to sb

réfléchi, e [ʀefleʃi] *adj* (*caractère*) thoughtful; (*action*) well-thought-out; (*LING*) reflexive

réfléchir [ʀefleʃiʀ] *vt* to reflect ♦ *vi* to think; ~ à *ou* sur to think about

reflet [ʀəflɛ] *nm* reflection; (*sur l'eau etc*) sheen *no pl*, glint

refléter [ʀəflete] *vt* to reflect; se ~ *vi* to be reflected

réflexe [ʀeflɛks(ə)] *nm, adj* reflex

réflexion [ʀeflɛksjɔ̃] *nf* (*de la lumière etc*, *pensée*) reflection; (*fait de penser*) thought; (*remarque*) remark; ~ faite, à la ~ on reflection

refluer [ʀəflye] *vi* to flow back; (*foule*) to surge back

reflux [ʀəfly] *nm* (*de la mer*) ebb

réforme [ʀefɔʀm(ə)] *nf* reform; (*REL*): la R~ the Reformation

réformer [ʀefɔʀme] *vt* to reform; (*MIL*) to declare unfit for service

refouler [ʀəfule] *vt* (*envahisseurs*) to drive back; (*liquide*) to force back; (*fig*) to suppress; (*PSYCH*) to repress

réfractaire [ʀefʀaktɛʀ] *adj*: être ~ à to resist

refrain [ʀəfʀɛ̃] *nm* (*MUS*) refrain, chorus; (*air, fig*) tune

refréner [ʀəfʀene] *vt* to curb, check

réfréner [ʀefʀene] *vt* = **refréner**

réfrigérateur [ʀefʀiʒeʀatœʀ] *nm* refrigerator, fridge

refroidir [ʀəfʀwadiʀ] *vt* to cool ♦ *vi* to cool (down); se ~ *vi* (*prendre froid*) to catch a chill; (*temps*) to get cooler *ou* colder; (*fig*) to cool (off); **refroidissement** *nm* (*grippe etc*) chill

refuge [ʀəfyʒ] *nm* refuge; (*pour piétons*) (traffic) island

réfugié, e [ʀefyʒje] *adj, nm/f* refugee

réfugier [ʀefyʒje]: se ~ *vi* to take refuge

refus [ʀəfy] *nm* refusal; **ce n'est pas de ~** I won't say no, it's welcome

refuser [ʀəfyze] *vt* to refuse; (*SCOL: candidat*) to fail; ~ qch à qn to refuse sb sth; ~ du monde to have to turn people away; se ~ à faire to refuse to do

réfuter [ʀefyte] *vt* to refute

regagner [ʀəgaɲe] *vt* (*argent, faveur*) to win back; (*lieu*) to get back to; ~ **le temps perdu** to make up (for) lost time

regain [ʀəgɛ̃] *nm* (*renouveau*): **un ~ de** renewed +*nom*

régal [ʀegal] *nm* treat

régaler [ʀegale]: se ~ *vi* to have a deli-

cious meal; (*fig*) to enjoy o.s.

regard [ʀəgaʀ] *nm* (*coup d'œil*) look, glance; (*expression*) look (in one's eye); **au ~ de** (*loi, morale*) from the point of view of; **en ~** (*vis à vis*) opposite; **en ~ de** in comparison with

regardant, e [ʀəgaʀdɑ̃, -ɑ̃t] *adj*: **très/peu ~ (sur)** quite fussy/very free (about); (*économe*) very tight-fisted/quite generous (with)

regarder [ʀəgaʀde] *vt* (*examiner, observer, lire*) to look at; (*film, télévision, match*) to watch; (*envisager: situation, avenir*) to view; (*considérer: son intérêt etc*) to be concerned with; (*être orienté vers*): ~ **(vers)** to face; (*concerner*) to concern ♦ *vi* to look; ~ à (*dépense*) to be fussy with *ou* over; ~ qn/ qch comme to regard sb/sth as

régie [ʀeʒi] *nf* (*COMM, INDUSTRIE*) state-owned company; (*THÉÂTRE, CINÉMA*) production; (*RADIO, TV*) control room

regimber [ʀəʒɛ̃be] *vi* to balk, jib

régime [ʀeʒim] *nm* (*POL*) régime; (*ADMIN: carcéral, fiscal etc*) system; (*MÉD*) diet; (*TECH*) (engine) speed; (*fig*) rate, pace; (*de bananes, dattes*) bunch; **se mettre au/ suivre un ~** to go on/be on a diet

régiment [ʀeʒimɑ̃] *nm* regiment; (*fig: fam*): **un ~ de** an army of

région [ʀeʒjɔ̃] *nf* region; **régional, e, aux** *adj* regional

régir [ʀeʒiʀ] *vt* to govern

régisseur [ʀeʒisœʀ] *nm* (*d'un domaine*) steward; (*CINÉMA, TV*) assistant director; (*THÉÂTRE*) stage manager

registre [ʀeʒistʀ(ə)] *nm* (*livre*) register; logbook; ledger; (*MUS, LING*) register

réglage [ʀeglaʒ] *nm* adjustment; tuning

règle [ʀɛgl(ə)] *nf* (*instrument*) ruler; (*loi, prescription*) rule; ~s *nfpl* (*PHYSIOL*) period *sg*; **en ~** (*papiers d'identité*) in order; **en ~ générale** as a (general) rule

réglé, e [ʀegle] *adj* well-ordered; steady; (*papier*) ruled; (*arrangé*) settled

règlement [ʀɛgləmɑ̃] *nm* (*paiement*) settlement; (*arrêté*) regulation; (*règles, statuts*) regulations *pl*, rules *pl*; ~ **de compte(s)** *nm* settling of old scores; **réglementaire** *adj* conforming to the regulations; (*tenue*) regulation *cpd*; **réglementer** [ʀɛgləmɑ̃te] *vt* to regulate

régler [ʀegle] *vt* (*mécanisme, machine*) to regulate, adjust; (*moteur*) to tune; (*thermostat etc*) to set, adjust; (*conflit, facture*) to settle; (*fournisseur*) to settle up with

réglisse [ʀeglis] *nf* liquorice

règne [ʀɛɲ] *nm* (*d'un roi etc, fig*) reign; (*BIO*): **le ~ végétal/animal** the vegetable/ animal kingdom

régner [ʀeɲe] *vi* (*roi*) to rule, reign; (*fig*) to reign

regorger [ʀəgɔʀʒe] *vi*: ~ **de** to overflow

with, be bursting with

regret [ʀəgʀɛ] nm regret; **à ~** with regret; **avec ~** regretfully; **être au ~ de devoir faire** to regret having to do

regrettable [ʀəgʀɛtabl(ə)] adj regrettable

regretter [ʀəgʀete] vt to regret; (personne) to miss; **je regrette** I'm sorry

regrouper [ʀəgʀupe] vt (grouper) to group together; (contenir) to include, comprise; **se ~** vi to gather (together)

régulier, ière [ʀegylje, -jɛʀ] adj (gén) regular; (vitesse, qualité) steady; (répartition, pression, paysage) even; (TRANSPORTS: ligne, service) scheduled, regular; (légal, réglementaire) lawful, in order; (fam: correct) straight, on the level; **régulièrement** adv regularly; steadily; evenly; normally

rehausser [ʀɔose] vt to heighten, raise

rein [ʀɛ̃] nm kidney; **~s** nmpl (dos) back sg

reine [ʀɛn] nf queen

reine-claude [ʀɛnklod] nf greengage

réintégrer [ʀeɛ̃tegʀe] vt (lieu) to return to; (fonctionnaire) to reinstate

rejaillir [ʀəʒajiʀ] vi to splash up; **~ sur** to splash up onto; (fig) to rebound on; to fall upon

rejet [ʀəʒɛ] nm (action, aussi MÉD) rejection

rejeter [ʀəʒte] vt (relancer) to throw back; (vomir) to bring ou throw up; (écarter) to reject; (déverser) to throw out, discharge; **la responsabilité de qch sur qn** to lay the responsibility for sth at sb's door

rejoindre [ʀəʒwɛ̃dʀ(ə)] vt (famille, régiment) to rejoin, return to; (lieu) to get (back) to; (suj: route etc) to meet, join; (rattraper) to catch up (with); **se ~** vi to meet; **je te rejoins au café** I'll see ou meet you at the café

réjouir [ʀeʒwiʀ] vt to delight; **se ~** vi to be delighted; to rejoice; **réjouissances** nfpl (joie) rejoicing sg; (fête) festivities

relâche [ʀəlɑʃ]: **sans ~** without respite ou a break

relâché, e [ʀəlɑʃe] adj loose, lax

relâcher [ʀəlɑʃe] vt to release; (étreinte) to loosen; **se ~** vi to loosen; (discipline) to become slack ou lax; (élève etc) to slacken off

relais [ʀəlɛ] nm (SPORT): **(course de) ~** relay (race); **équipe de ~** shift team; (SPORT) relay team; **prendre le ~ (de)** to take over (from); **~ routier** ≈ transport café (BRIT), ≈ truck stop (US)

relancer [ʀəlɑ̃se] vt (balle) to throw back; (moteur) to restart; (fig) to boost, revive; (personne): **~ qn** to pester sb

relater [ʀəlate] vt to relate, recount

relatif, ive [ʀəlatif, -iv] adj relative

relation [ʀəlasjɔ̃] nf (récit) account, report; (rapport) relation(ship); **~s** nfpl (rapports) relations; relationship sg; (connaissances) connections; **être/entrer en ~(s) avec** to be/get in contact with

relaxer [ʀəlakse] vt to relax; (JUR) to discharge; **se ~** vi to relax

relayer [ʀəleje] vt (collaborateur, coureur etc) to relieve; **se ~** vi (dans une activité) to take it in turns

reléguer [ʀəlege] vt to relegate

relent(s) [ʀəlɑ̃] nm(pl) (foul) smell

relevé, e [ʀəlve] adj (manches) rolled-up; (sauce) highly-seasoned ♦ nm (lecture) reading; (liste) statement; list; (facture) account; **~ de compte** bank statement

relève [ʀəlɛv] nf relief; relief team (ou troops pl); **prendre la ~** to take over

relever [ʀəlve] vt (statue, meuble) to stand up again; (personne tombée) to help up; (vitre, niveau de vie) to raise; (col) to turn up; (style, conversation) to elevate; (plat, sauce) to season; (sentinelle, équipe) to relieve; (fautes, points) to pick out; (constater: traces etc) to find, pick up; (répliquer à: remarque) to react to, reply to; (: défi) to accept, take up; (noter: adresse etc) to take down, note; (: plan) to sketch; (: cotes etc) to plot; (compteur) to read; (ramasser: cahiers) to collect, take in; **se ~** vi (se remettre debout) to get up; **~ de** (maladie) to be recovering from; (être du ressort de) to be a matter for; (ADMIN: dépendre de) to come under; (fig) to pertain to; **~ qn de** (fonctions) to relieve sb of; **~ la tête** to look up; to hold up one's head

relief [ʀəljɛf] nm relief; **~s** nmpl (restes) remains; **mettre en ~** (fig) to bring out, highlight

relier [ʀəlje] vt to link up; (livre) to bind; **~ qch à** to link sth to

religieuse [ʀəliʒjøz] nf nun; (gâteau) cream bun

religieux, euse [ʀəliʒjø, -øz] adj religious ♦ nm monk

religion [ʀəliʒjɔ̃] nf religion; (piété, dévotion) faith

relire [ʀəliʀ] vt (à nouveau) to reread, read again; (vérifier) to read over

reliure [ʀəljyʀ] nf binding

reluire [ʀəlɥiʀ] vi to gleam

remanier [ʀəmanje] vt to reshape, recast; (POL) to reshuffle

remarquable [ʀəmaʀkabl(ə)] adj remarkable

remarque [ʀəmaʀk(ə)] nf remark; (écrite) note

remarquer [ʀəmaʀke] vt (voir) to notice; **se ~** vi to be noticeable; **faire ~ (à qn) que** to point out (to sb) that; **faire ~ qch (à qn)** to point sth out (to sb); **remarquez, ... mind you ...**

remblai [ʀɑ̃blɛ] nm embankment

rembourrer [ʀɑ̃buʀe] vt to stuff; (dossier, vêtement, souliers) to pad

remboursement [ʀɑ̃buʀsəmɑ̃] nm repayment; **envoi contre ~** cash on delivery;

rembourser [ʀɑ̃buʀse] *vt* to pay back, repay

remède [ʀəmɛd] *nm* (*médicament*) medicine; (*traitement, fig*) remedy, cure

remémorer [ʀəmemɔʀe]: **se ~** *vt* to recall, recollect

remerciements [ʀəmɛʀsimɑ̃] *nmpl* thanks

remercier [ʀəmɛʀsje] *vt* to thank; (*congédier*) to dismiss; **~ qn de/d'avoir fait** to thank sb for/for having done

remettre [ʀəmɛtʀ(ə)] *vt* (*vêtement*): **~ qch** to put sth back on; (*replacer*): **~ qch quelque part** to put sth back somewhere; (*ajouter*): **~ du sel/un sucre** to add more salt/another lump of sugar; (*ajourner*): **~ qch (à)** to postpone sth (until); **se ~** *vi* to get better, recover; **se ~ de** to recover from, get over; **s'en ~ à** to leave it (up) to; **~ qch à qn** (*rendre, restituer*) to give sth back to sb; (*donner, confier: paquet, argent*) to hand over sth to sb, deliver sth to sb; (: *prix, décoration*) to present sb with sth

remise [ʀəmiz] *nf* delivery; presentation; (*rabais*) discount; (*local*) shed; **~ de peine** reduction of sentence; **~ en jeu** (*FOOTBALL*) throw-in

remontant [ʀəmɔ̃tɑ̃] *nm* tonic, pick-me-up

remonte-pente [ʀəmɔ̃tpɑ̃t] *nm* ski-lift

remonter [ʀəmɔ̃te] *vi* to go back up; (*jupe*) to ride up ♦ *vt* (*pente*) to go up; (*fleuve*) to sail (*ou* swim *etc*) up; (*manches, pantalon*) to roll up; (*col*) to turn up; (*niveau, limite*) to raise; (*fig: personne*) to buck up; (*moteur, meuble*) to put back together, reassemble; (*montre, mécanisme*) to wind up; **~ le moral à qn** to raise sb's spirits; **~ à** (*dater de*) to date *ou* go back to

remontrance [ʀəmɔ̃tʀɑ̃s] *nf* reproof, reprimand

remontrer [ʀəmɔ̃tʀe] *vt* (*fig*): **en ~ à** to prove one's superiority over

remords [ʀəmɔʀ] *nm* remorse *no pl*; **avoir des ~** to feel remorse

remorque [ʀəmɔʀk(ə)] *nf* trailer; **être en ~** to be on tow; **remorquer** *vt* to tow; **remorqueur** *nm* tug(boat)

remous [ʀəmu] *nm* (*d'un navire*) (back)wash *no pl*; (*de rivière*) swirl, eddy ♦ *nmpl* (*fig*) stir *sg*

remparts [ʀɑ̃paʀ] *nmpl* walls, ramparts

remplaçant, e [ʀɑ̃plasɑ̃, -ɑ̃t] *nm/f* replacement, stand-in; (*THÉÂTRE*) understudy; (*SCOL*) supply teacher

remplacement [ʀɑ̃plasmɑ̃] *nm* replacement; (*job*) replacement work *no pl*

remplacer [ʀɑ̃plase] *vt* to replace; (*tenir lieu de*) to take the place of; **~ qch/qn par** to replace sth/sb with

rempli, e [ʀɑ̃pli] *adj* (*emploi du temps*) full, busy; **~ de** full of, filled with

remplir [ʀɑ̃pliʀ] *vt* to fill (up); (*questionnaire*) to fill out *ou* up; (*obligations, fonc-*

tion, condition) to fulfil; **se ~** *vi* to fill up

remporter [ʀɑ̃pɔʀte] *vt* (*marchandise*) to take away; (*fig*) to win, achieve

remuant, e [ʀəmɥɑ̃, -ɑ̃t] *adj* restless

remue-ménage [ʀəmymenaʒ] *nm inv* commotion

remuer [ʀəmɥe] *vt* to move; (*café, sauce*) to stir ♦ *vi* to move; **se ~** *vi* to move

rémunérer [ʀemyneʀe] *vt* to remunerate

renard [ʀənaʀ] *nm* fox

renchérir [ʀɑ̃ʃeʀiʀ] *vi* (*fig*): **~ (sur)** to add something (to)

rencontre [ʀɑ̃kɔ̃tʀ(ə)] *nf* meeting; (*imprévue*) encounter; **aller à la ~ de qn** to go and meet sb

rencontrer [ʀɑ̃kɔ̃tʀe] *vt* to meet; (*mot, expression*) to come across; (*difficultés*) to meet with; **se ~** *vi* to meet; (*véhicules*) to collide

rendement [ʀɑ̃dmɑ̃] *nm* (*d'un travailleur, d'une machine*) output; (*d'une culture*) yield; (*d'un investissement*) return; **à plein ~** at full capacity

rendez-vous [ʀɑ̃devu] *nm* (*rencontre*) appointment; (: *d'amoureux*) date; (*lieu*) meeting place; **donner ~ à qn** to arrange to meet sb; **avoir/prendre ~ (avec)** to have/ make an appointment (with)

rendre [ʀɑ̃dʀ(ə)] *vt* (*livre, argent etc*) to give back, return; (*otages, visite etc*) to return; (*sang, aliments*) to bring up; (*exprimer, traduire*) to render; (*faire devenir*): **~ qn célèbre/qch possible** to make sb famous/ sth possible; **se ~** *vi* (*capituler*) to surrender, give o.s. up; (*aller*): **se ~ quelque part** to go somewhere; **se ~ compte de qch** to realize sth

rênes [ʀɛn] *nfpl* reins

renfermé, e [ʀɑ̃fɛʀme] *adj* (*fig*) withdrawn ♦ *nm*: **sentir le ~** to smell stuffy

renfermer [ʀɑ̃fɛʀme] *vt* to contain

renflement [ʀɑ̃fləmɑ̃] *nm* bulge

renflouer [ʀɑ̃flue] *vt* to refloat; (*fig*) to set back on its (*ou* his/her *etc*) feet

renfoncement [ʀɑ̃fɔ̃smɑ̃] *nm* recess

renforcer [ʀɑ̃fɔʀse] *vt* to reinforce

renfort [ʀɑ̃fɔʀ] : **~s** *nmpl* reinforcements; **à grand ~ de** with a great deal of

renfrogné, e [ʀɑ̃fʀɔɲe] *adj* sullen

rengaine [ʀɑ̃gɛn] *nf* (*péj*) old tune

renier [ʀənje] *vt* (*parents*) to disown, repudiate; (*foi*) to renounce

renifler [ʀənifle] *vi*, *vt* to sniff

renne [ʀɛn] *nm* reindeer *inv*

renom [ʀənɔ̃] *nm* reputation; (*célébrité*) renown; **renommée, e** *adj* celebrated, renowned; **renommée** *nf* fame

renoncer [ʀənɔ̃se]: **~ à** *vt* to give up; **~ à faire** to give up the idea of doing

renouer [ʀənwe] *vt*: **~ avec** (*tradition*) to revive; (*habitude*) to take up again; **~ avec qn** to take up with sb again

renouvelable [ʀ(ə)nuvlabl(ə)] *adj* (*énergie etc*) renewable

renouveler [ʀənuvle] *vt* to renew; (*exploit, méfait*) to repeat; **se ~** *vi* (*incident*) to recur, happen again; **renouvellement** *nm* renewal; recurrence

rénover [ʀenɔve] *vt* (*immeuble*) to renovate, do up; (*enseignement*) to reform; (*quartier*) to redevelop

renseignement [ʀɑ̃sɛɲmɑ̃] *nm* information *no pl*, piece of information; (**guichet des**) **~s** information desk

renseigner [ʀɑ̃sɛɲe] *vt*: **~ qn (sur)** to give information to sb (about); **se ~** *vi* to ask for information, make inquiries

rentabilité [ʀɑ̃tabilite] *nf* profitablity

rentable [ʀɑ̃tabl(ə)] *adj* profitable

rente [ʀɑ̃t] *nf* income; pension; government stock *ou* bond; **rentier, ière** *nm/f* person of private means

rentrée [ʀɑ̃tʀe] *nf*: **~ (d'argent)** cash *no pl* coming in; **la ~ (des classes)** the start of the new school year

rentrer [ʀɑ̃tʀe] *vi* (*entrer de nouveau*) to go (*ou* come) back in; (*entrer*) to go (*ou* come) in; (*revenir chez soi*) to go (*ou* come) (back) home; (*air, clou: pénétrer*) to go in; (*revenu, argent*) to come in ♦ *vt* (*foins*) to bring in; (*véhicule*) to put away; (*chemise dans pantalon ete*) to tuck in; (*griffes*) to draw in; (*fig: larmes, colère etc*) to hold back; **~ le ventre** to pull in one's stomach; **~ dans** (*heurter*) to crash into; **~ dans l'ordre** to be back to normal; **~ dans ses frais** to recover one's expenses

renversant, e [ʀɑ̃vɛʀsɑ̃, -ɑ̃t] *adj* astounding

renverse [ʀɑ̃vɛʀs(ə)]: **à la ~** *adv* backwards

renverser [ʀɑ̃vɛʀse] *vt* (*faire tomber: chaise, verre*) to knock over, overturn; (*piéton*) to knock down; (*liquide, contenu*) to spill, upset; (*retourner*) to turn upside down; (: *ordre des mots etc*) to reverse; (*fig: gouvernement etc*) to overthrow; (*stupéfier*) to bowl over; **se ~** *vi* to fall over; to overturn; to spill

renvoi [ʀɑ̃vwa] *nm* (*référence*) cross-reference; (*éructation*) belch

renvoyer [ʀɑ̃vwaje] *vt* to send back; (*congédier*) to dismiss; (*lumière*) to reflect; (*son*) to echo; (*ajourner*): **~ qch (à)** to put sth off *ou* postpone sth (until); **~ qn à** (*fig*) to refer sb to

repaire [ʀəpɛʀ] *nm* den

répandre [ʀepɑ̃dʀ(ə)] *vt* (*renverser*) to spill; (*étaler, diffuser*) to spread; (*lumière*) to shed; (*chaleur, odeur*) to give off; **se ~** *vi* to spill; to spread; **répandu, e** *adj* (*opinion, usage*) widespread

réparation [ʀepaʀɑsjɔ̃] *nf* repair

réparer [ʀepaʀe] *vt* to repair; (*fig: offense*)

to make up for, atone for; (: *oubli, erreur*) to put right

repartie [ʀəpaʀti] *nf* retort; **avoir de la ~** to be quick at repartee

repartir [ʀəpaʀtiʀ] *vi* to set off again; to leave again; (*fig*) to get going again; **~ à zéro** to start from scratch (again)

répartir [ʀepaʀtiʀ] *vt* (*pour attribuer*) to share out; (*pour disperser, disposer*) to divide up; (*poids, chaleur*) to distribute; **se ~** *vt* (*travail, rôles*) to share out between themselves; **répartition** *nf* sharing out; dividing up; distribution

repas [ʀəpa] *nm* meal

repasser [ʀəpase] *vi* to come (*ou* go) back ♦ *vt* (*vêtement, tissu*) to iron; (*examen*) to retake, resit; (*film*) to show again; (*leçon, rôle: revoir*) to go over (again)

repêcher [ʀəpeʃe] *vt* (*noyé*) to recover the body of; (*candidat*) to pass (*by inflating marks*)

repentir [ʀəpɑ̃tiʀ] *nm* repentance; **se ~** *vi* to repent; **se ~ de** to repent of

répercussions [ʀepɛʀkysjɔ̃] *nfpl* (*fig*) repercussions

répercuter [ʀepɛʀkyte] *vt* (*information, hausse des prix*) to pass on; **se ~** *vi* (*bruit*) to reverberate; (*fig*): **se ~ sur** to have repercussions on

repère [ʀəpɛʀ] *nm* mark; (*monument etc*) landmark

repérer [ʀəpeʀe] *vt* (*erreur, connaissance*) to spot; (*abri, ennemi*) to locate; **se ~** *vi* to find one's way about

répertoire [ʀepɛʀtwaʀ] *nm* (*liste*) (alphabetical) list; (*carnet*) index notebook; (*d'un artiste*) repertoire

répéter [ʀepete] *vt* to repeat; (*préparer: leçon: aussi vi*) to learn, go over; (*THÉÂTRE*) to rehearse; **se ~** *vi* (*redire*) to repeat o.s.; (*se reproduire*) to be repeated, recur

répétition [ʀepetisjɔ̃] *nf* repetition; (*THÉÂTRE*) rehearsal; **~ générale** final dress rehearsal

répit [ʀepi] *nm* respite

replet, ète [ʀəplɛ, -ɛt] *adj* chubby

replier [ʀəplije] *vt* (*rabattre*) to fold down *ou* over; **se ~** *vi* (*troupes, armée*) to withdraw, fall back

réplique [ʀeplik] *nf* (*repartie, fig*) reply; (*THÉÂTRE*) line; (*copie*) replica; **~r** [ʀeplike] *vi* to reply; (*riposter*) to retaliate

répondeur [ʀepɔ̃dœʀ] *nm*: **~ automatique** (*TÉL*) answering machine

répondre [ʀepɔ̃dʀ(ə)] *vi* to answer, reply; (*freins, mécanisme*) to respond; **~ à** to reply to, answer; (*affection, salut*) to return; (*provocation, suj: mécanisme etc*) to respond to; (*correspondre à: besoin*) to answer; (: *conditions*) to meet; (: *description*) to match; (*avec impertinence*): **~ à qn** to answer sb back; **~ de** to answer for

réponse [Repɔ̃s] *nf* answer, reply; **en ~ à** in reply to

reportage [Rəpɔrtaʒ] *nm* (*bref*) report; (*écrit: documentaire*) story; article; (*en direct*) commentary; (*genre, activité*): **le ~** reporting

reporter¹ [Rəpɔrtɛr] *nm* reporter

reporter² [Rəpɔrte] *vt* (*total*): **~ qch sur** to carry sth forward *ou* over to; (*ajourner*): **~ qch (à)** to postpone sth (until); (*transférer*): **~ qch sur** to transfer sth to; **se ~ à** (*époque*) to think back to; (*document*) to refer to

repos [Rəpo] *nm* rest; (*fig*) peace (and quiet); peace of mind; (*MIL*): **~!** stand at ease!; **en ~** at rest; **de tout ~** safe

reposant, e [Rəpozɑ̃, -ɑ̃t] *adj* restful

reposer [Rəpoze] *vt* (*verre, livre*) to put down; (*délasser*) to rest; (*problème*) to reformulate ♦ *vi* (*liquide, pâte*) to settle, rest; **se ~** *vi* to rest; **se ~ sur qn** to rely on sb; **~ sur** to be built on; (*fig*) to rest on

repoussant, e [Rəpusɑ̃, -ɑ̃t] *adj* repulsive

repousser [Rəpuse] *vi* to grow again ♦ *vt* to repel, repulse; (*offre*) to turn down, reject; (*tiroir, personne*) to push back; (*différer*) to put back

reprendre [Rəprɑ̃dr(ə)] *vt* (*prisonnier, ville*) to recapture; (*objet prêté, donné*) to take back; (*chercher*): **je viendrai te ~ à 4h** I'll come and fetch you at 4; (*se resservir de*): **~ du pain/un œuf** to take (*ou* eat) more bread/another egg; (*firme, entreprise*) to take over; (*travail, promenade*) to resume; (*emprunter: argument, idée*) to take up, use; (*refaire: article etc*) to go over again; (*jupe etc*) to alter; (*émission, pièce*) to put on again; (*réprimander*) to tell off; (*corriger*) to correct ♦ *vi* (*classes, pluie*) to start (up) again; (*activités, travaux, combats*) to resume, start (up) again; (*affaires, industrie*) to pick up; (*dire*): **reprit-il** he went on; **se ~** *vi* (*se ressaisir*) to recover; **s'y ~** to make another attempt; **~ des forces** to recover one's strength; **~ courage** to take new heart; **~ la route** to set off again; **~ haleine** *ou* **son souffle** to get one's breath back

représailles [Rəprezaj] *nfpl* reprisals

représentant, e [Rəprezɑ̃tɑ̃, -ɑ̃t] *nm/f* representative

représentation [Rəprezɑ̃tasjɔ̃] *nf* (*symbole, image*) representation; (*spectacle*) performance

représenter [Rəprezɑ̃te] *vt* to represent; (*donner: pièce, opéra*) to perform; **se ~** *vt* (*se figurer*) to imagine; to visualize

répression [Represjɔ̃] *nf* (*voir réprimer*) suppression; repression

réprimer [Reprime] *vt* (*émotions*) to suppress; (*peuple etc*) to repress

repris [Rəpri] *nm*: **~ de justice** ex-prisoner, ex-convict

reprise [Rəpriz] *nf* (*recommencement*) resumption; recovery; (*TV*) repeat; (*CINÉMA*) rerun; (*AUTO*) acceleration *no pl*; (*COMM*) trade-in, part exchange; **à plusieurs ~s** on several occasions

repriser [Rəprize] *vt* to darn; to mend

reproche [Rəprɔʃ] *nm* (*remontrance*) reproach; **faire des ~s à qn** to reproach sb; **sans ~(s)** beyond reproach

reprocher [Rəprɔʃe] *vt*: **~ qch à qn** to reproach *ou* blame sb for sth; **~ qch à** (*machine, théorie*) to have sth against

reproduction [Rəprɔdyksjɔ̃] *nf* reproduction

reproduire [Rəprɔdɥir] *vt* to reproduce; **se ~** *vi* (*BIO*) to reproduce; (*recommencer*) to recur, re-occur

reptile [Reptil] *nm* reptile

repu, e [Rəpy] *adj* satisfied, sated

républicain, e [Repyblikɛ̃, -ɛn] *adj, nm/f* republican

république [Repyblik] *nf* republic

répugnant, e [Repyɲɑ̃, -ɑ̃t] *adj* repulsive; loathsome

répugner [Repyɲe]: **~ à** *vt* to repel *ou* disgust sb; **~ à faire** to be loath *ou* reluctant to do

réputation [Repytasjɔ̃] *nf* reputation; **réputé, e** *adj* renowned

requérir [Rəkerir] *vt* (*nécessiter*) to require, call for; (*JUR: peine*) to call for, demand

requête [Rəkɛt] *nf* request; (*JUR*) petition

requin [Rəkɛ̃] *nm* shark

requis, e [Rəki, -iz] *adj* required

R.E.R. *sigle m* (= *réseau express régional*) Greater Paris high-speed train service

rescapé, e [Rɛskape] *nm/f* survivor

rescousse [Rɛskus] *nf*: **aller à la ~ de qn** to go to sb's aid *ou* rescue

réseau, x [Rezo] *nm* network

réservation [Rezɛrvasjɔ̃] *nf* booking, reservation

réserve [Rezɛrv(ə)] *nf* (*retenue*) reserve; (*entrepôt*) storeroom; (*restriction, d'Indiens*) reservation; (*de pêche, chasse*) preserve; **sous ~ de** subject to; **sans ~** unreservedly; **de ~** (*provisions etc*) in reserve

réservé, e [Rezɛrve] *adj* (*discret*) reserved; (*chasse, pêche*) private

réserver [Rezɛrve] *vt* (*gén*) to reserve; (*chambre, billet etc*) to book, reserve; (*garder*): **~ qch pour/à** to keep *ou* save sth for; **~ qch à qn** to reserve (*ou* book) sth for sb

réservoir [Rezɛrvwar] *nm* tank

résidence [Rezidɑ̃s] *nf* residence; **(en) ~ surveillée** (under) house arrest; **~ secondaire** second home

résidentiel, le [Rezidɑ̃sjɛl] *adj* residential

résider [Rezide] *vi*: **~ à/dans/en** to reside in; **~ dans** (*fig*) to lie in

résidu [Rezidy] *nm* residue *no pl*

résigner [Reziɲe]: se ~ *vi*: se ~ (à qch/à faire) to resign o.s. (to sth/to doing)

résilier [Rezilje] *vt* to terminate

résistance [Rezistɑ̃s] *nf* resistance; (*de réchaud, bouilloire*: fil) element

résistant, e [Rezistɑ̃, -ɑ̃t] *adj* (*personne*) robust, tough; (*matériau*) strong, hard-wearing

résister [Reziste] *vi* to resist; ~ à (*assaut, tentation*) to resist; (*effort, souffrance*) to withstand; (*désobéir à*) to stand up to, oppose

résolu, e [Rezɔly] *pp de* **résoudre** ♦ *adj*: être ~ à qch/faire to be set upon sth/doing

résolution [Rezɔlysjɔ̃] *nf* solving; (*fermeté, décision*) resolution

résolve *etc vb voir* **résoudre**

résonner [Rezɔne] *vi* (*cloche, pas*) to reverberate, resound; (*salle*) to be resonant; ~ de to resound with

résorber [Rezɔrbe]: se ~ *vi* (*fig*) to be reduced; to be absorbed

résoudre [Rezudr(ə)] *vt* to solve; se ~ à faire to bring o.s. to do

respect [Rɛspɛ] *nm* respect; tenir en ~ to keep at bay

respecter [Rɛspɛkte] *vt* to respect

respectueux, euse [Rɛspɛktɥø, -øz] *adj* respectful; ~ de respectful of

respiration [Rɛspirasjɔ̃] *nf* breathing *no pl*; ~ artificielle artificial respiration

respirer [Rɛspire] *vi* to breathe; (*fig*) to get one's breath; to breathe again ♦ *vt* to breathe (in), inhale; (*manifester*: santé, calme etc) to exude

resplendir [Rɛsplɑ̃dir] *vi* to shine; (*fig*): ~ (de) to be radiant (with)

responsabilité [Rɛspɔ̃sabilite] *nf* responsibility; (*légale*) liability

responsable [Rɛspɔ̃sabl(ə)] *adj* responsible ♦ *nm/f* (*du ravitaillement etc*) person in charge; (*de parti, syndicat*) official; ~ de responsible for; (*chargé de*) in charge of, responsible for

ressaisir [Rəsezir] : se ~ *vi* to regain one's self-control

ressasser [Rəsase] *vt* to keep going over

ressemblance [Rəsɑ̃blɑ̃s] *nf* resemblance, similarity, likeness

ressemblant, e [Rəsɑ̃blɑ̃, -ɑ̃t] *adj* (*portrait*) lifelike, true to life

ressembler [Rəsɑ̃ble]: ~ à *vt* to be like; to resemble; (*visuellement*) to look like; se ~ *vi* to be (ou look) alike

ressemeler [Rəsəmle] *vt* to (re)sole

ressentiment [Rəsɑ̃timɑ̃] *nm* resentment

ressentir [Rəsɑ̃tir] *vt* to feel; se ~ de to feel (ou show) the effects of

resserrer [Rəsere] *vt* (*nœud, boulon*) to tighten (up); (*fig: liens*) to strengthen; se ~ *vi* (*vallée*) to narrow

resservir [Rəservir] *vi* to do *ou* serve again

♦ *vt*: ~ qn (d'un plat) to give sb a second helping (of a dish)

ressort [Rəsɔr] *nm* (*pièce*) spring; (*force morale*) spirit; (*recours*): en dernier ~ as a last resort; (*compétence*): être du ~ de to fall within the competence of

ressortir [Rəsɔrtir] *vi* to go (*ou* come) out (again); (*contraster*) to stand out; ~ de to emerge from; faire ~ (*fig: souligner*) to bring out

ressortissant, e [Rəsɔrtisɑ̃, -ɑ̃t] *nm/f* national

ressource [Rəsurs(ə)] *nf*: avoir la ~ de to have the possibility of; ~s *nfpl* (*moyens*) resources; leur seule ~ était de the only course open to them was to

ressusciter [Rɛsysite] *vt* (*fig*) to revive, bring back ♦ *vi* to rise (from the dead)

restant, e [Rɛstɑ̃, -ɑ̃t] *adj* remaining ♦ *nm*: le ~ (de) the remainder (of); un ~ de (*de trop*) some left-over

restaurant [Rɛstɔrɑ̃] *nm* restaurant

restauration [Rɛstɔrasjɔ̃] *nf* restoration; (*hôtellerie*) catering; ~ rapide fast food

restaurer [Rɛstɔre] *vt* to restore; se ~ *vi* to have something to eat

reste [Rɛst(ə)] *nm* (*restant*): le ~ (de) the rest (of); (*de trop*) un ~ (de) some left-over; (*vestige*): un ~ de a remnant *ou* last trace of; (*MATH*) remainder; ~s *nmpl* (*nourriture*) left-overs; (*d'une cité etc, dépouille mortelle*) remains; du ~, au ~ besides, moreover

rester [Rɛste] *vi* to stay, remain; (*subsister*) to remain, be left; (*durer*) to last, live on ♦ *vb impers*: il reste du pain/2 œufs there's some bread/there are 2 eggs left (over); il me reste assez de temps I have enough time left; ce qui reste à faire what remains to be done; restons-en là let's leave it at that

restituer [Rɛstitɥe] *vt* (*objet, somme*): ~ qch (à qn) to return sth (to sb); (*TECH*) to release; (: *son*) to reproduce

restoroute [Rɛstɔrut] *nm* motorway (*BRIT*) *ou* highway (*US*) restaurant

restreindre [Rɛstrɛ̃dr(ə)] *vt* to restrict, limit

restriction [Rɛstriksjɔ̃] *nf* restriction

résultat [Rezylta] *nm* result; (*d'élection etc*) results *pl*

résulter [Rezylte] : ~ de *vt* to result from, be the result of

résumé [Rezyme] *nm* summary, résumé

résumer [Rezyme] *vt* (*texte*) to summarize; (*récapituler*) to sum up; se ~ à to come down to

résurrection [Rezyrɛksjɔ̃] *nf* resurrection; (*fig*) revival

rétablir [Retablir] *vt* to restore, re-establish; se ~ *vi* (*guérir*) to recover; (*silence, calme*) to return, be restored; **rétablissement** *nm* restoring; recovery; (*SPORT*) pull-up

retaper [Rətape] *vt* (*maison, voiture etc*) to do up; (*fam: revigorer*) to buck up; (*redactylographier*) to retype

retard [RətaR] *nm* (*d'une personne attendue*) lateness *no pl*; (*sur l'horaire, un programme*) delay; (*fig: scolaire, mental etc*) backwardness; **en** ~ (**de 2 heures**) (2 hours) late; **avoir du** ~ to be late; (*sur un programme*) to be behind (schedule); **prendre du** ~ (*train, avion*) to be delayed; (*montre*) to lose (time); **sans** ~ without delay

retardement [RətaRdəmɑ̃] : **à** ~ *adj* delayed action *cpd*; **bombe à** ~ time bomb

retarder [Rətarde] *vt* (*sur un horaire*): ~ **qn** (**d'une heure**) to delay sb (an hour); (*départ, date*): ~ **qch** (**de 2 jours**) to put sth back (2 days), delay sth (for *ou* by 2 days); (*horloge*) to put back ♦ *vi* (*montre*) to be slow; to lose (time)

retenir [Rətnir] *vt* (*garder, retarder*) to keep, detain; (*maintenir: objet qui glisse, fig: colère, larmes*) to hold back; (: *objet suspendu*) to hold; (*fig: empêcher d'agir*): ~ **qn** (**de faire**) to hold sb back (from doing); (*se rappeler*) to retain; (*réserver*) to reserve; (*accepter*) to accept; (*prélever*): ~ **qch** (**sur**) to deduct sth (from); **se** ~ *vi* (*se raccrocher*): **se** ~ **à** to hold onto; (*se contenir*): **se** ~ **de faire** to restrain o.s. from doing; ~ **son souffle** to hold one's breath

retentir [Rətɑ̃tiR] *vi* to ring out; (*salle*): ~ **de** to ring *ou* resound with

retentissant, e [Rətɑ̃tisɑ̃, -ɑ̃t] *adj* resounding; (*fig*) impact-making

retentissement [Rətɑ̃tismɑ̃] *nm* repercussion; effect, impact; stir

retenu, e [Rətny] *adj* (*place*) reserved; (*personne: empêché*) held up

retenue [Rətny] *nf* (*prélèvement*) deduction; (*SCOL*) detention; (*modération*) (self-) restraint; (*réserve*) reserve, reticence

réticence [Retisɑ̃s] *nf* hesitation, reluctance *no pl*

rétine [Retin] *nf* retina

retiré, e [RətiRe] *adj* secluded; remote

retirer [RətiRe] *vt* to withdraw; (*vêtement, lunettes*) to take off, remove; (*extraire*): ~ **qch de** to take sth out of, remove sth from; (*reprendre: bagages, billets*) to collect, pick up

retombées [Rətɔ̃be] *nfpl* (*radioactives*) fall-out *sg*; (*fig*) fallout; spin-offs

retomber [Rətɔ̃be] *vi* (*à nouveau*) to fall again; (*atterrir: après un saut etc*) to land; (*tomber, redescendre*) to fall back; (*pendre*) to fall, hang (down); (*échoir*): ~ **sur qn** to fall on sb

rétorquer [RetɔRke] *vt*: ~ (**à qn**) **que** to retort (to sb) that

retors, e [RətɔR, -ɔRs(ə)] *adj* wily

retoucher [Rətuʃe] *vt* (*photographie*) to touch up; (*texte, vêtement*) to alter

retour [RətuR] *nm* return; **au** ~ when we (*ou* they *etc*) get (*ou* got) back; (*en route*) on the way back; **être de** ~ (**de**) to be back (from); **par** ~ **du courrier** by return of post

retourner [Rəturne] *vt* (*dans l'autre sens: matelas, crêpe, foin, terre*) to turn (over); (: *caisse*) to turn upside down; (: *sac, vêtement*) to turn inside out; (*émouvoir: personne*) to shake; (*renvoyer, restituer*): ~ **qch à qn** to return sth to sb ♦ *vi* (*aller, revenir*): ~ **quelque part/à** to go back *ou* return somewhere/to; **se** ~ *vi* to turn over; (*tourner la tête*) to turn round; ~ **à** (*état, activité*) to return to, go back to; **se** ~ **contre** (*fig*) to turn against; **savoir de quoi il retourne** to know what it is all about

retracer [RətRase] *vt* to relate, recount

retrait [RətRɛ] *nm* (*voir retirer*) withdrawal; collection; **en** ~ set back; ~ **du permis (de conduire)** disqualification from driving (*BRIT*), revocation of driver's license (*US*)

retraite [RətRɛt] *nf* (*d'une armée, REL, refuge*) retreat; (*d'un employé*) retirement; (*revenu*) pension; **prendre sa** ~ to retire; ~ **anticipée** early retirement; **retraité, e** *adj* retired ♦ *nm/f* pensioner

retrancher [RətRɑ̃ʃe] *vt* (*passage, détails*) to take out, remove; (*nombre, somme*): ~ **qch de** to take *ou* deduct sth from; (*couper*) to cut off; **se** ~ **derrière/dans** to take refuge behind/in

retransmettre [RətRɑ̃smɛtR(ə)] *vt* (*RADIO*) to broadcast; (*TV*) to show

rétrécir [RetResiR] *vt* (*vêtement*) to take in ♦ *vi* to shrink; **se** ~ *vi* to narrow

rétribution [RetRibysjɔ̃] *nf* payment

rétro [Retro] *adj inv*: **la mode** ~ the nostalgia vogue

rétrograde [RetRogRad] *adj* reactionary, backward-looking

rétrograder [RetRogRade] *vi* (*économie*) to regress; (*AUTO*) to change down

rétroprojecteur [RetRopRɔʒɛktœR] *nm* overhead projector

rétrospective [RetRospɛktiv] *nf* retrospective exhibition/season; **rétrospectivement** *adv* in retrospect

retrousser [RətRuse] *vt* to roll up

retrouvailles [RətRuvaj] *nfpl* reunion *sg*

retrouver [RətRuve] *vt* (*fugitif, objet perdu*) to find; (*occasion*) to find again; (*calme, santé*) to regain; (*revoir*) to see again; (*rejoindre*) to meet (again), join; **se** ~ *vi* to meet; (*s'orienter*) to find one's way; **se** ~ **quelque part** to find o.s. somewhere; **s'y** ~ (*rentrer dans ses frais*) to break even

rétroviseur [RetRovizœR] *nm* (rear-view) mirror

réunion [Reynjɔ̃] *nf* bringing together; joining; (*séance*) meeting

réunir [ʀeyniʀ] *vt* (*convoquer*) to call together; (*rassembler*) to gather together; (*cumuler*) to combine; (*rapprocher*) to bring together (again), reunite; (*rattacher*) to join (together); **se** ~ *vi* (*se rencontrer*) to meet

réussi, e [ʀeysi] *adj* successful

réussir [ʀeysiʀ] *vi* to succeed, be successful; (*à un examen*) to pass; (*plante, culture*) to thrive, do well ♦ *vt* to make a success of; ~ **à faire** to succeed in doing; ~ **à qn** to go right for sb; (*aliment*) to agree with sb

réussite [ʀeysit] *nf* success; (*CARTES*) patience

revaloir [ʀəvalwaʀ] *vt*: **je vous revaudrai cela** I'll repay you some day; (*en mal*) I'll pay you back for this

revaloriser [ʀəvalɔʀize] *vt* (*monnaie*) to revalue; (*salaires*) to raise the level of

revanche [ʀəvɑ̃ʃ] *nf* revenge; **en** ~ on the other hand

rêve [ʀɛv] *nm* dream; (*activité psychique*): **le** ~ dreaming

revêche [ʀəvɛʃ] *adj* surly, sour-tempered

réveil [ʀevɛj] *nm* (*d'un dormeur*) waking up *no pl*; (*fig*) awakening; (*pendule*) alarm (clock); (*MIL*) reveille; **au** ~ on waking (up)

réveille-matin [ʀevɛjmatɛ̃] *nm inv* alarm clock

réveiller [ʀeveje] *vt* (*personne*) to wake up; (*fig*) to awaken, revive; **se** ~ *vi* to wake up; (*fig*) to reawaken

réveillon [ʀevɛjɔ̃] *nm* Christmas Eve; (*de la Saint-Sylvestre*) New Year's Eve; **réveillonner** *vi* to celebrate Christmas Eve (*ou* New Year's Eve)

révélateur, trice [ʀevelatœʀ, -tʀis] *adj*: ~ **(de qch)** revealing (sth) ♦ *nm* (*PHOTO*) developer

révéler [ʀevele] *vt* (*gén*) to reveal; (*faire connaître au public*): ~ **qn/qch** to make sb/sth widely known, bring sb/sth to the public's notice; **se** ~ *vi* to be revealed, reveal itself ♦ *vb +attrib* to prove (to be), to be revealed, reveal itself

revenant, e [ʀəvnɑ̃, -ɑ̃t] *nm/f* ghost

revendeur, euse [ʀəvɑ̃dœʀ, -øz] *nm/f* (*détaillant*) retailer; (*d'occasions*) secondhand dealer

revendication [ʀəvɑ̃dikasjɔ̃] *nf* claim, demand; **journée de** ~ day of action

revendiquer [ʀəvɑ̃dike] *vt* to claim, demand; (*responsabilité*) to claim

revendre [ʀəvɑ̃dʀ(ə)] *vt* (*d'occasion*) to resell; (*détailler*) to sell; **à** ~ (*en abondance*) to spare

revenir [ʀəvniʀ] *vi* to come back; (*CULIN*): **faire** ~ to brown; (*coûter*): ~ **cher/à 100 F (à qn)** to cost (sb) a lot/100 F; ~ **à** (*études, projet*) to return to, go back to; (*équivaloir à*) to amount to; ~ **à qn** (*part,*

honneur) to go to sb, be sb's; (*souvenir, nom*) to come back to sb; ~ **de** (*fig: maladie, étonnement*) to recover from; ~ **sur** (*question, sujet*) to go back over; (*engagement*) to go back on; ~ **à la charge** to return to the attack; ~ **à soi** to come round; **n'en pas** ~: **je n'en reviens pas** I can't get over it; ~ **sur ses pas** to retrace one's steps; **cela revient à dire que/au même** it amounts to saying that/the same thing

revenu [ʀəvny] *nm* income; (*de l'État*) revenue; (*d'un capital*) yield; ~**s** *nmpl* income *sg*

rêver [ʀeve] *vi, vt* to dream; ~ **de/à** to dream of

réverbère [ʀeveʀbɛʀ] *nm* street lamp *ou* light

réverbérer [ʀeveʀbeʀe] *vt* to reflect

révérence [ʀeveʀɑ̃s] *nf* (*salut*) bow; (: *de femme*) curtsey

rêverie [ʀɛvʀi] *nf* daydreaming *no pl*, daydream

revers [ʀəvɛʀ] *nm* (*de feuille, main*) back; (*d'étoffe*) wrong side; (*de pièce, médaille*) back, reverse; (*TENNIS, PING-PONG*) backhand; (*de veston*) lapel; (*de pantalon*) turnup; (*fig: échec*) setback

revêtement [ʀəvɛtmɑ̃] *nm* (*de paroi*) facing; (*des sols*) flooring; (*de chaussée*) surface; (*de tuyau etc: enduit*) coating

revêtir [ʀəvetiʀ] *vt* (*habit*) to don, put on; (*fig*) to take on; ~ **qn de** to endow *ou* invest sb with; ~ **qch de** to cover sth with; (*fig*) to cloak sth in

rêveur, euse [ʀevœʀ, -øz] *adj* dreamy ♦ *nm/f* dreamer

revient [ʀəvjɛ̃] *vb voir* **revenir**

revigorer [ʀəvigɔʀe] *vt* to invigorate, brace up; to revive, buck up

revirement [ʀəviʀmɑ̃] *nm* change of mind; (*d'une situation*) reversal

réviser [ʀevize] *vt* (*texte, SCOL: matière*) to revise; (*machine, installation, moteur*) to overhaul, service; (*JUR: procès*) to review

révision [ʀevizjɔ̃] *nf* revision; auditing *no pl*; overhaul; servicing *no pl*; review; **la** ~ **des 10000 km** (*AUTO*) the 10,000 km service

revivre [ʀəvivʀ(ə)] *vi* (*reprendre des forces*) to come alive again; (*traditions*) to be revived ♦ *vt* (*épreuve, moment*) to relive

revoir [ʀəvwaʀ] *vt* to see again; (*réviser*) to revise ♦ *nm*: **au** ~ goodbye

révoltant, e [ʀevɔltɑ̃, -ɑ̃t] *adj* revolting; appalling

révolte [ʀevɔlt(ə)] *nf* rebellion, revolt

révolter [ʀevɔlte] *vt* to revolt; to outrage, appal; **se** ~ **(contre)** to rebel (against)

révolu, e [ʀevɔly] *adj* past; (*ADMIN*): **âgé de 18 ans** ~**s** over 18 years of age; **après 3 ans** ~**s** when 3 full years have passed

révolution [ʀevɔlysjɔ̃] *nf* revolution; **révo-**

lutionnaire *adj, nm/f* revolutionary

revolver [ʀevɔlvɛʀ] *nm* gun; (*à barillet*) revolver

révoquer [ʀevɔke] *vt* (*fonctionnaire*) to dismiss; (*arrêt, contrat*) to revoke

revue [ʀəvy] *nf* (*inventaire, examen, MIL*) review; (*périodique*) review, magazine; (*de music-hall*) variety show; **passer en ~** to review; to go through

rez-de-chaussée [ʀedʃose] *nm inv* ground floor

RF *sigle* = **République Française**

Rhin [ʀɛ̃] *nm*: **le ~** the Rhine

rhinocéros [ʀinɔseʀɔs] *nm* rhinoceros

Rhône [ʀon] *nm*: **le ~** the Rhone

rhubarbe [ʀybaʀb(ə)] *nf* rhubarb

rhum [ʀɔm] *nm* rum

rhumatisme [ʀymatism(ə)] *nm* rheumatism *no pl*

rhume [ʀym] *nm* cold; **~ de cerveau** head cold; **le ~ des foins** hay fever

ri [ʀi] *pp de* **rire**

riant, e [ʀjɑ̃, -ɑ̃t] *adj* smiling, cheerful

ricaner [ʀikane] *vi* (*avec méchanceté*) to snigger; (*bêtement*) to giggle

riche [ʀiʃ] *adj* (*gén*) rich; (*personne, pays*) rich, wealthy; **~ en** rich in; **~ de** full of; rich in; **richesse** *nf* wealth; (*fig*) richness; **richesses** *nfpl* (*ressources, argent*) wealth *sg*; (*fig: trésors*) treasures

ricin [ʀisɛ̃] *nm*: **huile de ~** castor oil

ricocher [ʀikɔʃe] *vi*: **~ (sur)** to rebound (off); (*sur l'eau*) to bounce (on ou off)

ricochet [ʀikɔʃɛ] *nm*: **faire des ~s** to skip stones; **par ~** on the rebound; (*fig*) as an indirect result

rictus [ʀiktys] *nm* grin; (*snarling*) grimace

ride [ʀid] *nf* wrinkle; (*fig*) ripple

rideau, x [ʀido] *nm* curtain; (*POL*): **le ~ de fer** the Iron Curtain

rider [ʀide] *vt* to wrinkle; (*eau*) to ripple; **se ~** *vi* to become wrinkled

ridicule [ʀidikyl] *adj* ridiculous ♦ *nm*: **le ~** ridicule: **se ridiculiser** *vi* to make a fool of o.s.

─────────── **MOT CLÉ** ───────────

rien [ʀjɛ̃] *pron* **1**: **(ne) ... ~** nothing; *tournure negative + anything*; **qu'est-ce que vous avez? - ~** what have you got? - nothing; **il n'a ~ dit/fait** he said/did nothing; he hasn't said/done anything; **il n'a ~ (n'est pas blessé)** he's all right; **de ~!** not at all!

2 (*quelque chose*): **a-t-il jamais ~ fait pour nous?** has he ever done anything for us?

3: **~ d'intéressant** nothing interesting; **~ d'autre** nothing else; **~ du tout** nothing at all

4: **~ que** just, only; nothing but; **~ que pour lui faire plaisir** only *ou* just to please him; **~ que la vérité** nothing but the truth;

~ que cela that alone

♦ *nm*: **un petit ~** (*cadeau*) a little something; **des ~s** trivia *pl*; **un ~ de** a hint of; **en un ~ de temps** in no time at all

─────────────────────────

rieur, euse [ʀjœʀ, -øz] *adj* cheerful

rigide [ʀiʒid] *adj* stiff; (*fig*) rigid; strict

rigole [ʀigɔl] *nf* (*conduit*) channel; (*filet d'eau*) rivulet

rigoler [ʀigɔle] *vi* (*rire*) to laugh; (*s'amuser*) to have (some) fun; (*plaisanter*) to be joking *ou* kidding

rigolo, ote [ʀigɔlo, -ɔt] (*fam*) *adj* funny ♦ *nm/f* comic; (*péj*) fraud, phoney

rigoureux, euse [ʀiguʀø, -øz] *adj* (*morale*) rigorous, strict; (*personne*) stern, strict; (*climat, châtiment*) rigorous, harsh; (*interdiction, neutralité*) strict

rigueur [ʀigœʀ] *nf* rigour; strictness; harshness; **être de ~** to be the rule; **à la ~** at a pinch; possibly; **tenir ~ à qn de qch** to hold sth against sb

rime [ʀim] *nf* rhyme

rinçage [ʀɛ̃saʒ] *nm* rinsing (out); (*opération*) rinse

rincer [ʀɛ̃se] *vt* to rinse; (*récipient*) to rinse out

ring [ʀiŋ] *nm* (boxing) ring

ringard, e [ʀɛ̃gaʀ, -aʀd(ə)] *adj* old-fashioned

rions *vb voir* **rire**

riposter [ʀipɔste] *vi* to retaliate ♦ *vt*: **~ que** to retort that; **~ à** to counter; to reply to

rire [ʀiʀ] *vi* to laugh; (*se divertir*) to have fun ♦ *nm* laugh; **le ~** laughter; **~ de** to laugh at; **pour ~** (*pas sérieusement*) for a joke *ou* a laugh

risée [ʀize] *nf*: **être la ~ de** to be the laughing stock of

risible [ʀizibl(ə)] *adj* laughable

risque [ʀisk(ə)] *nm* risk; **le ~** danger; **à ses ~s et périls** at his own risk

risqué, e [ʀiske] *adj* risky; (*plaisanterie*) risqué, daring

risquer [ʀiske] *vt* to risk; (*allusion, question*) to venture, hazard; **ça ne risque rien** it's quite safe; **~ de: il risque de se tuer** he could get himself killed; **ce qui risque de se produire** what might *ou* could well happen; **il ne risque pas de recommencer** there's no chance of him doing that again; **se ~ à faire** (*tenter*) to venture *ou* dare to do

rissoler [ʀisɔle] *vi, vt*: **(faire) ~** to brown

ristourne [ʀistuʀn(ə)] *nf* rebate

rite [ʀit] *nm* rite; (*fig*) ritual

rivage [ʀivaʒ] *nm* shore

rival, e, aux [ʀival, -o] *adj, nm/f* rival

rivaliser [ʀivalize] *vi*: **~ avec** to rival, vie with; (*être comparable*) to hold its own against, compare with

rivalité [ʀivalite] *nf* rivalry

rive [Riv] nf shore; (de fleuve) bank
river [Rive] vt (clou, pointe) to clinch; (plaques) to rivet together
riverain, e [RivRɛ̃, -ɛn] nm/f riverside (ou lakeside) resident; local resident
rivet [Rive] nm rivet
rivière [RivjɛR] nf river
rixe [Riks(ə)] nf brawl, scuffle
riz [Ri] nm rice
R.N. sigle f = **route nationale**
robe [Rɔb] nf dress; (de juge, d'ecclésiastique) robe; (de professeur) gown; (pelage) coat; ~ **de chambre** dressing gown; ~ **de grossesse** maternity dress; ~ **de soirée/de mariée** evening/wedding dress
robinet [Rɔbinɛ] nm tap
robot [Rɔbo] nm robot
robuste [Rɔbyst(ə)] adj robust, sturdy
roc [Rɔk] nm rock
rocaille [Rɔkaj] nf loose stones pl; rocky ou stony ground; (jardin) rockery, rock garden
roche [Rɔʃ] nf rock
rocher [Rɔʃe] nm rock
rocheux, euse [Rɔʃø, -øz] adj rocky
rodage [Rɔdaʒ] nm: **en** ~ running in
roder [Rɔde] vt (AUTO) to run in
rôder [Rode] vi to roam about; (de façon suspecte) to lurk (about ou around); **rôdeur, euse** nm/f prowler
rogne [Rɔɲ] nf: **être en** ~ to be in a temper
rogner [Rɔɲe] vt to clip; ~ **sur** (fig) to cut down ou back on
rognons [Rɔɲɔ̃] nmpl kidneys
roi [Rwa] nm king; **le jour** ou **la fête des R~s**, **les R~s** Twelfth Night
roitelet [Rwatlɛ] nm wren
rôle [Rol] nm role; (contribution) part
romain, e [Rɔmɛ̃, -ɛn] adj, nm/f Roman
roman, e [Rɔmɑ̃, -an] adj (ARCHIT) Romanesque ♦ nm novel; ~ **d'espionnage** spy novel ou story; ~ **photo** romantic picture story
romance [Rɔmɑ̃s] nf ballad
romancer [Rɔmɑ̃se] vt to make into a novel; to romanticize
romancier, ière [Rɔmɑ̃sje, -jɛR] nm/f novelist
romanesque [Rɔmanɛsk(ə)] adj (fantastique) fantastic; storybook cpd; (sentimental) romantic
roman-feuilleton [Rɔmɑ̃fœjtɔ̃] nm serialized novel
romanichel, le [Rɔmaniʃɛl] nm/f gipsy
romantique [Rɔmɑ̃tik] adj romantic
romarin [RɔmaRɛ̃] nm rosemary
rompre [Rɔ̃pR(ə)] vt to break; (entretien, fiançailles) to break off ♦ vi (fiancés) to break it off; **se** ~ vi to break; (MÉD) to burst, rupture
rompu, e [Rɔ̃py] adj: ~ **à** with wide ex-

perience of; inured to
ronces [Rɔ̃s] nfpl brambles
ronchonner [Rɔ̃ʃɔne] (fam) vi to grouse, grouch
rond, e [Rɔ̃, Rɔ̃d] adj round; (joues, mollets) well-rounded; (fam: ivre) tight ♦ nm (cercle) ring; (fam: sou): **je n'ai plus un** ~ I haven't a penny left; **en** ~ (s'asseoir, danser) in a ring; **ronde** nf (gén: de surveillance) rounds pl, patrol; (danse) round (dance); (MUS) semibreve (BRIT), whole note (US); **à la ronde** (alentour): **à 10 km à la ronde** for 10 km round; **rondelet, te** adj plump
rondelle [Rɔ̃dɛl] nf (TECH) washer; (tranche) slice, round
rondement [Rɔ̃dmɑ̃] adv briskly; frankly
rondin [Rɔ̃dɛ̃] nm log
rond-point [Rɔ̃pwɛ̃] nm roundabout
ronflant, e [Rɑ̃flɑ̃, -ɑ̃t] (péj) adj high-flown, grand
ronfler [Rɑ̃fle] vi to snore; (moteur, poêle) to hum; to roar
ronger [Rɔ̃ʒe] vt to gnaw (at); (suj: vers, rouille) to eat into; **se** ~ **les sangs** to worry o.s. sick; **se** ~ **les ongles** to bite one's nails; **rongeur** nm rodent
ronronner [Rɔ̃Rɔne] vi to purr
roquet [Rɔkɛ] nm nasty little lap-dog
rosace [Rozas] nf (vitrail) rose window
rosbif [Rɔsbif] nm: **du** ~ roasting beef; (cuit) roast beef; **un** ~ a joint of beef
rose [Roz] nf rose ♦ adj pink
rosé, e [Roze] adj pinkish; (vin) ~ rosé
roseau, x [Rozo] nm reed
rosée [Roze] nf dew
roseraie [RozRɛ] nf rose garden
rosier [Rozje] nm rosebush, rose tree
rosse [Rɔs] nf (péj: cheval) nag ♦ adj nasty, vicious
rossignol [Rɔsiɲɔl] nm (ZOOL) nightingale
rot [Ro] nm belch; (de bébé) burp
rotatif, ive [Rɔtatif, -iv] adj rotary
rotation [Rɔtasjɔ̃] nf rotation; (fig) rotation, swap-around; turnover
roter [Rɔte] (fam) vi to burp, belch
rôti [Roti] nm: **du** ~ roasting meat; (cuit) roast meat; ~ **de bœuf/porc** joint of beef/pork
rotin [Rɔtɛ̃] nm rattan (cane); **fauteuil en** ~ cane (arm)chair
rôtir [RotiR] vi, vt (aussi: faire ~) to roast; **rôtisserie** nf steakhouse; roast meat counter (ou shop); **rôtissoire** nf (roasting) spit
rotule [Rɔtyl] nf kneecap, patella
roturier, ière [RɔtyRje, -jɛR] nm/f commoner
rouage [Rwaʒ] nm cog(wheel), gearwheel; (de montre) part; (fig) cog
roucouler [Rukule] vi to coo
roue [Ru] nf wheel; ~ **dentée** cogwheel; ~ **de secours** spare wheel
roué, e [Rwe] adj wily

rouer [ʀwe] *vt*: ~ **qn de coups** to give sb a thrashing

rouet [ʀwɛ] *nm* spinning wheel

rouge [ʀuʒ] *adj, nm/f* red ♦ *nm* red; (*fard*) rouge; (*vin*) ~ red wine; **sur la liste** ~ ex-directory (*BRIT*), unlisted (*US*); **passer au** ~ (*signal*) to go red; (*automobiliste*) to go through a red light; ~ **(à lèvres)** lipstick; **rouge-gorge** *nm* robin (redbreast)

rougeole [ʀuʒɔl] *nf* measles *sg*

rougeoyer [ʀuʒwaje] *vi* to glow red

rouget [ʀuʒɛ] *nm* mullet

rougeur [ʀuʒœʀ] *nf* redness

rougir [ʀuʒiʀ] *vi* (*de honte, timidité*) to blush, flush; (*de plaisir, colère*) to flush; (*fraise, tomate*) to go *ou* turn red; (*ciel*) to redden

rouille [ʀuj] *nf* rust

rouillé, e [ʀuje] *adj* rusty

rouiller [ʀuje] *vt* to rust ♦ *vi* to rust, go rusty; **se** ~ *vi* to rust

roulant, e [ʀulɑ̃, -ɑ̃t] *adj* (*meuble*) on wheels; (*surface, trottoir*) moving

rouleau, x [ʀulo] *nm* (*de papier, tissu, SPORT*) roll; (*de machine à écrire*) roller, platen; (*à mise en plis, à peinture, vague*) roller; ~ **compresseur** steamroller; ~ **à pâtisserie** rolling pin

roulement [ʀulmɑ̃] *nm* (*bruit*) rumbling *no pl*, rumble; (*rotation*) rotation; turnover; **par** ~ on a rota (*BRIT*) *ou* rotation (*US*) basis; ~ **(à billes)** ball bearings *pl*; ~ **de tambour** drum roll

rouler [ʀule] *vt* to roll; (*papier, tapis*) to roll up; (*CULIN: pâte*) to roll out; (*fam*) to do, con ♦ *vi* (*bille, boule*) to roll; (*voiture, train*) to go, run; (*automobiliste*) to drive; (*cycliste*) to ride; (*bateau*) to roll; (*tonnerre*) to rumble, roll; **se** ~ **dans** (*boue*) to roll in; (*couverture*) to roll o.s. (up) in

roulette [ʀulɛt] *nf* (*de table, fauteuil*) castor; (*de pâtissier*) pastry wheel; (*jeu*): **la** ~ roulette; **à** ~**s** on castors

roulis [ʀuli] *nm* roll(ing)

roulotte [ʀulɔt] *nf* caravan

Roumanie [ʀumani] *nf* Rumania

rouquin, e [ʀukɛ̃, -in] (*péj*) *nm/f* redhead

rouspéter [ʀuspete] (*fam*) *vi* to moan

rousse [ʀus] *adj voir* **roux**

roussi [ʀusi] *nm*: **ça sent le** ~ there's a smell of burning; (*fig*) I can smell trouble

roussir [ʀusiʀ] *vt* to scorch ♦ *vi* (*feuilles*) to go *ou* turn brown; (*CULIN*): **faire** ~ to brown

route [ʀut] *nf* road; (*fig: chemin*) way; (*itinéraire, parcours*) route; (*fig: voie*) road, path; **par (la)** ~ by road; **il y a 3h de** ~ it's a 3-hour ride *ou* journey; **en** ~ on the way; **mettre en** ~ to start up; **se mettre en** ~ to set off; **faire** ~ **vers** to head towards; ~ **nationale** ≈ A road (*BRIT*), ≈ state highway (*US*); **routier, ière** *adj* road *cpd* ♦ *nm*

(*camionneur*) (long-distance) lorry (*BRIT*) *ou* truck (*US*) driver; (*restaurant*) ≈ transport café (*BRIT*), ≈ truck stop (*US*); **routière** *nf* (*voiture*) touring car

routine [ʀutin] *nf* routine; **routinier, ière** (*péj*) *adj* humdrum; addicted to routine

rouvrir [ʀuvʀiʀ] *vt, vi* to reopen, open again; **se** ~ *vi* to reopen, open again

roux, rousse [ʀu, ʀus] *adj* red; (*personne*) red-haired ♦ *nm/f* redhead

royal, e, aux [ʀwajal, -o] *adj* royal; (*fig*) princely

royaume [ʀwajom] *nm* kingdom; (*fig*) realm; **le R~-Uni** the United Kingdom

royauté [ʀwajote] *nf* (*dignité*) kingship; (*régime*) monarchy

ruban [ʀybɑ̃] *nm* (*gén*) ribbon; (*d'acier*) strip; ~ **adhésif** adhesive tape

rubéole [ʀybeɔl] *nf* German measles *sg*, rubella

rubis [ʀybi] *nm* ruby

rubrique [ʀybʀik] *nf* (*titre, catégorie*) heading; (*PRESSE: article*) column

ruche [ʀyʃ] *nf* hive

rude [ʀyd] *adj* (*barbe, toile*) rough; (*métier, tâche*) hard, tough; (*climat*) severe, harsh; (*bourru*) harsh, rough; (*fruste*) rugged, tough; (*fam*) jolly good

rudement [ʀydmɑ̃] (*fam*) *adv* (*très*) terribly; (*beaucoup*) terribly hard

rudimentaire [ʀydimɑ̃tɛʀ] *adj* rudimentary, basic

rudoyer [ʀydwaje] *vt* to treat harshly

rue [ʀy] *nf* street

ruée [ʀɥe] *nf* rush

ruelle [ʀɥɛl] *nf* alley(-way)

ruer [ʀɥe] *vi* (*cheval*) to kick out; **se** ~ *vi*: **se** ~ **sur** to pounce on; **se** ~ **vers/dans/hors de** to rush *ou* dash towards/into/out of

rugby [ʀygbi] *nm* rugby (football)

rugir [ʀyʒiʀ] *vi* to roar

rugueux, euse [ʀygø, -øz] *adj* rough

ruine [ʀɥin] *nf* ruin; ~**s** *nfpl* (*de château etc*) ruins

ruiner [ʀɥine] *vt* to ruin

ruineux, euse [ʀɥinø, øz] *adj* ruinous

ruisseau, x [ʀɥiso] *nm* stream, brook

ruisseler [ʀɥisle] *vi* to stream

rumeur [ʀymœʀ] *nf* (*bruit confus*) rumbling, hubbub *no pl*; murmur(ing); (*nouvelle*) rumour

ruminer [ʀymine] *vt* (*herbe*) to ruminate; (*fig*) to ruminate on *ou* over, chew over

rupture [ʀyptyʀ] *nf* (*de câble, digue*) breaking; (*de tendon*) rupture, tearing; (*de négociations etc*) breakdown; (*de contrat*) breach; (*séparation, désunion*) break-up, split

rural, e, aux [ʀyʀal, -o] *adj* rural, country *cpd*

ruse [ʀyz] *nf*: **la** ~ cunning, craftiness;

trickery; **une ~** a trick, a ruse; **rusé, e** *adj* cunning, crafty

russe [ʀys] *adj, nm/f* Russian ♦ *nm* (*LING*) Russian

Russie [ʀysi] *nf*: **la ~** Russia

rustique [ʀystik] *adj* rustic

rustre [ʀystʀ(ə)] *nm* boor

rutilant, e [ʀytilɑ̃, -ɑ̃t] *adj* gleaming

rythme [ʀitm(ə)] *nm* rhythm; (*vitesse*) rate; (: *de la vie*) pace, tempo

S s

s' [s] *pron voir* **se**

sa [sa] *dét voir* **son**[1]

S.A. *sigle* (= *société anonyme*) ≈ Ltd (*BRIT*), ≈ Inc. (*US*)

sable [sabl(ə)] *nm* sand; **~s mouvants** quicksand(s)

sablé [suble] *nm* shortbread biscuit

sabler [suble] *vt* to sand; (*contre le verglas*) to grit; **~ le champagne** to drink champagne

sablier [sublije] *nm* hourglass; (*de cuisine*) egg timer

sablonneux, euse [sublɔnø, -øz] *adj* sandy

saborder [sabɔʀde] *vt* (*navire*) to scuttle; (*fig*) to wind up, shut down

sabot [sabo] *nm* clog; (*de cheval, bœuf*) hoof; **~ de frein** brake shoe

saboter [sabɔte] *vt* to sabotage

sac [sak] *nm* bag; (*à charbon etc*) sack; **mettre à ~** to sack; **~ à dos** rucksack; **~ à main** handbag; **~ à provisions/de voyage** shopping/travelling bag; **~ de couchage** sleeping bag

saccade [sakad] *nf* jerk

saccager [sakaʒe] *vt* (*piller*) to sack; (*dévaster*) to create havoc in

saccharine [sakaʀin] *nf* saccharin

sacerdoce [sasɛʀdɔs] *nm* priesthood; (*fig*) calling, vocation

sache *etc vb voir* **savoir**

sachet [saʃɛ] *nm* (small) bag; (*de lavande, poudre, shampooing*) sachet; **~ de thé** tea bag

sacoche [sakɔʃ] *nf* (*gén*) bag; (*de bicyclette*) saddlebag

sacre [sakʀ(ə)] *nm* coronation; consecration

sacré, e [sakʀe] *adj* sacred; (*fam: satané*) blasted; (: *fameux*): **un ~ ...** a heck of a ...

sacrement [sakʀəmɑ̃] *nm* sacrament

sacrifice [sakʀifis] *nm* sacrifice

sacrifier [sakʀifje] *vt* to sacrifice; **~ à** to conform to

sacristie [sakʀisti] *nf* sacristy; (*culte protestant*) vestry

sadique [sadik] *adj* sadistic

sage [saʒ] *adj* wise; (*enfant*) good ♦ *nm* wise man; sage

sage-femme [saʒfam] *nf* midwife

sagesse [saʒɛs] *nf* wisdom

Sagittaire [saʒitɛʀ] *nm*: **le ~** Sagittarius

Sahara [saaʀa] *nm*: **le ~** the Sahara (desert)

saignant, e [sɛɲɑ̃, -ɑ̃t] *adj* (*viande*) rare

saignée [seɲe] *nf* (*fig*) heavy losses *pl*

saigner [seɲe] *vi* to bleed ♦ *vt* to bleed; (*animal*) to kill (by bleeding); **~ du nez** to have a nosebleed

saillie [saji] *nf* (*sur un mur etc*) projection; (*trait d'esprit*) witticism

saillir [sajiʀ] *vi* to project, stick out; (*veine, muscle*) to bulge

sain, e [sɛ̃, sɛn] *adj* healthy; (*lectures*) wholesome; **~ d'esprit** sound in mind, sane; **~ et sauf** safe and sound, unharmed

saindoux [sɛ̃du] *nm* lard

saint, e [sɛ̃, sɛ̃t] *adj* holy; (*fig*) saintly ♦ *nm/f* saint; **le S~-Esprit** the Holy Spirit *ou* Ghost; **la S~e Vierge** the Blessed Virgin; **la S~-Sylvestre** New Year's Eve; **sainteté** *nf* holiness

sais *etc vb voir* **savoir**

saisie [sezi] *nf* seizure; **~ (de données)** (data) capture

saisir [seziʀ] *vt* to take hold of, grab; (*fig: occasion*) to seize; (*comprendre*) to grasp; (*entendre*) to get, catch; (*données*) to capture; (*suj: émotions*) to take hold of, come over; (*CULIN*) to fry quickly; (*JUR: biens, publication*) to seize; (: *juridiction*): **~ un tribunal d'une affaire** to submit *ou* refer a case to a court; **se ~ de** *vt* to seize; **saisissant, e** *adj* startling, striking

saison [sezɔ̃] *nf* season; **morte ~** slack season; **saisonnier, ière** *adj* seasonal

sait *vb voir* **savoir**

salade [salad] *nf* (*BOT*) lettuce *etc*; (*CULIN*) (green) salad; (*fam*) tangle, muddle; **~ de fruits** fruit salad; **saladier** *nm* (salad) bowl

salaire [salɛʀ] *nm* (*annuel, mensuel*) salary; (*hebdomadaire, journalier*) pay, wages *pl*; (*fig*) reward; **~ de base** basic salary (*ou* wage); **~ minimum interprofessionnel de croissance** index-linked guaranteed minimum wage

salarié, e [salaʀje] *nm/f* salaried employee; wage-earner

salaud [salo] (*fam!*) *nm* sod (*!*), bastard (*!*)

sale [sal] *adj* dirty, filthy

salé, e [sale] *adj* (*liquide, saveur*) salty; (*CULIN*) salted; (*fig*) spicy; steep

saler [sale] *vt* to salt
saleté [salte] *nf* (*état*) dirtiness; (*crasse*) dirt, filth; (*tache etc*) dirt *no pl*; (*fig*) dirty trick; rubbish *no pl*; filth *no pl*
salière [saljɛʀ] *nf* saltcellar
salin, e [salɛ̃, -in] *adj* saline; **saline** *nf* saltworks *sg*; salt marsh
salir [saliʀ] *vt* to (make) dirty; (*fig*) to soil the reputation of; **se ~** *vi* to get dirty; **salissant, e** *adj* (*tissu*) which shows the dirt; (*métier*) dirty, messy
salle [sal] *nf* room; (*d'hôpital*) ward; (*de restaurant*) dining room; (*d'un cinéma*) auditorium; (: *public*) audience; **faire ~ comble** to have a full house; **~ à manger** dining room; **~ commune** (*d'hôpital*) ward; **~ d'attente** waiting room; **~ de bain(s)** bathroom; **~ de classe** classroom; **~ de concert** concert hall; **~ de consultation** consulting room; **~ d'eau** shower-room; **~ d'embarquement** (*à l'aéroport*) departure lounge; **~ de jeux** games room; playroom; **~ d'opération** (*d'hôpital*) operating theatre; **~ de séjour** living room; **~ de spectacle** theatre; cinema; **~ des ventes** saleroom
salon [salɔ̃] *nm* lounge, sitting room; (*mobilier*) lounge suite; (*exposition*) exhibition, show; **~ de thé** tearoom
salopard [salɔpaʀ] (*fam!*) *nm* bastard (*!*)
salope [salɔp] (*fam!*) *nf* bitch (*!*)
saloperie [salɔpʀi] (*fam!*) *nf* filth *no pl*; dirty trick; rubbish *no pl*
salopette [salɔpɛt] *nf* dungarees *pl*; (*d'ouvrier*) overall(s)
salsifis [salsifi] *nm* salsify
salubre [salybʀ(ə)] *adj* healthy, salubrious
saluer [salɥe] *vt* (*pour dire bonjour, fig*) to greet; (*pour dire au revoir*) to take one's leave; (*MIL*) to salute
salut [saly] *nm* (*sauvegarde*) safety; (*REL*) salvation; (*geste*) wave; (*parole*) greeting; (*MIL*) salute ♦ *excl* (*fam*) hi (there)
salutations [salytasjɔ̃] *nfpl* greetings; **recevez, mes ~ distinguées** *ou* **respectueuses** yours faithfully
samedi [samdi] *nm* Saturday
SAMU [samy] *sigle m* (= *service d'assistance médicale d'urgence*) ≈ ambulance (service) (*BRIT*), ≈ paramedics *pl* (*US*)
sanction [sɑ̃ksjɔ̃] *nf* sanction; (*fig*) penalty; **sanctionner** *vt* (*loi, usage*) to sanction; (*punir*) to punish
sandale [sɑ̃dal] *nf* sandal
sandwich [sɑ̃dwitʃ] *nm* sandwich
sang [sɑ̃] *nm* blood; **en ~** covered in blood; **se faire du mauvais ~** to fret, get in a state
sang-froid [sɑ̃fʀwa] *nm* calm, sangfroid; **de ~** in cold blood
sanglant, e [sɑ̃glɑ̃, -ɑ̃t] *adj* bloody, covered in blood; (*combat*) bloody

sangle [sɑ̃gl(ə)] *nf* strap
sanglier [sɑ̃glije] *nm* (wild) boar
sanglot [sɑ̃glo] *nm* sob
sangsue [sɑ̃sy] *nf* leech
sanguin, e [sɑ̃gɛ̃, -in] *adj* blood *cpd*; (*fig*) fiery; **sanguinaire** [sɑ̃ginɛʀ] *adj* bloodthirsty; bloody
sanisette [sanizɛt] *nf* (automatic) public toilet
sanitaire [sanitɛʀ] *adj* health *cpd*; **~s** *nmpl* (*lieu*) bathroom *sg*
sans [sɑ̃] *prép* without; **~ qu'il s'en aperçoive** without him *ou* his noticing; **~-abri** *nmpl* homeless; **~-emploi** *n inv* unemployed person; **les ~-emploi** the unemployed; **~-façon** *adj inv* fuss-free; free and easy; **~-gêne** *adj inv* inconsiderate; **~-logis** *nmpl* homeless
santé [sɑ̃te] *nf* health; **en bonne ~** in good health; **boire à la ~ de qn** to drink (to) sb's health; **"à la ~ de"** "here's to"; **à ta/votre ~!** cheers!
saoudien, ne [saudjɛ̃, -jɛn] *adj* Saudi Arabian ♦ *nm/f*: **S~(ne)** Saudi Arabian
saoul, e [su, sul] *adj* = **soûl**
saper [sape] *vt* to undermine, sap
sapeur-pompier [sapœʀpɔ̃pje] *nm* fireman
saphir [safiʀ] *nm* sapphire
sapin [sapɛ̃] *nm* fir (tree); (*bois*) fir; **~ de Noël** Christmas tree
sarcastique [saʀkastik] *adj* sarcastic
sarcler [saʀkle] *vt* to weed
Sardaigne [saʀdɛɲ] *nf*: **la ~** Sardinia
sardine [saʀdin] *nf* sardine
SARL *sigle* (= *société à responsabilité limitée*) ≈ plc (*BRIT*), ≈ Inc. (*US*)
sas [sas] *nm* (*de sous-marin, d'engin spatial*) airlock; (*d'écluse*) lock
satané, e [satane] *adj* confounded
satellite [satelit] *nm* satellite
satin [satɛ̃] *nm* satin
satire [satiʀ] *nf* satire; **satirique** *adj* satirical
satisfaction [satisfaksjɔ̃] *nf* satisfaction
satisfaire [satisfɛʀ] *vt* to satisfy; **~ à** (*engagement*) to fulfil; (*revendications, conditions*) to satisfy, meet; to comply with; **satisfaisant, e** *adj* satisfactory; (*qui fait plaisir*) satisfying; **satisfait, e** *adj* satisfied; **satisfait de** happy *ou* satisfied with
saturer [satyʀe] *vt* to saturate
sauce [sos] *nf* sauce; (*avec un rôti*) gravy; **saucière** *nf* sauceboat
saucisse [sosis] *nf* sausage
saucisson [sosisɔ̃] *nm* (slicing) sausage
sauf, sauve [sof, sov] *adj* unharmed, unhurt; (*fig: honneur*) intact, saved ♦ *prép* except; **laisser la vie sauve à qn** to spare sb's life; **~ si** (*à moins que*) unless; **~ erreur** if I'm not mistaken; **~ avis contraire** unless you hear to the contrary

sauge [soʒ] nf sage
saugrenu, e [sogʀəny] adj preposterous
saule [sol] nm willow (tree)
saumon [somɔ̃] nm salmon inv
saumure [somyʀ] nf brine
saupoudrer [supudʀe] vt: ~ **qch de** to sprinkle sth with
saur [sɔʀ] adj m: **hareng** ~ smoked ou red herring, kipper
saurai etc vb voir **savoir**
saut [so] nm jump; (discipline sportive) jumping; **faire un** ~ **chez qn** to pop over to sb's (place); **au** ~ **du lit** on getting out of bed; ~ **à la corde** skipping; ~ **à la perche** pole vaulting; ~ **en hauteur/longueur** high/long jump; ~ **périlleux** somersault
saute [sot] nf sudden change
saute-mouton [sotmutɔ̃] nm: **jouer à** ~ to play leapfrog
sauter [sote] vi to jump, leap; (exploser) to blow up, explode; (: fusibles) to blow; (se rompre) to snap, burst; (se détacher) to pop out (ou off) ♦ vt to jump (over), leap (over); (omettre) to skip, miss (out); **faire** ~ to blow up; to burst open; (CULIN) to sauté; ~ **au cou de qn** to fly into sb's arms
sauterelle [sotʀɛl] nf grasshopper
sautiller [sotije] vi to hop; to skip
sautoir [sotwaʀ] nm: ~ **(de perles)** string of pearls
sauvage [sovaʒ] adj (gén) wild; (peuplade) savage; (farouche) unsociable; (barbare) wild, savage; (non officiel) unauthorized, unofficial ♦ nm/f savage; (timide) unsociable type
sauve [sov] f voir **sauf**
sauvegarde [sovgaʀd(ə)] nf safeguard; **sauvegarder** vt to safeguard; (INFORM: enregistrer) to save; (: copier) to back up
sauve-qui-peut [sovkipø] excl run for your life!
sauver [sove] vt to save; (porter secours à) to rescue; (récupérer) to salvage, rescue; **se** ~ vi (s'enfuir) to run away; (fam: partir) to be off; **sauvetage** nm rescue; **sauveteur** nm rescuer; **sauvette: à la sauvette** adv (vendre) without authorization; (se marier etc) hastily, hurriedly; **sauveur** nm saviour (BRIT), savior (US)
savais etc vb voir **savoir**
savamment [savamɑ̃] adv (avec érudition) learnedly; (habilement) skilfully, cleverly
savant, e [savɑ̃, -ɑ̃t] adj scholarly, learned; (calé) clever ♦ nm scientist
saveur [savœʀ] nf flavour; (fig) savour
savoir [savwaʀ] vt to know; (être capable de): **il sait nager** he can swim ♦ nm knowledge; **se** ~ vi (être connu) to be known; **à** ~ that is, namely; **faire** ~ **qch à qn** to let sb know sth; **pas que je sache** not as far as I know
savon [savɔ̃] nm (produit) soap; (morceau)

bar of soap; (fam): **passer un** ~ **à qn** to give sb a good dressing-down; **savonnette** nf bar of soap; **savonneux, euse** adj soapy
savons vb voir **savoir**
savourer [savuʀe] vt to savour
savoureux, euse [savuʀø, -øz] adj tasty; (fig) spicy, juicy
saxo(phone) [saksɔ(fɔn)] nm sax(ophone)
scabreux, euse [skabʀø, -øz] adj risky; (indécent) improper, shocking
scandale [skɑ̃dal] nm scandal; (tapage): **faire du** ~ to make a scene, create a disturbance; **faire** ~ to scandalize people; **scandaleux, euse** adj scandalous, outrageous
scandinave [skɑ̃dinav] adj, nm/f Scandinavian
Scandinavie [skɑ̃dinavi] nf Scandinavia
scaphandre [skafɑ̃dʀ(ə)] nm (de plongeur) diving suit; (de cosmonaute) space-suit
scarabée [skaʀabe] nm beetle
sceau, x [so] nm seal; (fig) stamp, mark
scélérat, e [seleʀa, -at] nm/f villain
sceller [sele] vt to seal
scénario [senaʀjo] nm (CINÉMA) scenario; script; (fig) scenario
scène [sɛn] nf (gén) scene; (estrade, fig: théâtre) stage; **entrer en** ~ to come on stage; **mettre en** ~ (THÉÂTRE) to stage; (CINÉMA) to direct; (fig) to present, introduce; ~ **de ménage** nf domestic scene
sceptique [sɛptik] adj sceptical
schéma [ʃema] nm (diagramme) diagram, sketch; (fig) outline; pattern; **~tique** adj diagrammatic(al), schematic; (fig) oversimplified
sciatique [sjatik] nf sciatica
scie [si] nf saw; ~ **à découper** fretsaw; ~ **à métaux** hacksaw
sciemment [sjamɑ̃] adv knowingly
science [sjɑ̃s] nf science; (savoir) knowledge; (savoir-faire) art, skill; ~**s naturelles** (SCOL) natural science sg, biology sg; ~**s po** nfpl political science ou studies pl; **scientifique** adj scientific ♦ nm/f scientist; science student
scier [sje] vt to saw; (retrancher) to saw off; **scierie** nf sawmill
scinder [sɛ̃de] vt to split up; **se** ~ vi to split up
scintiller [sɛ̃tije] vi to sparkle
scission [sisjɔ̃] nf split
sciure [sjyʀ] nf: ~ **(de bois)** sawdust
sclérose [skleʀoz] nf: ~ **en plaques** multiple sclerosis
scolaire [skɔlɛʀ] adj school cpd; (péj) schoolish; **scolariser** vt to provide with schooling (ou schools); **scolarité** nf schooling
scooter [skutœʀ] nm (motor) scooter
score [skɔʀ] nm score
scorpion [skɔʀpjɔ̃] nm (signe): **le S~** Scor-

pio
Scotch [skɔtʃ] (®) nm adhesive tape
scout, e [skut] adj, nm scout
script [skʀipt] nm printing; (CINÉMA) (shooting) script
script-girl [skʀiptgœʀl] nf continuity girl
scrupule [skʀypyl] nm scruple
scruter [skʀyte] vt to scrutinize; (l'obscurité) to peer into
scrutin [skʀytɛ̃] nm (vote) ballot; (ensemble des opérations) poll
sculpter [skylte] vt to sculpt; (suj: érosion) to carve; **sculpteur** nm sculptor
sculpture [skyltyʀ] nf sculpture; ~ sur bois wood carving

―――――――― MOT CLÉ ――――――――

se(s′) [s(ə)] pron **1** (emploi réfléchi) oneself; (: masc) himself; (: fém) herself; (: sujet non humain) itself; (: pl) themselves; **se voir comme l'on est** to see o.s. as one is
2 (réciproque) one another, each other; **ils s'aiment** they love one another ou each other
3 (passif): **cela se répare facilement** it is easily repaired
4 (possessif): **se casser la jambe/laver les mains** to break one's leg/wash one's hands

séance [seɑ̃s] nf (d'assemblée, récréative) meeting, session; (de tribunal) sitting, session; (musicale, CINÉMA, THÉÂTRE) performance; ~ **tenante** forthwith
seau, x [so] nm bucket, pail
sec, sèche [sɛk, sɛʃ] adj dry; (raisins, figues) dried; (cœur, personne: insensible) hard, cold ♦ nm: **tenir au** ~ to keep in a dry place ♦ adv hard; **je le bois** ~ I drink it straight ou neat; **à** ~ dried up
sécateur [sekatœʀ] nm secateurs pl (BRIT), shears pl
sèche [sɛʃ] adj f voir **sec**
sèche-cheveux [sɛʃʃəvø] nm inv hair-drier
sèche-linge [sɛʃlɛ̃ʒ] nm inv tumble dryer
sécher [seʃe] vt to dry; (dessécher: peau, blé) to dry (out); (: étang) to dry up ♦ vi to dry; to dry out; to dry up; (fam: candidat) to be stumped; **se** ~ (après le bain) to dry o.s.
sécheresse [sɛʃʀɛs] nf dryness; (absence de pluie) drought
séchoir [seʃwaʀ] nm drier
second, e [sɡɔ̃, -ɔ̃d] adj second ♦ nm (assistant) second in command; (NAVIG) first mate; **voyager en** ~**e** to travel second-class; **de** ~**e main** second-hand; **secondaire** adj secondary; **seconde** nf second; **seconder** vt to assist
secouer [səkwe] vt to shake; (passagers) to rock; (traumatiser) to shake (up)
secourir [səkuʀiʀ] vt (aller sauver) to (go and) rescue; (prodiguer des soins à) to help,

assist; (venir en aide à) to assist, aid; **se-courisme** nm first aid; life saving
secours [səkuʀ] nm help, aid, assistance ♦ nmpl aid sg; **au** ~! help!; **appeler au** ~ to shout ou call for help; **porter** ~ **à qn** to give sb assistance, help sb; **les premiers** ~ first aid sg
secousse [səkus] nf jolt, bump; (électrique) shock; (fig: psychologique) jolt, shock; ~ **sismique** ou **tellurique** earth tremor
secret, ète [səkʀɛ, -ɛt] adj secret; (fig: renfermé) reticent, reserved ♦ nm secret; (discrétion absolue): **le** ~ secrecy; **au** ~ in solitary confinement
secrétaire [səkʀetɛʀ] nm/f secretary ♦ nm (meuble) writing desk; ~ **de direction** private ou personal secretary; ~ **d'État** junior minister; ~ **général** nm (COMM) company secretary; **secrétariat** nm (profession) secretarial work; (bureau) office; (: d'organisation internationale) secretariat
secteur [sɛktœʀ] nm sector; (ADMIN) district; (ÉLEC): **branché sur le** ~ plugged into the mains (supply)
section [sɛksjɔ̃] nf section; (de parcours d'autobus) fare stage; (MIL: unité) platoon; **sectionner** vt to sever
Sécu [seky] abr f = **sécurité sociale**
séculaire [sekylɛʀ] adj secular; (très vieux) age-old
sécuriser [sekyʀize] vt to give (a feeling of) security to
sécurité [sekyʀite] nf safety; security; **système de** ~ safety system; **être en** ~ to be safe; **la** ~ **routière** road safety; **la** ~ **sociale** ≈ (the) Social Security (BRIT), ≈ Welfare (US)
sédition [sedisjɔ̃] nf insurrection; sedition
séduction [sedyksjɔ̃] nf seduction; (charme, attrait) appeal, charm
séduire [seduiʀ] vt to charm; (femme: abuser de) to seduce; **séduisant, e** adj (femme) seductive; (homme, offre) very attractive
ségrégation [segʀegɑsjɔ̃] nf segregation
seigle [sɛɡl(ə)] nm rye
seigneur [sɛɲœʀ] nm lord
sein [sɛ̃] nm breast; (entrailles) womb; **au** ~ **de** (équipe, institution) within; (flots, bonheur) in the midst of
séisme [seism(ə)] nm earthquake
seize [sɛz] num sixteen; **seizième** num sixteenth
séjour [seʒuʀ] nm stay; (pièce) living room; **séjourner** vi to stay
sel [sɛl] nm salt; (fig) wit; spice; ~ **de cuisine/de table** cooking/table salt
sélection [selɛksjɔ̃] nf selection; **sélectionner** vt to select
self-service [sɛlfsɛʀvis] adj, nm self-service
selle [sɛl] nf saddle; ~**s** nfpl (MÉD) stools; **seller** vt to saddle

sellette [sɛlɛt] *nf*: **être sur la** ~ to be on the carpet

selon [səlɔ̃] *prép* according to; (*en se conformant à*) in accordance with; ~ **que** according to whether; ~ **moi** as I see it

semaine [səmɛn] *nf* week; **en** ~ during the week, on weekdays

semblable [sɑ̃blabl(ə)] *adj* similar; (*de ce genre*): **de** ~**s mésaventures** such mishaps ♦ *nm* fellow creature *ou* man; ~ **à** similar to, like

semblant [sɑ̃blɑ̃] *nm*: **un** ~ **de vérité** a semblance of truth; **faire** ~ **(de faire)** to pretend (to do)

sembler [sɑ̃ble] *vb +attrib* to seem ♦ *vb impers*: **il semble (bien) que/inutile de** it (really) seems *ou* appears that/useless to; **il me semble que** it seems to me that; **I think (that)**; **comme bon lui semble** as he sees fit

semelle [səmɛl] *nf* sole; (*intérieure*) insole, inner sole

semence [səmɑ̃s] *nf* (*graine*) seed

semer [səme] *vt* to sow; (*fig: éparpiller*) to scatter; (: *confusion*) to spread; (: *poursuivants*) to lose, shake off; **semé de** (*difficultés*) riddled with

semestre [səmɛstʀ(ə)] *nm* half-year; (*SCOL*) semester

séminaire [seminɛʀ] *nm* seminar

semi-remorque [səmiʀəmɔʀk(ə)] *nm* articulated lorry (*BRIT*), semi(trailer) (*US*)

semonce [səmɔ̃s] *nf*: **un coup de** ~ a shot across the bows

semoule [səmul] *nf* semolina

sempiternel, le [sɛpitɛʀnɛl] *adj* eternal, never-ending

sénat [sena] *nm* Senate; **sénateur** *nm* Senator

sens [sɑ̃s] *nm* (*PHYSIOL, instinct*) sense; (*signification*) meaning, sense; (*direction*) direction; **à mon** ~ to my mind; **reprendre ses** ~ to regain consciousness; **dans le** ~ **des aiguilles d'une montre** clockwise; ~ **commun** common sense; ~ **dessus dessous** upside down; ~ **interdit** one-way street; ~ **unique** one-way street

sensass [sɑ̃sas] (*fam*) *adj* fantastic

sensation [sɑ̃sasjɔ̃] *nf* sensation; **à** ~ (*péj*) sensational

sensé, e [sɑ̃se] *adj* sensible

sensibiliser [sɑ̃sibilize] *vt*: ~ **qn à** to make sb sensitive to

sensibilité [sɑ̃sibilite] *nf* sensitivity

sensible [sɑ̃sibl(ə)] *adj* sensitive; (*aux sens*) perceptible; (*appréciable: différence, progrès*) appreciable, noticeable; **sensiblement** *adv* (*notablement*) appreciably, noticeably; (*à peu près*): **ils ont sensiblement le même poids** they weigh approximately the same; **sensiblerie** *nf* sentimentality; squeamishness

sensuel, le [sɑ̃sɥel] *adj* sensual; sensuous

sentence [sɑ̃tɑ̃s] *nf* (*jugement*) sentence; (*adage*) maxim

sentier [sɑ̃tje] *nm* path

sentiment [sɑ̃timɑ̃] *nm* feeling; **recevez mes** ~**s respectueux** yours faithfully; **sentimental, e, aux** *adj* sentimental; (*vie, aventure*) love *cpd*

sentinelle [sɑ̃tinɛl] *nf* sentry

sentir [sɑ̃tiʀ] *vt* (*par l'odorat*) to smell; (*par le goût*) to taste; (*au toucher, fig*) to feel; (*répandre une odeur de*) to smell of; (: *ressemblance*) to smell like; (*avoir la saveur de*) to taste of; to taste like ♦ *vi* to smell; ~ **mauvais** to smell bad; **se** ~ **bien** to feel good; **se** ~ **mal** (*être indisposé*) to feel unwell *ou* ill; **se** ~ **le courage/la force de faire** to feel brave/strong enough to do; **il ne peut pas le** ~ (*fam*) he can't stand him

séparation [separasjɔ̃] *nf* separation; (*cloison*) division, partition; ~ **de corps** legal separation

séparé, e [separe] *adj* (*appartements, pouvoirs*) separate; (*époux*) separated; ~**ment** *adv* separately

séparer [separe] *vt* (*gén*) to separate; (*suj: divergences etc*) to divide; to drive apart; (*suj: différences, obstacles*) to stand between; (*détacher*): ~ **qch de** to pull sth (off) from; (*diviser*): ~ **qch par** to divide sth (up) with; **se** ~ *vi* (*époux, amis, adversaires*) to separate, part; (*se diviser: route, tige etc*) to divide; (*se détacher*): **se** ~ **(de)** to split off (from); to come off; **se** ~ **de** (*époux*) to separate *ou* part from; (*employé, objet personnel*) to part with; ~ **une pièce en deux** to divide a room into two

sept [sɛt] *num* seven

septembre [sɛptɑ̃bʀ(ə)] *nm* September

septennat [septena] *nm* seven year term of office (of French President)

septentrional, e, aux [sɛptɑ̃tʀijɔnal, -o] *adj* northern

septicémie [sɛptisemi] *nf* blood poisoning, septicaemia

septième [sɛtjɛm] *num* seventh

septique [sɛptik] *adj*: **fosse** ~ septic tank

sépulture [sepyltyʀ] *nf* burial; burial place, grave

séquelles [sekɛl] *nfpl* after-effects; (*fig*) aftermath *sg*; consequences

séquestrer [sekɛstʀe] *vt* (*personne*) to confine illegally; (*biens*) to impound

serai *etc vb voir* **être**

serein, e [səʀɛ̃, -ɛn] *adj* serene; (*jugement*) dispassionate

serez *vb voir* **être**

sergent [sɛʀʒɑ̃] *nm* sergeant

série [seʀi] *nf* (*de questions, d'accidents*) series *inv*; (*de clés, casseroles,. outils*) set; (*catégorie: SPORT*) rank; class; **en** ~ in quick succession; (*COMM*) mass *cpd*; **de** ~

standard; **hors** ~ (*COMM*) custom-built; (*fig*) outstanding

sérieusement [seʀjøzmɑ̃] *adv* seriously; reliably; responsibly

sérieux, euse [seʀjø, -øz] *adj* serious; (*élève, employé*) reliable, responsible; (*client, maison*) reliable, dependable ♦ *nm* seriousness; reliability; **garder son** ~ to keep a straight face; **prendre qch/qn au** ~ to take sth/sb seriously

serin [səʀɛ̃] *nm* canary

seringue [səʀɛ̃g] *nf* syringe

serions *vb voir* être

serment [seʀmɑ̃] *nm* (*juré*) oath; (*promesse*) pledge, vow

sermon [seʀmɔ̃] *nm* sermon

séro-positif, ive [sero-] *adj* (*MED*) HIV-positive

serpent [seʀpɑ̃] *nm* snake

serpenter [seʀpɑ̃te] *vi* to wind

serpentin [seʀpɑ̃tɛ̃] *nm* (*tube*) coil; (*ruban*) streamer

serpillière [seʀpijɛʀ] *nf* floorcloth

serre [seʀ] *nf* (*AGR*) greenhouse; ~**s** *nfpl* (*griffes*) claws, talons

serré, e [seʀe] *adj* (*réseau*) dense; (*écriture*) close; (*habits*) tight; (*fig: lutte, match*) tight, close-fought; (*passagers etc*) (tightly) packed

serrer [seʀe] *vt* (*tenir*) to grip *ou* hold tight; (*comprimer, coincer*) to squeeze; (*poings, mâchoires*) to clench; (*suj: vêtement*) to be too tight for; (*à fit tightly*); (*rapprocher*) to close up, move closer together; (*ceinture, nœud, frein, vis*) to tighten ♦ *vi*: ~ **à droite** to keep *ou* get over to the right; **se** ~ *vi* (*se rapprocher*) to squeeze up; **se** ~ **contre qn** to huddle up to sb; ~ **la main à qn** to shake sb's hand; ~ **qn dans ses bras** to hug sb, clasp sb in one's arms

serrure [seʀyʀ] *nf* lock

serrurier [seʀyʀje] *nm* locksmith

sert *etc vb voir* servir

sertir [seʀtiʀ] *vt* (*pierre*) to set

servante [seʀvɑ̃t] *nf* (*maid*)servant

serveur, euse [seʀvœʀ, -øz] *nm/f* waiter(waitress)

serviable [seʀvjabl(ə)] *adj* obliging, willing to help

service [seʀvis] *nm* (*gén*) service; (*série de repas*): **premier** ~ first sitting; (*assortiment de vaisselle*) set, service; (*bureau: de la vente etc*) department, section; (*travail*): **pendant le** ~ on duty; ~**s** *nmpl* (*travail, ÉCON*) services; **faire le** ~ to serve; **rendre** ~ **à** to help; **rendre un** ~ **à qn** to do sb a favour; **mettre en** ~ to put into service *ou* operation; **hors** ~ out of order; ~ **après-vente** after-sales service; ~ **d'ordre** police (*ou* stewards) in charge of maintaining order; ~ **militaire** military service; ~**s secrets** secret service *sg*

serviette [seʀvjɛt] *nf* (*de table*) (table) napkin, serviette; (*de toilette*) towel; (*porte-documents*) briefcase; ~ **hygiénique** sanitary towel

servir [seʀviʀ] *vt* (*gén*) to serve; (*au restaurant*) to wait on; (*au magasin*) to serve, attend to; (*fig: aider*): ~ **qn** to aid sb; to serve sb's interests; (*COMM: rente*) to pay ♦ *vi* (*TENNIS*) to serve; (*CARTES*) to deal; **se** ~ *vi* (*prendre d'un plat*) to help o.s.; **se** ~ **de** (*plat*) to help o.s. to; (*voiture, outil, relations*) to use; **vous êtes servi?** are you being served?; ~ **à qn** (*diplôme, livre*) to be of use to sb; ~ **à qch/faire** (*outil etc*) to be used for sth/doing; **à quoi cela sert-il (de faire)?** what's the use (of doing)?; **cela ne sert à rien** it's no use; ~ (**à qn**) **de** to serve as (for sb); ~ **à dîner (à qn)** to serve dinner (to sb)

serviteur [seʀvitœʀ] *nm* servant

servitude [seʀvityd] *nf* servitude; (*fig*) constraint

ses [se] *dét voir* son[1]

seuil [sœj] *nm* doorstep; (*fig*) threshold

seul, e [sœl] *adj* (*sans compagnie*) alone; (*avec nuance affective: isolé*) lonely; (*unique*): **un** ~ **livre** only one book, a single book ♦ *adv* (*vivre*) alone, on one's own ♦ *nm, nf*: **il en reste un(e)** ~(**e**) there's only one left; **le** ~ **livre** the only book; ~ **ce livre, ce livre** ~ this book alone, only this book; **parler tout** ~ to talk to oneself; **faire qch (tout)** ~ to do sth (all) on one's own *ou* (all) by oneself; **à lui (tout)** ~ single-handed, on his own

seulement [sœlmɑ̃] *adv* only; **non** ~ ... **mais aussi** *ou* **encore** not only ... but also

sève [sɛv] *nf* sap

sévère [sevɛʀ] *adj* severe

sévices [sevis] *nmpl* (physical) cruelty *sg*, ill treatment *sg*

sévir [seviʀ] *vi* (*punir*) to use harsh measures, crack down; (*suj: fléau*) to rage, be rampant

sevrer [səvʀe] *vt* (*enfant etc*) to wean

sexe [sɛks(ə)] *nm* sex; (*organe mâle*) member

sexuel, le [sɛksɥɛl] *adj* sexual

seyant, e [sɛjɑ̃, -ɑ̃t] *adj* becoming

shampooing [ʃɑ̃pwɛ̃] *nm* shampoo; **se faire un** ~ to shampoo one's hair

short [ʃɔʀt] *nm* (pair of) shorts *pl*

--- MOT CLÉ

si [si] *nm* (*MUS*) B; (*en chantant la gamme*) ti

♦ *adv* **1** (*oui*) yes

2 (*tellement*) so; ~ **gentil/rapidement** so kind/fast; (**tant et**) ~ **bien que** so much so that; ~ **rapide qu'il soit** however fast he may be

♦ *conj* if; ~ **tu veux** if you want; **je me de-**

mande ~ I wonder if *ou* whether; ~ **seulement** if only

Sicile [sisil] *nf*: **la** ~ Sicily

SIDA [sida] *sigle m* (= *syndrome immunodéficitaire acquis*) AIDS *sg*

sidéré, e [sidere] *adj* staggered

sidérurgie [sideryrʒi] *nf* steel industry

siècle [sjɛkl(ə)] *nm* century; (*époque*) age

siège [sjɛʒ] *nm* seat; (*d'entreprise*) head office; (*d'organisation*) headquarters *pl*; (*MIL*) siege; ~ **social** registered office

siéger [sjeʒe] *vi* to sit

sien, ne [sjɛ̃, sjɛn] *pron*: **le(la)** ~**(ne)**, **les** ~**(ne)s** his; hers; its; **les** ~**s** (*sa famille*) one's family; **faire des** ~**nes** (*fam*) to be up to one's (usual) tricks

sieste [sjɛst(ə)] *nf* (afternoon) snooze *ou* nap, siesta; **faire la** ~ to have a snooze *ou* nap

sifflement [sifləmɑ̃] *nm* whistle, whistling *no pl*; wheezing *no pl*; hissing *no pl*

siffler [sifle] *vi* (*gén*) to whistle; (*en respirant*) to wheeze; (*serpent, vapeur*) to hiss ♦ *vt* (*chanson*) to whistle; (*chien etc*) to whistle for; (*fille*) to whistle at; (*pièce, orateur*) to hiss, boo; (*faute*) to blow one's whistle at; (*fin du match, départ*) to blow one's whistle for; (*fam: verre*) to guzzle

sifflet [sifle] *nm* whistle; **coup de** ~ whistle

siffloter [siflɔte] *vi*, *vt* to whistle

sigle [sigl(ə)] *nm* acronym

signal, aux [siɲal, -o] *nm* (*signe convenu, appareil*) signal; (*indice, écriteau*) sign; **donner le** ~ **de** to give the signal for; ~ **d'alarme** alarm signal; **signaux (lumineux)** (*AUTO*) traffic signals

signalement [siɲalmɑ̃] *nm* description, particulars *pl*

signaler [siɲale] *vt* to indicate; to announce; to report; (*faire remarquer*): ~ **qch à qn/(à qn) que** to point out sth to sb/(to sb) that; **se** ~ **(par)** to distinguish o.s. (by)

signature [siɲatyr] *nf* signature (*action*), signing

signe [siɲ] *nm* sign; (*TYPO*) mark; **faire un** ~ **de la main** to give a sign with one's hand; **faire** ~ **à qn** (*fig*) to get in touch with sb; **faire** ~ **à qn d'entrer** to motion (to) sb to come in; ~**s particuliers** *nmpl* distinguishing marks

signer [siɲe] *vt* to sign; **se** ~ *vi* to cross o.s.

signet [siɲe] *nm* bookmark

significatif, ive [siɲifikatif, -iv] *adj* significant

signification [siɲifikasjɔ̃] *nf* meaning

signifier [siɲifje] *vt* (*vouloir dire*) to mean; (*faire connaître*): ~ **qch (à qn)** to make sth known (to sb); (*JUR*): ~ **qch à qn** to serve notice of sth on sb

silence [silɑ̃s] *nm* silence; (*MUS*) rest; **gar-**

der le ~ to keep silent, say nothing; **passer sous** ~ to pass over (in silence); **silencieux, euse** *adj* quiet, silent ♦ *nm* silencer

silex [silɛks] *nm* flint

silhouette [silwet] *nf* outline, silhouette; (*lignes, contour*) outline; (*figure*) figure

silicium [silisjɔm] *nm* silicon; **plaquette de** ~ silicon chip

sillage [sijaʒ] *nm* wake; (*fig*) trail

sillon [sijɔ̃] *nm* furrow; (*de disque*) groove; **sillonner** *vt* to criss-cross

simagrées [simagre] *nfpl* fuss *sg*; airs and graces

similaire [similɛr] *adj* similar; **similicuir** *nm* imitation leather; **similitude** *nf* similarity

simple [sɛ̃pl(ə)] *adj* (*gén*) simple; (*non multiple*) single; ~**s** *nmpl* (*MÉD*) medicinal plants; ~ **d'esprit** *nm/f* simpleton; ~ **messieurs** *nm* (*TENNIS*) men's singles *sg*; **un** ~ **particulier** an ordinary citizen; ~ **soldat** private

simulacre [simylakr(ə)] *nm* (*péj*): **un** ~ **de** a pretence of

simuler [simyle] *vt* to sham, simulate

simultané, e [simyltane] *adj* simultaneous

sincère [sɛ̃sɛr] *adj* sincere; genuine; **sincérité** *nf* sincerity

sine qua non [sinekwanɔn] *adj*: **condition** ~ indispensable condition

singe [sɛ̃ʒ] *nm* monkey; (*de grande taille*) ape; ~**r** [sɛ̃ʒe] *vt* to ape, mimic

singeries [sɛ̃ʒri] *nfpl* antics; (*simagrées*) airs and graces

singulariser [sɛ̃gylarize] *vt* to mark out; **se** ~ *vi* to call attention to o.s.

singularité [sɛ̃gylarite] *nf* peculiarity

singulier, ière [sɛ̃gylje, -jɛr] *adj* remarkable, singular ♦ *nm* singular

sinistre [sinistr(ə)] *adj* sinister ♦ *nm* (*incendie*) blaze; (*catastrophe*) disaster; (*ASSURANCES*) damage (*giving rise to a claim*); **sinistré, e** *adj* disaster-stricken ♦ *nm/f* disaster victim

sinon [sinɔ̃] *conj* (*autrement, sans quoi*) otherwise, or else; (*sauf*) except, other than; (*si ce n'est*) if not

sinueux, euse [sinɥø, -øz] *adj* winding; (*fig*) tortuous

sinus [sinys] *nm* (*ANAT*) sinus; (*GÉOM*) sine; **sinusite** *nf* sinusitis

siphon [sifɔ̃] *nm* (*tube, d'eau gazeuse*) siphon; (*d'évier etc*) U-bend

sirène [siren] *nf* siren; ~ **d'alarme** air-raid siren; fire alarm

sirop [siro] *nm* (*à diluer: de fruit etc*) syrup; (*boisson*) fruit drink; (*pharmaceutique*) syrup, mixture

siroter [sirɔte] *vt* to sip

sismique [sismik] *adj* seismic

site [sit] *nm* (*paysage, environnement*) setting; (*d'une ville etc: emplacement*) site; ~

(pittoresque) beauty spot; **~s touristiques** places of interest

sitôt [sito] *adv*: **~ parti** as soon as he *etc* had left; **~ après** straight after; **pas de ~** not for a long time

situation [sitɥɑsjɔ̃] *nf* (*gén*) situation; (*d'un édifice, d'une ville*) situation, position; location; **~ de famille** *nf* marital status

situé, e [sitɥe] *adj*: **bien ~** well situated; **~ à** situated at

situer [sitɥe] *vt* to site, situate; (*en pensée*) to set, place; **se ~** *vi*: **se ~ à/près de** to be situated at/near

six [sis] *num* six; **sixième** *num* sixth

ski [ski] *nm* (*objet*) ski; (*sport*) skiing; **faire du ~** to ski; **~ de fond** cross-country skiing; **~ nautique** water-skiing; **~ de piste** downhill skiing; **~ de randonnée** cross-country skiing; **skier** *vi* to ski; **skieur, euse** *nm/f* skier

slip [slip] *nm* (*sous-vêtement*) pants *pl*, briefs *pl*; (*de bain: d'homme*) trunks *pl*; (: *du bikini*) (bikini) briefs *pl*

slogan [slɔgã] *nm* slogan

S.M.I.C. [s.nik] *sigle m* = **salaire minimum interprofessionnel de croissance**

smicard, e [smikar, -ard(ə)] (*fam*) *nm/f* minimum wage earner

smoking [smɔkiŋ] *nm* dinner *ou* evening suit

S.N.C.F. *sigle f* (= *société nationale des chemins de fer français*) French railways

snob [snɔb] *adj* snobbish ♦ *nm/f* snob

sobre [sɔbr(ə)] *adj* temperate, abstemious; (*élégance, style*) sober; **~ de** (*gestes, compliments*) sparing of

sobriquet [sɔbrikɛ] *nm* nickname

social, e, aux [sɔsjal, -o] *adj* social

socialisme [sɔsjalism(ə)] *nm* socialism; **socialiste** *nm/f* socialist

société [sɔsjete] *nf* society; (*sportive*) club; (*COMM*) company; **la ~ d'abondance/de consommation** the affluent/consumer society; **~ à responsabilité limitée** *type of limited liability company*; **~ anonyme** ≈ limited (*BRIT*) *ou* incorporated (*US*) company

sociologie [sɔsjɔlɔʒi] *nf* sociology

socle [sɔkl(ə)] *nm* (*de colonne, statue*) plinth, pedestal; (*de lampe*) base

socquette [sɔkɛt] *nf* ankle sock

sœur [sœr] *nf* sister; (*religieuse*) nun, sister

soi [swa] *pron* oneself; **cela va de ~** that *ou* it goes without saying; **soi-disant** *adj inv* so-called ♦ *adv* supposedly

soie [swa] *nf* silk; (*de porc, sanglier: poil*) bristle; **soierie** *nf* (*tissu*) silk

soif [swaf] *nf* thirst; **avoir ~** to be thirsty; **donner ~ à qn** to make sb thirsty

soigné, e [swaɲe] *adj* (*tenue*) well-groomed, neat; (*travail*) careful, meticulous; (*fam*) whopping; stiff

soigner [swaɲe] *vt* (*malade, maladie: suj:*

docteur) to treat; (*suj: infirmière, mère*) to nurse, look after; (*blessé*) to tend; (*travail, détails*) to take care over; (*jardin, chevelure, invités*) to look after

soigneux, euse [swaɲø, -øz] *adj* (*propre*) tidy, neat; (*méticuleux*) painstaking, careful; **~ de** careful with

soi-même [swamɛm] *pron* oneself

soin [swɛ̃] *nm* (*application*) care; (*propreté, ordre*) tidiness, neatness; **~s** *nmpl* (*à un malade, blessé*) treatment *sg*, medical attention *sg*; (*attentions, prévenance*) care and attention *sg*; (*hygiène*) care *sg*; **prendre ~ de** to take care of, look after; **prendre ~ de faire** to take care to do; **les premiers ~s** first aid *sg*; **aux bons ~s de** c/o, care of

soir [swar] *nm* evening; **ce ~** this evening, tonight; **demain ~** tomorrow evening, tomorrow night

soirée [sware] *nf* evening; (*réception*) party

soit [swa] *vb voir* **être** ♦ *conj* (*à savoir*) namely; (*ou*): **~ ... ~** either ... or ♦ *adv* so be it, very well; **~ que ... ~ que** *ou* **ou que** whether ... or whether

soixantaine [swasɑ̃tɛn] *nf*: **une ~ (de)** sixty or so, about sixty; **avoir la ~** (*âge*) to be around sixty

soixante [swasɑ̃t] *num* sixty; **soixante-dix** *num* seventy

soja [sɔʒa] *nm* soya; (*graines*) soya beans *pl*

sol [sɔl] *nm* ground; (*de logement*) floor; (*revêtement*) flooring *no pl*; (*territoire, AGR, GÉO*) soil; (*MUS*) G; (: *en chantant la gamme*) so(h)

solaire [sɔlɛr] *adj* solar, sun *cpd*

soldat [sɔlda] *nm* soldier

solde [sɔld(ə)] *nf* pay ♦ *nm* (*COMM*) balance; **~s** *nm ou f pl* sale goods; sales; **en ~** at sale price

solder [sɔlde] *vt* (*compte*) to settle; (*marchandise*) to sell at sale price, sell off; **se ~ par** (*fig*) to end in; **article soldé (à) 10 F** item reduced to 10 F

sole [sɔl] *nf* sole *inv* (*fish*)

soleil [sɔlɛj] *nm* sun; (*lumière*) sun(light); (*temps ensoleillé*) sun(shine); (*BOT*) sunflower; **il fait du ~** it's sunny; **au ~** in the sun

solennel, le [sɔlanɛl] *adj* solemn; ceremonial; **solennité** *nf* (*d'une fête*) solemnity

solfège [sɔlfɛʒ] *nm* rudiments *pl* of music; (*exercices*) ear training *no pl*

solidaire [sɔlidɛr] *adj* (*personnes*) who stand together, who show solidarity; (*pièces mécaniques*) interdependent; (*collègues*) to stand by; **solidarité** *nf* solidarity; interdependence; **par solidarité (avec)** in sympathy (with)

solide [sɔlid] *adj* solid; (*mur, maison, meuble*) solid, sturdy; (*connaissances, argument*) sound; (*personne, estomac*) robust, sturdy ♦

nm solid

soliste [sɔlist(ə)] *nm/f* soloist

solitaire [sɔlitɛʀ] *adj* (*sans compagnie*) solitary, lonely; (*lieu*) lonely ♦ *nm/f* recluse; loner

solitude [sɔlityd] *nf* loneliness; (*paix*) solitude

solive [sɔliv] *nf* joist

sollicitations [sɔlisitɑsjɔ̃] *nfpl* entreaties, appeals; enticements; (*TECH*) stress *sg*

solliciter [sɔlisite] *vt* (*personne*) to appeal to; (*emploi, faveur*) to seek; (*suj: occupations, attractions etc*): ~ **qn** to appeal to sb's curiosity *etc*; to entice sb; to make demands on sb's time

sollicitude [sɔlisityd] *nf* concern

soluble [sɔlybl(ə)] *adj* soluble

solution [sɔlysjɔ̃] *nf* solution; ~ **de facilité** easy way out

solvable [sɔlvabl(ə)] *adj* solvent

sombre [sɔ̃bʀ(ə)] *adj* dark; (*fig*) gloomy

sombrer [sɔ̃bʀe] *vi* (*bateau*) to sink; ~ **dans** (*misère, désespoir*) to sink into

sommaire [sɔmɛʀ] *adj* (*simple*) basic; (*expéditif*) summary ♦ *nm* summary

sommation [sɔmasjɔ̃] *nf* (*JUR*) summons *sg*; (*avant de faire feu*) warning

somme [sɔm] *nf* (*MATH*) sum; (*fig*) amount; (*argent*) sum, amount ♦ *nm*: **faire un** ~ to have a (short) nap; **en** ~ all in all; ~ **toute** all in all

sommeil [sɔmɛj] *nm* sleep; **avoir** ~ to be sleepy; **sommeiller** *vi* to doze; (*fig*) to lie dormant

sommelier [sɔməlje] *nm* wine waiter

sommer [sɔme] *vt*: ~ **qn de faire** to command *ou* order sb to do; (*JUR*) to summon sb to do

sommes *vb voir* **être**

sommet [sɔmɛ] *nm* top; (*d'une montagne*) summit, top; (*fig: de la perfection, gloire*) height

sommier [sɔmje] *nm* (*bed*) base

sommité [sɔmite] *nf* prominent person, leading light

somnambule [sɔmnɑ̃byl] *nm/f* sleepwalker

somnifère [sɔmnifɛʀ] *nm* sleeping drug *no pl* (*ou* pill)

somnoler [sɔmnɔle] *vi* to doze

somptueux, euse [sɔ̃ptɥø, -øz] *adj* sumptuous; lavish

son[1], sa [sɔ̃, sa] (*pl* **ses**) *dét* (*antécédent humain: mâle*) his; (: *femelle*) her; (: *valeur indéfinie*) one's, his/her; (*antécédent non humain*) its

son[2] [sɔ̃] *nm* sound; (*de blé*) bran

sondage [sɔ̃daʒ] *nm*: ~ (**d'opinion**) (opinion) poll

sonde [sɔ̃d] *nf* (*NAVIG*) lead *ou* sounding line; (*MÉD*) probe; catheter; feeding tube; (*TECH*) borer, driller; (*pour fouiller etc*) probe

sonder [sɔ̃de] *vt* (*NAVIG*) to sound; (*atmosphère, plaie, bagages etc*) to probe; (*TECH*) to bore, drill; (*fig*) to sound out; to probe

songe [sɔ̃ʒ] *nm* dream

songer [sɔ̃ʒe] *vi*: ~ **à** (*penser à*) to think of; ~ **que** to consider that; to think that; **songeur, euse** *adj* pensive

sonnant, e [sɔnɑ̃, -ɑ̃t] *adj*: **à 8 heures** ~**es** on the stroke of 8

sonné, e [sɔne] *adj* (*fam*) cracked; **il est midi** ~ it's gone twelve

sonner [sɔne] *vi* to ring ♦ *vt* (*cloche*) to ring; (*glas, tocsin*) to sound; (*portier, infirmière*) to ring for; (*messe*) to ring the bell for; ~ **faux** (*instrument*) to sound out of tune; (*rire*) to ring false; ~ **les heures** to strike the hours

sonnerie [sɔnʀi] *nf* (*son*) ringing; (*sonnette*) bell; (*mécanisme d'horloge*) striking mechanism; ~ **d'alarme** alarm bell

sonnette [sɔnɛt] *nf* bell; ~ **d'alarme** alarm bell

sono [sɔno] *abr f* = **sonorisation**

sonore [sɔnɔʀ] *adj* (*voix*) sonorous, ringing; (*salle, métal*) resonant; (*ondes, film, signal*) sound *cpd*

sonorisation [sɔnɔʀizasjɔ̃] *nf* (*installations*) public address system, P.A. system

sonorité [sɔnɔʀite] *nf* (*de piano, violon*) tone; (*de voix, mot*) sonority; (*d'une salle*) resonance; acoustics *pl*

sont *vb voir* **être**

sophistiqué, e [sɔfistike] *adj* sophisticated

sorbet [sɔʀbɛ] *nm* water ice, sorbet

sorcellerie [sɔʀsɛlʀi] *nf* witchcraft *no pl*

sorcier [sɔʀsje] *nm* sorcerer; **sorcière** *nf* witch *ou* sorceress

sordide [sɔʀdid] *adj* sordid; squalid

sornettes [sɔʀnɛt] *nfpl* twaddle *sg*

sort [sɔʀ] *nm* (*fortune, destinée*) fate; (*condition, situation*) lot; (*magique*) curse, spell; **tirer au** ~ to draw lots

sorte [sɔʀt(ə)] *nf* sort, kind; **de la** ~ in that way; **de (telle)** ~ **que, en** ~ **que** so that; so much so that; **faire en** ~ **que** to see to it that

sortie [sɔʀti] *nf* (*issue*) way out, exit; (*MIL*) sortie; (*fig: verbale*) outburst, sally; (*promenade*) outing; (*le soir: au restaurant etc*) night out; (*COMM: somme*): ~**s** items of expenditure; outgoings *sans sg*; ~ **de bain** (*vêtement*) bathrobe; ~ **de secours** emergency exit

sortilège [sɔʀtilɛʒ] *nm* (magic) spell

sortir [sɔʀtiʀ] *vi* (*gén*) to come out; (*partir, se promener, aller au spectacle*) to go out; (*numéro gagnant*) to come up ♦ *vt* (*gén*) to take out; (*produit, ouvrage, modèle*) to bring out; (*INFORM*) to output; (: *sur papier*) to print out; (*fam: expulser*) to throw out; **se** ~ **de** (*affaire, situation*) to get out of; **s'en** ~ (*malade*) to pull through; (*d'une* *difficulté etc*) to get through; ~ **de** (*gén*) to leave; (*endroit*) to go (*ou* come) out of, leave; (*rainure etc*) to come out of; (*cadre, compétence*) to be outside

sosie [sozi] *nm* double

sot, sotte [so, sɔt] *adj* silly, foolish ♦ *nm/f* fool; **sottise** *nf* silliness, foolishness; silly *ou* foolish thing

sou [su] *nm*: **près de ses ~s** tight-fisted; **sans le ~** penniless

soubresaut [subʀəso] *nm* start; jolt

souche [suʃ] *nf* (*d'arbre*) stump; (*de carnet*) counterfoil (*BRIT*), stub; **de vieille ~** of old stock

souci [susi] *nm* (*inquiétude*) worry; (*préoccupation*) concern; (*BOT*) marigold; **se faire du ~** to worry

soucier [susje] : **se ~ de** *vt* to care about

soucieux, euse [susjø, -øz] *adj* concerned, worried

soucoupe [sukup] *nf* saucer; ~ **volante** flying saucer

soudain, e [sudɛ̃, -ɛn] *adj* (*douleur, mort*) sudden ♦ *adv* suddenly, all of a sudden

soude [sud] *nf* soda

souder [sude] *vt* (*avec fil à souder*) to solder; (*par soudure autogène*) to weld; (*fig*) to bind together

soudoyer [sudwaje] (*péj*) *vt* to bribe

soudure [sudyʀ] *nf* soldering; welding; (*joint*) soldered joint; weld

souffert, e [sufɛʀ, -ɛʀt(ə)] *pp de* **souffrir**

souffle [sufl(ə)] *nm* (*en expirant*) breath; (*en soufflant*) puff, blow; (*respiration*) breathing; (*d'explosion, de ventilateur*) blast; (*du vent*) blowing; **être à bout de ~** to be out of breath; **un ~ d'air** *ou* **de vent** a breath of air, a puff of wind

soufflé, e [sufle] *adj* (*fam*: *stupéfié*) staggered ♦ *nm* (*CULIN*) soufflé

souffler [sufle] *vi* (*gén*) to blow; (*haleter*) to puff (and blow) ♦ *vt* (*feu, bougie*) to blow out; (*chasser*: *poussière etc*) to blow away; (*TECH*: *verre*) to blow; (*suj*: *explosion*) to destroy (with its blast); (*dire*): ~ **qch à qn** to whisper sth to sb; (*fam*: *voler*): ~ **qch à qn** to pinch sth from sb

soufflet [sufle] *nm* (*instrument*) bellows *pl*; (*gifle*) slap (in the face)

souffleur [suflœʀ] *nm* (*THÉÂTRE*) prompter

souffrance [sufʀɑ̃s] *nf* suffering; **en ~** (*marchandise*) awaiting delivery; (*affaire*) pending

souffrant, e [sufʀɑ̃, -ɑ̃t] *adj* unwell

souffre-douleur [sufʀədulœʀ] *nm inv* butt, underdog

souffrir [sufʀiʀ] *vi* to suffer; to be in pain ♦ *vt* to suffer, endure; (*supporter*) to bear, stand; (*admettre*: *exception etc*) to allow *ou* admit of; ~ **de** (*maladie, froid*) to suffer from

soufre [sufʀ(ə)] *nm* sulphur

souhait [swɛ] *nm* wish; **tous nos ~s de** good wishes *ou* best wishes for; **riche** *etc* **à ~** as rich *etc* as one could wish; **à vos ~s!** bless you!; **~able** [swɛtabl(ə)] *adj* desirable

souhaiter [swete] *vt* to wish for; ~ **la bonne année à qn** to wish sb a happy New Year

souiller [suje] *vt* to dirty, soil; (*fig*) to sully, tarnish

soûl, e [su, sul] *adj* drunk ♦ *nm*: **tout son ~** to one's heart's content

soulagement [sulaʒmɑ̃] *nm* relief

soulager [sulaʒe] *vt* to relieve

soûler [sule] *vt*: ~ **qn** to get sb drunk; (*suj*: *boisson*) to make sb drunk; (*fig*) to make sb's head spin *ou* reel; **se ~** *vi* to get drunk

soulever [sulve] *vt* to lift; (*vagues, poussière*) to send up; (*peuple*) to stir up (to revolt); (*enthousiasme*) to arouse; (*question, débat*) to raise; **se ~** *vi* (*peuple*) to rise up; (*personne couchée*) to lift o.s. up; **cela me soulève le cœur** it makes me feel sick

soulier [sulje] *nm* shoe

souligner [suliɲe] *vt* to underline; (*fig*) to emphasize; to stress

soumettre [sumɛtʀ(ə)] *vt* (*pays*) to subject, subjugate; (*rebelle*) to put down, subdue; **se ~ (à)** to submit (to); ~ **qn/qch à** to subject sb/sth to; ~ **qch à qn** (*projet etc*) to submit sth to sb

soumis, e [sumi, -iz] *adj* submissive; **revenus ~ à l'impôt** taxable income; **soumission** [sumisjɔ̃] *nf* submission; (*docilité*) submissiveness; (*COMM*) tender

soupape [supap] *nf* valve

soupçon [supsɔ̃] *nm* suspicion; (*petite quantité*): **un ~ de** a hint *ou* touch of; **soupçonner** *vt* to suspect; **soupçonneux, euse** *adj* suspicious

soupe [sup] *nf* soup; ~ **au lait** *adj inv* quick-tempered

souper [supe] *vi* to have supper ♦ *nm* supper

soupeser [supəze] *vt* to weigh in one's hand(s); (*fig*) to weigh up

soupière [supjɛʀ] *nf* (*soup*) tureen

soupir [supiʀ] *nm* sigh; (*MUS*) crotchet rest

soupirail, aux [supiʀaj, -o] *nm* (small) basement window

soupirer [supiʀe] *vi* to sigh; ~ **après qch** to yearn for sth

souple [supl(ə)] *adj* supple; (*fig*: *règlement, caractère*) flexible; (: *démarche, taille*) lithe, supple

source [suʀs(ə)] *nf* (*point d'eau*) spring; (*d'un cours d'eau, fig*) source; **de bonne ~** on good authority

sourcil [suʀsij] *nm* (eye)brow

sourciller [suʀsije] *vi*: **sans ~** without turning a hair *ou* batting an eyelid

sourcilleux, euse [suʀsijø, -øz] *adj* pernickety

sourd, e [suʀ, suʀd(ə)] *adj* deaf; *(bruit, voix)* muffled; *(douleur)* dull; *(lutte)* silent, hidden ♦ *nm/f* deaf person

sourdine [suʀdin] *nf (MUS)* mute; **en ~** softly, quietly

sourd-muet, sourde-muette [suʀmɥɛ, suʀdmɥɛt] *adj* deaf-and-dumb ♦ *nm/f* deaf-mute

souriant, e [suʀjɑ̃, -ɑ̃t] *adj* cheerful

souricière [suʀisjɛʀ] *nf* mousetrap; *(fig)* trap

sourire [suʀiʀ] *nm* smile ♦ *vi* to smile; **~ à qn** to smile at sb; *(fig)* to appeal to sb; to smile on sb; **garder le ~** to keep smiling

souris [suʀi] *nf* mouse

sournois, e [suʀnwa, -waz] *adj* deceitful, underhand

sous [su] *prép (gén)* under; **~ la pluie/le soleil** in the rain/sunshine; **~ terre** underground; **~ peu** shortly, before long

sous-bois [subwa] *nm inv* undergrowth

souscrire [suskʀiʀ]: **~ à** *vt* to subscribe to

sous: ~-directeur, trice *nm/f* assistant manager(manageress); **~-entendre** *vt* to imply, infer; **~-entendu, e** *adj* implied; *(LING)* understood ♦ *nm* innuendo, insinuation; **~-estimer** *vt* to under-estimate; **~-jacent, e** *adj* underlying; **~-louer** *vt* to sublet; **~-main** *nm inv* desk blotter; **en ~-main** secretly; **~-marin, e** *adj (flore, volcan)* submarine; *(navigation, pêche, explosif)* underwater ♦ *nm* submarine; **~-officier** ≈ non-commissioned officer (N.C.O.); **~-produit** *nm* by-product; *(fig: péj)* pale imitation; **~-signé, e** *adj:* **je ~signé** I the undersigned; **~-sol** *nm* basement; **~-titre** *nm* subtitle

soustraction [sustʀaksjɔ̃] *nf* subtraction

soustraire [sustʀɛʀ] *vt* to subtract, take away; *(dérober):* **~ qch à qn** to remove sth from sb; **se ~ à** *(autorité etc)* to elude, escape from; **~ qn à** *(danger)* to shield sb from

sous-traitant [sutʀɛtɑ̃] *nm* sub-contractor

sous-vêtements [suvɛtmɑ̃] *nmpl* underwear *sg*

soutane [sutan] *nf* cassock, soutane

soute [sut] *nf* hold

soutènement [sutɛnmɑ̃] *nm:* **mur de ~** retaining wall

souteneur [sutnœʀ] *nm* procurer

soutenir [sutniʀ] *vt* to support; *(assaut, choc)* to stand up to, withstand; *(intérêt, effort)* to keep up; *(assurer):* **~ que** to maintain that; **~ la comparaison avec** to bear *ou* stand comparison with; **soutenu, e** *adj (efforts)* sustained, unflagging; *(style)* elevated

souterrain, e [sutɛʀɛ̃, -ɛn] *adj* underground ♦ *nm* underground passage

soutien [sutjɛ̃] *nm* support; **~ de famille**

breadwinner; ~-gorge [sutjɛ̃gɔʀʒ(ə)] *nm* bra

soutirer [sutiʀe] *vt:* **~ qch à qn** to squeeze *ou* get sth out of sb

souvenir [suvniʀ] *nm (réminiscence)* memory; *(objet)* souvenir ♦ *vb:* **se ~ de** *vt* to remember; **se ~ que** to remember that; **en ~ de** in memory *ou* remembrance of

souvent [suvɑ̃] *adv* often; **peu ~** seldom, infrequently

souverain, e [suvʀɛ̃, -ɛn] *adj* sovereign; *(fig: mépris)* supreme ♦ *nm/f* sovereign, monarch

soviétique [sɔvjetik] *nm/f:* **Soviétique** Soviet citizen

soyeux, euse [swajø, øz] *adj* silky

soyons *etc vb voir* **être**

spacieux, euse [spasjø, -øz] *adj* spacious; roomy

spaghettis [spageti] *nmpl* spaghetti *sg*

sparadrap [spaʀadʀa] *nm* sticking plaster *(BRIT)*, Bandaid (®: *US)*

spatial, e, aux [spasjal, -o] *adj (AVIAT)* space *cpd*

speaker, ine [spikœʀ, -kʀin] *nm/f* announcer

spécial, e, aux [spesjal, -o] *adj* special; *(bizarre)* peculiar; **spécialement** *adv* especially, particularly; *(tout exprès)* specially

spécialiser [spesjalize]: **se ~** *vi* to specialize

spécialiste [spesjalist(ə)] *nm/f* specialist

spécialité [spesjalite] *nf* speciality; *(SCOL)* special field

spécifier [spesifje] *vt* to specify, state

spécimen [spesimɛn] *nm* specimen; *(revue etc)* specimen *ou* sample copy

spectacle [spɛktakl(ə)] *nm (tableau, scène)* sight; *(représentation)* show; *(industrie)* show business; **spectaculaire** *adj* spectacular

spectateur, trice [spɛktatœʀ, -tʀis] *nm/f (CINÉMA etc)* member of the audience; *(SPORT)* spectator; *(d'un événement)* onlooker, witness

spéculer [spekyle] *vi* to speculate; **~ sur** *(COMM)* to speculate in; *(réfléchir)* to speculate on

spéléologie [speleɔlɔʒi] *nf* potholing

sperme [spɛʀm(ə)] *nm* semen, sperm

sphère [sfɛʀ] *nf* sphere

spirale [spiʀal] *nf* spiral

spirituel, le [spiʀitɥɛl] *adj* spiritual; *(fin, piquant)* witty

spiritueux [spiʀitɥø] *nm* spirit

splendide [splɑ̃did] *adj* splendid; magnificent

spontané, e [spɔ̃tane] *adj* spontaneous

sport [spɔʀ] *nm* sport ♦ *adj inv (vêtement)* casual; **faire du ~** to do sport; **sportif, ive** *adj (journal, association, épreuve)* sports *cpd*; *(allure, démarche)* athletic; *(attitude, esprit)* sporting; ~s **d'hiver** winter sports

spot [spɔt] *nm* (*lampe*) spot(light); (*annonce*): ~ **(publicitaire)** commercial (break)

square [skwaʀ] *nm* public garden(s)

squelette [skəlɛt] *nm* skeleton; **squelettique** *adj* scrawny; (*fig*) skimpy

stabiliser [stabilize] *vt* to stabilize; (*terrain*) to consolidate

stable [stabl(ə)] *adj* stable, steady

stade [stad] *nm* (*SPORT*) stadium; (*phase, niveau*) stage

stage [staʒ] *nm* training period; training course; **stagiaire** *nm/f*, *adj* trainee

stalle [stal] *nf* stall, box

stand [stãd] *nm* (*d'exposition*) stand; (*de foire*) stall; ~ **de tir** (*à la foire, SPORT*) shooting range

standard [stãdaʀ] *adj inv* standard ♦ *nm* switchboard; **standardiste** *nm/f* switchboard operator

standing [stãdiŋ] *nm* standing; **immeuble de grand** ~ block of luxury flats (*BRIT*), condo(minium) (*US*)

starter [staʀtɛʀ] *nm* (*AUTO*) choke

station [stasjɔ̃] *nf* station; (*de bus*) stop; (*de villégiature*) resort; (*posture*): **la** ~ **debout** standing, an upright posture; ~ **de ski** ski resort; ~ **de taxis** taxi rank (*BRIT*) *ou* stand (*US*)

stationnement [stasjɔnmã] *nm* parking; **stationner** [stasjɔne] *vi* to park

station-service [stasjɔ̃sɛʀvis] *nf* service station

statistique [statistik] *nf* (*science*) statistics *sg*; (*rapport, étude*) statistic ♦ *adj* statistical

statue [staty] *nf* statue

statuer [statɥe] *vi*: ~ **sur** to rule on, give a ruling on

statut [staty] *nm* status; ~s *nmpl* (*JUR, ADMIN*) statutes; **statutaire** *adj* statutory

Sté *abr* = **société**

steak [stɛk] *nm* steak

sténo(dactylo) [stenɔ(daktilo)] *nf* shorthand typist (*BRIT*), stenographer (*US*)

sténo(graphie) [stenɔ(gʀafi)] *nf* shorthand

stéréo(phonique) [steʀeɔ(fɔnik)] *adj* stereo(phonic)

stérile [steʀil] *adj* sterile; (*terre*) barren; (*fig*) fruitless, futile

stérilet [steʀilɛ] *nm* coil, loop

stériliser [steʀilize] *vt* to sterilize

stigmates [stigmat] *nmpl* scars, marks

stimulant [stimylã] *nm* (*fig*) stimulus, incentive

stimuler [stimyle] *vt* to stimulate

stipuler [stipyle] *vt* to stipulate

stock [stɔk] *nm* stock; ~ **d'or** (*FINANCE*) gold reserves *pl*; **stocker** *vt* to stock

stop [stɔp] *nm* (*AUTO*) stop sign; (: *signal*) brake-light; ~**per** [stɔpe] *vt* to stop, halt; (*COUTURE*) to mend ♦ *vi* to stop, halt

store [stɔʀ] *nm* blind; (*de magasin*) shade,

awning

strabisme [stʀabism(ə)] *nm* squinting

strapontin [stʀapɔ̃tɛ̃] *nm* jump *ou* foldaway seat

stratégie [stʀateʒi] *nf* strategy; **stratégique** *adj* strategic

stressant, e [stʀɛsã, -ãt] *adj* stressful

strict, e [stʀikt(ə)] *adj* strict; (*tenue, décor*) severe, plain; **son droit le plus** ~ his most basic right; **le** ~ **nécessaire/minimum** the bare essentials/minimum

strie [stʀi] *nf* streak

strophe [stʀɔf] *nf* verse, stanza

structure [stʀyktyʀ] *nf* structure; ~s **d'accueil** reception facilities

studieux, euse [stydjø, -øz] *adj* studious; devoted to study

studio [stydjo] *nm* (*logement*) (one-roomed) flatlet (*BRIT*) *ou* apartment (*US*); (*d'artiste, TV etc*) studio

stupéfait, e [stypefɛ, -ɛt] *adj* astonished

stupéfiant [stypefjã] *nm* (*MÉD*) drug, narcotic

stupéfier [stypefje] *vt* to stupefy; (*étonner*) to stun, astonish

stupeur [stypœʀ] *nf* astonishment

stupide [stypid] *adj* stupid; **stupidité** *nf* stupidity; stupid thing (to do *ou* say)

style [stil] *nm* style; **meuble de** ~ piece of period furniture

stylé, e [stile] *adj* well-trained

styliste [stilist(ə)] *nm/f* designer

stylo [stilo] *nm*: ~ **(à encre)** (fountain) pen; ~ **(à) bille** ball-point pen

su, e [sy] *pp de* **savoir** ♦ *nm*: **au** ~ **de** with the knowledge of

suave [sɥav] *adj* sweet; (*goût*) mellow

subalterne [sybaltɛʀn(ə)] *adj* (*employé, officier*) junior; (*rôle*) subordinate, subsidiary ♦ *nm/f* subordinate

subconscient [sypkɔ̃sjã] *nm* subconscious

subir [sybiʀ] *vt* (*affront, dégâts*) to suffer; (*influence, charme*) to be under; (*opération, châtiment*) to undergo

subit, e [sybi, -it] *adj* sudden; **subitement** *adv* suddenly, all of a sudden

subjectif, ive [sybʒɛktif, -iv] *adj* subjective

subjonctif [sybʒɔ̃ktif] *nm* subjunctive

submerger [sybmɛʀʒe] *vt* to submerge; (*fig*) to overwhelm

subordonné, e [sybɔʀdɔne] *adj, nm/f* subordinate; ~ **à** subordinate to; subject to, depending on

subornation [sybɔʀnasjɔ̃] *nf* bribing

subrepticement [sybʀɛptismã] *adv* surreptitiously

subside [sypsid] *nm* grant

subsidiaire [sypsidjɛʀ] *adj*: **question** ~ deciding question

subsister [sybziste] *vi* (*rester*) to remain, subsist; (*vivre*) to live; (*survivre*) to live on

substance [sypstãs] *nf* substance

substituer [sypstitɥe] *vt*: ~ qn/qch à to substitute sb/sth for; **se** ~ **à qn** (*évincer*) to substitute o.s. for sb

substitut [sypstity] *nm* (*JUR*) deputy public prosecutor; (*succédané*) substitute

subterfuge [syptɛrfyʒ] *nm* subterfuge

subtil, e [syptil] *adj* subtle

subtiliser [syptilize] *vt*: ~ qch (à qn) to spirit sth away (from sb)

subvenir [sybvənir]: ~ **à** *vt* to meet

subvention [sybvɑ̃sjɔ̃] *nf* subsidy, grant; **subventionner** *vt* to subsidize

suc [syk] *nm* (*BOT*) sap; (*de viande, fruit*) juice

succédané [syksedane] *nm* substitute

succéder [syksede]: ~ **à** *vt* (*directeur, roi etc*) to succeed; (*venir après: dans une série*) to follow; succeed; **se** ~ *vi* (*accidents, années*) to follow one another

succès [syksɛ] *nm* success; **avoir du** ~ to be a success, be successful; **à** ~ successful; ~ **de librairie** bestseller; ~ (**féminins**) conquests

succession [syksesjɔ̃] *nf* (*série, POL*) succession; (*JUR: patrimoine*) estate, inheritance

succomber [sykɔ̃be] *vi* to die, succumb; (*fig*): ~ **à** to give way to, succumb to

succursale [sykyrsal] *nf* branch

sucer [syse] *vt* to suck

sucette [sysɛt] *nf* (*bonbon*) lollipop; (*de bébé*) dummy (*BRIT*), pacifier (*US*)

sucre [sykr(ə)] *nm* (*substance*) sugar; (*morceau*) lump of sugar, sugar lump *ou* cube; ~ **d'orge** barley sugar; ~ **en morceaux/cristallisé/en poudre** lump/granulated/caster sugar; **sucré, e** *adj* (*produit alimentaire*) sweetened; (*au goût*) sweet; (*péj*) sugary, honeyed; **sucrer** *vt* (*thé, café*) to sweeten, put sugar in; **sucreries** *nfpl* (*bonbons*) sweets, sweet things; **sucrier** *nm* (*récipient*) sugar bowl

sud [syd] *nm*: **le** ~ the south ♦ *adj inv* south; (*côte*) south, southern; **au** ~ (*situation*) in the south; (*direction*) to the south; **au** ~ **de** (to the) south of; **sud-africain, e** *adj, nm/f* South African; **sud-américain, e** *adj, nm/f* South American; **sud-est** [sydɛst] *nm* south-east ♦ *adj inv* south-east; **sud-ouest** [sydwɛst] *nm* south-west ♦ *adj inv* south-west

Suède [sɥɛd] *nf*: **la** ~ Sweden; **suédois, e** *adj* Swedish ♦ *nm/f*: **Suédois, e** Swede ♦ *nm* (*LING*) Swedish

suer [sɥe] *vi* to sweat; (*suinter*) to ooze

sueur [sɥœr] *nf* sweat; **en** ~ sweating, in a sweat

suffire [syfir] *vi* (*être assez*): ~ (**à qn/pour qch/pour faire**) to be enough *ou* sufficient (for sb/for sth/to do); **cela suffit pour les irriter/qu'ils se fâchent** it's enough to annoy them/for them to get angry; **il suffit d'une négligence** ... it only takes one act of carelessness ...; **il suffit qu'on oublie pour que** ... one only needs to forget for ...

suffisamment [syfizamɑ̃] *adv* sufficiently, enough; ~ **de** sufficient, enough

suffisant, e [syfizɑ̃, -ɑ̃t] *adj* (*temps, ressources*) sufficient; (*résultats*) satisfactory; (*vaniteux*) self-important, bumptious

suffixe [syfiks(ə)] *nm* suffix

suffoquer [syfɔke] *vt* to choke, suffocate; (*stupéfier*) to stagger, astound ♦ *vi* to choke, suffocate

suffrage [syfraʒ] *nm* (*POL: voix*) vote; (*du public etc*) approval *no pl*

suggérer [syʒere] *vt* to suggest; **suggestion** *nf* suggestion

suicide [sɥisid] *nm* suicide

suicider [sɥiside]: **se** ~ *vi* to commit suicide

suie [sɥi] *nf* soot

suinter [sɥɛ̃te] *vi* to ooze

suis *vb voir* **être; suivre**

suisse [sɥis] *adj* Swiss ♦ *nm*: **S~** Swiss *pl inv* ♦ *nf*: **la S~** Switzerland; **la S~ romande/allemande** French-speaking/German-speaking Switzerland; **Suissesse** *nf* Swiss (woman *ou* girl)

suite [sɥit] *nf* (*continuation: d'énumération etc*) rest, remainder; (: *de feuilleton*) continuation; (: *film etc sur le même thème*) sequel; (*série: de maisons, succès*): **une** ~ **de** a series *ou* succession of; (*MATH*) series *sg*; (*conséquence*) result; (*ordre, liaison logique*) coherence; (*appartement, MUS*) suite; (*escorte*) retinue, suite; ~**s** *nfpl* (*d'une maladie etc*) effects; **prendre la** ~ **de** (*directeur etc*) to succeed, take over from; **donner** ~ **à** (*requête, projet*) to follow up; **faire** ~ **à** to follow; (**faisant**) ~ **à votre lettre du** ... further to your letter of the ...; **de** ~ (*d'affilée*) in succession; (*immédiatement*) at once; **par la** ~ afterwards, subsequently; **à la** ~ one after the other; **à la** ~ **de** (*derrière*) behind; (*en conséquence de*) following; **par** ~ **de** owing to, as a result of

suivant, e [sɥivɑ̃, -ɑ̃t] *adj* next, following; (*ci-après*): **l'exercice** ~ the following exercise ♦ *prép* (*selon*) according to; **au** ~! next!

suivi, e [sɥivi] *adj* (*régulier*) regular; (*cohérent*) consistent; coherent; **très/peu** ~ (*cours*) well-/poorly-attended

suivre [sɥivr(ə)] *vt* (*gén*) to follow; (*SCOL: cours*) to attend; (: *programme*) to keep up with; (*COMM: article*) to continue to stock ♦ *vi* to follow; (*élève*) to attend; to keep up; **se** ~ *vi* (*accidents etc*) to follow one after the other; (*raisonnement*) to be coherent; **faire** ~ (*lettre*) to forward; ~ **son cours** (*suj: enquête etc*) to run *ou* take its course; **"à** ~**"** "to be continued"

sujet, te [syʒɛ, -ɛt] *adj*: **être** ~ **à** (*vertige* *etc*) to be liable *ou* subject to ♦ *nm/f* (*d'un souverain*) subject ♦ *nm* subject; **au ~ de** about; **~ à caution** questionable; **~ de conversation** topic *ou* subject of conversation; **~ d'examen** (*SCOL*) examination question; examination paper

summum [sɔmɔm] *nm*: **le ~ de** the height of

superbe [sypɛʀb(ə)] *adj* magnificent, superb

super(carburant) [sypɛʀ(kaʀbyʀɑ̃)] *nm* ≈ 4-star petrol (*BRIT*), ≈ high-octane gasoline (*US*)

supercherie [sypɛʀʃəʀi] *nf* trick

supérette [sypeʀɛt] *nf* (*COMM*) minimarket, superette (*US*)

superficie [sypɛʀfisi] *nf* (surface) area; (*fig*) surface

superficiel, le [sypɛʀfisjɛl] *adj* superficial

superflu, e [sypɛʀfly] *adj* superfluous

supérieur, e [sypeʀjœʀ] *adj* (*lèvre, étages, classes*) upper; (*plus élevé: température, niveau*): **~ (à)** higher (than); (*meilleur: qualité, produit*): **~ (à)** superior (to); (*excellent, hautain*) superior ♦ *nm, nf* superior; **à l'étage ~** on the next floor up; **supériorité** *nf* superiority

superlatif [sypɛʀlatif] *nm* superlative

supermarché [sypɛʀmaʀʃe] *nm* supermarket

superposer [sypɛʀpoze] *vt* (*faire chevaucher*) to superimpose; **lits superposés** bunk beds

superproduction [sypɛʀpʀɔdyksjɔ̃] *nf* (*film*) spectacular

superpuissance [sypɛʀpɥisɑ̃s] *nf* superpower

superstitieux, euse [sypɛʀstisjø, -øz] *adj* superstitious

superviser [sypɛʀvize] *vt* to supervise

suppléant, e [sypleɑ̃, -ɑ̃t] *adj* (*juge, fonctionnaire*) deputy *cpd*; (*professeur*) supply *cpd* ♦ *nm/f* deputy; supply teacher

suppléer [syplee] *vt* (*ajouter: mot manquant etc*) to supply, provide; (*compenser: lacune*) to fill in; (: *défaut*) to make up for; (*remplacer*) to stand in for; **~ à** to make up for; to substitute for

supplément [syplemɑ̃] *nm* supplement; (*de frites etc*) extra portion; **un ~ de travail** extra *ou* additional work; **ceci est en ~** (*au menu etc*) this is extra, there is an extra charge for this; **~aire** *adj* additional, further; (*train, bus*) relief *cpd*, extra

supplications [syplikasjɔ̃] *nfpl* pleas, entreaties

supplice [syplis] *nm* (*peine corporelle*) torture *no pl*; form of torture; (*douleur physique, morale*) torture, agony

supplier [syplije] *vt* to implore, beseech

supplique [syplik] *nf* petition

support [sypɔʀ] *nm* support; (*pour livre,*

outils) stand

supportable [sypɔʀtabl(ə)] *adj* (*douleur*) bearable

supporter¹ [sypɔʀtɛʀ] *nm* supporter, fan

supporter² [sypɔʀte] *vt* (*poids, poussée*) to support; (*conséquences, épreuve*) to bear, endure; (*défauts, personne*) to put up with; (*suj: chose: chaleur etc*) to withstand; (: *personne: chaleur, vin*) to be able to take

supposé, e [sypoze] *adj* (*nombre*) estimated; (*auteur*) supposed

supposer [sypoze] *vt* to suppose; (*impliquer*) to presuppose; **à ~ que** supposing (that)

suppositoire [sypozitwaʀ] *nm* suppository

suppression [sypʀesjɔ̃] *nf* (*voir supprimer*) removal; deletion; cancellation; suppression

supprimer [sypʀime] *vt* (*cloison, cause, anxiété*) to remove; (*clause, mot*) to delete; (*congés, service d'autobus etc*) to cancel; (*emplois, privilèges, témoin gênant*) to do away with

supputer [sypyte] *vt* to calculate

suprême [sypʀɛm] *adj* supreme

MOT CLÉ

sur *prép* **1** (*position*) on; (*par-dessus*) over; (*au-dessus*) above; **pose-le ~ la table** put it on the table; **je n'ai pas d'argent ~ moi** I haven't any money on me
2 (*direction*) towards; **en allant ~ Paris** going towards Paris; **~ votre droite** on *ou* to your right
3 (*à propos de*) on, about; **un livre/une conférence ~ Balzac** a book/lecture on *ou* about Balzac
4 (*proportion, mesures*) out of; by; **un ~ 10** one in 10; (*SCOL*) one out of 10; **4 m ~ 2** 4 m by 2
sur ce *adv* hereupon

---

sûr, e [syʀ] *adj* sure, certain; (*digne de confiance*) reliable; (*sans danger*) safe; **le plus ~ est de** the safest thing is to; **~ de soi** self-confident; **~ et certain** absolutely certain

suranné, e [syʀane] *adj* outdated, outmoded

surcharge [syʀʃaʀʒ(ə)] *nf* (*de passagers, marchandises*) excess load; (*correction*) alteration

surcharger [syʀʃaʀʒe] *vt* to overload

surchoix [syʀʃwa] *adj inv* top-quality

surclasser [syʀklase] *vt* to outclass

surcroît [syʀkʀwa] *nm*: **un ~ de** additional +*nom*; **par** *ou* **de ~** moreover; **en ~** in addition

surdité [syʀdite] *nf* deafness

surélever [syʀɛlve] *vt* to raise, heighten

sûrement [syʀmɑ̃] *adv* reliably; safely, securely; (*certainement*) certainly

surenchère [syʀɑ̃ʃɛʀ] *nf* (*aux enchères*)

higher bid; (sur prix fixe) overbid; (fig) overstatement; outbidding tactics pl; **surenchérir** vi to bid higher; (fig) to try and outbid each other

surent vb voir **savoir**

surestimer [syʀɛstime] vt to overestimate

sûreté [syʀte] nf (voir **sûr**) reliability; safety; (JUR) guaranty; surety; **mettre en ~** to put in a safe place; **pour plus de ~** as an extra precaution; to be on the safe side

surf [syʀf] nm surfing

surface [syʀfas] nf surface; (superficie) surface area; **faire ~** to surface; **en ~** near the surface; (fig) superficially

surfait, e [syʀfɛ, -ɛt] adj overrated

surfin, e [syʀfɛ̃, -in] adj superfine

surgelé, e [syʀʒəle] adj (deep-) frozen

surgir [syʀʒiʀ] vi to appear suddenly; (jaillir) to shoot up; (fig: problème, conflit) to arise

sur: **~humain, e** adj superhuman; **~impression** nf (PHOTO) double exposure; **en ~impression** superimposed; **~-le-champ** adv immediately; **~lendemain** nm: **le ~lendemain (soir)** two days later (in the evening); **le ~lendemain** two days after; **~mener** vt to overwork; **se ~mener** vi to overwork

surmonter [syʀmɔ̃te] vt (suj: coupole etc) to top; (vaincre) to overcome

surnager [syʀnaʒe] vi to float

surnaturel, le [syʀnatyʀɛl] adj, nm supernatural

surnom [syʀnɔ̃] nm nickname

surnombre [syʀnɔ̃bʀ(ə)] nm: **être en ~** to be too many (ou one too many)

surpeuplé, e [syʀpœple] adj overpopulated

sur-place [syʀplas] nm: **faire du ~** to mark time

surplomber [syʀplɔ̃be] vi to be overhanging ♦ vt to overhang; to tower above

surplus [syʀply] nm (COMM) surplus; (reste): **~ de bois** wood left over

surprenant, e [syʀpʀənɑ̃, -ɑ̃t] adj amazing

surprendre [syʀpʀɑ̃dʀ(ə)] vt (étonner, prendre à l'improviste) to surprise; (tomber sur: intrus etc) to catch; (fig) to detect; to chance upon; to overhear

surpris, e [syʀpʀi, -iz] adj: **~ (de/que)** surprised (at/that)

surprise [syʀpʀiz] nf surprise; **faire une ~ à qn** to give sb a surprise; **~-partie** [syʀpʀizpaʀti] nf party

sursaut [syʀso] nm start, jump; **~ de** (énergie, indignation) sudden fit ou burst of; **en ~** with a start; **sursauter** vi to (give a) start, jump

surseoir [syʀswaʀ] : **~ à** vt to defer

sursis [syʀsi] nm (JUR: gén) suspended sentence; (à l'exécution capitale, aussi fig) reprieve; (MIL) deferment

surtaxe [syʀtaks(ə)] nf surcharge

surtout [syʀtu] adv (avant tout, d'abord) above all; (spécialement, particulièrement) especially; **~, ne dites rien!** whatever you do don't say anything!; **~ pas!** certainly ou definitely not!; **~ que ...** especially as ...

surveillance [syʀvɛjɑ̃s] nf watch; (POLICE, MIL) surveillance; **sous ~ médicale** under medical supervision

surveillant, e [syʀvɛjɑ̃, -ɑ̃t] nm/f (de prison) warder; (SCOL) monitor; (de travaux) supervisor, overseer

surveiller [syʀveje] vt (enfant, élèves, bagages) to watch, keep an eye on; (malade) to watch over; (prisonnier, suspect) to keep (a) watch on; (territoire, bâtiment) to (keep) watch over; (travaux, cuisson) to supervise, (SCOL: examen) to invigilate; **se ~** vi to keep a check ou watch on o.s.; **~ son langage/sa ligne** to watch one's language/figure

survenir [syʀvəniʀ] vi (incident, retards) to occur, arise; (événement) to take place; (personne) to appear, arrive

survêt(ement) [syʀvɛt(mɑ̃)] nm tracksuit

survie [syʀvi] nf survival; (REL) afterlife

survivant, e [syʀvivɑ̃, -ɑ̃t] nm/f survivor

survivre [syʀvivʀ(ə)] vi to survive; **~ à** (accident etc) to survive; (personne) to outlive

survoler [syʀvɔle] vt to fly over; (fig: livre) to skim through

survolté, e [syʀvɔlte] adj (fig) worked up

sus [sy(s)]: **en ~ de** prép in addition to, over and above; **en ~** in addition; **~ à: ~ au tyran!** at the tyrant!

susceptible [syseptibl(ə)] adj touchy, sensitive; **~ d'amélioration** that can be improved, open to improvement; **~ de faire** able to do; liable to do

susciter [sysite] vt (admiration) to arouse; (obstacles, ennuis): **~ (à qn)** to create (for sb)

suspect, e [syspɛ(kt), -ɛkt(ə)] adj suspicious; (témoignage, opinions) suspect ♦ nm/f suspect

suspecter [syspɛkte] vt to suspect; (honnêteté de qn) to question, have one's suspicions about

suspendre [syspɑ̃dʀ(ə)] vt (accrocher: vêtement): **~ qch (à)** to hang sth up (on); (fixer: lustre etc): **~ qch à** to hang sth from; (interrompre, démettre) to suspend; (remettre) to defer; **se ~ à** to hang from

suspendu, e [syspɑ̃dy] adj (accroché): **~ à** hanging on (ou from); (perché): **~ au-dessus de** suspended over

suspens [syspɑ̃]: **en ~** adv (affaire) in abeyance; **tenir en ~** to keep in suspense

suspense [syspɑ̃s] nm suspense

suspension [syspɑ̃sjɔ̃] nf suspension; **~ d'audience** adjournment

sut vb voir **savoir**

suture [sytyʀ] nf (MÉD): **point de ~** stitch

svelte [svɛlt(ə)] *adj* slender, svelte
S.V.P. *sigle* (= *s'il vous plaît*) please
syllabe [silab] *nf* syllable
sylviculture [silvikyltyʀ] *nf* forestry
symbole [sɛ̃bɔl] *nm* symbol; **symbolique** *adj* symbolic(al); (*geste, offrande*) token *cpd*; (*salaire, dommage-intérêts*) nominal; **symboliser** *vt* to symbolize
symétrique [simetʀik] *adj* symmetrical
sympa [sɛ̃pa] *adj abr* = **sympathique**
sympathie [sɛ̃pati] *nf* (*inclination*) liking; (*affinité*) fellow feeling; (*condoléances*) sympathy; **accueillir avec ~** (*projet*) to receive favourably; **croyez à toute ma ~** you have my deepest sympathy
sympathique [sɛ̃patik] *adj* nice, friendly; likeable; pleasant
sympathisant, e [sɛ̃patizɑ̃, -ɑ̃t] *nm/f* sympathizer
sympathiser [sɛ̃patize] *vi* (*voisins etc*: *s'entendre*) to get on (*BRIT*) *ou* along (*US*) (well)
symphonie [sɛ̃fɔni] *nf* symphony
symptôme [sɛ̃ptom] *nm* symptom
synagogue [sinagɔg] *nf* synagogue
syncope [sɛ̃kɔp] *nf* (*MÉD*) blackout; **tomber en ~** to faint, pass out
syndic [sɛ̃dik] *nm* managing agent
syndical, e, aux [sɛ̃dikal, -o] *adj* (trade) union *cpd*; **syndicaliste** *nm/f* trade unionist
syndicat [sɛ̃dika] *nm* (*d'ouvriers, employés*) (trade) union; (*autre association d'intérêts*) union, association; **~ d'initiative** tourist office
syndiqué, e [sɛ̃dike] *adj* belonging to a (trade) union; **non ~** non-union
syndiquer [sɛ̃dike]: **se ~** *vi* to form a trade union; (*adhérer*) to join a trade union
synonyme [sinɔnim] *adj* synonymous ♦ *nm* synonym; **~ de** synonymous with
syntaxe [sɛ̃taks(ə)] *nf* syntax
synthèse [sɛ̃tɛz] *nf* synthesis
synthétique [sɛ̃tetik] *adj* synthetic
Syrie [siʀi] *nf*: **la ~** Syria
systématique [sistematik] *adj* systematic
système [sistɛm] *nm* system; **~ D** (*fam*) resourcefulness

T t

t' [t(ə)] *pron voir* **te**
ta [ta] *dét voir* **ton**[1]
tabac [taba] *nm* tobacco; tobacconist's (shop); **~ blond/brun** light/dark tobacco
tabagisme [tabaʒism] *nm*: **~ passif** passive smoking
table [tabl(ə)] *nf* table; **à ~!** dinner *etc* is ready!; **se mettre à ~** to sit down to eat; (*fig*: *fam*) to come clean; **mettre la ~** to lay the table; **faire ~ rase de** to make a clean sweep of; **~ de cuisson** (*à l'électricité*) hotplate; (*au gaz*) gas ring; **~ de nuit** *ou* **de chevet** bedside table; **~ des matières** (table of) contents *pl*
tableau, x [tablo] *nm* painting; (*reproduction, fig*) picture; (*panneau*) board; (*schéma*) table, chart; **~ d'affichage** notice board; **~ de bord** dashboard; (*AVIAT*) instrument panel; **~ noir** blackboard
tabler [table] *vi*: **~ sur** to bank on
tablette [tablɛt] *nf* (*planche*) shelf; **~ de chocolat** bar of chocolate
tableur [tablœʀ] *nm* spreadsheet
tablier [tablije] *nm* apron
tabouret [tabuʀɛ] *nm* stool
tac [tak] *nm*: **du ~ au ~** tit for tat
tache [taʃ] *nf* (*saleté*) stain, mark; (*ART, de couleur, lumière*) spot; splash, patch; **~ de rousseur** *nf* freckle
tâche [taʃ] *nf* task; **travailler à la ~** to do piecework
tacher [taʃe] *vt* to stain, mark; (*fig*) to sully, stain
tâcher [taʃe] *vi*: **~ de faire** to try *ou* endeavour to do
tacot [tako] (*péj*) *nm* banger (*BRIT*), (old) heap
tact [takt] *nm* tact; **avoir du ~** to be tactful
tactique [taktik] *adj* tactical ♦ *nf* (*technique*) tactics *sg*; (*plan*) tactic
taie [tɛ] *nf*: **~ (d'oreiller)** pillowslip, pillowcase
taille [taj] *nf* cutting; pruning; (*milieu du corps*) waist; (*hauteur*) height; (*grandeur*) size; **de ~ à faire** capable of doing; **de ~** sizeable
taille-crayon(s) [tajkʀɛjɔ̃] *nm* pencil sharpener
tailler [taje] *vt* (*pierre, diamant*) to cut; (*arbre, plante*) to prune; (*vêtement*) to cut

out; (*crayon*) to sharpen
tailleur [tɑjœʀ] *nm* (*couturier*) tailor; (*vêtement*) suit; **en ~** (*assis*) cross-legged
taillis [tɑji] *nm* copse
taire [tɛʀ] *vt* to keep to o.s., conceal ♦ *vi*: **faire ~ qn** to make sb be quiet; (*fig*) to silence sb; **se ~** *vi* to be silent *ou* quiet
talc [talk] *nm* talc, talcum powder
talent [talɑ̃] *nm* talent
talon [talɔ̃] *nm* heel; (*de chèque, billet*) stub, counterfoil (*BRIT*); **~s plats/aiguilles** flat/ stiletto heels
talonner [talɔne] *vt* to follow hard behind; (*fig*) to hound
talus [taly] *nm* embankment
tambour [tɑ̃buʀ] *nm* (*MUS, aussi TECH*) drum; (*musicien*) drummer; (*porte*) revolving door(s *pl*)
tamis [tami] *nm* sieve
Tamise [tamiz] *nf*: **la ~** the Thames
tamisé, e [tamize] *adj* (*fig*) subdued, soft
tamiser [tamize] *vt* to sieve, sift
tampon [tɑ̃pɔ̃] *nm* (*de coton, d'ouate*) wad, pad; (*amortisseur*) buffer; (*bouchon*) plug, stopper; (*cachet, timbre*) stamp; (**mémoire**) **~** (*INFORM*) buffer; **~** (**hygiénique**) tampon; **tamponner** *vt* (*timbres*) to stamp; (*heurter*) to crash *ou* ram into; **tamponneuse** *adj*: **autos tamponneuses** dodgems
tandis [tɑ̃di] : **~ que** *conj* while
tanguer [tɑ̃ge] *vi* to pitch (and toss)
tanière [tanjɛʀ] *nf* lair, den
tanné, e [tane] *adj* weather-beaten
tanner [tane] *vt* to tan
tant [tɑ̃] *adv* so much; **~ de** (*sable, eau*) so much; (*gens, livres*) so many; **~ que** as long as; (*comparatif*) as much as; **~ mieux** that's great; so much the better; **~ pis** never mind; too bad
tante [tɑ̃t] *nf* aunt
tantôt [tɑ̃to] *adv* (*parfois*): **~ ... ~** now ... now; (*cet après-midi*) this afternoon
tapage [tapaʒ] *nm* uproar, din
tapageur, euse [tapaʒœʀ, -øz] *adj* loud, flashy; noisy
tape [tap] *nf* slap
tape-à-l'œil [tapalœj] *adj inv* flashy, showy
taper [tape] *vt* (*porte*) to bang, slam; (*dactylographier*) to type (out); (*fam: emprunter*): **~ qn de 10 F** to touch sb for 10 F ♦ *vi* (*soleil*) to beat down; **~ sur qn** to thump sb; (*fig*) to run sb down; **~ sur qch** to hit sth; to bang on sth; **~ à** (*porte etc*) to knock on; **~ dans** (*se servir*) to dig into; **~ des mains/pieds** to clap one's hands/ stamp one's feet; **~** (**à la machine**) to type; **se ~ un travail** (*fam*) to land o.s. a job
tapi, e [tapi] *adj* crouching, cowering; hidden away
tapis [tapi] *nm* carpet; (*de table*) cloth; **mettre sur le ~** (*fig*) to bring up for discussion; **~ de sol** (*de tente*) groundsheet;

~ roulant conveyor belt
tapisser [tapise] *vt* (*avec du papier peint*) to paper; (*recouvrir*): **~ qch (de)** to cover sth (with)
tapisserie [tapisʀi] *nf* (*tenture, broderie*) tapestry; (*papier peint*) wallpaper
tapissier, ière [tapisje, -jɛʀ] *nm/f*: **~(- décorateur)** upholsterer (and decorator)
tapoter [tapɔte] *vt* to pat, tap
taquiner [takine] *vt* to tease
tarabiscoté, e [taʀabiskɔte] *adj* overornate, fussy
tard [taʀ] *adv* late; **plus ~** later (on); **au plus ~** at the latest; **sur le ~** late in life
tarder [taʀde] *vi* (*chose*) to be a long time coming; (*personne*): **~ à faire** to delay doing; **il me tarde d'être** I am longing to be; **sans (plus) ~** without (further) delay
tardif, ive [taʀdif, -iv] *adj* late
targuer [taʀge] : **se ~ de** *vt* to boast about
tarif [taʀif] *nm* (*liste*) price list; tariff; (*barème*) rates *pl*; fares *pl*; tariff; (*prix*) rate; fare
tarir [taʀiʀ] *vi* to dry up, run dry
tarte [taʀt(ə)] *nf* tart
tartine [taʀtin] *nf* slice of bread; **~ de miel** slice of bread and honey; **tartiner** *vt* to spread; **fromage à tartiner** cheese spread
tartre [taʀtʀ(ə)] *nm* (*des dents*) tartar; (*de chaudière*) fur, scale
tas [tɑ] *nm* heap, pile; (*fig*): **un ~ de** heaps of, lots of; **en ~** in a heap *ou* pile; **formé sur le ~** trained on the job
tasse [tɑs] *nf* cup; **~ à café** coffee cup
tassé, e [tɑse] *adj*: **bien ~** (*café etc*) strong
tasser [tɑse] *vt* (*terre, neige*) to pack down; (*entasser*): **~ qch dans** to cram sth into; **se ~** *vi* (*terrain*) to settle; (*fig*) to sort itself out, settle down
tâter [tɑte] *vt* to feel; (*fig*) to try out; **se ~** (*hésiter*) to be in two minds; **~ de** (*prison etc*) to have a taste of
tatillon, ne [tatijɔ̃, -ɔn] *adj* pernickety
tâtonnement [tɑtɔnmɑ̃] *nm*: **par ~s** (*fig*) by trial and error
tâtonner [tɑtɔne] *vi* to grope one's way along
tâtons [tɑtɔ̃] : **à ~: chercher/avancer à tâtons** *adv* to grope around for/grope one's way forward
tatouer [tatwe] *vt* to tattoo
taudis [todi] *nm* hovel, slum
taule [tol] (*fam*) *nf* nick (*fam*), prison
taupe [top] *nf* mole
taureau, x [tɔʀo] *nm* bull; (*signe*): **le T~** Taurus
tauromachie [tɔʀɔmaʃi] *nf* bullfighting
taux [to] *nm* rate; (*d'alcool*) level; **~ d'intérêt** interest rate
taxe [taks] *nf* tax; (*douanière*) duty; **~ à la valeur ajoutée** value added tax (*BRIT*); **~ de séjour** tourist tax

taxer [takse] *vt* (*personne*) to tax; (*produit*) to put a tax on, tax; (*fig*): ~ **qn de** to call sb +*attrib*; to accuse sb of, tax sb with

taxi [taksi] *nm* taxi

Tchécoslovaquie [tʃekɔslɔvaki] *nf* Czechoslovakia; **tchèque** *adj, nm/f* Czech ♦ *nm* (*LING*) Czech

te(t') [t(ə)] *pron* you; (*réfléchi*) yourself

technicien, ne [tɛknisjɛ̃, -jɛn] *nm/f* technician

technique [tɛknik] *adj* technical ♦ *nf* technique; **techniquement** *adv* technically

technologie [tɛknɔlɔʒi] *nf* technology; **technologique** *adj* technological

teck [tɛk] *nm* teak

teignais *etc vb voir* **teindre**

teindre [tɛ̃dʀ(ə)] *vt* to dye

teint, e [tɛ̃, tɛ̃t] *adj* dyed ♦ *nm* (*du visage*) complexion; colour ♦ *nf* shade; **grand** ~ *colourfast*

teinté, e [tɛ̃te] *adj*: ~ **de** (*fig*) tinged with

teinter [tɛ̃te] *vt* to tint; (*bois*) to stain; **teinture** *nf* dyeing; (*substance*) dye; (*MÉD*) tincture

teinturerie [tɛ̃tyʀʀi] *nf* dry cleaner's

teinturier [tɛ̃tyʀje] *nm* dry cleaner

tel, telle [tɛl] *adj* (*pareil*) such; (*comme*): ~ **un/des** ... like a/like ...; (*indéfini*) such-and-such a, a given; (*intensif*): **un** ~/**de** ~s ... such (a)/such ...; **rien de** ~ nothing like it, no such thing; ~ **que** like, such as; ~ **quel** as it is ou stands (*ou* was *etc*)

télé [tele] *abr f* (= *télévision*) TV, telly (*BRIT*); (*poste*) TV (set), telly; **à la** ~ on TV, on telly

télécabine [telekabin] *nf* (*benne*) cable car

télécarte [telekaʀt(ə)] *nf* phonecard

télé: ~**commande** *nf* remote control; ~**copie** *nf* fax; **envoyer qch par** ~**copie** to fax sth; ~**distribution** *nf* cable TV; ~**férique** *nm* = **téléphérique**; ~**gramme** *nm* telegram; ~**graphier** *vt* to telegraph, cable; ~**guider** *vt* to operate by remote control, radio-control; ~**journal** *nm* TV news magazine programme; ~**matique** *nf* telematics *sg*; ~**objectif** *nm* telephoto lens *sg*

téléphérique [teleferik] *nm* cable car

téléphone [telefɔn] *nm* telephone; **avoir le** ~ to be on the (tele)phone; **au** ~ on the phone; ~ **de voiture** car phone; **téléphoner** *vi* to telephone, ring; to make a phone call; **téléphoner à** to phone, call up; **téléphonique** *adj* (tele)phone *cpd*

télescope [telɛskɔp] *nm* telescope

télescoper [telɛskɔpe] *vt* to smash up; **se** ~ (*véhicules*) to concertina

télé: ~**scripteur** *nm* teleprinter; ~**siège** *nm* chairlift; ~**ski** *nm* ski-tow; ~**spectateur, trice** *nm/f* (television) viewer; ~**viseur** *nm* television set; ~**vision** *nf* television; **à la** ~**vision** on television

télex [telɛks] *nm* telex

telle [tɛl] *adj voir* **tel**

tellement [tɛlmã] *adv* (*tant*) so much; (*si*) so; ~ **de** (*sable, eau*) so much; (*gens, livres*) so many; **il s'est endormi** ~ **il était fatigué** he was so tired (that) he fell asleep; **pas** ~ not (all) that much; not (all) that +*adjectif*

téméraire [temeʀɛʀ] *adj* reckless, rash; **témérité** *nf* recklessness, rashness

témoignage [temwaɲaʒ] *nm* (*JUR: déclaration*) testimony *no pl*, evidence *no pl*; (: *faits*) evidence *no pl*; (*rapport, récit*) account; (*fig: d'affection etc*) token, mark; expression

témoigner [temwaɲe] *vt* (*intérêt, gratitude*) to show ♦ *vi* (*JUR*) to testify, give evidence; ~ **de** to bear witness to, testify to

témoin [temwɛ̃] *nm* witness; (*fig*) testimony ♦ *adj* control *cpd*, test *cpd*; **appartement** ~ show flat (*BRIT*); **être** ~ **de** to witness; ~ **oculaire** eyewitness

tempe [tãp] *nf* temple

tempérament [tãpeʀamã] *nm* temperament, disposition; **à** ~ (*vente*) on deferred (payment) terms; (*achat*) by instalments, hire purchase *cpd*

température [tãpeʀatyʀ] *nf* temperature; **avoir** *ou* **faire de la** ~ to be running *ou* have a temperature

tempéré, e [tãpeʀe] *adj* temperate

tempête [tãpɛt] *nf* storm; ~ **de sable/neige** sand/snowstorm

temple [tãpl(ə)] *nm* temple; (*protestant*) church

temporaire [tãpɔʀɛʀ] *adj* temporary

temps [tã] *nm* (*atmosphérique*) weather; (*durée*) time; (*époque*) time, times *pl*; (*LING*) tense; (*MUS*) beat; (*TECH*) stroke; **il fait beau/mauvais** ~ the weather is fine/bad; **avoir le** ~/**tout le** ~ to have time/plenty of time; **en** ~ **de paix/guerre** in peacetime/wartime; **en** ~ **utile** *ou* **voulu** in due time *ou* course; **de** ~ **en** ~, **de** ~ **à autre** from time to time; **à** ~ (*partir, arriver*) in time; **à** ~ **partiel** part-time; **dans le** ~ at one time; **de tout** ~ always; ~ **d'arrêt** pause, halt; ~ **mort** (*COMM*) slack period

tenable [tənabl(ə)] *adj* bearable

tenace [tənas] *adj* tenacious, persistent

tenailler [tənaje] *vt* (*fig*) to torment

tenailles [tənaj] *nfpl* pincers

tenais *etc vb voir* **tenir**

tenancier, ière [tənãsje, -jɛʀ] *nm/f* manager/manageress

tenant, e [tənã, -ãt] *nm/f* (*SPORT*): ~ **du titre** title-holder

tendance [tãdãs] *nf* (*opinions*) leanings *pl*, sympathies *pl*; (*inclination*) tendency; (*évolution*) trend; **avoir** ~ **à** to have a tendency to, tend to

tendeur [tãdœʀ] *nm* (*attache*) elastic strap

tendre [tãdʀ(ə)] *adj* tender; (*bois, roche,*

couleur) soft ♦ *vt (élastique, peau)* to stretch, draw tight; *(muscle)* to tense; *(donner)*: ~ **qch à qn** to hold sth out to sb; to offer sb sth; *(fig: piège)* to set, lay; **se ~** *vi (corde)* to tighten; *(relations)* to become strained; ~ **à qch/à faire** to tend towards sth/to do; ~ **l'oreille** to prick up one's ears; ~ **la main/le bras** to hold out one's hand/stretch out one's arm; **tendrement** *adv* tenderly; **tendresse** *nf* tenderness

tendu, e [tɑ̃dy] *pp de* **tendre** ♦ *adj* tight; tensed; strained

ténèbres [tenɛbʀ(ə)] *nfpl* darkness *sg*

teneur [tənœʀ] *nf* content; *(d'une lettre)* terms *pl*, content

tenir [tǝniʀ] *vt* to hold; *(magasin, hôtel)* to run; *(promesse)* to keep ♦ *vi* to hold; *(neige, gel)* to last; **se ~** *vi (avoir lieu)* to be held, take place; *(être: personne)* to stand; **se ~ droit** to stand *(ou* sit) up straight; **bien se ~** to behave well; **se ~ à qch** to hold on to sth; **s'en ~ à qch** to confine o.s. to sth; to stick to sth; ~ **à** to be attached to; to depend on; to stem from; ~ **à faire** to want to do; ~ **de** to partake of; to take after; **ça ne tient qu'à lui** it is entirely up to him; ~ **qn pour** to take sb for; ~ **qch de qn** *(histoire)* to have heard *ou* learnt sth from sb; *(qualité, défaut)* to have inherited *ou* got sth from sb; ~ **les comptes** to keep the books; ~ **le coup** to hold out; ~ **au chaud** to keep hot; **tiens/tenez, voilà le stylo** there's the pen!; **tiens, Alain!** look, here's Alain!; **tiens?** *(surprise)* really?

tennis [tenis] *nm* tennis; *(court)* tennis court ♦ *nm ou f pl (aussi: chaussures de ~)* tennis *ou* gym shoes; ~ **de table** table tennis; **tennisman** *nm* tennis player

tension [tɑ̃sjɔ̃] *nf* tension; *(fig)* tension; strain; *(MÉD)* blood pressure; **faire** *ou* **avoir de la ~** to have high blood pressure

tentation [tɑ̃tasjɔ̃] *nf* temptation

tentative [tɑ̃tativ] *nf* attempt, bid

tente [tɑ̃t] *nf* tent

tenter [tɑ̃te] *vt (éprouver, attirer)* to tempt; *(essayer)*: ~ **qch/de faire** to attempt *ou* try sth/to do; ~ **sa chance** to try one's luck

tenture [tɑ̃tyʀ] *nf* hanging

tenu, e [tǝny] *pp de* **tenir** ♦ *adj (maison, comptes)*: **bien ~** well-kept; *(obligé)*: ~ **de faire** under an obligation to do ♦ *nf (action de tenir)* running; keeping; holding; *(vêtements)* clothes *pl*, gear; dress *no pl*, appearance; *(comportement)* manners *pl*, behaviour; **en petite tenue** scantily dressed *ou* clad; **~e de route** *(AUTO)* road-holding; **~e de soirée** evening dress

ter [tɛʀ] *adj*: **16** ~ **16b** *ou* **B**

térébenthine [teʀebɑ̃tin] *nf*: **(essence de)** ~ (oil of) turpentine

terme [tɛʀm(ə)] *nm* term; *(fin)* end; **à**

court/long ~ short-/long-term *ou* -range ♦ *adv* in the short/long term; **avant** ~ *(MÉD)* prematurely; **mettre un** ~ **à** to put an end *ou* a stop to

terminaison [tɛʀminɛzɔ̃] *nf (LING)* ending

terminal, e, aux [tɛʀminal, -o] *adj* final ♦ *nm* terminal; **terminale** *nf (SCOL)* ≈ sixth form *ou* year *(BRIT)*, ≈ twelfth grade *(US)*

terminer [tɛʀmine] *vt* to end; *(travail, repas)* to finish; **se ~** *vi* to end

terne [tɛʀn(ə)] *adj* dull

ternir [tɛʀniʀ] *vt* to dull; *(fig)* to sully, tarnish; **se ~** *vi* to become dull

terrain [tɛʀɛ̃] *nm (sol, fig)* ground; *(COMM)* land *no pl*, plot of land; site; **sur le** ~ *(fig)* on the field; ~ **d'aviation** airfield; ~ **de camping** campsite; ~ **de football/rugby** football/rugby pitch *(BRIT)* ou field *(US)*; ~ **de golf** golf course; ~ **de jeu** games field; playground; ~ **de sport** sports ground; ~ **vague** waste ground *no pl*

terrasse [tɛʀas] *nf* terrace; **à la** ~ *(café)* outside; **~ment** [tɛʀasmɑ̃] *nm* earthmoving, earthworks *pl*; embankment; **~r** [tɛʀase] *vt (adversaire)* to floor; *(suj: maladie etc)* to lay low

terre [tɛʀ] *nf (gén, aussi ÉLEC)* earth; *(substance)* soil, earth; *(opposé à mer)* land *no pl*; *(contrée)* land; **~s** *nfpl (terrains)* lands, land *sg*; **en** ~ *(pipe, poterie)* clay *cpd*; **à** ~ *ou* **par** ~ *(mettre, être)* on the ground *(ou* floor); *(jeter, tomber)* to the ground, down; ~ **à** ~ *adj inv* down-to-earth; ~ **cuite** earthenware; terracotta; **la** ~ **ferme** dry land; ~ **glaise** clay

terreau [tɛʀo] *nm* compost

terre-plein [tɛʀplɛ̃] *nm* platform

terrer [tɛʀe]: **se** ~ *vi* to hide away; to go to ground

terrestre [tɛʀɛstʀ(ə)] *adj (surface)* earth's, of the earth; *(BOT, ZOOL, MIL)* land *cpd*; *(REL)* earthly, worldly

terreur [tɛʀœʀ] *nf* terror *no pl*

terrible [tɛʀibl(ə)] *adj* terrible, dreadful; *(fam)* terrific

terrien, ne [tɛʀjɛ̃, -jɛn] *adj*: **propriétaire** ~ landowner ♦ *nm/f (non martien etc)* earthling

terrier [tɛʀje] *nm* burrow, hole; *(chien)* terrier

terril [tɛʀil] *nm* slag heap

terrine [tɛʀin] *nf (récipient)* terrine; *(CULIN)* pâté

territoire [tɛʀitwaʀ] *nm* territory

terroir [tɛʀwaʀ] *nm (AGR)* soil; region

terrorisme [tɛʀɔʀism(ə)] *nm* terrorism; **terroriste** *nm/f* terrorist

tertiaire [tɛʀsjɛʀ] *adj* tertiary ♦ *nm (ÉCON)* service industries *pl*

tertre [tɛʀtʀ(ə)] *nm* hillock, mound

tes [te] *dét voir* **ton**[1]

tesson [tesɔ̃] *nm*: ~ **de bouteille** piece of

broken bottle

test [tɛst] nm test

testament [tɛstamɑ̃] nm (JUR) will; (REL) Testament; (fig) legacy

tester [tɛste] vt to test

testicule [tɛstikyl] nm testicle

tétanos [tetanos] nm tetanus

têtard [tɛtaʀ] nm tadpole

tête [tɛt] nf head; (cheveux) hair no pl; (visage) face; **de ~** (wagon etc) front cpd ♦ adv (calculer) in one's head, mentally; **tenir ~ à qn** to stand up to sb; **la ~ en bas** with one's head down; **la ~ la première** (tomber) headfirst; **faire une ~** (FOOTBALL) to head the ball; **faire la ~** (fig) to sulk; **en ~** (SPORT) in the lead; at the front; **en ~ à ~** in private, alone together; **de la ~ aux pieds** from head to toe; **~ de lecture** (playback) head; **~ de liste** (POL) chief candidate; **~ de série** (TENNIS) seeded player, seed

tête-à-queue [tɛtakø] nm inv: **faire un ~** to spin round

téter [tete] vt: **~ (sa mère)** to suck at one's mother's breast, feed

tétine [tetin] nf teat; (sucette) dummy (BRIT), pacifier (US)

têtu, e [tety] adj stubborn, pigheaded

texte [tɛkst(ə)] nm text

textile [tɛkstil] adj textile cpd ♦ nm textile; textile industry

texture [tɛkstyʀ] nf texture

TGV sigle m (= train à grande vitesse) high-speed train

thé [te] nm tea; **prendre le ~** to have tea; **faire le ~** to make the tea

théâtral, e, aux [teatʀal, -o] adj theatrical

théâtre [teatʀ(ə)] nm theatre; (œuvres) plays pl, dramatic works pl; (fig: lieu): **le ~ de** the scene of; (péj) histrionics pl, playacting; **faire du ~** to be on the stage; to do some acting

théière [tejɛʀ] nf teapot

thème [tɛm] nm theme; (SCOL: traduction) prose (composition)

théologie [teɔlɔʒi] nf theology

théorie [teɔʀi] nf theory; **théorique** adj theoretical

thérapie [teʀapi] nf therapy

thermal, e, aux [tɛʀmal, -o] adj: **station ~e** spa; **cure ~e** water cure

thermes [tɛʀm(ə)] nmpl thermal baths

thermomètre [tɛʀmɔmɛtʀ(ə)] nm thermometer

thermos [tɛʀmos] (®) nm ou nf: (bouteille) **~** vacuum ou Thermos (®) flask

thermostat [tɛʀmɔsta] nm thermostat

thèse [tɛz] nf thesis

thon [tɔ̃] nm tuna (fish)

thym [tɛ̃] nm thyme

tibia [tibja] nm shinbone, tibia; shin

tic [tik] nm tic, (nervous) twitch; (de lan-

gage etc) mannerism

ticket [tikɛ] nm ticket; **~ de caisse** nm receipt; **~ de quai** platform ticket

tiède [tjɛd] adj lukewarm; tepid; (vent, air) mild, warm; **tiédir** vi to cool; to grow warmer

tien, ne [tjɛ̃, tjɛn] pron: **le(la) ~(ne)**, **les ~(ne)s** yours; **à la ~ne!** cheers!

tiens [tjɛ̃] vb, excl voir **tenir**

tierce [tjɛʀs(ə)] adj voir **tiers**

tiercé [tjɛʀse] nm system of forecast betting giving first 3 horses

tiers, tierce [tjɛʀ, tjɛʀs(ə)] adj third ♦ nm (JUR) third party; (fraction) third; **le ~ monde** the Third World

tige [tiʒ] nf stem; (baguette) rod

tignasse [tiɲas] (péj) nf mop of hair

tigre [tigʀ(ə)] nm tiger

tigré, e [tigʀe] adj striped; spotted

tilleul [tijœl] nm lime (tree), linden (tree); (boisson) lime(-blossom) tea

timbale [tɛ̃bal] nf (metal) tumbler; **~s** nfpl (MUS) timpani, kettledrums

timbre [tɛ̃bʀ(ə)] nm (tampon) stamp; (aussi: **~-poste**) (postage) stamp; (MUS: de voix, instrument) timbre, tone

timbré, e [tɛ̃bʀe] (fam) adj daft

timide [timid] adj shy; timid; (timoré) timid, timorous; **timidement** adv shyly; timidly; **timidité** nf shyness; timidity

tins etc vb voir **tenir**

tintamarre [tɛ̃tamaʀ] nm din, uproar

tinter [tɛ̃te] vi to ring, chime; (argent, clefs) to jingle

tir [tiʀ] nm (sport) shooting; (fait ou manière de tirer) firing no pl; (stand) shooting gallery; **~ à l'arc** archery; **~ au pigeon** clay pigeon shooting

tirage [tiʀaʒ] nm (action) printing; (PHOTO) print; (de journal) circulation; (de livre) (print-)run; edition; (de loterie) draw; **~ au sort** drawing lots

tirailler [tiʀaje] vt to pull at, tug at ♦ vi to fire at random

tirant [tiʀɑ̃] nm: **~ d'eau** draught

tire [tiʀ] nf: **vol à la ~** pickpocketing

tiré, e [tiʀe] adj (traits) drawn ♦ nm (COMM) drawee; **~ par les cheveux** far-fetched

tire-au-flanc [tiʀoflɑ̃] (péj) nm inv skiver

tire-bouchon [tiʀbuʃɔ̃] nm corkscrew

tirelire [tiʀliʀ] nf moneybox

tirer [tiʀe] vt (gén) to pull; (extraire): **~ qch de** to take ou pull sth out of; to get sth out of; to extract sth from; (tracer: ligne, trait) to draw, trace; (fermer: rideau) to draw, close; (choisir: carte, conclusion, aussi COMM: chèque) to draw; (en faisant feu: balle, coup) to fire; (: animal) to shoot; (journal, livre, photo) to print; (FOOTBALL: corner etc) to take ♦ vi (faire feu) to fire; (faire du tir, FOOTBALL) to shoot; (cheminée) to draw; **se ~** *vi* (*fam*) to push off; **s'en ~** to pull through, get off; **~ sur** to pull on *ou* at; to shoot *ou* fire at; (*pipe*) to draw on; (*fig: avoisiner*) to verge *ou* border on; **~ qn de** (*embarras etc*) to help *ou* get sb out of; **~ à l'arc/la carabine** to shoot with a bow and arrow/with a rifle

tiret [tiʀɛ] *nm* dash

tireur, euse [tiʀœʀ, -øz] *nm/f* (*COMM*) drawer ♦ *nm* gunman; **~ d'élite** marksman

tiroir [tiʀwaʀ] *nm* drawer; **tiroir-caisse** *nm* till

tisane [tizan] *nf* herb tea

tisonnier [tizɔnje] *nm* poker

tisser [tise] *vt* to weave; **tisserand** *nm* weaver

tissu [tisy] *nm* fabric, material, cloth *no pl*; (*ANAT, BIO*) tissue

tissu-éponge [tisyepɔ̃ʒ] *nm* (terry) towelling *no pl*

titre [titʀ(ə)] *nm* (*gén*) title; (*de journal*) headline; (*diplôme*) qualification; (*COMM*) security; **en ~** (*champion*) official; **à juste ~** with just cause, rightly; **à quel ~?** on what grounds?; **à aucun ~** on no account; **au même ~ (que)** in the same way (as); **à ~ d'information** for (your) information; **à ~ gracieux** free of charge; **à ~ d'essai** on a trial basis; **à ~ privé** in a private capacity; **~ de propriété** title deed; **~ de transport** ticket

tituber [titybe] *vi* to stagger (along)

titulaire [titylɛʀ] *adj* (*ADMIN*) appointed, with tenure ♦ *nm/f* incumbent; **être ~ de** (*poste*) to hold; (*permis*) to be the holder of

toast [tost] *nm* slice *ou* piece of toast; (*de bienvenue*) (welcoming) toast; **porter un ~ à qn** to propose *ou* drink a toast to sb

toboggan [tɔbɔgɑ̃] *nm* toboggan; (*jeu*) slide

tocsin [tɔksɛ̃] *nm* alarm (bell)

toge [tɔʒ] *nf* toga; (*de juge*) gown

toi [twa] *pron* you

toile [twal] *nf* (*matériau*) cloth *no pl*; (*bâche*) piece of canvas; (*tableau*) canvas; **~ cirée** oilcloth; **~ d'araignée** cobweb; **~ de fond** (*fig*) backdrop

toilette [twalɛt] *nf* wash; (*habits*) outfit; dress *no pl*; **~s** *nfpl* (w.-c.) toilet *sg*; **faire sa ~** to have a wash, get washed; **articles de ~** toiletries

toi-même [twamɛm] *pron* yourself

toiser [twaze] *vt* to eye up and down

toison [twazɔ̃] *nf* (*de mouton*) fleece; (*cheveux*) mane

toit [twa] *nm* roof; **~ ouvrant** sunroof

toiture [twatyʀ] *nf* roof

tôle [tol] *nf* (*plaque*) steel *ou* iron sheet; **~ ondulée** corrugated iron

tolérable [tɔleʀabl(ə)] *adj* tolerable, bearable

tolérant, e [tɔleʀɑ̃, -ɑ̃t] *adj* tolerant

tolérer [tɔleʀe] *vt* to tolerate; (*ADMIN: hors taxe etc*) to allow

tollé [tɔle] *nm* outcry

tomate [tɔmat] *nf* tomato

tombe [tɔ̃b] *nf* (*sépulture*) grave; (*avec monument*) tomb

tombeau, x [tɔ̃bo] *nm* tomb

tombée [tɔ̃be] *nf*: **à la ~ de la nuit** at the close of day, at nightfall

tomber [tɔ̃be] *vi* to fall; **laisser ~** to drop; **~ sur** (*rencontrer*) to come across; (*attaquer*) to set about; **~ de fatigue/sommeil** to drop from exhaustion/be falling asleep on one's feet; **ça tombe bien** that's come at the right time; **il est bien tombé** he's been lucky

tome [tɔm] *nm* volume

ton¹, ta [tɔ̃, ta] (*pl* **tes**) *dét* your

ton² [tɔ̃] *nm* (*gén*) tone; (*MUS*) key; (*couleur*) shade, tone; **de bon ton** in good taste

tonalité [tɔnalite] *nf* (*au téléphone*) dialling tone; (*MUS*) key; (*fig*) tone

tondeuse [tɔ̃døz] *nf* (*à gazon*) (lawn)mower; (*du coiffeur*) clippers *pl*; (*pour la tonte*) shears *pl*

tondre [tɔ̃dʀ(ə)] *vt* (*pelouse, herbe*) to mow; (*haie*) to cut, clip; (*mouton, toison*) to shear; (*cheveux*) to crop

tonifier [tɔnifje] *vt* (*peau, organisme*) to tone up

tonique [tɔnik] *adj* fortifying ♦ *nm* tonic

tonne [tɔn] *nf* metric ton, tonne

tonneau, x [tɔno] *nm* (*à vin, cidre*) barrel; (*NAVIG*) ton; **faire des ~x** (*voiture, avion*) to roll over

tonnelle [tɔnɛl] *nf* bower, arbour

tonner [tɔne] *vi* to thunder; **il tonne** it is thundering, there's some thunder

tonnerre [tɔnɛʀ] *nm* thunder

tonus [tɔnys] *nm* dynamism

top [tɔp] *nm*: **au 3ème ~** at the 3rd stroke

topinambour [tɔpinɑ̃buʀ] *nm* Jerusalem artichoke

toque [tɔk] *nf* (*de fourrure*) fur hat; **~ de cuisinier** chef's hat; **~ de jockey/juge** jockey's/judge's cap

toqué, e [tɔke] (*fam*) *adj* cracked

torche [tɔʀʃ(ə)] *nf* torch

torchon [tɔʀʃɔ̃] *nm* cloth, duster; (*à vaisselle*) tea towel *ou* cloth

tordre [tɔʀdʀ(ə)] *vt* (*chiffon*) to wring; (*barre, fig: visage*) to twist; **se ~** *vi* (*barre*) to bend; (*roue*) to twist, buckle; (*ver, serpent*) to writhe; **se ~ le pied/bras** to twist one's foot/arm; **tordu, e** [tɔʀdy] *adj* (*fig*) warped, twisted

tornade [tɔʀnad] *nf* tornado

torpille [tɔʀpij] *nf* torpedo

torréfier [tɔʀefje] *vt* to roast

torrent [tɔʀɑ̃] *nm* torrent

torse [tɔʀs(ə)] *nm* (*ANAT*) torso; chest

torsion [tɔʀsjɔ̃] *nf* twisting; torsion

tort [tɔʀ] *nm* (*défaut*) fault; (*préjudice*) wrong *no pl*; ~**s** *nmpl* (*JUR*) fault *sg*; **avoir** ~ to be wrong; **être dans son** ~ to be in the wrong; **donner** ~ **à qn** to lay the blame on sb; (*fig*) to prove sb wrong; **causer du** ~ **à** to harm; to be harmful *ou* detrimental to; **à** ~ wrongly; **à** ~ **et à travers** wildly

torticolis [tɔʀtikɔli] *nm* stiff neck

tortiller [tɔʀtije] *vt* to twist; to twiddle; **se** ~ *vi* to wriggle, squirm

tortionnaire [tɔʀsjɔnɛʀ] *nm* torturer

tortue [tɔʀty] *nf* tortoise

tortueux, euse [tɔʀtɥø, -øz] *adj* (*rue*) twisting; (*fig*) tortuous

torture [tɔʀtyʀ] *nf* torture; **torturer** *vt* to torture; (*fig*) to torment

tôt [to] *adv* early; ~ **ou tard** sooner or later; **si** ~ **so** early; (*déjà*) so soon; **au plus** ~ at the earliest; **il eut** ~ **fait de faire** he soon did

total, e, aux [tɔtal, -o] *adj, nm* total; **au** ~ in total *ou* all; **faire le** ~ to work out the total, add up; **totalement** *adv* totally, completely; **totaliser** *vt* to total (up)

totalité [tɔtalite] *nf*: **la** ~ **de** all of, the total amount (*ou* number) of; the whole +*sg*; **en** ~ entirely

toubib [tubib] (*fam*) *nm* doctor

touchant, e [tuʃɑ̃, -ɑ̃t] *adj* touching

touche [tuʃ] *nf* (*de piano, de machine à écrire*) key; (*PEINTURE etc*) stroke, touch; (*fig: de nostalgie*) touch, hint; (*FOOTBALL: aussi: remise en* ~) throw-in; (*aussi: ligne de* ~) touch-line

toucher [tuʃe] *nm* touch ♦ *vt* to touch; (*palper*) to feel; (*atteindre: d'un coup de feu etc*) to hit; (*concerner*) to concern, affect; (*contacter*) to reach, contact; (*recevoir: récompense*) to receive, get; (: *salaire*) to draw, get; (: *chèque*) to cash; **se** ~ (*être en contact*) to touch; **au** ~ to the touch; ~ **à** to touch; (*concerner*) to have to do with, concern; **je vais lui en** ~ **un mot** I'll have a word with him about it; ~ **à sa fin** to be drawing to a close

touffe [tuf] *nf* tuft

touffu, e [tufy] *adj* thick, dense

toujours [tuʒuʀ] *adv* always; (*encore*) still; (*constamment*) forever; ~ **plus** more and more; **pour** ~ forever; ~ **est-il que** the fact remains that; **essaie** ~ (you can) try anyway

toupet [tupɛ] (*fam*) *nm* cheek

toupie [tupi] *nf* (spinning) top

tour [tuʀ] *nf* tower; (*immeuble*) high-rise block (*BRIT*) *ou* building (*US*); (*ÉCHECS*) castle, rook ♦ *nm* (*excursion*) stroll, walk; run, ride; trip; (*SPORT: aussi:* ~ **de piste**) lap; (*d'être servi ou de jouer etc*) turn; (*de roue etc*) revolution; (*circonférence*): **de 3 m**

de ~ **3 m** round, with a circumference *ou* girth of 3 m; (*POL: aussi:* ~ **de scrutin**) ballot; (*ruse, de prestidigitation*) trick; (*de potier*) wheel; (*à bois, métaux*) lathe; **faire le** ~ **de** to go round; (*à pied*) to walk round; **c'est au** ~ **de Renée** it's Renée's turn; **à** ~ **de rôle,** ~ **à** ~ in turn; ~ **de chant** song recital; ~ **de contrôle** *nf* control tower; ~ **de garde** spell of duty; ~ **d'horizon** (*fig*) general survey; ~ **de taille/tête** waist/head measurement

tourbe [tuʀb(ə)] *nf* peat

tourbillon [tuʀbijɔ̃] *nm* whirlwind; (*d'eau*) whirlpool; (*fig*) whirl, swirl; **tourbillonner** *vi* to whirl (round)

tourelle [tuʀɛl] *nf* turret

tourisme [tuʀism(ə)] *nm* tourism; **agence de** ~ tourist agency; **faire du** ~ to go sightseeing; to go touring; **touriste** *nm/f* tourist; **touristique** *adj* tourist *cpd*; (*région*) touristic

tourment [tuʀmɑ̃] *nm* torment

tourmenter [tuʀmɑ̃te] *vt* to torment; **se** ~ *vi* to fret, worry o.s.

tournant [tuʀnɑ̃] *nm* (*de route*) bend; (*fig*) turning point

tournebroche [tuʀnəbʀɔʃ] *nm* roasting spit

tourne-disque [tuʀnədisk(ə)] *nm* record player

tournée [tuʀne] *nf* (*du facteur etc*) round; (*d'artiste, politicien*) tour; (*au café*) round (of drinks)

tournemain [tuʀnəmɛ̃] : **en un** ~ *adv* (as) quick as a flash

tourner [tuʀne] *vt* to turn; (*sauce, mélange*) to stir; (*contourner*) to get round; (*CINÉMA*) to shoot; to make ♦ *vi* to turn; (*moteur*) to run; (*compteur*) to tick away; (*lait etc*) to turn (sour); **se** ~ *vi* to turn round; **se** ~ **vers** to turn to; to turn towards; **bien** ~ to turn out well; ~ **autour de** to go round; (*péj*) to hang round; ~ **à/en** to turn into; ~ **le dos à** to turn one's back on; to have one's back to; ~ **de l'œil** to pass out

tournesol [tuʀnəsɔl] *nm* sunflower

tournevis [tuʀnəvis] *nm* screwdriver

tourniquet [tuʀnikɛ] *nm* (*pour arroser*) sprinkler; (*portillon*) turnstile; (*présentoir*) revolving stand, spinner

tournoi [tuʀnwa] *nm* tournament

tournoyer [tuʀnwaje] *vi* to whirl round; to swirl round

tournure [tuʀnyʀ] *nf* (*LING*) turn of phrase; form; phrasing; (*évolution*): **la** ~ **de qch** the way sth is developing; (*aspect*): **la** ~ **de** the look of; ~ **d'esprit** turn *ou* cast of mind; **la** ~ **des événements** the turn of events

tourte [tuʀt(ə)] *nf* pie

tous [tu] *adj tu, pron* tus] *adj, pron voir* **tout**

Toussaint [tusɛ̃] *nf*: **la** ~ All Saints' Day

tousser [tuse] *vi* to cough

──────── MOT CLÉ ────────

tout, e [tu, tut] (*mpl* **tous,** *fpl* **toutes**) *adj* **1**
(*avec article singulier*) all; ~ **le lait** all the
milk; **~e la nuit** all night, the whole night;
~ **le livre** the whole book; ~ **un pain** a
whole loaf; ~ **le temps** all the time; the
whole time; **c'est** ~ **le contraire** it's quite
the opposite
2 (*avec article pluriel*) every; all; **tous les livres** all the books; **~es les nuits** every
night; **~es les fois** every time; **~es les
trois/deux semaines** every third/other *ou*
second week, every three/two weeks; **tous
les deux** both *ou* each of us (*ou* them *ou*
you); **~es les trois** all three of us (*ou* them
ou you)
3 (*sans article*): **à** ~ **âge** at any age; **pour**
~**e nourriture, il avait** ... his only food
was ...
♦ *pron* everything, all; **Il a** ~ **fait** he's done
everything; **je les vois tous** I can see them
all *ou* all of them; **nous y sommes tous
allés** all of us went, we all went; **en** ~ in
all; ~ **ce qu'il sait** all he knows
♦ *nm* whole; **le** ~ all of it (*ou* them); **le** ~
est de ... the main thing is to ...; **pas du** ~
not at all
♦ *adv* **1** (*très, complètement*) very; ~ **près**
very near; **le** ~ **premier** the very first; ~
seul all alone; **le livre** ~ **entier** the whole
book; ~ **en haut** right at the top; ~ **droit**
straight ahead
2: ~ **en** while; ~ **en travaillant** while
working, as he *etc* works
3 ~ **d'abord** first of all; ~ **à coup** suddenly; ~ **à fait** absolutely; ~ **à l'heure** a
short while ago; (*futur*) in a short while,
shortly; **à** ~ **à l'heure!** see you later!; ~ **de
même** all the same; ~ **le monde** everybody; ~ **de suite** immediately, straight
away; ~ **terrain** *ou* **tous terrains** all-terrain

toutefois [tutfwa] *adv* however
toutes [tut] *adj, pron voir* **tout**
toux [tu] *nf* cough
toxicomane [tɔksikɔman] *nm/f* drug addict
trac [tRak] *nm* nerves *pl*
tracasser [tRakase] *vt* to worry, bother; to
harass; **tracasseries** [tRakasRi] *nfpl* (*chi-
canes*) annoyances
trace [tRas] *nf* (*empreintes*) tracks *pl*; (*mar-
ques, aussi fig*) mark; (*restes, vestige*) trace;
(*indice*) sign; ~**s de pas** footprints
tracé [tRase] *nm* line; layout
tracer [tRase] *vt* to draw; (*mot*) to trace; to
(*piste*) to open up
tract [tRakt] *nm* tract, pamphlet
tractations [tRaktɑsjɔ̃] *nfpl* dealings, bar-
gaining *sg*
tracteur [tRaktœR] *nm* tractor
traction [tRaksjɔ̃] *nf*: ~ **avant/arrière**

front-wheel/rear-wheel drive
tradition [tRadisjɔ̃] *nf* tradition; **tradition-
nel, le** *adj* traditional
traducteur, trice [tRadyktœR, -tRis] *nm/f*
translator
traduction [tRadyksjɔ̃] *nf* translation
traduire [tRaduiR] *vt* to translate; (*exprimer*)
to render, convey
trafic [tRafik] *nm* traffic; ~ **d'armes** arms
dealing; **trafiquant, e** *nm/f* trafficker; dealer; **trafiquer** (*péj*) *vt* to doctor, tamper
with
tragédie [tRaʒedi] *nf* tragedy
tragique [tRaʒik] *adj* tragic
trahir [tRaiR] *vt* to betray; (*fig*) to give
away, reveal; **trahison** *nf* betrayal; (*JUR*)
treason
train [tRɛ̃] *nm* (*RAIL*) train; (*allure*) pace;
(*fig: ensemble*) set; **mettre qch en** ~ to get
sth under way; **mettre qn en** ~ to put sb
in good spirits; **se mettre en** ~ to get
started; to warm up; **se sentir en** ~ to feel
in good form; ~ **d'atterrissage** undercarriage; ~ **de vie** style of living; ♦ **électrique**
(*jouet*) (electric) train set; ~**-autos-
couchettes** car-sleeper train
traîne [tRɛn] *nf* (*de robe*) train; **être à la** ~
to be in tow; to lag behind
traîneau, x [tRɛno] *nm* sleigh, sledge
traînée [tRene] *nf* streak, trail; (*péj*) slut
traîner [tRene] *vt* (*remorque*) to pull; (*enfant, chien*) to drag *ou* trail along ♦ *vi* (*être
en désordre*) to lie around; (*marcher*) to
dawdle (along); (*vagabonder*) to hang
about; (*agir lentement*) to idle about; (*durer*) to drag on; **se** ~ *vi* to drag o.s. along;
~ **les pieds** to drag one's feet
train-train [tRɛ̃tRɛ̃] *nm* humdrum routine
traire [tRɛR] *vt* to milk
trait [tRɛ] *nm* (*ligne*) line; (*de dessin*)
stroke; (*caractéristique*) feature, trait; ~**s**
nmpl (*du visage*) features; **d'un** ~ (*boire*) in
one gulp; **de** ~ (*animal*) draught; **avoir** ~ **à**
to concern; ~ **d'union** hyphen; (*fig*) link
traitant, e [tRɛtɑ̃, -ɑ̃t] *adj*: **votre médecin**
~ your usual *ou* family doctor; **crème** ~**e**
conditioning cream
traite [tRɛt] *nf* (*COMM*) draft; (*AGR*) milk-
ing; **d'une** ~ without stopping; **la** ~ **des
noirs** the slave trade
traité [tRɛte] *nm* treaty
traitement [tRɛtmɑ̃] *nm* treatment; processing; (*salaire*) salary; ~ **de données/
texte** data/word processing
traiter [tRɛte] *vt* (*gén*) to treat; (*TECH, IN-
FORM*) to process; (*affaire*) to deal with,
handle; (*qualifier*): ~ **qn d'idiot** to call sb a
fool ♦ *vi* to deal; ~ **de** to deal with
traiteur [tRɛtœR] *nm* caterer
traître, esse [tRɛtR(ə), -tRɛs] *adj* (*dangereux*) treacherous ♦ *nm* traitor
trajectoire [tRaʒɛktwaR] *nf* path

trajet [traʒɛ] nm journey; (*itinéraire*) route; (*fig*) path, course

trame [tram] nf (*de tissu*) weft; (*fig*) framework; texture

tramer [trame] vt to plot, hatch

tramway [tramwɛ] nm tram(way); tram(car) (*BRIT*), streetcar (*US*)

tranchant, e [trɑ̃ʃɑ̃, -ɑ̃t] adj sharp; (*fig*) peremptory ♦ nm (*d'un couteau*) cutting edge; (*de la main*) edge

tranche [trɑ̃ʃ] nf (*morceau*) slice; (*arête*) edge; (*partie*) section; (*série*) block; issue; bracket

tranché, e [trɑ̃ʃe] adj (*couleurs*) distinct, sharply contrasted; (*opinions*) clear-cut, definite; **tranchée** nf trench

trancher [trɑ̃ʃe] vt to cut, sever; (*fig: résoudre*) to settle ♦ vi to take a decision; ~ **avec** to contrast sharply with

tranquille [trɑ̃kil] adj calm, quiet; (*enfant, élève*) quiet; (*rassuré*) easy in one's mind, with one's mind at rest; **se tenir** ~ (*enfant*) to be quiet; **laisse-moi/laisse-ça** ~ leave me/it alone; **tranquillité** nf quietness; peace (and quiet)

transat [trɑ̃zat] nm deckchair

transborder [trɑ̃sbɔrde] vt to tran(s)ship

trans: ~**férer** vt to transfer; ~**fert** nm transfer; ~**figurer** vt to transform; ~**formation** nf transformation; (*RUGBY*) conversion

transformer [trɑ̃sfɔrme] vt to transform, alter; (*matière première, appartement, RUGBY*) to convert; ~ **en** to transform into; to turn into; to convert into

transfusion [trɑ̃sfyzjɔ̃] nf: ~ **sanguine** blood transfusion

transgresser [trɑ̃sgrese] vt to contravene, disobey

transi, e [trɑ̃zi] adj numb (with cold), chilled to the bone

transiger [trɑ̃ziʒe] vi to compromise

transit [trɑ̃zit] nm transit; **transiter** vi to pass in transit

transitif, ive [trɑ̃zitif, -iv] adj transitive

transition [trɑ̃zisjɔ̃] nf transition; **transitoire** adj transitional; transient

translucide [trɑ̃slysid] adj translucent

transmetteur [trɑ̃smɛtœr] nm transmitter

transmettre [trɑ̃smɛtr(ə)] vt (*passer*): ~ **qch à qn** to pass sth on to sb; (*TECH, TÉL, MÉD*) to transmit; (*TV, RADIO*: re~) to broadcast

trans: ~**mission** nf transmission; ~**paraître** vi to show (through); ~**parence** nf transparence; **par** ~**parence** (*regarder*) against the light; (*voir*) showing through; ~**parent, e** adj transparent; ~**percer** vt to go through, pierce; ~**piration** nf perspiration; ~**pirer** vi to perspire; ~**planter** vt (*MÉD, BOT*) to transplant; (*personne*) to uproot; ~**port** nm transport; ~**ports en**

commun public transport sg

transporter [trɑ̃spɔrte] vt to carry, move; (*COMM*) to transport, convey; **transporteur** nm haulage contractor (*BRIT*), trucker (*US*)

transversal, e, aux [trɑ̃svɛrsal, -o] adj transverse, cross(-); cross-country; running at right angles

trapèze [trapɛz] nm (*au cirque*) trapeze

trappe [trap] nf trap door

trapu, e [trapy] adj squat, stocky

traquenard [traknar] nm trap

traquer [trake] vt to track down; (*harceler*) to hound

traumatiser [tromatize] vt to traumatize

travail, aux [travaj, -o] nm (*gén*) work; (*tâche, métier*) work no pl, job; (*ÉCON, MÉD*) labour; **être sans** ~ (*employé*) to be out of work ou unemployed; *voir aussi* **travaux**; ~ **(au) noir** moonlighting

travailler [travaje] vi to work; (*bois*) to warp ♦ vt (*bois, métal*) to work; (*objet d'art, discipline, fig: influencer*) to work on; **cela le travaille** it is on his mind; ~ **à** to work on; (*fig: contribuer à*) to work towards; **travailleur, euse** adj hard-working ♦ nm/f worker; **travailliste** adj ≈ Labour (*BRIT*) cpd

travaux [travo] nmpl (*de réparation, agricoles etc*) work sg; (*sur route*) roadworks pl; (*de construction*) building (work); ~ **des champs** farmwork sg; ~ **dirigés** (*SCOL*) supervised practical work sg; ~ **forcés** hard labour sg; ~ **manuels** (*SCOL*) handicrafts; ~ **ménagers** housework sg

travée [trave] nf row; (*ARCHIT*) bay; span

travers [travɛr] nm fault, failing; **en** ~ **(de)** across; **au** ~ **(de)** through; **de** ~ askew ♦ adv sideways; (*fig*) the wrong way; **à** ~ through; **regarder de** ~ (*fig*) to look askance at

traverse [travɛrs(ə)] nf (*de voie ferrée*) sleeper; **chemin de** ~ shortcut

traversée [travɛrse] nf crossing

traverser [travɛrse] vt (*gén*) to cross; (*ville, tunnel, aussi: percer, fig*) to go through; (*suj: ligne, trait*) to run across

traversin [travɛrsɛ̃] nm bolster

travestir [travɛstir] vt (*vérité*) to misrepresent; **se** ~ vi to dress up; to dress as a woman

trébucher [trebyʃe] vi: ~ **(sur)** to stumble (over), trip (against)

trèfle [trɛfl(ə)] nm (*BOT*) clover; (*CARTES: couleur*) clubs pl; (*: carte*) club

treille [trɛj] nf vine arbour; climbing vine

treillis [trɛji] nm (*métallique*) wire-mesh

treize [trɛz] num thirteen; **treizième** num thirteenth

tréma [trema] nm diaeresis

tremblement [trɑ̃bləmɑ̃] nm: ~ **de terre** earthquake

trembler [tʀɑ̃ble] *vi* to tremble, shake; ~ **de** (*froid, fièvre*) to shiver *ou* tremble with; (*peur*) to shake *ou* tremble with; ~ **pour qn** to fear for sb

trémousser [tʀemuse] : **se** ~ *vi* to jig about, wriggle about

trempe [tʀɑ̃p] *nf* (*fig*): **de cette/sa** ~ of this/his calibre

trempé, e [tʀɑ̃pe] *adj* soaking (wet), drenched; (*TECH*) tempered

tremper [tʀɑ̃pe] *vt* to soak, drench; (*aussi*: **faire** ~, **mettre à** ~) to soak; (*plonger*): ~ **qch dans** to dip sth in(to) ♦ *vi* to soak; (*fig*): ~ **dans** to be involved *ou* have a hand in; **se** ~ *vi* to have a quick dip; **trempette** *nf*: **faire trempette** to go paddling

tremplin [tʀɑ̃plɛ̃] *nm* springboard; (*SKI*) ski-jump

trentaine [tʀɑ̃tɛn] *nf*: **une** ~ (**de**) thirty or so, about thirty; **avoir la** ~ (*âge*) to be around thirty

trente [tʀɑ̃t] *num* thirty; **trentième** *num* thirtieth

trépidant, e [tʀepidɑ̃, -ɑ̃t] *adj* (*fig: rythme*) pulsating; (: *vie*) hectic

trépied [tʀepje] *nm* tripod

trépigner [tʀepiɲe] *vi* to stamp (one's feet)

très [tʀɛ] *adv* very; much +*pp*, highly +*pp*

trésor [tʀezɔʀ] *nm* treasure; (*ADMIN*) finances *pl*; funds *pl*; **T~** (**public**) public revenue

trésorerie [tʀezɔʀʀi] *nf* (*gestion*) accounts *pl*; (*bureaux*) accounts department; **difficultés de** ~ cash problems, shortage of cash *ou* funds

trésorier, ière [tʀezɔʀje, -jɛʀ] *nm/f* treasurer

tressaillir [tʀesajiʀ] *vi* to shiver, shudder; to quiver

tressauter [tʀesote] *vi* to start, jump

tresse [tʀɛs] *nf* braid, plait

tresser [tʀese] *vt* (*cheveux*) to braid, plait; (*fil, jonc*) to plait; (*corbeille*) to weave; (*corde*) to twist

tréteau, x [tʀeto] *nm* trestle

treuil [tʀœj] *nm* winch

trêve [tʀɛv] *nf* (*MIL, POL*) truce; (*fig*) respite; ~ **de ...** enough of this ...

tri [tʀi] *nm* sorting out *no pl*; selection; (*POSTES*) sorting; sorting office

triangle [tʀijɑ̃gl(ə)] *nm* triangle

tribord [tʀibɔʀ] *nm*: **à** ~ to starboard, on the starboard side

tribu [tʀiby] *nf* tribe

tribunal, aux [tʀibynal, -o] *nm* (*JUR*) court; (*MIL*) tribunal

tribune [tʀibyn] *nf* (*estrade*) platform, rostrum; (*débat*) forum; (*d'église, de tribunal*) gallery; (*de stade*) stand

tribut [tʀiby] *nm* tribute

tributaire [tʀibytɛʀ] *adj*: **être** ~ **de** to be dependent on

tricher [tʀiʃe] *vi* to cheat

tricolore [tʀikɔlɔʀ] *adj* three-coloured; (*français*) red, white and blue

tricot [tʀiko] *nm* (*technique, ouvrage*) knitting *no pl*; (*tissu*) knitted fabric; (*vêtement*) jersey, sweater

tricoter [tʀikɔte] *vt* to knit

trictrac [tʀiktʀak] *nm* backgammon

tricycle [tʀisikl(ə)] *nm* tricycle

triennal, e, aux [tʀienal, -o] *adj* three-yearly; three-year

trier [tʀije] *vt* to sort out; (*POSTES, fruits*) to sort

trimestre [tʀimɛstʀ(ə)] *nm* (*SCOL*) term; (*COMM*) quarter; **trimestriel, le** *adj* quarterly; (*SCOL*) end-of-term

tringle [tʀɛ̃gl(ə)] *nf* rod

trinquer [tʀɛ̃ke] *vi* to clink glasses

triomphe [tʀijɔ̃f] *nm* triumph

triompher [tʀijɔ̃fe] *vi* to triumph, win; ~ **de** to triumph over, overcome

tripes [tʀip] *nfpl* (*CULIN*) tripe *sg*

triple [tʀipl(ə)] *adj* triple; treble ♦ *nm*: **le** ~ (**de**) (*comparaison*) three times as much (as); **en** ~ **exemplaire** in triplicate; **tripler** *vi, vt* to triple, treble

triplés, ées [tʀiple] *nm/fpl* triplets

tripoter [tʀipɔte] *vt* to fiddle with

trique [tʀik] *nf* cudgel

triste [tʀist(ə)] *adj* sad; (*péj*): ~ **personnage/affaire** sorry individual/affair; **tristesse** *nf* sadness

trivial, e, aux [tʀivjal, -o] *adj* coarse, crude; (*commun*) mundane

troc [tʀɔk] *nm* barter

trognon [tʀɔɲɔ̃] *nm* (*de fruit*) core; (*de légume*) stalk

trois [tʀwɑ] *num* three; **troisième** *num* third; **trois quarts** *nmpl*: **les trois quarts de** three-quarters of

trombe [tʀɔ̃b] *nf*: **des** ~**s d'eau** a downpour; **en** ~ like a whirlwind

trombone [tʀɔ̃bɔn] *nm* (*MUS*) trombone; (*de bureau*) paper clip

trompe [tʀɔ̃p] *nf* (*d'éléphant*) trunk; (*MUS*) trumpet, horn

tromper [tʀɔ̃pe] *vt* to deceive; (*vigilance, poursuivants*) to elude; **se** ~ *vi* to make a mistake, be mistaken; **se** ~ **de voiture/jour** to take the wrong car/get the day wrong; **se** ~ **de 3 cm/20 F** to be out by 3 cm/20 F; ~**ie** *nf* deception, trickery *no pl*

trompette [tʀɔ̃pɛt] *nf* trumpet; **en** ~ (*nez*) turned-up

tronc [tʀɔ̃] *nm* (*BOT, ANAT*) trunk; (*d'église*) collection box

tronçon [tʀɔ̃sɔ̃] *nm* section

tronçonner [tʀɔ̃sɔne] *vt* to saw up

trône [tʀon] *nm* throne

trop [tʀo] *adv* (+*vb*) too much; (+*adjectif, adverbe*) too; ~ (**nombreux**) too many; ~

peu (nombreux) too few; ~ **(souvent)** too often; ~ **(longtemps)** (for) too long; ~ **de** *(nombre)* too many; *(quantité)* too much; **de** ~, **en** ~: **des livres en** ~ a few books too many; **du lait en** ~ too much milk; **3 livres/3 F de** ~ 3 books too many/3 F too much

tropical, e, aux [tʀɔpikal, -o] *adj* tropical

tropique [tʀɔpik] *nm* tropic

trop-plein [tʀɔplɛ̃] *nm (tuyau)* overflow *ou* outlet (pipe); *(liquide)* overflow

troquer [tʀɔke] *vt*: ~ **qch contre** to barter *ou* trade sth for; *(fig)* to swap sth for

trot [tʀo] *nm* trot; ~**ter** [tʀɔte] *vi* to trot; *(fig)* to scamper along *(ou* about)

trottiner [tʀɔtine] *vi (fig)* to scamper along *(ou* about); **trottinette** [tʀɔtinɛt] *nf* (child's) scooter

trottoir [tʀɔtwaʀ] *nm* pavement; **faire le** ~ *(péj)* to walk the streets; ~ **roulant** moving walkway, travellator

trou [tʀu] *nm* hole; *(fig)* gap; *(COMM)* deficit; ~ **d'air** air pocket; ~ **d'ozone** ozone hole; **le** ~ **de la serrure** the keyhole; ~ **de mémoire** blank, lapse of memory

trouble [tʀubl(ə)] *adj (liquide)* cloudy; *(image, mémoire)* indistinct, hazy; *(affaire)* shady, murky ♦ *nm (désarroi)* agitation; *(embarras)* confusion; *(zizanie)* unrest, discord; ~**s** *nmpl (POL)* disturbances, troubles, unrest *sg*; *(MÉD)* trouble *sg*, disorders

troubler [tʀuble] *vt (embarrasser)* to confuse, disconcert; *(émouvoir)* to agitate; to disturb; *(perturber: ordre etc)* to disrupt; *(liquide)* to make cloudy; **se** ~ *vi (personne)* to become flustered *ou* confused

trouée [tʀue] *nf* gap; *(MIL)* breach

trouer [tʀue] *vt* to make a hole *(ou* holes) in; *(fig)* to pierce

trouille [tʀuj] *(fam) nf*: **avoir la** ~ to be scared to death

troupe [tʀup] *nf* troop; ~ **(de théâtre)** (theatrical) company

troupeau, x [tʀupo] *nm (de moutons)* flock; *(de vaches)* herd

trousse [tʀus] *nf* case, kit; *(d'écolier)* pencil case; *(de docteur)* instrument case; **aux** ~**s de** *(fig)* on the heels *ou* tail of; ~ **à outils** toolkit; ~ **de toilette** toilet bag

trousseau, x [tʀuso] *nm (de mariée)* trousseau; ~ **de clefs** bunch of keys

trouvaille [tʀuvaj] *nf* find

trouver [tʀuve] *vt* to find; *(rendre visite)*: **aller/venir** ~ **qn** to go/come and see sb; **se** ~ *vi (être)* to be; *(être soudain)* to find o.s.; **il se trouve que** it happens that, it turns out that; **se** ~ **bien** to feel well; **se** ~ **mal** to pass out; **je trouve que** I find *ou* think that; ~ **à boire/critiquer** to find something to drink/criticize

truand [tʀyɑ̃] *nm* villain, crook

truander [tʀyɑ̃de] *vt* to cheat

truc [tʀyk] *nm (astuce)* way, device; *(de cinéma, prestidigitateur)* trick effect; *(chose)* thing, thingumajig; **avoir le** ~ to have the knack

truchement [tʀyʃmɑ̃] *nm*: **par le** ~ **de qn** through (the intervention of) sb

truelle [tʀyɛl] *nf* trowel

truffe [tʀyf] *nf* truffle; *(nez)* nose

truffé, e [tʀyfe] *adj*: ~ **de** *(fig)* peppered with; bristling with

truie [tʀɥi] *nf* sow

truite [tʀɥit] *nf* trout *inv*

truquer [tʀyke] *vt (élections, serrure, dés)* to fix; *(CINÉMA)* to use special effects in

T.S.V.P. *sigle* (= *tournez s.v.p.*) P.T.O.

T.T.C. *sigle* = **toutes taxes comprises**

tu[1] [ty] *pron* you

tu[2]**, e** [ty] *pp de* **taire**

tuba [tyba] *nm (MUS)* tuba; *(SPORT)* snorkel

tube [tyb] *nm* tube; pipe; *(chanson, disque)* hit song *ou* record

tuer [tɥe] *vt* to kill; **se** ~ *vi* to be killed; *(suicide)* to kill o.s.; **tuerie** *nf* slaughter *no pl*

tue-tête [tytɛt] : **à** ~ *adv* at the top of one's voice

tueur [tɥœʀ] *nm* killer; ~ **à gages** hired killer

tuile [tɥil] *nf* tile; *(fam)* spot of bad luck, blow

tulipe [tylip] *nf* tulip

tuméfié, e [tymefje] *adj* puffy, swollen

tumeur [tymœʀ] *nf* growth, tumour

tumulte [tymylt(ə)] *nm* commotion

tumultueux, euse [tymyltɥø, -øz] *adj* stormy, turbulent

tunique [tynik] *nf* tunic

Tunisie [tynizi] *nf*: **la** ~ Tunisia; **tunisien, ne** *adj, nm/f* Tunisian

tunnel [tynɛl] *nm* tunnel

turbulences [tyʀbylɑ̃s] *nfpl (AVIAT)* turbulence *sg*

turbulent, e [tyʀbylɑ̃, -ɑ̃t] *adj* boisterous, unruly

turc, turque [tyʀk(ə)] *adj* Turkish ♦ *nm/f*: **T~, Turque** Turk/Turkish woman ♦ *nm (LING)* Turkish

turf [tyʀf] *nm* racing; **turfiste** *nm/f* racegoer

Turquie [tyʀki] *nf*: **la** ~ Turkey

turquoise [tyʀkwaz] *nf* turquoise ♦ *adj inv* turquoise

tus *etc vb voir* **taire**

tutelle [tytɛl] *nf (JUR)* guardianship; *(POL)* trusteeship; **sous la** ~ **de** *(fig)* under the supervision of

tuteur [tytœʀ] *nm (JUR)* guardian; *(de plante)* stake, support

tutoyer [tytwaje] *vt*: ~ **qn** to address sb as "tu"

tuyau, x [tɥijo] *nm* pipe; *(flexible)* tube; *(fam)* tip; *gen no pl*; ~ **d'arrosage** hose-

pipe; ~ **d'échappement** exhaust pipe; **~te-
rie** *nf* piping *no pl*
T.V.A. *sigle f* (= *taxe à la valeur ajoutée*)
VAT
tympan [tɛ̃pɑ̃] *nm* (*ANAT*) eardrum
type [tip] *nm* type; (*fam*) chap, guy ♦ *adj*
typical, standard
typé, e [tipe] *adj* ethnic
typhoïde [tifɔid] *nf* typhoid
typique [tipik] *adj* typical
tyran [tirɑ̃] *nm* tyrant
tzigane [dzigan] *adj* gypsy ♦ *nm/f* gypsy

U u

ulcère [ylsɛr] *nm* ulcer; **ulcérer** [ylsere] *vt*
(*fig*) to sicken, appal
ultérieur, e [ylterjœr] *adj* later, subsequent; **remis à une date ~e** postponed to
a later date
ultime [yltim] *adj* final
ultra... [yltra] *préfixe*: **ultramoderne/-
rapide** ultra-modern/-fast

─────── *MOT CLÉ*

un, une [œ̃, yn] *art indéf* a; (*devant voyelle*)
an; ~ **garçon/vieillard** a boy/an old man;
une fille a girl
♦ *pron* one; **l'~ des meilleurs** one of the
best; **l'~ ..., l'autre** (the) one ..., the other;
les ~s ..., les autres some ..., others; **l'~ et
l'autre** both (of them); **l'~ ou l'autre** either
(of them); **l'~ l'autre, les ~s les autres**
each other, one another; **pas ~ seul** not a
single one; ~ **par** ~ one by one
♦ *num* one; **une pomme seulement** one
apple only

unanime [ynanim] *adj* unanimous; **unanimité** *nf*: **à l'unanimité** unanimously
uni, e [yni] *adj* (*ton, tissu*) plain; (*surface*)
smooth, even; (*famille*) close(-knit); (*pays*)
united
unifier [ynifje] *vt* to unite, unify
uniforme [ynifɔrm(ə)] *adj* (*mouvement*) regular, uniform; (*surface, ton*) even; (*objets,
maisons*) uniform ♦ *nm* uniform; **uniformi-
ser** *vt* to make uniform; (*systèmes*) to
standardize
union [ynjɔ̃] *nf* union; ~ **de consomma-
teurs** consumers' association; **l'U~ soviétique** the Soviet Union
unique [ynik] *adj* (*seul*) only; (*le même*): **un**

prix/système ~ a single price/system; (*exceptionnel*) unique; **fils/fille** ~ only son/
daughter, only child; **uniquement** *adv*
only, solely; (*juste*) only, merely
unir [ynir] *vt* (*nations*) to unite; (*éléments,
couleurs*) to combine; (*en mariage*) to unite,
join together; **s'~** to unite; (*en mariage*) to
be joined together; ~ **qch à** to unite sth
with; to combine sth with
unité [ynite] *nf* (*harmonie, cohésion*) unity;
(*COMM, MIL, de mesure, MATH*) unit
univers [yniver] *nm* universe
universel, le [yniversɛl] *adj* universal;
(*esprit*) all-embracing
universitaire [yniversiter] *adj* university
cpd; (*diplôme, études*) academic, university
cpd ♦ *nm/f* academic
université [yniversite] *nf* university
urbain, e [yrbɛ̃, -ɛn] *adj* urban, city *cpd*,
town *cpd*; (*poli*) urbane; **urbanisme** *nm*
town planning
urgence [yrʒɑ̃s] *nf* urgency; (*MÉD etc*)
emergency; **d'~** emergency *cpd* ♦ *adv* as a
matter of urgency
urgent, e [yrʒɑ̃, -ɑ̃t] *adj* urgent
urine [yrin] *nf* urine; **urinoir** *nm* (public)
urinal
urne [yrn(ə)] *nf* (*électorale*) ballot box;
(*vase*) urn
urticaire [yrtiker] *nf* nettle rash
us [ys] *nmpl*: ~ **et coutumes** (habits and)
customs
USA *sigle mpl*: **les** ~ the USA
usage [yzaʒ] *nm* (*emploi, utilisation*) use;
(*coutume*) custom; (*LING*): **l'~** usage; **à l'~
de** (*pour*) for (use of); **en** ~ in use; **hors
d'~** out of service; wrecked; **à** ~ **interne**
to be taken; **à** ~ **externe** for external use
only; **usagé, e** [yzaʒe] *adj* (*usé*) worn;
(*d'occasion*) used; **usager, ère** [yzaʒe, -ɛr]
nm/f user
usé, e [yze] *adj* worn; (*banal*) hackneyed
user [yze] *vt* (*outil*) to wear down;
(*vêtement*) to wear out; (*matière*) to wear
away; (*consommer: charbon etc*) to use; **s'~**
vi to wear; to wear out; (*fig*) to decline; ~
de (*moyen, procédé*) to use, employ; (*droit*)
to exercise
usine [yzin] *nf* factory; ~ **marémotrice** tidal power station
usité, e [yzite] *adj* common
ustensile [ystɑ̃sil] *nm* implement; ~ **de
cuisine** kitchen utensil
usuel, le [yzɥɛl] *adj* everyday, common
usure [yzyr] *nf* wear; worn state
ut [yt] *nm* (*MUS*) C
utérus [yterys] *nm* uterus, womb
utile [ytil] *adj* useful
utilisation [ytilizasjɔ̃] *nf* use
utiliser [ytilize] *vt* to use
utilitaire [ytiliter] *adj* utilitarian; (*objets*)
practical

utilité [ytilite] *nf* usefulness *no pl*; use; **re-connu d'~ publique** state-approved

V v

va *vb voir* aller
vacance [vakɑ̃s] *nf* (*ADMIN*) vacancy; **~s** *nfpl* holiday(s *pl*), vacation *sg*; **prendre des/ses ~s** to take a holiday/one's holiday(s); **aller en ~s** to go on holiday; **vacancier, ière** *nm/f* holiday-maker
vacant, e [vakɑ̃, -ɑ̃t] *adj* vacant
vacarme [vakaʀm(ə)] *nm* row, din
vaccin [vaksɛ̃] *nm* vaccine; (*opération*) vaccination; **vaccination** *nf* vaccination; **vacciner** *vt* to vaccinate; (*fig*) to make immune
vache [vaʃ] *nf* (*ZOOL*) cow; (*cuir*) cowhide ♦ *adj* (*fam*) rotten, mean; **~ment** (*fam*) *adv* damned, hellish
vaciller [vasije] *vi* to sway, wobble; (*bougie, lumière*) to flicker; (*fig*) to be failing, falter
va-et-vient [vaevjɛ̃] *nm inv* (*de personnes, véhicules*) comings and goings *pl*, to-ings and fro-ings *pl*
vagabond [vagabɔ̃] *nm* (*rôdeur*) tramp, vagrant; (*voyageur*) wanderer; **~er** [vagabɔ̃de] *vi* to roam, wander
vagin [vaʒɛ̃] *nm* vagina
vague [vag] *nf* wave ♦ *adj* vague; (*regard*) faraway; (*manteau, robe*) loose(-fitting); (*quelconque*): **un ~ bureau/cousin** some office/cousin or other; **~ de fond** ground swell
vaillant, e [vajɑ̃, -ɑ̃t] *adj* (*courageux*) gallant; (*robuste*) hale and hearty
vaille *vb voir* valoir
vain, e [vɛ̃, vɛn] *adj* vain; **en ~** in vain
vaincre [vɛ̃kʀ(ə)] *vt* to defeat; (*fig*) to conquer, overcome; **vaincu, e** *nm/f* defeated party; **vainqueur** *nm* victor; (*SPORT*) winner
vais *vb voir* aller
vaisseau, x [vɛso] *nm* (*ANAT*) vessel; (*NAVIG*) ship, vessel; **~ spatial** spaceship
vaisselier [vɛsəlje] *nm* dresser
vaisselle [vɛsɛl] *nf* (*service*) crockery; (*plats etc à laver*) (dirty) dishes *pl*; (*lavage*) washing-up (*BRIT*), dishes *pl*
val [val] (*pl* **vaux** *ou* **~s**) *nm* valley
valable [valabl(ə)] *adj* valid; (*acceptable*) decent, worthwhile
valent *etc vb voir* valoir

valet [valɛ] *nm* valet; (*CARTES*) jack
valeur [valœʀ] *nf* (*gén*) value; (*mérite*) worth, merit; (*COMM: titre*) security; **mettre en ~** (*terrain, région*) to develop; (*fig*) to highlight; to show off to advantage; **avoir de la ~** to be valuable; **sans ~** worthless; **prendre de la ~** to go up *ou* gain in value
valide [valid] *adj* (*en bonne santé*) fit; (*valable*) valid; **valider** *vt* to validate
valions *vb voir* valoir
valise [valiz] *nf* (suit)case
vallée [vale] *nf* valley
vallon [valɔ̃] *nm* small valley
valoir [valwaʀ] *vi* (*être valable*) to hold, apply ♦ *vt* (*prix, valeur, effort*) to be worth; (*causer*): **~ qch à qn** to earn sb sth; **se ~** *vi* to be of equal merit; (*péj*) to be two of a kind; **faire ~** (*droits, prérogatives*) to assert; **faire ~ que** to point out that; **à ~ sur** to be deducted from; **vaille que vaille** somehow or other; **cela ne me dit rien qui vaille** I don't like the look of it at all; **ce climat ne me vaut rien** this climate doesn't suit me; **~ la peine** to be worth the trouble *ou* worth it; **~ mieux: il vaut mieux se taire** it's better to say nothing; **ça ne vaut rien** it's worthless; **que vaut ce candidat?** how good is this applicant?
valoriser [valɔʀize] *vt* (*ÉCON*) to develop (the economy of); (*PSYCH*) to increase the standing of
valse [vals(ə)] *nf* waltz
valu, e [valy] *pp de* valoir
vandalisme [vɑ̃dalism(ə)] *nm* vandalism
vanille [vanij] *nf* vanilla
vanité [vanite] *nf* vanity; **vaniteux, euse** *adj* vain, conceited
vanne [van] *nf* gate; (*fig*) joke
vannerie [vanʀi] *nf* basketwork
vantard, e [vɑ̃taʀ, -aʀd(ə)] *adj* boastful
vanter [vɑ̃te] *vt* to speak highly of, vaunt; **se ~** *vi* to boast, brag; **se ~ de** to pride o.s. on; (*péj*) to boast of
vapeur [vapœʀ] *nf* steam; (*émanation*) vapour, fumes *pl*; **~s** *nfpl* (*bouffées*) vapours; **à ~** steam-powered, steam *cpd*; **cuit à la ~** steamed
vaporeux, euse [vapɔʀø, -øz] *adj* (*flou*) hazy, misty; (*léger*) filmy
vaporisateur [vapɔʀizatœʀ] *nm* spray; **vaporiser** [vapɔʀize] *vt* (*parfum etc*) to spray
varappe [vaʀap] *nf* rock climbing
vareuse [vaʀøz] *nf* (*blouson*) pea jacket; (*d'uniforme*) tunic
variable [vaʀjabl(ə)] *adj* variable; (*temps, humeur*) changeable; (*divers: résultats*) varied, various
varice [vaʀis] *nf* varicose vein
varicelle [vaʀisɛl] *nf* chickenpox
varié, e [vaʀje] *adj* varied; (*divers*) various
varier [vaʀje] *vi* to vary; (*temps, humeur*) to change ♦ *vt* to vary

variété [vaʀjete] *nf* variety; **~s** *nfpl*: **spectacle/émission de ~s** variety show

variole [vaʀjɔl] *nf* smallpox

vas *vb voir* **aller**

vase [vaz] *nm* vase ♦ *nf* silt, mud

vaseux, euse [vazø, -øz] *adj* silty, muddy; *(fig: confus)* woolly, hazy; *(: fatigué)* peaky; woozy

vasistas [vazistas] *nm* fanlight

vaste [vast(ə)] *adj* vast, immense

vaudrai *etc vb voir* **valoir**

vaurien, ne [voʀjɛ̃, -ɛn] *nm/f* good-for-nothing, guttersnipe

vaut *vb voir* **valoir**

vautour [votuʀ] *nm* vulture

vautrer [votʀe]: **se ~** *vi*: **se ~ dans/sur** to wallow in/sprawl on

vaux [vo] *nmpl de* **val** ♦ *vb voir* **valoir**

va-vite [vavit]: **à la ~** *adv* in a rush *ou* hurry

veau, x [vo] *nm (ZOOL)* calf; *(CULIN)* veal; *(peau)* calfskin

vécu, e [veky] *pp de* **vivre**

vedette [vədɛt] *nf (artiste etc)* star; *(canot)* patrol boat; launch

végétal, e, aux [veʒetal, -o] *adj* vegetable ♦ *nm* vegetable, plant

végétarien, ne [veʒetaʀjɛ̃, -ɛn] *adj, nm/f* vegetarian

végétation [veʒetasjɔ̃] *nf* vegetation; **~s** *nfpl (MÉD)* adenoids

véhicule [veikyl] *nm* vehicle; **~ utilitaire** commercial vehicle

veille [vɛj] *nf (garde)* watch; *(PSYCH)* wakefulness; *(jour)*: **la ~ (de)** the day before; **la ~ au soir** the previous evening; **à la ~ de** on the eve of

veillée [veje] *nf (soirée)* evening; *(réunion)* evening gathering; **~ (mortuaire)** watch

veiller [veje] *vi* to stay up; to be awake; to be on watch ♦ *vt (malade, mort)* to watch over, sit up with; **~ à** to attend to, see to; **~ à ce que** to make sure that; **~ sur** to keep a watch on

veilleur [vɛjœʀ] *nm*: **~ de nuit** night watchman

veilleuse [vɛjøz] *nf (lampe)* night light; *(AUTO)* sidelight; *(flamme)* pilot light; **en ~** *(lampe)* dimmed

veine [vɛn] *nf (ANAT, du bois etc)* vein; *(filon)* vein, seam; *(fam: chance)*: **avoir de la ~** to be lucky

véliplanchiste [veliplɑ̃ʃist(ə)] *nm/f* windsurfer

velléités [veleite] *nfpl* vague impulses

vélo [velo] *nm* bike, cycle; **faire du ~** to go cycling; **~ tout-terrain** mountain bike

vélomoteur [velomɔtœʀ] *nm* moped

velours [vəluʀ] *nm* velvet; **~ côtelé** corduroy

velouté, e [vəlute] *adj (au toucher)* velvety; *(à la vue)* soft, mellow; *(au goût)* smooth,
mellow

velu, e [vəly] *adj* hairy

venais *etc vb voir* **venir**

venaison [vənɛzɔ̃] *nf* venison

vendange [vɑ̃dɑ̃ʒ] *nf (opération, période: aussi: ~s)* grape harvest; *(raisins)* grape crop, grapes *pl*; **~r** [vɑ̃dɑ̃ʒe] *vi* to harvest the grapes

vendeur, euse [vɑ̃dœʀ, -øz] *nm/f (de magasin)* shop assistant; *(COMM)* salesman(woman) ♦ *nm (JUR)* vendor, seller; **~ de journaux** newspaper seller

vendre [vɑ̃dʀ(ə)] *vt* to sell; **~ qch à qn** to sell sb sth; **"à ~"** "for sale"

vendredi [vɑ̃dʀədi] *nm* Friday; **V~ saint** Good Friday

vendu, e [vɑ̃dy] *adj (péj: corrompu)* corrupt

vénéneux, euse [venenø, -øz] *adj* poisonous

vénérien, ne [veneʀjɛ̃, -ɛn] *adj* venereal

vengeance [vɑ̃ʒɑ̃s] *nf* vengeance *no pl*, revenge *no pl*

venger [vɑ̃ʒe] *vt* to avenge; **se ~** *vi* to avenge o.s.; **se ~ de qch** to avenge o.s. for sth; to take one's revenge for sth; **se ~ de qn** to take revenge on sb; **se ~ sur** to take revenge on; to take it out on

venimeux, euse [vənimø, -øz] *adj* poisonous, venomous; *(fig: haineux)* venomous, vicious

venin [vənɛ̃] *nm* venom, poison

venir [vəniʀ] *vi* to come; **~ de** to come from; **~ de faire: je viens d'y aller/de le voir** I've just been there/seen him; **s'il vient à pleuvoir** if it should rain; **j'en viens à croire que** I have come to believe that; **faire ~ *(docteur, plombier)* to call (out)

vent [vɑ̃] *nm* wind; **il y a du ~** it's windy; **c'est du ~** it's all hot air; **au ~** to windward; **sous le ~** to leeward; **avoir le ~ debout/arrière** to head into the wind/have the wind astern; **dans le ~** *(fam)* trendy

vente [vɑ̃t] *nf* sale; **la ~** *(activité)* selling; *(secteur)* sales *pl*; **mettre en ~** to put on sale; *(objets personnels)* to put up for sale; **~ aux enchères** auction sale; **~ de charité** jumble sale

venteux, euse [vɑ̃tø, -øz] *adj* windy

ventilateur [vɑ̃tilatœʀ] *nm* fan

ventiler [vɑ̃tile] *vt* to ventilate; *(total, statistiques)* to break down

ventouse [vɑ̃tuz] *nf (de caoutchouc)* suction pad; *(ZOOL)* sucker

ventre [vɑ̃tʀ(ə)] *nm (ANAT)* stomach; *(fig)* belly; **avoir mal au ~** to have stomach ache *(BRIT)* ou a stomach ache *(US)*

ventriloque [vɑ̃tʀilɔk] *nm/f* ventriloquist

venu, e [vəny] *pp de* **venir** ♦ *adj*: **être mal ~ à ou de faire** to have no grounds for doing, be in no position to do

ver [vɛʀ] *nm* worm; *(des fruits etc)* maggot; *(du bois)* woodworm *no pl*; *voir aussi* **vers**;

~ **à soie** silkworm; ~ **de terre** earthworm; ~ **luisant** glow-worm; ~ **solitaire** tapeworm

verbaliser [vɛʀbalize] vi (POLICE) to book ou report an offender

verbe [vɛʀb(ə)] nm verb

verdeur [vɛʀdœʀ] nf (vigueur) vigour, vitality; (crudité) forthrightness

verdict [vɛʀdik(t)] nm verdict

verdir [vɛʀdiʀ] vi, vt to turn green

verdure [vɛʀdyʀ] nf greenery

véreux, euse [veʀø, -øz] adj worm-eaten; (malhonnête) shady, corrupt

verge [vɛʀʒ(ə)] nf (ANAT) penis; (baguette) stick, cane

verger [vɛʀʒe] nm orchard

verglacé, e [vɛʀglase] adj icy, iced-over

verglas [vɛʀgla] nm (black) ice

vergogne [vɛʀgɔɲ]: **sans** ~ adv shamelessly

véridique [veʀidik] adj truthful

vérification [veʀifikasjɔ̃] nf checking no pl, check

vérifier [veʀifje] vt to check; (corroborer) to confirm, bear out

véritable [veʀitabl(ə)] adj real; (ami, amour) true

vérité [veʀite] nf truth; (d'un portrait romanesque) lifelikeness; (sincérité) truthfulness, sincerity

vermeil, le [vɛʀmɛj] adj ruby red

vermine [vɛʀmin] nf vermin pl

vermoulu, e [vɛʀmuly] adj worm-eaten, with woodworm

verni, e [vɛʀni] adj (fam) lucky; **cuir** ~ patent leather

vernir [vɛʀniʀ] vt (bois, tableau, ongles) to varnish; (poterie) to glaze

vernis [vɛʀni] nm (enduit) varnish; glaze; (fig) veneer; ~ **à ongles** nail polish ou varnish; **~sage** [vɛʀnisaʒ] nm varnishing, glazing; (d'une exposition) preview

vérole [veʀɔl] nf (variole) smallpox

verrai etc vb voir **voir**

verre [vɛʀ] nm glass; (de lunettes) lens sg; **boire** ou **prendre un** ~ to have a drink; **~s de contact** contact lenses; **verrerie** [vɛʀi] nf (fabrique) glassworks sg; (activité) glass-making; (objets) glassware; **verrière** [vɛʀjɛʀ] nf (grand vitrage) window; (toit vitré) glass roof

verrons etc vb voir **voir**

verrou [vɛʀu] nm (targette) bolt; (fig) constriction; **mettre qn sous les ~s** to put sb behind bars; **verrouillage** nm locking; **verrouiller** vt to bolt; to lock

verrue [vɛʀy] nf wart

vers [vɛʀ] nm line ♦ nmpl (poésie) verse sg ♦ prép (en direction de) toward(s); (près de) around (about); (temporel) about, around

versant [vɛʀsɑ̃] nm slopes pl, side

versatile [vɛʀsatil] adj fickle, changeable

verse [vɛʀs(ə)]: **à** ~ adv: **il pleut à** ~ it's pouring (with rain)

Verseau [vɛʀso] nm: **le** ~ Aquarius

versement [vɛʀsəmɑ̃] nm payment; **en 3 ~s** in 3 instalments

verser [vɛʀse] vt (liquide, grains) to pour; (larmes, sang) to shed; (argent) to pay ♦ vi (véhicule) to overturn; (fig): ~ **dans** to lapse into

verset [vɛʀsɛ] nm verse

version [vɛʀsjɔ̃] nf version; (SCOL) translation (into the mother tongue)

verso [vɛʀso] nm back; **voir au** ~ see over(leaf)

vert, e [vɛʀ, vɛʀt(ə)] adj green; (vin) young; (vigoureux) sprightly; (cru) forthright ♦ nm green

vertèbre [vɛʀtɛbʀ(ə)] nf vertebra

vertement [vɛʀtəmɑ̃] adv (réprimander) sharply

vertical, e, aux [vɛʀtikal, -o] adj vertical; ~**e** nf vertical; **à la** ~**e** vertically; ~**ement** adv vertically

vertige [vɛʀtiʒ] nm (peur du vide) vertigo; (étourdissement) dizzy spell; (fig) fever; **vertigineux, euse** adj breathtaking

vertu [vɛʀty] nf virtue; **en** ~ **de** in accordance with; **vertueux, euse** adj virtuous

verve [vɛʀv(ə)] nf witty eloquence; **être en** ~ to be in brilliant form

verveine [vɛʀvɛn] nf (BOT) verbena, vervain; (infusion) verbena tea

vésicule [vezikyl] nf vesicle; ~ **biliaire** gall-bladder

vessie [vesi] nf bladder

veste [vɛst(ə)] nf jacket; ~ **droite/croisée** single-/double-breasted jacket

vestiaire [vɛstjɛʀ] nm (au théâtre etc) cloakroom; (de stade etc) changing-room (BRIT), locker-room (US)

vestibule [vɛstibyl] nm hall

vestige [vɛstiʒ] nm relic; (fig) vestige; ~**s** nmpl remains

vestimentaire [vɛstimɑ̃tɛʀ] adj (détail) of dress; (élégance) sartorial; **dépenses ~s** spending on clothes

veston [vɛstɔ̃] nm jacket

vêtement [vɛtmɑ̃] nm garment, item of clothing; ~**s** nmpl clothes

vétérinaire [veteʀinɛʀ] nm/f vet, veterinary surgeon

vêtir [vetiʀ] vt to clothe, dress

veto [veto] nm veto; **opposer un** ~ **à** to veto

vêtu, e [vety] pp de **vêtir**

vétuste [vetyst(ə)] adj ancient, timeworn

veuf, veuve [vœf, vœv] adj widowed ♦ nm widower

veuille etc vb voir **vouloir**

veuillez vb voir **vouloir**

veule [vøl] adj spineless

veuve [vœv] nf widow

veux vb voir **vouloir**

vexations [vɛksɑsjɔ̃] nfpl humiliations

vexer [vɛkse] vt to hurt, upset; **se ~** vi to be hurt, get upset

viabiliser [vjabilize] vt to provide with services (water etc)

viable [vjabl(ə)] adj viable; (économie, industrie etc) sustainable

viager, ère [vjaʒe, -ɛʀ] adj: **rente viagère** life annuity

viande [vjɑ̃d] nf meat

vibrer [vibʀe] vi to vibrate; (son, voix) to be vibrant; (fig) to be stirred; **faire ~** to (cause to) vibrate; to stir, thrill

vice [vis] nm vice; (défaut) fault ♦ préfixe: **~ ... vice-**; **~ de forme** legal flaw ou irregularity

vichy [viʃi] nm (toile) gingham

vicié, e [visje] adj (air) polluted, tainted; (JUR) invalidated

vicieux, euse [visjø, -øz] adj (pervers) dirty(-minded); nasty; (fautif) incorrect, wrong

vicinal, e, aux [visinal, -o] adj: **chemin ~** by-road, byway

victime [viktim] nf victim; (d'accident) casualty

victoire [viktwaʀ] nf victory

victuailles [viktɥaj] nfpl provisions

vidange [vidɑ̃ʒ] nf (d'un fossé, réservoir) emptying; (AUTO) oil change; (de lavabo: bonde) waste outlet; **~s** nfpl (matières) sewage sg; **vidanger** vt to empty

vide [vid] adj empty ♦ nm (PHYSIQUE) vacuum; (espace) (empty) space, gap; (futilité, néant) void; **avoir peur du ~** to be afraid of heights; **emballé sous ~** vacuum packed; **à ~** (sans occupants) empty; (sans charge) unladen

vidéo [video] nf video ♦ adj: **cassette ~** video cassette

vide-ordures [vidɔʀdyʀ] nm inv (rubbish) chute

vide-poches [vidpɔʃ] nm inv tidy; (AUTO) glove compartment

vider [vide] vt to empty; (CULIN: volaille, poisson) to gut, clean out; **se ~** vi to empty; **~ les lieux** to quit ou vacate the premises; **videur** nm (de boîte de nuit) bouncer

vie [vi] nf life; **être en ~** to be alive; **sans ~** lifeless; **à ~** for life

vieil [vjɛj] adj m voir **vieux**

vieillard [vjɛjaʀ] nm old man; **les ~s** old people, the elderly

vieille [vjɛj] adj, nf voir **vieux**

vieilleries [vjɛjʀi] nfpl old things

vieillesse [vjɛjɛs] nf old age

vieillir [vjɛjiʀ] vi (prendre de l'âge) to grow old; (population, vin) to age; (doctrine, auteur) to become dated ♦ vt to age; **vieillissement** nm growing old; ageing

Vienne [vjɛn] nf Vienna

viens vb voir **venir**

vierge [vjɛʀʒ(ə)] adj virgin; (page) clean, blank ♦ nf virgin; (signe): **la V~** Virgo; **~ de** (sans) free from, unsullied by

Vietnam [vjɛtnam] nm = **Viêt-nam**

Viêt-nam [vjɛtnam] nm Vietnam

vietnamien, ne [vjɛtnamjɛ̃, -jɛn] adj, nm/f Vietnamese

vieux(vieil), vieille [vjø, vjɛj] adj old ♦ nm/f old man(woman) ♦ nmpl old people; **mon vieux/ma vieille** (fam) old man/girl; **prendre un coup de vieux** to put years on; **vieux garçon** bachelor; **vieux jeu** adj inv old-fashioned

vif, vive [vif, viv] adj (animé) lively; (alerte, brusque, aigu) sharp; (lumière, couleur) brilliant; (air) crisp; (vent, émotion) keen; (fort: regret, déception) great, deep; (vivant): **brûlé ~** burnt alive; **de vive voix** personally; **piquer qn au ~** to cut sb to the quick; **à ~** (plaie) open; **avoir les nerfs à ~** to be on edge

vigie [viʒi] nf look-out; look-out post

vigne [viɲ] nf (plante) vine; (plantation) vineyard

vigneron [viɲʀɔ̃] nm wine grower

vignette [viɲɛt] nf (motif) vignette; (de marque) manufacturer's label ou seal; (ADMIN) ≈ (road) tax disc (BRIT), ≈ license plate sticker (US); price label (used for reimbursement)

vignoble [viɲɔbl(ə)] nm (plantation) vineyard; (vignes d'une région) vineyards pl

vigoureux, euse [viguʀø, -øz] adj vigorous, robust

vigueur [vigœʀ] nf vigour; **entrer en ~** to come into force; **en ~** current

vil, e [vil] adj vile, base; **à ~ prix** at a very low price

vilain, e [vilɛ̃, -ɛn] adj (laid) ugly; (affaire, blessure) nasty; (pas sage: enfant) naughty

villa [vila] nf (detached) house; **~ en multipropriété** time-share villa

village [vilaʒ] nm village; **villageois, e** adj village cpd ♦ nm/f villager

ville [vil] nf town; (importante) city; (administration): **la ~** ≈ the Corporation; ≈ the (town) council

villégiature [vileʒjatyʀ] nf holiday; (holiday) resort

vin [vɛ̃] nm wine; **avoir le ~ gai** to get happy after a few drinks; **~ d'honneur** reception (with wine and snacks); **~ de pays** local wine; **~ ordinaire** table wine

vinaigre [vinɛgʀ(ə)] nm vinegar; **vinaigrette** nf vinaigrette, French dressing

vindicatif, ive [vɛ̃dikatif, -iv] adj vindictive

vineux, euse [vinø, -øz] adj win(e)y

vingt [vɛ̃, vɛ̃t] num twenty; **~aine** nf: **une ~aine (de)** about twenty, twenty or so; **~ième** num twentieth

vinicole [vinikɔl] *adj* wine *cpd*, wine-growing

vins *etc vb voir* **venir**

vinyle [vinil] *nm* vinyl

viol [vjɔl] *nm* (*d'une femme*) rape; (*d'un lieu sacré*) violation

violacé, e [vjɔlase] *adj* purplish, mauvish

violemment [vjɔlamɑ̃] *adv* violently

violence [vjɔlɑ̃s] *nf* violence

violent, e [vjɔlɑ̃, -ɑ̃t] *adj* violent; (*remède*) drastic

violer [vjɔle] *vt* (*femme*) to rape; (*sépulture, loi, traité*) to violate

violet, te [vjɔlɛ, -ɛt] *adj, nm* purple, mauve; **violette** *nf* (*fleur*) violet

violon [vjɔlɔ̃] *nm* violin; (*fam: prison*) lock-up

violoncelle [vjɔlɔ̃sɛl] *nm* cello

violoniste [vjɔlɔnist(ə)] *nm/f* violinist

vipère [vipɛʀ] *nf* viper, adder

virage [viʀaʒ] *nm* (*d'un véhicule*) turn; (*d'une route, piste*) bend; (*fig: POL*) about-turn

virée [viʀe] *nf* (*courte*) run; (: *à pied*) walk; (*longue*) trip; hike, walking tour

virement [viʀmɑ̃] *nm* (*COMM*) transfer

virent *vb voir* **voir**

virer [viʀe] *vt* (*COMM*): ~ **qch (sur)** to transfer sth (into) ♦ *vi* to turn; (*CHIMIE*) to change colour; ~ **de bord** to tack

virevolter [viʀvɔlte] *vi* to twirl around

virgule [viʀgyl] *nf* comma; (*MATH*) point

viril, e [viʀil] *adj* (*propre à l'homme*) masculine; (*énergique, courageux*) manly, virile

virtuel, le [viʀtɥɛl] *adj* potential; (*théorique*) virtual

virtuose [viʀtɥoz] *nm/f* (*MUS*) virtuoso; (*gén*) master

virus [viʀys] *nm* (*aussi: COMPUT*) virus

vis[1] [vi] *vb voir* **voir; vivre**

vis[2] [vis] *nf* screw

visa [viza] *nm* (*sceau*) stamp; (*validation de passeport*) visa

visage [vizaʒ] *nm* face

vis-à-vis [vizavi] *adv* face to face ♦ *nm* person opposite; house *etc* opposite; ~ **de** opposite; (*fig*) vis-à-vis; **en** ~ facing each other

viscéral, e, aux [viseʀal, -o] *adj* (*fig*) deep-seated, deep-rooted

visée [vize] : ~**s** *nfpl* (*intentions*) designs

viser [vize] *vi* to aim ♦ *vt* to aim at; (*concerner*) to be aimed *ou* directed at; (*apposer un visa sur*) to stamp, visa; ~ **à qch/faire** to aim at sth/at doing *ou* to do; **viseur** [vizœʀ] *nm* (*d'arme*) sights *pl*; (*PHOTO*) viewfinder

visibilité [vizibilite] *nf* visibility

visible [vizibl(ə)] *adj* visible; (*disponible*): **est-il** ~? can he see me?, will he see visitors?

visière [vizjɛʀ] *nf* (*de casquette*) peak; (*qui s'attache*) eyeshade

vision [vizjɔ̃] *nf* vision; (*sens*) (eye)sight, vision; (*fait de voir*): **la** ~ **de** the sight of

visionneuse [vizjɔnøz] *nf* viewer

visite [vizit] *nf* visit; (*visiteur*) visitor; (*médicale, à domicile*) visit, call; **la** ~ (*MÉD*) medical examination; **faire une** ~ **à qn** to call on sb, pay sb a visit; **rendre** ~ **à qn** to visit sb, pay sb a visit; **être en** ~ (**chez qn**) to be visiting (sb); **heures de** ~ (*hôpital, prison*) visiting hours

visiter [vizite] *vt* to visit; (*musée, ville*) to visit, go round; **visiteur, euse** *nm/f* visitor

vison [vizɔ̃] *nm* mink

visser [vise] *vt*: ~ **qch** (*fixer, serrer*) to screw sth on

visuel, le [vizɥɛl] *adj* visual

vit *vb voir* **voir; vivre**

vital, e, aux [vital, -o] *adj* vital

vitamine [vitamin] *nf* vitamin

vite [vit] *adv* (*rapidement*) quickly, fast; (*sans délai*) quickly; soon; **faire** ~ to act quickly; to be quick

vitesse [vites] *nf* speed; (*AUTO: dispositif*) gear; **prendre qn de** ~ to outstrip sb; get ahead of sb; **prendre de la** ~ to pick up *ou* gather speed; **à toute** ~ at full *ou* top speed

viticole [vitikɔl] *adj* wine *cpd*, wine-growing

viticulteur [vitikyltœʀ] *nm* wine grower

vitrage [vitʀaʒ] *nm* glass *no pl*; (*rideau*) net curtain

vitrail, aux [vitʀaj, -o] *nm* stained-glass window

vitre [vitʀ(ə)] *nf* (window) pane; (*de portière, voiture*) window

vitré, e [vitʀe] *adj* glass *cpd*

vitrer [vitʀe] *vt* to glaze

vitreux, euse [vitʀø, -øz] *adj* (*terne*) glassy

vitrine [vitʀin] *nf* (*devanture*) (shop) window; (*étalage*) display; (*petite armoire*) display cabinet; ~ **publicitaire** display case, showcase

vitupérer [vitypeʀe] *vi* to rant and rave

vivace [vivas] *adj* (*arbre, plante*) hardy; (*fig*) indestructible, inveterate

vivacité [vivasite] *nf* liveliness, vivacity; sharpness; brilliance

vivant, e [vivɑ̃, -ɑ̃t] *adj* (*qui vit*) living, alive; (*animé*) lively; (*preuve, exemple*) living ♦ *nm*: **du** ~ **de qn** in sb's lifetime

vivats [viva] *nmpl* cheers

vive [viv] *adj voir* **vif** ♦ *vb voir* **vivre** ♦ *excl*: ~ **le roi!** long live the king!; **vivement** *adv* vivaciously; sharply ♦ *excl*: **vivement les vacances!** roll on the holidays!

viveur [vivœʀ] (*péj*) *nm* high liver, pleasure-seeker

vivier [vivje] *nm* fish tank; fishpond

vivifiant, e [vivifjɑ̃, -ɑ̃t] *adj* invigorating

vivions *vb voir* **vivre**

vivoter [vivɔte] *vi* (*personne*) to scrape a

living, get by; (*fig: affaire etc*) to struggle along

vivre [vivʀ(ə)] *vi*, *vt* to live; **il vit encore** he is still alive; **se laisser** ~ to take life as it comes; **ne plus** ~ (*être anxieux*) to live on one's nerves; **il a vécu** (*eu une vie aventureuse*) he has seen life; **être facile à** ~ to be easy to get on with; **faire** ~ **qn** (*pourvoir à sa subsistance*) to provide (a living) for sb; **vivres** *nmpl* provisions, food supplies

vlan [vlɑ̃] *excl* wham!, bang!

vocable [vɔkabl(ə)] *nm* term

vocabulaire [vɔkabylɛʀ] *nm* vocabulary

vocation [vɔkasjɔ̃] *nf* vocation, calling

vociférer [vɔsifeʀe] *vi*, *vt* to scream

vœu, x [vø] *nm* wish; (*à Dieu*) vow; **faire** ~ **de** to take a vow of; ~**x de bonne année** best wishes for the New Year

vogue [vɔg] *nf* fashion, vogue

voguer [vɔge] *vi* to sail

voici [vwasi] *prép* (*pour introduire, désigner*) here is +*sg*, here are +*pl*; **et** ~ **que ...** and now it (*ou* he) ...; *voir aussi* **voilà**

voie [vwa] *nf* way; (*RAIL*) track, line; (*AUTO*) lane; **être en bonne** ~ to be going well; **mettre qn sur la** ~ to put sb on the right track; **être en** ~ **d'achèvement/de renovation** to be nearing completion/in the process of renovation; **par** ~ **buccale** *ou* **orale** orally; **à** ~ **étroite** narrow-gauge; ~ **d'eau** (*NAVIG*) leak; ~ **de garage** (*RAIL*) siding; ~ **ferrée** track; railway line

voilà [vwala] *prép* (*en désignant*) there is +*sg*, there are +*pl*; **les** ~ *ou* **voici** here *ou* there they are; **en** ~ *ou* **voici un** here's one, there's one; ~ *ou* **voici deux ans** two years ago; ~ *ou* **voici deux ans que** it's two years since; **et** ~! there we are!; ~ **tout** that's all; "~ *ou* **voici**" (*en offrant etc*) "there *ou* here you are"

voile [vwal] *nm* veil; (*tissu léger*) net ♦ *nf* sail; (*sport*) sailing

voiler [vwale] *vt* to veil; (*fausser: roue*) to buckle; (: *bois*) to warp; **se** ~ *vi* (*lune, regard*) to mist over; (*voix*) to become husky; (*roue, disque*) to buckle; (*planche*) to warp

voilier [vwalje] *nm* sailing ship; (*de plaisance*) sailing boat

voilure [vwalyʀ] *nf* (*de voilier*) sails *pl*

voir [vwaʀ] *vi*, *vt* to see; **se** ~ *vt*: **se** ~ **critiquer/transformer** to be criticized/transformed; **cela se voit** (*cela arrive*) it happens; (*c'est visible*) that's obvious, it shows; ~ **venir** (*fig*) to wait and see; **faire** ~ **qch à qn** to show sb sth; **en faire** ~ **à qn** (*fig*) to give sb a hard time; **ne pas pouvoir** ~ **qn** not to be able to stand sb; **voyons!** let's see now; (*indignation etc*) come (along) now!; **avoir quelque chose à** ~ **avec** to have something to do with

voire [vwaʀ] *adv* indeed; nay; or even

voisin, e [vwazɛ̃, -in] *adj* (*proche*) neighbouring; (*contigu*) next; (*ressemblant*) connected ♦ *nm/f* neighbour; **voisinage** *nm* (*proximité*) proximity; (*environs*) vicinity; (*quartier, voisins*) neighbourhood

voiture [vwatyʀ] *nf* (*wagon*) coach, carriage; ~ **d'enfant** pram (*BRIT*), baby carriage (*US*); ~ **de sport** sports car; ~**-lit** *nf* sleeper

voix [vwa] *nf* voice; (*POL*) vote; **à haute** ~ aloud; **à** ~ **basse** in a low voice; **à 2/4** ~ (*MUS*) in 2/4 parts; **avoir** ~ **au chapitre** to have a say in the matter

vol [vɔl] *nm* (*mode de locomotion*) flying; (*trajet, voyage, groupe d'oiseaux*) flight; (*larcin*) theft; **à** ~ **d'oiseau** as the crow flies; **au** ~: **attraper qch au** ~ to catch sth as it flies past; **en** ~ in flight; ~ **à main armée** armed robbery; ~ **à voile** gliding; ~ **libre** hang-gliding

volage [vɔlaʒ] *adj* fickle

volaille [vɔlaj] *nf* (*oiseaux*) poultry *pl*; (*viande*) poultry *no pl*; (*oiseau*) fowl

volant, e [vɔlɑ̃, -ɑ̃t] *adj voir* **feuille** *etc* ♦ *nm* (*d'automobile*) (steering) wheel; (*de commande*) wheel; (*objet lancé*) shuttlecock; (*bande de tissu*) flounce

volcan [vɔlkɑ̃] *nm* volcano

volée [vɔle] *nf* (*TENNIS*) volley; **à la** ~: **rattraper à la** ~ to catch in mid-air; **à toute** ~ (*sonner les cloches*) vigorously; (*lancer un projectile*) with full force; ~ **de coups/de flèches** volley of blows/arrows

voler [vɔle] *vi* (*avion, oiseau, fig*) to fly; (*voleur*) to steal ♦ *vt* (*objet*) to steal; (*personne*) to rob; ~ **qch à qn** to steal sth from sb

volet [vɔlɛ] *nm* (*de fenêtre*) shutter; (*de feuillet, document*) section

voleur, euse [vɔlœʀ, -øz] *nm/f* thief ♦ *adj* thieving

volontaire [vɔlɔ̃tɛʀ] *adj* voluntary; (*caractère, personne: décidé*) self-willed ♦ *nm/f* volunteer

volonté [vɔlɔ̃te] *nf* (*faculté de vouloir*) will; (*énergie, fermeté*) will(power); (*souhait, désir*) wish; **à** ~ as much as one likes; **bonne** ~ goodwill, willingness; **mauvaise** ~ lack of goodwill, unwillingness

volontiers [vɔlɔ̃tje] *adv* (*de bonne grâce*) willingly; (*avec plaisir*) willingly, gladly; (*habituellement, souvent*) readily, willingly

volt [vɔlt] *nm* volt

volte-face [vɔltəfas] *nf inv* about-turn

voltige [vɔltiʒ] *nf* (*ÉQUITATION*) trick riding; (*au cirque*) acrobatics *sg*; ~**r** [vɔltiʒe] *vi* to flutter (about)

volume [vɔlym] *nm* volume; (*GÉOM: solide*) solid; **volumineux, euse** *adj* voluminous, bulky

volupté [vɔlypte] *nf* sensual delight *ou* pleasure

vomir [vɔmiʀ] *vi* to vomit, be sick ♦ *vt* to vomit, bring up; *(fig)* to belch out, spew out; *(exécrer)* to loathe, abhor

vont [vɔ̃] *vb voir* **aller**

vos [vo] *dét voir* **votre**

vote [vɔt] *nm* vote; ~ **par correspondance/procuration** postal/proxy vote

voter [vɔte] *vi* to vote ♦ *vt (loi, décision)* to vote for

votre [vɔtʀ(ə)] *(pl* **vos)** *dét* your

vôtre [votʀ(ə)] *pron:* **le ~, la ~, les ~s** yours; **les ~s** *(fig)* your family *ou* folks; **à la ~** *(toast)* your (good) health!

voudrai *etc vb voir* **vouloir**

voué, e [vwe] *adj:* ~ **à** doomed to

vouer [vwe] *vt:* ~ **qch à** *(Dieu/un saint)* to dedicate sth to; ~ **sa vie à** *(étude, cause etc)* to devote one's life to; ~ **une amitié éternelle à qn** to vow undying friendship to sb

---

MOT CLÉ

vouloir [vulwaʀ] *nm:* **le bon ~ de qn** sb's goodwill; sb's pleasure

♦ *vt* **1** *(exiger, désirer)* to want; ~ **faire/que qn fasse** to want to do/sb to do; **voulez-vous du thé?** would you like *ou* do you want some tea?; **que me veut-il?** what does he want with me?; **sans le ~** *(involontairement)* without meaning to, unintentionally; **je voudrais ceci/faire** I would *ou* I'd like this/to do

2 *(consentir):* **je veux bien** *(bonne volonté)* I'll be happy to; *(concession)* fair enough, that's fine; **oui, si on veut** *(en quelque sorte)* yes, if you like; **veuillez attendre** please wait; **veuillez agréer ...** *(formule épistolaire)* yours faithfully

3: **en ~ à qn** to bear sb a grudge; **s'en ~ (de)** to be annoyed with o.s. (for); **il en veut à mon argent** he's after my money

4: ~ **de: l'entreprise ne veut plus de lui** the firm doesn't want him any more; **elle ne veut pas de son aide** she doesn't want his help

5: ~ **dire** to mean

---

voulu, e [vuly] *adj (requis)* required, requisite; *(délibéré)* deliberate, intentional; *voir aussi* **vouloir**

vous [vu] *pron* you; *(objet indirect)* (to) you; *(réfléchi: sg)* yourself; (: *pl)* yourselves; *(réciproque)* each other; **~-même** yourself; **~-mêmes** yourselves

voûte [vut] *nf* vault

voûter [vute] *vt:* **se ~** *vi (dos, personne)* to become stooped

vouvoyer [vuvwaje] *vt:* ~ **qn** to address sb as "vous"

voyage [vwajaʒ] *nm* journey, trip; *(fait de voyager):* **le ~** travel(ling); **partir/être en ~** to go off/be away on a journey *ou* trip; **faire bon ~** to have a good journey; ~ **d'agrément/d'affaires** pleasure/business trip; ~ **de noces** honeymoon; ~ **organisé** package tour

voyager [vwajaʒe] *vi* to travel; **voyageur, euse** *nm/f* traveller; *(passager)* passenger

voyant, e [vwajɑ̃, -ɑ̃t] *adj (couleur)* loud, gaudy ♦ *nm (signal)* (warning) light.

voyante [vwajɑ̃t] *nf* clairvoyant

voyelle [vwajɛl] *nf* vowel

voyons *etc vb voir* **voir**

voyou [vwaju] *nm* lout, hoodlum; *(enfant)* guttersnipe

vrac [vʀak] : **en ~** *adv* higgledy-piggledy; *(COMM)* in bulk

vrai, e [vʀɛ] *adj (véridique: récit, faits)* true; *(non factice, authentique)* real; **à ~ dire** to tell the truth

vraiment [vʀɛmɑ̃] *adv* really

vraisemblable [vʀɛsɑ̃blabl(ə)] *adj* likely, probable

vraisemblance [vʀɛsɑ̃blɑ̃s] *nf* likelihood; *(romanesque)* verisimilitude

vrille [vʀij] *nf (de plante)* tendril; *(outil)* gimlet; *(spirale)* spiral; *(AVIAT)* spin

vrombir [vʀɔ̃biʀ] *vi* to hum

vu, e [vy] *pp de* **voir** ♦ *adj:* **bien/mal ~** *(fig)* well/poorly thought of; good/bad form ♦ *prép (en raison de)* in view of; ~ **que** in view of the fact that

vue [vy] *nf (fait de voir):* **la ~ de** the sight of; *(sens, faculté)* (eye)sight; *(panorama, image, photo)* view; **~s** *nfpl (idées)* views; *(dessein)* designs; **hors de ~** out of sight; **tirer à ~** to shoot on sight; **à ~ d'œil** visibly; at a quick glance; **en ~** *(visible)* in sight; *(COMM)* in the public eye; **en ~ de faire** with a view to doing

vulgaire [vylgɛʀ] *adj (grossier)* vulgar, coarse; *(trivial)* commonplace, mundane; *(péj: quelconque):* **de ~s touristes** common tourists; *(BOT, ZOOL: non latin)* common; **vulgariser** *vt* to popularize

vulnérable [vylneʀabl(ə)] *adj* vulnerable

W w

wagon [vagɔ̃] *nm (de voyageurs)* carriage; *(de marchandises)* truck, wagon; **wagon-lit** *nm* sleeper, sleeping car; **wagon-restaurant** *nm* restaurant *ou* dining car

wallon, ne [valɔ̃, -ɔn] *adj* Walloon

waters [watɛʀ] *nmpl* toilet *sg*
watt [wat] *nm* watt
w.-c. [vese] *nmpl* toilet *sg*, lavatory *sg*
week-end [wikɛnd] *nm* weekend
western [wɛstɛʀn] *nm* western
whisky [wiski] (*pl* **whiskies**) *nm* whisky

xérès [gzeʀɛs] *nm* sherry
xylophone [ksilɔfɔn] *nm* xylophone

y [i] *adv* (*à cet endroit*) there; (*dessus*) on it (*ou* them); (*dedans*) in it (*ou* them) ♦ *pron* (about *ou* on *ou* of) it (*d'après le verbe employé*); **j'~ pense** I'm thinking about it; *voir aussi* **aller; avoir**
yacht [jɔt] *nm* yacht
yaourt [jauʀt] *nm* yoghourt
yeux [jø] *nmpl de* **œil**

yoghourt [jɔguʀt] *nm* = **yaourt**
yougoslave [jugɔslav] *nm/f* Yugoslav(ian)
Yougoslavie [jugɔslavi] *nf* Yugoslavia

zèbre [zɛbʀ(ə)] *nm* (*ZOOL*) zebra
zébré, e [zebʀe] *adj* striped, streaked
zèle [zɛl] *nm* zeal; **faire du ~** (*péj*) to be over-zealous
zéro [zeʀo] *nm* zero, nought (*BRIT*); **au-dessous de ~** below zero (Centigrade) *ou* freezing; **partir de ~** to start from scratch; **trois (buts) à ~** 3 (goals to) nil
zeste [zɛst(ə)] *nm* peel, zest
zézayer [zezeje] *vi* to have a lisp
zigzag [zigzag] *nm* zigzag
zinc [zɛ̃g] *nm* (*CHIMIE*) zinc; (*comptoir*) bar, counter
zizanie [zizani] *nf*: **semer la ~** to stir up ill-feeling
zodiaque [zɔdjak] *nm* zodiac
zona [zona] *nm* shingles *sg*
zone [zon] *nf* zone, area; (*quartiers*): **la ~** the slum belt; **~ bleue** ≈ restricted parking area; **~ industrielle** *nf* industrial estate
zoo [zoo] *nm* zoo
zoologie [zɔɔlɔʒi] *nf* zoology; **zoologique** *adj* zoological
zut [zyt] *excl* dash (it)! (*BRIT*), nuts! (*US*)

ENGLISH - FRENCH
ANGLAIS - FRANÇAIS

A a

A [eɪ] *n* (*MUS*) la *m*

a [eɪ, ə] (*before vowel or silent h: an*) *indef art* **1** un(e); **~ book** un livre; **an apple** une pomme; **she's ~ doctor** elle est médecin
2 (*instead of the number 'one'*) un(e); **~ year ago** il y a un an; **~ hundred/ thousand** *etc* **pounds** cent/mille *etc* livres
3 (*in expressing ratios, prices etc*): **3 ~ day/week** 3 par jour/semaine; **10 km ~n hour** 10 km à l'heure; **30p ~ kilo** 30p le kilo

A.A. *n abbr* = **Alcoholics Anonymous;** (*BRIT*: = *Automobile Association*) ≈ TCF *m*
A.A.A. (*US*) *n abbr* (= *American Automobile Association*) ≈ TCF *m*
aback [ə'bæk] *adv*: **to be taken ~** être stupéfait(e), être décontenancé(e)
abandon [ə'bændən] *vt* abandonner ♦ *n*: **with ~** avec désinvolture
abate [ə'beɪt] *vi* s'apaiser, se calmer
abbey ['æbɪ] *n* abbaye *f*
abbot ['æbət] *n* père supérieur
abbreviation [əbriːvɪ'eɪʃən] *n* abréviation *f*
abdicate ['æbdɪkeɪt] *vt, vi* abdiquer
abdomen ['æbdəmən] *n* abdomen *m*
abduct [æb'dʌkt] *vt* enlever
aberration [æbə'reɪʃən] *n* anomalie *f*
abet [ə'bet] *vt see* **aid**
abeyance [ə'beɪəns] *n*: **in ~** (*law*) tombé(e) en désuétude; (*matter*) en suspens
abide [ə'baɪd] *vt*: **I can't ~ it/him** je ne peux pas le souffrir *or* supporter; **~ by** *vt fus* observer, respecter
ability [ə'bɪlɪtɪ] *n* compétence *f*; capacité *f*; (*skill*) talent *m*
abject ['æbdʒekt] *adj* (*poverty*) sordide; (*apology*) plat(e)
ablaze [ə'bleɪz] *adj* en feu, en flammes
able ['eɪbl] *adj* capable, compétent(e); **to be**

~ to do sth être capable de faire qch, pouvoir faire qch; **~-bodied** *adj* robuste; **ably** ['eɪblɪ] *adv* avec compétence *or* talent, habilement
abnormal [æb'nɔːməl] *adj* anormal(e)
aboard [ə'bɔːd] *adv* à bord ♦ *prep* à bord de
abode [ə'bəud] *n* (*LAW*): **of no fixed ~** sans domicile fixe
abolish [ə'bɒlɪʃ] *vt* abolir
aborigine [æbə'rɪdʒɪniː] *n* aborigène *m/f*
abort [ə'bɔːt] *vt* faire avorter; **~ion** [ə'bɔːʃən] *n* avortement *m*; **to have an ~ion** se faire avorter; **~ive** *adj* manqué(e)
abound [ə'baund] *vi* abonder; **to ~ in** *or* **with** abonder en, regorger de

about [ə'baut] *adv* **1** (*approximately*) environ, à peu près; **~ a hundred/thousand** *etc* environ cent/mille *etc*, une centaine (de)/un millier (de) *etc*; **it takes ~ 10 hours** ça prend environ *or* à peu près 10 heures; **at ~ 2 o'clock** vers 2 heures; **I've just ~ finished** j'ai presque fini
2 (*referring to place*) çà et là, deci delà; **to run ~** courir çà et là; **to walk ~** se promener, aller et venir
3: **to be ~ to do sth** être sur le point de faire qch
♦ *prep* **1** (*relating to*) au sujet de, à propos de; **a book ~ London** un livre sur Londres; **what is it ~?** de quoi s'agit-il?; **we talked ~ it** nous en avons parlé; **what** *or* **how ~ doing this?** et si nous faisions ceci?
2 (*referring to place*) dans; **to walk ~ the town** se promener dans la ville

about-face [ə'baut'feɪs] *n* demi-tour *m*
about-turn [ə'baut'tɜːn] *n* (*MIL*) demi-tour *m*; (*fig*) volte-face *f*

above [ə'bʌv] *adv* au-dessus ♦ *prep* au-dessus de; (*more*) plus de; **mentioned ~** mentionné ci-dessus; **~ all** par-dessus tout, surtout; **~board** *adj* franc(franche); honnête

abrasive [ə'breɪzɪv] *adj* abrasif(ive); (*fig*) caustique, agressif(ive)

abreast [ə'brest] *adv* de front; **to keep ~ of** se tenir au courant de

abridge [ə'brɪdʒ] *vt* abréger

abroad [ə'brɔːd] *adv* à l'étranger

abrupt [ə'brʌpt] *adj* (*steep, blunt*) abrupt(e); (*sudden, gruff*) brusque; **~ly** *adv* (*speak, end*) brusquement

abscess ['æbsɪs] *n* abcès *m*

abscond [əb'skɒnd] *vi* disparaître, s'enfuir

absence ['æbsəns] *n* absence *f*

absent ['æbsənt] *adj* absent(e); **~ee** [æbsən'tiː] *n* absent(e); (*habitual*) absentéiste *m/f*; **~-minded** *adj* distrait(e)

absolute ['æbsəluːt] *adj* absolu(e); **~ly** [æbsə'luːtlɪ] *adv* absolument

absolve [əb'zɒlv] *vt*: **to ~ sb (from)** (*blame, responsibility, sin*) absoudre qn (de)

absorb [əb'zɔːb] *vt* absorber; **to be ~ed in a book** être plongé(e) dans un livre; **~ent cotton** (*US*) *n* coton *m* hydrophile; **absorption** [əb'zɔːpʃən] *n* absorption *f*; (*fig*) concentration *f*

abstain [əb'steɪn] *vi*: **to ~ (from)** s'abstenir (de)

abstract ['æbstrækt] *adj* abstrait(e)

absurd [əb'sɜːd] *adj* absurde

abuse [*n* ə'bjuːs, *vb* ə'bjuːz] *n* abus *m*; (*insults*) insultes *fpl*, injures *fpl* ♦ *vt* abuser de; (*insult*) insulter; **abusive** [ə'bjuːsɪv] *adj* grossier(ère), injurieux(euse)

abysmal [ə'bɪzməl] *adj* exécrable; (*ignorance etc*) sans bornes

abyss [ə'bɪs] *n* abîme *m*, gouffre *m*

AC *abbr* (= *alternating current*) courant alternatif

academic [ækə'demɪk] *adj* universitaire; (*person: scholarly*) intellectuel(le); (*pej: issue*) oiseux(euse), purement théorique ♦ *n* universitaire *m/f*; **~ year** année *f* universitaire

academy [ə'kædəmɪ] *n* (*learned body*) académie *f*; (*school*) collège *m*; **~ of music** conservatoire *m*

accelerate [æk'seləreɪt] *vt, vi* accélérer; **accelerator** [æk'seləreɪtə*] *n* accélérateur *m*

accent ['æksent] *n* accent *m*

accept [ək'sept] *vt* accepter; **~able** *adj* acceptable; **~ance** *n* acceptation *f*

access ['ækses] *n* accès *m*; (*JUR: in divorce*) droit *m* de visite; **~ible** [æk'sesɪbl] *adj* accessible

accessory [æk'sesərɪ] *n* accessoire *m*; (*LAW*): **~ to** complice de

accident ['æksɪdənt] *n* accident *m*; (*chance*) hasard *m*; **by ~** accidentellement; par hasard; **~al** [æksɪ'dentl] *adj* accidentel(le); **~ally** [æksɪ'dentəlɪ] *adv* accidentellement; **~-prone** *adj* sujet(te) aux accidents

acclaim [ə'kleɪm] *n* acclamations *fpl* ♦ *vt* acclamer

accommodate [ə'kɒmədeɪt] *vt* loger, recevoir; (*oblige, help*) obliger; (*car etc*) contenir; **accommodating** [ə'kɒmədeɪtɪŋ] *adj* obligeant(e), arrangeant(e); **accommodation** [əkɒmə'deɪʃən] (*US* **~s**) *n* logement *m*

accompany [ə'kʌmpənɪ] *vt* accompagner

accomplice [ə'kʌmplɪs] *n* complice *m/f*

accomplish [ə'kʌmplɪʃ] *vt* accomplir; **~ment** *n* accomplissement *m*; réussite *f*; (*skill: gen pl*) talent *m*

accord [ə'kɔːd] *n* accord *m* ♦ *vt* accorder; **of his own ~** de son plein gré; **~ance** *n*: **in ~ance with** conformément à; **~ing: ~ing to** *prep* selon; **~ingly** *adv* en conséquence

accordion [ə'kɔːdɪən] *n* accordéon *m*

accost [ə'kɒst] *vt* aborder

account [ə'kaʊnt] *n* (*COMM*) compte *m*; (*report*) compte rendu; récit *m*; **~s** *npl* (*COMM*) comptabilité *f*, comptes; **of no ~** sans importance; **on ~** en acompte; **on no ~** en aucun cas; **on ~ of** à cause de; **to take into ~, take ~ of** tenir compte de; **~ for** *vt fus* expliquer, rendre compte de; **~able** *adj*: **~able (to)** responsable (devant); **~ancy** [ə'kaʊntənsɪ] *n* comptabilité *f*; **~ant** [ə'kaʊntənt] *n* comptable *m/f*; **~ number** *n* (*at bank etc*) numéro *m* de compte

accrued interest [əkruːd-] *n* intérêt *m* cumulé

accumulate [ə'kjuːmjʊleɪt] *vt* accumuler, amasser ♦ *vi* s'accumuler, s'amasser

accuracy ['ækjʊrəsɪ] *n* exactitude *f*, précision *f*

accurate ['ækjʊrɪt] *adj* exact(e), précis(e); **~ly** *adv* avec précision

accusation [ækjuː'zeɪʃən] *n* accusation *f*

accuse [ə'kjuːz] *vt*: **to ~ sb (of sth)** accuser qn (de qch); **~d** *n*: **the ~d** l'accusé(e)

accustom [ə'kʌstəm] *vt* accoutumer, habituer; **~ed** *adj* (*usual*) habituel(le); (*in the habit*): **~ed to** habitué(e) or accoutumé(e) à

ace [eɪs] *n* as *m*

ache [eɪk] *n* mal *m*, douleur *f* ♦ *vi* (*yearn*): **to ~ to do sth** mourir d'envie de faire qch; **my head ~s** j'ai mal à la tête

achieve [ə'tʃiːv] *vt* (*aim*) atteindre; (*victory, success*) remporter, obtenir; **~ment** *n* exploit *m*, réussite *f*

acid ['æsɪd] *adj* acide ♦ *n* acide *m*; **~ rain** *n* pluies *fpl* acides

acknowledge [ək'nɒlɪdʒ] *vt* (*letter: also:* **~ receipt of**) accuser réception de; (*fact*) reconnaître; **~ment** *n* (*of letter*) accusé *m* de

réception
acne ['ækni] *n* acné *m*
acorn ['eikɔːn] *n* gland *m*
acoustic [ə'kuːstik] *adj* acoustique; **~s** *n, npl* acoustique *f*
acquaint [ə'kweint] *vt*: **to ~ sb with sth** mettre qn au courant de qch; **to be ~ed with** connaître; **~ance** *n* connaissance *f*
acquiesce [ækwi'es] *vi*: **to ~ to** acquiescer *or* consentir à
acquire [ə'kwaiə*] *vt* acquérir
acquit [ə'kwit] *vt* acquitter; **to ~ o.s. well** bien se comporter, s'en tirer très honorablement
acre ['eikə*] *n* acre *f* (= 4047 m^2)
acrid ['ækrid] *adj* âcre
acrobat ['ækrəbæt] *n* acrobate *m/f*
across [ə'krɔs] *prep* (*on the other side*) de l'autre côté de; (*crosswise*) en travers de ♦ *adv* de l'autre côté; en travers; **to run/ swim ~** traverser en courant/à la nage; **~ from** en face de
acrylic [ə'krilik] *adj* acrylique
act [ækt] *n* acte *m*, action *f*; (*of play*) acte *m*; (*in music-hall etc*) numéro *m*; (*LAW*) loi *f* ♦ *vi* agir; (*THEATRE*) jouer; (*pretend*) jouer la comédie ♦ *vt* (*part*) jouer, tenir; **in the ~ of** en train de; **to ~ as** servir de; **~ing** *adj* suppléant(e), par intérim ♦ *n* (*activity*): **to do some ~ing** faire du théâtre (*or* du cinéma)
action ['ækʃən] *n* action *f*; (*MIL*) combat(s) *m(pl)*; (*LAW*) procès *m*, action en justice; **out of ~** hors de combat; (*machine*) hors d'usage; **to take ~** agir, prendre des mesures; **~ replay** *n* (*TV*) ralenti *m*
activate ['æktiveit] *vt* (*mechanism*) actionner, faire fonctionner
active ['æktiv] *adj* actif(ive); (*volcano*) en activité; **~ly** *adv* activement
activity [æk'tiviti] *n* activité *f*
actor ['æktə*] *n* acteur *m*
actress ['æktris] *n* actrice *f*
actual ['æktjuəl] *adj* réel(le), véritable; **~ly** *adv* (*really*) réellement, véritablement; (*in fact*) en fait
acumen ['ækjumen] *n* perspicacité *f*
acute [ə'kjuːt] *adj* aigu(ë); (*mind, observer*) pénétrant(e), perspicace
ad [æd] *n abbr* = **advertisement**
A.D. *adv abbr* (= *anno Domini*) ap. J.-C.
adamant ['ædəmənt] *adj* inflexible
adapt [ə'dæpt] *vt* adapter ♦ *vi*: **to ~ (to)** s'adapter (à); **~able** *adj* (*device*) adaptable; (*person*) qui s'adapte facilement; **~er,** *or* **~or** *n* (*ELEC*) adaptateur *m*, adaptateur *m*
add [æd] *vt* ajouter; (*figures: also:* **to ~ up**) additionner ♦ *vi*: **to ~ to** (*increase*) ajouter à, accroître
adder ['ædə*] *n* vipère *f*
addict ['ædikt] *n* intoxiqué(e); (*fig*) fanatique *m/f*; **~ed** [ə'diktid] *adj*: **to be ~ed to**

(*drugs, drink etc*) être adonné(e) à; (*fig: football etc*) être un(e) fanatique de; **~ion** [ə'dikʃən] *n* (*MED*) dépendance *f*; **~ive** *adj* qui crée une dépendance
addition [ə'diʃən] *n* addition *f*; (*thing added*) ajout *m*; **in ~** de plus; de surcroît; **in ~ to** en plus de; **~al** *adj* supplémentaire
additive ['æditiv] *n* additif *m*
address [ə'dres] *n* adresse *f*; (*talk*) discours *m*, allocution *f* ♦ *vt* adresser; (*speak to*) s'adresser à; **to ~ (o.s. to) a problem** s'attaquer à un problème
adept ['ædept] *adj*: **~ at** expert(e) à *or* en
adequate ['ædikwit] *adj* adéquat(e); suffisant(e)
adhere [əd'hiə*] *vi*: **to ~ to** adhérer à; (*fig: rule, decision*) se tenir à
adhesive [əd'hiːziv] *n* adhésif *m*; **~ tape** *n* (*BRIT*) ruban adhésif; (*US: MED*) sparadrap *m*
ad hoc [æd'hɔk] *adj* improvisé(e), ad hoc
adjective ['ædʒektiv] *n* adjectif *m*
adjoining [ə'dʒɔiniŋ] *adj* voisin(e), adjacent(e), attenant(e)
adjourn [ə'dʒɜːn] *vt* ajourner ♦ *vi* suspendre la séance; lever la séance; clore la session
adjust [ə'dʒʌst] *vt* ajuster, régler; rajuster ♦ *vi*: **to ~ (to)** s'adapter (à); **~able** *adj* réglable; **~ment** *n* (*PSYCH*) adaptation *f*; (*to machine*) ajustage *m*, réglage *m*; (*of prices, wages*) rajustement *m*
ad-lib [æd'lib] *vt, vi* improviser; **ad lib** *adv* à volonté, à loisir
administer [əd'ministə*] *vt* administrer; (*justice*) rendre
administration [ədminis'treiʃən] *n* administration *f*
administrative [əd'ministrətiv] *adj* administratif(ive)
admiral ['ædmərəl] *n* amiral *m*; **A~ty** ['ædmərəlti] (*BRIT*) (*also:* **A~ty Board**): **the A~ty** ministère *m* de la Marine
admire [əd'maiə*] *vt* admirer
admission [əd'miʃən] *n* admission *f*; (*to exhibition, night club etc*) entrée *f*; (*confession*) aveu *m*
admit [əd'mit] *vt* laisser entrer; admettre; (*agree*) reconnaître, admettre; **~ to** *vt fus* reconnaître, avouer; **~tance** *n* admission *f*, (droit *m* d')entrée *f*; **~tedly** *adv* il faut en convenir
admonish [əd'mɔniʃ] *vt* donner un avertissement à; réprimander
ad nauseam [æd'nɔːsiæm] *adv* (*repeat, talk*) à n'en plus finir
ado [ə'duː] *n*: **without (any) more ~** sans plus de cérémonies
adolescence [ædə'lesns] *n* adolescence *f*; **adolescent** [ædə'lesnt] *adj, n* adolescent(e)
adopt [ə'dɔpt] *vt* adopter; **~ed** *adj* adoptif(ive), adopté(e); **~ion** [ə'dɔpʃən] *n* adop-

tion *f*

adore [ə'dɔ:*] *vt* adorer

adorn [ə'dɔ:n] *vt* orner

Adriatic (Sea) [eɪdrɪ'ætɪk-] *n* Adriatique *f*

adrift [ə'drɪft] *adv* à la dérive

adult ['ædʌlt] *n* adulte *m/f* ♦ *adj* adulte; (*literature, education*) pour adultes

adultery [ə'dʌltərɪ] *n* adultère *m*

advance [əd'vɑ:ns] *n* avance *f* ♦ *adj*: ~ **booking** réservation *f* ♦ *vt* avancer ♦ *vi* avancer, s'avancer; ~ **notice** avertissement *m*; **to make** ~**s (to sb)** faire des propositions (à qn); (*amorously*) faire des avances (à qn); **in** ~ à l'avance, d'avance; ~**d** *adj* avancé(e); (*SCOL: studies*) supérieur(e)

advantage [əd'vɑ:ntɪdʒ] *n* (*also TENNIS*) avantage *m*; **to take** ~ **of** (*person*) exploiter

advent ['ædvent] *n* avènement *m*, venue *f*; **A**~ Avent *m*

adventure [əd'ventʃə*] *n* aventure *f*

adverb ['ædvɜ:b] *n* adverbe *m*

adverse ['ædvɜ:s] *adj* défavorable, contraire

advert ['ædvɜ:t] (*BRIT*) *n* abbr = **advertisement**

advertise ['ædvətaɪz] *vi(vt)* faire de la publicité (pour); mettre une annonce (pour vendre); **to** ~ **for** (*staff, accommodation*) faire paraître une annonce pour trouver; ~**ment** [əd'vɜ:tɪsmənt] *n* (*COMM*) réclame *f*, publicité *f*; (*in classified ads*) annonce *f*; ~**r** ['ædvətaɪzə*] *n* (*in newspaper etc*) annonceur *m*; **advertising** ['ædvətaɪzɪŋ] *n* publicité *f*

advice [əd'vaɪs] *n* conseils *mpl*; (*notification*) avis *m*; **piece of** ~ conseil; **to take legal** ~ consulter un avocat

advisable [əd'vaɪzəbl] *adj* conseillé(e), indiqué(e)

advise [əd'vaɪz] *vt* conseiller; **to** ~ **sb of sth** aviser *or* informer qn de qch; **to** ~ **against sth/doing sth** déconseiller qch/conseiller de ne pas faire qch; ~**dly** [əd'vaɪzədlɪ] *adv* (*deliberately*) délibérément; ~**r** *n* conseiller(ère); **advisor** *n* = ~**r**; **advisory** [əd'vaɪzərɪ] *adj* consultatif(ive)

advocate [*vb* 'ædvəkeɪt, *n* 'ædvəkət] *n* (*upholder*) défenseur *m*, avocat(e), partisan(e); (*LAW*) avocat(e) ♦ *vt* recommander, prôner

aerial ['ɛərɪəl] *n* antenne *f* ♦ *adj* aérien(ne)

aerobics [ɛər'əubɪks] *n* aérobic *f*

aeroplane ['ɛərəpleɪn] (*BRIT*) *n* avion *m*

aerosol ['ɛərəsɒl] *n* aérosol *m*

aesthetic [ɪs'θetɪk] *adj* esthétique

afar [ə'fɑ:*] *adv*: **from** ~ de loin

affair [ə'fɛə*] *n* affaire *f*; (*also: love* ~) liaison *f*, aventure *f*

affect [ə'fekt] *vt* affecter; (*disease*) atteindre; ~**ed** *adj* affecté(e)

affection [ə'fekʃən] *n* affection *f*; ~**ate** [ə'fekʃənɪt] *adj* affectueux(euse)

affinity [ə'fɪnɪtɪ] *n* (*bond, rapport*): **to have**

an ~ **with/for** avoir une affinité avec/pour; (*resemblance*): **to have an** ~ **with** avoir une ressemblance avec

afflict [ə'flɪkt] *vt* affliger

affluence ['æfluəns] *n* abondance *f*, opulence *f*

affluent ['æfluənt] *adj* (*person, family, surroundings*) aisé(e), riche; **the** ~ **society** la société d'abondance

afford [ə'fɔ:d] *vt* se permettre; avoir les moyens d'acheter *or* d'entretenir; (*provide*) fournir, procurer

afield [ə'fi:ld] *adv*: (**from**) **far** ~ (de) loin

afloat [ə'fləut] *adj*, *adv* à flot; **to stay** ~ surnager

afoot [ə'fut] *adv*: **there is something** ~ il se prépare quelque chose

afraid [ə'freɪd] *adj* effrayé(e); **to be** ~ **of** *or* **to** avoir peur de; **I am** ~ **that** ... je suis désolé(e), mais ...; **I am** ~ **so/not** hélas oui/non

afresh [ə'freʃ] *adv* de nouveau

Africa ['æfrɪkə] *n* Afrique *f*; ~**n** *adj* africain(e) ♦ *n* Africain(e)

aft [ɑ:ft] *adv* à l'arrière, vers l'arrière

after ['ɑ:ftə*] *prep*, *adv* après ♦ *conj* après que, après avoir *or* être +*pp*; **what/who are you** ~? que/qui cherchez-vous?; ~ **he left/having done** après qu'il fut parti/après avoir fait; **ask** ~ **him** demander de ses nouvelles; **to name sb** ~ **sb** donner le nom de qn; **twenty** ~ **eight** (*US*) huit heures vingt; ~ **all** après tout; ~ **you!** après vous, Monsieur (*or* Madame *etc*); ~**effects** *npl* (*of disaster, radiation, drink etc*) répercussions *fpl*; (*of illness*) séquelles *fpl*, suites *fpl*; ~**math** *n* conséquences *fpl*, suites *fpl*; ~**noon** *n* après-midi *m or f*; ~**s** (*inf*) *n* (*dessert*) dessert *m*; ~**sales service** (*BRIT*) *n* (*for car, washing machine etc*) service *m* après-vente; ~**-shave (lotion)** *n* after-shave *m*; ~**thought** *n*: **I had an** ~**thought** il m'est venu une idée après coup; ~**wards** (*US* ~**ward**) *adv* après

again [ə'gen] *adv* de nouveau; encore (une fois); **to do sth** ~ refaire qch; **not** ... ~ ne ... plus; ~ **and** ~ à plusieurs reprises

against [ə'genst] *prep* contre; (*compared to*) par rapport à

age [eɪdʒ] *n* âge *m* ♦ *vt*, *vi* vieillir; **it's been** ~**s since** ça fait une éternité que ... ne; **he is 20 years of** ~ il a 20 ans; **to come of** ~ atteindre sa majorité; ~**d**[1] *adj*: ~**d 10** âgé(e) de 10 ans; ~**d**[2] ['eɪdʒɪd] *npl*: **the** ~**d** les personnes âgées; ~ **group** *n* tranche *f* d'âge; ~ **limit** *n* limite *f* d'âge

agency ['eɪdʒənsɪ] *n* agence *f*; (*government body*) organisme *m*, office *m*

agenda [ə'dʒendə] *n* ordre *m* du jour

agent ['eɪdʒənt] *n* agent *m*, représentant *m*; (*firm*) concessionnaire *m*

aggravate ['ægrəveɪt] *vt* aggraver; (*annoy*)

exaspérer

aggregate ['ægrɪgɪt] *n* ensemble *m*, total *m*

aggressive [ə'gresɪv] *adj* agressif(ive)

aggrieved [ə'griːvd] *adj* chagriné(e), affligé(e)

aghast [ə'gɑːst] *adj* consterné(e), atterré(e)

agitate ['ædʒɪteɪt] *vt* (*person*) agiter, émouvoir, troubler ♦ *vi*: **to ~ for/against** faire campagne pour/contre

AGM *n abbr* (= *annual general meeting*) AG *f*, assemblée générale

ago [ə'gəʊ] *adv*: **2 days ~** il y a deux jours; **not long ~** il n'y a pas longtemps; **how long ~?** il y a combien de temps (de cela)?

agog [ə'gɒg] *adj* en émoi

agonizing ['ægənaɪzɪŋ] *adj* angoissant(e); déchirant(e)

agony ['ægənɪ] *n* (*pain*) douleur *f* atroce; **to be in ~** souffrir le martyre

agree [ə'griː] *vt* (*price*) convenir de ♦ *vi*: **to ~ with** (*person*) être d'accord avec; (*statements etc*) concorder avec; (*LING*) s'accorder avec; **to ~ to do** accepter de *or* consentir à faire; **to ~ to sth** consentir à qch; **to ~ that** (*admit*) convenir *or* reconnaître que; **garlic doesn't ~ with me** je ne supporte pas l'ail; **~able** *adj* agréable; (*willing*) consentant(e), d'accord; **~d** *adj* (*time, place*) convenu(e); **~ment** *n* accord *m*; **in ~ment** d'accord

agricultural [ægrɪ'kʌltʃərəl] *adj* agricole

agriculture ['ægrɪkʌltʃə*] *n* agriculture *f*

aground [ə'graʊnd] *adv*: **to run ~** échouer, s'échouer

ahead [ə'hed] *adv* (*in front: of position, place*) devant; (: *at the head*) en avant; (*look, plan, think*) en avant; **~ of** devant; (*fig: schedule etc*) en avance sur; **~ of time** en avance; **go right** *or* **straight ~** allez tout droit; **go ~!** (*fig: permission*) allez-y!

aid [eɪd] *n* aide *f*; (*device*) appareil *m* ♦ *vt* aider; **in ~ of** en faveur de; **to ~ and abet** (*LAW*) se faire le complice de; *see also* **hearing**

aide [eɪd] *n* (*person*) aide *mf*, assistant(e)

AIDS [eɪdz] *n abbr* (= *acquired immune deficiency syndrome*) SIDA *m*

ailing ['eɪlɪŋ] *adj* malade

ailment ['eɪlmənt] *n* affection *f*

aim [eɪm] *vt*: **to ~ sth (at)** (*gun, camera*) braquer *or* pointer qch (sur); (*missile*) lancer qch (à *or* contre *or* en direction de); (*blow*) allonger qch (à); (*remark*) destiner *or* adresser qch (à) ♦ *vi* (*also: to take ~*) viser ♦ *n* but *m*; (*skill*): **his ~ is bad** il vise mal; **to ~ at** viser; (*fig*) viser (à); **to ~ to do** avoir l'intention de faire; **~less** *adj* sans but

ain't [eɪnt] (*inf*) = **am not; aren't; isn't**

air [ɛə*] *n* air *m* ♦ *vt* (*room, bed, clothes*) aérer; (*grievances, views, ideas*) exposer, faire connaître ♦ *cpd* (*currents, attack etc*) aérien(ne); **to throw sth into the ~** jeter qch en l'air; **by ~** (*travel*) par avion; **to be on the ~** (*RADIO, TV: programme*) être diffusé(e); (: *station*) diffuser; **~bed** *n* matelas *m* pneumatique; **~borne** *adj* en vol; **~-conditioned** *adj* climatisé(e); **~ conditioning** *n* climatisation *f*; **~craft** *n inv* avion *m*; **~craft carrier** *n* porte-avions *m inv*; **~field** *n* terrain *m* d'aviation; **A~ Force** *n* armée *f* de l'air; **~ freshener** *n* désodorisant *m*; **~gun** *n* fusil *m* à air comprimé; **~ hostess** *n* (*BRIT*) hôtesse *f* de l'air; **~ letter** *n* (*BRIT*) aérogramme *m*; **~lift** *n* pont aérien; **~line** *n* ligne aérienne, compagnie *f* d'aviation; **~liner** *n* avion *m* de ligne; **~mail** *n*: **by ~mail** par avion; **~plane** *n* (*US*) avion *m*; **~port** *n* aéroport *m*; **~ raid** *n* attaque *or* raid aérien(ne); **~sick** *adj*: **to be ~sick** avoir le mal de l'air; **air space** espace aérien; **~ terminal** *n* aérogare *f*; **~tight** *adj* hermétique; **~-traffic controller** *n* aiguilleur *m* du ciel; **~y** *adj* bien aéré(e); (*manners*) dégagé(e)

aisle [aɪl] *n* (*of church*) allée centrale; nef latérale; (*of theatre etc*) couloir *m*, passage *m*, allée

ajar [ə'dʒɑː*] *adj* entrouvert(e)

akin [ə'kɪn] *adj*: **~ to** (*similar*) qui tient de *or* ressemble à

alarm [ə'lɑːm] *n* alarme *f* ♦ *vt* alarmer; **~ call** *n* coup de fil *m* pour réveiller; **~ clock** *n* réveille-matin *m inv*, réveil *m*

alas [ə'læs] *excl* hélas!

albeit [ɔːl'biːɪt] *conj* (*although*) bien que +*sub*, encore que +*sub*

album ['ælbəm] *n* album *m*

alcohol ['ælkəhɒl] *n* alcool *m*; **~ic** [ælkə'hɒlɪk] *adj* alcoolique ♦ *n* alcoolique *m/f*; **A~ics Anonymous** Alcooliques anonymes

ale [eɪl] *n* bière *f*

alert [ə'lɜːt] *adj* alerte, vif(vive); vigilant(e) ♦ *n* alerte *f* ♦ *vt* alerter; **on the ~** sur le qui-vive; (*MIL*) en état d'alerte

algebra ['ældʒɪbrə] *n* algèbre *m*

Algeria [æl'dʒɪərɪə] *n* Algérie *f*

alias ['eɪlɪəs] *adv* alias ♦ *n* faux nom, nom d'emprunt; (*writer*) pseudonyme *m*

alibi ['ælɪbaɪ] *n* alibi *m*

alien ['eɪlɪən] *n* étranger(ère); (*from outer space*) extraterrestre *mf* ♦ *adj*: **~ (to)** étranger(ère) (à); **~ate** *vt* aliéner; s'aliéner

alight [ə'laɪt] *adj, adv* en feu ♦ *vi* mettre pied à terre; (*passenger*) descendre; (*bird*) se poser

alike [ə'laɪk] *adj* semblable, pareil(le) ♦ *adv* de même; **to look ~** se ressembler

alimony ['ælɪmənɪ] *n* (*payment*) pension *f* alimentaire

alive [ə'laɪv] *adj* vivant(e); (*lively*) plein(e) de vie

─────── KEYWORD ───────

all [ɔːl] *adj* (*singular*) tout(e); (*plural*) tous(toutes); ~ **day** toute la journée; ~ **night** toute la nuit; ~ **men** tous les hommes; ~ **five** tous les cinq; ~ **the food** toute la nourriture; ~ **the books** tous les livres; ~ **the time** tout le temps; ~ **his life** toute sa vie

♦ *pron 1* tout; **I ate it** ~, **I ate** ~ **of it** j'ai tout mangé; ~ **of us went** nous y sommes tous allés; ~ **of the boys went** tous les garçons y sont allés

2 (*in phrases*): **above** ~ surtout, par-dessus tout; **after** ~ après tout; **at** ~: **not at** ~ (*in answer to question*) pas du tout; (*in answer to thanks*) je vous en prie!; **I'm not at** ~ **tired** je ne suis pas du tout fatigué(e); **anything at** ~ **will do** n'importe quoi fera l'affaire; ~ **in** ~ tout bien considéré, en fin de compte

♦ *adv*: ~ **alone** tout(e) seul(e); **it's not as hard as** ~ **that** ce n'est pas si difficile que ça; ~ **the more/the better** d'autant plus/mieux; ~ **but** presque, pratiquement; **the score is 2** ~ le score est de 2 partout

───────────────────────

allay [əˈleɪ] *vt* (*fears*) apaiser, calmer

allege [əˈledʒ] *vt* alléguer, prétendre; ~**dly** [əˈledʒɪdlɪ] *adv* à ce que l'on prétend, paraît-il

allegiance [əˈliːdʒəns] *n* allégeance *f*, fidélité *f*, obéissance *f*

allergic [əˈlɜːdʒɪk] *adj*: ~ **to** allergique à; **allergy** [ˈælədʒɪ] *n* allergie *f*

alleviate [əˈliːvɪeɪt] *vt* soulager, adoucir

alley [ˈælɪ] *n* ruelle *f*

alliance [əˈlaɪəns] *n* alliance *f*

allied [ˈælaɪd] *adj* allié(e)

all-in [ˈɔːlɪn] (*BRIT*) *adj* (*also adv*: *charge*) tout compris; ~ **wrestling** *n* lutte *f* libre

all-night [ˈɔːlˈnaɪt] *adj* ouvert(e) *or* qui dure toute la nuit

allocate [ˈæləkeɪt] *vt* (*share out*) répartir, distribuer; (*duties*): **to** ~ **sth to** assigner *or* attribuer qch à; (*sum, time*): **to** ~ **sth to** allouer qch à

allot [əˈlɒt] *vt*: **to** ~ **(to)** (*money*) répartir (entre), distribuer (à); (*time*) allouer (à); ~**ment** *n* (*share*) part *f*; (*garden*) lopin *m* de terre (*loué à la municipalité*)

all-out [ˈɔːlˈaut] *adj* (*effort etc*) total(e) ♦ *adv*: **all out** à fond

allow [əˈlau] *vt* (*practice, behaviour*) permettre, autoriser; (*sum to spend etc*) accorder; allouer; (*sum, time estimated*) compter, prévoir; (*claim, goal*) admettre; (*concede*): **to** ~ **that** convenir que; **to** ~ **sb to do** permettre à qn de faire, autoriser qn à faire; **he is** ~**ed to** ... on lui permet de ...; ~ **for** *vt fus* tenir compte de; ~**ance** *n* (*money received*) allocation *f*; subside *m*; indemnité *f*;

(*TAX*) somme *f* déductible du revenu imposable, abattement *m*; **to make** ~**ances for** tenir compte de

alloy [ˈælɔɪ] *n* alliage *m*

all: ~ **right** *adv* (*feel, work*) bien; (*as answer*) d'accord; ~**-rounder** *n*: **to be a good** ~**-rounder** être doué(e) en tout; ~**-time** *adj* (*record*) sans précédent, absolu(e)

allude [əˈluːd] *vi*: **to** ~ **to** faire allusion à

alluring [əˈljuərɪŋ] *adj* séduisant(e)

ally [*n* ˈælaɪ, *vb* əˈlaɪ] *n* allié *m* ♦ *vt*: **to** ~ **o.s. with** s'allier avec

almighty [ɔːlˈmaɪtɪ] *adj* tout-puissant; (*tremendous*) énorme

almond [ˈɑːmənd] *n* amande *f*

almost [ˈɔːlməust] *adv* presque

alms [ɑːmz] *npl* aumône *f*

aloft [əˈlɒft] *adv* en l'air

alone [əˈləun] *adj, adv* seul(e); **to leave sb** ~ laisser qn tranquille; **to leave sth** ~ ne pas toucher à qch; **let** ~ ... sans parler de ...; encore moins ...

along [əˈlɒŋ] *prep* le long de ♦ *adv*: **is he coming** ~ **with us?** vient-il avec nous?; **he was hopping/limping** ~ il avançait en sautillant/boitant; ~ **with** (*together with: person*) en compagnie de; (: *thing*) avec, en plus de; **all** ~ (*all the time*) depuis le début; ~**side** *prep* le long de; à côté de ♦ *adv* bord à bord

aloof [əˈluːf] *adj* distant(e) ♦ *adv*: **to stand** ~ se tenir à distance *or* à l'écart

aloud [əˈlaud] *adv* à haute voix

alphabet [ˈælfəbet] *n* alphabet *m*; ~**ical** [ælfəˈbetɪkl] *adj* alphabétique

alpine [ˈælpaɪn] *adj* alpin(e), alpestre

Alps [ælps] *npl*: **the** ~ les Alpes *fpl*

already [ɔːlˈredɪ] *adv* déjà

alright [ɔːlˈraɪt] (*BRIT*) *adv* = **all right**

Alsatian [ælˈseɪʃən] (*BRIT*) *n* (*dog*) berger allemand

also [ˈɔːlsəu] *adv* aussi

altar [ˈɔːltə*] *n* autel *m*

alter [ˈɔːltə*] *vt, vi* changer

alternate [*adj* ɒlˈtɜːnɪt, *vb* ˈɒltɜːneɪt] *adj* alterné(e), alternant(e), alternatif(ive) ♦ *vi* alterner; **on** ~ **days** un jour sur deux, tous les deux jours; **alternating current** *n* courant alternatif

alternative [ɒlˈtɜːnətɪv] *adj* (*solutions*) possible, au choix; (*plan*) autre, de rechange; (*lifestyle, medicine*) parallèle ♦ *n* (*choice*) alternative *f*; (*other possibility*) solution *f* de remplacement *or* de rechange, autre possibilité *f*; **an** ~ **comedian** un nouveau comique; ~**ly** *adv*: ~**ly one could** une autre *or* l'autre solution serait de, on pourrait aussi

alternator [ˈɒltɜːneɪtə*] *n* (*AUT*) alternateur *m*

although [ɔːlˈðəu] *conj* bien que +*sub*

altitude [ˈæltɪtjuːd] *n* altitude *f*

alto [ˈæltəu] *n* (*female*) contralto *m*; (*male*)

haute-contre *f*

altogether [ɔːltəˈgeðə*] *adv* entièrement, tout à fait; *(on the whole)* tout compte fait; *(in all)* en tout

aluminium [æljʊˈmɪnɪəm] *(BRIT)*, **aluminum** [əˈluːmɪnəm] *(US)* n aluminium *m*

always [ˈɔːlweɪz] *adv* toujours

Alzheimer's (disease) [ælts'haɪməz] *n* maladie *f* d'Alzheimer

am [æm] *vb see* be

a.m. *adv abbr* (= *ante meridiem*) du matin

amalgamate [əˈmælgəmeɪt] *vt, vi* fusionner

amateur [ˈæmətɜ:*] *n* amateur *m*; **~ish** *(pej)* adj d'amateur

amaze [əˈmeɪz] *vt* stupéfier; **to be ~d (at)** être stupéfait(e) (de); **~ment** *n* stupéfaction *f*, stupeur *f*; **amazing** [əˈmeɪzɪŋ] *adj* étonnant(e); exceptionnel(le)

ambassador [æmˈbæsədə*] *n* ambassadeur *m*

amber [ˈæmbə*] *n* ambre *m*; **at ~** *(BRIT: AUT)* à l'orange

ambiguous [æmˈbɪgjuəs] *adj* ambigu(ë)

ambition [æmˈbɪʃən] *n* ambition *f*

ambitious [æmˈbɪʃəs] *adj* ambitieux(euse)

amble [ˈæmbl] *vi (also: to ~ along)* aller d'un pas tranquille

ambulance [ˈæmbjʊləns] *n* ambulance *f*

ambush [ˈæmbʊʃ] *n* embuscade *f* ♦ *vt* tendre une embuscade à

amenable [əˈmiːnəbl] *adj*: **~ to** *(advice etc)* disposé(e) à écouter

amend [əˈmend] *vt (law)* amender; *(text)* corriger; **to make ~s** réparer ses torts, faire amende honorable

amenities [əˈmiːnɪtɪz] *npl* aménagements *mpl*, équipements *mpl*

America [əˈmerɪkə] *n* Amérique *f*; **~n** *adj* américain(e) ♦ *n* Américain(e)

amiable [ˈeɪmɪəbl] *adj* aimable, affable

amicable [ˈæmɪkəbl] *adj* amical(e); *(JUR)* à l'amiable

amid(st) [əˈmɪd(st)] *prep* parmi, au milieu de

amiss [əˈmɪs] *adj, adv*: **there's something ~** il y a quelque chose qui ne va pas *or* qui cloche; **to take sth ~** prendre qch mal *or* de travers

ammonia [əˈməʊnɪə] *n (gas)* ammoniac *m*; *(liquid)* ammoniaque *f*

ammunition [æmjʊˈnɪʃən] *n* munitions *fpl*

amok [əˈmɔk] *adv*: **to run ~** être pris(e) d'un accès de folie furieuse

among(st) [əˈmʌŋ(st)] *prep* parmi, entre

amorous [ˈæmərəs] *adj* amoureux(euse)

amount [əˈmaʊnt] *n (sum)* somme *f*, montant *m*; *(quantity)* quantité *f*, nombre *m* ♦ *vi*: **to ~ to** *(total)* s'élever à; *(be same as)* équivaloir à, revenir à

amp(ere) [ˈæmp(ɛə*)] *n* ampère *m*

ample [ˈæmpl] *adj* ample; spacieux(euse); *(enough)*: **this is ~** c'est largement suffi-

sant; **to have ~ time/room** avoir bien assez de temps/place

amplifier [ˈæmplɪfaɪə*] *n* amplificateur *m*

amuse [əˈmjuːz] *vt* amuser, divertir; **~ment** *n* amusement *m*; **~ment arcade** *n* salle *f* de jeu

an [æn] *indef art see* a

anaemic [əˈniːmɪk] *(US* **anemic***)* adj anémique

anaesthetic [ænɪsˈθetɪk] *n* anesthésique *m*

analog(ue) [ˈænəlɔg] *adj (watch, computer)* analogique

analyse [ˈænəlaɪz] *(US* **analyze***)* vt analyser; **analysis** [əˈnælɪsɪs] *(pl* **analyses***)* n analyse *f*; **analyst** [ˈænəlɪst] *n (POL etc)* spécialiste *m/f*; *(US)* psychanalyste *m/f*

analyze [ˈænəlaɪz] *(US)* vt = **analyse**

anarchist [ˈænəkɪst] *n* anarchiste *m/f*

anarchy [ˈænəkɪ] *n* anarchie *f*

anatomy [əˈnætəmɪ] *n* anatomie *f*

ancestor [ˈænsestə*] *n* ancêtre *m*, aïeul *m*

anchor [ˈæŋkə*] *n* ancre *f* ♦ *vi (also: to drop ~)* jeter l'ancre, mouiller ♦ *vt* mettre à l'ancre; *(fig)*: **to ~ sth to** fixer qch à; **to weigh ~** lever l'ancre

anchovy [ˈæntʃəvɪ] *n* anchois *m*

ancient [ˈeɪnʃənt] *adj* ancien(ne), antique; *(person)* d'un âge vénérable; *(car)* antédiluvien(ne)

ancillary [ænˈsɪlərɪ] *adj* auxiliaire

and [ænd] *conj* et; **~ so on** et ainsi de suite; **try ~ come** tâchez de venir; **he talked ~ talked** il n'a pas arrêté de parler; **better ~ better** de mieux en mieux

anew [əˈnjuː] *adv* à nouveau

angel [ˈeɪndʒəl] *n* ange *m*

anger [ˈæŋgə*] *n* colère *f*

angina [ænˈdʒaɪnə] *n* angine *f* de poitrine

angle [ˈæŋgl] *n* angle *m*; **from their ~** de leur point de vue

angler [ˈæŋglə*] *n* pêcheur(euse) à la ligne

Anglican [ˈæŋglɪkən] *adj, n* anglican(e)

angling [ˈæŋglɪŋ] *n* pêche *f* à la ligne

angrily [ˈæŋgrɪlɪ] *adv* avec colère

angry [ˈæŋgrɪ] *adj* en colère, furieux(euse); *(wound)* enflammé(e); **to be ~ with sb/at sth** être furieux contre qn/de qch; **to get ~** se fâcher, se mettre en colère

anguish [ˈæŋgwɪʃ] *n (physical)* supplice *m*; *(mental)* angoisse *f*

angular [ˈæŋgjʊlə*] *adj* anguleux(euse)

animal [ˈænɪməl] *n* animal *m* ♦ *adj* animal(e)

animate [*vb* ˈænɪmeɪt, *adj* ˈænɪmət] *vt* animer ♦ *adj* animé(e), vivant(e); **~d** *adj* animé(e)

aniseed [ˈænɪsiːd] *n* anis *m*

ankle [ˈæŋkl] *n* cheville *f*; **~ sock** *n* socquette *f*

annex [*n* ˈæneks, *vb* əˈneks] *n (also: BRIT: ~e)* annexe *f* ♦ *vt* annexer

anniversary [ænɪˈvɜːsərɪ] *n* anniversaire *m*

announce [ə'naʊns] *vt* annoncer; *(birth, death)* faire part de; **~ment** *n* annonce *f*; *(for births etc: in newspaper)* avis *m* de faire-part; (: *letter, card)* faire-part *m*; **~r** *n* (RADIO, TV: *between programmes)* speaker(ine)

annoy [ə'nɔɪ] *vt* agacer, ennuyer, contrarier; **don't get ~ed!** ne vous fâchez pas!; **~ance** *n* mécontentement *m*, contrariété *f*; **~ing** *adj* agaçant(e), contrariant(e)

annual ['ænjʊəl] *adj* annuel(le) ♦ *n* (BOT) plante annuelle; *(children's book)* album *m*

annul [ə'nʌl] *vt* annuler

annum ['ænəm] *n see* per

anonymous [ə'nɒnɪməs] *adj* anonyme

anorak ['ænəræk] *n* anorak *m*

another [ə'nʌðə*] *adj:* **~ book** *(one more)* un autre livre, encore un livre, un livre de plus; *(a different one)* un autre livre ♦ *pron* un(e) autre, encore un(e), un(e) de plus; *see also* **one**

answer ['ɑːnsə*] *n* réponse *f*; *(to problem)* solution *f* ♦ *vi* répondre ♦ *vt* (reply to) répondre à; *(problem)* résoudre; *(prayer)* exaucer; **in ~ to your letter** en réponse à votre lettre; **to ~ the phone** répondre (au téléphone); **to ~ the bell** *or* **the door** aller *or* venir ouvrir (la porte); **~ back** *vi* répondre, répliquer; **~ for** *vt fus* (person) répondre de, se porter garant de; *(crime, one's actions)* être responsable de; **~ to** *vt fus* (description) répondre *or* correspondre à; **~able** *adj:* **~able (to sb/for sth)** responsable (devant qn/de qch); **~ing machine** *n* répondeur *m* automatique

ant [ænt] *n* fourmi *f*

antagonism [æn'tægənɪzəm] *n* antagonisme *m*

antagonize [æn'tægənaɪz] *vt* éveiller l'hostilité de, contrarier

Antarctic [ænt'ɑːktɪk] *n:* **the ~** l'Antarctique *m*

antenatal [æntɪ'neɪtl] *adj* prénatal(e); **~ clinic** *n* service *m* de consultation prénatale

anthem ['ænθəm] *n:* **national ~** hymne national

anti: **~-aircraft** [æntɪ'ɛəkrɑːft] *adj* (missile) anti-aérien(ne); **~biotic** ['æntɪbaɪ'ɒtɪk] *n* antibiotique *m*; **~body** ['æntɪbɒdɪ] *n* anticorps *m*

anticipate [æn'tɪsɪpeɪt] *vt* s'attendre à; prévoir; *(wishes, request)* aller au devant de, devancer

anticipation [æntɪsɪ'peɪʃən] *n* attente *f*; **with ~** impatiemment

anticlimax ['æntɪ'klaɪmæks] *n* déception *f*, douche froide *(col)*

anticlockwise ['æntɪ'klɒkwaɪz] *adj, adv* dans le sens inverse des aiguilles d'une montre

antics ['æntɪks] *npl* singeries *fpl*

antifreeze ['æntɪfriːz] *n* antigel *m*

antihistamine [æntɪ'hɪstəmiːn] *n* antihistaminique *m*

antiquated ['æntɪkweɪtɪd] *adj* vieilli(e), suranné(e), vieillot(te)

antique [æn'tiːk] *n* objet *m* d'art ancien, meuble ancien *or* d'époque, antiquité *f* ♦ *adj* ancien(ne); **~ dealer** *n* antiquaire *m*; **~ shop** *n* magasin *m* d'antiquités

anti: **~-Semitism** [æntɪ'semɪtɪzəm] *n* antisémitisme *m*; **~septic** [æntɪ'septɪk] *n* antiseptique *m*; **~social** [æntɪ'səʊʃl] *adj* peu liant(e), sauvage, insociable; *(against society)* antisocial(e)

antlers ['æntləz] *npl* bois *mpl*, ramure *f*

anvil ['ænvɪl] *n* enclume *f*

anxiety [æŋ'zaɪətɪ] *n* anxiété *f*; *(keenness):* **~ to do** grand désir *or* impatience *f* de faire

anxious ['æŋkʃəs] *adj* anxieux(euse), angoissé(e); *(worrying: time, situation)* inquiétant(e); *(keen):* **~ to do/that** qui tient beaucoup à faire/à ce que; impatient(e) de faire/que

KEYWORD

any ['enɪ] *adj* **1** *(in questions etc: singular)* du, de l', de la; *(in questions etc: plural)* des; **have you ~ butter/children/ink?** avez-vous du beurre/des enfants/de l'encre?

2 *(with negative)* de, d'; **I haven't ~ money/books** je n'ai pas d'argent/de livres

3 *(no matter which)* n'importe quel(le); **choose ~ book you like** vous pouvez choisir n'importe quel livre

4 *(in phrases):* **in ~ case** de toute façon; **~ day now** d'un jour à l'autre; **at ~ moment** à tout moment, d'un instant à l'autre; **at ~ rate** en tout cas

♦ *pron* **1** *(in questions etc)* en; **have you got ~?** est-ce que vous en avez?; **can ~ of you sing?** est-ce que parmi vous il y en a qui chantent?

2 *(with negative)* en; **I haven't ~ (of them)** je n'en ai pas, je n'en ai aucun

3 *(no matter which one(s))* n'importe lequel *(or* laquelle); **take ~ of those books (you like)** vous pouvez prendre n'importe lequel de ces livres

♦ *adv* **1** *(in questions etc):* **do you want ~ more soup/sandwiches?** voulez-vous encore de la soupe/des sandwichs?; **are you feeling ~ better?** est-ce que vous vous sentez mieux?

2 *(with negative):* **I can't hear him ~ more** je ne l'entends plus; **don't wait ~ longer** n'attendez pas plus longtemps

any: **~body** ['enɪbɒdɪ] *pron* n'importe qui; *(in interrogative sentences)* quelqu'un; *(in negative sentences):* **I don't see ~** je ne vois personne; **~how** adv (at any rate) de toute façon, quand même; (haphazard) n'importe comment; **~one** [-wʌn] pron = **anybody**; **~thing** pron n'importe quoi, quelque chose, ne ... rien; **~way** adv de toute façon; **~where** adv n'importe où, quelque part; **I don't see him** ~ je ne le vois nulle part

apart [ə'pɑːt] adv (to one side) à part; de côté; à l'écart; (separately) séparément; **10 miles** ~ à 10 miles l'un de l'autre; **to take** ~ démonter; **~ from** à part, excepté

apartheid [ə'pɑːteɪt] n apartheid m

apartment [ə'pɑːtmənt] n (US) appartement m, logement m; (room) chambre f; **~ building** (US) n immeuble m; maison divisée en appartements

ape [eɪp] n (grand) singe ♦ vt singer

apéritif [ə'pɛrɪtiːf] n apéritif m

aperture ['æpətjuə*] n orifice m, ouverture f; (PHOT) ouverture (du diaphragme)

apex ['eɪpeks] n sommet m

apiece [ə'piːs] adv chacun(e)

apologetic [əpɒlə'dʒetɪk] adj (tone, letter) d'excuse; (person): **to be** ~ s'excuser

apologize [ə'pɒlədʒaɪz] vi: **to** ~ **(for sth to sb)** s'excuser (de qch auprès de qn), présenter des excuses (à qn pour qch)

apology [ə'pɒlədʒɪ] n excuses fpl

apostrophe [ə'pɒstrəfɪ] n apostrophe f

appal [ə'pɔːl] vt consterner; **~ling** [ə'pɔːlɪŋ] adj épouvantable; (stupidity) consternant(e)

apparatus [æpə'reɪtəs] n appareil m, dispositif m; (in gymnasium) agrès mpl; (of government) dispositif m

apparel [ə'pærəl] (US) n habillement m

apparent [ə'pærənt] adj apparent(e); **~ly** adv apparemment

appeal [ə'piːl] vi (LAW) faire or interjeter appel ♦ n appel m; (request) prière f; appel m; (charm) attrait m, charme m; **to** ~ **for** lancer un appel pour; **to** ~ **to** (beg) faire appel à; (be attractive) plaire à; **it doesn't** ~ **to me** cela ne m'attire pas; **~ing** adj (attractive) attrayant(e)

appear [ə'pɪə*] vi apparaître, se montrer; (LAW) comparaître; (publication) paraître, sortir, être publié(e); (seem) paraître, sembler; **it would** ~ **that** il semble que; **to** ~ **in Hamlet** jouer dans Hamlet; **to** ~ **on TV** passer à la télé; **~ance** n apparition f, parution f; (look, aspect) apparence f, aspect m

appease [ə'piːz] vt apaiser, calmer

appendicitis [əpendɪ'saɪtɪs] n appendicite f; **appendix** [ə'pendɪks] (pl **appendices**) n appendice m

appetite ['æpɪtaɪt] n appétit m

appetizer ['æpətaɪzə*] n amuse-gueule m; (drink) apéritif m

applaud [ə'plɔːd] vt, vi applaudir

applause [ə'plɔːz] n applaudissements mpl

apple ['æpl] n pomme f; ~ **tree** n pommier m

appliance [ə'plaɪəns] n appareil m

applicable [ə'plɪkəbl] adj (relevant): **to be** ~ **to** valoir pour

applicant ['æplɪkənt] n: ~ **(for)** candidat(e) (à)

application [æplɪ'keɪʃən] n application f; (for a job, grant etc) demande f; candidature f; ~ **form** n formulaire m de demande

applied [ə'plaɪd] adj appliqué(e)

apply [ə'plaɪ] vt (paint, ointment): **to** ~ **(to)** appliquer (sur); (law etc): **to** ~ **(to)** appliquer (à) ♦ vi: **to** ~ **to** (be suitable for, relevant to) s'appliquer à; (ask) s'adresser à; **to** ~ **(for)** (permit, grant) faire une demande (en vue d'obtenir); (job) poser sa candidature (pour), faire une demande d'emploi (concernant); **to** ~ **o.s. to** s'appliquer à

appoint [ə'pɔɪnt] vt nommer, engager; **~ed** adj: **at the ~ed time** à l'heure dite; **~ment** n nomination f; (meeting) rendez-vous m; **to make an ~ment (with)** prendre rendez-vous (avec)

appraisal [ə'preɪzl] n évaluation f

appreciate [ə'priːʃɪeɪt] vt (like) apprécier; (be grateful for) être reconnaissant(e) de; (understand) comprendre; se rendre compte de ♦ vi (FINANCE) prendre de la valeur

appreciation [əpriːʃɪ'eɪʃən] n appréciation f; (gratitude) reconnaissance f; (COMM) hausse f, valorisation f

appreciative [ə'priːʃɪətɪv] adj (person) sensible; (comment) élogieux(euse)

apprehensive [æprɪ'hensɪv] adj inquiet(ète), appréhensif(ive)

apprentice [ə'prentɪs] n apprenti m; **~ship** n apprentissage m

approach [ə'prəʊtʃ] vi approcher ♦ vt (come near) approcher de; (ask, apply to) s'adresser à; (situation, problem) aborder ♦ n approche f; (access) accès m; **~able** adj accessible

appropriate [adj ə'prəʊprɪət, vb ə'prəʊprɪeɪt] adj (moment, remark) opportun(e); (tool etc) approprié(e) ♦ vt (take) s'approprier

approval [ə'pruːvəl] n approbation f; **on** ~ (COMM) à l'examen

approve [ə'pruːv] vt approuver; ~ **of** vt fus approuver

approximate [adj ə'prɒksɪmɪt, vb ə'prɒksɪmeɪt] adj approximatif(ive) ♦ vt se rapprocher de, être proche de; **~ly** adv approximativement

apricot ['eɪprɪkɒt] n abricot m

April ['eɪprəl] n avril m; ~ **Fool's Day** le premier avril

apron ['eɪprən] n tablier m

apt [æpt] adj (suitable) approprié(e); (likely): ~ **to do** susceptible de faire; qui a tendance à faire

Aquarius [ə'kwɛərɪəs] *n* le Verseau
Arab ['ærəb] *adj* arabe ♦ *n* Arabe *m/f*; **~ian** [ə'reɪbɪən] *adj* arabe; **~ic** ['ærəbɪk] *adj* arabe ♦ *n* arabe *m*
arbitrary ['ɑːbɪtrərɪ] *adj* arbitraire
arbitration [ɑːbɪ'treɪʃən] *n* arbitrage *m*
arcade [ɑː'keɪd] *n* arcade *f*; (*passage with shops*) passage *m*, galerie marchande
arch [ɑːtʃ] *n* arc *m*; (*of foot*) cambrure *f*, voûte *f* plantaire ♦ *vt* arquer, cambrer
archaeologist [ɑːkɪ'ɒlədʒɪst] *n* archéologue *m/f*; **archaeology** [ɑːkɪ'ɒlədʒɪ] *n* archéologie *f*
archbishop ['ɑːtʃ'bɪʃəp] *n* archevêque *m*
archenemy ['ɑːtʃ'enɪmɪ] *n* ennemi *m* de toujours *or* juré
archeology *etc* (*US*) = **archaeology** *etc*
archery [ɑːtʃərɪ] *n* tir *m* à l'arc
architect ['ɑːkɪtekt] *n* architecte *m*; **~ure** *n* architecture *f*
archives ['ɑːkaɪvz] *npl* archives *fpl*
Arctic ['ɑːktɪk] *adj* arctique ♦ *n*: **the ~** l'Arctique *m*
ardent ['ɑːdənt] *adj* fervent(e)
are [ɑː*] *vb see* **be**
area ['ɛərɪə] *n* (GEOM) superficie *f*, (*zone*) région *f*; (: *smaller*) secteur *m*, partie *f*; (*in room*) coin *m*; (*knowledge, research*) domaine *m*
aren't [ɑːnt] = **are not**
Argentina [ɑːdʒən'tiːnə] *n* Argentine *f*; **Argentinian** [ɑːdʒən'tɪnɪən] *adj* argentin(e) ♦ *n* Argentin(e)
arguably ['ɑːgjʊəblɪ] *adv*: **it is ~ ...** on peut soutenir que c'est ...
argue ['ɑːgjuː] *vi* (*quarrel*) se disputer; (*reason*) argumenter; **to ~ that** objecter *or* alléguer que
argument ['ɑːgjʊmənt] *n* (*reasons*) argument *m*; (*quarrel*) dispute *f*; **~ative** [ɑːgjʊ'mentətɪv] *adj* ergoteur(euse), raisonneur(euse)
Aries ['ɛəriːz] *n* le Bélier
arise [ə'raɪz] (*pt* **arose**, *pp* **arisen**) *vi* survenir, se présenter
aristocrat ['ærɪstəkræt] *n* aristocrate *m/f*
arithmetic [ə'rɪθmətɪk] *n* arithmétique *f*
ark [ɑːk] *n*: **Noah's A~** l'Arche *f* de Noé
arm [ɑːm] *n* bras *m* ♦ *vt* armer; **~s** *npl* (*weapons, HERALDRY*) armes *fpl*; **~ in ~** bras dessus bras dessous
armaments ['ɑːməmənts] *npl* armement *m*
arm: **~chair** *n* fauteuil *m*; **~ed** *adj* armé(e); **~ed robbery** *n* vol *m* à main armée
armour ['ɑːmə*] (*US* **armor**) *n* armure *f*; (*MIL: tanks*) blindés *mpl*; **~ed car** *n* véhicule blindé
armpit ['ɑːmpɪt] *n* aisselle *f*
armrest ['ɑːmrest] *n* accoudoir *m*
army ['ɑːmɪ] *n* armée *f*
aroma [ə'rəʊmə] *n* arôme *m*

arose [ə'rəʊz] *pt of* **arise**
around [ə'raʊnd] *adv* autour; (*nearby*) dans les parages ♦ *prep* autour de; (*near*) près de; (*fig: about*) environ; (: *date, time*) vers
arouse [ə'raʊz] *vt* (*sleeper*) éveiller; (*curiosity, passions*) éveiller, susciter; (*anger*) exciter
arrange [ə'reɪndʒ] *vt* arranger; **to ~ to do sth** prévoir de faire qch; **~ment** *n* arrangement *m*; **~ments** *npl* (*plans etc*) arrangements *mpl*, dispositions *fpl*
array [ə'reɪ] *n*: **~ of** déploiement *m or* étalage *m* de
arrears [ə'rɪəz] *npl* arriéré *m*; **to be in ~ with one's rent** devoir un arriéré de loyer
arrest [ə'rest] *vt* arrêter; (*sb's attention*) retenir, attirer ♦ *n* arrestation *f*; **under ~** en état d'arrestation
arrival [ə'raɪvəl] *n* arrivée *f*; **new ~** nouveau venu, nouvelle venue; (*baby*) nouveau-né(e)
arrive [ə'raɪv] *vi* arriver
arrogant ['ærəgənt] *adj* arrogant(e)
arrow ['ærəʊ] *n* flèche *f*
arse [ɑːs] (*BRIT: inf!*) *n* cul *m* (!)
arson ['ɑːsn] *n* incendie criminel
art [ɑːt] *n* art *m*; **A~s** *npl* (*SCOL*) les lettres *fpl*
artery ['ɑːtərɪ] *n* artère *f*
artful ['ɑːtfʊl] *adj* astucieux(euse), rusé(e)
art gallery *n* musée *m* d'art; (*small and private*) galerie *f* de peinture
arthritis [ɑː'θraɪtɪs] *n* arthrite *f*
artichoke ['ɑːtɪtʃəʊk] *n* (*also: globe ~*) artichaut *m*; (: *Jerusalem ~*) topinambour *m*
article ['ɑːtɪkl] *n* article *m*; **~s** *npl* (*BRIT: LAW: training*) ≈ stage *m*; **~ of clothing** vêtement *m*
articulate [*adj* ɑː'tɪkjʊlɪt, *vb* ɑː'tɪkjʊleɪt] *adj* (*person*) qui s'exprime bien; (*speech*) bien articulé(e), prononcé(e) clairement ♦ *vt* exprimer; **~d lorry** (*BRIT*) *n* (camion *m*) semi-remorque *m*
artificial [ɑːtɪ'fɪʃəl] *adj* artificiel(le)
artist ['ɑːtɪst] *n* artiste *m/f*; **~ic** [ɑː'tɪstɪk] *adj* artistique; **~ry** *n* art *m*, talent *m*
art school *n* ≈ école *f* des beaux-arts

───────────── *KEYWORD*

as [æz] *conj* **1** (*referring to time*) comme, alors que; à mesure que; **he came in ~ I was leaving** il est arrivé comme je partais; **~ the years went by** à mesure que les années passaient; **~ from tomorrow** à partir de demain
2 (*in comparisons*): **~ big ~** aussi grand que; **twice ~ big ~** deux fois plus grand que; **~ much** *or* **many ~** autant que; **~ much money/many books** autant d'argent/de livres que; **~ soon ~** dès que
3 (*since, because*) comme, puisque; **~ he had to be home by 10 ...** comme il *or*

puisqu'il devait être de retour avant 10h ...
4 (referring to manner, way) comme; **do ~ you wish** faites comme vous voudrez
5 (concerning): ~ **for** or **to that** quant à cela, pour ce qui est de cela
6: ~ **if** or **though** comme si; **he looked ~ if he was ill** il avait l'air d'être malade; *see also* **long; such; well**

♦ *prep*: **he works ~ a driver** il travaille comme chauffeur; ~ **chairman of the company, he ...** en tant que président de la compagnie, il ...; **dressed up ~ a cowboy** déguisé en cowboy; **he gave me it ~ a present** il me l'a offert, il m'en a fait cadeau

a.s.a.p. *abbr* (= *as soon as possible*) dès que possible
asbestos [æz'bɛstəs] *n* amiante *f*
ascend [ə'send] *vt* gravir; (*throne*) monter sur
ascent [ə'sent] *n* ascension *f*
ascertain [æsə'teɪn] *vt* vérifier
ascribe [ə'skraɪb] *vt*: **to ~ sth to** attribuer qch à
ash [æʃ] *n* (*dust*) cendre *f*; (*also*: ~ *tree*) frêne *m*
ashamed [ə'ʃeɪmd] *adj* honteux(euse), confus(e); **to be ~ of** avoir honte de
ashen ['æʃən] *adj* (*pale*) cendreux(euse), blême
ashore [ə'ʃɔː*] *adv* à terre
ashtray ['æʃtreɪ] *n* cendrier *m*
Ash Wednesday *n* mercredi *m* des cendres
Asia ['eɪʃə] *n* Asie *f*; ~**n** *n* Asiatique *m/f* ♦ *adj* asiatique
aside [ə'saɪd] *adv* de côté; à l'écart ♦ *n* aparté *m*
ask [ɑːsk] *vt* demander; (*invite*) inviter; **to ~ sb sth/to do sth** demander qch à qn/à qn de faire qch; **to ~ sb about sth** questionner qn sur qch; se renseigner auprès de qn sur qch; **to ~ (sb) a question** poser une question (à qn); **to ~ sb out to dinner** inviter qn au restaurant; ~ **after** *vt fus* demander des nouvelles de; ~ **for** *vt fus* demander; (*trouble*) chercher
askance [əs'kɑːns] *adv*: **to look ~ at sb** regarder qn de travers or d'un œil désapprobateur
asking price ['ɑːskɪŋ] *n*: **the ~** le prix de départ
asleep [ə'sliːp] *adj* endormi(e); **to fall ~** s'endormir
asparagus [əs'pærəgəs] *n* asperges *fpl*
aspect ['æspekt] *n* aspect *m*; (*direction in which a building etc faces*) orientation *f*, exposition *f*
aspersions [əs'pɜːʃənz] *npl*: **to cast ~ on** dénigrer
aspire [əs'paɪə*] *vi*: **to ~ to** aspirer à

aspirin ['æsprɪn] *n* aspirine *f*
ass [æs] *n* âne *m*; (*inf*) imbécile *m/f*; (*US: inf!*) cul *m* (*!*)
assailant [ə'seɪlənt] *n* agresseur *m*; assaillant *m*
assassinate [ə'sæsɪneɪt] *vt* assassiner; **assassination** [əsæsɪ'neɪʃən] *n* assassinat *m*
assault [ə'sɔːlt] *n* (*MIL*) assaut *m*; (*gen: attack*) agression *f* ♦ *vt* attaquer; (*sexually*) violenter
assemble [ə'sembl] *vt* assembler ♦ *vi* s'assembler, se rassembler
assembly [ə'semblɪ] *n* assemblée *f*, réunion *f*; (*institution*) assemblée; (*construction*) assemblage *m*; ~ **line** *n* chaîne *f* de montage
assent [ə'sent] *n* assentiment *m*, consentement *m*
assert [ə'sɜːt] *vt* affirmer, déclarer; (*one's authority*) faire valoir; (*one's innocence*) protester de
assess [ə'ses] *vt* évaluer; (*tax, payment*) établir or fixer le montant de; (*property etc: for tax*) calculer la valeur imposable de; (*person*) juger la valeur de; ~**ment** *n* évaluation *f*, fixation *f*, calcul *m* de la valeur imposable de, jugement *m*; ~**or** *n* expert *m* (*impôt et assurance*)
asset ['æset] *n* avantage *m*, atout *m*; ~**s** *npl* (*FINANCE*) capital *m*; avoir(s) *m(pl)*; actif *m*
assign [ə'saɪn] *vt* (*date*) fixer; (*task*) assigner à; (*resources*) affecter à; ~**ment** [ə'saɪnmənt] *n* tâche *f*, mission *f*
assist [ə'sɪst] *vt* aider, assister; ~**ance** *n* aide *f*, assistance *f*; ~**ant** *n* assistant(e), adjoint(e); (*BRIT: also: shop ~ant*) vendeur(euse)
associate [*adj, n* ə'səʊʃɪɪt, *vb* ə'səʊʃɪeɪt] *adj, n* associé(e) ♦ *vt* associer ♦ *vi*: **to ~ with sb** fréquenter qn; **association** [əsəʊsɪ'eɪʃən] *n* association *f*
assorted [ə'sɔːtɪd] *adj* assorti(e)
assortment [ə'sɔːtmənt] *n* assortiment *m*
assume [ə'sjuːm] *vt* supposer; (*responsibilities etc*) assumer; (*attitude, name*) prendre, adopter; ~**d name** *n* nom *m* d'emprunt; **assumption** [ə'sʌmpʃən] *n* supposition *f*, hypothèse *f*; (*of power*) assomption *f*, prise *f*
assurance [ə'ʃʊərəns] *n* assurance *f*
assure [ə'ʃʊə*] *vt* assurer
asthma ['æsmə] *n* asthme *m*
astonish [əs'tonɪʃ] *vt* étonner, stupéfier; ~**ment** *n* étonnement *m*
astound [əs'taʊnd] *vt* stupéfier, sidérer
astray [əs'treɪ] *adv*: **to go ~** s'égarer; (*fig*) quitter le droit chemin; **to lead ~** détourner du droit chemin
astride [əs'traɪd] *prep* à cheval sur
astrology [əs'trolədʒɪ] *n* astrologie *f*
astronaut ['æstrənɔːt] *n* astronaute *m/f*
astronomy [əs'tronəmɪ] *n* astronomie *f*
astute [əs'tjuːt] *adj* astucieux(euse)

asylum [ə'saɪləm] *n* asile *m*

─────── *KEYWORD* ───────

at [æt] *prep* **1** (*referring to position, direction*) à; ~ **the top** au sommet; ~ **home/school** à la maison *or* chez soi/à l'école; ~ **the baker's** à la boulangerie, chez le boulanger; **to look** ~ **sth** regarder qch
2 (*referring to time*): ~ **4 o'clock** à 4 heures; ~ **Christmas** à Noël; ~ **night** la nuit; ~ **times** par moments, parfois
3 (*referring to rates, speed etc*) à; ~ **£1 a kilo** une livre au kilo; **two** ~ **a time** deux à la fois; ~ **50 km/h** à 50 km/h
4 (*referring to manner*): ~ **a stroke** d'un seul coup; ~ **peace** en paix
5 (*referring to activity*): **to be** ~ **work** être à l'œuvre, travailler; **to play** ~ **cowboys** jouer aux cowboys; **to be good** ~ **sth** être bon en qch
6 (*referring to cause*): **shocked/surprised/annoyed** ~ **sth** choqué par/étonné de/agacé par qch; **I went** ~ **his suggestion** j'y suis allé sur son conseil

ate [et, eɪt] *pt of* **eat**
atheist [eɪθɪɪst] *n* athée *m/f*
Athens ['æθɪnz] *n* Athènes
athlete ['æθliːt] *n* athlète *m/f*
athletic [æθ'letɪk] *adj* athlétique; **~s** *n* athlétisme *m*
Atlantic [ət'læntɪk] *adj* atlantique ♦ *n*: **the** ~ **(Ocean)** l'Atlantique *m*, l'océan *m* Atlantique
atlas ['ætləs] *n* atlas *m*
atmosphere ['ætməsfɪə*] *n* atmosphère *f*
atom ['ætəm] *n* atome *m*; **~ic** [ə'tɒmɪk] *adj* atomique; **~(ic) bomb** *n* bombe *f* atomique; **~izer** ['ætəmaɪzə*] *n* atomiseur *m*
atone [ə'təʊn] *vi*: **to** ~ **for** expier, racheter
atrocious [ə'trəʊʃəs] *adj* (*very bad*) atroce, exécrable
attach [ə'tætʃ] *vt* attacher; (*document, letter*) joindre; **to be ~ed to sb/sth** être attaché à qn/qch
attaché case [ə'tæʃeɪ-] *n* mallette *f*, attaché-case *m*
attachment [ə'tætʃmənt] *n* (*tool*) accessoire *m*; (*love*): ~ **(to)** affection *f* (pour), attachement *m* (à)
attack [ə'tæk] *vt* attaquer; (*task etc*) s'attaquer à ♦ *n* attaque *f*; (*also: heart* ~) crise *f* cardiaque
attain [ə'teɪn] *vt* (*also: to* ~ *to*) parvenir à, atteindre; (: *knowledge*) acquérir; **~ments** *npl* connaissances *fpl*, résultats *mpl*
attempt [ə'tempt] *n* tentative *f* ♦ *vt* essayer, tenter; **to make an** ~ **on sb's life** attenter à la vie de qn; **~ed** *adj*: **~ed murder/suicide** tentative *f* de meurtre/suicide
attend [ə'tend] *vt* (*course*) suivre; (*meeting, talk*) assister à; (*school, church*) aller à, fré-

quenter; (*patient*) soigner, s'occuper de; ~ **to** *vt fus* (*needs, affairs etc*) s'occuper de; (*customer, patient*) s'occuper de; **~ance** *n* (*being present*) présence *f*; (*people present*) assistance *f*; **~ant** *n* employé(e) ♦ *adj* (*dangers*) inhérent(e), concomitant(e)
attention [ə'tenʃən] *n* attention *f*; **~!** (*MIL*) garde-à-vous!; **for the** ~ **of** (*ADMIN*) à l'attention de
attentive [ə'tentɪv] *adj* attentif(ive); (*kind*) prévenant(e)
attest [ə'test] *vi*: **to** ~ **to** (*demonstrate*) démontrer; (*confirm*) témoigner
attic ['ætɪk] *n* grenier *m*
attitude ['ætɪtjuːd] *n* attitude *f*; pose *f*, maintien *m*
attorney [ə'tɜːnɪ] *n* (*US: lawyer*) avoué *m*; **A~ General** *n* (*BRIT*) ≈ procureur général; (*US*) ≈ garde *m* des Sceaux, ministre *m* de la Justice
attract [ə'trækt] *vt* attirer; **~ion** [ə'trækʃən] *n* (*gen pl: pleasant things*) attraction *f*, attrait *m*; (*PHYSICS*) attraction *f*; (*fig: towards sb or sth*) attirance *f*; **~ive** *adj* attrayant(e); (*person*) séduisant(e)
attribute [*n* 'ætrɪbjuːt, *vb* ə'trɪbjuːt] *n* attribut *m* ♦ *vt*: **to** ~ **sth to** attribuer qch à
attrition [ə'trɪʃən] *n*: **war of** ~ guerre *f* d'usure
aubergine ['əʊbəʒiːn] *n* aubergine *f*
auction ['ɔːkʃən] *n* (*also: sale by* ~) vente *f* aux enchères ♦ *vt* (: *to sell by* ~) vendre aux enchères; (: *to put up for* ~) mettre aux enchères; **~eer** [ɔːkʃə'nɪə*] *n* commissaire-priseur *m*
audience ['ɔːdɪəns] *n* (*people*) assistance *f*; public *m*; spectateurs *mpl*; (*interview*) audience *f*
audiovisual ['ɔːdɪəʊ'vɪzjʊəl] *adj* audiovisuel(le); ~ **aids** *npl* supports *or* moyens audiovisuels
audit ['ɔːdɪt] *vt* vérifier
audition [ɔː'dɪʃən] *n* audition *f*
auditor ['ɔːdɪtə*] *n* vérificateur *m* des comptes
augur ['ɔːgə*] *vi*: **it ~s well** c'est bon signe *or* de bon augure
August ['ɔːgəst] *n* août *m*
aunt [ɑːnt] *n* tante *f*; **~ie** *n* dimin of **aunt**; **~y** *n* dimin of **aunt**
au pair ['əʊ'pɛə*] *n* (*also:* ~ *girl*) jeune fille *f* au pair
auspicious [ɔːs'pɪʃəs] *adj* de bon augure, propice
Australia [ɒs'treɪlɪə] *n* Australie *f*; **~n** *adj* australien(ne) ♦ *n* Australien(ne)
Austria ['ɒstrɪə] *n* Autriche *f*; **~n** *adj* autrichien(ne) ♦ *n* Autrichien(ne)
authentic [ɔː'θentɪk] *adj* authentique
author ['ɔːθə*] *n* auteur *m*
authoritarian [ɔːθɒrɪ'tɛərɪən] *adj* autoritaire

authoritative [ɔːˈθɒrɪtətɪv] *adj* (*account*) digne de foi; (*study, treatise*) qui fait autorité; (*person, manner*) autoritaire

authority [ɔːˈθɒrɪtɪ] *n* autorité *f*; (*permission*) autorisation (formelle); **the authorities** *npl* (*ruling body*) les autorités *fpl*, l'administration *f*

authorize [ˈɔːθəraɪz] *vt* autoriser

auto [ˈɔːtəʊ] (*US*) *n* auto *f*, voiture *f*

auto: ~**biography** [ɔːtəʊbaɪˈɒɡrəfɪ] *n* autobiographie *f*; ~**graph** [ˈɔːtəɡrɑːf] *n* autographe *m* ♦ *vt* signer, dédicacer; ~**mated** [ˈɔːtəmeɪtɪd] *adj* automatisé(e), automatique; ~**matic** [ɔːtəˈmætɪk] *adj* automatique ♦ *n* (*gun*) automatique *m*; (*washing machine*) machine *f* à laver automatique; (*BRIT: AUT*) voiture *f* à transmission automatique; ~**matically** *adv* automatiquement; ~**mation** [ɔːtəˈmeɪʃən] *n* automatisation *f* (électronique); ~**mobile** [ˈɔːtəməbiːl] (*US*) *n* automobile *f*; ~**nomy** [ɔːˈtɒnəmɪ] *n* autonomie *f*

autumn [ˈɔːtəm] *n* automne *m*; **in** ~ en automne

auxiliary [ɔːɡˈzɪlɪərɪ] *adj* auxiliaire ♦ *n* auxiliaire *m/f*

avail [əˈveɪl] *vt*: **to** ~ **o.s. of** profiter de ♦ *n*: **to no** ~ sans résultat, en vain, en pure perte

availability [əveɪləˈbɪlɪtɪ] *n* disponibilité *f*

available [əˈveɪləbl] *adj* disponible

avalanche [ˈævəlɑːnʃ] *n* avalanche *f*

Ave *abbr* = **avenue**

avenge [əˈvendʒ] *vt* venger

avenue [ˈævənjuː] *n* avenue *f*; (*fig*) moyen *m*

average [ˈævərɪdʒ] *n* moyenne *f*; (*fig*) moyen *m* ♦ *adj* moyen(ne) ♦ *vt* (*a certain figure*) atteindre *or* faire une moyenne de; **on** ~ en moyenne; ~ **out** *vi*: **to** ~ **out at** représenter en moyenne, donner une moyenne de

averse [əˈvɜːs] *adj*: **to be** ~ **to sth/doing sth** éprouver une forte répugnance envers qch/à faire qch

avert [əˈvɜːt] *vt* prévenir, écarter; (*one's eyes*) détourner

aviary [ˈeɪvɪərɪ] *n* volière *f*

avocado [ævəˈkɑːdəʊ] *n* (*also: BRIT:* ~ **pear**) avocat *m*

avoid [əˈvɔɪd] *vt* éviter

await [əˈweɪt] *vt* attendre

awake [əˈweɪk] (*pt* **awoke**, *pp* **awoken**) *adj* éveillé(e) ♦ *vt* éveiller ♦ *vi* s'éveiller; ~ **to** (*dangers, possibilities*) conscient(e) de; **to be** ~ être réveillé(e); **he was still** ~ il ne dormait pas encore; ~**ning** *n* réveil *m*

award [əˈwɔːd] *n* récompense *f*, prix *m*; (*LAW: damages*) dommages-intérêts *mpl* ♦ *vt* (*prize*) décerner; (*LAW: damages*) accorder

aware [əˈwɛə*] *adj*: ~ (**of**) (*conscious*)

conscient(e) (de); (*informed*) au courant (de); **to become** ~ **of/that** prendre conscience de/que; se rendre compte de/ que; ~**ness** *n* conscience *f*, connaissance *f*

awash [əˈwɒʃ] *adj*: ~ (**with**) inondé(e) (de)

away [əˈweɪ] *adj, adv* (au) loin; absent(e); **two kilometres** ~ à (une distance de) deux kilomètres, à deux kilomètres de distance; **two hours** ~ **by car** à deux heures de voiture *or* de route; **the holiday was two weeks** ~ il restait deux semaines jusqu'aux vacances; ~ **from** loin de; **he's** ~ **for a week** il est parti (pour) une semaine; **to pedal/work/laugh** ~ être en train de pédaler/travailler/rire; **to fade** ~ (*sound*) s'affaiblir; (*colour*) s'estomper; **to wither** ~ (*plant*) se dessécher; **to take** ~ emporter; (*subtract*) enlever; ~ **game** *n* (*SPORT*) match *m* à l'extérieur

awe [ɔː] *n* respect mêlé de crainte; ~**inspiring** *adj* impressionnant(e); ~**some** *adj* impressionnant(e)

awful [ˈɔːfʊl] *adj* affreux(euse); **an** ~ **lot (of)** un nombre incroyable (de); ~**ly** *adv* (*very*) terriblement, vraiment

awhile [əˈwaɪl] *adv* un moment, quelque temps

awkward [ˈɔːkwəd] *adj* (*clumsy*) gauche, maladroit(e); (*inconvenient*) peu pratique; (*embarrassing*) gênant(e), délicat(e)

awning [ˈɔːnɪŋ] *n* (*of tent*) auvent *m*; (*of shop*) store *m*; (*of hotel etc*) marquise *f*

awoke [əˈwəʊk] *pt of* **awake**; ~**n** [əˈwəʊkən] *pp of* **awake**

awry [əˈraɪ] *adj, adv* de travers; **to go** ~ mal tourner

axe [æks] (*US* **ax**) *n* hache *f* ♦ *vt* (*project etc*) abandonner; (*jobs*) supprimer; **axes** [ˈæksɪz] *npl of* **axe**

axis [ˈæksɪs, *pl* -siːz] (*pl* **axes**) *n* axe *m*

axle [ˈæksl] *n* (*also:* ~**-tree**: *AUT*) essieu *m*

ay(e) [aɪ] *excl* (*yes*) oui

B b

B [biː] *n* (*MUS*) si *m*

B.A. *abbr* = **Bachelor of Arts**

babble [ˈbæbl] *vi* bredouiller; (*baby, stream*) gazouiller

baby [ˈbeɪbɪ] *n* bébé *m*; (*US: inf: darling*): **come on,** ~! viens ma belle/mon gars!; ~ **carriage** (*US*) *n* voiture *f* d'enfant; ~**sit** *vi* garder les enfants; ~**-sitter** *n* babysitter *m/f*

bachelor ['bætʃələ*] *n* célibataire *m*; **B~ of Arts/Science** ≈ licencié(e) ès *or* en lettres/sciences

back [bæk] *n* (*of person, horse, book*) dos *m*; (*of hand*) dos, revers *m*; (*of house*) derrière *m*; (*of car, train*) arrière *m*; (*of chair*) dossier *m*; (*of page*) verso *m*; (*of room, audience*) fond *m*; (SPORT) arrière *m* ♦ *vt* (*candidate: also:* ~ **up**) soutenir, appuyer; (*horse: at races*) parier *or* miser sur; (*car*) (*faire*) reculer ♦ *vi* (*also:* ~ **up**) reculer; (: *car etc*) faire marche arrière ♦ *adj* (*in compounds*) de derrière, à l'arrière ♦ *adv* (*not forward*) en arrière; (*returned*): **he's** ~ il est rentré, il est de retour; (*restitution*): **throw the ball** ~ renvoie la balle; (*again*): **he called** ~ il a rappelé; ~ **seat/wheels** (AUT) sièges *mpl*/roues *fpl* arrières; ~ **payments/rent** arriéré *m* de paiements/loyer; **he ran** ~ il est revenu en courant; ~ **down** *vi* rabattre de ses prétentions; ~ **out** *vi* (*of promise*) se dédire; ~ **up** *vt* (*candidate etc*) soutenir, appuyer; (COMPUT) sauvegarder; **~bencher** (BRIT) *n* membre *du parlement sans portefeuille*; **~bone** *n* colonne vertébrale, épine dorsale; **~cloth** (BRIT) *n* toile *f* de fond; **~date** *vt* (*letter*) antidater; **~dated pay rise** augmentation *f* avec effet rétroactif; **~drop** *n* = **backcloth**; **~fire** *vi* (AUT) pétarader; (*plans*) mal tourner; **~ground** *n* arrière-plan *m*; (*of events*) situation *f*, conjoncture *f*; (*basic knowledge*) éléments *mpl* de base; (*experience*) formation *f*, **family ~ground** milieu familial; **~hand** *n* (TENNIS: *also:* **~hand stroke**) revers *m*; **~hander** (BRIT) *n* (*bribe*) pot-de-vin *m*; **~ing** *n* (*fig*) soutien *m*, appui *m*; **~lash** *n* contre-coup *m*, répercussion *f*; **~log** *n*: **~log of work** travail *m* en retard; ~ **number** *n* (*of magazine etc*) vieux numéro; **~pack** *n* sac *m* à dos; **~ pay** *n* rappel *m* de salaire; **~side** (*inf*) *n* derrière *m*, postérieur *m*; **~stage** *adv* derrière la scène, dans la coulisse; **~stroke** *n* dos crawlé; **~up** *adj* (*train, plane*) supplémentaire, de réserve; (COMPUT) de sauvegarde ♦ *n* (*support*) appui *m*, soutien *m*; (*also:* ~**up disk/file**) sauvegarde *f*; **~ward** *adj* (*movement*) en arrière; (*person, country*) arriéré(e); attardé(e); **~wards** *adv* (*move, go*) en arrière; (*read a list*) à l'envers, à rebours; (*fall*) à la renverse; (*walk*) à reculons; **~water** *n* (*fig*) coin reculé; bled perdu (*péj*); **~yard** *n* arrière-cour *f*

bacon ['beɪkən] *n* bacon *m*, lard *m*

bacteria [bæk'tɪərɪə] *npl* bactéries *fpl*

bad [bæd] *adj* mauvais(e); (*child*) vilain(e); (*mistake, accident etc*) grave; (*meat, food*) gâté(e), avarié(e); **his** ~ **leg** sa jambe malade; **to go** ~ (*meat, food*) se gâter

bade [bæd] *pt of* **bid**

badge [bædʒ] *n* insigne *m*; (*of policeman*) plaque *f*

badger ['bædʒə*] *n* blaireau *m*

badly ['bædlɪ] *adv* (*work, dress etc*) mal; ~ **wounded** grièvement blessé; **he needs it** ~ il en a absolument besoin; ~ **off** *adj, adv* dans la gêne

badminton ['bædmɪntən] *n* badminton *m*

bad-tempered ['bæd'tempəd] *adj* (*person: by nature*) ayant mauvais caractère; (: *on one occasion*) de mauvaise humeur

baffle ['bæfl] *vt* (*puzzle*) déconcerter

bag [bæg] *n* sac *m* ♦ *vt* (*inf: take*) empocher; s'approprier; **~s of** (*inf: lots of*) des masses de; **~gage** *n* bagages *mpl*; **~gy** *adj* avachi(e), qui fait des poches; **~pipes** *npl* cornemuse *f*

bail [beɪl] *n* (*payment*) caution *f*; (*release*) mise *f* en liberté sous caution ♦ *vt* (*prisoner: also: grant* ~ **to**) mettre en liberté sous caution; (*boat: also:* ~ **out**) écoper; **on** ~ (*prisoner*) sous caution; *see also* **bale**; ~ **out** *vt* (*prisoner*) payer la caution de

bailiff ['beɪlɪf] *n* (BRIT) ≈ huissier *m*; (US) ≈ huissier-audiencier *m*

bait [beɪt] *n* appât *m* ♦ *vt* appâter; (*fig: tease*) tourmenter

bake [beɪk] *vt* (*faire*) cuire au four ♦ *vi* (*bread etc*) cuire (au four); (*make cakes etc*) faire de la pâtisserie; **~d beans** *npl* haricots blancs à la sauce tomate; **~r** *n* boulanger *m*; **~ry** *n* boulangerie *f*, boulangerie industrielle; **baking** *n* cuisson *f*; **baking powder** *n* levure *f* (chimique)

balance ['bæləns] *n* équilibre *m*; (COMM: sum) solde *m*; (*remainder*) reste *m*; (*scales*) balance *f* ♦ *vt* mettre ou faire tenir en équilibre; (*pros and cons*) peser; (*budget*) équilibrer; (*account*) balancer; ~ **of trade/payments** balance commerciale/des comptes *or* paiements; **~d** *adj* (*personality, diet*) équilibré(e); (*report*) objectif(ive); ~ **sheet** *n* bilan *m*

balcony ['bælkənɪ] *n* balcon *m*; (*in theatre*) deuxième balcon

bald [bɔːld] *adj* chauve; (*tyre*) lisse

bale [beɪl] *n* balle *f*, ballot *m*; ~ **out** *vi* (*of a plane*) sauter en parachute

ball [bɔːl] *n* boule *f*; (*football*) ballon *m*; (*for tennis, golf*) balle *f*; (*of wool*) pelote *f*; (*of string*) bobine *f*; (*dance*) bal *m*; **to play** ~ (**with sb**) (*fig*) coopérer (avec qn)

ballast ['bæləst] *n* lest *m*

ball bearings *npl* roulement *m* à billes

ballerina [bælə'riːnə] *n* ballerine *f*

ballet ['bæleɪ] *n* ballet *m*; (*art*) danse *f* (classique); ~ **dancer** *n* danseur(euse) *m/f* de ballet

balloon [bə'luːn] *n* ballon *m*; (*in comic strip*) bulle *f*

ballot ['bælət] *n* scrutin *m*; ~ **paper** *n* bulletin *m* de vote

ballpoint (pen) ['bɔːlpɔɪnt-] *n* stylo *m* à bille

ballroom ['bɔːlrʊm] *n* salle *f* de bal

balm [bɑːm] *n* baume *m*

ban [bæn] *n* interdiction *f* ♦ *vt* interdire

banana [bə'nɑːnə] *n* banane *f*

band [bænd] *n* bande *f*; (*at a dance*) orchestre *m*; (*MIL*) musique *f*, fanfare *f*; ~ **together** *vi* se liguer

bandage ['bændɪdʒ] *n* bandage *m*, pansement *m* ♦ *vt* bander

Bandaid ['bændeɪd] (*US* ®) *n* pansement adhésif

bandwagon ['bændwægən] *n*: **to jump on the ~** (*fig*) monter dans *or* prendre le train en marche

bandy ['bændɪ] *vt* (*jokes, insults, ideas*) échanger

bandy-legged ['bændɪ'legɪd] *adj* aux jambes arquées

bang [bæŋ] *n* détonation *f*; (*of door*) claquement *m*; (*blow*) coup (violent) ♦ *vt* frapper (violemment); (*door*) claquer ♦ *vi* détoner; claquer ♦ *excl* pan!

bangs [bæŋz] (*US*) *npl* (*fringe*) frange *f*

banish ['bænɪʃ] *vt* bannir

banister(s) ['bænɪstə(z)] *n(pl)* rampe *f* (d'escalier)

bank [bæŋk] *n* banque *f*; (*of river, lake*) bord *m*, rive *f*; (*of earth*) talus *m*, remblai *m* ♦ *vi* (*AVIAT*) virer sur l'aile; ~ **on** *vt fus* miser *or* tabler sur; ~ **account** *n* compte *m* en banque; ~ **card** *n* carte *f* d'identité bancaire; ~**er** *n* banquier *m*; ~**er's card** (*BRIT*) *n* = bank card; ~ **holiday** (*BRIT*) *n* jour férié (*les banques sont fermées*); ~**ing** *n* opérations *fpl* bancaires; profession *f* de banquier; ~**note** *n* billet *m* de banque; ~ **rate** *n* taux *m* de l'escompte

bankrupt ['bæŋkrʌpt] *adj* en faillite; **to go ~** faire faillite; ~**cy** *n* faillite *f*

bank statement *n* relevé *m* de compte

banner ['bænə*] *n* bannière *f*

bannister(s) ['bænɪstə(z)] *n(pl)* = **banister(s)**

banns [bænz] *npl* bans *mpl*

baptism ['bæptɪzəm] *n* baptême *m*

bar [bɑː*] *n* (*pub*) bar *m*; (*counter: in pub*) comptoir *m*, bar; (*rod: of metal etc*) barre *f*; (*on window etc*) barreau *m*; (*of chocolate*) tablette *f*, plaque *f*; (*fig*) obstacle *m*; (*prohibition*) mesure *f* d'exclusion; (*MUS*) mesure *f* ♦ *vt* (*road*) barrer; (*window*) munir de barreaux; (*person*) exclure; (*activity*) interdire; ~ **of soap** savonnette *f*; **the B~** (*LAW*) le barreau; **behind ~s** (*prisoner*) sous les verrous; ~ **none** sans exception

barbaric [bɑː'bærɪk] *adj* barbare

barbecue ['bɑːbɪkjuː] *n* barbecue *m*

barbed wire ['bɑːbd-] *n* fil *m* de fer barbelé

barber ['bɑːbə*] *n* coiffeur *m* (pour hommes)

bar code *n* (*on goods*) code *m* à barres

bare [bɛə*] *adj* nu(e) ♦ *vt* mettre à nu, dénuder; (*teeth*) montrer; **the ~ necessities** le strict nécessaire; ~**back** *adv* à cru, sans selle; ~**faced** *adj* impudent(e), effronté(e); ~**foot** *adj, adv* nu-pieds, (les) pieds nus; ~**ly** *adv* à peine

bargain ['bɑːgɪn] *n* (*transaction*) marché *m*; (*good buy*) affaire *f*, occasion *f* ♦ *vi* (*haggle*) marchander; (*negotiate*): **to ~ (with sb)** négocier (avec qn), traiter (avec qn); **into the ~** par-dessus le marché; ~ **for** *vt fus*: **he got more than he ~ed for** il ne s'attendait pas à un coup pareil

barge [bɑːdʒ] *n* péniche *f*; ~ **in** *vi* (*walk in*) faire irruption; (*interrupt talk*) intervenir mal à propos

bark [bɑːk] *n* (*of tree*) écorce *f*; (*of dog*) aboiement *m* ♦ *vi* aboyer

barley ['bɑːlɪ] *n* orge *f*; ~ **sugar** *n* sucre *m* d'orge

barmaid ['bɑːmeɪd] *n* serveuse *f* (de bar), barmaid *f*

barman ['bɑːmən] (*irreg*) *n* serveur *m* (de bar), barman *m*

barn [bɑːn] *n* grange *f*

barometer [bə'rɒmɪtə*] *n* baromètre *m*

baron ['bærən] *n* baron *m*; ~**ess** *n* baronne *f*

barracks ['bærəks] *npl* caserne *f*

barrage ['bærɑːʒ] *n* (*MIL*) tir *m* de barrage; (*dam*) barrage *m*; (*fig*) pluie *f*

barrel ['bærəl] *n* tonneau *m*; (*of oil*) baril *m*; (*of gun*) canon *m*

barren ['bærən] *adj* stérile

barricade [bærɪ'keɪd] *n* barricade *f*

barrier ['bærɪə*] *n* barrière *f*; (*fig: to progress etc*) obstacle *m*

barring ['bɑːrɪŋ] *prep* sauf

barrister ['bærɪstə*] (*BRIT*) *n* avocat (plaidant)

barrow ['bærəʊ] *n* (*wheel~*) charrette *f* à bras

bartender ['bɑːtendə*] (*US*) *n* barman *m*

barter ['bɑːtə*] *vt*: **to ~ sth for** échanger qch contre

base [beɪs] *n* base *f*; (*of tree, post*) pied *m* ♦ *vt*: **to ~ sth on** baser *or* fonder qch sur ♦ *adj* vil(e), bas(se)

baseball ['beɪsbɔːl] *n* base-ball *m*

basement ['beɪsmənt] *n* sous-sol *m*

bases[1] ['beɪsɪz] *npl of* base

bases[2] ['beɪsiːz] *npl of* basis

bash [bæʃ] (*inf*) *vt* frapper, cogner

bashful ['bæʃfʊl] *adj* timide; modeste

basic ['beɪsɪk] *adj* fondamental(e), de base; (*minimal*) rudimentaire; ~**ally** *adv* fondamentalement, à la base; (*in fact*) en fait, au fond; ~**s** *npl*: **the ~s** l'essentiel *m*

basil ['bæzl] *n* basilic *m*

basin ['beɪsn] *n* (*vessel, also GEO*) cuvette *f*,

bassin *m*; (*also*: *wash~*) lavabo *m*

basis ['beɪsɪs] (*pl* **bases**) *n* base *f*; **on a trial ~** à titre d'essai; **on a part-time ~** à temps partiel

bask [bɑːsk] *vi*: **to ~ in the sun** se chauffer au soleil

basket ['bɑːskɪt] *n* corbeille *f*; (*with handle*) panier *m*; **~ball** *n* basket-ball *m*

bass [beɪs] *n* (*MUS*) basse *f*

bassoon [bə'suːn] *n* (*MUS*) basson *m*

bastard ['bɑːstəd] *n* enfant naturel(le), bâtard(e); (*infl*) salaud *m* (*l*)

bat [bæt] *n* chauve-souris *f*; (*for baseball etc*) batte *f*; (*BRIT: for table tennis*) raquette *f* ♦ *vt*: **he didn't ~ an eyelid** il n'a pas sourcillé *or* bronché

batch [bætʃ] *n* (*of bread*) fournée *f*; (*of papers*) liasse *f*

bated ['beɪtɪd] *adj*: **with ~ breath** en retenant son souffle

bath [bɑːθ, *pl* bɑːðz] *n* bain *m*; (*~tub*) baignoire *f* ♦ *vt* baigner, donner un bain à; **to have a ~** prendre un bain; *see also* **baths**

bathe [beɪð] *vi* se baigner ♦ *vt* (*wound*) laver

bathing ['beɪðɪŋ] *n* baignade *f*; **~ cap** *n* bonnet *m* de bain; **~ costume** (*US* **~ suit**) *n* maillot *m* (de bain)

bath: **~robe** *n* peignoir *m* de bain; **~room** *n* salle *f* de bains; **~s** [bɑːðz] *npl* (*also: swimming ~*) piscine *f*; **~ towel** *n* serviette *f* de bain

baton ['bætən] *n* bâton *m*; (*MUS*) baguette *f*; (*club*) matraque *f*

batter ['bætə*] *vt* battre ♦ *n* pâte *f* à frire; **~ed** (*hat, pan*) cabossé(e)

battery ['bætərɪ] *n* batterie *f*; (*of torch*) pile *f*

battle ['bætl] *n* bataille *f*, combat *m* ♦ *vi* se battre, lutter; **~field** *n* champ *m* de bataille; **~ship** *n* cuirassé *m*

bawdy ['bɔːdɪ] *adj* paillard(e)

bawl [bɔːl] *vi* hurler; (*child*) brailler

bay [beɪ] *n* (*of sea*) baie *f*; **to hold sb at ~** tenir qn à distance *or* en échec; **~ leaf** *n* laurier *m*; **~ window** *n* baie vitrée

bazaar [bə'zɑː*] *n* bazar *m*; vente *f* de charité

B & B *n abbr* = **bed and breakfast**

BBC *n abbr* (= *British Broadcasting Corporation*) office de la radiodiffusion et télévision britannique

B.C. *adv abbr* (= *before Christ*) av. J.-C.

--- **KEYWORD** ---

be [biː] (*pt* **was, were**, *pp* **been**) *aux vb* **1** (*with present participle: forming continuous tenses*): **what are you doing?** que faites-vous?; **they're coming tomorrow** ils viennent demain; **I've been waiting for you for 2 hours** je t'attends depuis 2 heures

2 (*with pp: forming passives*) être; **to ~**

killed être tué(e); **he was nowhere to ~ seen** on ne le voyait nulle part

3 (*in tag questions*): **it was fun, wasn't it?** c'était drôle, n'est-ce pas?; **she's back, is she?** elle est rentrée, n'est-ce pas *or* alors?

4 (*+to +infinitive*): **the house is to ~ sold** la maison doit être vendue; **he's not to open it** il ne doit pas l'ouvrir

♦ *vb + complement* **1** (*gen*) être; **I'm English** je suis anglais(e); **I'm tired** je suis fatigué(e); **I'm hot/cold** j'ai chaud/froid; **he's a doctor** il est médecin; **2 and 2 are 4** 2 et 2 font 4

2 (*of health*) aller; **how are you?** comment allez-vous?; **he's fine now** il va bien maintenant; **he's very ill** il est très malade

3 (*of age*) avoir; **how old are you?** quel âge avez-vous?; **I'm sixteen (years old)** j'ai seize ans

4 (*cost*) coûter; **how much was the meal?** combien a coûté le repas?; **that'll ~ £5, please** ça fera 5 livres, s'il vous plaît

♦ *vi* **1** (*exist, occur etc*) être, exister; **the prettiest girl that ever was** la fille la plus jolie qui ait jamais existé; **~ that as it may** quoi qu'il en soit; **so ~ it** soit

2 (*referring to place*) être, se trouver; **I won't ~ here tomorrow** je ne serai pas là demain; **Edinburgh is in Scotland** Édimbourg est *or* se trouve en Écosse

3 (*referring to movement*) aller; **where have you been?** où êtes-vous allé(s)?

♦ *impers vb* **1** (*referring to time, distance*) être; **it's 5 o'clock** il est 5 heures; **it's the 28th of April** c'est le 28 avril; **it's 10 km to the village** le village est à 10 km

2 (*referring to the weather*) faire; **it's too hot/cold** il fait trop chaud/froid; **it's windy** il y a du vent

3 (*emphatic*): **it's me/the postman** c'est moi/le facteur

beach [biːtʃ] *n* plage *f* ♦ *vt* échouer

beacon ['biːkən] *n* (*lighthouse*) fanal *m*; (*marker*) balise *f*

bead [biːd] *n* perle *f*

beak [biːk] *n* bec *m*

beaker ['biːkə*] *n* gobelet *m*

beam [biːm] *n* poutre *f*; (*of light*) rayon *m* ♦ *vi* rayonner

bean [biːn] *n* haricot *m*; (*of coffee*) grain *m*; **runner ~** haricot *m* (à rames); **broad ~** fève *f*; **~sprouts** *npl* germes *mpl* de soja

bear [bɛə*] (*pt* **bore**, *pp* **borne**) *n* ours *m* ♦ *vt* porter; (*endure*) supporter ♦ *vi*: **to ~ right/left** obliquer à droite/gauche, se diriger vers la droite/gauche; **~ out** *vt* corroborer, confirmer; **~ up** *vi* (*person*) tenir le coup

beard [bɪəd] *n* barbe *f*; **~ed** *adj* barbu(e)

bearer ['bɛərə*] *n* porteur *m*; (*of passport*) titulaire *m/f*

bearing ['bɛərɪŋ] *n* maintien *m*, allure *f*; (*connection*) rapport *m*; ~s *npl* (*also*: ball ~s) roulement *m* (à billes); **to take a** ~ faire le point

beast [biːst] *n* bête *f*; (*inf*: *person*) brute *f*; ~ly *adj* infect(e)

beat [biːt] (*pt* beat, *pp* beaten) *n* battement *m*; (*MUS*) temps *m*, mesure *f*; (*of policeman*) ronde *f* ♦ *vt* battre; **off the** ~en **track** hors des chemins *or* sentiers battus; ~ **it!** (*inf*) fiche(-moi) le camp!; ~ **off** *vt* repousser; ~ **up** *vt* (*inf*: *person*) tabasser; (*eggs*) battre; ~**ing** *n* raclée *f*

beautiful ['bjuːtɪful] *adj* beau(belle); ~ly *adv* admirablement

beauty ['bjuːtɪ] *n* beauté *f*; ~ **salon** *n* institut *m* de beauté; ~ **spot** (*BRIT*) *n* (*TOURISM*) site naturel (d'une grande beauté)

beaver ['biːvə*] *n* castor *m*

became [bɪ'keɪm] *pt of* **become**

because [bɪ'kɒz] *conj* parce que; ~ **of** *prep* à cause de

beck [bek] *n*: **to be at sb's** ~ **and call** être à l'entière disposition de qn

beckon ['bekən] *vt* (*also*: ~ **to**) faire signe (de venir) à

become [bɪ'kʌm] (*irreg*: *like* come) *vi* devenir; **to** ~ **fat/thin** grossir/maigrir

becoming [bɪ'kʌmɪŋ] *adj* (*behaviour*) convenable, bienséant(e); (*clothes*) seyant(e)

bed [bed] *n* lit *m*; (*of flowers*) parterre *m*; (*of coal, clay*) couche *f*; (*of sea*) fond *m*; **to go to** ~ aller se coucher; ~ **and breakfast** *n* (*terms*) chambre et petit déjeuner; (*place*) ≈ chambre *f* d'hôte; ~**clothes** *npl* couvertures *fpl* et draps *mpl*; ~**ding** *n* literie *f*

bedraggled [bɪ'drægld] *adj* (*person, clothes*) débraillé(e); (*hair: wet*) trempé(e)

bed: ~**ridden** *adj* cloué(e) au lit; ~**room** *n* chambre *f* (à coucher); ~**side** *n*: **at sb's** ~**side** au chevet de qn; ~**sit(ter)** (*BRIT*) *n* chambre meublée, studio *m*; ~**spread** *n* couvre-lit *m*, dessus-de-lit *m inv*; ~**time** *n* heure *f* du coucher

bee [biː] *n* abeille *f*

beech [biːtʃ] *n* hêtre *m*

beef [biːf] *n* boeuf *m*; **roast** ~ rosbif *m*; ~**burger** *n* hamburger *m*; ~**eater** *n* hallebardier de la Tour de Londres

beehive ['biːhaɪv] *n* ruche *f*

beeline ['biːlaɪn] *n*: **to make a** ~ **for** se diriger tout droit vers

been [biːn] *pp of* **be**

beer [bɪə*] *n* bière *f*

beet [biːt] *n* (*vegetable*) betterave *f*; (*US: also*: red ~) betterave (potagère)

beetle ['biːtl] *n* scarabée *m*

beetroot ['biːtruːt] (*BRIT*) *n* betterave *f*

before [bɪ'fɔː*] *prep* (*in time*) avant; (*in space*) devant ♦ *conj* avant que +*sub*; avant

de ♦ *adv* avant; devant; ~ **going** avant de partir; ~ **she goes** avant qu'elle ne parte; **the week** ~ la semaine précédente *or* d'avant; **I've seen it** ~ je l'ai déjà vu; ~**hand** *adv* au préalable, à l'avance

beg [beg] *vi* mendier ♦ *vt* mendier; (*forgiveness, mercy etc*) demander; (*entreat*) supplier; *see also* **pardon**

began [bɪ'gæn] *pt of* **begin**

beggar ['begə*] *n* mendiant(e)

begin [bɪ'gɪn] (*pt* began, *pp* begun) *vt, vi* commencer; **to** ~ **doing** *or* **to do sth** commencer à *or* de faire qch; ~**ner** *n* débutant(e); ~**ning** *n* commencement *m*, début *m*

behalf [bɪ'hɑːf] *n*: **on** ~ **of**, (*US*) **in** ~ **of** (*representing*) de la part de; (*for benefit of*) pour le compte de; **on my/his** ~ pour moi/lui

behave [bɪ'heɪv] *vi* se conduire, se comporter; (*well*: *also*: ~ **o.s.**) se conduire bien *or* comme il faut

behaviour [bɪ'heɪvjə*] (*US* **behavior**) *n* comportement *m*, conduite *f*

behead [bɪ'hed] *vt* décapiter

beheld [bɪ'held] *pt, pp of* **behold**

behind [bɪ'haɪnd] *prep* derrière; (*time, progress*) en retard sur; (*work, studies*) en retard dans ♦ *adv* derrière ♦ *n* derrière *m*; **to be** ~ (**schedule**) avoir du retard; ~ **the scenes** dans les coulisses

behold [bɪ'həʊld] (*irreg*: *like* hold) *vt* apercevoir, voir

beige [beɪʒ] *adj* beige

Beijing ['beɪ'dʒɪŋ] *n* Bei-jing, Pékin

being [biːɪŋ] *n* être *m*

Beirut [beɪ'ruːt] *n* Beyrouth

belated [bɪ'leɪtɪd] *adj* tardif(ive)

belch [beltʃ] *vi* avoir un renvoi, roter ♦ *vt* (*also*: ~ **out**: smoke etc) vomir, cracher

belfry ['belfrɪ] *n* beffroi *m*

Belgian ['beldʒən] *adj* belge, de Belgique ♦ *n* Belge *m/f*

Belgium ['beldʒəm] *n* Belgique *f*

belie [bɪ'laɪ] *vt* démentir

belief [bɪ'liːf] *n* (*opinion*) conviction *f*; (*trust, faith*) foi *f*

believe [bɪ'liːv] *vt, vi* croire; **to** ~ **in** (*God*) croire en; (*method, ghosts*) croire à; ~**r** *n* (*in idea, activity*): ~**r** **in** partisan(e) de; (*REL*) croyant(e)

belittle [bɪ'lɪtl] *vt* déprécier, rabaisser

bell [bel] *n* cloche *f*; (*small*) clochette *f*, grelot *m*; (*on door*) sonnette *f*; (*electric*) sonnerie *f*

belligerent [bɪ'lɪdʒərənt] *adj* (*person, attitude*) agressif(ive)

bellow ['beləʊ] *vi* (*bull*) meugler; (*person*) brailler

belly ['belɪ] *n* ventre *m*

belong [bɪ'lɒŋ] *vi*: **to** ~ **to** appartenir à; (*club etc*) faire partie de; **this book** ~s here ce livre va ici; **~ings** *npl* affaires *fpl*, possessions *fpl*

beloved [bɪ'lʌvɪd] *adj* (bien-)aimé(e)

below [bɪ'ləʊ] *prep* sous, au-dessous de ♦ *adv* en dessous; **see ~** voir plus bas *or* plus loin *or* ci-dessous

belt [belt] *n* ceinture *f*; (*of land*) région *f*; (TECH) courroie *f* ♦ *vt* (*thrash*) donner une raclée à; **~way** (US) *n* (AUT) route *f* de ceinture; (: *motorway*) périphérique *m*

bemused [bɪ'mju:zd] *adj* stupéfié(e)

bench [bentʃ] *n* (*gen, also* BRIT: POL) banc *m*; (*in workshop*) établi *m*; **the B~** (LAW: *judge*) le juge; (: *judges collectively*) la magistrature, la Cour

bend [bend] (*pt, pp* **bent**) *vt* courber; (*leg, arm*) plier ♦ *vi* se courber ♦ *n* (BRIT: *in road*) virage *m*, tournant *m*; (*in pipe, river*) coude *m*; **~ down** *vi* se baisser; **~ over** *vi* se pencher

beneath [bɪ'ni:θ] *prep* sous, au-dessous de; (*unworthy of*) indigne de ♦ *adv* dessous, au-dessous, en bas

benefactor ['benɪfæktə*] *n* bienfaiteur *m*

beneficial [benɪ'fɪʃl] *adj* salutaire; avantageux(euse); **~ to the health** bon(ne) pour la santé

benefit ['benɪfɪt] *n* avantage *m*, profit *m*; (*allowance of money*) allocation *f* ♦ *vt* faire du bien à, profiter à ♦ *vi*: **he'll ~ from it** cela lui fera du bien, il y gagnera *or* s'en trouvera bien

Benelux ['benɪlʌks] *n* Bénélux *m*

benevolent [bɪ'nevələnt] *adj* bienveillant(e); (*organization*) bénévole

benign [bɪ'naɪn] *adj* (*person, smile*) bienveillant(e), affable; (MED) bénin(igne)

bent [bent] *pt, pp of* **bend** ♦ *n* inclination *f*, penchant *m*; **to be ~ on** être résolu(e) à

bequest [bɪ'kwest] *n* legs *m*

bereaved [bɪ'ri:vd] *n*: **the ~** la famille du disparu

beret ['beɪ] *n* béret *m*

Berlin [bə:'lɪn] *n* Berlin

berm [bə:m] (US) *n* (AUT) accotement *m*

berry ['berɪ] *n* baie *f*

berserk [bə'sə:k] *adj*: **to go ~** (*madman, crowd*) se déchaîner

berth [bə:θ] *n* (*bed*) couchette *f*; (*for ship*) poste *m* d'amarrage, mouillage *m* ♦ *vi* (*in harbour*) venir à quai; (*at anchor*) mouiller

beseech [bɪ'si:tʃ] (*pt, pp* **besought**) *vt* implorer, supplier

beset [bɪ'set] (*pt, pp* **beset**) *vt* assaillir

beside [bɪ'saɪd] *prep* à côté de; **to be ~ o.s. (with anger)** être hors de soi; **that's ~ the point** cela n'a rien à voir; **~s** [-z] *adv* en outre, de plus; (*in any case*) d'ailleurs ♦ *prep* (*as well as*) en plus de

besiege [bɪ'si:dʒ] *vt* (*town*) assiéger; (*fig*) assaillir

besought [bɪ'sɔ:t] *pt, pp of* **beseech**

best [best] *adj* meilleur(e) ♦ *adv* le mieux; **the ~ part of** (*quantity*) le plus clair de, la plus grande partie de; **at ~** au mieux; **to make the ~ of sth** s'accommoder de qch (du mieux que l'on peut); **to do one's ~** faire de son mieux; **to the ~ of my knowledge** pour autant que je sache; **to the ~ of my ability** du mieux que je pourrai; **~ man** *n* garçon *m* d'honneur

bestow [bɪ'stəʊ] *vt*: **to ~ sth on sb** accorder qch à qn; (*title*) conférer qch à qn

bet [bet] (*pt, pp* **bet** *or* **betted**) *n* pari *m* ♦ *vt, vi* parier

betray [bɪ'treɪ] *vt* trahir; **~al** *n* trahison *f*

better ['betə*] *adj* meilleur(e) ♦ *adv* mieux ♦ *vt* améliorer ♦ *n*: **to get the ~ of** triompher de, l'emporter sur; **you had ~ do it** vous feriez mieux de le faire; **he thought ~ of it** il s'est ravisé; **to get ~** aller mieux; s'améliorer; **~ off** *adj* plus à l'aise financièrement; (*fig*): **you'd be ~ off this way** vous vous en trouveriez mieux ainsi

betting ['betɪŋ] *n* paris *mpl*; **~ shop** (BRIT) *n* bureau *m* de paris

between [bɪ'twi:n] *prep* entre ♦ *adv*: **(in) ~** au milieu; dans l'intervalle; (*in time*) dans l'intervalle

beverage ['bevərɪdʒ] *n* boisson *f* (*gén sans alcool*)

beware [bɪ'weə*] *vi*: **to ~ (of)** prendre garde (à); **"~ of the dog"** "(attention) chien méchant"

bewildered [bɪ'wɪldəd] *adj* dérouté(e), ahuri(e)

beyond [bɪ'jɒnd] *prep* (*in space, time*) au-delà de; (*exceeding*) au-dessus de ♦ *adv* au-delà; **~ doubt** hors de doute; **~ repair** irréparable

bias ['baɪəs] *n* (*prejudice*) préjugé *m*, parti pris; **~(s)ed** *adj* partial(e), montrant un parti pris

bib [bɪb] *n* bavoir *m*, bavette *f*

Bible ['baɪbl] *n* Bible *f*

bicarbonate of soda [baɪ'kɑ:bənɪt-] *n* bicarbonate *m* de soude

bicker ['bɪkə*] *vi* se chamailler

bicycle ['baɪsɪkl] *n* bicyclette *f*

bid [bɪd] (*pt* **bid** *or* **bade**, *pp* **bid(den)**) *n* offre *f*; (*at auction*) enchère *f*; (*attempt*) tentative *f* ♦ *vi* faire une enchère *or* offre ♦ *vt* faire une enchère *or* offre de; **to ~ sb good day** souhaiter le bonjour à qn; **~der** *n*: **the highest ~der** le plus offrant; **~ding** *n* enchères *fpl*

bide [baɪd] *vt*: **to ~ one's time** attendre son heure

bifocals [baɪ'fəʊkəlz] *npl* verres *mpl* à double foyer, lunettes bifocales

big [bɪg] *adj* grand(e); gros(se)

bigheaded ['bɪg'hedɪd] *adj* prétentieux(euse)

bigot ['bɪgət] *n* fanatique *m/f*, sectaire *m/f*;

~**ed** adj fanatique, sectaire; ~**ry** n fanatisme
m, sectarisme m
big top n grand chapiteau
bike [baɪk] n vélo m, bécane f
bikini [bɪ'ki:nɪ] n bikini m
bilingual [baɪ'lɪŋgwəl] adj bilingue
bill [bɪl] n note f, facture f, (POL) projet m
de loi; (US: banknote) billet m (de banque);
(of bird) bec m; (THEATRE): **on the ~** à
l'affiche; "**post no ~s**" "défense d'afficher"; **to fit** or **fill the ~** (fig) faire l'affaire;
~**board** n panneau m d'affichage
billet ['bɪlɪt] n cantonnement m (chez l'habitant)
billfold ['bɪlfəʊld] (US) n portefeuille m
billiards ['bɪljədz] n (jeu m de) billard m
billion ['bɪljən] n (BRIT) billion m (million
de millions); (US) milliard m
bin [bɪn] n boîte f; (also: dust~) poubelle f;
(for coal) coffre m
bind [baɪnd] (pt, pp **bound**) vt attacher;
(book) relier; (oblige) obliger, contraindre ♦
n (inf: nuisance) scie f; ~**ing** adj (contract)
constituant une obligation
binge [bɪndʒ] (inf) n: **to go on a/the ~**
(inf) aller faire la bringue
bingo ['bɪŋgəʊ] n jeu de loto pratiqué dans
des établissements publics
binoculars [bɪ'nɒkjʊləz] npl jumelles fpl
bio... prefix: ~**chemistry** n biochimie f;
~**graphy** n biographie f; ~**logical** adj bio-
logique; ~**logy** n biologie f
birch [bɜ:tʃ] n bouleau m
bird [bɜ:d] n oiseau m; (BRIT: inf: girl) nana
f; ~**'s-eye view** n vue f à vol d'oiseau;
(fig) vue d'ensemble or générale; ~-
watcher n ornithologue m/f amateur
Biro ['baɪrəʊ] (®) n stylo m à bille
birth [bɜ:θ] n naissance f; **to give ~ to**
(subj: woman) donner naissance à; (: animal) mettre bas; ~ **certificate** n acte m de
naissance; ~ **control** n (policy) limitation f
des naissances; (method) méthode(s)
contraceptive(s); ~**day** n anniversaire m ♦
cpd d'anniversaire; ~**place** n lieu m de
naissance; (fig) berceau m; ~ **rate** n (taux
m de) natalité f
biscuit ['bɪskɪt] n (BRIT) biscuit m; (US) petit pain au lait
bisect [baɪ'sɛkt] vt couper or diviser en
deux
bishop ['bɪʃəp] n évêque m; (CHESS) fou m
bit [bɪt] pt of **bite** ♦ n morceau m; (of tool)
mèche f; (of horse) mors m; (COMPUT) élément m binaire; **a ~ of** un peu de; **a ~**
mad un peu fou; ~ **by** ~ petit à petit
bitch [bɪtʃ] n (dog) chienne f; (inf!) salope f
(!), garce f
bite [baɪt] (pt **bit**, pp **bitten**) vt, vi mordre;
(insect) piquer ♦ n (insect ~) piqûre f;
(mouthful) bouchée f; **let's have a ~ (to**
eat) (inf) mangeons un morceau; **to ~**

one's nails se ronger les ongles
bitter ['bɪtə*] adj amer(ère); (weather, wind)
glacial(e); (criticism) cinglant(e); (struggle)
acharné(e) ♦ n (BRIT: beer) bière f (forte);
~**ness** n amertume f; (taste) goût amer
blab [blæb] vi jaser, trop parler
black [blæk] adj noir(e) ♦ n (colour) noir m;
(person): B~ noir(e) ♦ vt (BRIT: INDUSTRY)
boycotter; **to give sb a ~ eye** pocher l'œil
à qn, faire un œil au beurre noir à qn; ~
and blue couvert(e) de bleus; **to be in the**
~ (in credit) être créditeur(trice); ~**berry**
n mûre f; ~**bird** n merle m; ~**board** n tableau noir; ~ **coffee** n café noir; ~**cur-**
rant n cassis m; ~**en** vt noircir; ~ **ice** n
verglas m; ~**leg** n (BRIT) briseur m de
grève, jaune m; ~**list** n liste noire; ~**mail**
n chantage m ♦ vt faire chanter, soumettre
au chantage; ~ **market** n marché noir;
~**out** n panne f d'électricité; (TV etc) interruption f d'émission; (fainting) syncope f,
étourdissement m; B~ **Sea** n: **the B~ Sea** la mer Noire; ~
sheep n brebis galeuse; ~**smith** n forge-
ron m; ~ **spot** n (AUT) point noir
bladder ['blædə*] n vessie f
blade [bleɪd] n lame f; (of propeller) pale f;
~ **of grass** brin m d'herbe
blame [bleɪm] n faute f, blâme m ♦ vt: **to ~**
sb/sth for sth attribuer à qn/qch la responsabilité de qch; reprocher qch à qn/
qch; **who's to ~?** qui est le fautif or coupable or responsable?; ~**less** adj irréprochable
bland [blænd] adj (taste, food) doux(douce),
fade
blank [blæŋk] adj blanc(blanche); (look)
sans expression, dénué(e) d'expression ♦ n
espace m vide, blanc m; (cartridge) cartouche f à blanc; **his mind was a ~** il avait la
tête vide; ~ **cheque** n chèque m en blanc
blanket ['blæŋkɪt] n couverture f; (of snow,
cloud) couche f
blare [blɛə*] vi beugler
blast [blɑ:st] n souffle m; (of explosive) explosion f ♦ vt faire sauter or exploser; ~-
off n (SPACE) lancement m
blatant ['bleɪtənt] adj flagrant(e), criant(e)
blaze [bleɪz] n (fire) incendie m; (fig) flam-
boiement m ♦ vi (fire) flamber; (fig: eyes)
flamboyer; (: guns) crépiter ♦ vt: **to ~ a**
trail (fig) montrer la voie
blazer ['bleɪzə*] n blazer m
bleach [bli:tʃ] n (also: household ~) eau f
de Javel ♦ vt (linen etc) blanchir; ~**ed** adj
(hair) oxygéné(e), décoloré(e); ~**ers**
['bli:tʃəz] (US) npl (SPORT) gradins mpl (en
plein soleil)
bleak [bli:k] adj morne; (countryside) dé-
solé(e)
bleary-eyed ['blɪərɪ'aɪd] adj aux yeux
pleins de sommeil
bleat [bli:t] vi bêler

bleed [bliːd] (*pt, pp* **bled**) *vt, vi* saigner; **my nose is ~ing** je saigne du nez

bleeper ['bliːpə*] *n* (*device*) bip *m*

blemish ['blemɪʃ] *n* défaut *m*; (*on fruit, reputation*) tache *f*

blend [blend] *n* mélange *m* ♦ *vt* mélanger ♦ *vi* (*colours etc: also:* ~ **in**) se mélanger, se fondre

bless [bles] (*pt, pp* **blessed** *or* **blest**) *vt* bénir; ~ **you!** (*after sneeze*) à vos souhaits!; ~**ing** *n* bénédiction *f*; (*godsend*) bienfait *m*

blew [bluː] *pt of* **blow**

blight [blaɪt] *vt* (*hopes etc*) anéantir; (*life*) briser

blimey ['blaɪmɪ] (*BRIT: inf*) *excl* mince alors!

blind [blaɪnd] *adj* aveugle ♦ *n* (*for window*) store *m* ♦ *vt* aveugler; ~ **alley** *n* impasse *f*; ~ **corner** (*BRIT*) *n* virage *m* sans visibilité; ~**fold** *n* bandeau *m* ♦ *adj, adv* les yeux bandés ♦ *vt* bander les yeux à; ~**ly** *adv* aveuglément; ~**ness** *n* cécité *f*; ~ **spot** *n* (*AUT etc*) angle mort; **that is her ~ spot** (*fig*) elle refuse d'y voir clair sur ce point

blink [blɪŋk] *vi* cligner des yeux; (*light*) clignoter; ~**ers** *npl* œillères *fpl*

bliss [blɪs] *n* félicité *f*, bonheur *m* sans mélange

blister ['blɪstə*] *n* (*on skin*) ampoule *f*, cloque *f*; (*on paintwork, rubber*) boursouflure *f* ♦ *vi* (*paint*) se boursoufler, se cloquer

blithely ['blaɪðlɪ] *adv* (*unconcernedly*) tranquillement

blizzard ['blɪzəd] *n* blizzard *m*, tempête *f* de neige

bloated ['bləʊtɪd] *adj* (*face*) bouffi(e); (*stomach, person*) gonflé(e)

blob [blɒb] *n* (*drop*) goutte *f*; (*stain, spot*) tache *f*

block [blɒk] *n* bloc *m*; (*in pipes*) obstruction *f*; (*toy*) cube *m*; (*of buildings*) pâté *m* (de maisons) *m* ♦ *vt* bloquer; (*fig*) faire obstacle à; ~ **of flats** (*BRIT*) *n* immeuble (locatif); **mental ~** trou *m* de mémoire; ~**ade** *n* blocus *m*; ~**age** *n* obstruction *f*; ~**buster** *n* (*film, book*) grand succès; ~ **letters** *npl* majuscules *fpl*

bloke [bləʊk] (*BRIT: inf*) *n* type *m*

blond(e) [blɒnd] *adj, n* blond(e)

blood [blʌd] *n* sang *m*; ~ **donor** *n* donneur(euse) *de* sang; ~ **group** *n* groupe sanguin; ~**hound** *n* limier *m*; ~ **poisoning** *n* empoisonnement *m* du sang; ~ **pressure** *n* tension *f* (artérielle); ~**shed** *n* effusion *f* de sang, carnage *m*; ~**shot** *adj*: ~**shot eyes** yeux injectés de sang; ~**stream** *n* sang *m*, système sanguin; ~ **test** *n* prise *f* de sang; ~**thirsty** *adj* sanguinaire; ~ **vessel** *n* vaisseau sanguin; ~**y** *adj* sanglant(e); (*nose*) en sang; (*BRIT: inf!*): **this ~y ...** ce foutu ... (*!*), ce putain de ... (*!*); ~**y strong/good** vachement *or* sacré-

ment fort/bon; ~**y-minded** (*BRIT: inf*) *adj* contrariant(e), obstiné(e)

bloom [bluːm] *n* fleur *f* ♦ *vi* être en fleur

blossom ['blɒsəm] *n* fleur(s) *f(pl)* ♦ *vi* être en fleurs; (*fig*) s'épanouir; **to ~ into** devenir

blot [blɒt] *n* tache *f* ♦ *vt* tacher; ~ **out** *vt* (*memories*) effacer; (*view*) cacher, masquer

blotchy ['blɒtʃɪ] *adj* (*complexion*) couvert(e) de marbrures

blotting paper ['blɒtɪŋ-] *n* buvard *m*

blouse [blaʊz] *n* chemisier *m*, corsage *m*

blow [bləʊ] (*pt* **blew**, *pp* **blown**) *n* coup *m* ♦ *vi* souffler ♦ *vt* souffler; (*fuse*) faire sauter; (*instrument*) jouer de; **to ~ one's nose** se moucher; **to ~ a whistle** siffler; ~ **away** *vt* chasser, faire s'envoler; ~ **down** *vt* faire tomber, renverser; ~ **off** *vt* emporter; ~ **out** *vi* (*fire, flame*) s'éteindre; ~ **over** *vi* s'apaiser; ~ **up** *vt* faire sauter; (*tyre*) gonfler; (*PHOT*) agrandir ♦ *vi* exploser, sauter; ~**dry** *n* brushing *m*; ~**lamp** (*BRIT*) *n* chalumeau *m*; ~**-out** *n* (*of tyre*) éclatement *m*; ~**-torch** *n* = **blowlamp**

blue [bluː] *adj* bleu(e); (*fig*) triste; ~**s** *n* (*MUS*): **the ~s** le blues; ~ **film/joke** film *m*/histoire *f* pornographique; **to come out of the ~** (*fig*) être complètement inattendu; ~**bell** *n* jacinthe *f* des bois; ~**bottle** *n* mouche *f* à viande; ~**print** *n* (*fig*) projet *m*, plan directeur

bluff [blʌf] *vi* bluffer ♦ *n* bluff *m*; **to call sb's ~** mettre qn au défi d'exécuter ses menaces

blunder ['blʌndə*] *n* gaffe *f*, bévue *f* ♦ *vi* faire une gaffe *or* une bévue

blunt [blʌnt] *adj* (*person*) brusque, ne mâchant pas ses mots; (*knife*) émoussé(e), peu tranchant(e); (*pencil*) mal taillé

blur [blɜː*] *n* tache *f* ou masse floue *or* confuse ♦ *vt* brouiller

blurb [blɜːb] *n* notice *f* publicitaire; (*for book*) texte *m* de présentation

blurt out [blɜːt-] *vt* (*reveal*) lâcher

blush [blʌʃ] *vi* rougir ♦ *n* rougeur *f*

blustery ['blʌstərɪ] *adj* (*weather*) à bourrasques

boar [bɔː*] *n* sanglier *m*

board [bɔːd] *n* planche *f*; (*on wall*) panneau *m*; (*for chess*) échiquier *m*; (*cardboard*) carton *m*; (*committee*) conseil *m*, comité *m*; (*in firm*) conseil d'administration; (*NAUT, AVIAT*): **on ~** à bord ♦ *vt* (*ship*) monter à bord de; (*train*) monter dans; **full ~** (*BRIT*) pension complète; **half ~** demi-pension *f*; ~ **and lodging** chambre *f* avec pension; **which goes by the ~** (*fig*) qu'on laisse tomber, qu'on abandonne; ~ **up** *vt* (*door, window*) boucher; ~**er** *n* (*SCOL*) interne *m/f*, pensionnaire; ~**ing card** *n* = **boarding pass**; ~**ing house** *n* pension *f*; ~**ing pass** *n* (*AVIAT, NAUT*) carte *f* d'embarquement; ~**ing school** *n* internat *m*, pensionnat *m*; ~ **room** *n* salle *f* du conseil d'administration

boast [bəust] *vi*: **to ~ (about *or* of)** se vanter (de)

boat [bəut] *n* bateau *m*; (*small*) canot *m*; barque *f*; ~**er** *n* (*hat*) canotier *m*

bob [bɒb] *vi* (*boat, cork on water: also:* ~ **up** *and down*) danser, se balancer

bobby ['bɒbɪ] (*BRIT: inf*) *n* ≈ agent *m* (de police)

bobsleigh ['bɒbsleɪ] *n* bob *m*

bode [bəud] *vi*: **to ~ well/ill (for)** être de bon/mauvais augure (pour)

bodily ['bɒdɪlɪ] *adj* corporel(le) ♦ *adv* dans ses bras

body ['bɒdɪ] *n* corps *m*; (*of car*) carrosserie *f*; (*of plane*) fuselage *m*; (*fig: society*) organe *m*, organisme *m*; (*: quantity*) ensemble *m*, masse *f*; (*of wine*) corps *m*; ~-**building** *n* culturisme *m*; ~**guard** *n* garde *m* du corps; ~**work** *n* carrosserie *f*

bog [bɒg] *n* tourbière *f* ♦ *vt*: **to get ~ged down** (*fig*) s'enliser

boggle ['bɒgl] *vi*: **the mind ~s** c'est incroyable, on en reste sidéré

bogus ['bəugəs] *adj* bidon *inv*; fantôme

boil [bɔɪl] *vt* (faire) bouillir ♦ *vi* bouillir ♦ *n* (*MED*) furoncle *m*; **to come to the** (*BRIT*) ~ *or* **a** (*US*) ~ bouillir; ~ **down to** *vt fus* (*fig*) se réduire *or* ramener à; ~ **over** *vi* déborder; ~**ed egg** *n* œuf *m* à la coque; ~**ed potatoes** *npl* pommes *fpl* à l'anglaise *or* à l'eau; ~**er** *n* chaudière *f*; ~**ing point** *n* point *m* d'ébullition

boisterous ['bɔɪstərəs] *adj* bruyant(e), tapageur(euse)

bold [bəuld] *adj* hardi(e), audacieux(euse); (*pej*) effronté(e); (*outline, colour*) franc(franche), tranché(e), marqué(e); (*pattern*) grand(e)

bollard ['bɒləd] (*BRIT*) *n* (*AUT*) borne lumineuse *or* de signalisation

bolster ['bəulstə*] : ~ **up** *vt* soutenir

bolt [bəult] *n* (*lock*) verrou *m*; (*with nut*) boulon *m* ♦ *adv*: ~ **upright** droit(e) comme un piquet ♦ *vt* verrouiller; (*TECH: also:* ~ **on**, ~ **together**) boulonner; (*food*) engloutir ♦ *vi* (*horse*) s'emballer

bomb [bɒm] *n* bombe *f* ♦ *vt* bombarder

bombastic [bɒm'bæstɪk] *adj* pompeux(euse)

bomb: ~ **disposal unit** *n* section *f* de déminage; ~**er** *n* (*AVIAT*) bombardier *m*; ~**shell** *n* (*fig*) bombe *f*

bona fide ['bəunə'faɪdɪ] *adj* (*traveller*) véritable

bond [bɒnd] *n* lien *m*; (*binding promise*) engagement *m*, obligation *f*; (*COMM*) obligation; **in ~** (*of goods*) en douane

bondage ['bɒndɪdʒ] *n* esclavage *m*

bone [bəun] *n* os *m*; (*of fish*) arête *f* ♦ *vt* désosser; ôter les arêtes de; ~ **idle** *adj* fainéant(e)

bonfire ['bɒnfaɪə*] *n* feu *m* (de joie); (*for rubbish*) feu

bonnet ['bɒnɪt] *n* bonnet *m*; (*BRIT: of car*) capot *m*

bonus ['bəunəs] *n* prime *f*, gratification *f*

bony ['bəunɪ] *adj* (*arm, face, MED: tissue*) osseux(euse); (*meat*) plein(e) d'os; (*fish*) plein d'arêtes

boo [bu:] *excl* hou!, peuh! ♦ *vt* huer

booby trap ['bu:bɪ-] *n* engin piégé

book [buk] *n* livre *m*; (*of stamps, tickets*) carnet *m* ♦ *vt* (*ticket*) prendre; (*seat, room*) réserver; (*driver*) dresser un procès-verbal à; (*football player*) prendre le nom de; ~**s** *npl* (*accounts*) comptes *mpl*, comptabilité *f*; ~**case** *n* bibliothèque *f* (*meuble*); ~**ing office** (*BRIT*) *n* bureau *m* de location; ~**keeping** *n* comptabilité *f*; ~**let** *n* brochure *f*; ~**maker** *n* bookmaker *m*; ~**seller** *n* libraire *m/f*; ~**shop** *n* librairie *f*; ~**store** *n* librairie *f*

boom [bu:m] *n* (*noise*) grondement *m*; (*in prices, population*) forte augmentation ♦ *vi* gronder; prospérer

boon [bu:n] *n* bénédiction *f*, grand avantage

boost [bu:st] *n* stimulant *m*, remontant *m* ♦ *vt* stimuler; ~**er** *n* (*MED*) rappel *m*

boot [bu:t] *n* botte *f*; (*for hiking*) chaussure *f* (de marche); (*for football etc*) soulier *m*; (*BRIT: of car*) coffre *m* ♦ *vt* (*COMPUT*) amorcer, initialiser; **to ~** (*in addition*) pardessus le marché

booth [bu:ð] *n* (*at fair*) baraque (foraine); (*telephone etc*) cabine *f*; (*also: voting* ~) isoloir *m*

booty ['bu:tɪ] *n* butin *m*

booze [bu:z] (*inf*) *n* boissons *fpl* alcooliques, alcool *m*

border ['bɔ:də*] *n* bordure *f*; bord *m*; (*of a country*) frontière *f* ♦ *vt* border; (*on: country*) être limitrophe de; **B~s** *n* (*GEO*): **the B~s** la région frontière entre l'Écosse et l'Angleterre; ~ **on** *vt fus* être voisin(e) de, toucher à; ~**line** *n* (*fig*) ligne *f* de démarcation; ~**line case** *n* cas *m* limite

bore [bɔ:*] *pt of* **bear** ♦ *vt* (*hole*) percer; (*oil well, tunnel*) creuser; (*person*) ennuyer, raser ♦ *n* raseur(euse); (*of gun*) calibre *m*; **to be ~d** s'ennuyer; ~**dom** *n* ennui *m*; **boring** *adj* ennuyeux(euse)

born [bɔ:n] *adj*: **to be ~** naître; **I was ~ in 1960** je suis né en 1960

borne [bɔ:n] *pp of* **bear**

borough ['bʌrə] *n* municipalité *f*

borrow ['bɒrəu] *vt*: **to ~ sth (from sb)** emprunter qch (à qn)

Bosnia (and) Herzegovina [bɒznɪə (ənd) herzəgəuvi:nə] *n* Bosnie-Herzégovine *f*

bosom ['buzəm] *n* poitrine *f*, (*fig*) sein *m*; ~ **friend** *n* ami(e) intime

boss [bɒs] n patron(ne) ♦ vt (also: ~ around/about) commander; **~y** adj autoritaire

bosun ['bəʊsn] n maître m d'équipage

botany ['bɒtənɪ] n botanique f

botch [bɒtʃ] vt (also: ~ up) saboter, bâcler

both [bəʊθ] adj les deux, l'un(e) et l'autre ♦ pron: ~ (of them) les deux, tous(toutes) (les) deux, l'un(e) et l'autre; **they sell ~ the fabric and the finished curtains** ils vendent (et) le tissu et les rideaux (finis), ils vendent à la fois le tissu et les rideaux (finis); ~ of us went, we ~ went nous y sommes allés (tous) les deux

bother ['bɒðə*] vt (worry) tracasser; (disturb) déranger ♦ vi (also: ~ o.s.) se tracasser, se faire du souci ♦ n: **it is a ~ to have to do** c'est vraiment ennuyeux d'avoir à faire; **it's no ~** aucun problème; **to ~ doing** prendre la peine de faire

bottle ['bɒtl] n bouteille f; (baby's) biberon m ♦ vt mettre en bouteille(s); ~ up vt refouler, contenir; ~ **bank** n conteneur m à verre; **~neck** n étranglement m; **~-opener** n ouvre-bouteille m

bottom ['bɒtəm] n (of container, sea etc) fond m; (buttocks) derrière m; (of page, list) bas m ♦ adj du fond; du bas; **the ~ of the class** le dernier de la classe; **~less** adj (funds) inépuisable

bough [baʊ] n branche f, rameau m

bought [bɔːt] pt, pp of **buy**

boulder ['bəʊldə*] n gros rocher

bounce [baʊns] vi (ball) rebondir; (cheque) être refusé(e) (étant sans provision) ♦ vt faire rebondir ♦ n (rebound) rebond m; **~r** (inf) n (at dance, club) videur m

bound [baʊnd] pt, pp of **bind** ♦ n (gen pl) limite f; (leap) bond m ♦ vi (leap) bondir ♦ vt (limit) borner ♦ adj: **to be ~ to do sth** (obliged) être obligé(e) or avoir obligation de faire qch; **he's ~ to fail** (likely) il est sûr d'échouer, son échec est inévitable or assuré; ~ **by** (law, regulation) engagé(e) par; ~ **for** à destination de; **out of ~s** dont l'accès est interdit

boundary ['baʊndərɪ] n frontière f

boundless ['baʊndlɪs] adj sans bornes

bout [baʊt] n période f; (of malaria etc) accès m, crise f, attaque f; (BOXING etc) combat m, match m

bow[1] [bəʊ] n nœud m; (weapon) arc m; (MUS) archet m

bow[2] [baʊ] n (with body) révérence f, inclination f (du buste or corps); (NAUT: also: ~s) proue f ♦ vi faire une révérence, s'incliner; (yield): **to ~ to or before** s'incliner devant, se soumettre à

bowels ['baʊəlz] npl intestins mpl; (fig) entrailles fpl

bowl [bəʊl] n (for eating) bol m; (ball) boule f ♦ vi (CRICKET, BASEBALL) lancer (la balle)

bow-legged ['bəʊ'legɪd] adj aux jambes arquées

bowler ['bəʊlə*] n (CRICKET, BASEBALL) lanceur m (de la balle); (BRIT: also: ~ hat) (chapeau m) melon m

bowling ['bəʊlɪŋ] n (game) jeu m de boules; jeu m de quilles; ~ **alley** n bowling m; ~ **green** n terrain m de boules (gazonné et carré)

bowls [bəʊlz] n (game) (jeu m de) boules fpl

bow tie ['bəʊ-] n nœud m papillon

box [bɒks] n boîte f; (also: cardboard ~) carton m; (THEATRE) loge f ♦ vt mettre en boîte; (SPORT) boxer avec ♦ vi boxer, faire de la boxe; **~er** n (person) boxeur m; **~ing** n (SPORT) boxe f; **B~ing Day** (BRIT) n le lendemain de Noël; **~ing gloves** npl gants mpl de boxe; **~ing ring** n ring m; ~ **office** n bureau m de location; **~room** n débarras m; chambrette f

boy [bɔɪ] n garçon m

boycott ['bɔɪkɒt] n boycottage m ♦ vt boycotter

boyfriend ['bɔɪfrend] n (petit) ami

boyish ['bɔɪɪʃ] adj (behaviour) de garçon; (girl) garçonnier(ière)

BR abbr = **British Rail**

bra [brɑː] n soutien-gorge m

brace [breɪs] n (on teeth) appareil m (dentaire); (tool) vilbrequin m ♦ vt (knees, shoulders) appuyer; ~**s** npl (BRIT: for trousers) bretelles fpl; **to ~ o.s.** (lit) s'arcbouter; (fig) se préparer mentalement

bracelet ['breɪslɪt] n bracelet m

bracing ['breɪsɪŋ] adj tonifiant(e), tonique

bracket ['brækɪt] n (TECH) tasseau m, support m; (group) classe f, tranche f, catégorie f; (also: brace ~) accolade f; (: round ~) parenthèse f; (: square ~) crochet m ♦ vt mettre entre parenthèse(s); (fig: also: ~ together) regrouper

brag [bræg] vi se vanter

braid [breɪd] n (trimming) galon m; (of hair) tresse f

brain [breɪn] n cerveau m; ~**s** npl (intellect, CULIN) cervelle f; **he's got ~s** il est intelligent; **~child** n invention personnelle; **~wash** vt faire subir un lavage de cerveau à; **~wave** n idée géniale; **~y** adj intelligent(e), doué(e)

braise [breɪz] vt braiser

brake [breɪk] n (on vehicle, also fig) frein m ♦ vi freiner; ~ **fluid** n liquide m de freins; ~ **light** n feu m de stop

bran [bræn] n son m

branch [brɑːntʃ] n branche f; (COMM) succursale f ♦ vi bifurquer; ~ **out** vi (fig): **to ~ out into** étendre ses activités à

brand [brænd] n marque (commerciale) ♦ vt (cattle) marquer (au fer rouge); **~-new** adj

tout(e) neuf(neuve), flambant neuf(neuve)
brandy ['brændɪ] *n* cognac *m*, fine *f*
brash [bræʃ] *adj* effronté(e)
brass [brɑːs] *n* cuivre *m* (jaune), laiton *m*;
the ~ (*MUS*) les cuivres; ~ **band** *n* fanfare
f
brassière ['bræsɪə*] *n* soutien-gorge *m*
brat [bræt] (*pej*) *n* mioche *m/f*, môme *m/f*
brave [breɪv] *adj* courageux(euse), brave ♦
n guerrier indien ♦ *vt* braver, affronter; ~**ry**
n bravoure *f*, courage *m*
brawl [brɔːl] *n* rixe *f*, bagarre *f*
bray [breɪ] *vi* braire
brazen ['breɪzn] *adj* impudent(e), effron-
té(e) ♦ *vt*: **to** ~ **it out** payer d'effronterie,
crâner
brazier ['breɪzɪə*] *n* brasero *m*
Brazil [brə'zɪl] *n* Brésil *m*
breach [briːtʃ] *vt* ouvrir une brèche dans ♦
n (*gap*) brèche *f*; (*breaking*): ~ **of contract**
rupture *f* de contrat; ~ **of the peace** attent-
tat *m* à l'ordre public
bread [bred] *n* pain *m*; ~ **and butter** *n*
tartines (beurrées); (*fig*) subsistance *f*; ~**bin**
(*BRIT*) *n* boîte *f* à pain; (*bigger*) huche *f* à
pain; ~**box** (*US*) *n* = ~**bin**; ~**crumbs** *npl*
miettes *fpl* de pain; (*CULIN*) chapelure *f*,
panure *f*; ~**line** *n*: **to be on the ~line** être
sans le sou *or* dans l'indigence
breadth [bretθ] *n* largeur *f*, (*fig*) ampleur *f*
breadwinner ['bredwɪnə*] *n* soutien *m* de
famille
break [breɪk] (*pt* **broke**, *pp* **broken**) *vt* casser, briser; (*promise*) rompre; (*law*) violer ♦
vi (se) casser, se briser; (*weather*) tourner;
(*story, news*) se répandre; (*day*) se lever ♦ *n*
(*gap*) brèche *f*, (*fracture*) cassure *f*; (*pause,
interval*) interruption *f*, arrêt *m*; (: *short*)
pause *f*; (: *at school*) récréation *f*, (*chance*)
chance *f*, occasion *f* favorable; **to** ~ **one's
leg** *etc* se casser la jambe *etc*; **to** ~ **a record** battre un record; **to** ~ **the news to sb**
annoncer la nouvelle à qn; ~ **even** rentrer
dans ses frais; ~ **free** *or* **loose** se dégager,
s'échapper; ~ **open** (*door etc*) forcer, frac-
turer; ~ **down** *vt* (*figures, data*) décomposer, analyser ♦ *vi* s'effondrer; (*MED*) faire
une dépression (nerveuse); (*AUT*) tomber
en panne; ~ **in** *vt* (*horse etc*) dresser ♦ *vi*
(*burglar*) entrer par effraction; (*interrupt*) interrompre; ~ **into** *vt fus* (*house*) s'introduire *or* pénétrer par effraction dans; ~ **off** *vi*
(*speaker*) s'interrompre; (*branch*) se rompre;
~ **out** *vi* éclater, se déclarer; (*prisoner*)
s'évader; **to** ~ **out in spots** *or* **a rash** avoir
une éruption de boutons; ~ **up** *vi* (*ship*) se
disloquer; (*crowd, meeting*) se disperser, se
séparer; (*marriage*) se briser; (*SCOL*) entrer
en vacances ♦ *vt* casser; (*fight etc*) interrompre, faire cesser; ~**age** *n* casse *f*;
~**down** *n* (*AUT*) panne *f*; (*in communica-
tions, marriage*) rupture *f*, (*MED*: also: ner-

vous ~) dépression (nerveuse); (*of statistics*)
ventilation *f*; ~**down van** (*BRIT*) *n* dépanneuse *f*; ~**er** *n* brisant *m*
breakfast ['brekfəst] *n* petit déjeuner
break: ~**-in** *n* cambriolage *m*; ~**ing and
entering** *n* (*LAW*) effraction *f*; ~**through**
n percée *f*; ~**water** *n* brise-lames *m inv*, digue *f*
breast [brest] *n* (*of woman*) sein *m*; (*chest,
of meat*) poitrine *f*; ~**-feed** (*irreg: like* **feed**)
vt, *vi* allaiter; ~**stroke** *n* brasse *f*
breath [breθ] *n* haleine *f*; **out of** ~ à bout
de souffle, essoufflé(e)
Breathalyser ['breθəlaɪzə*] (®) *n* Alcoo-
test *m* (®)
breathe [briːð] *vt*, *vi* respirer; ~ **in** *vt*, *vi*
aspirer, inspirer; ~ **out** *vt*, *vi* expirer; ~**r** *n*
moment *m* de repos *or* de répit; **breathing**
['briːðɪŋ] *n* respiration *f*; **breathing space**
n (*fig*) (moment *m* de) répit *m*
breathless ['breθlɪs] *adj* essoufflé(e), hale-
tant(e); oppressé(e)
breathtaking ['breθteɪkɪŋ] *adj* stupé-
fiant(e), à vous couper le souffle
breed [briːd] (*pt*, *pp* **bred**) *vt* élever, faire
l'élevage de ♦ *vi* se reproduire ♦ *n* race *f*,
variété *f*; ~**ing** *n* (*upbringing*) éducation *f*
breeze [briːz] *n* brise *f*; **breezy** ['briːzɪ] *adj*
frais(fraîche); aéré(e); (*manner etc*) désinvolte, jovial(e)
brevity ['brevɪtɪ] *n* brièveté *f*
brew [bruː] *vt* (*tea*) faire infuser; (*beer*)
brasser ♦ *vi* (*fig*) se préparer, couver; ~**ery**
n brasserie *f* (*fabrique*)
bribe ['braɪb] *n* pot-de-vin *m* ♦ *vt* acheter;
soudoyer; ~**ry** *n* corruption *f*
brick [brɪk] *n* brique *f*; ~**layer** *n* maçon *m*
bridal ['braɪdl] *adj* nuptial(e)
bride [braɪd] *n* mariée *f*, épouse *f*; ~**groom**
n marié *m*, époux *m*; ~**smaid** *n* demoiselle
f d'honneur
bridge [brɪdʒ] *n* pont *m*; (*NAUT*) passerelle
f (de commandement); (*of nose*) arête *f*;
(*CARDS, DENTISTRY*) bridge *m* ♦ *vt* (*fig:
gap, gulf*) combler
bridle ['braɪdl] *n* bride *f*; ~ **path** *n* piste *or*
allée cavalière
brief [briːf] *adj* bref(brève) ♦ *n* (*LAW*) dossier *m*, cause *f*; (*gen*) tâche *f* ♦ *vt* mettre au
courant; ~**s** *npl* (*undergarment*) slip *m*;
~**case** *n* serviette *f*, porte-documents *m
inv*; ~**ly** *adv* brièvement
bright [braɪt] *adj* brillant(e); (*room, weather*) clair(e); (*clever: person, idea*) intelli-
gent(e); (*cheerful: colour, person*) vif(vive)
brighten (*also* ~ **up**) *vt* (*room*) éclaircir,
égayer; (*event*) égayer ♦ *vi* s'éclaircir; (*person*) retrouver un peu de sa gaieté; (*face*)
s'éclairer; (*prospects*) s'améliorer
brilliance ['brɪljəns] *n* éclat *m*
brilliant ['brɪljənt] *adj* brillant(e); (*sunshine,
light*) éclatant(e); (*inf: holiday etc*) super

brim [brɪm] *n* bord *m*

brine [braɪn] *n* (*CULIN*) saumure *f*

bring [brɪŋ] (*pt, pp* **brought**) *vt* apporter; (*person*) amener; ~ **about** *vt* provoquer, entraîner; ~ **back** *vt* rapporter; ramener; (*restore: hanging*) réinstaurer; ~ **down** *vt* (*price*) faire baisser; (*enemy plane*) descendre; (*government*) faire tomber; ~ **forward** *vt* avancer; ~ **off** *vt* (*task, plan*) réussir, mener à bien; ~ **out** *vt* (*meaning*) faire ressortir; (*book*) publier; (*object*) sortir; ~ **round** *vt* (*unconscious person*) ranimer; ~ **to** *vt* = ~ **round**; ~ **up** *vt* (*child*) élever; (*carry up*) monter; (*question*) soulever; (*food: vomit*) vomir, rendre

brink [brɪŋk] *n* bord *m*

brisk [brɪsk] *adj* vif(vive)

bristle [brɪsl] *n* poil *m* ♦ *vi* se hérisser

Britain ['brɪtən] *n* (*also: Great* ~) Grande-Bretagne *f*

British ['brɪtɪʃ] *adj* britannique ♦ *npl*: **the** ~ les Britanniques *mpl*; ~ **Isles** *npl*: **the** ~ **Isles** les Iles *fpl* Britanniques; ~ **Rail** *n* compagnie ferroviaire britannique

Briton ['brɪtən] *n* Britannique *m/f*

Brittany ['brɪtənɪ] *n* Bretagne *f*

brittle ['brɪtl] *adj* cassant(e), fragile

broach [brəʊtʃ] *vt* (*subject*) aborder

broad [brɔːd] *adj* large; (*general: outlines*) grand(e); (: *distinction*) général(e); (*accent*) prononcé(e); **in** ~ **daylight** en plein jour; ~**cast** (*pt, pp* ~**cast**) *n* émission *f* ♦ *vt* radiodiffuser; télévisér ♦ *vi* émettre; ~**en** *vt* élargir ♦ *vi* s'élargir; **to** ~**en one's mind** élargir ses horizons; ~**ly** *adv* en gros, généralement; ~**-minded** *adj* large d'esprit

broccoli ['brɒkəlɪ] *n* brocoli *m*

brochure ['brəʊʃʊə*] *n* prospectus *m*, dépliant *m*

broil [brɔɪl] *vt* griller

broke [brəʊk] *pt of* **break** ♦ *adj* (*inf*) fauché(e)

broken ['brəʊkən] *pp of* **break** ♦ *adj* cassé(e); (*machine: also:* ~ **down**) fichu(e); **in** ~ **English/French** dans un anglais/français approximatif ou hésitant; ~ **leg** *etc* jambe *etc* cassée; ~**-hearted** *adj* (ayant) le cœur brisé

broker ['brəʊkə*] *n* courtier *m*

brolly ['brɒlɪ] (*BRIT: inf*) *n* pépin *m*, parapluie *m*

bronchitis [brɒŋ'kaɪtɪs] *n* bronchite *f*

bronze [brɒnz] *n* bronze *m*

brooch [brəʊtʃ] *n* broche *f*

brood [bruːd] *n* couvée *f* ♦ *vi* (*person*) méditer (sombrement), ruminer

broom [bruːm] *n* balai *m*; (*BOT*) genêt *m*; ~**stick** *n* manche *m* à balai

Bros. *abbr* = **Brothers**

broth [brɒθ] *n* bouillon *m* de viande et de légumes

brothel ['brɒθl] *n* maison close, bordel *m*

brother ['brʌðə*] *n* frère *m*; ~**-in-law** *n* beau-frère *m*

brought [brɔːt] *pt, pp of* **bring**

brow [braʊ] *n* front *m*; (*eye~*) sourcil *m*; (*of hill*) sommet *m*

brown [braʊn] *adj* brun(e), marron *inv*; (*hair*) châtain *inv*; brun; (*eyes*) marron *inv*; (*tanned*) bronzé(e) ♦ *n* (*colour*) brun *m* ♦ *vt* (*CULIN*) faire dorer; ~ **bread** *n* pain *m* bis; **B~ie** ['braʊnɪ] *n* (*also:* ~ *Guide*) jeannette *f*, éclaireuse (cadette); ~**ie** ['braʊnɪ] (*US*) *n* (*cake*) gâteau *m* au chocolat et aux noix; ~ **paper** *n* papier *m* d'emballage; ~ **sugar** *n* cassonade *f*

browse [braʊz] *vi* (*among books*) bouquiner, feuilleter les livres; **to** ~ **through a book** feuilleter un livre

bruise [bruːz] *n* bleu *m*, contusion *f* ♦ *vt* contusionner, meurtrir

brunette [bruː'net] *n* (femme) brune

brunt [brʌnt] *n*: **the** ~ **of** (*attack, criticism etc*) le plus gros de

brush [brʌʃ] *n* brosse *f*; (*painting*) pinceau *m*; (*shaving*) blaireau *m*; (*quarrel*) accrochage *m*, prise *f* de bec ♦ *vt* brosser; (*also:* ~ *against*) effleurer, frôler; ~ **aside** *vt* écarter, balayer; ~ **up** *vt* (*knowledge*) rafraîchir, réviser; ~**wood** *n* broussailles *fpl*, taillis *m*

Brussels ['brʌslz] *n* Bruxelles; ~ **sprout** *n* chou *m* de Bruxelles

brutal ['bruːtl] *adj* brutal(e)

brute [bruːt] *n* brute *f* ♦ *adj*: **by** ~ **force** par la force

BSc *abbr* = **Bachelor of Science**

bubble ['bʌbl] *n* bulle *f* ♦ *vi* bouillonner, faire des bulles; (*sparkle*) pétiller; ~ **bath** *n* bain moussant; ~ **gum** *n* bubblegum *m*

buck [bʌk] *n* mâle *m* (*d'un lapin, daim etc*); (*US: inf*) dollar *m* ♦ *vi* ruer, lancer une ruade; **to pass the** ~ **(to sb)** se décharger de la responsabilité (sur qn); ~ **up** *vi* (*cheer up*) reprendre du poil de la bête, se remonter

bucket ['bʌkɪt] *n* seau *m*

buckle ['bʌkl] *n* boucle *f* ♦ *vt* (*belt etc*) boucler, attacher ♦ *vi* (*warp*) tordre, gauchir; (: *wheel*) se voiler; se déformer

bud [bʌd] *n* bourgeon *m*; (*of flower*) bouton *m* ♦ *vi* bourgeonner; (*flower*) éclore

Buddhism ['bʊdɪzəm] *n* bouddhisme *m*

budding ['bʌdɪŋ] *adj* (*poet etc*) en herbe; (*passion etc*) naissant(e)

buddy ['bʌdɪ] (*US*) *n* copain *m*

budge [bʌdʒ] *vt* faire bouger; (*fig: person*) faire changer d'avis ♦ *vi* bouger; changer d'avis

budgerigar ['bʌdʒərɪgɑː*] (*BRIT*) *n* perruche *f*

budget ['bʌdʒɪt] *n* budget *m* ♦ *vi*: **to** ~ **for sth** inscrire qch au budget

budgie ['bʌdʒɪ] (*BRIT*) *n* = **budgerigar**

buff [bʌf] *adj* (couleur *f*) chamois *m* ♦ *n* (*inf: enthusiast*) mordu(e); **he's a ...** ~ c'est un mordu de ...

buffalo ['bʌfələu] (*pl* ~ *or* ~**es**) *n* buffle *m*; (*US*) bison *m*

buffer ['bʌfə*] *n* tampon *m*; (*COMPUT*) mémoire *f* tampon

buffet[1] ['bʌfɪt] *vt* secouer, ébranler

buffet[2] ['bufeɪ] *n* (*food, BRIT: bar*) buffet *m*; ~ **car** (*BRIT*) *n* (*RAIL*) voiture-buffet *f*

bug [bʌg] *n* (*insect*) punaise *f*; (: *gen*) insecte *m*, bestiole *f*; (*fig: germ*) virus *m*, microbe *m*; (*COMPUT*) erreur *f*; (*fig: spy device*) dispositif *m* d'écoute (électronique) ♦ *vt* garnir de dispositifs d'écoute; (*inf: annoy*) embêter

bugle ['bjuːgl] *n* clairon *m*

build [bɪld] (*pt, pp* built) *n* (*of person*) carrure *f*, charpente *f* ♦ *vt* construire, bâtir; ~ **up** *vt* accumuler, amasser; accroître; ~**er** *n* entrepreneur *m*; ~**ing** *n* (*trade*) construction *f*; (*house, structure*) bâtiment *m*, construction; (*offices, flats*) immeuble *m*; ~**ing society** (*BRIT*) *n* société *f* de crédit immobilier

built [bɪlt] *pt, pp of* build; ~-**in** *adj* (*cupboard, device*) encastré(e); (*device*) incorporé(e); intégré(e); ~-**up area** *n* zone urbanisée

bulb [bʌlb] *n* (*BOT*) bulbe *m*, oignon *m*; (*ELEC*) ampoule *f*

bulge [bʌldʒ] *n* renflement *m*, gonflement *m* ♦ *vi* (*pocket, file etc*) être plein(e) à craquer; (*cheeks*) être gonflé(e)

bulk [bʌlk] *n* masse *f*, volume *m*; (*of person*) corpulence *f*; **in** ~ (*COMM*) en vrac; **the** ~ **of** la plus grande *or* grosse partie de; ~**y** *adj* volumineux(euse), encombrant(e)

bull [bul] *n* taureau *m*; (*male elephant/ whale*) mâle *m*; ~**dog** *n* bouledogue *m*

bulldozer ['buldəuzə*] *n* bulldozer *m*

bullet ['bulɪt] *n* balle *f* (*de fusil etc*)

bulletin ['bulɪtɪn] *n* bulletin *m*, communiqué *m*; (*news* ~) (bulletin d')informations *fpl*

bulletproof ['bulɪtpruːf] *adj* (*car*) blindé(e); (*vest etc*) pare-balles *inv*

bullfight ['bulfaɪt] *n* corrida *f*, course *f* de taureaux; ~**er** *n* torero *m*; ~**ing** *n* tauromachie *f*

bullion ['buliən] *n* or *m or* argent *m* en lingots

bull: ~**ock** ['bulək] *n* bœuf *m*; ~**ring** ['bulrɪŋ] *n* arènes *fpl*; ~'**s-eye** ['bulzaɪ] *n* centre *m* (*de la cible*)

bully ['buli] *n* brute *f*, tyran *m* ♦ *vt* tyranniser, rudoyer

bum [bʌm] *n* (*inf: backside*) derrière *m*; (*esp US: tramp*) vagabond(e), traîne-savates *m/f inv*

bumblebee ['bʌmblbiː] *n* bourdon *m*

bump [bʌmp] *n* (*in car: minor accident*) accrochage *m*; (*jolt*) cahot *m*; (*on road etc, on head*) bosse *f* ♦ *vt* heurter, cogner; ~ **into**

vt fus rentrer dans, tamponner; (*meet*) tomber sur; ~**er** *n* pare-chocs *m inv* ♦ *adj*: ~**er crop/harvest** récolte/moisson exceptionnelle; ~**er cars** *npl* autos tamponneuses

bumpy ['bʌmpi] *adj* cahoteux(euse)

bun [bʌn] *n* petit pain au lait; (*of hair*) chignon *m*

bunch [bʌntʃ] *n* (*of flowers*) bouquet *m*; (*of keys*) trousseau *m*; (*of bananas*) régime *m*; (*of people*) groupe *m*; ~**es** *npl* (*in hair*) couettes *fpl*; ~ **of grapes** grappe *f* de raisin

bundle ['bʌndl] *n* paquet *m* ♦ *vt* (*also*: ~ *up*) faire un paquet de; (*put*): **to** ~ **sth/sb into** fourrer *or* enfourner qch/qn dans

bungalow ['bʌŋgələu] *n* bungalow *m*

bungle ['bʌŋgl] *vt* bâcler, gâcher

bunion ['bʌnjən] *n* oignon *m* (*au pied*)

bunk [bʌŋk] *n* couchette *f*; ~ **beds** *npl* lits superposés

bunker ['bʌŋkə*] *n* (*coal store*) soute *f* à charbon; (*MIL, GOLF*) bunker *m*

bunny ['bʌni] *n* (*also*: ~ *rabbit*) Jeannot *m* lapin

bunting ['bʌntɪŋ] *n* pavoisement *m*, drapeaux *mpl*

buoy [bɔɪ] *n* bouée *f*; ~ **up** *vt* faire flotter; (*fig*) soutenir, épauler; ~**ant** *adj* capable de flotter; (*carefree*) gai(e), plein(e) d'entrain; (*economy*) ferme, actif

burden ['bɜːdn] *n* fardeau *m* ♦ *vt* (*trouble*) accabler, surcharger

bureau ['bjuərəu] (*pl* ~**x**) *n* (*BRIT: writing desk*) bureau *m*, secrétaire *m*; (*US: chest of drawers*) commode *f*; (*office*) bureau, office *m*; ~**cracy** [bju'rɒkrəsɪ] *n* bureaucratie *f*

burglar ['bɜːglə*] *n* cambrioleur *m*; ~ **alarm** *n* sonnerie *f* d'alarme; ~**y** *n* cambriolage *m*

Burgundy ['bɜːgəndi] *n* Bourgogne *f*

burial ['beriəl] *n* enterrement *m*

burly ['bɜːli] *adj* de forte carrure, costaud(e)

Burma ['bɜːmə] *n* Birmanie *f*

burn [bɜːn] (*pt, pp* burned *or* burnt) *vt, vi* brûler ♦ *n* brûlure *f*; ~ **down** *vt* incendier, détruire par le feu; ~**er** *n* brûleur *m*; ~**ing** *adj* brûlant(e); (*house*) en flammes; (*ambition*) dévorant(e)

burrow ['bʌrəu] *n* terrier *m* ♦ *vt* creuser

bursary ['bɜːsəri] (*BRIT*) *n* bourse *f* (d'études)

burst [bɜːst] (*pt, pp* burst) *vt* crever; faire éclater; (*subj: river: banks etc*) rompre ♦ *vi* éclater; (*tyre*) crever ♦ *n* (*of gunfire*) rafale *f* (de tir); (*also*: ~ *pipe*) rupture *f*, fuite *f*; **a** ~ **of enthusiasm/energy** un accès d'enthousiasme/d'énergie; **to** ~ **into flames** s'enflammer soudainement; **to** ~ **out laughing** éclater de rire; **to** ~ **into tears** fondre en larmes; **to be** ~**ing with** être plein (à craquer) de; (*fig*) être débordant(e) de; ~ **into** *vt fus* (*room etc*) faire irruption dans

bury ['bɛrɪ] vt enterrer

bus [bʌs, pl '-ɪz] (pl ~es) n autobus m

bush [buʃ] n buisson m; (scrubland) brousse f; **to beat about the** ~ tourner autour du pot; ~**y** ['buʃɪ] adj broussailleux(euse), touffu(e)

busily ['bɪzɪlɪ] adv activement

business ['bɪznɪs] n (matter, firm) affaire f; (trading) affaires fpl; (job, duty) travail m; **to be away on** ~ être en déplacement d'affaires; **it's none of my** ~ cela ne me regarde pas, ce ne sont pas mes affaires; **he means** ~ il ne plaisante pas, il est sérieux; ~**like** adj sérieux(euse); efficace; ~**man** (irreg) n homme m d'affaires; ~ **trip** n voyage m d'affaires; ~**woman** (irreg) n femme f d'affaires

busker ['bʌskə*] (BRIT) n musicien ambulant

bus stop n arrêt m d'autobus

bust [bʌst] n buste m; (measurement) tour m de poitrine ♦ adj (inf: broken) fichu(e), fini(e); **to go** ~ faire faillite

bustle ['bʌsl] n remue-ménage m, affairement ♦ vi s'affairer, se démener; **bustling** adj (town) bruyant(e), affairé(e)

busy ['bɪzɪ] adj occupé(e); (shop, street) très fréquenté(e) ♦ vt: **to** ~ **o.s.** s'occuper; ~**body** n mouche f du coche, âme f charitable; ~ **signal** (US) n (TEL) tonalité f occupé inv

but [bʌt] conj mais; **I'd love to come,** ~ **I'm busy** j'aimerais venir mais je suis occupé ♦ prep (apart from, except) sauf, excepté; **we've had nothing** ~ **trouble** nous n'avons eu que des ennuis; **no-one** ~ **him can do it** lui seul peut le faire; ~ **for you/your help** sans toi/ton aide; **anything** ~ **that** tout sauf or excepté ça, tout mais pas ça ♦ adv (just, only) ne ... que; **she's** ~ **a child** elle n'est qu'une enfant; **had I** ~ **known** si seulement j'avais su; **all** ~ **finished** pratiquement terminé

butcher ['butʃə*] n boucher m ♦ vt massacrer; (cattle etc for meat) tuer; ~'**s (shop)** n boucherie f

butler ['bʌtlə*] n maître m d'hôtel

butt [bʌt] n (large barrel) gros tonneau; (of gun) crosse f; (of cigarette) mégot m; (BRIT: fig: target) cible f ♦ vt donner un coup de tête à; ~ **in** vi (interrupt) s'immiscer dans la conversation

butter ['bʌtə*] n beurre m ♦ vt beurrer; ~**cup** n bouton m d'or; ~**fly** n papillon m; (SWIMMING: also: ~fly stroke) brasse f papillon

buttocks ['bʌtəks] npl fesses fpl

button ['bʌtn] n bouton m; (US: badge) pin

m ♦ vt (also: ~ up) boutonner ♦ vi se boutonner

buttress ['bʌtrɪs] n contrefort m

buxom ['bʌksəm] adj aux formes avantageuses or épanouies

buy [baɪ] (pt, pp bought) vt acheter ♦ n achat m; **to** ~ **sb sth/sth from sb** acheter qch à qn; **to** ~ **sb a drink** offrir un verre or à boire à qn; ~**er** n acheteur(euse)

buzz [bʌz] n bourdonnement m; (inf: phone call): **to give sb a** ~ passer un coup m de fil à qn ♦ vi bourdonner; ~**er** ['bʌzə*] n timbre m électrique; ~ **word** (inf) n mot m à la mode

by [baɪ] prep **1** (referring to cause, agent) par, de; **killed** ~ **lightning** tué par la foudre; **surrounded** ~ **a fence** entouré d'une barrière; **a painting** ~ **Picasso** un tableau de Picasso

2 (referring to method, manner, means): ~ **bus/car** en autobus/voiture; ~ **train** par le or en train; **to pay** ~ **cheque** payer par chèque; ~ **saving hard, he ...** à force d'économiser, il ...

3 (via, through) par; **we came** ~ **Dover** nous sommes venus par Douvres

4 (close to, past) à côté de; **the house** ~ **the school** la maison à côté de l'école; **a holiday** ~ **the sea** des vacances au bord de la mer; **she sat** ~ **his bed** elle était assise à son chevet; **she went** ~ **me** elle est passée à côté de moi; **I go** ~ **the post office every day** je passe devant la poste tous les jours

5 (with time: not later than) avant; (: during) ~ **daylight** à la lumière du jour; ~ **night** la nuit, de nuit; ~ **4 o'clock** avant 4 heures; ~ **this time tomorrow** d'ici demain à la même heure; ~ **the time I got here it was too late** lorsque je suis arrivé il était déjà trop tard

6 (amount) à; ~ **the kilo/metre** au kilo/au mètre; **paid** ~ **the hour** payé à l'heure

7 (MATH, measure): **to divide/multiply** ~ **3** diviser/multiplier par 3; **a room 3 metres** ~ **4** une pièce de 3 mètres sur 4; **it's broader** ~ **a metre** c'est plus large d'un mètre; **one** ~ **one** un à un; **little** ~ **little** petit à petit, peu à peu

8 (according to) d'après, selon; **it's 3 o'clock** ~ **my watch** il est 3 heures à ma montre; **it's all right** ~ **me** je n'ai rien contre

9: (all) ~ **oneself** etc tout(e) seul(e)

10: ~ **the way** au fait, à propos

♦ adv **1** see go; pass etc

2: **and** ~ un peu plus tard, bientôt; ~ **and large** dans l'ensemble

bye(-bye) ['baɪ('baɪ)] excl au revoir!, salut!

by(e)-law ['baɪlɔː] n arrêté municipal
by: ~**-election** (BRIT) n élection (législative) partielle; ~**gone** adj passé(e) ♦ n: **let** ~**gones be** ~**gones** passons l'éponge, oublions le passé; ~**pass** n (route f de) contournement m; (MED) pontage m ♦ vt éviter; ~**-product** n sous-produit m, dérivé m; (fig) conséquence f secondaire, retombée f; ~**stander** ['baɪstændə*] n spectateur(trice), badaud(e)
byte [baɪt] n (COMPUT) octet m
byword ['baɪwɜːd] n: **to be a** ~ **for** être synonyme de (fig)
by-your-leave ['baɪjɔː'liːv] n: **without so much as a** ~ sans même demander la permission

——————— *C c*

C [slɪ] n (MUS) do m
CA abbr = **chartered accountant**
cab [kæb] n taxi m; (of train, truck) cabine f
cabaret ['kæbəreɪ] n (show) spectacle m de cabaret
cabbage ['kæbɪdʒ] n chou m
cabin ['kæbɪn] n (house) cabane f, hutte f; (on ship) cabine f; (on plane) compartiment m; ~ **cruiser** n cruiser m
cabinet ['kæbɪnɪt] n (POL) cabinet m; (furniture) petit meuble à tiroirs et rayons; (also: display ~) vitrine f, petite armoire vitrée
cable ['keɪbl] n câble m ♦ vt câbler, télégraphier; ~**-car** n téléphérique m; ~ **television** n télévision f par câble
cache [kæʃ] n stock m
cackle ['kækl] vi caqueter
cactus ['kæktəs, pl -taɪ] (pl **cacti**) n cactus m
cadet [kə'det] n (MIL) élève m officier
cadge [kædʒ] (inf) vt: **to** ~ (**from** or **off**) se faire donner (par)
café ['kæfɪ] n ≈ café(-restaurant) m (sans alcool)
cage [keɪdʒ] n cage f
cagey ['keɪdʒɪ] (inf) adj réticent(e); méfiant(e)
cagoule [kə'guːl] n K-way m (®)
cajole [kə'dʒəʊl] vt couvrir de flatteries or de gentillesses
cake [keɪk] n gâteau m; ~ **of soap** savonnette f; ~**d** adj: ~**d with** raidi(e) par, couvert(e) d'une croûte de
calculate ['kælkjʊleɪt] vt calculer; (estimate:

chances, effect) évaluer; **calculation** [kælkjʊ'leɪʃən] n calcul m; **calculator** n machine f à calculer, calculatrice f; (pocket) calculette f
calendar ['kælɪndə*] n calendrier m; ~ **year** n année civile
calf [kɑːf] (pl **calves**) n (of cow) veau m; (of other animals) petit m; (also: ~**skin**) veau m, vachette f; (ANAT) mollet m
calibre ['kælɪbə*] (US **caliber**) n calibre m
call [kɔːl] vt appeler; (meeting) convoquer ♦ vi appeler; (visit: also: ~ **in**, ~ **round**) passer ♦ n (shout) appel m, cri m; (also: telephone ~) coup m de téléphone; (visit) visite f; **she's** ~**ed Suzanne** elle s'appelle Suzanne; **to be on** ~ être de permanence; ~ **back** vi (return) repasser; (TEL) rappeler; ~ **for** vt fus (demand) demander; (fetch) passer prendre; ~ **off** vt annuler; ~ **on** vt fus (visit) rendre visite à, passer voir; (request): **to** ~ **on sb to do** inviter qn à faire; ~ **out** vi pousser un cri or des cris; ~ **up** vt (MIL) appeler, mobiliser; (TEL) appeler; ~**box** (BRIT) n (TEL) cabine f téléphonique; ~**er** n (TEL) personne f qui appelle; (visitor) visiteur m; ~ **girl** n call-girl f; ~**-in** (US) n (RADIO, TV: phone-in) programme m à ligne ouverte; ~**ing** n vocation f; (trade, occupation) état m; ~**ing card** (US) n carte f de visite
callous ['kæləs] adj dur(e), insensible
calm [kɑːm] adj calme ♦ n calme m ♦ vt calmer, apaiser; ~ **down** vi se calmer ♦ vt calmer, apaiser
Calor gas ['kælə-] (®) n butane m, butagaz m (®)
calorie ['kælərɪ] n calorie f
calves [kɑːvz] npl of **calf**
camber ['kæmbə*] n (of road) bombement m
Cambodia [kæm'bəʊdjə] n Cambodge m
camcorder ['kæmkɔːdə*] n camescope m
came [keɪm] pt of **come**
camel ['kæməl] n chameau m
camera ['kæmərə] n (PHOT) appareil-photo m; (also: cine-~, movie ~) caméra f; **in** ~ à huis clos; ~**man** (irreg) n caméraman m
camouflage ['kæməflɑːʒ] n camouflage m ♦ vt camoufler
camp [kæmp] n camp m ♦ vi camper ♦ adj (man) efféminé(e)
campaign [kæm'peɪn] n (MIL, POL etc) campagne f ♦ vi faire campagne
camp: ~**bed** (BRIT) n lit m de camp; ~**er** n campeur(euse); (vehicle) camping-car m; ~**ing** n camping m; **to go** ~**ing** faire du camping; ~**site** ['kæmpsaɪt] n campement m, (terrain m de) camping m
campus ['kæmpəs] n campus m
can[1] [kæn] n (of milk, oil, water) bidon m; (tin) boîte f de conserve ♦ vt mettre en conserve

—————— KEYWORD ——————

can² [kæn] (negative **cannot, can't**; conditional and pt **could**) aux vb **1** (be able to) pouvoir; **you ~ do it if you try** vous pouvez le faire si vous essayez; **I ~'t hear you** je ne t'entends pas

2 (know how to) savoir; **I ~ swim/play tennis/drive** je sais nager/jouer au tennis/conduire; **~ you speak French?** parlez-vous français?

3 (may) pouvoir; **~ I use your phone?** puis-je me servir de votre téléphone?

4 (expressing disbelief, puzzlement etc): **it ~'t be true!** ce n'est pas possible!; **what CAN he want?** qu'est-ce qu'il peut bien vouloir?

5 (expressing possibility, suggestion etc): **he could be in the library** il est peut-être dans la bibliothèque; **she could have been delayed** il se peut qu'elle ait été retardée

Canada ['kænədə] n Canada m; **Canadian** [kə'neɪdɪən] adj canadien(ne) ♦ n Canadien(ne)

canal [kə'næl] n canal m

canary [kə'nɛərɪ] n canari m, serin m

cancel ['kænsəl] vt annuler; (train) supprimer; (party, appointment) décommander; (cross out) barrer, rayer; **~lation** [kænsə'leɪʃən] n annulation f; suppression f

cancer ['kænsə*] n (MED) cancer m; **C~** (ASTROLOGY) le Cancer

candid ['kændɪd] adj (très) franc(franche), sincère

candidate ['kændɪdeɪt] n candidat(e)

candle ['kændl] n bougie f; (of tallow) chandelle f; (in church) cierge m; **~light** n: **by ~light** à la lumière d'une bougie; (dinner) aux chandelles; **~stick** n (also: **~ holder**) bougeoir m; (bigger, ornate) chandelier m

candour ['kændə*] (US **candor**) n (grande) franchise or sincérité

candy ['kændɪ] n sucre candi; (US) bonbon m; **~-floss** (BRIT) n barbe f à papa

cane [keɪn] n canne f; (for furniture, baskets etc) rotin m ♦ vt (BRIT: SCOL) administrer des coups de bâton à

canister ['kænɪstə*] n boîte f; (of gas, pressurized substance) bombe f

cannabis ['kænəbɪs] n (drug) cannabis m

canned [kænd] adj (food) en boîte, en conserve

cannon ['kænən] (pl ~ or ~s) n (gun) canon m

cannot ['kænɒt] = **can not**

canoe [kə'nuː] n pirogue f; (SPORT) canoë m

canon ['kænən] n (clergyman) chanoine m; (standard) canon m

can-opener [-'əʊpnə*] n ouvre-boîte m

canopy ['kænəpɪ] n baldaquin m; dais m

can't [kɑːnt] = **can not**

cantankerous [kæn'tæŋkərəs] adj querelleur(euse), acariâtre

canteen [kæn'tiːn] n cantine f; (BRIT: of cutlery) ménagère f

canter ['kæntə*] vi (horse) aller au petit galop

canvas ['kænvəs] n toile f

canvass ['kænvəs] vi (POL): **to ~ for** faire campagne pour ♦ vt (investigate: opinions etc) sonder

canyon ['kænjən] n cañon m, gorge (profonde)

cap [kæp] n casquette f; (of pen) capuchon m; (of bottle) capsule f; (contraceptive: also: Dutch ~) diaphragme m; (for toy gun) amorce f ♦ vt (outdo) surpasser; (put limit on) plafonner

capability [keɪpə'bɪlɪtɪ] n aptitude f, capacité f

capable ['keɪpəbl] adj capable

capacity [kə'pæsɪtɪ] n capacité f; (capability) aptitude f; (of factory) rendement m

cape [keɪp] n (garment) cape f; (GEO) cap m

caper ['keɪpə*] n (CULIN: gen: ~s) câpre f; (prank) farce f

capital ['kæpɪtl] n (also: ~ city) capitale f; (money) capital m; (also: ~ letter) majuscule f; **~ gains tax** n (COMM) impôt m sur les plus-values; **~ism** n capitalisme m; **~ist** adj capitaliste ♦ n capitaliste m/f; **~ize** vi: **to ~ize on** tirer parti de; **~ punishment** n peine capitale

Capricorn ['kæprɪkɔːn] n (ASTROLOGY) le Capricorne

capsize [kæp'saɪz] vt faire chavirer ♦ vi chavirer

capsule ['kæpsjuːl] n capsule f

captain ['kæptɪn] n capitaine m

caption ['kæpʃən] n légende f

captive ['kæptɪv] adj, n captif(ive)

capture ['kæptʃə*] vt capturer, prendre; (attention) capter; (COMPUT) saisir ♦ n capture f; (data ~) saisie f de données

car [kɑː*] n voiture f, auto f; (RAIL) wagon m, voiture

caramel ['kærəməl] n caramel m

caravan ['kærəvæn] n caravane f; **~ site** (BRIT) n camping m pour caravanes

carbohydrate [kɑːbəʊ'haɪdreɪt] n hydrate m de carbone; (food) féculent m

carbon ['kɑːbən] n carbone m; **~ dioxide** n gaz m carbonique; **~ monoxide** n oxyde m de carbone; **~ paper** n papier m carbone

carburettor ['kɑːbjʊretə*] (US **carburetor**) n carburateur m

card [kɑːd] n carte f; (material) carton m; **~board** n carton m; **~ game** n jeu m de cartes

cardiac ['kɑːdɪæk] adj cardiaque

cardigan ['kɑ:dɪgən] n cardigan m
cardinal ['kɑ:dɪnl] adj cardinal(e) ♦ n cardinal m
card index n fichier m
care [kɛə*] n soin m, attention f; (worry) souci m; (charge) charge f, garde f; to ~ **about** se soucier de, s'intéresser à; (person) être attaché(e) à; ~ **of** chez, aux bons soins de; **in sb's** ~ à la garde de qn, confié(e) à qn; **to take** ~ **(to do)** faire attention (à faire); **to take** ~ **of** s'occuper de; **I don't** ~ ça m'est bien égal; **I couldn't** ~ **less** je m'en fiche complètement (inf); ~ **for** vt fus s'occuper de; (like) aimer
career [kə'rɪə*] n carrière f ♦ vi (also: ~ *along*) aller à toute allure; ~ **woman** (irreg) n femme ambitieuse
care: ~**free** ['kɛəfri:] adj sans souci, insouciant(e); ~**ful** ['kɛəful] adj (thorough) soigneux(euse); (cautious) prudent(e); **(be)** ~**ful!** (fais) attention!; ~**fully** adv avec soin, soigneusement; prudemment; ~**less** ['kɛəlɪs] adj négligent(e); (heedless) insouciant(e); ~**r** [kɛərə*] n (MED) aide f
caress [kə'rɛs] n caresse f ♦ vt caresser
caretaker ['kɛəteɪkə*] n gardien(ne), concierge m/f
car-ferry ['kɑ:fɛrɪ] n (on sea) ferry(-boat) m
cargo ['kɑ:gəu] (pl ~es) n cargaison f, chargement m
car hire n location f de voitures
Caribbean [kærɪ'bi:ən] adj: **the** ~ **(Sea)** la mer des Antilles or Caraïbes
caring ['kɛərɪŋ] adj (person) bienveillant(e); (society, organization) humanitaire
carnal ['kɑ:nl] adj charnel(le)
carnation [kɑ:'neɪʃən] n œillet m
carnival ['kɑ:nɪvəl] n (public celebration) carnaval m; (US: funfair) fête foraine
carol ['kærl] n: **(Christmas)** ~ chant m de Noël
carp [kɑ:p] n (fish) carpe f; ~ **at** vt fus critiquer
car park (BRIT) n parking m, parc m de stationnement
carpenter ['kɑ:pɪntə*] n charpentier m; **carpentry** ['kɑ:pɪntrɪ] n menuiserie f
carpet ['kɑ:pɪt] n tapis m ♦ vt recouvrir d'un tapis; ~ **slippers** npl pantoufles fpl; ~ **sweeper** n balai m mécanique
car phone n (TEL) téléphone m de voiture
carriage ['kærɪdʒ] n voiture f; (of goods) transport m; (: cost) port m; ~**way** (BRIT) n (part of road) chaussée f
carrier ['kærɪə*] n transporteur m, camionneur m; (company) entreprise f de transport; (MED) porteur(euse); ~ **bag** (BRIT) n sac m en papier or en plastique
carrot ['kærət] n carotte f
carry ['kærɪ] vt (subj: person) porter; (: vehicle) transporter; (involve: responsibilities etc) comporter, impliquer ♦ vi (sound) porter;

to get carried away (fig) s'emballer, s'enthousiasmer; ~ **on** vi: **to** ~ **on with sth/doing** continuer qch/de faire ♦ vt poursuivre; ~ **out** vt (orders) exécuter; (investigation) mener; ~**cot** (BRIT) n porte-bébé m; ~**-on** (inf) n (fuss) histoires fpl
cart [kɑ:t] n charrette f ♦ vt (inf) transporter, trimballer (inf)
carton ['kɑ:tən] n (box) carton m; (of yogurt) pot m; (of cigarettes) cartouche f
cartoon [kɑ:'tu:n] n (PRESS) dessin m (humoristique), caricature f; (BRIT: comic strip) bande dessinée; (CINEMA) dessin animé
cartridge ['kɑ:trɪdʒ] n cartouche f
carve [kɑ:v] vt (meat) découper; (wood, stone) tailler, sculpter; ~ **up** vt découper; (fig: country) morceler; **carving** ['kɑ:vɪŋ] n sculpture f; **carving knife** n couteau m à découper
car wash n station f de lavage (de voitures)
case [keɪs] n cas m; (LAW) affaire f, procès m; (box) caisse f, boîte f, étui m; (BRIT: also: suit~) valise f; **in** ~ **of** en cas de; **in** ~ **he ...** au cas où il ...; **just in** ~ à tout hasard; **in any** ~ en tout cas, de toute façon
cash [kæʃ] n argent m; (COMM) argent liquide, espèces fpl ♦ vt encaisser; **to pay (in)** ~ payer comptant; ~ **on delivery** payable or paiement à la livraison; ~**-book** n livre m de caisse; ~ **card** (BRIT) n carte f de retrait; ~ **desk** (BRIT) n caisse f; ~ **dispenser** (BRIT) n distributeur m automatique de billets, billeterie f
cashew [kæ'ʃu:] n (also: ~ nut) noix f de cajou
cashier [kæ'ʃɪə*] n caissier(ère)
cashmere ['kæʃmɪə*] n cachemire m
cash register n caisse (enregistreuse)
casing ['keɪsɪŋ] n revêtement (protecteur), enveloppe (protectrice)
casino [kə'si:nəu] n casino m
casket ['kɑ:skɪt] n coffret m; (US: coffin) cercueil m
casserole ['kæsərəul] n (container) cocotte f; (food) ragoût m (en cocotte)
cassette [kæ'sɛt] n cassette f, musicassette f; ~ **player** n lecteur m de cassettes; ~ **recorder** n magnétophone m à cassettes
cast [kɑ:st] (pt, pp cast) vt (throw) jeter; (shed) perdre; se dépouiller de; (statue) mouler; (THEATRE): **to** ~ **sb as Hamlet** attribuer à qn le rôle de Hamlet ♦ n (THEATRE) distribution f; (also: plaster ~) plâtre m; **to** ~ **one's vote** voter; ~ **off** vi (NAUT) larguer les amarres; (KNITTING) arrêter les mailles; ~ **on** vi (KNITTING) monter les mailles
castaway ['kɑ:stəweɪ] n naufragé(e)
caster sugar ['kɑ:stə-] (BRIT) n sucre m semoule

casting vote ['kɑːstɪŋ-] (*BRIT*) n voix prépondérante (*pour départager*)

cast iron n fonte f

castle ['kɑːsl] n château (fort); (*CHESS*) tour f

castor ['kɑːstə*] n (*wheel*) roulette f; ~ **oil** n huile f de ricin

castrate [kæs'treɪt] vt châtrer

casual ['kæʒjʊl] adj (*by chance*) de hasard, fait(e) au hasard, fortuit(e); (*irregular: work etc*) temporaire; (*unconcerned*) désinvolte; ~**ly** adv avec désinvolture, négligemment; (*dress*) de façon décontractée

casualty ['kæʒjʊltɪ] n accidenté(e), blessé(e); (*dead*) victime f, mort(e); (*MED: department*) urgences fpl

casual wear n vêtements mpl décontractés

cat [kæt] n chat m

catalogue ['kætəlɒg] (*US* catalog) n catalogue m ♦ vt cataloguer

catalyst ['kætəlɪst] n catalyseur m

catalytic converter [kætə'lɪtɪk kən'vɜːtə*] n pot m catalytique

catapult ['kætəpʌlt] (*BRIT*) n (*sling*) lance-pierres m inv, fronde m

catarrh [kə'tɑː*] n rhume m chronique, catarrhe m

catastrophe [kə'tæstrəfɪ] n catastrophe f

catch [kætʃ] (pt, pp **caught**) vt attraper; (*person: by surprise*) prendre, surprendre; (*understand, hear*) saisir ♦ vi (*fire*) prendre; (*become trapped*) se prendre, s'accrocher ♦ n prise f; (*trick*) attrape f; (*of lock*) loquet m; **to ~ sb's attention** or **eye** attirer l'attention de qn; **to ~ one's breath** retenir son souffle; **to ~ fire** prendre feu; **to ~ sight of** apercevoir; ~ **on** vi saisir; (*grow popular*) prendre; ~ **up** vi se rattraper, combler son retard ♦ vt (*also: ~ up with*) rattraper; ~**ing** adj (*MED*) contagieux(euse); ~**ment area** ['kætʃmənt-] (*BRIT*) n (*SCOL*) secteur m de recrutement; (*of hospital*) circonscription hospitalière; ~ **phrase** n slogan m; expression f (à la mode); ~**y** adj (*tune*) facile à retenir

category ['kætɪgərɪ] n catégorie f

cater ['keɪtə*] vi (*provide food*): **to ~ (for)** préparer les repas (pour), se charger de la restauration (pour); ~ **for** (*BRIT*) vt fus (*needs*) satisfaire, pourvoir à; (*readers, consumers*) s'adresser à, pourvoir aux besoins de; ~**er** n traiteur m; fournisseur m; ~**ing** n restauration f; approvisionnement m, ravitaillement m

caterpillar ['kætəpɪlə*] n chenille f; ~ **track** ® n chenille f

cathedral [kə'θiːdrəl] n cathédrale f

catholic ['kæθəlɪk] adj (*tastes*) éclectique, varié(e); **C~** adj catholique ♦ n catholique m/f

Catseye ['kætsaɪ] (®: *BRIT*) n (*AUT*) catadioptre m

cattle ['kætl] npl bétail m

catty ['kætɪ] adj méchant(e)

caucus ['kɔːkəs] n (*POL: group*) comité local d'un parti politique; (*US: POL*) comité électoral (pour désigner des candidats)

caught [kɔːt] pt, pp of **catch**

cauliflower ['kɒlɪflaʊə*] n chou-fleur m

cause [kɔːz] n cause f ♦ vt causer

caution ['kɔːʃən] n prudence f; (*warning*) avertissement m ♦ vt avertir, donner un avertissement à

cautious ['kɔːʃəs] adj prudent(e)

cavalry ['kævəlrɪ] n cavalerie f

cave [keɪv] n caverne f, grotte f; ~ **in** vi (*roof etc*) s'effondrer; ~**man** (*irreg*) n homme m des cavernes

caviar(e) ['kævɪɑː*] n caviar m

cavort [kə'vɔːt] vi cabrioler, faire des cabrioles

CB n abbr (= Citizens' Band (Radio)) CB f

CBI n abbr (= Confederation of British Industries) groupement du patronat

cc abbr = **carbon copy**; **cubic centimetres**

CD n abbr (= compact disc (player)) CD m; ~**-ROM** n abbr (= compact disc read-only memory) CD-ROM m

cease [siːs] vt, vi cesser; ~**fire** n cessez-le-feu m; ~**less** adj incessant(e), continuel(le)

cedar ['siːdə*] n cèdre m

ceiling ['siːlɪŋ] n plafond m

celebrate ['selɪbreɪt] vt, vi célébrer; ~**d** adj célèbre; **celebration** [selɪ'breɪʃən] n célébration f

celery ['selərɪ] n céleri m (à côtes)

cell [sel] n cellule f; (*ELEC*) élément m (de pile)

cellar ['selə*] n cave f

cello ['tʃeləʊ] n violoncelle m

cellphone [sel'fəʊn] n téléphone m cellulaire

Celt [kelt, selt] n Celte m/f; ~**ic** ['keltɪk, 'seltɪk] adj celte

cement [sɪ'ment] n ciment m; ~ **mixer** n bétonnière f

cemetery ['semɪtrɪ] n cimetière m

censor ['sensə*] n censeur m ♦ vt censurer; ~**ship** n censure f

censure ['senʃə*] vt blâmer, critiquer

census ['sensəs] n recensement m

cent [sent] n (*US etc: coin*) cent m (= un centième du dollar); see also **per**

centenary [sen'tiːnərɪ] n centenaire m

center ['sentə*] (*US*) n = **centre**

centigrade ['sentɪgreɪd] adj centigrade

centimetre ['sentɪmiːtə*] (*US* **centimeter**) n centimètre m

centipede ['sentɪpiːd] n mille-pattes m inv

central ['sentrəl] adj central(e); **C~ America** n Amérique centrale; ~ **heating** n chauffage central; ~ **reservation** (*BRIT*) n (*AUT*) terre-plein central

centre ['sentə*] (*US* **center**) n centre m ♦ vt

centrer; **~-forward** n (SPORT) avant-centre m; **~-half** n (SPORT) demi-centre m
century ['sentʃʊrɪ] n siècle m; **20th** ~ XXe siècle
ceramic [sɪ'ræmɪk] adj céramique
cereal ['sɪərɪəl] n céréale f
ceremony ['serɪmənɪ] n cérémonie f; **to stand on** ~ faire des façons
certain ['sɜːtən] adj certain(e); **for** ~ certainement, sûrement; **~ly** adv certainement; **~ty** n certitude f
certificate [sə'tɪfɪkɪt] n certificat m
certified mail ['sɜːtɪfaɪd-] (US) n: **by** ~ en recommandé, avec avis de réception
certified public accountant (US) n expert-comptable m
certify ['sɜːtɪfaɪ] vt certifier; (award diploma to) conférer un diplôme etc à; (declare insane) déclarer malade mental(e)
cervical ['sɜːvɪkl] adj: ~ **cancer** cancer m du col de l'utérus; ~ **smear** frottis vaginal
cervix ['sɜːvɪks] n col m de l'utérus
cf. abbr (= compare) cf., voir
CFC n abbr (= chlorofluorocarbon) CFC m (gen pl)
ch. abbr (= chapter) chap.
chafe [tʃeɪf] vt irriter, frotter contre
chain [tʃeɪn] n chaîne f ♦ vt (also: ~ up) enchaîner, attacher (avec une chaîne); ~ **reaction** n réaction f en chaîne; **~-smoke** vi fumer cigarette sur cigarette; ~ **store** n magasin m à succursales multiples
chair [tʃeə*] n chaise f; (arm~) fauteuil m; (of university) chaire f; (of meeting, committee) présidence f ♦ vt (meeting) présider; **~lift** n télésiège m; **~man** (irreg) n président m
chalet ['ʃæleɪ] n chalet m
chalice ['tʃælɪs] n calice m
chalk ['tʃɔːk] n craie f
challenge ['tʃælɪndʒ] n défi m ♦ vt défier; (statement, right) mettre en question, contester; **to** ~ **sb to do** mettre qn au défi de faire; **challenging** ['tʃælɪndʒɪŋ] adj (tone, look) de défi, provocateur(trice); (task, career) qui représente un défi or une gageure
chamber ['tʃeɪmbə*] n chambre f; ~ **of commerce** chambre de commerce; **~maid** n femme f de chambre; ~ **music** n musique f de chambre
champagne [ʃæm'peɪn] n champagne m
champion ['tʃæmpɪən] n champion(ne); **~ship** n championnat m
chance [tʃɑːns] n (opportunity) occasion f, possibilité f; (hope, likelihood) chance f; (risk) risque m ♦ vt: **to** ~ **it** risquer (le coup), essayer ♦ adj fortuit(e), de hasard; **to take a** ~ prendre un risque; **by** ~ par hasard
chancellor ['tʃɑːnsələ*] n chancelier m; **C~ of the Exchequer** (BRIT) n chancelier

m de l'Échiquier, ≈ ministre m des Finances
chandelier [ʃændɪ'lɪə*] n lustre m
change [tʃeɪndʒ] vt (alter, replace, COMM: money) changer; (hands, trains, clothes, one's name) changer de; (transform): **to** ~ **sb into** changer or transformer qn en ♦ vi (gen) changer; (one's clothes) se changer; (be transformed): **to** ~ **into** se changer or transformer en ♦ n changement m; (money) monnaie f; **to** ~ **gear** (AUT) changer de vitesse; **to** ~ **one's mind** changer d'avis; **a** ~ **of clothes** des vêtements de rechange; **for a** ~ pour changer; **~able** (of weather) variable; ~ **machine** n distributeur m de monnaie; **~over** n (to new system) changement m, passage m
changing ['tʃeɪndʒɪŋ] adj changeant(e); ~ **room** (BRIT) n (in shop) salon m d'essayage; (SPORT) vestiaire m
channel ['tʃænl] n (TV) chaîne f; (navigable passage) chenal m; (irrigation) canal m ♦ vt canaliser; **the (English) C~** la Manche; **the C~ Islands** les îles de la Manche, les îles Anglo-Normandes
chant [tʃɑːnt] n chant m; (REL) psalmodie f ♦ vt chanter, scander
chaos ['keɪɒs] n chaos m
chap [tʃæp] (BRIT: inf) n (man) type m
chapel ['tʃæpəl] n chapelle f; (BRIT: nonconformist ~) église f
chaplain ['tʃæplɪn] n aumônier m
chapped ['tʃæpt] adj (skin, lips) gercé(e)
chapter ['tʃæptə*] n chapitre m
char [tʃɑː*] vt (burn) carboniser
character ['kærɪktə*] n caractère m; (in novel, film) personnage m; (eccentric) numéro m, phénomène m; **~istic** [kærɪktə'rɪstɪk] adj caractéristique ♦ n caractéristique f
charcoal ['tʃɑːkəʊl] n charbon m de bois; (for drawing) charbon m
charge [tʃɑːdʒ] n (cost) prix (demandé); (accusation) accusation f; (LAW) inculpation f ♦ vt: **to** ~ **sb (with)** inculper qn (de); (battery, enemy) charger; (customer, sum) faire payer ♦ vi foncer; **~s** npl (costs) frais mpl; **to reverse the ~s** (TEL) téléphoner en P.C.V.; **to take** ~ **of** se charger de; **to be in** ~ **of** être responsable de, s'occuper de; **how much do you** ~? combien prenez-vous?; **to** ~ **an expense (up) to sb** mettre une dépense sur le compte de qn; ~ **card** n carte f de client
charity ['tʃærɪtɪ] n charité f; (organization) institution f charitable or de bienfaisance, œuvre f (de charité)
charm [tʃɑːm] n charme m; (on bracelet) breloque f ♦ vt charmer, enchanter; **~ing** adj charmant(e)
chart [tʃɑːt] n tableau m, diagramme m; graphique m; (map) carte marine ♦ vt dresser or établir la carte de; **~s** npl (hit pa-

rade) hit-parade *m*

charter ['tʃɑːtə*] *vt* (*plane*) affréter ♦ *n* (*document*) charte *f*; **~ed accountant** (*BRIT*) *n* expert-comptable *m*; ~ **flight** *n* charter *m*

chase [tʃeɪs] *vt* poursuivre, pourchasser; (*also:* ~ *away*) chasser ♦ *n* poursuite *f*, chasse *f*

chasm ['kæzəm] *n* gouffre *m*, abîme *m*

chat [tʃæt] *vi* (*also: have a* ~) bavarder, causer ♦ *n* conversation *f*; ~ **show** (*BRIT*) *n* causerie télévisée

chatter ['tʃætə*] *vi* (*person*) bavarder; (*animal*) jacasser ♦ *n* bavardage *m*; jacassement *m*; **my teeth are** ~ing je claque des dents; ~**box** (*inf*) *n* moulin *m* à paroles

chatty ['tʃætɪ] *adj* (*style*) familier(ère); (*person*) bavard(e)

chauffeur ['ʃəʊfə*] *n* chauffeur *m* (de maître)

chauvinist ['ʃəʊvɪnɪst] *n* (*male* ~) phallocrate *m*; (*nationalist*) chauvin(e)

cheap [tʃiːp] *adj* bon marché *inv*, pas cher(chère); (*joke*) facile, d'un goût douteux; (*poor quality*) à bon marché, de qualité médiocre ♦ *adv* à bon marché, pour pas cher; ~**er** *adj* moins cher(chère); ~**ly** *adv* à bon marché, à bon compte

cheat [tʃiːt] *vi* tricher ♦ *vt* tromper, duper; (*rob*): **to** ~ **sb out of sth** escroquer qch à qn ♦ *n* tricheur(euse); escroc *m*

check [tʃek] *vt* vérifier; (*passport, ticket*) contrôler; (*halt*) arrêter; (*restrain*) maîtriser ♦ *n* vérification *f*; contrôle *m*; (*curb*) frein *m*; (*US: bill*) addition *f*; (*pattern: gen pl*) carreaux *mpl*; (*US*) = **cheque** ♦ *adj* (*pattern, cloth*) à carreaux; ~ **in** *vi* (*in hotel*) remplir sa fiche (d'hôtel); (*at airport*) se présenter à l'enregistrement ♦ *vt* (*luggage*) (faire) enregistrer; ~ **out** *vi* (*in hotel*) régler sa note; ~ **up** *vi*: **to** ~ **up (on sth)** vérifier (qch); **to** ~ **up on sb** se renseigner sur le compte de qn; ~**ered** (*US*) *adj* = **chequered**; ~**ers** (*US*) *npl* jeu *m* de dames; ~**in (desk)** *n* enregistrement *m*; ~**ing account** (*US*) *n* (*current account*) compte courant; ~**mate** *n* échec et mat *m*; ~**out** *n* (*in shop*) caisse *f*; ~**point** *n* contrôle *m*; ~**room** (*US*) *n* (*left-luggage office*) consigne *f*; ~**up** *n* (*MED*) examen médical, check-up *m*

cheek [tʃiːk] *n* joue *f*; (*impudence*) toupet *m*, culot *m*; (*impudence*) toupet *m*, culot *m*; ~**bone** *n* pommette *f*; ~**y** *adj* effronté(e), culotté(e)

cheep [tʃiːp] *vi* piauler

cheer [tʃɪə*] *vt* acclamer, applaudir; (*gladden*) réjouir, réconforter ♦ *vi* applaudir ♦ *n* (*gen pl*) acclamations *fpl*, applaudissements *mpl*; bravos *mpl*, hourras *mpl*; ~**s!** à la vôtre!; ~ **up** *vi* se dérider, reprendre courage ♦ *vt* remonter le moral *à or* de, dérider; ~**ful** *adj* gai(e), joyeux(euse)

cheerio ['tʃɪərɪ'əʊ] (*BRIT*) *excl* salut!, au revoir!

cheese [tʃiːz] *n* fromage *m*; ~**board** *n* plateau *m* de fromages

cheetah ['tʃiːtə] *n* guépard *m*

chef [ʃef] *n* chef (cuisinier)

chemical ['kemɪkəl] *adj* chimique ♦ *n* produit *m* chimique

chemist ['kemɪst] *n* (*BRIT: pharmacist*) pharmacien(ne); (*scientist*) chimiste *m/f*; ~**ry** *n* chimie *f*; ~**'s (shop)** (*BRIT*) *n* pharmacie *f*

cheque [tʃek] (*BRIT*) *n* chèque *m*; ~**book** *n* chéquier *m*, carnet *m* de chèques; ~ **card** *n* carte *f* (d'identité) bancaire

chequered ['tʃekəd] (*US* **checkered**) *adj* (*fig*) varié(e)

cherish ['tʃerɪʃ] *vt* chérir; ~**ed** *adj* (*dream, memory*) cher(chère)

cherry ['tʃerɪ] *n* cerise *f*; (*also:* ~ *tree*) cerisier *m*

chess [tʃes] *n* échecs *mpl*; ~**board** *n* échiquier *m*

chest [tʃest] *n* poitrine *f*; (*box*) coffre *m*, caisse *f*; ~ **of drawers** *n* commode *f*

chestnut ['tʃesnʌt] *n* châtaigne *f*; (*also:* ~ *tree*) châtaignier *m*

chew [tʃuː] *vt* mâcher; ~**ing gum** *n* chewing-gum *m*

chic [ʃiːk] *adj* chic *inv*, élégant(e)

chick [tʃɪk] *n* poussin *m*; (*inf*) nana *f*

chicken ['tʃɪkɪn] *n* poulet *m*; (*inf: coward*) poule mouillée; ~ **out** (*inf*) *vi* se dégonfler; ~**pox** ['tʃɪkɪnpɒks] *n* varicelle *f*

chicory ['tʃɪkərɪ] *n* (*for coffee*) chicorée *f*; (*salad*) endive

chief [tʃiːf] *n* chef ♦ *adj* principal(e); ~ **executive** (*US* **chief executive officer**) *n* directeur(trice) général(e); ~**ly** *adv* principalement, surtout

chiffon ['ʃɪfɒn] *n* mousseline *f* de soie

chilblain ['tʃɪlbleɪn] *n* engelure *f*

child [tʃaɪld] (*pl* ~**ren**) *n* enfant *m/f*; ~**birth** *n* accouchement *m*; ~**hood** *n* enfance *f*; ~**ish** *adj* puéril(e), enfantin(e); ~**like** *adj* d'enfant, innocent(e); ~ **minder** (*BRIT*) *n* garde *f* d'enfants

Chile ['tʃɪlɪ] *n* Chili *m*

chill [tʃɪl] *n* (*of water*) froid *m*; (*of air*) fraîcheur *f*; (*MED*) refroidissement *m*, coup *m* de froid ♦ *vt* (*person*) faire frissonner; (*CULIN*) mettre au frais, rafraîchir

chil(l)i ['tʃɪlɪ] *n* piment *m* (rouge)

chilly ['tʃɪlɪ] *adj* froid(e), glacé(e); (*sensitive to cold*) frileux(euse); **to feel** ~ avoir froid

chime [tʃaɪm] *n* carillon *m* ♦ *vi* carillonner, sonner

chimney ['tʃɪmnɪ] *n* cheminée *f*; ~ **sweep** *n* ramoneur *m*

chimpanzee [tʃɪmpæn'ziː] *n* chimpanzé *m*

chin [tʃɪn] *n* menton *m*

China ['tʃaɪnə] *n* Chine *f*

china ['tʃaɪnə] *n* porcelaine *f*; (*crockery*) (vaisselle *f* en) porcelaine

Chinese [tʃaɪ'niːz] *adj* chinois(e) ♦ *n inv* (*person*) Chinois(e); (*LING*) chinois *m*

chink [tʃɪŋk] *n* (*opening*) fente *f*, fissure *f*; (*noise*) tintement *m*

chip [tʃɪp] *n* (*gen pl*: *CULIN*: *BRIT*) frite *f*; (: *US*: *potato* ~) chip *m*; (*of wood*) copeau *m*; (*of glass, stone*) éclat *m*; (*also*: *micro*~) puce *f* ♦ *vt* (*cup, plate*) ébrécher; ~ **in** *vi* mettre son grain de sel; (*contribute*) contribuer

chiropodist [kɪ'rɒpədɪst] (*BRIT*) *n* pédicure *m/f*

chirp [tʃɜːp] *vi* pépier, gazouiller

chisel ['tʃɪzl] *n* ciseau *m*

chit [tʃɪt] *n* mot *m*, note *f*

chitchat ['tʃɪtʃæt] *n* bavardage *m*

chivalry ['ʃɪvəlrɪ] *n* esprit *m* chevaleresque, galanterie *f*

chives [tʃaɪvz] *npl* ciboulette *f*, civette *f*

chock-a-block ['tʃɒkə'blɒk], **chock-full** [tʃɒk'ful] *adj* plein(e) à craquer

chocolate ['tʃɒklɪt] *n* chocolat *m*

choice [tʃɔɪs] *n* choix *m* ♦ *adj* de choix

choir ['kwaɪə*] *n* chœur *m*, chorale *f*; ~**boy** *n* jeune choriste *m*

choke [tʃəʊk] *vi* étouffer ♦ *vt* étrangler; étouffer ♦ *n* (*AUT*) starter *m*; **street** ~**d with traffic** rue engorgée *or* embouteillée

cholesterol [kə'lestərɒl] *n* cholestérol *m*

choose [tʃuːz] (*pt* **chose**, *pp* **chosen**) *vt* choisir; **to** ~ **to do** décider de faire, juger bon de faire

choosy ['tʃuːzɪ] *adj*: (**to be**) ~ (faire le/la) difficile

chop [tʃɒp] *vt* (*wood*) couper (à la hache); (*CULIN*: *also*: ~ *up*) couper (fin), émincer, hacher (en morceaux) ♦ *n* (*CULIN*) côtelette *f*; ~**s** *npl* (*jaws*) mâchoires *fpl*

chopper ['tʃɒpə*] *n* (*helicopter*) hélicoptère *m*, hélico *m*

choppy ['tʃɒpɪ] *adj* (*sea*) un peu agité(e)

chopsticks ['tʃɒpstɪks] *npl* baguettes *fpl*

chord [kɔːd] *n* (*MUS*) accord *m*

chore [tʃɔː*] *n* travail *m* de routine; **household** ~**s** travaux *mpl* du ménage

chortle ['tʃɔːtl] *vi* glousser

chorus ['kɔːrəs] *n* chœur *m*; (*repeated part of song*: *also*: *fig*) refrain *m*

chose [tʃəʊz] *pt of* **choose**

chosen ['tʃəʊzn] *pp of* **choose**

Christ [kraɪst] *n* Christ *m*

christen ['krɪsn] *vt* baptiser

Christian ['krɪstɪən] *adj*, *n* chrétien(ne); ~**ity** [krɪstɪ'ænɪtɪ] *n* christianisme *m*; ~ **name** *n* prénom *m*

Christmas ['krɪsməs] *n* Noël *m or f*; **Happy** *or* **Merry** ~! joyeux Noël!; ~ **card** *n* carte *f* de Noël; ~ **Day** *n* le jour de Noël; ~ **Eve** *n* la veille de Noël; la nuit de Noël; ~ **tree** *n* arbre *m* de Noël

chrome [krəʊm] *n* chrome *m*

chromium ['krəʊmɪəm] *n* chrome *m*

chronic ['krɒnɪk] *adj* chronique

chronicle ['krɒnɪkl] *n* chronique *f*

chronological [krɒnə'lɒdʒɪkəl] *adj* chronologique

chrysanthemum [krɪ'sænθəməm] *n* chrysanthème *m*

chubby ['tʃʌbɪ] *adj* potelé(e), rondelet(te)

chuck [tʃʌk] (*inf*) *vt* (*throw*) lancer, jeter; (*BRIT*: *also*: ~ *up*: *job*) lâcher; (: *person*) plaquer; ~ **out** *vt* flanquer dehors *or* à la porte; (*rubbish*) jeter

chuckle ['tʃʌkl] *vi* glousser

chug [tʃʌg] *vi* faire teuf-teuf; (*also*: ~ *along*) avancer en faisant teuf-teuf

chum [tʃʌm] *n* copain(copine)

chunk [tʃʌŋk] *n* gros morceau

church [tʃɜːtʃ] *n* église *f*; ~**yard** *n* cimetière *m*

churn [tʃɜːn] *n* (*for butter*) baratte *f*; (*also*: *milk* ~) (grand) bidon à lait; ~ **out** *vt* débiter

chute [ʃuːt] *n* glissoire *f*; (*also*: *rubbish* ~) vide-ordures *m inv*

chutney ['tʃʌtnɪ] *n* condiment *m* à base de fruits au vinaigre

CIA (*US*) *n abbr* (= *Central Intelligence Agency*) CIA *f*

CID (*BRIT*) *n abbr* (= *Criminal Investigation Department*) ≈ P.J. *f*

cider ['saɪdə*] *n* cidre *m*

cigar [sɪ'gɑː*] *n* cigare *m*

cigarette [sɪgə'ret] *n* cigarette *f*; ~ **case** *n* étui *m* à cigarettes; ~ **end** *n* mégot *m*

Cinderella [sɪndə'relə] *n* Cendrillon

cinders ['sɪndəz] *npl* cendres *fpl*

cine-camera ['sɪnɪ'kæmərə] (*BRIT*) *n* caméra *f*

cinema ['sɪnəmə] *n* cinéma *m*

cinnamon ['sɪnəmən] *n* cannelle *f*

circle ['sɜːkl] *n* cercle *m*; (*in cinema, theatre*) balcon *m* ♦ *vi* faire *or* décrire des cercles ♦ *vt* (*move round*) faire le tour de, tourner autour de; (*surround*) entourer, encercler

circuit ['sɜːkɪt] *n* circuit *m*; ~**ous** [sɜː'kjuːɪtəs] *adj* indirect(e), qui fait un détour

circular ['sɜːkjʊlə*] *adj* circulaire ♦ *n* circulaire *f*

circulate ['sɜːkjʊleɪt] *vi* circuler ♦ *vt* faire circuler; **circulation** [sɜːkjʊ'leɪʃən] *n* circulation *f*; (*of newspaper*) tirage *m*

circumflex ['sɜːkəmfleks] *n* (*also*: ~ *accent*) accent *m* circonflexe

circumstances ['sɜːkəmstənsəz] *npl* circonstances *fpl*; (*financial condition*) moyens *mpl*, situation financière

circumvent [sɜːkəm'vent] *vt* (*rule, difficulty*) tourner

circus ['sɜːkəs] *n* cirque *m*

CIS *n abbr* (= *Commonwealth of Indepen-*

dent States) CEI *f*

cistern ['sɪstən] *n* réservoir *m* (d'eau); (*in toilet*) réservoir de la chasse d'eau

citizen ['sɪtɪzn] *n* citoyen(ne); (*resident*): **the ~s of this town** les habitants de cette ville; **~ship** *n* citoyenneté *f*

citrus fruit ['sɪtrəs-] *n* agrume *m*

city ['sɪtɪ] *n* ville *f*, cité *f*; **the C~** la Cité de Londres (*centre des affaires*)

civic ['sɪvɪk] *adj* civique; (*authorities*) municipal(e); **~ centre** (*BRIT*) *n* centre administratif (municipal)

civil ['sɪvl] *adj* civil(e); (*polite*) poli(e), courtois(e); (*disobedience, defence*) passif(ive); **~ engineer** *n* ingénieur *m* des travaux publics; **~ian** [sɪ'vɪlɪən] *adj, n* civil(e)

civilization [sɪvɪlaɪ'zeɪʃən] *n* civilisation *f*

civilized ['sɪvɪlaɪzd] *adj* civilisé(e); (*fig*) où règnent les bonnes manières

civil: **~ law** *n* code civil; (*study*) droit civil; **~ servant** *n* fonctionnaire *m/f*; **C~ Service** *n* fonction publique, administration *f*; **~ war** *n* guerre civile

clad [klæd] *adj*: **~ (in)** habillé(e) (de)

claim [kleɪm] *vt* revendiquer; (*rights, inheritance*) demander, prétendre à; (*assert*) déclarer, prétendre ♦ *vi* (*for insurance*) faire une déclaration de sinistre ♦ *n* revendication *f*; demande *f*; prétention *f*, déclaration *f*; (*right*) droit *m*, titre *m*; **~ant** *n* (*ADMIN, LAW*) requérant(e)

clairvoyant [kleə'vɔɪənt] *n* voyant(e), extra-lucide *m/f*

clam [klæm] *n* palourde *f*

clamber ['klæmbə*] *vi* grimper, se hisser

clammy ['klæmɪ] *adj* humide (et froid(e)), moite

clamour ['klæmə*] (*US* clamor) *vi*: **to ~ for** réclamer à grands cris

clamp [klæmp] *n* agrafe *f*, crampon *m* ♦ *vt* serrer; (*sth to sth*) fixer; **~ down on** *vt fus* sévir *or* prendre des mesures draconiennes contre

clan [klæn] *n* clan *m*

clang [klæŋ] *vi* émettre un bruit *or* fracas métallique

clap [klæp] *vi* applaudir; **~ping** *n* applaudissements *mpl*

claret ['klærɪt] *n* (vin *m* de) bordeaux *m* (rouge)

clarinet [klærɪ'net] *n* clarinette *f*

clarity ['klærɪtɪ] *n* clarté *f*

clash [klæʃ] *n* choc *m*; (*fig*) conflit *m* ♦ *vi* se heurter; être *or* entrer en conflit; (*colours*) jurer; (*two events*) tomber en même temps

clasp [klɑːsp] *n* (*of necklace, bag*) fermoir *m*; (*hold, embrace*) étreinte *f* ♦ *vt* serrer, étreindre

class [klɑːs] *n* classe *f* ♦ *vt* classer, classifier

classic ['klæsɪk] *adj* classique ♦ *n* (*author, work*) classique *m*; **~al** *adj* classique

classified ['klæsɪfaɪd] *adj* (*information*) secret(ète); **~ advertisement** *n* petite annonce

classmate ['klɑːsmeɪt] *n* camarade *m/f* de classe

classroom ['klɑːsrum] *n* (salle *f* de) classe *f*

clatter ['klætə*] *n* cliquetis *m* ♦ *vi* cliqueter

clause [klɔːz] *n* clause *f*; (*LING*) proposition *f*

claw [klɔː] *n* griffe *f*; (*of bird of prey*) serre *f*; (*of lobster*) pince *f*; **~ at** *vt fus* essayer de s'agripper à *or* griffer

clay [kleɪ] *n* argile *f*

clean [kliːn] *adj* propre; (*clear, smooth*) net(te); (*record, reputation*) sans tache; (*joke, story*) correct(e) ♦ *vt* nettoyer; **~ out** *vt* nettoyer (à fond); **~ up** *vt* nettoyer; (*fig*) remettre de l'ordre dans; **~-cut** *adj* (*person*) net(te), soigné(e); **~er** *n* (*person*) nettoyeur(euse), femme *f* de ménage; (*product*) détachant *m*; **~er's** *n* (*also*: dry ~er's) teinturier *m*; **~ing** *n* nettoyage *m*; **~liness** ['klenlɪnɪs] *n* propreté *f*

cleanse [klenz] *vt* nettoyer; (*purify*) purifier; **~r** *n* (*for face*) démaquillant *m*

clean-shaven ['kliːn'ʃeɪvn] *adj* rasé(e) de près

cleansing department ['klenzɪŋ-] (*BRIT*) *n* service *m* de voirie

clear ['klɪə*] *adj* clair(e); (*glass, plastic*) transparent(e); (*road, way*) libre, dégagé(e); (*conscience*) net(te) ♦ *vt* (*room*) débarrasser; (*of people*) faire évacuer; (*cheque*) compenser; (*LAW: suspect*) innocenter; (*obstacle*) franchir *or* sauter sans heurter ♦ *vi* (*weather*) s'éclaircir; (*fog*) se dissiper ♦ *adv*: **~ of** à distance de, à l'écart de; **to ~ the table** débarrasser la table, desservir; **~ up** *vt* ranger, mettre en ordre; (*mystery*) éclaircir, résoudre; **~ance** ['klɪərns] *n* (*removal*) déblaiement *m*; (*permission*) autorisation *f*; **~-cut** *adj* clair(e), nettement défini(e); **~ing** *n* (*in forest*) clairière *f*; **~ing bank** (*BRIT*) *n* banque qui appartient à une chambre de compensation; **~ly** *adv* clairement; (*evidently*) de toute évidence; **~way** (*BRIT*) *n* route *f* à stationnement interdit

clef [klef] *n* (*MUS*) clé *f*

cleft [kleft] *n* (*in rock*) crevasse *f*, fissure *f*

clench [klentʃ] *vt* serrer

clergy ['klɜːdʒɪ] *n* clergé *m*; **~man** (*irreg*) *n* ecclésiastique *m*

clerical ['klerɪkəl] *adj* de bureau, d'employé de bureau; (*REL*) clérical(e), du clergé

clerk [klɑːk, (*US*) klɜːk] *n* employé(e) de bureau; (*US: salesperson*) vendeur(euse)

clever ['klevə*] *adj* (*mentally*) intelligent(e); (*deft, crafty*) habile, adroit(e); (*device, arrangement*) ingénieux(euse), astucieux(euse)

clew [kluː] (*US*) *n* = **clue**

click [klɪk] *vi* faire un bruit sec *or* un déclic ♦ *vt*: **to ~ one's tongue** faire claquer sa

langue; **to ~ one's heels** claquer des talons
client ['klaɪənt] n client(e)
cliff [klɪf] n falaise f
climate ['klaɪmɪt] n climat m
climax ['klaɪmæks] n apogée m, point culminant; (*sexual*) orgasme m
climb [klaɪm] vi grimper, monter ♦ vt gravir, escalader, monter sur ♦ n montée f, escalade f; **~-down** n reculade f, dérobade f; **~er** n (*mountaineer*) grimpeur(euse), varappeur(euse); (*plant*) plante grimpante; **~ing** n (*mountaineering*) escalade f, varappe f
clinch [klɪntʃ] vt (*deal*) conclure, sceller
cling [klɪŋ] (*pt, pp* **clung**) vi: **to ~ (to)** se cramponner (à), s'accrocher (à); (*of clothes*) coller (à)
clinic ['klɪnɪk] n centre médical; **~al** adj clinique; (*attitude*) froid(e), détaché(e)
clink [klɪŋk] vi tinter, cliqueter
clip [klɪp] n (*for hair*) barrette f; (*also: paper* ~) trombone m ♦ vt (*fasten*) attacher; (*hair, nails*) couper; (*hedge*) tailler; **~pers** npl (*for hedge*) sécateur m; (*also: nail ~pers*) coupe-ongles m inv; **~ping** n (*from newspaper*) coupure f de journal
cloak [kləʊk] n grande cape ♦ vt (*fig*) masquer, cacher; **~room** n (*for coats etc*) vestiaire m; (*BRIT: WC*) toilettes fpl
clock [klɒk] n (*large*) horloge f; (*small*) pendule f; ~ **in** (*BRIT*) vi pointer (en arrivant); ~ **off** (*BRIT*) vi pointer (en partant); ~ **on** (*BRIT*) vi = **clock in**; ~ **out** (*BRIT*) vi = **clock off**; **~wise** adv dans le sens des aiguilles d'une montre; **~work** n rouages mpl, mécanisme m; (*of clock*) mouvement m (d'horlogerie) ♦ adj mécanique
clog [klɒg] n sabot m ♦ vt boucher ♦ vi (*also:* ~ up) se boucher
cloister ['klɔɪstə*] n cloître m
close[1] [kləʊs] adj (*near*): ~ **(to)** près (de), proche (de); (*contact, link*) étroit(e); (*contest*) très serré(e); (*watch*) étroit(e), strict(e); (*examination*) attentif(ive), minutieux(euse); (*weather*) lourd(e), étouffant(e) ♦ adv près, à proximité; ~ **to** près de; ~ **by** adj proche ♦ adv tout(e) près; ~ **at hand** = **by**; **a ~ friend** un ami intime; **to have a ~ shave** (*fig*) l'échapper belle
close[2] [kləʊz] vt fermer ♦ vi (*shop etc*) fermer; (*lid, door etc*) se fermer; (*end*) se terminer, se conclure ♦ n (*end*) conclusion f, fin f; ~ **down** vt, vi fermer (définitivement)
closed [kləʊzd] adj fermé(e); **~ shop** n organisation f qui n'admet que des travailleurs syndiqués
close-knit [kləʊs'nɪt] adj (*family, community*) très uni(e)
closely ['kləʊslɪ] adv (*examine, watch*) de près
closet ['klɒzɪt] n (*cupboard*) placard m, réduit m

close-up ['kləʊsʌp] n gros plan
closure ['kləʊʒə*] n fermeture f
clot [klɒt] n (*gen: blood* ~) caillot m; (*inf: person*) ballot m ♦ vi (*blood*) se coaguler
cloth [klɒθ] n (*material*) tissu m, étoffe f; (*also: tea~*) torchon m; lavette f
clothe [kləʊð] vt habiller, vêtir; **~s** npl vêtements mpl, habits mpl; **~s brush** n brosse f à habits; **~s line** n corde f (à linge); **~s peg** (*US* **~s pin**) n pince f à linge
clothing ['kləʊðɪŋ] n = **clothes**
cloud [klaʊd] n nuage m; **~burst** n grosse averse; **~y** adj nuageux(euse), couvert(e); (*liquid*) trouble
clout [klaʊt] vt flanquer une taloche à
clove [kləʊv] n (*CULIN: spice*) clou m de girofle; ~ **of garlic** gousse f d'ail
clover ['kləʊvə*] n trèfle m
clown [klaʊn] n clown m ♦ vi (*also:* ~ about, ~ around) faire le clown
cloying ['klɔɪɪŋ] adj (*taste, smell*) écœurant(e)
club [klʌb] n (*society, place: also: golf* ~) club m; (*weapon*) massue f, matraque f ♦ vt matraquer ♦ vi: **to ~ together** s'associer; **~s** npl (*CARDS*) trèfle m; ~ **car** (*US*) n (*RAIL*) wagon-restaurant m; **~house** n club m
cluck [klʌk] vi glousser
clue [kluː] n indice m; (*in crosswords*) définition f; **I haven't a ~** je n'en ai pas la moindre idée
clump [klʌmp] n: ~ **of trees** bouquet m d'arbres; **a ~ of buildings** un ensemble de bâtiments
clumsy ['klʌmzɪ] adj gauche, maladroit(e)
clung [klʌŋ] pt, pp of **cling**
cluster ['klʌstə*] n (*of people*) (petit) groupe; (*of flowers*) grappe f; (*of stars*) amas m ♦ vi se rassembler
clutch [klʌtʃ] n (*grip, grasp*) étreinte f, prise f; (*AUT*) embrayage m ♦ vt (*grasp*) agripper; (*hold tightly*) serrer fort; (*hold on to*) se cramponner à
clutter ['klʌtə*] vt (*also:* ~ up) encombrer
CND n abbr (= Campaign for Nuclear Disarmament) mouvement pour le désarmement nucléaire
Co. abbr = **county**; **company**
c/o abbr (= care of) c/o, aux bons soins de
coach [kəʊtʃ] n (*bus*) autocar m; (*horsedrawn*) diligence f; (*of train*) voiture f, wagon m; (*SPORT: trainer*) entraîneur(euse); (*SCOL: tutor*) répétiteur(trice) ♦ vt entraîner; (*student*) faire travailler; ~ **trip** n excursion f en car
coal [kəʊl] n charbon m; ~ **face** n front m de taille; **~field** n bassin houiller
coalition [kəʊə'lɪʃən] n coalition f
coal: **~man** ['kəʊlmən] (*irreg*) n charbonnier m, marchand m de charbon; ~ **merchant** n = **~man**; **~mine** ['kəʊlmaɪn]

n mine *f* de charbon

coarse [kɔːs] *adj* grossier(ère), rude

coast [kəust] *n* côte *f* ♦ *vi* (*car, cycle etc*) descendre en roue libre; **~al** *adj* côtier(ère); **~guard** *n* garde-côte *m*; (*service*) gendarmerie *f* maritime; **~line** *n* côte *f*, littoral *m*

coat [kəut] *n* manteau *m*; (*of animal*) pelage *m*, poil *m*; (*of paint*) couche *f* ♦ *vt* couvrir; **~ hanger** *n* cintre *m*; **~ing** *n* couche *f*, revêtement *m*; **~ of arms** *n* blason *m*, armoiries *fpl*

coax [kəuks] *vt* persuader par des cajoleries

cob [kɒb] *n* see **corn**

cobbler [ˈkɒblə*] *n* cordonnier *m*

cobbles [ˈkɒblz] (*also:* **cobblestones**) *npl* pavés (ronds)

cobweb [ˈkɒbweb] *n* toile *f* d'araignée

cocaine [kəˈkeɪn] *n* cocaïne *f*

cock [kɒk] *n* (*rooster*) coq *m*; (*male bird*) mâle *m* ♦ *vt* (*gun*) armer; **~erel** *n* jeune coq *m*; **~-eyed** *adj* (*idea, method*) absurde, qui ne tient pas debout

cockle [ˈkɒkl] *n* coque *f*

cockney [ˈkɒknɪ] *n* cockney *m*, habitant des quartiers populaires de l'East End de Londres, ≈ faubourien(ne)

cockpit [ˈkɒkpɪt] *n* (*in aircraft*) poste *m* de pilotage, cockpit *m*

cockroach [ˈkɒkrəutʃ] *n* cafard *m*

cocktail [ˈkɒkteɪl] *n* cocktail *m* (*fruit ~ etc*) salade *f*; **~ cabinet** *n* (meuble-)bar *m*; **~ party** *n* cocktail *m*

cocoa [ˈkəukəu] *n* cacao *m*

coconut [ˈkəukənʌt] *n* noix *f* de coco

COD *abbr* = **cash on delivery**

cod [kɒd] *n* morue fraîche, cabillaud *m*

code [kəud] *n* code *m*

cod-liver oil [ˈkɒdlɪvər-] *n* huile *f* de foie de morue

coercion [kəuˈɜːʃən] *n* contrainte *f*

coffee [ˈkɒfɪ] *n* café *m*; **~ bar** (*BRIT*) *n* café *m*; **~ bean** *n* grain *m* de café; **~ break** *n* pause-café *f*; **~pot** *n* cafetière *f*; **~ table** *n* (petite) table basse

coffin [ˈkɒfɪn] *n* cercueil *m*

cog [kɒg] *n* dent *f* (d'engrenage); (*wheel*) roue dentée

cogent [ˈkəudʒənt] *adj* puissant(e), convaincant(e)

coil [kɔɪl] *n* rouleau *m*, bobine *f*; (*contraceptive*) stérilet *m* ♦ *vt* enrouler

coin [kɔɪn] *n* pièce *f* de monnaie ♦ *vt* (*word*) inventer; **~age** *n* monnaie *f*, système *m* monétaire; **~ box** (*BRIT*) *n* cabine *f* téléphonique

coincide [kəuɪnˈsaɪd] *vi* coïncider; **~nce** [kəuˈɪnsɪdəns] *n* coïncidence *f*

Coke [kəuk] (®) *n* coca *m*

coke [kəuk] *n* coke *m*

colander [ˈkɒləndə*] *n* passoire *f*

cold [kəuld] *adj* froid(e) ♦ *n* froid *m*; (*MED*)

rhume *m*; **it's ~** il fait froid; **to be** *or* **feel ~** (*person*) avoir froid; **to catch ~** prendre *or* attraper froid; **to catch a ~** attraper un rhume; **in ~ blood** de sang-froid; **~-shoulder** *vt* se montrer froid(e) envers, snober; **~ sore** *n* bouton *m* de fièvre

coleslaw [ˈkəulslɔː] *n* sorte de salade de chou cru

colic [ˈkɒlɪk] *n* colique(s) *f(pl)*

collapse [kəˈlæps] *vi* s'effondrer, s'écrouler ♦ *n* effondrement *m*, écroulement *m*; **collapsible** [kəˈlæpsəbl] *adj* pliant(e); télescopique

collar [ˈkɒlə*] *n* (*of coat, shirt*) col *m*; (*for animal*) collier *m*; **~bone** *n* clavicule *f*

collateral [kɒˈlætərəl] *n* nantissement *m*

colleague [ˈkɒliːg] *n* collègue *m/f*

collect [kəˈlekt] *vt* rassembler; ramasser; (*as a hobby*) collectionner; (*BRIT: call and pick up*) (passer) prendre; (*mail*) faire la levée de, ramasser; (*money owed*) encaisser; (*donations, subscriptions*) recueillir ♦ *vi* (*people*) se rassembler; (*things*) s'amasser; **to call ~** (*US: TEL*) téléphoner en P.C.V.; **~ion** [kəˈlekʃən] *n* collection *f*; (*of mail*) levée *f*; (*for money*) collecte *f*, quête *f*; **~or** [kəˈlektə*] *n* collectionneur *m*

college [ˈkɒlɪdʒ] *n* collège *m*

collide [kəˈlaɪd] *vi* entrer en collision

collie [ˈkɒlɪ] *n* (*dog*) colley *m*

colliery [ˈkɒlɪərɪ] (*BRIT*) *n* mine *f* de charbon, houillère *f*

collision [kəˈlɪʒən] *n* collision *f*

colloquial [kəˈləukwɪəl] *adj* familier(ère)

colon [ˈkəulɒn] *n* (*sign*) deux-points *m inv*; (*MED*) côlon *m*

colonel [ˈkɜːnl] *n* colonel *m*

colony [ˈkɒlənɪ] *n* colonie *f*

colour [ˈkʌlə*] (*US* **color**) *n* couleur *f* ♦ *vt* (*paint*) peindre; (*dye*) teindre; (*news*) fausser, exagérer ♦ *vi* (*blush*) rougir; **~s** *npl* (*of party, club*) couleurs *fpl*; **~ in** *vt* colorier; **~ bar** *n* discrimination raciale (*dans un établissement*); **~-blind** *adj* daltonien(ne); **~ed** *adj* (*person*) de couleur; (*illustration*) en couleur; **~ film** *n* (*for camera*) pellicule *f* (en) couleur; **~ful** *adj* coloré(e), vif(vive); (*personality*) pittoresque, haut(e) en couleurs; **~ing** *n* colorant *m*; (*complexion*) teint *m*; **~ scheme** *n* combinaison *f* de(s) couleurs; **~ television** *n* télévision *f* (en) couleur

colt [kəult] *n* poulain *m*

column [ˈkɒləm] *n* colonne *f*; **~ist** [ˈkɒləmnɪst] *n* chroniqueur(euse)

coma [ˈkəumə] *n* coma *m*

comb [kəum] *n* peigne *m* ♦ *vt* (*hair*) peigner; (*area*) ratisser, passer au peigne fin

combat [ˈkɒmbæt] *n* combat *m* ♦ *vt* combattre, lutter contre

combination [kɒmbɪˈneɪʃən] *n* combinaison *f*

combine [*vb* kəm'baɪn, *n* 'kɒmbaɪn] *vt*: **to ~ sth with sth** combiner qch avec qch; (*one quality with another*) joindre *or* allier qch à qch ♦ *vi* s'associer; (*CHEM*) se combiner ♦ *n* (*ECON*) trust *m*; **~ (harvester)** *n* moissonneuse-batteuse(-lieuse) *f*

come [kʌm] (*pt* **came**, *pp* **come**) *vi* venir, arriver; **to ~ to** (*decision etc*) parvenir *or* arriver à; **to ~ undone/loose** se défaire/ desserrer; **~ about** *vi* se produire, arriver; **~ across** *vt fus* rencontrer par hasard, tomber sur; **~ along** *vi* = **to come on; ~ away** *vi* partir, s'en aller, se détacher; **~ back** *vi* revenir; **~ by** *vt fus* (*acquire*) obtenir, se procurer; **~ down** *vi* descendre; (*prices*) baisser; (*buildings*) s'écrouler, être démoli(e); **~ forward** *vi* s'avancer, se présenter, s'annoncer; **~ from** *vt fus* être originaire de, venir de; **~ in** *vi* entrer; **~ in for** *vi* (*criticism etc*) être l'objet de; **~ into** *vt fus* (*money*) hériter de; **~ off** *vi* (*button*) se détacher; (*stain*) s'enlever; (*attempt*) réussir; **~ on** *vi* (*pupil, work, project*) faire des progrès, s'avancer; (*lights, electricity*) s'allumer; (*central heating*) se mettre en marche; **~ on!** viens!, allons!, allez!; **~ out** *vi* sortir; (*book*) paraître; (*strike*) cesser le travail, se mettre en grève; **~ round** *vi* (*after faint, operation*) revenir à soi, reprendre connaissance; **~ to** *vi* revenir à soi; **~ up** *vi* monter; **~ up against** *vt fus* (*resistance, difficulties*) rencontrer; **~ up with** *vt fus*: **he came up with an idea** il a eu une idée, il a proposé quelque chose; **~ upon** *vt fus* tomber sur; **~back** ['kʌmbæk] *n* (*THEATRE etc*) rentrée *f*

comedian [kə'miːdɪən] *n* (*in music hall etc*) comique *m*; (*THEATRE*) comédien *m*

comedy ['kɒmədɪ] *n* comédie *f*

comeuppance [kʌm'ʌpəns] *n*: **to get one's ~** recevoir ce qu'on mérite

comfort ['kʌmfət] *n* confort *m*, bien-être *m*; (*relief*) soulagement *m*, réconfort *m* ♦ *vt* consoler, réconforter; **the ~s of home** les commodités *fpl* de la maison; **~able** *adj* confortable; (*person*) à l'aise; (*patient*) dont l'état est stationnaire; (*walk etc*) facile; **~ably** *adv* (*sit*) confortablement; (*live*) à l'aise; **~ station** (*US*) *n* toilettes *fpl*

comic ['kɒmɪk] *adj* (*also*: **~al**) comique ♦ *n* comique *m*; (*BRIT*: *magazine*) illustré *m*; **~ strip** *n* bande dessinée

coming ['kʌmɪŋ] *n* arrivée *f* ♦ *adj* prochain(e), à venir; **~(s) and going(s)** *n(pl)* va-et-vient *m inv*

comma ['kɒmə] *n* virgule *f*

command [kə'mɑːnd] *n* ordre *m*, commandement *m*; (*MIL*: *authority*) commandement *m*; (*mastery*) maîtrise *f* ♦ *vt* (*troops*) commander; **to ~ sb to do** ordonner à qn de faire; **~eer** [kɒmən'dɪə*] *vt* réquisitionner; **~er** *n* (*MIL*) commandant *m*

commando [kə'mɑːndəʊ] *n* commando *m*; membre *m* d'un commando

commemorate [kə'meməreɪt] *vt* commémorer

commence [kə'mens] *vt, vi* commencer

commend [kə'mend] *vt* louer; (*recommend*) recommander

commensurate [kə'mensjʊrɪt] *adj*: **~ with** *or* **to** en proportion de, proportionné(e) à

comment ['kɒment] *n* commentaire *m* ♦ *vi*: **to ~ (on)** faire des remarques (sur); **"no ~"** "je n'ai rien à dire"; **~ary** ['kɒməntrɪ] *n* commentaire *m*; (*SPORT*) reportage *m* (en direct); **~ator** ['kɒməntɛɪtə*] *n* commentateur *m*; reporter *m*

commerce ['kɒmɜːs] *n* commerce *m*

commercial [kə'mɜːʃəl] *adj* commercial(e) ♦ *n* (*TV, RADIO*) annonce *f* publicitaire, spot *m* (publicitaire); **~ radio** *n* radio privée; **~ television** *n* télévision privée

commiserate [kə'mɪzəreɪt] *vi*: **to ~ with sb** témoigner de la sympathie pour qn

commission [kə'mɪʃən] *n* (*order for work*) commande *f*; (*committee, fee*) commission *f* ♦ *vt* (*work of art*) commander, charger un artiste de l'exécution de; **out of ~** (*not working*) hors service; **~aire** [kəmɪʃə'nɛə*] (*BRIT*) *n* (*at shop, cinema etc*) portier *m* (en uniforme); **~er** *n* (*POLICE*) préfet *m* (de police)

commit [kə'mɪt] *vt* (*act*) commettre; (*resources*) consacrer; (*to sb's care*) confier (à); **to ~ o.s. (to do)** s'engager (à faire); **to ~ suicide** se suicider; **~ment** *n* engagement *m*; (*obligation*) responsabilité(s) *f(pl)*

committee [kə'mɪtɪ] *n* comité *m*

commodity [kə'mɒdɪtɪ] *n* produit *m*, marchandise *f*, article *m*

common ['kɒmən] *adj* commun(e); (*usual*) courant(e) ♦ *n* terrain communal; **the C~s** *npl* la chambre des Communes; **in ~** en commun; **~er** *n* roturier(ière); **~ law** *n* droit coutumier; **~ly** *adv* communément, généralement; couramment; **C~ Market** *n*: **the C~ Market** le Marché commun; **~place** *adj* banal(e), ordinaire; **~ room** *n* salle commune; **~ sense** *n* bon sens; **C~wealth** (*BRIT*) *n*: **the C~wealth** le Commonwealth

commotion [kə'məʊʃən] *n* désordre *m*, tumulte *m*

communal ['kɒmjuːnl] *adj* (*life*) communautaire; (*for common use*) commun(e)

commune [*n* 'kɒmjuːn, *vb* kə'mjuːn] *n* (*group*) communauté *f* ♦ *vi*: **to ~ with** communier avec

communicate [kə'mjuːnɪkeɪt] *vt, vi* communiquer

communication [kəmjuːnɪ'keɪʃən] *n* communication *f*; **~ cord** (*BRIT*) *n* sonnette *f* d'alarme

communion [kə'mjuːnɪən] *n* (*also: Holy*

C~) communion *f*

communism ['kɒmjʊnɪzəm] *n* communisme *m*; **communist** ['kɒmjʊnɪst] *adj* communiste ♦ *n* communiste *m/f*

community [kə'mjuːnɪtɪ] *n* communauté *f*; ~ **centre** *n* centre *m* de loisirs; ~ **chest** (US) *n* fonds commun; ~ **home** *n* (*school*) centre *m* d'éducation surveillée

commutation ticket [kɒmjuː'teɪʃən-] (US) *n* carte *f* d'abonnement

commute [kə'mjuːt] *vi* faire un trajet journalier (de son domicile à son bureau) ♦ *vt* (LAW) commuer; ~**r** *n* banlieusard(e) (qui ... *see vi*)

compact [*adj* kəm'pækt, *n* 'kɒmpækt] *adj* compact(e) ♦ *n* (*also*: *powder* ~) poudrier *m*; ~ **disc** *n* disque compact; ~ **disc player** *n* lecteur *m* de disque compact

companion [kəm'pænɪən] *n* compagnon(compagne); ~**ship** *n* camaraderie *f*

company ['kʌmpənɪ] *n* compagnie *f*; **to keep sb** ~ tenir compagnie à qn; ~ **secretary** (BRIT) *n* (COMM) secrétaire général (d'une société)

comparative [kəm'pærətɪv] *adj* (*study*) comparatif(ive); (*relative*) relatif(ive); ~**ly** *adv* (*relatively*) relativement

compare [kəm'pɛə*] *vt*: **to** ~ **sth/sb with/to** comparer qch/qn avec *or* et/à ♦ *vi*: **to** ~ (**with**) se comparer (à); être comparable (à); **comparison** [kəm'pærɪsn] *n* comparaison *f*

compartment [kəm'pɑːtmənt] *n* compartiment *m*

compass ['kʌmpəs] *n* boussole *f*; ~**es** *npl* (GEOM: *also*: *pair of* ~*es*) compas *m*

compassion [kəm'pæʃən] *n* compassion *f*, ~**ate** *adj* compatissant(e)

compatible [kəm'pætɪbl] *adj* compatible

compel [kəm'pel] *vt* contraindre, obliger; ~**ling** *adj* (*fig*: *argument*) irrésistible

compensate ['kɒmpenseɪt] *vt* indemniser, dédommager ♦ *vi*: **to** ~ **for** compenser; **compensation** [kɒmpen'seɪʃn] *n* compensation *f*; (*money*) dédommagement *m*, indemnité *f*

compère ['kɒmpɛə*] *n* (TV) animateur(trice)

compete [kəm'piːt] *vi*: **to** ~ (**with**) rivaliser (avec), faire concurrence (à)

competent ['kɒmpɪtənt] *adj* compétent(e), capable

competition [kɒmpɪ'tɪʃən] *n* (*contest*) compétition *f*, concours *m*; (ECON) concurrence *f*

competitive [kəm'petɪtɪv] *adj* (ECON) concurrentiel(le); (*sport*) de compétition; (*person*) qui a l'esprit de compétition

competitor [kəm'petɪtə*] *n* concurrent(e)

complacency [kəm'pleɪsnsɪ] *n* suffisance *f*, vaine complaisance

complain [kəm'pleɪn] *vi*: **to** ~ (**about**) se plaindre (de); (*in shop etc*) réclamer (au sujet de); (*of pain*) se plaindre de; ~**t** *n* plainte *f*, réclamation *f*; (MED) affection *f*

complement [*n* 'kɒmplɪmənt, *vb* 'kɒmplɪment] *n* complément *m*; (*especially of ship's crew etc*) effectif complet ♦ *vt* (*enhance*) compléter; ~**ary** [kɒmplɪ'mentərɪ] *adj* complémentaire

complete [kəm'pliːt] *adj* complet(ète) ♦ *vt* achever, parachever; (*set*, *group*) compléter; (*a form*) remplir; ~**ly** *adv* complètement; **completion** [kəm'pliːʃən] *n* achèvement *m*; (*of contract*) exécution *f*

complex ['kɒmpleks] *adj* complexe ♦ *n* complexe *m*

complexion [kəm'plekʃən] *n* (*of face*) teint *m*

compliance [kəm'plaɪəns] *n* (*submission*) docilité *f*; (*agreement*): ~ **with** le fait de se conformer à; **in** ~ **with** en accord avec

complicate ['kɒmplɪkeɪt] *vt* compliquer; ~**d** *adj* compliqué(e); **complication** [kɒmplɪ'keɪʃn] *n* complication *f*

compliment [*n* 'kɒmplɪmənt, *vb* 'kɒmplɪment] *n* compliment *m* ♦ *vt* complimenter; ~**s** *npl* (*respects*) compliments *mpl*, hommages *mpl*; **to pay sb a** ~ faire *or* adresser un compliment à qn; ~**ary** [kɒmplɪ'mentəri] *adj* flatteur(euse); (*free*) (offert(e)) à titre gracieux; ~**ary ticket** *n* billet *m* de faveur

comply [kəm'plaɪ] *vi*: **to** ~ **with** se soumettre à, se conformer à

component [kəm'pəʊnənt] *n* composant *m*, élément *m*

compose [kəm'pəʊz] *vt* composer; (*form*): **to be** ~**d of** se composer de; **to** ~ **o.s.** se calmer, se maîtriser; prendre une contenance; ~**d** *adj* calme, posé(e); ~**r** *n* (MUS) compositeur *m*; **composition** [kɒmpə'zɪʃən] *n* composition *f*; **composure** [kəm'pəʊʒə*] *n* calme *m*, maîtrise *f* de soi

compound ['kɒmpaʊnd] *n* composé *m*; (*enclosure*) enclos *m*, enceinte *f*; ~ **fracture** *n* fracture compliquée; ~ **interest** *n* intérêt composé

comprehend [kɒmprɪ'hend] *vt* comprendre; **comprehension** [kɒmprɪ'henʃən] *n* compréhension *f*

comprehensive [kɒmprɪ'hensɪv] *adj* (très) complet(ète); ~ **policy** *n* (INSURANCE) assurance *f* tous risques; ~ (**school**) (BRIT) *n* école secondaire polyvalente, ≈ C.E.S. *m*

compress [*vb* kəm'pres, *n* 'kɒmpres] *vt* comprimer; (*text*, *information*) condenser ♦ *n* (MED) compresse *f*

comprise [kəm'praɪz] *vt* (*also*: *be* ~*d of*) comprendre; (*constitute*) constituer, représenter

compromise ['kɒmprəmaɪz] *n* compromis *m* ♦ *vt* compromettre ♦ *vi* transiger, accepter un compromis

compulsion [kəm'pʌlʃən] *n* contrainte *f*, force *f*

compulsive [kəm'pʌlsɪv] *adj* (*PSYCH*) compulsif(ive); (*book, film etc*) captivant(e)

compulsory [kəm'pʌlsərɪ] *adj* obligatoire

computer [kəm'pju:tə*] *n* ordinateur *m*; ~ **game** *n* jeu *m* vidéo; ~**ize** *vt* informatiser; ~ **programmer** *n* programmeur(euse); ~ **programming** *n* programmation *f*; ~ **science** *n* informatique *f*; **computing** *n* = ~ **science**

comrade ['kɒmrɪd] *n* camarade *m/f*

con [kɒn] *vt* duper; (*cheat*) escroquer ♦ *n* escroquerie *f*

conceal [kən'si:l] *vt* cacher, dissimuler

conceit [kən'si:t] *n* vanité *f*, suffisance *f*, prétention *f*; ~**ed** *adj* vaniteux(euse), suffisant(e)

conceive [kən'si:v] *vt*, *vi* concevoir

concentrate ['kɒnsəntreɪt] *vi* se concentrer ♦ *vt* concentrer

concentration [kɒnsən'treɪʃən] *n* concentration *f*; ~ **camp** *n* camp *m* de concentration

concept ['kɒnsept] *n* concept *m*

concern [kən'sɜ:n] *n* affaire *f*; (*COMM*) entreprise *f*, firme *f*; (*anxiety*) inquiétude *f*, souci *m* ♦ *vt* concerner; **to be ~ed (about)** s'inquiéter (de), être inquiet(e) (au sujet de); ~**ing** *prep* en ce qui concerne, à propos de

concert ['kɒnsət] *n* concert *m*; ~**ed** *adj* concerté(e); ~ **hall** *n* salle *f* de concert

concerto [kən'tʃɜːtəʊ] *n* concerto *m*

concession [kən'seʃən] *n* concession *f*; **tax ~** dégrèvement fiscal

conclude [kən'klu:d] *vt* conclure; **conclusion** [kən'klu:ʒən] *n* conclusion *f*; **conclusive** [kən'klu:sɪv] *adj* concluant(e), définitif(ive)

concoct [kən'kɒkt] *vt* confectionner, composer; (*fig*) inventer; ~**ion** [kən'kɒkʃən] *n* mélange *m*

concourse ['kɒŋkɔ:s] *n* (*hall*) hall *m*, salle *f* des pas perdus

concrete ['kɒŋkri:t] *n* béton *m* ♦ *adj* concret(ète); (*floor etc*) en béton

concur [kən'kɜ:*] *vi* (*agree*) être d'accord

concurrently [kən'kʌrəntlɪ] *adv* simultanément

concussion [kɒn'kʌʃən] *n* (*MED*) commotion (cérébrale)

condemn [kən'dem] *vt* condamner

condensation [kɒnden'seɪʃən] *n* condensation *f*

condense [kən'dens] *vi* se condenser ♦ *vt* condenser; ~**d milk** *n* lait concentré (sucré)

condition [kən'dɪʃən] *n* condition *f*; (*MED*) état *m* ♦ *vt* déterminer, conditionner; **on ~ that** à condition que +*sub*, à condition de; ~**al** *adj* conditionnel(le); ~**er** *n* (*for hair*)

baume après-shampooing *m*; (*for fabrics*) assouplissant *m*

condolences [kən'dəʊlənsɪz] *npl* condoléances *fpl*

condom ['kɒndəm] *n* préservatif *m*

condominium [kɒndə'mɪnɪəm] (*US*) *n* (*building*) immeuble *m* (en copropriété)

condone [kən'dəʊn] *vt* fermer les yeux sur, approuver (tacitement)

conducive [kən'dju:sɪv] *adj*: ~ **to** favorable à, qui contribue à

conduct [*n* 'kɒndʌkt, *vb* kən'dʌkt] *n* conduite *f* ♦ *vt* conduire; (*MUS*) diriger; **to ~ o.s.** se conduire, se comporter; ~**ed tour** *n* voyage organisé; (*of building*) visite guidée; ~**or** [kən'dʌktə*] *n* (*of orchestra*) chef *m* d'orchestre; (*on bus*) receveur *m*, (*US: on train*) chef *m* de train; (*ELEC*) conducteur *m*; ~**ress** [kən'dʌktrɪs] *n* (*on bus*) receveuse *f*

cone [kəʊn] *n* cône *m*; (*for ice-cream*) cornet *m*; (*BOT*) pomme *f* de pin, cône

confectioner [kən'fekʃənə*] *n* confiseur(euse); ~'**s (shop)** *n* confiserie *f*; ~**y** *n* confiserie *f*

confer [kən'fɜ:*] *vt*: **to ~ sth on** conférer qch à ♦ *vi* conférer, s'entretenir

conference ['kɒnfərəns] *n* conférence *f*

confess [kən'fes] *vt* confesser, avouer ♦ *vi* se confesser; ~**ion** [kən'feʃən] *n* confession *f*

confetti [kən'fetɪ] *n* confettis *mpl*

confide [kən'faɪd] *vi*: **to ~ in** se confier à

confidence ['kɒnfɪdəns] *n* confiance *f*; (*also: self-~*) assurance *f*, confiance en soi; (*secret*) confidence *f*; **in ~** (*speak, write*) en confidence, confidentiellement; ~ **trick** *n* escroquerie *f*; **confident** ['kɒnfɪdənt] *adj* sûr(e), assuré(e); **confidential** [kɒnfɪ'denʃəl] *adj* confidentiel(le)

confine [kən'faɪn] *vt* limiter, borner; (*shut up*) confiner, enfermer; ~**d** *adj* (*space*) restreint(e), réduit(e); ~**ment** *n* emprisonnement *m*, détention *f*; ~**s** ['kɒnfaɪnz] *npl* confins *mpl*, bornes *fpl*

confirm [kən'fɜ:m] *vt* confirmer; (*appointment*) ratifier; ~**ation** [kɒnfə'meɪʃən] *n* confirmation *f*; ~**ed** *adj* invétéré(e), incorrigible

confiscate ['kɒnfɪskeɪt] *vt* confisquer

conflict [*n* 'kɒnflɪkt, *vb* kən'flɪkt] *n* conflit *m*, lutte *f* ♦ *vi* être *or* entrer en conflit; (*opinions*) s'opposer, se heurter; ~**ing** [kən'flɪktɪŋ] *adj* contradictoire

conform [kən'fɔ:m] *vi*: **to ~ (to)** se conformer (à)

confound [kən'faʊnd] *vt* confondre

confront [kən'frʌnt] *vt* confronter, mettre en présence; (*enemy, danger*) affronter, faire face à; ~**ation** [kɒnfrən'teɪʃən] *n* confrontation *f*

confuse [kən'fju:z] *vt* (*person*) troubler; (*si-*

tuation) embrouiller; (one thing with another) confondre; **~d** adj (person) dérouté(e), désorienté(e); **confusing** adj peu clair(e), déroutant(e); **confusion** [kən'fjuːʒən] n confusion f

congeal [kən'dʒiːl] vi (blood) se coaguler; (oil etc) se figer

congenial [kən'dʒiːnɪəl] adj sympathique, agréable

congested [kən'dʒestɪd] adj (MED) congestionné(e); (area) surpeuplé(e); (road) bloqué(e)

congestion [kən'dʒestʃən] n congestion f; (fig) encombrement m

congratulate [kən'grætjʊleɪt] vt: **to ~ sb (on)** féliciter qn (de); **congratulations** [kəngrætjʊ'leɪʃənz] npl félicitations fpl

congregate ['kɒŋgrɪgeɪt] vi se rassembler, se réunir

congregation [kɒŋgrɪ'geɪʃən] n assemblée f (des fidèles)

congress ['kɒŋgres] n congrès m; **~man** (irreg: US) n membre m du Congrès

conjunction [kən'dʒʌŋkʃən] n (LING) conjonction f

conjunctivitis [kəndʒʌŋktɪ'vaɪtɪs] n conjonctivite f

conjure ['kʌndʒə*] vi faire des tours de passe-passe; **~ up** vt (ghost, spirit) faire apparaître; (memories) évoquer; **~r** n prestidigitateur m, illusionniste m/f

conk out [kɒŋk-] (inf) vi tomber or rester en panne

con man (irreg) n escroc m

connect [kə'nekt] vt joindre, relier; (ELEC) connecter; (TEL: caller) mettre en connection (with avec); (: new subscriber) brancher; (fig) établir un rapport entre, faire un rapprochement entre ♦ vi (train): **to ~ with** assurer la correspondance avec; **to be ~ed with** (fig) avoir un rapport avec; avoir des rapports avec, être en relation avec; **~ion** [kə'nekʃə] n relation f, lien m; (ELEC) connexion f; (train, plane etc) correspondance f; (TEL) branchement m, communication f

connive [kə'naɪv] vi: **to ~ at** se faire le complice de

conquer ['kɒŋkə*] vt conquérir; (feelings) vaincre, surmonter

conquest ['kɒŋkwest] n conquête f

cons [kɒnz] npl see **convenience; pro**

conscience ['kɒnʃəns] n conscience f; **conscientious** [kɒnʃɪ'enʃəs] adj consciencieux(euse)

conscious ['kɒnʃəs] adj conscient(e); **~ness** n conscience f; (MED) connaissance f

conscript ['kɒnskrɪpt] n conscrit m

consent [kən'sent] n consentement m ♦ vi: **to ~ (to)** consentir (à)

consequence ['kɒnsɪkwəns] n conséquence

f, suites fpl; (significance) importance f

consequently ['kɒnsɪkwəntlɪ] adv par conséquent, donc

conservation [kɒnsə'veɪʃən] n préservation f, protection f

conservative [kən'sɜːvətɪv] adj conservateur(trice); **at a ~ estimate** au bas mot; **C~** (BRIT) adj, n (POL) conservateur(trice)

conservatory [kən'sɜːvətrɪ] n (greenhouse) serre f

conserve [kən'sɜːv] vt conserver, préserver; (supplies, energy) économiser ♦ n confiture f

consider [kən'sɪdə*] vt (study) considérer, réfléchir à; (take into account) penser à, prendre en considération; (regard, judge) considérer, estimer; **to ~ doing sth** envisager de faire qch; **~able** [kən'sɪdərəbl] adj considérable; **~ably** adv nettement; **~ate** [kən'sɪdərɪt] adj prévenant(e), plein(e) d'égards; **~ation** [kənsɪdə'reɪʃən] n considération f; **~ing** [kən'sɪdərɪŋ] prep étant donné

consign [kən'saɪn] vt expédier; (to sb's care) confier; (fig) livrer; **~ment** n arrivage m, envoi m

consist [kən'sɪst] vi: **to ~ of** consister en, se composer de

consistency [kən'sɪstənsɪ] n consistance f; (fig) cohérence f

consistent [kən'sɪstənt] adj logique, cohérent(e)

consolation [kɒnsə'leɪʃən] n consolation f

console ['kɒnsəʊl] n (COMPUT) console f

consonant ['kɒnsənənt] n consonne f

conspicuous [kən'spɪkjʊəs] adj voyant(e), qui attire l'attention

conspiracy [kən'spɪrəsɪ] n conspiration f, complot m

constable ['kʌnstəbl] (BRIT) n ≈ agent m de police, gendarme m; **chief ~** ≈ préfet m de police

constabulary [kən'stæbjʊlərɪ] (BRIT) n ≈ police f, gendarmerie f

constant ['kɒnstənt] adj constant(e); incessant(e); **~ly** adv constamment, sans cesse

constipated ['kɒnstɪpeɪtəd] adj constipé(e); **constipation** [kɒnstɪ'peɪʃən] n constipation f

constituency [kən'stɪtjʊənsɪ] n circonscription électorale

constituent [kən'stɪtjʊənt] n (POL) électeur(trice); (part) élément constitutif, composant m

constitution [kɒnstɪ'tjuːʃən] n constitution f; **~al** adj constitutionnel(le)

constraint [kən'streɪnt] n contrainte f

construct [kən'strʌkt] vt construire; **~ion** [kən'strʌkʃən] n construction f; **~ive** adj constructif(ive)

construe [kən'struː] vt interpréter, expliquer

consul ['kɒnsl] n consul m; **~ate** ['kɒnsjʊlət] n consulat m

consult [kən'sʌlt] vt consulter; **~ant** n (MED) médecin consultant; (other specialist) consultant m, (expert-) conseil m; **~ing room** (BRIT) n cabinet m de consultation

consume [kən'sju:m] vt consommer; **~r** n consommateur(trice); **~r goods** npl biens mpl de consommation; **~r society** n société f de consommation

consummate ['kɒnsʌmeɪt] vt consommer

consumption [kən'sʌmpʃən] n consommation f

cont. abbr (= continued) suite

contact ['kɒntækt] n contact m; (person) connaissance f, relation ♦ vt contacter, se mettre en contact or en rapport avec; **~ lenses** npl verres mpl de contact, lentilles fpl

contagious [kən'teɪdʒəs] adj contagieux(euse)

contain [kən'teɪn] vt contenir; **to ~ o.s.** se contenir, se maîtriser; **~er** n récipient m; (for shipping etc) container m

contaminate [kən'tæmɪneɪt] vt contaminer

cont'd abbr (= continued) suite

contemplate ['kɒntəmpleɪt] vt contempler; (consider) envisager

contemporary [kən'tempərərɪ] adj contemporain(e); (design, wallpaper) moderne ♦ n contemporain(e)

contempt [kən'tempt] n mépris m, dédain m; **~ of court** (LAW) outrage m à l'autorité de la justice; **~uous** adj dédaigneux(euse), méprisant(e)

contend [kən'tend] vt: **to ~ that** soutenir or prétendre que ♦ vi: **to ~ with** (compete) rivaliser avec; (struggle) lutter avec; **~er** n concurrent(e); (POL) candidat(e)

content [adj, vb kən'tent, n 'kɒntent] adj content(e), satisfait(e) ♦ vt contenter, satisfaire ♦ n contenu m; (of fat, moisture) teneur f; **~s** npl (of container etc) contenu m; **(table of) ~s** table f des matières; **~ed** adj content(e), satisfait(e)

contention [kən'tenʃən] n dispute f, contestation f; (argument) assertion f, affirmation f

contest [n 'kɒntest, vb kən'test] n combat m, lutte f; (competition) concours m ♦ vt (decision, statement) contester, discuter; (compete for) disputer; **~ant** [kən'testənt] n concurrent(e); (in fight) adversaire m/f

context ['kɒntekst] n contexte m

continent ['kɒntɪnənt] n continent m; **the C~** (BRIT) l'Europe continentale; **~al** [kɒntɪ'nentl] adj continental(e); **~al quilt** (BRIT) n couette f

contingency [kən'tɪndʒənsɪ] n éventualité f, événement imprévu

continual [kən'tɪnjuəl] adj continuel(le)

continuation [kəntɪnju'eɪʃən] n continua-

tion f; (after interruption) reprise f; (of story) suite f

continue [kən'tɪnju:] vi, vt continuer; (after interruption) reprendre, poursuivre

continuity [kɒntɪ'nju:ɪtɪ] n continuité f; (TV etc) enchaînement m

continuous [kən'tɪnjuəs] adj continu(e); (LING) progressif(ive); **~ stationery** n papier m en continu

contort [kən'tɔ:t] vt tordre, crisper

contour ['kɒntuə*] n contour m, profil m; (on map: also: **~ line**) courbe f de niveau

contraband ['kɒntrəbænd] n contrebande f

contraceptive [kɒntrə'septɪv] adj contraceptif(ive), anticonceptionnel(le) ♦ n contraceptif m

contract [n 'kɒntrækt, vb kən'trækt] n contrat m ♦ vi (become smaller) se contracter, se resserrer; (COMM): **to ~ to do sth** s'engager (par contrat) à faire qch; **~ion** [kən'trækʃən] n contraction f; **~or** [kən'træktə*] n entrepreneur m

contradict [kɒntrə'dɪkt] vt contredire

contraption [kən'træpʃən] (pej) n machin m, truc m

contrary¹ ['kɒntrərɪ] adj contraire, opposé(e) ♦ n contraire m; **on the ~** au contraire; **unless you hear to the ~** sauf avis contraire

contrary² [kən'treərɪ] adj (perverse) contrariant(e), entêté(e)

contrast [n 'kɒntrɑ:st, vb kən'trɑ:st] n contraste m ♦ vt mettre en contraste, contraster; **in ~ to** or **with** contrairement à

contravene [kɒntrə'vi:n] vt enfreindre, violer, contrevenir à

contribute [kən'trɪbju:t] vi contribuer ♦ vt: **to ~ £10/an article to** donner 10 livres/un article à; **to ~ to** contribuer à; (newspaper) collaborer à; **contribution** [kɒntrɪ'bju:ʃən] n contribution f; **contributor** [kən'trɪbjutə*] n (to newspaper) collaborateur(trice)

contrive [kən'traɪv] vi: **to ~ to do** s'arranger pour faire, trouver le moyen de faire

control [kən'trəul] vt maîtriser, commander; (check) contrôler ♦ n contrôle m, autorité f; maîtrise f; **~s** npl (of machine etc) commandes fpl; (on radio, TV) boutons mpl de réglage; **everything is under ~** tout va bien, j'ai (or il a etc) la situation en main; **to be in ~ of** être maître de, maîtriser; **the car went out of ~** j'ai (or il a etc) perdu le contrôle du véhicule; **~ panel** n tableau m de commande; **~ room** n salle f des commandes; **~ tower** n (AVIAT) tour f de contrôle

controversial [kɒntrə'vɜ:ʃəl] adj (topic) discutable, controversé(e); (person) qui fait beaucoup parler de lui; **controversy** ['kɒntrəvɜ:sɪ] n controverse f, polémique f

convalesce [kɒnvə'les] vi relever de maladie, se remettre (d'une maladie)

convector [kən'vɛktə*] *n* (*heater*) radiateur *m* (à convexion)

convene [kən'viːn] *vt* convoquer, assembler ♦ *vi* se réunir, s'assembler

convenience [kən'viːnɪəns] *n* commodité *f*; **at your ~** quand *or* comme cela vous convient; **all modern ~s**, (*BRIT*) **all mod cons** avec tout le confort moderne, tout confort

convenient [kən'viːnɪənt] *adj* commode

convent ['kɔnvənt] *n* couvent *m*

convention [kən'vɛnʃən] *n* convention *f*; **~al** *adj* conventionnel(le)

conversant [kən'vɜːsənt] *adj*: **to be ~ with** s'y connaître en; être au courant de

conversation [kɔnvə'seɪʃən] *n* conversation *f*

converse [*n* 'kɔnvɜːs, *vb* kən'vɜːs] *n* contraire *m*, inverse *m* ♦ *vi* s'entretenir; **~ly** [kɔn'vɜːslɪ] *adv* inversement, réciproquement

convert [*vb* kən'vɜːt, *n* 'kɔnvɜːt] *vt* (*REL, COMM*) convertir; (*alter*) transformer; (*house*) aménager ♦ *n* converti(e); **~ible** *n* (voiture *f*) décapotable *f*

convey [kən'veɪ] *vt* transporter; (*thanks*) transmettre; (*idea*) communiquer; **~or belt** *n* convoyeur *m*, tapis roulant

convict [*vb* kən'vɪkt, *n* 'kɔnvɪkt] *vt* déclarer (*or* reconnaître) coupable ♦ *n* forçat *m*, détenu *m*; **~ion** [kən'vɪkʃən] *n* (*LAW*) condamnation *f*; (*belief*) conviction *f*

convince [kən'vɪns] *vt* convaincre, persuader; **convincing** *adj* persuasif(ive), convaincant(e)

convoluted [kɔnvə'luːtɪd] *adj* (*argument*) compliqué(e)

convulse [kən'vʌls] *vt*: **to be ~d with laughter/pain** se tordre de rire/douleur

coo [kuː] *vi* roucouler

cook [kuk] *vt* (faire) cuire ♦ *vi* cuire; (*person*) faire la cuisine ♦ *n* cuisinier(ière); **~book** *n* livre *m* de cuisine; **~er** *n* cuisinière *f*; **~ery** *n* cuisine *f*; **~ery book** (*BRIT*) *n* = **cookbook**; **~ie** (*US*) *n* biscuit *m*, petit gâteau sec; **~ing** *n* cuisine *f*

cool [kuːl] *adj* frais(fraîche); (*calm, unemotional*) calme; (*unfriendly*) froid(e) ♦ *vt*, *vi* rafraîchir, refroidir

coop [kuːp] *n* poulailler *m*; (*for rabbits*) clapier *m* ♦ *vt*: **to ~ up** (*fig*) cloîtrer, enfermer

cooperate [kəu'ɔpəreɪt] *vi* coopérer, collaborer; **cooperation** [kəuɔpə'reɪʃən] *n* coopération *f*, collaboration *f*; **cooperative** [kəu'ɔpərətɪv] *adj* coopératif(ive) ♦ *n* coopérative *f*

coordinate [*vb* kəu'ɔːdɪneɪt, *n* kəu'ɔːdɪnət] *vt* coordonner ♦ *n* (*MATH*) coordonnée *f*; **~s** *npl* (*clothes*) ensemble *m*, coordonnés *mpl*

co-ownership ['kəu'əunəʃɪp] *n* copropriété *f*

cop [kɔp] (*inf*) *n* flic *m*

cope [kəup] *vi*: **to ~ with** faire face à; (*solve*) venir à bout de

copper ['kɔpə*] *n* cuivre *m*; (*BRIT*: *inf*: *policeman*) flic *m*; **~s** *npl* (*coins*) petite monnaie; **~ sulphate** *n* sulfate *m* de cuivre

copy ['kɔpɪ] *n* copie *f*; (*of book etc*) exemplaire *m* ♦ *vt* copier; **~right** *n* droit *m* d'auteur, copyright *m*

coral ['kɔrəl] *n* corail *m*; **~ reef** *n* récif *m* de corail

cord [kɔːd] *n* corde *f*; (*fabric*) velours côtelé; (*ELEC*) cordon *m*, fil *m*

cordial ['kɔːdɪəl] *adj* cordial(e), chaleureux(euse) ♦ *n* cordial *m*

cordon ['kɔːdn] *n* cordon *m*; **~ off** *vt* boucler (*par cordon de police*)

corduroy ['kɔːdərɔɪ] *n* velours côtelé

core [kɔː*] *n* noyau *m*; (*of fruit*) trognon *m*, cœur *m*; (*of building, problem*) cœur *m* ♦ *vt* enlever le trognon *or* le cœur de

cork [kɔːk] *n* liège *m*; (*of bottle*) bouchon *m*; **~screw** *n* tire-bouchon *m*

corn [kɔːn] *n* (*BRIT*: *wheat*) blé *m*; (*US*: *maize*) maïs *m*; (*on foot*) cor *m*; **~ on the cob** (*CULIN*) épi *m* de maïs; **~ed beef** ['kɔːnd-] *n* corned-beef *m*

corner ['kɔːnə*] *n* coin *m*; (*AUT*) tournant *m*, virage *m*; (*FOOTBALL*: *also*: **~ kick**) corner *m* ♦ *vt* acculer, mettre au pied du mur; coincer; (*COMM*: *market*) accaparer ♦ *vi* prendre un virage; **~stone** *n* pierre *f* angulaire

cornet ['kɔːnɪt] *n* (*MUS*) cornet *m* à pistons; (*BRIT*: *of ice-cream*) cornet (de glace)

cornflakes ['kɔːnfleɪks] *npl* corn-flakes *mpl*

cornflour ['kɔːnflauə*] (*BRIT*), **cornstarch** ['kɔːnstɑːtʃ] (*US*) *n* farine *f* de maïs, maïzena *f* ®

Cornwall ['kɔːnwəl] *n* Cornouailles *f*

corny ['kɔːnɪ] (*inf*) *adj* rebattu(e)

coronary ['kɔrənərɪ] *n* (*also*: **~ thrombosis**) infarctus *m* (du myocarde), thrombose *f* coronarienne

coronation [kɔrə'neɪʃən] *n* couronnement *m*

coroner ['kɔrənə*] *n* officiel chargé de déterminer les causes d'un décès

corporal ['kɔːpərəl] *n* caporal *m*, brigadier *m* ♦ *adj*: **~ punishment** châtiment corporel

corporate ['kɔːpərɪt] *adj* en commun, collectif(ive); (*COMM*) de l'entreprise

corporation [kɔːpə'reɪʃən] *n* (*of town*) municipalité *f*, conseil municipal; (*COMM*) société *f*

corps [kɔː*, *pl* kɔːz] (*pl* **corps**) *n* corps *m*

corpse [kɔːps] *n* cadavre *m*

correct [kə'rɛkt] *adj* (*accurate*) correct(e), exact(e); (*proper*) correct, convenable ♦ *vt* corriger; **~ion** [kə'rɛkʃən] *n* correction *f*

correspond [kɔrɪs'pɔnd] *vi* correspondre;

~ence *n* correspondance *f*; **~ence course** *n* cours *m* par correspondance; **~ent** *n* correspondant(e)

corridor ['kɒrɪdɔː*] *n* couloir *m*, corridor *m*

corrode [kə'rəud] *vt* corroder, ronger ♦ *vi* se corroder

corrugated ['kɒrəɡeɪtɪd] *adj* plissé(e); ondulé(e); **~ iron** *n* tôle ondulée

corrupt [kə'rʌpt] *adj* corrompu(e) ♦ *vt* corrompre; **~ion** [kə'rʌpʃən] *n* corruption *f*

Corsica ['kɔːsɪkə] *n* Corse *f*

cosmetic [kɒz'metɪk] *n* produit *m* de beauté, cosmétique *m*

cosset ['kɒsɪt] *vt* choyer, dorloter

cost [kɒst] (*pt, pp* **cost**) *n* coût *m* ♦ *vi* coûter ♦ *vt* établir *or* calculer le prix de revient de; **~s** *npl* (COMM) frais *mpl*; (LAW) dépens *mpl*; **it ~s £5/too much** cela coûte cinq livres/c'est trop cher; **at all ~s** coûte que coûte, à tout prix

co-star ['kəustɑː*] *n* partenaire *m/f*

cost-effective ['kɒstɪ'fektɪv] *adj* rentable

costly ['kɒstlɪ] *adj* coûteux(euse)

cost-of-living ['kɒstəv'lɪvɪŋ] *adj*: **~ allowance** indemnité *f* de vie chère; **~ index** index *m* du coût de la vie

cost price (BRIT) *n* prix coûtant *or* de revient

costume ['kɒstjuːm] *n* costume *m*; (*lady's suit*) tailleur *m*; (BRIT: *also*: **swimming ~**) maillot *m* (de bain); **~ jewellery** *n* bijoux *mpl* fantaisie

cosy ['kəuzɪ] (US **cozy**) *adj* douillet(te); (*person*) à l'aise, au chaud

cot [kɒt] *n* (BRIT: *child's*) lit *m* d'enfant, petit lit; (US: *campbed*) lit de camp

cottage ['kɒtɪdʒ] *n* petite maison (à la campagne), cottage *m*; **~ cheese** *n* fromage blanc (*maigre*)

cotton ['kɒtn] *n* coton *m*; **~ on** (*inf*) *vi*: **to ~ on to** (*inf*) vi comprendre; **~ candy** (US) *n* barbe *f* à papa; **~ wool** (BRIT) *n* ouate *f*, coton *m* hydrophile

couch [kautʃ] *n* canapé *m*; divan *m*

couchette [kuː'ʃet] *n* couchette *f*

cough [kɒf] *vi* tousser ♦ *n* toux *f*; **~ drop** *n* pastille *f* pour *or* contre la toux

could [kud] *pt of* **can²**; **~n't = could not**

council ['kaunsl] *n* conseil *m*; **city** *or* **town ~** conseil municipal; **~ estate** (BRIT) *n* (zone *f* de) logements loués à/par la municipalité; **~ house** (BRIT) *n* maison *f* (à loyer modéré) louée par la municipalité; **~lor** ['kaunsɪlə*] *n* conseiller(ère)

counsel ['kaunsl] *n* (*lawyer*) avocat(e); (*advice*) conseil *m*, consultation *f*; **~lor** *n* conseiller(ère); (US: *lawyer*) avocat(e)

count [kaunt] *vt, vi* compter ♦ *n* compte *m*; (*nobleman*) comte *m*; **~ on** *vt fus* compter sur; **~down** *n* compte *m* à rebours

countenance ['kauntɪnəns] *n* expression *f* ♦ *vt* approuver

counter ['kauntə*] *n* comptoir *m*; (*in post office, bank*) guichet *m*; (*in game*) jeton *m* ♦ *vt* aller à l'encontre de, opposer ♦ *adv*: **~ to** contrairement à; **~act** [kauntə'rækt] *vt* neutraliser, contrebalancer; **~feit** ['kauntəfiːt] *n* faux *m*, contrefaçon *f* ♦ *vt* contrefaire ♦ *adj* faux(fausse); **~foil** ['kauntəfɔɪl] *n* talon *m*, souche *f*; **~mand** ['kauntəmɑːnd] *vt* annuler; **~part** ['kauntəpɑːt] *n* (*of person etc*) homologue *m/f*

countess ['kauntɪs] *n* comtesse *f*

countless ['kauntlɪs] *adj* innombrable

country ['kʌntrɪ] *n* pays *m*; (*native land*) patrie *f*; (*as opposed to town*) campagne *f*; (*region*) région *f*, pays; **~ dancing** (BRIT) *n* danse *f* folklorique; **~ house** *n* manoir *m*, (petit) château; **~man** (*irreg*) *n* (*compatriot*) compatriote *m*; (*country dweller*) habitant *m* de la campagne, campagnard *m*; **~side** *n* campagne *f*

county ['kauntɪ] *n* comté *m*

coup [kuː] (*pl* **~s**) *n* beau coup; (*also*: **~ d'état**) coup d'État

couple ['kʌpl] *n* couple *m*; **a ~ of** deux; (*a few*) quelques

coupon ['kuːpɒn] *n* coupon *m*, bon-prime *m*, bon-réclame *m*; (COMM) coupon

courage ['kʌrɪdʒ] *n* courage *m*

courier ['kurɪə*] *n* messager *m*, courrier *m*; (*for tourists*) accompagnateur(trice), guide *m/f*

course [kɔːs] *n* cours *m*; (*of ship*) route *f*; (*for golf*) terrain *m*; (*part of meal*) plat *m*; **first ~** entrée *f*; **of ~** bien sûr; **~ of conduct** parti *m*, ligne *f* de conduite; **~ of treatment** (MED) traitement *m*

court [kɔːt] *n* cour *f*; (LAW) cour, tribunal *m*; (TENNIS) court *m* ♦ *vt* (*woman*) courtiser, faire la cour à; **to take to ~** actionner *or* poursuivre en justice

courteous ['kɜːtɪəs] *adj* courtois(e), poli(e)

courtesy ['kɜːtəsɪ] *n* courtoisie *f*, politesse *f*; **(by) ~ of** avec l'aimable autorisation de

court: **~-house** ['kɔːthaus] (US) *n* palais *m* de justice; **~ier** ['kɔːtɪə*] *n* courtisan *m*, dame *f* de cour; **~ martial** (*pl* **~s martial**) *n* cour martiale, conseil *m* de guerre; **~room** ['kɔːtrum] *n* salle *f* de tribunal; **~yard** ['kɔːtjɑːd] *n* cour *f*

cousin ['kʌzn] *n* cousin(e); **first ~** cousin(e) germain(e)

cove [kəuv] *n* petite baie, anse *f*

covenant ['kʌvənənt] *n* engagement *m*

cover ['kʌvə*] *vt* couvrir ♦ *n* couverture *f*; (*of pan*) couvercle *m*; (*over furniture*) housse *f*; (*shelter*) abri *m*; **to take ~** se mettre à l'abri; **under ~** à l'abri; **under ~ of darkness** à la faveur de la nuit; **under separate ~** (COMM) sous pli séparé; **to ~ up for sb** couvrir qn; **~age** *n* (TV, PRESS) reportage *m*; **~ charge** *n* couvert *m* (*supplément à* *payer*); **~ing** *n* couche *f*; **~ing letter** (*US* ~ **letter**) *n* lettre explicative; ~ **note** *n* (*INSURANCE*) police *f* provisoire

covert ['kʌvət] *adj* (*threat*) voilé(e), caché(e); (*glance*) furtif(ive)

cover-up ['kʌvərʌp] *n* tentative *f* pour étouffer une affaire

covet ['kʌvɪt] *vt* convoiter

cow [kau] *n* vache *f* ♦ *vt* effrayer, intimider

coward ['kauəd] *n* lâche *m/f*; **~ice** ['kauədɪs] *n* lâcheté *f*; **~ly** *adj* lâche

cowboy ['kaubɔɪ] *n* cow-boy *m*

cower ['kauə*] *vi* se recroqueviller

coy [kɔɪ] *adj* faussement effarouché(e) *or* timide

cozy ['kəuzɪ] (*US*) *adj* = **cosy**

CPA (*US*) *n abbr* = **certified public accountant**

crab [kræb] *n* crabe *m*; ~ **apple** *n* pomme *f* sauvage

crack [kræk] *n* fente *f*, fissure *f*; fêlure *f*; lézarde *f*; (*noise*) craquement *m*, coup (sec); (*drug*) crack *m* ♦ *vt* fendre, fissurer; fêler; lézarder; (*whip*) faire claquer; (*nut*) casser; (*code*) déchiffrer; (*problem*) résoudre ♦ *adj* (*athlete*) de première classe, d'élite; ~ **down on** *vt fus* mettre un frein à; ~ **up** *vi* être au bout du rouleau, s'effondrer; **~er** *n* (*Christmas ~er*) pétard *m*; (*biscuit*) biscuit (salé)

crackle ['krækl] *vi* crépiter, grésiller

cradle ['kreɪdl] *n* berceau *m*

craft [krɑ:ft] *n* métier (artisanal); (*pl inv: boat*) embarcation *f*, barque *f*; (*: plane*) appareil *m*; **~sman** (*irreg*) *n* artisan *m*, ouvrier (qualifié); **~smanship** *n* travail *m*; **~y** *adj* rusé(e), malin(igne)

crag [kræg] *n* rocher escarpé

cram [kræm] *vt* (*fill*): **to ~ sth with** bourrer qch de; (*put*): **to ~ sth into** fourrer qch dans ♦ *vi* (*for exams*) bachoter

cramp [kræmp] *n* crampe *f* ♦ *vt* gêner, entraver; **~ed** *adj* à l'étroit, très serré(e)

cranberry ['krænbərɪ] *n* canneberge *f*

crane [kreɪn] *n* grue *f*

crank [kræŋk] *n* manivelle *f*; (*person*) excentrique *m/f*; **~shaft** *n* vilebrequin *m*

cranny ['krænɪ] *n see* **nook**

crash [kræʃ] *n* fracas *m*; (*of car*) collision *f*; (*of plane*) accident *m* ♦ *vt* avoir un accident avec ♦ *vi* (*plane*) s'écraser; (*two cars*) se percuter, s'emboutir; (*COMM*) s'effondrer; **to ~ into** se jeter *or* se fracasser contre; ~ **course** *n* cours intensif; ~ **helmet** *n* casque (protecteur); ~ **landing** *n* atterrissage forcé *or* en catastrophe

crate [kreɪt] *n* cageot *m*; (*for bottles*) caisse *f*

cravat(e) [krə'væt] *n* foulard (noué autour du cou)

crave [kreɪv] *vt*, *vi*: **to ~ (for)** avoir une envie irrésistible de

crawl [krɔ:l] *vi* ramper; (*vehicle*) avancer au pas ♦ *n* (*SWIMMING*) crawl *m*

crayfish ['kreɪfɪʃ] *n inv* (*freshwater*) écrevisse *f*; (*saltwater*) langoustine *f*

crayon ['kreɪən] *n* crayon *m* (de couleur)

craze [kreɪz] *n* engouement *m*

crazy ['kreɪzɪ] *adj* fou(folle)

creak [kri:k] *vi* grincer; craquer

cream [kri:m] *n* crème *f* ♦ *adj* (*colour*) crème *inv*; ~ **cake** *n* (petit) gâteau à la crème; ~ **cheese** *n* fromage *m* à la crème, fromage blanc; **~y** *adj* crémeux(euse)

crease [kri:s] *n* pli *m* ♦ *vt* froisser, chiffonner ♦ *vi* se froisser, se chiffonner

create [kri:'eɪt] *vt* créer; **creation** [kri:'eɪʃən] *n* création *f*; **creative** [kri:'eɪtɪv] *adj* (*artistic*) créatif(ive); (*ingenious*) ingénieux(euse)

creature ['kri:tʃə*] *n* créature *f*

crèche [kreʃ] *n* garderie *f*, crèche *f*

credence ['kri:dəns] *n*: **to lend** *or* **give ~ to** ajouter foi à

credentials [krɪ'denʃəlz] *npl* (*references*) références *fpl*; (*papers of identity*) pièce *f* d'identité

credit ['kredɪt] *n* crédit *m*; (*recognition*) honneur *m* ♦ *vt* (*COMM*) créditer; (*believe: also: give ~ to*) ajouter foi à, croire; **~s** *npl* (*CINEMA, TV*) générique *m*; **to be in ~** (*person, bank account*) être créditeur(trice); **to ~ sb with** (*fig*) prêter *or* attribuer à qn; ~ **card** *n* carte *f* de crédit; **~or** *n* créancier(ière)

creed [kri:d] *n* croyance *f*, credo *m*

creek [kri:k] *n* crique *f*, anse *f*; (*US: stream*) ruisseau *m*, petit cours d'eau

creep [kri:p] (*pt, pp crept*) *vi* ramper; **~er** *n* plante grimpante; **~y** *adj* (*frightening*) qui fait frissonner, qui donne la chair de poule

cremate [krɪ'meɪt] *vt* incinérer

crematorium [kremə'tɔ:rɪəm] (*pl ~ia*) *n* four *m* crématoire

crêpe [kreɪp] *n* crêpe *m*; ~ **bandage** (*BRIT*) *n* bande *f* Velpeau (®)

crept [krept] *pt, pp of* **creep**

crescent ['kresnt] *n* croissant *m*; (*street*) rue *f* (en arc de cercle)

cress [kres] *n* cresson *m*

crest [krest] *n* crête *f*; **~fallen** *adj* déconfit(e), découragé(e)

crevice ['krevɪs] *n* fissure *f*, lézarde *f*, fente *f*

crew [kru:] *n* équipage *m*; (*CINEMA*) équipe *f*; **~-cut** *n*: **to have a ~-cut** avoir les cheveux en brosse; **~-neck** *n* col ras du cou

crib [krɪb] *n* lit *m* d'enfant; (*for baby*) berceau *m* ♦ *vt* (*inf*) copier

crick [krɪk] *n*: ~ **in the neck** torticolis *m*; ~ **in the back** tour *m* de reins

cricket ['krɪkɪt] *n* (*insect*) grillon *m*, cri-cri *m inv*; (*game*) cricket *m*

crime [kraɪm] *n* crime *m*; **criminal** ['krɪmɪnl] *adj, n* criminel(le)

crimson ['krɪmzn] *adj* cramoisi(e)

cringe [krɪndʒ] *vi* avoir un mouvement de recul

crinkle ['krɪŋkl] *vt* froisser, chiffonner

cripple ['krɪpl] *n* boiteux(euse), infirme *m/f* ♦ *vt* estropier

crisis ['kraɪsɪs] (*pl* **crises**) *n* crise *f*

crisp [krɪsp] *adj* croquant(e); (*weather*) vif(vive); (*manner etc*) brusque; **~s** (*BRIT*) *npl* (pommes) chips *fpl*

crisscross ['krɪskrɒs] *adj* entrecroisé(e)

criterion [kraɪ'tɪərɪən] (*pl* **~ia**) *n* critère *m*

critic ['krɪtɪk] *n* critique *m*; **~al** *adj* critique; **~ally** *adv* (*examine*) d'un œil critique; (*speak etc*) sévèrement; **~ally III** gravement malade; **~ism** ['krɪtɪsɪzəm] *n* critique *f*; **~ize** ['krɪtɪsaɪz] *vt* critiquer

croak [krəʊk] *vi* (*frog*) coasser; (*raven*) croasser; (*person*) parler d'une voix rauque

Croatia [krəʊ'eɪʃə] *n* Croatie *f*

crochet ['krəʊʃeɪ] *n* travail *m* au crochet

crockery ['krɒkərɪ] *n* vaisselle *f*

crocodile ['krɒkədaɪl] *n* crocodile *m*

crocus ['krəʊkəs] *n* crocus *m*

croft [krɒft] (*BRIT*) *n* petite ferme

crony ['krəʊnɪ] (*inf: pej*) *n* copain(copine)

crook [krʊk] *n* escroc *m*; (*of shepherd*) houlette *f*; **~ed** ['krʊkɪd] *adj* courbé(e), tordu(e); (*action*) malhonnête

crop [krɒp] *n* (*produce*) culture *f*; (*amount produced*) récolte *f*; (*riding ~*) cravache *f* ♦ *vt* (*hair*) tondre; **~ up** *vi* surgir, se présenter, survenir

cross [krɒs] *n* croix *f*; (*BIO etc*) croisement *m* ♦ *vt* (*street etc*) traverser; (*arms, legs, BIO*) croiser; (*cheque*) barrer ♦ *adj* en colère, fâché(e); **~ out** *vt* barrer, biffer; **~ over** *vt* traverser; **~bar** *n* barre (transversale); **~-country** (*race*) *n* cross(-country) *m*; **~-examine** *vt* (*LAW*) faire subir un examen contradictoire à; **~-eyed** *adj* qui louche; **~fire** *n* feux croisés; **~ing** *n* (*sea passage*) traversée *f*; (*also: pedestrian* **~ing**) passage clouté; **~ing guard** (*US*) *n* contractuel(le) qui fait traverser la rue aux enfants; **~ purposes** *npl*: **to be at ~ purposes with sb** comprendre qn de travers; **~-reference** *n* renvoi *m*, référence *f*; **~roads** *n* carrefour *m*; **~ section** *n* (*of object*) coupe transversale; (*in population*) échantillon *m*; **~walk** (*US*) *n* passage clouté; **~wind** *n* vent *m* de travers; **~word** *n* mots *mpl* croisés

crotch [krɒtʃ] *n* (*ANAT, of garment*) entre-jambes *m inv*

crouch [kraʊtʃ] *vi* s'accroupir; se tapir

crow [krəʊ] *n* (*bird*) corneille *f*; (*of cock*) chant *m* du coq, cocorico *m* ♦ *vi* (*cock*) chanter

crowbar ['krəʊbɑː*] *n* levier *m*

crowd [kraʊd] *n* foule *f* ♦ *vt* remplir ♦ *vi* affluer, s'attrouper, s'entasser; **to ~ in** entrer

en foule; **~ed** *adj* bondé(e), plein(e)

crown [kraʊn] *n* couronne *f*; (*of head*) sommet *m* de la tête; (*of hill*) sommet ♦ *vt* couronner; **~ jewels** *npl* joyaux *mpl* de la Couronne; **~ prince** *n* prince héritier

crow's-feet ['krəʊzfiːt] *npl* pattes *fpl* d'oie

crucial ['kruːʃəl] *adj* crucial(e), décisif(ive)

crucifix ['kruːsɪfɪks] *n* (*REL*) crucifix *m*; **~ion** [kruːsɪ'fɪkʃən] *n* (*REL*) crucifixion *f*

crude [kruːd] *adj* (*materials*) brut(e); non raffiné(e); (*fig: basic*) rudimentaire, sommaire; (: *vulgar*) cru(e), grossier(ère); **~ (oil)** *n* (pétrole) brut *m*

cruel ['kruəl] *adj* cruel(le); **~ty** *n* cruauté *f*

cruise [kruːz] *n* croisière *f* ♦ *vi* (*ship*) croiser; (*car*) rouler; **~r** *n* croiseur *m*; (*motorboat*) yacht *m* de croisière

crumb [krʌm] *n* miette *f*

crumble ['krʌmbl] *vt* émietter ♦ *vi* (*plaster etc*) s'effriter; (*land, earth*) s'ébouler; (*building*) s'écrouler, crouler; (*fig*) s'effondrer; **crumbly** ['krʌmblɪ] *adj* friable

crumpet ['krʌmpɪt] *n* petite crêpe (épaisse)

crumple ['krʌmpl] *vt* froisser, friper

crunch [krʌntʃ] *vt* croquer; (*underfoot*) faire craquer *or* crisser, écraser ♦ *n* (*fig*) instant *m or* moment *m* critique, moment de vérité; **~y** *adj* croquant(e), croustillant(e)

crusade [kruː'seɪd] *n* croisade *f*

crush [krʌʃ] *n* foule *f*, cohue *f*; (*love*): **to have a ~ on sb** avoir le béguin pour qn (*inf*); (*drink*): **lemon ~** citron pressé ♦ *vt* écraser; (*crumple*) froisser; (*fig: hopes*) anéantir

crust [krʌst] *n* croûte *f*

crutch [krʌtʃ] *n* béquille *f*

crux [krʌks] *n* point crucial

cry [kraɪ] *vi* pleurer; (*shout: also: ~ out*) crier ♦ *n* cri *m*; **~ off** (*inf*) *vi* se dédire; se décommander

cryptic ['krɪptɪk] *adj* énigmatique

crystal ['krɪstl] *n* cristal *m*; **~-clear** *adj* clair(e) comme de l'eau de roche

cub [kʌb] *n* petit *m* (*d'un animal*); (*also: C~ scout*) louveteau *m*

Cuba ['kjuːbə] *n* Cuba *m*

cubbyhole ['kʌbɪhəʊl] *n* cagibi *m*

cube [kjuːb] *n* cube *m* ♦ *vt* (*MATH*) élever au cube; **cubic** ['kjuːbɪk] *adj* cubique; **cubic metre** *etc* mètre *m etc* cube; **cubic capacity** *n* cylindrée *f*

cubicle ['kjuːbɪkl] *n* (*in hospital*) box *m*; (*at pool*) cabine *f*

cuckoo ['kʊkuː] *n* coucou *m*; **~ clock** *n* (pendule *f* à) coucou *m*

cucumber ['kjuːkʌmbə*] *n* concombre *m*

cuddle ['kʌdl] *vt* câliner, caresser ♦ *vi* se blottir l'un contre l'autre

cue [kjuː] *n* (*snooker ~*) queue *f* de billard; (*THEATRE etc*) signal *m*

cuff [kʌf] *n* (*BRIT: of shirt, coat etc*) poignet *m*, manchette *f*; (*US: of trousers*) revers *m*;

(*blow*) tape *f*; **off the ~** à l'improviste; **~ links** *npl* boutons *mpl* de manchette

cul-de-sac ['kʌldəsæk] *n* cul-de-sac *m*, impasse *f*

cull [kʌl] *vt* sélectionner ♦ *n* (*of animals*) massacre *m*

culminate ['kʌlmɪneɪt] *vi*: **to ~ in** finir *or* se terminer par; (*end in*) mener à; **culmination** [kʌlmɪ'neɪʃən] *n* point culminant

culottes [kju:'lɒts] *npl* jupe-culotte *f*

culprit ['kʌlprɪt] *n* coupable *m/f*

cult [kʌlt] *n* culte *m*

cultivate ['kʌltɪveɪt] *vt* cultiver; **cultivation** [kʌltɪ'veɪʃən] *n* culture *f*

cultural ['kʌltʃərəl] *adj* culturel(le)

culture ['kʌltʃə*] *n* culture *f*; **~d** *adj* (*person*) cultivé(e)

cumbersome ['kʌmbəsəm] *adj* encombrant(e), embarrassant(e)

cunning ['kʌnɪŋ] *n* ruse *f*, astuce *f* ♦ *adj* rusé(e), malin(igne); (*device, idea*) astucieux(euse)

cup [kʌp] *n* tasse *f*; (*as prize*) coupe *f*; (*of bra*) bonnet *m*

cupboard ['kʌbəd] *n* armoire *f*; (*built-in*) placard *m*

cup tie (*BRIT*) *n* match *m* de coupe

curate ['kjuərɪt] *n* vicaire *m*

curator [kju'reɪtə*] *n* conservateur *m* (*d'un musée etc*)

curb [kɜ:b] *vt* refréner, mettre un frein à ♦ *n* (*fig*) frein *m*, restriction *f*; (*US: kerb*) bord *m* du trottoir

curdle ['kɜ:dl] *vi* se cailler

cure [kjuə*] *vt* guérir; (*CULIN: salt*) saler; (: *smoke*) fumer; (: *dry*) sécher ♦ *n* remède *m*

curfew ['kɜ:fju:] *n* couvre-feu *m*

curio ['kjuərɪəu] *n* bibelot *m*, curiosité *f*

curiosity [kjuərɪ'ɒsɪtɪ] *n* curiosité *f*

curious ['kjuərɪəs] *adj* curieux(euse)

curl [kɜ:l] *n* boucle *f* (de cheveux) ♦ *vt*, *vi* boucler; (*tightly*) friser; **~ up** s'enrouler; se pelotonner; **~er** *n* bigoudi *m*, rouleau *m*; **~y** *adj* bouclé(e); frisé(e)

currant ['kʌrənt] *n* (*dried*) raisin *m* de Corinthe, raisin sec; (*bush*) groseiller *m*; (*fruit*) groseille *f*

currency ['kʌrənsɪ] *n* monnaie *f*, **to gain ~** (*fig*) s'accréditer

current ['kʌrənt] *n* courant *m* ♦ *adj* courant(e); **~ account** *n* compte courant; **~ affairs** *npl* (questions *fpl* d')actualité *f*; **~ly** *adv* actuellement

curriculum [kə'rɪkjuləm] (*pl* **~s** *or* **curricula**) *n* programme *m* d'études; **~ vitae** *n* curriculum vitae *m*

curry ['kʌrɪ] *n* curry *m* ♦ *vt*: **to ~ favour with** chercher à s'attirer les bonnes grâces de

curse [kɜ:s] *vi* jurer, blasphémer ♦ *vt* maudire ♦ *n* (*spell*) malédiction *f*; (*problem, scourge*) fléau *m*; (*swearword*) juron *m*

cursor ['kɜ:sə*] *n* (*COMPUT*) curseur *m*

cursory ['kɜ:sərɪ] *adj* superficiel(le), hâtif(ive)

curt [kɜ:t] *adj* brusque, sec(sèche)

curtail [kɜ:'teɪl] *vt* (*visit etc*) écourter; (*expenses, freedom etc*) réduire

curtain ['kɜ:tn] *n* rideau *m*

curts(e)y ['kɜ:tsɪ] *vi* faire une révérence

curve [kɜ:v] *n* courbe *f*, (*in the road*) tournant *m*, virage *m* ♦ *vi* se courber; (*road*) faire une courbe

cushion ['kuʃən] *n* coussin *m* ♦ *vt* (*fall, shock*) amortir

custard ['kʌstəd] *n* (*for pouring*) crème anglaise

custody ['kʌstədɪ] *n* (*of child*) garde *f*, **to take sb into ~** (*suspect*) placer qn en détention préventive

custom ['kʌstəm] *n* coutume *f*, usage *m*; (*COMM*) clientèle *f*; **~ary** *adj* habituel(le)

customer ['kʌstəmə*] *n* client(e)

customized ['kʌstəmaɪzd] *adj* (*car etc*) construit(e) sur commande

custom-made ['kʌstəm'meɪd] *adj* (*clothes*) fait(e) sur mesure; (*other goods*) hors série, fait(e) sur commande

customs ['kʌstəmz] *npl* douane *f*; **~ officer** *n* douanier(ière)

cut [kʌt] (*pt, pp cut*) *vt* couper; (*meat*) découper; (*reduce*) réduire ♦ *vi* couper ♦ *n* coupure *f*, (*of clothes*) coupe *f*; (*in salary etc*) réduction *f*; (*of meat*) morceau *m*; **to ~ one's hand** se couper la main; **to ~ a tooth** percer une dent; **~ down** *vt fus* (*tree etc*) couper, abattre; (*consumption*) réduire; **~ off** *vt* couper; (*fig*) isoler; **~ out** *vt* découper; (*stop*) arrêter; (*remove*) ôter; **~ up** *vt* (*paper, meat*) découper; **~back** *n* réduction *f*

cute [kju:t] *adj* mignon(ne), adorable

cuticle remover ['kju:tɪkl-] *n* (*on nail*) repousse-peaux *m inv*

cutlery ['kʌtlərɪ] *n* couverts *mpl*

cutlet ['kʌtlɪt] *n* côtelette *f*

cut-: **~out** *n* (*switch*) coupe-circuit *m inv*; (*cardboard ~out*) découpage *m*; **~-price** (*US* **~-rate**) *adj* au rabais, à prix réduit; **~throat** *n* assassin *m* ♦ *adj* acharné(e)

cutting ['kʌtɪŋ] *adj* tranchant(e), coupant(e); (*fig*) cinglant(e), mordant(e) ♦ *n* (*BRIT: from newspaper*) coupure *f* (de journal); (*from plant*) bouture *f*

CV *n abbr* = **curriculum vitae**

cwt *abbr* = **hundredweight(s)**

cyanide ['saɪənaɪd] *n* cyanure *m*

cycle ['saɪkl] *n* cycle *m*; (*bicycle*) bicyclette *f*, vélo *m* ♦ *vi* faire de la bicyclette; **cycling** ['saɪklɪŋ] *n* cyclisme *m*; **cyclist** ['saɪklɪst] *n* cycliste *m/f*

cygnet ['sɪgnɪt] *n* jeune cygne *m*

cylinder ['sɪlɪndə*] *n* cylindre *m*; **~-head gasket** *n* joint *m* de culasse

cymbals ['sɪmbəlz] *npl* cymbales *fpl*
cynic ['sɪnɪk] *n* cynique *m/f*; **~al** *adj* cynique; **~ism** ['sɪnɪsɪzəm] *n* cynisme *m*
Cypriot ['sɪprɪət] *adj* cypriote, chypriote ♦ *n* Cypriote *m/f*, Chypriote *m/f*
Cyprus ['saɪprəs] *n* Chypre *f*
cyst [sɪst] *n* kyste *m*
cystitis [sɪs'taɪtɪs] *n* cystite *f*
czar [zɑː*] *n* tsar *m*
Czech [tʃek] *adj* tchèque ♦ *n* Tchèque *m/f*; (*LING*) tchèque *m*
Czechoslovak [tʃekə'sləuvæk] *adj, n* = **Czechoslovakian**
Czechoslovakia [tʃekəslə'vækɪə] *n* Tchécoslovaquie *f*; **~n** *adj* tchécoslovaque ♦ *n* Tchécoslovaque *m/f*

D d

D [diː] *n* (*MUS*) ré *m*
dab [dæb] *vt* (*eyes, wound*) tamponner; (*paint, cream*) appliquer (par petites touches *or* rapidement)
dabble ['dæbl] *vi*: **to ~ in** faire *or* se mêler *or* s'occuper un peu de
dad [dæd] *n* papa *m*
daddy ['dædɪ] *n* papa *m*
daffodil ['dæfədɪl] *n* jonquille *f*
daft [dɑːft] *adj* idiot(e), stupide
dagger ['dægə*] *n* poignard *m*
daily ['deɪlɪ] *adj* quotidien(ne), journalier(ère) ♦ *n* quotidien *m* ♦ *adv* tous les jours
dainty ['deɪntɪ] *adj* délicat(e), mignon(ne)
dairy ['dɛərɪ] *n* (*BRIT: shop*) crémerie *f*, laiterie *f*; (*on farm*) laiterie *f*; **~ products** *npl* produits laitiers; **~ store** (*US*) *n* crémerie *f*, laiterie *f*
dais ['deɪɪs] *n* estrade *f*
daisy ['deɪzɪ] *n* pâquerette *f*; **~ wheel** *n* (*on printer*) marguerite *f*
dale [deɪl] *n* vallon *m*
dam [dæm] *n* barrage *m* ♦ *vt* endiguer
damage ['dæmɪdʒ] *n* dégâts *mpl*, dommages *mpl*; (*fig*) tort *m* ♦ *vt* endommager, abîmer; (*fig*) faire du tort à; **~s** *npl* (*LAW*) dommages-intérêts *mpl*
damn [dæm] *vt* condamner; (*curse*) maudire ♦ *n* (*inf*): **I don't give a ~** je m'en fous ♦ *adj* (*inf: also:* **~ed**): **this ~ ...** ce sacré *or* foutu ...; **~ (it)!** zut!; **~ing** *adj* accablant(e)
damp [dæmp] *adj* humide ♦ *n* humidité *f* ♦ *vt* (*also:* **~en:** *cloth, rag*) humecter; (: *enthu-*

siasm) refroidir
damson ['dæmzən] *n* prune *f* de Damas
dance [dɑːns] *n* danse *f*; (*social event*) bal *m* ♦ *vi* danser; **~ hall** *n* salle *f* de bal, dancing *m*; **~r** *n* danseur(euse); **dancing** ['dɑːnsɪŋ] *n* danse *f*
dandelion ['dændɪlaɪən] *n* pissenlit *m*
dandruff ['dændrəf] *n* pellicules *fpl*
Dane [deɪn] *n* Danois(e)
danger ['deɪndʒə*] *n* danger *m*; **there is a ~ of fire** il y a un (un) risque d'incendie; **in ~** en danger; **he was in ~ of falling** il risquait de tomber; **~ous** *adj* dangereux(euse)
dangle ['dæŋgl] *vt* balancer ♦ *vi* pendre
Danish ['deɪnɪʃ] *adj* danois(e) ♦ *n* (*LING*) danois *m*
dapper ['dæpə*] *adj* pimpant(e)
dare [dɛə*] *vt*: **to ~ sb to do** défier qn de faire ♦ *vi*: **to ~ (to) do sth** oser faire qch; **I ~ say** (*I suppose*) il est probable (que); **~devil** *n* casse-cou *m inv*; **daring** ['dɛərɪŋ] *adj* hardi(e), audacieux(euse); (*dress*) osé(e) ♦ *n* audace *f*, hardiesse *f*
dark [dɑːk] *adj* (*night, room*) obscur(e), sombre; (*colour, complexion*) foncé(e), sombre ♦ *n*: **in the ~** dans le noir; **in the ~ about** (*fig*) ignorant tout de; **after ~** après la tombée de la nuit; **~en** *vt* obscurcir, assombrir ♦ *vi* s'obscurcir, s'assombrir; **~ glasses** *npl* lunettes noires; **~ness** *n* obscurité *f*; **~room** *n* chambre noire
darling ['dɑːlɪŋ] *adj* chéri(e); (*favourite*): **to be the ~ of** être la coqueluche de
darn [dɑːn] *vt* repriser, raccommoder
dart [dɑːt] *n* fléchette *f*; (*sewing*) pince *f* ♦ *vi*: **to ~ towards** (*also:* **make a ~ towards**) se précipiter *or* s'élancer vers; **~s** *n* (jeu *m* de) fléchettes *fpl*; **to ~ away/along** partir/ passer comme une flèche; **~board** *n* cible *f* (de jeu de fléchettes)
dash [dæʃ] *n* (*sign*) tiret *m*; (*small quantity*) goutte *f*, larme *f* ♦ *vt* (*missile*) jeter *or* lancer violemment; (*hopes*) anéantir ♦ *vi*: **to ~ towards** (*also:* **make a ~ towards**) se précipiter *or* se ruer vers; **~ away** *vi* partir à toute allure, filer; **~ off** *vi* = **~ away**
dashboard ['dæʃbɔːd] *n* (*AUT*) tableau *m* de bord
dashing ['dæʃɪŋ] *adj* fringant(e)
data ['deɪtə] *npl* données *fpl*; **~base** *n* (*COMPUT*) base *f* de données; **~ processing** *n* traitement *m* de données
date [deɪt] *n* date *f*; (*with sb*) rendez-vous *m*; (*fruit*) datte *f* ♦ *vt* dater; (*person*) sortir avec; **~ of birth** date de naissance; **to ~** (*until now*) ce jour; **out of ~** (*passport*) périmé(e); (*theory etc*) dépassé(e); (*clothes etc*) démodé(e); **up to ~** moderne; (*news*) très récent; **~d** *adj* démodé(e)
daub [dɔːb] *vt* barbouiller
daughter ['dɔːtə*] *n* fille *f*; **~-in-law** *n*

belle-fille f, bru f

daunting ['dɔːntɪŋ] *adj* décourageant(e)

dawdle ['dɔːdl] *vi* traîner, lambiner

dawn [dɔːn] *n* aube f, aurore f ♦ *vi* (*day*) se lever, poindre; (*fig*): **it ~ed on him that ...** il lui vint à l'esprit que ...

day [deɪ] *n* jour m; (*as duration*) journée f; (*period of time, age*) époque f, temps m; **the ~ before** la veille, le jour précédent; **the ~ after, the following ~** le lendemain, le jour suivant; **the ~ after tomorrow** après-demain; **the ~ before yesterday** avant-hier; **by ~** de jour; **~break** *n* point m du jour; **~dream** *vi* rêver (tout éveillé); **~light** *n* (lumière f du) jour m; **~ return** (*BRIT*) *n* billet m d'aller-retour (valable pour la journée); **~time** *n* jour m, journée f; **~-to-day** *adj* quotidien(ne); (*event*) journalier(ère)

daze [deɪz] *vt* (*stun*) étourdir ♦ *n*: **in a ~** étourdi(e), hébété(e)

dazzle ['dæzl] *vt* éblouir, aveugler

DC *abbr* (= *direct current*) courant continu

D-day ['diːdeɪ] *n* le jour J

dead [ded] *adj* mort(e); (*numb*) engourdi(e), insensible; (*battery*) à plat; (*telephone*): **the line is ~** la ligne est coupée ♦ *adv* absolument, complètement ♦ *npl*: **the ~** les morts; **he was shot ~** il a été tué d'un coup de revolver; **~ on time** à l'heure pile; **~ tired** éreinté(e), complètement fourbu(e); **to stop ~** s'arrêter pile *or* net; **~en** *vt* (*blow, sound*) amortir; (*pain*) calmer; **~ end** *n* impasse f; **~ heat** *n* (*SPORT*): **to finish in a ~ heat** terminer ex æquo; **~line** *n* date f *or* heure f limite; **~lock** *n* (*fig*) impasse f; **~ loss** *n*: **to be a ~ loss** (*inf*: *person*) n'être bon(ne) à rien; **~ly** *adj* mortel(le); (*weapon*) meurtrier(ère); (*accuracy*) extrême; **~pan** *adj* impassible; **D~ Sea** *n*: **the D~ Sea** la mer Morte

deaf [def] *adj* sourd(e); **~en** *vt* rendre sourd; **~-mute** *n* sourd(e)-muet(te); **~ness** *n* surdité f

deal [diːl] (*pt, pp dealt*) *n* affaire f, marché m ♦ *vt* (*blow*) porter; (*cards*) donner, distribuer; **a great ~ (of)** beaucoup (de); **~ in** *vt fus* faire le commerce de; **~ with** *vt fus* (*person, problem*) s'occuper *or* se charger de; (*be about: book etc*) traiter de; **~er** *n* marchand m; **~ings** *npl* (*COMM*) transactions fpl; (*relations*) relations fpl, rapports mpl

dean [diːn] *n* (*REL, BRIT: SCOL*) doyen m; (*US*) conseiller(ère) (principal(e)) d'éducation

dear [dɪə*] *adj* cher(chère); (*expensive*) cher, coûteux(euse) ♦ *n*: **my ~** mon cher/ ma chère; **~ me!** mon Dieu!; **D~ Sir/ Madam** (*in letter*) Monsieur/Madame; **D~ Mr/Mrs X** Cher Monsieur/Chère Madame; **~ly** *adv* (*love*) tendrement; (*pay*) cher

death [deθ] *n* mort f; (*fatality*) mort m; (*ADMIN*) décès m; **~ certificate** *n* acte m de décès; **~ly** *adj* de mort; **~ penalty** *n* peine f de mort; **~ rate** *n* (taux m de) mortalité f; **~ toll** *n* nombre m de morts

debar [dɪˈbɑː*] *vt*: **to ~ sb from doing** interdire à qn de faire

debase [dɪˈbeɪs] *vt* (*value*) déprécier, dévaloriser

debatable [dɪˈbeɪtəbl] *adj* discutable

debate [dɪˈbeɪt] *n* discussion f, débat m ♦ *vt* discuter, débattre

debit ['debɪt] *n* débit m ♦ *vt*: **to ~ a sum to sb** *or* **to sb's account** porter une somme au débit de qn, débiter qn d'une somme; *see also* **direct**

debt [det] *n* dette f; **to be in ~** avoir des dettes, être endetté(e); **~or** *n* débiteur(trice)

debunk [diːˈbʌŋk] *vt* (*theory, claim*) montrer le ridicule de

decade ['dekeɪd] *n* décennie f, décade f

decadence ['dekədəns] *n* décadence f

decaffeinated [diːˈkæfɪneɪtɪd] *adj* décaféiné(e)

decanter [dɪˈkæntə*] *n* carafe f

decay [dɪˈkeɪ] *n* (*of building*) délabrement m; (*also: tooth ~*) carie f (dentaire) ♦ *vi* (*rot*) se décomposer, pourrir; (: *teeth*) se carier

deceased [dɪˈsiːst] *n* défunt(e)

deceit [dɪˈsiːt] *n* tromperie f, supercherie f; **~ful** *adj* trompeur(euse); **deceive** [dɪˈsiːv] *vt* tromper

December [dɪˈsembə*] *n* décembre m

decent ['diːsənt] *adj* décent(e), convenable; **they were very ~ about it** ils se sont montrés très chic

deception [dɪˈsepʃən] *n* tromperie f

deceptive [dɪˈseptɪv] *adj* trompeur(euse)

decide [dɪˈsaɪd] *vt* (*person*) décider; (*question, argument*) trancher, régler ♦ *vi* se décider, décider; **to ~ to do/that** décider de faire/que; **to ~ on** se décider pour, décider pour; **~d** *adj* (*resolute*) résolu(e), décidé(e); (*clear, definite*) net(te), marqué(e); **~dly** [dɪˈsaɪdɪdlɪ] *adv* résolument; (*distinctly*) incontestablement, nettement

deciduous [dɪˈsɪdjʊəs] *adj* à feuilles caduques

decimal ['desɪməl] *adj* décimal(e) ♦ *n* décimale f; **~ point** *n* ≈ virgule f

decipher [dɪˈsaɪfə*] *vt* déchiffrer

decision [dɪˈsɪʒən] *n* décision f

decisive [dɪˈsaɪsɪv] *adj* décisif(ive); (*person*) décidé(e)

deck [dek] *n* (*NAUT*) pont m; (*of bus*): **top ~** impériale f; (*of cards*) jeu m; (*record ~*) platine f; **~chair** *n* chaise longue

declare [dɪˈklɛə*] *vt* déclarer

decline [dɪˈklaɪn] *n* (*decay*) déclin m; (*lessening*) baisse f ♦ *vt* refuser, décliner ♦ *vi* décliner; (*business*) baisser

decoder [di:ˈkəʊdə*] *n* (*TV*) décodeur *m*

decorate [ˈdekəreɪt] *vt* (*adorn, give a medal to*) décorer; (*paint and paper*) peindre et tapisser; **decoration** [dekəˈreɪʃən] *n* (*medal etc, adornment*) décoration *f*; **decorator** [ˈdekəreɪtə*] *n* peintre-décorateur *m*

decoy [ˈdiːkɔɪ] *n* piège *m*; (*person*) compère *m*

decrease [*n* ˈdiːkriːs, *vb* diːˈkriːs] *n*: ~ (**in**) diminution *f* (de) ♦ *vt, vi* diminuer

decree [dɪˈkriː] *n* (*POL, REL*) décret *m*; (*LAW*) arrêt *m*, jugement *m*; ~ **nisi** [-ˈnaɪsaɪ] *n* jugement *m* provisoire de divorce

dedicate [ˈdedɪkeɪt] *vt* consacrer; (*book etc*) dédier; **dedication** [dedɪˈkeɪʃən] *n* (*devotion*) dévouement *m*; (*in book*) dédicace *f*

deduce [dɪˈdjuːs] *vt* déduire, conclure

deduct [dɪˈdʌkt] *vt*: **to ~ sth (from)** déduire qch (de), retrancher qch (de); ~**ion** [dɪˈdʌkʃən] *n* (*deducting, deducing*) déduction *f*; (*from wage etc*) prélèvement *m*, retenue *f*

deed [diːd] *n* action *f*, acte *m*; (*LAW*) acte notarié, contrat *m*

deem [diːm] *vt* (*formal*) juger

deep [diːp] *adj* profond(e); (*voice*) grave ♦ *adv*: **spectators stood 20 ~** il y avait 20 rangs de spectateurs; **4 metres ~** de 4 mètres de profondeur; ~**en** *vt* approfondir ♦ *vi* (*fig*) s'épaissir; ~**freeze** *n* congélateur *m*; ~**fry** *vt* faire frire (en friteuse); ~**ly** *adv* profondément; (*interested*) vivement; ~**-sea diver** *n* sous-marin(e); ~**-sea diving** *n* plongée sous-marine; ~**-sea fishing** *n* grande pêche; ~**-seated** *adj* profond(e), profondément enraciné(e)

deer [dɪə*] *n inv*: (**red**) ~ cerf *m*, biche *f*; (**fallow**) ~ daim *m*; (**roe**) ~ chevreuil *m*; ~**skin** *n* daim

deface [dɪˈfeɪs] *vt* dégrader; (*notice, poster*) barbouiller

default [dɪˈfɔːlt] *n* (*COMPUT: also*: ~ *value*) valeur *f* par défaut; **by ~** (*LAW*) par défaut, par contumace; (*SPORT*) par forfait

defeat [dɪˈfiːt] *n* défaite *f* ♦ *vt* (*team, opponents*) battre

defect [*n* ˈdiːfekt, *vb* dɪˈfekt] *n* défaut *m* ♦ *vi*: **to ~ to the enemy/the West** passer à l'ennemi/à l'Ouest; ~**ive** [dɪˈfektɪv] *adj* défectueux(euse)

defence [dɪˈfens] (*US* **defense**) *n* défense *f*; ~**less** *adj* sans défense

defend [dɪˈfend] *vt* défendre; ~**ant** *n* défendeur(deresse); (*in criminal case*) accusé(e), prévenu(e); ~**er** *n* défenseur *m*

defer [dɪˈfɜː*] *vt* (*postpone*) différer, ajourner

defiance [dɪˈfaɪəns] *n* défi *m*; **in ~ of** au mépris de; **defiant** [dɪˈfaɪənt] *adj* provocant(e), de défi; (*person*) rebelle, intraitable

deficiency [dɪˈfɪʃənsɪ] *n* insuffisance *f*, défi-

cience *f*; **deficient** *adj* (*inadequate*) insuffisant(e); **to be deficient in** manquer de

deficit [ˈdefɪsɪt] *n* déficit *m*

defile [*vb* dɪˈfaɪl, *n* ˈdiːfaɪl] *vt* souiller, profaner

define [dɪˈfaɪn] *vt* définir

definite [ˈdefɪnɪt] *adj* (*fixed*) défini(e), (bien) déterminé(e); (*clear, obvious*) net(te), manifeste; (*certain*) sûr(e); **he was ~ about it** il a été catégorique; ~**ly** *adv* sans aucun doute

definition [defɪˈnɪʃən] *n* définition *f*; (*clearness*) netteté *f*

deflate [diːˈfleɪt] *vt* dégonfler

deflect [dɪˈflekt] *vt* détourner, faire dévier

deformed [dɪˈfɔːmd] *adj* difforme

defraud [dɪˈfrɔːd] *vt* frauder; **to ~ sb of sth** escroquer qch à qn

defrost [diːˈfrɒst] *vt* dégivrer; (*food*) décongeler; ~**er** (*US*) *n* (*demister*) dispositif *m* anti-buée *inv*

deft [deft] *adj* adroit(e), preste

defunct [dɪˈfʌŋkt] *adj* défunt(e)

defuse [diːˈfjuːz] *vt* désamorcer

defy [dɪˈfaɪ] *vt* défier; (*efforts etc*) résister à

degenerate [*vb* dɪˈdʒenəreɪt, *adj* dɪˈdʒenərɪt] *vi* dégénérer ♦ *adj* dégénéré(e)

degree [dɪˈgriː] *n* degré *m*; (*SCOL*) diplôme *m* (universitaire); **a (first)** ~ **in maths** une licence en maths; **by ~s** (*gradually*) par degrés; **to some ~, to a certain** ~ jusqu'à un certain point, dans une certaine mesure

dehydrated [diːhaɪˈdreɪtɪd] *adj* déshydraté(e); (*milk, eggs*) en poudre

de-ice [diːˈaɪs] *vt* (*windscreen*) dégivrer

deign [deɪn] *vi*: **to ~ to do** daigner faire

dejected [dɪˈdʒektɪd] *adj* abattu(e), déprimé(e)

delay [dɪˈleɪ] *vt* retarder ♦ *vi* s'attarder ♦ *n* délai *m*, retard *m*; **to be ~ed** être en retard

delectable [dɪˈlektəbl] *adj* délicieux(euse)

delegate [*n* ˈdelɪgɪt, *vb* ˈdelɪgeɪt] *n* délégué(e) ♦ *vt* déléguer

delete [dɪˈliːt] *vt* rayer, supprimer

deliberate [*adj* dɪˈlɪbərɪt, *vb* dɪˈlɪbəreɪt] *adj* (*intentional*) délibéré(e); (*slow*) mesuré(e) ♦ *vi* délibérer, réfléchir; ~**ly** *adv* (*on purpose*) exprès, délibérément

delicacy [ˈdelɪkəsɪ] *n* délicatesse *f*; (*food*) mets fin *or* délicat, friandise *f*

delicate [ˈdelɪkɪt] *adj* délicat(e)

delicatessen [delɪkəˈtesn] *n* épicerie fine

delicious [dɪˈlɪʃəs] *adj* délicieux(euse)

delight [dɪˈlaɪt] *n* (grande) joie, grand plaisir ♦ *vt* enchanter; **to take (a)** ~ **in** prendre grand plaisir à; ~**ed** *adj*: ~**ed (at** *or* **with/to do)** ravi(e) (de/de faire); ~**ful** *adj* (*person*) adorable; (*meal, evening*) merveilleux(euse)

delinquent [dɪˈlɪŋkwənt] *adj, n* délinquant(e)

delirious [dɪˈlɪrɪəs] *adj*: **to be ~** délirer

deliver [dɪ'lɪvə*] vt (mail) distribuer; (goods) livrer; (message) remettre; (speech) prononcer; (MED: baby) mettre au monde; ~**y** n distribution f; livraison f; (of speaker) élocution f; (MED) accouchement m; **to take** ~**y of** prendre livraison de

delude [dɪ'luːd] vt tromper, leurrer

delusion [dɪ'luːʒən] n illusion f

delve [delv] vi: **to** ~ **into** fouiller dans; (subject) approfondir

demand [dɪ'mɑːnd] vt réclamer, exiger ♦ n exigence f; (claim) revendication f; (ECON) demande f; **in** ~ demandé(e), recherché(e); **on** ~ sur demande; ~**ing** adj (person) exigeant(e); (work) astreignant(e)

demean [dɪ'miːn] vt: **to** ~ **o.s.** s'abaisser

demeanour [dɪ'miːnə*] (US **demeanor**) n comportement m; maintien m

demented [dɪ'mentɪd] adj dément(e), fou(folle)

demise [dɪ'maɪz] n mort f

demister [diː'mɪstə*] (BRIT) n (AUT) dispositif m anti-buée inv

demo [demɔu] (inf) n abbr (= *demonstration*) manif f

democracy [dɪ'mɒkrəsɪ] n démocratie f; **democrat** ['deməkræt] n démocrate m/f; **democratic** [demə'krætɪk] adj démocratique

demolish [dɪ'mɒlɪʃ] vt démolir

demonstrate ['demənstreɪt] vt démontrer, prouver; (show) faire une démonstration de ♦ vi: **to** ~ **(for/against)** manifester (en faveur de/contre); **demonstration** [demən'streɪʃən] n démonstration f, manifestation f; **demonstrator** ['demənstreɪtə*] n (POL) manifestant(e)

demote [dɪ'məut] vt rétrograder

demure [dɪ'mjuə*] adj sage, réservé(e)

den [den] n tanière f, antre m

denatured alcohol [diː'neɪtʃəd-] (US) n alcool m à brûler

denial [dɪ'naɪəl] n démenti m; (refusal) dénégation f

denim ['denɪm] n jean m; ~**s** npl (jeans) (blue-)jean(s) m(pl)

Denmark ['denmɑːk] n Danemark m

denomination [dɪnɒmɪ'neɪʃən] n (of money) valeur f; (REL) confession f

denounce [dɪ'naʊns] vt dénoncer

dense [dens] adj dense; (stupid) obtus(e), bouché(e); ~**ly** adv: ~**ly populated** à forte densité de population

density ['densɪtɪ] n densité f; **double/high-** ~ **diskette** disquette f double densité/haute densité

dent [dent] n bosse f ♦ vt (also: **make a** ~ **in**) cabosser

dental ['dentl] adj dentaire; ~ **surgeon** (chirurgien(ne)) dentiste

dentist ['dentɪst] n dentiste m/f

dentures ['dentʃəz] npl dentier m sg

deny [dɪ'naɪ] vt nier; (refuse) refuser

deodorant [diː'əudərənt] n déodorant m, désodorisant m

depart [dɪ'pɑːt] vi partir; **to** ~ **from** (fig: differ from) s'écarter de

department [dɪ'pɑːtmənt] n (COMM) rayon m; (SCOL) section f; (POL) ministère m, département m; ~ **store** n grand magasin

departure [dɪ'pɑːtʃə*] n départ m; **a new** ~ une nouvelle voie; ~ **lounge** n (at airport) salle f d'embarquement

depend [dɪ'pend] vi: **to** ~ **on** dépendre de; (rely on) compter sur; **it** ~**s** cela dépend; ~**ing on the result** selon le résultat; ~**able** adj (person) sérieux(euse), sûr(e); (car, watch) solide, fiable; ~**ant** n personne f à charge; ~**ent** adj: **to be** ~**ent (on)** dépendre (de) ♦ n = **dependant**

depict [dɪ'pɪkt] vt (in picture) représenter; (in words) dépeindre, décrire

depleted [dɪ'pliːtɪd] adj (considérablement) réduit(e) or diminué(e)

deport [dɪ'pɔːt] vt expulser

deposit [dɪ'pɒzɪt] n (CHEM, COMM, GEO) dépôt m; (of ore, oil) gisement m; (part payment) arrhes fpl, acompte m; (on bottle etc) consigne f; (for hired goods etc) cautionnement m, garantie f ♦ vt déposer; ~ **account** n compte m sur livret

depot ['depəu] n dépôt m; (US: RAIL) gare f

depress [dɪ'pres] vt déprimer; (press down) appuyer sur, abaisser; (prices, wages) faire baisser; ~**ed** adj (person) déprimé(e); (area) en déclin, touché(e) par le sous-emploi; ~**ing** adj déprimant(e); ~**ion** [dɪ'preʃən] n dépression f; (hollow) creux m

deprivation [deprɪ'veɪʃən] n privation f; (loss) perte f

deprive [dɪ'praɪv] vt: **to** ~ **sb of** priver qn de; ~**d** adj déshérité(e)

depth [depθ] n profondeur f; **in the** ~**s of despair** au plus profond du désespoir; **to be out of one's** ~ avoir perdu pied, nager

deputize ['depjutaɪz] vi: **to** ~ **for** assurer l'intérim de

deputy ['depjutɪ] adj adjoint(e) ♦ n (second in command) adjoint(e); (US: also ~ sheriff) shérif adjoint; ~ **head** directeur adjoint, sous-directeur m

derail [dɪ'reɪl] vt: **to be** ~**ed** dérailler

deranged [dɪ'reɪndʒd] adj: **to be (mentally)** ~ avoir le cerveau dérangé

derby ['dɑːbɪ] (US) n (bowler hat) (chapeau m) melon m

derelict ['derɪlɪkt] adj abandonné(e), à l'abandon

derisory [dɪ'raɪsərɪ] adj (sum) dérisoire; (smile, person) moqueur(euse)

derive [dɪ'raɪv] vt: **to** ~ **sth from** tirer qch de; trouver qch dans: **to** ~ **from** provenir de, dériver de

derogatory [dɪ'rɒgətərɪ] adj désobligeant(e); péjoratif(ive)

descend [dɪ'send] *vt, vi* descendre; **to ~ from** descendre de, être issu(e) de; **to ~ to (doing) sth** s'abaisser à (faire) qch; **descent** [dɪ'sent] *n* descente *f*; (*origin*) origine *f*

describe [dɪs'kraɪb] *vt* décrire; **description** [dɪs'krɪpʃən] *n* description *f*; (*sort*) sorte *f*, espèce *f*

desecrate ['desɪkreɪt] *vt* profaner

desert [*n* 'dezət, *vb* dɪ'zɜːt] *n* désert *m* ♦ *vt* déserter, abandonner ♦ *vi* (*MIL*) déserter; **~s** *npl*: **to get one's just ~s** n'avoir que ce qu'on mérite; **~er** *n* déserteur *m*; **~ion** [dɪ'zɜːʃən] *n* (*MIL*) désertion *f*; (*LAW: of spouse*) abandon *m* du domicile conjugal; **~ island** *n* île déserte

deserve [dɪ'zɜːv] *vt* mériter; **deserving** [dɪ'zɜːvɪŋ] *adj* (*person*) méritant(e); (*action, cause*) méritoire

design [dɪ'zaɪn] *n* (*sketch*) plan *m*, dessin *m*; (*layout, shape*) conception *f*, ligne *f*; (*pattern*) dessin *m*, motif(s) *m(pl)*; (*COMM, art*) design *m*, stylisme *m*; (*intention*) dessein *m* ♦ *vt* dessiner; élaborer; **~er** [dɪ'zaɪnə*] *n* (*TECH*) concepteur-projeteur *m*; (*ART*) dessinateur(trice), designer *m*; (*fashion*) styliste *m/f*

desire [dɪ'zaɪə*] *n* désir *m* ♦ *vt* désirer

desk [desk] *n* (*in office*) bureau *m*; (*for pupil*) pupitre *m*; (*BRIT: in shop, restaurant*) caisse *f*; (*in hotel, at airport*) réception *f*

desolate ['desəlɪt] *adj* désolé(e); (*person*) affligé(e)

despair [dɪs'peə*] *n* désespoir *m* ♦ *vi*: **to ~ of** désespérer de

despatch [dɪs'pætʃ] *n, vt* = **dispatch**

desperate ['despərɪt] *adj* désespéré(e); (*criminal*) prêt(e) à tout; **to be ~ for sth/ to do sth** avoir désespérément besoin de qch/de faire qch; **~ly** ['despərɪtlɪ] *adv* désespérément; (*very*) terriblement, extrêmement

desperation [despə'reɪʃən] *n* désespoir *m*; **in (sheer) ~** en désespoir de cause

despicable [dɪs'pɪkəbl] *adj* méprisable

despise [dɪs'paɪz] *vt* mépriser

despite [dɪs'paɪt] *prep* malgré, en dépit de

despondent [dɪs'pɒndənt] *adj* découragé(e), abattu(e)

dessert [dɪ'zɜːt] *n* dessert *m*; **~spoon** *n* cuiller *f* à dessert

destination [destɪ'neɪʃən] *n* destination *f*

destined ['destɪnd] *adj*: **to be ~ to do/for sth** être destiné(e) à faire/à qch

destiny ['destɪnɪ] *n* destinée *f*, destin *m*

destitute ['destɪtjuːt] *adj* indigent(e)

destroy [dɪs'trɔɪ] *vt* détruire; (*injured horse*) abattre; (*dog*) faire piquer; **~er** *n* (*NAUT*) contre-torpilleur *m*

destruction [dɪs'trʌkʃən] *n* destruction *f*

detach [dɪ'tætʃ] *vt* détacher; **~ed** *adj* (*attitude, person*) détaché(e); **~ed house** *n* pavillon *m*, maison(nette) (individuelle); **~ment** *n* (*MIL*) détachement *m*; (*fig*) détachement, indifférence *f*

detail ['diːteɪl] *n* détail *m* ♦ *vt* raconter en détail, énumérer; **in ~** en détail; **~ed** *adj* détaillé(e)

detain [dɪ'teɪn] *vt* retenir; (*in captivity*) détenir; (*in hospital*) hospitaliser

detect [dɪ'tekt] *vt* déceler, percevoir; (*MED, POLICE*) dépister; (*MIL, RADAR, TECH*) détecter; **~ion** [dɪ'tekʃən] *n* découverte *f*; **~ive** *n* agent *m* de la sûreté, policier *m*; **private ~ive** détective privé; **~ive story** *n* roman policier

detention [dɪ'tenʃən] *n* détention *f*, (*SCOL*) retenue *f*, consigne *f*

deter [dɪ'tɜː*] *vt* dissuader

detergent [dɪ'tɜːdʒənt] *n* détergent *m*, détersif *m*

deteriorate [dɪ'tɪərɪəreɪt] *vi* se détériorer, se dégrader

determine [dɪ'tɜːmɪn] *vt* déterminer; **to ~ to do** se résoudre de faire, se déterminer à faire; **~d** *adj* (*person*) déterminé(e), décidé(e)

deterrent [dɪ'terənt] *n* effet *m* de dissuasion; force *f* de dissuasion

detonate ['detəneɪt] *vt* faire détoner *or* exploser

detour ['diːtuə*] *n* détour *m*; (*US: AUT: diversion*) déviation *f*

detract [dɪ'trækt] *vt*: **to ~ from** (*quality, pleasure*) diminuer; (*reputation*) porter atteinte à

detriment ['detrɪmənt] *n*: **to the ~ of** au détriment de, au préjudice de; **~al** [detrɪ'mentl] *adj*: **~al to** préjudiciable *or* nuisible à

devaluation [diːvæljuː'eɪʃən] *n* dévaluation *f*

devastate ['devəsteɪt] *vt* (*also fig*) dévaster; **devastating** *adj* dévastateur(trice); (*news*) accablant(e)

develop [dɪ'veləp] *vt* (*gen*) développer; (*disease*) commencer à souffrir de; (*resources*) mettre en valeur, exploiter ♦ *vi* se développer; (*situation, disease: evolve*) évoluer; (*facts, symptoms: appear*) se manifester, se produire; **~ing country** pays *m* en voie de développement; **the machine has ~ed a fault** un problème s'est manifesté dans cette machine; **~er** *n* (*also: property ~er*) promoteur *m*; **~ment** *n* développement *m*; (*of affair, case*) rebondissement *m*, fait(s) nouveau(x)

device [dɪ'vaɪs] *n* (*apparatus*) engin *m*, dispositif *m*

devil ['devl] *n* diable *m*; démon *m*

devious ['diːvɪəs] *adj* (*person*) sournois(e), dissimulé(e)

devise [dɪ'vaɪz] *vt* imaginer, concevoir

devoid [dɪ'vɔɪd] *adj*: **~ of** dépourvu(e) de, dénué(e) de

devolution [diːvə'luːʃən] n (POL) décentralisation f

devote [dɪ'vəʊt] vt: **to ~ sth to** consacrer qch à; **~d** adj dévoué(e); **to be ~d to** (book etc) être consacré(e) à; (person) être très attaché(e) à; **~e** [devəʊ'tiː] n (REL) adepte m/f; (MUS, SPORT) fervent(e)

devotion [dɪ'vəʊʃən] n dévouement m, attachement m; (REL) dévotion f, piété f

devour [dɪ'vaʊə*] vt dévorer

devout [dɪ'vaʊt] adj pieux(euse), dévot(e)

dew [djuː] n rosée f

diabetes [daɪə'biːtiːz] n diabète m; **diabetic** [daɪə'betɪk] adj diabétique ♦ n diabétique m/f

diabolical [daɪə'bɒlɪkl] (inf) adj (weather) atroce; (behaviour) infernal(e)

diagnosis [daɪəg'nəʊsɪs, pl daɪəg'nəʊsiːz] (pl **diagnoses**) n diagnostic m

diagonal [daɪ'ægənl] adj diagonal(e) ♦ n diagonale f

diagram ['daɪəgræm] n diagramme m, schéma m

dial ['daɪəl] n cadran m ♦ vt (number) faire, composer; **~ code** (US) n = **dialling code**

dialect ['daɪəlekt] n dialecte m

dialling code ['daɪəlɪŋ-] (BRIT) n indicatif m (téléphonique)

dialling tone ['daɪəlɪŋ-] (BRIT) n tonalité f

dialogue ['daɪəlɒg] n dialogue m

dial tone (US) n = **dialling tone**

diameter [daɪ'æmɪtə*] n diamètre m

diamond ['daɪəmənd] n diamant m; (shape) losange m; **~s** npl (CARDS) carreau m

diaper ['daɪəpə*] (US) n couche f

diaphragm ['daɪəfræm] n diaphragme m

diarrhoea [daɪə'riːə] (US **diarrhea**) n diarrhée f

diary ['daɪərɪ] n (daily account) journal m; (book) agenda m

dice [daɪs] n inv dé m ♦ vt (CULIN) couper en dés or en cubes

dictate [vb dɪk'teɪt] vt dicter

dictation [dɪk'teɪʃən] n dictée f

dictator [dɪk'teɪtə*] n dictateur m; **~ship** n dictature f

dictionary ['dɪkʃənrɪ] n dictionnaire m

did [dɪd] pt of do; **~n't** = did not

die [daɪ] vi mourir; **to be dying for sth** avoir une envie folle de qch; **to be dying to do sth** mourir d'envie de faire qch; **~ away** vi s'éteindre; **~ down** vi se calmer, s'apaiser; **~ out** vi disparaître

die-hard ['daɪhɑːd] n réactionnaire m/f, jusqu'au-boutiste m/f

diesel ['diːzəl] n (vehicle) diesel m; (also: **~ oil**) carburant m diesel, gas-oil m; **~ engine** n moteur m diesel

diet ['daɪət] n alimentation f; (restricted food) régime m ♦ vi (also: **be on a ~**) suivre un régime

differ ['dɪfə*] vi (be different): **to ~ (from)**

être différent (de); différer (de); (disagree): **to ~ (from sb over sth)** ne pas être d'accord (avec qn au sujet de qch); **~ence** n différence f; (quarrel) différend m, désaccord m; **~ent** adj différent(e); **~entiate** [dɪfə'renʃɪeɪt] vi: **to ~entiate (between)** faire une différence (entre)

difficult ['dɪfɪkəlt] adj difficile; **~y** n difficulté f

diffident ['dɪfɪdənt] adj qui manque de confiance or d'assurance

dig [dɪg] (pt, pp **dug**) vt (hole) creuser; (garden) bêcher ♦ n (prod) coup m de coude; (fig) coup de griffe or de patte; (archeological) fouilles fpl; **~ in** vi (MIL: also: **~ o.s. in**) se retrancher; **~ into** vt fus (savings) puiser dans; **to ~ one's nails into sth** enfoncer ses ongles dans qch; **~ up** vt déterrer

digest [vb daɪ'dʒest, n 'daɪdʒest] vt digérer ♦ n sommaire m, résumé m; **~ion** n digestion f

digit ['dɪdʒɪt] n (number) chiffre m; (finger) doigt m; **~al** adj digital(e), à affichage numérique or digital; **~al computer** calculateur m numérique

dignified ['dɪgnɪfaɪd] adj digne

dignity ['dɪgnɪtɪ] n dignité f

digress [daɪ'gres] vi: **to ~ from** s'écarter de, s'éloigner de

digs [dɪgz] (BRIT: inf) npl piaule f, chambre meublée

dilapidated [dɪ'læpɪdeɪtɪd] adj délabré(e)

dilemma [daɪ'lemə] n dilemme m

diligent ['dɪlɪdʒənt] adj appliqué(e), assidu(e)

dilute [daɪ'luːt] vt diluer

dim [dɪm] adj (light) faible; (memory, outline) vague, indécis(e); (figure) vague, indistinct(e); (room) sombre; (stupid) borné(e), obtus(e) ♦ vt (light) réduire, baisser; (US: AUT) mettre en code

dime [daɪm] (US) n = **10 cents**

dimension [dɪ'menʃən] n dimension f

diminish [dɪ'mɪnɪʃ] vt, vi diminuer

diminutive [dɪ'mɪnjʊtɪv] adj minuscule, tout(e) petit(e)

dimmers ['dɪməz] (US) npl (AUT) phares mpl code inv; feux mpl de position

dimple ['dɪmpl] n fossette f

din [dɪn] n vacarme m

dine [daɪn] vi dîner; **~r** n (person) dîneur(euse); (US: restaurant) petit restaurant

dinghy ['dɪŋgɪ] n youyou m; (also: rubber **~**) canot m pneumatique; (: sailing **~**) voilier m, dériveur m

dingy ['dɪndʒɪ] adj miteux(euse), minable

dining car ['daɪnɪŋ-] (BRIT) n wagon-restaurant m

dining room ['daɪnɪŋ-] n salle f à manger

dinner ['dɪnə*] n dîner m; (lunch) déjeuner

m; (*public*) banquet *m*; ~ **jacket** *n* smoking *m*; ~ **party** *n* dîner *m*; ~ **time** *n* heure *f* du dîner; (*midday*) heure du déjeuner

dint [dɪnt] *n*: **by ~ of (doing)** à force de (faire)

dip [dɪp] *n* déclivité *f*, (*in sea*) baignade *f*, bain ≈; (*CULIN*) ≈ sauce *f* ♦ *vt* tremper, plonger; (*BRIT: AUT: lights*) mettre en code, baisser ♦ *vi* plonger

diploma [dɪ'pləʊmə] *n* diplôme *m*

diplomacy [dɪ'pləʊməsɪ] *n* diplomatie *f*

diplomat ['dɪpləmæt] *n* diplomate *m*; **~ic** [dɪplə'mætɪk] *adj* diplomatique

dipstick ['dɪpstɪk] *n* (*AUT*) jauge *f* de niveau d'huile

dipswitch ['dɪpswɪtʃ] (*BRIT*) *n* (*AUT*) interrupteur *m* de lumière réduite

dire [daɪə*] *adj* terrible, extrême, affreux(euse)

direct [daɪ'rɛkt] *adj* direct(e) ♦ *vt* diriger, orienter (*letter, remark*) adresser; (*film, programme*) réaliser; (*play*) mettre en scène; (*order*): **to ~ sb to do sth** ordonner à qn de faire qch ♦ *adv* directement; **can you ~ me to ...?** pouvez-vous m'indiquer le chemin de ...?; ~ **debit** (*BRIT*) *n* prélèvement *m* automatique

direction [dɪ'rɛkʃən] *n* direction *f*, ~**s** *npl* (*advice*) indications *fpl*; **sense of ~** sens *m* de l'orientation; ~**s for use** mode *m* d'emploi

directly [dɪ'rɛktlɪ] *adv* (*in a straight line*) directement, tout droit; (*at once*) tout de suite, immédiatement

director [dɪ'rɛktə*] *n* directeur *m*; (*THEATRE*) metteur *m* en scène; (*CINEMA, TV*) réalisateur(trice)

directory [dɪ'rɛktərɪ] *n* annuaire *m*; (*COMPUT*) répertoire *m*

dirt [dɜːt] *n* saleté *f*; crasse *f*; (*earth*) terre *f*, boue *f*; ~**-cheap** *adj* très bon marché *inv*; ~**y** *adj* sale ♦ *vt* salir; ~**y trick** coup tordu

disability [dɪsə'bɪlɪtɪ] *n* invalidité *f*, infirmité *f*

disabled [dɪs'eɪbld] *adj* infirme, invalide ♦ *npl*: **the ~** les handicapés

disadvantage [dɪsəd'vɑːntɪdʒ] *n* désavantage *m*, inconvénient *m*

disagree [dɪsə'griː] *vi* (*be different*) ne pas concorder; (*be against, think otherwise*): **to ~ (with)** ne pas être d'accord (avec); ~**able** *adj* désagréable; ~**ment** *n* désaccord *m*, différend *m*

disallow ['dɪsə'laʊ] *vt* rejeter

disappear [dɪsə'pɪə*] *vi* disparaître; ~**ance** *n* disparition *f*

disappoint [dɪsə'pɔɪnt] *vt* décevoir; ~**ed** *adj* déçu(e); ~**ing** *adj* décevant(e); ~**ment** *n* déception *f*

disapproval [dɪsə'pruːvəl] *n* désapprobation *f*

disapprove [dɪsə'pruːv] *vi*: **to ~ (of)** désapprouver

disarmament [dɪs'ɑːməmənt] *n* désarmement *m*

disarray ['dɪsə'reɪ] *n*: **in ~** (*army*) en déroute; (*organization*) en désarroi; (*hair, clothes*) en désordre

disaster [dɪ'zɑːstə*] *n* catastrophe *f*, désastre *m*

disband [dɪs'bænd] *vt* démobiliser; disperser ♦ *vi* se séparer; se disperser

disbelief ['dɪsbə'liːf] *n* incrédulité *f*

disc [dɪsk] *n* disque *m*; (*COMPUT*) = **disk**

discard [dɪs'kɑːd] *vt* (*old things*) se débarrasser de; (*fig*) écarter, renoncer à

discern [dɪ'sɜːn] *vt* discerner, distinguer; ~**ing** *adj* perspicace

discharge [*vb* dɪs'tʃɑːdʒ, *n* 'dɪstʃɑːdʒ] *vt* décharger; (*duties*) s'acquitter de; (*patient*) renvoyer (chez lui); (*employee*) congédier, licencier; (*soldier*) rendre à la vie civile, réformer; (*defendant*) relaxer, élargir ♦ *n* décharge *f*; (*dismissal*) renvoi *m*; licenciement *m*; élargissement *m*; (*MED*) écoulement *m*

discipline ['dɪsɪplɪn] *n* discipline *f*

disc jockey *n* disc-jockey *m*

disclaim [dɪs'kleɪm] *vt* nier

disclose [dɪs'kləʊz] *vt* révéler, divulguer; **disclosure** [dɪs'kləʊʒə*] *n* révélation *f*

disco ['dɪskəʊ] *n abbr* = **discotheque**

discomfort [dɪs'kʌmfət] *n* malaise *m*, gêne *f*; (*lack of comfort*) manque *m* de confort

disconcert [dɪskən'sɜːt] *vt* déconcerter

disconnect ['dɪskə'nɛkt] *vt* (*ELEC, RADIO, pipe*) débrancher; (*TEL, water*) couper

discontent [dɪskən'tɛnt] *n* mécontentement *m*; ~**ed** *adj* mécontent(e)

discontinue [dɪskən'tɪnjuː] *vt* cesser, interrompre; "~**d**" (*COMM*) "fin de série"

discord ['dɪskɔːd] *n* discorde *f*, dissension *f*; (*MUS*) dissonance *f*

discotheque ['dɪskəʊtɛk] *n* discothèque *f*

discount [*n* 'dɪskaʊnt, *vb* dɪs'kaʊnt] *n* remise *f*, rabais *m* ♦ *vt* (*sum*) faire une remise de; (*fig*) ne pas tenir compte de

discourage [dɪs'kʌrɪdʒ] *vt* décourager

discover [dɪs'kʌvə*] *vt* découvrir; ~**y** *n* découverte *f*

discredit [dɪs'krɛdɪt] *vt* (*idea*) mettre en doute; (*person*) discréditer

discreet [dɪs'kriːt] *adj* discret(ète)

discrepancy [dɪs'krɛpənsɪ] *n* divergence *f*, contradiction *f*

discretion [dɪs'krɛʃən] *n* discrétion *f*; **use your own ~** à vous de juger

discriminate [dɪs'krɪmɪneɪt] *vi*: **to ~ between** établir une distinction entre, faire la différence entre; **to ~ against** pratiquer une discrimination contre; **discriminating** *adj* qui a du discernement; **discrimination** [dɪskrɪmɪ'neɪʃən] *n* discrimination *f*; (*judgment*) discernement *m*

discuss [dɪs'kʌs] *vt* discuter de; *(debate)* discuter; **~ion** [dɪs'kʌʃən] *n* discussion *f*

disdain [dɪs'deɪn] *n* dédain *m*

disease [dɪ'ziːz] *n* maladie *f*

disembark [dɪsɪm'bɑːk] *vt, vi* débarquer

disengage [dɪsɪn'geɪdʒ] *vt*: **to ~ the clutch** *(AUT)* débrayer

disentangle [dɪsɪn'tæŋgl] *vt (wool, wire)* démêler, débrouiller; *(from wreckage)* dégager

disfigure [dɪs'fɪgə*] *vt* défigurer

disgrace [dɪs'greɪs] *n* honte *f*; *(disfavour)* disgrâce *f* ♦ *vt* déshonorer, couvrir de honte; **~ful** *adj* scandaleux(euse), honteux(euse)

disgruntled [dɪs'grʌntld] *adj* mécontent(e)

disguise [dɪs'gaɪz] *n* déguisement *m* ♦ *vt* déguiser; **in ~** déguisé(e)

disgust [dɪs'gʌst] *n* dégoût *m*, aversion *f* ♦ *vt* dégoûter, écœurer; **~ing** *adj* dégoûtant(e), révoltant(e)

dish [dɪʃ] *n* plat *m*; **to do** *or* **wash the ~es** faire la vaisselle; **~ out** *vt* servir, distribuer; **~ up** *vt* servir; **~cloth** *n (for washing)* lavette *f*

dishearten [dɪs'hɑːtn] *vt* décourager

dishevelled [dɪ'ʃevəld] *(US* **disheveled)** *adj* ébouriffé(e); décoiffé(e); débraillé(e)

dishonest [dɪs'ɒnɪst] *adj* malhonnête

dishonour [dɪs'ɒnə*] *(US* **dishonor)** *n* déshonneur *m*; **~able** *adj (behaviour)* déshonorant(e); *(person)* peu honorable

dishtowel ['dɪʃtauəl] *(US)* *n* torchon *m*

dishwasher ['dɪʃwɒʃə*] *n* lave-vaisselle *m*

disillusion [dɪsɪ'luːʒən] *vt* désabuser, désillusionner

disincentive ['dɪsɪn'sentɪv] *n*: **to be a ~** être démotivant(e)

disinfect [dɪsɪn'fekt] *vt* désinfecter; **~ant** *n* désinfectant *m*

disintegrate [dɪs'ɪntɪgreɪt] *vi* se désintégrer

disinterested [dɪs'ɪntrɪstɪd] *adj* désintéressé(e)

disjointed [dɪs'dʒɔɪntɪd] *adj* décousu(e), incohérent(e)

disk [dɪsk] *n (COMPUT)* disque *m*; *(: floppy ~)* disquette *f*; **single/double-sided ~** disquette simple/double face; **~ drive** *n* lecteur *m* de disquettes; **~ette** [dɪs'ket] *n* disquette *f*, disque *m* souple

dislike [dɪs'laɪk] *n* aversion *f*, antipathie *f* ♦ *vt* ne pas aimer

dislocate ['dɪsləukeɪt] *vt* disloquer; déboîter

dislodge [dɪs'lɒdʒ] *vt* déplacer, faire bouger

disloyal ['dɪs'lɔɪəl] *adj* déloyal(e)

dismal ['dɪzməl] *adj* lugubre, maussade

dismantle [dɪs'mæntl] *vt* démonter

dismay [dɪs'meɪ] *n* consternation *f*

dismiss [dɪs'mɪs] *vt* congédier, renvoyer; *(soldiers)* faire rompre les rangs à; *(idea)* écarter; *(LAW)*: **to ~ a case** rendre une fin de non-recevoir; **~al** *n* renvoi *m*

dismount [dɪs'maunt] *vi* mettre pied à terre, descendre

disobedient [dɪsə'biːdɪənt] *adj* désobéissant(e)

disobey ['dɪsə'beɪ] *vt* désobéir à

disorder [dɪs'ɔːdə*] *n* désordre *m*; *(rioting)* désordres *mpl*; *(MED)* troubles *mpl*; **~ly** [dɪs'ɔːdəlɪ] *adj* en désordre; désordonné(e)

disorientated [dɪs'ɔːrɪenteɪtɪd] *adj* désorienté(e)

disown [dɪs'əun] *vt* renier

disparaging [dɪs'pærɪdʒɪŋ] *adj* désobligeant(e)

dispassionate [dɪs'pæʃnɪt] *adj* calme, froid(e); impartial(e), objectif(ive)

dispatch [dɪs'pætʃ] *vt* expédier, envoyer ♦ *n* envoi *m*, expédition *f*; *(MIL, PRESS)* dépêche *f*

dispel [dɪs'pel] *vt* dissiper, chasser

dispense [dɪs'pens] *vt* distribuer, administrer; **~ with** *vt fus* se passer de; **~r** *n (machine)* distributeur *m*; **dispensing chemist** *(BRIT)* *n* pharmacie *f*

disperse [dɪs'pɜːs] *vt* disperser ♦ *vi* se disperser

dispirited [dɪs'pɪrɪtɪd] *adj* découragé(e), déprimé(e)

displace [dɪs'pleɪs] *vt* déplacer

display [dɪs'pleɪ] *n* étalage *m*; déploiement *m*; affichage *m*; *(screen)* écran *m*, visuel *m*; *(of feeling)* manifestation *f* ♦ *vt* montrer; *(goods)* mettre à l'étalage, exposer; *(results, departure times)* afficher; *(pej)* faire étalage de

displease [dɪs'pliːz] *vt* mécontenter, contrarier; **~d** *adj*: **~d with** mécontent(e) de; **displeasure** [dɪs'pleʒə*] *n* mécontentement *m*

disposable [dɪs'pəuzəbl] *adj (pack etc)* jetable, à jeter; *(income)* disponible; **~ nappy** *(BRIT)* *n* couche *f* à jeter, couche-culotte *f*

disposal [dɪs'pəuzəl] *n (of goods for sale)* vente *f*; *(of property)* disposition *f*, cession *f*; *(of rubbish)* enlèvement *m*; destruction *f*; **at one's ~** à sa disposition

dispose [dɪs'pəuz] *vt* disposer; **~ of** *vt fus (unwanted goods etc)* se débarrasser de, se défaire de; *(problem)* expédier; **~d** [dɪs'pəuzd] *adj*: **to be ~d to do sth** être disposé(e) à faire qch; **disposition** [dɪspə'zɪʃən] *n* disposition *f*; *(temperament)* naturel *m*

disprove [dɪs'pruːv] *vt* réfuter

dispute [dɪs'pjuːt] *n* discussion *f*; *(also: industrial ~)* conflit *m* ♦ *vt* contester; *(matter)* discuter; *(victory)* disputer

disqualify [dɪs'kwɒlɪfaɪ] *vt (SPORT)* disqualifier; **to ~ sb for sth/from doing** rendre qn inapte à qch/à faire

disquiet [dɪs'kwaɪət] *n* inquiétude *f*, trouble *m*

disregard [dɪsrɪ'gɑːd] *vt* ne pas tenir compte de

disrepair [ˌdɪsrɪˈpɛə*] *n*: **to fall into ~** (*building*) tomber en ruine

disreputable [dɪsˈrepjʊtəbl] *adj* (*person*) de mauvaise réputation; (*behaviour*) déshonorant(e)

disrespectful [dɪsrɪˈspɛktful] *adj* irrespectueux(euse)

disrupt [dɪsˈrʌpt] *vt* (*plans*) déranger; (*conversation*) interrompre

dissatisfied [dɪsˈsætɪsfaɪd] *adj*: **~ (with)** insatisfait(e) (de)

dissect [dɪˈsɛkt] *vt* disséquer

dissent [dɪˈsent] *n* dissentiment *m*, différence *f* d'opinion

dissertation [dɪsəˈteɪʃən] *n* mémoire *m*

disservice [dɪsˈsɜːvɪs] *n*: **to do sb a ~** rendre un mauvais service à qn

dissimilar [ˈdɪˈsɪmɪlə*] *adj*: **~ (to)** dissemblable (à), différent(e) (de)

dissipate [ˈdɪsɪpeɪt] *vt* dissiper; (*money, efforts*) disperser

dissolute [ˈdɪsəluːt] *adj* débauché(e), dissolu(e)

dissolve [dɪˈzɒlv] *vt* dissoudre ♦ *vi* se dissoudre, fondre; **to ~ in(to) tears** fondre en larmes

distance [ˈdɪstəns] *n* distance *f*; **in the ~** au loin

distant [ˈdɪstənt] *adj* lointain(e), éloigné(e); (*manner*) distant(e), froid(e)

distaste [dɪsˈteɪst] *n* dégoût *m*; **~ful** *adj* déplaisant(e), désagréable

distended [dɪsˈtendɪd] *adj* (*stomach*) dilaté(e)

distil, (*US*) **distill** [dɪsˈtɪl] *vt* distiller; **~lery** *n* distillerie *f*

distinct [dɪsˈtɪŋkt] *adj* distinct(e); (*clear*) marqué(e); **as ~ from** par opposition à; **~ion** [dɪsˈtɪŋkʃən] *n* distinction *f*; (*in exam*) mention *f* très bien; **~ive** *adj* distinctif(ive)

distinguish [dɪsˈtɪŋgwɪʃ] *vt* distinguer; **~ed** *adj* (*eminent*) distingué(e); **~ing** *adj* (*feature*) distinctif(ive), caractéristique

distort [dɪsˈtɔːt] *vt* déformer

distract [dɪsˈtrækt] *vt* distraire, déranger; **~ed** *adj* distrait(e); (*anxious*) éperdu(e), égaré(e); **~ion** [dɪsˈtrækʃən] *n* distraction *f*; égarement *m*

distraught [dɪsˈtrɔːt] *adj* éperdu(e)

distress [dɪsˈtres] *n* détresse *f* ♦ *vt* affliger; **~ing** *adj* douloureux(euse), pénible

distribute [dɪsˈtrɪbjuːt] *vt* distribuer; **distribution** [dɪstrɪˈbjuːʃən] *n* distribution *f*; **distributor** [dɪsˈtrɪbjʊtə*] *n* distributeur *m*

district [ˈdɪstrɪkt] *n* (*of country*) région *f*; (*of town*) quartier *m*; (*ADMIN*) district *m*; **~ attorney** (*US*) *n* ≈ procureur *m* de la République; **~ nurse** (*BRIT*) *n* infirmière visiteuse

distrust [dɪsˈtrʌst] *n* méfiance *f* ♦ *vt* se méfier de

disturb [dɪsˈtɜːb] *vt* troubler; (*inconvenience*) déranger; **~ance** *n* dérangement *m*; (*violent event, political etc*) troubles *mpl*; **~ed** *adj* (*worried, upset*) agité(e), troublé(e); **to be emotionally ~ed** avoir des problèmes affectifs; **~ing** *adj* troublant(e), inquiétant(e)

disuse [ˈdɪsˈjuːs] *n*: **to fall into ~** tomber en désuétude

disused [ˈdɪsˈjuːzd] *adj* désaffecté(e)

ditch [dɪtʃ] *n* fossé *m*; (*irrigation*) rigole *f* ♦ *vt* (*inf*) abandonner; (*person*) plaquer

dither [ˈdɪðə*] *vi* hésiter

ditto [ˈdɪtəʊ] *adv* idem

dive [daɪv] *n* plongeon *m*; (*of submarine*) plongée *f* ♦ *vi* plonger; **to ~ into** (*bag, drawer etc*) plonger la main dans; (*shop, car etc*) se précipiter dans; **~r** *n* plongeur *m*

diversion [daɪˈvɜːʃən] *n* (*BRIT: AUT*) déviation *f*; (*distraction, MIL*) diversion *f*

divert [daɪˈvɜːt] *vt* (*funds, BRIT: traffic*) dévier; (*river, attention*) détourner

divide [dɪˈvaɪd] *vt* diviser; (*separate*) séparer ♦ *vi* se diviser; **~d highway** (*US*) *n* route *f* à quatre voies

dividend [ˈdɪvɪdend] *n* dividende *m*

divine [dɪˈvaɪn] *adj* divin(e)

diving [ˈdaɪvɪŋ] *n* plongée (sous-marine); **~ board** *n* plongeoir *m*

divinity [dɪˈvɪnɪtɪ] *n* divinité *f*; (*SCOL*) théologie *f*

division [dɪˈvɪʒən] *n* division *f*

divorce [dɪˈvɔːs] *n* divorce *m* ♦ *vt* divorcer d'avec; (*dissociate*) séparer; **~d** *adj* divorcé(e); **~e** [dɪvɔːˈsiː] *n* divorcé(e)

D.I.Y. (*BRIT*) *n abbr* = **do-it-yourself**

dizzy [ˈdɪzɪ] *adj*: **to make sb ~** donner le vertige à qn; **to feel ~** avoir la tête qui tourne

DJ *n abbr* = **disc jockey**

─────────────── *KEYWORD*

do [duː] (*pt* **did**, *pp* **done**) *n* (*inf: party etc*) soirée *f*, fête *f*

♦ *vb* **1** (*in negative constructions*) non traduit; **I ~n't understand** je ne comprends pas

2 (*to form questions*) non traduit; **didn't you know?** vous ne le saviez pas?; **why didn't you come?** pourquoi n'êtes-vous pas venu?

3 (*for emphasis, in polite expressions*): **she does seem rather late** je trouve qu'elle est bien en retard; **~ sit down/help yourself** asseyez-vous/servez-vous je vous en prie

4 (*used to avoid repeating vb*): **she swims better than I** – elle nage mieux que moi; **~ you agree?** - **yes, I ~/no, I ~n't** vous êtes d'accord? - oui/non; **she lives in Glasgow - so ~ I** elle habite Glasgow - moi aussi; **who broke it? - I did** qui l'a cassé? - c'est moi

5 (*in question tags*): **he laughed, didn't he?** il a ri, n'est-ce pas?; **I ~n't know him, ~ I?** je ne le connais pas, je crois
♦ *vt* (*gen: carry out, perform etc*) faire; **what are you ~ing tonight?** qu'est-ce que vous faites ce soir?; **to ~ the cooking/ washing-up** faire la cuisine/la vaisselle; **to ~ one's teeth/hair/nails** se brosser les dents/se coiffer/se faire les ongles; **the car was ~ing 100** la voiture faisait du 100 (à l'heure)
♦ *vi* **1** (*act, behave*) faire; **~ as I ~** faites comme moi
2 (*get on, fare*) marcher; **the firm is ~ing well** l'entreprise marche bien; **how ~ you ~?** comment allez-vous?; (*on being introduced*) enchanté(e)!
3 (*suit*) aller; **will it ~?** est-ce que ça ira?
4 (*be sufficient*) suffire, aller; **will £10 ~?** est-ce que 10 livres suffiront?; **that'll ~** ça suffit, ça ira; **that'll ~!** (*in annoyance*) ça va *ou* suffit comme ça!; **to make ~ (with)** se contenter (de)
do away with *vt fus* supprimer
do up *vt* (*laces, dress*) attacher; (*buttons*) boutonner; (*zip*) fermer; (*renovate: room*) refaire; (: *house*) remettre à neuf
do with *vt fus* (*need*): **I could do with a drink/some help** quelque chose à boire/un peu d'aide ne serait pas de refus; (*be connected*): **that has nothing to ~ with you** cela ne vous concerne pas; **I won't have anything to ~ with it** je ne veux pas m'en mêler
do without *vi* s'en passer ♦ *vt fus* se passer de

dock [dɒk] *n* dock *m*; (*LAW*) banc *m* des accusés ♦ *vi* se mettre à quai; (*SPACE*) s'arrimer; **~er** *n* docker *m*; **~yard** *n* chantier *m* de construction navale
doctor ['dɒktə*] *n* médecin *m*, docteur *m*; (*PhD etc*) docteur ♦ *vt* (*drink*) frelater; **D~ of Philosophy** *n* (*degree*) doctorat *m*; (*person*) Docteur *m* en Droit *or* Lettres *etc*, titulaire *m/f* d'un doctorat
document ['dɒkjumənt] *n* document *m*; **~ary** [dɒkju'mentəri] *adj* documentaire ♦ *n* documentaire *m*
dodge [dɒdʒ] *n* truc *m*; combine *f* ♦ *vt* esquiver, éviter
dodgems ['dɒdʒəmz] (*BRIT*) *npl* autos tamponneuses
doe [dəʊ] *n* (*deer*) biche *f*; (*rabbit*) lapine *f*
does [dʌz] *vb see* do; **~n't = does not**
dog [dɒg] *n* chien(ne) ♦ *vt* suivre de près; poursuivre, harceler; **~ collar** *n* collier *m* de chien; (*fig*) faux-col *m* d'ecclésiastique; **~-eared** *adj* corné(e)
dogged ['dɒgɪd] *adj* obstiné(e), opiniâtre
dogsbody ['dɒgzbɒdɪ] *n* bonne *f* à tout faire, tâcheron *m*

doings ['duːɪŋz] *npl* activités *fpl*
do-it-yourself ['duːɪtjɔ'self] *n* bricolage *m*
doldrums ['dɒldrəmz] *npl*: **to be in the ~** avoir le cafard; (*business*) être dans le marasme
dole [dəʊl] *n* (*BRIT: payment*) allocation *f* de chômage; **on the ~** au chômage; **~ out** *vt* donner au compte-goutte
doleful ['dəʊlful] *adj* plaintif(ive), lugubre
doll [dɒl] *n* poupée *f*
dollar ['dɒlə*] *n* dollar *m*
dolled up [dɒld-] (*inf*) *adj*: **(all) ~** sur son trente et un
dolphin ['dɒlfɪn] *n* dauphin *m*
dome [dəʊm] *n* dôme *m*
domestic [də'mestɪk] *adj* (*task, appliances*) ménager(ère); (*of country: trade, situation etc*) intérieur(e); (*animal*) domestique; **~ated** *adj* (*animal*) domestiqué(e); (*husband*) pantouflard(e)
dominate ['dɒmɪneɪt] *vt* dominer
domineering [dɒmɪ'nɪərɪŋ] *adj* dominateur(trice), autoritaire
dominion [də'mɪnɪən] *n* (*territory*) territoire *m*; **to have ~ over** contrôler
domino ['dɒmɪnəʊ] (*pl* **~es**) *n* domino *m*; **~s** *n* (*game*) dominos *mpl*
don [dɒn] (*BRIT*) *n* professeur *m* d'université
donate [də'neɪt] *vt* faire don de, donner
done [dʌn] *pp of* do
donkey ['dɒŋkɪ] *n* âne *m*
donor ['dəʊnə*] *n* (*of blood etc*) donneur(euse); (*to charity*) donateur(trice)
don't [dəʊnt] *vb* = do not
donut (*US*) *n* = doughnut
doodle ['duːdl] *vi* griffonner, gribouiller
doom [duːm] *n* destin *m* ♦ *vt*: **to be ~ed (to failure)** être voué(e) à l'échec; **~sday** *n* le Jugement dernier
door [dɔː*] *n* porte *f*; (*RAIL, car*) portière *f*; **~bell** *n* sonnette *f*; **~handle** *n* poignée *f* de la porte; (*car*) poignée de portière; **~man** (*irreg*) *n* (*in hotel*) portier *m*; **~mat** *n* paillasson *m*; **~step** *n* pas *m* de (la) porte, seuil *m*; **~way** *n* (embrasure *f* de la) porte *f*
dope [dəʊp] *n* (*inf: drug*) drogue *f*; (: *person*) andouille *f* ♦ *vt* (*horse etc*) doper
dopey ['dəʊpɪ] (*inf*) *adj* à moitié endormi(e)
dormant ['dɔːmənt] *adj* assoupi(e), en veilleuse
dormitory ['dɔːmɪtrɪ] *n* dortoir *m*; (*US: building*) résidence *f* universitaire
dormouse ['dɔːmaus, *pl* 'dɔːmaɪs] (*pl* **dormice**) *n* loir *m*
dose [dəʊs] *n* dose *f*
doss house ['dɒs-] (*BRIT*) *n* asile *m* de nuit
dot [dɒt] *n* point *m*; (*on material*) pois *m* ♦ *vt*: **~ted with** parsemé(e) de; **on the ~** à l'heure tapante *or* pile
dote [dəʊt]: **to ~ on** *vt fus* être fou(folle)

de

dot-matrix printer [dɒt'meɪtrɪks-] *n* imprimante matricielle

dotted line *n* pointillé(s) *m(pl)*

double ['dʌbl] *adj* double ♦ *adv* (*twice*): **to cost** ~ (**sth**) coûter le double (de qch) *or* deux fois plus (que qch) ♦ *n* double *m* ♦ *vt* doubler; (*fold*) plier en deux ♦ *vi* doubler; ~**s** *n* (*TENNIS*) double *m*; **on** *or* (*BRIT*) **at the** ~ au pas de course; ~ **bass** (*BRIT*) *n* contrebasse *f*; ~ **bed** *n* grand lit; ~ **bend** (*BRIT*) *n* virage *m* en S; ~**-breasted** *adj* croisé(e); ~**cross** *vt* doubler, trahir; ~**decker** *n* autobus *m* à impériale; ~ **glazing** (*BRIT*) *n* double vitrage *m*; ~ **room** *n* chambre *f* pour deux personnes; **doubly** ['dʌblɪ] *adv* doublement, deux fois plus

doubt [daʊt] *n* doute *m* ♦ *vt* douter de; **to** ~ **that** douter que; ~**ful** *adj* douteux(euse); (*person*) incertain(e); ~**less** *adv* sans doute, sûrement

dough [dəʊ] *n* pâte *f*, ~**nut** (*US* **donut**) *n* beignet *m*

douse [daʊz] *vt* (*drench*) tremper, inonder; (*extinguish*) éteindre

dove [dʌv] *n* colombe *f*

Dover ['dəʊvə*] *n* Douvres

dovetail ['dʌvteɪl] *vi* (*fig*) concorder

dowdy ['daʊdɪ] *adj* démodé(e); mal fagoté(e) (*inf*)

down [daʊn] *n* (*soft feathers*) duvet *m* ♦ *adv* en bas, vers le bas; (*on the ground*) par terre ♦ *prep* en bas de; (*along*) le long de ♦ *vt* (*inf*: *drink, food*) s'envoyer; ~ **with X!** à bas X!; ~**-and-out** *n* clochard(e); ~**-at-heel** *adj* éculé(e); (*fig*) miteux(euse); ~**cast** *adj* démoralisé(e); ~**fall** *n* chute *f*, ruine *f*; ~**hearted** *adj* découragé(e); ~**hill** *adv*: **to go** ~**hill** descendre; (*fig*) péricliter, ~ **payment** *n* acompte *m*; ~**pour** *n* pluie torrentielle, déluge *m*; ~**right** *adj* (*lie etc*) effronté(e); (*refusal*) catégorique

Down's syndrome [daʊnz-] *n* (*MED*) trisomie *f*

down: ~**stairs** *adv* au rez-de-chaussée; à l'étage inférieur; ~**stream** *adv* en aval; ~**to-earth** *adj* terre à terre *inv*; ~**town** *adv* en ville; ~ **under** *adv* en Australie (*or* Nouvelle-Zélande); ~**ward** *adj*, *adv* vers le bas; ~**wards** *adv* vers le bas

dowry ['daʊrɪ] *n* dot *f*

doz. *abbr* = **dozen**

doze [dəʊz] *vi* sommeiller; ~ **off** *vi* s'assoupir

dozen ['dʌzn] *n* douzaine *f*; **a** ~ **books** une douzaine de livres; ~**s of** des centaines de

Dr. *abbr* = **doctor; drive**

drab [dræb] *adj* terne, morne

draft [drɑːft] *n* ébauche *f*; (*of letter, essay etc*) brouillon *m*; (*COMM*) traite *f*; (*US: call-up*) conscription *f* ♦ *vt* faire le brouillon

or un projet de; (*MIL: send*) détacher; *see also* **draught**

draftsman ['drɑːftsmən] (*irreg*: *US*) *n* = **draughtsman**

drag [dræg] *vt* traîner; (*river*) draguer ♦ *vi* traîner ♦ *n* (*inf*) casse-pieds *m/f*; (*women's clothing*): **in** ~ (en) travesti; ~ **on** *vi* s'éterniser

dragon ['drægən] *n* dragon *m*

dragonfly ['drægənflaɪ] *n* libellule *f*

drain [dreɪn] *n* égout *m*, canalisation *f*; (*on resources*) saignée *f* ♦ *vt* (*land, marshes etc*) drainer, assécher; (*vegetables*) égoutter; (*glass*) vider ♦ *vi* (*water*) s'écouler; ~**age** *n* drainage *m*; système *m* d'égouts *or* de canalisations; ~**ing board** (*US* ~**board**) *n* égouttoir *m*; ~**pipe** *n* tuyau *m* d'écoulement

drama ['drɑːmə] *n* (*art*) théâtre *m*, art *m* dramatique; (*play*) pièce *f* (de théâtre); (*event*) drame *m*; ~**tic** [drə'mætɪk] *adj* dramatique; spectaculaire; ~**tist** ['dræmətɪst] *n* auteur *m* dramatique; ~**tize** *vt* (*events*) dramatiser; (*adapt: for TV/cinema*) adapter pour la télévision/pour l'écran

drank [dræŋk] *pt of* **drink**

drape [dreɪp] *vt* draper; ~**s** (*US*) *npl* rideaux *mpl*

drastic ['dræstɪk] *adj* sévère, énergique; (*change*) radical(e)

draught [drɑːft] (*US* **draft**) *n* courant *m* d'air; (*NAUT*) tirant *m* d'eau; **on** ~ (*beer*) à la pression; ~**board** (*BRIT*) *n* damier *m*; ~**s** (*BRIT*) *n* (jeu *m* de) dames *fpl*

draughtsman ['drɑːftsmən] (*irreg*) *n* dessinateur(trice) (industriel(le))

draw [drɔː] (*pt* **drew**, *pp* **drawn**) *vt* tirer; (*tooth*) arracher, extraire; (*attract*) attirer; (*picture*) dessiner; (*line, circle*) tracer; (*money*) retirer; (*wages*) toucher ♦ *vi* (*SPORT*) faire match nul ♦ *n* match nul; (*lottery*) tirage *m* au sort; loterie *f*; **to** ~ **near** s'approcher; approcher; ~ **out** *vi* (*lengthen*) s'allonger ♦ *vt* (*money*) retirer; ~ **up** *vi* (*stop*) s'arrêter ♦ *vt* (*chair*) approcher; (*document*) établir, dresser; ~**back** *n* inconvénient *m*, désavantage *m*; ~**bridge** *n* pont-levis *m*; ~**er** [drɔː*] *n* tiroir *m*

drawing ['drɔːɪŋ] *n* dessin *m*; ~ **board** *n* planche *f* à dessin; ~ **pin** (*BRIT*) *n* punaise *f*; ~ **room** *n* salon *m*

drawl [drɔːl] *n* accent traînant

drawn [drɔːn] *pp of* **draw**

dread [dred] *n* terreur *f*, effroi *m* ♦ *vt* redouter, appréhender; ~**ful** *adj* affreux(euse)

dream [driːm] (*pt, pp* **dreamed** *or* **dreamt**) *n* rêve *m* ♦ *vt, vi* rêver; ~**y** *adj* rêveur(euse); (*music*) langoureux(euse)

dreary ['drɪərɪ] *adj* morne; monotone

dredge [dredʒ] *vt* draguer

dregs [dregz] *npl* lie *f*

drench [drentʃ] *vt* tremper

dress [dres] *n* robe *f*; (*no pl: clothing*) habillement *m*, tenue *f* ♦ *vi* s'habiller ♦ *vt* habiller; (*wound*) panser; **to get ~ed** s'habiller; **~ up** *vi* s'habiller; (*in fancy ~*) se déguiser; **~ circle** (*BRIT*) *n* (*THEATRE*) premier balcon; **~er** *n* (*furniture*) vaisselier *m*; (: *US*) coiffeuse *f*, commode *f*; **~ing** *n* (*MED*) pansement *m*; (*CULIN*) sauce *f*, assaisonnement *m*; **~ing gown** (*BRIT*) *n* robe *f* de chambre; **~ing room** *n* (*THEATRE*) loge *f*; (*SPORT*) vestiaire *m*; **~ing table** *n* coiffeuse *f*; **~maker** *n* couturière *f*; **~ rehearsal** *n* (répétition) générale *f*

drew [druː] *pt of* **draw**

dribble ['drɪbl] *vi* (*baby*) baver ♦ *vt* (*ball*) dribbler

dried [draɪd] *adj* (*fruit, beans*) sec(sèche); (*eggs, milk*) en poudre

drier ['draɪə*] *n* = **dryer**

drift [drɪft] *n* (*of current etc*) force *f*, direction *f*, mouvement *m*; (*of snow*) rafale *f*; (: *on ground*) congère *f*; (*general meaning*) sens (général) ♦ *vi* (*boat*) aller à la dérive, dériver; (*sand, snow*) s'amonceler, s'entasser; **~wood** *n* bois flotté

drill [drɪl] *n* perceuse *f*; (*~ bit*) foret *m*, mèche *f*; (*of dentist*) roulette *f*, fraise *f*; (*MIL*) exercice *m* ♦ *vt* percer; (*troops*) entraîner ♦ *vi* (*for oil*) faire un *or* des forage(s)

drink [drɪŋk] (*pt* **drank**, *pp* **drunk**) *n* boisson *f*; (*alcoholic*) verre *m* ♦ *vt, vi* boire; **to have a ~** boire quelque chose, boire un verre; prendre l'apéritif; **a ~ of water** un verre d'eau; **~er** *n* buveur(euse); **~ing water** *n* eau *f* potable

drip [drɪp] *n* goutte *f*; (*MED*) goutte-à-goutte *m inv*; perfusion *f* ♦ *vi* tomber goutte à goutte; (*tap*) goutter; **~-dry** *adj* (*shirt*) sans repassage; **~ping** *n* graisse *f* (de rôti)

drive [draɪv] (*pt* **drove**, *pp* **driven**) *n* promenade *f or* trajet *m* en voiture; (*also: ~way*) allée *f*; (*energy*) dynamisme *m*, énergie *f*; (*push*) effort (concerté), campagne *f* (*also: disk ~*) lecteur *m* de disquettes ♦ *vt* conduire; (*push*) chasser, pousser; (*TECH: motor, wheel*) faire fonctionner; entraîner; (*nail, stake etc*): **to ~ sth into sth** enfoncer qch dans qch ♦ *vi* (*AUT: at controls*) conduire; (: *travel*) aller en voiture; **left-/right-hand ~** conduite *f* à gauche/droite; **to ~ sb mad** rendre qn fou(folle); **to ~ sb home/to the airport** reconduire qn chez lui/conduire qn à l'aéroport

drivel ['drɪvl] (*inf*) *n* idioties *fpl*

driver ['draɪvə*] *n* conducteur(trice); (*of taxi, bus*) chauffeur *m*; **~'s license** (*US*) *n* permis *m* de conduire

driveway ['draɪvweɪ] *n* allée *f*

driving ['draɪvɪŋ] *n* conduite *f*; **~ instructor** *n* moniteur *m* d'auto-école; **~ lesson** *n* leçon *f* de conduite; **~ licence** (*BRIT*) *n* permis *m* de conduire; **~ school** *n* auto-

école *f*; **~ test** *n* examen *m* du permis de conduire

drizzle ['drɪzl] *n* bruine *f*, crachin *m*

drone [drəʊn] *n* bourdonnement *m*; (*male bee*) faux bourdon

drool [druːl] *vi* baver

droop [druːp] *vi* (*shoulders*) tomber; (*head*) pencher; (*flower*) pencher la tête

drop [drɒp] *n* goutte *f*; (*fall*) baisse *f*; (*also: parachute ~*) saut *m* ♦ *vt* laisser tomber; (*voice, eyes, price*) baisser; (*set down from car*) déposer ♦ *vi* tomber; **~s** *npl* (*MED*) gouttes; **~ off** *vi* (*sleep*) s'assoupir ♦ *vt* (*passenger*) déposer; **~ out** *vi* (*withdraw*) se retirer; (*student etc*) abandonner, décrocher; **~out** *n* marginal(e); **~per** *n* compte-gouttes *m inv*; **~pings** *npl* crottes *fpl*

drought [draʊt] *n* sécheresse *f*

drove [drəʊv] *pt of* **drive**

drown [draʊn] *vt* noyer ♦ *vi* se noyer

drowsy ['draʊzɪ] *adj* somnolent(e)

drudgery ['drʌdʒərɪ] *n* corvée *f*

drug [drʌg] *n* médicament *m*; (*narcotic*) drogue *f* ♦ *vt* droguer; **to be on ~s** se droguer; **~ addict** *n* toxicomane *m/f*; **~gist** (*US*) *n* pharmacien(ne)-droguiste; **~store** (*US*) *n* pharmacie-droguerie *f*, drugstore *m*

drum [drʌm] *n* tambour *m*; (*for oil, petrol*) bidon *m*; **~s** *npl* (*kit*) batterie *f*; **~mer** *n* (joueur *m* de) tambour *m*

drunk [drʌŋk] *pp of* **drink** ♦ *adj* ivre, soûl(e) ♦ *n* (*also: ~ard*) ivrogne *m/f*; **~en** *adj* (*person*) ivre, soûl(e); (*rage, stupor*) ivrogne, d'ivrogne

dry [draɪ] *adj* sec(sèche); (*day*) sans pluie; (*humour*) pince-sans-rire *inv*; (*lake, riverbed, well*) à sec ♦ *vt* sécher; (*clothes*) faire sécher ♦ *vi* tarir; **~ up** *vi* tarir; **~-cleaner's** *n* teinturerie *f*; **~er** *n* séchoir *m*; (*spin-~er*) essoreuse *f*; **~ness** *n* sécheresse *f*; **~ rot** *n* pourriture sèche (*du bois*)

dual ['djuəl] *adj* double; **~ carriageway** (*BRIT*) *n* route *f* à quatre voies *or* à chaussées séparées; **~ purpose** *adj* à double usage

dubbed [dʌbd] *adj* (*CINEMA*) doublé(e)

dubious ['djuːbɪəs] *adj* hésitant(e), incertain(e); (*reputation, company*) douteux(euse)

duchess ['dʌtʃɪs] *n* duchesse *f*

duck [dʌk] *n* canard *m* ♦ *vi* se baisser vivement, baisser subitement la tête; **~ling** *n* caneton *m*

duct [dʌkt] *n* conduite *f*, canalisation *f*; (*ANAT*) conduit *m*

dud [dʌd] *n* (*object, tool*): **it's a ~** c'est de la camelote, ça ne marche pas ♦ *adj* : **~ cheque** (*BRIT*) chèque sans provision

due [djuː] *adj* dû(due); (*expected*) attendu(e); (*fitting*) qui convient ♦ *n*: **to give sb his** (*or* **her**) **~** être juste envers qn ♦ *adv*: **~ north** droit vers le nord; **~s** *npl* (*for club*, *union*) cotisation f; (*in harbour*) droits mpl (de port); **in ~ course** en temps utile *or* voulu; finalement; **~ to** dû(due) à; causé(e) par; **he's ~ to finish tomorrow** normalement il doit finir demain

duet [dju:'et] n duo m

duffel bag [dʌfl] n sac m marin

duffel coat n duffel-coat m

dug [dʌg] pt, pp of **dig**

duke [dju:k] n duc m

dull [dʌl] adj terne, morne; (*boring*) ennuyeux(euse); (*sound, pain*) sourd(e); (*weather, day*) gris(e), maussade ♦ vt (*pain, grief*) atténuer; (*mind, senses*) engourdir

duly ['dju:lɪ] adv (*on time*) en temps voulu; (*as expected*) comme il se doit

dumb [dʌm] adj muet(te); (*stupid*) bête; **~founded** [dʌm'faundɪd] adj sidéré(e)

dummy ['dʌmɪ] n (*tailor's model*) mannequin m; (*mock-up*) factice m, maquette f; (*BRIT: for baby*) tétine f ♦ adj faux(fausse), factice

dump [dʌmp] n (*also: rubbish dump*) décharge (publique); (*pej*) trou m ♦ vt (*put down*) déposer; déverser; (*get rid of*) se débarrasser de; (*COMPUT: data*) vider, transférer

dumpling ['dʌmplɪŋ] n boulette f (de pâte)

dumpy ['dʌmpɪ] adj boulot(te)

dunce [dʌns] n âne m, cancre m.

dune [dju:n] n dune f

dung [dʌŋ] n fumier m

dungarees [dʌŋgə'ri:z] npl salopette f, bleu(s) m(pl)

dungeon ['dʌndʒən] n cachot m

duplex ['dju:pleks] (*US*) n maison jumelée; (*apartment*) duplex m

duplicate [n 'dju:plɪkɪt, vb 'dju:plɪkeɪt] n double m ♦ vt faire un double de; (*on machine*) polycopier; photocopier; **in ~** en deux exemplaires

durable ['djuərəbl] adj durable; (*clothes, metal*) résistant(e), solide

duration [djuə'reɪʃən] n durée f

duress [djuə'res] n: **under ~** sous la contrainte

during ['djuərɪŋ] prep pendant, au cours de

dusk [dʌsk] n crépuscule m

dust [dʌst] n poussière f ♦ vt (*furniture*) épousseter, essuyer; (*cake etc*): **to ~ with** saupoudrer de; **~bin** (*BRIT*) n poubelle f; **~er** n chiffon m; **~man** (*BRIT irreg*) n boueux m, éboueur m; **~y** adj poussiéreux(euse)

Dutch [dʌtʃ] adj hollandais(e), néerlandais(e) ♦ n (*LING*) hollandais m ♦ adv (*inf*): **to go ~** partager les frais; **the ~** npl (*people*) les Hollandais; **~man** (*irreg*) n Hollandais; **~woman** (*irreg*) n Hollandaise f

dutiful ['dju:tɪful] adj (*child*) respectueux(euse)

duty ['dju:tɪ] n devoir m; (*tax*) droit m, taxe

f; **on ~** de service; (*at night etc*) de garde; **off ~** libre, pas de service *or* de garde; **~-free** adj exempté(e) de douane, hors taxe inv

duvet ['du:veɪ] (*BRIT*) n couette f

dwarf [dwɔ:f] (*pl* **dwarves**) n nain(e) ♦ vt écraser

dwell [dwel] (*pt, pp* **dwelt**) vi demeurer; **~ on** vt fus s'appesantir sur; **~ing** n habitation f, demeure f

dwindle ['dwɪndl] vi diminuer, décroître

dye [daɪ] n teinture f ♦ vt teindre

dying ['daɪɪŋ] adj mourant(e), agonisant(e)

dyke [daɪk] (*BRIT*) n digue f

dynamic [daɪ'næmɪk] adj dynamique

dynamite ['daɪnəmaɪt] n dynamite f

dynamo ['daɪnəməu] n dynamo f

dyslexia [dɪs'leksɪə] n dyslexie f

─────── *E e*

E [i:] n (*MUS*) mi m

each [i:tʃ] adj chaque ♦ pron chacun(e); **~ other** l'un(e) l'autre; **they hate ~ other** ils se détestent (mutuellement); **you are jealous of ~ other** vous êtes jaloux l'un de l'autre; **they have 2 books ~** ils ont 2 livres chacun

eager ['i:gə*] adj (*keen*) avide; **to be ~ to do sth** avoir très envie de faire qch; **to be ~ for** désirer vivement, être avide de

eagle ['i:gl] n aigle m

ear [ɪə*] n oreille f; (*of corn*) épi m; **~ache** n mal m aux oreilles; **~drum** n tympan m

earl [ɜ:l] (*BRIT*) n comte m

earlier ['ɜ:lɪə*] adj (*date etc*) plus rapproché(e); (*edition, fashion etc*) plus ancien(ne), antérieur(e) ♦ adv plus tôt

early ['ɜ:lɪ] adv tôt, de bonne heure; (*ahead of time*) en avance; (*near the beginning*) au début ♦ adj qui se manifeste (*or* se fait) tôt *or* de bonne heure; (*work*) de jeunesse; (*settler, Christian*) premier(ère); (*reply*) rapide; (*death*) prématuré(e); **to have an ~ night** se coucher tôt *or* de bonne heure; **in the ~ or ~ in the spring/19th century** au début du printemps/19ème siècle; **~ retirement** n: **to take ~ retirement** prendre sa retraite anticipée

earmark ['ɪəmɑ:k] vt: **to ~ sth for** réserver *or* destiner qch à

earn [ɜ:n] vt gagner; (*COMM: yield*) rapporter

earnest ['ɜːnɪst] *adj* sérieux(euse); **in ~** *adv* sérieusement

earnings ['ɜːnɪŋz] *npl* salaire *m*; (*of company*) bénéfices *mpl*

earphones ['ɪəfəunz] *npl* écouteurs *mpl*

earring ['ɪərɪŋ] *n* boucle *f* d'oreille

earshot ['ɪəʃɒt] *n*: **within ~** à portée de voix

earth [ɜːθ] *n* (*gen, also BRIT*: *ELEC*) terre *f* ♦ *vt* relier à la terre; **~enware** *n* poterie *f*; faïence *f*; **~quake** *n* tremblement *m* de terre, séisme *m*; **~y** ['ɜːθɪ] *adj* (*vulgar*: *humour*) truculent(e)

ease [iːz] *n* facilité *f*, aisance *f*; (*comfort*) bien-être *m* ♦ *vt* (*soothe*) calmer; (*loosen*) relâcher, détendre; **to ~ sth in/out** faire pénétrer/sortir qch délicatement *or* avec douceur; faciliter la pénétration/la sortie de qch; **at ~!** (*MIL*) repos!; **~ off** *vi* diminuer; (*slow down*) ralentir; **~ up** *vi* = **ease off**

easel ['iːzl] *n* chevalet *m*

easily ['iːzɪlɪ] *adv* facilement

east [iːst] *n* est *m* ♦ *adj* (*wind*) d'est; (*side*) est *inv* ♦ *adv* à l'est, vers l'est; **the E~** l'Orient *m*; (*POL*) les pays *mpl* de l'Est

Easter ['iːstə*] *n* Pâques *fpl*; **~ egg** *n* œuf *m* de Pâques

east: **~erly** ['iːstəlɪ] *adj* (*wind*) d'est; (*direction*) est *inv*; (*point*) à l'est; **~ern** ['iːstən] *adj* de l'est, oriental(e); **~ward(s)** ['iːstwəd(z)] *adv* vers l'est, à l'est

easy ['iːzɪ] *adj* facile; (*manner*) aisé(e) ♦ *adv*: **to take it** *or* **things ~** ne pas se fatiguer; (*not worry*) ne pas (trop) s'en faire; **~ chair** *n* fauteuil *m*; **~-going** *adj* accommodant(e), facile à vivre

eat [iːt] (*pt* **ate**, *pp* **eaten**) *vt, vi* manger; **~ away at** *vt fus* ronger, attaquer; (*savings*) entamer; **~ into** *vt fus* = **eat away at**

eaves [iːvz] *npl* avant-toit *m*

eavesdrop ['iːvzdrɒp] *vi*: **to ~ (on a conversation)** écouter (une conversation) de façon indiscrète

ebb [eb] *n* reflux *m* ♦ *vi* refluer; (*fig*: *also*: **~ away**) décliner

ebony ['ebənɪ] *n* ébène *f*

EC *n abbr* (= *European Community*) C.E. *f*

eccentric [ɪk'sentrɪk] *adj* excentrique ♦ *n* excentrique *m/f*

echo ['ekəu] (*pl* **~es**) *n* écho *m* ♦ *vt* répéter ♦ *vi* résonner, faire écho

eclipse [ɪ'klɪps] *n* éclipse *f*

ecology [ɪ'kɒlədʒɪ] *n* écologie *f*

economic [iːkə'nɒmɪk] *adj* économique; (*business etc*) rentable; **~al** *adj* économique; (*person*) économe; **~s** *n* économie *f* politique ♦ *npl* (*of project, situation*) aspect *m* financier

economize [ɪ'kɒnəmaɪz] *vi* économiser, faire des économies

economy [ɪ'kɒnəmɪ] *n* économie *f*; **~ class** *n* classe *f* touriste; **~ size** *n* format

m économique

ecstasy ['ekstəsɪ] *n* extase *f*; **ecstatic** *adj* extatique

ECU [eiːkjuː] *n abbr* (= *European Currency Unit*) ECU *m*

eczema ['eksɪmə] *n* eczéma *m*

edge [edʒ] *n* bord *m*; (*of knife etc*) tranchant *m*, fil *m* ♦ *vt* border; **on ~** (*fig*) crispé(e), tendu(e); **to ~ away from** s'éloigner furtivement de; **~ways** *adv*: **he couldn't get a word in ~ways** il ne pouvait pas placer un mot

edgy ['edʒɪ] *adj* crispé(e), tendu(e)

edible ['edɪbl] *adj* comestible

edict ['iːdɪkt] *n* décret *m*

Edinburgh ['edɪnbərə] *n* Édimbourg

edit ['edɪt] *vt* (*text, book*) éditer; (*report*) préparer; (*film*) monter; (*broadcast*) réaliser; **~ion** [ɪ'dɪʃən] *n* édition *f*; **~or** *n* (*of column*) rédacteur(trice); (*of newspaper*) rédacteur(trice) en chef; (*of sb's work*) éditeur(trice); **~orial** [edɪ'tɔːrɪəl] *adj* de la rédaction, éditorial(e) ♦ *n* éditorial *m*

educate ['edjukeɪt] *vt* (*teach*) instruire; (*instruct*) éduquer

education [edju'keɪʃən] *n* éducation *f*; (*studies*) études *fpl*; (*teaching*) enseignement *m*, instruction *f*; **~al** *adj* (*experience, toy*) pédagogique; (*institution*) scolaire; (*policy*) d'éducation

eel [iːl] *n* anguille *f*

eerie ['ɪərɪ] *adj* inquiétant(e)

effect [ɪ'fekt] *n* effet *m* ♦ *vt* effectuer; **to take ~** (*law*) entrer en vigueur, prendre effet; (*drug*) agir, faire son effet; **in ~** en fait; **~ive** *adj* efficace; (*actual*) véritable; **~ively** *adv* efficacement; (*in reality*) effectivement; **~iveness** *n* efficacité *f*

effeminate [ɪ'femɪnɪt] *adj* efféminé(e)

effervescent [efə'vesnt] *adj* (*drink*) gazeux(euse)

efficiency [ɪ'fɪʃənsɪ] *n* efficacité *f*; (*of machine*) rendement *m*

efficient [ɪ'fɪʃənt] *adj* efficace; (*machine*) qui a un bon rendement

effort ['efət] *n* effort *m*; **~less** *adj* (*style*) aisé(e); (*achievement*) facile

effusive [ɪ'fjuːsɪv] *adj* chaleureux(euse)

e.g. *adv abbr* (= *exempli gratia*) par exemple, p. ex.

egg [eg] *n* œuf *m*; **hard-boiled/soft-boiled ~** œuf dur/à la coque; **~ on** *vt* pousser; **~cup** *n* coquetier *m*; **~plant** *n* (*esp US*) aubergine *f*; **~shell** *n* coquille *f* d'œuf

ego ['iːgəu] *n* (*self-esteem*) amour-propre *m*

egotism ['egəutɪzəm] *n* égotisme *m*

egotist ['egəutɪst] *n* égocentrique *m/f*

Egypt ['iːdʒɪpt] *n* Égypte *f*; **~ian** [ɪ'dʒɪpʃən] *adj* égyptien(ne) ♦ *n* Égyptien(ne)

eiderdown ['aɪdədaun] *n* édredon *m*

eight [eɪt] *num* huit; **~een** *num* dix-huit; **~h** [eɪtθ] *num* huitième; **~y** *num* quatre-vingt(s)

Eire ['ɛərə] n République f d'Irlande

either ['aɪðə*] adj l'un ou l'autre; (both, each) chaque ◊ pron: ~ **(of them)** l'un ou l'autre ◊ adv non plus ◊ conj: ~ **good or bad** ou bon ou mauvais, soit bon soit mauvais; **on ~ side** de chaque côté; **I don't like ~** je n'aime ni l'un ni l'autre; **no, I don't ~** moi non plus

eject [ɪ'dʒɛkt] vt (tenant etc) expulser; (object) éjecter

eke [iːk] : **to ~ out** vt faire durer

elaborate [adj ɪ'læbərɪt, vb ɪ'læbəreɪt] adj compliqué(e), recherché(e) ◊ vt élaborer ◊ vi: **to ~ (on)** entrer dans les détails (de)

elapse [ɪ'læps] vi s'écouler, passer

elastic [ɪ'læstɪk] adj élastique ◊ n élastique m; ~ **band** n élastique m

elated [ɪ'leɪtɪd] adj transporté(e) de joie

elation [ɪ'leɪʃən] n allégresse f

elbow ['elbəʊ] n coude m

elder ['eldə*] adj aîné(e) ◊ n (tree) sureau m; **one's ~s** ses aînés; **~ly** adj âgé(e) ◊ npl: **the ~ly** les personnes âgées

eldest ['eldɪst] adj, n: **the ~ (child)** l'aîné(e) (des enfants)

elect [ɪ'lekt] vt élire ◊ adj: **the president ~** le président désigné; **to ~ to do** choisir de faire; **~ion** [ɪ'lekʃən] n élection f; **~eering** [ɪlekʃə'nɪərɪŋ] n propagande électorale, manœuvres électorales; **~or** n électeur(trice); **~orate** n électorat m

electric [ɪ'lektrɪk] adj électrique; **~al** adj électrique; ~ **blanket** n couverture chauffante; ~ **fire** (BRIT) n radiateur m électrique; **~ian** [ɪlek'trɪʃən] n électricien m

electricity [ɪlek'trɪsɪtɪ] n électricité f

electrify [ɪ'lektrɪfaɪ] vt (RAIL, fence) électrifier; (audience) électriser

electronic [ɪlek'trɒnɪk] adj électronique; **~s** n électronique f

elegant ['elɪgənt] adj élégant(e)

element ['elɪmənt] n (gen) élément m; (of heater, kettle etc) résistance f; **~ary** [elɪ'mentərɪ] adj élémentaire; (school, education) primaire

elephant ['elɪfənt] n éléphant m

elevation [elɪ'veɪʃən] n (raising, promotion) avancement m, promotion f; (height) hauteur f

elevator ['elɪveɪtə*] n (in warehouse etc) élévateur m, monte-charge m inv; (US: lift) ascenseur m

eleven [ɪ'levn] num onze; **~ses** npl ≈ pause-café f; **~th** num onzième

elicit [ɪ'lɪsɪt] vt: **to ~ (from)** obtenir (de), arracher (à)

eligible ['elɪdʒəbl] adj: **to be ~ for** remplir les conditions requises pour; **an ~ young man/woman** un beau parti

elm [elm] n orme m

elongated ['iːlɒŋgeɪtɪd] adj allongé(e)

elope [ɪ'ləʊp] vi (lovers) s'enfuir (ensemble); **~ment** [ɪ'ləʊpmənt] n fugue amoureuse

eloquent ['eləkwənt] adj éloquent(e)

else [els] adv d'autre; **something ~** quelque chose d'autre, autre chose; **somewhere ~** ailleurs, autre part; **everywhere ~** partout ailleurs; **nobody ~** personne d'autre; **where ~?** à quel autre endroit?; **little ~** pas grand-chose d'autre; **~where** adv ailleurs, autre part

elude [ɪ'luːd] vt échapper à

elusive [ɪ'luːsɪv] adj insaisissable

emaciated [ɪ'meɪsɪeɪtɪd] adj émacié(e), décharné(e)

emancipate [ɪ'mænsɪpeɪt] vt émanciper

embankment [ɪm'bæŋkmənt] n (of road, railway) remblai m, talus m; (of river) berge f, quai m

embark [ɪm'bɑːk] vi embarquer; **to ~ on** (journey) entreprendre; (fig) se lancer or s'embarquer dans; **~ation** [embɑːˈkeɪʃən] n embarquement m

embarrass [ɪm'bærəs] vt embarrasser, gêner; **~ed** adj gêné(e); **~ing** adj gênant(e), embarrassant(e); **~ment** n embarras m, gêne f

embassy ['embəsɪ] n ambassade f

embedded [ɪm'bedɪd] adj enfoncé(e)

embellish [ɪm'belɪʃ] vt orner, décorer; (fig: account) enjoliver

embers ['embəz] npl braise f

embezzle [ɪm'bezl] vt détourner

embezzlement [ɪm'bezlmənt] n détournement m de fonds

embitter [ɪm'bɪtə*] vt (person) aigrir; (relations) envenimer

embody [ɪm'bɒdɪ] vt (features) réunir, comprendre; (ideas) formuler, exprimer

embossed [ɪm'bɒst] adj (metal) estampé(e); (leather) frappé(e); ~ **wallpaper** papier gaufré

embrace [ɪm'breɪs] vt embrasser, étreindre; (include) embrasser ◊ vi s'étreindre, s'embrasser ◊ n étreinte f

embroider [ɪm'brɔɪdə*] vt broder; **~y** n broderie f

emerald ['emərəld] n émeraude f

emerge [ɪ'mɜːdʒ] vi apparaître; (from room, car) surgir; (from sleep, imprisonment) sortir

emergency [ɪ'mɜːdʒənsɪ] n urgence f; **in an ~** en cas d'urgence; ~ **cord** n sonnette f d'alarme; ~ **exit** n sortie f de secours; ~ **landing** n atterrissage forcé; ~ **services** npl: **the ~ services** (fire, police, ambulance) les services mpl d'urgence

emergent [ɪ'mɜːdʒənt] adj (nation) en voie de développement; (group) en développement

emery board ['emərɪ-] n lime f à ongles (en carton émerisé)

emigrate ['emɪgreɪt] vi émigrer

eminent ['emɪnənt] adj éminent(e)

emissions [ɪ'mɪʃənz] *npl* émissions *fpl*
emit [ɪ'mɪt] *vt* émettre
emotion [ɪ'məuʃən] *n* émotion *f*; ~**al** *adj*
(*person*) émotif(ive), très sensible; (*needs,
exhaustion*) affectif(ive); (*scene*) émou-
vant(e); (*tone, speech*) qui fait appel aux
sentiments
emotive [ɪ'məutɪv] *adj* chargé(e) d'émotion;
(*subject*) sensible
emperor ['empərə*] *n* empereur *m*
emphasis ['emfəsɪs] (*pl* -**ases**) *n* (*stress*)
accent *m*; (*importance*) insistance *f*
emphasize ['emfəsaɪz] *vt* (*syllable, word,
point*) appuyer *or* insister sur; (*feature*) souligner, accentuer
emphatic [ɪm'fætɪk] *adj* (*strong*) énergique,
vigoureux(euse); (*unambiguous, clear*) catégorique; ~**ally** [ɪm'fætɪkəlɪ] *adv* avec vigueur *or* énergie; catégoriquement
empire ['empaɪə*] *n* empire *m*
employ [ɪm'plɔɪ] *vt* employer; ~**ee** *n* em-
ployé(e); ~**er** *n* employeur(euse); ~**ment** *n*
emploi *m*; ~**ment agency** *n* agence *f or*
bureau *m* de placement
empower [ɪm'pauə*] *vt*: **to** ~ **sb to do** autoriser *or* habiliter qn à faire
empress ['emprɪs] *n* impératrice *f*
emptiness ['emptɪnəs] *n* (*of area, region*)
aspect *m* désertique; (*of life*) vide *m*, va-
cuité *f*
empty ['emptɪ] *adj* vide; (*threat, promise*)
en l'air, vain(e) ♦ *vt* vider ♦ *vi* se vider; (*liquid*) s'écouler; ~**-handed** *adj* les mains
vides
emulate ['emjuleɪt] *vt* rivaliser avec, imiter
emulsion [ɪ'mʌlʃən] *n* émulsion *f*; ~
(**paint**) *n* peinture mate
enable [ɪ'neɪbl] *vt*: **to** ~ **sb to do** permettre
à qn de faire
enact [ɪn'ækt] *vt* (*law*) promulguer; (*play*)
jouer
enamel [ɪ'næməl] *n* émail *m*; (*also*: ~ **paint**)
peinture laquée
enamoured [ɪn'æməd] *adj*: **to be** ~ **of** être
entiché(e) de
encased [ɪn'keɪst] *adj*: ~ **in** enfermé(e) *or*
enchassé(e) dans
enchant [ɪn'tʃɑːnt] *vt* enchanter; ~**ing** *adj*
ravissant(e), enchanteur(teresse)
encl. *abbr* = **enclosed**
enclose [ɪn'kləuz] *vt* (*land*) clôturer; (*space,
object*) entourer; (*letter etc*) **to** ~ (**with**)
joindre (à); **please find** ~**d** veuillez trouver
ci-joint
enclosure [ɪn'kləuʒə*] *n* enceinte *f*
encompass [ɪn'kʌmpəs] *vt* (*include*) contenir, inclure
encore ['ɒŋkɔː*] *excl* bis ♦ *n* bis *m*
encounter [ɪn'kauntə*] *n* rencontre *f* ♦ *vt*
rencontrer
encourage [ɪn'kʌrɪdʒ] *vt* encourager;
~**ment** *n* encouragement *m*

encroach [ɪn'krəutʃ] *vi*: **to** ~ (**up)on** empiéter sur
encyclop(a)edia [ensaɪkləu'piːdɪə] *n* encyclopédie *f*
end [end] *n* (*gen, also*: *aim*) fin *f*; (*of table,
street, rope etc*) bout *m*, extrémité *f* ♦ *vt* terminer; (*also*: **bring to an** ~, **put an** ~ **to**)
mettre fin à ♦ *vi* se terminer, finir; **in the**
~ finalement; **on** ~ (*object*) debout, dres-
sé(e); **to stand on** ~ (*hair*) se dresser sur la
tête; **for hours on** ~ pendant des heures et
des heures; ~ **up** *vi*: **to** ~ **up in** (*condition*)
finir *or* se terminer par; (*place*) finir *or*
aboutir à
endanger [ɪn'deɪndʒə*] *vt* mettre en danger
endearing [ɪn'dɪərɪŋ] *adj* attachant(e)
endeavour [ɪn'devə*] (*US* **endeavor**) *n*
tentative *f*, effort *m* ♦ *vi*: **to** ~ **to do** tenter
or s'efforcer de faire
ending ['endɪŋ] *n* dénouement *m*, fin *f*;
(*LING*) terminaison *f*
endive ['endaɪv] *n* chicorée *f*; (*smooth*) endive *f*
endless ['endlɪs] *adj* sans fin, interminable
endorse [ɪn'dɔːs] *vt* (*cheque*) endosser; (*approve*) appuyer, approuver, sanctionner;
~**ment** *n* (*approval*) appui *m*, aval *m*;
(*BRIT: on driving licence*) contravention portée au permis de conduire
endow [ɪn'dau] *vt*: **to** ~ (**with**) doter (de)
endure [ɪn'djuə*] *vt* supporter, endurer ♦ *vi*
durer
enemy ['enɪmɪ] *adj, n* ennemi(e)
energetic [enə'dʒetɪk] *adj* énergique; (*activity*) qui fait se dépenser (physiquement)
energy ['enədʒɪ] *n* énergie *f*
enforce [ɪn'fɔːs] *vt* (*LAW*) appliquer, faire
respecter
engage [ɪn'geɪdʒ] *vt* engager; (*attention etc*)
retenir ♦ *vi* (*TECH*) s'enclencher, s'engrener;
to ~ **in** se lancer dans; ~**d** *adj* (*BRIT: busy,
in use*) occupé(e); (*betrothed*) fiancé(e); **to
get** ~**d** se fiancer; ~**d tone** *n* (*TEL*) tonalité *f* occupé *inv or* pas libre; ~**ment** *n* obligation *f*, engagement *m*; rendez-vous *m inv*;
(*to marry*) fiançailles *fpl*; ~**ment ring** *n*
bague *f* de fiançailles
engaging [ɪn'geɪdʒɪŋ] *adj* engageant(e), at-
tirant(e)
engender [ɪn'dʒendə*] *vt* produire, causer
engine ['endʒɪn] *n* (*AUT*) moteur *m*; (*RAIL*)
locomotive *f*; ~ **driver** *n* mécanicien *m*
engineer [endʒɪ'nɪə*] *n* ingénieur *m*; (*BRIT:
repairer*) dépanneur *m*; (*NAVY, US RAIL*)
mécanicien *m*; ~**ing** [-'nɪərɪŋ] *n* engineering *m*, ingénierie *f*; (*of bridges, ships*) génie
m; (*of machine*) mécanique *f*
England ['ɪŋɡlənd] *n* Angleterre *f*
English ['ɪŋɡlɪʃ] *adj* anglais(e) ♦ *n* (*LING*)
anglais *m*; **the** ~ *npl* (*people*) les Anglais;
the ~ **Channel** la Manche; ~**man** (*irreg*) *n*
Anglais; ~**woman** (*irreg*) *n* Anglaise *f*

engraving [ɪnˈgreɪvɪŋ] n gravure f
engrossed [ɪnˈgrəʊst] adj: ~ **in** absorbé(e) par, plongé(e) dans
engulf [ɪnˈgʌlf] vt engloutir
enhance [ɪnˈhɑːns] vt rehausser, mettre en valeur
enjoy [ɪnˈdʒɔɪ] vt aimer, prendre plaisir à; (have: health, fortune) jouir de; (: success) connaître; **to ~ o.s.** s'amuser; **~able** adj agréable; **~ment** n plaisir m
enlarge [ɪnˈlɑːdʒ] vt accroître; (PHOT) agrandir ♦ vi: **to ~ on** (subject) s'étendre sur; **~ment** n (PHOT) agrandissement m
enlighten [ɪnˈlaɪtn] vt éclairer; **~ed** adj éclairé(e); **~ment** n: **the E~ment** (HISTORY) ≈ le Siècle des lumières
enlist [ɪnˈlɪst] vt recruter; (support) s'assurer ♦ vi s'engager
enmity [ˈenmɪtɪ] n inimitié f
enormous [ɪˈnɔːməs] adj énorme
enough [ɪˈnʌf] adj, pron: ~ **time/books** assez or suffisamment de temps/livres ♦ adv: **big** ~ assez or suffisamment grand; **have you got ~?** en avez-vous assez?; **he has not worked** ~ il n'a pas assez or suffisamment travaillé; **~ to eat** assez à manger; **~! assez!**, ça suffit!; **that's ~, thanks** cela suffit or c'est assez, merci; **I've had ~ of him** j'en ai assez de lui; ... **which, funnily or oddly** ~ ... qui, chose curieuse
enquire [ɪnˈkwaɪə*] vt, vi = **inquire**
enrage [ɪnˈreɪdʒ] vt mettre en fureur or en rage, rendre furieux(euse)
enrol [ɪnˈrəʊl] (US **-l**) vt inscrire ♦ vi s'inscrire; **~ment** (US **~ment**) n inscription f
ensue [ɪnˈsjuː] vi s'ensuivre, résulter
ensure [ɪnˈʃʊə*] vt assurer; garantir; **to ~ that** s'assurer que
entail [ɪnˈteɪl] vt entraîner, occasionner
entangled [ɪnˈtæŋgld] adj: **to become ~ (in)** s'empêtrer dans
enter [ˈentə*] vt (room) entrer dans, pénétrer dans; (club, army) entrer à; (competition) s'inscrire à or pour; (sb for a competition) (faire) inscrire; (write down) inscrire, noter; (COMPUT) entrer, introduire ♦ vi entrer; **~ for** vt fus s'inscrire à, se présenter pour or à; **~ into** vt fus (explanation) se lancer dans; (discussion, negotiations) entamer; (agreement) conclure
enterprise [ˈentəpraɪz] n entreprise f; (initiative) (esprit m d')initiative f; **free ~** libre entreprise; **private ~** entreprise privée
enterprising [ˈentəpraɪzɪŋ] adj entreprenant(e), dynamique; (scheme) audacieux(euse)
entertain [entəˈteɪn] vt amuser, distraire; (invite) recevoir (à dîner); (idea, plan) envisager; **~er** n artiste m/f de variétés; **~ing** adj amusant(e), distrayant(e); **~ment** n (amusement) divertissement m, amusement m; (show) spectacle m

enthralled [ɪnˈθrɔːld] adj captivé(e)
enthusiasm [ɪnˈθuːzɪæzəm] n enthousiasme m
enthusiast [ɪnˈθuːzɪæst] n enthousiaste m/f; **~ic** [ɪnθuːzɪˈæstɪk] adj enthousiaste; **to be ~ic about** être enthousiasmé(e) par
entice [ɪnˈtaɪs] vt attirer, séduire
entire [ɪnˈtaɪə*] adj (tout) entier(ère); **~ly** adv entièrement, complètement; **~ty** [ɪnˈtaɪərətɪ] n: **in its ~ty** dans sa totalité
entitle [ɪnˈtaɪtl] vt: **to ~ sb to sth** donner droit à qch à qn; **~d** adj (book) intitulé(e); **to be ~d to do** avoir le droit de or être habilité à faire
entrance [n ˈentrəns, vb ɪnˈtrɑːns] n entrée f ♦ vt enchanter, ravir; **to gain ~ to** (university etc) être admis à; **~ examination** n examen m d'entrée; **~ fee** n (to museum etc) prix m d'entrée; (to join club etc) droit m d'inscription; **~ ramp** (US) n (AUT) bretelle f d'accès
entrant [ˈentrənt] n participant(e); concurrent(e); (BRIT: in exam) candidat(e)
entrenched [ɪnˈtrentʃt] adj retranché(e); (ideas) arrêté(e)
entrepreneur [ɒntrəprəˈnɜː*] n entrepreneur m
entrust [ɪnˈtrʌst] vt: **to ~ sth to** confier qch à
entry [ˈentrɪ] n entrée f; (in register) inscription f, **no ~** défense d'entrer, entrée interdite; (AUT) sens interdit; **~ form** n feuille f d'inscription; **~ phone** (BRIT) n interphone m
enunciate [ɪˈnʌnsɪeɪt] vt énoncer; (word) articuler, prononcer
envelop [ɪnˈveləp] vt envelopper
envelope [ˈenvələʊp] n enveloppe f
envious [ˈenvɪəs] adj envieux(euse)
environment [ɪnˈvaɪərənmənt] n environnement m; (social, moral) milieu m; **~al** [ɪnvaɪərənˈmentl] adj écologique; du milieu; **~-friendly** adj écologique
envisage [ɪnˈvɪzɪdʒ] vt (foresee) prévoir
envoy [ˈenvɔɪ] n (diplomat) ministre m plénipotentiaire
envy [ˈenvɪ] n envie f ♦ vt envier; **to ~ sb sth** envier qch à qn
epic [ˈepɪk] n épopée f ♦ adj épique
epidemic [epɪˈdemɪk] n épidémie f
epilepsy [ˈepɪlepsɪ] n épilepsie f
episode [ˈepɪsəʊd] n épisode m
epitome [ɪˈpɪtəmɪ] n modèle m; **epitomize** [ɪˈpɪtəmaɪz] vt incarner
equable [ˈekwəbl] adj égal(e); de tempérament égal
equal [ˈiːkwl] adj égal(e) ♦ n égal(e) ♦ vt égaler; **~ to** (task) à la hauteur de; **~ity** [ɪˈkwɒlɪtɪ] n égalité f; **~ize** vi (SPORT) égaliser; **~ly** adv également; (just as) tout aussi
equanimity [ekwəˈnɪmɪtɪ] n égalité f d'hu-

meur

equate [ɪ'kweɪt] *vt*: **to ~ sth with** comparer qch à; assimiler qch à; **equation** [ɪ'kweɪʒən] *n* (MATH) équation *f*

equator [ɪ'kweɪtə*] *n* équateur *m*

equilibrium [iːkwɪ'lɪbrɪəm] *n* équilibre *m*

equip [ɪ'kwɪp] *vt*: **to ~ (with)** équiper (de); **to be well ~ped** (office etc) être bien équipé(e); **he is well ~ped for the job** il a les compétences requises pour ce travail; **~ment** *n* équipement *m*; (electrical etc) appareillage *m*, installation *f*

equities [ɪ'kwɪtɪz] (BRIT) *npl* (COMM) actions cotées en Bourse

equivalent [ɪ'kwɪvələnt] *adj*: **~ (to)** équivalent(e) (à) ♦ *n* équivalent *m*

equivocal [ɪ'kwɪvəkəl] *adj* équivoque; (open to suspicion) douteux (euse)

era ['ɪərə] *n* ère *f*, époque *f*

eradicate [ɪ'rædɪkeɪt] *vt* éliminer

erase [ɪ'reɪz] *vt* effacer; **~r** *n* gomme *f*

erect [ɪ'rekt] *adj* droit(e) ♦ *vt* construire; (monument) ériger; élever; (tent etc) dresser; **~ion** [ɪ'rekʃən] *n* érection *f*

ERM *n abbr* (= Exchange Rate Mechanism) SME *m*

erode [ɪ'rəʊd] *vt* éroder; (metal) ronger

erotic [ɪ'rɒtɪk] *adj* érotique

err [ɜː*] *vi* (formal: make a mistake) se tromper

errand ['erənd] *n* course *f*, commission *f*

erratic [ɪ'rætɪk] *adj* irrégulier(ère); inconstant(e)

error ['erə*] *n* erreur *f*

erupt [ɪ'rʌpt] *vi* entrer en éruption; (fig) éclater; **~ion** [ɪ'rʌpʃən] *n* éruption *f*

escalate ['eskəleɪt] *vi* s'intensifier

escalator ['eskəleɪtə*] *n* escalier roulant

escapade [eskə'peɪd] *n* fredaine *f*, équipée *f*

escape [ɪs'keɪp] *n* fuite *f*; (from prison) évasion *f* ♦ *vi* s'échapper, fuir; (from jail) s'évader; (fig) s'en tirer; (leak) s'échapper ♦ *vt* échapper à; **to ~ from** (person) échapper à; (place) s'échapper de; (fig) fuir; **escapism** [-ɪzəm] *n* (fig) évasion *f*

escort [*n* 'eskɔːt, *vb* ɪs'kɔːt] *n* escorte *f* ♦ *vt* escorter

Eskimo ['eskɪməʊ] *n* Esquimau(de)

esophagus [iː'sɒfəgəs] (US) *n* = **oesophagus**

especially [ɪs'peʃəlɪ] *adv* (particularly) particulièrement; (above all) surtout

espionage ['espɪɒnɑːʒ] *n* espionnage *m*

Esquire [ɪs'kwaɪə*] *n*: **J Brown, ~** Monsieur J. Brown

essay ['eseɪ] *n* (SCOL) dissertation *f*, (LITERATURE) essai *m*

essence ['esns] *n* essence *f*

essential [ɪ'senʃəl] *adj* essentiel(le); (basic) fondamental(e) ♦ *n*: **~s** éléments essentiels; **~ly** *adv* essentiellement

establish [ɪs'tæblɪʃ] *vt* établir; (business) fonder, créer; (one's power etc) asseoir, affermir; **~ed** *adj* bien établi(e); **~ment** *n* établissement *m*; (founding) création *f*; **the E~ment** les pouvoirs établis; l'ordre établi; les milieux dirigeants

estate [ɪs'teɪt] *n* (land) domaine *m*, propriété *f*; (LAW) biens *mpl*, succession *f*; (BRIT: also: housing ~) lotissement *m*, cité *f*; **~ agent** *n* agent immobilier; **~ car** (BRIT) *n* break *m*

esteem [ɪs'tiːm] *n* estime *f*

esthetic [ɪs'θetɪk] (US) *adj* = **aesthetic**

estimate [*n* 'estɪmət, *vb* 'estɪmeɪt] *n* estimation *f*; (COMM) devis *m* ♦ *vt* estimer; **estimation** [estɪ'meɪʃən] *n* opinion *f*; (calculation) estimation *f*

estranged [ɪ'streɪndʒd] *adj* séparé(e); dont on s'est séparé(e)

etc. *abbr* (= et cetera) etc

etching ['etʃɪŋ] *n* eau-forte *f*

eternal [ɪ'tɜːnl] *adj* éternel(le)

eternity [ɪ'tɜːnɪtɪ] *n* éternité *f*

ethical ['eθɪkəl] *adj* moral(e); **ethics** ['eθɪks] *n* éthique *f* ♦ *npl* moralité *f*

Ethiopia [iːθɪ'əʊpɪə] *n* Éthiopie *f*

ethnic ['eθnɪk] *adj* ethnique; (music etc) folklorique

ethos ['iːθɒs] *n* génie *m*

etiquette ['etɪket] *n* convenances *fpl*, étiquette *f*

Eurocheque ['jʊərəʊ'tʃek] *n* eurochèque *m*

Europe ['jʊərəp] *n* Europe *f*; **~an** [jʊərə'piːən] *adj* européen(ne) ♦ *n* Européen(ne)

evacuate [ɪ'vækjueɪt] *vt* évacuer

evade [ɪ'veɪd] *vt* échapper à; (question etc) éluder; (duties) se dérober à; **to ~ tax** frauder le fisc

evaporate [ɪ'væpəreɪt] *vi* s'évaporer; **~d milk** *n* lait condensé non sucré

evasion [ɪ'veɪʒən] *n* dérobade *f*; **tax ~** fraude fiscale

eve [iːv] *n*: **on the ~ of** à la veille de

even ['iːvən] *adj* (level, smooth) régulier(ère); (equal) égal(e); (number) pair(e) ♦ *adv* même; **~ if** même si +indic; **~ though** alors même que +cond; **~ more** encore plus; **~ so** quand même; **not ~** pas même; **to get ~ with sb** prendre sa revanche sur qn; **~ out** *vi* s'égaliser

evening ['iːvnɪŋ] *n* soir *m*; (as duration, event) soirée *f*; **in the ~** le soir; **~ class** *n* cours *m* du soir; **~ dress** *n* tenue *f* de soirée

event [ɪ'vent] *n* événement *m*; (SPORT) épreuve *f*; **in the ~ of** en cas de; **~ful** *adj* mouvementé(e)

eventual [ɪ'ventʃʊəl] *adj* final(e); **~ity** [ɪventʃʊ'ælɪtɪ] *n* possibilité *f*, éventualité *f*; **~ly** *adv* finalement

ever ['evə*] *adv* jamais; (at all times) toujours; **the best** ~ le meilleur qu'on ait jamais vu; **have you** ~ **seen it?** l'as-tu déjà vu?, as-tu eu l'occasion *or* t'est-il arrivé de le voir?; **why** ~ **not?** mais enfin, pourquoi pas?; ~ **since** *adv* depuis ♦ *conj* depuis que; ~**green** *n* arbre *m* à feuilles persistantes; ~**lasting** *adj* éternel(le)

every ['evrɪ] *adj* chaque; ~ **day** tous les jours, chaque jour; ~ **other/third day** tous les deux/trois jours; ~ **other car** une voiture sur deux; ~ **now and then** de temps en temps; ~**body** *pron* tout le monde, tous *pl*; ~**day** *adj* quotidien(ne); de tous les jours; ~**one** *pron* = **everybody**; ~**thing** *pron* tout; ~**where** *adv* partout

evict [ɪ'vɪkt] *vt* expulser; ~**ion** [ɪ'vɪkʃən] *n* expulsion *f*

evidence ['evɪdəns] *n* (*proof*) preuve(s) *f(pl)*; (*of witness*) témoignage *m*; (*sign*): **to show** ~ **of** présenter des signes de; **to give** ~ témoigner, déposer

evident ['evɪdənt] *adj* évident(e); ~**ly** *adv* de toute évidence; (*apparently*) apparamment

evil ['iːvl] *adj* mauvais(e) ♦ *n* mal *m*

evoke [ɪ'vəʊk] *vt* évoquer

evolution [iːvə'luːʃən] *n* évolution *f*

evolve [ɪ'vɒlv] *vt* élaborer ♦ *vi* évoluer

ewe [juː] *n* brebis *f*

ex- [eks] *prefix* ex-

exact [ɪg'zækt] *adj* exact(e) ♦ *vt*: **to** ~ **sth (from)** extorquer qch (à); exiger qch (de); ~**ing** *adj* exigeant(e); (*work*) astreignant(e); ~**ly** *adv* exactement

exaggerate [ɪg'zædʒəreɪt] *vt, vi* exagérer; **exaggeration** [ɪgzædʒə'reɪʃən] *n* exagération *f*

exalted [ɪg'zɔːltɪd] *adj* (*prominent*) élevé(e); (: *person*) haut placé(e)

exam [ɪg'zæm] *n abbr* (*SCOL*) = **examination**

examination [ɪgzæmɪ'neɪʃən] *n* (*SCOL, MED*) examen *m*

examine [ɪg'zæmɪn] *vt* (*gen*) examiner; (*SCOL: person*) interroger; ~**r** *n* examinateur(trice)

example [ɪg'zɑːmpl] *n* exemple *m*; **for** ~ par exemple

exasperate [ɪg'zɑːspəreɪt] *vt* exaspérer; **exasperation** [ɪgzɑːspə'reɪʃən] *n* exaspération *f*, irritation *f*

excavate ['ekskəveɪt] *vt* excaver; **excavation** [ekskə'veɪʃən] *n* fouilles *fpl*

exceed [ɪk'siːd] *vt* dépasser; (*one's powers*) outrepasser; ~**ingly** *adv* extrêmement

excellent ['eksələnt] *adj* excellent(e)

except [ɪk'sept] *prep* (*also*: ~ **for**, ~**ing**) sauf, excepté ♦ *vt* excepter; ~ **if/when** sauf si/quand; ~ **that** sauf que, si ce n'est que; ~**ion** [ɪk'sepʃən] *n* exception *f*; **to take** ~**ion to** s'offusquer de; ~**ional** [ɪk'sepʃənl] *adj* exceptionnel(le)

excerpt ['eksɜːpt] *n* extrait *m*

excess [ek'ses] *n* excès *m*; ~ **baggage** *n* excédent *m* de bagages; ~ **fare** (*BRIT*) *n* supplément *m*; ~**ive** *adj* excessif(ive)

exchange [ɪks'tʃeɪndʒ] *n* échange *m*; (*also*: *telephone* ~) central *m* ♦ *vt*: **to** ~ **(for)** échanger (contre); ~ **rate** *n* taux *m* de change

Exchequer [ɪks'tʃekə*] (*BRIT*) *n*: **the** ~ l'Échiquier *m*, ≈ le ministère des Finances

excise [*n* 'eksaɪz, *vb* ek'saɪz] *n* taxe *f* ♦ *vt* exciser

excite [ɪk'saɪt] *vt* exciter; **to get** ~**d** s'exciter; ~**ment** *n* excitation *f*; **exciting** *adj* passionnant(e)

exclaim [ɪks'kleɪm] *vi* s'exclamer; **exclamation** [eksklə'meɪʃən] *n* exclamation *f*; **exclamation mark** *n* point *m* d'exclamation

exclude [ɪks'kluːd] *vt* exclure

exclusive [ɪks'kluːsɪv] *adj* exclusif(ive); (*club, district*) sélect(e); (*item of news*) en exclusivité; ~ **of VAT** TVA non comprise; **mutually** ~ qui s'excluent l'un(e) l'autre

excruciating [ɪks'kruːʃɪeɪtɪŋ] *adj* atroce

excursion [ɪks'kɜːʃən] *n* excursion *f*

excuse [*n* ɪks'kjuːs, *vb* ɪks'kjuːz] *n* excuse *f* ♦ *vt* excuser; **to** ~ **sb from** (*activity*) dispenser qn de; ~ **me!** excusez-moi!, pardon!; **now if you will** ~ **me,** ... maintenant, si vous (le) permettez ...

ex-directory ['eksdaɪ'rektərɪ] (*BRIT*) *adj* sur la liste rouge

execute ['eksɪkjuːt] *vt* exécuter

execution [eksɪ'kjuːʃən] *n* exécution *f*; ~**er** *n* bourreau *m*

executive [ɪg'zekjʊtɪv] *n* (*COMM*) cadre *m*; (*of organization, political party*) bureau *m* ♦ *adj* exécutif(ive)

exemplify [ɪg'zemplɪfaɪ] *vt* illustrer; (*typify*) incarner

exempt [ɪg'zempt] *adj*: ~ **from** exempté(e) *or* dispensé(e) de ♦ *vt*: **to** ~ **sb from** exempter *or* dispenser qn de

exercise ['eksəsaɪz] *n* exercice *m* ♦ *vt* exercer; (*patience etc*) faire preuve de; (*dog*) promener ♦ *vi* prendre de l'exercice; ~ **bike** *n* vélo *m* d'appartement; ~ **book** *n* cahier *m*

exert [ɪg'zɜːt] *vt* exercer, employer; **to** ~ **o.s.** se dépenser; ~**ion** [ɪg'zɜːʃən] *n* effort *m*

exhale [eks'heɪl] *vt* exhaler ♦ *vi* expirer

exhaust [ɪg'zɔːst] *n* (*also*: ~ *fumes*) gaz *mpl* d'échappement; (: ~ *pipe*) tuyau *m* d'échappement ♦ *vt* épuiser; ~**ed** *adj* épuisé(e); ~**ion** [ɪg'zɔːstʃən] *n* épuisement *m*; **nervous** ~**ion** fatigue nerveuse; surmenage mental; ~**ive** *adj* très complet(ète)

exhibit [ɪg'zɪbɪt] *n* (*ART*) pièce exposée, objet exposé; (*LAW*) pièce à conviction ♦ *vt* exposer; (*courage, skill*) faire preuve de;

~ion [eksɪˈbɪʃən] *n* exposition *f*; *(of ill-temper, talent etc)* démonstration *f*

exhilarating [ɪgˈzɪləreɪtɪŋ] *adj* grisant(e); stimulant(e)

exile [ˈeksaɪl] *n* exil *m*; *(person)* exilé(e) ♦ *vt* exiler

exist [ɪgˈzɪst] *vi* exister; **~ence** *n* existence *f*; **~ing** *adj* actuel(le)

exit [ˈeksɪt] *n* sortie *f* ♦ *vi (COMPUT, THEATRE)* sortir; **~ ramp** *n (AUT)* bretelle *f* d'accès

exodus [ˈeksədəs] *n* exode *m*

exonerate [ɪgˈzɒnəreɪt] *vt*: **to ~ from** disculper de

exotic [ɪgˈzɒtɪk] *adj* exotique

expand [ɪksˈpænd] *vt* agrandir; accroître ♦ *vi (trade etc)* se développer, s'accroître; *(gas, metal)* se dilater

expanse [ɪksˈpæns] *n* étendue *f*

expansion [ɪksˈpænʃən] *n* développement *m*, accroissement *m*

expect [ɪksˈpekt] *vt (anticipate)* s'attendre à, s'attendre à ce que +*sub*; *(count on)* compter sur, escompter; *(require)* demander, exiger; *(suppose)* supposer; *(await, also baby)* attendre ♦ *vi*: **to be ~ing** être enceinte; **~ancy** *n (anticipation)* attente *f*; **life ~ancy** espérance *f* de vie; **~ant mother** *n* future maman; **~ation** [ekspekˈteɪʃən] *n* attente *f*, espérance(s) *f(pl)*

expedient [ɪksˈpiːdɪənt] *adj* indiqué(e), opportun(e) ♦ *n* expédient *m*

expedition [ekspɪˈdɪʃən] *n* expédition *f*

expel [ɪksˈpel] *vt* chasser, expulser; *(SCOL)* renvoyer

expend [ɪksˈpend] *vt* consacrer; *(money)* dépenser; **~able** *adj* remplaçable; **~iture** [ɪkˈspendɪtʃə*] *n* dépense *f*; dépenses *fpl*

expense [ɪksˈpens] *n* dépense *f*, frais *mpl*; *(high cost)* coût *m*; **~s** *npl (COMM)* frais *mpl*; **at the ~ of** aux dépens de; **~ account** *n* (note *f* de) frais *mpl*

expensive [ɪksˈpensɪv] *adj* cher(chère), coûteux(euse); **to be ~** coûter cher

experience [ɪksˈpɪərɪəns] *n* expérience *f* ♦ *vt* connaître, faire l'expérience de; *(feeling)* éprouver; **~d** *adj* expérimenté(e)

experiment [*n* ɪksˈperɪmənt, *vb* ɪksˈperɪment] *n* expérience *f* ♦ *vi* faire une expérience; **to ~ with** expérimenter

expert [ˈekspɜːt] *adj* expert(e) ♦ *n* expert *m*; **~ise** [ekspəˈtiːz] *n* (grande) compétence *f*

expire [ɪksˈpaɪə*] *vi* expirer; **expiry** *n* expiration *f*

explain [ɪksˈpleɪn] *vt* expliquer; **explanation** [ekspləˈneɪʃən] *n* explication *f*; **explanatory** [ɪksˈplænətərɪ] *adj* explicatif(ive)

explicit [ɪksˈplɪsɪt] *adj* explicite; *(definite)* formel(le)

explode [ɪksˈpləʊd] *vi* exploser

exploit [*n* ˈeksplɔɪt, *vb* ɪksˈplɔɪt] *n* exploit *m* ♦ *vt* exploiter; **~ation** [eksplɔɪˈteɪʃən] *n* ex-

ploitation *f*

exploratory [eksˈplɒrətərɪ] *adj (expedition)* d'exploration; *(fig: talks)* préliminaire; **~ operation** *n (MED)* sondage *m*

explore [ɪksˈplɔː*] *vt* explorer; *(possibilities)* étudier, examiner; **~r** *n* explorateur(trice)

explosion [ɪksˈpləʊʒən] *n* explosion *f*; **explosive** [ɪksˈpləʊzɪv] *adj* explosif(ive) ♦ *n* explosif *m*

exponent [eksˈpəʊnənt] *n (of school of thought etc)* interprète *m*, représentant *m*

export [*vb* eksˈpɔːt, *n* ˈekspɔːt] *vt* exporter ♦ *n* exportation *f* ♦ *cpd* d'exportation; **~er** *n* exportateur *m*

expose [ɪksˈpəʊz] *vt* exposer; *(unmask)* démasquer, dévoiler; **~d** [ɪksˈpəʊzd] *adj (position, house)* exposé(e)

exposure [ɪksˈpəʊʒə*] *n* exposition *f*; *(publicity)* couverture *f*; *(PHOT)* (temps *m* de) pose *f*; (: *shot*) pose; **to die from ~** *(MED)* mourir de froid; **~ meter** *n* posemètre *m*

express [ɪksˈpres] *adj (definite)* formel(le), exprès(esse); *(BRIT: letter etc)* exprès *inv* ♦ *n (train)* rapide *m*; *(bus)* car *m* express ♦ *vt* exprimer; **~ion** [ɪksˈpreʃən] *n* expression *f*; **~ly** *adv* expressément, formellement; **~way** *(US)* *n (urban motorway)* voie *f* express (à plusieurs files)

exquisite [eksˈkwɪzɪt] *adj* exquis(e)

extend [ɪksˈtend] *vt (visit, street)* prolonger; *(building)* agrandir; *(offer)* présenter, offrir; *(hand, arm)* tendre ♦ *vi* s'étendre

extension [ɪksˈtenʃən] *n* prolongation *f*; agrandissement *m*; *(building)* annexe *f*; *(to wire, table)* rallonge *f*; *(telephone: in offices)* poste *m*; (: *in private house)* téléphone *m* supplémentaire

extensive [ɪksˈtensɪv] *adj* étendu(e), vaste; *(damage, alterations)* considérable; *(inquiries)* approfondi(e); **~ly** *adv*: **he's travelled ~ly** il a beaucoup voyagé

extent [ɪksˈtent] *n* étendue *f*; **to some ~** dans une certaine mesure; **to what ~?** dans quelle mesure?; **to the ~ of ...** au point de ...; **to such an ~ that ...** à tel point que ...

extenuating [eksˈtenjʊeɪtɪŋ] *adj*: **~ circumstances** circonstances atténuantes

exterior [eksˈtɪərɪə*] *adj* extérieur(e) ♦ *n* extérieur *m*; dehors *m*

external [eksˈtɜːnl] *adj* externe

extinct [ɪksˈtɪŋkt] *adj* éteint(e)

extinguish [ɪksˈtɪŋgwɪʃ] *vt* éteindre; **~er** *n (also: fire ~er)* extincteur *m*

extort [ɪksˈtɔːt] *vt*: **to ~ sth (from)** extorquer qch (à); **~ionate** [ɪksˈtɔːʃənɪt] *adj* exorbitant(e)

extra [ˈekstrə] *adj* supplémentaire, de plus ♦ *adv (in addition)* en plus ♦ *n* supplément *m*; *(perk)* à-côté *m*; *(THEATRE)* figurant(e) ♦ *prefix* extra...

extract [*vb* ɪksˈtrækt, *n* ˈekstrækt] *vt* extrai-

re; (*tooth*) arracher; (*money, promise*) soutirer ♦ *n* extrait *m*
extracurricular ['ekstrəkə'rıkjolə*] *adj* pa-
rascolaire
extradite ['ekstrədaıt] *vt* extrader
extra: ~**marital** [ekstrə'mærıtl] *adj* extra-
conjugal(e); ~**mural** [ekstrə'mjʊərl] *adj*
hors faculté *inv*; (*lecture*) public(que); ~**ordinary** [ıks'trɔːdnrı] *adj* extraordinaire
extravagance [ıks'trævəgəns] *n* prodigali-
tés *fpl*; (*thing bought*) folie *f*, dépense excessive; **extravagant** [ıks'trævəgənt] *adj* ex-
travagant(e); (*in spending: person*) prodigue,
dépensier(ère); (: *tastes*) dispendieux(euse)
extreme [ıks'triːm] *adj* extrême ♦ *n* extrême
m; ~**ly** *adv* extrêmement
extricate ['ekstrıkeıt] *vt*: **to ~ sth (from)**
dégager qch (de)
extrovert ['ekstrəʊvɜːt] *n* extraverti(e)
eye [aı] *n* œil *m* (*pl yeux*); (*of needle*) trou
m, chas *m* ♦ *vt* examiner; **to keep an ~ on**
surveiller; ~**ball** *n* globe *m* oculaire;
~**bath** (*BRIT*) *n* œillère *f* (*pour bains d'œil*);
~**brow** *n* sourcil *m*; ~**brow pencil** *n*
crayon *m* à sourcils; ~**drops** *npl* gouttes
fpl pour les yeux; ~**lash** *n* cil *m*; ~**lid** *n*
paupière *f*; ~**liner** *n* eye-liner *m*; ~-
opener *n* révélation *f*, ~**shadow** *n* ombre
f à paupières; ~**sight** *n* vue *f*; ~**sore** *n*
horreur *f*; ~ **witness** *n* témoin *m* oculaire

<hr/>

F f

F [ef] *n* (*MUS*) fa *m* ♦ *abbr* = Fahrenheit
fable ['feıbl] *n* fable *f*
fabric ['fæbrık] *n* tissu *m*
fabrication [fæbrı'keıʃən] *n* (*lies*) inven-
tion(s) *f(pl)*, fabulation *f*; (*making*) fabrication *f*
fabulous ['fæbjʊləs] *adj* fabuleux(euse); (*inf:
super*) formidable
face [feıs] *n* visage *m*, figure *f*; (*expression*)
expression *f*; (*of clock*) cadran *m*; (*of cliff*)
paroi *f*; (*of mountain*) face *f*; (*of building*)
façade *f* ♦ *vt* faire face à; ~ **down** (*person*)
à plat ventre; (*card*) face en dessous; **to
lose/save** ~ perdre/sauver la face; **to
make** *or* **pull a** ~ faire une grimace; **in the**
~ **of** (*difficulties etc*) face à, devant; **on the**
~ **of it** à première vue; ~ **to** ~ face à face;
~ **up to** *vt fus* faire face à, affronter; ~
cloth (*BRIT*) *n* gant *m* de toilette; ~
cream *n* crème *f* pour le visage; ~ **lift**

lifting *m*; (*of building etc*) ravalement *m*, re-
tapage *m*; ~ **powder** *n* poudre *f* de riz; ~
value *n* (*of coin*) valeur nominale; **to take
sth at** ~ **value** (*fig*) prendre qch pour argent comptant
facilities [fə'sılıtız] *npl* installations *fpl*,
équipement *m*; **credit** ~ facilités *fpl* de
paiement
facing ['feısıŋ] *prep* face à, en face de
facsimile [fæk'sımılı] *n* (*exact replica*) fac-
similé *m*; (*fax*) télécopie *f*
fact [fækt] *n* fait *m*; **in** ~ en fait
factor ['fæktə*] *n* facteur *m*
factory ['fæktərı] *n* usine *f*, fabrique *f*
factual ['fæktjʊəl] *adj* basé(e) sur les faits
faculty ['fækəltı] *n* faculté *f*; (*US: teaching
staff*) corps enseignant
fad [fæd] *n* (*craze*) engouement *m*
fade [feıd] *vi* se décolorer, passer; (*light,
sound*) s'affaiblir; (*flower*) se faner
fag [fæg] (*BRIT: inf*) *n* (*cigarette*) sèche *f*
fail [feıl] *vt* (*exam*) échouer à; (*candidate*)
recaler; (*subj: courage, memory*) faire défaut
à ♦ *vi* échouer; (*brakes*) lâcher; (*eyesight,
health, light*) baisser, s'affaiblir; **to** ~ **to do
sth** (*neglect*) négliger de faire qch; (*be unable*) ne pas arriver *or* parvenir à faire qch;
without ~ à coup sûr; sans faute; ~**ing** *n*
défaut *m* ♦ *prep* faute de; ~**ure** *n* échec *m*;
(*person*) raté(e); (*mechanical etc*) défaillance
f
faint [feınt] *adj* faible; (*recollection*) vague;
(*mark*) à peine visible ♦ *n* évanouissement
m ♦ *vi* s'évanouir; **to feel** ~ défaillir
fair [feə*] *adj* équitable, juste, impartial(e);
(*hair*) blond(e); (*skin, complexion*) pâle,
blanc(blanche); (*weather*) beau(belle);
(*good enough*) assez bon(ne); (*sizeable*)
considérable ♦ *adv*: **to play** ~ jouer franc-
jeu ♦ *n* foire *f*; (*BRIT: fun~*) fête (foraine);
~**ly** *adv* équitablement; (*quite*) assez;
~**ness** *n* justice *f*, équité *f*, impartialité *f*
fairy ['feərı] *n* fée *f*; ~ **tale** *n* conte *m* de
fées
faith [feıθ] *n* foi *f*; (*trust*) confiance *f*; (*specific religion*) religion *f*; ~**ful** *adj* fidèle;
~**fully** *adv* see **yours**
fake [feık] *n* (*painting etc*) faux *m*; (*person*)
imposteur *m* ♦ *adj* faux(fausse) ♦ *vt* simuler;
(*painting*) faire un faux de
falcon ['fɔːlkən] *n* faucon *m*
fall [fɔːl] (*pt* **fell**, *pp* **fallen**) *n* chute *f*; (*US:
autumn*) automne *m* ♦ *vi* tomber; (*price,
temperature, dollar*) baisser; ~**s** *npl* (*waterfall*) chute *f* d'eau, cascade *f*; **to** ~ **flat** (*on
one's face*) tomber de tout son long, s'éta-
ler; (*joke*) tomber à plat; (*plan*) échouer; ~
back *vi* reculer, se retirer; ~ **back on** *vt
fus* se rabattre sur; ~ **behind** *vi* prendre
du retard; ~ **down** *vi* (*person*) tomber;
(*building*) s'effondrer, s'écrouler; ~ **for** *vt
fus* (*trick, story etc*) se laisser prendre à;

(*person*) tomber amoureux de; ~ **in** *vi* s'effondrer; (*MIL*) se mettre en rangs; ~ **off** *vi* tomber; (*diminish*) baisser, diminuer; ~ **out** *vi* (*hair, teeth*) tomber; (*MIL*) rompre les rangs; (*friends etc*) se brouiller; ~ **through** *vi* (*plan, project*) tomber à l'eau

fallacy ['fæləsɪ] *n* erreur *f*, illusion *f*

fallout ['fɔːlaut] *n* retombées (radioactives); ~ **shelter** *n* abri *m* antiatomique

fallow ['fæləu] *adj* en jachère; en friche

false [fɔːls] *adj* faux(fausse); ~ **alarm** *n* fausse alerte; ~ **pretences** *npl*: **under** ~ **pretences** sous un faux prétexte; ~ **teeth** (*BRIT*) *npl* fausses dents

falter ['fɔːltə*] *vi* chanceler, vaciller

fame [feɪm] *n* renommée *f*, renom *m*

familiar [fə'mɪlɪə*] *adj* familier(ère); **to be** ~ **with** (*subject*) connaître

family ['fæmɪlɪ] *n* famille *f* ♦ *cpd* (*business, doctor etc*) de famille; **has he any** ~? (*children*) a-t-il des enfants?

famine ['fæmɪn] *n* famine *f*

famished ['fæmɪʃt] (*inf*) *adj* affamé(e)

famous ['feɪməs] *adj* célèbre; ~**ly** *adv* (*get on*) fameusement, à merveille

fan [fæn] *n* (*folding*) éventail *m*; (*ELEC*) ventilateur *m*; (*of person*) fan *m*, admirateur(trice); (*of team, sport etc*) supporter *m/f* ♦ *vt* éventer; (*fire, quarrel*) attiser; ~ **out** *vi* se déployer (en éventail)

fanatic [fə'nætɪk] *n* fanatique *m/f*

fan belt *n* courroie *f* de ventilateur

fanciful ['fænsɪful] *adj* fantaisiste

fancy ['fænsɪ] *n* fantaisie *f*, envie *f*; imagination *f* ♦ *adj* (*de*) fantaisie *inv* ♦ *vt* (*feel like, want*) avoir envie de; (*imagine, think*) imaginer; **to take a** ~ **to** se prendre d'affection pour; s'enticher de; **he fancies her** (*inf*) elle lui plaît; ~ **dress** *n* déguisement *m*, travesti *m*; ~-**dress ball** *n* bal masqué *or* costumé

fang [fæŋ] *n* croc *m*; (*of snake*) crochet *m*

fantastic [fæn'tæstɪk] *adj* fantastique

fantasy ['fæntəzɪ] *n* imagination *f*, fantaisie *f*; (*dream*) chimère *f*

far [fɑː*] *adj* lointain(e), éloigné(e) ♦ *adv* loin; ~ **away** *or* **off** au loin, dans le lointain; **at the** ~ **side/end** à l'autre côté/bout; ~ **better** beaucoup mieux; ~ **from** loin de; **by** ~ de loin, de beaucoup; **go as** ~ **as the farm** allez jusqu'à la ferme; **as** ~ **as I know** pour autant que je sache; **how** ~ **is it to ...?** combien y a-t-il jusqu'à ...?; **how** ~ **have you got?** où en êtes-vous?; ~**away** *adj* lointain(e); (*look*) distrait(e)

farce [fɑːs] *n* farce *f*

farcical ['fɑːsɪkəl] *adj* grotesque

fare [fɛə*] *n* (*on trains, buses*) prix *m* du billet; (*in taxi*) prix de la course; (*food*) table *f*, chère *f*; **half** ~ demi-tarif; **full** ~ plein tarif

Far East *n*: **the** ~ l'Extrême-Orient *m*

farewell [fɛə'wel] *excl* adieu ♦ *n* adieu

farm [fɑːm] *n* ferme *f* ♦ *vt* cultiver; ~**er** *n* fermier(ère); cultivateur(trice); ~**hand** *n* ouvrier(ère) agricole; ~**house** *n* (maison *f* de) ferme *f*; ~**ing** *n* agriculture *f*; (*of animals*) élevage *m*; ~**land** *n* terres cultivées; ~ **worker** *n* = **farmhand**; ~**yard** *n* cour *f* de ferme

far-reaching ['fɑː'riːtʃɪŋ] *adj* d'une grande portée

fart [fɑːt] (*inf!*) *vi* péter

farther ['fɑːðə*] *adv* plus loin ♦ *adj* plus éloigné(e), plus lointain(e)

farthest ['fɑːðɪst] *superl of* **far**

fascinate ['fæsɪneɪt] *vt* fasciner; **fascinating** *adj* fascinant(e)

fascism ['fæʃɪzəm] *n* fascisme *m*

fashion ['fæʃən] *n* mode *f*; (*manner*) façon *f*, manière *f* ♦ *vt* façonner; **in** ~ à la mode; **out of** ~ démodé(e); ~**able** *adj* à la mode; ~ **show** *n* défilé *m* de mannequins *or* de mode

fast [fɑːst] *adj* rapide; (*clock*): **to be** ~ avancer; (*dye, colour*) grand *or* bon teint *inv* ♦ *adv* vite, rapidement; (*stuck, held*) solidement ♦ *n* jeûne *m* ♦ *vi* jeûner; ~ **asleep** profondément endormi

fasten ['fɑːsn] *vt* attacher, fixer; (*coat*) attacher, fermer ♦ *vi* se fermer, s'attacher; ~**er** *n* attache *f*; ~**ing** *n* = **fastener**

fast food *n* fast food *m*, restauration *f* rapide

fastidious [fæs'tɪdɪəs] *adj* exigeant(e), difficile

fat [fæt] *adj* gros(se) ♦ *n* graisse *f*; (*on meat*) gras *m*; (*for cooking*) matière grasse

fatal ['feɪtl] *adj* (*injury etc*) mortel(le); (*mistake*) fatal(e); ~**ity** [fə'tælɪtɪ] *n* (*road death etc*) victime *f*, décès *m*

fate [feɪt] *n* destin *m*; (*of person*) sort *m*; ~**ful** *adj* fatidique

father ['fɑːðə*] *n* père *m*; ~-**in-law** *n* beau-père *m*; ~**ly** *adj* paternel(le)

fathom ['fæðəm] *n* brasse *f* (= 1828 mm) ♦ *vt* (*mystery*) sonder, pénétrer

fatigue [fə'tiːg] *n* fatigue *f*

fatten ['fætn] *vt, vi* engraisser

fatty ['fætɪ] *adj* (*food*) gras(se) ♦ *n* (*inf*) gros(se)

fatuous ['fætjuəs] *adj* stupide

faucet ['fɔːsɪt] (*US*) *n* robinet *m*

fault [fɔːlt] *n* faute *f*; (*defect*) défaut *m*; (*GEO*) faille *f* ♦ *vt* trouver des défauts à; **it's my** ~ c'est de ma faute; **to find** ~ **with** trouver à redire *or* à critiquer à; **at** ~ fautif(ive), coupable; ~**y** *adj* défectueux(euse)

fauna ['fɔːnə] *n* faune *f*

faux pas ['fəu'pɑː] *n inv* impair *m*, bévue *f*, gaffe *f*

favour ['feɪvə*] (*US* **favor**) *n* faveur *f*; (*help*) service *m* ♦ *vt* (*proposition*) être en faveur de; (*pupil etc*) favoriser; (*team, horse*) donner gagnant; **to do sb a ~** rendre un service à qn; **to find ~ with** trouver grâce aux yeux de; **in ~ of** en faveur de; **~able** adj favorable; **~ite** ['feɪvərɪt] adj, n favori(te)

fawn [fɔːn] n faon m ♦ adj (also: ~-coloured) fauve ♦ vi: **to ~ (up)on** flatter servilement

fax [fæks] n (document) télécopie f; (machine) télécopieur m ♦ vt envoyer par télécopie

FBI ['efbiː'aɪ] n abbr (US: = Federal Bureau of Investigation) F.B.I. m

fear [fɪə*] n crainte f, peur f ♦ vt craindre; **for ~ of** de peur que +sub, de peur de +infin; **~ful** adj craintif(ive); (sight, noise) affreux(euse), épouvantable; **~less** adj intrépide

feasible ['fiːzəbl] adj faisable, réalisable

feast [fiːst] n festin m, banquet m; (REL: also: ~ day) fête f ♦ vi festoyer

feat [fiːt] n exploit m, prouesse f

feather ['feðə*] n plume f

feature ['fiːtʃə*] n caractéristique f; (article) chronique f, rubrique f ♦ vt (subj: film) avoir pour vedette(s) ♦ vi: **to ~ in** figurer (en bonne place) dans; (in film) jouer dans; **~s** npl (of face) traits mpl; **~ film** n long métrage

February ['februərɪ] n février m

fed [fed] pt, pp of **feed**

federal ['fedərəl] adj fédéral(e)

fed up adj: **to be ~** en avoir marre, en avoir plein le dos

fee [fiː] n rémunération f; (of doctor, lawyer) honoraires mpl; (for examination) droits mpl; **school ~s** frais mpl de scolarité

feeble ['fiːbl] adj faible; (pathetic: attempt, excuse) pauvre; (:joke) piteux(euse)

feed [fiːd] (pt, pp **fed**) n (of baby) tétée f; (of animal) fourrage m; pâture f; (on printer) mécanisme m d'alimentation ♦ vt (person) nourrir; (BRIT: baby) allaiter; (: with bottle) donner le biberon à; (horse etc) donner à manger à; (machine) alimenter; (data, information): **to ~ sth into** fournir qch à; **~ on** vt fus se nourrir de; **~back** n feed-back m inv; **~ing bottle** (BRIT) n biberon m

feel [fiːl] (pt, pp **felt**) n sensation f; (impression) impression f ♦ vt toucher; (explore) tâter, palper; (cold, pain) sentir; (grief, anger) ressentir, éprouver; (think, believe) trouver; **to ~ hungry/cold** avoir faim/froid; **to ~ lonely/better** se sentir seul/mieux; **I don't ~ well** je ne me sens pas bien; **it ~s soft** c'est doux(douce) au toucher; **to ~ like** (want) avoir envie de; **~ about** vi fouiller, tâtonner; **~er** n (of insect) antenne f; **to put out ~ers** or a **~er** tâter le terrain; **~ing** n (physical) sensation f; (emotional) sentiment m

feet [fiːt] npl of **foot**

feign [feɪn] vt feindre, simuler

fell [fel] pt of **fall** ♦ vt (tree, person) abattre

fellow ['feləu] n type m; (comrade) compagnon m; (of learned society) membre m ♦ cpd: **their ~ prisoners/students** leurs camarades prisonniers/d'étude; **~ citizen** n concitoyen(ne) m/f; **~ countryman** (irreg) n compatriote m; **~ men** npl semblables mpl; **~ship** n (society) association f; (comradeship) amitié f, camaraderie f; (grant) sorte de bourse universitaire

felony ['feiənɪ] n crime m, forfait m

felt [felt] pt, pp of **feel** ♦ n feutre m; **~-tip pen** n stylo-feutre m

female ['fiːmeɪl] n (ZOOL) femelle f; (pej: woman) bonne femme ♦ adj (BIO) femelle; (sex, character) féminin(e); (vote etc) des femmes

feminine ['femɪnɪn] adj féminin(e)

feminist ['femɪnɪst] n féministe m/f

fence [fens] n barrière f ♦ vt (also: ~ in) clôturer ♦ vi faire de l'escrime; **fencing** ['fensɪŋ] n escrime m

fend [fend] vi: **to ~ for o.s.** se débrouiller (tout seul); **~ off** vt (attack etc) parer

fender ['fendə*] n garde-feu m inv; (on boat) défense f; (US: of car) aile f

ferment [vb fə'ment, n 'fɜːment] vi fermenter ♦ n agitation f, effervescence f

fern [fɜːn] n fougère f

ferocious [fə'rəuʃəs] adj féroce

ferret ['ferɪt] n furet m

ferry ['ferɪ] n (small) bac m; (large: also: ~boat) ferry(-boat) m ♦ vt transporter

fertile ['fɜːtaɪl] adj fertile; (BIO) fécond(e); **fertilizer** ['fɜːtɪlaɪzə*] n engrais m

fester ['festə*] vi suppurer

festival ['festɪvəl] n (REL) fête f; (ART, MUS) festival m

festive ['festɪv] adj de fête; **the ~ season** (BRIT: Christmas) la période des fêtes; **festivities** [fes'tɪvɪtɪz] npl réjouissances fpl

festoon [fes'tuːn] vt: **to ~ with** orner de

fetch [fetʃ] vt aller chercher; (sell for) rapporter

fetching ['fetʃɪŋ] adj charmant(e)

fête [feɪt] n fête f, kermesse f

fetish ['fetɪʃ] n: **to make a ~ of** être obsédé(e) par

feud [fjuːd] n dispute f, dissension f

fever ['fiːvə*] n fièvre f; **~ish** adj fiévreux(euse), fébrile

few [fjuː] adj (not many) peu de; **a ~** adj quelques ♦ pron quelques-uns(unes); **~er** adj moins de; moins (nombreux); **~est** adj le moins (de)

fiancé, e [fɪ'ɑːnseɪ] n fiancé(e) m/f

fib [fɪb] n bobard m

fibre ['faɪbə*] (US **fiber**) n fibre f; **~-glass** ® n fibre de verre

fickle ['fɪkl] adj inconstant(e), volage, capricieux(euse)

fiction ['fɪkʃən] n romans mpl, littérature f

romanesque; (*invention*) fiction f; ~**al** *adj* fictif(ive)

fictitious [fɪk'tɪʃəs] *adj* fictif(ive), imaginaire

fiddle ['fɪdl] *n* (*MUS*) violon m; (*cheating*) combine f, escroquerie f ♦ *vt* (*BRIT*: *accounts*) falsifier, maquiller; ~ **with** *vt fus* tripoter

fidget ['fɪdʒɪt] *vi* se trémousser, remuer

field [fiːld] *n* champ m; (*fig*) domaine m, champ; (*SPORT*: *ground*) terrain m; ~ **marshal** *n* maréchal m; ~**work** *n* travaux *mpl* pratiques (sur le terrain)

fiend [fiːnd] *n* démon m; ~**ish** *adj* diabolique, abominable

fierce [fɪəs] *adj* (*look, animal*) féroce, sauvage; (*wind, attack, person*) (très) violent(e); (*fighting, enemy*) acharné(e)

fiery ['faɪərɪ] *adj* ardent(e), brûlant(e); (*temperament*) fougueux(euse)

fifteen [fɪf'tiːn] *num* quinze

fifth [fɪfθ] *num* cinquième

fifty ['fɪftɪ] *num* cinquante; ~-**fifty** *adj*: a ~-**fifty chance** *etc* une chance *etc* sur deux ♦ *adv* moitié-moitié

fig [fɪg] *n* figue f

fight [faɪt] (*pt, pp* **fought**) *n* (*MIL*) combat m; (*between persons*) bagarre f; (*against cancer etc*) lutte f ♦ *vt* se battre contre; (*cancer, alcoholism, emotion*) combattre, lutter contre; (*election*) se présenter à ♦ *vi* se battre; ~**er** *n* (*fig*) lutteur m; (*plane*) chasseur m; ~**ing** *n* combats *mpl* (*brawl*) bagarres *fpl*

figment ['fɪgmənt] *n*: a ~ **of the imagination** une invention

figurative ['fɪgərətɪv] *adj* figuré(e)

figure ['fɪgə*] *n* figure f; (*number, cipher*) chiffre m; (*body, outline*) silhouette f; (*shape*) ligne f, formes *fpl* ♦ *vt* (*think: esp US*) supposer ♦ *vi* (*appear*) figurer; ~ **out** *vt* (*work out*) calculer; ~**head** *n* (*NAUT*) figure f de proue; (*pej*) prête-nom m; ~ **of speech** *n* figure f de rhétorique

file [faɪl] *n* (*dossier*) dossier m; (*folder*) dossier, chemise f, (: *with hinges*) classeur m; (*COMPUT*) fichier m; (*row*) file f; (*tool*) lime f ♦ *vt* (*nails, wood*) limer; (*papers*) classer; (*LAW: claim*) faire enregistrer; déposer ♦ *vi*: **to** ~ **in/out** entrer/sortir l'un derrière l'autre; **to** ~ **for divorce** faire une demande en divorce; **filing cabinet** *n* classeur m (*meuble*)

fill [fɪl] *vt* remplir; (*need*) répondre à ♦ *n*: **to eat one's** ~ manger à sa faim; **to** ~ **with** remplir de; ~ **in** *vt* (*hole*) boucher; (*form*) remplir; ~ **up** *vt* remplir; ~ **it up, please** (*AUT*) le plein, s'il vous plaît

fillet ['fɪlɪt] *n* filet m; ~ **steak** *n* filet m de bœuf, tournedos m

filling ['fɪlɪŋ] *n* (*CULIN*) garniture f, farce f; (*for tooth*) plombage m; ~ **station** *n*

station-service f

film [fɪlm] *n* film m; (*PHOT*) pellicule f, film; (*of powder, liquid*) couche f, pellicule ♦ *vt* (*scene*) filmer ♦ *vi* tourner; ~ **star** *n* vedette f de cinéma

filter ['fɪltə*] *n* filtre m ♦ *vt* filtrer; ~ **lane** *n* (*AUT*) voie f de sortie; ~-**tipped** *adj* à bout filtre

filth [fɪlθ] *n* saleté f; ~**y** *adj* sale, dégoûtant(e); (*language*) ordurier(ère)

fin [fɪn] *n* (*of fish*) nageoire f

final ['faɪnl] *adj* final(e); (*definitive*) définitif(ive) ♦ *n* (*SPORT*) finale f; ~**s** *npl* (*SCOL*) examens *mpl* de dernière année; ~**e** [fɪ'nɑːlɪ] *n* finale m; ~**ize** *vt* mettre au point; ~**ly** *adv* (*eventually*) enfin, finalement; (*lastly*) en dernier lieu

finance [faɪ'næns] *n* finance f ♦ *vt* financer; ~**s** *npl* (*financial position*) finances *fpl*; **financial** [faɪ'nænʃəl] *adj* financier(ère)

find [faɪnd] (*pt, pp* **found**) *vt* trouver; (*lost object*) retrouver ♦ *n* trouvaille f, découverte f; **to** ~ **sb guilty** (*LAW*) déclarer qn coupable; ~ **out** *vt* (*truth, secret*) découvrir; (*person*) démasquer ♦ *vi*: **to** ~ **out about** (*make enquiries*) se renseigner; (*by chance*) apprendre; ~**ings** *npl* (*LAW*) conclusions *fpl*, verdict m; (*of report*) conclusions

fine [faɪn] *adj* (*excellent*) excellent(e); (*thin, not coarse, subtle*) fin(e); (*weather*) beau(belle) ♦ *adv* (*well*) très bien ♦ *n* (*LAW*) amende f; contravention f ♦ *vt* (*LAW*) condamner à une amende; donner une contravention à; **to be** ~ (*person*) aller bien; (*weather*) être beau; ~ **arts** *npl* beaux-arts *mpl*

finery ['faɪnərɪ] *n* parure f

finger ['fɪŋgə*] *n* doigt m ♦ *vt* palper, toucher; **little** ~ auriculaire m, petit doigt; **index** ~ index m; ~**nail** *n* ongle m (de la main); ~**print** *n* empreinte digitale; ~**tip** *n* bout m du doigt

finicky ['fɪnɪkɪ] *adj* tatillon(ne), méticuleux(euse); minutieux(euse)

finish ['fɪnɪʃ] *n* fin f; (*SPORT*) arrivée f; (*polish etc*) finition f ♦ *vt* finir, terminer ♦ *vi* finir, se terminer; **to** ~ **doing sth** finir de faire qch; **to** ~ **third** arriver or terminer troisième; ~ **off** *vt* finir, terminer; (*kill*) achever; ~ **up** *vi, vt* finir; ~**ing line** *n* ligne f d'arrivée; ~**ing school** *n* institution privée (*pour jeunes filles*)

finite ['faɪnaɪt] *adj* fini(e); (*verb*) conjugué(e)

Finland ['fɪnlənd] *n* Finlande f

Finn [fɪn] *n* Finnois(e); Finlandais(e); ~**ish** *adj* finnois(e), finlandais(e) ♦ *n* (*LING*) finnois m

fir [fəː*] *n* sapin m

fire [faɪə*] *n* feu m; (*accidental*) incendie m; (*heater*) radiateur m ♦ *vt* (*discharge*): **to** ~ **a gun** tirer un coup de feu; (*fig*) enflammer, animer; (*inf: dismiss*) mettre à la porte, renvoyer ♦ *vi* (*shoot*) tirer, faire feu; **on ~** en feu; **~ alarm** *n* avertisseur *m* d'incendie; **~arm** *n* arme *f* à feu; **~ brigade** *n* (sapeurs-)pompiers *mpl*; **~ department** (*US*) *n* = fire brigade; **~ engine** *n* (*vehicle*) voiture *f* des pompiers; **~ escape** *n* escalier *m* de secours; **~ extinguisher** *n* extincteur *m*; **~man** *n* pompier *m*; **~place** *n* cheminée *f*; **~side** *n* foyer *m*, coin *m* du feu; **~ station** *n* caserne *f* de pompiers; **~wood** *n* bois *m* de chauffage; **~works** *npl* feux *mpl* d'artifice; (*display*) feu(x) d'artifice

firing squad ['faɪərɪŋ-] *n* peloton *m* d'exécution

firm [fɜːm] *adj* ferme ♦ *n* compagnie *f*, firme *f*

first [fɜːst] *adj* premier(ère) ♦ *adv* (*before all others*) le premier, la première; (*before all other things*) en premier, d'abord; (*when listing reasons etc*) en premier lieu, premièrement ♦ *n* (*person: in race*) premier(ère); (*BRIT: SCOL*) mention *f* très bien; (*AUT*) première *f*; **at ~** au commencement, au début; **~ of all** tout d'abord, pour commencer; **~ aid** *n* premiers secours *or* soins; **~-aid kit** *n* trousse *f* à pharmacie; **~-class** *adj* de première classe; (*excellent*) excellent(e), exceptionnel(le); **~-hand** *adj* de première main; **~ lady** (*US*) *n* femme *f* du président; **~ly** *adv* premièrement, en premier lieu; **~ name** *n* prénom *m*; **~-rate** *adj* excellent(e)

fish [fɪʃ] *n inv* poisson *m* ♦ *vt, vi* pêcher; **to go ~ing** aller à la pêche; **~erman** *n* pêcheur *m*; **~ farm** *n* établissement *m* piscicole; **~ fingers** (*BRIT*) *npl* bâtonnets de poisson (congelés); **~ing boat** *n* barque *f* *or* bateau *m* de pêche; **~ing line** *n* ligne *f* (de pêche); **~ing rod** *n* canne *f* à pêche; **~monger's (shop)** *n* poissonnerie *f*; **~ sticks** (*US*) *npl* = fish fingers; **~y** (*inf*) *adj* suspect(e), louche

fist [fɪst] *n* poing *m*

fit [fɪt] *adj* (*healthy*) en (bonne) forme; (*proper*) convenable; approprié(e) ♦ *vt* (*subj: clothes*) aller à; (*put in, attach*) installer, poser; adapter; (*equip*) équiper, garnir, munir; (*suit*) convenir à ♦ *vi* (*clothes*) aller; (*parts*) s'adapter; (*in space, gap*) entrer, s'adapter ♦ *n* (*MED*) accès *m*, crise *f*; (*of anger*) accès; (*of hysterics, jealousy*) crise; **~ to** en état de; **~ for** digne de; apte à; **~ of coughing** quinte *f* de toux; **a ~ of giggles** le fou rire; **this dress is a good ~** cette robe (me) va très bien; **by ~s and starts** par à-coups; **~ in** *vi* s'accorder; s'adapter; **~ful** *adj* (*sleep*) agité(e); **~ment** *n* meuble encastré, élément *m*; **~ness** *n* (*MED*) forme *f* physique; **~ted carpet** *n* moquette *f*; **~ted kitchen** (*BRIT*) *n* cuisine équipée; **~ter** *n* monteur

m; **~ting** *adj* approprié(e) ♦ *n* (*of dress*) essayage *m*; (*of piece of equipment*) pose *f*, installation *f*; **~tings** *npl* (*in building*) installations *fpl*; **~ting room** *n* cabine *f* d'essayage

five [faɪv] *num* cinq; **~r** (*BRIT*) *n* billet *m* de cinq livres; (*US*) billet *m* de cinq dollars

fix [fɪks] *vt* (*date, amount etc*) fixer; (*organize*) arranger; (*mend*) réparer; (*meal, drink*) préparer ♦ *n*: **to be in a ~** être dans le pétrin; **~ up** *vt* (*meeting*) arranger; **to ~ sb up with sth** faire avoir qch à qn; **~ation** [fɪkˈseɪʃən] *n* (*PSYCH*) fixation *f*; (*fig*) obsession *f*; **~ed** [fɪkst] *adj* (*prices etc*) fixe; (*smile*) figé(e); **~ture** [ˈfɪkstʃə*] *n* installation *f* (fixe); (*SPORT*) rencontre *f* (au programme)

fizzle [ˈfɪzl] *vi*: **~ out** *vi* (*interest*) s'estomper; (*strike, film*) se terminer en queue de poisson

fizzy [ˈfɪzɪ] *adj* pétillant(e); gazeux(euse)

flabbergasted [ˈflæbəɡɑːstɪd] *adj* sidéré(e), ahuri(e)

flabby [ˈflæbɪ] *adj* mou(molle)

flag [flæɡ] *n* drapeau *m*; (*also: ~stone*) dalle *f* ♦ *vi* faiblir; fléchir; **~ down** *vt* héler, faire signe (de s'arrêter) à; **~pole** [ˈflæɡpəʊl] *n* mât *m*; **~ship** *n* vaisseau *m* amiral; (*fig*) produit *m* vedette

flair [flɛə*] *n* flair *m*

flak [flæk] *n* (*MIL*) tir antiaérien; (*inf: criticism*) critiques *fpl*

flake [fleɪk] *n* (*of rust, paint*) écaille *f*; (*of snow, soap powder*) flocon *m* ♦ *vi* (*also: ~ off*) s'écailler

flamboyant [flæmˈbɔɪənt] *adj* flamboyant(e), éclatant(e); (*person*) haut(e) en couleur

flame [fleɪm] *n* flamme *f*

flamingo [fləˈmɪŋɡəʊ] *n* flamant *m* (rose)

flammable [ˈflæməbl] *adj* inflammable

flan [flæn] (*BRIT*) *n* tarte *f*

flank [flæŋk] *n* flanc *m* ♦ *vt* flanquer

flannel [ˈflænl] *n* (*fabric*) flanelle *f*; (*BRIT: also: face ~*) gant *m* de toilette; **~s** *npl* (*trousers*) pantalon *m* de flanelle

flap [flæp] *n* (*of pocket, envelope*) rabat *m* ♦ *vt* (*wings*) battre (de) ♦ *vi* (*sail, flag*) claquer; (*inf: also: be in a ~*) paniquer

flare [flɛə*] *n* (*signal*) signal lumineux; (*in skirt etc*) évasement *m*; **~ up** *vi* s'embraser; (*fig: person*) se mettre en colère, s'emporter; (*: revolt etc*) éclater

flash [flæʃ] *n* éclair *m*; (*also: news ~*) flash *m* (d'information); (*PHOT*) flash ♦ *vt* (*light*) projeter; (*send: message*) câbler; (*look*) jeter; (*smile*) lancer ♦ *vi* (*light*) clignoter; **a ~ of lightning** un éclair; **in a ~** en un clin d'œil; **to ~ one's headlights** faire un appel de phares; **to ~ by or past** (*person*) passer comme un éclair (devant); **~bulb** *n* ampoule *f* de flash; **~cube** *n* cube-flash *m*; **~light** *n* lampe *f* de poche

flashy ['flæʃɪ] (*pej*) *adj* tape-à-l'œil *inv*, tapageur(euse)

flask [flɑːsk] *n* flacon *m*, bouteille *f*; **(vacuum)** ~ thermos *m or f* ®

flat [flæt] *adj* plat(e); (*tyre*) dégonflé(e), à plat; (*beer*) éventé(e); (*denial*) catégorique; (*MUS*) bémol *inv*; (: *voice*) faux(fausse); (*fee, rate*) fixe ♦ *n* (*BRIT: apartment*) appartement *m*; (*AUT*) crevaison *f*; (*MUS*) bémol *m*; **to work** ~ **out** travailler d'arrache-pied; **~ly** *adv* catégoriquement; **~ten** *vt* (*also*: **~ten out**) aplatir; (*crop*) coucher; (*building(s)*) raser

flatter ['flætə*] *vt* flatter; **~ing** *adj* flatteur(euse); **~y** *n* flatterie *f*

flaunt [flɔːnt] *vt* faire étalage de

flavour ['fleɪvə*] (*US* **flavor**) *n* goût *m*, saveur *f*; (*of ice cream etc*) parfum *m* ♦ *vt* parfumer; **vanilla-flavoured** à l'arôme de vanille, à la vanille; **~ing** *n* arôme *m*

flaw [flɔː] *n* défaut *m*; **~less** *adj* sans défaut

flax [flæks] *n* lin *m*; **~en** *adj* blond(e)

flea [fliː] *n* puce *f*

fleck [flek] *n* tacheture *f*; moucheture *f*

flee [fliː] (*pt, pp* **fled**) *vt* fuir ♦ *vi* fuir, s'enfuir

fleece [fliːs] *n* toison *f* ♦ *vt* (*inf*) voler, filouter

fleet [fliːt] *n* flotte *f*; (*of lorries etc*) parc *m*, convoi *m*

fleeting ['fliːtɪŋ] *adj* fugace, fugitif(ive); (*visit*) très bref(brève)

Flemish ['flemɪʃ] *adj* flamand(e)

flesh [fleʃ] *n* chair *f*; ~ **wound** *n* blessure superficielle

flew [fluː] *pt of* **fly**

flex [fleks] *n* fil *m or* câble *m* électrique ♦ *vt* (*knee*) fléchir; (*muscles*) tendre

flexible *adj* flexible

flick [flɪk] *n* petite tape; chiquenaude *f*; (*of duster*) petit coup ♦ *vt* donner un petit coup à; (*switch*) appuyer sur; ~ **through** *vt fus* feuilleter

flicker ['flɪkə*] *vi* (*light*) vaciller; **his eyelids ~ed** il a cillé

flier ['flaɪə*] *n* aviateur *m*

flight [flaɪt] *n* vol *m*; (*escape*) fuite *f*; (*also*: ~ **of steps**) escalier *m*; ~ **attendant** (*US*) *n* steward *m*, hôtesse *f* de l'air; ~ **deck** *n* (*AVIAT*) poste *m* de pilotage; (*NAUT*) pont *m* d'envol

flimsy ['flɪmzɪ] *adj* peu solide; (*clothes*) trop léger(ère); (*excuse*) pauvre, mince

flinch [flɪntʃ] *vi* tressaillir; **to ~ from** se dérober à, reculer devant

fling [flɪŋ] (*pt, pp* **flung**) *vt* jeter, lancer

flint [flɪnt] *n* silex *m*; (*in lighter*) pierre *f* (à briquet)

flip [flɪp] *vt* (*throw*) lancer (d'une chiquenaude); **to ~ a coin** jouer à pile ou face; **to ~ sth over** retourner qch

flippant ['flɪpənt] *adj* désinvolte, irrévérencieux(euse)

flipper ['flɪpə*] *n* (*of seal etc*) nageoire *f*; (*for swimming*) palme *f*

flirt [flɜːt] *vi* flirter ♦ *n* flirteur(euse) *m/f*

flit [flɪt] *vi* voleter

float [fləut] *n* flotteur *m*; (*in procession*) char *m*; (*money*) réserve *f* ♦ *vi* flotter

flock [flɒk] *n* troupeau *m*; (*of birds*) vol *m*; (*REL*) ouailles *fpl* ♦ *vi*: **to ~ to** se rendre en masse à

flog [flɒg] *vt* fouetter

flood [flʌd] *n* inondation *f*; (*of letters, refugees etc*) flot *m* ♦ *vt* inonder ♦ *vi* (*people*): **to ~ into** envahir; **~ing** *n* inondation *f*; **~light** *n* projecteur *m*

floor [flɔː*] *n* sol *m*; (*storey*) étage *m*; (*of sea, valley*) fond *m* ♦ *vt* (*subj: question*) décontenancer; (: *blow*) terrasser; **on the ~** par terre; **ground ~**, (*US*) **first ~** rez-de-chaussée *m inv*; **first ~**, (*US*) **second ~** premier étage; **~board** *n* planche *f* (*du plancher*); ~ **show** *n* spectacle *m* de variétés

flop [flɒp] *n* fiasco *m* ♦ *vi* être un fiasco; (*fall: into chair*) s'affaler, s'effondrer

floppy ['flɒpɪ] *adj* lâche, flottant(e); ~ **(disk)** *n* (*COMPUT*) disquette *f*

flora ['flɔːrə] *n* flore *f*

floral ['flɔːrəl] *adj* (*dress*) à fleurs

florid ['flɒrɪd] *adj* (*complexion*) coloré(e); (*style*) plein(e) de fioritures

florist ['flɒrɪst] *n* fleuriste *m/f*

flounce [flauns]: **to ~ out** *vi* sortir dans un mouvement d'humeur

flounder ['flaundə*] *vi* patauger ♦ *n* (*ZOOL*) flet *m*

flour ['flauə*] *n* farine *f*

flourish ['flʌrɪʃ] *vi* prospérer ♦ *n* (*gesture*) moulinet *m*

flout [flaut] *vt* se moquer de, faire fi de

flow [fləu] *n* (*ELEC, of river*) courant *m*; (*of blood in veins*) circulation *f*; (*of tide*) flux *m*; (*of orders, data*) flot *m* ♦ *vi* couler; (*traffic*) s'écouler; (*robes, hair*) flotter; **the ~ of traffic** l'écoulement *m* de la circulation; ~ **chart** *n* organigramme *m*

flower ['flauə*] *n* fleur *f* ♦ *vi* fleurir; ~ **bed** *n* plate-bande *f*; **~pot** *n* pot *m* (de fleurs); **~y** *adj* fleuri(e)

flown [fləun] *pp of* **fly**

flu [fluː] *n* grippe *f*

fluctuate ['flʌktjueɪt] *vi* varier, fluctuer

fluent ['fluːənt] *adj* (*speech*) coulant(e), aisé(e); **he speaks ~ French, he's ~ in French** il parle couramment le français

fluff [flʌf] *n* duvet *m*; (*on jacket, carpet*) peluche *f*; **~y** *adj* duveteux(euse); (*toy*) en peluche

fluid ['fluːɪd] *adj* fluide ♦ *n* fluide *m*

fluke [fluːk] (*inf*) *n* (*luck*) coup *m* de veine

flung [flʌŋ] *pt, pp of* **fling**

fluoride ['fluəraɪd] n fluorure f; ~ **tooth-paste** n dentifrice m au fluor

flurry ['flʌrɪ] n (of snow) rafale f, bourrasque f; ~ of activity/excitement affairement m/excitation f soudain(e)

flush [flʌʃ] n (on face) rougeur f; (fig: of youth, beauty etc) éclat m ♦ vt nettoyer à grande eau ♦ vi rougir ♦ adj: ~ with au ras de, de niveau avec; **to ~ the toilet** tirer la chasse (d'eau); ~ **out** vt (game, birds) débusquer; ~ed adj (tout(e)) rouge

flustered ['flʌstəd] adj énervé(e)

flute [flu:t] n flûte f

flutter ['flʌtə*] n (of panic, excitement) agitation f, (of wings) battement m ♦ vi (bird) battre des ailes, voleter

flux [flʌks] n: **in a state of ~** fluctuant sans cesse

fly [flaɪ] (pt **flew**, pp **flown**) n (insect) mouche f; (on trousers: also: **flies**) braguette f ♦ vt piloter; (passengers, cargo) transporter (par avion); (distances) parcourir ♦ vi voler; (passengers) aller en avion; (escape) s'enfuir, fuir; (flag) se déployer; ~ **away** vi (bird, insect) s'envoler; ~ **off** vi = **fly away**; ~**ing** n (activity) aviation f, (action) vol m ♦ adj: **a ~ing visit** une visite éclair; **with ~ing colours** haut la main; ~**ing saucer** n soucoupe volante; ~**ing start** n: **to get off to a ~ing start** prendre un excellent départ; ~**over** (BRIT) n (bridge) saut-de-mouton m; ~**sheet** n (for tent) double toit m

foal [fəul] n poulain m

foam [fəum] n écume f; (on beer) mousse f; (also: ~ **rubber**) caoutchouc m mousse ♦ vi (liquid) écumer; (soapy water) mousser

fob [fɒb] vt: **to ~ sb off** se débarrasser de qn

focal point ['fəukəl–] n (fig) point central

focus ['fəukəs] (pl ~**es**) n foyer m; (of interest) centre m ♦ vt (field glasses etc) mettre au point ♦ vi: **to ~ (on)** (with camera) régler la mise au point (sur); (person) fixer son regard (sur); **out of/in ~** (picture) flou(e)/net(te); (camera) pas au point/au point

fodder ['fɒdə*] n fourrage m

foe [fəu] n ennemi m

fog [fɒg] n brouillard m; ~**gy** adj: **it's ~gy** il y a du brouillard; ~ **lamp** n (AUT) phare m antibrouillard; ~ **light** (US) n = **fog lamp**

foil [fɔɪl] vt déjouer, contrecarrer ♦ n feuille f de métal; (kitchen ~) papier m d'alu(minium); (complement) repoussoir m; (FENCING) fleuret m

fold [fəuld] n (bend, crease) pli m; (AGR) parc m à moutons; (fig) bercail m ♦ vt plier; (arms) croiser; ~ **up** vi (map, table etc) se plier; (business) fermer boutique ♦ vt (map, clothes) plier; ~**er** n (for papers)

chemise f; (: with hinges) classeur m; ~**ing** adj (chair, bed) pliant(e)

foliage ['fəulɪɪdʒ] n feuillage m

folk [fəuk] npl gens mpl ♦ cpd folklorique; ~**s** npl (parents) parents mpl; ~**lore** ['fəuklɔ:*] n folklore m; ~ **song** n chanson f folklorique

follow ['fɒləu] vt suivre ♦ vi suivre; (result) s'ensuivre; **to ~ suit** (fig) faire de même; ~ **up** vt (letter, offer) donner suite à; (case) suivre; ~**er** n disciple m/f, partisan(e); ~**ing** adj suivant(e) ♦ n partisans mpl, disciples mpl

folly ['fɒlɪ] n inconscience f, folie f

fond [fɒnd] adj (memory, look) tendre; (hopes, dreams) un peu fou(folle); **to be ~ of** aimer beaucoup

fondle ['fɒndl] vt caresser

font [fɒnt] n (in church: for baptism) fonts baptismaux; (TYP) fonte f

food [fu:d] n nourriture f; ~ **mixer** n mixer m; ~ **poisoning** n intoxication f alimentaire; ~ **processor** n robot m de cuisine; ~**stuffs** npl denrées fpl alimentaires

fool [fu:l] n idiot(e); (CULIN) mousse f de fruits ♦ vt berner, duper ♦ vi faire l'idiot or l'imbécile; ~**hardy** adj téméraire, imprudent(e); ~**ish** adj idiot(e), stupide; (rash) imprudent(e); insensé; ~**proof** adj (plan etc) infaillible

foot [fut] (pl **feet**) n pied m; (of animal) patte f, (measure) pied (= 30,48 cm; 12 inches) ♦ vt (bill) payer; **on ~** à pied; ~**age** n (CINEMA: length) ≈ métrage m; (: material) séquences fpl; ~**ball** n ballon m (de football); (sport: BRIT) football m, foot m; (: US) football américain; ~**ball player** (BRIT) n (also: **footballer**) joueur m de football; ~**brake** n frein m à pédale; ~**bridge** n passerelle f; ~**hills** npl contreforts mpl; ~**hold** n prise f (de pied); ~**ing** n (fig) position f; **to lose one's ~ing** perdre pied; ~**lights** npl rampe f; ~**man** (irreg) n valet m de pied; ~**note** n note f (en bas de page); ~**path** n sentier m; (in street) trottoir m; ~**print** n trace f (de pas); ~**step** n pas m; ~**wear** n chaussure(s) f(pl)

for [fɔ:*] prep **1** (indicating destination, intention, purpose) pour; **the train ~ London** le train pour or (à destination) de Londres; **he went ~ the paper** il est allé chercher le journal; **it's time ~ lunch** c'est l'heure du déjeuner; **what's it ~?** ça sert à quoi?; **what ~?** (why) pourquoi?

2 (on behalf of, representing) pour; **the MP ~ Hove** le député de Hove; **to work ~ sb/sth** travailler pour qn/qch; **G ~ George** G comme Georges

3 (because of) pour; ~ **this reason** pour cette raison; ~ **fear of being criticized** de peur d'être critiqué

4 (*with regard to*) pour; **it's cold ~ July** il fait froid pour juillet; **a gift ~ languages** un don pour les langues

5 (*in exchange for*): **I sold it ~ £5** je l'ai vendu 5 livres; **to pay 50 pence ~ a ticket** payer un billet 50 pence

6 (*in favour of*) pour; **are you ~ or against us?** êtes-vous pour ou contre nous?

7 (*referring to distance*) pendant, sur; **there are roadworks ~ 5 km** il y a des travaux sur 5 km; **we walked ~ miles** nous avons marché pendant des kilomètres

8 (*referring to time*) pendant; depuis; pour; **he was away ~ 2 years** il a été absent pendant 2 ans; **she will be away ~ a month** elle sera absente (pendant) un mois; **I have known her ~ years** je la connais depuis des années; **can you do it ~ tomorrow?** est-ce que tu peux le faire pour demain?

9 (*with infinitive clauses*): **it is not ~ me to decide** ce n'est pas à moi de décider; **it would be best ~ you to leave** le mieux serait que vous partiez; **there is still time ~ you to do it** vous avez encore le temps de le faire; **~ this to be possible ...** pour que cela soit possible ...

10 (*in spite of*): **~ all his work/efforts** malgré tout son travail/tous ses efforts; **~ all his complaints, he's very fond of her** il a beau se plaindre, il l'aime beaucoup

♦ *conj* (*since, as: rather formal*) car

forage ['fɒrɪdʒ] *vi* fourrager

foray ['fɒreɪ] *n* incursion *f*

forbid [fə'bɪd] (*pt* forbad(e), *pp* forbidden) *vt* défendre, interdire; **to ~ sb to do** défendre *or* interdire à qn de faire; **~ding** *adj* sévère, sombre

force [fɔːs] *n* force *f* ♦ *vt* forcer; (*push*) pousser (de force); **the F~s** *npl* (*MIL*) l'armée *f*; **in ~** en vigueur; **~-feed** *vt* nourrir de force; **~ful** *adj* énergique, volontaire

forcibly ['fɔːsəblɪ] *adv* par la force, de force; (*express*) énergiquement

ford [fɔːd] *n* gué *m*

fore [fɔː*] *n*: **to come to the ~** se faire remarquer

fore: **~arm** ['fɔːrɑːm] *n* avant-bras *m inv*; **~boding** [fɔː'bəʊdɪŋ] *n* pressentiment *m* (néfaste); **~cast** ['fɔːkɑːst] (*irreg: like* cast) *n* prévision *f* ♦ *vt* prévoir; **~court** ['fɔːkɔːt] *n* (*of garage*) devant *m*; **~fathers** ['fɔːfɑːðəz] *npl* ancêtres *mpl*; **~finger** ['fɔːfɪŋgə*] *n* index *m*

forefront ['fɔːfrʌnt] *n*: **in the ~ of** au premier rang *or* plan de

forego [fɔː'gəʊ] (*irreg: like* go) *vt* renoncer à; **~ne** ['fɔːgɒn] *adj*: **it's a ~ne conclusion** c'est couru d'avance

foreground ['fɔːgraʊnd] *n* premier plan

forehead ['fɒrɪd] *n* front *m*

foreign ['fɒrɪn] *adj* étranger(ère); (*trade*) extérieur(e); **~er** étranger(ère); **~ exchange** *n* change *m*; **F~ Office** (*BRIT*) *n* ministère *m* des affaires étrangères; **F~ Secretary** (*BRIT*) *n* ministre *m* des affaires étrangères

foreleg ['fɔːleg] *n* (*cat, dog*) patte *f* de devant; (*horse*) jambe antérieure

foreman ['fɔːmən] (*irreg*) *n* (*factory, building site*) contremaître *m*, chef *m* d'équipe

foremost ['fɔːməʊst] *adj* le(la) plus en vue; premier(ère) ♦ *adv*: **first and ~** avant tout, tout d'abord

forensic [fə'rensɪk] *adj*: **~ medicine** médecine légale; **~ scientist** *n* médecin *m* légiste

forerunner ['fɔːrʌnə*] *n* précurseur *m*

foresee [fɔː'siː] (*irreg: like* see) *vt* prévoir; **~able** *adj* prévisible

foreshadow [fɔː'ʃædəʊ] *vt* présager, annoncer, laisser prévoir

foresight ['fɔːsaɪt] *n* prévoyance *f*

forest ['fɒrɪst] *n* forêt *f*

forestall [fɔː'stɔːl] *vt* devancer

forestry ['fɒrɪstrɪ] *n* sylviculture *f*

foretaste ['fɔːteɪst] *n* avant-goût *m*

foretell [fɔː'tel] (*irreg: like* tell) *vt* prédire

foretold [fɔː'təʊld] *pt, pp of* **foretell**

forever [fə'revə*] *adv* pour toujours; (*fig*) continuellement

forewent [fɔː'went] *pt of* **forego**

foreword ['fɔːwɜːd] *n* avant-propos *m inv*

forfeit ['fɔːfɪt] *vt* (*lose*) perdre

forgave [fə'geɪv] *pt of* **forgive**

forge [fɔːdʒ] *n* forge *f* ♦ *vt* (*signature*) contrefaire; (*wrought iron*) forger; **to ~ money** (*BRIT*) fabriquer de la fausse monnaie; **~ ahead** *vi* prendre de l'avant, prendre de l'avance; **~r** *n* faussaire *m*; **~ry** *n* faux *m*, contrefaçon *f*

forget [fə'get] (*pt* forgot, *pp* forgotten) *vt, vi* oublier; **~ful** *adj* distrait(e), étourdi(e); **~-me-not** *n* myosotis *m*

forgive [fə'gɪv] (*pt* forgave, *pp* forgiven) *vt* pardonner; **to ~ sb for sth/for doing sth** pardonner qch à qn/à qn de faire qch; **~ness** *n* pardon *m*

forgo [fɔː'gəʊ] (*pt* forwent, *pp* forgone) *vt* = **forego**

fork [fɔːk] *n* (*for eating*) fourchette *f*; (*for gardening*) fourche *f*; (*of roads*) bifurcation *f*; (*of railways*) embranchement *m* ♦ *vi* (*road*) bifurquer; **~ out** *vt* (*inf*) allonger; **~-lift truck** *n* chariot élévateur

forlorn [fə'lɔːn] *adj* (*deserted*) abandonné(e); (*attempt, hope*) désespéré(e)

form [fɔːm] *n* forme *f*; (*SCOL*) classe *f*; (*questionnaire*) formulaire *m* ♦ *vt* former; (*habit*) contracter; **in top ~** en pleine forme

formal ['fɔːməl] *adj* (*offer, receipt*) en bonne et due forme; (*person*) cérémonieux(euse);

(*dinner*) officiel(le); (*clothes*) de soirée; (*garden*) à la française; (*education*) à proprement parler; ~**ly** *adv* officiellement; cérémonieusement

format ['fɔːmæt] *n* format *m* ♦ *vt* (*COMPUT*) formater

formative ['fɔːmətɪv] *adj*: ~ **years** années *fpl* d'apprentissage *or* de formation

former ['fɔːmə*] *adj* ancien(ne) (*before n*), précédent(e); **the** ~ **... the latter** le premier ... le second, celui-là ... celui-ci; ~**ly** *adv* autrefois

formidable ['fɔːmɪdəbl] *adj* redoutable

formula ['fɔːmjulə] (*pl* ~**s** *or* **formulae**) *n* formule *f*

forsake [fə'seɪk] (*pt* **forsook**, *pp* **forsaken**) *vt* abandonner

fort [fɔːt] *n* fort *m*

forte ['fɔːtɪ] *n* (point) fort *m*

forth [fɔːθ] *adv* en avant; **to go back and** ~ aller et venir; **and so** ~ et ainsi de suite; ~**coming** *adj* (*event*) qui va avoir lieu prochainement; (*character*) ouvert(e), communicatif(ive); (*available*) disponible; ~**right** *adj* franc(franche), direct(e); ~**with** *adv* sur-le-champ

fortify ['fɔːtɪfaɪ] *vt* fortifier

fortitude ['fɔːtɪtjuːd] *n* courage *m*

fortnight ['fɔːtnaɪt] (*BRIT*) *n* quinzaine *f*, quinze jours *mpl*; ~**ly** (*BRIT*) *adj* bimensuel(le) ♦ *adv* tous les quinze jours

fortunate ['fɔːtʃənɪt] *adj* heureux(euse); (*person*) chanceux (euse); **it is** ~ **that** c'est une chance que; ~**ly** *adv* heureusement

fortune ['fɔːtʃən] *n* chance *f*; (*wealth*) fortune *f*; ~-**teller** *n* diseuse *f* de bonne aventure

forty ['fɔːtɪ] *num* quarante

forward ['fɔːwəd] *adj* (*ahead of schedule*) en avance; (*movement, position*) en avant, vers l'avant; (*not shy*) direct(e); effronté(e) ♦ *n* (*SPORT*) avant *m* ♦ *vt* (*letter*) faire suivre; (*parcel, goods*) expédier; (*fig*) promouvoir, avancer; ~(**s**) *adv* en avant; **to move** ~ avancer

fossil ['fɔsl] *n* fossile *m*

foster ['fɔstə*] *vt* encourager, favoriser; (*child*) élever (*sans obligation d'adopter*); ~ **child** *n* enfant adoptif(ive)

fought [fɔːt] *pt*, *pp* of **fight**

foul [faul] *adj* (*weather, smell, food*) infect(e); (*language*) ordurier(ère) ♦ *n* (*SPORT*) faute *f* ♦ *vt* (*dirty*) salir, encrasser; **he's got a** ~ **temper** il a un caractère de chien; ~ **play** *n* (*LAW*) acte criminel

found [faund] *pt*, *pp* of **find** ♦ *vt* (*establish*) fonder; ~**ation** [faun'deɪʃən] *n* (*act*) fondation *f*; (*base*) fondement *m*; (*also*: ~**ation cream**) fond *m* de teint; ~**ations** *npl* (*of building*) fondations *fpl*

founder ['faundə*] *n* fondateur *m* ♦ *vi* couler, sombrer

foundry ['faundrɪ] *n* fonderie *f*

fountain ['fauntɪn] *n* fontaine *f*; ~ **pen** *n* stylo *m* (à encre)

four [fɔː*] *num* quatre; **on all** ~**s** à quatre pattes; ~-**poster** *n* (*also*: ~-poster bed) lit *m* à baldaquin; ~**some** *n* (*game*) partie *f* à quatre; (*outing*) sortie *f* à quatre

fourteen [fɔː'tiːn] *num* quatorze

fourth [fɔːθ] *num* quatrième

fowl [faul] *n* volaille *f*

fox [fɔks] *n* renard *m* ♦ *vt* mystifier

foyer ['fɔɪeɪ] *n* (*hotel*) hall *m*; (*THEATRE*) foyer *m*

fraction ['frækʃən] *n* fraction *f*

fracture ['fræktʃə*] *n* fracture *f*

fragile ['frædʒaɪl] *adj* fragile

fragment ['frægmənt] *n* fragment *m*

fragrant ['freɪɡrənt] *adj* parfumé(e), odorant(e)

frail [freɪl] *adj* fragile, délicat(e)

frame [freɪm] *n* charpente *f*, (*of picture, bicycle*) cadre *m*; (*of door, window*) encadrement *m*, chambranle *m*; (*of spectacles*: *also*: ~**s**) monture *f* ♦ *vt* encadrer; ~ **of mind** disposition *f* d'esprit; ~**work** *n* structure *f*

France [frɑːns] *n* France *f*

franchise ['fræntʃaɪz] *n* (*POL*) droit *m* de vote; (*COMM*) franchise *f*

frank [fræŋk] *adj* franc(franche) ♦ *vt* (*letter*) affranchir; ~**ly** *adv* franchement

frantic ['fræntɪk] *adj* (*hectic*) frénétique; (*distraught*) hors de soi

fraternity [frə'tɜːnɪtɪ] *n* (*spirit*) fraternité *f*; (*club*) communauté *f*, confrérie *f*

fraud [frɔːd] *n* supercherie *f*, fraude *f*, tromperie *f*; (*person*) imposteur *m*

fraught [frɔːt] *adj*: ~ **with** chargé(e) de, plein(e) de

fray [freɪ] *n* bagarre *f* ♦ *vi* s'effilocher; **tempers were** ~**ed** les gens commençaient à s'énerver

freak [friːk] *n* (*also cpd*) phénomène *m*, créature *or* événement exceptionnel(le) par sa rareté

freckle ['frekl] *n* tache *f* de rousseur

free [friː] *adj* libre; (*gratis*) gratuit(e) ♦ *vt* (*prisoner etc*) libérer; (*jammed object or person*) dégager; ~ (**of charge**), **for** ~ gratuitement; ~**dom** ['friːdəm] *n* liberté *f*; ~**for-all** *n* mêlée générale; ~ **gift** *n* prime *f*; ~**hold** *n* propriété foncière libre; ~ **kick** *n* coup franc; ~**lance** *adj* indépendant(e); ~**ly** *adv* librement; (*liberally*) libéralement; **F~mason** *n* franc-maçon *m*; **F~post** (®) *n* port payé; ~**range** *adj* (*hen, eggs*) de ferme; ~ **trade** *n* libre-échange *m*; ~**way** (*US*) *n* autoroute *f*; ~ **will** *n* libre arbitre *m*; **of one's own** ~ **will** de son plein gré

freeze [friːz] (*pt* **froze**, *pp* **frozen**) *vi* geler ♦ *vt* geler; (*food*) congeler; (*prices, salaries*) bloquer, geler ♦ *n* gel *m*; (*fig*) blocage *m*; ~-**dried** *adj* lyophilisé(e); ~**r** *n* congélateur *m*

freezing ['fri:zɪŋ] *adj:* ~ **(cold)** *(weather, water)* glacial(e) ♦ *n* **3 degrees below** ~ **3** degrés au-dessous de zéro; ~ **point** *n* point *m* de congélation

freight [freɪt] *n (goods)* fret *m*, cargaison *f*; *(money charged)* fret, prix *m* du transport; ~ **train** *n* train *m* de marchandises

French [frentʃ] *adj* français(e) ♦ *n* (LING) français *m*; **the** ~ *npl (people)* les Français; ~ **bean** *n* haricot vert; ~ **fried (potatoes)**, ~ **fries** *(US) npl* (pommes de terre *fpl*) frites *fpl*; ~**man** *(irreg) n* Français *m*; ~ **window** *n* porte-fenêtre *f*; ~**woman** *(irreg) n* Française *f*

frenzy ['frenzɪ] *n* frénésie *f*

frequency ['fri:kwənsɪ] *n* fréquence *f*

frequent [*adj* 'fri:kwənt, *vb* fri:'kwent] *adj* fréquent(e) ♦ *vt* fréquenter; ~**ly** *adv* fréquemment

fresh [freʃ] *adj* frais(fraîche); *(new)* nouveau(nouvelle); *(cheeky)* familier(ère), culotté(e); ~ **en** *vi (wind, air)* fraîchir; ~**en up** *vi* faire un brin de toilette; ~**er** *(BRIT: inf) n (SCOL)* bizuth *m*, étudiant(e) de 1ère année; ~**ly** *adv* nouvellement, récemment; ~**man** *(US: irreg) n* = **fresher**; ~**ness** *n* fraîcheur *f*; ~**water** *adj (fish)* d'eau douce

fret [fret] *vi* s'agiter, se tracasser

friar ['fraɪə*] *n* moine *m*, frère *m*

friction ['frɪkʃən] *n* friction *f*

Friday ['fraɪdeɪ] *n* vendredi *m*

fridge [frɪdʒ] *(BRIT) n* frigo *m*, frigidaire *m* (®)

fried [fraɪd] *adj* frit(e); ~ **egg** œuf *m* sur le plat

friend [frend] *n* ami(e); ~**ly** *adj* amical(e); gentil(le); *(place)* accueillant(e); ~**ship** *n* amitié *f*

frieze [fri:z] *n* frise *f*

fright [fraɪt] *n* peur *f*, effroi *m*; **to take** ~ prendre peur, s'effrayer; ~**en** *vt* effrayer, faire peur à; ~**ened** *adj:* **to be** ~**ened (of)** avoir peur (de); ~**ening** *adj* effrayant(e); ~**ful** *adj* affreux(euse)

frigid ['frɪdʒɪd] *adj (woman)* frigide

frill [frɪl] *n (of dress)* volant *m*; *(of shirt)* jabot *m*

fringe [frɪndʒ] *n (BRIT: of hair)* frange *f*; *(edge: of forest etc)* bordure *f*; ~ **benefits** *npl* avantages sociaux *or* en nature

frisk [frɪsk] *vt* fouiller

fritter ['frɪtə*] *n* beignet *m*; ~ **away** *vt* gaspiller

frivolous ['frɪvələs] *adj* frivole

frizzy ['frɪzɪ] *adj* crépu(e)

fro [frəʊ] *adv:* **to go to and** ~ aller et venir

frock [frɒk] *n* robe *f*

frog [frɒg] *n* grenouille *f*; ~**man** *n* homme-grenouille *m*

frolic ['frɒlɪk] *vi* folâtrer, batifoler

from [frɒm] *prep* **1** *(indicating starting place, origin etc)* de; **where do you come** ~?, **where are you** ~? d'où venez-vous?; **London to Paris** de Londres à Paris; **a letter** ~ **my sister** une lettre de ma sœur; **to drink** ~ **the bottle** boire à (même) la bouteille

2 *(indicating time)* (à partir) de; ~ **one o'clock to** *or* **until** *or* **till two** d'une heure à deux heures; ~ **January (on)** à partir de janvier

3 *(indicating distance)* de; **the hotel is one kilometre** ~ **the beach** l'hôtel est à un kilomètre de la plage

4 *(indicating price, number etc)* de; **the interest rate was increased** ~ **9% to 10%** le taux d'intérêt a augmenté de 9 à 10%

5 *(indicating difference)* **he can't tell red** ~ **green** il ne peut pas distinguer le rouge du vert

6 *(because of, on the basis of):* ~ **what he says** d'après ce qu'il dit; **weak** ~ **hunger** affaibli par la faim

front [frʌnt] *n (of house, dress)* devant *m*; *(of coach, train)* avant *m*; *(promenade: also:* **sea** ~) bord *m* de mer; *(MIL, METEOROLOGY)* front *m*; *(fig: appearances)* contenance *f*, façade *f* ♦ *adj* de devant; *(seat)* avant *inv*; **in** ~ **(of)** devant; ~**age** ['frʌntɪdʒ] *n (of building)* façade *f*; ~ **door** *n* porte *f* d'entrée; *(of car)* portière *f* avant; ~**ier** ['frʌntɪə*] *n* frontière *f*; ~ **page** *n* première page; ~ **room** *(BRIT) n* pièce *f* de devant, salon *m*; ~-**wheel drive** *n* traction *f* avant

frost [frɒst] *n* gel *m*, gelée *f*; *(also: hoar~)* givre *m*; ~**bite** *n* gelures *fpl*; ~**ed** *adj (glass)* dépoli(e); ~**y** *adj (weather, welcome)* glacial(e)

froth [frɒθ] *n* mousse *f*, écume *f*

frown [fraʊn] *vi* froncer les sourcils

froze [frəʊz] *pt of* **freeze**

frozen ['frəʊzn] *pp of* **freeze**

fruit [fru:t] *n inv* fruit *m*; ~**erer** *n* fruitier *m*, marchand(e) de fruits; ~**ful** *adj (fig)* fructueux(euse); ~**ion** [fru:'ɪʃən] *n:* **to come to** ~**ion** se réaliser; ~ **juice** *n* jus *m* de fruit; ~ **machine** *(BRIT) n* machine *f* à sous; ~ **salad** *n* salade *f* de fruits

frustrate [frʌs'treɪt] *vt* frustrer

fry [fraɪ] *(pt, pp* **fried***) vt* (faire) frire; *see also* **small**; ~**ing pan** *n* poêle *f* (à frire)

ft. *abbr* = **foot**; **feet**

fuddy-duddy ['fʌdɪdʌdɪ] *(pej) n* vieux schnock

fudge [fʌdʒ] *n (CULIN)* caramel *m*

fuel [fjuəl] *n (for heating)* combustible *m*; *(for propelling)* carburant *m*; ~ **oil** *n* mazout *m*; ~ **tank** *n (in vehicle)* réservoir *m*

fugitive ['fju:dʒɪtɪv] *n* fugitif(ive)

fulfil [fʊl'fɪl] (*US* **~l**) *vt* (*function, condition*) remplir; (*order*) exécuter; (*wish, desire*) satisfaire, réaliser; **~ment** *n* (*of wishes etc*) réalisation *f*; (*feeling*) contentement *m*

full [fʊl] *adj* plein(e); (*details, information*) complet(ète); (*skirt*) ample, large ♦ *adv*: **to know ~ well that** savoir fort bien que; **I'm ~** (**up**) j'ai bien mangé; **a ~ two hours** deux bonnes heures; **at ~ speed** à toute vitesse; **in ~** (*reproduce, quote*) intégralement; (*write*) en toutes lettres; **~ employment** plein emploi; **to pay in ~** tout payer; **~-length** *adj* (*film*) long métrage; (*portrait, mirror*) en pied; (*coat*) long(ue); **~ moon** *n* pleine lune; **~-scale** *adj* (*attack, war*) complet(ète), total(e); (*model*) grandeur nature *inv*; **~ stop** *n* point *m*; **~-time** *adj, adv* (*work*) à plein temps; **~y** *adv* entièrement, complètement; (*at least*) au moins; **~y-fledged** *adj* (*teacher, barrister*) diplômé(e); (*citizen, member*) à part entière

fumble ['fʌmbl] *vi*: **~ with** tripoter

fume [fjuːm] *vi* rager; **~s** *npl* vapeurs *fpl*, émanations *fpl*, gaz *mpl*

fun [fʌn] *n* amusement *m*, divertissement *m*; **to have ~** s'amuser; **for ~** pour rire; **to make ~ of** se moquer de

function ['fʌŋkʃən] *n* fonction *f*; (*social occasion*) cérémonie *f*, soirée officielle ♦ *vi* fonctionner; **~al** *adj* fonctionnel(le)

fund [fʌnd] *n* caisse *f*, fonds *m*; (*source, store*) source *f*, mine *f*; **~s** *npl* (*money*) fonds *mpl*

fundamental [fʌndə'mentl] *adj* fondamental(e)

funeral ['fjuːnərəl] *n* enterrement *m*, obsèques *fpl*; **~ parlour** *n* entreprise *f* de pompes funèbres; **~ service** *n* service *m* funèbre

funfair ['fʌnfɛə*] (*BRIT*) *n* fête (foraine)

fungus ['fʌŋgəs] (*pl* **fungi**) *n* champignon *m*; (*mould*) moisissure *f*

funnel ['fʌnl] *n* entonnoir *m*; (*of ship*) cheminée *f*

funny ['fʌnɪ] *adj* amusant(e), drôle; (*strange*) curieux(euse), bizarre

fur [fɜː*] *n* fourrure *f*; (*BRIT: in kettle etc*) (dépôt *m* de) tartre *m*; **~ coat** *n* manteau *m* de fourrure

furious ['fjʊərɪəs] *adj* furieux(euse); (*effort*) acharné(e)

furlong ['fɜːlɒŋ] *n* = 201,17 m

furlough ['fɜːləʊ] *n* permission *f*, congé *m*

furnace ['fɜːnɪs] *n* fourneau *m*

furnish ['fɜːnɪʃ] *vt* meubler; (*supply*): **to ~ sb with** fournir qch à qn; **~ings** *npl* mobilier *m*, ameublement *m*

furniture ['fɜːnɪtʃə*] *n* meubles *mpl*, mobilier *m*; **piece of ~** meuble *m*

furrow ['fʌrəʊ] *n* sillon *m*

furry ['fɜːrɪ] *adj* (*animal*) à fourrure; (*toy*) en peluche

further ['fɜːðə*] *adj* (*additional*) supplémentaire, autre; nouveau (nouvelle) ♦ *adv* plus loin; (*more*) davantage; (*moreover*) de plus ♦ *vt* faire avancer *or* progresser, promouvoir; **~ education** *n* enseignement *m* postscolaire; **~more** *adv* de plus, en outre

furthest ['fɜːðɪst] *superl of* **far**

fury ['fjʊərɪ] *n* fureur *f*

fuse [fjuːz] (*US* **fuze**) *n* fusible *m*; (*for bomb etc*) amorce *f*, détonateur *m* ♦ *vt, vi* (*metal*) fondre; **to ~ the lights** (*BRIT*) faire sauter les plombs; **~ box** *n* boîte *f* à fusibles

fuss [fʌs] *n* (*excitement*) agitation *f*; (*complaining*) histoire(s) *f(pl)*; **to make a ~** faire des histoires; **to make a ~ of sb** être aux petits soins pour qn; **~y** *adj* (*person*) tatillon(ne), difficile; (*dress, style*) tarabiscoté(e)

future ['fjuːtʃə*] *adj* futur(e) ♦ *n* avenir *m*; (*LING*) futur *m*; **in ~** à l'avenir

fuze [fjuːz] (*US*) *n, vt, vi* = **fuse**

fuzzy ['fʌzɪ] *adj* (*PHOT*) flou(e); (*hair*) crépu(e)

G g

G [dʒiː] *n* (*MUS*) sol *m*

G7 *n abbr* (= *Group of 7*) le groupe des 7

gabble ['gæbl] *vi* bredouiller

gable ['geɪbl] *n* pignon *m*

gadget ['gædʒɪt] *n* gadget *m*

Gaelic ['geɪlɪk] *adj* gaélique ♦ *n* (*LING*) gaélique *m*

gag [gæg] *n* (*on mouth*) bâillon *m*; (*joke*) gag *m* ♦ *vt* bâillonner

gaiety ['geɪətɪ] *n* gaieté *f*

gain [geɪn] *n* (*improvement*) gain *m*; (*profit*) gain, profit *m*; (*increase*): **~ (in)** augmentation *f* (de) ♦ *vt* gagner ♦ *vi* (*watch*) avancer; **to ~ 3 lbs (in weight)** prendre 3 livres; **to ~ on sb** (*catch up*) rattraper qn; **to ~ from/by** gagner de/à

gait [geɪt] *n* démarche *f*

gal. *abbr* = **gallon**

gale [geɪl] *n* rafale *f* de vent; coup *m* de vent

gallant ['gælənt] *adj* vaillant(e), brave; (*towards ladies*) galant

gall bladder ['gɔːl-] *n* vésicule *f* biliaire

gallery ['gælərɪ] *n* galerie *f*; (*also: art ~*) musée *m*; (: *private*) galerie

galley ['gælɪ] *n* (*ship's kitchen*) cambuse *f*

gallon ['gælən] *n* gallon *m* (*BRIT* = 4,5 l; *US*

= 3,8 l)

gallop ['gæləp] n galop m ♦ vi galoper

gallows ['gæləuz] n potence f

gallstone ['gɔːlstəun] n calcul m biliaire

galore [gə'lɔː*] adv en abondance, à gogo

Gambia n: (The) ~ la Gambie

gambit ['gæmbɪt] n (fig): (opening) ~ ma-nœuvre f stratégique

gamble ['gæmbl] n pari m, risque calculé ♦ vt, vi jouer; **to ~ on** (fig) miser sur; **~r** n joueur m; **gambling** ['gæmblɪŋ] n jeu m

game [geɪm] n jeu m; (match) match m; (strategy, scheme) plan m; projet m; (HUN-TING) gibier m ♦ adj (willing): **to be ~ (for)** être prêt(e) (à or pour); **big ~** gros gibier; **~keeper** n garde-chasse m

gammon ['gæmən] n (bacon) quartier m de lard fumé; (ham) jambon fumé

gamut ['gæmət] n gamme f

gang [gæŋ] n bande f, (of workmen) équipe f; ~ **up** vi: **to ~ up on sb** se liguer contre qn; **~ster** ['gæŋstə*] n gangster m; **~way** n passerelle f, (BRIT: of bus, plane) couloir central; (: in cinema) allée centrale

gaol [dʒeɪl] (BRIT) n = **jail**

gap [gæp] n trou m; (in time) intervalle m; (difference) ~ **between** écart m entre

gape [geɪp] vi (person) être or rester bou-che bée; (hole, shirt) être ouvert(e); **gaping** ['geɪpɪŋ] adj (hole) béant(e)

garage ['gærɑːʒ] n garage m

garbage ['gɑːbɪdʒ] n (US: rubbish) ordures fpl, détritus mpl; (inf: nonsense) foutaises fpl; ~ **can** (US) n poubelle f, boîte f à or-dures

garbled ['gɑːbld] adj (account, message) embrouillé(e)

garden ['gɑːdn] n jardin m; ~**s** npl jardin public; ~**er** n jardinier m; ~**ing** n jardina-ge m

gargle ['gɑːgl] vi se gargariser

garish ['gɛərɪʃ] adj criard(e), voyant(e); (light) cru(e)

garland ['gɑːlənd] n guirlande f, couronne f

garlic ['gɑːlɪk] n ail m

garment ['gɑːmənt] n vêtement m

garrison ['gærɪsən] n garnison f

garrulous ['gærʊləs] adj volubile, loquace

garter ['gɑːtə*] n jarretière f, (US) jarretelle f

gas [gæs] n gaz m; (US: ~oline) essence f ♦ vt asphyxier; ~ **cooker** (BRIT) n cuisinière f à gaz; ~ **cylinder** n bouteille f de gaz; ~ **fire** (BRIT) n radiateur m à gaz

gash [gæʃ] n entaille f; (on face) balafre f

gasket ['gæskɪt] n (AUT) joint m de culasse

gas mask n masque m à gaz

gas meter n compteur m à gaz

gasoline ['gæsəliːn] (US) n essence f

gasp [gɑːsp] vi haleter; ~ **out** vt (say) dire dans un souffle or d'une voix entrecoupée

gas station (US) n station-service f

gas tap n bouton m (de cuisinière à gaz); (on pipe) robinet m à gaz

gastric adj gastrique; ~ **flu** grippe f intesti-nale

gate [geɪt] n (of garden) portail m; (of field) barrière f, (of building, at airport) porte f; ~**crash** vt s'introduire sans invitation dans; ~**way** n porte f

gather ['gæðə*] vt (flowers, fruit) cueillir; (pick up) ramasser; (assemble) rassembler, réunir; recueillir; (understand) comprendre; (SEWING) froncer ♦ vi (assemble) se ras-sembler; **to ~ speed** prendre de la vitesse; ~**ing** n rassemblement m

gaudy ['gɔːdɪ] adj voyant(e)

gauge [geɪdʒ] n (instrument) jauge f ♦ vt jauger

gaunt [gɔːnt] adj (thin) décharné(e); (grim, desolate) désolé(e)

gauntlet ['gɔːntlɪt] n (glove) gant m; (fig): **to run the ~ through an angry crowd** se frayer un passage à travers une foule hosti-le; **to throw down the ~** jeter le gant

gauze [gɔːz] n gaze f

gave [geɪv] pt of **give**

gay [geɪ] adj (homosexual) homosexuel(le); (cheerful) gai(e), réjoui(e); (colour etc) gai, vif(vive)

gaze [geɪz] n regard m fixe ♦ vi: **to ~ at** fixer du regard

gazump (BRIT) vi revenir sur une promesse de vente (pour accepter une offre plus inté-ressante)

GB abbr = Great Britain

GCE n abbr (BRIT) = General Certificate of Education

GCSE n abbr (BRIT) = General Certificate of Secondary Education

gear [gɪə*] n matériel m, équipement m; at-tirail m; (TECH) engrenage m; (AUT) vitesse f ♦ vt (fig: adapt): **to ~ sth to** adapter qch à; **top** (or US **high**) ~ quatrième (or cin-quième) vitesse; **low** ~ première vitesse; **in** ~ en prise; ~ **box** n boîte f de vitesses; ~ **lever** (US ~ **shift**) n levier m de vitesse

geese [giːs] npl of **goose**

gel [dʒel] n gel m

gelignite ['dʒelɪgnaɪt] n plastic m

gem [dʒem] n pierre précieuse

Gemini ['dʒemɪniː] n les Gémeaux mpl

gender ['dʒendə*] n genre m

general ['dʒenərəl] n général m ♦ adj géné-ral(e); **in** ~ en général; ~ **delivery** n poste restante; ~ **election** n élection(s) législati-ve(s); ~**ly** adv généralement; ~ **practitio-ner** n généraliste m

generate ['dʒenəreɪt] vt engendrer; (electri-city etc) produire

generation [dʒenə'reɪʃən] n génération f, (of electricity etc) production f

generator ['dʒenəreɪtə*] n générateur m

generosity [dʒenə'rɒsɪtɪ] n générosité f;

generous ['dʒenərəs] *adj* généreux(euse); (*copious*) copieux(euse)
genetic engineering [dʒɪ'netɪk-] *n* ingénierie *f* génétique
genetics [dʒɪ'netɪks] *n* génétique *f*
Geneva [dʒɪ'niːvə] *n* Genève
genial ['dʒiːnɪəl] *adj* cordial(e), chaleureux(euse)
genitals ['dʒenɪtlz] *npl* organes génitaux
genius ['dʒiːnɪəs] *n* génie *m*
genteel [dʒen'tiːl] *adj* de bon ton, distingué(e)
gentle ['dʒentl] *adj* doux(douce)
gentleman ['dʒentlmən] *n* monsieur *m*; (*well-bred man*) gentleman *m*
gently ['dʒentlɪ] *adv* doucement
gentry ['dʒentrɪ] *n inv*: **the ~** la petite noblesse
gents [dʒents] *n* W.-C. *mpl* (pour hommes)
genuine ['dʒenjʊɪn] *adj* véritable, authentique; (*person*) sincère
geography [dʒɪ'ɒɡrəfɪ] *n* géographie *f*
geology [dʒɪ'ɒlədʒɪ] *n* géologie *f*
geometric(al) [dʒɪə'metrɪk(l)] *adj* géométrique
geometry [dʒɪ'ɒmɪtrɪ] *n* géométrie *f*
geranium [dʒɪ'reɪnɪəm] *n* géranium *m*
geriatric [dʒerɪ'ætrɪk] *adj* gériatrique
germ [dʒɜːm] *n* (*MED*) microbe *m*
German ['dʒɜːmən] *adj* allemand(e) ♦ *n* Allemand(e); (*LING*) allemand *m*; **~ measles** (*BRIT*) *n* rubéole *f*
Germany ['dʒɜːmənɪ] *n* Allemagne *f*
gesture ['dʒestʃə*] *n* geste *m*

───────────── *KEYWORD* ─────────────

get [get] (*pt, pp* **got**, *pp* **gotten** (*US*)) *vi* **1** (*become, be*) devenir; **to ~ old/tired** devenir vieux/fatigué, vieillir/se fatiguer; **to ~ drunk** s'enivrer; **to ~ killed** se faire tuer; **when do I ~ paid?** quand est-ce que je serai payé?; **it's ~ting late** il se fait tard
2 (*go*): **to ~ to/from** aller à/de; **to ~ home** rentrer chez soi; **how did you ~ here?** comment es-tu arrivé ici?
3 (*begin*) commencer *or* se mettre à; **I'm ~ting to like him** je commence à l'apprécier; **let's ~ going** *or* **started** allons-y
4 (*modal aux vb*): **you've got to do it** il faut que vous le fassiez; **I've got to tell the police** je dois le dire à la police
♦ *vt* **1**: **to ~ sth done** (*do*) faire qch; (*have done*) faire faire qch; **to ~ one's hair cut** se faire couper les cheveux; **to ~ sb to do sth** faire faire qch à qn; **to ~ sb drunk** enivrer qn
2 (*obtain*: *money, permission, results*) obtenir, avoir; (*find*: *job, flat*) trouver; (*fetch*: *person, doctor, object*) aller chercher; **to ~ sth for sb** procurer qch à qn; **~ me Mr Jones, please** (*on phone*) passez-moi Mr Jones, s'il vous plaît; **can I ~ you a drink?**

est-ce que je peux vous servir à boire?
3 (*receive*: *present, letter*) recevoir, avoir; (*acquire*: *reputation*) avoir; (: *prize*) obtenir; **what did you ~ for your birthday?** qu'est-ce que tu as eu pour ton anniversaire?
4 (*catch*) prendre, saisir, attraper; (*hit*: *target etc*) atteindre; **to ~ sb by the arm/throat** prendre *or* saisir *or* attraper qn par le bras/à la gorge; **~ him!** arrête-le!
5 (*take, move*) faire parvenir; **do you think we'll ~ it through the door?** on arrivera à le faire passer par la porte?; **I'll ~ you there somehow** je me débrouillerai pour t'y emmener
6 (*catch, take*: *plane, bus etc*) prendre
7 (*understand*) comprendre, saisir; (*hear*) entendre; **I've got it!** j'ai compris!; **I didn't ~ your name** je n'ai pas entendu votre nom
8 (*have, possess*): **to have got** avoir; **how many have you got?** vous en avez combien?

get about *vi* se déplacer; (*news*) se répandre
get along *vi* (*agree*) s'entendre; (*depart*) s'en aller; (*manage*) = **get by**
get at *vt fus* (*attack*) s'en prendre à; (*reach*) attraper, atteindre
get away *vi* partir, s'en aller; (*escape*) s'échapper
get away with *vt fus* en être quitte pour; se faire passer *or* pardonner
get back *vi* (*return*) rentrer ♦ *vt* récupérer, recouvrer
get by *vi* (*pass*) passer; (*manage*) se débrouiller
get down *vi, vt fus* descendre ♦ *vt* descendre; (*depress*) déprimer
get down to *vt fus* (*work*) se mettre à (faire)
get in *vi* rentrer; (*train*) arriver; **get into** *vt fus* entrer dans; (*car, train etc*) monter dans; (*clothes*) mettre, enfiler, endosser; **to get into bed/a rage** se mettre au lit/en colère
get off *vi* (*from train etc*) descendre; (*depart*: *person, car*) s'en aller; (*escape*) s'en tirer ♦ *vt* (*remove*: *clothes, stain*) enlever ♦ *vt fus* (*train, bus*) descendre de
get on *vi* (*at exam etc*) se débrouiller; (*agree*): **to get on (with)** s'entendre (avec) ♦ *vt fus* monter dans; (*horse*) monter sur
get out *vi* sortir; (*of vehicle*) descendre ♦ *vt* sortir
get out of *vt fus* sortir de; (*duty etc*) échapper à, se soustraire à
get over *vt fus* (*illness*) se remettre de
get round *vt fus* contourner; (*fig*: *person*) entortiller
get through *vi* (*TEL*) avoir la communication; **to get through to sb** atteindre qn

get together *vi* se réunir ♦ *vt* assembler
get up *vi* (*rise*) se lever ♦ *vt fus* monter
get up to *vt fus* (*reach*) arriver à; (*prank etc*) faire

getaway ['getəweɪ] *n*: **to make one's ~** filer
geyser ['giːzə*] *n* (GEO) geyser *m*; (BRIT: *water heater*) chauffe-eau *m inv*
Ghana ['gɑːnə] *n* Ghana *m*
ghastly ['gɑːstlɪ] *adj* atroce, horrible; (*pale*) livide, blême
gherkin ['gɜːkɪn] *n* cornichon *m*
ghetto blaster ['getəʊ-] *n* stéréo *f* portable
ghost [gəʊst] *n* fantôme *m*, revenant *m*
giant ['dʒaɪənt] *n* géant(e) ♦ *adj* géant(e), énorme
gibberish ['dʒɪbərɪʃ] *n* charabia *m*
giblets ['dʒɪblɪts] *npl* abats *mpl*
Gibraltar [dʒɪ'brɔːltə*] *n* Gibraltar
giddy ['gɪdɪ] *adj* (*dizzy*): **to be** or **feel ~** avoir le vertige
gift [gɪft] *n* cadeau *m*; (*donation, ability*) don *m*; **~ed** *adj* doué(e); **~ token** *n* chèque-cadeau *m*
gigantic [dʒaɪ'gæntɪk] *adj* gigantesque
giggle ['gɪgl] *vi* pouffer (de rire), rire sottement
gill [dʒɪl] *n* (*measure*) = 0.25 pints (BRIT = 0.15 l, US = 0.12 l)
gills [gɪlz] *npl* (*of fish*) ouïes *fpl*, branchies *fpl*
gilt [gɪlt] *adj* doré(e) ♦ *n* dorure *f*; **~-edged** *adj* (COMM) de premier ordre
gimmick ['gɪmɪk] *n* truc *m*
gin [dʒɪn] *n* (*liquor*) gin *m*
ginger ['dʒɪndʒə*] *n* gingembre *m*; **~ ale** *n* boisson gazeuse au gingembre; **~ beer** *n* = **ginger ale**; **~bread** *n* pain *m* d'épices
gingerly ['dʒɪndʒəlɪ] *adv* avec précaution
gipsy ['dʒɪpsɪ] *n* = **gypsy**
giraffe [dʒɪ'rɑːf] *n* girafe *f*
girder ['gɜːdə*] *n* poutrelle *f*
girdle ['gɜːdl] *n* (*corset*) gaine *f*
girl [gɜːl] *n* fille *f*, fillette *f*; (*young unmarried woman*) jeune fille; (*daughter*) fille; **an English ~** une jeune Anglaise; **~friend** *n* (*of girl*) amie *f*, (*of boy*) petite amie; **~ish** *adj* de petite *or* de jeune fille; (*for a boy*) efféminé(e)
giro ['dʒaɪrəʊ] *n* (*bank ~*) virement *m* bancaire; (*post office ~*) mandat *m*; (BRIT: *welfare cheque*) mandat d'allocation chômage
girth [gɜːθ] *n* circonférence *f*; (*of horse*) sangle *f*
gist [dʒɪst] *n* essentiel *m*
give [gɪv] (*pt* **gave**, *pp* **given**) *vt* donner ♦ *vi* (*break*) céder; (*stretch: fabric*) se prêter; **to ~ sb sth**, **~ sth to sb** donner qch à qn; **to ~ a cry/sigh** pousser un cri/un soupir; **~ away** *vt* donner; (~ *free*) faire cadeau de; (*betray*) donner, trahir; (*disclose*) révé-

ler; (*bride*) conduire à l'autel; **~ back** *vt* rendre; **~ in** *vi* céder ♦ *vt* donner; **~ off** *vt* dégager; **~ out** *vt* distribuer; annoncer; **~ up** *vi* renoncer ♦ *vt* renoncer à; **to ~ up smoking** arrêter de fumer; **to ~ o.s. up** se rendre; **~ way** (BRIT) *vi* céder; (AUT) céder la priorité
glacier ['glæsɪə*] *n* glacier *m*
glad [glæd] *adj* content(e); **~ly** *adv* volontiers
glamorous ['glæmərəs] *adj* (*person*) séduisant(e); (*job*) prestigieux (euse)
glamour ['glæmə*] *n* éclat *m*, prestige *m*
glance [glɑːns] *n* coup *m* d'œil ♦ *vi*: **to ~ at** jeter un coup d'œil à; **~ off** *vt fus* (*bullet*) ricocher sur; **glancing** ['glɑːnsɪŋ] *adj* (*blow*) oblique
gland [glænd] *n* glande *f*
glare [gleə*] *n* (*of anger*) regard furieux; (*of light*) lumière éblouissante; (*of publicity*) feux *mpl* ♦ *vi* briller d'un éclat aveuglant; **to ~ at** lancer un regard furieux à; **glaring** ['gleərɪŋ] *adj* (*mistake*) criant(e), qui saute aux yeux
glass [glɑːs] *n* verre *m*; **~es** *npl* (*spectacles*) lunettes *fpl*; **~house** (BRIT) *n* (*for plants*) serre *f*; **~ware** *n* verrerie *f*
glaze [gleɪz] *vt* (*door, window*) vitrer; (*pottery*) vernir ♦ *n* (*on pottery*) vernis *m*; **~d** *adj* (*pottery*) verni(e); (*eyes*) vitreux(euse); **glazier** ['gleɪzɪə*] *n* vitrier *m*
gleam [gliːm] *vi* luire, briller
glean [gliːn] *vt* (*information*) glaner
glee [gliː] *n* joie *f*
glib [glɪb] *adj* (*person*) qui a du bagou; (*response*) désinvolte, facile
glide [glaɪd] *vi* glisser; (AVIAT, *birds*) planer; **~r** *n* (AVIAT) planeur *m*; **gliding** ['glaɪdɪŋ] *n* (SPORT) vol *m* à voile
glimmer ['glɪmə*] *n* lueur *f*
glimpse [glɪmps] *n* vision passagère, aperçu *m* ♦ *vt* entrevoir, apercevoir
glint [glɪnt] *vi* étinceler
glisten ['glɪsn] *vi* briller, luire
glitter ['glɪtə*] *vi* scintiller, briller
gloat [gləʊt] *vi*: **to ~ (over)** jubiler (à propos de)
global ['gləʊbl] *adj* mondial(e)
globe [gləʊb] *n* globe *m*
gloom [gluːm] *n* obscurité *f*; (*sadness*) tristesse *f*, mélancolie *f*; **~y** *adj* sombre, triste, lugubre
glorious ['glɔːrɪəs] *adj* glorieux(euse); splendide
glory ['glɔːrɪ] *n* gloire *f*; (*splendour*) splendeur *f*
gloss [glɒs] *n* (*shine*) brillant *m*, vernis *m*; (*also*: **~ paint**) peinture brillante *or* laquée; **~ over** *vt fus* glisser sur
glossary ['glɒsərɪ] *n* glossaire *m*
glossy ['glɒsɪ] *adj* brillant(e); **~ magazine** magazine *m* de luxe

glove [glʌv] *n* gant *m*; ~ **compartment** *n* (*AUT*) boîte *f* à gants, vide-poches *m inv*

glow [gləʊ] *vi* rougeoyer; (*face*) rayonner; (*eyes*) briller

glower ['glaʊə*] *vi*: **to ~ (at)** lancer des regards mauvais (à)

glucose ['gluːkəʊz] *n* glucose *m*

glue [gluː] *n* colle *f* ♦ *vt* coller

glum [glʌm] *adj* sombre, morne

glut [glʌt] *n* surabondance *f*

glutton ['glʌtn] *n* glouton(ne); **a ~ for work** un bourreau de travail; **a ~ for punishment** un masochiste (*fig*)

gnarled [nɑːld] *adj* noueux(euse)

gnat [næt] *n* moucheron *m*

gnaw [nɔː] *vt* ronger

go [gəʊ] (*pt* **went**, *pp* **gone**; *pl* ~**es**) *vi* aller; (*depart*) partir, s'en aller; (*work*) marcher; (*be sold*): **to ~ for £10** se vendre 10 livres; (*fit, suit*): **to ~ with** aller avec; (*become*): **to ~ pale/mouldy** pâlir/moisir; (*break etc*) céder ♦ *n*: **to have a ~ (at)** essayer (de faire); **to be on the ~** être en mouvement; **whose ~ is it?** à qui est-ce de jouer?; **he's ~ing to do it** il va faire, il est sur le point de faire; **to ~ for a walk** aller se promener; **to ~ dancing** aller danser; **how did it ~?** comment est-ce que ça s'est passé?; **to ~ round the back/by the shop** passer par derrière/devant le magasin; ~ **about** *vi* (*rumour*) se répandre ♦ *vt fus*: **how do I ~ about this?** comment dois-je m'y prendre (pour faire ceci)?; ~ **ahead** *vi* (*make progress*) avancer; (*get going*) y aller; ~ **along** *vi* aller, avancer ♦ *vt fus* longer, parcourir; ~ **away** *vi* partir, s'en aller; ~ **back** *vi* rentrer; revenir; (*go again*) retourner; ~ **back on** *vt fus* (*promise*) revenir sur; ~ **by** *vi* (*years, time*) passer, s'écouler ♦ *vt fus* s'en tenir à; en croire; ~ **down** *vi* descendre; (*ship*) couler; (*sun*) se coucher ♦ *vt fus* descendre; ~ **for** *vt fus* (*fetch*) aller chercher; (*like*) aimer; (*attack*) s'en prendre à, attaquer; ~ **in** *vi* entrer; ~ **in for** *vt fus* (*competition*) se présenter à; (*like*) aimer; ~ **into** *vt fus* entrer dans; (*investigate*) étudier, examiner; (*embark on*) se lancer dans; ~ **off** *vi* partir, s'en aller; (*food*) se gâter; (*explode*) sauter; (*event*) se dérouler ♦ *vt fus* ne plus aimer; **the gun went off** le coup est parti; ~ **on** *vi* continuer; (*happen*) se passer; **to ~ on doing** continuer à faire; ~ **out** *vi* sortir; (*fire, light*) s'éteindre; ~ **over** *vt fus* (*check*) revoir, vérifier; ~ **through** *vt fus* (*town etc*) traverser; ~ **up** *vi* monter; (*price*) augmenter ♦ *vt fus* gravir; ~ **without** *vt fus* se passer de

goad [gəʊd] *vt* aiguillonner

go-ahead ['gəʊhed] *adj* dynamique, entreprenant(e) ♦ *n* feu vert

goal [gəʊl] *n* but *m*; ~**keeper** *n* gardien *m* de but; ~**post** *n* poteau *m* de but

goat [gəʊt] *n* chèvre *f*

gobble ['gɒbl] *vt* (*also*: ~ **down**, ~ **up**) engloutir

go-between ['gəʊ-] *n* intermédiaire *m/f*

god [gɒd] *n* dieu *m*; **G~** *n* Dieu *m*; ~**child** *n* filleul(e); ~**daughter** *n* filleule *f*; ~**dess** *n* déesse *f*; ~**father** *n* parrain *m*; ~**forsaken** *adj* maudit(e); ~**mother** *n* marraine *f*; ~**send** *n* aubaine *f*; ~**son** *n* filleul *m*

goggles ['gɒglz] *npl* (*for skiing etc*) lunettes protectrices

going ['gəʊɪŋ] *n* (*conditions*) état *m* du terrain ♦ *adj*: **the ~ rate** le tarif (en vigueur)

gold [gəʊld] *n* or *m* ♦ *adj* en or; (*reserves*) d'or; ~**en** *adj* (*made of gold*) en or; (*gold in colour*) doré(e); ~**fish** *n* poisson *m* rouge; ~**-plated** *adj* plaqué(e or *inv*); ~**smith** *n* orfèvre *m*

golf [gɒlf] *n* golf *m*; ~ **ball** *n* balle *f* de golf; (*on typewriter*) boule *m*; ~ **club** *n* club *m* de golf; (*stick*) club *m*, crosse *f* de golf; ~ **course** *n* (*terrain m de*) golf *m*; ~**er** *n* joueur(euse) de golf

gone [gɒn] *pp of* **go**

gong [gɒŋ] *n* gong *m*

good [gʊd] *adj* bon(ne); (*kind*) gentil(le); (*child*) sage ♦ *n* bien *m*; ~**s** *npl* (*COMM*) marchandises *fpl*, articles *mpl*; ~**!** bon!, très bien!; **to be ~ at** être bon en; **to be ~ for** être bon pour; **would you be ~ enough to ...?** auriez-vous la bonté or l'amabilité de ...?; **a ~ deal (of)** beaucoup (de); **a ~ many** beaucoup (de); **to make ~** *vi* (*succeed*) faire son chemin, réussir ♦ *vt* (*deficit*) combler; (*losses*) compenser; **it's no ~ complaining** cela ne sert à rien de se plaindre; **for ~** pour de bon, une fois pour toutes; ~ **morning/afternoon!** bonjour!; ~ **evening!** bonsoir!; ~ **night!** bonsoir!; (*on going to bed*) bonne nuit!; ~**bye** *excl* au revoir!; **G~ Friday** *n* Vendredi saint; ~**-looking** *adj* beau(belle), bien *inv*; ~**-natured** *adj* (*person*) qui a un bon naturel; ~**ness** *n* (*of person*) bonté *f*; **for ~ness sake!** je vous en prie!; ~**ness gracious!** mon Dieu!; ~**s train** *n* (*BRIT*) train *m* de marchandises; ~**will** *n* bonne volonté *f*

goose [guːs] (*pl* **geese**) *n* oie *f*

gooseberry ['gʊzbərɪ] *n* groseille *f* à maquereau; **to play ~** (*BRIT*) tenir la chandelle

gooseflesh ['guːsfleʃ] *n*, **goose pimples** *npl* chair *f* de poule

gore [gɔː*] *vt* encorner ♦ *n* sang *m*

gorge [gɔːdʒ] *n* gorge *f* ♦ *vt*: **to ~ o.s. (on)** se gorger (de)

gorgeous ['gɔːdʒəs] *adj* splendide, superbe

gorilla [gə'rɪlə] *n* gorille *m*

gorse [gɔːs] *n* ajoncs *mpl*

gory ['gɔːrɪ] *adj* sanglant(e); (*details*) horrible

go-slow ['gəu'sləu] (*BRIT*) *n* grève perlée
gospel ['gɒspəl] *n* évangile *m*
gossip ['gɒsɪp] *n* (*chat*) bavardages *mpl*;
commérage *m*, cancans *mpl*; (*person*)
commère *f* ♦ *vi* bavarder; (*maliciously*) can-
caner, faire des commérages
got [gɒt] *pt, pp of* **get**
gotten ['gɒtn] (*US*) *pp of* **get**
gout [gaut] *n* goutte *f*
govern ['gʌvən] *vt* gouverner; **~ess**
['gʌvənɪs] *n* gouvernante *f*; **~ment**
['gʌvnmənt] *n* gouvernement *m*; (*BRIT*: *mi-
nisters*) ministère *m*; **~or** ['gʌvənə*] *n* (*of
state, bank*) gouverneur *m*; (*of school, hospital*) ≈ membre *m/f* du conseil d'établissement; (*BRIT*: *of prison*) directeur(trice)
gown [gaun] *n* robe *f*; (*of teacher, BRIT*: *of
judge*) toge *f*
GP *n abbr* = **general practitioner**
grab [græb] *vt* saisir, empoigner ♦ *vi*: **to ~
at** essayer de saisir
grace [greɪs] *n* grâce *f* ♦ *vt* honorer; (*adorn*)
orner; **5 days'** ~ cinq jours de répit; **~ful**
adj gracieux(euse), élégant(e); **gracious**
['greɪʃəs] *adj* bienveillant(e)
grade [greɪd] *n* (*COMM*) qualité *f*; (*in hierarchy*) catégorie *f*, grade *m*, échelon *m*;
(*SCOL*) note *f*; (*US*: *school class*) classe *f* ♦
vt classer; **~ crossing** (*US*) *n* passage *m* à
niveau; **~ school** (*US*) *n* école *f* primaire
gradient ['greɪdɪənt] *n* inclinaison *f*, pente *f*
gradual ['grædjuəl] *adj* graduel(le), progres-
sif(ive); **~ly** *adv* peu à peu, graduellement
graduate [*n* 'grædjuɪt, *vb* 'grædjueɪt] *n* di-
plômé(e), licencié(e); (*US*: *of high school*)
bachelier(ère) ♦ *vi* obtenir son diplôme;
(*US*) obtenir son baccalauréat; **graduation**
[grædu'eɪʃən] *n* (cérémonie *f* de) remise *f*
des diplômes
graffiti [grə'fiːtɪ] *npl* graffiti *mpl*
graft [grɑːft] *n* (*AGR, MED*) greffe *f*; (*bribery*) corruption *f* ♦ *vt* greffer; **hard ~** (*BRIT*:
inf) boulot acharné
grain [greɪn] *n* grain *m*
gram [græm] *n* gramme *m*
grammar ['græmə*] *n* grammaire *f*; **~
school** (*BRIT*) *n* ≈ lycée *m*; **grammatical**
[grə'mætɪkl] *adj* grammatical(e)
gramme [græm] *n* = **gram**
grand [grænd] *adj* magnifique, splendide;
(*gesture etc*) noble; **~children** *npl* petits-
enfants *mpl*; **~dad** (*inf*) *n* grand-papa *m*;
~daughter *n* petite-fille *f*; **~father** *n*
grand-père *m*; **~ma** (*inf*) *n* grand-maman *f*;
~mother *n* grand-mère *f*; **~pa** (*inf*) *n* =
~dad; **~parents** *npl* grands-parents *mpl*;
~ piano *n* piano *m* à queue; **~son** *n*
petit-fils *m*; **~stand** *n* (*SPORT*) tribune *f*
granite ['grænɪt] *n* granit *m*
granny ['grænɪ] (*inf*) *n* grand-maman *f*
grant [grɑːnt] *vt* accorder; (*a request*) accéder à; (*admit*) concéder ♦ *n* (*SCOL*) bourse

f; (*ADMIN*) subside *m*, subvention *f*; **to take
it for ~ed that** trouver tout naturel que
+*sub*; **to take sb for ~ed** considérer qn
comme faisant partie du décor
granulated sugar ['grænjuleɪtɪd-] *n* sucre
m en poudre
grape [greɪp] *n* raisin *m*; **~fruit** ['greɪpfruːt]
n pamplemousse *m*
graph [grɑːf] *n* graphique *m*; **~ic** ['græfɪk]
adj graphique; (*account, description*) vi-
vant(e); **~ics** *n* arts *mpl* graphiques; gra-
phisme *m* ♦ *npl* représentations *fpl* graphiques
grapple ['græpl] *vi*: **to ~ with** être aux prises avec
grasp [grɑːsp] *vt* saisir ♦ *n* (*grip*) prise *f*;
(*understanding*) compréhension *f*, connaissance *f*; **~ing** *adj* cupide
grass [grɑːs] *n* herbe *f*; (*lawn*) gazon *m*;
~hopper *n* sauterelle *f*; **~-roots** *adj* de la
base, du peuple
grate [greɪt] *n* grille *f* de cheminée ♦ *vi*
grincer ♦ *vt* (*CULIN*) râper
grateful ['greɪtful] *adj* reconnaissant(e)
grater ['greɪtə*] *n* râpe *f*
gratifying ['grætɪfaɪɪŋ] *adj* agréable
grating ['greɪtɪŋ] *n* (*iron bars*) grille *f* ♦ *adj*
(*noise*) grinçant(e)
gratitude ['grætɪtjuːd] *n* gratitude *f*
gratuity [grə'tjuːɪtɪ] *n* pourboire *m*
grave [greɪv] *n* tombe *f* ♦ *adj* grave, sé-
rieux(euse)
gravel ['grævəl] *n* gravier *m*
gravestone ['greɪvstəun] *n* pierre tombale
graveyard ['greɪvjɑːd] *n* cimetière *m*
gravity ['grævɪtɪ] *n* (*PHYSICS*) gravité *f*; pesanteur *f*; (*seriousness*) gravité
gravy ['greɪvɪ] *n* jus *m* (de viande); sauce *f*
gray [greɪ] (*US*) *adj* = **grey**
graze [greɪz] *vi* paître, brouter ♦ *vt* (*touch
lightly*) frôler, effleurer; (*scrape*) écorcher ♦
n écorchure *f*
grease [griːs] *n* (*fat*) graisse *f*; (*lubricant*) lubrifiant *m* ♦ *vt* graisser; lubrifier; **~proof
paper** (*BRIT*) *n* papier sulfurisé; **greasy**
['griːsɪ] *adj* gras(se), graisseux(euse)
great [greɪt] *adj* grand(e); (*inf*) formidable;
G~ Britain *n* Grande-Bretagne *f*; **~-
grandfather** *n* arrière-grand-père *m*; **~-
grandmother** *n* arrière-grand-mère *f*; **~ly**
adv très, grandement; (*with verbs*) beaucoup; **~ness** *n* grandeur *f*
Greece [griːs] *n* Grèce *f*
greed [griːd] *n* (*also*: **~iness**) avidité *f*; (*for
food*) gourmandise *f*, gloutonnerie *f*; **~y** *adj*
avide; gourmand(e), glouton(ne)
Greek [griːk] *adj* grec(grecque) ♦ *n*
Grec(Grecque); (*LING*) grec *m*
green [griːn] *adj* vert(e); (*inexperienced*)
(bien) jeune, naïf(naïve); (*POL*) vert(e), écologiste; (*ecological*) écologique ♦ *n* vert *m*;
(*stretch of grass*) pelouse *f*; **~s** *npl* (*vegeta-*

bles) légumes verts; *(POL)*: **the G~s** les Verts *mpl*; **The G~ belt** *(BRIT: POL)* le parti écologiste; ~ **belt** *n (round town)* ceinture verte; ~ **card** *n (AUT)* carte verte; *(US)* permis *m* de travail; ~**ery** *n* verdure *f*, ~**grocer** *(BRIT) n* marchand *m* de fruits et légumes; ~**house** *n* serre *f*; ~**house effect** *n* effet *m* de serre; ~**house gas** *n* gas *m* à effet de serre; ~**ish** *adj* verdâtre

Greenland ['gri:nlənd] *n* Groenland *m*

greet [gri:t] *vt* accueillir; ~**ing** *n* salutation *f*; ~**ing(s) card** *n* carte *f* de vœux

gregarious [grɪ'gʊərɪəs] *adj (person)* sociable

grenade [grɪ'neɪd] *n* grenade *f*

grew [gru:] *pt* of **grow**

grey [greɪ] *(US* **gray)** *adj* gris(e); *(dismal)* sombre; ~**haired** *adj* grisonnant(e); ~**hound** *n* lévrier *m*

grid [grɪd] *n* grille *f*; *(ELEC)* réseau *m*

grief [gri:f] *n* chagrin *m*, douleur *f*

grievance ['gri:vəns] *n* doléance *f*, grief *m*

grieve [gri:v] *vi* avoir du chagrin; se désoler ♦ *vt* faire de la peine à, affliger; **to** ~ **for sb** *(dead person)* pleurer qn

grievous ['gri:vəs] *adj (LAW)*: ~ **bodily harm** coups *mpl* et blessures *fpl*

grill [grɪl] *n (on cooker)* gril *m*; *(food: also* **mixed** ~) grillade(s) *f(pl)* ♦ *vt (BRIT)* griller; *(inf: question)* cuisiner

grille [grɪl] *n* grille *f*, grillage *m*; *(AUT)* calandre *f*

grim [grɪm] *adj* sinistre, lugubre; *(serious, stern)* sévère

grimace [grɪ'meɪs] *n* grimace *f* ♦ *vi* grimacer, faire une grimace

grime [graɪm] *n* crasse *f*, saleté *f*

grin [grɪn] *n* large sourire *m* ♦ *vi* sourire

grind [graɪnd] *(pt, pp* **ground)** *vt* écraser; *(coffee, pepper etc)* moudre; *(US: meat)* hacher; *(make sharp)* aiguiser ♦ *n (work)* corvée *f*

grip [grɪp] *n (hold)* prise *f*, étreinte *f*; *(control)* emprise *f*; *(grasp)* connaissance *f*; *(handle)* poignée *f*; *(holdall)* sac *m* de voyage ♦ *vt* saisir, empoigner; **to come to** ~**s with** en venir aux prises avec; ~**ping** *adj* prenant(e), palpitant(e)

grisly ['grɪzlɪ] *adj* sinistre, macabre

gristle ['grɪsl] *n* cartilage *m*

grit [grɪt] *n* gravillon *m*; *(courage)* cran *m* ♦ *vt (road)* sabler; **to** ~ **one's teeth** serrer les dents

groan [grəun] *n (of pain)* gémissement *m* ♦ *vi* gémir

grocer ['grəusə*] *n* épicier *m*; ~**ies** *npl* provisions *fpl*; ~**'s (shop)** *n* épicerie *f*

groin [grɔɪn] *n* aine *f*

groom [gru:m] *n* palefrenier *m*; *(also:* **bride**~) marié *m* ♦ *vt (horse)* panser; *(fig)*: **to** ~ **sb for** former qn pour; **well-groomed** très soigné(e)

groove [gru:v] *n* rainure *f*

grope [grəup] *vi*: **to** ~ **for** chercher à tâtons

gross [grəus] *adj* grossier(ère); *(COMM)* brut(e); ~**ly** *adv (greatly)* très, grandement

grotto ['grotəu] *n* grotte *f*

grotty ['grotɪ] *(inf) adj* minable, affreux(euse)

ground [graund] *pt, pp* of **grind** ♦ *n* sol *m*, terre *f*; *(land)* terrain *m*, terres *fpl*; *(SPORT)* terrain; *(US: also:* ~ **wire)** terre; *(reason: gen pl)* raison *f* ♦ *vt (plane)* empêcher de décoller, retenir au sol; *(US: ELEC)* équiper d'une prise de terre; ~**s** *npl (of coffee etc)* marc *m*; *(gardens etc)* parc *m*, domaine *m*; **on the** ~, **to the** ~ par terre; **to gain/lose** ~ gagner/perdre du terrain; ~ **cloth** *(US)* *n* = **groundsheet**; ~**ing** *n (in education)* connaissances *fpl* de base; ~**less** *adj* sans fondement; ~**sheet** *(BRIT)* *n* tapis *m* de sol; ~ **staff** *n* personnel *m* au sol; ~**swell** *n* lame *f* *or* vague *f* de fond; ~**work** *n* préparation *f*

group [gru:p] *n* groupe *m* ♦ *vt (also:* ~ **together)** grouper ♦ *vi* se grouper

grouse [graus] *n inv (bird)* grouse *f* ♦ *vi (complain)* rouspéter, râler

grove [grəuv] *n* bosquet *m*

grovel ['grovl] *vi (fig)* ramper

grow [grəu] *(pt* **grew**, *pp* **grown)** *vi* pousser, croître; *(person)* grandir; *(increase)* augmenter, se développer; *(become)*: **to** ~ **rich/weak** s'enrichir/s'affaiblir; *(develop)*: **he's** ~**n out of his jacket** sa veste est (devenue) trop petite pour lui; **he'll** ~ **out of it!** ça lui passera! ♦ *vt* cultiver, faire pousser; *(beard)* laisser pousser; ~ **up** *vi* grandir; ~**er** *n* producteur *m*; ~**ing** *adj (fear, amount)* croissant(e), grandissant(e)

growl [graul] *vi* grogner

grown [grəun] *pp* of **grow**; ~-**up** *n* adulte *m/f*, grande personne

growth [grəuθ] *n* croissance *f*, développement *m*; *(what has grown)* pousse *f*, poussée *f*; *(MED)* grosseur *f*, tumeur *f*

grub [grʌb] *n* larve *f*; *(inf: food)* bouffe *f*

grubby ['grʌbɪ] *adj* crasseux(euse)

grudge [grʌdʒ] *n* rancune *f* ♦ *vt*: **to** ~ **sb sth** *(in giving)* donner qch à qn à contrecœur; *(resent)* reprocher qch à qn; **to bear sb a** ~ **(for)** garder rancune *or* en vouloir à qn (de)

gruelling ['gruəlɪŋ] *(US* **grueling)** *adj* exténuant(e)

gruesome ['gru:səm] *adj* horrible

gruff [grʌf] *adj* bourru(e)

grumble ['grʌmbl] *vi* rouspéter, ronchonner

grumpy ['grʌmpɪ] *adj* grincheux(euse)

grunt [grʌnt] *vi* grogner

G-string ['dʒi:-] *n (garment)* cache-sexe *m inv*

guarantee [gærən'tiː] *n* garantie *f* ♦ *vt* garantir

guard [gɑːd] *n* garde *f*; (*one man*) garde *m*; (*BRIT: RAIL*) chef *m* de train; (*on machine*) dispositif *m* de sûreté; (*also: fire~*) garde-feu *m* ♦ *vt* garder, surveiller; (*protect*): **to ~ against** *vt* (*prevent*) empêcher, se protéger de; **~ed** *adj* (*fig*) prudent(e); **~ian** *n* gardien(ne), (*of minor*) tuteur(trice); **~'s van** (*BRIT*) *n* (*RAIL*) fourgon *m*

guerrilla [gə'rɪlə] *n* guérillero *m*

guess [ges] *vt* deviner; (*estimate*) évaluer; (*US*) croire, penser ♦ *vi* deviner ♦ *n* supposition *f*, hypothèse *f*; **to take *or* have a ~** essayer de deviner; **~work** *n* hypothèse *f*

guest [gest] *n* invité(e); (*in hotel*) client(e); **~-house** *n* pension *f*; **~ room** *n* chambre *f* d'amis

guffaw [gʌ'fɔː] *vi* pouffer de rire

guidance ['gaɪdəns] *n* conseils *mpl*

guide [gaɪd] *n* (*person, book etc*) guide *m*; (*BRIT: also: girl ~*) guide *f* ♦ *vt* guider; **~book** *n* guide *m*; **~ dog** *n* chien *m* d'aveugle; **~lines** *npl* (*fig*) instructions (générales), conseils *mpl*

guild [gɪld] *n* corporation *f*; cercle *m*, association *f*

guile [gaɪl] *n* astuce *f*

guillotine [gɪlə'tiːn] *n* guillotine *f*

guilt [gɪlt] *n* culpabilité *f*; **~y** *adj* coupable

guinea pig ['gɪnɪ-] *n* cobaye *m*

guise [gaɪz] *n* aspect *m*, apparence *f*

guitar [gɪ'tɑː*] *n* guitare *f*

gulf [gʌlf] *n* golfe *m*; (*abyss*) gouffre *m*

gull [gʌl] *n* mouette *f*; (*larger*) goéland *m*

gullet ['gʌlɪt] *n* gosier *m*

gullible ['gʌlɪbl] *adj* crédule

gully ['gʌlɪ] *n* ravin *m*; ravine *f*, couloir *m*

gulp [gʌlp] *vi* avaler sa salive ♦ *vt* (*also: ~ down*) avaler

gum [gʌm] *n* (*ANAT*) gencive *f*; (*glue*) colle *f*; (*sweet: also ~drop*) boule *f* de gomme; (*also: chewing ~*) chewing-gum *m* ♦ *vt* coller; **~boots** (*BRIT*) *npl* bottes *fpl* en caoutchouc

gun [gʌn] *n* (*small*) revolver *m*, pistolet *m*; (*rifle*) fusil *m*, carabine *f*; (*cannon*) canon *m*; **~boat** *n* canonnière *f*; **~fire** *n* fusillade *f*; **~man** *n* bandit armé; **~point** *n*: **at ~point** sous la menace du pistolet (*or* fusil); **~powder** *n* poudre *f* à canon; **~shot** *n* coup *m* de feu

gurgle ['gɜːgl] *vi* gargouiller; (*baby*) gazouiller

gush [gʌʃ] *vi* jaillir; (*fig*) se répandre en effusions

gust [gʌst] *n* (*of wind*) rafale *f*; (*of smoke*) bouffée *f*

gusto ['gʌstəu] *n* enthousiasme *m*

gut [gʌt] *n* intestin *m*, boyau *m*; **~s** *npl* (*inf: courage*) cran *m*

gutter ['gʌtə*] *n* (*in street*) caniveau *m*; (*of roof*) gouttière *f*

guy [gaɪ] *n* (*inf: man*) type *m*; (*also: ~rope*) corde *f*; (*BRIT: figure*) effigie de Guy Fawkes (*brûlée en plein air le 5 novembre*)

guzzle ['gʌzl] *vt* avaler gloutonnement

gym [dʒɪm] *n* (*also: ~nasium*) gymnase *m*; (*also: ~nastics*) gym *f*; **~nast** ['dʒɪmnæst] *n* gymnaste *m/f*; **~nastics** [dʒɪm'næstɪks] *n, npl* gymnastique *f*; **~ shoes** *npl* chaussures *fpl* de gym; **~slip** (*BRIT*) *n* tunique *f* (d'écolière)

gynaecologist [gaɪnɪ'kɒlədʒɪst] (*US* **gynecologist**) *n* gynécologue *m/f*

gypsy ['dʒɪpsɪ] *n* gitan(e), bohémien(ne)

H h

haberdashery [hæbə'dæʃərɪ] (*BRIT*) *n* mercerie *f*

habit ['hæbɪt] *n* habitude *f*; (*REL: costume*) habit *m*

habitual [hə'bɪtjuəl] *adj* habituel(le); (*drinker, liar*) invétéré(e)

hack [hæk] *vt* hacher, tailler ♦ *n* (*pej: writer*) nègre *m*; **~er** *n* (*COMPUT*) pirate *m* (informatique); (: *enthusiast*) passionné(e) *m/f* des ordinateurs

hackneyed ['hæknɪd] *adj* usé(e), rebattu(e)

had [hæd] *pt, pp* of **have**

haddock ['hædɒk] (*pl ~ or ~s*) *n* églefin *m*; **smoked ~** haddock *m*

hadn't ['hædnt] = **had not**

haemorrhage ['hemərɪdʒ] (*US* **hemorrhage**) *n* hémorragie *f*

haemorroids ['hemərɔɪdz] (*US* **hemorroids**) *npl* hémorroïdes *fpl*

haggle ['hægl] *vi* marchander

Hague [heɪg] *n*: **The ~** La Haye

hail [heɪl] *n* grêle *f* ♦ *vt* (*call*) héler; (*acclaim*) acclamer ♦ *vi* grêler; **~stone** *n* grêlon *m*

hair [hɛə*] *n* cheveux *mpl*; (*of animal*) pelage *m*; (*single hair: on head*) cheveu *m*; (: *on body; of animal*) poil *m*; **to do one's ~** se coiffer; **~brush** *n* brosse *f* à cheveux; **~cut** *n* coupe *f* (de cheveux); **~do** *n* coiffure *f*; **~dresser** *n* coiffeur(euse); **~dresser's** *n* salon *m* de coiffure, coiffeur *m*; **~ dryer** *n* sèche-cheveux *m*; **~grip** *n* pince *f* à cheveux; **~net** *n* filet *m* à cheveux; **~piece** *n* perruque *f*; **~pin** *n* épingle *f* à cheveux; **~pin bend** (*US* **~pin curve**) *n* virage m en épingle à cheveux; ~-**raising** adj à (vous) faire dresser les cheveux sur la tête; ~ **removing cream** n crème f dépilatoire; ~ **spray** n laque f (pour les cheveux); ~**style** n coiffure f; ~**y** adj poilu(e); (inf: fig) effrayant(e)

hake [heɪk] (pl ~ or ~s) n colin m, merlu m

half [hɑːf] (pl **halves**) n moitié f; (of beer: also: ~ **pint**) ≈ demi m; (RAIL, bus also: ~ **fare**) demi-tarif m ♦ adj demi(e) ♦ adv (à) moitié, à demi; ~ **a dozen** une demi-douzaine; ~ **a pound** une demi-livre, ≈ 250 g; **two and a** ~ deux et demi; **to cut sth in** ~ couper qch en deux; ~-**baked** adj (plan) qui ne tient pas debout; ~-**caste** n métis(se); ~-**hearted** adj tiède, sans enthousiasme; ~-**hour** n demi-heure f; **half-mast: at** ~-**mast** adv (flag) en berne; ~**penny** ['heɪpnɪ] (BRIT) n demi-penny m; ~-**price** adj, adv: (**at**) ~-**price** à moitié prix; ~ **term** (BRIT) n (SCOL) congé m de demi-trimestre; ~-**time** n mi-temps f; ~**way** adv à mi-chemin

hall [hɔːl] n salle f; (entrance way) hall m, entrée f

hallmark ['hɔːlmɑːk] n poinçon m; (fig) marque f

hallo [hʌ'ləʊ] excl = **hello**

hall of residence (BRIT: pl **halls of residence**) n résidence f universitaire

Hallowe'en ['hæləʊ'iːn] n veille f de la Toussaint

hallucination [həluːsɪ'neɪʃən] n hallucination f

hallway ['hɔːlweɪ] n vestibule m

halo ['heɪləʊ] n (of saint etc) auréole f

halt [hɔːlt] n halte f, arrêt m ♦ vt (progress etc) interrompre ♦ vi faire halte, s'arrêter

halve [hɑːv] vt (apple etc) partager or diviser en deux; (expense) réduire de moitié; ~**s** [hɑːvz] npl of **half**

ham [hæm] n jambon m

hamburger ['hæmbɜːgə*] n hamburger m

hamlet ['hæmlɪt] n hameau m

hammer ['hæmə*] n marteau m ♦ vt (nail) enfoncer; (fig) démolir ♦ vi (on door) frapper à coups redoublés; **to** ~ **an idea into sb** faire entrer de force une idée dans la tête de qn

hammock ['hæmək] n hamac m

hamper ['hæmpə*] vt gêner ♦ n panier m (d'osier)

hamster ['hæmstə*] n hamster m

hand [hænd] n main f; (of clock) aiguille f; (handwriting) écriture f; (worker) ouvrier(ère); (at cards) jeu m ♦ vt passer, donner; **to give** or **lend sb a** ~ donner un coup de main à qn; **at** ~ à portée de la main; **in** ~ (time) à disposition; (job, situation) en main; **to be on** ~ (person) être disponible; (emergency services) se tenir

prêt(e) (à intervenir); **to** ~ (information etc) sous la main, à portée de la main; **on the one** ~ ..., **on the other** ~ d'une part ..., d'autre part; ~ **in** vt remettre; ~ **out** vt distribuer; ~ **over** vt transmettre; céder; ~**bag** n sac m à main; ~**book** n manuel m; ~**brake** n frein m à main; ~**cuffs** npl menottes fpl; ~**ful** n poignée f

handicap ['hændɪkæp] n handicap m ♦ vt handicaper; **mentally/physically** ~**ped** handicapé(e) mentalement/physiquement

handicraft ['hændɪkrɑːft] n (travail m d')artisanat m, technique artisanale; (object) objet artisanal

handiwork ['hændɪwɜːk] n ouvrage m

handkerchief ['hæŋkətʃɪf] n mouchoir m

handle ['hændl] n (of door etc) poignée f; (of cup etc) anse f; (of knife etc) manche m; (of saucepan) queue f; (for winding) manivelle f ♦ vt toucher, manier; (deal with) s'occuper de; (treat: people) prendre; "~ **with care**" "fragile"; **to fly off the** ~ s'énerver; ~**bar(s)** n(pl) guidon m

hand: ~luggage n bagages mpl à main; ~**made** adj fait(e) à la main; ~**out** n (from government, parents) aide f, don m; (leaflet) documentation f, prospectus m; (summary of lecture) polycopié m; ~**rail** n rampe f, main courante f; ~**shake** n poignée f de main

handsome ['hænsəm] adj beau (belle); (profit, return) considérable

handwriting ['hændraɪtɪŋ] n écriture f

handy ['hændɪ] adj (person) adroit(e); (close at hand) sous la main; (convenient) pratique; ~**man** ['hændɪmən] (irreg) n bricoleur m; (servant) homme m à tout faire

hang [hæŋ] (pt, pp **hung**) vt accrocher; (criminal: pt, pp: **hanged**) pendre ♦ vi pendre; (hair, drapery) tomber; **to get the** ~ **of (doing) sth** (inf) attraper le coup pour faire qch; ~ **about** vi traîner; ~ **around** vi = **hang about**; ~ **on** vi (wait) attendre; ~ **up** vi (TEL): **to** ~ **up (on sb)** raccrocher (au nez de qn) ♦ vt (coat, painting etc) accrocher, suspendre

hangar ['hæŋə*] n hangar m

hanger ['hæŋə*] n cintre m, portemanteau m; ~-**on** ['hæŋər'ɒn] n parasite m

hang: ~gliding ['hæŋglaɪdɪŋ] n deltaplane m, vol m libre; ~**over** ['hæŋəʊvə*] n (after drinking) gueule f de bois; ~-**up** ['hæŋʌp] n complexe m

hanker ['hæŋkə*] vi: **to** ~ **after** avoir envie de

hankie, hanky ['hæŋkɪ] n abbr = **handkerchief**

haphazard ['hæp'hæzəd] adj fait(e) au hasard, fait(e) au petit bonheur

happen ['hæpən] vi arriver; se passer, se produire; **it so** ~**s that** il se trouve que; **as it** ~**s** justement; ~**ing** n événement m

happily ['hæpılı] *adv* heureusement; *(cheerfully)* joyeusement
happiness ['hæpınıs] *n* bonheur *m*
happy ['hæpı] *adj* heureux(euse); ~ **with** *(arrangements etc)* satisfait(e) de; **to be ~ to do** faire volontiers; ~ **birthday!** bon anniversaire!; ~**-go-lucky** *adj* insouciant(e)
harass ['hærəs] *vt* accabler, tourmenter; ~**ment** *n* tracasseries *fpl*
harbour ['hɑ:bə*] *(US* **harbor)** *n* port *m* ♦ *vt* héberger, abriter; *(hope, fear etc)* entretenir
hard [hɑ:d] *adj* dur(e); *(question, problem)* difficile, dur(e); *(facts, evidence)* concret(ète) ♦ *adv (work)* dur; *(think, try)* sérieusement; **to look ~ at** regarder fixement; *(thing)* regarder de près; **no ~ feelings!** sans rancune!; **to be ~ of hearing** être dur(e) d'oreille; **to be ~ done by** être traité(e) injustement; ~ **cash** *n* espèces *fpl*; ~ **disk** *n (COMPUT)* disque dur; ~**en** *vt* durcir; *(fig)* endurcir ♦ *vi* durcir; ~**-headed** *adj* réaliste; décidé(e); ~ **labour** *n* travaux forcés
hardly ['hɑ:dlı] *adv (scarcely, no sooner)* à peine; ~ **anywhere/ever** presque nulle part/jamais
hard: ~**ship** *n* épreuves *fpl*; ~ **up** *(inf) adj* fauché(e); ~**ware** *n* quincaillerie *f*; *(COMPUT, MIL)* matériel *m*; ~**ware shop** *n* quincaillerie *f*; ~**-wearing** *adj* solide; ~**-working** *adj* travailleur(euse)
hardy ['hɑ:dı] *adj* robuste; *(plant)* résistant(e) au gel
hare [heə*] *n* lièvre *m*; ~**-brained** *adj* farfelu(e)
harm [hɑ:m] *n* mal *m*; *(wrong)* tort *m* ♦ *vt (person)* faire du mal *or* du tort à; *(thing)* endommager; **out of ~'s way** à l'abri du danger, en lieu sûr; ~**ful** *adj* nuisible; ~**less** *adj* inoffensif(ive); sans méchanceté
harmony ['hɑ:mənı] *n* harmonie *f*
harness ['hɑ:nıs] *n* harnais *m*; *(safety ~)* harnais de sécurité ♦ *vt (horse)* harnacher; *(resources)* exploiter
harp [hɑ:p] *n* harpe *f* ♦ *vi*: **to ~ on about** rabâcher
harrowing ['hærəʊıŋ] *adj* déchirant(e), très pénible
harsh [hɑ:ʃ] *adj (hard)* dur(e); *(severe)* sévère; *(unpleasant: sound)* discordant(e); *(: light)* cru(e)
harvest ['hɑ:vıst] *n (of corn)* moisson *f*; *(of fruit)* récolte *f*; *(of grapes)* vendange *f* ♦ *vt* moissonner; récolter; vendanger
has [hæz] *vb see* **have**
hash [hæʃ] *n (CULIN)* hachis *m*; *(fig: mess)* gâchis *m*
hasn't ['hæznt] = **has not**
hassle ['hæsl] *n (inf: bother)* histoires *fpl*, tracas *mpl*
haste [heıst] *n* hâte *f*; précipitation *f*; ~**n**
['heısn] *vt* hâter, accélérer ♦ *vi* se hâter, s'empresser; **hastily** ['heıstılı] *adv* à la hâte; précipitamment; **hasty** ['heıstı] *adj* hâtif(ive); précipité(e)
hat [hæt] *n* chapeau *m*
hatch [hætʃ] *n (NAUT: also:* ~**way)** écoutille *f*; *(also: service* ~**)** passe-plats *m inv* ♦ *vi* éclore
hatchback ['hætʃbæk] *n (AUT)* modèle *m* avec hayon arrière
hatchet ['hætʃıt] *n* hachette *f*
hate [heıt] *vt* haïr, détester ♦ *n* haine *f*; ~**ful** *adj* odieux(euse), détestable; **hatred** ['heıtrıd] *n* haine *f*
haughty ['hɔ:tı] *adj* hautain(e), arrogant(e)
haul [hɔ:l] *vt* traîner, tirer ♦ *n (of fish)* prise *f*; *(of stolen goods etc)* butin *m*; ~**age** *n* transport routier; *(costs)* frais *mpl* de transport; ~**ier** *(US* **hauler)** *n (company)* transporteur (routier); *(driver)* camionneur *m*
haunch [hɔ:ntʃ] *n* hanche *f*; *(of meat)* cuissot *m*
haunt [hɔ:nt] *vt* hanter ♦ *n* repaire *m*

─────── *KEYWORD*

have [hæv] *(pt, pp* **had)** *aux vb* **1** *(gen)* avoir; être; **to ~ arrived/gone** être arrivé(e)/allé(e); **to ~ eaten/slept** avoir mangé/dormi; **he has been promoted** il a eu une promotion
2 *(in tag questions)*: **you've done it,** ~**n't you?** vous l'avez fait, n'est-ce pas?
3 *(in short answers and questions)*: **no I** ~**n't/yes we have!** mais non!/mais si!; **so I** ~! ah oui!, oui c'est vrai!; **I've been there before,** ~ **you?** j'y suis déjà allé, et vous?
♦ *modal aux vb (be obliged)*: **to ~ (got) to do sth** devoir faire qch; être obligé(e) de faire qch; **she has (got) to do it** elle doit le faire, il faut qu'elle le fasse; **you** ~**n't to tell her** vous ne devez pas le lui dire
♦ *vt* **1** *(possess, obtain)* avoir; **he has (got) blue eyes/dark hair** il a les yeux bleus/les cheveux bruns; **may I ~ your address?** puis-je avoir votre adresse?
2 *(+noun: take, hold etc)*: **to ~ breakfast/a bath/a shower** prendre le petit déjeuner/un bain/une douche; **to ~ dinner/lunch** dîner/déjeuner; **to ~ a swim** nager; **to ~ a meeting** se réunir; **to ~ a party** organiser une fête
3: **to ~ sth done** faire faire qch; **to ~ one's hair cut** se faire couper les cheveux; **to ~ sb do sth** faire faire qch à qn
4 *(experience, suffer)* avoir; **to ~ a cold/flu** avoir un rhume/la grippe; **to ~ an operation** se faire opérer
5 *(inf: dupe)* avoir; **he's been had** il s'est fait avoir *or* rouler
have out *vt*: **to have it out with sb** *(settle a problem etc)* s'expliquer (franchement)

avec qn

haven ['heɪvn] n port m; (*fig*) havre m

haven't ['hævnt] = **have not**

havoc ['hævək] n ravages mpl

hawk [hɔːk] n faucon m

hay [heɪ] n foin m; ~ **fever** n rhume m des foins; ~**stack** n meule f de foin

haywire ['heɪwaɪə*] (*inf*) adj: **to go** ~ (*machine*) se détraquer; (*plans*) mal tourner

hazard ['hæzəd] n (*danger*) danger m, risque m ♦ vt risquer, hasarder; ~ (**warning**) **lights** npl (*AUT*) feux mpl de détresse

haze [heɪz] n brume f

hazelnut ['heɪzlnʌt] n noisette f

hazy ['heɪzɪ] adj brumeux(euse); (*idea*) vague

he [hiː] pron il; **it is** ~ **who ...** c'est lui qui ...

head [hed] n tête f; (*leader*) chef m; (*of school*) directeur(trice) ♦ vt (*list*) être en tête de; (*group*) être à la tête de; ~**s** (**or tails**) pile (ou face); ~ **first** la tête la première; ~ **over heels in love** follement or éperdument amoureux(euse); **to** ~ **a ball** faire une tête; ~ **for** vt fus se diriger vers; ~**ache** n mal m de tête; ~**dress** (*BRIT*) n (*of Red Indian etc*) coiffure f; ~**ing** n titre m; ~**lamp** (*BRIT*) n = **headlight**; ~**land** n promontoire m, cap m; ~**light** n phare m; ~**line** n titre m; ~**long** adv (*fall*) la tête la première; (*rush*) tête baissée; ~**master** n directeur m; ~**mistress** n directrice f; ~**office** n bureau central, siège m; ~**-on** adj (*collision*) de plein fouet; (*confrontation*) en face à face; ~**phones** npl casque m (à écouteurs); ~**quarters** npl bureau or siège central; (*MIL*) quartier général; ~**rest** n appui-tête m; ~**room** n (*in car*) hauteur f de plafond; (*under bridge*) hauteur limite; ~**scarf** n foulard m; ~**strong** adj têtu(e), entêté(e); ~ **waiter** n maître m d'hôtel; ~**way** n: **to make** ~**way** avancer, faire des progrès; ~**wind** n vent m contraire; (*NAUT*) vent debout; ~**y** adj capiteux(euse); enivrant(e); (*experience*) grisant(e)

heal [hiːl] vt, vi guérir

health [helθ] n santé f; ~ **food** n aliment(s) naturel(s); ~ **food shop** n magasin m diététique; **H~ Service** (*BRIT*) n: **the H~ Service** ≈ la Sécurité sociale; ~**y** adj (*person*) en bonne santé; (*climate, food, attitude etc*) sain(e), bon(ne) pour la santé

heap [hiːp] n tas m ♦ vt: **to** ~ (**up**) entasser, amonceler; **she** ~**ed her plate with cakes** elle a chargé son assiette de gâteaux

hear [hɪə*] (*pt, pp* heard) vt entendre; (*news*) apprendre ♦ vi entendre; **to** ~ **about** entendre parler de; avoir des nouvelles de; **to** ~ **from sb** recevoir or avoir des nouvelles de qn; ~**ing** ['hɪərɪŋ] n (*sense*) ouïe f, (*of witnesses*) audition f, (*of a case*)

audience f; ~**ing aid** n appareil m acoustique; ~**say** ['hɪəseɪ]: **by** ~**say** adv par ouï-dire m

hearse [hɜːs] n corbillard m

heart [hɑːt] n cœur m; ~**s** npl (*CARDS*) cœur; **to lose/take** ~ perdre/prendre courage; **at** ~ au fond; **by** ~ (*learn, know*) par cœur; ~ **attack** n crise f cardiaque; ~**beat** n battement m du cœur; ~**breaking** adj déchirant(e), qui fend le cœur; ~**broken** adj: **to be** ~**broken** avoir beaucoup de chagrin or le cœur brisé; ~**burn** n brûlures fpl d'estomac; ~ **failure** n arrêt m du cœur; ~**felt** adj sincère

hearth [hɑːθ] n foyer m, cheminée f

heartily ['hɑːtɪlɪ] adv chaleureusement; (*laugh*) de bon cœur; (*eat*) de bon appétit; **to agree** ~ être entièrement d'accord

heartland ['hɑːtlænd] n (*of country, region*) centre m

hearty ['hɑːtɪ] adj chaleureux(euse); (*appetite*) robuste; (*dislike*) cordial(e)

heat [hiːt] n chaleur f; (*fig*) feu m, agitation f, (*SPORT: also: qualifying* ~) éliminatoire f ♦ vt chauffer; ~ **up** vi (*water*) chauffer; (*room*) se réchauffer ♦ vt réchauffer; ~**ed** adj chauffé(e); (*fig*) passionné(e), échauffé(e); ~**er** n appareil m de chauffage; radiateur m; (*in car*) chauffage m; (*water* ~) chauffe-eau m

heath [hiːθ] (*BRIT*) n lande f

heather ['heðə*] n bruyère f

heating ['hiːtɪŋ] n chauffage m

heatstroke ['hiːtstrəuk] n (*MED*) coup m de chaleur

heatwave n vague f de chaleur

heave [hiːv] vt soulever (avec effort); (*drag*) traîner ♦ vi se soulever; (*retch*) avoir un haut-le-cœur; **to** ~ **a sigh** pousser un soupir

heaven ['hevn] n ciel m, paradis m; (*fig*) paradis; ~**ly** adj céleste, divin(e)

heavily ['hevɪlɪ] adv lourdement; (*drink, smoke*) beaucoup; (*sleep, sigh*) profondément

heavy ['hevɪ] adj lourd(e); (*work, sea, rain, eater*) gros(se); (*snow*) beaucoup de; (*drinker, smoker*) grand(e); (*breathing*) bruyant(e); (*schedule, week*) chargé(e); ~ **goods vehicle** n poids lourd; ~**weight** n (*SPORT*) poids lourd

Hebrew ['hiːbruː] adj hébraïque ♦ n (*LING*) hébreu m

Hebrides ['hebrɪdiːz] npl: **the** ~ les Hébrides fpl

heckle ['hekl] vt interpeller (*un orateur*)

hectic ['hektɪk] adj agité(e), trépidant(e)

he'd [hiːd] = **he would**; **he had**

hedge [hedʒ] n haie f ♦ vi se dérober; **to** ~ **one's bets** (*fig*) se couvrir

hedgehog ['hedʒhɒg] n hérisson m

heed [hiːd] vt (*also: take* ~ *of*) tenir compte

de; **~less** *adj* insouciant(e)

heel [hiːl] *n* talon *m* ♦ *vt* (*shoe*) retalonner

hefty ['heftɪ] *adj* (*person*) costaud(e); (*parcel*) lourd(e); (*profit*) gros(se)

heifer ['hefə*] *n* génisse *f*

height [haɪt] *n* (*of person*) taille *f*, grandeur *f*; (*of object*) hauteur *f*; (*of plane, mountain*) altitude *f*; (*high ground*) hauteur, éminence *f*; (*fig: of glory*) sommet *m*; (: *of luxury, stupidity*) comble *m*; **~en** *vt* (*fig*) augmenter

heir [ɛə*] *n* héritier *m*; **~ess** ['ɛərɪs] *n* héritière *f*; **~loom** *n* héritage *m*, meuble *m* (*or* bijou *m* or tableau *m*) de famille

held [held] *pt, pp of* **hold**

helicopter ['helɪkɒptə*] *n* hélicoptère *m*

hell [hel] *n* enfer *m*; **~!** (*inf!*) merde!

he'll [hiːl] = **he will; he shall**

hellish ['helɪʃ] (*inf*) *adj* infernal(e)

hello [hʌ'ləʊ] *excl* bonjour!; (*to attract attention*) hé!; (*surprise*) tiens!

helm [helm] *n* (*NAUT*) barre *f*

helmet ['helmɪt] *n* casque *m*

help [help] *n* aide *f*, (*cleaner*) femme *f* de ménage ♦ *vt* aider; **~!** au secours!; **~ yourself** servez-vous; **he can't ~ it** il n'y peut rien; **~er** *n* aide *m/f*, assistant(e), **~ful** *adj* serviable, obligeant(e); (*useful*) utile; **~ing** *n* portion *f*; **~less** *adj* impuissant(e); (*defenceless*) faible

hem [hem] *n* ourlet *m* ♦ *vt* ourler; **~ in** *vt* cerner

hemorrhage ['hemərɪdʒ] (*US*) *n* = **haemorrhage**

hemorrhoids ['hemərɔɪdz] (*US*) *npl* = **haemorrhoids**

hen [hen] *n* poule *f*

hence [hens] *adv* (*therefore*) d'où, de là; **2 years ~** d'ici 2 ans, dans 2 ans; **~forth** *adv* dorénavant

henchman ['hentʃmən] (*pej: irreg*) *n* acolyte *m*

her [hɜː*] *pron* (*direct*) la, l'; (*indirect*) lui; (*stressed, after prep*) elle ♦ *adj* son(sa), ses *pl; see also* **me; my**

herald ['herəld] *n* héraut *m* ♦ *vt* annoncer; **~ry** ['herəldrɪ] *n* (*study*) héraldique *f*; (*coat of arms*) blason *m*

herb [hɜːb] *n* herbe *f*

herd [hɜːd] *n* troupeau *m*

here [hɪə*] *adv* ici; (*time*) alors ♦ *excl* tiens!, tenez!; **~! présent!; ~ is, ~ are** voici; **~ he/she is!** le/la voici!; **~after** *adv* après, plus tard; **~by** *adv* (*formal: in letter*) par la présente

hereditary [hɪ'redɪtərɪ] *adj* héréditaire

heresy ['herəsɪ] *n* hérésie *f*

heritage ['herɪtɪdʒ] *n* (*of country*) patrimoine *m*

hermit ['hɜːmɪt] *n* ermite *m*

hernia ['hɜːnɪə] *n* hernie *f*

hero ['hɪərəʊ] (*pl* **~es**) *n* héros *m*

heroin ['herəʊɪn] *n* héroïne *f*

heroine ['herəʊɪn] *n* héroïne *f*

heron ['herən] *n* héron *m*

herring ['herɪŋ] *n* hareng *m*

hers [hɜːz] *pron* le(la) sien(ne), les siens(siennes); *see also* **mine**[1]

herself [hɜː'self] *pron* (*reflexive*) se; (*emphatic*) elle-même; (*after prep*) elle; *see also* **oneself**

he's [hiːz] = **he is; he has**

hesitant ['hezɪtənt] *adj* hésitant(e), indécis(e)

hesitate ['hezɪteɪt] *vi* hésiter; **hesitation** [hezɪ'teɪʃən] *n* hésitation *f*

hew [hjuː] (*pp* **hewed** *or* **hewn**) *vt* (*stone*) tailler; (*wood*) couper

heyday ['heɪdeɪ] *n*: **the ~ of** l'âge *m* d'or de, les beaux jours de

HGV *n abbr* = **heavy goods vehicle**

hi [haɪ] *excl* salut!; (*to attract attention*) hé!

hiatus [haɪ'eɪtəs] *n* (*gap*) lacune *f*, (*interruption*) pause *f*

hibernate ['haɪbəneɪt] *vi* hiberner

hiccough, hiccup ['hɪkʌp] *vi* hoqueter; **~s** *npl* hoquet *m*

hide [haɪd] (*pt* **hid**, *pp* **hidden**) *n* (*skin*) peau *f* ♦ *vt* cacher ♦ *vi*: **to ~ (from sb)** se cacher (de qn); **~-and-seek** *n* cache-cache *m*; **~away** *n* cachette *f*

hideous ['hɪdɪəs] *adj* hideux(euse)

hiding ['haɪdɪŋ] *n* (*beating*) correction *f*, volée *f* de coups; **to be in ~** (*concealed*) se tenir caché(e)

hierarchy ['haɪərɑːkɪ] *n* hiérarchie *f*

hi-fi ['haɪfaɪ] *n* hi-fi *f inv* ♦ *adj* hi-fi *inv*

high [haɪ] *adj* haut(e); (*speed, respect, number*) grand(e); (*price*) élevé(e); (*wind*) fort(e), violent(e); (*voice*) aigu(aiguë) ♦ *adv* haut; **20 m ~** haut(e) de 20 m; **~brow** *adj, n* intellectuel(le); **~chair** *n* (*child's*) chaise haute; **~er education** *n* études supérieures; **~-handed** *adj* très autoritaire; très cavalier(ère); **~ jump** *n* (*SPORT*) saut *m* en hauteur; **~lands** *npl*: **the H~lands** les Highlands *mpl*; **~light** *n* (*fig: of event*) point culminant ♦ *vt* faire ressortir, souligner; **~lights** *npl* (*in hair*) reflets *mpl*; **~ly** *adv* très, fort, hautement; **to speak/think ~ly of sb** dire/penser beaucoup de bien de qn; **~ly paid** *adj* très bien payé(e); **~ly strung** *adj* nerveux(euse), toujours tendu(e); **~ness** *n*: **Her** (*or* **His**) **H~ness** Son Altesse *f*; **~-pitched** *adj* aigu(aiguë); **~-rise** *adj*: **~-rise block, ~-rise flats** tour *f* (d'habitation); **~ school** *n* lycée *m*; (*US*) établissement *m* d'enseignement supérieur; **~ season** (*BRIT*) *n* haute saison; **~ street** (*BRIT*) *n* grand-rue *f*; **~way** ['haɪweɪ] *n* route nationale; **H~way Code** (*BRIT*) *n* code *m* de la route

hijack ['haɪdʒæk] *vt* (*plane*) détourner; **~er** *n* pirate *m* de l'air

hike [haɪk] *vi* aller *or* faire des excursions à

pied ♦ *n* excursion *f* à pied, randonnée *f*; ~**r** *n* promeneur(euse), excursionniste *m/f*

hilarious [hɪ'lɛərɪəs] *adj* (*account, event*) désopilant(e)

hill [hɪl] *n* colline *f*; (*fairly high*) montagne *f*; (*on road*) côte *f*; ~**side** *n* (flanc *m* de) coteau *m*; ~**y** *adj* vallonné(e); montagneux(euse)

hilt [hɪlt] *n* (*of sword*) garde *f*; **to the** ~ (*fig: support*) à fond

him [hɪm] *pron* (*direct*) le, l'; (*stressed, indirect, after prep*) lui; *see also* **me**; ~**self** [hɪm'sɛlf] *pron* (*reflexive*) se; (*emphatic*) lui-même; (*after prep*) lui; *see also* **oneself**

hind [haɪnd] *adj* de derrière

hinder ['hɪndə*] *vt* gêner; (*delay*) retarder; **hindrance** ['hɪndrəns] *n* gêne *f*, obstacle *m*

hindsight ['haɪndsaɪt] *n*: **with** ~ avec du recul, rétrospectivement

Hindu ['hɪnduː] *adj* hindou(e)

hinge [hɪndʒ] *n* charnière *f* ♦ *vi* (*fig*): **to** ~ **on** dépendre de

hint [hɪnt] *n* allusion *f*; (*advice*) conseil *m* ♦ *vt*: **to** ~ **that** insinuer que ♦ *vi*: **to** ~ **at** faire une allusion à

hip [hɪp] *n* hanche *f*

hippopotamus [hɪpə'pɒtəməs] (*pl* ~**es** *or* **hippopotami**) *n* hippopotame *m*

hire ['haɪə*] *vt* (*BRIT: car, equipment*) louer; (*worker*) embaucher, engager ♦ *n* location *f*; **for** ~ à louer; (*taxi*) libre; ~ **purchase** (*BRIT*) *n* achat *m* (*or* vente *f*) à tempérament *or* crédit

his [hɪz] *pron* le(la) sien(ne), les siens(siennes) ♦ *adj* son(sa), ses *pl*; *see also* **my**; **mine**[1]

hiss [hɪs] *vi* siffler

historic [hɪs'tɒrɪk] *adj* historique

historical [hɪs'tɒrɪkəl] *adj* historique

history ['hɪstərɪ] *n* histoire *f*

hit [hɪt] (*pt, pp* **hit**) *vt* frapper; (*reach: target*) atteindre, toucher; (*collide with: car*) entrer en collision avec, heurter; (*fig: affect*) toucher ♦ *n* coup *m*; (*success*) succès *m*; (: *song*) tube *m*; **to** ~ **it off with sb** bien s'entendre avec qn; ~**-and-run driver** *n* chauffard *m* (coupable du délit de fuite)

hitch [hɪtʃ] *vt* (*fasten*) accrocher, attacher; (*also*: ~ **up**) remonter d'une saccade ♦ *n* (*difficulty*) anicroche *f*, contretemps *m*; **to** ~ **a lift** faire du stop

hitchhike ['hɪtʃhaɪk] *vi* faire de l'auto-stop; ~**r** *n* auto-stoppeur(euse)

hi-tech ['haɪ'tɛk] *adj* de pointe

hitherto [hɪðə'tuː] *adv* jusqu'ici

HIV: ~**-negative/-positive** *adj* séro-négatif (ive)/-positif(ive)

hive [haɪv] *n* ruche *f*; ~ **off** (*inf*) *vt* mettre à part, séparer

HMS *abbr* = **Her (His) Majesty's Ship**

hoard [hɔːd] *n* (*of food*) provisions *fpl*, réserves *fpl*; (*of money*) trésor *m* ♦ *vt* amas-

ser; ~**ing** ['hɔːdɪŋ] (*BRIT*) *n* (*for posters*) panneau *m* d'affichage *or* publicitaire

hoarse [hɔːs] *adj* enroué(e)

hoax [həʊks] *n* canular *m*

hob [hɒb] *n* plaque (chauffante)

hobble ['hɒbl] *vi* boitiller

hobby ['hɒbɪ] *n* passe-temps favori; ~**horse** *n* (*fig*) dada *m*

hobo ['həʊbəʊ] (*US*) *n* vagabond *m*

hockey ['hɒkɪ] *n* hockey *m*

hog [hɒg] *n* porc (châtré) ♦ *vt* (*fig*) accaparer; **to go the whole** ~ aller jusqu'au bout

hoist [hɔɪst] *n* (*apparatus*) palan *m* ♦ *vt* hisser

hold [həʊld] (*pt, pp* **held**) *vt* tenir; (*contain*) contenir; (*believe*) considérer; (*possess*) avoir; (*detain*) détenir ♦ *vi* (*withstand pressure*) tenir (bon); (*be valid*) valoir ♦ *n* (*also fig*) prise *f*; (*NAUT*) cale *f*; ~ **the line!** (*TEL*) ne quittez pas!; **to** ~ **one's own** (*fig*) (bien) se défendre; **to catch** *or* **get (a)** ~ **of** saisir; **to get** ~ **of** (*fig*) trouver; ~ **back** *vt* retenir; (*secret*) taire; ~ **down** *vt* (*person*) maintenir à terre; (*job*) occuper; ~ **off** *vt* tenir à distance; ~ **on** *vi* tenir bon; (*wait*) attendre; ~ **on!** (*TEL*) ne quittez pas!; ~ **on to** *vt fus* se cramponner à; (*keep*) conserver, garder; ~ **out** *vt* offrir ♦ *vi* (*resist*) tenir bon; ~ **up** *vt* (*raise*) lever; (*support*) soutenir; (*delay*) retarder; (*rob*) braquer; ~**all** (*BRIT*) *n* fourre-tout *m inv*; ~**er** *n* (*of ticket, record*) détenteur(trice); (*of office, title etc*) titulaire *m/f*; (*container*) support *m*; ~**ing** (*share*) intérêts *mpl*; (*farm*) ferme *f*; ~**-up** *n* (*robbery*) hold-up *m*; (*delay*) retard *m*; (*BRIT: in traffic*) bouchon *m*

hole [həʊl] *n* trou *m*

holiday ['hɒlədɪ] *n* vacances *fpl*; (*day off*) jour *m* de congé; (*public*) jour férié; **on** ~ en congé; ~ **camp** *n* (*also*: ~ **centre**) camp *m* de vacances; ~**-maker** (*BRIT*) *n* vacancier(ère); ~ **resort** *n* centre *m* de villégiature *or* de vacances

Holland ['hɒlənd] *n* Hollande *f*

hollow ['hɒləʊ] *adj* creux(euse) ♦ *n* creux *m* ♦ *vt*: **to** ~ **out** creuser, évider

holly ['hɒlɪ] *n* houx *m*

holocaust ['hɒləkɔːst] *n* holocauste *m*

holster ['həʊlstə*] *n* étui *m* de revolver

holy ['həʊlɪ] *adj* saint(e); (*bread, water*) bénit(e); (*ground*) sacré(e); **H~ Ghost** *n* Saint-Esprit *m*

homage ['hɒmɪdʒ] *n* hommage *m*; **to pay** ~ **to** rendre hommage à

home [həʊm] *n* foyer *m*, maison *f*; (*country*) pays natal, patrie *f*; (*institution*) maison ♦ *adj* de famille; (*ECON, POL*) national(e), intérieur(e); (*SPORT: game*) sur leur (*or* notre) terrain; (*team*) qui reçoit ♦ *adv* chez soi, à la maison; au pays natal; (*right in: nail etc*) à fond; **at** ~ chez soi, à la maison; **make yourself at** ~ faites comme chez vous; ~ **address** *n* domicile permanent; ~**land** *n* patrie *f*; ~**less** *adj* sans foyer; sans abri; ~**ly** *adj* (*plain*) simple, sans prétention; ~**-made** *adj* fait(e) à la maison; **H~ Office** (*BRIT*) *n* ministère *m* de l'Intérieur; ~ **rule** *n* autonomie *f*; **H~ Secretary** (*BRIT*) *n* ministre *m* de l'Intérieur; ~**sick** *adj*: **to be** ~**sick** avoir le mal du pays; s'ennuyer de sa famille; ~ **town** *n* ville natale; ~**ward** *adj* (*journey*) du retour; ~**work** *n* devoirs *mpl*

homogeneous [hɔmə'dʒiːnɪəs] *adj* homogène

homosexual ['hɔməʊ'seksjʊəl] *adj, n* homosexuel(le)

honest ['ɒnɪst] *adj* honnête; (*sincere*) franc(franche); ~**ly** *adv* honnêtement; franchement; ~**y** *n* honnêteté *f*

honey ['hʌnɪ] *n* miel *m*; ~**comb** *n* rayon *m* de miel; ~**moon** *n* lune *f* de miel, voyage *m* de noces; ~**suckle** ['hʌnɪsʌkl] (*BOT*) *n* chèvrefeuille *m*

honk [hɔŋk] *vi* (*AUT*) klaxonner

honorary ['ɒnərərɪ] *adj* honoraire; (*duty, title*) honorifique

honour ['ɒnə*] (*US* honor) *vt* honorer ♦ *n* honneur *m*; **hono(u)rable** *adj* honorable; **hono(u)rs degree** (*SCOL*) licence avec mention

hood [hʊd] *n* capuchon *m*; (*of cooker*) hotte *f*; (*AUT: BRIT*) capote *f*; (: *US*) capot *m*

hoof [huːf] (*pl* hooves) *n* sabot *m*

hook [hʊk] *n* crochet *m*; (*on dress*) agrafe *f*; (*for fishing*) hameçon *m* ♦ *vt* accrocher; (*fish*) prendre

hooligan ['huːlɪgən] *n* voyou *m*

hoop [huːp] *n* cerceau *m*

hooray [huː'reɪ] *excl* hourra

hoot [huːt] *vi* (*AUT*) klaxonner; (*siren*) mugir; (*owl*) hululer; ~**er** *n* (*BRIT: AUT*) klaxon *m*; (*NAUT, factory*) sirène *f*

Hoover ['huːvə*] (®:*BRIT*) *n* aspirateur *m* ♦ *vt*: **h~** passer l'aspirateur dans *or* sur

hooves [huːvz] *npl of* hoof

hop [hɔp] *vi* (*on one foot*) sauter à cloche-pied; (*bird*) sautiller

hope [həʊp] *vt, vi* espérer ♦ *n* espoir *m*; **I ~ so** je l'espère; **I ~ not** j'espère que non; ~**ful** *adj* (*person*) plein(e) d'espoir, (*situation*) prometteur(euse), encourageant(e); ~**fully** *adv* (*expectantly*) avec espoir, avec optimisme; (*one hopes*) avec un peu de chance; ~**less** *adj* désespéré(e); (*useless*) nul(le)

hops [hɔps] *npl* houblon *m*

horizon [hə'raɪzn] *n* horizon *m*; ~**tal** [hɔrɪ'zɒntl] *adj* horizontal(e)

horn [hɔːn] *n* corne *f*; (*MUS: also:* French ~) cor *m*; (*AUT*) klaxon *m*

hornet ['hɔːnɪt] *n* frelon *m*

horny ['hɔːnɪ] (*inf*) *adj* (*aroused*) en rut, excité(e)

horoscope ['hɒrəskəʊp] *n* horoscope *m*

horrendous [hə'rendəs] *adj* horrible, affreux(euse)

horrible ['hɒrɪbl] *adj* horrible, affreux(euse)

horrid ['hɒrɪd] *adj* épouvantable

horrify ['hɒrɪfaɪ] *vt* horrifier

horror ['hɒrə*] *n* horreur *f*; ~ **film** *n* film *m* d'épouvante

hors d'œuvre [ɔː'dəːvrə] *n* (*CULIN*) hors-d'œuvre *m inv*

horse [hɔːs] *n* cheval *m*; ~**back** *n*: **on** ~**back** à cheval; ~ **chestnut** *n* marron *m* (d'Inde); ~**man** (*irreg*) *n* cavalier *m*; ~**power** *n* puissance *f* (en chevaux); ~**racing** *n* courses *fpl* de chevaux; ~**radish** *n* raifort *m*; ~**shoe** *n* fer *m* à cheval

hose [həʊz] *n* (*also:* ~**pipe**) tuyau *m*; (: *garden* ~) tuyau d'arrosage

hospitable [hɒs'pɪtəbl] *adj* hospitalier(ère)

hospital ['hɒspɪtl] *n* hôpital *m*; **in** ~ à l'hôpital

hospitality [hɒspɪ'tælɪtɪ] *n* hospitalité *f*

host [həʊst] *n* hôte *m*; (*TV, RADIO*) animateur(trice); (*REL*) hostie *f*; (*large number*): **a ~ of** une foule de

hostage ['hɒstɪdʒ] *n* otage *m*

hostel ['hɒstl] *n* foyer *m*; (*also:* youth ~) auberge *f* de jeunesse

hostess ['həʊstes] *n* hôtesse *f*; (*TV, RADIO*) animatrice *f*

hostile ['hɒstaɪl] *adj* hostile; **hostility** [hɒs'tɪlɪtɪ] *n* hostilité *f*

hot [hɒt] *adj* chaud(e); (*as opposed to only warm*) très chaud; (*spicy*) fort(e); (*contest etc*) acharné(e); (*temper*) passionné(e); **to be** ~ (*person*) avoir chaud; (*object*) être (très) chaud; **it is** ~ (*weather*) il fait chaud; ~**bed** *n* (*fig*) foyer *m*, pépinière *f*; ~ **dog** *n* hot-dog *m*

hotel [həʊ'tel] *n* hôtel *m*

hot: ~**-headed** *adj* impétueux(euse); ~**house** *n* serre (chaude); ~**line** (*POL*) téléphone *m* rouge, ligne directe; ~**ly** *adv* passionnément, violemment; ~**plate** *n* (*on cooker*) plaque chauffante; ~**-water bottle** *n* bouillotte *f*

hound [haʊnd] *vt* poursuivre avec acharnement ♦ *n* chien courant

hour ['aʊə*] *n* heure *f*; ~**ly** *adj, adv* toutes les heures; (*rate*) horaire

house [*n* haus, *pl* 'hauzɪz, *vb* hauz] *n* maison *f*; (*POL*) chambre *f*; (*THEATRE*) salle *f*, auditoire *m* ♦ *vt* (*person*) loger, héberger; (*objects*) abriter; **on the** ~ (*fig*) aux frais de la maison; ~ **arrest** *n* assignation *f* à résidence; ~**boat** *n* bateau *m* (aménagé en habitation); ~**bound** *adj* confiné(e) chez soi; ~**breaking** *n* cambriolage *m* (avec effraction); ~**coat** *n* peignoir *m*; ~**hold** *n* (*persons*) famille *f*, maisonnée *f*; (*ADMIN etc*) ménage *m*; ~**keeper** *n* gouvernante *f*; ~**keeping** *n* (*work*) ménage *m*; ~**keeping**

(money) argent *m* du ménage; **~-warming (party)** *n* pendaison *f* de crémaillère; **~wife** *(irreg)* *n* ménagère *f*; femme *f* au foyer; **~work** *n* (travaux *mpl* du) ménage *m*

housing ['hauzɪŋ] *n* logement *m*; **~ development**, **~ estate** *n* lotissement *m*

hovel ['hɒvəl] *n* taudis *m*

hover ['hɒvə*] *vi* planer; **~craft** *n* aéroglisseur *m*

how [hau] *adv* comment; **~ are you?** comment allez-vous?; **~ do you do?** bonjour; enchanté(e); **~ far is it to?** combien y a-t-il jusqu'à ...?; **~ long have you been here?** depuis combien de temps êtes-vous là?; **~ lovely!** que *or* comme c'est joli!; **~ many/much?** combien?; **~ many people/much milk?** combien de gens/lait?; **~ old are you?** quel âge avez-vous?

however [hau'evə*] *adv* de quelque façon *or* manière *que +subj*; *(+adj)* quelque *or* si ... *que +subj*; *(In questions)* comment ♦ *conj* pourtant, cependant

howl [haul] *vi* hurler

H.P. *abbr* = hire purchase

h.p. *abbr* = horsepower

HQ *abbr* = headquarters

hub [hʌb] *n (of wheel)* moyeu *m*; *(fig)* centre *m*, foyer *m*

hubbub ['hʌbʌb] *n* brouhaha *m*

hubcap ['hʌbkæp] *n* enjoliveur *m*

huddle ['hʌdl] *vi*: **to ~ together** se blottir les uns contre les autres

hue [hju:] *n* teinte *f*, nuance *f*; **~ and cry** *n* tollé (général), clameur *f*

huff [hʌf] *n*: **in a ~** fâché(e)

hug [hʌg] *vt* serrer dans ses bras; *(shore, kerb)* serrer

huge [hju:dʒ] *adj* énorme, immense

hulk [hʌlk] *n (ship)* épave *f*; *(car, building)* carcasse *f*; *(person)* mastodonte *m*

hull [hʌl] *n* coque *f*

hullo [hʌ'ləu] *excl* = hello

hum [hʌm] *vt (tune)* fredonner ♦ *vi* fredonner; *(insect)* bourdonner; *(plane, tool)* vrombir

human ['hju:mən] *adj* humain(e) ♦ *n* **~ (being)** être humain; **~e** [hju:'meɪn] *adj* humain(e), humanitaire; **~itarian** [hju:mænɪ'tɛərɪən] *adj* humanitaire; **~ity** [hju:'mænɪtɪ] *n* humanité *f*

humble ['hʌmbl] *adj* humble, modeste ♦ *vt* humilier

humbug ['hʌmbʌg] *n* fumisterie *f*, *(BRIT)* bonbon *m* à la menthe

humdrum ['hʌmdrʌm] *adj* monotone, banal(e)

humid ['hju:mɪd] *adj* humide

humiliate [hju:'mɪlɪeɪt] *vt* humilier; **humiliation** *n* humiliation *f*

humorous ['hju:mərəs] *adj* humoristique; *(person)* plein(e) d'humour

humour ['hju:mə*] *(US* humor*)* *n* humour *m*; *(mood)* humeur *f* ♦ *vt (person)* faire plaisir à; se prêter aux caprices de

hump [hʌmp] *n* bosse *f*

humpbacked ['hʌmpbækt] *adj*: **~ bridge** pont *m* en dos d'âne

hunch [hʌntʃ] *n (premonition)* intuition *f*; **~back** *n* bossu(e); **~ed** *adj* voûté(e)

hundred ['hʌndrɪd] *num* cent; **~s of** des centaines de; **~weight** *n (BRIT)* = 50.8 kg; *(US)* = 45.3 kg

hung [hʌŋ] *pt, pp of* hang

Hungary ['hʌŋgərɪ] *n* Hongrie *f*

hunger ['hʌŋgə*] *n* faim *f* ♦ *vi*: **to ~ for** avoir faim de, désirer ardemment

hungry ['hʌŋgrɪ] *adj* affamé(e); *(keen)*: **~ for** avide de; **to be ~** avoir faim

hunk [hʌŋk] *n (of bread etc)* gros morceau

hunt [hʌnt] *vt* chasser; *(criminal)* pourchasser ♦ *vi* chasser; *(search)*: **to ~ for** chercher (partout) ♦ *n* chasse *f*; **~er** *n* chasseur *m*; **~ing** *n* chasse *f*

hurdle ['hɜ:dl] *n (SPORT)* haie *f*; *(fig)* obstacle *m*

hurl [hɜ:l] *vt* lancer (avec violence); *(abuse, insults)* lancer

hurrah [hu'rɑ:] *excl* = hooray

hurray [hu'reɪ] *excl* = hooray

hurricane ['hʌrɪkən] *n* ouragan *m*

hurried ['hʌrɪd] *adj* pressé(e), précipité(e); *(work)* fait(e) à la hâte; **~ly** *adv* précipitamment, à la hâte

hurry ['hʌrɪ] *(vb: also: ~ up)* *n* hâte *f*, précipitation *f* ♦ *vi* se presser, se dépêcher ♦ *vt (person)* faire presser, faire se dépêcher; *(work)* presser; **to be in a ~** être pressé(e); **to do sth in a ~** faire qch en vitesse; **to ~ in/out** entrer/sortir précipitamment

hurt [hɜ:t] *(pt, pp* hurt*)* *vt (cause pain to)* faire mal à; *(injure, fig)* blesser ♦ *vi* faire mal ♦ *adj* blessé(e); **~ful** *adj (remark)* blessant(e)

hurtle ['hɜ:tl] *vi*: **to ~ past** passer en trombe; **to ~ down** dégringoler

husband ['hʌzbənd] *n* mari *m*

hush [hʌʃ] *n* calme *m*, silence *m* ♦ *vt* faire taire; **~!** chut!; **~ up** *vt (scandal)* étouffer

husk [hʌsk] *n (of wheat)* balle *f*; *(of rice, maize)* enveloppe *f*

husky ['hʌskɪ] *adj* rauque ♦ *n* chien *m* esquimau *or* de traîneau

hustle ['hʌsl] *vt* pousser, bousculer ♦ *n*: **~ and bustle** tourbillon *m* (d'activité)

hut [hʌt] *n* hutte *f*; *(shed)* cabane *f*

hutch [hʌtʃ] *n* clapier *m*

hyacinth ['haɪəsɪnθ] *n* jacinthe *f*

hydrant ['haɪdrənt] *n (also: fire ~)* bouche *f* d'incendie

hydraulic [haɪ'drɒlɪk] *adj* hydraulique

hydroelectric [haɪdrəu'lektrɪk] *adj* hydroélectrique

hydrofoil ['haɪdrəufɔɪl] *n* hydrofoil *m*

hydrogen ['haɪdrɪdʒən] *n* hydrogène *m*
hyena [haɪ'iːnə] *n* hyène *f*
hygiene ['haɪdʒiːn] *n* hygiène *f*
hymn [hɪm] *n* hymne *m*; cantique *m*
hype [haɪp] (*inf*) *n* battage *m* publicitaire
hypermarket ['haɪpə'mɑːkɪt] (*BRIT*) *n* hyper-marché *m*
hyphen ['haɪfən] *n* trait *m* d'union
hypnotize ['hɪpnətaɪz] *vt* hypnotiser
hypocrisy [hɪ'pɒkrɪsɪ] *n* hypocrisie *f*; **hypocrite** ['hɪpəkrɪt] *n* hypocrite *m/f*; **hypocritical** *adj* hypocrite
hypothesis [haɪ'pɒθɪsɪs] (*pl* ~es) *n* hypothèse *f*
hysterical [hɪs'terɪkəl] *adj* hystérique; (*funny*) hilarant(e); ~ **laughter** fou rire *m*
hysterics [hɪs'terɪks] *npl*: **to be in/have** ~ (*anger, panic*) avoir une crise de nerfs; (*laughter*) attraper un fou rire

——————— **I i**

I [aɪ] *pron* je; (*before vowel*) j'; (*stressed*) moi
ice [aɪs] *n* glace *f*, (*on road*) verglas *m* ♦ *vt* (*cake*) glacer ♦ *vi* (*also*: ~ **over**, ~ **up**) geler; (: *window*) se givrer; ~**berg** *n* iceberg *m*; ~**box** *n* (*US*) réfrigérateur *m*; (*BRIT*) compartiment *m* à glace; (*insulated box*) glacière *f*; ~ **cream** *n* glace *f*; ~ **cube** *n* glaçon *m*; ~**d** *adj* glacé(e); ~ **hockey** *n* hockey *m* sur glace; **I**~**land** ['aɪslənd] *n* Islande *f*; ~ **lolly** *n* (*BRIT*) esquimau *m* (glace); ~ **rink** *n* patinoire *f*; ~**skating** *n* patinage *m* (sur glace)
icicle ['aɪsɪkl] *n* glaçon *m* (*naturel*)
icing ['aɪsɪŋ] *n* (*CULIN*) glace *f*, ~ **sugar** (*BRIT*) *n* sucre *m* glace
icy ['aɪsɪ] *adj* glacé(e); (*road*) verglacé(e); (*weather, temperature*) glacial(e)
I'd [aɪd] = **I would; I had**
idea [aɪ'dɪə] *n* idée *f*
ideal [aɪ'dɪəl] *n* idéal *m* ♦ *adj* idéal(e)
identical [aɪ'dentɪkəl] *adj* identique
identification [aɪdentɪfɪ'keɪʃən] *n* identification *f*; **means of** ~ pièce *f* d'identité
identify [aɪ'dentɪfaɪ] *vt* identifier
Identikit picture [aɪ'dentɪkɪt-] ® *n* portrait-robot *m*
identity [aɪ'dentɪtɪ] *n* identité *f*; ~ **card** *n* carte *f* d'identité
ideology [aɪdɪ'ɒlədʒɪ] *n* idéologie *f*
idiom ['ɪdɪəm] *n* expression *f* idiomatique; (*style*) style *m*

idiosyncrasy [ɪdɪə'sɪŋkrəsɪ] *n* (*of person*) particularité *f*, petite manie
idiot ['ɪdɪət] *n* idiot(e), imbécile *m/f*; ~**ic** [ɪdɪ'ɒtɪk] *adj* idiot(e), bête, stupide
idle ['aɪdl] *adj* sans occupation, désœuvré(e); (*lazy*) oisif(ive), paresseux(euse); (*unemployed*) au chômage; (*question, pleasures*) vain(e), futile ♦ *vi* (*engine*) tourner au ralenti; **to lie** ~ être arrêté(e), ne pas fonctionner; ~ **away** *vt*: **to** ~ **away the time** passer son temps à ne rien faire
idol ['aɪdl] *n* idole *f*; ~**ize** *vt* idolâtrer, adorer
i.e. *adv abbr* (= *id est*) c'est-à-dire
if [ɪf] *conj* si; ~ **so** si c'est le cas; ~ **not** sinon; ~ **only** si seulement
ignite [ɪg'naɪt] *vt* mettre le feu à, enflammer ♦ *vi* s'enflammer
ignition [ɪg'nɪʃən] *n* (*AUT*) allumage *m*; **to switch on/off the** ~ mettre/couper le contact; ~ **key** *n* clé *f* de contact
ignorant ['ɪgnərənt] *adj* ignorant(e); **to be** ~ **of** (*subject*) ne rien connaître à; (*events*) ne pas être au courant de
ignore [ɪg'nɔː*] *vt* ne tenir aucun compte de; (*person*) faire semblant de ne pas reconnaître, ignorer; (*fact*) méconnaître
ill [ɪl] *adj* (*sick*) malade; (*bad*) mauvais(e) ♦ *n* mal *m* ♦ *adv*: **to speak/think** ~ **of** dire/penser du mal de; ~**s** *npl* (*misfortunes*) maux *mpl*, malheurs *mpl*; **to be taken** ~ tomber malade; ~**-advised** *adj* (*decision*) peu judicieux(euse); (*person*) malavisé(e); ~**-at-ease** *adj* mal à l'aise
I'll [aɪl] = **I will; I shall**
illegal [ɪ'liːgəl] *adj* illégal(e)
illegible [ɪ'ledʒəbl] *adj* illisible
illegitimate [ɪlɪ'dʒɪtɪmət] *adj* illégitime
ill: ~**-fated** [ɪl'feɪtɪd] *adj* malheureux(euse); (*day*) néfaste; ~ **feeling** *n* ressentiment *m*, rancune *f*
illiterate [ɪ'lɪtərət] *adj* illettré(e); (*letter*) plein(e) de fautes
ill: ~**-mannered** [ɪl'mænəd] *adj* (*child*) mal élevé(e); ~**ness** [ɪl'nɪs] *n* maladie *f*; ~**treat** [ɪl'triːt] *vt* maltraiter
illuminate [ɪ'luːmɪneɪt] *vt* (*room, street*) éclairer; (*for special effect*) illuminer; **illumination** [ɪluːmɪ'neɪʃən] *n* éclairage *m*; illumination *f*
illusion [ɪ'luːʒən] *n* illusion *f*
illustrate ['ɪləstreɪt] *vt* illustrer; **illustration** [ɪləs'treɪʃən] *n* illustration *f*
ill will *n* malveillance *f*
I'm [aɪm] = **I am**
image ['ɪmɪdʒ] *n* image *f*; (*public face*) image de marque; ~**ry** *n* images *fpl*
imaginary [ɪ'mædʒɪnərɪ] *adj* imaginaire
imagination [ɪmædʒɪ'neɪʃən] *n* imagination *f*
imaginative [ɪ'mædʒɪnətɪv] *adj* imaginatif(ive); (*person*) plein(e) d'imagination

imagine [ɪ'mædʒɪn] vt imaginer, s'imaginer; (suppose) imaginer, supposer

imbalance [ɪm'bæləns] n déséquilibre m

imbue [ɪm'bjuː] vt: **to ~ sb/sth with** imprégner qn/qch de

imitate ['ɪmɪteɪt] vt imiter; **imitation** [ɪmɪ'teɪʃən] n imitation f

immaculate [ɪ'mækjʊlɪt] adj impeccable; (REL) immaculé(e)

immaterial [ɪmə'tɪərɪəl] adj sans importance, insignifiant(e)

immature [ɪmə'tjuə*] adj (fruit) (qui n'est pas mûr(e); (person) qui manque de maturité

immediate [ɪ'miːdɪət] adj immédiat(e); ~**ly** adv (at once) immédiatement; ~**ly next to** juste à côté de

immense [ɪ'mens] adj immense; énorme

immerse [ɪ'mɜːs] vt immerger, plonger; **immersion heater** [ɪ'mɜːʃən-] (BRIT) n chauffe-eau m électrique

immigrant ['ɪmɪgrənt] n immigrant(e); immigré(e); **immigration** [ɪmɪ'greɪʃən] n immigration f

imminent ['ɪmɪnənt] adj imminent(e)

immoral [ɪ'mɒrəl] adj immoral(e)

immortal [ɪ'mɔːtl] adj, n immortel(le)

immune [ɪ'mjuːn] adj: **~ (to)** immunisé(e) (contre); (fig) à l'abri de; **immunity** [ɪ'mjuːnɪtɪ] n immunité f

imp [ɪmp] n lutin m; (child) petit diable

impact ['ɪmpækt] n choc m, impact m; (fig) impact

impair [ɪm'peə*] vt détériorer, diminuer

impart [ɪm'pɑːt] vt communiquer, transmettre; (flavour) donner

impartial [ɪm'pɑːʃəl] adj impartial(e)

impassable [ɪm'pɑːsəbl] adj infranchissable; (road) impraticable

impassive [ɪm'pæsɪv] adj impassible

impatience [ɪm'peɪʃəns] n impatience f

impatient [ɪm'peɪʃənt] adj impatient(e); **to get** or **grow ~** s'impatienter

impeccable [ɪm'pekəbl] adj impeccable, parfait(e)

impede [ɪm'piːd] vt gêner

impediment [ɪm'pedɪmənt] n obstacle m; (also: speech **~**) défaut m d'élocution

impending [ɪm'pendɪŋ] adj imminent(e)

imperative [ɪm'perətɪv] adj (need) urgent(e), pressant(e); (tone) impérieux(euse) ♦ n (LING) impératif m

imperfect [ɪm'pɜːfɪkt] adj imparfait(e); (goods etc) défectueux(euse)

imperial [ɪm'pɪərɪəl] adj impérial(e); (BRIT: measure) légal(e)

impersonal [ɪm'pɜːsnl] adj impersonnel(le)

impersonate [ɪm'pɜːsəneɪt] vt se faire passer pour; (THEATRE) imiter

impertinent [ɪm'pɜːtɪnənt] adj impertinent(e), insolent(e)

impervious [ɪm'pɜːvɪəs] adj (fig): **~ to** insensible à

impetuous [ɪm'petjuəs] adj impétueux(euse), fougueux(euse)

impetus ['ɪmpɪtəs] n impulsion f; (of runner) élan m

impinge [ɪm'pɪndʒ]: **to ~ on** vt fus (person) affecter, toucher; (rights) empiéter sur

implement [n 'ɪmplɪmənt, vb 'ɪmplɪment] n outil m, instrument m; (for cooking) ustensile m ♦ vt exécuter

implicit [ɪm'plɪsɪt] adj implicite; (complete) absolu(e), sans réserve

imply [ɪm'plaɪ] vt suggérer, laisser entendre; indiquer, supposer

impolite [ɪmpə'laɪt] adj impoli(e)

import [vb ɪm'pɔːt, n 'ɪmpɔːt] vt importer ♦ n (COMM) importation f

importance [ɪm'pɔːtəns] n importance f

important [ɪm'pɔːtənt] adj important(e)

importer [ɪm'pɔːtə*] n importateur(trice)

impose [ɪm'pəʊz] vt imposer ♦ vi: **to ~ on sb** abuser de la gentillesse de qn; **imposing** [ɪm'pəʊzɪŋ] adj imposant(e), impressionnant(e); **imposition** [ɪmpə'zɪʃən] n (of tax etc) imposition f; **to be an imposition on** (person) abuser de la gentillesse or la bonté de

impossible [ɪm'pɒsəbl] adj impossible

impotent ['ɪmpətənt] adj impuissant(e)

impound [ɪm'paʊnd] vt confisquer, saisir

impoverished [ɪm'pɒvərɪʃt] adj appauvri(e), pauvre

impractical [ɪm'præktɪkəl] adj pas pratique; (person) qui manque d'esprit pratique

impregnable [ɪm'pregnəbl] adj (fortress) imprenable

impress [ɪm'pres] vt impressionner, faire impression sur; (mark) imprimer, marquer; **to ~ sth on sb** faire bien comprendre qch à qn

impression [ɪm'preʃən] n impression f; (of stamp, seal) empreinte f; (imitation) imitation f; **to be under the ~ that** avoir l'impression que; ~**ist** n (ART) impressionniste m/f; (entertainer) imitateur(trice) m/f

impressive [ɪm'presɪv] adj impressionnant(e)

imprint ['ɪmprɪnt] n (outline) marque f, empreinte f

imprison [ɪm'prɪzn] vt emprisonner, mettre en prison

improbable [ɪm'prɒbəbl] adj improbable; (excuse) peu plausible

improper [ɪm'prɒpə*] adj (unsuitable) déplacé(e), de mauvais goût; indécent(e); (dishonest) malhonnête

improve [ɪm'pruːv] vt améliorer ♦ vi s'améliorer; (pupil etc) faire des progrès; ~**ment** n amélioration f (in de); progrès m

improvise ['ɪmprəvaɪz] vt, vi improviser

impudent ['ɪmpjʊdənt] adj impudent(e)

impulse ['ɪmpʌls] n impulsion f; **on ~** impulsivement, sur un coup de tête; **impulsive** [ɪm'pʌlsɪv] *adj* impulsif(ive)

in [ɪn] *prep* **1** (*indicating place, position*) dans; ~ **the house/the fridge** dans la maison/le frigo; ~ **the garden** dans le *or* au jardin; ~ **town** en ville; ~ **the country** à la campagne; ~ **school** à l'école; ~ **here/there** ici/là
2 (*with place names: of town, region, country*): ~ **London** à Londres; ~ **England** en Angleterre; ~ **Japan** au Japon; ~ **the United States** aux États-Unis
3 (*indicating time: during*): ~ **spring** au printemps; ~ **summer** en été; ~ **May/1992** en mai/1992; ~ **the afternoon** (dans) l'après-midi; **at 4 o'clock** ~ **the afternoon** à 4 heures de l'après-midi
4 (*indicating time: in the space of*) en; (*: future*) dans; **I did it** ~ **3 hours/days** je l'ai fait en 3 heures/jours; **I'll see you** ~ **2 weeks** *or* ~ **2 weeks' time** je te verrai dans 2 semaines
5 (*indicating manner etc*) à; ~ **a loud/soft voice** à voix haute/basse; ~ **pencil** au crayon; ~ **French** en français; **the boy** ~ **the blue shirt** le garçon à *or* avec la chemise bleue
6 (*indicating circumstances*): ~ **the sun** au soleil; ~ **the shade** à l'ombre; ~ **the rain** sous la pluie
7 (*indicating mood, state*): ~ **tears** en larmes; ~ **anger** sous le coup de la colère; ~ **despair** au désespoir; ~ **good condition** en bon état; **to live** ~ **luxury** vivre dans le luxe
8 (*with ratios, numbers*): **1** ~ **10** (**households**), **1** (**household**) ~ **10** 1 (ménage) sur 10; **20 pence** ~ **the pound** 20 pence par livre sterling; **they lined up** ~ **twos** ils se mirent en rangs (deux) par deux; ~ **hundreds** par centaines
9 (*referring to people, works*) chez; **the disease is common** ~ **children** c'est une maladie courante chez les enfants; ~ (**the works of**) **Dickens** chez Dickens, dans (l'œuvre de) Dickens
10 (*indicating profession etc*) dans; **to be** ~ **teaching** être dans l'enseignement
11 (*after superlative*) de; **the best pupil** ~ **the class** le meilleur élève de la classe
12 (*with present participle*): ~ **saying this** en disant ceci
♦ *adv*: **to be** ~ (*person: at home, work*) être là; (*train, ship, plane*) être arrivé(e); (*in fashion*) être à la mode; **to ask sb** ~ inviter qn à entrer; **to run/limp** *etc* ~ entrer en courant/boitant *etc*
♦ *n*: **the** ~**s and outs (of)** (*of proposal, situation etc*) les tenants et aboutissants (de)

in. *abbr* = **inch**
inability [ɪnə'bɪlɪtɪ] *n* incapacité *f*
inaccurate [ɪn'ækjʊrɪt] *adj* inexact(e); (*person*) qui manque de précision
inadequate [ɪn'ædɪkwət] *adj* insuffisant(e), inadéquat(e)
inadvertently [ɪnəd'vɜːtəntlɪ] *adv* par mégarde
inadvisable [ɪnəd'vaɪzəbl] *adj* (*action*) à déconseiller
inane [ɪ'neɪn] *adj* inepte, stupide
inanimate [ɪn'ænɪmət] *adj* inanimé(e)
inappropriate [ɪnə'prəʊprɪət] *adj* inopportun(e), mal à propos; (*word, expression*) impropre
inarticulate [ɪnɑː'tɪkjʊlət] *adj* (*person*) qui s'exprime mal; (*speech*) indistinct(e)
inasmuch as [ɪnəz'mʌtʃəz] *adv* (*insofar as*) dans la mesure où; (*seeing that*) attendu que
inauguration [ɪnɔːgjʊ'reɪʃən] *n* inauguration *f*; (*of president*) investiture *f*
inborn ['ɪn'bɔːn] *adj* (*quality*) inné(e)
inbred ['ɪn'bred] *adj* inné(e), naturel(le); (*family*) consanguin(e)
inc. *abbr* = **incorporated**
incapable [ɪn'keɪpəbl] *adj* incapable
incapacitate [ɪnkə'pæsɪteɪt] *vt*: **to** ~ **sb from doing** rendre qn incapable de faire
incense [*n* 'ɪnsens, *vb* ɪn'sens] *n* encens *m*
♦ *vt* (*anger*) mettre en colère
incentive [ɪn'sentɪv] *n* encouragement *m*, raison *f* de se donner de la peine
incessant [ɪn'sesnt] *adj* incessant(e); ~**ly** *adv* sans cesse, constamment
inch [ɪntʃ] *n* pouce *m* (= 25 mm; 12 in a foot); **within an** ~ **of** à deux doigts de; **he didn't give an** ~ (*fig*) il n'a pas voulu céder d'un pouce; ~ **forward** *vi* avancer petit à petit
incident ['ɪnsɪdənt] *n* incident *m*
incidental [ɪnsɪ'dentl] *adj* (*additional*) accessoire; ~ **to** qui accompagne; ~**ly** *adv* (*by the way*) à propos
inclination [ɪnklɪ'neɪʃən] *n* (*fig*) inclination *f*
incline [*n* 'ɪnklaɪn, *vb* ɪn'klaɪn] *n* pente *f* ♦ *vt* incliner ♦ *vi* (*surface*) s'incliner; **to be** ~**d to do** avoir tendance à faire
include [ɪn'kluːd] *vt* inclure, comprendre; **including** [ɪn'kluːdɪŋ] *prep* y compris
inclusive [ɪn'kluːsɪv] *adj* inclus(e), compris(e); ~ **of tax** *etc* taxes *etc* comprises
income ['ɪnkʌm] *n* revenu *m*; ~ **tax** *n* impôt *m* sur le revenu
incoming ['ɪnkʌmɪŋ] *adj* qui arrive; (*president*) entrant(e); ~ **mail** courrier *m* du jour; ~ **tide** marée montante
incompetent [ɪn'kɒmpɪtənt] *adj* incompétent(e), incapable

incomplete [ɪnkəm'pliːt] *adj* incomplet(ète)

incongruous [ɪn'kɒŋgruəs] *adj* incongru(e)

inconsiderate [ɪnkən'sɪdərɪt] *adj* (*person*) qui manque d'égards; (*action*) inconsidéré(e)

inconsistency [ɪnkən'sɪstənsɪ] *n* (*of actions etc*) inconséquence *f*; (*of work*) irrégularité *f*; (*of statement etc*) incohérence *f*

inconsistent [ɪnkən'sɪstənt] *adj* inconséquent(e); irrégulier(ère); peu cohérent(e); ~ **with** incompatible avec

inconspicuous [ɪnkən'spɪkjuəs] *adj* qui passe inaperçu(e); (*colour, dress*) discret(ète)

inconvenience [ɪnkən'viːnɪəns] *n* inconvénient *m*; (*trouble*) dérangement *m* ♦ *vt* déranger

inconvenient [ɪnkən'viːnɪənt] *adj* (*house*) malcommode; (*time, place*) mal choisi(e), qui ne convient pas; (*visitor*) importun(e)

incorporate [ɪn'kɔːpəreɪt] *vt* incorporer; (*contain*) contenir; ~**d company** (*US*) *n* ≈ société *f* anonyme

incorrect [ɪnkə'rekt] *adj* incorrect(e)

increase [*n* 'ɪnkriːs, *vb* ɪn'kriːs] *n* augmentation *f* ♦ *vi, vt* augmenter; **increasing** [ɪn'kriːsɪŋ] *adj* (*number*) croissant(e); **increasingly** [ɪn'kriːsɪŋlɪ] *adv* de plus en plus

incredible [ɪn'kredəbl] *adj* incroyable

incredulous [ɪn'kredjuləs] *adj* incrédule

incubator ['ɪnkjubeɪtə*] *n* (*for babies*) couveuse *f*

incumbent [ɪn'kʌmbənt] *n* (*president*) président *m* en exercice; (*REL*) titulaire *m/f* ♦ *adj*: **it is ~ on him to ...** il lui incombe *or* appartient de ...

incur [ɪn'kɜː*] *vt* (*expenses*) encourir; (*anger, risk*) s'exposer à; (*debt*) contracter; (*loss*) subir

indebted [ɪn'detɪd] *adj*: **to be ~ to sb (for)** être redevable à qn (de)

indecent [ɪn'diːsnt] *adj* indécent(e), inconvenant(e); ~ **assault** (*BRIT*) *n* attentat *m* à la pudeur; ~ **exposure** *n* outrage *m* (public) à la pudeur

indecisive [ɪndɪ'saɪsɪv] *adj* (*person*) indécis(e)

indeed [ɪn'diːd] *adv* vraiment; en effet; (*furthermore*) d'ailleurs; **yes ~!** certainement!

indefinitely [ɪn'defɪnɪtlɪ] *adv* (*wait*) indéfiniment

indemnity [ɪn'demnɪtɪ] *n* (*safeguard*) assurance *f*, garantie *f*; (*compensation*) indemnité *f*

independence [ɪndɪ'pendəns] *n* indépendance *f*; **independent** [ɪndɪ'pendənt] *adj* indépendant(e); (*school*) privé(e); (*radio*) libre

index ['ɪndeks] *n* (*pl*: ~**es**: *in book*) index *m*; (: *in library etc*) catalogue *m*; (*pl*: *indices*: *ratio, sign*) indice *m*; ~ **card** *n* fiche *f*; ~-**finger** *n* index *m*; ~-**linked** *adj* indexé(e)

(sur le coût de la vie *etc*)

India ['ɪndɪə] *n* Inde *f*; ~**n** *adj* indien(ne) ♦ *n* Indien(ne); (**American**) ~**n** Indien(ne) (d'Amérique)

indicate ['ɪndɪkeɪt] *vt* indiquer; **indication** [ɪndɪ'keɪʃən] *n* indication *f*, signe *m*; **indicative** [ɪn'dɪkətɪv] *adj*: **indicative of** symptomatique de ♦ *n* (*LING*) indicatif *m*; **indicator** ['ɪndɪkeɪtə*] *n* (*sign*) indicateur *m*; (*AUT*) clignotant *m*

indices ['ɪndɪsiːz] *npl of* **index**

indictment [ɪn'daɪtmənt] *n* accusation *f*

indifferent [ɪn'dɪfrənt] *adj* indifférent(e); (*poor*) médiocre, quelconque

indigenous [ɪn'dɪdʒɪnəs] *adj* indigène

indigestion [ɪndɪ'dʒestʃən] *n* indigestion *f*, mauvaise digestion

indignant [ɪn'dɪgnənt] *adj*: ~ (**at sth/with sb**) indigné(e) (de qch/contre qn)

indignity [ɪn'dɪgnɪtɪ] *n* indignité *f*, affront *m*

indirect [ɪndɪ'rekt] *adj* indirect(e)

indiscreet [ɪndɪs'kriːt] *adj* indiscret(ète); (*rash*) imprudent(e)

indiscriminate [ɪndɪs'krɪmɪnət] *adj* (*person*) qui manque de discernement; (*killings*) commis(e) au hasard

indisputable [ɪndɪs'pjuːtəbl] *adj* incontestable, indiscutable

individual [ɪndɪ'vɪdjuəl] *n* individu *m* ♦ *adj* individuel(le); (*characteristic*) particulier(ère), original(e)

indoctrination [ɪndɒktrɪ'neɪʃən] *n* endoctrinement *m*

Indonesia [ɪndəʊ'niːzɪə] *n* Indonésie *f*

indoor ['ɪndɔː*] *adj* (*plant*) d'appartement; (*swimming pool*) couvert(e); (*sport, games*) pratiqué(e) en salle; ~**s** [ɪn'dɔːz] *adv* à l'intérieur

induce [ɪn'djuːs] *vt* (*persuade*) persuader; (*bring about*) provoquer; ~**ment** *n* (*incentive*) récompense *f*; (*pej: bribe*) pot-de-vin *m*

indulge [ɪn'dʌldʒ] *vt* (*whim*) céder à, satisfaire; (*child*) gâter ♦ *vi*: **to ~ in sth** (*luxury*) se permettre qch; (*fantasies etc*) se livrer à qch; ~**nce** *n* fantaisie *f* (que l'on s'offre); (*leniency*) indulgence *f*; ~**nt** *adj* indulgent(e)

industrial [ɪn'dʌstrɪəl] *adj* industriel(le); (*injury*) du travail; ~ **action** *n* action revendicative; ~ **estate** (*BRIT*) *n* zone industrielle; ~**ist** *n* industriel *m*; ~ **park** (*US*) *n* = **industrial estate**

industrious [ɪn'dʌstrɪəs] *adj* travailleur(euse)

industry ['ɪndəstrɪ] *n* industrie *f*; (*diligence*) zèle *m*, application *f*

inebriated [ɪ'niːbrɪeɪtɪd] *adj* ivre

inedible [ɪn'edɪbl] *adj* immangeable; (*plant etc*) non comestible

ineffective [ɪnɪ'fektɪv], **ineffectual** [ɪnɪ'fektjuəl] *adj* inefficace

inefficient [ɪnɪ'fɪʃənt] *adj* inefficace
inequality [ɪnɪ'kwɒlɪtɪ] *n* inégalité *f*
inescapable [ɪnɪs'keɪpəbl] *adj* inéluctable,
inévitable
inevitable [ɪn'evɪtəbl] *adj* inévitable; **inevitably** *adv* inévitablement
inexhaustible [ɪnɪg'zɔːstəbl] *adj* inépuisable
inexpensive [ɪnɪks'pensɪv] *adj* bon marché
inv
inexperienced [ɪnɪks'pɪərɪənst] *adj* inexpé-
rimenté(e)
infallible [ɪn'fæləbl] *adj* infaillible
infamous ['ɪnfəməs] *adj* infâme, abominable
infancy ['ɪnfənsɪ] *n* petite enfance, bas âge
infant ['ɪnfənt] *n* (*baby*) nourrisson *m*;
(*young child*) petit(e) enfant; ~ **school**
(*BRIT*) *n* classes *fpl* préparatoires (*entre 5 et
7 ans*)
infatuated [ɪn'fætjʊeɪtɪd] *adj*: ~ **with** enti-
ché(e) de; **infatuation** [ɪnfætjʊ'eɪʃən] *n* engouement *m*
infect [ɪn'fekt] *vt* infecter, contaminer;
~**ion** [ɪn'fekʃən] *n* infection *f*; (*contagion*)
contagion *f*; ~**ious** [ɪn'fekʃəs] *adj* infec-
tieux(euse); (*also fig*) contagieux(euse)
infer [ɪn'fɜː*] *vt* conclure, déduire; (*imply*)
suggérer
inferior [ɪn'fɪərɪə*] *adj* inférieur(e); (*goods*)
de qualité inférieure ♦ *n* inférieur(e); (*in
rank*) subalterne *m/f*; ~**ity** [ɪnfɪərɪ'ɒrɪtɪ] *n*
infériorité *f*; ~**ity complex** *n* complexe *m*
d'infériorité
inferno [ɪn'fɜːnəʊ] *n* (*blaze*) brasier *m*
infertile [ɪn'fɜːtaɪl] *adj* stérile
infighting ['ɪnfaɪtɪŋ] *n* querelles *fpl* internes
infinite ['ɪnfɪnɪt] *adj* infini(e)
infinitive [ɪn'fɪnɪtɪv] *n* infinitif *m*
infinity [ɪn'fɪnɪtɪ] *n* infinité *f*; (*also MATH*)
infini *m*
infirmary [ɪn'fɜːmərɪ] *n* (*hospital*) hôpital *m*
inflamed [ɪn'fleɪmd] *adj* enflammé(e)
inflammable [ɪn'flæməbl] (*BRIT*) *adj* inflammable
inflammation [ɪnflə'meɪʃən] *n* inflammation *f*
inflatable [ɪn'fleɪtəbl] *adj* gonflable
inflate [ɪn'fleɪt] *vt* (*tyre, balloon*) gonfler;
(*price*) faire monter; **inflation** [ɪn'fleɪʃən] *n*
(*ECON*) inflation *f*; **inflationary**
[ɪn'fleɪʃnərɪ] *adj* inflationniste
inflict [ɪn'flɪkt] *vt*: **to** ~ **on** infliger à
influence ['ɪnflʊəns] *n* influence *f* ♦ *vt* influencer; **under the** ~ **of alcohol** en état
d'ébriété; **influential** [ɪnflʊ'enʃəl] *adj* in-
fluent(e)
influenza [ɪnflʊ'enzə] *n* grippe *f*
influx ['ɪnflʌks] *n* afflux *m*
inform [ɪn'fɔːm] *vt*: **to** ~ **sb (of)** informer
or avertir qn (de) ♦ *vi*: **to** ~ **on sb** dénoncer qn

informal [ɪn'fɔːməl] *adj* (*person, manner,
party*) simple; (*visit, discussion*) dénué(e) de
formalités; (*announcement, invitation*) non
officiel(le); (*colloquial*) familier(ère); ~**ity**
[ɪnfɔː'mælɪtɪ] *n* simplicité *f*, absence *f* de cérémonie; caractère non officiel
informant [ɪn'fɔːmənt] *n* informateur(trice)
information [ɪnfə'meɪʃən] *n* information *f*,
renseignements *mpl*; (*knowledge*) connaissances *fpl*; **a piece of** ~ un renseignement;
~ **office** *n* bureau *m* de renseignements
informative [ɪn'fɔːmətɪv] *adj* instructif(ive)
informer [ɪn'fɔːmə*] *n* (*also: police* ~) indi-
cateur(trice)
infringe [ɪn'frɪndʒ] *vt* enfreindre ♦ *vi*: **to** ~
on empiéter sur; ~**ment** *n*: ~**ment (of)** infraction *f* (à)
infuriating [ɪn'fjʊərɪeɪtɪŋ] *adj* exaspérant(e)
ingenious [ɪn'dʒiːnɪəs] *adj* ingénieux(euse);
ingenuity [ɪndʒɪ'njuːɪtɪ] *n* ingéniosité *f*
ingenuous [ɪn'dʒenjʊəs] *adj* naïf(naïve), in-
génu(e)
ingot ['ɪŋgət] *n* lingot *m*
ingrained [ɪn'greɪnd] *adj* enraciné(e)
ingratiate [ɪn'greɪʃɪeɪt] *vt*: **to** ~ **o.s. with**
s'insinuer dans les bonnes grâces de, se fai-
re bien voir de
ingredient [ɪn'griːdɪənt] *n* ingrédient *m*;
(*fig*) élément *m*
inhabit [ɪn'hæbɪt] *vt* habiter; ~**ant**
[ɪn'hæbɪtnt] *n* habitant(e)
inhale [ɪn'heɪl] *vt* respirer; (*smoke*) avaler ♦
vi aspirer; (*in smoking*) avaler la fumée
inherent [ɪn'hɪərənt] *adj*: ~ **(in or to)** inhé-
rent(e) (à)
inherit [ɪn'herɪt] *vt* hériter (de); ~**ance** *n*
héritage *m*
inhibit [ɪn'hɪbɪt] *vt* (*PSYCH*) inhiber;
(*growth*) freiner; ~**ion** [ɪnhɪ'bɪʃən] *n* inhibition *f*
inhuman [ɪn'hjuːmən] *adj* inhumain(e)
initial [ɪ'nɪʃəl] *adj* initial(e) ♦ *n* initiale *f* ♦
vt parafer; ~**s** *npl* (*letters*) initiales *fpl*; (*as
signature*) parafe *m*; ~**ly** *adv* initialement,
au début
initiate [ɪ'nɪʃɪeɪt] *vt* (*start*) entreprendre;
amorcer; lancer; (*person*) initier; **to** ~ **proceedings against sb** intenter une action à
qn
initiative [ɪ'nɪʃətɪv] *n* initiative *f*
inject [ɪn'dʒekt] *vt* injecter; (*person*): **to** ~
sb with sth faire une piqûre de qch à qn;
~**ion** [ɪn'dʒekʃən] *n* injection *f*, piqûre *f*
injure ['ɪndʒə*] *vt* blesser; (*reputation etc*)
compromettre; ~**d** *adj* blessé(e); **injury**
['ɪndʒərɪ] *n* blessure *f*; **injury time** *n*
(*SPORT*) arrêts *mpl* de jeu
injustice [ɪn'dʒʌstɪs] *n* injustice *f*
ink [ɪŋk] *n* encre *f*
inkling ['ɪŋklɪŋ] *n*: **to have an/no** ~ **of**
avoir une (vague) idée de/n'avoir aucune
idée de

inlaid ['ɪn'leɪd] *adj* incrusté(e); (*table etc*) marqueté(e)

inland [*adj* 'ɪnlənd, *adv* 'ɪnlænd] *adj* intérieur(e) ♦ *adv* à l'intérieur, dans les terres; **I~ Revenue** (*BRIT*) *n* fisc *m*

in-laws ['ɪnlɔːz] *npl* beaux-parents *mpl*; belle famille

inlet ['ɪnlet] *n* (*GEO*) crique *f*

inmate ['ɪnmeɪt] *n* (*in prison*) détenu(e); (*in asylum*) interné(e)

inn [ɪn] *n* auberge *f*

innate [ɪ'neɪt] *adj* inné(e)

inner ['ɪnə*] *adj* intérieur(e); ~ **city** *n* centre *m* de zone urbaine; ~ **tube** *n* (*of tyre*) chambre *f* à air

innings ['ɪnɪŋz] *n* (*CRICKET*) tour *m* de batte

innocent ['ɪnəsnt] *adj* innocent(e)

innocuous [ɪ'nɒkjuəs] *adj* inoffensif(ive)

innuendo [ɪnjuˈendəu] (*pl* ~es) *n* insinuation *f*, allusion (malveillante)

innumerable [ɪ'njuːmərəbl] *adj* innombrable

inordinately [ɪ'nɔːdɪnɪtlɪ] *adv* démesurément

inpatient ['ɪnpeɪʃənt] *n* malade hospitalisé(e)

input ['ɪnput] *n* (*resources*) ressources *fpl*; (*COMPUT*) entrée *f* (de données); (: *data*) données *fpl*

inquest ['ɪnkwest] *n* enquête *f*; (*coroner's*) ~ enquête judiciaire

inquire [ɪn'kwaɪə*] *vi* demander ♦ *vt* demander; **to** ~ **about** se renseigner sur; ~ **into** *vt fus* faire une enquête sur; **inquiry** [ɪn'kwaɪərɪ] *n* demande *f* de renseignements; (*investigation*) enquête *f*, investigation *f*; **inquiry office** (*BRIT*) *n* bureau *m* de renseignements

inquisitive [ɪn'kwɪzɪtɪv] *adj* curieux(euse)

inroads ['ɪnrəudz] *npl*: **to make** ~ **into** (*savings etc*) entamer

ins *abbr* = **inches**

insane [ɪn'seɪn] *adj* fou(folle); (*MED*) aliéné(e); **insanity** [ɪn'sænɪtɪ] *n* folie *f*; (*MED*) aliénation (mentale)

inscription [ɪn'skrɪpʃən] *n* inscription *f*; (*in book*) dédicace *f*

inscrutable [ɪn'skruːtəbl] *adj* impénétrable; (*comment*) obscur(e)

insect ['ɪnsekt] *n* insecte *m*; ~**icide** [ɪn'sektɪsaɪd] *n* insecticide *m*

insecure [ɪnsɪ'kjuə*] *adj* peu solide; peu sûr(e); (*person*) anxieux(euse)

insensitive [ɪn'sensɪtɪv] *adj* insensible

insert [ɪn'sɜːt] *vt* insérer; ~**ion** [ɪn'sɜːʃən] *n* insertion *f*

in-service ['ɪn'sɜːvɪs] *adj* (*training*) continu(e), en cours d'emploi; (*course*) de perfectionnement; de recyclage

inshore ['ɪn'ʃɔː*] *adj* côtier(ère) ♦ *adv* près de la côte; (*move*) vers la côte

inside ['ɪn'saɪd] *n* intérieur *m* ♦ *adj* intérieur(e) ♦ *adv* à l'intérieur, dedans ♦ *prep* à l'intérieur de; (*of time*): ~ **10 minutes** en moins de 10 minutes; ~**s** *npl* (*inf*) intestins *mpl*; ~ **information** *n* renseignements obtenus à la source; ~ **lane** *n* (*AUT: BRIT*) voie *f* de gauche; (: *US, Europe etc*) voie de droite; ~ **out** *adv* à l'envers; (*know*) à fond

insider dealing, insider trading *n* (*St Ex*) délit *m* d'initié

insight ['ɪnsaɪt] *n* perspicacité *f*; (*glimpse, idea*) aperçu *m*

insignificant [ɪnsɪg'nɪfɪkənt] *adj* insignifiant(e)

insincere [ɪnsɪn'sɪə*] *adj* hypocrite

insinuate [ɪn'sɪnjueɪt] *vt* insinuer

insist [ɪn'sɪst] *vi* insister; **to** ~ **on doing** insister pour faire; **to** ~ **on sth** exiger qch; **to** ~ **that** insister pour que; (*claim*) maintenir *or* soutenir que; ~**ent** *adj* insistant(e), pressant(e); (*noise, action*) ininterrompu(e)

insole ['ɪnsəul] *n* (*removable*) semelle intérieure

insolent ['ɪnsələnt] *adj* insolent(e)

insolvent [ɪn'sɒlvənt] *adj* insolvable

insomnia [ɪn'sɒmnɪə] *n* insomnie *f*

inspect [ɪn'spekt] *vt* inspecter; (*ticket*) contrôler; ~**ion** [ɪn'spekʃən] *n* inspection *f*; contrôle *m*; ~**or** *n* inspecteur(trice); (*BRIT: on buses, trains*) contrôleur(euse)

inspire [ɪn'spaɪə*] *vt* inspirer

install [ɪn'stɔːl] *vt* installer; ~**ation** [ɪnstə'leɪʃən] *n* installation *f*

instalment [ɪn'stɔːlmənt] (*US* **Installment**) *n* acompte *m*, versement partiel; (*of TV serial etc*) épisode *m*; **in** ~**s** (*pay*) à tempérament; (*receive*) en plusieurs fois

instance ['ɪnstəns] *n* exemple *m*; **for** ~ par exemple; **in the first** ~ tout d'abord, en premier lieu

instant ['ɪnstənt] *n* instant *m* ♦ *adj* immédiat(e); (*coffee, food*) instantané(e), en poudre; ~**ly** *adv* immédiatement, tout de suite

instead [ɪn'sted] *adv* au lieu de cela; ~ **of** au lieu de; ~ **of sb** à la place de qn

instep ['ɪnstep] *n* cou-de-pied *m*; (*of shoe*) cambrure *f*

instigate ['ɪnstɪgeɪt] *vt* (*rebellion*) fomenter, provoquer; (*talks etc*) promouvoir

instil [ɪn'stɪl] *vt*: **to** ~ (**into**) inculquer (à); (*courage*) insuffler (à)

instinct ['ɪnstɪŋkt] *n* instinct *m*

institute ['ɪnstɪtjuːt] *n* institut *m* ♦ *vt* instituer, établir; (*inquiry*) ouvrir; (*proceedings*) entamer

institution [ɪnstɪ'tjuːʃən] *n* institution *f*; (*educational*) établissement *m* (scolaire); (*mental home*) établissement (psychiatrique)

instruct [ɪn'strʌkt] *vt*: **to** ~ **sb in sth** enseigner qch à qn; **to** ~ **sb to do** charger qn *or* ordonner à qn de faire; ~**ion** [ɪn'strʌkʃən] *n* instruction *f*; ~**ions** *npl* (*or-*

ders) directives *fpl*; **~ions (for use)** mode *m* d'emploi; **~or** *n* professeur *m*; (*for skiing, driving*) moniteur *m*

instrument ['ɪnstrumənt] *n* instrument *m*; **~al** [ɪnstru'mentl] *adj*: **to be ~al in** contribuer à; **~ panel** *n* tableau *m* de bord

insufficient [ɪnsə'fɪʃənt] *adj* insuffisant(e)

insular ['ɪnsjələ*] *adj* (*outlook*) borné(e); (*person*) aux vues étroites

insulate ['ɪnsjuleɪt] *vt* isoler; (*against sound*) insonoriser; **insulating tape** *n* ruban isolant; **insulation** [ɪnsju'leɪʃən] *n* isolation *f*, insonorisation *f*

insulin ['ɪnsjulɪn] *n* insuline *f*

insult [*n* 'ɪnsʌlt, *vb* ɪn'sʌlt] *n* insulte *f*, affront *m* ♦ *vt* insulter, faire affront à

insurance [ɪn'ʃuərəns] *n* assurance *f*; **fire/ life ~** assurance-incendie/-vie; **~ policy** *n* police *f* d'assurance

insure [ɪn'ʃuə*] *vt* assurer; **to ~ (o.s.) against** (*fig*) parer à

intact [ɪn'tækt] *adj* intact(e)

intake ['ɪnteɪk] *n* (*of food, oxygen*) consommation *f*; (*BRIT: SCOL*): **an ~ of 200 a year** 200 admissions *fpl* par an

integral ['ɪntɪɡrəl] *adj* (*part*) intégrant(e)

integrate ['ɪntɪɡreɪt] *vt* intégrer ♦ *vi* s'intégrer

intellect ['ɪntɪlekt] *n* intelligence *f*; **~ual** [ɪntɪ'lektjuəl] *adj, n* intellectuel(le)

intelligence [ɪn'telɪdʒəns] *n* intelligence *f*; (*MIL etc*) informations *fpl*, renseignements *mpl*; **~ service** *n* services secrets; **intelligent** [ɪn'telɪdʒənt] *adj* intelligent(e)

intend [ɪn'tend] *vt* (*gift etc*): **to ~ sth for** destiner qch à; **to ~ to do** avoir l'intention de faire; **~ed** *adj* (*journey*) projeté(e); (*effect*) voulu(e); (*insult*) intentionnel(le)

intense [ɪn'tens] *adj* intense; (*person*) véhément(e); **~ly** *adv* intensément; profondément

intensive [ɪn'tensɪv] *adj* intensif(ive); **~ care unit** *n* service *m* de réanimation

intent [ɪn'tent] *n* intention *f* ♦ *adj* attentif(ive); (*absorbed*): **~ (on)** absorbé(e) (par); **to all ~s and purposes** en fait, pratiquement; **to be ~ on doing sth** être (bien) décidé à faire qch

intention [ɪn'tenʃən] *n* intention *f*; **~al** *adj* intentionnel(le), délibéré(e)

intently [ɪn'tentlɪ] *adv* attentivement

interact [ɪntər'ækt] *vi* avoir une action réciproque; (*people*) communiquer; **~ive** *adj* (*COMPUT*) interactif(ive)

interchange [*n* 'ɪntətʃeɪndʒ, *vb* ɪntə'tʃeɪndʒ] *n* (*exchange*) échange *m*; (*on motorway*) échangeur *m*; **~able** [ɪntə'tʃeɪndʒəbl] *adj* interchangeable

intercom ['ɪntəkɔm] *n* interphone *m*

intercourse ['ɪntəkɔːs] *n* (*sexual*) rapports *mpl*

interest ['ɪntrest] *n* intérêt *m*; (*pastime*):

my main ~ ce qui m'intéresse le plus; (*COMM*) intérêts *mpl* ♦ *vt* intéresser; **to be ~ed in sth** s'intéresser à qch; **I am ~ed in going** ça m'intéresse d'y aller; **~ing** *adj* intéressant(e); **~ rate** *n* taux *m* d'intérêt

interface ['ɪntəfeɪs] *n* (*COMPUT*) interface *f*

interfere [ɪntə'fɪə*] *vi*: **to ~ in** (*quarrel*) s'immiscer dans; (*other people's business*) se mêler de; **to ~ with** (*object*) toucher à; (*plans*) contrecarrer; (*duty*) être en conflit avec; **~nce** [ɪntə'fɪərəns] *n* (*in affairs*) ingérance *f*; (*RADIO, TV*) parasites *mpl*

interim ['ɪntərɪm] *adj* provisoire ♦ *n*: **in the ~** dans l'intérim, entre-temps

interior [ɪn'tɪərɪə*] *n* intérieur *m* ♦ *adj* intérieur(e); (*minister, department*) de l'Intérieur; **~ designer** *n* styliste *m/f*, designer *m/f*

interjection [ɪntə'dʒekʃən] *n* (*interruption*) interruption *f*; (*LING*) interjection *f*

interlock [ɪntə'lɔk] *vi* s'enclencher

interlude ['ɪntəluːd] *n* intervalle *m*; (*THEATRE*) intermède *m*

intermediate [ɪntə'miːdɪət] *adj* intermédiaire; (*SCOL: course, level*) moyen(ne)

intermission [ɪntə'mɪʃən] *n* pause *f*; (*THEATRE, CINEMA*) entracte *m*

intern [*vb* ɪn'təːn, *n* 'ɪntəːn] *vt* interner ♦ *n* (*US*) interne *m/f*

internal [ɪn'təːnl] *adj* interne; (*politics*) intérieur(e); **~ly** *adv*: "**not to be taken ~ly**" "pour usage externe"; **I~ Revenue Service** (*US*) *n* fisc *m*

international [ɪntə'næʃnəl] *adj* international(e)

interplay ['ɪntəpleɪ] *n* effet *m* réciproque, interaction *f*

interpret [ɪn'təːprɪt] *vt* interpréter ♦ *vi* servir d'interprète; **~er** *n* interprète *m/f*

interrelated [ɪntərɪ'leɪtɪd] *adj* en corrélation, en rapport étroit

interrogate [ɪn'terəgeɪt] *vt* interroger; (*suspect etc*) soumettre à un interrogatoire; **interrogation** [ɪntərə'geɪʃən] *n* interrogation *f*; interrogatoire *m*

interrupt [ɪntə'rʌpt] *vt, vi* interrompre; **~ion** *n* interruption *f*

intersect [ɪntə'sekt] *vi* (*roads*) se croiser, se couper; **~ion** [ɪntə'sekʃən] *n* (*of roads*) croisement *m*

intersperse [ɪntə'spəːs] *vt*: **to ~ with** parsemer de

intertwine [ɪntə'twaɪn] *vi* s'entrelacer

interval ['ɪntəvəl] *n* intervalle *m*; (*BRIT: THEATRE*) entracte *m*; (: *SPORT*) mi-temps *f*; **at ~s** par intervalles

intervene [ɪntə'viːn] *vi* (*person*) intervenir; (*event*) survenir; (*time*) s'écouler (entretemps); **intervention** [ɪntə'venʃən] *n* intervention *f*

interview ['ɪntəvjuː] *n* (*RADIO, TV etc*) interview *f*; (*for job*) entrevue *f* ♦ *vt* interviewer; avoir une entrevue avec; ~**er** *n* (*RADIO, TV*) interviewer *m*

intestine [ɪn'testɪn] *n* intestin *m*

intimacy ['ɪntɪməsɪ] *n* intimité *f*

intimate [*adj* 'ɪntɪmət, *vb* 'ɪntɪmeɪt] *adj* intime; (*friendship*) profond(e); (*knowledge*) approfondi(e) ♦ *vt* (*hint*) suggérer, laisser entendre

into ['ɪntʊ] *prep* dans; ~ **pieces/French** en morceaux/français

intolerant [ɪn'tɒlərənt] *adj*: ~ (**of**) intolérant(e) (de)

intoxicated [ɪn'tɒksɪkeɪtɪd] *adj* (*drunk*) ivre; **intoxication** [ɪntɒksɪ'keɪʃən] *n* ivresse *f*

intractable [ɪn'træktəbl] *adj* (*child*) indocile, insoumis(e); (*problem*) insoluble

intransitive [ɪn'trænsɪtɪv] *adj* intransitif(ive)

intravenous [ɪntrə'viːnəs] *adj* intraveineux(euse)

in-tray ['ɪntreɪ] *n* courrier *m* "arrivée"

intricate ['ɪntrɪkət] *adj* complexe, compliqué(e)

intrigue [ɪn'triːg] *n* intrigue *f* ♦ *vt* intriguer; **intriguing** [ɪn'triːgɪŋ] *adj* fascinant(e)

intrinsic [ɪn'trɪnsɪk] *adj* intrinsèque

introduce [ɪntrə'djuːs] *vt* introduire; (*TV show, people to each other*) présenter; **to ~ sb to** (*pastime, technique*) initier qn à; **introduction** [ɪntrə'dʌkʃən] *n* introduction *f*; (*of person*) présentation *f*; (*to new experience*) initiation *f*; **introductory** [ɪntrə'dʌktərɪ] *adj* préliminaire, d'introduction; **introductory offer** *n* (*COMM*) offre *f* de lancement

intrude [ɪn'truːd] *vi* (*person*) être importun(e); **to ~ on** (*conversation etc*) s'immiscer dans; ~**r** *n* intrus(e)

intuition [ɪntjuː'ɪʃən] *n* intuition *f*

inundate ['ɪnʌndeɪt] *vt*: **to ~ with** inonder de

invade [ɪn'veɪd] *vt* envahir

invalid [*n* 'ɪnvəlɪd, *adj* ɪn'vælɪd] *n* malade *m/f*; (*with disability*) invalide *m/f* ♦ *adj* (*not valid*) non valide *or* valable

invaluable [ɪn'væljuəbl] *adj* inestimable, inappréciable

invariably [ɪn'vɛərɪəblɪ] *adv* invariablement; toujours

invent [ɪn'vent] *vt* inventer; ~**ion** [ɪn'venʃən] *n* invention *f*; ~**ive** *adj* inventif(ive); ~**or** *n* inventeur(trice)

inventory ['ɪnvəntrɪ] *n* inventaire *m*

invert [ɪn'vɜːt] *vt* intervertir; (*cup, object*) retourner; ~**ed commas** (*BRIT*) *npl* guillemets *mpl*

invest [ɪn'vest] *vt* investir ♦ *vi*: **to ~ in sth** placer son argent dans qch; (*fig*) s'offrir qch

investigate [ɪn'vestɪgeɪt] *vt* (*crime etc*) faire une enquête sur; **investigation** [ɪnvestɪ'geɪʃən] *n* (*of crime*) enquête *f*

investment [ɪn'vestmənt] *n* investissement *m*, placement *m*

investor [ɪn'vestə*] *n* investisseur *m*; actionnaire *m/f*

invigilator [ɪn'vɪdʒɪleɪtə*] *n* surveillant(e)

invigorating [ɪn'vɪgəreɪtɪŋ] *adj* vivifiant(e); (*fig*) stimulant(e)

invisible [ɪn'vɪzəbl] *adj* invisible

invitation [ɪnvɪ'teɪʃən] *n* invitation *f*

invite [ɪn'vaɪt] *vt* inviter; (*opinions etc*) demander; **inviting** [ɪn'vaɪtɪŋ] *adj* engageant(e), attrayant(e)

invoice ['ɪnvɔɪs] *n* facture *f*

involuntary [ɪn'vɒləntərɪ] *adj* involontaire

involve [ɪn'vɒlv] *vt* (*entail*) entraîner, nécessiter; (*concern*) concerner; (*associate*): **to ~ sb (in)** impliquer qn (dans), mêler qn (à); faire participer qn (à); ~**d** *adj* (*complicated*) complexe; **to be ~d in** participer à; (*engrossed*) être absorbé(e) par; ~**ment** *n*: ~**ment (in)** participation *f* (à); rôle *m* (dans); (*enthusiasm*) enthousiasme *m* (pour)

inward ['ɪnwəd] *adj* (*thought, feeling*) profond(e), intime; (*movement*) vers l'intérieur; ~**(s)** *adv* vers l'intérieur

I/O *abbr* (*COMPUT*: = *input/output*) E/S

iodine ['aɪədiːn] *n* iode *m*

iota [aɪ'əʊtə] *n* (*fig*) brin *m*, grain *m*

IOU *n abbr* (= *I owe you*) reconnaissance *f* de dette

IQ *n abbr* (= *intelligence quotient*) Q.I. *m*

IRA *n abbr* (= *Irish Republican Army*) IRA *f*

Iran [ɪ'rɑːn] *n* Iran *m*

Iraq [ɪ'rɑːk] *n* Irak *m*

irate [aɪ'reɪt] *adj* courroucé(e)

Ireland ['aɪələnd] *n* Irlande *f*

iris ['aɪrɪs] (*pl* ~**es**) *n* iris *m*

Irish ['aɪrɪʃ] *adj* irlandais(e) ♦ *npl*: **the ~** les Irlandais; ~**man** (*irreg*) *n* Irlandais *m*; ~ **Sea** *n* mer *f* d'Irlande; ~**woman** (*irreg*) *n* Irlandaise *f*

iron ['aɪən] *n* fer, *m*; (*for clothes*) fer *m* à repasser ♦ *cpd* de *or* en fer; (*fig*) de fer ♦ *vt* (*clothes*) repasser; ~ **out** *vt* (*fig*) aplanir; faire disparaître; **the I~ Curtain** *n* le rideau de fer

ironic(al) [aɪ'rɒnɪk(əl)] *adj* ironique

ironing ['aɪənɪŋ] *n* repassage *m*; ~ **board** *n* planche *f* à repasser

ironmonger's (shop) ['aɪənmʌŋgəz-] *n* quincaillerie *f*

irony ['aɪərənɪ] *n* ironie *f*

irrational [ɪ'ræʃənl] *adj* irrationnel(le)

irregular [ɪ'regjulə*] *adj* irrégulier(ère); (*surface*) inégal(e)

irrelevant [ɪ'reləvənt] *adj* sans rapport, hors de propos

irresistible [ɪrɪ'zɪstəbl] *adj* irrésistible

irrespective [ɪrɪ'spektɪv]: ~ **of** *prep* sans tenir compte de

irresponsible [ɪrɪ'spɒnsəbl] *adj* (*act*) irréfléchi(e); (*person*) irresponsable, inconscient(e)

irrigate ['ɪrɪgeɪt] *vt* irriguer; **irrigation** [ɪrɪ'geɪʃən] *n* irrigation *f*

irritate ['ɪrɪteɪt] *vt* irriter; **irritating** *adj* irritant(e); **irritation** [ɪrɪ'teɪʃən] *n* irritation *f*

IRS *n abbr* = **Internal Revenue Service**

is [ɪz] *vb see* **be**

Islam ['ɪzlɑːm] *n* Islam *m*

island ['aɪlənd] *n* île *f*; **~er** *n* habitant(e) d'une île, insulaire *m/f*

isle [aɪl] *n* île *f*

isn't ['ɪznt] = **is not**

isolate ['aɪsəʊleɪt] *vt* isoler; **~d** *adj* isolé(e); **isolation** [aɪsəʊ'leɪʃən] *n* isolation *f*

Israel ['ɪzreɪəl] *n* Israël *m*; **~i** [ɪz'reɪlɪ] *adj* israélien(ne) ♦ *n* Israélien(ne)

issue ['ɪʃuː] *n* question *f*, problème *m*; (*of book*) publication *f*, parution *f*; (*of banknotes etc*) émission *f*; (*of newspaper etc*) numéro *m* ♦ *vt* (*rations, equipment*) distribuer; (*statement*) publier, faire; (*banknotes etc*) émettre, mettre en circulation; **at ~** en jeu, en cause; **to take ~ with sb (over)** exprimer son désaccord avec qn (sur); **to make an ~ of sth** faire une montagne de qch

---
KEYWORD

it [ɪt] *pron* **1** (*specific: subject*) il(elle); (*: direct object*) le(la, l'); (*: indirect object*) lui; **~'s on the table** c'est *or* il (*or* elle) est sur la table; **about/from/of ~** en; **I spoke to him about ~** je lui en ai parlé; **what did you learn from ~?** qu'est-ce que vous en avez retiré?; **I'm proud of ~** j'en suis fier; **in/to ~** y; **put the book in ~** mettez-y le livre; **he agreed to ~** il y a consenti; **did you go to ~?** (*party, concert etc*) est-ce que vous y êtes allé(s)?

2 (*impersonal*) il; ce; **~'s raining** il pleut; **~'s Friday tomorrow** demain c'est vendredi *or* nous sommes vendredi; **~'s 6 o'clock** il est 6 heures; **who is ~? - ~'s me** qui est-ce? - c'est moi

---

Italian [ɪ'tæljən] *adj* italien(ne) ♦ *n* Italien(ne); (*LING*) italien *m*

italics [ɪ'tælɪks] *npl* italiques *fpl*

Italy ['ɪtəlɪ] *n* Italie *f*

itch [ɪtʃ] *n* démangeaison *f* ♦ *vi* (*person*) éprouver des démangeaisons; (*part of body*) démanger; **I'm ~ing to do** l'envie me démange de faire; **~y** *adj* qui démange; **to be ~y** avoir des démangeaisons

it'd ['ɪtd] = **it would; it had**

item ['aɪtəm] *n* article *m*; (*on agenda*) question *f*, point *m*; (*also: news ~*) nouvelle *f*; **~ize** *vt* détailler, faire une liste de

itinerary [aɪ'tɪnərərɪ] *n* itinéraire *m*

it: **~'ll** ['ɪtl] = **it will; it shall**; **~s** [ɪts] *adj* son(sa), ses *pl*; **~'s** [ɪts] = **it is; it has**; **~self** [ɪt'self] *pron* (*reflexive*) se; (*emphatic*) lui-même(elle-même)

ITV *n abbr* (*BRIT:* = *Independent Television*)

chaîne privée

IUD *n abbr* (= *intra-uterine device*) DIU *m*, stérilet *m*

I've [aɪv] = **I have**

ivory ['aɪvərɪ] *n* ivoire *m*

ivy ['aɪvɪ] *n* lierre *m*

J j

jab [dʒæb] *vt*: **to ~ sth into** enfoncer *or* planter qch dans ♦ *n* (*inf: injection*) piqûre *f*

jack [dʒæk] *n* (*AUT*) cric *m*; (*CARDS*) valet *m*; **~ up** *vt* soulever (au cric)

jackal ['dʒækəl] *n* chacal *m*

jackdaw ['dʒækdɔː] *n* choucas *m*

jacket ['dʒækɪt] *n* veste *f*, veston *m*; (*of book*) jaquette *f*, couverture *f*

jackknife ['dʒæknaɪf] *vi*: **the lorry ~d** la remorque (du camion) s'est mise en travers

jack plug *n* (*ELEC*) prise jack mâle *f*

jackpot ['dʒækpɒt] *n* gros lot

jaded ['dʒeɪdɪd] *adj* éreinté(e), fatigué(e)

jagged ['dʒægɪd] *adj* dentelé(e)

jail [dʒeɪl] *n* prison *f* ♦ *vt* emprisonner, mettre en prison

jam [dʒæm] *n* confiture *f*; (*also: traffic ~*) embouteillage *m* ♦ *vt* (*passage etc*) encombrer, obstruer; (*mechanism, drawer etc*) bloquer, coincer; (*RADIO*) brouiller ♦ *vi* se coincer, se bloquer; (*gun*) s'enrayer; **to be in a ~** (*inf*) être dans le pétrin; **to ~ sth into** entasser qch dans; enfoncer qch dans

jangle ['dʒæŋgl] *vi* cliqueter

janitor ['dʒænɪtə*] *n* concierge *m*

January ['dʒænjʊərɪ] *n* janvier *m*

Japan [dʒə'pæn] *n* Japon *m*; **~ese** *adj* [dʒæpə'niːz] japonais(e) ♦ *n inv* Japonais(e); (*LING*) japonais *m*

jar [dʒɑː*] *n* (*stone, earthenware*) pot *m*; (*glass*) bocal *m* ♦ *vi* (*sound discordant*) produire un son grinçant *or* discordant; (*colours etc*) jurer

jargon ['dʒɑːgən] *n* jargon *m*

jaundice ['dʒɔːndɪs] *n* jaunisse *f*; **~d** *adj* (*fig*) envieux(euse), désapprobateur(trice)

javelin ['dʒævlɪn] *n* javelot *m*

jaw [dʒɔː] *n* mâchoire *f*

jay [dʒeɪ] *n* geai *m*; **~walker** ['dʒeɪwɔːkə*] *n* piéton indiscipliné

jazz [dʒæz] *n* jazz *m*; **~ up** *vt* animer, égayer

jealous ['dʒeləs] *adj* jaloux(ouse); **~y** *n* jalousie *f*

jeans [dʒiːnz] npl jean m
jeer [dʒɪə*] vi: **to ~ (at)** se moquer cruellement (de), railler
jelly ['dʒelɪ] n gelée f; **~fish** n méduse f
jeopardy ['dʒepədɪ] n: **to be in ~** être en danger or péril
jerk [dʒɜːk] n secousse f; saccade f; sursaut m, spasme m; (inf: idiot) pauvre type m ♦ vt (pull) tirer brusquement ♦ vi (vehicles) cahoter
jersey ['dʒɜːzɪ] n (pullover) tricot m; (fabric) jersey m
Jesus ['dʒiːzəs] n Jésus
jet [dʒet] n (gas, liquid) jet m; (AVIAT) avion m à réaction, jet m; **~-black** adj (d'un noir) de jais; **~ engine** n moteur m à réaction; **~ lag** n (fatigue due au) décalage m horaire
jettison ['dʒetɪsn] vt jeter par-dessus bord
jetty ['dʒetɪ] n jetée f, digue f
Jew [dʒuː] n Juif m
jewel ['dʒuːəl] n bijou m, joyau m; (in watch) rubis m; **~ler** (US **~er**) n bijoutier(ère), joaillier m; **~ler's (shop)** n bijouterie f, joaillerie f; **~lery** (US **~ry**) n bijoux mpl
Jewess ['dʒuːɪs] n Juive f
Jewish ['dʒuːɪʃ] adj juif(juive)
jibe [dʒaɪb] n sarcasme m
jiffy ['dʒɪfɪ] (inf) n: **in a ~** en un clin d'œil
jigsaw ['dʒɪgsɔː] n (also: **~ puzzle**) puzzle m
jilt [dʒɪlt] vt laisser tomber, plaquer
jingle ['dʒɪŋgl] n (for advert) couplet m publicitaire ♦ vi cliqueter, tinter
jinx [dʒɪŋks] (inf) n (mauvais) sort m
jitters ['dʒɪtəz] (inf) npl: **to get the ~** (inf) avoir la trouille or la frousse
job [dʒɒb] n (chore, task) travail m, tâche f; (employment) emploi m, poste m, place f; **it's a good ~ that ...** c'est heureux or c'est une chance que ...; **just the ~!** (c'est) juste or exactement ce qu'il faut!; **~ centre** (BRIT) n agence f pour l'emploi; **~less** adj sans travail, au chômage
jockey ['dʒɒkɪ] n jockey m ♦ vi: **to ~ for position** manœuvrer pour être bien placé
jocular ['dʒɒkjulə*] adj jovial(e), enjoué(e); facétieux(euse)
jog [dʒɒg] vt secouer ♦ vi (SPORT) faire du jogging; **to ~ sb's memory** rafraîchir la mémoire de qn; **~ along** vi cheminer, trotter; **~ging** n jogging m
join [dʒɔɪn] vt (put together) unir, assembler; (become member of) s'inscrire à; (meet) rejoindre, retrouver; (queue) se joindre à ♦ vi (roads, rivers) se rejoindre, se rencontrer ♦ n raccord m; **~ in** vi se mettre de la partie, participer ♦ vt fus participer à, se mêler à; **~ up** vi (meet) se rejoindre; (MIL) s'engager; **~er** ['dʒɔɪnə*] (BRIT) n menuisier m

joint [dʒɔɪnt] n (TECH) jointure f; joint m; (ANAT) articulation f, jointure; (BRIT: CULIN) rôti m; (inf: place) boîte f; (: of cannabis) joint m ♦ adj commun(e); **~ account** n (with bank etc) compte joint
joke [dʒəʊk] n plaisanterie f; (also: practical **~**) farce f ♦ vi plaisanter; **to play a ~ on** jouer un tour à, faire une farce à; **~r** n (CARDS) joker m
jolly ['dʒɒlɪ] adj gai(e), enjoué(e); (enjoyable) amusant(e), plaisant(e) ♦ adv (BRIT: inf) rudement, drôlement
jolt [dʒəʊlt] n cahot m, secousse f; (shock) choc m ♦ vt cahoter, secouer
Jordan ['dʒɔːdən] n (country) Jordanie f
jostle ['dʒɒsl] vt bousculer, pousser
jot [dʒɒt] n: **not one ~** pas un brin; **~ down** vt noter; **~ter** (BRIT) n cahier m (de brouillon); (pad) bloc-notes m
journal ['dʒɜːnl] n journal m; **~ism** n journalisme m; **~ist** n journaliste m/f
journey ['dʒɜːnɪ] n voyage m; (distance covered) trajet m
joy [dʒɔɪ] n joie f; **~ful** adj joyeux(euse); **~rider** n personne qui fait une virée dans une voiture volée; **~stick** n (AVIAT, COMPUT) manche m à balai
JP n abbr = **Justice of the Peace**
Jr abbr = **junior**
jubilant ['dʒuːbɪlənt] adj triomphant(e); réjoui(e)
judge [dʒʌdʒ] n juge m ♦ vt juger; **judg(e)ment** n jugement m
judicial [dʒuːˈdɪʃəl] adj judiciaire
judiciary [dʒuːˈdɪʃɪərɪ] n (pouvoir m) judiciaire m
judo ['dʒuːdəʊ] n judo m
jug [dʒʌg] n pot m, cruche f
juggernaut ['dʒʌgənɔːt] (BRIT) n (huge truck) énorme poids lourd
juggle ['dʒʌgl] vi jongler; **~r** n jongleur m
Jugoslav etc = **Yugoslav** etc
juice [dʒuːs] n jus m; **juicy** ['dʒuːsɪ] adj juteux(euse)
jukebox ['dʒuːkbɒks] n juke-box m
July [dʒuːˈlaɪ] n juillet m
jumble ['dʒʌmbl] n fouillis m ♦ vt (also: **~ up**) mélanger, brouiller; **~ sale** (BRIT) n vente f de charité
jumbo (jet) ['dʒʌmbəʊ-] n jumbo-jet m, gros porteur
jump [dʒʌmp] vi sauter, bondir; (start) sursauter; (increase) monter en flèche ♦ vt sauter, franchir ♦ n saut m, bond m; sursaut m; **to ~ the queue** (BRIT) passer avant son tour
jumper ['dʒʌmpə*] n (BRIT: pullover) pullover m; (US: dress) robe-chasuble f
jumper cables (US), **jump leads** (BRIT) npl câbles mpl de démarrage
jumpy ['dʒʌmpɪ] adj nerveux(euse), agité(e)
Jun. abbr = **junior**

junction ['dʒʌŋkʃən] (*BRIT*) *n* (*of roads*) carrefour *m*; (*of rails*) embranchement *m*

juncture ['dʒʌŋktʃə*] *n*: **at this ~** à ce moment-là, sur ces entrefaites

June [dʒuːn] *n* juin *m*

jungle ['dʒʌŋgl] *n* jungle *f*

junior ['dʒuːnɪə*] *adj*, *n*: **he's ~ to me (by 2 years), he's my ~ (by 2 years)** il est mon cadet (de 2 ans), il est plus jeune que moi (de 2 ans); **he's ~ to me** (*seniority*) il est en dessous de moi (dans la hiérarchie), j'ai plus d'ancienneté que lui; **~ school** (*BRIT*) *n* ≈ école *f* primaire

junk [dʒʌŋk] *n* (*rubbish*) camelote *f*; (*cheap goods*) bric-à-brac *m inv*; **~ food** *n* aliments *mpl* sans grande valeur nutritive; **~ mail** *n* prospectus *mpl* (*non sollicités*); **~ shop** *n* (boutique *f* de) brocanteur *m*

Junr *abbr* = **junior**

juror ['dʒuərə*] *n* juré *m*

jury ['dʒuəri] *n* jury *m*

just [dʒʌst] *adj* juste ♦ *adv*: **he's ~ done it/left** il vient de le faire/partir; **~ right/two o'clock** exactement *or* juste ce qu'il faut/deux heures; **she's ~ as clever as you** elle est tout aussi intelligente que vous; **it's ~ as well (that)** ... heureusement que ...; **~ as he was leaving** au moment *or* à l'instant précis où il partait; **~ before/enough/here** juste avant/assez/ici; **it's ~ me/a mistake** ce n'est que moi/(rien) qu'une erreur; **~ missed/caught** manqué/attrapé de justesse; **~ listen to this!** écoutez un peu ça!

justice ['dʒʌstɪs] *n* justice *f*; (*US*: *judge*) juge *m* de la Cour suprême; **J~ of the Peace** *n* juge *m* de paix

justify ['dʒʌstɪfaɪ] *vt* justifier

jut [dʒʌt] *vi* (*also*: **~ out**) dépasser, faire saillie

juvenile ['dʒuːvənaɪl] *adj* juvénile; (*court, books*) pour enfants ♦ *n* adolescent(e)

K k

K *abbr* (= *one thousand*) K; (= *kilobyte*) Ko

kangaroo [kæŋgə'ruː] *n* kangourou *m*

karate [kə'rɑːtɪ] *n* karaté *m*

kebab [kə'bæb] *n* kébab *m*

keel [kiːl] *n* quille *f*

keen [kiːn] *adj* (*eager*) plein(e) d'enthousiasme; (*interest, desire, competition*) vif(vive); (*eye, intelligence*) pénétrant(e); (*edge*) effilé(e); **to be ~ to do** *or* **on doing sth** désirer vivement faire qch, tenir beaucoup à faire qch; **to be ~ on sth/sb** aimer beaucoup qch/qn

keep [kiːp] (*pt*, *pp* **kept**) *vt* (*retain, preserve*) garder; (*detain*) retenir; (*shop, accounts, diary, promise*) tenir; (*house*) avoir; (*support*) entretenir; (*chickens, bees etc*) élever ♦ *vi* (*remain*) rester; (*food*) se conserver ♦ *n* (*of castle*) donjon *m*; (*food etc*): **enough for his ~** assez pour (assurer) sa subsistance; (*inf*): **for ~s** pour de bon, pour toujours; **to ~ doing sth** ne pas arrêter de faire qch; **to ~ sb from doing sth** empêcher qn de faire *or* que qn ne fasse; **to ~ sb happy/a place tidy** faire que qn soit content/qu'un endroit reste propre; **to ~ sth to o.s.** garder qch pour soi, tenir qch secret; **to ~ sth (back) from sb** cacher qch à qn; **to ~ time** (*clock*) être à l'heure, ne pas retarder; **well kept** bien entretenu(e); **~ on** *vi*: **to ~ on doing** continuer à faire; **don't ~ on about it!** arrête (de m'en parler)!; **~ out** *vt* empêcher d'entrer; **"~ out"** "défense d'entrer"; **~ up** *vt* continuer, maintenir ♦ *vi*: **to ~ up with sb** (*in race etc*) aller aussi vite que qn; (*in work etc*) se maintenir au niveau de qn; **~er** *n* gardien(ne); **~-fit** *n* gymnastique *f* d'entretien; **~ing** *n* (*care*) garde *f*, in **~ing with** en accord avec; **~sake** *n* souvenir *m*

kennel ['kenl] *n* niche *f*, **~s** *npl* (*boarding ~s*) chenil *m*

kerb [kɜːb] (*BRIT*) *n* bordure *f* du trottoir

kernel ['kɜːnl] *n* (*of nut*) amande *f*, (*fig*) noyau *m*

kettle ['ketl] *n* bouilloire *f*; **~drum** *n* timbale *f*

key [kiː] *n* (*gen*, *MUS*) clé *f*; (*of piano, typewriter*) touche *f* ♦ *cpd* clé ♦ *vt* (*also*: **~ in**) introduire (au clavier), saisir; **~board** *n* clavier *m*; **~ed up** *adj* (*person*) surexcité(e); **~hole** *n* trou *m* de la serrure; **~note** *n* (*of speech*) note dominante; (*MUS*) tonique *f*; **~ ring** *n* porte-clés *m*

khaki ['kɑːkɪ] *n* kaki *m*

kick [kɪk] *vt* donner un coup de pied à ♦ *vi* (*horse*) ruer ♦ *n* coup *m* de pied; (*thrill*): **he does it for ~s** il le fait parce que ça l'excite, il le fait pour le plaisir; **to ~ the habit** (*inf*) arrêter; **~ off** *vi* (*SPORT*) donner le coup d'envoi

kid [kɪd] *n* (*inf*: *child*) gamin(e), gosse *m/f*; (*animal, leather*) chevreau *m* ♦ *vi* (*inf*) plaisanter, blaguer

kidnap ['kɪdnæp] *vt* enlever, kidnapper; **~per** *n* ravisseur(euse); **~ping** *n* enlèvement *m*

kidney ['kɪdnɪ] *n* (*ANAT*) rein *m*; (*CULIN*) rognon *m*

kill [kɪl] *vt* tuer ♦ *n* mise *f* à mort; **~er** *n* tueur(euse); meurtrier(ère), **~ing** *n* meurtre *m*; (*of group of people*) tuerie *f*, massacre m; **to make a ~ing** (inf) réussir un beau coup (de filet); **~joy** n rabat-joie m/f

kiln [kıln] n four m

kilo ['kiːləʊ] n kilo m; **~byte** n (COMPUT) kilo-octet m; **~gram(me)** ['kıləʊgræm] n kilogramme m; **~metre** ['kıləmiːtə*] (US **~meter**) n kilomètre m; **~watt** n kilowatt m

kilt [kılt] n kilt m

kin [kın] n see next; kith

kind [kaınd] adj gentil(le), aimable ♦ n sorte f, espèce f, genre m; **to be two of a ~** se ressembler; **in ~** (COMM) en nature

kindergarten ['kındəgɑːtn] n jardin m d'enfants

kind-hearted ['kaınd'hɑːtıd] adj bon(bonne)

kindle ['kındl] vt allumer, enflammer

kindly ['kaındlı] adj bienveillant(e), plein(e) de gentillesse ♦ adv avec bonté; **will you ~ ...!** auriez-vous la bonté or l'obligeance de ...?

kindness ['kaındnəs] n bonté f, gentillesse f

kindred ['kındrıd] adj: **~ spirit** âme f sœur

kinetic [kı'netık] adj cinétique

king [kıŋ] n roi m; **~dom** n royaume m; **~fisher** n martin-pêcheur m; **~-size bed** n grand lit (de 1,95 m de large); **~-size(d)** adj format géant inv; (cigarettes) long(longue)

kinky ['kıŋkı] (pej) adj (person) excentrique; (sexually) aux goûts spéciaux

kiosk ['kiːɒsk] n kiosque m; (BRIT: TEL) cabine f (téléphonique)

kipper ['kıpə*] n hareng fumé et salé

kiss [kıs] n baiser m ♦ vt embrasser; **to ~ (each other)** s'embrasser; **~ of life** (BRIT) n bouche à bouche m

kit [kıt] n équipement m, matériel m; (set of tools etc) trousse f; (for assembly) kit m

kitchen ['kıtʃın] n cuisine f; **~ sink** n évier m

kite [kaıt] n (toy) cerf-volant m

kith [kıθ] n: **~ and kin** parents et amis mpl

kitten ['kıtn] n chaton m, petit chat

kitty ['kıtı] n (money) cagnotte f

knack [næk] n: **to have the ~ of doing** avoir le coup pour faire

knapsack ['næpsæk] n musette f

knead [niːd] vt pétrir

knee [niː] n genou m; **~cap** n rotule f

kneel [niːl] (pt, pp knelt) vi (also: **~ down**) s'agenouiller

knew [njuː] pt of know

knickers ['nıkəz] (BRIT) npl culotte f (de femme)

knife [naıf] (pl knives) n couteau m ♦ vt poignarder, frapper d'un coup de couteau

knight [naıt] n chevalier m; (CHESS) cavalier m; **~hood** (BRIT) n (title): **to get a ~hood** être fait chevalier

knit [nıt] vt tricoter ♦ vi tricoter; (broken bones) se ressouder; **to ~ one's brows** froncer les sourcils; **~ting** n tricot m; **~ting needle** n aiguille f à tricoter; **~wear** n tricots mpl, lainages mpl

knives [naıvz] npl of knife

knob [nɒb] n bouton m

knock [nɒk] vt frapper; (bump into) heurter; (inf) dénigrer ♦ vi (at door etc): **to ~ at or on frapper à** ♦ n coup m; **~ down** vt renverser; **~ off** vi (inf: finish) s'arrêter (de travailler) ♦ vt (from price) faire un rabais de; (inf: steal) piquer; **~ out** vt assommer; (BOXING) mettre k.-o.; (defeat) éliminer; **~ over** vt renverser, faire tomber; **~er** n (on door) heurtoir m; **~out** n (BOXING) knock-out m, K.-O. m; **~out competition** n compétition f avec épreuves éliminatoires

knot [nɒt] n (gen) nœud m ♦ vt nouer; **~ty** adj (fig) épineux(euse)

know [nəʊ] (pt knew, pp known) vt savoir; (person, place) connaître; **to ~ how to do** savoir (comment) faire; **to ~ how to swim** savoir nager; **to ~ about or of sth** être au courant de qch; **to ~ about or of sb** avoir entendu parler de qn; **~-all** (pej) n je-sais-tout m/f; **~-how** n savoir-faire m; **~ing** adj (look etc) entendu(e); **~ingly** adv sciemment; (smile, look) d'un air entendu

knowledge ['nɒlıdʒ] n connaissance f; (learning) connaissances, savoir m; **~able** adj bien informé(e)

knuckle ['nʌkl] n articulation f (des doigts), jointure f

Koran [kɔː'rɑːn] n Coran m

Korea [kə'rıə] n Corée f

kosher ['kəʊʃə*] adj kascher inv

L l

L abbr (= lake, large) L; (= left) g; (= BRIT: AUT: = learner) signale un conducteur débutant

lab [læb] n abbr (= laboratory) labo m

label ['leıbl] n étiquette f ♦ vt étiqueter

labor etc (US) = labour etc

laboratory [lə'bɒrətərı] n laboratoire m

labour ['leıbə*] (US labor) n (work) travail m; (workforce) main-d'œuvre f ♦ vi: **to ~ (at)** travailler dur (à), peiner (sur) ♦ vt: **to ~ a point** insister sur un point; **in ~** (MED) en travail, en train d'accoucher; **L~, the L~ party** (BRIT) le parti travailliste, les travaillistes mpl; **~ed** adj (breathing) pénible, difficile; **~er** *n* manœuvre *m*; **farm ~er** ouvrier *m* agricole

lace [leɪs] *n* dentelle *f*; (*of shoe etc*) lacet *m* ♦ *vt* (*shoe: also:* ~ **up**) lacer

lack [læk] *n* manque *m* ♦ *vt* manquer de; **through** *or* **for ~ of** faute de, par manque de; **to be ~ing** manquer, faire défaut; **to be ~ing in** manquer de

lacquer ['lækə*] *n* laque *f*

lad [læd] *n* garçon *m*, gars *m*

ladder ['lædə*] *n* échelle *f*, (*BRIT: in tights*) maille filée

laden ['leɪdn] *adj*: ~ **(with)** chargé(e) (de)

ladle ['leɪdl] *n* louche *f*

lady ['leɪdɪ] *n* dame *f*; (*in address*): **ladies and gentlemen** Mesdames (et) Messieurs; **young ~** jeune fille *f*; (*married*) jeune femme *f*; **the ladies' (room)** les toilettes *fpl* (pour dames); **~bird** *n* coccinelle *f*, **~bug** (*US*) *n* = **ladybird**; **~like** *adj* distingué(e); **~ship** *n*: **your ~ship** Madame la comtesse (*or* la baronne *etc*)

lag [læg] *n* retard *m* ♦ *vi* (*also:* ~ *behind*) rester en arrière, traîner; (*fig*) rester en traîne ♦ *vt* (*pipes*) calorifuger

lager ['lɑːgə*] *n* bière blonde

lagoon [lə'guːn] *n* lagune *f*

laid [leɪd] *pt, pp of* **lay**; **~-back** (*inf*) *adj* relaxe, décontracté(e); ~ **up** *adj* alité(e)

lain [leɪn] *pp of* **lie**

lake [leɪk] *n* lac *m*

lamb [læm] *n* agneau *m*; ~ **chop** *n* côtelette *f* d'agneau

lame [leɪm] *adj* boiteux(euse)

lament [lə'ment] *n* lamentation *f* ♦ *vt* pleurer, se lamenter sur

laminated ['læmɪneɪtɪd] *adj* laminé(e); (*windscreen*) (en verre) feuilleté

lamp [læmp] *n* lampe *f*; **~post** (*BRIT*) *n* réverbère *m*; **~shade** *n* abat-jour *m inv*

lance [lɑːns] *vt* (*MED*) inciser

land [lænd] *n* (*as opposed to sea*) terre *f* (ferme); (*soil*) terre; terrain *m*; (*estate*) terre(s), domaine(s) *m(pl)*; (*country*) pays *m* ♦ *vi* (*AVIAT*) atterrir; (*fig*) (re)tomber ♦ *vt* (*passengers, goods*) débarquer; **to ~ sb with sth** (*inf*) coller qch à qn; ~ **up** *vi* atterrir, (finir par) se retrouver; **~fill site** *n* décharge *f*; **~ing** *n* (*AVIAT*) atterrissage *m*; (*of staircase*) palier *m*; (*of troops*) débarquement *m*; **~ing gear** *n* train *m* d'atterrissage; **~ing strip** *n* piste *f* d'atterrissage; **~lady** *n* propriétaire *f*, logeuse *f*; (*of pub*) patronne *f*; **~locked** *adj* sans littoral; **~lord** *n* propriétaire *m*, logeur *m*; (*of pub etc*) patron *m*; **~mark** *n* (point *m* de) repère *m*; **to be a ~mark** (*fig*) faire date *or* époque; **~owner** *n* propriétaire foncier *or* terrien; **~scape** ['lændskeɪp] *n* paysage *m*; **~scape gardener** *n* jardinier(ère) paysagiste; **~slide** ['lændslaɪd] *n* (*GEO*) glissement *m* (de terrain); (*fig: POL*) raz-de-

marée (électoral)

lane [leɪn] *n* (*in country*) chemin *m*; (*AUT*) voie *f*, file *f*; (*in race*) couloir *m*

language ['læŋgwɪdʒ] *n* langue *f*, (*way one speaks*) langage *m*; **bad ~** grossièretés *fpl*, langage grossier; ~ **laboratory** *n* laboratoire *m* de langues

lank [læŋk] *adj* (*hair*) raide et terne

lanky ['læŋkɪ] *adj* grand(e) et maigre, efflanqué(e)

lantern ['læntən] *n* lanterne *f*

lap [læp] *n* (*of track*) tour *m* (de piste); (*of body*): **in** *or* **on one's ~** sur les genoux ♦ *vt* (*also:* ~ **up**) laper ♦ *vi* (*waves*) clapoter; ~ **up** *vt* (*fig*) accepter béatement, gober

lapel [lə'pel] *n* revers *m*

Lapland ['læplænd] *n* Laponie *f*

lapse [læps] *n* défaillance *f*, (*in behaviour*) écart *m* de conduite ♦ *vi* (*LAW*) cesser d'être en vigueur; (*contract*) expirer; **to ~ into bad habits** prendre de mauvaises habitudes; ~ **of time** laps *m* de temps, intervalle *m*

laptop (computer) ['læptɒp-] *n* portable *m*

larceny ['lɑːsənɪ] *n* vol *m*

larch [lɑːtʃ] *n* mélèze *m*

lard [lɑːd] *n* saindoux *m*

larder ['lɑːdə*] *n* garde-manger *m inv*

large [lɑːdʒ] *adj* grand(e); (*person, animal*) gros(se); **at ~** (*free*) en liberté; (*generally*) en général; *see also* **by**; **~ly** *adv* en grande partie; (*principally*) surtout; **~scale** *adj* (*action*) d'envergure; (*map*) à grande échelle

lark [lɑːk] *n* (*bird*) alouette *f*; (*joke*) blague *f*, farce *f*; ~ **about** *vi* faire l'idiot, rigoler

laryngitis [lærɪn'dʒaɪtɪs] *n* laryngite *f*

laser ['leɪzə*] *n* laser *m*; ~ **printer** *n* imprimante *f* laser

lash [læʃ] *n* coup *m* de fouet; (*also:* **eye~**) cil *m* ♦ *vt* fouetter; (*tie*) attacher; ~ **out** *vi*: **to ~ out at** *or* **against** attaquer violemment

lass [læs] (*BRIT*) *n* (jeune) fille *f*

lasso [læ'suː] *n* lasso *m*

last [lɑːst] *adj* dernier(ère) ♦ *adv* en dernier; (*finally*) finalement ♦ *vi* durer; ~ **week** la semaine dernière; ~ **night** (*evening*) hier soir; (*night*) la nuit dernière; **at ~** enfin; ~ **but one** avant-dernier(ère); **~-ditch** *adj* (*attempt*) ultime, désespéré(e); **~ing** *adj* durable; **~ly** *adv* en dernier lieu, pour finir; **~-minute** *adj* de dernière minute

latch [lætʃ] *n* loquet *m*

late [leɪt] *adj* (*not on time*) en retard; (*far on in day etc*) tardif(ive); (*edition, delivery*) dernier(ère); (*former*) ancien(ne) ♦ *adv* tard; (*behind time, schedule*) en retard; **of ~** dernièrement; **in ~ May** vers la fin (du mois) de mai, fin mai; **the ~ Mr X** feu M. X; **~comer** *n* retardataire *m/f*; **~ly** *adv* ré-

cemment; ~r ['leɪtə*] adj (date etc) ulté-
rieur(e); (version etc) plus récent(e) ♦ adv
plus tard; ~r on plus tard; ~st ['leɪtɪst] adj
tout(e) dernier(ère); at the ~st au plus
tard

lathe [leɪð] n tour m

lather ['lɑːðə*] n mousse f (de savon) ♦ vt
savonner

Latin ['lætɪn] n latin m ♦ adj latin(e); ~
America n Amérique latine; ~ **American**
adj latino-américain(e)

latitude ['lætɪtjuːd] n latitude f

latter ['lætə*] adj deuxième, dernier(ère) ♦
n: the ~ ce dernier, celui-ci; ~**ly** adv dernièrement, récemment

laudable ['lɔːdəbl] adj louable

laugh [lɑːf] n rire m ♦ vi rire; ~ at vt fus
se moquer de; rire de; ~ off vt écarter par
une plaisanterie or par une boutade; ~**able**
adj risible, ridicule; ~**ing stock** n: the
~**ing stock of** la risée de; ~**ter** n rire m ;
rires mpl

launch [lɔːntʃ] n lancement m; (motorboat)
vedette f ♦ vt lancer; ~ **into** vt fus se lancer dans

Launderette [lɔːn'dret] (BRIT: ®), **Laun-
dromat** ['lɔːndrəmæt] (US: ®) n laverie f
(automatique)

laundry ['lɔːndrɪ] n (clothes) linge m; (business) blanchisserie f; (room) buanderie f

laureate ['lɔːrɪət] adj see **poet**

laurel ['lɒrəl] n laurier m

lava ['lɑːvə] n lave f

lavatory ['lævətrɪ] n toilettes fpl

lavender ['lævɪndə*] n lavande f

lavish ['lævɪʃ] adj (amount) copieux(euse);
(person): ~ **with** prodigue de ♦ vt: to ~
sth on sb prodiguer qch à qn; (money) dépenser qch sans compter pour qn/qch

law [lɔː] n loi f; (science) droit m; ~-
abiding adj respectueux(euse) des lois; ~
and order n l'ordre public; ~ **court** n tribunal m, cour f de justice; ~**ful** adj lé-
gal(e); ~**less** adj (action) illégal(e)

lawn [lɔːn] n pelouse f; ~**mower** n tondeuse f à gazon; ~ **tennis** n tennis m

law school (US) n faculté f de droit

lawsuit ['lɔːsuːt] n procès m

lawyer ['lɔːjə*] n (consultant, with company)
juriste m; (for sales, wills etc) notaire m;
(partner, in court) avocat m

lax [læks] adj relâché(e)

laxative ['læksətɪv] n laxatif m

lay [leɪ] (pt, pp **laid**) pt of **lie** ♦ adj laïque;
(not expert) profane ♦ vt poser, mettre;
(eggs) pondre; to ~ **the table** mettre la table; ~ **aside** vt mettre de côté; ~ **by** vt =
lay aside; ~ **down** vt poser; to ~ **down
the law** faire la loi; to ~ **down one's life**
sacrifier sa vie; ~ **off** vt (workers) licencier;
~ **on** vt (provide) fournir; ~ **out** vt (display) disposer, étaler; ~**about** (inf) n fai-

néant(e); ~**-by** (BRIT) n aire f de stationnement (sur le bas-côté)

layer ['leɪə*] n couche f

layman ['leɪmən] (irreg) n profane m

layout ['leɪaʊt] n disposition f, plan m,
agencement m; (PRESS) mise f en page

laze [leɪz] vi (also: ~ **about**) paresser

lazy ['leɪzɪ] adj paresseux(euse)

lb abbr = **pound** (weight)

lead¹ [liːd] (pt, pp **led**) n (distance, time
ahead) avance f; (clue) piste f; (THEATRE)
rôle principal; (ELEC) fil m; (for dog) laisse
f ♦ vt mener, conduire; (be leader of) être à
la tête de ♦ vi (street etc) mener, conduire;
(SPORT) mener, être en tête; in the ~ en
tête; to ~ **the way** montrer le chemin; ~
away vt emmener; ~ **back** vt: to ~ **back**
to ramener à; ~ **on** vt (tease) faire marcher; ~ **to** vt fus mener à; conduire à; ~
up to vt fus conduire à

lead² [led] n (metal) plomb m; (in pencil)
mine f; ~**en** ['ledn] adj (sky, sea) de plomb

leader ['liːdə*] n chef m; dirigeant(e), leader m; (SPORT: in league) leader; (: in race)
coureur m de tête; ~**ship** n direction f;
(quality) qualités fpl de chef

lead-free ['led'friː] adj (petrol) sans plomb

leading ['liːdɪŋ] adj principal(e); de premier
plan; (in race) de tête; ~ **lady** n (THEATRE)
vedette (féminine); ~ **light** n (person) vedette f, sommité f; ~ **man** (irreg) n vedette
(masculine)

lead singer [liːd-] n (in pop group) (chanteur m) vedette f

leaf [liːf] (pl **leaves**) n feuille f ♦ vi: to ~
through feuilleter; **to turn over a new** ~
changer de conduite or d'existence

leaflet ['liːflɪt] n prospectus m, brochure f;
(POL, REL) tract m

league [liːg] n ligue f; (FOOTBALL) championnat m; **to be in** ~ **with** avoir partie
liée avec, être de mèche avec

leak [liːk] n fuite f ♦ vi (pipe, liquid etc) fuir;
(shoes) prendre l'eau; (ship) faire eau ♦ vt
(information) divulguer

lean [liːn] (pt, pp **leaned** or **leant**) adj maigre ♦ vt: to ~ **sth on sth** appuyer qch sur
qch ♦ vi (slope) pencher; (rest): to ~
against s'appuyer contre; être appuyé(e)
contre; to ~ **on** s'appuyer sur; to ~ **back/
forward** se pencher en arrière/avant; ~
out vi se pencher au dehors; ~ **over** vi se
pencher; ~**ing** n: ~**ing (towards)** tendance
f (à), penchant m (pour)

leap [liːp] (pt, pp **leaped** or **leapt**) n bond
m, saut m ♦ vi bondir, sauter; ~**frog** n
saute-mouton m; ~ **year** n année f bissextile

learn [lɜːn] (pt, pp ~**ed** or **learnt**) vt, vi apprendre; to ~ **to do sth** apprendre à faire
qch; to ~ **about** or of sth (hear, read) apprendre qch; ~**ed** ['lɜːnɪd] adj érudit(e), sa-

vant(e); **~er** (BRIT) n (also: ~er driver) (conducteur(trice)) débutant(e); **~ing** n (knowledge) savoir m

lease [liːs] n bail m ♦ vt louer à bail

leash [liːʃ] n laisse f

least [liːst] adj: the ~ (+noun) le(la) plus petit(e), le(la) moindre; (: smallest amount of) le moins de ♦ adv (+verb) le moins; (+adj): the ~ le(la) moins; at ~ au moins; (or rather) du moins; not in the ~ pas le moins du monde

leather ['leðəʳ] n cuir m

leave [liːv] (pt, pp left) vt laisser; (go away from) quitter; (forget) oublier ♦ vi partir, s'en aller ♦ n (time off) congé m; (MIL also: consent) permission f; **to be left** rester; **there's some milk left over** il reste du lait; **on ~** en permission; ~ **behind** vt (person, object) laisser; (forget) oublier; ~ **out** vt oublier, omettre; ~ **of absence** n congé exceptionnel; (MIL) permission spéciale

leaves [liːvz] npl of leaf

Lebanon ['lebənən] n Liban m

lecherous ['letʃərəs] (pej) adj lubrique

lecture ['lektʃəʳ] n conférence f; (SCOL) cours m ♦ vi donner des cours; enseigner ♦ vt (scold) sermonner, réprimander; **to give a ~ on** faire une conférence sur; donner un cours sur; ~**r** ['lektʃərəʳ] (BRIT) n (at university) professeur m (d'université)

led [led] pt, pp of lead

ledge [ledʒ] n (of window, on wall) rebord m; (of mountain) saillie f, corniche f

ledger ['ledʒəʳ] n (COMM) registre m, grand livre

leech [liːtʃ] n (also fig) sangsue f

leek [liːk] n poireau m

leer [lɪəʳ] vi: **to ~ at sb** regarder qn d'un air mauvais or concupiscent

leeway ['liːweɪ] n (fig): **to have some ~** avoir une certaine liberté d'action

left [left] pt, pp of leave ♦ adj (not right) gauche ♦ n gauche f ♦ adv à gauche; **on the ~, to the ~** à gauche; **the L~** (POL) la gauche; ~**-handed** adj gaucher(ère); ~**-hand side** n gauche f, côté m gauche; ~**-luggage (office)** (BRIT) n consigne f; ~**overs** npl restes mpl; ~**-wing** adj (POL) de gauche

leg [leg] n jambe f; (of animal) patte f; (of furniture) pied m; (CULIN: of chicken, pork) \cuisse f; (: of lamb) gigot m; (of journey) étape f; **1st/2nd ~** (SPORT) match m aller/retour

legacy ['legəsɪ] n héritage m, legs m

legal ['liːɡəl] adj légal(e); ~ **holiday** (US) n jour férié; ~ **tender** n monnaie légale

legend ['ledʒənd] n légende f

legible ['ledʒəbl] adj lisible

legislation [ledʒɪs'leɪʃən] n législation f; **legislature** ['ledʒɪsleɪtʃəʳ] n (corps) m législatif

legitimate [lɪ'dʒɪtɪmət] adj légitime

leg-room ['legrʊm] n place f pour les jambes

leisure ['leʒəʳ] n loisir m, temps m libre; loisirs mpl; **at ~** (tout) à loisir; à tête reposée; ~ **centre** n centre m de loisirs; ~**ly** adj tranquille; fait(e) sans se presser

lemon ['lemən] n citron m; ~**ade** n limonade f; ~ **tea** n thé m au citron

lend [lend] (pt, pp lent) vt: **to ~ sth (to sb)** prêter qch (à qn)

length [leŋθ] n longueur f; (section: of road, pipe etc) morceau m, bout m; (of time) durée f; **at ~** (at last) enfin, à la fin; (lengthily) longuement; ~**en** vt allonger, prolonger ♦ vi s'allonger; ~**ways** adv dans le sens de la longueur, en long; ~**y** adj (très) long(longue)

lenient ['liːnɪənt] adj indulgent(e), clément(e)

lens [lenz] n lentille f; (of spectacles) verre m; (of camera) objectif m

Lent [lent] n Carême m

lent [lent] pt, pp of lend

lentil ['lentl] n lentille f

Leo ['liːəʊ] n le Lion

leotard ['liːətɑːd] n maillot m (de danseur etc), collant m

leprosy ['leprəsɪ] n lèpre f

lesbian ['lezbɪən] n lesbienne f

less [les] adj moins de ♦ pron, adv moins ♦ prep moins; ~ **than that/you** moins que cela/vous; ~ **than half** moins de la moitié; ~ **than ever** moins que jamais; ~ **and** ~ de moins en moins; **the ~ he works ...** moins il travaille ...

lessen ['lesn] vi diminuer, s'atténuer ♦ vt diminuer, réduire, atténuer

lesser ['lesəʳ] adj moindre; **to a ~ extent** à un degré moindre

lesson ['lesn] n leçon f; **to teach sb a ~** (fig) donner une bonne leçon à qn

lest [lest] conj de peur que +sub

let [let] (pt, pp let) vt laisser; (BRIT: lease) louer; **to ~ sb do sth** laisser qn faire qch; **to ~ sb know sth** faire savoir qch à qn, prévenir qn de qch; ~**'s go** allons-y; ~ **him come** qu'il vienne; **"to ~"** "à louer"; ~ **down** vt (tyre) dégonfler; (person) décevoir, faire faux bond à; ~ **go** vi lâcher prise ♦ vt lâcher; ~ **in** vt laisser entrer; (visitor etc) faire entrer; ~ **off** vt (culprit) ne pas punir; (firework etc) faire partir; ~ **on** (inf) vi dire; ~ **out** vt laisser sortir; (scream) laisser échapper; ~ **up** vi diminuer; (cease) s'arrêter

lethal ['liːθəl] adj mortel(le), fatal(e)

letter ['letəʳ] n lettre f; ~ **bomb** n lettre piégée; ~**box** (BRIT) n boîte f aux or à lettres; ~**ing** n lettres fpl; caractères mpl

lettuce ['letɪs] n laitue f, salade f

let-up ['letʌp] n répit m, arrêt m

leukaemia [luːˈkiːmɪə] (*US* **leukemia**) *n* leucémie *f*

level [ˈlɛvl] *adj* plat(e), plan(e), uni(e); horizontal(e) ♦ *n* niveau *m* ♦ *vt* niveler, aplanir; **to be ~ with** être au même niveau que; **to draw ~ with** (*person, vehicle*) arriver à la hauteur de; **"A" ~s** (*BRIT*) ≈ baccalauréat *m*; **"O" ~s** (*BRIT*) ≈ B.E.P.C.; **on the ~** (*fig: honest*) régulier(ère); **~ off** *vi* (*prices etc*) se stabiliser; **~ out** *vi* = **level off**; **~ crossing** (*BRIT*) *n* passage *m* à niveau; **~-headed** *adj* équilibré(e)

lever [ˈliːvə*] *n* levier *m*; **~age** *n*: **~age (on** *or* **with) prise** *f* (sur)

levity [ˈlɛvɪtɪ] *n* légèreté *f*

levy [ˈlɛvɪ] *n* taxe *f*, impôt *m* ♦ *vt* prélever, imposer, percevoir

lewd [luːd] *adj* obscène, lubrique

liability [laɪəˈbɪlɪtɪ] *n* responsabilité *f*; (*handicap*) handicap *m*; **liabilities** *npl* (*on balance sheet*) passif *m*

liable [ˈlaɪəbl] *adj* (*subject*): **~ to** sujet(te) à; passible de; (*responsible*): **~ (for)** responsable (de); (*likely*): **~ to do** susceptible de faire

liaise [lɪˈeɪz] *vi*: **to ~ with** assurer la liaison avec; **liaison** [lɪːˈeɪzɒn] *n* liaison *f*

liar [ˈlaɪə*] *n* menteur(euse)

libel [ˈlaɪbl] *n* diffamation *f*; (*document*) écrit *m* diffamatoire ♦ *vt* diffamer

liberal [ˈlɪbərəl] *adj* libéral(e); (*generous*): **~ with** prodigue de, généreux(euse) avec; **the L~ Democrats** (*BRIT*) le parti libéral-démocrate

liberation [lɪbəˈreɪʃən] *n* libération *f*

liberty [ˈlɪbətɪ] *n* liberté *f*; **to be at ~ to do** être libre de faire

Libra [ˈliːbrə] *n* la Balance

librarian [laɪˈbrɛərɪən] *n* bibliothécaire *m/f*

library [ˈlaɪbrərɪ] *n* bibliothèque *f*

libretto [lɪˈbrɛtəu] *n* livret *m*

Libya [ˈlɪbɪə] *n* Libye *f*

lice [laɪs] *npl of* **louse**

licence [ˈlaɪsəns] (*US* **license**) *n* autorisation *f*, permis *m*; (*RADIO, TV*) redevance *f*; **driving ~,** (*US*) **driver's license** permis *m* (de conduire); **~ number** *n* numéro *m* d'immatriculation; **~ plate** *n* plaque *f* minéralogique

license [ˈlaɪsəns] *n* (*US*) = **licence** ♦ *vt* donner une licence à; **~d** *adj* (*car*) muni(e) de la vignette; (*to sell alcohol*) patenté(e) pour la vente des spiritueux, qui a une licence de débit de boissons

lick [lɪk] *vt* lécher; (*inf: defeat*) écraser; **to ~ one's lips** (*fig*) se frotter les mains

licorice [ˈlɪkərɪs] (*US*) *n* = **liquorice**

lid [lɪd] *n* couvercle *m*; (*eye~*) paupière *f*

lie [laɪ] (*pt* **lay,** *pp* **lain**) *vi* (*rest*) être étendu(e) *or* allongé(e) *or* couché(e); (*in grave*) être enterré(e), reposer; (*be situated*) se trouver, être; (*be untruthful: pt, pp* **lied**)

mentir ♦ *n* mensonge *m*; **to ~ low** (*fig*) se cacher; **~ about** *vi* traîner; **~ around** *vi* = **lie about; ~-down** (*BRIT*) *n*: **to have a ~-down** s'allonger, se reposer; **~-in** (*BRIT*) *n*: **to have a ~-in** faire la grasse matinée

lieutenant [lɛfˈtɛnənt, (*US*) luːˈtɛnənt] *n* lieutenant *m*

life [laɪf] (*pl* **lives**) *n* vie *f*; **to come to ~** (*fig*) s'animer; **~ assurance** (*BRIT*) *n* = **life insurance; ~belt** (*BRIT*) *n* bouée *f* de sauvetage; **~boat** *n* canot *m* *or* chaloupe *f* de sauvetage; **~buoy** *n* bouée *f* de sauvetage; **~guard** *n* surveillant *m* de baignade; **~ insurance** *n* assurance-vie *f*; **~ jacket** *n* gilet *m* *or* ceinture *f* de sauvetage; **~less** *adj* sans vie, inanimé(e); (*dull*) qui manque de vie *or* de vigueur; **~like** *adj* qui semble vrai(e) *or* vivant(e); (*painting*) réaliste; **~line** *n*: **it was his ~line** ça l'a sauvé; **~long** *adj* de toute une vie, de toujours; **~ preserver** (*US*) *n* = **lifebelt** *or* **life jacket; ~ sentence** *n* condamnation *f* à perpétuité; **~-size(d)** *adj* grandeur nature *inv*; **~ span** *n* (*durée f de*) vie *f*; **~ style** *n* style *m* *or* mode *m* de vie; **~-support system** *n* (*MED*) respirateur artificiel; **~time** *n* vie *f*; **in his ~time** de son vivant

lift [lɪft] *vt* soulever, lever; (*end*) supprimer, lever ♦ *vi* (*fog*) se lever ♦ *n* (*BRIT: elevator*) ascenseur *m*; **to give sb a ~** (: *AUT*) emmener *or* prendre qn en voiture; **~-off** *n* décollage *m*

light [laɪt] (*pt, pp* **lit**) *n* lumière *f*; (*lamp*) lampe *f*; (*AUT: rear ~*) feu *m*; (: *head~*) phare *m*; (*for cigarette etc*): **have you got a ~?** avez-vous du feu? ♦ *vt* (*candle, cigarette, fire*) allumer; (*room*) éclairer ♦ *adj* (*room, colour*) clair(e); (*not heavy*) léger(ère); (*not strenuous*) peu fatigant(e); **~s** *npl* (*AUT: traffic ~s*) feux *mpl*; **to come to ~** être dévoilé(e) *or* découvert(e); **~ up** *vi* (*face*) s'éclairer ♦ *vt* (*illuminate*) éclairer, illuminer; **~ bulb** *n* ampoule *f*; **~en** *vt* (*make less heavy*) alléger; **~er** *n* (*also: cigarette ~er*) briquet *m*; **~-headed** *adj* étourdi(e); (*excited*) grisé(e); **~-hearted** *adj* gai(e), joyeux(euse), enjoué(e); **~house** *n* phare *m*; **~ing** *n* (*on road*) éclairage *m*; (*in theatre*) éclairages *mpl*; **~ly** *adv* légèrement; **to get off ~ly** s'en tirer à bon compte; **~ness** *n* (*in weight*) légèreté *f*

lightning [ˈlaɪtnɪŋ] *n* éclair *m*, foudre *f*; **~ conductor** *n* paratonnerre *m*; **~ rod** (*US*) *n* = **lightning conductor**

light pen *n* crayon *m* optique

lightweight [ˈlaɪtweɪt] *adj* (*suit*) léger(ère) ♦ *n* (*BOXING*) poids léger

like [laɪk] *vt* aimer (bien) ♦ *prep* comme ♦ *adj* semblable, pareil(le) ♦ *n*: **and the ~** et d'autres du même genre; **his ~s and dislikes** ses goûts *mpl* *or* préférences *fpl*; **I would ~, I'd ~** je voudrais, j'aimerais;

would you ~ a coffee? voulez-vous du café?; **to be/look ~ sb/sth** ressembler à qn/qch; **what does it look ~?** de quoi est-ce que ça a l'air?; **what does it taste ~?** quel goût est-ce que ça a?; **that's just ~ him** c'est bien de lui, ça lui ressemble; **do it ~ this** fais-le comme ceci; **it's nothing ~ ...** ce n'est pas du tout comme ...; **~able** *adj* sympathique, agréable

likelihood ['laɪklɪhʊd] *n* probabilité *f*

likely ['laɪklɪ] *adj* probable; plausible; **he's ~ to leave** il va sûrement partir, il risque fort de partir; **not ~!** (*inf*) pas de danger!

likeness ['laɪknɪs] *n* ressemblance *f*; **that's a good ~** c'est très ressemblant

likewise ['laɪkwaɪz] *adv* de même, pareillement

liking ['laɪkɪŋ] *n* (*for person*) affection *f*, (*for thing*) penchant *m*, goût *m*

lilac ['laɪlək] *n* lilas *m*

lily ['lɪlɪ] *n* lis *m*; **~ of the valley** *n* muguet *m*

limb [lɪm] *n* membre *m*

limber up ['lɪmbə*-] *vi* se dégourdir, faire des exercices d'assouplissement

limbo ['lɪmbəʊ] *n*: **to be in ~** (*fig*) être tombé(e) dans l'oubli

lime [laɪm] *n* (*tree*) tilleul *m*; (*fruit*) lime *f*, citron vert; (*GEO*) chaux *f*

limelight ['laɪmlaɪt] *n*: **in the ~** (*fig*) en vedette, au premier plan

limerick ['lɪmərɪk] *n* poème *m* humoristique (de 5 vers)

limestone ['laɪmstəʊn] *n* pierre *f* à chaux; (*GEO*) calcaire *m*

limit ['lɪmɪt] *n* limite *f* ♦ *vt* limiter; **~ed** *adj* limité(e), restreint(e); **to be ~ed to** se limiter à, ne concerner que; **~ed (liability) company** (*BRIT*) *n* ≈ société *f* anonyme

limp [lɪmp] *n*: **to have a ~** boiter ♦ *vi* boiter ♦ *adj* mou(molle)

limpet ['lɪmpɪt] *n* patelle *f*

line [laɪn] *n* ligne *f*; (*stroke*) trait *m*; (*wrinkle*) ride *f*; (*rope*) corde *f*; (*wire*) fil *m*; (*of poem*) vers *m*; (*row, series*) rangée *f*; (*of people*) file *f*, queue *f*; (*railway track*) voie *f*, (*COMM: series of goods*) article(s) *m(pl)*; (*work*) métier *m*, type *m* d'activité; (*attitude, policy*) position *f* ♦ *vt*: **to ~ (with)** (*clothes*) doubler (de); (*box*) garnir *or* tapisser (de); (*subj: trees, crowd*) border; **in a ~** aligné(e); **in his ~ of business** dans sa partie, dans son rayon; **in ~ with** en accord avec; **~ up** *vi* s'aligner, se mettre en rang(s) ♦ *vt* aligner; (*event*) prévoir, préparer

lined [laɪnd] *adj* (*face*) ridé(e), marqué(e); (*paper*) réglé(e)

linen ['lɪnɪn] *n* linge *m* (de maison); (*cloth*) lin *m*

liner ['laɪnə*] *n* paquebot *m* (de ligne); (*for bin*) sac *m* à poubelle

linesman ['laɪnzmən] (*irreg*) *n* juge *m* de touche; (*TENNIS*) juge *m* de ligne

line-up ['laɪnʌp] *n* (*US: queue*) file *f*, (*SPORT*) composition *f* de l')équipe *f*

linger ['lɪŋgə*] *vi* s'attarder; traîner; (*smell, tradition*) persister

lingo ['lɪŋgəʊ] (*inf: pl* **~es**) *n pej* jargon *m*

linguist ['lɪŋgwɪst] *n*: **to be a good ~** être doué(e) par les langues

linguistics [lɪŋ'gwɪstɪks] *n* linguistique *f*

lining ['laɪnɪŋ] *n* doublure *f*

link [lɪŋk] *n* lien *m*, rapport *m*; (*of a chain*) maillon *m* ♦ *vt* relier, lier, unir; **~s** *npl* (*GOLF*) (terrain *m* de) golf *m*; **~ up** *vt* relier ♦ *vi* se rejoindre; s'associer

lino ['laɪnəʊ] *n* = **linoleum**

linoleum [lɪ'nəʊlɪəm] *n* linoléum *m*

lion ['laɪən] *n* lion *m*; **~ess** *n* lionne *f*

lip [lɪp] *n* lèvre *f*; **~-read** *vi* lire sur les lèvres; **~ salve** *n* pommade *f* rosat *or* pour les lèvres; **~ service** *n*: **to pay ~ service to sth** ne reconnaître le mérite de qch que pour la forme; **~stick** *n* rouge *m* à lèvres

liqueur [lɪ'kjʊə*] *n* liqueur *f*

liquid ['lɪkwɪd] *adj* liquide ♦ *n* liquide *m*; **~ize** ['lɪkwɪdaɪz] *vt* (*CULIN*) passer au mixer; **~izer** *n* mixer *m*

liquor ['lɪkə*] (*US*) *n* spiritueux *m*, alcool *m*

liquorice ['lɪkərɪs] (*BRIT*) *n* réglisse *f*

liquor store (*US*) *n* magasin *m* de vins et spiritueux

lisp [lɪsp] *vi* zézayer

list [lɪst] *n* liste *f* ♦ *vt* (*write down*) faire une *or* la liste de; (*mention*) énumérer; **~ed building** (*BRIT*) *n* monument classé

listen ['lɪsn] *vi* écouter; **to ~ to** écouter; **~er** *n* auditeur(trice)

listless ['lɪstləs] *adj* indolent(e), apathique

lit [lɪt] *pt, pp of* **light**

liter ['li:tə*] (*US*) *n* = **litre**

literacy ['lɪtərəsɪ] *n* degré *m* d'alphabétisation, fait *m* de savoir lire et écrire

literal ['lɪtərəl] *adj* littéral(e); **~ly** *adv* littéralement; (*really*) réellement

literary ['lɪtərərɪ] *adj* littéraire

literate ['lɪtərət] *adj* qui sait lire et écrire, instruit(e)

literature ['lɪtrətʃə*] *n* littérature *f*, (*brochures etc*) documentation *f*

lithe [laɪð] *adj* agile, souple

litigation [lɪtɪ'geɪʃən] *n* litige *m*; contentieux *m*

litre ['li:tə*] (*US* **liter**) *n* litre *m*

litter ['lɪtə*] *n* (*rubbish*) détritus *mpl*, ordures *fpl*; (*young animals*) portée *f*; **~ bin** (*BRIT*) *n* boîte *f* à ordures, poubelle *f*; **~ed** *adj*: **~ed with** jonché(e) de, couvert(e) de

little ['lɪtl] *adj* (*small*) petit(e) ♦ *adv* peu; **milk/time** peu de lait/temps; **a ~** un peu (de); **a ~ bit** un peu; **~ by ~** petit à petit, peu à peu

live[1] [laɪv] *adj* (*animal*) vivant(e), en vie;

(wire) sous tension; *(bullet, bomb)* non explosé(e); *(broadcast)* en direct; *(performance)* en public

live² [lɪv] *vi* vivre; *(reside)* vivre, habiter; ~ **down** *vt* faire oublier (avec le temps); ~ **on** *vt fus* *(food, salary)* vivre de; ~ **together** *vi* vivre ensemble, cohabiter; ~ **up to** *vt fus* se montrer à la hauteur de

livelihood ['laɪvlɪhʊd] *n* moyens *mpl* d'existence

lively ['laɪvlɪ] *adj* vif(vive), plein(e) d'entrain; *(place, book)* vivant(e)

liven up ['laɪvn-] *vt* animer ♦ *vi* s'animer

liver ['lɪvə*] *n* foie *m*

lives [laɪvz] *npl of* **life**

livestock ['laɪvstɒk] *n* bétail *m*, cheptel *m*

livid ['lɪvɪd] *adj* livide, blafard(e); *(inf: furious)* furieux(euse), furibond(e)

living ['lɪvɪŋ] *adj* vivant(e), en vie ♦ *n*: to **earn** *or* **make a** ~ gagner sa vie; ~ **conditions** *npl* conditions *fpl* de vie; ~ **room** *n* salle *f* de séjour; ~ **standards** *npl* niveau *m* de vie; ~ **wage** *n* salaire *m* permettant de vivre (décemment)

lizard ['lɪzəd] *n* lézard *m*

load [ləʊd] *n* *(weight)* poids *m*; *(thing carried)* chargement *m*, charge *f* ♦ *vt* *(also: ~ up)*: to ~ **(with)** charger (de); *(gun, camera)* charger (avec); *(COMPUT)* charger; **a** ~ **of**, ~**s of** *(fig)* un *or* des tas de, des masses de; **to talk a** ~ **of rubbish** dire des bêtises; ~**ed** *adj* *(question)* insidieux(euse); *(inf: rich)* bourré(e) de fric

loaf [ləʊf] *(pl* **loaves)** *n* pain *m*, miche *f*

loan [ləʊn] *n* prêt *m* ♦ *vt* prêter; **on** ~ prêté(e), en prêt

loath [ləʊθ] *adj*: **to be** ~ **to do** répugner à faire

loathe [ləʊð] *vt* détester, avoir en horreur

loaves [ləʊvz] *npl of* **loaf**

lobby ['lɒbɪ] *n* hall *m*, entrée *f*; *(POL)* groupe *m* de pression, lobby *m* ♦ *vt* faire pression sur

lobster ['lɒbstə*] *n* homard *m*

local ['ləʊkəl] *adj* local(e) ♦ *n* *(BRIT: pub)* pub *m* *or* café *m* du coin; **the** ~**s** *npl* *(inhabitants)* les gens *mpl* du pays *or* du coin; ~ **anaesthetic** *n* anesthésie locale; ~ **call** *n* communication urbaine; ~ **government** *n* administration locale *or* municipale; ~**ity** [ləʊˈkælɪtɪ] *n* région *f*, environs *mpl*; *(position)* lieu *m*

locate [ləʊˈkeɪt] *vt* *(find)* trouver, repérer; *(situate)*: **to be** ~**d in** être situé(e) à *or* en

location [ləʊˈkeɪʃən] *n* emplacement *m*; **on** ~ *(CINEMA)* en extérieur

loch [lɒx] *n* lac *m*, loch *m*

lock [lɒk] *n* *(of door, box)* serrure *f*; *(of canal)* écluse *f*; *(of hair)* mèche *f*, boucle *f* ♦ *vt* *(with key)* fermer à clé ♦ *vi* *(door etc)* fermer à clé; *(wheels)* se bloquer; ~ **in** *vt* enfermer; ~ **out** *vt* enfermer dehors; *(delibe-*

rately) mettre à la porte; ~ **up** *vt* *(person)* enfermer; *(house)* fermer à clé ♦ *vi* tout fermer (à clé)

locker ['lɒkə*] *n* casier *m*; *(in station)* consigne *f* automatique

locket ['lɒkɪt] *n* médaillon *m*

locksmith ['lɒksmɪθ] *n* serrurier *m*

lockup ['lɒkʌp] *n* *(prison)* prison *f*

locum ['ləʊkəm] *n* *(MED)* suppléant(e) (de médecin)

lodge [lɒdʒ] *n* pavillon *m* (de gardien); *(hunting* ~*)* pavillon de chasse ♦ *vi* *(person)*: **to** ~ **(with)** être logé(e) (chez), être en pension (chez); *(bullet)* se loger ♦ *vt*: **to** ~ **a complaint** porter plainte; ~**r** *n* locataire *m/f*; *(with meals)* pensionnaire *m/f*; **lodgings** ['lɒdʒɪŋz] *npl* chambre *f*; meublé *m*

loft [lɒft] *n* grenier *m*

lofty ['lɒftɪ] *adj* *(noble)* noble, élevé(e); *(haughty)* hautain(e)

log [lɒg] *n* *(of wood)* bûche *f*; *(book)* = **logbook** ♦ *vt* *(record)* noter

logbook ['lɒgbʊk] *n* *(NAUT)* livre *m* *or* journal *m* de bord; *(AVIAT)* carnet *m* de vol; *(of car)* ≈ carte grise

loggerheads ['lɒgəhedz] *npl*: **at** ~ **(with)** à couteaux tirés (avec)

logic ['lɒdʒɪk] *n* logique *f*; ~**al** *adj* logique

loin [lɔɪn] *n* *(CULIN)* filet *m*, longe *f*

loiter ['lɔɪtə*] *vi* traîner

loll [lɒl] *vi* *(also:* ~ *about)* se prélasser, fainéanter

lollipop ['lɒlɪpɒp] *n* sucette *f*; ~ **man/lady** *(BRIT: irreg)* *n* contractuel(le) qui fait traverser la rue aux enfants

London ['lʌndən] *n* Londres *m*; ~**er** *n* Londonien(ne)

lone [ləʊn] *adj* solitaire

loneliness ['ləʊnlɪnəs] *n* solitude *f*, isolement *m*; **lonely** ['ləʊnlɪ] *adj* seul(e); solitaire, isolé(e)

long [lɒŋ] *adj* long(longue) ♦ *adv* longtemps ♦ *vi*: **to** ~ **for sth** avoir très envie de qch; attendre qch avec impatience; **so** *or* **as** ~ **as** pourvu que; **don't be** ~! dépêchez-vous!; **how** ~ **is this river/course?** quelle est la longueur de ce fleuve/la durée de ce cours?; **6 metres** ~ (long) de 6 mètres; **6 months** ~ qui dure 6 mois, de 6 mois; **all night** ~ toute la nuit; **he no** ~**er comes** il ne vient plus; ~ **before/after** longtemps avant/après; **before** ~ *(+future)* avant peu, dans peu de temps; *(+past)* peu de (temps) après; **at** ~ **last** enfin; ~-**distance** *adj* *(call)* interurbain(e); ~**hand** *n* écriture normale *or* courante; ~**ing** *n* désir *m*, envie *f*, nostalgie *f*

longitude ['lɒŋgɪtjuːd] *n* longitude *f*

long: ~ **jump** *n* saut *m* en longueur; ~-**life** *adj* longue durée *inv*; *(milk)* upérisé(e); ~-**lost** *adj* *(person)* perdu(e) de vue depuis longtemps; ~-**playing record** *n* (disque *m*)

33 tours *inv*; ~**-range** *adj* à longue portée; ~**-sighted** *adj* (*MED*) presbyte; ~**standing** *adj* de longue date; ~**-suffering** *adj* empreint(e) d'une patience résignée; extrêmement patient(e); ~**-term** *adj* à long terme; ~ **wave** *n* grandes ondes; ~**-winded** *adj* intarissable, interminable

loo [luː] *n* (*BRIT: inf*) *n* W.-C. *mpl*, petit coin

look [lʊk] *vi* regarder; (*seem*) sembler, paraître, avoir l'air; (*building etc*): **to ~ south/(out) onto the sea** donner au sud/sur la mer ♦ *n* regard *m*; (*appearance*) air *m*, allure *f*, aspect *m*; ~**s** *npl* (*good ~s*) physique *m*, beauté *f*; **to have a ~** regarder; ~**!** regardez!; ~ (*here*)! (*annoyance*) écoutez!; ~ **after** *vt fus* (*care for, deal with*) s'occuper de; ~ **at** *vt fus*, regarder (*problem etc*) examiner; ~ **back** *vi*: **to ~ back on** (*event etc*) évoquer, repenser à; ~ **down on** *vt fus* (*fig*) regarder de haut, dédaigner; ~ **for** *vt fus* chercher; ~ **forward to** *vt fus* attendre avec impatience; **we ~ forward to hearing from you** (*in letter*) dans l'attente de vous lire; ~ **into** *vt fus* examiner, étudier; ~ **on** *vi* regarder (en spectateur); ~ **out** *vi* (*beware*): **to ~ out (for)** prendre garde (à), faire attention (à); ~ **out for** *vt fus* être à la recherche de; guetter; ~ **round** *vi* regarder derrière soi, se retourner; ~ **to** *vt fus* (*rely on*) compter sur; ~ **up** *vi* lever les yeux; (*improve*) s'améliorer ♦ *vt* (*word, name*) chercher; ~ **up to** *vt fus* avoir du respect pour; ~**out** *n* poste *m* de guet; (*person*) guetteur *m*; **to be on the ~out (for)** guetter

loom [luːm] *vi* (*also*: ~ **up**) surgir; (*approach: event etc*) être imminent(e); (*threaten*) menacer ♦ *n* (*for weaving*) métier *m* à tisser

loony [ˈluːnɪ] (*inf*) *adj, n* timbré(e), cinglé(e)

loop [luːp] *n* boucle *f*; ~**hole** *n* (*fig*) porte *f* de sortie; échappatoire *f*

loose [luːs] *adj* (*knot, screw*) desserré(e); (*clothes*) ample, lâche; (*hair*) dénoué(e), épars(e); (*not firmly fixed*) pas solide; (*morals, discipline*) relâché(e) ♦ *n*: **on the ~** en liberté; ~ **change** *n* petite monnaie; ~ **chippings** *npl* (*on road*) gravillons *mpl*; ~ **end** *n*: **to be at a ~ end** *or* (*US*) **at ~ ends** ne pas trop savoir quoi faire; ~**ly** *adv* sans serrer; (*imprecisely*) approximativement; ~**n** *vt* desserrer

loot [luːt] *n* (*inf: money*) pognon *m*, fric *m* ♦ *vt* piller

lopsided [ˈlɒpˈsaɪdɪd] *adj* de travers, asymétrique

lord [lɔːd] *n* seigneur *m*; **L~ Smith** lord Smith; **the L~** le Seigneur; **good L~!** mon Dieu!; **the (House of) L~s** (*BRIT*) la Chambre des lords; **my L~** = **your lordship**; **L~ship** *n*: **your L~ship** Monsieur le comte (*or* le baron *or* le juge); (*to bishop*) Monsei-

gneur

lore [lɔː*] *n* tradition(s) *f(pl)*

lorry [ˈlɒrɪ] (*BRIT*) *n* camion *m*; ~ **driver** (*BRIT*) *n* camionneur *m*, routier *m*

lose [luːz] (*pt, pp* lost) *vt, vi* perdre; **to ~ (time)** (*clock*) retarder; **to get lost** *vi* se perdre; ~**r** *n* perdant(e)

loss [lɒs] *n* perte *f*; **to be at a ~** être perplexe *or* embarrassé(e)

lost [lɒst] *pt, pp of* **lose** ♦ *adj* perdu(e); ~ **and found** (*US*), ~ **property** *n* objets trouvés

lot [lɒt] *n* (*set*) lot *m*; **the ~** le tout; **a ~ (of)** beaucoup (de); ~**s of** des tas de; **to draw ~s (for sth)** tirer (qch) au sort

lotion [ˈləʊʃən] *n* lotion *f*

lottery [ˈlɒtərɪ] *n* loterie *f*

loud [laʊd] *adj* bruyant(e), sonore; (*voice*) fort(e); (*support, condemnation*) vigoureux(euse); (*gaudy*) voyant(e), tapageur(euse) ♦ *adv* (*speak etc*) fort; **out ~** tout haut; ~**-hailer** (*BRIT*) *n* porte-voix *m inv*; ~**ly** *adv* fort, bruyamment; ~ **speaker** *n* haut-parleur *m*

lounge [laʊndʒ] *n* salon *m*; (*at airport*) salle *f*; (*BRIT: also*: ~ **bar**) (salle de) café *m or* bar *m* ♦ *vi* (*also*: ~ **about** *or* **around**) se prélasser, paresser; ~ **suit** (*BRIT*) *n* complet *m*; (*on invitation*) "tenue de ville"

louse [laʊs] (*pl* lice) *n* pou *m*

lousy [ˈlauzɪ] (*inf*) *adj* infect(e), moche; **I feel ~** je suis mal fichu(e)

lout [laʊt] *n* rustre *m*, butor *m*

lovable [ˈlʌvəbl] *adj* adorable; très sympathique

love [lʌv] *n* amour *m* ♦ *vt* aimer; (*caringly, kindly*) aimer beaucoup; "~ **(from) Anne**" "affectueusement, Anne"; **I ~ chocolate** j'adore le chocolat; **to be/fall in ~ with** être/tomber amoureux(euse) de; **to make ~** faire l'amour; "**15 ~**" (*TENNIS*) "15 à rien *or* zéro"; ~ **affair** *n* liaison (amoureuse); ~ **life** *n* vie sentimentale

lovely [ˈlʌvlɪ] *adj* (très) joli(e), ravissant(e); (*delightful: person*) charmant(e); (*holiday etc*) (très) agréable

lover [ˈlʌvə*] *n* amant *m*; (*person in love*) amoureux(euse); (*amateur*): **a ~ of** un amateur de; un(e) amoureux(euse) de

loving [ˈlʌvɪŋ] *adj* affectueux(euse), tendre

low [ləʊ] *adj* bas(basse); (*quality*) mauvais(e), inférieur(e); (*person: depressed*) déprimé(e); (*: ill*) bas(basse), affaibli(e) ♦ *adv* bas ♦ *n* (*METEOROLOGY*) dépression *f*; **to be ~ on** être à court de; **to feel ~** se sentir déprimé(e); **to reach an all-time ~** être au plus bas; ~**-alcohol** *adj* peu alcoolisé(e); ~**-cut** *adj* (*dress*) décolleté(e)

lower [ˈləʊə*] *adj* inférieur(e) ♦ *vt* abaisser, baisser

low: ~**-fat** *adj* maigre; ~**lands** *npl* (*GEO*) plaines *fpl*; ~**ly** *adj* humble, modeste

loyalty ['lɔɪəltɪ] *n* loyauté *f*, fidélité *f*
lozenge ['lɔzɪndʒ] *n* (*MED*) pastille *f*
LP *n abbr* = **long-playing record**
L-plates ['elpleɪts] (*BRIT*) *npl* plaques *fpl* d'apprenti conducteur
Ltd *abbr* (= *limited*) ≈ S.A.
lubricant ['luːbrɪkənt] *n* lubrifiant *m*
lubricate ['luːbrɪkeɪt] *vt* lubrifier, graisser
luck [lʌk] *n* chance *f*; **bad** ~ malchance *f*, malheur *m*; **bad** *or* **hard** *or* **tough** ~! pas de chance!; **good** ~! bonne chance!; ~**ily** *adv* heureusement, par bonheur; ~**y** *adj* (*person*) qui a de la chance; (*coincidence, event*) heureux(euse); (*object*) porte-bonheur *inv*
ludicrous ['luːdɪkrəs] *adj* ridicule, absurde
lug [lʌg] (*inf*) *vt* traîner, tirer
luggage ['lʌgɪdʒ] *n* bagages *mpl*; ~ **rack** *n* (*on car*) galerie *f*
lukewarm ['luːkwɔːm] *adj* tiède
lull [lʌl] *n* accalmie *f*; (*in conversation*) pause *f* ♦ *vt*: **to** ~ **sb to sleep** bercer qn pour qu'il s'endorme; **to be** ~**ed into a false sense of security** s'endormir dans une fausse sécurité
lullaby ['lʌləbaɪ] *n* berceuse *f*
lumbago [lʌm'beɪgəʊ] *n* lumbago *m*
lumber ['lʌmbə*] *n* (*wood*) bois *m* de charpente; (*junk*) bric-à-brac *m inv* ♦ *vt*: **to be** ~**ed with** (*inf*) se farcir; ~**jack** *n* bûcheron *m*
luminous ['luːmɪnəs] *adj* lumineux(euse)
lump [lʌmp] *n* morceau *m*; (*swelling*) grosseur *f* ♦ *vt*: **to** ~ **together** réunir, mettre en tas; ~ **sum** *n* somme globale *or* forfaitaire; ~**y** *adj* (*sauce*) avec des grumeaux; (*bed*) défoncé(e), peu confortable
lunar ['luːnə*] *adj* lunaire
lunatic ['luːnətɪk] *adj* fou(folle), cinglé(e) (*inf*)
lunch [lʌntʃ] *n* déjeuner *m*
luncheon ['lʌntʃən] *n* déjeuner *m* (*chic*); ~ **meat** *n* sorte de mortadelle; ~ **voucher** (*BRIT*) *n* chèque-repas *m*
lung [lʌŋ] *n* poumon *m*
lunge [lʌndʒ] *vi* (*also*: ~ *forward*) faire un mouvement brusque en avant; **to** ~ **at** envoyer *or* assener un coup à
lurch [lɜːtʃ] *vi* vaciller, tituber ♦ *n* écart *m* brusque; **to leave sb in the** ~ laisser qn se débrouiller *or* se dépêtrer tout(e) seul(e)
lure [ljʊə*] *n* (*attraction*) attrait *m*, charme *m* ♦ *vt* attirer *or* persuader par la ruse
lurid ['ljʊərɪd] *adj* affreux(euse), atroce; (*pej*: *colour, dress*) criard(e)
lurk [lɜːk] *vi* se tapir, se cacher
luscious ['lʌʃəs] *adj* succulent(e); appétissant(e)
lush [lʌʃ] *adj* luxuriant(e)
lust [lʌst] *n* (*sexual*) luxure *f*; lubricité *f*; désir *m*; (*fig*): ~ **for** soif *f* de; ~ **after**, ~ **for** *vt fus* (*sexually*) convoiter, désirer; ~**y**

['lʌstɪ] *adj* vigoureux(euse), robuste
Luxembourg ['lʌksəmbɜːg] *n* Luxembourg *m*
luxurious [lʌg'zjʊərɪəs] *adj* luxueux(euse); **luxury** ['lʌkʃərɪ] *n* luxe *m* ♦ *cpd* de luxe
lying ['laɪɪŋ] *n* mensonge(s) *m(pl)* ♦ *vb see* **lie**
lyrical *adj* lyrique
lyrics ['lɪrɪks] *npl* (*of song*) paroles *fpl*

M m

m. *abbr* = **metre**; **mile**; **million**
M.A. *abbr* = **Master of Arts**
mac [mæk] (*BRIT*) *n* imper(méable) *m*
macaroni [mækə'rəʊnɪ] *n* macaroni *mpl*
machine [mə'ʃiːn] *n* machine *f* ♦ *vt* (*TECH*) façonner à la machine; (*dress etc*) coudre à la machine; ~ **gun** *n* mitrailleuse *f*; ~ **language** *n* (*COMPUT*) langage-machine *m*; ~**ry** *n* machinerie *f*, machines *fpl*; (*fig*) mécanisme(s) *m(pl)*
mackerel ['mækrəl] *n inv* maquereau *m*
mackintosh ['mækɪntɔʃ] (*BRIT*) *n* imperméable *m*
mad [mæd] *adj* fou(folle); (*foolish*) insensé(e); (*angry*) furieux(euse); (*keen*): **to be** ~ **about** être fou(folle) de
madam ['mædəm] *n* madame *f*
madden ['mædn] *vt* exaspérer
made [meɪd] *pt, pp of* **make**
Madeira [mə'dɪərə] *n* (*GEO*) Madère *f*; (*wine*) madère *m*
made-to-measure ['meɪdtə'meʒə*] (*BRIT*) *adj* fait(e) sur mesure
madly ['mædlɪ] *adv* follement; ~ **in love** éperdument amoureux(euse)
madman ['mædmən] (*irreg*) *n* fou *m*
madness ['mædnəs] *n* folie *f*
magazine ['mægəziːn] *n* (*PRESS*) magazine *m*, revue *f*; (*RADIO, TV*: *also*: ~ *programme*) magazine
maggot ['mægət] *n* ver *m*, asticot *m*
magic ['mædʒɪk] *n* magie *f* ♦ *adj* magique; ~**al** *adj* magique; (*experience, evening*) merveilleux (euse); ~**ian** [mə'dʒɪʃən] *n* magicien (ne); (*conjurer*) prestidigitateur *m*
magistrate ['mædʒɪstreɪt] *n* magistrat *m*; juge *m*
magnet ['mægnɪt] *n* aimant *m*; ~**ic** [mæg'netɪk] *adj* magnétique
magnificent [mæg'nɪfɪsənt] *adj* superbe, magnifique; (*splendid*: *robe, building*) somp-

tueux(euse), magnifique

magnify ['mægnifai] *vt* grossir; (*sound*) amplifier; ~**ing glass** *n* loupe *f*

magnitude ['mægnitjuːd] *n* ampleur *f*

magpie ['mægpai] *n* pie *f*

mahogany [mə'hɒgəni] *n* acajou *m*

maid [meid] *n* bonne *f*; **old** ~ (*pej*) vieille fille

maiden ['meidn] *n* jeune fille *f* ◆ *adj* (*aunt etc*) non mariée; (*speech, voyage*) inaugural(e); ~ **name** *n* nom *m* de jeune fille

mail [meil] *n* poste *f*; (*letters*) courrier *m* ◆ *vt* envoyer (par la poste); ~**box** (*US*) *n* boîte *f* aux lettres; ~**ing list** *n* liste *f* d'adresses; ~-**order** *n* vente *f* or achat *m* par correspondance

maim [meim] *vt* mutiler

main [mein] *adj* principal(e) ◆ *n*: **the** ~(**s**) *n(pl)* (*gas, water*) conduite principale, canalisation *f*; **the** ~**s** *npl* (*ELEC*) le secteur; **in the** ~ dans l'ensemble; ~**frame** *n* (*COMPUT*) (gros) ordinateur, unité centrale; ~**land** *n* continent *m*; ~**ly** *adv* principalement, surtout; ~ **road** *n* grand-route *f*, ~**stay** *n* (*fig*) pilier *m*; ~**stream** *n* courant principal

maintain [mein'tein] *vt* entretenir; (*continue*) maintenir; (*affirm*) soutenir; **maintenance** ['meintənəns] *n* entretien *m*; (*alimony*) pension *f* alimentaire

maize [meiz] *n* maïs *m*

majestic [mə'dʒestik] *adj* majestueux(euse)

majesty ['mædʒisti] *n* majesté *f*

major ['meidʒə*] *n* (*MIL*) commandant *m* ◆ *adj* (*important*) important(e); (*most important*) principal(e); (*MUS*) majeur(e)

Majorca [mə'jɔːkə] *n* Majorque *f*

majority [mə'dʒɒriti] *n* majorité *f*

make [meik] (*pt, pp* **made**) *vt* faire; (*manufacture*) faire, fabriquer; (*earn*) gagner; (*cause to be*): **to** ~ **sb sad** *etc* rendre qn triste *etc*; (*force*): **to** ~ **sb do sth** obliger qn à faire qch, faire faire qch à qn; (*equal*): **2 and 2** ~ **4** 2 et 2 font 4 ◆ *n* fabrication *f*; (*brand*) marque *f*; **to** ~ **a fool of sb** (*ridicule*) ridiculiser qn; (*trick*) avoir or duper qn; **to** ~ **a profit** faire un or des bénéfice(s); **to** ~ **a loss** essuyer une perte; **to** ~ **it** (*arrive*) arriver; (*achieve sth*) parvenir à qch, réussir; **what time do you** ~ **it?** quelle heure avez-vous?; **to** ~ **do with** se contenter de; se débrouiller avec; ~ **for** *vt fus* (*place*) se diriger vers; ~ **out** *vt* (*write out: cheque*) faire; (*decipher*) déchiffrer; (*understand*) comprendre; (*see*) distinguer; ~ **up** *vt* (*constitute*) constituer; (*invent*) inventer, imaginer; (*parcel, bed*) faire ◆ *vi* se réconcilier; (*with cosmetics*) se maquiller; ~ **up for** *vt fus* compenser; ~-**believe** *n*: **it's just** ~-**believe** (*game*) c'est pour faire semblant; (*invention*) c'est de l'invention pure; ~**r** *n* fabricant *m*; ~**shift** *adj* provisoire,

improvisé(e); ~-**up** *n* maquillage *m*; ~-**up remover** *n* démaquillant *m*

making ['meikiŋ] *n* (*fig*): **in the** ~ en formation *or* en gestation; **to have the** ~**s of** (*actor, athlete etc*) avoir l'étoffe de

malaria [mə'lɛəriə] *n* malaria *f*

Malaysia [mə'leiziə] *n* Malaisie *f*

male [meil] *n* (*BIO*) mâle *m* ◆ *adj* mâle; (*sex, attitude*) masculin(e); (*child etc*) du sexe masculin

malevolent [mə'levələnt] *adj* malveillant(e)

malfunction [mæl'fʌŋkʃən] *n* fonctionnement défectueux

malice ['mælis] *n* méchanceté *f*, malveillance *f*; **malicious** [mə'liʃəs] *adj* méchant(e), malveillant(e)

malign [mə'lain] *vt* diffamer, calomnier

malignant [mə'lignənt] *adj* (*MED*) malin(igne)

mall [mɔːl] *n* (*also: shopping* ~) centre commercial

mallet ['mælit] *n* maillet *m*

malpractice ['mæl'præktis] *n* faute professionnelle; négligence *f*

malt [mɔːlt] *n* malt *m* ◆ *cpd* (*also*: ~ *whisky*) pur malt

Malta ['mɔːltə] *n* Malte *f*

mammal ['mæməl] *n* mammifère *m*

mammoth ['mæməθ] *n* mammouth *m* ◆ *adj* géant(e), monstre

man [mæn] (*pl* **men**) *n* homme *m* ◆ *vt* (*NAUT: ship*) garnir d'hommes; (*MIL: gun*) servir; (: *post*) être de service à; (*machine*) assurer le fonctionnement de; **an old** ~ un vieillard; ~ **and wife** mari et femme

manage ['mænidʒ] *vi* se débrouiller ◆ *vt* (*be in charge of*) s'occuper de; (: *business etc*) gérer; (*control: ship*) manier, manœuvrer; (: *person*) savoir s'y prendre avec; **to** ~ **to do** réussir à faire; ~**able** *adj* (*task*) faisable; (*number*) raisonnable; ~**ment** *n* gestion *f*, administration *f*, direction *f*; ~**r** *n* directeur *m*; administrateur *m*; (*SPORT*) manager *m*; (*of artist*) impresario *m*; ~**ress** [mænidʒə'res] *n* directrice *f*, gérante *f*; ~**rial** [mænə'dʒiəriəl] *adj* directorial(e); (*skills*) de cadre, de gestion; **managing director** ['mænidʒiŋ] *n* directeur général

mandarin ['mændərin] *n* (*also*: ~ *orange*) mandarine *f*; (*person*) mandarin *m*

mandatory ['mændətəri] *adj* obligatoire

mane [mein] *n* crinière *f*

maneuver (*US*) *vt, vi, n* = **manoeuvre**

manfully ['mænfuli] *adv* vaillamment

mangle ['mæŋgl] *vt* déchiqueter; mutiler

mango ['mæŋgəu] (*pl* ~**es**) *n* mangue *f*

mangy ['meindʒi] *adj* galeux(euse)

manhandle ['mænhændl] *vt* malmener

man: ~**hole** ['mænhəul] *n* trou *m* d'homme; ~**hood** ['mænhud] *n* âge *m* d'homme; virilité *f*; ~-**hour** ['mæn'auə*] *n* heure *f* de main-d'œuvre; ~**hunt** ['mænhʌnt] *n* (*POLI-*

CE) chasse *f* à l'homme

mania ['meɪnɪə] *n* manie *f*; ~**c** ['meɪnɪæk] *n* maniaque *m/f*; (*fig*) fou(folle) *m/f*; **manic** ['mænɪk] *adj* maniaque

manicure ['mænɪkjʊə*] *n* manucure *f*; ~ **set** *n* trousse *f* à ongles

manifest ['mænɪfest] *vt* manifester ♦ *adj* manifeste, évident(e)

manifesto [mænɪ'festəʊ] *n* manifeste *m*

manipulate [mə'nɪpjʊleɪt] *vt* manipuler; (*system, situation*) exploiter

man: ~**kind** [mæn'kaɪnd] *n* humanité *f*, genre humain; ~**ly** ['mænlɪ] *adj* viril(e); ~**made** ['mæn'meɪd] *adj* artificiel(le); (*fibre*) synthétique

manner ['mænə*] *n* manière *f*, façon *f*; (*behaviour*) attitude *f*, comportement *m*; (*sort*): **all** ~ **of** toutes sortes de; ~**s** *npl* (*behaviour*) manières *f*; ~**ism** *n* particularité *f* de langage (*or* de comportement), tic *m*

manoeuvre [mə'nu:və*] (*US* **maneuver**) *vt* (*move*) manœuvrer; (*manipulate: person*) manipuler; (: *situation*) exploiter ♦ *vi* manœuvrer ♦ *n* manœuvre *f*

manor ['mænə*] *n* (*also:* ~ **house**) manoir *m*

manpower ['mænpaʊə*] *n* main-d'œuvre *f*

mansion ['mænʃən] *n* château *m*, manoir *m*

manslaughter ['mænslɔ:tə*] *n* homicide *m* involontaire

mantelpiece ['mæntlpi:s] *n* cheminée *f*

manual ['mænjʊəl] *adj* manuel(le) ♦ *n* manuel *m*

manufacture [mænjʊ'fæktʃə*] *vt* fabriquer ♦ *n* fabrication *f*; ~**r** *n* fabricant *m*

manure [mə'njʊə*] *n* fumier *m*

manuscript ['mænjʊskrɪpt] *n* manuscrit *m*

many ['menɪ] *adj* beaucoup de, de nombreux(euses) ♦ *pron* beaucoup, un grand nombre; **a great** ~ un grand nombre (de); ~ **a** ... bien des ..., plus d'un(e) ...

map [mæp] *n* carte *f*; (*of town*) plan *m*; ~ **out** *vt* tracer; (*task*) planifier

maple ['meɪpl] *n* érable *m*

mar [mɑ:*] *vt* gâcher, gâter

marathon ['mærəθən] *n* marathon *m*

marble ['mɑ:bl] *n* marbre *m*; (*toy*) bille *f*

March [mɑ:tʃ] *n* mars *m*

march [mɑ:tʃ] *vi* marcher au pas; (*fig: protesters*) défiler ♦ *n* marche *f*; (*demonstration*) manifestation *f*

mare [mɛə*] *n* jument *f*

margarine [mɑ:dʒə'ri:n] *n* margarine *f*

margin ['mɑ:dʒɪn] *n* marge *f*; ~**al (seat)** *n* (*POL*) siège disputé

marigold ['mærɪgəʊld] *n* souci *m*

marijuana [mærɪ'wɑ:nə] *n* marijuana *f*

marina [mə'ri:nə] *n* (*harbour*) marina *f*

marine [mə'ri:n] *adj* marin(e) ♦ *n* fusilier marin; (*US*) marine *m*; ~ **engineer** *n* ingénieur *m* en génie maritime

marital ['mærɪtl] *adj* matrimonial(e); ~ **status** situation *f* de famille

marjoram ['mɑ:dʒərəm] *n* marjolaine *f*

mark [mɑ:k] *n* marque *f*; (*of skid etc*) trace *f*; (*BRIT: SCOL*) note *f*; (*currency*) mark *m* ♦ *vt* marquer; (*stain*) tacher; (*BRIT: SCOL*) noter; corriger; **to** ~ **time** marquer le pas; ~**er** *n* (*sign*) jalon *m*; (*bookmark*) signet *m*

market ['mɑ:kɪt] *n* marché *m* ♦ *vt* (*COMM*) commercialiser; ~ **garden** (*BRIT*) *n* jardin maraîcher; ~**ing** *n* marketing *m*; ~**place** *n* place *f* du marché; (*COMM*) marché *m*; ~ **research** *n* étude *f* de marché

marksman ['mɑ:ksmən] (*irreg*) *n* tireur *m* d'élite

marmalade ['mɑ:məleɪd] *n* confiture *f* d'oranges

maroon [mə'ru:n] *vt*: **to be** ~**ed** être abandonné(e); (*fig*) être bloqué(e) ♦ *adj* bordeaux *inv*

marquee [mɑ:'ki:] *n* chapiteau *m*

marriage ['mærɪdʒ] *n* mariage *m*; ~ **bureau** *n* agence matrimoniale; ~ **certificate** *n* extrait *m* d'acte de mariage

married ['mærɪd] *adj* marié(e); (*life, love*) conjugal(e)

marrow ['mærəʊ] *n* moelle *f*; (*vegetable*) courge *f*

marry ['mærɪ] *vt* épouser, se marier avec; (*subj: father, priest etc*) marier ♦ *vi* (*also: get married*) se marier

Mars [mɑ:z] *n* (*planet*) Mars *f*

marsh [mɑ:ʃ] *n* marais *m*, marécage *m*

marshal ['mɑ:ʃəl] *n* maréchal *m*; (*US: fire, police*) ≈ capitaine *m*; (*SPORT*) membre *m* du service d'ordre ♦ *vt* rassembler

marshy ['mɑ:ʃɪ] *adj* marécageux(euse)

martyr ['mɑ:tə*] *n* martyr(e); ~**dom** *n* martyre *m*

marvel ['mɑ:vəl] *n* merveille *f* ♦ *vi*: **to** ~ **(at)** s'émerveiller (de); ~**lous** (*US* ~**ous**) *adj* merveilleux(euse)

Marxist ['mɑ:ksɪst] *adj* marxiste ♦ *n* marxiste *m/f*

marzipan [mɑ:zɪ'pæn] *n* pâte *f* d'amandes

mascara [mæs'kɑ:rə] *n* mascara *m*

masculine ['mæskjʊlɪn] *adj* masculin(e)

mash [mæʃ] *vt* écraser, réduire en purée; ~**ed potatoes** *npl* purée *f* de pommes de terre

mask [mɑ:sk] *n* masque *m* ♦ *vt* masquer

mason ['meɪsn] *n* (*also: stone~*) maçon *m*; (: *free~*) franc-maçon *m*; ~**ry** *n* maçonnerie *f*

masquerade [mæskə'reɪd] *vi*: **to** ~ **as** se faire passer pour

mass [mæs] *n* multitude *f*, masse *f*; (*PHYSICS*) masse; (*REL*) messe *f* ♦ *cpd* (*communication*) de masse; (*unemployment*) massif(ive) ♦ *vi* se masser; **the** ~**es** les masses; ~**es of** des tas de

massacre ['mæsəkə*] *n* massacre *m*

massage ['mæsɑːʒ] *n* massage *m* ♦ *vt* masser

massive ['mæsɪv] *adj* énorme, massif(ive)

mass media *n inv* mass-media *mpl*

mass production *n* fabrication *f* en série

mast [mɑːst] *n* mât *m*; (*RADIO*) pylône *m*

master ['mɑːstə*] *n* maître *m*; (*in secondary school*) professeur *m*; (*title for boys*): **M~ X** Monsieur X ♦ *vt* maîtriser; (*learn*) apprendre à fond; **~ly** *adj* magistral(e); **~mind** *n* esprit supérieur ♦ *vt* diriger, être le cerveau de; **M~ of Arts/Science** *n* ≈ maîtrise *f* (en lettres/sciences); **~piece** *n* chef-d'œuvre *m*; **~plan** *n* stratégie *f* d'ensemble; **~y** *n* maîtrise *f*; connaissance parfaite

mat [mæt] *n* petit tapis; (*also: door~*) paillasson *m*; (: *table~*) napperon *m* ♦ *adj* = **matt**

match [mætʃ] *n* allumette *f*; (*game*) match *m*, partie *f*; (*fig*) égal(e) ♦ *vt* (*also: ~ up*) assortir; (*go well with*) aller bien avec, s'assortir à; (*equal*) égaler, valoir ♦ *vi* être assorti(e); **to be a good ~** être bien assorti(e); **~box** *n* boîte *f* d'allumettes; **~ing** *adj* assorti(e)

mate [meɪt] *n* (*inf*) copain(copine); (*animal*) partenaire *m/f*, mâle/femelle; (*in merchant navy*) second *m* ♦ *vi* s'accoupler

material [mə'tɪərɪəl] *n* (*substance*) matière *f*, matériau *m*; (*cloth*) tissu *m*, étoffe *f*; (*information, data*) données *fpl* ♦ *adj* matériel(le); (*relevant: evidence*) pertinent(e); **~s** *npl* (*equipment*) matériaux *mpl*

maternal [mə'tɜːnl] *adj* maternel(le)

maternity [mə'tɜːnɪtɪ] *n* maternité *f*; **~ dress** *n* robe *f* de grossesse; **~ hospital** *n* maternité *f*

mathematical [mæθə'mætɪkl] *adj* mathématique; **mathematics** [mæθə'mætɪks] *n* mathématiques *fpl*

maths [mæθs] (*US* **math**) *n* math(s) *fpl*

matinée ['mætɪneɪ] *n* matinée *f*

mating call ['meɪtɪŋ-] *n* appel *m* du mâle

matrices ['meɪtrɪsiːz] *npl* of **matrix**

matriculation [mətrɪkjʊ'leɪʃən] *n* inscription *f*

matrimonial [mætrɪ'məʊnɪəl] *adj* matrimonial(e), conjugal(e)

matrimony ['mætrɪmənɪ] *n* mariage *m*

matrix ['meɪtrɪks] (*pl* **matrices**) *n* matrice *f*

matron ['meɪtrən] *n* (*in hospital*) infirmière-chef *f*; (*in school*) infirmière

matt(t) [mæt] *adj* mat(e)

matted ['mætɪd] *adj* emmêlé(e)

matter ['mætə*] *n* question *f*, (*PHYSICS*) matière *f*; (*content*) contenu *m*, fond *m*; (*MED: pus*) pus *m* ♦ *vi* importer; **~s** *npl* (*affairs, situation*) la situation; **it doesn't ~** cela n'a pas d'importance; (*I don't mind*) cela ne fait rien; **what's the ~?** qu'est-ce qu'il y a?, qu'est-ce qui ne va pas?; **no ~ what** quoiqu'il arrive; **as a ~ of course**

tout naturellement; **as a ~ of fact** en fait; **~-of-fact** *adj* terre à terre; (*voice*) neutre

mattress ['mætrəs] *n* matelas *m*

mature [mə'tjʊə*] *adj* mûr(e); (*cheese*) fait(e); (*wine*) arrivé(e) à maturité ♦ *vi* (*person*) mûrir; (*wine, cheese*) se faire

maul [mɔːl] *vt* lacérer

mausoleum [mɔːsə'lɪəm] *n* mausolée *m*

mauve [məʊv] *adj* mauve

maverick ['mævərɪk] *n* (*fig*) non-conformiste *m/f*

maximum ['mæksɪməm] (*pl* **maxima**) *adj* maximum ♦ *n* maximum *m*

May [meɪ] *n* mai *m*; **~ Day** *n* le Premier Mai; *see also* **mayday**

may [meɪ] (*conditional* **might**) *vi* (*indicating possibility*): **he ~ come** il se peut qu'il vienne; (*be allowed to*): **~ I smoke?** puis-je fumer?; (*wishes*): **~ God bless you!** (que) Dieu vous bénisse!; **you ~ as well go** à votre place, je partirais

maybe ['meɪbɪ] *adv* peut-être; **~ he'll ...** peut-être qu'il ...

mayday ['meɪdeɪ] *n* SOS *m*

mayhem ['meɪhem] *n* grabuge *m*

mayonnaise [meɪə'neɪz] *n* mayonnaise *f*

mayor [mεə*] *n* maire *m*; **~ess** *n* épouse *f* du maire

maze [meɪz] *n* labyrinthe *m*, dédale *m*

MD *n abbr* (= *Doctor of Medicine*) titre universitaire; = **managing director**

me [miː] *pron* me, m' +*vowel*; (*stressed, after prep*) moi; **he heard ~** il m'a entendu(e); **give ~ a book** donnez-moi un livre; **after ~** après moi

meadow ['medəʊ] *n* prairie *f*, pré *m*

meagre ['miːgə*] (*US* **meager**) *adj* maigre

meal [miːl] *n* repas *m*; (*flour*) farine *f*; **~time** *n* l'heure *f* du repas

mean [miːn] (*pt, pp* **meant**) *adj* (*with money*) avare, radin(e); (*unkind*) méchant(e); (*shabby*) misérable; (*average*) moyen(ne) ♦ *vt* signifier, vouloir dire; (*refer to*) faire allusion à, parler de; (*intend*): **to ~ to do** avoir l'intention de faire ♦ *n* moyenne *f*; **~s** *npl* (*way, money*) moyens *mpl*; **by ~s of** par l'intermédiaire de; au moyen de; **by all ~s!** je vous en prie!; **to ~t for sb/sth** être destiné(e) à qn/qch; **do you ~ it?** vous êtes sérieux?; **what do you ~?** que voulez-vous dire?

meander [mɪ'ændə*] *vi* faire des méandres

meaning ['miːnɪŋ] *n* signification *f*, sens *m*; **~ful** *adj* significatif(ive); (*relationship, occasion*) important(e); **~less** *adj* dénué(e) de sens

meanness ['miːnnɪs] *n* (*with money*) avarice *f*; (*unkindness*) méchanceté *f*; (*shabbiness*) médiocrité *f*

meant [ment] *pt, pp of* **mean**

meantime ['miːntaɪm] *adv* (*also: in the ~*) pendant ce temps

meanwhile ['miːnwaɪl] *adv* = **meantime**
measles ['miːzlz] *n* rougeole *f*
measly ['miːzlɪ] (*inf*) *adj* minable
measure ['meʒə*] *vt, vi* mesurer ♦ *n* mesure *f*, (*ruler*) règle (graduée); **~ments** *npl* mesures *fpl*; **chest/hip ~ment** tour *m* de poitrine/hanches
meat [miːt] *n* viande *f*; **~ball** *n* boulette *f* de viande
Mecca ['mekə] *n* la Mecque
mechanic [mɪ'kænɪk] *n* mécanicien *m*; **~al** *adj* mécanique; **~s** *n* (*PHYSICS*) mécanique *f* ♦ *npl* (*of reading, government etc*) mécanisme *m*
mechanism ['mekənɪzəm] *n* mécanisme *m*
medal ['medl] *n* médaille *f*; **~lion** *n* médaillon *m*; **~list** (*US* **~ist**) *n* (*SPORT*) médaillé(e)
meddle ['medl] *vi*: **to ~ in** se mêler de, s'occuper de; **to ~ with** toucher à
media ['miːdɪə] *npl* media *mpl*
mediaeval [medɪ'iːvəl] *adj* = **medieval**
median ['miːdɪən] (*US*) *n* (*also*: **~ strip**) bande médiane
mediate ['miːdɪeɪt] *vi* servir d'intermédiaire
Medicaid ['medɪkeɪd] (®:*US*) *n* assistance médicale aux indigents
medical ['medɪkəl] *adj* médical(e) ♦ *n* visite médicale
Medicare ['medɪkeə*] (®:*US*) *n* assistance médicale aux personnes âgées
medication [medɪ'keɪʃən] *n* (*drugs*) médicaments *mpl*
medicine ['medsɪn] *n* médecine *f*; (*drug*) médicament *m*
medieval [medɪ'iːvəl] *adj* médiéval(e)
mediocre [miːdɪ'əukə*] *adj* médiocre
meditate ['medɪteɪt] *vi* méditer
Mediterranean [medɪtə'reɪnɪən] *adj* méditerranéen(ne); **the ~ (Sea)** la (mer) Méditerranée
medium ['miːdɪəm] (*pl* **media**) *adj* moyen(ne) ♦ *n* (*means*) moyen *m*; (*pl* **mediums: person**) médium *m*; **the happy ~** le juste milieu; **~ wave** *n* ondes moyennes
medley ['medlɪ] *n* mélange *m*; (*MUS*) pot-pourri *m*
meek [miːk] *adj* doux(douce), humble
meet [miːt] (*pt, pp* **met**) *vt* rencontrer; (*by arrangement*) retrouver, rejoindre; (*for the first time*) faire la connaissance de; (*go and fetch*): **I'll ~ you at the station** j'irai te chercher à la gare; (*opponent, danger*) faire face à; (*obligations*) satisfaire à ♦ *vi* (*friends*) se rencontrer, se retrouver; (*in session*) se réunir; (*join: lines, roads*) se rejoindre; **~ with** *vt fus* rencontrer; **~ing** *n* rencontre *f*; (*session: of club etc*) réunion *f*; (*POL*) meeting *m*; **she's at a ~ing** (*COMM*) elle est en conférence
megabyte ['megəbaɪt] *n* (*COMPUT*) méga-octet *m*

megaphone ['megəfəun] *n* porte-voix *m inv*
melancholy ['melənkəlɪ] *n* mélancolie *f* ♦ *adj* mélancolique
mellow ['meləu] *adj* velouté(e); doux(douce); (*sound*) mélodieux(euse) ♦ *vi* (*person*) s'adoucir
melody ['melədɪ] *n* mélodie *f*
melon ['melən] *n* melon *m*
melt [melt] *vi* fondre ♦ *vt* faire fondre; (*metal*) fondre; **~ away** *vi* fondre complètement; **~ down** *vt* fondre; **~down** *n* fusion *f* (du cœur d'un réacteur nucléaire); **~ing pot** *n* (*fig*) creuset *m*
member ['membə*] *n* membre *m*; **M~ of Parliament** (*BRIT*) député *m*; **M~ of the European Parliament** Eurodéputé *m*; **~ship** *n* adhésion *f*; statut *m* de membre; (*members*) membres *mpl*, adhérents *mpl*; **~ship card** *n* carte *f* de membre
memento [mə'mentəu] *n* souvenir *m*
memo ['meməu] *n* note *f* (de service)
memoirs ['memwɑːz] *npl* mémoires *mpl*
memorandum [memə'rændəm] (*pl* **memoranda**) *n* note *f* (de service)
memorial [mɪ'mɔːrɪəl] *n* mémorial *m* ♦ *adj* commémoratif(ive)
memorize ['meməraɪz] *vt* apprendre par cœur; retenir
memory ['memərɪ] *n* mémoire *f*; (*recollection*) souvenir *m*
men [men] *npl* of **man**
menace ['menɪs] *n* menace *f*; (*nuisance*) plaie *f* ♦ *vt* menacer; **menacing** *adj* menaçant(e)
mend [mend] *vt* réparer; (*darn*) raccommoder, repriser ♦ *n*: **on the ~** en voie de guérison; **to ~ one's ways** s'amender; **~ing** *n* réparation *f*; (*clothes*) raccommodage *m*
menial ['miːnɪəl] *adj* subalterne
meningitis [menɪn'dʒaɪtɪs] *n* méningite *f*
menopause ['menəupɔːz] *n* ménopause *f*
menstruation [menstru'eɪʃən] *n* menstruation *f*
mental ['mentl] *adj* mental(e); **~ity** [men'tælɪtɪ] *n* mentalité *f*
mention ['menʃən] *n* mention *f* ♦ *vt* mentionner, faire mention de; **don't ~ it!** je vous en prie, il n'y a pas de quoi!
menu ['menjuː] *n* (*set ~, COMPUT*) menu *m*; (*list of dishes*) carte *f*
MEP *n abbr* = **Member of the European Parliament**
mercenary ['mɜːsɪnərɪ] *adj* intéressé(e), mercenaire ♦ *n* mercenaire *m*
merchandise ['mɜːtʃəndaɪz] *n* marchandises *fpl*
merchant ['mɜːtʃənt] *n* négociant *m*, marchand *m*; **~ bank** (*BRIT*) *n* banque *f* d'affaires; **~ navy** (*US* **~ marine**) *n* marine marchande
merciful ['mɜːsɪful] *adj* miséricor-

dieux(euse), clément(e); **a ~ release** une délivrance

merciless ['mɜːsɪləs] *adj* impitoyable, sans pitié

mercury ['mɜːkjʊrɪ] *n* mercure *m*

mercy ['mɜːsɪ] *n* pitié *f*, indulgence *f*; (*REL*) miséricorde *f*; **at the ~ of** à la merci de

mere [mɪə*] *adj* simple; (*chance*) pur(e); **a ~ two hours** seulement deux heures; **~ly** *adv* simplement, purement

merge [mɜːdʒ] *vt* unir ♦ *vi* (*colours, shapes, sounds*) se mêler; (*roads*) se joindre; (*COMM*) fusionner; **~r** *n* (*COMM*) fusion *f*

meringue [mə'ræŋ] *n* meringue *f*

merit ['merɪt] *n* mérite *m*, valeur *f*

mermaid ['mɜːmeɪd] *n* sirène *f*

merry ['merɪ] *adj* gai(e); **M~ Christmas!** Joyeux Noël!; **~-go-round** *n* manège *m*

mesh [meʃ] *n* maille *f*

mesmerize ['mezməraɪz] *vt* hypnotiser; fasciner

mess·[mes] *n* désordre *m*, fouillis *m*, pagaille *f*; (*muddle: of situation*) gâchis *m*; (*dirt*) saleté *f*; (*MIL*) mess *m*, cantine *f*; **~ about** (*inf*) *vi* perdre son temps; **~ about with** (*inf*) *vt fus* tripoter; **~ around** (*inf*) *vi* = **mess about**; **~ around with** *vt fus* = **mess about with**; **~ up** *vt* (*dirty*) salir; (*spoil*) gâcher

message ['mesɪdʒ] *n* message *m*

messenger ['mesɪndʒə*] *n* messager *m*

Messrs ['mesəz] *abbr* (*on letters*) MM

messy ['mesɪ] *adj* sale; en désordre

met [met] *pt, pp of* **meet**

metal ['metl] *n* métal *m*; **~lic** *adj* métallique

meteorology [miːtɪə'rɒlədʒɪ] *n* météorologie *f*

mete out [miːt-] *vt* infliger; (*justice*) rendre

meter ['miːtə*] *n* (*instrument*) compteur *m*; (*also: parking ~*) parcomètre *m*; (*US: unit*) = **metre**

method ['meθəd] *n* méthode *f*, **~ical** *adj* méthodique; **M~ist** ['meθədɪst] *n* méthodiste *m/f*

meths [meθs] (*BRIT*), **methylated spirit** ['meθɪleɪtɪd-] (*BRIT*) *n* alcool *m* à brûler

metre ['miːtə*] (*US* **meter**) *n* mètre *m*

metric ['metrɪk] *adj* métrique

metropolitan [metrə'pɒlɪtən] *adj* métropolitain(e); **the M~ Police** (*BRIT*) la police londonienne

mettle ['metl] *n*: **to be on one's ~** être d'attaque

mew [mjuː] *vi* (*cat*) miauler

mews [mjuːz] (*BRIT*) *n*: **~ cottage** cottage aménagé dans une ancienne écurie

Mexico ['meksɪkəʊ] *n* Mexique *m*

miaow [miː'aʊ] *vi* miauler

mice [maɪs] *npl of* **mouse**

micro ['maɪkrəʊ] *n* (*also: ~computer*) micro-ordinateur *m*

microchip ['maɪkrəʊtʃɪp] *n* puce *f*

microphone ['maɪkrəfəʊn] *n* microphone *m*

microscope ['maɪkrəskəʊp] *n* microscope *m*

microwave ['maɪkrəʊweɪv] *n* (*also: ~ oven*) four *m* à micro-ondes

mid [mɪd] *adj*: **in ~ May** à la mi-mai; **~ afternoon** le milieu de l'après-midi; **in ~ air** en plein ciel; **~day** *n* midi *m*

middle ['mɪdl] *n* milieu *m*; (*waist*) taille *f* ♦ *adj* du milieu; (*average*) moyen(ne); **in the ~ of the night** au milieu de la nuit; **~-aged** *adj* d'un certain âge; **M~ Ages** *npl*: **the M~ Ages** le moyen âge; **~-class** *adj* bourgeois(e); **~ class(es)** *n(pl)*: **the ~ class(es)** ≈ les classes moyennes; **M~ East** *n* Proche-Orient *m*, Moyen-Orient *m*; **~man** (*irreg*) *n* intermédiaire *m*; **~ name** *n* deuxième nom *m*; **~-of-the-road** *adj* (*politician*) modéré(e); (*music*) neutre; **~weight** *n* (*BOXING*) poids moyen; **middling** ['mɪdlɪŋ] *adj* moyen(ne)

midge [mɪdʒ] *n* moucheron *m*

midget ['mɪdʒɪt] *n* nain(e)

Midlands ['mɪdləndz] *npl comtés du centre de l'Angleterre*

midnight ['mɪdnaɪt] *n* minuit *m*

midriff ['mɪdrɪf] *n* estomac *m*, taille *f*

midst [mɪdst] *n*: **in the ~ of** au milieu de

midsummer ['mɪd'sʌmə*] *n* milieu *m* de l'été

midway ['mɪd'weɪ] *adj, adv*: **~ (between)** à mi-chemin (entre); **~ through ...** au milieu de ..., en plein(e) ...

midweek ['mɪd'wiːk] *n* milieu *m* de la semaine

midwife ['mɪdwaɪf] (*pl* **midwives**) *n* sagefemme *f*

midwinter ['mɪd'wɪntə*] *n*: **in ~** en plein hiver

might [maɪt] *vb see* **may** ♦ *n* puissance *f*, force *f*; **~y** *adj* puissant(e)

migraine ['miːgreɪn] *n* migraine *f*

migrant ['maɪgrənt] *adj* (*bird*) migrateur(trice); (*worker*) saisonnier(ère)

migrate [maɪ'greɪt] *vi* émigrer

mike [maɪk] *n abbr* (= **microphone**) micro *m*

mild [maɪld] *adj* doux(douce); (*reproach, infection*) léger(ère); (*illness*) bénin(igne); (*interest*) modéré(e); (*taste*) peu relevé(e)

mildly ['maɪldlɪ] *adv* doucement; légèrement; **to put it ~** c'est le moins qu'on puisse dire

mile [maɪl] *n* mil(l)e *m* (= 1609 *m*); **~age** *n* distance *f* en milles, ≈ kilométrage *m*; **~ometer** [maɪ'lɒmɪtə*] *n* compteur *m* (kilométrique); **~stone** *n* borne *f*; (*fig*) jalon *m*

militant ['mɪlɪtnt] *adj* militant(e)

military ['mɪlɪtərɪ] *adj* militaire

militate ['mɪlɪteɪt] *vi:* **to ~ against** (*prevent*) empêcher

militia [mɪ'lɪʃə] *n* milice(s) *f(pl)*

milk [mɪlk] *n* lait *m* ♦ *vt* (*cow*) traire; (*fig: person*) dépouiller, plumer; (: *situation*) exploiter à fond; **~ chocolate** *n* chocolat *m* au lait; **~man** (*irreg*) *n* laitier *m*; **~ shake** *n* milk-shake *m*; **~y** *adj* (*drink*) au lait; (*colour*) laiteux(euse); **M~y Way** *n* voie lactée

mill [mɪl] *n* moulin *m*; (*steel ~*) aciérie *f*; (*spinning ~*) filature *f*; (*flour ~*) minoterie *f* ♦ *vt* moudre, broyer ♦ *vi* (*also:* **~ about**) grouiller; **~er** *n* meunier *m*

milligram(me) ['mɪlɪɡræm] *n* milligramme *m*

millimetre ['mɪlɪmiːtə*] (*US* **millimeter**) *n* millimètre *m*

millinery ['mɪlɪnərɪ] *n* chapellerie *f*

million ['mɪljən] *n* million *m*; **~aire** [mɪljə'nɛə*] *n* millionnaire *m*

milometer [maɪ'lɒmɪtə*] *n* ≈ compteur *m* kilométrique

mime [maɪm] *n* mime *m* ♦ *vt, vi* mimer

mimic ['mɪmɪk] *n* imitateur(trice) ♦ *vt* imiter, contrefaire

min. *abbr* = **minute(s); minimum**

mince [mɪns] *vt* hacher ♦ *vi* (*in walking*) marcher à petits pas maniérés ♦ *n* (*BRIT: CULIN*) viande hachée, hachis *m*; **~meat** *n* (*fruit*) hachis de fruits secs utilisé en pâtisserie; (*US: meat*) viande hachée, hachis; **~ pie** *n* (*sweet*) sorte de tarte aux fruits secs; **~r** *n* hachoir *m*

mind [maɪnd] *n* esprit *m* ♦ *vt* (*attend to, look after*) s'occuper de; (*be careful*) faire attention à; (*object to*): **I don't ~ the noise** le bruit ne me dérange pas; **I don't ~ cela ne me dérange pas; it is on my ~** cela me préoccupe; **to my ~** à mon avis *or* sens; **to be out of one's ~** ne plus avoir toute sa raison; **to keep** *or* **bear sth in ~** tenir compte de qch; **to make up one's ~** se décider; **~ you, ... remarquez ...; never ~** ça ne fait rien; (*don't worry*) ne vous en faites pas; "**~ the step**" "attention à la marche"; **~er** *n* (*child-~er*) gardienne *f*; (*inf: bodyguard*) ange gardien (*fig*); **~ful** *adj*: **~ful of** attentif(ive) à, soucieux(euse) de; **~less** *adj* irréfléchi(e); (*boring: job*) idiot(e)

mine¹ [maɪn] *pron* le(la) mien(ne), les miens(miennes) ♦ *adj*: **this book is mine** ce livre est à moi

mine² [maɪn] *n* mine *f* ♦ *vt* (*coal*) extraire; (*ship, beach*) miner; **~field** *n* champ *m* de mines; (*fig*) situation (très délicate); **~r** *n* mineur *m*

mineral ['mɪnərəl] *adj* minéral(e) ♦ *n* minéral *m*; **~s** *npl* (*BRIT: soft drinks*) boissons gazeuses; **~ water** *n* eau minérale

mingle ['mɪŋɡl] *vi*: **to ~ with** se mêler à

miniature ['mɪnɪtʃə*] *adj* (en) miniature ♦

n miniature *f*

minibus ['mɪnɪbʌs] *n* minibus *m*

minim ['mɪnɪm] *n* (*MUS*) blanche *f*

minimal ['mɪnɪməl] *adj* minime

minimize ['mɪnɪmaɪz] *vt* (*reduce*) réduire au minimum; (*play down*) minimiser

minimum ['mɪnɪməm] (*pl* **minima**) *adj, n* minimum *m*

mining ['maɪnɪŋ] *n* exploitation minière

miniskirt ['mɪnɪskɜːt] *n* mini-jupe *f*

minister ['mɪnɪstə*] *n* (*BRIT: POL*) ministre *m*; (*REL*) pasteur *m* ♦ *vi*: **to ~ to sb's needs** pourvoir aux besoins de qn; **~ial** [mɪnɪs'tɪərɪəl] (*BRIT*) *adj* (*POL*) ministériel(le)

ministry ['mɪnɪstrɪ] *n* (*BRIT: POL*) ministère *m*; (*REL*): **to go into the ~** devenir pasteur

mink [mɪŋk] *n* vison *m*

minor ['maɪnə*] *adj* petit(e), de peu d'importance; (*MUS, poet, problem*) mineur(e) ♦ *n* (*LAW*) mineur(e)

minority [maɪ'nɒrɪtɪ] *n* minorité *f*

mint [mɪnt] *n* (*plant*) menthe *f*; (*sweet*) bonbon *m* à la menthe ♦ *vt* (*coins*) battre; **the (Royal) M~**, (*US*) **the (US) M~** ≈ l'Hôtel *m* de la Monnaie; **in ~ condition** à l'état de neuf

minus ['maɪnəs] *n* (*also:* **~ sign**) signe *m* moins ♦ *prep* moins

minute¹ [maɪ'njuːt] *adj* minuscule; (*detail, search*) minutieux(euse)

minute² ['mɪnɪt] *n* minute *f*; **~s** *npl* (*official record*) procès-verbal, compte rendu

miracle ['mɪrəkl] *n* miracle *m*

mirage ['mɪrɑːʒ] *n* mirage *m*

mirror ['mɪrə*] *n* miroir *m*, glace *f*; (*in car*) rétroviseur *m*

mirth [mɜːθ] *n* gaieté *f*

misadventure [mɪsəd'ventʃə*] *n* mésaventure *f*

misapprehension ['mɪsæprɪ'henʃən] *n* malentendu *m*, méprise *f*

misappropriate [mɪsə'prəʊprɪeɪt] *vt* détourner

misbehave ['mɪsbɪ'heɪv] *vi* se conduire mal

miscalculate [mɪs'kælkjʊleɪt] *vt* mal calculer

miscarriage ['mɪskærɪdʒ] *n* (*MED*) fausse couche *f*; **~ of justice** erreur *f* judiciaire

miscellaneous [mɪsɪ'leɪnɪəs] *adj* (*items*) divers(es); (*selection*) varié(e)

mischief ['mɪstʃɪf] *n* (*naughtiness*) sottises *fpl*; (*fun*) farce *f*; (*playfulness*) espièglerie *f*; (*maliciousness*) méchanceté *f*; **mischievous** ['mɪstʃɪvəs] *adj* (*playful, naughty*) coquin(e), espiègle

misconception ['mɪskən'sepʃən] *n* idée fausse

misconduct [mɪs'kɒndʌkt] *n* inconduite *f*; **professional ~** faute professionnelle

misdemeanour [mɪsdɪ'miːnə*] (*US* **misdemeanor**) *n* écart *m* de conduite; infraction *f*

miser ['maɪzə*] n avare m/f
miserable ['mɪzərəbl] adj (person, expression) malheureux(euse); (conditions) misérable; (weather) maussade; (offer, donation) minable; (failure) pitoyable
miserly ['maɪzəlɪ] adj avare
misery ['mɪzərɪ] n (unhappiness) tristesse f; (pain) souffrances fpl; (wretchedness) misère f
misfire ['mɪs'faɪə*] vi rater
misfit ['mɪsfɪt] n (person) inadapté(e)
misfortune [mɪs'fɔ:tʃən] n malchance f, malheur m
misgiving [mɪs'gɪvɪŋ] n (apprehension) craintes fpl; **to have ~s about** avoir des doutes quant à
misguided ['mɪs'gaɪdɪd] adj malavisé(e)
mishandle ['mɪs'hændl] vt (mismanage) mal s'y prendre pour faire or résoudre etc
mishap ['mɪshæp] n mésaventure f
misinform [mɪsɪn'fɔ:m] vt mal renseigner
misinterpret ['mɪsɪn'tɜ:prɪt] vt mal interpréter
misjudge ['mɪs'dʒʌdʒ] vt méjuger
mislay [mɪs'leɪ] (irreg: like **lay**) vt égarer
mislead [mɪs'li:d] (irreg: like **lead**) vt induire en erreur; **~ing** adj trompeur(euse)
mismanage [mɪs'mænɪdʒ] vt mal gérer
misnomer ['mɪs'nəʊmə*] n terme or qualificatif trompeur or peu approprié
misplace ['mɪs'pleɪs] vt égarer
misprint ['mɪsprɪnt] n faute f d'impression
Miss [mɪs] n Mademoiselle
miss [mɪs] vt (fail to get, attend or see) manquer, rater; (regret the absence of): **I ~ him/it** il/cela me manque ♦ vi manquer ♦ n (shot) coup manqué; **~ out** (BRIT) vt oublier
misshapen ['mɪs'ʃeɪpən] adj difforme
missile ['mɪsaɪl] n (MIL) missile m; (object thrown) projectile m
missing ['mɪsɪŋ] adj manquant(e); (after escape, disaster: person) disparu(e); **to go ~** disparaître; **to be ~** avoir disparu
mission ['mɪʃən] n mission f; **~ary** n missionnaire m/f
misspent ['mɪs'spent] adj: **his ~ youth** sa folle jeunesse
mist [mɪst] n (light) brume f; (heavy) brouillard m ♦ vi (also: **~ over**: eyes) s'embuer; **~ over** vi (windows etc) s'embuer; **~ up** vi = **mist over**
mistake [mɪs'teɪk] (irreg: like **take**) n erreur f, faute f ♦ vt (meaning, remark) mal comprendre; se méprendre sur; **to make a ~** se tromper, faire une erreur; **by ~** par erreur, par inadvertance; **to ~ for** prendre pour; **~n** pp of **mistake** ♦ adj (idea etc) erroné(e); **to be ~n** faire erreur, se tromper
mister ['mɪstə*] n (inf) Monsieur m; see also **Mr**

mistletoe ['mɪsltəʊ] n gui m
mistook [mɪs'tʊk] pt of **mistake**
mistress ['mɪstrɪs] n maîtresse f; (BRIT: in primary school) institutrice f; (: in secondary school) professeur m
mistrust ['mɪs'trʌst] vt se méfier de
misty ['mɪstɪ] adj brumeux(euse); (glasses, window) embué(e)
misunderstand ['mɪsʌndə'stænd] (irreg) vt, vi mal comprendre; **~ing** n méprise f, malentendu m
misuse [n 'mɪs'ju:s, vb 'mɪs'ju:z] n mauvais emploi; (of power) abus m ♦ vt mal employer; abuser de; **~ of funds** détournement m de fonds
mitigate ['mɪtɪgeɪt] vt atténuer
mitt(en) ['mɪt(n)] n mitaine f; moufle f
mix [mɪks] vt mélanger; (sauce, drink etc) préparer ♦ vi se mélanger; (socialize): **he doesn't ~ well** il est peu sociable ♦ n mélange m; **to ~ with** (people) fréquenter; **~ up** vt mélanger; (confuse) confondre; **~ed** adj (feelings, reactions) contradictoire; (salad) mélangé(e); (school, marriage) mixte; **~ed grill** n assortiment m de grillades; **~ed-up** adj (confused) désorienté(e), embrouillé(e); **~er** n (for food) batteur m, mixer m; (person): **he is a good ~er** il est très liant; **~ture** n assortiment m, mélange m; (MED) préparation f; **~-up** n confusion f
mm abbr (= millimeter) mm
moan [məʊn] n gémissement m ♦ vi gémir; (inf: complain): **to ~ (about)** se plaindre (de)
moat [məʊt] n fossé m, douves fpl
mob [mɒb] n foule f; (disorderly) cohue f ♦ vt assaillir
mobile ['məʊbaɪl] adj mobile ♦ n mobile m; **~ home** n (grande) caravane; **~ phone** n téléphone portatif
mock [mɒk] vt ridiculiser; (laugh at) se moquer de ♦ adj faux(fausse); **~ exam** examen blanc; **~ery** n moquerie f, raillerie f; **to make a ~ery of** tourner en dérision; **~-up** n maquette f
mod [mɒd] adj see **convenience**
mode [məʊd] n mode m
model ['mɒdl] n modèle m; (person: for fashion) mannequin m; (: for artist) modèle m ♦ vt (with clay etc) modeler ♦ vi travailler comme mannequin ♦ adj (railway: toy) modèle réduit inv; (child, factory) modèle; **to ~ clothes** présenter des vêtements; **to ~ o.s. on** imiter
modem ['məʊdem] (COMPUT) n modem m
moderate [adj, n 'mɒdərət, vb 'mɒdəreɪt] adj modéré(e); (amount, change) peu important(e) ♦ vi se calmer ♦ vt modérer
modern ['mɒdən] adj moderne; **~ize** vt moderniser
modest ['mɒdɪst] adj modeste; **~y** n mo-

destie f

modicum ['mɒdɪkəm] n: **a ~ of** un minimum de

modify ['mɒdɪfaɪ] vt modifier

mogul ['məʊgəl] n (fig) nabab m

mohair ['məʊhɛə*] n mohair m

moist [mɔɪst] adj humide, moite; **~en** ['mɔɪsən] vt humecter, mouiller légèrement; **~ure** ['mɔɪstʃə*] n humidité f; **~urizer** ['mɔɪstʃəraɪzə*] n produit hydratant

molar ['məʊlə*] n molaire f

molasses [mə'læsɪz] n mélasse f

mold [məʊld] (US) n, vt = **mould**

mole [məʊl] n (animal, fig: spy) taupe f; (spot) grain m de beauté

molest [məʊ'lest] vt (harass) molester; (JUR: sexually) attenter à la pudeur de

mollycoddle ['mɒlɪkɒdl] vt chouchouter, couver

molt [məʊlt] (US) vi = **moult**

molten ['məʊltən] adj fondu(e); (rock) en fusion

mom [mɒm] (US) n = **mum**

moment ['məʊmənt] n moment m, instant m; **at the ~** en ce moment; **at that ~** à ce moment-là; **~ary** adj momentané(e), passager(ère); **~ous** [məʊ'mentəs] adj important(e), capital(e)

momentum [məʊ'mentəm] n élan m, vitesse acquise; (fig) dynamique f; **to gather ~** prendre de la vitesse

mommy ['mɒmɪ] (US) n = **mummy**

Monaco ['mɒnəkəʊ] n Monaco m

monarch ['mɒnək] n monarque m; **~y** n monarchie f

monastery ['mɒnəstrɪ] n monastère m

Monday ['mʌndeɪ] n lundi m

monetary ['mʌnɪtərɪ] adj monétaire

money ['mʌnɪ] n argent m; **to make ~** gagner de l'argent; **~ order** n mandat m; **~-spinner** (inf) n mine f d'or (fig)

mongrel ['mʌŋgrəl] n (dog) bâtard m

monitor ['mɒnɪtə*] n (TV, COMPUT) moniteur m ♦ vt contrôler; (broadcast) être à l'écoute de; (progress) suivre (de près)

monk [mʌŋk] n moine m

monkey ['mʌŋkɪ] n singe m; **~ nut** (BRIT) n cacahuète f; **~ wrench** n clé f à molette

monopoly [mə'nɒpəlɪ] n monopole m

monotone ['mɒnətəʊn] n ton m (or voix f) monocorde

monotonous [mə'nɒtənəs] adj monotone

monsoon [mɒn'suːn] n mousson f

monster ['mɒnstə*] n monstre m

monstrous ['mɒnstrəs] adj monstrueux(euse); (huge) gigantesque

month [mʌnθ] n mois m; **~ly** adj mensuel(le) ♦ adv mensuellement

monument ['mɒnjumənt] n monument m

moo [muː] vi meugler, beugler

mood [muːd] n humeur f, disposition f; **to be in a good/bad ~** être de bonne/ mauvaise humeur; **~y** adj (variable) d'humeur changeante, lunatique; (sullen) morose, maussade

moon [muːn] n lune f; **~light** n clair m de lune; **~lighting** n travail m au noir; **~lit** adj: **a ~lit night** une nuit de lune

moor [mʊə*] n lande f ♦ vt (ship) amarrer ♦ vi mouiller; **~land** ['mʊələnd] n lande f

moose [muːs] n inv élan m

mop [mɒp] n balai m à laver; (for dishes) lavette f (à vaisselle) ♦ vt essuyer; **~ of hair** tignasse f; **~ up** vt éponger

mope [məʊp] vi avoir le cafard, se morfondre

moped ['məʊped] n cyclomoteur m

moral ['mɒrəl] adj moral(e) ♦ n morale f; **~s** npl (attitude, behaviour) moralité f

morale [mɒ'rɑːl] n moral m

morality [mə'rælɪtɪ] n moralité f

morass [mə'ræs] n marais m, marécage m

KEYWORD

more [mɔː*] adj **1** (greater in number etc) plus (de), davantage; **people/work (than)** plus de gens/de travail (que) **2** (additional) encore (de); **do you want some) ~ tea?** voulez-vous encore du thé?; **I have no** or **I don't have any ~ money** je n'ai plus d'argent; **it'll take a few ~ weeks** ça prendra encore quelques semaines

♦ pron plus, davantage; **~ than 10** plus de 10; **it cost ~ than we expected** cela a coûté plus que prévu; **I want ~** j'en veux plus or davantage; **is there any ~?** est-ce qu'il en reste?; **there's no ~** il n'y en a plus; **a little ~** un peu plus; **many/much ~** beaucoup plus, bien davantage

♦ adv: **~ dangerous/easily (than)** plus dangereux/facilement (que); **~ and ~ expensive** de plus en plus cher; **~ or less** plus ou moins; **~ than ever** plus que jamais

---

moreover [mɔː'rəʊvə*] adv de plus

morning ['mɔːnɪŋ] n matin m; matinée f ♦ cpd matinal(e); (paper) du matin; **in the ~** le matin; **7 o'clock in the ~** 7 heures du matin; **~ sickness** n nausées matinales

Morocco [mə'rɒkəʊ] n Maroc m

moron ['mɔːrɒn] (inf) n idiot(e)

Morse [mɔːs] n: **~ (code)** morse m

morsel ['mɔːsl] n bouchée f

mortar ['mɔːtə*] n mortier m

mortgage ['mɔːgɪdʒ] n hypothèque f; (loan) prêt m (or crédit m) hypothécaire ♦ vt hypothéquer; **~ company** (US) n société f de crédit immobilier

mortuary ['mɔːtjʊərɪ] n morgue f

mosaic [məʊ'zeɪɪk] n mosaïque f

Moscow ['mɒskəʊ] n Moscou m

Moslem ['mɒzləm] adj, n = **Muslim**

mosque [mɒsk] n mosquée f
mosquito [mɒsˈkiːtəʊ] (pl ~es) n moustique m
moss [mɒs] n mousse f
most [məʊst] adj la plupart de; le plus de ♦ pron la plupart ♦ adv le plus; (very) très, extrêmement; **the ~** (also: + adjective) le plus; ~ **of** la plus grande partie de; ~ **of them** la plupart d'entre eux; **I saw (the) ~** j'en ai vu la plupart; c'est moi qui en ai vu le plus; **at the (very) ~** au plus; **to make the ~ of** profiter au maximum de; ~**ly** adv (chiefly) surtout; (usually) généralement
MOT n abbr (BRIT: = Ministry of Transport): **the ~ (test)** la visite technique (annuelle) obligatoire des véhicules à moteur
motel [məʊˈtel] n motel m
moth [mɒθ] n papillon m de nuit; (in clothes) mite f; ~**ball** n boule f de naphtaline
mother [ˈmʌðə*] n mère f ♦ vt (act as mother to) servir de mère à; (pamper, protect) materner; ~ **country** mère patrie; ~**hood** n maternité f; ~**-in-law** n belle-mère f; ~**ly** adj maternel(le); ~**-of-pearl** n nacre f; ~**-to-be** n future maman; ~ **tongue** n langue maternelle
motion [ˈməʊʃən] n mouvement m; (gesture) geste m; (at meeting) motion f ♦ vt, vi: **to ~ (to) sb to do** faire signe à qn de faire; ~**less** adj immobile, sans mouvement; ~ **picture** n film m
motivated [ˈməʊtɪveɪtɪd] adj motivé(e)
motive [ˈməʊtɪv] n motif m, mobile m
motley [ˈmɒtlɪ] adj hétéroclite
motor [ˈməʊtə*] n moteur m; (BRIT: inf: vehicle) auto f ♦ cpd (industry, vehicle) automobile; ~**bike** n moto f; ~**boat** n bateau m à moteur; ~**car** (BRIT) n automobile f; ~**cycle** n vélomoteur m; ~**cycle racing** n course f de motos; ~**cyclist** n motocycliste m/f; ~**ing** (BRIT) n tourisme m automobile; ~**ist** [ˈməʊtərɪst] n automobiliste m/f; ~ **mechanic** n mécanicien m garagiste; ~ **racing** (BRIT) n course f automobile; ~ **trade** n secteur m de l'automobile; ~**way** (BRIT) n autoroute f
mottled [ˈmɒtld] adj tacheté(e), marbré(e)
motto [ˈmɒtəʊ] (pl ~es) n devise f
mould [məʊld] (US **mold**) n moule m; (mildew) moisissure f ♦ vt mouler, modeler; (fig) façonner; **mo(u)ldy** adj moisi(e); (smell) de moisi
moult [məʊlt] (US **molt**) vi muer
mound [maʊnd] n monticule m, tertre m; (heap) monceau m, tas m
mount [maʊnt] n mont m, montagne f ♦ vt monter ♦ vi (inflation, tension) augmenter; (also: ~ **up**: problems etc) s'accumuler; ~ **up** vi (bills, costs, savings) s'accumuler
mountain [ˈmaʊntɪn] n montagne f ♦ cpd de montagne; ~ **bike** n VTT m, vélo tout-terrain; ~**eer** [maʊntɪˈnɪə*] n alpiniste m/f;

~**eering** n alpinisme m; ~**ous** adj montagneux(euse); ~ **rescue team** n équipe f de secours en montagne; ~**side** n flanc m or versant m de la montagne
mourn [mɔːn] vt pleurer ♦ vi: **to ~ (for)** (person) pleurer (la mort de); ~**er** n parent(e) or ami(e) du défunt; personne f en deuil; ~**ful** adj triste, lugubre; ~**ing** n deuil m; **in ~ing** en deuil
mouse [maʊs] (pl **mice**) n (also COMPUT) souris f; ~**trap** n souricière f
mousse [muːs] n mousse f
moustache [məsˈtɑːʃ] (US **mustache**) n moustache(s) f(pl)
mousy [ˈmaʊsɪ] adj (hair) d'un châtain terne
mouth [maʊθ, pl maʊðz] (pl ~**s**) n bouche f; (of dog, cat) gueule f; (of river) embouchure f; (of hole, cave) ouverture f; ~**ful** n bouchée f; ~ **organ** n harmonica m; ~**piece** n (of musical instrument) embouchure f; (spokesman) porte-parole m inv; ~**wash** n eau f dentifrice; ~**-watering** adj qui met l'eau à la bouche
movable [ˈmuːvəbl] adj mobile
move [muːv] n (movement) mouvement m; (in game) coup m; (: turn to play) tour m; (change: of house) déménagement m; (: of job) changement m d'emploi ♦ vt déplacer, bouger; (emotionally) émouvoir; (POL: resolution etc) proposer; (in game) jouer ♦ vi (gen) bouger, remuer; (traffic) circuler; (also: ~ **house**) déménager; (situation) progresser; **that was a good ~** bien joué!; **to ~ sb to do sth** pousser or inciter qn à faire qch; **to get a ~ on** se dépêcher, se remuer; ~ **about** vi (fidget) remuer; (travel) voyager, se déplacer; (change residence, job) ne pas rester au même endroit; ~ **along** vi se pousser; ~ **around** vi = **move about**; ~ **away** vi s'en aller; ~ **back** vi revenir, retourner; ~ **forward** vi avancer; ~ **in** vi (to a house) emménager; (police, soldiers) intervenir; ~ **on** vi se remettre en route; ~ **out** vi (of house) déménager; ~ **over** vi se pousser, se déplacer; ~ **up** vi (pupil) passer dans la classe supérieure; (employee) avoir de l'avancement; ~**able** adj = **movable**
movement [ˈmuːvmənt] n mouvement m
movie [ˈmuːvɪ] n film m; **the ~s** le cinéma; ~ **camera** n caméra f
moving [ˈmuːvɪŋ] adj en mouvement; (emotional) émouvant(e)
mow [məʊ] (pt **mowed**, pp **mowed** or **mown**) vt faucher; (lawn) tondre; ~ **down** vt faucher; ~**er** n (also: lawnmower) tondeuse f à gazon
MP n abbr = **Member of Parliament**
mph abbr = **miles per hour**
Mr [ˈmɪstə*] (US **Mr.**) n: ~ **Smith** Monsieur Smith, M. Smith
Mrs [ˈmɪsɪz] (US **Mrs.**) n: ~ **Smith** Madame

Smith, Mme Smith

Ms [mɪz] (US **Ms.**) n (= Miss or Mrs): ~ Smith ≈ Madame Smith, Mme Smith

MSc abbr = Master of Science

much [mʌtʃ] adj beaucoup de ♦ adv, n, pron beaucoup; **how** ~ **is it?** combien est-ce que ça coûte?; **too** ~ trop (de); **as** ~ **as** autant de

muck [mʌk] n (dirt) saleté f; ~ **about** (or) **around** (inf) vi faire l'imbécile; ~ **up** (inf) vt (exam, interview) se planter à (fam); ~**y** adj (très) sale; (book, film) cochon(ne)

mud [mʌd] n boue f

muddle ['mʌdl] n (mess) pagaille f, désordre m; (mix-up) confusion f ♦ vt (also: ~ up) embrouiller; ~ **through** vi se débrouiller

muddy ['mʌdɪ] adj boueux(euse); **mudguard** ['mʌdgɑːd] n garde-boue m inv

muffin ['mʌfɪn] n muffin m

muffle ['mʌfl] vt (sound) assourdir, étouffer; (against cold) emmitoufler; ~**d** adj (sound) étouffé(e); (person) emmitouflé(e); ~**r** (US) n (AUT) silencieux m

mug [mʌg] n (cup) grande tasse (sans soucoupe); (: for beer) chope f; (inf: face) bouille f; (: fool) poire f ♦ vt (assault) agresser; ~**ging** n agression f

muggy ['mʌgɪ] adj lourd(e), moite

mule [mjuːl] n mule f

mull over [mʌl-] vt réfléchir à

multi-level ['mʌltɪlevl] (US) adj = **multistorey**

multiple ['mʌltɪpl] adj multiple ♦ n multiple m; ~ **sclerosis** n sclérose f en plaques

multiplication [mʌltɪplɪ'keɪʃən] n multiplication f, **multiply** ['mʌltɪplaɪ] vt multiplier ♦ vi se multiplier

multistorey ['mʌltɪ'stɔːrɪ] (BRIT) adj (building) à étages; (car park) à étages or niveaux multiples

mum [mʌm] (BRIT: inf) n maman f ♦ adj: **to keep** ~ ne pas souffler mot

mumble ['mʌmbl] vt, vi marmotter, marmonner

mummy ['mʌmɪ] n (BRIT: mother) maman f; (embalmed) momie f

mumps [mʌmps] n oreillons mpl

munch [mʌntʃ] vt, vi mâcher

mundane [mʌn'deɪn] adj banal(e), terre à terre inv

municipal [mjuː'nɪsɪpəl] adj municipal(e)

murder ['mɜːdə*] n meurtre m, assassinat m ♦ vt assassiner; ~**er** n meurtrier m, assassin m; ~**ous** adj meurtrier(ère)

murky ['mɜːkɪ] adj sombre, ténébreux(euse); (water) trouble

murmur ['mɜːmə*] n murmure m ♦ vt, vi murmurer

muscle ['mʌsl] n muscle m; (fig) force f; ~ **in** vi (on territory) envahir; (on success) exploiter

muscular ['mʌskjulə*] adj musculaire; (person, arm) musclé(e)

muse [mjuːz] vi méditer, songer

museum [mjuː'zɪəm] n musée m

mushroom ['mʌʃruːm] n champignon m ♦ vi pousser comme un champignon

music ['mjuːzɪk] n musique f; ~**al** adj musical(e); (person) musicien(ne) ♦ n (show) comédie musicale; ~**al instrument** n instrument m de musique; ~**ian** [mjuː'zɪʃən] n musicien(ne)

Muslim ['mʌzlɪm] adj, n musulman(e)

muslin ['mʌzlɪn] n mousseline f

mussel ['mʌsl] n moule f

must [mʌst] aux vb (obligation): **I** ~ **do it** je dois le faire, il faut que je le fasse; (probability): **he** ~ **be there by now** il doit y être maintenant, il y est probablement maintenant; (suggestion, invitation): **you** ~ **come and see me** il faut que vous veniez me voir; (indicating sth unwelcome): **why** ~ **he behave so badly?** qu'est-ce qui le pousse à se conduire si mal? ♦ n nécessité f, impératif m; **it's a** ~ c'est indispensable

mustache (US) n = **moustache**

mustard ['mʌstəd] n moutarde f

muster ['mʌstə*] vt rassembler

mustn't ['mʌsnt] = **must not**

mute [mjuːt] adj muet(te)

muted ['mjuːtɪd] adj (colour) sourd(e); (reaction) voilé(e)

mutiny ['mjuːtɪnɪ] n mutinerie f ♦ vi se mutiner

mutter ['mʌtə*] vt, vi marmonner, marmotter

mutton ['mʌtn] n mouton m

mutual ['mjuːtjuəl] adj mutuel(le), réciproque; (benefit, interest) commun(e); ~**ly** adv mutuellement

muzzle ['mʌzl] n museau m; (protective device) muselière f; (of gun) gueule f ♦ vt museler

my [maɪ] adj mon(ma), mes pl; ~ **house/car/gloves** ma maison/mon auto/mes gants; **I've washed** ~ **hair/cut** ~ **finger** je me suis lavé les cheveux/coupé le doigt; ~**self** [maɪ'self] pron (reflexive) me; (emphatic) moi-même; (after prep) moi; see also **oneself**

mysterious [mɪs'tɪərɪəs] adj mystérieux(euse)

mystery ['mɪstərɪ] n mystère m

mystify ['mɪstɪfaɪ] vt mystifier; (puzzle) ébahir

myth [mɪθ] n mythe m; ~**ology** [mɪ'θɒlədʒɪ] n mythologie f

N n

n/a *abbr* = not applicable

nag [næg] *vt* (*scold*) être toujours après, reprendre sans arrêt; ~**ging** *adj* (*doubt, pain*) persistant(e)

nail [neɪl] *n* (*human*) ongle *m*; (*metal*) clou *m* ♦ *vt* clouer; **to ~ sb down to a date/price** contraindre qn à accepter *or* donner une date/un prix; ~**brush** *n* brosse *f* à ongles; ~**file** *n* lime *f* à ongles; ~ **polish** *n* vernis *m* à ongles; ~ **polish remover** *n* dissolvant *m*; ~ **scissors** *npl* ciseaux *mpl* à ongles; ~ **varnish** (*BRIT*) *n* = nail polish

naïve [naɪ'iːv] *adj* naïf(ïve)

naked ['neɪkɪd] *adj* nu(e)

name [neɪm] *n* nom *m*; (*reputation*) réputation *f* ♦ *vt* nommer; (*identify: accomplice etc*) citer; (*price, date*) fixer, donner; **by ~** par son nom; **in the ~ of** au nom de; **what's your ~?** comment vous appelez-vous?; ~**less** *adj* sans nom; (*witness, contributor*) anonyme; ~**ly** *adv* à savoir; ~**sake** *n* homonyme *m*

nanny ['nænɪ] *n* bonne *f* d'enfants

nap [næp] *n* (*sleep*) (petit) somme ♦ *vi*: **to be caught ~ping** être pris à l'improviste *or* en défaut

nape [neɪp] *n*: ~ **of the neck** nuque *f*

napkin ['næpkɪn] *n* serviette *f* (de table)

nappy ['næpɪ] (*BRIT*) *n* couche *f* (*gen pl*); ~ **rash** *n*: **to have ~ rash** avoir les fesses rouges

narcissus [nɑː'sɪsəs, *pl* nɑː'sɪsaɪ] (*pl* **narcissi**) *n* narcisse *m*

narcotic [nɑː'kɒtɪk] *n* (*drug*) stupéfiant *m*; (*MED*) narcotique *m*

narrative ['nærətɪv] *n* récit *m*

narrow ['nærəʊ] *adj* étroit(e); (*fig*) restreint(e), limité(e) ♦ *vi* (*road*) devenir plus étroit, se rétrécir; (*gap, difference*) se réduire; **to have a ~ escape** l'échapper belle; **to ~ sth down to** réduire qch à; ~**ly** *adv*: **he ~ly missed injury/the tree** il a failli se blesser/rentrer dans l'arbre; ~**-minded** *adj* à l'esprit étroit, borné(e); (*attitude*) borné

nasty ['nɑːstɪ] *adj* (*person: malicious*) méchant(e); (*: rude*) très désagréable; (*smell*) dégoûtant(e); (*wound, situation, disease*) mauvais(e)

nation ['neɪʃən] *n* nation *f*

national ['næʃənl] *adj* national(e) ♦ *n* (*abroad*) ressortissant(e); (*when home*) national(e); ~ **dress** *n* costume national; **N~ Health Service** (*BRIT*) *n* service national de santé; ≈ Sécurité Sociale; **N~ Insurance** (*BRIT*) *n* ≈ Sécurité Sociale; ~**ism** ['næʃnəlɪzəm] *n* nationalisme *m*; ~**ist** ['næʃnəlɪst] *adj* nationaliste ♦ *n* nationaliste *m/f*; ~**ity** [næʃə'nælɪtɪ] *n* nationalité *f*; ~**ize** *vt* nationaliser; ~**ly** *adv* (*as a nation*) du point de vue national; (*nationwide*) dans le pays entier

nationwide ['neɪʃənwaɪd] *adj* s'étendant à l'ensemble du pays; (*problem*) à l'échelle du pays entier ♦ *adv* à travers *or* dans tout le pays

native ['neɪtɪv] *n* autochtone *m/f*, habitant(e) du pays ♦ *adj* du pays, indigène; (*country*) natal(e); (*ability*) inné(e); **a ~ of Russia** une personne originaire de Russie; **a ~ speaker of French** une personne de langue maternelle française; ~ **language** *n* langue maternelle

NATO ['neɪtəʊ] *n abbr* (= *North Atlantic Treaty Organization*) OTAN *f*

natural ['nætʃrəl] *adj* naturel(le); ~ **gas** *n* gaz naturel; ~**ize** *vt* naturaliser; (*plant*) acclimater; **to become ~ized** (*person*) se naturaliser; ~**ly** *adv* naturellement

nature ['neɪtʃə*] *n* nature *f*; **by ~** par tempérament, de nature

naught [nɔːt] *n* = nought

naughty ['nɔːtɪ] *adj* (*child*) vilain(e), pas sage

nausea ['nɔːsɪə] *n* nausée *f*; **nauseate** ['nɔːsɪeɪt] *vt* écœurer, donner la nausée à

naval ['neɪvl] *adj* naval(e); ~ **officer** *n* officier *m* de marine

nave [neɪv] *n* nef *f*

navel ['neɪvl] *n* nombril *m*

navigate ['nævɪgeɪt] *vt* (*steer*) diriger; (*plot course*) naviguer ♦ *vi* naviguer; **navigation** [nævɪ'geɪʃən] *n* navigation *f*

navvy ['nævɪ] (*BRIT*) *n* terrassier *m*

navy ['neɪvɪ] *n* marine *f*; ~**(-blue)** *adj* bleu marine *inv*

Nazi ['nɑːtsɪ] *n* Nazi(e)

NB *abbr* (= *nota bene*) NB

near [nɪə*] *adj* proche ♦ *adv* près ♦ *prep* (*also*: ~ **to**) près de ♦ *vt* approcher de; ~**by** *adj* proche ♦ *adv* tout près, à proximité; ~**ly** *adv* presque; **I ~ly fell** j'ai failli tomber; ~ **miss** *n* (*AVIAT*) quasi-collision *f*; **that was a ~ miss** (*gen*) il s'en est fallu de peu; (*of shot*) c'est passé très près; ~**side** *n* (*AUT: BRIT*) côté *m* gauche; (*: in US, Europe*) côté droit; ~**-sighted** *adj* myope

neat [niːt] *adj* (*person, work*) soigné(e); (*room etc*) bien tenu(e) *or* rangé(e); (*skilful*) habile; (*spirits*) pur(e); ~**ly** *adv* avec soin *or* ordre; habilement

necessarily ['nesɪsərɪlɪ] *adv* nécessairement

necessary ['nesɪsərɪ] adj nécessaire
necessity [nɪ'sesɪtɪ] n nécessité f; (thing needed) chose nécessaire or essentielle; **necessities** npl nécessaire m
neck [nek] n cou m; (of animal, garment) encolure f; (of bottle) goulot m ♦ vi (inf) se peloter; ~ **and** ~ à égalité; ~**lace** ['neklɪs] n collier m; ~**line** n encolure f; ~**tie** n cravate f
need [ni:d] n besoin m ♦ vt avoir besoin de; **to** ~ **to do** devoir faire; avoir besoin de faire; **you don't** ~ **to go** vous n'avez pas besoin or vous n'êtes pas obligé de partir
needle ['ni:dl] n aiguille f ♦ vt asticoter, tourmenter
needless ['ni:dlɪs] adj inutile
needlework ['ni:dlwɜ:k] n (activity) travaux mpl d'aiguille; (object(s)) ouvrage m
needn't ['ni:dnt] = need not
needy ['ni:dɪ] adj nécessiteux(euse)
negative ['negətɪv] n (PHOT, ELEC) négatif m; (LING) terme m de négation ♦ adj négatif(ive)
neglect [nɪ'glekt] vt négliger ♦ n (of person, duty, garden) le fait de négliger; (state) abandon m
negligee ['neglɪʒeɪ] n déshabillé m
negotiate [nɪ'gəʊʃɪeɪt] vi, vt négocier; **negotiation** [nɪgəʊʃɪ'eɪʃən] n négociation f, pourparlers mpl
Negro ['ni:grəʊ] (!; pl ~**es**) n Noir(e)
neigh [neɪ] vi hennir
neighbour ['neɪbə*] (US **neighbor**) n voisin(e); ~**hood** n (place) quartier m; (people) voisinage m; ~**ing** adj voisin(e), avoisinant(e); ~**ly** adj obligeant(e); (action etc) amical(e)
neither ['naɪðə*] adj, pron aucun(e) (des deux), ni l'un(e) ni l'autre ♦ conj: **I didn't move and** ~ **did Claude** je n'ai pas bougé, (et) Claude non plus; ..., ~ **did I refuse** ..., (et or mais) je n'ai pas non plus refusé ... ♦ adv: ~ **good nor bad** ni bon ni mauvais
neon ['ni:ɒn] n néon m; ~ **light** n lampe f au néon
nephew ['nefju:] n neveu m
nerve [nɜ:v] n nerf m; (fig: courage) sang-froid m, courage m; (: impudence) aplomb m, toupet m; **to have a fit of** ~**s** avoir le trac; ~**-racking** adj angoissant(e)
nervous ['nɜ:vəs] adj nerveux(euse); (anxious) inquiet(ète), plein(e) d'appréhension; (timid) intimidé(e); ~ **breakdown** n dépression nerveuse
nest [nest] n nid m ♦ vi (se) nicher, faire son nid; ~ **egg** n (fig) bas m de laine, magot m
nestle ['nesl] vi se blottir
net [net] n filet m ♦ adj net(te) ♦ vt (fish etc) prendre au filet; (profit) rapporter; ~**ball** n netball m; ~ **curtains** npl voilages

mpl
Netherlands ['neðələndz] npl: **the** ~ les Pays-Bas mpl
nett [net] adj = net
netting ['netɪŋ] n (for fence etc) treillis m, grillage m
nettle ['netl] n ortie f
network ['netwɜ:k] n réseau m
neurotic [njʊə'rɒtɪk] adj, n névrosé(e)
neuter ['nju:tə*] adj neutre ♦ vt (cat etc) châtrer, couper
neutral ['nju:trəl] adj neutre ♦ n (AUT) point mort; ~**ize** vt neutraliser
never ['nevə*] adv (ne ...) jamais; ~ **again** plus jamais; ~ **in my life** jamais de ma vie; see also **mind**; ~**-ending** adj interminable; ~**theless** [nevəðə'les] adv néanmoins, malgré tout
new [nju:] adj nouveau(nouvelle); (brand new) neuf(neuve); ~**-born** adj nouveau-né(e); ~**comer** ['nju:kʌmə*] n nouveau venu/nouvelle venue; ~**-fangled** (pej) adj ultramoderne (et farfelu(e)); ~**-found** adj (enthusiasm) de fraîche date; (friend) nouveau(nouvelle); ~**ly** adv nouvellement, récemment; ~**ly-weds** npl jeunes mariés mpl
news [nju:z] n nouvelle(s) f(pl); (RADIO, TV) informations fpl, actualités fpl; **a piece of** ~ une nouvelle; ~ **agency** n agence f de presse; ~**agent** (BRIT) n marchand m de journaux; ~**caster** n présentateur(trice); ~**dealer** (US) n = newsagent; ~ **flash** n flash m d'information; ~**letter** n bulletin m; ~**paper** n journal m; ~**print** n papier m (de) journal; ~**reader** n = newscaster; ~**reel** n actualités (filmées) fpl; ~ **stand** n kiosque m à journaux
newt [nju:t] n triton m
New Year n Nouvel An; ~**'s Day** n le jour de l'An; ~**'s Eve** n la Saint-Sylvestre
New Zealand [-'zi:lənd] n la Nouvelle-Zélande; ~**er** n Néo-zélandais(e)
next [nekst] adj (seat, room) voisin(e), d'à côté; (meeting, bus stop) suivant(e); (in time) prochain(e) ♦ adv (place) à côté; (time) la fois suivante, la prochaine fois; (afterwards) ensuite; **the** ~ **day** le lendemain, le jour suivant or d'après; ~ **year** l'année prochaine; ~ **time** la prochaine fois; ~ **to** à côté de; ~ **to nothing** presque rien; ~, **please!** (at doctor's) au suivant!; ~ **door** adv à côté ♦ adj d'à côté; ~**-of-kin** n parent m le plus proche
NHS n abbr = **National Health Service**
nib [nɪb] n (bec m de) plume f
nibble ['nɪbl] vt grignoter
nice [naɪs] adj (pleasant, likeable) agréable; (pretty) joli(e); (kind) gentil(le); ~**ly** adv agréablement; joliment; gentiment
niceties ['naɪsɪtɪz] npl subtilités fpl
nick [nɪk] n (indentation) encoche f; (wound) entaille f ♦ vt (BRIT: inf) faucher,

piquer; **in the ~ of time** juste à temps
nickel ['nɪkl] *n* nickel *m*; (*US*) pièce *f* de 5 cents
nickname ['nɪkneɪm] *n* surnom *m* ♦ *vt* surnommer
niece [niːs] *n* nièce *f*
Nigeria [naɪ'dʒɪərɪə] *n* Nigéria *m or f*
niggling ['nɪglɪŋ] *adj* (*person*) tatillon(ne); (*detail*) insignifiant(e); (*doubts, injury*) persistant(e)
night [naɪt] *n* nuit *f*; (*evening*) soir *m*; **at ~** la nuit; **by ~** de nuit; **the ~ before last** avant-hier soir; **~cap** *n* boisson prise avant le coucher; **~ club** *n* boîte *f* de nuit; **~dress** *n* chemise *f* de nuit; **~fall** *n* tombée *f* de la nuit; **~gown** *n* chemise *f* de nuit; **~ie** ['naɪtɪ] *n* chemise *f* de nuit; **~ingale** ['naɪtɪŋgeɪl] *n* rossignol *m*; **~life** ['naɪtlaɪf] *n* vie *f* nocturne; **~ly** ['naɪtlɪ] *adj* de chaque nuit or soir; (*by night*) nocturne ♦ *adv* chaque nuit or soir; **~mare** ['naɪtmɛə*] *n* cauchemar *m*; **~ porter** *n* gardien *m* de nuit, concierge *m* de service la nuit; **~ school** *n* cours *mpl* du soir; **~-shift** *n* équipe *f* de nuit; **~-time** *n* nuit *f*; **~ watchman** *n* veilleur *m* or gardien *m* de nuit
nil [nɪl] *n* rien *m*; (*BRIT: SPORT*) zéro *m*
Nile [naɪl] *n*: **the ~** le Nil
nimble ['nɪmbl] *adj* agile
nine [naɪn] *num* neuf; **~teen** *num* dix-neuf; **~ty** *num* quatre-vingt-dix
ninth [naɪnθ] *num* neuvième
nip [nɪp] *vt* pincer
nipple ['nɪpl] *n* (*ANAT*) mamelon *m*, bout *m* du sein
nitrogen ['naɪtrədʒən] *n* azote *m*

──────────── KEYWORD ────────────

no [nəʊ] (*pl* **~es**) *adv* (*opposite of "yes"*) non; **are you coming? - ~ (I'm not)** est-ce que vous venez? - non; **would you like some more? - ~ thank you** vous en voulez encore? - non merci
♦ *adj* (*not any*) pas de, aucun(e) (*used with "ne"*); **I have ~ money/books** je n'ai pas d'argent/de livres; **~ student would have done it** aucun étudiant ne l'aurait fait; **"~ smoking"** "défense de fumer"; **"~ dogs"** "les chiens ne sont pas admis"
♦ *n* non *m*

nobility [nəʊ'bɪlɪtɪ] *n* noblesse *f*
noble ['nəʊbl] *adj* noble
nobody ['nəʊbədɪ] *pron* personne
nod [nɒd] *vi* faire un signe de tête (*affirmatif ou amical*); (*sleep*) somnoler ♦ *vt*: **to ~ one's head** faire un signe de (la) tête; (*in agreement*) faire signe que oui ♦ *n* signe *m* de (la) tête; **~ off** *vi* s'assoupir
noise [nɔɪz] *n* bruit *m*; **noisy** ['nɔɪzɪ] *adj* bruyant(e)

nominal ['nɒmɪnl] *adj* (*rent, leader*) symbolique
nominate ['nɒmɪneɪt] *vt* (*propose*) proposer; (*appoint*) nommer; **nominee** [nɒmɪ'niː] *n* candidat agréé; personne nommée
non... *prefix* non-; **~-alcoholic** *adj* non-alcoolisé(e); **~-committal** *adj* évasif(ive)
nondescript ['nɒndɪskrɪpt] *adj* quelconque, indéfinissable
none [nʌn] *pron* aucun(e); **~ of you** aucun d'entre vous, personne parmi vous; **I've ~ left** je n'en ai plus; **he's ~ the worse for it** il ne s'en porte pas plus mal
nonentity [nɒ'nentɪtɪ] *n* personne insignifiante
nonetheless ['nʌnðə'les] *adv* néanmoins
non-existent [nɒnɪg'zɪstənt] *adj* inexistant(e)
non-fiction [nɒn'fɪkʃən] *n* littérature *f* non-romanesque
nonplussed ['nɒn'plʌst] *adj* perplexe
nonsense ['nɒnsəns] *n* absurdités *fpl*, idioties *fpl*; **~!** ne dites pas d'idioties!
non-: ~-smoker *n* non-fumeur *m*; **~-stick** *adj* qui n'attache pas; **~-stop** *adj* direct(e), sans arrêt (or escale) ♦ *adv* sans arrêt
noodles ['nuːdlz] *npl* nouilles *fpl*
nook [nʊk] *n*: **~s and crannies** recoins *mpl*
noon [nuːn] *n* midi *m*
no one ['nəʊwʌn] *pron* = **nobody**
noose [nuːs] *n* nœud coulant; (*hangman's*) corde *f*
nor [nɔː*] *conj* = **neither** ♦ *adv see* **neither**
norm [nɔːm] *n* norme *f*
normal ['nɔːməl] *adj* normal(e); **~ly** *adv* normalement
Normandy ['nɔːməndɪ] *n* Normandie *f*
north [nɔːθ] *n* nord *m* ♦ *adj* du nord, nord *inv* ♦ *adv* au or vers le nord; **N~ America** *n* Amérique *f* du Nord; **~-east** *n* nord-est *m*; **~erly** ['nɔːðəlɪ] *adj* du nord; **~ern** ['nɔːðən] *adj* du nord, septentrional(e); **N~ern Ireland** *n* Irlande *f* du Nord; **N~ Pole** *n* pôle *m* Nord; **N~ Sea** *n* mer *f* du Nord; **~ward(s)** ['nɔːθwəd(z)] *adv* vers le nord; **~-west** *n* nord-ouest *m*
Norway ['nɔːweɪ] *n* Norvège *f*
Norwegian [nɔː'wiːdʒən] *adj* norvégien(ne) ♦ *n* Norvégien(ne); (*LING*) norvégien *m*
nose [nəʊz] *n* nez *m*; **~ about, around** *vi* fouiner or fureter (partout); **~bleed** *n* saignement *m* du nez; **~-dive** *n* (descente *f* en) piqué *m*; **~y** (*inf*) *adj* = **nosy**
nostalgia [nɔs'tældʒɪə] *n* nostalgie *f*
nostril ['nɒstrɪl] *n* narine *f*; (*of horse*) naseau *m*
nosy ['nəʊzɪ] (*inf*) *adj* curieux(euse)
not [nɒt] *adv* (ne ...) pas; **he is ~ or isn't here** il n'est pas ici; **you must ~ or you mustn't do that** tu ne dois pas faire ça; **it's too late, isn't it or is it ~?** c'est trop tard, n'est-ce pas?; **~ yet/now** pas

encore/maintenant; *see also* **all; only**

notably ['nəʊtəblɪ] *adv* (*particularly*) en particulier; (*markedly*) spécialement

notary ['nəʊtərɪ] *n* notaire *m*

notch [nɒtʃ] *n* encoche *f*

note [nəʊt] *n* note *f*; (*letter*) mot *m*; (*banknote*) billet *m* ♦ *vt* (*also*: ~ **down**) noter; (*observe*) constater; **~book** *n* carnet *m*; **~d** ['nəʊtɪd] *adj* réputé(e); **~pad** *n* bloc-notes *m*; **~paper** *n* papier *m* à lettres

nothing ['nʌθɪŋ] *n* rien *m*; **he does** ~ il ne fait rien; ~ **new** rien de nouveau; **for** ~ pour rien

notice ['nəʊtɪs] *n* (*announcement, warning*) avis *m*; (*period of time*) délai *m*; (*resignation*) démission *f*; (*dismissal*) congé *m* ♦ *vt* remarquer, s'apercevoir de; **to take** ~ **of** prêter attention à; **to bring sth to sb's** ~ porter qch à la connaissance de qn; **at short** ~ dans un délai très court; **until further** ~ jusqu'à nouvel ordre; **to hand in one's** ~ donner sa démission, démissionner; **~able** *adj* visible; ~ **board** (*BRIT*) *n* panneau *m* d'affichage

notify ['nəʊtɪfaɪ] *vt*: **to** ~ **sth to sb** notifier qch à qn; **to** ~ **sb (of sth)** avertir qn (de qch)

notion ['nəʊʃən] *n* idée *f*; (*concept*) notion *f*

notorious [nəʊ'tɔːrɪəs] *adj* notoire (*souvent en mal*)

notwithstanding [nɒtwɪθ'stændɪŋ] *adv* néanmoins ♦ *prep* en dépit de

nought [nɔːt] *n* zéro *m*

noun [naʊn] *n* nom *m*

nourish ['nʌrɪʃ] *vt* nourrir; **~ing** *adj* nourrissant(e); **~ment** *n* nourriture *f*

novel ['nɒvəl] *n* roman *m* ♦ *adj* nouveau(nouvelle), original(e); **~ist** *n* romancier *m*; **~ty** *n* nouveauté *f*

November [nəʊ'vembə*] *n* novembre *m*

now [naʊ] *adv* maintenant ♦ *conj*: ~ **(that)** maintenant que; **right** ~ tout de suite; **by** ~ à l'heure qu'il est; **just** ~: **that's the fashion just** ~ c'est la mode en ce moment; ~ **and then**, ~ **and again** de temps en temps; **from** ~ **on** dorénavant; **~adays** ['naʊədeɪz] *adv* de nos jours

nowhere ['nəʊwɛə*] *adv* nulle part

nozzle ['nɒzl] *n* (*of hose etc*) ajutage *m*; (*of vacuum cleaner*) suceur *m*

nuclear ['njuːklɪə*] *adj* nucléaire

nucleus ['njuːklɪəs, *pl* 'njuːklɪaɪ] (*pl* **nuclei**) *n* noyau *m*

nude [njuːd] *adj* nu(e) ♦ *n* nu *m*; **in the** ~ (tout(e)) nu(e)

nudge [nʌdʒ] *vt* donner un (petit) coup de coude à

nudist ['njuːdɪst] *n* nudiste *m/f*

nuisance ['njuːsns] *n*: **it's a** ~ c'est (très) embêtant; **he's a** ~ il est assommant *or* casse-pieds; **what a** ~! quelle barbe!

null [nʌl] *adj*: ~ **and void** nul(le) et non

avenu(e)

numb [nʌm] *adj* engourdi(e); (*with fear*) paralysé(e)

number ['nʌmbə*] *n* nombre *m*; (*numeral*) chiffre *m*; (*of house, bank account etc*) numéro *m* ♦ *vt* numéroter; (*amount to*) compter; **a** ~ **of** un certain nombre de; **to be ~ed among** compter parmi; **they were seven in** ~ ils étaient (au nombre de) sept; ~ **plate** *n* (*AUT*) plaque *f* minéralogique *or* d'immatriculation

numeral ['njuːmərəl] *n* chiffre *m*

numerate ['njuːmərɪt] (*BRIT*) *adj*: **to be** ~ avoir des notions d'arithmétique

numerical [njuː'merɪkəl] *adj* numérique

numerous ['njuːmərəs] *adj* nombreux(euse)

nun [nʌn] *n* religieuse *f*, sœur *f*

nurse [nɜːs] *n* infirmière *f* ♦ *vt* (*patient, cold*) soigner

nursery ['nɜːsərɪ] *n* (*room*) nursery *f*; (*institution*) crèche *f*; (*for plants*) pépinière *f*; ~ **rhyme** *n* comptine *f*, chansonnette *f* pour enfants; ~ **school** *n* école maternelle; ~ **slope** *n* (*SKI*) piste *f* pour débutants

nursing ['nɜːsɪŋ] *n* (*profession*) profession *f* d'infirmière; (*care*) soins *mpl*; ~ **home** *n* clinique *f*; maison *f* de convalescence; ~ **mother** *n* mère *f* qui allaite

nut [nʌt] *n* (*of metal*) écrou *m*; (*fruit*) noix *f*; noisette *f*; cacahuète *f*; **~crackers** ['nʌtkrækəz] *npl* casse-noix *m inv*, casse-noisette(s) *m*

nutmeg ['nʌtmeg] *n* (noix *f*) muscade *f*

nutritious [njuː'trɪʃəs] *adj* nutritif(ive), nourrissant(e)

nuts (*inf*) *adj* dingue

nutshell ['nʌtʃel] *n*: **in a** ~ en un mot

nylon ['naɪlɒn] *n* nylon *m* ♦ *adj* de *or* en nylon

O o

oak [əʊk] *n* chêne *m* ♦ *adj* de *or* en (bois de) chêne

OAP (*BRIT*) *n abbr* = **old age pensioner**

oar [ɔː*] *n* aviron *m*, rame *f*

oasis [əʊ'eɪsɪs, *pl* əʊ'eɪsiːz] (*pl* **oases**) *n* oasis *f*

oath [əʊθ] *n* serment *m*; (*swear word*) juron *m*; **under** ~, (*BRIT*) **on** ~ sous serment

oatmeal ['əʊtmiːl] *n* flocons *mpl* d'avoine

oats [əʊts] *n* avoine *f*

obedience [ə'biːdɪəns] *n* obéissance *f*; **ob-**

edient [ə'biːdiənt] *adj* obéissant(e)

obey [ə'beɪ] *vt* obéir à; (*instructions*) se conformer à

obituary [ə'bɪtjuərɪ] *n* nécrologie *f*

object [*n* 'ɒbdʒɪkt, *vb* əb'dʒekt] *n* objet *m*; (*purpose*) but *m*, objet; (*LING*) complément *m* d'objet ♦ *vi*: **to ~ to** (*attitude*) désapprouver; (*proposal*) protester contre; **expense is no ~** l'argent n'est pas un problème; **he ~ed that ...** il a fait valoir *or* a objecté que ...; **I ~!** je proteste!; **~ion** [əb'dʒekʃən] *n* objection *f*; **~ionable** [əb'dʒekʃnəbl] *adj* très désagréable; (*language*) choquant(e); **~ive** [əb'dʒektɪv] *n* objectif *m* ♦ *adj* objectif(ive)

obligation [ɒblɪ'geɪʃən] *n* obligation *f*, devoir *m*; **without ~** sans engagement

oblige [ə'blaɪdʒ] *vt* (*force*): **to ~ sb to do** obliger *or* forcer qn à faire; (*do a favour*) rendre service à, obliger; **to be ~d to sb for sth** être obligé(e) à qn de qch; **obliging** [ə'blaɪdʒɪŋ] *adj* obligeant(e), serviable

oblique [ə'bliːk] *adj* oblique; (*allusion*) indirect(e)

obliterate [ə'blɪtəreɪt] *vt* effacer

oblivion [ə'blɪvɪən] *n* oubli *m*; **oblivious** [ə'blɪvɪəs] *adj*: **oblivious of** oublieux(euse) de

oblong ['ɒblɒŋ] *adj* oblong(ue) ♦ *n* rectangle *m*

obnoxious [əb'nɒkʃəs] *adj* odieux (euse); (*smell*) nauséabond(e)

oboe ['əubəu] *n* hautbois *m*

obscene [əb'siːn] *adj* obscène

obscure [əb'skjuə*] *adj* obscur(e) ♦ *vt* obscurcir; (*hide: sun*) cacher

observant [əb'zɜːvənt] *adj* observateur(trice)

observation [ɒbzə'veɪʃən] *n* (*remark*) observation *f*; (*watching*) surveillance *f*; **observatory** [əb'zɜːvətrɪ] *n* observatoire *m*

observe [əb'zɜːv] *vt* observer; (*remark*) faire observer *or* remarquer; **~r** *n* observateur(trice)

obsess [əb'ses] *vt* obséder; **~ive** *adj* obsédant(e)

obsolescence [ɒbsə'lesns] *n* vieillissement *m*

obsolete ['ɒbsəliːt] *adj* dépassé(e); démodé(e)

obstacle ['ɒbstəkl] *n* obstacle *m*; **~ race** *n* course *f* d'obstacles

obstinate ['ɒbstɪnət] *adj* obstiné(e)

obstruct [əb'strʌkt] *vt* (*block*) boucher, obstruer; (*hinder*) entraver

obtain [əb'teɪn] *vt* obtenir; **~able** *adj* qu'on peut obtenir

obvious ['ɒbvɪəs] *adj* évident(e), manifeste; **~ly** *adv* manifestement; **~ly not!** bien sûr que non!

occasion [ə'keɪʒən] *n* occasion *f*; (*event*) événement *m*; **~al** *adj* pris(e) *or* fait(e) *etc*

de temps en temps; occasionnel(le); **~ally** *adv* de temps en temps, quelquefois

occupation [ɒkju'peɪʃən] *n* occupation *f*; (*job*) métier *m*, profession *f*; **~al hazard** *n* risque *m* du métier

occupier ['ɒkjupaɪə*] *n* occupant(e)

occupy ['ɒkjupaɪ] *vt* occuper; **to ~ o.s. in** *or* **with doing** s'occuper à faire

occur [ə'kɜː*] *vi* (*event*) se produire; (*phenomenon, error*) se rencontrer; **to ~ to sb** venir à l'esprit de qn; **~rence** *n* (*existence*) présence *f*, existence *f*; (*event*) cas *m*, fait *m*

ocean ['əuʃən] *n* océan *m*; **~-going** *adj* de haute mer

o'clock [ə'klɒk] *adv*: **it is 5 ~** il est 5 heures

OCR *n abbr* = **optical character reader; optical character recognition**

October [ɒk'təubə*] *n* octobre *m*

octopus ['ɒktəpəs] *n* pieuvre *f*

odd [ɒd] *adj* (*strange*) bizarre, curieux(euse); (*number*) impair(e); (*not of a set*) dépareillé(e); **60-odd** 60 et quelques; **at ~ times** de temps en temps; **the ~ one out** l'exception *f*; **~ity** *n* (*person*) excentrique *m/f*; (*thing*) curiosité *f*; **~-job man** *n* homme *m* à tout faire; **~ jobs** *npl* petits travaux divers; **~ly** *adv* bizarrement, curieusement; **~ments** *npl* (*COMM*) fins *fpl* de série; **~s** *npl* (*in betting*) cote *f*; **it makes no ~s** cela n'a pas d'importance; **at ~s** en désaccord; **~s and ends** de petites choses

odour ['əudə*] (*US* **odor**) *n* odeur *f*

──────────── **KEYWORD**

of [ɒv, əv] *prep* **1** (*gen*) de; **a friend ~ ours** un de nos amis; **a boy ~ 10** un garçon de 10 ans; **that was kind ~ you** c'était gentil de votre part

2 (*expressing quantity, amount, dates etc*) de; **a kilo ~ flour** un kilo de farine; **how much ~ this do you need?** combien vous en faut-il?; **there were 3 ~ them** (*people*) ils étaient 3; (*objects*) il y en avait 3; **3 ~ us went** 3 d'entre nous y sont allé(e)s; **the 5th ~ July** le 5 juillet

3 (*from, out of*) en, de; **a statue ~ marble** une statue de *or* en marbre; **made ~ wood** (fait) en bois

──────────────────────────

off [ɒf] *adj, adv* (*engine*) coupé(e); (*tap*) fermé(e); (*BRIT: food: bad*) mauvais(e); (: *milk*) tourné(e); (*absent*) absent(e); (*cancelled*) annulé(e) ♦ *prep* de; sur; **to be ~** (*to leave*) partir, s'en aller; **to be ~ sick** être absent pour cause de maladie; **a day ~** un jour de congé; **to have an ~ day** n'être pas en forme; **he had his coat ~** il avait enlevé son manteau; **10% ~** (*COMM*) 10% de rabais; **~ the coast** au large de la côte; **I'm ~ meat** je ne mange plus de viande, je n'aime plus la viande; **on the ~ chance** à tout hasard

offal ['ɒfəl] *n* (*CULIN*) abats *mpl*

off-colour ['ɒf'kʌlə*] (*BRIT*) *adj* (*ill*) malade, mal fichu(e)

offence [ə'fɛns] (*US* **offense**) *n* (*crime*) délit *m*, infraction *f*; **to take ~ at** se vexer de, s'offenser de

offend [ə'fɛnd] *vt* (*person*) offenser, blesser; **~er** *n* délinquant(e)

offense [ə'fɛns] (*US*) *n* = **offence**

offensive [ə'fɛnsɪv] *adj* offensant(e), choquant(e); (*smell etc*) très déplaisant(e); (*weapon*) offensif(ive) ♦ *n* (*MIL*) offensive *f*

offer ['ɒfə*] *n* offre *f*, proposition *f* ♦ *vt* offrir, proposer; **"on ~"** (*COMM*) "en promotion"; **~ing** *n* offrande *f*

offhand ['ɒf'hænd] *adj* désinvolte ♦ *adv* spontanément

office ['ɒfɪs] *n* (*place, room*) bureau *m*; (*position*) charge *f*, fonction *f*; **doctor's ~** (*US*) cabinet (médical); **to take ~** entrer en fonctions; **~ automation** *n* bureautique *f*; **~ block** (*US* **~ building**) *n* immeuble *m* de bureaux; **~ hours** *npl* heures *fpl* de bureau; (*US: MED*) heures de consultation

officer ['ɒfɪsə*] *n* (*MIL etc*) officier *m*; (*also: police ~*) agent *m* (de police); (*of organization*) membre *m* du bureau directeur

office worker *n* employé(e) de bureau

official [ə'fɪʃəl] *adj* officiel(le) ♦ *n* officiel *m*; (*civil servant*) fonctionnaire *m/f*; employé(e); **~dom** *n* administration *f*, bureaucratie *f*

officiate [ə'fɪʃɪeɪt] *vi* (*REL*) officier; **to ~ at a marriage** célébrer un mariage

officious [ə'fɪʃəs] *adj* trop empressé(e)

offing ['ɒfɪŋ] *n*: **in the ~** (*fig*) en perspective

off: **~-licence** (*BRIT*) *n* (*shop*) débit *m* de vins et de spiritueux; **~-line** *adj, adv* (*COMPUT*) (en mode) autonome; (: *switched off*) non connecté(e); **~-peak** *adj* aux heures creuses; (*electricity, heating, ticket*) au tarif heures creuses; **~-putting** (*BRIT*) *adj* (*remark*) rébarbatif(ive); (*person*) rebutant(e), peu engageant(e); **~-season** *adj, adv* hors-saison *inv*

offset ['ɒfsɛt] (*irreg*) *vt* (*counteract*) contrebalancer, compenser

offshoot ['ɒfʃuːt] *n* (*fig*) ramification *f*, antenne *f*

offshore ['ɒf'ʃɔ:*] *adj* (*breeze*) de terre; (*fishing*) côtier(ère)

offside ['ɒf'saɪd] *adj* (*SPORT*) hors jeu; (*AUT: with right-hand drive*) de droite; (: *with left-hand drive*) de gauche

offspring ['ɒfsprɪŋ] *n inv* progéniture *f*

off: **~stage** *adv* dans les coulisses; **~-the-peg** (*US* **~-the-rack**) *adv* en prêt-à-porter; **~-white** *adj* blanc cassé *inv*

often ['ɒfən] *adv* souvent; **how ~ do you**

go? vous y allez tous les combien?; **how ~ have you gone there?** vous y êtes allé combien de fois?

ogle ['əʊgl] *vt* lorgner

oh [əʊ] *excl* ô!, oh!, ah!

oil [ɔɪl] *n* huile *f*; (*petroleum*) pétrole *m*; (*for central heating*) mazout *m* ♦ *vt* (*machine*) graisser; **~can** *n* burette *f* de graissage; (*for storing*) bidon *m* à huile; **~field** *n* gisement *m* de pétrole; **~ filter** *n* (*AUT*) filtre *m* à huile; **~ painting** *n* peinture *f* à l'huile; **~ refinery** *n* raffinerie *f*; **~ rig** *n* derrick *m*; (*at sea*) plate-forme pétrolière; **~skins** *npl* ciré *m*; **~ tanker** *n* (*ship*) pétrolier *m*; (*truck*) camion-citerne *m*; **~ well** *n* puits *m* de pétrole; **~y** *adj* huileux(euse); (*food*) gras(se)

ointment ['ɔɪntmənt] *n* onguent *m*

O.K., okay ['əʊ'keɪ] *excl* d'accord! ♦ *adj* (*average*) pas mal ♦ *vt* approuver, donner son accord à; **is it ~?, are you ~?** ça va?

old [əʊld] *adj* vieux(vieille); (*person*) vieux, âgé(e); (*former*) ancien(ne), vieux; **how ~ are you?** quel âge avez-vous?; **he's 10 years ~** il a 10 ans, il est âgé de 10 ans; **~er brother/sister** frère/sœur aîné(e); **~ age** *n* vieillesse *f*; **~ age pensioner** (*BRIT*) *n* retraité(e); **~-fashioned** *adj* démodé(e); (*person*) vieux jeu *inv*

olive ['ɒlɪv] *n* (*fruit*) olive *f*; (*tree*) olivier *m* ♦ *adj* (*also: ~-green*) (vert) olive *inv*; **~ oil** *n* huile *f* d'olive

Olympic [əʊ'lɪmpɪk] *adj* olympique; **the ~ Games, the ~s** les Jeux *mpl* olympiques

omelet(te) ['ɒmlət] *n* omelette *f*

omen ['əʊmən] *n* présage *m*

ominous ['ɒmɪnəs] *adj* menaçant(e), inquiétant(e); (*event*) de mauvais augure

omit [əʊ'mɪt] *vt* omettre; **to ~ to do** omettre de faire

KEYWORD

on [ɒn] *prep* **1** (*indicating position*) sur; **~ the table** sur la table; **~ the wall** sur le *or* au mur; **~ the left** à gauche

2 (*indicating means, method, condition etc*): **~ foot** à pied; **~ the train/plane** (*be*) dans le train/l'avion; (*go*) en train/avion; **~ the telephone/radio/television** au téléphone/à la radio/à la télévision; **to be ~ drugs** se droguer; **~ holiday** en vacances

3 (*referring to time*): **~ Friday** vendredi; **~ Fridays** le vendredi; **~ June 20th** le 20 juin; **a week ~ Friday** vendredi en huit; **~ arrival** à l'arrivée; **~ seeing this** en voyant cela

4 (*about, concerning*) sur, de; **a book ~ Balzac/physics** un livre sur Balzac/de physique

♦ *adv* **1** (*referring to dress, covering*): **to have one's coat ~** avoir (mis) son manteau; **to put one's coat ~** mettre son manteau; **what's she got ~?** qu'est-ce qu'elle

porte?; **screw the lid** ~ **tightly** vissez bien le couvercle
2 (*further, continuously*): **to walk** etc ~ continuer à marcher *etc*; ~ **and off** de temps à autre
♦ *adj* **1** (*in operation: machine*) en marche; (: *radio, TV, light*) allumé(e); (: *tap, gas*) ouvert(e); (: *brakes*) mis(e); **is the meeting still** ~? (*not cancelled*) est-ce que la réunion a bien lieu?; (*in progress*) la réunion dure-t-elle encore?; **when is this film** ~? quand passe ce film?
2 (*inf*): **that's not** ~! (*not acceptable*) cela ne se fait pas!; (*not possible*) pas question!

once [wʌns] *adv* une fois; (*formerly*) autrefois ♦ *conj* une fois que; ~ **he had left/it was done** une fois qu'il fut parti/que ce fut terminé; **at** ~ tout de suite, immédiatement; (*simultaneously*) à la fois; ~ **a week** une fois par semaine; ~ **more** encore une fois; ~ **and for all** une fois pour toutes; ~ **upon a time** il y avait une fois, il était une fois

oncoming [ˈɒnkʌmɪŋ] *adj* (*traffic*) venant en sens inverse

KEYWORD
---

one [wʌn] *num* un(e); ~ **hundred and fifty** cent cinquante; ~ **day** un jour
♦ *adj* **1** (*sole*) seul(e), unique; **the** ~ **book which** l'unique *or* le seul livre qui; **the** ~ **man who** le seul (homme) qui
2 (*same*) même; **they came in the** ~ **car** ils sont venus dans la même voiture
♦ *pron* **1**: **this** ~ celui-ci(celle-ci); **that** ~ celui-là(celle-là); **I've already got** ~/**a red** ~ j'en ai déjà une(e)/un(e) rouge; ~ **by** ~ un(e) à *or* par un(e)
2: ~ **another** l'un(e) l'autre; **to look at** ~ **another** se regarder
3 (*impersonal*) on; ~ **never knows** on ne sait jamais; **to cut** ~**'s finger** se couper le doigt

one: ~**-day excursion** (*US*) *n* billet *m* d'aller-retour (valable pour la journée); ~**-man** *adj* (*business*) dirigé(e) *etc* par un seul homme; ~**-man band** *n* homme-orchestre *m*; ~**-off** (*BRIT: inf*) *n* exemplaire *m* unique
oneself [wʌnˈself] *pron* (*reflexive*) se; (*after prep*) soi(-même); (*emphatic*) soi-même; **to hurt** ~ se faire mal; **to keep sth for** ~ garder qch pour soi; **to talk to** ~ se parler à soi-même
one: ~**-sided** *adj* (*argument*) unilatéral; ~**-to-** ~ *adj* (*relationship*) univoque; ~**-upmanship** *n*: **the art of** ~**-upmanship** l'art de faire mieux que les autres; ~**-way** *adj* (*street, traffic*) à sens unique
ongoing [ˈɒngəʊɪŋ] *adj* en cours; (*relationship*) suivi(e)

onion [ˈʌnjən] *n* oignon *m*
on-line [ˈɒnˈlaɪn] *adj, adv* (*COMPUT*) en ligne; (: *switched on*) connecté(e)
onlooker [ˈɒnlʊkə*] *n* spectateur (trice)
only [ˈəʊnlɪ] *adv* seulement ♦ *adj* seul(e), unique ♦ *conj* seulement, mais; **an** ~ **child** un enfant unique; **not** ~ ... **but also** non seulement ... mais aussi
onset [ˈɒnset] *n* début *m*; (*of winter, old age*) approche *f*
onshore [ˈɒnʃɔː*] *adj* (*wind*) du large
onslaught [ˈɒnslɔːt] *n* attaque *f*, assaut *m*
onto [ˈɒntʊ] *prep* = **on to**
onus [ˈəʊnəs] *n* responsabilité *f*
onward(s) [ˈɒnwəd(z)] *adv* (*move*) en avant; **from that time** ~ à partir de ce moment
ooze [uːz] *vi* suinter
opaque [əʊˈpeɪk] *adj* opaque
OPEC [ˈəʊpek] *n abbr* (= *Organization of Petroleum Exporting Countries*) O.P.E.P. *f*
open [ˈəʊpən] *adj* ouvert(e); (*car*) découvert(e); (*road, view*) dégagé(e); (*meeting*) public(ique); (*admiration*) manifeste ♦ *vt* ouvrir ♦ *vi* (*flower, eyes, door, debate*) s'ouvrir; (*shop, bank, museum*) ouvrir; (*book etc*: *commence*) commencer, débuter; **in the** ~ (*air*) en plein air; ~ **on to** *vt fus* (*subj: room, door*) donner sur; ~ **up** *vt* ouvrir; (*blocked road*) dégager ♦ *vi* s'ouvrir; ~**ing** *n* ouverture *f*, (*opportunity*) occasion *f* ♦ *adj* (*remarks*) préliminaire; ~**ly** *adv* ouvertement; ~**-minded** *adj* à l'esprit ouvert; ~**-necked** *adj* à col ouvert; ~**-plan** *adj* sans cloisons
opera [ˈɒpərə] *n* opéra *m*; ~ **singer** *n* chanteur(euse) d'opéra
operate [ˈɒpəreɪt] *vt* (*machine*) faire marcher, faire fonctionner ♦ *vi* fonctionner; (*MED*): **to** ~ (**on sb**) opérer (qn)
operatic [ɒpəˈrætɪk] *adj* d'opéra
operating: ~**-table** *n* table *f* d'opération; ~ **theatre** *n* salle *f* d'opération
operation [ɒpəˈreɪʃən] *n* opération *f*, (*of machine*) fonctionnement *m*; **to be in** ~ (*system, law*) être en vigueur; **to have an** ~ (*MED*) se faire opérer
operative [ˈɒpərətɪv] *adj* (*measure*) en vigueur
operator [ˈɒpəreɪtə*] *n* (*of machine*) opérateur(trice); (*TEL*) téléphoniste *m/f*
opinion [əˈpɪnjən] *n* opinion *f*, avis *m*; **in my** ~ à mon avis; ~**ated** *adj* aux idées bien arrêtées; ~ **poll** *n* sondage *m* (d'opinion)
opponent [əˈpəʊnənt] *n* adversaire *m/f*
opportunity [ɒpəˈtjuːnɪtɪ] *n* occasion *f*; **to take the** ~ **of doing** profiter de l'occasion pour faire; **chercher profiter pour faire**
oppose [əˈpəʊz] *vt* s'opposer à; ~**d to** opposé(e) à; **as** ~**d to** par opposition à; **opposing** [əˈpəʊzɪŋ] *adj* (*side*) opposé(e)

opposite ['ɒpəzɪt] adj opposé(e); (house etc) d'en face ♦ adv en face ♦ prep en face de ♦ n opposé m, contraire m; **the ~ sex** l'autre sexe, le sexe opposé
opposition [ɒpə'zɪʃən] n opposition f
oppress [ə'prɛs] vt opprimer
oppressive adj (political regime) oppressif(ive); (weather) lourd(e); (heat) accablant(e)
opt [ɒpt] vi: **to ~ for** opter pour; **to ~ to do** choisir de faire; **~ out** vi: **to ~ out of** choisir de ne pas participer à or de ne pas faire
optical ['ɒptɪkəl] adj optique; (instrument) d'optique; **~ character recognition/reader** n lecture f/lecteur m optique
optician [ɒp'tɪʃən] n opticien(ne)
optimist ['ɒptɪmɪst] n optimiste m/f; **~ic** adj optimiste
option ['ɒpʃən] n choix m, option f; (SCOL) matière f à option; (COMM) option; **~al** adj facultatif(ive); (COMM) en option
or [ɔː*] conj ou; (with negative): **he hasn't seen ~ heard anything** il n'a rien vu ni entendu; **~ else** sinon; ou bien
oral ['ɔːrəl] adj oral(e) ♦ n oral m
orange ['ɒrɪndʒ] n (fruit) orange f ♦ adj orange inv
orator ['ɒrətə*] n orateur(trice)
orbit ['ɔːbɪt] n orbite f ♦ vt graviter autour de
orchard ['ɔːtʃəd] n verger m
orchestra ['ɔːkɪstrə] n orchestre m; (US: seating) (fauteuils mpl d')orchestre
orchid ['ɔːkɪd] n orchidée f
ordain [ɔː'deɪn] vt (REL) ordonner
ordeal [ɔː'diːl] n épreuve f
order ['ɔːdə*] n ordre m; (COMM) commande f ♦ vt ordonner; (COMM) commander; **in ~** en ordre; (document) en règle; **in (working) ~** en état de marche; **out of ~** (not in correct order) en désordre; (not working) en dérangement; **in ~ to do/that** pour faire/que +sub; **on ~** (COMM) en commande; **to ~ sb to do** ordonner à qn de faire; **~ form** n bon m de commande; **~ly** n (MIL) ordonnance f, (MED) garçon m de salle ♦ adj (room) en ordre; (person) qui a de l'ordre
ordinary ['ɔːdnrɪ] adj ordinaire, normal(e); (pej) ordinaire, quelconque; **out of the ~** exceptionnel(le)
Ordnance Survey map n ≈ carte f d'Etat-Major
ore [ɔː*] n minerai m
organ ['ɔːgən] n organe m; (MUS) orgue m, orgues fpl; **~ic** [ɔː'gænɪk] adj organique
organization [ɔːgənaɪ'zeɪʃən] n organisation f
organize ['ɔːgənaɪz] vt organiser; **~r** n organisateur(trice)
orgasm ['ɔːgæzəm] n orgasme m

Orient ['ɔːrɪənt] n: **the ~** l'Orient m; **o~al** [ɔːrɪ'entəl] adj oriental(e)
origin ['ɒrɪdʒɪn] n origine f
original [ə'rɪdʒɪnl] adj original(e); (earliest) originel(le) ♦ n original m; **~ly** adv (at first) à l'origine
originate [ə'rɪdʒɪneɪt] vi: **to ~ from** (person) être originaire de; (suggestion) provenir de; **to ~ in** prendre naissance dans; avoir son origine dans
Orkneys ['ɔːknɪz] npl: **the ~** (also: the Orkney Islands) les Orcades fpl
ornament ['ɔːnəmənt] n ornement m; (trinket) bibelot m; **~al** [ɔːnə'mentl] adj décoratif(ive); (garden) d'agrément
ornate [ɔː'neɪt] adj très orné(e)
orphan ['ɔːfən] n orphelin(e); **~age** n orphelinat m
orthopaedic [ɔːθəʊ'piːdɪk] (US orthopedic) adj orthopédique
ostensibly [ɒs'tensəblɪ] adv en apparence
ostentatious [ɒsten'teɪʃəs] adj prétentieux(euse)
ostracize ['ɒstrəsaɪz] vt frapper d'ostracisme
ostrich ['ɒstrɪtʃ] n autruche f
other ['ʌðə*] adj autre ♦ pron: **the ~ (one)** l'autre; **~s** (~ people) d'autres; **~ than** autrement que; à part; **~wise** adv, conj autrement
otter ['ɒtə*] n loutre f
ouch [aʊtʃ] excl aïe!
ought [ɔːt] (pt ought) aux vb: **I ~ to do it** je devrais le faire, il faudrait que je le fasse; **this ~ to have been corrected** cela aurait dû être corrigé; **he ~ to win** il devrait gagner
ounce [aʊns] n once f (= 28.35g; 16 in a pound)
our [aʊə*] adj notre, nos pl; see also **my**; **~s** pron le(la) nôtre, les nôtres; see also **mine**[1]; **~selves** pron pl (reflexive, after preposition) nous; (emphatic) nous-mêmes; see also **oneself**
oust [aʊst] vt évincer
out [aʊt] adv dehors; (published, not at home etc) sorti(e); (light, fire) éteint(e); **~ here** ici; **~ there** là-bas; **he's ~** (absent) il est sorti; (unconscious) il est sans connaissance; **to be ~ in one's calculations** s'être trompé dans ses calculs; **to run/back** etc **~** sortir en courant/en reculant etc; **~ loud** à haute voix; **~ of** (outside) en dehors de; (because of: anger etc) par; (from among): **~ of 10** sur 10; **~ of:** (without): **~ of petrol** sans essence, à court d'essence; **~ of order** (machine) en panne; (TEL: line) en dérangement; **~-and-out** adj (liar, thief etc) véritable
outback ['aʊtbæk] n (in Australia): **the ~** l'intérieur m
outboard ['aʊtbɔːd] n (also: ~ motor) (mo-

teur m) hors-bord m;

out: ~**break** ['aʊtbreɪk] n (of war, disease) début m; (of violence) éruption f; ~**burst** ['aʊtbɜːst] n explosion f, accès m; ~**cast** ['aʊtkɑːst] n exilé(e); (socially) paria m; ~**come** ['aʊtkʌm] n issue f, résultat m; ~**crop** ['aʊtkrɒp] n (of rock) affleurement m; ~**cry** ['aʊtkraɪ] n tollé (général); ~**dated** [aʊt'deɪtɪd] adj démodé(e); ~**do** [aʊt'duː] (irreg) vt surpasser

outdoor ['aʊtdɔː*] adj de or en plein air; ~**s** adv dehors; au grand air

outer ['aʊtə*] adj extérieur(e); ~ **space** n espace m cosmique

outfit ['aʊtfɪt] n (clothes) tenue f

outgoing ['aʊtgəʊɪŋ] adj (character) ouvert(e), extraverti(e); (retiring) sortant(e); ~**s** npl (expenses) dépenses fpl

outgrow [aʊt'grəʊ] (irreg) vt (clothes) devenir trop grand(e) pour

outhouse ['aʊthaʊs] n appentis m, remise f

outing ['aʊtɪŋ] n sortie f; excursion f

outlandish [aʊt'lændɪʃ] adj étrange

outlaw ['aʊtlɔː] n hors-la-loi m inv ♦ vt mettre hors-la-loi

outlay ['aʊtleɪ] n dépenses fpl; (investment) mise f de fonds

outlet ['aʊtlet] n (for liquid etc) issue f, sortie f; (US: ELEC) prise f de courant; (also: retail ~) point m de vente

outline ['aʊtlaɪn] n (shape) contour m; (summary) esquisse f, grandes lignes ♦ vt (fig: theory, plan) exposer à grands traits

out: ~**live** [aʊt'lɪv] vt survivre à; ~**look** ['aʊtlʊk] n perspective f; ~**lying** ['aʊtlaɪɪŋ] adj écarté(e); ~**moded** [aʊt'məʊdɪd] adj démodé(e); dépassé(e); ~**number** [aʊt'nʌmbə*] vt surpasser en nombre

out-of-date [aʊtəv'deɪt] adj (passport) périmé(e); (theory etc) dépassé(e); (clothes etc) démodé(e)

out-of-the-way [aʊtəvðə'weɪ] adj (place) loin de tout

outpatient ['aʊtpeɪʃənt] n malade m/f en consultation externe

outpost ['aʊtpəʊst] n avant-poste m

output ['aʊtpʊt] n rendement m, production f; (COMPUT) sortie f

outrage ['aʊtreɪdʒ] n (anger) indignation f; (violent act) atrocité f; (scandal) scandale m ♦ vt outrager; ~**ous** [aʊt'reɪdʒəs] adj atroce; scandaleux(euse)

outright [adv 'aʊtraɪt, adj aʊt'raɪt] adv complètement; (deny, refuse) catégoriquement; (ask) carrément; (kill) sur le coup ♦ adj complet(ète); catégorique

outset ['aʊtset] n début m

outside ['aʊt'saɪd] n extérieur m ♦ adj extérieur(e) ♦ adv (au) dehors, à l'extérieur ♦ prep hors de, à l'extérieur de; **at the** ~ (fig) au plus or maximum; ~ **lane** n (AUT: in Britain) voie f de droite; (: in US, Europe)

voie de gauche; ~ **line** n (TEL) ligne extérieure; ~**r** n (stranger) étranger(ère)

out: ~**size** ['aʊtsaɪz] adj énorme; (clothes) grande taille inv; ~**skirts** ['aʊtskɜːts] npl faubourgs mpl; ~**spoken** [aʊt'spəʊkən] adj très franc(franche)

outstanding [aʊt'stændɪŋ] adj remarquable, exceptionnel(le); (unfinished) en suspens; (debt) impayé(e); (problem) non réglé(e)

outstay [aʊt'steɪ] vt: **to** ~ **one's welcome** abuser de l'hospitalité de son hôte

out: ~**stretched** ['aʊtstretʃt] adj (hand) tendu(e); ~**strip** [aʊt'strɪp] vt (competitors, demand) dépasser; ~ **tray** n courrier m "départ"

outward ['aʊtwəd] adj (sign, appearances) extérieur(e); (journey) (d')aller; ~**ly** adv extérieurement; en apparence

outweigh [aʊt'weɪ] vt l'emporter sur

outwit [aʊt'wɪt] vt se montrer plus malin que

oval ['əʊvəl] adj ovale ♦ n ovale m

ovary ['əʊvərɪ] n ovaire m

oven ['ʌvn] n four m; ~**proof** adj allant au four

over ['əʊvə*] adv (par-)dessus ♦ adj (finished) fini(e), terminé(e); (too much) en plus ♦ prep sur; par-dessus; (above) au-dessus de; (on the other side of) de l'autre côté de; (more than) plus de; (during) pendant; ~ **here** ici; ~ **there** là-bas; **all** ~ (everywhere) partout; (finished) fini(e); ~ **and** ~ **(again)** à plusieurs reprises; ~ **and above** en plus de; **to ask sb** ~ inviter qn (à passer)

overall [adj, n 'əʊvərɔːl, adv əʊvər'ɔːl] adj (length, cost etc) total(e); (study) d'ensemble ♦ n (BRIT) blouse f ♦ adv dans l'ensemble, en général; ~**s** npl bleus mpl (de travail)

overawe [əʊvər'ɔː] vt impressionner

over: ~**balance** [əʊvə'bæləns] vi basculer; ~**bearing** [əʊvə'beərɪŋ] adj impérieux(euse), autoritaire; ~**board** ['əʊvəbɔːd] adv (NAUT) par-dessus bord; ~**book** [əʊvə'bʊk] vt faire du surbooking; ~**cast** ['əʊvəkɑːst] adj couvert(e)

overcharge ['əʊvə'tʃɑːdʒ] vt: **to** ~ **sb for sth** faire payer qch trop cher à qn

overcoat ['əʊvəkəʊt] n pardessus m

overcome [əʊvə'kʌm] (irreg) vt (defeat) triompher de; (difficulty) surmonter

overcrowded [əʊvə'kraʊdɪd] adj bondé(e)

overdo [əʊvə'duː] (irreg) vt exagérer; (overcook) trop cuire; **to** ~ **it** (work etc) se surmener

overdose ['əʊvədəʊs] n dose excessive

overdraft ['əʊvədrɑːft] n découvert m; **overdrawn** ['əʊvə'drɔːn] adj (account) à découvert; (person) dont le compte est à découvert

overdue ['əʊvə'djuː] adj en retard; (change,

reform) qui tarde

overestimate [əuvər'ɛstɪmeɪt] *vt* surestimer

overexcited [əuvərɪk'saɪtɪd] *adj* surexcité(e)

overflow [*vb* əuvə'fləu, *n* 'əuvəfləu] *vi* déborder ♦ *n* (*also:* ~ *pipe*) tuyau *m* d'écoulement, trop-plein *m*

overgrown ['əuvə'grəun] *adj* (*garden*) envahi(e) par la végétation

overhaul [*vb* əuvə'hɔːl, *n* 'əuvəhɔːl] *vt* réviser ♦ *n* révision *f*

overhead [*adv* əuvə'hed, *adj, n* 'əuvəhed] *adv* au-dessus ♦ *adj* aérien(ne); (*lighting*) vertical(e) ♦ ~**s** *npl*, (*US*) *n* frais généraux

overhear [əuvə'hɪə*] (*irreg*) *vt* entendre (par hasard)

overheat [əuvə'hiːt] *vi* (*engine*) chauffer

overjoyed [əuvə'dʒɔɪd] *adj:* ~ (*at*) ravi(e) (de), enchanté(e) (de)

overkill ['əuvəkɪl] *n:* **that would be** ~ ce serait trop

overland *adj, adv* par voie de terre

overlap [*vb* əuvə'læp, *n* 'əuvəlæp] *vi* se chevaucher

overleaf [əuvə'liːf] *adv* au verso

overload ['əuvə'ləud] *vt* surcharger

overlook [əuvə'luk] *vt* (*have view of*) donner sur; (*miss: by mistake*) oublier; (*forgive*) fermer les yeux sur

overnight [*adv* 'əuvə'naɪt, *adj* 'əuvənaɪt] *adv* (*happen*) durant la nuit; (*fig*) soudain ♦ *adj* d'une (*or* de) nuit; **he stayed there** ~ il y a passé la nuit

overpass *n* pont autoroutier

overpower [əuvə'pauə*] *vt* vaincre; (*fig*) accabler; ~**ing** *adj* (*heat, stench*) suffocant(e)

overrate ['əuvə'reɪt] *vt* surestimer

override [əuvə'raɪd] (*irreg: like ride*) *vt* (*order, objection*) passer outre à; **overriding** [əuvə'raɪdɪŋ] *adj* prépondérant(e)

overrule [əuvə'ruːl] *vt* (*decision*) annuler; (*claim*) rejeter; (*person*) rejeter l'avis de

overrun [əuvə'rʌn] (*irreg: like run*) *vt* (*country*) occuper; (*time limit*) dépasser

overseas ['əuvə'siːz] *adv* outre-mer; (*abroad*) à l'étranger ♦ *adj* (*trade*) extérieur(e); (*visitor*) étranger(ère)

overshadow [əuvə'ʃædəu] *vt* (*fig*) éclipser

oversight ['əuvəsaɪt] *n* omission *f*, oubli *m*

oversleep ['əuvə'sliːp] (*irreg*) *vi* se réveiller (trop) tard

overstate *vt* exagérer

overstep ['əuvə'step] *vt:* **to** ~ **the mark** dépasser la mesure

overt [əu'vɜːt] *adj* non dissimulé(e)

overtake [əuvə'teɪk] (*irreg*) *vt* (*AUT*) dépasser, doubler

overthrow [əuvə'θrəu] (*irreg*) *vt* (*government*) renverser

overtime ['əuvətaɪm] *n* heures *fpl* supplémentaires

overtone ['əuvətəun] *n* (*also:* ~**s**) note *f,*

sous-entendus *mpl*

overture ['əuvətʃuə*] *n* (*MUS, fig*) ouverture *f*

overturn [əuvə'tɜːn] *vt* renverser ♦ *vi* se retourner

overweight ['əuvə'weɪt] *adj* (*person*) trop gros(se)

overwhelm [əuvə'welm] *vt* (*subj: emotion*) accabler; (*enemy, opponent*) écraser; ~**ing** *adj* (*victory, defeat*) écrasant(e); (*desire*) irrésistible

overwork ['əuvə'wɜːk] *n* surmenage *m*

overwrought ['əuvə'rɔːt] *adj* excédé(e)

owe [əu] *vt:* **to** ~ **sb sth, to** ~ **sth to sb** devoir qch à qn; **owing to** ['əuɪŋ-] *prep* à cause de, en raison de

owl [aul] *n* hibou *m*

own [əun] *vt* posséder ♦ *adj* propre; **a room of my** ~ une chambre à moi, ma propre chambre; **to get one's** ~ **back** prendre sa revanche; **on one's** ~ tout(e) seul(e); ~ **up** *vi* avouer; ~**er** *n* propriétaire *m/f*; ~**ership** *n* possession *f*

ox [ɒks] (*pl* **oxen**) *n* bœuf *m*

oxtail ['ɒksteɪl] *n:* ~ **soup** soupe *f* à la queue de bœuf

oxygen ['ɒksɪdʒən] *n* oxygène *m*; ~ **mask** *n* masque *m* à oxygène

oyster ['ɔɪstə*] *n* huître *f*

oz. *abbr* = **ounce(s)**

ozone hole *n* trou *m* d'ozone

ozone layer *n* couche *f* d'ozone

P p

p [piː] *abbr* = **penny; pence**

PA *n abbr* = **personal assistant; public address system**

pa [pɑː] (*inf*) *n* papa *m*

p.a. *abbr* = **per annum**

pace [peɪs] *n* pas *m*; (*speed*) allure *f*; vitesse *f* ♦ *vi:* **to** ~ **up and down** faire les cent pas; **to keep** ~ **with** aller à la même vitesse que; ~**maker** *n* (*MED*) stimulateur *m* cardiaque; (*SPORT: also:* **pacesetter**) meneur(euse) de train

Pacific *n:* **the** ~ (**Ocean**) le Pacifique, l'océan *m* Pacifique

pack [pæk] *n* (*packet; US: of cigarettes*) paquet *m*; (*of hounds*) meute *f*; (*of thieves etc*) bande *f*; (*back pack*) sac *m* à dos; (*of cards*) jeu *m* ♦ *vt* (*goods*) empaqueter, emballer; (*box*) remplir; (*cram*) entasser; **to** ~ **one's**

suitcase faire sa valise; **to ~ (one's bags)** faire ses bagages; **to ~ sb off** to expédier qn à; **~ it in!** laisse tomber!, écrase!

package ['pækɪdʒ] n paquet m; (also: **~ deal**) forfait m; **~ tour** (BRIT) n voyage organisé

packed lunch ['pækt-] (BRIT) n repas froid

packet ['pækɪt] n paquet m

packing ['pækɪŋ] n emballage m; **~ case** n caisse f (d'emballage)

pact [pækt] n pacte m; traité m

pad [pæd] n bloc(-notes) m; (to prevent friction) tampon m; (inf: home) piaule f ♦ vt rembourrer; **~ding** n rembourrage m

paddle ['pædl] n (oar) pagaie f; (US: for table tennis) raquette f de ping-pong ♦ vt: **to ~ a canoe** etc pagayer ♦ vi barboter, faire trempette; **~ steamer** n bateau m à aubes; **paddling pool** (BRIT) n petit bassin

paddock ['pædək] n enclos m; (RACING) paddock m

paddy field ['pædɪ-] n rizière f

padlock ['pædlɒk] n cadenas m

paediatrics [piːdɪ'ætrɪks] (US **pediatrics**) n pédiatrie f

pagan ['peɪgən] adj, n païen(ne)

page [peɪdʒ] n (of book) page f; (also: **~ boy**) groom m, chasseur m; (at wedding) garçon m d'honneur ♦ vt (in hotel etc) (faire) appeler

pageant ['pædʒənt] n spectacle m historique; **~ry** n apparat m, pompe f

pager, paging device n (TEL) récepteur m d'appels

paid [peɪd] pt, pp of **pay** ♦ adj (work, official) rémunéré(e); (holiday) payé(e); **to put ~ to** (BRIT) mettre fin à, régler; **~ gunman** n tueur m à gages

pail [peɪl] n seau m

pain [peɪn] n douleur f; **to be in ~** souffrir, avoir mal; **to take ~s to do se** donner du mal pour faire; **~ed** adj peiné(e), chagrin(e); **~ful** adj douloureux(euse); (fig) difficile, pénible; **~fully** adv (fig: very) terriblement; **~killer** n analgésique m; **~less** adj indolore

painstaking ['peɪnzteɪkɪŋ] adj (person) soigneux(euse); (work) soigné(e)

paint [peɪnt] n peinture f ♦ vt peindre; **to ~ the door blue** peindre la porte en bleu; **~brush** n pinceau m; **~er** n peintre m; **~ing** n peinture f; (picture) tableau m; **~work** n peinture f

pair [pɛə*] n (of shoes, gloves etc) paire f; (of people) couple m; **~ of scissors** (paire de) ciseaux mpl; **~ of trousers** pantalon m

pajamas [pə'dʒɑːməz] (US) npl pyjama(s) m(pl)

Pakistan [pɑːkɪ'stɑːn] n Pakistan m; **~i** adj pakistanais(e) ♦ n Pakistanais(e)

pal [pæl] (inf) n copain(copine)

palace ['pæləs] n palais m

palatable ['pælətəbl] adj bon(bonne), agréable au goût

palate ['pælɪt] n palais m (ANAT)

pale [peɪl] adj pâle ♦ n: **beyond the ~** (behaviour) inacceptable; **to grow ~** pâlir

Palestine ['pælɪstaɪn] n Palestine f; **Palestinian** adj palestinien(ne) ♦ n Palestinien(ne)

palette ['pælɪt] n palette f

pall [pɔːl] n (of smoke) voile m ♦ vi devenir lassant(e)

pallet ['pælɪt] n (for goods) palette f

pallid ['pælɪd] adj blême

palm [pɑːm] n (of hand) paume f; (also: **~ tree**) palmier m ♦ vt: **to ~ sth off on sb** (inf) refiler qch à qn; **P~ Sunday** n le dimanche des Rameaux

palpable ['pælpəbl] adj évident(e), manifeste

paltry ['pɔːltrɪ] adj dérisoire

pamper ['pæmpə*] vt gâter, dorloter

pamphlet ['pæmflət] n brochure f

pan [pæn] n (also: **sauce~**) casserole f; (: frying ~) poêle f

pancake ['pænkeɪk] n crêpe f

panda ['pændə] n panda m; **~ car** (BRIT) n ≈ voiture f de police

pandemonium [pændɪ'məunɪəm] n tohu-bohu m

pander ['pændə*] vi: **to ~ to** flatter bassement; obéir servilement à

pane [peɪn] n carreau m, vitre f

panel ['pænl] n (of wood, cloth etc) panneau m; (RADIO, TV) experts mpl; (for interview, exams) jury m; **~ling** (US **~ing**) n boiseries fpl

pang [pæŋ] n: **~s of remorse/jealousy** affres mpl du remords/de la jalousie; **~s of hunger/conscience** tiraillements mpl d'estomac/de la conscience

panic ['pænɪk] n panique f, affolement m ♦ vi s'affoler, paniquer; **~ky** adj (person) qui panique or s'affole facilement; **~-stricken** adj affolé(e)

pansy ['pænzɪ] n (BOT) pensée f; (inf: pej) tapette f, pédé m

pant [pænt] vi haleter

panther ['pænθə*] n panthère f

panties ['pæntɪz] npl slip m

pantomime ['pæntəmaɪm] (BRIT) n spectacle m de Noël

pantry ['pæntrɪ] n garde-manger m inv

pants [pænts] npl (BRIT: woman's) slip m; (: man's) slip, caleçon m; (US: trousers) pantalon m

pantyhose ['pæntɪhəuz] (US) npl collant m

paper ['peɪpə*] n papier m; (also: **wall~**) papier peint; (: news~) journal m; (academic essay) article m; (exam) épreuve écrite ♦ adj en or de papier ♦ vt tapisser (de papier peint); **~s** npl (also: identity **~s**) papiers (d'identité); **~back** n livre m de poche; livre broché or non relié; **~ bag** n sac

m en papier; ~ **clip** *n* trombone *m*; ~
hankie *n* mouchoir *m* en papier; ~**weight**
n presse-papiers *m inv*; ~**work** *n* papiers
mpl; (*péj*) paperasserie *f*

par [pɑː*] *n* pair *m*; (GOLF) normale *f* du
parcours; **on a ~ with** à égalité avec, au
même niveau que

parable ['pærəbl] *n* parabole *f* (REL)

parachute ['pærəʃuːt] *n* parachute *m*

parade [pə'reɪd] *n* défilé *m* ♦ *vt* (*fig*) faire
étalage de ♦ *vi* défiler

paradise ['pærədaɪs] *n* paradis *m*

paradox ['pærədɔks] *n* paradoxe *m*; ~**ical-
ly** [pærə'dɔksɪkəlɪ] *adv* paradoxalement

paraffin ['pærəfɪn] (BRIT) *n* (*also*: ~ *oil*) pétrole (lampant)

paragon ['pærəgən] *n* modèle *m*

paragraph ['pærəgrɑːf] *n* paragraphe *m*

parallel ['pærəlel] *adj* parallèle; (*fig*) semblable ♦ *n* (*line*) parallèle *f*; (*fig*, GEO) parallèle *m*

paralyse ['pærəlaɪz] (BRIT) *vt* paralyser

paralysis [pə'ræləsɪs] *n* paralysie *f*

paralyze ['pærəlaɪz] (US) *vt* = **paralyse**

paramount ['pærəmaunt] *adj*: **of ~ importance** de la plus haute *or* grande importance

paranoid ['pærənɔɪd] *adj* (PSYCH) para-
noïaque

paraphernalia ['pærəfə'neɪlɪə] *n* attirail *m*

parasol ['pærəsɔl] *n* ombrelle *f*; (*over table*)
parasol *m*

paratrooper ['pærətruːpə*] *n* parachutiste
m (*soldat*)

parcel ['pɑːsl] *n* paquet *m*, colis *m* ♦ *vt*
(*also*: ~ *up*) empaqueter

parch [pɑːtʃ] *vt* dessécher; ~**ed** *adj* (*person*) assoiffé(e)

parchment ['pɑːtʃmənt] *n* parchemin *m*

pardon ['pɑːdn] *n* pardon *m*; grâce *f* ♦ *vt*
pardonner à; ~ **me!, I beg your ~!** pardon!, je suis désolé!; (**I beg your**) ~?, (US)
~ **me?** pardon?

parent ['pɛərənt] *n* père *m or* mère *f*; ~**s**
npl parents *mpl*

Paris ['pærɪs] *n* Paris

parish ['pærɪʃ] *n* paroisse *f*; (BRIT: *civil*) ≈
commune *f*

Parisian [pə'rɪzɪən] *adj* parisien(ne) ♦ *n* Pa-
risien(ne)

park [pɑːk] *n* parc *m*, jardin public ♦ *vt* garer ♦ *vi* se garer

parking ['pɑːkɪŋ] *n* stationnement *m*; "**no
~**" "stationnement interdit"; ~ **lot** (US) *n*
parking *m*, parc *m* de stationnement; ~
meter *n* parcomètre *m*; ~ **ticket** *n* P.V. *m*

parlance ['pɑːləns] *n* langage *m*

parliament ['pɑːləmənt] *n* parlement *m*;
~**ary** [pɑːlə'mɛntərɪ] *adj* parlementaire

parlour ['pɑːlə*] (US **parlor**) *n* salon *m*

parochial [pə'rəukɪəl] (*péj*) *adj* à l'esprit de
clocher

parody ['pærədɪ] *n* parodie *f*

parole [pə'rəul] *n*: **on ~** en liberté condi-
tionnelle

parrot ['pærət] *n* perroquet *m*

parry ['pærɪ] *vt* (*blow*) esquiver

parsley ['pɑːslɪ] *n* persil *m*

parsnip ['pɑːsnɪp] *n* panais *m*

parson ['pɑːsn] *n* ecclésiastique *m*; (*Church
of England*) pasteur *m*

part [pɑːt] *n* partie *f*; (*of machine*) pièce *f*;
(THEATRE *etc*) rôle *m*; (*of serial*) épisode *m*;
(US: *in hair*) raie *f* ♦ *adv* = **partly** ♦ *vt* séparer ♦ *vi* (*people*) se séparer; (*crowd*) s'ouvrir; **to take ~ in** participer à, prendre part
à; **to take sth in good ~** prendre qch du
bon côté; **to take sb's ~** prendre le parti
de qn, prendre parti pour qn; **for my ~** en
ce qui me concerne; **for the most ~** dans
la plupart des cas; ~ **with** *vt fus* se séparer
de; ~ **exchange** (BRIT) *n*: **in ~ exchange**
en reprise

partial ['pɑːʃəl] *adj* (*not complete*) par-
tiel(le); **to be ~ to** avoir un faible pour

participate [pɑː'tɪsɪpeɪt] *vi*: **to ~ (in)** participer (à), prendre part (à); **participation**
[pɑːtɪsɪ'peɪʃən] *n* participation *f*

participle ['pɑːtɪsɪpl] *n* participe *m*

particle ['pɑːtɪkl] *n* particule *f*

particular [pə'tɪkjulə*] *adj* particulier(ère);
(*special*) spécial(e); (*fussy*) difficile; méti-
culeux(euse); ~**s** *npl* (*details*) détails *mpl*;
(*personal*) nom, adresse *etc*; **in ~** en particulier; ~**ly** *adv* particulièrement

parting ['pɑːtɪŋ] *n* séparation *f*, (BRIT: *in
hair*) raie *f* ♦ *adj* d'adieu

partisan [pɑːtɪ'zæn] *n* partisan(e) ♦ *adj* par-
tisan(e); de parti

partition [pɑː'tɪʃən] *n* (*wall*) cloison *f*;
(POL) partition *f*, division *f*

partly ['pɑːtlɪ] *adv* en partie, partiellement

partner ['pɑːtnə*] *n* partenaire *m/f*; (*in marriage*) conjoint(e); (*boyfriend, girlfriend*)
ami(e); (COMM) associé(e); (*at dance*) cava-
lier(ère); ~**ship** *n* association *f*

partridge ['pɑːtrɪdʒ] *n* perdrix *f*

part-time ['pɑːt'taɪm] *adj*, *adv* à mi-temps,
à temps partiel

party ['pɑːtɪ] *n* (POL) parti *m*; (*group*) groupe *m*; (LAW) partie *f*; (*celebration*) réception
f, soirée *f*; fête *f* ♦ *cpd* (POL) de ou du parti;
~ **dress** *n* robe habillée; ~ **line** *n* (TEL) ligne partagée

pass [pɑːs] *vt* passer; (*place*) passer devant;
(*friend*) croiser; (*overtake*) dépasser; (*exam*)
être reçu(e) à, réussir; (*approve*) approuver,
accepter ♦ *vi* passer; (SCOL) être reçu(e) *or*
admis(e), réussir ♦ *n* (*permit*) laissez-passer
m inv; carte *f* d'accès ou d'abonnement; (*in
mountains*) col *m*; (SPORT) passe *f*; (SCOL:
also: ~ *mark*): **to get a ~** être reçu(e) (sans
mention); **to make a ~ at sb** (*inf*) faire des
avances à qn; ~ **away** *vi* mourir; ~ **by** *vi*

passer ♦ vt négliger; ~ **on** vt *(news, object)* transmettre; *(illness)* passer; ~ **out** vi s'évanouir; ~ **up** vt *(opportunity)* laisser passer; ~**able** *adj (road)* praticable; *(work)* acceptable

passage ['pæsɪdʒ] n *(also: ~way)* couloir m; *(gen, in book)* passage m; *(by boat)* traversée f

passbook ['pɑːsbʊk] n livret m

passenger ['pæsɪndʒə*] n passager(ère)

passer-by ['pɑːsə'baɪ] *(pl* ~**s-by)** n passant(e)

passing ['pɑːsɪŋ] *adj (fig)* passager(ère); **in** ~ en passant

passing place n *(AUT)* aire f de croisement

passion ['pæʃən] n passion f; ~**ate** *adj* passionné(e)

passive ['pæsɪv] *adj (also LING)* passif(ive); ~ **smoking** n tabagisme m passif

Passover ['pɑːsəʊvə*] n Pâque f *(Juive)*

passport ['pɑːspɔːt] n passeport m; ~ **control** n contrôle m des passeports

password ['pɑːswɜːd] n mot m de passe

past [pɑːst] *prep (in front of)* devant; *(further than)* au delà de, plus loin que; après; *(later than)* après ♦ *adj* passé(e); *(president etc)* ancien(ne) ♦ n passé m; **he's** ~ **forty** il a dépassé la quarantaine, il a plus de or passé quarante ans; **for the** ~ **few/3 days** depuis quelques/3 jours; **ces derniers/3 derniers jours**; **ten/quarter** ~ **eight** huit heures dix/un or et quart

pasta ['pæstə] n pâtes fpl

paste [peɪst] n pâte f; *(meat ~)* pâté m (à tartiner); *(tomato ~)* purée f, concentré m; *(glue)* colle f (de pâte) ♦ vt coller

pasteurized ['pæstəraɪzd] *adj* pasteurisé(e)

pastille ['pæstl] n pastille f

pastime ['pɑːstaɪm] n passe-temps m inv

pastry ['peɪstrɪ] n pâte f; *(cake)* pâtisserie f

pasture ['pɑːstʃə*] n pâturage m

pasty [n 'pæstɪ, adj 'peɪstɪ] n petit pâté (en croûte) ♦ *adj (complexion)* terreux(euse)

pat [pæt] vt tapoter; *(dog)* caresser

patch [pætʃ] n *(of material)* pièce f; *(eye ~)* cache m; *(spot)* tache f; *(on tyre)* rustine f ♦ vt *(clothes)* rapiécer; **(to go through) a bad** ~ (passer par) une période difficile; ~ **up** vt réparer (grossièrement); **to** ~ **up a quarrel** se raccommoder; ~**y** *adj* inégal(e); *(incomplete)* fragmentaire

pâté ['pæteɪ] n pâté m, terrine f

patent ['peɪtənt] n brevet m (d'invention) ♦ vt faire breveter ♦ *adj* patent(e), manifeste; ~ **leather** n cuir verni

paternal [pə'tɜːnl] *adj* paternel(le)

path [pɑːθ] n chemin m, sentier m; *(in garden)* allée f; *(trajectory)* trajectoire f

pathetic [pə'θetɪk] *adj (pitiful)* pitoyable; *(very bad)* lamentable, minable

pathological [pæθə'lɒdʒɪkl] *adj* pathologi-

que

pathos ['peɪθɒs] n pathétique m

pathway ['pɑːθweɪ] n sentier m, passage m

patience ['peɪʃəns] n patience f; *(BRIT: CARDS)* réussite f

patient ['peɪʃənt] n patient(e); malade m/f ♦ *adj* patient(e)

patriotic [pætrɪ'ɒtɪk] *adj* patriotique; *(person)* patriote

patrol [pə'trəʊl] n patrouille f ♦ vt patrouiller dans; ~ **car** n voiture f de police; ~**man** *(irreg: US)* n agent m de police

patron ['peɪtrən] n *(in shop)* client(e); *(of charity)* patron(ne); ~ **of the arts** mécène m; ~**ize** vt *(pej)* traiter avec condescendance; *(shop, club)* être (un) client or un habitué de

patter ['pætə*] n crépitement m, tapotement m; *(sales talk)* boniment m

pattern ['pætən] n *(design)* motif m; *(SEWING)* patron m

paunch [pɔːntʃ] n gros ventre, bedaine f

pauper ['pɔːpə*] n indigent(e)

pause [pɔːz] n pause f, arrêt m ♦ vi faire une pause, s'arrêter

pave [peɪv] vt paver, daller; **to** ~ **the way for** ouvrir la voie à; ~**ment** ['peɪvmənt] *(BRIT)* n trottoir m

pavilion [pə'vɪlɪən] n pavillon m; tente f

paving ['peɪvɪŋ] n *(material)* pavé m, dalle f, ~ **stone** n pavé m

paw [pɔː] n patte f

pawn [pɔːn] n *(CHESS, also fig)* pion m ♦ vt mettre en gage; ~**broker** n prêteur m sur gages; ~**shop** n mont-de-piété m

pay [peɪ] *(pt, pp **paid**)* n salaire m; paie f ♦ vt payer ♦ vi payer; *(be profitable)* être rentable; **to** ~ **attention (to)** prêter attention (à); **to** ~ **sb a visit** rendre visite à qn; **to** ~ **one's respects to sb** présenter ses respects à qn; ~ **back** vt rembourser; ~ **for** vt fus payer; ~ **in** vt verser; ~ **off** vt régler, acquitter; *(person)* rembourser ♦ vi *(scheme, decision)* se révéler payant(e); ~ **up** vt *(money)* payer; ~**able** *adj; ~**able to sb** *(cheque)* à l'ordre de qn; ~**ee** [peɪ'iː] n bénéficiaire m/f; ~ **envelope** *(US)* n = **pay packet**; ~**ment** n paiement m; règlement m; **monthly** ~**ment** mensualité f; ~ **packet** *(BRIT)* n paie f; ~ **phone** n cabine f téléphonique, téléphone public; ~**roll** n registre m du personnel; ~ **slip** *(BRIT)* n bulletin m de paie; ~ **television** n chaînes fpl payantes

PC n abbr = **personal computer**

p.c. abbr = **per cent**

pea [piː] n (petit) pois

peace [piːs] n paix f; *(calm)* calme m, tranquillité f; ~**ful** *adj* paisible, calme

peach [piːtʃ] n pêche f

peacock ['piːkɒk] n paon m

peak [piːk] n *(mountain)* pic m, cime f; *(of*

cap) visière f; (*fig: highest level*) maximum m; (: *of career, fame*) apogée m; ~ **hours** npl heures fpl de pointe

peal [pi:l] n (*of bells*) carillon m; ~ **of laughter** éclat m de rire

peanut ['pi:nʌt] n arachide f, cacahuète f

pear [peə*] n poire f

pearl [pɜ:l] n perle f

peasant ['pezənt] n paysan(ne)

peat [pi:t] n tourbe f

pebble ['pebl] n caillou m, galet m

peck [pek] vt (*also*: ~ **at**) donner un coup de bec à ♦ n coup m de bec; (*kiss*) bise f; ~**ing order** n ordre m des préséances; ~**ish** (*BRIT: inf*) adj: **I feel ~ish** je mangerais bien quelque chose

peculiar [pɪ'kju:lɪə*] adj étrange, bizarre, curieux(euse); ~ **to** particulier(ère) à

pedal ['pedl] n pédale f ♦ vi pédaler

pedantic [pɪ'dæntɪk] adj pédant(e)

peddler ['pedlə*] n (*of drugs*) revendeur(euse)

pedestal ['pedɪstl] n piédestal m

pedestrian [pɪ'destrɪən] n piéton m; ~ **crossing** (*BRIT*) n passage clouté

pediatrics [pi:dɪ'ætrɪks] (*US*) n = **paediatrics**

pedigree ['pedɪgri:] n ascendance f; (*of animal*) pedigree m ♦ cpd (*animal*) de race

pee [pi:] (*inf*) vi faire pipi, pisser

peek [pi:k] vi jeter un coup d'œil (furtif)

peel [pi:l] n pelure f, épluchure f; (*of orange, lemon*) écorce f ♦ vt peler, éplucher ♦ vi (*paint etc*) s'écailler; (*wallpaper*) se décoller; (*skin*) peler

peep [pi:p] n (*BRIT: look*) coup d'œil furtif; (*sound*) pépiement m ♦ vi (*BRIT*) jeter un coup d'œil (furtif); ~ **out** (*BRIT*) vi se montrer (furtivement); ~**hole** n judas m

peer [pɪə*] vi: **to ~ at** regarder attentivement, scruter ♦ n (*noble*) pair m; (*equal*) pair, égal(e); ~**age** n pairie f

peeved [pi:vd] adj irrité(e), fâché(e)

peg [peg] n (*for coat etc*) patère f; (*BRIT: also: clothes ~*) pince f à linge

Peking [pi:'kɪŋ] n Pékin; **Pekin(g)ese** [pi:kɪ'ni:z] n (*dog*) pékinois m

pelican ['pelɪkən] n pélican m; ~ **crossing** (*BRIT*) n (*AUT*) feu m à commande manuelle

pellet ['pelɪt] n boulette f; (*of lead*) plomb m

pelt [pelt] vt: **to ~ sb (with)** bombarder qn (de) ♦ vi (*rain*) tomber à seaux; (*inf: run*) courir à toutes jambes ♦ n peau f

pelvis ['pelvɪs] n bassin m

pen [pen] n (*for writing*) stylo m; (*for sheep*) parc m

penal ['pi:nl] adj pénal(e); (*system, colony*) pénitentiaire; ~**ize** vt pénaliser

penalty ['penltɪ] n pénalité f; sanction f; (*fine*) amende f; (*SPORT*) pénalisation f;

(*FOOTBALL*) penalty m; (*RUGBY*) pénalité f

penance ['penəns] n pénitence f

pence [pens] (*BRIT*) npl of **penny**

pencil ['pensl] n crayon m; ~ **case** n trousse f (d'écolier); ~ **sharpener** n taille-crayon(s) m inv

pendant ['pendənt] n pendentif m

pending ['pendɪŋ] prep en attendant ♦ adj en suspens

pendulum ['pendjʊləm] n (*of clock*) balancier m

penetrate ['penɪtreɪt] vt pénétrer dans; pénétrer

penfriend ['penfrend] (*BRIT*) n correspondant(e)

penguin ['peŋgwɪn] n pingouin m

penicillin [penɪ'sɪlɪn] n pénicilline f

peninsula [pɪ'nɪnsjʊlə] n péninsule f

penis ['pi:nɪs] n pénis m, verge f

penitentiary [penɪ'tenʃərɪ] n prison f

penknife ['pennaɪf] n canif m

pen name n nom m de plume, pseudonyme m

penniless ['penɪləs] adj sans le sou

penny ['penɪ] (*pl* **pennies** *or* (*BRIT*) **pence**) n penny m; (*US*) = **cent**

penpal ['penpæl] n correspondant(e)

pension ['penʃən] n pension f; (*from company*) retraite f; ~**er** (*BRIT*) n retraité(e); ~ **fund** n caisse f de retraite

Pentecost ['pentɪkɒst] n Pentecôte f

penthouse ['penthaʊs] n appartement m (de luxe) (en attique)

pent-up ['pentʌp] adj (*feelings*) refoulé(e)

penultimate [pɪ'nʌltɪmɪt] adj avant-dernier(ère)

people ['pi:pl] npl gens mpl; personnes fpl; (*inhabitants*) population f; (*POL*) peuple m ♦ n (*nation, race*) peuple m; **several ~ came** plusieurs personnes sont venues; ~ **say that ...** on dit que ...

pep [pep] (*inf*) n entrain m, dynamisme m; ~ **up** vt remonter

pepper ['pepə*] n poivre m; (*vegetable*) poivron m ♦ vt (*fig*): **to ~ with** bombarder de; ~**mint** n (*sweet*) pastille f de menthe

peptalk ['peptɔ:k] (*inf*) n (petit) discours d'encouragement

per [pɜ:*] prep par; ~ **hour** (*miles etc*) à l'heure; (*fee*) (de) l'heure; ~ **kilo** etc le kilo etc; ~ **annum** adv par an; ~ **capita** adj, adv par personne, par habitant

perceive [pə'si:v] vt percevoir; (*notice*) remarquer, s'apercevoir de

per cent [pə'sent] adv pour cent

percentage [pə'sentɪdʒ] n pourcentage m

perception [pə'sepʃən] n perception f; (*insight*) perspicacité f

perceptive [pə'septɪv] adj pénétrant(e); (*person*) perspicace

perch [pɜ:tʃ] n (*fish*) perche f; (*for bird*) perchoir m ♦ vi: **to ~ on** se percher sur

percolator ['pɜːkəleɪtə*] n cafetière f (électrique)

perennial [pə'renɪəl] adj perpétuel(le); (BOT) vivace

perfect [adj. n 'pɜːfɪkt, vb pə'fekt] adj parfait(e) ♦ n (also: ~ tense) parfait m ♦ vt parfaire; mettre au point; ~**ly** adv parfaitement

perforate ['pɜːfəreɪt] vt perforer, percer; **perforation** [pɜːfə'reɪʃən] n perforation f

perform [pə'fɔːm] vt (carry out) exécuter; (concert etc) jouer, donner ♦ vi jouer; ~**ance** n représentation f, spectacle m; (of an artist) interprétation f; (SPORT) performance f; (of car, engine) fonctionnement m; (of company, economy) résultats mpl; ~**er** n artiste m/f, interprète m/f

perfume ['pɜːfjuːm] n parfum m

perfunctory [pə'fʌŋktərɪ] adj négligent(e), pour la forme

perhaps [pə'hæps] adv peut-être

peril ['perɪl] n péril m

perimeter [pə'rɪmɪtə*] n périmètre m

period ['pɪərɪəd] n période f; (HISTORY) époque f; (SCOL) cours m; (full stop) point m; (MED) règles fpl ♦ adj (costume, furniture) d'époque; ~**ic(al)** [pɪərɪ'ɒdɪk(əl)] adj périodique; ~**ical** n périodique m

peripheral [pə'rɪfərəl] adj périphérique ♦ n (COMPUT) périphérique m

perish ['perɪʃ] vi périr; (decay) se détériorer; ~**able** adj périssable

perjury ['pɜːdʒərɪ] n parjure m, faux serment

perk [pɜːk] n avantage m; accessoire, à-côté m; ~ **up** vi (cheer up) se ragaillardir; ~**y** adj (cheerful) guilleret(te)

perm [pɜːm] n (for hair) permanente f

permanent ['pɜːmənənt] adj permanent(e)

permeate ['pɜːmɪeɪt] vi s'infiltrer ♦ vt s'infiltrer dans; pénétrer

permissible [pə'mɪsəbl] adj permis(e), acceptable

permission [pə'mɪʃən] n permission f, autorisation f

permissive [pə'mɪsɪv] adj tolérant(e), permissif(ive)

permit [n 'pɜːmɪt, vb pə'mɪt] n permis m ♦ vt permettre

perpendicular [pɜːpən'dɪkjulə*] adj perpendiculaire

perplex [pə'pleks] vt (person) rendre perplexe

persecute ['pɜːsɪkjuːt] vt persécuter

persevere [pɜːsɪ'vɪə*] vi persévérer

Persian ['pɜːʃən] adj persan(e) ♦ n (LING) persan m; **the** ~ **Gulf** le golfe Persique

persist [pə'sɪst] vi: **to** ~ (**in doing**) persister or s'obstiner (à faire); ~**ent** adj persistant(e), tenace

person ['pɜːsn] n personne f; **in** ~ en personne; ~**al** adj personnel(le); ~**al assis-**

tant n secrétaire privé(e); ~**al call** n communication privée; ~**al column** n annonces personnelles; ~**al computer** n ordinateur personnel; ~**ality** [pɜːsə'nælɪtɪ] n personnalité f; ~**ally** adv personnellement; **to take sth** ~**ally** se sentir visé(e) (par qch); ~**al organizer** n filofax m (®); ~**al stereo** n balladeur m

personnel [pɜːsə'nel] n personnel m

perspective [pə'spektɪv] n perspective f; **to get things into** ~ faire la part des choses

Perspex ['pɜːspeks] (®) n plexiglas m (®)

perspiration [pɜːspə'reɪʃən] n transpiration f

persuade [pə'sweɪd] vt: **to** ~ **sb to do sth** persuader qn de faire qch

persuasion [pə'sweɪʒən] n persuasion f; (creed) religion f

pertaining [pɜː'teɪnɪŋ] : ~ **to** prep relatif(ive) à

peruse [pə'ruːz] vt lire (attentivement)

pervade [pɜː'veɪd] vt se répandre dans, envahir

perverse [pə'vɜːs] adj pervers(e); (contrary) contrariant(e); **pervert** [n 'pɜːvɜːt, vb pə'vɜːt] n perverti(e) ♦ vt pervertir; (words) déformer

pessimist ['pesɪmɪst] n pessimiste m/f; ~**ic** [pesɪ'mɪstɪk] adj pessimiste

pest [pest] n animal m (or insecte m) nuisible; (fig) fléau m

pester ['pestə*] vt importuner, harceler

pet [pet] n animal familier ♦ cpd (favourite) favori(te) ♦ vt (stroke) caresser, câliner ♦ vi (inf) se peloter; **teacher's** ~ chouchou m du professeur; ~ **hate** bête noire

petal ['petl] n pétale m

peter out ['piːtə-] vi (stream, conversation) tarir; (meeting) tourner court; (road) se perdre

petite [pə'tiːt] adj menu(e)

petition [pə'tɪʃən] n pétition f

petrified ['petrɪfaɪd] adj (fig) mort(e) de peur

petrol ['petrəl] (BRIT) n essence f; **two-star** ~ essence f ordinaire; **four-star** ~ super m; ~ **can** n bidon m à essence

petroleum [pɪ'trəuliəm] n pétrole m

petrol: ~ **pump** (BRIT) n pompe f à essence; ~ **station** (BRIT) n station-service f; ~ **tank** (BRIT) n réservoir m (d'essence)

petticoat ['petɪkəut] n combinaison f

petty ['petɪ] adj (mean) mesquin(e); (unimportant) insignifiant(e), sans importance; ~ **cash** n caisse f des dépenses courantes; ~ **officer** n second-maître m

petulant ['petjulənt] adj boudeur(euse), irritable

pew [pjuː] n banc m d'église

pewter ['pjuːtə*] n étain m

phantom ['fæntəm] n fantôme m

pharmacy ['fɑːməsɪ] n pharmacie f

phase [feɪz] n phase f ♦ vt: **to ~ sth in/out** introduire/supprimer qch progressivement

PhD abbr = **Doctor of Philosophy** n (title) ≈ docteur m (en droit or lettres etc) ≈ doctorat m; titulaire m/f d'un doctorat

pheasant ['feznt] n faisan m

phenomenon [fɪ'nɒmɪnən] (pl **phenomena**) n phénomène m

philosophical [fɪlə'sɒfɪkl] adj philosophique

philosophy [fɪ'lɒsəfɪ] n philosophie f

phobia ['fəʊbjə] n phobie f

phone [fəʊn] n téléphone m ♦ vt téléphoner; **to be on the ~** avoir le téléphone; (be calling) être au téléphone; **~ back** vt, vi rappeler; **~ up** vt téléphoner à ♦ vi téléphoner; **~ book** n annuaire m; **~ booth** n = **phone box**; **box** (BRIT) n cabine f téléphonique; **~ call** n coup m de fil or de téléphone; **~card** n carte f de téléphone; **~-in** (BRIT) n (RADIO, TV) programme m à ligne ouverte

phonetics [fə'netɪks] n phonétique f

phoney ['fəʊnɪ] adj faux(fausse), factice; (person) pas franc(he), poseur(euse)

photo ['fəʊtəʊ] n photo f

photo...: **~copier** [-'kɒpɪə*] n photocopieuse f; **~copy** [-kɒpɪ] n photocopie f ♦ vt photocopier; **~graph** [-grɑːf] n photographie f ♦ vt photographier; **~grapher** [-grəfə*] n photographe m/f; **~graphy** [-grəfɪ] n photographie f

phrase [freɪz] n expression f; (LING) locution f ♦ vt exprimer; **~ book** n recueil m d'expressions (pour touristes)

physical ['fɪzɪkəl] adj physique; **~ education** n éducation f physique; **~ly** adv physiquement

physician [fɪ'zɪʃən] n médecin m

physicist ['fɪzɪsɪst] n physicien(ne)

physics ['fɪzɪks] n physique f

physiotherapy [fɪzɪə'θerəpɪ] n kinésithérapie f

physique [fɪ'ziːk] n physique m; constitution f

pianist ['pɪənɪst] n pianiste m/f

piano [pɪ'ænəʊ] n piano m

pick [pɪk] n (tool: also: ~axe) pic m, pioche f ♦ vt choisir; (fruit etc) cueillir; (remove) prendre; (lock) forcer; **take your ~** faites votre choix; **the ~ of** le(la) meilleur(e) de; **to ~ one's nose** se mettre les doigts dans le nez; **to ~ one's teeth** se curer les dents; **to ~ a quarrel with sb** chercher noise à qn; **~ at** vt fus: **to ~ at one's food** manger du bout des dents, chipoter; **~ on** vt fus (person) harceler; **~ out** vt choisir; (distinguish) distinguer; **~ up** vi (improve) s'améliorer ♦ vt ramasser; (collect) passer prendre; (AUT: give lift to) prendre, emmener; (learn) apprendre; (RADIO) capter; **to ~ up speed** prendre de la vitesse; **to ~**

o.s. up se relever

picket ['pɪkɪt] n (in strike) piquet m de grève ♦ vt mettre un piquet de grève devant

pickle ['pɪkl] n (also: ~s: as condiment) pickles mpl, petits légumes macérés dans du vinaigre ♦ vt conserver dans du vinaigre or dans de la saumure; **to be in a ~** (mess) être dans le pétrin

pickpocket ['pɪkpɒkɪt] n pickpocket m

pick-up ['pɪkʌp] n (small truck) pick-up m inv

picnic ['pɪknɪk] n pique-nique m

picture ['pɪktʃə*] n image f; (painting) peinture f, tableau m; (etching) gravure f; (photograph) photo(graphie) f; (drawing) dessin m; (film) film m; (fig) description f, tableau m ♦ vt se représenter; **the ~s** (BRIT: inf) le cinéma; **~ book** n livre m d'images

picturesque [pɪktʃə'resk] adj pittoresque

pie [paɪ] n tourte f; (of fruit) tarte f; (of meat) pâté m en croûte

piece [piːs] n morceau m; (item): **a ~ of furniture/advice** un meuble/conseil ♦ vt: **to ~ together** rassembler; **to take to ~s** démonter; **~meal** adv (irregularly) au coup par coup; (bit by bit) par bouts; **~work** n travail m aux pièces

pie chart n graphique m circulaire, camembert m

pier [pɪə*] n jetée f

pierce [pɪəs] vt percer, transpercer

pig [pɪg] n cochon m, porc m

pigeon ['pɪdʒən] n pigeon m; **~hole** n casier m

piggy bank ['pɪgɪ-] n tirelire f

pig: **~headed** [-'hedɪd] adj entêté(e), têtu(e); **~let** n porcelet m, petit cochon; **~skin** [-skɪn] n peau m de porc; **~sty** [-staɪ] n porcherie f; **~tail** [-teɪl] n natte f, tresse f

pike [paɪk] n (fish) brochet m

pilchard ['pɪltʃəd] n pilchard m (sorte de sardine)

pile [paɪl] n (pillar, of books) pile f; (heap) tas m; (of carpet) poils mpl ♦ vt (also: ~ up) empiler, entasser ♦ vi (also: ~up) s'entasser, s'accumuler; **to ~ into** (car) s'entasser dans

piles [paɪlz] npl hémorroïdes fpl

pile-up ['paɪlʌp] n (AUT) télescopage m, collision f en série

pilfering ['pɪlfərɪŋ] n chapardage m

pilgrim ['pɪlgrɪm] n pèlerin m

pill [pɪl] n pilule f

pillage ['pɪlɪdʒ] vt piller

pillar ['pɪlə*] n pilier m; **~ box** (BRIT) n boîte f aux lettres

pillion ['pɪljən] n: **to ride ~** (on motorcycle) monter derrière

pillow ['pɪləʊ] n oreiller m; **~case** n taie f d'oreiller

pilot ['paɪlət] n pilote m ♦ cpd (scheme etc)

pilote, expérimental(e) ♦ vt piloter; ~ **light** n veilleuse f

pimp [pɪmp] n souteneur m, maquereau m

pimple ['pɪmpl] n bouton m

pin [pɪn] n épingle f; (TECH) cheville f ♦ vt épingler; ~**s and needles** fourmis fpl; **to ~ sb down** (fig) obliger qn à répondre; **to ~ sth on sb** (fig) mettre qch sur le dos de qn

pinafore ['pɪnəfɔ:*] n tablier m

pinball ['pɪnbɔ:l] n flipper m

pincers ['pɪnsəz] npl tenailles fpl; (of crab etc) pinces fpl

pinch [pɪntʃ] n (of salt etc) pincée f ♦ vt pincer; (inf: steal) piquer, chiper; **at a ~** à la rigueur

pincushion ['pɪnkuʃən] n pelote f à épingles

pine [paɪn] n (also: ~ tree) pin m ♦ vi: **to ~ for** s'ennuyer de, désirer ardemment; ~ **away** vi dépérir

pineapple ['paɪnæpl] n ananas m

ping [pɪŋ] n (noise) tintement m; ~**-pong** (®) n ping-pong m (®)

pink [pɪŋk] adj rose ♦ n (colour) rose m; (BOT) œillet m, mignardise f

PIN (number) n code m confidentiel

pinpoint ['pɪnpɔɪnt] vt indiquer or localiser (avec précision); (problem) mettre le doigt sur

pint [paɪnt] n pinte f (BRIT = 0.57l; US = 0.47l); (BRIT: inf) ≈ demi m

pioneer [paɪə'nɪə*] n pionnier m

pious ['paɪəs] adj pieux(euse)

pip [pɪp] n (seed) pépin m; **the ~s** npl (BRIT: time signal on radio) le(s) top(s) sonore(s)

pipe [paɪp] n tuyau m, conduite f; (for smoking) pipe f ♦ vt amener par tuyau; ~**s** npl (also: bag~s) cornemuse f; ~ **down** (inf) vi se taire; ~ **cleaner** n cure-pipe m; ~ **dream** n chimère f, château m en Espagne; ~**line** n pipe-line m; ~**r** n joueur(euse) de cornemuse

piping ['paɪpɪŋ] adv: ~ **hot** très chaud(e)

pique [pi:k] n dépit m

pirate ['paɪərɪt] n pirate m

Pisces ['paɪsi:z] n les Poissons mpl

piss [pɪs] (inf!) vi pisser; ~**ed** (inf!) adj (drunk) bourré(e)

pistol ['pɪstl] n pistolet m

piston ['pɪstən] n piston m

pit [pɪt] n trou m, fosse f; (also: coal ~) puits m de mine; (quarry) carrière f ♦ vt: **to ~ one's wits against sb** se mesurer à qn; ~**s** npl (AUT) aire f de service

pitch [pɪtʃ] n (MUS) ton m; (BRIT: SPORT) terrain m; (tar) poix f; (fig) degré m; point m ♦ vt (throw) lancer ♦ vi (fall) tomber; **to ~ a tent** dresser une tente; ~**-black** adj noir(e) (comme du cirage); ~**ed battle** n bataille rangée

piteous ['pɪtɪəs] adj pitoyable

pitfall ['pɪtfɔ:l] n piège m

pith [pɪθ] n (of orange etc) intérieur m de l'écorce

pithy ['pɪθɪ] adj piquant(e)

pitiful ['pɪtɪful] adj (touching) pitoyable

pitiless ['pɪtɪləs] adj impitoyable

pittance ['pɪtəns] n salaire m de misère

pity ['pɪtɪ] n pitié f ♦ vt plaindre; **what a ~!** quel dommage!

pizza ['pi:tsə] n pizza f

placard ['plækɑ:d] n affiche f, (in march) pancarte f

placate [plə'keɪt] vt apaiser, calmer

place [pleɪs] n endroit m, lieu m; (proper position, job, rank, seat) place f; (home): **at/to his ~** chez lui ♦ vt (object) placer, mettre; (identify) situer; reconnaître; **to take ~** avoir lieu; **out of ~** (not suitable) déplacé(e), inopportun(e); **to change ~s with sb** changer de place avec qn; **in the first ~** d'abord, en premier

plague [pleɪg] n fléau m; (MED) peste f ♦ vt (fig) tourmenter

plaice [pleɪs] n inv carrelet m

plaid [plæd] n tissu écossais

plain [pleɪn] adj (in one colour) uni(e); (simple) simple; (clear) clair(e), évident(e); (not handsome) quelconque, ordinaire ♦ adv franchement, carrément ♦ n plaine f; ~ **chocolate** n chocolat m à croquer; ~ **clothes** adj (police officer) en civil; ~**ly** adv clairement; (frankly) carrément, sans détours

plaintiff ['pleɪntɪf] n plaignant(e)

plait [plæt] n tresse f, natte f

plan [plæn] n plan m; (scheme) projet m ♦ vt (think in advance) projeter; (prepare) organiser; (house) dresser les plans de, concevoir ♦ vi faire des projets; **to ~ to do** prévoir de faire

plane [pleɪn] n (AVIAT) avion m; (ART, MATH etc) plan m; (fig) niveau m, plan; (tool) rabot m; (also: ~ tree) platane m ♦ vt raboter

planet ['plænɪt] n planète f

plank [plæŋk] n planche f

planner ['plænə*] n planificateur(trice); (town) urbaniste m/f

planning ['plænɪŋ] n planification f; **family ~ planning** familial; ~ **permission** n permis m de construire

plant [plɑ:nt] n plante f; (machinery) matériel m; (factory) usine f ♦ vt planter; (bomb) poser; (microphone, incriminating evidence) cacher

plaster ['plɑ:stə*] n plâtre m; (also: ~ of Paris) plâtre à mouler; (BRIT: also: sticking ~) pansement adhésif ♦ vt plâtrer; (cover): **to ~ with** couvrir de; ~**ed** (inf) adj soûl(e)

plastic ['plæstɪk] n plastique m ♦ adj (made of ~) en plastique; ~ **bag** n sac m en plastique

Plasticine ['plæstɪsiːn] (®) *n* pâte *f* à modeler

plastic surgery *n* chirurgie *f* esthétique

plate [pleɪt] *n* (*dish*) assiette *f*; (*in book*) gravure *f*, planche *f*; (*dental ~*) dentier *m*

plateau ['plætəʊ] (*pl* **~s** *or* **~x**) *n* plateau *m*

plate glass *n* verre *m* (de vitrine)

platform ['plætfɔːm] *n* plate-forme *f*; (*at meeting*) tribune *f*; (*stage*) estrade *f*; (*RAIL*) quai *m*

platinum ['plætɪnəm] *n* platine *m*

platter ['plætə*] *n* plat *m*

plausible ['plɔːzɪbl] *adj* plausible; (*person*) convaincant(e)

play [pleɪ] *n* (*THEATRE*) pièce *f* (de théâtre) ♦ *vt* (*game*) jouer à; (*team, opponent*) jouer contre; (*instrument*) jouer de; (*part, piece of music, note*) jouer; (*record etc*) passer ♦ *vi* jouer; **to ~ safe** ne prendre aucun risque; **~ down** *vt* minimiser; **~ up** *vi* (*cause trouble*) faire des siennes; **~boy** *n* playboy *m*; **~er** *n* joueur(euse); (*THEATRE*) acteur(trice); (*MUS*) musicien(ne); **~ful** *adj* enjoué(e); **~ground** *n* cour *f* de récréation; (*in park*) aire *f* de jeux; **~group** *n* garderie *f*; **~ing card** *n* carte *f* à jouer; **~ing field** *n* terrain *m* de sport; **~mate** *n* camarade *m/f*, copain(copine); **~-off** *n* (*SPORT*) belle *f*; **~pen** *n* parc *m* (pour bébé); **~thing** *n* jouet *m*; **~time** *n* récréation *f*; **~wright** *n* dramaturge *m*

plc *abbr* (= *public limited company*) ≈ SARL *f*

plea [pliː] *n* (*request*) appel *m*; (*LAW*) défense *f*

plead [pliːd] *vt* plaider; (*give as excuse*) invoquer ♦ *vi* (*LAW*) plaider; (*beg*): **to ~ with sb** implorer qn

pleasant ['plɛznt] *adj* agréable; **~ries** *npl* (*polite remarks*) civilités *fpl*

please [pliːz] *excl* s'il te (*or* vous) plaît ♦ *vt* plaire à ♦ *vi* plaire; (*think fit*): **do as you ~** faites comme il vous plaira; **~ yourself!** à ta (*or* votre) guise!; **~d** *adj*: **~d (with)** content(e) (de); **~d to meet you** enchanté (de faire votre connaissance); **pleasing** ['pliːzɪŋ] *adj* plaisant(e), qui fait plaisir

pleasure ['plɛʒə*] *n* plaisir *m*; "**it's a ~**" "je vous en prie"; **~ boat** *n* bateau *m* de plaisance

pleat [pliːt] *n* pli *m*

pledge [plɛdʒ] *n* (*promise*) promesse *f* ♦ *vt* engager; promettre

plentiful ['plɛntɪful] *adj* abondant(e), copieux(euse)

plenty ['plɛntɪ] *n*: **~ of** beaucoup de; (*bien*) assez de

pliable ['plaɪəbl] *adj* flexible; (*person*) malléable

pliers ['plaɪəz] *npl* pinces *fpl*

plight [plaɪt] *n* situation *f* critique

plimsolls ['plɪmsəlz] (*BRIT*) *npl* chaussures *fpl* de tennis, tennis *mpl*

plinth [plɪnθ] *n* (*of statue*) socle *m*

PLO *n abbr* (= *Palestine Liberation Organization*) OLP *f*

plod [plɒd] *vi* avancer péniblement; (*fig*) peiner

plonk [plɒŋk] (*inf*) *n* (*BRIT: wine*) pinard *m*, piquette *f* ♦ *vt*: **to ~ sth down** poser brusquement qch

plot [plɒt] *n* complot *m*, conspiration *f*; (*of story, play*) intrigue *f*; (*of land*) lot *m* de terrain, lopin *m* ♦ *vt* (*sb's downfall*) comploter; (*mark out*) pointer; relever, déterminer ♦ *vi* comploter

plough [plaʊ] (*US* **plow**) *n* charrue *f* ♦ *vt* (*earth*) labourer; **to ~ money into** investir dans; **~ through** *vt fus* (*snow etc*) avancer péniblement dans; **~man's lunch** (*BRIT*) *n* assiette froide avec du pain, du fromage et des pickles

ploy [plɔɪ] *n* stratagème *m*

pluck [plʌk] *vt* (*fruit*) cueillir; (*musical instrument*) pincer; (*bird*) plumer; (*eyebrow*) épiler ♦ *n* courage *m*, cran *m*; **to ~ up courage** prendre son courage à deux mains

plug [plʌg] *n* (*ELEC*) prise *f* de courant; (*stopper*) bouchon *m*, bonde *f*; (*AUT: also: spark(ing) ~*) bougie *f* ♦ *vt* (*hole*) boucher; (*inf: advertise*) faire du battage pour; **~ in** *vt* (*ELEC*) brancher

plum [plʌm] *n* (*fruit*) prune *f* ♦ *cpd*: **~ job** (*inf*) travail *m* en or

plumb [plʌm] *vt*: **to ~ the depths** (*fig*) toucher le fond (du désespoir)

plumber ['plʌmə*] *n* plombier *m*

plumbing ['plʌmɪŋ] *n* (*trade*) plomberie *f*; (*piping*) tuyauterie *f*

plummet ['plʌmɪt] *vi*: **to ~ (down)** plonger, dégringoler

plump [plʌmp] *adj* rondelet(te), dodu(e), bien en chair ♦ *vi*: **to ~ for** (*col: choose*) se décider pour

plunder ['plʌndə*] *n* pillage *m* (*loot*) butin *m* ♦ *vt* piller

plunge [plʌndʒ] *n* plongeon *m*; (*fig*) chute *f* ♦ *vt* plonger ♦ *vi* (*dive*) plonger (*fall*) tomber, dégringoler; **to take the ~** se jeter à l'eau; **~r** *n* (*for drain*) (débouchoir *m* à) ventouse *f*; **plunging** *adj*: **plunging neckline** décolleté plongeant

pluperfect [pluː'pɜːfɪkt] *n* plus-que-parfait *m*

plural ['plʊərəl] *adj* pluriel(le) ♦ *n* pluriel *m*

plus [plʌs] *n* (*also: ~ sign*) signe *m* plus ♦ *prep* plus; **ten/twenty ~** plus de dix/vingt

plush [plʌʃ] *adj* somptueux(euse)

ply [plaɪ] *vt* (*a trade*) exercer ♦ *vi* (*ship*) faire la navette ♦ *n* (*of wool, rope*) fil *m*, brin *m*; **to ~ sb with drink** donner continuellement à boire à qn; **to ~ sb with questions** presser qn de questions; **~wood** *n* contre-plaqué *m*

PM *abbr* = Prime Minister

p.m. *adv abbr* (= *post meridiem*) de l'après-midi

pneumatic drill [nju:'mætɪk-] *n* marteau-piqueur *m*

pneumonia [nju:'məʊnɪə] *n* pneumonie *f*

poach [pəʊtʃ] *vt* (*cook*) pocher; (*steal*) pêcher (*or* chasser) sans permis ♦ *vi* braconner; **~ed egg** *n* œuf poché; **~er** *n* braconnier *m*

P.O. Box *n abbr* = Post Office Box

pocket ['pɒkɪt] *n* poche *f* ♦ *vt* empocher; **to be out of ~** (*BRIT*) en être de sa poche; **~book** (*US*) *n* (*wallet*) portefeuille *m*; **~ knife** *n* canif *m*; **~ money** *n* argent *m* de poche

pod [pɒd] *n* cosse *f*

podgy ['pɒdʒɪ] *adj* rondelet(te)

podiatrist [pɒ'di:ətrɪst] (*US*) *n* pédicure *m/f*, podologue *m/f*

poem ['pəʊəm] *n* poème *m*

poet ['pəʊɪt] *n* poète *m*; **~ic** *adj* poétique; **~ laureate** *n* poète lauréat (*nommé par la Cour royal*); **~ry** *n* poésie *f*

poignant ['pɔɪnjənt] *adj* poignant(e); (*sharp*) vif(vive)

point [pɔɪnt] *n* point *m*; (*tip*) pointe *f*; (*in time*) moment *m*; (*in space*) endroit *m*; (*subject, idea*) point, sujet *m*; (*purpose*) sens *m*; (*ELEC*) prise *f*; (*also: decimal ~*): **2 → 3 (2.3)** 2 virgule 3 (2,3) ♦ *vt* (*show*) indiquer; (*gun etc*): **to ~ sth at** braquer *or* diriger qch sur ♦ *vi*: **to ~ at** montrer du doigt; **~s** *npl* (*AUT*) vis platinées; (*RAIL*) aiguillage *m*; **to be on the ~ of doing sth** être sur le point de faire qch; **to make a ~ of doing** ne pas manquer de faire; **to get the ~** comprendre, saisir; **to miss the ~** ne pas comprendre; **to come to the ~** en venir au fait; **there's no ~ (in doing)** cela ne sert à rien (de faire); **~ out** *vt* faire remarquer, souligner; **~ to** *vt fus* (*fig*) indiquer; **~-blank** *adv* (*fig*) catégoriquement; (*also: at ~-blank range*) à bout portant; **~ed** *adj* (*shape*) pointu(e); (*remark*) plein(e) de sous-entendus; **~er** *n* (*needle*) aiguille *f*; (*piece of advice*) conseil *m*; (*clue*) indice *m*; **~less** *adj* inutile, vain(e); **~ of view** *n* point *m* de vue

poise [pɔɪz] *n* (*composure*) calme *m*

poison ['pɔɪzn] *n* poison *m* ♦ *vt* empoisonner; **~ous** *adj* (*snake*) venimeux(euse); (*plant*) vénéneux(euse); (*fumes etc*) toxique

poke [pəʊk] *vt* (*fire*) tisonner; (*jab with finger, stick etc*) piquer; pousser du doigt; (*put*): **to ~ sth in(to)** fourrer *or* enfoncer qch dans; **~ about** *vi* fureter

poker ['pəʊkə*] *n* tisonnier *m*; (*CARDS*) poker *m*

poky ['pəʊkɪ] *adj* exigu(ë)

Poland ['pəʊlənd] *n* Pologne *f*

polar ['pəʊlə*] *adj* polaire; **~ bear** *n* ours blanc

Pole [pəʊl] *n* Polonais(e)

pole [pəʊl] *n* poteau *m*; (*of wood*) mât *m*, perche *f*; (*GEO*) pôle *m*; **~ bean** (*US*) *n* haricot *m* (à rames); **~ vault** *n* saut *m* à la perche

police [pə'li:s] *npl* police *f* ♦ *vt* maintenir l'ordre dans; **~ car** *n* voiture *f* de police; **~man** (*irreg*) *n* agent *m* de police, policier *m*; **~ station** *n* commissariat *m* de police; **~woman** (*irreg*) *n* femme-agent *f*

policy ['pɒlɪsɪ] *n* politique *f*; (*also: insurance ~*) police *f* (d'assurance)

polio ['pəʊlɪəʊ] *n* polio *f*

Polish ['pəʊlɪʃ] *adj* polonais(e) ♦ *n* (*LING*) polonais *m*

polish ['pɒlɪʃ] *n* (*for shoes*) cirage *m*; (*for floor*) cire *f*, encaustique *f*; (*shine*) éclat *m*, poli *m*; (*fig: refinement*) raffinement *m* ♦ *vt* (*put polish on shoes, wood*) cirer; (*make shiny*) astiquer, faire briller; **~ off** *vt* (*work*) expédier; (*food*) liquider; **~ed** *adj* (*fig*) raffiné(e)

polite [pə'laɪt] *adj* poli(e); **in ~ society** dans la bonne société; **~ness** *n* politesse *f*

political [pə'lɪtɪkəl] *adj* politique

politician [pɒlɪ'tɪʃən] *n* homme *m* politique, politicien *m*

politics ['pɒlɪtɪks] *npl* politique *f*

poll [pəʊl] *n* scrutin *m*, vote *m*; (*also: opinion ~*) sondage *m* (d'opinion) ♦ *vt* obtenir

pollen ['pɒlən] *n* pollen *m*

polling day ['pəʊlɪŋ-] (*BRIT*) *n* jour *m* des élections

polling station (*BRIT*) *n* bureau *m* de vote

pollute [pə'lu:t] *vt* polluer; **pollution** *n* pollution *f*

polo ['pəʊləʊ] *n* polo *m*; **~-necked** *adj* à col roulé; **~ shirt** *n* polo *m*

poltergeist ['pɒltəgaɪst] *n* esprit frappeur

polyester [pɒlɪ'estə*] *n* polyester *m*

polytechnic [pɒlɪ'teknɪk] (*BRIT*) *n* (*college*) I.U.T. *m*, Institut *m* Universitaire de Technologie

polythene ['pɒlɪθi:n] *n* polyéthylène *m*; **~ bag** *n* sac *m* en plastique

pomegranate ['pɒməgrænɪt] *n* grenade *f*

pomp [pɒmp] *n* pompe *f*, faste *f*, apparat *m*; **~ous** ['pɒmpəs] *adj* pompeux(euse)

pond [pɒnd] *n* étang *m*; mare *f*

ponder ['pɒndə*] *vt* considérer, peser; **~ous** *adj* pesant(e), lourd(e)

pong [pɒŋ] (*BRIT: inf*) *n* puanteur *f*

pony ['pəʊnɪ] *n* poney *m*; **~tail** *n* queue *f* de cheval; **~ trekking** (*BRIT*) *n* randonnée *f* à cheval

poodle ['pu:dl] *n* caniche *m*

pool [pu:l] *n* (*of rain*) flaque *f*; (*pond*) mare *f*; (*also: swimming ~*) piscine *f*; (*billiards*) poule *f* ♦ *vt* mettre en commun; **~s** *npl* (*football pools*) ≈ loto sportif

poor [pʊə*] *adj* pauvre; (*mediocre*) médiocre, faible, mauvais(e) ♦ *npl*: **the** ~ les pauvres *mpl*; ~**ly** *adj* souffrant(e), malade ♦ *adv* mal; médiocrement

pop [pɒp] *n* (*MUS*) musique *f* pop; (*drink*) boisson gazeuse; (*US: inf: father*) papa *m*; (*noise*) bruit sec ♦ *vt* (*put*) mettre (rapidement) ♦ *vi* éclater; (*cork*) sauter; ~ **in** *vi* entrer en passant; ~ **out** *vi* sortir (brièvement); ~ **up** *vi* apparaître, surgir

pope [pəʊp] *n* pape *m*

poplar ['pɒplə*] *n* peuplier *m*

popper ['pɒpə*] (*BRIT*: *inf*) *n* bouton-pression *m*

poppy ['pɒpɪ] *n* coquelicot *m*; pavot *m*

Popsicle ['pɒpsɪkl] (®: *US*) *n* esquimau *m* (*glace*)

popular ['pɒpjʊlə*] *adj* populaire; (*fashionable*) à la mode

population [pɒpjʊ'leɪʃən] *n* population *f*

porcelain ['pɔːslɪn] *n* porcelaine *f*

porch [pɔːtʃ] *n* porche *m*; (*US*) véranda *f*

porcupine ['pɔːkjʊpaɪn] *n* porc-épic *m*

pore [pɔː*] *n* pore *m* ♦ *vi*: **to** ~ **over** s'absorber dans, être plongé(e) dans

pork [pɔːk] *n* porc *m*

pornography [pɔː'nɒɡrəfɪ] *n* pornographie *f*

porpoise ['pɔːpəs] *n* marsouin *m*

porridge ['pɒrɪdʒ] *n* porridge *m*

port [pɔːt] *n* (*harbour*) port *m*; (*NAUT: left side*) bâbord *m*; (*wine*) porto *m*; ~ **of call** escale *f*

portable ['pɔːtəbl] *adj* portatif(ive)

porter ['pɔːtə*] *n* (*for luggage*) porteur *m*; (*doorkeeper*) gardien/ne; portier *m*

portfolio [pɔːt'fəʊlɪəʊ] *n* portefeuille *m*; (*of artist*) portfolio *m*

porthole ['pɔːthəʊl] *n* hublot *m*

portion ['pɔːʃən] *n* portion *f*, part *f*

portly ['pɔːtlɪ] *adj* corpulent(e)

portrait ['pɔːtrɪt] *n* portrait *m*

portray [pɔː'treɪ] *vt* faire le portrait de; (*in writing*) dépeindre, représenter; (*subj: actor*) jouer; ~**al** *n* portrait *m*, représentation *f*

Portugal ['pɔːtjʊɡəl] *n* Portugal *m*

Portuguese [pɔːtjʊ'ɡiːz] *adj* portugais(e) ♦ *n inv* Portugais(e); (*LING*) portugais *m*

pose [pəʊz] *n* pose *f* ♦ *vi* (*pretend*): **to** ~ **as** se poser en ♦ *vt* poser; (*problem*) créer

posh [pɒʃ] (*inf*) *adj* chic *inv*

position [pə'zɪʃən] *n* position *f*; (*job*) situation *f* ♦ *vt* placer

positive ['pɒzɪtɪv] *adj* positif(ive); (*certain*) sûr(e), certain(e); (*definite*) formel(le), catégorique

posse ['pɒsɪ] (*US*) *n* détachement *m*

possess [pə'zes] *vt* posséder; ~**ion** [pə'zeʃən] *n* possession *f*

possibility [pɒsə'bɪlɪtɪ] *n* possibilité *f*, éventualité *f*

possible ['pɒsəbl] *adj* possible; **as big as** ~ aussi gros que possible

possibly ['pɒsəblɪ] *adv* (*perhaps*) peut-être; **if you** ~ **can** si cela vous est possible; **I cannot** ~ **come** il m'est impossible de venir

post [pəʊst] *n* poste *f*; (*BRIT: letters, delivery*) courrier *m*; (*job, situation, MIL*) poste *m*; (*pole*) poteau *m* ♦ *vt* (*BRIT: send by* ~) poster; (: *appoint*): **to** ~ **to** affecter à; ~**age** *n* tarifs *mpl* d'affranchissement; ~**al order** *n* mandat(-poste) *m*; ~**box** (*BRIT*) *n* boîte *f* aux lettres; ~**card** *n* carte postale; ~**code** (*BRIT*) *n* code postal

poster ['pəʊstə*] *n* affiche *f*

poste restante ['pəʊst'restɑ̃ːnt] (*BRIT*) *n* poste restante

postgraduate ['pəʊst'ɡrædjʊɪt] *n* ≈ étudiant(e) de troisième cycle

posthumous ['pɒstjʊməs] *adj* posthume

postman ['pəʊstmən] (*irreg*) *n* facteur *m*

postmark ['pəʊstmɑːk] *n* cachet *m* (de la poste)

postmortem ['pəʊst'mɔːtəm] *n* autopsie *f*

post office *n* (*building*) poste *f*; (*organization*): **the Post Office** les Postes; **Post Office Box** *n* boîte postale

postpone [pə'spəʊn] *vt* remettre (à plus tard)

posture ['pɒstʃə*] *n* posture *f*; (*fig*) attitude *f*

postwar ['pəʊst'wɔː*] *adj* d'après-guerre

posy ['pəʊzɪ] *n* petit bouquet

pot [pɒt] *n* pot *m*; (*for cooking*) marmite *f*, casserole *f*; (*tea*~) théière *f*; (*coffee*~) cafetière *f*; (*inf: marijuana*) herbe *f* ♦ *vt* (*plant*) mettre en pot; **to go to** ~ (*inf: work, performance*) aller à vau-l'eau

potato [pə'teɪtəʊ] (*pl* ~**es**) *n* pomme *f* de terre; ~ **peeler** *n* épluche-légumes *m inv*

potent ['pəʊtənt] *adj* puissant(e); (*drink*) fort(e), très alcoolisé(e); (*man*) viril

potential [pəʊ'tenʃəl] *adj* potentiel(le) ♦ *n* potentiel *m*

pothole ['pɒthəʊl] *n* (*in road*) nid *m* de poule; (*BRIT: underground*) gouffre *m*, caverne *f*; **potholing** ['pɒthəʊlɪŋ] (*BRIT*) *n*: **to go potholing** faire de la spéléologie

potluck [pɒt'lʌk] *n*: **to take** ~ tenter sa chance

potted ['pɒtɪd] *adj* (*food*) en conserve; (*plant*) en pot; (*abbreviated*) abrégé(e)

potter ['pɒtə*] *n* potier *m* ♦ *vi*: **to** ~ **around**, ~ **about** (*BRIT*) bricoler; ~**y** *n* poterie *f*

potty ['pɒtɪ] *adj* (*inf: mad*) dingue ♦ *n* (*child's*) pot *m*

pouch [paʊtʃ] *n* (*ZOOL*) poche *f*; (*for tobacco*) blague *f*; (*for money*) bourse *f*

poultry ['pəʊltrɪ] *n* volaille *f*

pounce [paʊns] *vi*: **to** ~ **(on)** bondir (sur), sauter (sur)

pound [paʊnd] *n* (*unit of money*) livre *f*; (*unit of weight*) livre ♦ *vt* (*beat*) bourrer de

coups, marteler; (*crush*) piler, pulvériser ◆
vi (*heart*) battre violemment, taper

pour [pɔː*] *vt* verser ◆ *vi* couler à flots; **to**
~ **(with rain)** pleuvoir à verse; **to** ~ **sb a**
drink verser or servir à boire à qn; ~
away *vt* vider; ~ **in** *vi* (*people*) affluer, se
précipiter; (*news, letters etc*) arriver en masse; ~ **off** *vt* = **pour away**; ~ **out** *vi* (*people*) sortir en masse ◆ *vt* vider; (*fig*) déverser; (*serve: a drink*) verser; ~**ing** *adj*: ~**ing**
rain pluie torrentielle

pout [paʊt] *vi* faire la moue

poverty ['pɒvətɪ] *n* pauvreté *f*, misère *f*; ~-
stricken *adj* pauvre, déshérité(e)

powder ['paʊdə*] *n* poudre *f* ◆ *vt*: **to** ~
one's face se poudrer; ~ **compact** *n* poudrier *m*; ~**ed milk** *n* lait *m* en poudre; ~
puff *n* houppette *f*; ~ **room** *n* toilettes *fpl*
(pour dames)

power ['paʊə*] *n* (*strength*) puissance *f*,
force *f*; (*ability, authority*) pouvoir *m*; (*of
speech, thought*) faculté *f*; (*ELEC*) courant
m; **to be in** ~ (*POL etc*) être au pouvoir; ~
cut (*BRIT*) *n* coupure *f* de courant; ~**ed**
adj: ~**ed by** actionné(e) par, fonctionnant
à; ~ **failure** *n* panne *f* de courant; ~**ful**
adj puissant(e); ~**less** *adj* impuissant(e); ~
point (*BRIT*) *n* prise *f* de courant; ~ **station** *n* centrale *f* électrique

p.p. *abbr* (= *per procurationem*): ~ **J. Smith**
pour M. J. Smith

PR *n abbr* = **public relations**

practical ['præktɪkəl] *adj* pratique; ~**ities**
npl (*of situation*) aspect *m* pratique; ~**ity**
(*no pl*) *n* (*of person*) sens *m* pratique; ~
joke *n* farce *f*; ~**ly** *adv* (*almost*) pratiquement

practice ['præktɪs] *n* pratique *f*; (*of profession*) exercice *m*; (*at football etc*) entraînement *m*; (*business*) cabinet *m* ◆ *vt, vi*
(*US*) = **practise**; **in** ~ (*in reality*) en pratique; **out of** ~ rouillé(e)

practise ['præktɪs] (*US* **practice**) *vt* (*musical
instrument*) travailler; (*train for: sport*) s'entraîner à; (*a sport, religion*) pratiquer; (*profession*) exercer ◆ *vi* s'exercer, travailler;
(*train*) s'entraîner; (*lawyer, doctor*) exercer;
practising ['præktɪsɪŋ] *adj* (*Christian etc*)
pratiquant(e); (*lawyer*) en exercice

practitioner [præk'tɪʃənə*] *n* praticien(ne)

prairie ['prɛərɪ] *n* steppe *f*, prairie *f*

praise [preɪz] *n* éloge(s) *m(pl)*, louange(s)
f(pl) ◆ *vt* louer, faire l'éloge de; ~**worthy**
adj digne d'éloges

pram [præm] (*BRIT*) *n* landau *m*, voiture *f*
d'enfant

prance [prɑːns] *vi* (*also: to* ~ *about: person*)
se pavaner

prank [præŋk] *n* farce *f*

prawn [prɔːn] *n* crevette *f* (rose)

pray [preɪ] *vi* prier; ~**er** [prɛə*] *n* prière
f

preach [priːtʃ] *vt, vi* prêcher

precaution [prɪ'kɔːʃən] *n* précaution *f*

precede [prɪ'siːd] *vt* précéder

precedent ['presɪdənt] *n* précédent *m*

precinct ['priːsɪŋkt] *n* (*US*) circonscription
f, arrondissement *m*; ~**s** *npl* (*neighbourhood*) alentours *mpl*, environs *mpl*; **pedestrian** ~ (*BRIT*) zone piétonnière; **shopping**
~ (*BRIT*) centre commercial

precious ['preʃəs] *adj* précieux(euse)

precipitate [*vb* prɪ'sɪpɪteɪt] *vt* précipiter

precise [prɪ'saɪs] *adj* précis(e); ~**ly** *adv* précisément

preclude [prɪ'kluːd] *vt* exclure

precocious [prɪ'kəʊʃəs] *adj* précoce

precondition ['priːkən'dɪʃən] *n* condition *f*
nécessaire

predecessor ['priːdɪsesə*] *n* prédécesseur
m

predicament [prɪ'dɪkəmənt] *n* situation *f*
difficile

predict [prɪ'dɪkt] *vt* prédire; ~**able** *adj* prévisible

predominantly [prɪ'dɒmɪnəntlɪ] *adv* en
majeure partie; surtout

preempt *vt* anticiper, devancer

preen [priːn] *vt*: **to** ~ **itself** (*bird*) se lisser
les plumes; **to** ~ **o.s.** s'admirer

prefab ['priːfæb] *n* bâtiment préfabriqué

preface ['prefɪs] *n* préface *f*

prefect ['priːfekt] (*BRIT*) *n* (*in school*) élève
chargé(e) de certaines fonctions de discipline

prefer [prɪ'fɜː*] *vt* préférer; ~**ably** *adv* de
préférence; ~**ence** *n* préférence *f*; ~**ential**
adj: ~**ential treatment** traitement *m* de faveur or préférentiel

prefix ['priːfɪks] *n* préfixe *m*

pregnancy ['pregnənsɪ] *n* grossesse *f*

pregnant ['pregnənt] *adj* enceinte; (*animal*)
pleine

prehistoric ['priːhɪs'tɒrɪk] *adj* préhistorique

prejudice ['predʒʊdɪs] *n* préjugé *m*; ~**d** *adj*
(*person*) plein(e) de préjugés; (*in a matter*)
partial(e)

premarital ['priː'mærɪtl] *adj* avant le mariage

premature ['premətʃʊə*] *adj* prématuré(e)

premier ['premɪə*] *adj* premier(ère), princi-
pal(e) ◆ *n* (*POL*) Premier ministre

première [premɪ'ɛə*] *n* première *f*

premise ['premɪs] *n* prémisse *f*; ~**s** *npl*
(*building*) locaux *mpl*; **on the** ~**s** sur les
lieux; sur place

premium ['priːmɪəm] *n* prime *f*; **to be at a**
~ faire prime; ~ **bond** (*BRIT*) *n* bon *m* à
lot, obligation *f* à prime

premonition [premə'nɪʃən] *n* prémonition
f

preoccupied [priː'ɒkjʊpaɪd] *adj* préoc-
cupé(e)

prep [prep] *n* (*SCOL: study*) étude *f*

prepaid ['pri:'peɪd] adj payé(e) d'avance

preparation ['prepə'reɪʃən] n préparation f; ~s npl (for trip, war) préparatifs mpl

preparatory [prɪ'pærətərɪ] adj préliminaire; ~ **school** (BRIT) n école primaire privée

prepare [prɪ'pɛə*] vt préparer ♦ vi: **to ~ for** se préparer à; ~**d to** prêt(e) à

preposition [prepə'zɪʃən] n préposition f

preposterous [prɪ'pɒstərəs] adj absurde

prep school n = preparatory school

prerequisite ['pri:'rekwɪzɪt] n condition f préalable

prescribe [prɪs'kraɪb] vt prescrire

prescription [prɪs'krɪpʃən] n (MED) ordonnance f; (: medicine) médicament (obtenu sur ordonnance)

presence ['prezns] n présence f; ~ **of mind** présence d'esprit

present [adj, n 'preznt, vb prɪ'zent] adj présent(e) ♦ n (gift) cadeau m; (actuality) présent m ♦ vt présenter; (prize, medal) remettre; (give): **to ~ sb with sth** or **sth to sb** offrir qch à qn; **to give sb a ~** offrir un cadeau à qn; **at ~** en ce moment; ~**ation** n présentation f; (ceremony) remise f du cadeau (or de la médaille etc); ~**-day** adj contemporain(e), actuel(le); ~**er** n (RADIO, TV) présentateur(trice); ~**ly** adv (with verb in past) peu après; (soon) tout à l'heure, bientôt; (at present) en ce moment

preservative [prɪ'zɜ:vətɪv] n agent m de conservation

preserve [prɪ'zɜ:v] vt (keep safe) préserver, protéger; (maintain) conserver, garder; (food) mettre en conserve ♦ n (often pl: jam) confiture f

president ['prezɪdənt] n président(e); ~**ial** adj présidentiel(le)

press [pres] n presse f; (for wine) pressoir m ♦ vt (squeeze) presser, serrer; (push) appuyer sur; (clothes: iron) repasser; (put pressure on) faire pression sur; (insist): **to ~ sth on sb** presser qn d'accepter qch ♦ vi appuyer, peser; **to ~ for sth** faire pression pour obtenir qch; **we are ~ed for time/money** le temps/l'argent nous manque; ~ **on** vi continuer; ~ **conference** n conférence f de presse; ~**ing** adj urgent(e), pressant(e); ~ **stud** (BRIT) n bouton-pression m; ~**-up** (BRIT) n traction f

pressure ['preʃə*] n pression f; (stress) tension f; **to put ~ on sb (to do)** faire pression sur qn (pour qu'il/elle fasse); ~ **cooker** n cocotte-minute f; ~ **gauge** n manomètre m; ~ **group** n groupe m de pression

prestige [pres'ti:ʒ] n prestige m

presumably [prɪ'zju:məblɪ] adv vraisemblablement

presume [prɪ'zju:m] vt présumer, supposer

pretence [prɪ'tens] (US **pretense**) n (claim) prétention f; **under false ~s** sous des prétextes fallacieux

pretend [prɪ'tend] vt (feign) feindre, simuler ♦ vi faire semblant

pretext ['pri:tekst] n prétexte m

pretty ['prɪtɪ] adj joli(e) ♦ adv assez

prevail [prɪ'veɪl] vi (be usual) avoir cours; (win) l'emporter, prévaloir; ~**ing** adj dominant(e)

prevalent ['prevələnt] adj répandu(e), courant(e)

prevent [prɪ'vent] vt: **to ~ (from doing)** empêcher (de faire); ~**ative** adj = **preventive**; ~**ive** adj préventif(ive)

preview ['pri:vju:] n (of film etc) avant-première f

previous ['pri:vɪəs] adj précédent(e); antérieur(e); ~**ly** adv précédemment, auparavant

prewar ['pri:'wɔ:*] adj d'avant-guerre

prey [preɪ] n proie f ♦ vi: **to ~ on** s'attaquer à; **it was ~ing on his mind** cela le travaillait

price [praɪs] n prix m ♦ vt (goods) fixer le prix de; ~**less** adj sans prix, inestimable; ~ **list** n liste f des prix, tarif m

prick [prɪk] n piqûre f ♦ vt piquer; **to ~ up one's ears** dresser or tendre l'oreille

prickle ['prɪkl] n (of plant) épine f; (sensation) picotement m; **prickly** ['prɪklɪ] adj piquant(e), épineux(euse); **prickly heat** n fièvre f miliaire

pride [praɪd] n orgueil m; fierté f ♦ vt: **to ~ o.s. on** se flatter de; s'enorgueillir de

priest [pri:st] n prêtre m; ~**hood** n prêtrise f, sacerdoce m

prim [prɪm] adj collet monté inv, guindé(e)

primarily ['praɪmərɪlɪ] adv principalement, essentiellement

primary ['praɪmərɪ] adj (first in importance) premier(ère), primordial(e), principal(e) ♦ n (US: election) (élection f) primaire f; ~ **school** (BRIT) n école primaire f

prime [praɪm] adj primordial(e), fondamental(e); (excellent) excellent(e) ♦ n: **in the ~ of life** dans la fleur de l'âge ♦ vt (wood) apprêter; (fig) mettre au courant; **P~ Minister** n Premier ministre m

primeval [praɪ'mi:vəl] adj primitif(ive); ~ **forest** forêt f vierge

primitive ['prɪmɪtɪv] adj primitif(ive)

primrose ['prɪmrəuz] n primevère f

primus (stove) ['praɪməs-] (®:BRIT) n réchaud m de camping

prince [prɪns] n prince m

princess [prɪn'ses] n princesse f

principal ['prɪnsəpl] adj principal(e) ♦ n (headmaster) directeur(trice), principal m

principle ['prɪnsəpl] n principe m; **in/on ~** en/par principe

print [prɪnt] n (mark) empreinte f; (letters) caractères mpl; (ART) gravure f, estampe f; (: photograph) photo f ♦ vt imprimer;

(publish) publier; *(write in block letters)* écrire en caractères d'imprimerie; **out of** ~ épuisé(e); ~**ed matter** *n* imprimé(s) *m(pl)*; ~**er** *n* imprimeur *m*; *(machine)* imprimante *f*; ~**ing** *n* impression *f*; ~**-out** *n* copie *f* papier

prior ['praɪə*] *adj* antérieur(e), précédent(e); *(more important)* prioritaire ♦ *adv*: ~ **to doing** avant de faire

priority [praɪ'ɒrɪtɪ] *n* priorité *f*

prise [praɪz] *vt*: **to** ~ **open** forcer

prison ['prɪzn] *n* prison *f* ♦ *cpd* pénitentiaire; ~**er** *n* prisonnier(ère)

pristine ['prɪstiːn] *adj* parfait(e)

privacy ['prɪvəsɪ] *n* intimité *f*, solitude *f*

private ['praɪvɪt] *adj* privé(e); *(personal)* personnel(le); *(house, lesson)* particulier(ère); *(quiet: place)* tranquille; *(reserved: person)* secret(ète) ♦ *n* soldat *m* de deuxième classe; "~" *(on envelope)* "personnelle"; **in** ~ en privé; ~ **enterprise** *n* l'entreprise privée; ~ **eye** *n* détective privé; ~ **property** *n* propriété privée; **privatize** *vt* privatiser

privet ['prɪvɪt] *n* troène *m*

privilege ['prɪvɪlɪdʒ] *n* privilège *m*

privy ['prɪvɪ] *adj*: **to be** ~ **to** être au courant de

prize [praɪz] *n* prix *m* ♦ *adj* *(example, idiot)* parfait(e); *(bull, novel)* primé(e) ♦ *vt* priser, faire grand cas de; ~-**giving** *n* distribution *f* des prix; ~**winner** *n* gagnant(e)

pro [prəʊ] *n* *(SPORT)* professionnel(le); **the** ~**s and cons** le pour et le contre

probability [prɒbə'bɪlɪtɪ] *n* probabilité *f*; **probable** ['prɒbəbl] *adj* probable; **probably** *adv* probablement

probation [prə'beɪʃən] *n*: **on** ~ *(LAW)* en liberté surveillée, en sursis; *(employee)* à l'essai

probe [prəʊb] *n* *(MED, SPACE)* sonde *f*; *(enquiry)* enquête *f*, investigation *f* ♦ *vt* sonder, explorer

problem ['prɒbləm] *n* problème *m*

procedure [prə'siːdʒə*] *n* *(ADMIN, LAW)* procédure *f*; *(method)* marche *f* à suivre, façon *f* de procéder

proceed [prə'siːd] *vi* continuer; *(go forward)* avancer; **to** ~ **(with)** continuer, poursuivre; **to** ~ **to do** se mettre à faire; ~**ings** *npl* *(LAW)* poursuites *fpl*; *(meeting)* réunion *f*, séance *f*; ~**s** ['prəʊsiːdz] *npl* produit *m*, recette *f*

process ['prəʊses] *n* processus *m*; *(method)* procédé *m* ♦ *vt* traiter; ~**ing** *n* *(PHOT)* développement *m*; ~**ion** [prə'seʃən] *n* défilé *m*, cortège *m*; *(REL)* procession *f*; **funeral** ~**ion** *(on foot)* cortège *m* funèbre; *(in cars)* convoi *m* mortuaire

proclaim [prə'kleɪm] *vt* déclarer, proclamer

procrastinate [prəʊ'kræstɪneɪt] *vi* faire traîner les choses, vouloir tout remettre au lendemain

procure [prə'kjʊə*] *vt* obtenir

prod [prɒd] *vt* pousser

prodigal ['prɒdɪgəl] *adj* prodigue

prodigy ['prɒdɪdʒɪ] *n* prodige *m*

produce [*n* 'prɒdjuːs, *vb* prə'djuːs] *n* *(AGR)* produits *mpl* ♦ *vt* produire; *(to show)* présenter; *(cause)* provoquer, causer; *(THEATRE)* monter, mettre en scène; ~**r** *n* producteur *m*; *(THEATRE)* metteur *m* en scène

product ['prɒdʌkt] *n* produit *m*

production [prə'dʌkʃən] *n* production *f*; *(THEATRE)* mise *f* en scène; ~ **line** *n* chaîne *f* (de fabrication)

productivity [prɒdʌk'tɪvɪtɪ] *n* productivité *f*

profession [prə'feʃən] *n* profession *f*; ~**al** *n* professionnel(le) ♦ *adj* professionnel(le); *(work)* de professionnel

professor [prə'fesə*] *n* professeur *m* *(titulaire d'une chaire)*

proficiency [prə'fɪʃənsɪ] *n* compétence *f*, aptitude *f*

profile ['prəʊfaɪl] *n* profil *m*

profit ['prɒfɪt] *n* bénéfice *m*; profit *m* ♦ *vi*: **to** ~ **(by** or **from)** profiter (de); ~**able** *adj* lucratif(ive), rentable

profound [prə'faʊnd] *adj* profond(e)

profusely [prə'fjuːslɪ] *adv* abondamment; avec effusion

prognosis [prɒg'nəʊsɪs] *(pl* **prognoses)** *n* pronostic *m*

programme ['prəʊgræm] *(US* **program)** *n* programme *m*; *(RADIO, TV)* émission *f* ♦ *vt* programmer; ~**r** *(US* **programer)** *n* programmeur(euse)

progress [*n* 'prəʊgres, *vb* prə'gres] *n* progrès *m(pl)* ♦ *vi* progresser, avancer; **in** ~ en cours; ~**ive** *adj* progressif(ive); *(person)* progressiste

prohibit [prə'hɪbɪt] *vt* interdire, défendre

project [*n* 'prɒdʒekt, *vb* prə'dʒekt] *n* *(plan)* projet *m*, plan *m*; *(venture)* opération *f*, entreprise *f*; *(research)* étude *f*, dossier *m* ♦ *vt* projeter ♦ *vi* *(stick out)* faire saillie, s'avancer; ~**ion** [prə'dʒekʃən] *n* projection *f*; *(overhang)* saillie *f*; ~**or** [prə'dʒektə*] *n* projecteur *m*

prolong [prə'lɒŋ] *vt* prolonger

prom [prɒm] *n abbr* = **promenade;** *(US: ball)* bal *m* d'étudiants

promenade [prɒmɪ'nɑːd] *n* *(by sea)* esplanade *f*, promenade *f*; ~ **concert** *(BRIT)* *n* concert *m* populaire (de musique classique)

prominent ['prɒmɪnənt] *adj* *(standing out)* proéminent(e); *(important)* important(e)

promiscuous [prə'mɪskjʊəs] *adj* *(sexually)* de mœurs légères

promise ['prɒmɪs] *n* promesse *f* ♦ *vt, vi* promettre; **promising** ['prɒmɪsɪŋ] *adj* prometteur(euse)

promote [prə'məʊt] *vt* promouvoir; *(new product)* faire la promotion de; ~**r** *n* *(of* *event*) organisateur(trice); (*of cause, idea*) promoteur(trice); **promotion** [prə'məʊʃən] *n* promotion *f*

prompt [prɒmpt] *adj* rapide ♦ *adv* (*punctually*) à l'heure ♦ *n* (COMPUT) message *m* (de guidage) ♦ *vt* provoquer; (*person*) inciter, pousser; (THEATRE) souffler (son rôle *or* ses répliques) à; ~**ly** *adv* rapidement, sans délai; ponctuellement

prone [prəʊn] *adj* (*lying*) couché(e) (face contre terre); ~ **to** enclin(e) à

prong [prɒŋ] *n* (*of fork*) dent *f*

pronoun ['prəʊnaʊn] *n* pronom *m*

pronounce [prə'naʊns] *vt* prononcer

pronunciation [prənʌnsɪ'eɪʃən] *n* prononciation *f*

proof [pruːf] *n* preuve *f*; (TYP) épreuve *f* ♦ *adj*: ~ **against** à l'épreuve de

prop [prɒp] *n* support *m*, étai *m*; (*fig*) soutien *m* ♦ *vt* (*also*: ~ *up*) étayer, soutenir; (*lean*): **to** ~ **sth against** appuyer qch contre *or* à

propaganda [prɒpə'gændə] *n* propagande *f*

propel [prə'pel] *vt* propulser, faire avancer; ~**ler** *n* hélice *f*

propensity [prə'pensɪtɪ] *n*: **a** ~ **for** *or* **to/ to do** une propension à/à faire

proper ['prɒpə*] *adj* (*suited, right*) approprié(e), bon(bonne); (*seemly*) correct(e), convenable; (*authentic*) vrai(e), véritable; (*referring to place*): **the village** ~ le village proprement dit; ~**ly** *adv* correctement, convenablement; ~ **noun** *n* nom *m* propre

property ['prɒpətɪ] *n* propriété *f*; (*things owned*) biens *mpl*; propriété(s) *f(pl)*; (*land*) terres *fpl*

prophecy ['prɒfɪsɪ] *n* prophétie *f*

prophesy ['prɒfɪsaɪ] *vt* prédire

prophet ['prɒfɪt] *n* prophète *m*

proportion [prə'pɔːʃən] *n* proportion *f*; (*share*) part *f*, partie *f*; ~**al**, ~**ate** *adj* proportionnel(le)

proposal [prə'pəʊzl] *n* proposition *f*, offre *f*; (*plan*) projet *m*; (*of marriage*) demande *f* en mariage

propose [prə'pəʊz] *vt* proposer, suggérer ♦ *vi* faire sa demande en mariage; **to** ~ **to do** avoir l'intention de faire; **proposition** [prɒpə'zɪʃən] *n* proposition *f*

propriety [prə'praɪətɪ] *n* (*seemliness*) bienséance *f*, convenance *f*

prose [prəʊz] *n* (*not poetry*) prose *f*

prosecute ['prɒsɪkjuːt] *vt* poursuivre; **prosecution** [prɒsɪ'kjuːʃen] *n* poursuites *fpl* judiciaires; (*accusing side*) partie plaignante; **prosecutor** ['prɒsɪkjuːtə*] *n* (US: *plaintiff*) plaignant(e); (*also*: **public** ~) procureur *m*, ministère public

prospect [*n* 'prɒspekt, *vb* prə'spekt] *n* perspective *f* ♦ *vt, vi* prospecter; ~**s** *npl* (*for work etc*) possibilités *fpl* d'avenir, débouchés *mpl*; ~**ing** *n* (*for gold, oil etc*) pros-

pection *f*; ~**ive** *adj* (*possible*) éventuel(le); (*future*) futur(e)

prospectus [prə'spektəs] *n* prospectus *m*

prosperity [prɒ'sperɪtɪ] *n* prospérité *f*

prostitute ['prɒstɪtjuːt] *n* prostitué(e)

protect [prə'tekt] *vt* protéger; ~**ion** *n* protection *f*; ~**ive** *adj* protecteur(trice); (*clothing*) de protection

protein ['prəʊtiːn] *n* protéine *f*

protest [*n* 'prəʊtest, *vb* prə'test] *n* protestation *f* ♦ *vi, vt*: **to** ~ **(that)** protester (que)

Protestant ['prɒtɪstənt] *adj, n* protestant(e)

protester [prə'testə*] *n* manifestant(e)

protracted [prə'træktɪd] *adj* prolongé(e)

protrude [prə'truːd] *vi* avancer, dépasser

proud [praʊd] *adj* fier(ère); (*pej*) orgueilleux(euse)

prove [pruːv] *vt* prouver, démontrer ♦ *vi*: **to** ~ **(to be) correct** *etc* s'avérer juste *etc*; **to** ~ **o.s.** montrer ce dont on est capable

proverb ['prɒvɜːb] *n* proverbe *m*

provide [prə'vaɪd] *vt* fournir; **to** ~ **sb with sth** fournir qch à qn; ~ **for** *vt fus* (*person*) subvenir aux besoins de; (*future event*) prévoir; ~**d (that)** *conj* à condition que +*sub*; **providing** [prə'vaɪdɪŋ] *conj*: **providing (that)** à condition que +*sub*

province ['prɒvɪns] *n* province *f*; (*fig*) domaine *m*; **provincial** [prə'vɪnʃəl] *adj* provincial(e)

provision [prə'vɪʒən] *n* (*supplying*) fourniture *f*; approvisionnement *m*; (*stipulation*) disposition *f*; ~**s** *npl* (*food*) provisions *fpl*; ~**al** *adj* provisoire

proviso [prə'vaɪzəʊ] *n* condition *f*

provocative [prə'vɒkətɪv] *adj* provocateur(trice), provocant(e)

provoke [prə'vəʊk] *vt* provoquer

prow [praʊ] *n* proue *f*

prowess ['praʊɪs] *n* prouesse *f*

prowl [praʊl] *vi* (*also*: ~ *about*, ~ *around*) rôder ♦ *n*: **on the** ~ à l'affût; ~**er** *n* rôdeur(euse)

proxy ['prɒksɪ] *n* procuration *f*

prudent ['pruːdənt] *adj* prudent(e)

prune [pruːn] *n* pruneau *m* ♦ *vt* élaguer

pry [praɪ] *vi*: **to** ~ **into** fourrer son nez dans

PS *n abbr* (= *postscript*) p.s.

psalm [sɑːm] *n* psaume *m*

pseudo- ['sjuːdəʊ] *prefix* pseudo-; ~**nym** ['sjuːdənɪm] *n* pseudonyme *m*

psyche ['saɪkɪ] *n* psychisme *m*

psychiatrist [saɪ'kaɪətrɪst] *n* psychiatre *m/f*

psychic ['saɪkɪk] *adj* (*also*: ~**al**) (méta)psychique; (*person*) doué(e) d'un sixième sens

psychoanalyst [saɪkəʊ'ænəlɪst] *n* psychanalyste *m/f*

psychological [saɪkə'lɒdʒɪkəl] *adj* psychologique; **psychologist** [saɪ'kɒlədʒɪst] *n* psychologue *m/f*; **psychology** [saɪ'kɒlədʒɪ] *n* psychologie f

PTO *abbr* (= *please turn over*) T.S.V.P.

pub [pʌb] *n* (= *public house*) pub *m*

public ['pʌblɪk] *adj* public(ique) ♦ *n* public *m*; **in ~** en public; **to make ~** rendre public; **~ address system** *n* (système *m* de) sonorisation *f*, hauts-parleurs *mpl*

publican ['pʌblɪkən] *n* patron *m* de pub

public: **~ company** *n* société *f* anonyme (*cotée en Bourse*); **~ convenience** (*BRIT*) *n* toilettes *fpl*; **~ holiday** *n* jour férié; **~ house** (*BRIT*) *n* pub *m*

publicity [pʌb'lɪsɪtɪ] *n* publicité *f*

publicize ['pʌblɪsaɪz] *vt* faire connaître, rendre public(ique)

public: **~ opinion** *n* opinion publique; **~ relations** *n* relations publiques; **~ school** *n* (*BRIT*) école (secondaire) privée; (*US*) école publique; **~-spirited** *adj* qui fait preuve de civisme; **~ transport** *n* transports *mpl* en commun

publish ['pʌblɪʃ] *vt* publier; **~er** *n* éditeur *m*; **~ing** *n* édition *f*

pucker ['pʌkə*] *vt* plisser

pudding ['pʊdɪŋ] *n* pudding *m*; (*BRIT*: *sweet*) dessert *m*, entremets *m*; **black ~**, (*US*) **blood ~** boudin (noir)

puddle ['pʌdl] *n* flaque *f* (d'eau)

puff [pʌf] *n* bouffée *f* ♦ *vt*: **to ~ one's pipe** tirer sur sa pipe ♦ *vi* (*pant*) haleter; **~ out** *vt* (*fill with air*) gonfler; **~ed (out)** (*inf*) *adj* (*out of breath*) tout(e) essoufflé(e); **~ pastry** (*US* = **paste**) *n* pâte feuilletée; **~y** *adj* bouffi(e), boursouflé(e)

pull [pʊl] *n* (*tug*): **to give sth a ~** tirer sur qch ♦ *vt* tirer; (*trigger*) presser ♦ *vi* tirer; **to ~ to pieces** mettre en morceaux; **to ~ one's punches** ménager son adversaire; **to ~ one's weight** faire sa part (du travail); **to ~ o.s. together** se ressaisir; **to ~ sb's leg** (*fig*) faire marcher qn; **~ apart** *vt* (*break*) mettre en pièces, démantibuler; **~ down** *vt* (*house*) démolir; **~ in** *vi* (*AUT*) entrer; (*RAIL*) entrer en gare; **~ off** *vt* enlever, ôter; (*deal etc*) mener à bien, conclure; **~ out** *vi* démarrer, partir ♦ *vt* sortir; arracher; **~ over** *vi* (*AUT*) se ranger; **~ through** *vi* s'en sortir; **~ up** *vi* (*stop*) s'arrêter ♦ *vt* remonter; (*uproot*) déraciner, arracher

pulley ['pʊlɪ] *n* poulie *f*

pullover ['pʊləʊvə*] *n* pull(-over) *m*, tricot *m*

pulp [pʌlp] *n* (*of fruit*) pulpe *f*

pulpit ['pʊlpɪt] *n* chaire *f*

pulsate [pʌl'seɪt] *vi* battre, palpiter; (*music*) vibrer

pulse [pʌls] *n* (*of blood*) pouls *m*; (*of heart*) battement *m*; (*of music, engine*) vibrations *fpl*; (*BOT, CULIN*) légume sec

pump [pʌmp] *n* pompe *f*; (*shoe*) escarpin *m* ♦ *vt* pomper; **~ up** *vt* gonfler

pumpkin ['pʌmpkɪn] *n* potiron *m*, citrouille *f*

pun [pʌn] *n* jeu *m* de mots, calembour *m*

punch [pʌntʃ] *n* (*blow*) coup *m* de poing; (*tool*) poinçon *m*; (*drink*) punch *m* ♦ *vt* (*hit*): **to ~ sb/sth** donner un coup de poing à qn/sur qch; **~line** *n* (*of joke*) conclusion *f*; **~-up** *vt* (*BRIT*: *inf*) *n* bagarre *f*

punctual ['pʌŋktjʊəl] *adj* ponctuel(le)

punctuation [pʌŋktjʊ'eɪʃən] *n* ponctuation *f*

puncture ['pʌŋktʃə*] *n* crevaison *f*

pundit ['pʌndɪt] *n* individu *m* qui pontifie, pontife *m*

pungent ['pʌndʒənt] *adj* piquant(e), âcre

punish ['pʌnɪʃ] *vt* punir; **~ment** *n* punition *f*, châtiment *m*

punk [pʌŋk] *n* (*also*: **~ rocker**) punk *m/f*; (: **~ rock**) le punk rock; (*US*: *inf*: *hoodlum*) voyou *m*

punt [pʌnt] *n* (*boat*) bachot *m*

punter ['pʌntə*] (*BRIT*) *n* (*gambler*) parieur(euse); (*inf*): **the ~s** le public

puny ['pju:nɪ] *adj* chétif(ive); (*effort*) piteux(euse)

pup [pʌp] *n* chiot *m*

pupil ['pju:pl] *n* (*SCOL*) élève *m/f*; (*of eye*) pupille *f*

puppet ['pʌpɪt] *n* marionnette *f*, pantin *m*

puppy ['pʌpɪ] *n* chiot *m*, jeune chien(ne)

purchase ['pɜ:tʃɪs] *n* achat *m* ♦ *vt* acheter; **~r** *n* acheteur(euse)

pure [pjʊə*] *adj* pur(e); **~ly** ['pjʊəlɪ] *adv* purement

purge [pɜ:dʒ] *n* purge *f*

purple ['pɜ:pl] *adj* violet(te); (*face*) cramoisi(e)

purport [pɜ:'pɔ:t] *vi*: **to ~ to be/do** prétendre être/faire

purpose ['pɜ:pəs] *n* intention *f*, but *m*; **on ~** exprès; **~ful** *adj* déterminé(e), résolu(e)

purr [pɜ:*] *vi* ronronner

purse [pɜ:s] *n* (*BRIT*: *for money*) porte-monnaie *m inv*; (*US*: *handbag*) sac *m* à main ♦ *vt* serrer, pincer

purser ['pɜ:sə*] *n* (*NAUT*) commissaire *m* du bord

pursue [pə'sju:] *vt* poursuivre

pursuit [pə'sju:t] *n* poursuite *f*; (*occupation*) occupation *f*, activité *f*

push [pʊʃ] *n* poussée *f* ♦ *vt* pousser; (*button*) appuyer sur; (*thrust*): **to ~ sth (into)** enfoncer qch (dans); (*product*) faire de la publicité pour ♦ *vi* pousser; (*demand*): **to ~ for** exiger, demander avec insistance; **~ aside** *vt* écarter; **~ off** (*inf*) *vi* filer, ficher le camp; **~ on** *vi* (*continue*) continuer; **~ through** *vi* se frayer un chemin ♦ *vt* (*measure*) faire accepter; **~ up** *vt* (*total, prices*) faire monter; **~chair** (*BRIT*) *n* poussette *f*; **~er** *n* (*drug ~er*) revendeur(euse) (de drogue), ravitailleur(euse) (en drogue); **~over**

(inf) n: **it's a** ~**over** c'est un jeu d'enfant;
~**-up** *(US) n* traction *f*; ~**y** *(pej) adj* arriviste
puss [pʊs] *(inf) n* minet *m*
pussy (cat) ['pʊsɪ (kæt)] *(inf) n* minet *m*
put [pʊt] *(pt, pp put) vt* mettre, poser, placer; *(say)* dire, exprimer; *(a question)* poser;
(case, view) exposer, présenter; *(estimate)*
estimer; ~ **about** *vt (rumour)* faire courir;
~ **across** *vt (ideas etc)* communiquer; ~
away *vt (store)* ranger; ~ **back** *vt (replace)*
remettre, replacer; *(postpone)* remettre; *(delay)* retarder; ~ **by** *vt (money)* mettre de
côté, économiser; ~ **down** *vt (parcel etc)*
poser, déposer; *(in writing)* mettre par écrit,
inscrire; *(suppress: revolt etc)* réprimer, faire
cesser; *(animal)* abattre; *(dog, cat)* faire piquer; *(attribute)* attribuer; ~ **forward** *vt
(ideas)* avancer; ~ **in** *vt (gas, electricity)*
installer; *(application, complaint)* soumettre;
(time, effort) consacrer; ~ **off** *vt (light etc)*
éteindre; *(postpone)* remettre à plus tard,
ajourner; *(discourage)* dissuader; ~ **on** *vt
(clothes, lipstick, record)* mettre; *(light etc)*
allumer; *(play etc)* monter; *(food: cook)*
mettre à cuire *or* à chauffer; *(gain)*: **to** ~
on weight prendre du poids, grossir; **to** ~
the brakes on freiner; **to** ~ **the kettle on**
mettre l'eau à chauffer; ~ **out** *vt (take out)*
mettre dehors; *(one's hand)* tendre; *(light
etc)* éteindre; *(person: inconvenience)* déranger, gêner; ~ **through** *vt (TEL: call)* passer;
(: person) mettre en communication; *(plan)*
faire accepter; ~ **up** *vt (raise)* lever, relever, remonter; *(pin up)* afficher; *(hang)* accrocher; *(build)* construire, ériger; *(tent)*
monter; *(umbrella)* ouvrir; *(increase)* augmenter; *(accommodate)* loger; ~ **up with**
vt fus supporter
putt [pʌt] *n* coup roulé; ~**ing green** *n*
green *m*
putty ['pʌtɪ] *n* mastic *m*
put-up ['pʊtʌp] *(BRIT) adj*: ~ **job** coup
monté
puzzle ['pʌzl] *n* énigme *f*, mystère *m*; *(jigsaw)* puzzle *m* ♦ *vt* intriguer, rendre perplexe ♦ *vi* se creuser la tête; **puzzling** *adj*
déconcertant(e)
pyjamas [pɪ'dʒɑːməz] *(BRIT) npl* pyjama(s)
m(pl)
pyramid ['pɪrəmɪd] *n* pyramide *f*
Pyrenees [pɪrɪ'niːz] *npl*: **the** ~ les Pyrénées
fpl

Q q

quack [kwæk] *n (of duck)* coin-coin *m inv*;
(pej: doctor) charlatan *m*
quad [kwɒd] *n abbr* = **quadrangle** ♦ *abbr* =
quadruplet
quadrangle ['kwɒdræŋgl] *n (courtyard)*
cour *f*
quadruple [kwɒ'druːpl] *vt, vi* quadrupler;
~**ts** [kwɒ'druːpləts] *npl* quadruplés
quagmire ['kwægmaɪə*] *n* bourbier *m*
quail [kweɪl] *n (ZOOL)* caille *f* ♦ *vi*: **to** ~ **at**
or **before** reculer devant
quaint [kweɪnt] *adj* bizarre; *(house, village)*
au charme vieillot, pittoresque
quake [kweɪk] *vi* trembler
qualification [kwɒlɪfɪ'keɪʃən] *n (often pl:
degree etc)* diplôme *m*; *(: training)* qualification(s) *f(pl)*, expérience *f*; *(ability)* compétence(s) *f(pl)*; *(limitation)* réserve *f*, restriction *f*
qualified ['kwɒlɪfaɪd] *adj (trained)* qualifié(e); *(professionally)* diplômé(e); *(fit,
competent)* compétent(e), qualifié(e); *(limited)* conditionnel(le)
qualify ['kwɒlɪfaɪ] *vt* qualifier; *(modify)* atténuer, nuancer ♦ *vi*: **to** ~ **(as)** obtenir son
diplôme (de); **to** ~ **(for)** remplir les conditions requises (pour); *(SPORT)* se qualifier
(pour)
quality ['kwɒlɪtɪ] *n* qualité *f*
qualm [kwɑːm] *n* doute *m*; scrupule *m*
quandary ['kwɒndərɪ] *n*: **in a** ~ devant un
dilemme, dans l'embarras
quantity ['kwɒntɪtɪ] *n* quantité *f*; ~ **surveyor** *n* métreur *m* vérificateur
quarantine ['kwɒrəntiːn] *n* quarantaine *f*
quarrel ['kwɒrəl] *n* querelle *f*, dispute *f* ♦ *vi*
se disputer, se quereller; ~**some** *adj* querelleur(euse)
quarry ['kwɒrɪ] *n (for stone)* carrière *f*; *(animal)* proie *f*, gibier *m*
quart [kwɔːt] *n* ≈ litre *m*
quarter ['kwɔːtə*] *n* quart *m*; *(US: coin: 25
cents)* quart de dollar; *(of year)* trimestre *m*;
(district) quartier *m* ♦ *vt (divide)* partager en
quartiers *or* en quatre; ~**s** *npl (living* ~*)* logement *m*; *(MIL)* quartiers *mpl*, cantonnement *m*; **a** ~ **of an hour** un quart d'heure;
~ **final** *n* quart *m* de finale; ~**ly** *adj* trimestriel(le) ♦ *adv* tous les trois mois

quartet(te) [kwɔːˈtet] *n* quatuor *m*; (*jazz players*) quartette *m*

quartz [kwɔːts] *n* quartz *m*

quash [kwɒʃ] *vt* (*verdict*) annuler

quaver ['kweɪvə*] *n* (*BRIT: MUS*) croche *f* ♦ *vi* trembler

quay [kiː] *n* (*also:* ~side) quai *m*

queasy ['kwiːzɪ] *adj*: **to feel ~** avoir mal au cœur

queen [kwiːn] *n* reine *f*; (*CARDS etc*) dame *f*; ~ **mother** *n* reine mère *f*

queer [kwɪə*] *adj* étrange, curieux(euse); (*suspicious*) louche ♦ *n* (*infl*) homosexuel *m*

quell [kwel] *vt* réprimer, étouffer

quench [kwentʃ] *vt*: **to ~ one's thirst** se désaltérer

querulous ['kwerʊləs] *adj* (*person*) récriminateur(trice); (*voice*) plaintif(ive)

query ['kwɪərɪ] *n* question *f* ♦ *vt* remettre en question, mettre en doute

quest [kwest] *n* recherche *f*, quête *f*

question ['kwestʃən] *n* question *f* ♦ *vt* (*person*) interroger; (*plan, idea*) remettre en question, mettre en doute; **beyond** ~ sans aucun doute; **out of the** ~ hors de question; ~**able** *adj* discutable; ~ **mark** *n* point *m* d'interrogation; ~**naire** [kwestʃəˈnɛə*] *n* questionnaire *m*

queue [kjuː] *n* (*BRIT*) queue *f*, file *f* ♦ *vi* (*also:* ~ **up**) faire la queue

quibble ['kwɪbl] *vi*: ~ (**about**) *or* (**over**) *or* (**with sth**) ergoter (sur qch)

quick [kwɪk] *adj* rapide; (*agile*) agile, vif(vive) ♦ *n*: **cut to the** ~ (*fig*) touché(e) au vif; **be** ~! dépêche-toi!; ~**en** *vt* accélérer, presser ♦ *vi* s'accélérer, devenir plus rapide; ~**ly** *adv* vite, rapidement; ~**sand** *n* sables mouvants; ~**-witted** *adj* à l'esprit vif

quid [kwɪd] (*BRIT: inf*) *n, pl inv* livre *f*

quiet ['kwaɪət] *adj* tranquille, calme; (*voice*) bas(se); (*ceremony, colour*) discret(ète) ♦ *n* tranquillité *f*, calme *m*; (*silence*) silence *m* ♦ *vt, vi* (*US*) = **quieten**; **keep** ~! tais-toi!; ~**en** *vi* (*also:* ~ **down**) se calmer, s'apaiser ♦ *vt* calmer, apaiser; ~**ly** *adv* tranquillement, calmement; (*silently*) silencieusement; ~**ness** *n* tranquillité *f*, calme *m*; (*silence*) silence *m*

quilt [kwɪlt] *n* édredon *m*; (*continental* ~) couette *f*

quin [kwɪn] *n abbr* = **quintuplet**

quintuplets [kwɪnˈtjuːpləts] *npl* quintuplé(e)s

quip [kwɪp] *n* remarque piquante *or* spirituelle, pointe *f*

quirk [kwɜːk] *n* bizarrerie *f*

quit [kwɪt] (*pt, pp* ~ *or* ~ted) *vt* quitter; (*smoking, grumbling*) arrêter de ♦ *vi* (*give up*) abandonner, renoncer; (*resign*) démissionner

quite [kwaɪt] *adv* (*rather*) assez, plutôt; (*en-*

tirely) complètement, tout à fait; (*following a negative = almost*): **that's not** ~ **big enough** ce n'est pas tout à fait assez grand; **I** ~ **understand** je comprends très bien; ~ **a few of them** un assez grand nombre d'entre eux; ~ (**so**)! exactement!

quits [kwɪts] *adj*: ~ (**with**) quitte (envers); **let's call it** ~ restons-en là

quiver ['kwɪvə*] *vi* trembler, frémir

quiz [kwɪz] *n* (*game*) jeu-concours *m* ♦ *vt* interroger; ~**zical** *adj* narquois(e)

quota ['kwəʊtə] *n* quota *m*

quotation [kwəʊˈteɪʃən] *n* citation *f*; (*estimate*) devis *m*; ~ **marks** *npl* guillemets *mpl*

quote [kwəʊt] *n* citation *f*; (*estimate*) devis *m* ♦ *vt* citer; (*price*) indiquer; ~**s** *npl* guillemets *mpl*

R r

rabbi ['ræbaɪ] *n* rabbin *m*

rabbit ['ræbɪt] *n* lapin *m*; ~ **hutch** *n* clapier *m*

rabble ['ræbl] (*pej*) *n* populace *f*

rabies ['reɪbiːz] *n* rage *f*

RAC *n abbr* (*BRIT*) = Royal Automobile Club

rac(c)oon [rəˈkuːn] *n* raton laveur

race [reɪs] *n* (*species*) race *f*; (*competition, rush*) course *f* ♦ *vt* (*horse*) faire courir ♦ *vi* (*compete*) faire la course, courir; (*hurry*) aller à toute vitesse, courir; (*engine*) s'emballer; (*pulse*) augmenter; ~ **car** (*US*) *n* = **racing car**; ~ **car driver** (*US*) *n* = **racing driver**; ~**course** *n* champ *m* de courses; ~**horse** *n* cheval *m* de course; ~**track** *n* piste *f*

racial ['reɪʃəl] *adj* racial(e)

racing ['reɪsɪŋ] *n* courses *fpl*; ~ **car** (*BRIT*) *n* voiture *f* de course; ~ **driver** (*BRIT*) *n* pilote *m* de course

racism ['reɪsɪzəm] *n* racisme *m*; **racist** *adj* raciste ♦ *n* raciste *m/f*

rack [ræk] *n* (*for guns, tools*) râtelier *m*; (*also: luggage* ~) porte-bagages *m inv*, filet *m* à bagages; (: *roof* ~) galerie *f*; (*dish* ~) égouttoir *m* de vaisselle; **to** ~ **one's brains** se creuser la cervelle

racket ['rækɪt] *n* (*for tennis*) raquette *f*; (*noise*) tapage *m*; vacarme *m*; (*swindle*) escroquerie *f*

racquet ['rækɪt] *n* raquette *f*

racy ['reɪsɪ] *adj* plein(e) de verve; (*slightly indecent*) osé(e)

radar ['reɪdɑː*] *n* radar *m*

radial ['reɪdɪəl] *adj* (*also: ~-ply*) à carcasse radiale

radiant ['reɪdɪənt] *adj* rayonnant(e)

radiate ['reɪdɪeɪt] *vt* (*heat*) émettre, dégager; (*emotion*) rayonner de ♦ *vi* (*lines*) rayonner

radiation [reɪdɪ'eɪʃən] *n* rayonnement *m*; (*radioactive*) radiation *f*

radiator ['reɪdɪeɪtə*] *n* radiateur *m*

radical ['rædɪkəl] *adj* radical(e)

radii ['reɪdɪaɪ] *npl of* radius

radio ['reɪdɪəʊ] *n* radio *f* ♦ *vt* appeler par radio; **on the ~** à la radio; **~active** [reɪdɪəʊ'æktɪv] *adj* radioactif(ive); **~ station** *n* station *f* de radio

radish ['rædɪʃ] *n* radis *m*

radius ['reɪdɪəs] (*pl* **radii**) *n* rayon *m*

RAF *n abbr* = **Royal Air Force**

raffle ['ræfl] *n* tombola *f*

raft [rɑːft] *n* (*craft; also: life ~*) radeau *m*

rafter ['rɑːftə*] *n* chevron *m*

rag [ræg] *n* chiffon *m*; (*pej: newspaper*) feuille *f* de chou, torchon *m*; (*student ~*) attractions organisées au profit d'œuvres de charité; **~s** *npl* (*torn clothes etc*) haillons *mpl*; **~ doll** *n* poupée *f* de chiffon

rage [reɪdʒ] *n* (*fury*) rage *f*, fureur *f* ♦ *vi* (*person*) être fou(folle) de rage; (*storm*) faire rage, être déchaîné(e); **it's all the ~** cela fait fureur

ragged ['rægɪd] *adj* (*edge*) inégal(e); (*clothes*) en loques; (*appearance*) déguenillé(e)

raid [reɪd] *n* (*attack, also: MIL*) raid *m*; (*criminal*) hold-up *m inv*; (*by police*) descente *f*, rafle *f* ♦ *vt* faire un raid sur *or* un hold-up *or* une descente dans

rail [reɪl] *n* (*on stairs*) rampe *f*; (*on bridge, balcony*) balustrade *f*; (*of ship*) bastingage *m*; **~s** *npl* (*track*) rails *mpl*, voie ferrée; **by ~** par chemin de fer, en train; **~ing(s)** *n(pl)* grille *f*, **~road** (*US*), **~way** (*BRIT*) *n* (*track*) voie ferrée; (*company*) chemin *m* de fer; **~way** (*BRIT*) *n* ligne *f* de chemin de fer; **~wayman** (*BRIT: irreg*) *n* cheminot *m*; **~way station** (*BRIT*) *n* gare *f*

rain [reɪn] *n* pluie *f* ♦ *vi* pleuvoir; **in the ~** sous la pluie; **it's ~ing** il pleut; **~bow** *n* arc-en-ciel *m*; **~coat** *n* imperméable *m*; **~drop** *n* goutte *f* de pluie; **~fall** *n* chute *f* de pluie; (*measurement*) hauteur *f* des précipitations; **~forest** *n* forêt *f* tropicale humide; **~y** *adj* pluvieux(euse)

raise [reɪz] *n* augmentation *f* ♦ *vt* (*lift*) lever; hausser; (*increase*) augmenter; (*morale*) remonter; (*standards*) améliorer; (*question, doubt*) provoquer, soulever; (*cattle, family*) élever; (*crop*) faire pousser; (*funds*) rassembler; (*loan*) obtenir; (*army*) lever; **to ~ one's voice** élever la voix

raisin ['reɪzən] *n* raisin sec

rake [reɪk] *n* (*tool*) râteau *m* ♦ *vt* (*garden, leaves*) ratisser; (*with machine gun*) balayer

rally ['rælɪ] *n* (*POL etc*) meeting *m*, rassemblement *m*; (*AUT*) rallye *m*; (*TENNIS*) échange *m* ♦ *vt* (*support*) gagner ♦ *vi* (*sick person*) aller mieux; (*Stock Exchange*) reprendre; **~ round** *vt fus* venir en aide à

RAM [ræm] *n abbr* (= *random access memory*) mémoire vive

ram [ræm] *n* bélier *m* ♦ *vt* enfoncer; (*crash into*) emboutir; percuter

ramble ['ræmbl] *n* randonnée *f* ♦ *vi* (*walk*) se promener, faire une randonnée; (*talk: also: ~ on*) discourir, pérorer; **~r** *n* promeneur(euse), randonneur(euse); (*BOT*) rosier grimpant

rambling ['ræmblɪŋ] *adj* (*speech*) décousu(e); (*house*) plein(e) de coins et de recoins; (*BOT*) grimpant(e)

ramp [ræmp] *n* (*incline*) rampe *f*; dénivellation *f*; **on ~, off ~** (*US: AUT*) bretelle *f* d'accès

rampage [ræm'peɪdʒ] *n*: **to be on the ~** se déchaîner

rampant ['ræmpənt] *adj* (*disease etc*) qui sévit

ramshackle ['ræmʃækl] *adj* (*house*) délabré(e); (*car etc*) déglingué(e)

ran [ræn] *pt of* run

ranch [rɑːntʃ] *n* ranch *m*; **~er** *n* propriétaire *m* de ranch

rancid ['rænsɪd] *adj* rance

rancour ['ræŋkə*] (*US* rancor) *n* rancune *f*

random ['rændəm] *adj* fait(e) *or* établi(e) au hasard; (*MATH*) aléatoire ♦ *n*: **at ~** au hasard; **~ access** *n* (*COMPUT*) accès sélectif

randy ['rændɪ] (*BRIT: inf*) *adj* excité(e); lubrique

rang [ræŋ] *pt of* ring

range [reɪndʒ] *n* (*of mountains*) chaîne *f*; (*of missile, voice*) portée *f*; (*of products*) choix *m*, gamme *f*; (*MIL: also: shooting ~*) champ *m* de tir; (*indoor*) stand *m* de tir; (*also: kitchen ~*) fourneau *m* (de cuisine) ♦ *vt* (*place in a line*) mettre en rang, ranger ♦ *vi*: **to ~ over** (*extend*) couvrir; **to ~ from ... to** aller de ... à; **a ~ of** (*series: of proposals etc*) divers(es)

ranger ['reɪndʒə*] *n* garde forestier

rank [ræŋk] *n* rang *m*; (*MIL*) grade *m*; (*BRIT: also: taxi ~*) station *f* de taxis ♦ *vi*: **to ~ among** compter *or* se classer parmi ♦ *adj* (*stinking*) fétide, puant(e); **the ~ and file** (*fig*) la masse, la base

rankle ['ræŋkl] *vi* (*insult*) rester sur le cœur

ransack ['rænsæk] *vt* fouiller (à fond); (*plunder*) piller

ransom ['rænsəm] *n* rançon *f*; **to hold to ~** (*fig*) exercer un chantage sur

rant [rænt] *vi* fulminer

rap [ræp] *vt* frapper sur *or* à; taper sur; *n*: (*music*) rap *m*

rape [reɪp] *n* viol *m*; (*BOT*) colza *m* ♦ *vt*

violer; ~**(seed) oil** *n* huile *f* de colza

rapid ['ræpɪd] *adj* rapide; ~**s** *npl* (GEO) rapides *mpl*

rapist ['reɪpɪst] *n* violeur *m*

rapport [ræ'pɔː*] *n* entente *f*

rapture ['ræptʃə*] *n* extase *f*, ravissement *m*; **rapturous** ['ræptʃərəs] *adj* enthousiaste, frénétique

rare [rɛə*] *adj* rare; (CULIN: *steak*) saignant(e)

raring ['rɛərɪŋ] *adj*: ~ **to go** (*inf*) très impatient(e) de commencer

rascal ['rɑːskəl] *n* vaurien *m*

rash [ræʃ] *adj* imprudent(e), irréfléchi(e) ♦ *n* (MED) rougeur *f*, éruption *f*; (*spate: of events*) série (noire)

rasher ['ræʃə*] *n* fine tranche (de lard)

raspberry ['rɑːzbərɪ] *n* framboise *f*; ~ **bush** *n* framboisier *m*

rasping ['rɑːspɪŋ] *adj*: ~ **noise** grincement *m*

rat [ræt] *n* rat *m*

rate [reɪt] *n* taux *m*; (*speed*) vitesse *f*, rythme *m*; (*price*) tarif *m* ♦ *vt* classer; évaluer; ~**s** *npl* (BRIT: *tax*) impôts locaux; (*fees*) tarifs *mpl*; **to** ~ **sb/sth as** considérer qn/qch comme; ~**able value** (BRIT) *n* valeur locative imposable; ~**payer** (BRIT) *n* contribuable *m/f* (*payant les impôts locaux*)

rather ['rɑːðə*] *adv* plutôt; **it's** ~ **expensive** c'est assez cher; (*too much*) c'est un peu cher; **there's** ~ **a lot** il y en a beaucoup; **I would** *or* **I'd** ~ **go** j'aimerais mieux *or* je préférerais partir

rating ['reɪtɪŋ] *n* (*assessment*) évaluation *f*; (*score*) classement *m*; (NAUT: BRIT: *sailor*) matelot *m*; ~**s** *npl* (RADIO, TV) indice *m* d'écoute

ratio ['reɪʃɪəʊ] *n* proportion *f*

ration ['ræʃən] *n* (*gen pl*) ration(s) *f(pl)*

rational ['ræʃənl] *adj* raisonnable, sensé(e); (*solution, reasoning*) logique; ~**e** [ræʃə'nɑːl] *n* raisonnement *m*; ~**ize** ['ræʃnəlaɪz] *vt* rationaliser; (*conduct*) essayer d'expliquer *or* de motiver

rat race *n* foire *f* d'empoigne

rattle ['rætl] *n* (*of door, window*) battement *m*; (*of coins, chain*) cliquetis *m*; (*of train, engine*) bruit *m* de ferraille; (*object: for baby*) hochet *m* ♦ *vi* cliqueter; (*car, bus*): **to** ~ **along** rouler dans un bruit de ferraille ♦ *vt* agiter (bruyamment); (*unnerve*) décontenancer; ~**snake** *n* serpent *m* à sonnettes

raucous ['rɔːkəs] *adj* rauque; (*noisy*) bruyant(e), tapageur(euse)

rave [reɪv] *vi* (*in anger*) s'emporter; (*with enthusiasm*) s'extasier; (MED) délirer

raven ['reɪvn] *n* corbeau *m*

ravenous ['rævənəs] *adj* affamé(e)

ravine [rə'viːn] *n* ravin *m*

raving ['reɪvɪŋ] *adj*: ~ **lunatic** *n* fou(folle) furieux(euse)

ravishing ['rævɪʃɪŋ] *adj* enchanteur(eresse)

raw [rɔː] *adj* (*uncooked*) cru(e); (*not processed*) brut(e); (*sore*) à vif, irrité(e); (*inexperienced*) inexpérimenté(e); (*weather, day*) froid(e) et humide; ~ **deal** (*inf*) *n* sale coup *m*; ~ **material** *n* matière première

ray [reɪ] *n* rayon *m*; ~ **of hope** lueur *f* d'espoir

raze [reɪz] *vt* (*also*: ~ **to the ground**) raser, détruire

razor ['reɪzə*] *n* rasoir *m*; ~ **blade** *n* lame *f* de rasoir

Rd *abbr* = **road**

re [riː] *prep* concernant

reach [riːtʃ] *n* portée *f*, atteinte *f*; (*of river etc*) étendue *f* ♦ *vt* atteindre; (*conclusion, decision*) parvenir à ♦ *vi* s'étendre, étendre le bras; **out of/within** ~ hors de/à portée; **within** ~ **of the shops** pas trop loin des *or* à proximité des magasins; ~ **out** *vt* tendre ♦ *vi*: **to** ~ **out (for)** allonger le bras (pour prendre)

react [riː'ækt] *vi* réagir; ~**ion** [riː'ækʃən] *n* réaction *f*

reactor [riː'æktə*] *n* réacteur *m*

read[1] [riːd] (*pt, pp* **read**) *vi* lire ♦ *vt* lire; (*understand*) comprendre, interpréter; (*study*) étudier; (*meter*) relever; ~ **out** *vt* lire à haute voix; ~**able** *adj* facile *or* agréable à lire; (*writing*) lisible; ~**er** *n* lecteur(trice); (*book*) livre *m* de lecture; (BRIT: *at university*) chargé(e) d'enseignement; ~**ership** *n* (*of paper etc*) (nombre *m* de) lecteurs *mpl*

read[2] [red] *pt, pp of* **read**[1]

readily ['redɪlɪ] *adv* volontiers, avec empressement; (*easily*) facilement

readiness ['redɪnəs] *n* empressement *m*; **in** ~ (*prepared*) prêt(e)

reading ['riːdɪŋ] *n* lecture *f*; (*understanding*) interprétation *f*; (*on instrument*) indications *fpl*

ready ['redɪ] *adj* prêt(e); (*willing*) prêt, disposé(e); (*available*) disponible ♦ *n*: **at the** ~ (MIL) prêt à faire feu; **to get** ~ se préparer ♦ *vt* préparer; ~**-made** *adj* tout(e) fait(e); ~ **money** *n* (argent *m*) liquide *m*; ~**-to-wear** *adj* prêt(e) à porter

real [rɪəl] *adj* véritable; réel(le); **in** ~ **terms** dans la réalité; ~ **estate** *n* biens fonciers *or* immobiliers; ~**istic** *adj* réaliste; ~**ity** [riː'ælɪtɪ] *n* réalité *f*

realization [rɪəlaɪ'zeɪʃən] *n* (*awareness*) prise *f* de conscience; (*fulfilment; also: of asset*) réalisation *f*

realize ['rɪəlaɪz] *vt* (*understand*) se rendre compte de; (*a project, COMM: asset*) réaliser

really ['rɪəlɪ] *adv* vraiment; ~? vraiment?, c'est vrai?

realm [relm] *n* royaume *m*; (*fig*) domaine *m*

realtor ['rɪəltɔː*] (®:*US*) *n* agent immobilier

reap [riːp] *vt* moissonner; (*fig*) récolter

reappear ['riːə'pɪə*] vi réapparaître, reparaître

rear [rɪə*] adj de derrière, arrière inv; (AUT: wheel etc) arrière ♦ n arrière m ♦ vt (cattle, family) élever ♦ vi (also: ~ up: animal) se cabrer; **~guard** n (MIL) arrière-garde f

rear-view mirror ['rɪəvjuː-] n (AUT) rétroviseur m

reason ['riːzn] n raison f ♦ vi: **to ~ with sb** raisonner qn, faire entendre raison à qn; **to have ~ to think** avoir lieu de penser; **it stands to ~ that** il va sans dire que; **~able** adj raisonnable; (not bad) acceptable; **~ably** adv raisonnablement; **~ing** n raisonnement m

reassurance ['riːə'ʃuərəns] n réconfort m; (factual) assurance f, garantie f; **reassure** ['riːə'ʃuə*] vt rassurer

rebate ['riːbeɪt] n (on tax etc) dégrèvement m

rebel [n 'rebl, vb rɪ'bel] n rebelle m/f ♦ vi se rebeller, se révolter; **~lious** adj rebelle

rebound [vb rɪ'baund, n 'riːbaund] vi (ball) rebondir ♦ n rebond m; **to marry on the ~** se marier immédiatement après une déception amoureuse

rebuff [rɪ'bʌf] n rebuffade f

rebuke [rɪ'bjuːk] vt réprimander

rebut [rɪ'bʌt] vt réfuter

recall [rɪ'kɔːl] vt rappeler; (remember) se rappeler, se souvenir de ♦ n rappel m; (ability to remember) mémoire f

recant [rɪ'kænt] vi se rétracter; (REL) abjurer

recap ['riːkæp], **recapitulate** [riːkə'pɪtjuleɪt] vt, vi récapituler

rec'd abbr = **received**

recede [rɪ'siːd] vi (tide) descendre; (disappear) disparaître peu à peu; (memory, hope) s'estomper; **receding** [rɪ'siːdɪŋ] adj (chin) fuyant(e); **receding hairline** front dégarni

receipt [rɪ'siːt] n (document) reçu m; (for parcel etc) accusé m de réception; (act of receiving) réception f; **~s** npl (COMM) recettes fpl

receive [rɪ'siːv] vt recevoir

receiver [rɪ'siːvə*] n (TEL) récepteur m, combiné m; (RADIO) récepteur m; (of stolen goods) receleur m; (LAW) administrateur m judiciaire

recent ['riːsnt] adj récent(e); **~ly** adv récemment

receptacle [rɪ'septəkl] n récipient m

reception [rɪ'sepʃən] n réception f; (welcome) accueil m, réception; **~ desk** n réception f; **~ist** n réceptionniste m/f

recess [rɪ'ses] n (in room) renfoncement m, alcôve f; (secret place) recoin m; (POL etc: holiday) vacances fpl

recession [rɪ'seʃən] n récession f

recipe ['resɪpɪ] n recette f

recipient [rɪ'sɪpɪənt] n (of payment) bénéfi-

ciaire m/f; (of letter) destinataire m/f

recital [rɪ'saɪtl] n récital m

recite [rɪ'saɪt] vt (poem) réciter

reckless ['rekləs] adj (driver etc) imprudent(e)

reckon ['rekən] vt (count) calculer, compter; (think): **I ~ that ...** je pense que ...; **~ on** vt fus compter sur, s'attendre à; **~ing** n compte m, calcul m; estimation f

reclaim [rɪ'kleɪm] vt (demand back) réclamer (le remboursement or la restitution de); (land: from sea) assécher; (waste materials) récupérer

recline [rɪ'klaɪn] vi être allongé(e) or étendu(e); **reclining** [rɪ'klaɪnɪŋ] adj (seat) à dossier réglable

recluse [rɪ'kluːs] n reclus(e), ermite m

recognition [rekəg'nɪʃən] n reconnaissance f; **to gain ~** être reconnu(e); **transformed beyond ~** méconnaissable

recognize ['rekəgnaɪz] vt: **to ~ (by/as)** reconnaître (à/comme étant)

recoil [rɪ'kɔɪl] vi (person): **to ~ (from sth/doing sth)** reculer (devant qch/l'idée de faire qch) ♦ n (of gun) recul m

recollect [rekə'lekt] vt se rappeler, se souvenir de; **~ion** [rekə'lekʃən] n souvenir m

recommend [rekə'mend] vt recommander

reconcile ['rekənsaɪl] vt (two people) réconcilier; (two facts) concilier, accorder; **to ~ o.s. to** se résigner à

recondition ['riːkən'dɪʃən] vt remettre à neuf; réviser entièrement

reconnoitre [rekə'nɔɪtə*] (US **reconnoiter**) vt (MIL) reconnaître

reconstruct ['riːkən'strʌkt] vt (building) reconstruire; (crime, policy, system) reconstituer

record [n 'rekɔːd, vb rɪ'kɔːd] n rapport m, récit m; (of meeting etc) procès-verbal m; (register) registre m; (file) dossier m; (also: criminal ~) casier m judiciaire; (MUS: disc) disque m; (SPORT) record m; (COMPUT) article m ♦ vt (set down) noter; (MUS: song etc) enregistrer; **in ~ time** en un temps record; **off the ~** adj officieux(euse) ♦ adv officieusement; **~ card** n (in file) fiche f; **~ed delivery** [rɪ'kɔːdɪd-] n (BRIT: POST): **~ed delivery letter** etc lettre etc recommandée; **~er** [rɪ'kɔːdə*] n (MUS) flûte f à bec; **~ holder** n (SPORT) détenteur(trice) du record; **~ing** [rɪ'kɔːdɪŋ] n (MUS) enregistrement m; **~ player** n tourne-disque m

recount [rɪ'kaunt] vt raconter

re-count ['riːkaunt] n (POL: of votes) deuxième compte m ♦ vt recompter

recoup [rɪ'kuːp] vt: **to ~ one's losses** récupérer ce qu'on a perdu, se refaire

recourse [rɪ'kɔːs] n: **to have ~ to** avoir recours à

recover [rɪ'kʌvə*] vt récupérer ♦ vi: **to ~ (from)** (illness) se rétablir (de); (from shock) se remettre (de); **~y** [rɪ'kʌvərɪ] *n* récupération *f*; rétablissement *m*; (*ECON*) redressement *m*

recreation [rekrɪ'eɪʃən] *n* récréation *f*, détente *f*; **~al** *adj* pour la détente, récréatif(ive)

recruit [rɪ'kruːt] *n* recrue *f* ♦ *vt* recruter

rectangle ['rektæŋgl] *n* rectangle *m*; **rectangular** [rek'tæŋgjʊlə*] *adj* rectangulaire

rectify ['rektɪfaɪ] *vt* (*error*) rectifier, corriger

rector ['rektə*] *n* (*REL*) pasteur *m*

recuperate [rɪ'kuːpəreɪt] *vi* récupérer; (*from illness*) se rétablir

recur [rɪ'kɜː*] *vi* se reproduire; (*symptoms*) réapparaître; **~rence** *n* répétition *f*, réapparition *f*; **~rent** *adj* périodique, fréquent(e)

recycle *vt* recycler

red [red] *n* rouge *m*; (*POL: pej*) rouge *m/f* ♦ *adj* rouge; (*hair*) roux(rousse); **in the ~** (*account*) à découvert; (*business*) en déficit; **~ carpet treatment** *n* réception *f* en grande pompe; **R~ Cross** *n* Croix-Rouge *f*; **~currant** *n* groseille *f* (rouge); **~den** *vt, vi* rougir; **~dish** *adj* rougeâtre; (*hair*) qui tirent sur le roux

redeem [rɪ'diːm] *vt* (*debt*) rembourser; (*sth in pawn*) dégager; (*fig, also REL*) racheter; **~ing** *adj* (*feature*) qui sauve, qui rachète (le reste)

redeploy [riːdɪ'plɔɪ] *vt* (*resources*) réorganiser

redevelopment [riːdɪ'vɛləpmənt] *n* rénovation *f*, reconstruction *f*

red: ~-haired ['hɛəd] *adj* roux(rousse); **~-handed** [-'hændɪd] *adj*: **to be caught ~-handed** être pris(e) en flagrant délit *or* la main dans le sac; **~head** [-'hed] *n* roux-(rousse); **~ herring** *n* (*fig*) diversion *f*, fausse piste; **~-hot** [-'hɒt] *adj* chauffé(e) au rouge, brûlant(e)

redirect [riːdaɪ'rekt] *vt* (*mail*) faire suivre

red light *n*: **to go through a ~** (*AUT*) brûler un feu rouge; **red-light district** *n* quartier *m* des prostituées

redo ['riː'duː] (*irreg*) *vt* refaire

redolent ['redəʊlənt] *adj*: **~ of** qui sent; (*fig*) qui évoque

redress [rɪ'dres] *n* réparation *f* ♦ *vt* redresser

Red Sea *n*: **the ~** la mer Rouge

redskin ['redskɪn] *n* Peau-Rouge *m/f*

red tape *n* (*fig*) paperasserie (administrative)

reduce [rɪ'djuːs] *vt* réduire; (*lower*) abaisser; **"~ speed now"** (*AUT*) "ralentir"; **reduction** [rɪ'dʌkʃən] *n* réduction *f*; (*discount*) rabais *m*

redundancy [rɪ'dʌndənsɪ] (*BRIT*) *n* licenciement *m*, mise *f* au chômage

redundant [rɪ'dʌndənt] *adj* (*BRIT: worker*) mis(e) au chômage, licencié(e); (*detail, ob-*

ject) superflu(e); **to be made ~** être licencié(e), être mis(e) au chômage

reed [riːd] *n* (*BOT*) roseau *m*; (*MUS: of clarinet etc*) hanche *f*

reef [riːf] *n* (*at sea*) récif *m*, écueil *m*

reek [riːk] *vi*: **to ~ (of)** puer, empester

reel [riːl] *n* bobine *f*; (*FISHING*) moulinet *m*; (*CINEMA*) bande *f*; (*dance*) quadrille écossais ♦ *vi* (*sway*) chanceler; **~ in** *vt* (*fish, line*) ramener

ref [ref] (*inf*) *n abbr* (= *referee*) arbitre *m*

refectory [rɪ'fektərɪ] *n* réfectoire *m*

refer [rɪ'fɜː*] *vt*: **to ~ sb to** (*inquirer: for information, patient: to specialist*) adresser qn à; (*reader: to text*) renvoyer qn à; (*dispute, decision*): **to ~ sth to** soumettre qch à ♦ *vi*: **~ to** (*allude to*) parler de, faire allusion à; (*consult*) se reporter à

referee [refə'riː] *n* arbitre *m*; (*TENNIS*) juge-arbitre *m*; (*BRIT: for job application*) répondant(e)

reference ['refrəns] *n* référence *f*, renvoi *m*; (*mention*) allusion *f*, mention *f*; (*for job application: letter*) références, lettre *f* de recommandation; **with ~ to** (*COMM: in letter*) me référant à, suite à; **~ book** *n* ouvrage *m* de référence

refill [*vb* 'riː'fɪl, *n* 'riː:fɪl] *vt* remplir à nouveau; (*pen, lighter etc*) recharger ♦ *n* (*for pen etc*) recharge *f*

refine [rɪ'faɪn] *vt* (*sugar, oil*) raffiner; (*taste*) affiner; (*theory, idea*) fignoler (*inf*); **~d** *adj* (*person, taste*) raffiné(e)

reflect [rɪ'flekt] *vt* (*light, image*) réfléchir, refléter; (*fig*) refléter ♦ *vi* (*think*) réfléchir, méditer; **it ~s badly on him** cela le discrédite; **it ~s well on him** c'est tout à son honneur; **~ion** [rɪ'flekʃən] *n* réflexion *f*; (*image*) reflet *m*; (*criticism*): **~ion on** critique *f* de, atteinte *f* à; **on ~ion** réflexion faite

reflex ['riːfleks] *adj* réflexe ♦ *n* réflexe *m*; **~ive** [rɪfleksɪv] *adj* (*LING*) réfléchi(e)

reform [rɪ'fɔːm] *n* réforme *f* ♦ *vt* réformer; **R~ation** [refə'meɪʃən] *n*: **the R~ation** la Réforme; **~atory** (*US*) *n* ≈ centre *m* d'éducation surveillée

refrain [rɪ'freɪn] *vi*: **to ~ from doing** s'abstenir de faire ♦ *n* refrain *m*

refresh [rɪ'freʃ] *vt* rafraîchir; (*subj: sleep*) reposer; **~er course** (*BRIT*) *n* cours *m* de recyclage; **~ing** *adj* (*drink*) rafraîchissant(e); (*sleep*) réparateur(trice); **~ments** *npl* rafraîchissements *mpl*

refrigerator [rɪ'frɪdʒəreɪtə*] *n* réfrigérateur *m*, frigidaire *m* (®)

refuel ['riː'fjʊəl] *vi* se ravitailler en carburant

refuge ['refjuːdʒ] *n* refuge *m*; **to take ~ in** se réfugier dans

refugee [refju'dʒiː] *n* réfugié(e)

refund [*n* 'riː:fʌnd, *vb* rɪ'fʌnd] *n* remboursement m ♦ vt rembourser

refurbish [ˈriːˈfɜːbɪʃ] vt remettre à neuf

refusal [rɪˈfjuːzəl] n refus m; **to have first ~ on** avoir droit de préemption sur

refuse[1] [rɪˈfjuːz] vt, vi refuser

refuse[2] [ˈrefjuːs] n ordures fpl, détritus mpl; ~ **collection** n ramassage m d'ordures

regain [rɪˈgeɪn] vt regagner; retrouver

regal [ˈriːɡəl] adj royal(e)

regard [rɪˈɡɑːd] n respect m, estime f, considération f ♦ vt considérer; **to give one's ~s to** faire ses amitiés à; **"with kindest ~s"** "bien amicalement"; **as ~s, with ~ to = regarding; ~ing** prep en ce qui concerne; **~less** adv quand même; **~less of** sans se soucier de

régime [reɪˈʒiːm] n régime m

regiment [n ˈredʒɪmənt, vb ˈredʒɪment] n régiment m; **~al** [redʒɪˈmentl] adj d'un or du régiment

region [ˈriːdʒən] n région f; **in the ~ of** (fig) aux alentours de; **~al** adj régional(e)

register [ˈredʒɪstə*] n registre m; (also: electoral ~) liste électorale ♦ vt enregistrer; (birth, death) déclarer; (vehicle) immatriculer; (POST: letter) envoyer en recommandé; (subj: instrument) marquer ♦ vi s'inscrire; (at hotel) signer le registre; (make impression) être (bien) compris(e); **~ed** adj (letter, parcel) recommandé(e); **~ed trademark** n marque déposée; **registrar** [redʒɪsˈtrɑː*] n officier m de l'état civil; **registration** [redʒɪsˈtreɪʃən] n enregistrement m; (BRIT AUT: also: ~ number) numéro m d'immatriculation

registry [ˈredʒɪstrɪ] n bureau m de l'enregistrement; ~ **office** (BRIT) n bureau m de l'état civil; **to get married in a ~ office** ≈ se marier à la mairie

regret [rɪˈɡret] n regret m ♦ vt regretter; **~fully** adv à or avec regret

regular [ˈreɡjʊlə*] adj régulier(ère); (usual) habituel(le); (soldier) de métier ♦ n (client etc) habitué(e); **~ly** adv régulièrement

regulate [ˈreɡjʊleɪt] vt régler; **regulation** [reɡjʊˈleɪʃən] n (rule) règlement m; (adjustment) réglage m

rehabilitation [ˈriːhəbɪlɪˈteɪʃən] n (of offender) réinsertion f; (of addict) réadaptation f

rehearsal [rɪˈhɜːsəl] n répétition f

rehearse [rɪˈhɜːs] vt répéter

reign [reɪn] n règne m ♦ vi régner

reimburse [riːɪmˈbɜːs] vt rembourser

rein [reɪn] n (for horse) rêne f

reindeer [ˈreɪndɪə*] n, pl inv renne m

reinforce [riːɪnˈfɔːs] vt renforcer; **~d concrete** n béton armé; **~ments** npl (MIL) renfort(s) m(pl)

reinstate [riːɪnˈsteɪt] vt rétablir, réintégrer

reject [n ˈriːdʒekt, vb rɪˈdʒekt] n (COMM) article m de rebut ♦ vt refuser; (idea) reje-

ter; **~ion** [rɪˈdʒekʃən] n rejet m, refus m

rejoice [rɪˈdʒɔɪs] vi: **to ~ (at or over)** se réjouir (de)

rejuvenate [rɪˈdʒuːvɪneɪt] vt rajeunir

relapse [rɪˈlæps] n (MED) rechute f

relate [rɪˈleɪt] vt (tell) raconter; (connect) établir un rapport entre ♦ vi: **this ~s to** cela se rapporte à; **to ~ to sb** entretenir des rapports avec qn; **~d** adj apparenté(e); **relating to** prep concernant

relation [rɪˈleɪʃən] n (person) parent(e); (link) rapport m, lien m; **~ship** n rapport m, lien m; (personal ties) relations fpl, rapports; (also: family ~ship) lien de parenté

relative [ˈrelətɪv] n parent(e) ♦ adj relatif(ive); **all her ~s** toute sa famille; **~ly** adv relativement

relax [rɪˈlæks] vi (muscle) se relâcher; (person: unwind) se détendre ♦ vt relâcher; (mind, person) détendre; **~ation** [riːlækˈseɪʃən] n relâchement m; (of mind) détente f, relaxation f; (recreation) détente f, délassement m; **~ed** adj détendu(e); **~ing** adj délassant(e)

relay [ˈriːleɪ] n (SPORT) course f de relais ♦ vt (message) retransmettre, relayer

release [rɪˈliːs] n (from prison, obligation) libération f; (of gas etc) émission f; (of film etc) sortie f; (new recording) disque m ♦ vt (prisoner) libérer; (gas etc) émettre, dégager; (free: from wreckage etc) dégager; (TECH: catch, spring etc) faire jouer; (book, film) sortir; (report, news) rendre public, publier

relegate [ˈreləɡeɪt] vt reléguer; (BRIT SPORT): **to be ~d** descendre dans une division inférieure

relent [rɪˈlent] vi se laisser fléchir; **~less** adj implacable; (unceasing) continuel(le)

relevant [ˈreləvənt] adj (question) pertinent(e); (fact) significatif(ive); (information) utile; **~ to** ayant rapport à, approprié à

reliable [rɪˈlaɪəbl] adj (person, firm) sérieux(euse), fiable; (method, machine) fiable; (news, information) sûr(e); **reliably** adv: **to be reliably informed** savoir de source sûre

reliance [rɪˈlaɪəns] n: **~ (on)** (person) confiance f (en); (drugs, promises) besoin m (de), dépendance f (de)

relic [ˈrelɪk] n (REL) relique f; (of the past) vestige m

relief [rɪˈliːf] n (from pain, anxiety etc) soulagement m; (help, supplies) secours m(pl); (ART, GEO) relief m

relieve [rɪˈliːv] vt (pain, patient) soulager; (fear, worry) dissiper; (bring help) secourir; (take over from: gen) relayer; (: guard) relever; **to ~ sb of sth** débarrasser qn de qch; **to ~ o.s.** se soulager

religion [rɪˈlɪdʒən] n religion f; **religious** [rɪˈlɪdʒəs] adj religieux(euse); (book) de piété

relinquish [rɪˈlɪŋkwɪʃ] vt abandonner;

(*plan, habit*) renoncer à

relish ['relɪʃ] *n* (*CULIN*) condiment *m*; (*enjoyment*) délectation *f* ♦ *vt* (*food etc*) savourer; **to ~ doing** se délecter à faire

relocate ['riːləʊ'keɪt] *vt* installer ailleurs ♦ *vi* déménager, s'installer ailleurs

reluctance [rɪ'lʌktəns] *n* répugnance *f*

reluctant [rɪ'lʌktənt] *adj* peu disposé(e), qui hésite; **~ly** *adv* à contrecœur

rely on [rɪlaɪ] *vt fus* (*be dependent*) dépendre de; (*trust*) compter sur

remain [rɪ'meɪn] *vi* rester; **~der** *n* reste *m*; **~ing** *adj* qui reste; **~s** *npl* restes *mpl*

remand [rɪ'mɑːnd] *n*: **on ~** en détention préventive ♦ *vt*: **to be ~ed in custody** être placé(e) en détention préventive; **~ home** (*BRIT*) *n* maison *f* d'arrêt

remark [rɪ'mɑːk] *n* remarque *f*, observation *f* ♦ *vt* (faire) remarquer, dire; **~able** *adj* remarquable

remedial [rɪ'miːdɪəl] *adj* (*tuition, classes*) de rattrapage; **~ exercises** gymnastique corrective

remedy ['remədɪ] *n*: **~ (for)** remède *m* (contre *or* à) ♦ *vt* remédier à

remember [rɪ'membə*] *vt* se rappeler, se souvenir de; (*send greetings*): **~ me to him** saluez-le de ma part; **remembrance** [rɪ'membrəns] *n* souvenir *m*; mémoire *f*

remind [rɪ'maɪnd] *vt*: **to ~ sb of** rappeler à qn; **to ~ sb to do** faire penser à qn à faire, rappeler à qn qu'il doit faire; **~er** *n* (*souvenir*) souvenir *m*; (*letter*) rappel *m*

reminisce [remɪ'nɪs] *vi*: **to ~ (about)** évoquer ses souvenirs (de)

reminiscent [remɪ'nɪsnt] *adj*: **to be ~ of** rappeler, faire penser à

remiss [rɪ'mɪs] *adj* négligent(e)

remission [rɪ'mɪʃən] *n* (*of illness, sins*) rémission *f*; (*of debt, prison sentence*) remise *f*

remit [rɪ'mɪt] *vt* (*send: money*) envoyer; **~tance** *n* paiement *m*

remnant ['remnənt] *n* reste *m*, restant *m*; (*of cloth*) coupon *m*; **~s** *npl* (*COMM*) fins *fpl* de série

remorse [rɪ'mɔːs] *n* remords *m*; **~ful** *adj* plein(e) de remords; **~less** *adj* (*fig*) impitoyable

remote [rɪ'məʊt] *adj* éloigné(e), lointain(e); (*person*) distant(e); (*possibility*) vague; **~ control** *n* télécommande *f*; **~ly** *adv* au loin; (*slightly*) très vaguement

remould ['riːməʊld] (*BRIT*) *n* (*tyre*) pneu rechapé

removable [rɪ'muːvəbl] *adj* (*detachable*) amovible

removal [rɪ'muːvəl] *n* (*taking away*) enlèvement *m*; suppression *f*; (*BRIT: from house*) déménagement *m*; (*from office: dismissal*) renvoi *m*; (*of stain*) nettoyage *m*; (*MED*) ablation *f*; **~ van** (*BRIT*) *n* camion *m* de déménagement

remove [rɪ'muːv] *vt* enlever, retirer; (*employee*) renvoyer; (*stain*) faire partir; (*abuse*) supprimer; (*doubt*) chasser

render ['rendə*] *vt* rendre; **~ing** *n* (*MUS etc*) interprétation *f*

rendezvous *n* rendez-vous *m inv*

renew [rɪ'njuː] *vt* renouveler; (*negotiations*) reprendre; (*acquaintance*) renouer; **~able** *adj* (*energy*) renouvelable; **~al** *n* renouvellement *m*; reprise *f*

renounce [rɪ'naʊns] *vt* renoncer à

renovate ['renəveɪt] *vt* rénover; (*art work*) restaurer

renown [rɪ'naʊn] *n* renommée *f*; **~ed** *adj* renommé(e)

rent [rent] *n* loyer *m* ♦ *vt* louer; **~al** *n* (*for television, car*) (prix *m* de) location *f*

rep [rep] *n abbr* = **representative**; = **repertory**

repair [rɪ'pɛə*] *n* réparation *f* ♦ *vt* réparer; **in good/bad ~** en bon/mauvais état; **~ kit** *n* trousse *f* de réparation

repatriate [riː'pætrɪeɪt] *vt* rapatrier

repay [riː'peɪ] (*irreg*) *vt* (*money, creditor*) rembourser; (*sb's efforts*) récompenser; **~ment** *n* remboursement *m*

repeal [rɪ'piːl] *n* (*of law*) abrogation *f* ♦ *vt* (*law*) abroger

repeat [rɪ'piːt] *n* (*RADIO, TV*) reprise *f* ♦ *vt* répéter; (*COMM: order*) renouveler; (*SCOL: a class*) redoubler ♦ *vi* répéter; **~edly** *adv* souvent, à plusieurs reprises

repel [rɪ'pel] *vt* repousser; **~lent** *adj* repoussante(e) ♦ *n*: **insect ~lent** insectifuge *m*

repent [rɪ'pent] *vi*: **to ~ (of)** se repentir (de); **~ance** *n* repentir *m*

repertory ['repətərɪ] *n* (*also*: **~ theatre**) théâtre *m* de répertoire

repetition [repə'tɪʃən] *n* répétition *f*

repetitive [rɪ'petɪtɪv] *adj* (*movement, work*) répétitif(ive); (*speech*) plein(e) de redites

replace [rɪ'pleɪs] *vt* (*put back*) remettre, replacer; (*take the place of*) remplacer; **~ment** *n* (*substitution*) remplacement *m*; (*person*) remplaçant(e)

replay ['riːpleɪ] *n* (*of match*) match rejoué; (*of tape, film*) répétition *f*

replenish [rɪ'plenɪʃ] *vt* (*glass*) remplir (de nouveau); (*stock etc*) réapprovisionner

replica ['replɪkə] *n* réplique *f*, copie exacte

reply [rɪ'plaɪ] *n* réponse *f* ♦ *vi* répondre; **~ coupon** *n* coupon-réponse *m*

report [rɪ'pɔːt] *n* rapport *m*; (*PRESS etc*) reportage *m*; (*BRIT: also: school ~*) bulletin *m* (scolaire); (*of gun*) détonation *f* ♦ *vt* rapporter, faire un compte rendu de; (*PRESS etc*) faire un reportage sur; (*bring to notice: occurrence*) signaler ♦ *vi* (*make a ~*) faire un rapport (*or* un reportage); (*present o.s.*): **to ~ (to sb)** se présenter (chez qn); (*be responsible to*): **to ~ to sb** être sous les ordres de qn; ~ **card** (*US, SCOTTISH*) n bulletin *m* scolaire; **~edly** adv: **she is ~edly living in ...** elle habiterait ...; **he ~edly told them to ...** il leur aurait ordonné de ...; **~er** n reporter *m*

repose [rɪ'pəuz] n: **in ~** en or au repos

represent [reprɪ'zent] vt représenter; (*view, belief*) présenter, expliquer; (*describe*): **to ~ sth as** présenter or décrire qch comme; **~ation** [reprɪzen'teɪʃən] n représentation *f*; **~ations** npl (*protest*) démarche *f*; **~ative** n représentant(e); (*US: POL*) député *m* ♦ adj représentatif(ive), caractéristique

repress [rɪ'pres] vt réprimer; **~ion** [rɪ'preʃən] n répression *f*

reprieve [rɪ'priːv] n (*LAW*) grâce *f*; (*fig*) sursis *m*, délai *m*

reprisal [rɪ'praɪzəl] n: **~s** npl représailles *fpl*

reproach [rɪ'prəutʃ] vt: **to ~ sb with sth** reprocher qch à qn; **~ful** adj de reproche

reproduce [riːprə'djuːs] vt reproduire ♦ vi se reproduire; **reproduction** [riːprə'dʌkʃən] n reproduction *f*

reproof [rɪ'pruːf] n reproche *m*

reptile ['reptaɪl] n reptile *m*

republic [rɪ'pʌblɪk] n république *f*; **~an** adj républicain(e)

repudiate [rɪ'pjuːdɪeɪt] vt répudier, rejeter

repulsive [rɪ'pʌlsɪv] adj repoussant(e), répulsif(ive)

reputable ['repjutəbl] adj de bonne réputation; (*occupation*) honorable

reputation [repju'teɪʃən] n réputation *f*

reputed [rɪ'pjuːtɪd] adj (*supposed*) supposé(e); **~ly** adv d'après ce qu'on dit

request [rɪ'kwest] n demande *f*; (*formal*) requête *f* ♦ vt: **to ~ (of or from sb)** demander (à qn); **~ stop** (*BRIT*) n (*for bus*) arrêt facultatif

require [rɪ'kwaɪə*] vt (*need: subj: person*) avoir besoin de; (: *thing, situation*) demander; (*want*) exiger; (*order*): **to ~ sb to do sth/sth of sb** exiger que qn fasse qch/qch de qn; **~ment** n exigence *f*; besoin *m*; condition requise

requisite ['rekwɪzɪt] n chose *f* nécessaire ♦ adj requis(e), nécessaire; **toilet ~s** accessoires *mpl* de toilette

requisition [rekwɪ'zɪʃən] n: **~ (for)** demande *f* (de) ♦ vt (*MIL*) réquisitionner

rescue ['reskjuː] n (*from accident*) sauvetage *m*; (*help*) secours *mpl* ♦ vt sauver; **~ party** n équipe *f* de sauvetage; **~r** n sauveteur *m*

research [rɪ'sɜːtʃ] n recherche(s) *f(pl)* ♦ vt faire des recherches sur

resemblance [rɪ'zembləns] n ressemblance *f*

resemble [rɪ'zembl] vt ressembler à

resent [rɪ'zent] vt être contrarié(e) par; **~ful** adj irrité(e), plein(e) de ressentiment; **~ment** n ressentiment *m*

reservation [rezə'veɪʃən] n (*booking*) réservation *f*; (*doubt*) réserve *f*; (*for tribe*) réserve; **to make a ~** (in a hotel/a restaurant/on a plane) réserver or retenir une chambre/une table/une place

reserve [rɪ'zɜːv] n réserve *f*; (*SPORT*) remplaçant(e) ♦ vt (*seats etc*) réserver, retenir; **~s** npl (*MIL*) réservistes *mpl*; **in ~** en réserve; **~d** adj réservé(e)

reshuffle ['riː'ʃʌfl] n: **Cabinet ~** (*POL*) remaniement ministériel

residence ['rezɪdəns] n résidence *f*; **~ permit** (*BRIT*) n permis *m* de séjour

resident ['rezɪdənt] n résident(e) ♦ adj résidant(e); **~ial** [rezɪ'denʃəl] adj (*area*) résidentiel(le); (*course*) avec hébergement sur place; **~ial school** n internat *m*

residue ['rezɪdjuː] n reste *m*; (*CHEM, PHYSICS*) résidu *m*

resign [rɪ'zaɪn] vt (*one's post*) démissionner de ♦ vi démissionner; **to ~ o.s. to** se résigner à; **~ation** [rezɪg'neɪʃən] n (*of post*) démission *f*; (*state of mind*) résignation *f*; **~ed** adj résigné(e)

resilient [rɪ'zɪlɪənt] adj (*material*) élastique; (*person*) qui réagit, qui a du ressort

resist [rɪ'zɪst] vt résister à; **~ance** n résistance *f*

resolution [rezə'luːʃən] n résolution *f*

resolve [rɪ'zɒlv] n résolution *f* ♦ vt (*problem*) résoudre ♦ vi: **to ~ to do** résoudre or décider de faire

resort [rɪ'zɔːt] n (*town*) station *f*; (*recourse*) recours *m* ♦ vi: **to ~ to** avoir recours à; **in the last ~** en dernier ressort

resound [rɪ'zaund] vi: **to ~ (with)** retentir or résonner (de); **~ing** [rɪ'zaundɪŋ] adj retentissant(e)

resource [rɪ'sɔːs] n ressource *f*; **~s** npl (*supplies, wealth etc*) ressources; **~ful** adj ingénieux(euse), débrouillard(e)

respect [rɪs'pekt] n respect *m* ♦ vt respecter; **~s** npl (*compliments*) respects, hommages *mpl*; **with ~ to** en ce qui concerne; **in this ~** à cet égard; **~able** adj respectable; **~ful** adj respectueux(euse)

respite ['respaɪt] n répit *m*

resplendent [rɪs'plendənt] adj resplendissant(e)

respond [rɪs'pɒnd] vi répondre; (*react*) réagir; **response** [rɪs'pɒns] n réponse *f*, réaction *f*

responsibility [rɪspɒnsə'bɪlɪtɪ] n responsabilité *f*

responsible [rɪs'pɒnsəbl] adj (*liable*): **~ (for)** responsable (de); (*person*) digne de confiance; (*job*) qui comporte des responsabilités

responsive [rɪs'pɒnsɪv] adj qui réagit; (*person*) qui n'est pas réservé(e) or indifférent(e)

rest [rest] n repos *m*; (*stop*) arrêt *m*, pause *f*; (*MUS*) silence *m*; (*support*) support *m*, appui *m*; (*remainder*) reste *m*, restant *m* ♦ *vi* se reposer; (*be supported*): **to ~ on** appuyer *or* reposer sur; (*remain*) rester ♦ *vt* (*lean*): **to ~ sth on/against** appuyer qch sur/contre; **the ~ of them** les autres; **it ~s with him to ...** c'est à lui de ...

restaurant ['rɛstərɒŋ] *n* restaurant *m*; **~ car** (*BRIT*) *n* wagon-restaurant *m*

restful ['rɛstful] *adj* reposant(e)

restive ['rɛstɪv] *adj* agité(e), impatient(e); (*horse*) rétif(ive)

restless ['rɛstləs] *adj* agité(e)

restoration [rɛstə'reɪʃən] *n* restauration *f*; restitution *f*; rétablissement *m*

restore [rɪ'stɔ:*] *vt* (*building*) restaurer; (*sth stolen*) restituer; (*peace, health*) rétablir; **to ~ to** (*former state*) ramener à

restrain [rɪs'treɪn] *vt* contenir; (*person*): **to ~** (*from doing*) retenir (de faire); **~ed** *adj* (*style*) sobre; (*manner*) mesuré(e); **~t** *n* (*restriction*) contrainte *f*; (*moderation*) retenue *f*

restrict [rɪs'trɪkt] *vt* restreindre, limiter; **~ion** [rɪs'trɪkʃən] *n* restriction *f*, limitation *f*

rest room (*US*) *n* toilettes *fpl*

result [rɪ'zʌlt] *n* résultat *m* ♦ *vi*: **to ~ in** aboutir à, se terminer par; **as a ~ of** à la suite de

resume [rɪ'zju:m] *vt, vi* (*work, journey*) reprendre

résumé ['reɪzju:meɪ] *n* résumé *m*; (*US*) curriculum vitae *m*

resumption [rɪ'zʌmpʃən] *n* reprise *f*

resurgence [rɪ'sɜ:dʒəns] *n* (*of energy, activity*) regain *m*

resurrection [rɛzə'rekʃən] *n* résurrection *f*

resuscitate [rɪ'sʌsɪteɪt] *vt* (*MED*) réanimer

retail [*n, adj* 'ri:teɪl, *vb* ri:'teɪl] *adj* de *or* au détail ♦ *adv* au détail; **~er** ['ri:teɪlə*] *n* détaillant(e); **~ price** *n* prix *m* de détail

retain [rɪ'teɪn] *vt* (*keep*) garder, conserver; **~er** *n* (*fee*) acompte *m*, provision *f*

retaliate [rɪ'tælieɪt] *vi*: **to ~** (**against**) se venger (de); **retaliation** [rɪtæli'eɪʃən] *n* représailles *fpl*, vengeance *f*

retarded [rɪ'tɑ:dɪd] *adj* retardé(e)

retch [retʃ] *vi* avoir des haut-le-cœur

retentive [rɪ'tentɪv] *adj*: **~ memory** excellente mémoire

retina ['retɪnə] *n* rétine *f*

retire [rɪ'taɪə*] *vi* (*give up work*) prendre sa retraite; (*withdraw*) se retirer, partir; (*go to bed*) (aller) se coucher; **~d** *adj* (*person*) retraité(e); **~ment** *n* retraite *f*; **retiring** [rɪ'taɪərɪŋ] *adj* (*shy*) réservé(e); (*leaving*) sortant(e)

retort [rɪ'tɔ:t] *vi* riposter

retrace [rɪ'treɪs] *vt*: **to ~ one's steps** revenir sur ses pas

retract [rɪ'trækt] *vt* (*statement, claws*) rétracter; (*undercarriage, aerial*) rentrer, escamoter

retrain [ri:'treɪn] *vt* (*worker*) recycler

retread ['ri:tred] *n* (*tyre*) pneu rechapé

retreat [rɪ'tri:t] *n* retraite *f* ♦ *vi* battre en retraite

retribution [retrɪ'bju:ʃən] *n* châtiment *m*

retrieval [rɪ'tri:vəl] *n* (*see vb*) récupération *f*, réparation *f*

retrieve [rɪ'tri:v] *vt* (*sth lost*) récupérer; (*situation, honour*) sauver; (*match*) réparer; (*error, loss*) réparer; **~r** *n* chien *m* d'arrêt

retrospect ['retrəuspekt] *n*: **in ~** rétrospectivement, après coup; **~ive** [retrəu'spektɪv] *adj* rétrospectif(ive); (*law*) rétroactif(ive)

return [rɪ'tɜ:n] *n* (*going or coming back*) retour *m*; (*of sth stolen etc*) restitution *f*; (*FINANCE: from land, shares*) rendement *m*, rapport *m* ♦ *cpd* (*journey*) de retour; (*BRIT: ticket*) aller et retour; (*match*) retour ♦ *vi* (*come back*) revenir; (*go back*) retourner ♦ *vt* rendre; (*bring back*) rapporter; (*send back; also: ball*) renvoyer; (*put back*) remettre; (*POL: candidate*) élire; **~s** *npl* (*COMM*) recettes *fpl*; (*FINANCE*) bénéfices *mpl*; **in ~** (**for**) en échange (de); **by ~ (of post)** par retour (du courrier); **many happy ~s (of the day)!** bon anniversaire!

reunion [ri:'ju:njən] *n* réunion *f*

reunite [ri:ju:'naɪt] *vt* réunir

rev [rev] *n abbr* (*AUT*: = *revolution*) tour *m* ♦ *vt* (*also*: **~ up**) emballer

revamp ['ri:'væmp] *vt* (*firm, system etc*) réorganiser

reveal [rɪ'vi:l] *vt* (*make known*) révéler; (*display*) laisser voir; **~ing** *adj* révélateur(trice); (*dress*) au décolleté généreux *or* suggestif

revel ['revl] *vi*: **to ~ in sth/in doing** se délecter de qch/à faire

revelry ['revlrɪ] *n* festivités *fpl*

revenge [rɪ'vendʒ] *n* vengeance *f*; **to take ~ on** (*enemy*) se venger sur

revenue ['revənju:] *n* revenu *m*

reverberate [rɪ'vɜ:bəreɪt] *vi* (*sound*) retentir, se répercuter; (*fig: shock etc*) se propager

reverence ['revərəns] *n* vénération *f*, révérence *f*

Reverend ['revərənd] *adj* (*in titles*): **the ~ John Smith** (*Anglican*) le révérend John Smith; (*Catholic*) l'abbé (John) Smith; (*Protestant*) le pasteur (John) Smith

reversal [rɪ'vɜ:səl] *n* (*of opinion*) revirement *m*; (*of order*) renversement *m*; (*of direction*) changement *m*

reverse [rɪ'vɜ:s] *n* contraire *m*, opposé *m*; (*back*) dos *m*, envers *m*; (*of paper*) verso *m*; (*of coin; also: setback*) revers *m*; (*AUT: also:* **~ gear**) marche *f* arrière ♦ *adj* (*order, direction*) opposé(e), inverse ♦ *vt* (*order, position*) changer, inverser; (*direction, policy*) changer complètement de; (*decision*) annuler; (*roles*) renverser; (*car*) faire marche arrière avec ♦ *vi* (*BRIT: AUT*) faire marche arrière; **he** ~**d (the car) into a wall** il a embouti un mur en marche arrière; ~**d charge call** (BRIT) n (TEL) communication f en PCV; **reversing lights** (BRIT) npl (AUT) feux mpl de marche arrière or de recul

revert [rɪ'vɜ:t] vi: **to ~ to** revenir à, retourner à

review [rɪ'vju:] n revue f, (of book, film) critique f, compte rendu; (of situation, policy) examen m, bilan m ♦ vt passer en revue; faire la critique de; examiner; ~**er** n critique m

revile [rɪ'vaɪl] vt injurier

revise [rɪ'vaɪz] vt réviser, modifier; (manuscript) revoir, corriger ♦ vi (study) réviser; **revision** [rɪ'vɪʒən] n révision f

revival [rɪ'vaɪvəl] n reprise f, (recovery) rétablissement m; (of faith) renouveau m

revive [rɪ'vaɪv] vt (person) ranimer; (custom) rétablir; (economy) relancer; (hope, courage) raviver, faire renaître; (play) reprendre ♦ vi (person) reprendre connaissance; (: from ill health) se rétablir; (hope etc) renaître; (activity) reprendre

revoke [rɪ'vəuk] vt révoquer; (law) abroger

revolt [rɪ'vəult] n révolte f ♦ vi se révolter, se rebeller ♦ vt révolter, dégoûter; ~**ing** adj dégoûtant(e)

revolution [revə'lu:ʃən] n révolution f; (of wheel etc) tour m, révolution; ~**ary** adj révolutionnaire ♦ n révolutionnaire m/f

revolve [rɪ'vɒlv] vi tourner

revolver [rɪ'vɒlvə*] n revolver m

revolving [rɪ'vɒlvɪŋ] adj tournant(e); (chair) pivotant(e); ~ **door** n (porte f à) tambour m

revulsion [rɪ'vʌlʃən] n dégoût m, répugnance f

reward [rɪ'wɔ:d] n récompense f ♦ vt: **to ~ (for)** récompenser (de); ~**ing** adj (fig) qui (en) vaut la peine, gratifiant(e)

rewind [ri:'waɪnd] (irreg) vt (tape) rembobiner

rewire [ri:'waɪə*] vt (house) refaire l'installation électrique de

rheumatism ['ru:mətɪzəm] n rhumatisme m

Rhine [raɪn] n: **the ~** le Rhin

rhinoceros [raɪ'nɒsərəs] n rhinocéros m

Rhone [rəun] n: **the ~** le Rhône

rhubarb ['ru:bɑ:b] n rhubarbe f

rhyme [raɪm] n rime f; (verse) vers mpl

rhythm ['rɪðəm] n rythme m

rib [rɪb] n (ANAT) côte f

ribbon ['rɪbən] n ruban m; **in ~s** (torn) en lambeaux

rice [raɪs] n riz m; ~ **pudding** n riz au lait

rich [rɪtʃ] adj riche; (gift, clothes) somptueux(euse) ♦ npl: **the ~** les riches mpl; ~**es** npl richesses fpl; ~**ly** adv richement; (deserved, earned) largement

rickets ['rɪkɪts] n rachitisme m

rickety ['rɪkɪtɪ] adj branlant(e)

rickshaw ['rɪkʃɔ:] n pousse-pousse m inv

rid [rɪd] (pt, pp rid) vt: **to ~ sb of** débarrasser qn de; **to get ~ of** se débarrasser de

riddle ['rɪdl] n (puzzle) énigme f ♦ vt: **to be ~d with** être criblé(e) de; (fig: guilt, corruption, doubts) être en proie à

ride [raɪd] (pt rode, pp ridden) n promenade f, tour m; (distance covered) trajet m ♦ vi (as sport) monter (à cheval), faire du cheval; (go somewhere: on horse, bicycle) aller (à cheval or bicyclette etc); (journey: on bicycle, motorcycle, bus) rouler ♦ vt (a certain horse) monter; (distance) parcourir, faire; **to take sb for a ~** (fig) faire marcher qn; **to ~ a horse/bicycle** monter à cheval/à bicyclette; ~**r** n cavalier(ère); (in race) jockey m; (on bicycle) cycliste m/f; (on motorcycle) motocycliste m/f

ridge [rɪdʒ] n (of roof, mountain) arête f; (of hill) faîte m; (on object) strie f

ridicule ['rɪdɪkju:l] n ridicule m; dérision f

ridiculous [rɪ'dɪkjuləs] adj ridicule

riding ['raɪdɪŋ] n équitation f; ~ **school** n manège m, école f d'équitation

rife [raɪf] adj répandu(e); ~ **with** abondant(e) en, plein(e) de

riffraff ['rɪfræf] n racaille f

rifle ['raɪfl] n fusil m (à canon rayé) ♦ vt vider, dévaliser; ~ **through** vt (belongings) fouiller; (papers) feuilleter; ~ **range** n champ m de tir; (at fair) stand m de tir

rift [rɪft] n fente f, fissure f; (fig: disagreement) désaccord m

rig [rɪg] n (also: oil ~: at sea) plate-forme pétrolière ♦ vt (election etc) truquer; ~ **out** (BRIT) vt: **to ~ out as/in** habiller en/de; ~ **up** vt arranger, faire avec des moyens de fortune; ~**ging** n (NAUT) gréement m

right [raɪt] adj (correctly chosen: answer, road etc) bon(bonne); (true) juste, exact(e); (suitable) approprié(e), convenable; (just) juste, équitable; (morally good) bien inv; (not left) droit(e) ♦ n (what is morally right) bien m; (title, claim) droit m; (not left) droite f ♦ adv (answer) correctement, juste; (treat) bien, comme il faut; (not on the left) à droite ♦ vt redresser ♦ excl bon!; **to be ~** (person) avoir raison; (answer) être juste or correct(e); (clock) être à l'heure (juste); **by ~s** en toute justice; **on the ~** à droite; **to be in the ~** avoir raison; ~ **now** en ce moment même; tout de suite; ~ **in the middle** en plein milieu; ~ **away** immédiatement; ~ **angle** n (MATH) angle droit; ~**eous** ['raɪtʃəs] adj droit(e), vertueux(euse); (anger) justifié(e); ~**ful** adj légitime; ~-**handed** adj (person) droitier(ère); ~-**hand man** n bras droit (fig); ~-**hand side** n côté droit; ~**ly** adv (with reason) à juste titre; ~ **of way** n droit m de passage; (AUT) priorité f; ~-**wing** adj (POL) de droite

rigid ['rɪdʒɪd] adj rigide; (principle, control) strict(e)

rigmarole ['rɪgmərəʊl] n comédie f

rigorous ['rɪgərəs] adj rigoureux(euse)

rile [raɪl] vt agacer

rim [rɪm] n bord m; (of spectacles) monture f; (of wheel) jante f

rind [raɪnd] n (of bacon) couenne f; (of lemon etc) écorce f, zeste m; (of cheese) croûte f

ring [rɪŋ] (pt **rang**, pp **rung**) n anneau m; (on finger) bague f; (also: wedding ~) alliance f; (of people, objects) cercle m; (of spies) réseau m; (of smoke etc) rond m; (arena) piste f, arène f; (for boxing) ring m; (sound of bell) sonnerie f ♦ vi (telephone, bell) sonner; (person: by telephone) téléphoner; (also: ~ out: voice, words) retentir; (ears) bourdonner ♦ vt (BRIT: TEL: also: ~ up) téléphoner à, appeler; (bell) faire sonner; **to** ~ **the bell** sonner; **to give sb a** ~ (BRIT: TEL) appeler qn; ~ **back** (BRIT) vt, vi (TEL) rappeler; ~ **off** (BRIT) vi (TEL) raccrocher; ~ **up** (BRIT) vt (TEL) appeler; ~**ing** n (of telephone) sonnerie f; (of bell) tintement m; (in ears) bourdonnement m; ~**ing tone** (BRIT) n (TEL) sonnerie f; ~**leader** n (of gang) chef m, meneur m

ringlets ['rɪŋlɪts] npl anglaises fpl

ring road: (BRIT) n route f de ceinture; (motorway) périphérique m

rink [rɪŋk] n (also: ice ~) patinoire f

rinse [rɪns] vt rincer

riot ['raɪət] n émeute f; (of flowers, colour) profusion f ♦ vi faire une émeute, manifester avec violence; **to run** ~ se déchaîner; ~**ous** adj (mob, assembly) séditieux(euse), déchaîné(e); (living, behaviour) débauché(e); (party) très animé(e); (welcome) délirant(e)

rip [rɪp] n déchirure f ♦ vt déchirer ♦ vi se déchirer; ~**cord** ['rɪpkɔːd] n poignée f d'ouverture

ripe [raɪp] adj (fruit) mûr(e); (cheese) fait(e); ~**n** vt mûrir ♦ vi mûrir

ripple ['rɪpl] n ondulation f; (of applause, laughter) cascade f ♦ vi onduler

rise [raɪz] (pt **rose**, pp **risen**) n (slope) côte f, pente f; (hill) hauteur f; (increase: in wages: BRIT) augmentation f; (: in prices, temperature) hausse f, augmentation; (fig: to power etc) ascension f ♦ vi s'élever, monter; (prices, numbers) augmenter; (waters) monter; (sun; person: from chair, bed) se lever; (also: ~ up: tower, building) s'élever; (: rebel) se révolter; se rebeller; (in rank) s'élever; **to give** ~ **to** donner lieu à; **to** ~ **to the occasion** se montrer à la hauteur; **rising** adj (increasing: number, prices) en hausse; (tide) montant(e); (sun, moon) levant(e)

risk [rɪsk] n risque m ♦ vt risquer; **at** ~ en danger; **at one's own** ~ à ses risques et périls; ~**y** adj risqué(e)

rissole ['rɪsəʊl] n croquette f

rite [raɪt] n rite m; **last** ~**s** derniers sacrements; **ritual** ['rɪtjʊəl] adj rituel(le) ♦ n rituel m

rival ['raɪvəl] adj, n rival(e); (in business) concurrent(e) ♦ vt (match) égaler; ~**ry** n rivalité f, concurrence f

river ['rɪvə*] n rivière f; (major, also fig) fleuve m ♦ cpd (port, traffic) fluvial(e); **up/down** ~ en amont/aval; ~**bank** n rive f, berge f

rivet ['rɪvɪt] n rivet m ♦ vt (fig) river, fixer

Riviera [rɪvɪ'eərə] n: **the (French)** ~ la Côte d'Azur; **the Italian** ~ la Riviera (italienne)

road [rəʊd] n route f; (in town) rue f; (fig) chemin, voie f; **major/minor** ~ route principale or à priorité/voie secondaire; ~ **accident** n accident m de la circulation; ~**block** n barrage routier; ~**hog** n chauffard m; ~ **map** n carte routière; ~ **safety** n sécurité routière; ~**side** n bord m de la route, bas-côté m; ~**sign** n panneau m de signalisation; ~**way** n chaussée f; ~ **works** npl travaux mpl (de réfection des routes); ~**worthy** adj en bon état de marche

roam [rəʊm] vi errer, vagabonder

roar [rɔː*] n rugissement m; (of crowd) hurlements mpl; (of vehicle, thunder, storm) grondement m ♦ vi rugir; hurler; gronder; **to** ~ **with laughter** éclater de rire; **to do a** ~**ing trade** faire des affaires d'or

roast [rəʊst] n rôti m ♦ vt (faire) rôtir; (coffee) griller, torréfier; ~ **beef** n rôti m de bœuf, rosbif m

rob [rɒb] vt (person) voler; (bank) dévaliser; **to** ~ **sb of sth** voler or dérober qch à qn; (fig: deprive) priver qn de qch; ~**ber** n bandit m, voleur m; ~**bery** n vol m

robe [rəʊb] n (for ceremony etc) robe f; (also: bath~) peignoir m; (US) couverture f

robin ['rɒbɪn] n rouge-gorge m

robust [rəʊ'bʌst] adj robuste; (material, appetite) solide

rock [rɒk] n (substance) roche f, roc m; (boulder) rocher m; (US: small stone) caillou m; (BRIT: sweet) ≈ sucre m d'orge ♦ vt (swing gently: cradle) balancer; (: child) bercer; (shake) ébranler, secouer ♦ vi (se) balancer; être ébranlé(e) or secoué(e); **on the** ~**s** (drink) avec des glaçons; (marriage etc) en train de craquer; ~ **and roll** n rock (and roll) m, rock'n'roll m; ~-**bottom** adj (fig: prices) sacrifié(e); ~**ery** n (jardin m de) rocaille f

rocket ['rɒkɪt] n fusée f; (MIL) fusée, roquette f

rocking chair ['rɒkɪŋ-] n fauteuil m à bascule

rocking horse *n* cheval *m* à bascule

rocky ['rɒkɪ] *adj* (*hill*) rocheux(euse); (*path*) rocailleux(euse)

rod [rɒd] *n* (*wooden*) baguette *f*; (*metallic*) tringle *f*; (*TECH*) tige *f*; (*also: fishing* ~) canne *f* à pêche

rode [rəʊd] *pt of* ride

rodent ['rəʊdənt] *n* rongeur *m*

rodeo ['rəʊdɪəʊ] (*US*) *n* rodéo *m*

roe [rəʊ] *n* (*species: also:* ~ deer) chevreuil *m*; (*of fish, also: hard* ~) œufs *mpl* de poisson; **soft** ~ laitance *f*

rogue [rəʊg] *n* coquin(e)

role [rəʊl] *n* rôle *m*

roll [rəʊl] *n* rouleau *m*; (*of banknotes*) liasse *f*; (*also: bread* ~) petit pain; (*register*) liste *f*; (*sound: of drums etc*) roulement *m* ♦ *vt* rouler; (*also:* ~ up: string) enrouler; (: *sleeves*) retrousser; (: ~ out: pastry) étendre au rouleau, abaisser ♦ *vi* rouler; ~ **about** *vi* rouler ça et là; (*person*) se rouler par terre; ~ **around** *vi* = **roll about**; ~ **by** *vi* (*time*) s'écouler, passer; ~ **in** *vi* (*mail, cash*) affluer; ~ **over** *vi* se retourner; ~ **up** *vi* (*inf: arrive*) arriver, s'amener ♦ *vt* rouler; ~ **call** *n* appel *m*; ~**er** *n* rouleau *m*; (*wheel*) roulette *f*; (*for road*) rouleau compresseur; ~**er coaster** *n* montagnes *fpl* russes; ~**er skates** *npl* patins *mpl* à roulettes; ~**ing** ['rəʊlɪŋ] *adj* (*landscape*) onduleux(euse); ~**ing pin** *n* rouleau *m* à pâtisserie; ~**ing stock** *n* (*RAIL*) matériel roulant

ROM [rɒm] *n abbr* (= *read only memory*) mémoire morte

Roman ['rəʊmən] *adj* romain(e); ~ **Catholic** *adj*, *n* catholique (*m/f*)

romance [rə'mæns] *n* (*love affair*) idylle *f*; (*charm*) poésie *f*; (*novel*) roman *m* à l'eau de rose

Romania [rəʊ'meɪnɪə] *n* Roumanie *f*; ~**n** *adj* roumain(e) ♦ *n* Roumain(e); (*LING*) roumain *m*

Roman numeral *n* chiffre romain

romantic [rə'mæntɪk] *adj* romantique; sentimental(e)

Rome [rəʊm] *n* Rome

romp [rɒmp] *n* jeux bruyants ♦ *vi* (*also:* ~ about) s'ébattre, jouer bruyamment; ~**ers** ['rɒmpəz] *npl* barboteuse *f*

roof [ruːf] (*pl* ~**s**) *n* toit *m* ♦ *vt* couvrir (d'un toit); **the** ~ **of the mouth** la voûte du palais; ~**ing** *n* toiture *f*; ~ **rack** *n* (*AUT*) galerie *f*

rook [rʊk] *n* (*bird*) freux *m*; (*CHESS*) tour *f*

room [rʊm] *n* (*in house*) pièce *f*; (*also: bed*~) chambre *f* (à coucher); (*in school etc*) salle *f*; (*space*) place *f*; ~**s** *npl* (*lodging*) meublé *m*; "~**s to let**" (*BRIT*) or "~**s for rent**" (*US*) "chambres à louer"; **single/double** ~ chambre pour une personne/deux personnes; **there is** ~ **for improvement** cela lais-

se à désirer; ~**ing house** (*US*) *n* maison *f* or immeuble *m* de rapport; ~**mate** *n* camarade *m/f* de chambre; ~ **service** *n* service *m* des chambres (*dans un hôtel*); ~**y** *adj* spacieux(euse); (*garment*) ample

roost [ruːst] *vi* se jucher

rooster ['ruːstə*] *n* (*esp US*) coq *m*

root [ruːt] *n* (*BOT, MATH*) racine *f*; (*fig: of problem*) origine *f*, fond *m* ♦ *vi* (*plant*) s'enraciner; ~ **about** *vi* (*fig*) fouiller; ~ **for** *vt fus* encourager, applaudir; ~ **out** *vt* (*find*) dénicher

rope [rəʊp] *n* corde *f*; (*NAUT*) cordage *m* ♦ *vt* (*tie up or together*) attacher; (*climbers: also:* ~ together) encorder; (*area:* ~ off) interdire l'accès de; (*divide off*) séparer; **to know the** ~**s** (*fig*) être au courant, connaître les ficelles; ~ **in** *vt* (*fig: person*) embringuer

rosary ['rəʊzərɪ] *n* chapelet *m*

rose [rəʊz] *pt of* **rise** ♦ *n* rose *f*; (*also:* ~bush) rosier *m*; (*on watering can*) pomme *f*

rosé ['rəʊzeɪ] *n* rosé *m*

rosebud ['rəʊzbʌd] *n* bouton *m* de rose

rosemary ['rəʊzmərɪ] *n* romarin *m*

roster ['rɒstə*] *n*: **duty** ~ tableau *m* de service

rostrum ['rɒstrəm] *n* tribune *f* (*pour un orateur etc*)

rosy ['rəʊzɪ] *adj* rose; **a** ~ **future** un bel avenir

rot [rɒt] *n* (*decay*) pourriture *f*; (*fig: pej*) idioties *fpl* ♦ *vt, vi* pourrir

rota ['rəʊtə] *n* liste *f*, tableau *m* de service; **on a** ~ **basis** par roulement

rotary ['rəʊtərɪ] *adj* rotatif(ive)

rotate [rəʊ'teɪt] *vt* (*revolve*) faire tourner; (*change round: jobs*) faire à tour de rôle ♦ *vi* (*revolve*) tourner; **rotating** *adj* (*movement*) tournant(e)

rote [rəʊt] *n*: **by** ~ machinalement, par cœur

rotten ['rɒtn] *adj* (*decayed*) pourri(e); (*dishonest*) corrompu(e); (*inf: bad*) mauvais(e), moche; **to feel** ~ (*ill*) être mal fichu(e)

rotund [rəʊ'tʌnd] *adj* (*person*) rondelet(te)

rough [rʌf] *adj* (*cloth, skin*) rêche, rugueux(euse); (*terrain*) accidenté(e); (*path*) rocailleux(euse); (*voice*) rauque, rude; (*person, manner: coarse*) rude, fruste; (: *violent*) brutal(e); (*district, weather*) mauvais(e); (*sea*) houleux(euse); (*plan etc*) ébauché(e); (*guess*) approximatif(ive) ♦ *n* (*GOLF*) rough *m*; **to** ~ **it** vivre à la dure; **to sleep** ~ (*BRIT*) coucher à la dure; ~**age** *n* fibres *fpl* alimentaires; ~**-and-ready** *adj* rudimentaire; ~ **copy**, ~**-draft** *n* brouillon *m*; ~**ly** *adv* (*handle*) rudement, brutalement; (*speak*) avec brusquerie; (*make*) grossièrement; (*approximately*) à peu près, en gros

roulette [ruː'let] *n* roulette *f*

Roumania [ruˈmeɪnɪə] *n* = **Romania**

round [raʊnd] *adj* rond(e) ♦ *n* (BRIT: *of toast*) tranche *f*; (*duty: of policeman, milkman etc*) tournée *f*; (: *of doctor*) visites *fpl*; (*game: of cards, in competition*) partie *f*; (BOXING) round *m*; (*of talks*) série *f* ♦ *vt* (*corner*) tourner ♦ *prep* autour de ♦ *adv*: **all ~** tout autour; **the long way ~** (par) le chemin le plus long; **all the year ~** toute l'année; **it's just ~ the corner** (fig) c'est tout près; **~ the clock** 24 heures sur 24; **to go ~ to sb's (house)** aller chez qn; **go ~ the back** passez par derrière; **to go ~ a house** visiter une maison, faire le tour d'une maison; **enough to go ~** assez pour tout le monde; **~ of ammunition** cartouche *f*; **~ of applause** ban *m*, applaudissements *mpl*; **~ of drinks** tournée *f*; **~ of sandwiches** sandwich *m*; **~ off** *vt* (*speech etc*) terminer; **~ up** *vt* rassembler; (*criminals*) effectuer une rafle de; (*price, figure*) arrondir (au chiffre supérieur); **~about** *n* (BRIT: AUT) rond-point *m* (à sens giratoire); (: *at fair*) manège *m* (de chevaux de bois) ♦ *adj* (*route, means*) détourné(e); **~ers** *n* (*game*) sorte de baseball; **~ly** *adv* (fig) tout net, carrément; **~-shouldered** *adj* au dos rond; **~ trip** *n* (voyage *m*) aller et retour *m*; **~up** *n* rassemblement *m*; (*of criminals*) rafle *f*

rouse [raʊz] *vt* (*wake up*) réveiller; (*stir up*) susciter; provoquer; éveiller.

rousing [ˈraʊzɪŋ] *adj* (*welcome*) enthousiaste

rout [raʊt] *n* (MIL) déroute *f*

route [ruːt] *n* itinéraire *m*; (*of bus*) parcours *m*; (*of trade, shipping*) route *f*; **~ map** (BRIT) *n* (*for journey*) croquis *m* d'itinéraire

routine [ruːˈtiːn] *adj* (*work*) ordinaire, courant(e); (*procedure*) d'usage ♦ *n* (*habits*) habitudes *fpl*; (*pej*) train-train *m*; (THEATRE) numéro *m*

rove [rəʊv] *vt* (*area, streets*) errer dans

row[1] [rəʊ] *n* (*line*) rangée *f*; (*of people, seats, KNITTING*) rang *m*; (*behind one another: of cars, people*) file *f* ♦ *vi* (*in boat*) ramer; (*as sport*) faire de l'aviron ♦ *vt* (*boat*) faire aller à la rame *or* à l'aviron; **in a row** (fig) d'affilée

row[2] [raʊ] *n* (*noise*) vacarme *m*; (*dispute*) dispute *f*, querelle *f*; (*scolding*) réprimande *f*, savon *m* ♦ *vi* se disputer, se quereller

rowboat [ˈrəʊbəʊt] (US) *n* canot *m* (à rames)

rowdy [ˈraʊdɪ] *adj* chahuteur(euse); (*occasion*) tapageur(euse)

rowing [ˈrəʊɪŋ] *n* canotage *m*; (*as sport*) aviron *m*; **~ boat** (BRIT) *n* canot *m* (à rames)

royal [ˈrɔɪəl] *adj* royal(e); **R~ Air Force** (BRIT) *n* armée de l'air britannique

royalty [ˈrɔɪəltɪ] *n* (*royal persons*) (membres *mpl* de la) famille royale; (*payment: to author*) droits *mpl* d'auteur; (: *to inventor*) royalties *fpl*

rpm *abbr* (AUT: = *revs per minute*) tr/mn

RSVP *abbr* (= *répondez s'il vous plaît*) R.S.V.P.

Rt Hon. *abbr* (BRIT: = *Right Honourable*) titre donné aux députés de la Chambre des communes

rub [rʌb] *vt* frotter; frictionner; (*hands*) se frotter ♦ *n* (*with cloth*) coup *m* chiffon *or* de torchon; **to give sth a ~** donner un coup de chiffon *or* de torchon à; **to ~ sb up** (BRIT) *or* **to ~ sb** (US) **the wrong way** prendre qn à rebrousse-poil; **~ off** *vi* partir; **~ off on** *vt fus* déteindre sur; **~ out** *vt* effacer

rubber [ˈrʌbə*] *n* caoutchouc *m*; (BRIT: *eraser*) gomme *f* (à effacer); **~ band** *n* élastique *m*; **~ plant** *n* caoutchouc *m* (*plante verte*)

rubbish [ˈrʌbɪʃ] *n* (*from household*) ordures *fpl*; (fig: *pej*) camelote *f*; (: *nonsense*) bêtises *fpl*, idioties *fpl*; **~ bin** (BRIT) *n* poubelle *f*; **~ dump** *n* décharge publique, dépotoir *m*

rubble [ˈrʌbl] *n* décombres *mpl*; (*smaller*) gravats *mpl*; (CONSTR) blocage *m*

ruby [ˈruːbɪ] *n* rubis *m*

rucksack [ˈrʌksæk] *n* sac *m* à dos

rudder [ˈrʌdə*] *n* gouvernail *m*

ruddy [ˈrʌdɪ] *adj* (*face*) coloré(e); (*inf: damned*) sacré(e), fichu(e)

rude [ruːd] *adj* (*impolite*) impoli(e); (*coarse*) grossier(ère); (*shocking*) indécent(e), inconvenant(e)

ruffian [ˈrʌfɪən] *n* brute *f*, voyou *m*

ruffle [ˈrʌfl] *vt* (*hair*) ébouriffer; (*clothes*) chiffonner; (fig: *person*): **to get ~d** s'énerver

rug [rʌg] *n* petit tapis; (BRIT: *blanket*) couverture *f*

rugby [ˈrʌgbɪ] *n* (*also: ~ football*) rugby *m*

rugged [ˈrʌgɪd] *adj* (*landscape*) accidenté(e); (*features, character*) rude

rugger [ˈrʌgə*] (BRIT: *inf*) *n* rugby *m*

ruin [ˈruːɪn] *n* ruine *f* ♦ *vt* ruiner; (*spoil, clothes*) abîmer; (*event*) gâcher; **~s** *npl* (*of building*) ruine(s)

rule [ruːl] *n* règle *f*; (*regulation*) règlement *m*; (*government*) autorité *f*, gouvernement *m* ♦ *vt* (*country*) gouverner; (*person*) dominer ♦ *vi* commander; (LAW) statuer; **as a ~** normalement, en règle générale; **~ out** *vt* exclure; **~d** *adj* (*paper*) réglé(e); **~r** *n* (*sovereign*) souverain(e); (*for measuring*) règle *f*; **ruling** *adj* (*party*) au pouvoir; (*class*) dirigeant(e) ♦ *n* (LAW) décision *f*

rum [rʌm] *n* rhum *m*

Rumania [ruːˈmeɪnɪə] *n* = **Romania**

rumble [ˈrʌmbl] *vi* gronder; (*stomach, pipe*) gargouiller

rummage ['rʌmɪdʒ] *vi* fouiller

rumour ['ruːmə*] (*US* **rumor**) *n* rumeur *f*, bruit *m* (qui court) ♦ *vt*: **it is ~ed that** le bruit court que

rump [rʌmp] *n* (*of animal*) croupe *f*; (*inf: of person*) postérieur *m*; **~ steak** *n* rumsteck *m*

rumpus ['rʌmpəs] (*inf*) *n* tapage *m*, chahut *m*

run [rʌn] (*pt* **ran**, *pp* **run**) *n* (*fast pace*) (pas *m* de) course *f*; (*outing*) tour *m* or promenade *f* (en voiture); (*distance travelled*) parcours *m*, trajet *m*; (*series*) suite *f*, série *f*; (*THEATRE*) série de représentations; (*SKI*) piste *f*; (*CRICKET, BASEBALL*) point *m*; (*in tights, stockings*) maille filée, échelle *f* ♦ *vt* (*operate: business*) diriger; (*: competition, course*) organiser; (*: hotel, house*) tenir; (*race*) participer à; (*COMPUT*) exécuter; (*to pass: hand, finger*) passer, (*water, bath*) faire couler; (*PRESS: feature*) publier ♦ *vi* courir; (*flee*) s'enfuir; (*work: machine, factory*) marcher; (*bus, train*) circuler, (*continue: play*) se jouer; (*: contract*) être valide; (*flow: river, bath; nose*) couler; (*colours, washing*) déteindre; (*in election*) être candidat, se présenter; **to go for a ~** faire un peu de course à pied; **there was a ~ en ...** (*meat, tickets*) les gens se sont rués sur ...; **in the long ~** à longue échéance; à la longue; en fin de compte; **on the ~** en fuite; **I'll ~ you to the station** je vais vous emmener *or* conduire à la gare; **to ~ a risk** courir un risque; **~ about** *vi* (*children*) courir çà et là; **~ across** *vt fus* (*find*) trouver par hasard; **~ around** *vi* = **run about**; **~ down** *vt* (*production*) réduire progressivement; (*factory*) réduire progressivement la production de; (*AUT*) renverser; (*criticize*) critiquer, dénigrer; **to be ~ down** (*person: tired*) être fatigué(e) *or* à plat; **~ in** (*BRIT*) *vt* (*car*) roder; **~ into** *vt fus* (*meet: person*) rencontrer par hasard; (*: trouble*) se heurter à; (*collide with*) heurter; **~ off** *vi* s'enfuir ♦ *vt* (*water*) laisser s'écouler; (*copies*) tirer; **~ out** *vi* (*person*) sortir en courant; (*liquid*) couler; (*lease*) expirer; (*money*) être épuisé(e); **~ out of** *vt fus* se trouver à court de; **~ over** *vt* (*AUT*) écraser ♦ *vt fus* (*revise*) revoir, reprendre; **~ through** *vt fus* (*recapitulate*) reprendre; (*play*) répéter; **~ up** *vt*: **to ~ up against** (*difficulties*) se heurter à; **to ~ up a debt** s'endetter; **~away** *adj* (*horse*) emballé(e); (*truck*) fou(folle); (*person*) fugitif(ive); (*teenager*) fugueur(euse)

rung [rʌŋ] *pp of* **ring** ♦ *n* (*of ladder*) barreau *m*

runner ['rʌnə*] *n* (*in race: person*) coureur(euse); (*: horse*) partant *m*; (*on sledge*) patin *m*; (*for drawer etc*) coulisseau *m*; **~ bean** (*BRIT*) *n* haricot *m* (à rames); **~-up**

n second(e)

running ['rʌnɪŋ] *n* course *f*; (*of business, organization*) gestion *f*, direction *f* ♦ *adj* (*water*) courant(e); **to be in/out of the ~ for sth** être/ne pas être sur les rangs pour qch; **6 days ~** 6 jours de suite; **~ commentary** *n* commentaire détaillé; **~ costs** *npl* frais *mpl* d'exploitation

runny ['rʌnɪ] *adj* qui coule

run-of-the-mill ['rʌnəvðə'mɪl] *adj* ordinaire, banal(e)

runt [rʌnt] (*also pej*) *n* avorton *m*

run-up ['rʌnʌp] *n*: **~ to sth** (*election etc*) période *f* précédant qch

runway ['rʌnweɪ] *n* (*AVIAT*) piste *f*

rupee [ruː'piː] *n* roupie *f*

rupture ['rʌptʃə*] *n* (*MED*) hernie *f*

rural ['ruərəl] *adj* rural(e)

rush [rʌʃ] *n* (*hurry*) hâte *f*, précipitation *f*; (*of crowd; COMM: sudden demand*) ruée *f*; (*current*) flot *m*; (*of emotion*) vague *f*; (*BOT*) jonc *m* ♦ *vt* (*hurry*) transporter *or* envoyer d'urgence ♦ *vi* se précipiter; **~ hour** *n* heures *fpl* de pointe

rusk [rʌsk] *n* biscotte *f*

Russia ['rʌʃə] *n* Russie *f*; **~n** *adj* russe ♦ *n* Russe *m/f*; (*LING*) russe *m*

rust [rʌst] *n* rouille *f* ♦ *vi* rouiller

rustic ['rʌstɪk] *adj* rustique

rustle ['rʌsl] *vi* bruire, produire un bruissement ♦ *vt* (*paper*) froisser; (*US: cattle*) voler

rustproof ['rʌstpruːf] *adj* inoxydable

rusty ['rʌstɪ] *adj* rouillé(e)

rut [rʌt] *n* ornière *f*; (*ZOOL*) rut *m*; **to be in a ~** suivre l'ornière, s'encroûter

ruthless ['ruːθləs] *adj* sans pitié, impitoyable

rye [raɪ] *n* seigle *m*; **~ bread** *n* pain de seigle

S s

Sabbath ['sæbəθ] *n* (*Jewish*) sabbat *m*; (*Christian*) dimanche *m*

sabotage ['sæbətɑːʒ] *n* sabotage *m* ♦ *vt* saboter

saccharin(e) ['sækərɪn] *n* saccharine *f*

sachet ['sæʃeɪ] *n* sachet *m*

sack [sæk] *n* (*bag*) sac *m* ♦ *vt* (*dismiss*) renvoyer, mettre à la porte; (*plunder*) piller, mettre à sac; **to get the ~** être renvoyé(e), être mis(e) à la porte; **~ing** *n* (*material*) toile *f* à sac; (*dismissal*) renvoi *m*

sacrament ['sækrəmənt] n sacrement m

sacred ['seɪkrɪd] adj sacré(e)

sacrifice ['sækrɪfaɪs] n sacrifice m ♦ vt sacrifier

sad [sæd] adj triste; (deplorable) triste, fâcheux(euse)

saddle ['sædl] n selle f ♦ vt (horse) seller; **to be ~d with sth** (inf) avoir qch sur les bras; **~bag** n sacoche f

sadistic [sə'dɪstɪk] adj sadique

sadly adv tristement; (unfortunately) malheureusement; (seriously) fort

sadness ['sædnəs] n tristesse f

s.a.e. n abbr = **stamped addressed envelope**

safe [seɪf] adj (out of danger) hors de danger, en sécurité; (not dangerous) sans danger; (unharmed) indemne; **~ journey!** bon voyage!; (cautious) prudent(e); (sure: bet etc) assuré(e) ♦ n coffre-fort m; **~ from** à l'abri de; **~ and sound** sain(e) et sauf(sauve); **(just) to be on the ~ side** pour plus de sûreté, par précaution; **~-conduct** n sauf-conduit m; **~-deposit** n (vault) dépôt m de coffres-forts; (box) coffre-fort m; **~guard** n sauvegarde f, protection f ♦ vt sauvegarder, protéger; **~keeping** n bonne garde f; **~ly** adv (assume, say) sans risque d'erreur; (drive, arrive) sans accident; **~ sex** n rapports mpl sexuels sans risque, sexe m sans risques

safety ['seɪftɪ] n sécurité f; **~ belt** n ceinture f de sécurité; **~ pin** n épingle f de sûreté or de nourrice; **~ valve** n soupape f de sûreté

sag [sæg] vi s'affaisser; (hem, breasts) pendre

sage [seɪdʒ] n (herb) sauge f; (person) sage m

Sagittarius [sædʒɪ'teərɪəs] n le Sagittaire

Sahara [sə'hɑːrə] n: **the ~ (Desert)** le (désert du) Sahara

said [sed] pt, pp of **say**

sail [seɪl] n (on boat) voile f; (trip): **to go for a ~** faire un tour en bateau ♦ vt (boat) manœuvrer, piloter ♦ vi (travel: ship) avancer, naviguer; (set off) partir, prendre la mer; (SPORT) faire de la voile; **they ~ed into Le Havre** ils sont entrés dans le port du Havre; **~ through** vi, vt fus (fig) réussir haut la main; **~boat** n (US) bateau m à voiles, voilier m; **~ing** n (SPORT) voile f; **to go ~ing** faire de la voile; **~ing boat** n bateau m à voiles, voilier m; **~ing ship** n grand voilier; **~or** n marin m, matelot m

saint [seɪnt] n saint(e)

sake [seɪk] n: **for the ~ of** pour (l'amour de), dans l'intérêt de; par égard pour

salad ['sæləd] n salade f; **~ bowl** n saladier m; **~ cream** (BRIT) n (sorte f de) mayonnaise f; **~ dressing** n vinaigrette f

salary ['sælərɪ] n salaire m

sale [seɪl] n vente f; (at reduced prices) soldes mpl; **"for ~"** "à vendre"; **on ~** en vente; **on ~ or return** vendu(e) avec faculté de retour; **~room** n salle f des ventes; **~s assistant** n vendeur(euse); **~s clerk** (US) n vendeur(euse); **~sman** (irreg) n vendeur m; (representative) représentant m de commerce; **~swoman** (irreg) n vendeuse f; (representative) représentante f de commerce

sallow ['sæləʊ] adj cireux(euse)

salmon ['sæmən] n inv saumon m

saloon [sə'luːn] n (US) bar m; (BRIT: AUT) berline f; (ship's lounge) salon m

salt [sɔːlt] n sel m ♦ vt saler; **~ cellar** n salière f; **~water** adj de mer; **~y** adj salé(e)

salute [sə'luːt] n salut m ♦ vt saluer

salvage ['sælvɪdʒ] n (saving) sauvetage m; (things saved) biens sauvés or récupérés ♦ vt sauver, récupérer

salvation [sæl'veɪʃən] n salut m; **S~ Army** n armée f du Salut

same [seɪm] adj même ♦ pron: **the ~** le(la) même, les mêmes; **the ~ book as** le même livre que; **at the ~ time** en même temps; **all or just the ~** tout de même, quand même; **to do the ~** faire de même, en faire autant; **to do the ~ as sb** faire comme qn; **the ~ to you!** à vous de même!; (after insult) toi-même!

sample ['sɑːmpl] n échantillon m; (blood) prélèvement m ♦ vt (food, wine) goûter

sanctimonious [sæŋktɪ'məʊnɪəs] adj moralisateur(trice)

sanction ['sæŋkʃən] n approbation f, sanction f

sanctity ['sæŋktɪtɪ] n sainteté f, caractère sacré

sanctuary ['sæŋktjʊərɪ] n (holy place) sanctuaire m; (refuge) asile m; (for wild life) réserve f

sand [sænd] n sable m ♦ vt (furniture: also: **~ down**) poncer

sandal ['sændl] n sandale f

sand: **~box** (US) n tas m de sable; **~castle** n château m de sable; **~paper** n papier m de verre; **~pit** (BRIT) n (for children) tas m de sable; **~stone** n grès m

sandwich ['sænwɪdʒ] n sandwich m; **cheese/ham ~** sandwich au fromage/jambon; **~ course** (BRIT) n cours m de formation professionnelle

sandy ['sændɪ] adj sablonneux(euse); (colour) sable inv, blond roux inv

sane [seɪn] adj (person) sain(e) d'esprit; (outlook) sensé(e), sain(e)

sang [sæŋ] pt of **sing**

sanitary ['sænɪtərɪ] adj (system, arrangements) sanitaire; (clean) hygiénique; **~ towel** (US **~ napkin**) n serviette f hygiénique

sanitation [sænɪ'teɪʃən] n (in house) installations fpl sanitaires; (in town) système m sanitaire; **~ department** (US) n service m de voirie

sanity ['sænɪtɪ] *n* santé mentale; *(common sense)* bon sens

sank [sæŋk] *pt of* sink

Santa Claus [sæntə'klɔːz] *n* le père Noël

sap [sæp] *n (of plants)* sève *f* ♦ *vt (strength)* saper, miner

sapling ['sæplɪŋ] *n* jeune arbre *m*

sapphire ['sæfaɪə*] *n* saphir *m*

sarcasm ['saːkæzəm] *n* sarcasme *m*, raillerie *f*

sardine [saː'diːn] *n* sardine *f*

Sardinia [saɪ'dɪnɪə] *n* Sardaigne *f*

sash [sæʃ] *n* écharpe *f*

sat [sæt] *pt, pp of* sit

satchel ['sætʃəl] *n* cartable *m*

satellite ['sætəlaɪt] *n* satellite *m*; ~ **dish** *n* antenne *f* parabolique; ~ **television** *n* télévision *f* par câble

satin ['sætɪn] *n* satin *m* ♦ *adj* en or de satin, satiné(e)

satisfaction [sætɪs'fækʃən] *n* satisfaction *f*, **satisfactory** [sætɪs'fæktərɪ] *adj* satisfaisant(e)

satisfy ['sætɪsfaɪ] *vt* satisfaire, contenter; *(convince)* convaincre, persuader; ~**ing** *adj* satisfaisant(e)

Saturday ['sætədeɪ] *n* samedi *m*

sauce [sɔːs] *n* sauce *f*; ~**pan** *n* casserole *f*

saucer ['sɔːsə*] *n* soucoupe *f*

saucy ['sɔːsɪ] *adj* impertinent(e)

Saudi ['saʊdɪ]: ~ **Arabia** *n* Arabie Saoudite; ~ **(Arabian)** *adj* saoudien(ne)

sauna ['sɔːnə] *n* sauna *m*

saunter ['sɔːntə*] *vi*: **to** ~ **along/in/out** *etc* marcher/entrer/sortir *etc* d'un pas nonchalant

sausage ['sɒsɪdʒ] *n* saucisse *f*, *(cold meat)* saucisson *m*; ~ **roll** *n* ≈ friand *m*

savage ['sævɪdʒ] *adj (cruel, fierce)* brutal(e), féroce; *(primitive)* primitif(ive), sauvage ♦ *n* sauvage *m/f*

save [seɪv] *vt (person, belongings)* sauver; *(money)* mettre de côté, économiser; *(time)* (faire) gagner, *(keep)* garder; *(COMPUT)* sauvegarder; *(SPORT: stop)* arrêter; *(avoid: trouble)* éviter ♦ *vi (also:* ~ **up**) mettre de l'argent de côté ♦ *n (SPORT)* arrêt *m* (du ballon) ♦ *prep* sauf, à l'exception de

saving ['seɪvɪŋ] *n* économie *f* ♦ *adj*: **the** ~ **grace of sth** ce qui rachète qch; ~**s** *npl (money saved)* économies *fpl*; ~**s account** *n* compte *m* d'épargne; ~**s bank** *n* caisse *f* d'épargne

saviour ['seɪvjə*] *(US* **savior**) *n* sauveur *m*

savour ['seɪvə*] *(US* **savor**) *vt* savourer; ~**y** *(US* **savory**) *adj (dish: not sweet)* salé(e)

saw [sɔː] *(pt* ~**ed**, *pp* ~**ed** *or* **sawn**) *vt* scier ♦ *n (tool)* scie *f* ♦ *pt of* see; ~**dust** *n* sciure *f*, ~**mill** *n* scierie *f*; ~**n-off** *adj*: ~**n-off shotgun** carabine *f* à canon scié

saxophone ['sæksəfəʊn] *n* saxophone *m*

say [seɪ] *(pt, pp* **said**) *n*: **to have one's** ~ dire ce qu'on a à dire ♦ *vt* dire; **to have a** *or* **some** ~ **in sth** avoir voix au chapitre; **could you** ~ **that again?** pourriez-vous répéter ce que vous venez de dire?; **that goes without** ~**ing** cela va sans dire, cela va de soi; ~**ing** *n* dicton *m*, proverbe *m*

scab [skæb] *n* croûte *f*; *(pej)* jaune *m*

scaffold ['skæfəʊld] *n* échafaud *m*; ~**ing** *n* échafaudage *m*

scald [skɔːld] *n* brûlure *f* ♦ *vt* ébouillanter

scale [skeɪl] *n (of fish)* écaille *f*; *(MUS)* gamme *f*; *(of ruler, thermometer etc)* graduation *f*, échelle (graduée); *(of salaries, fees etc)* barème *m*; *(of map, also size, extent)* échelle ♦ *vt (mountain)* escalader; ~**s** *npl (for weighing)* balance *f*; *(also: bathroom* ~) pèse-personne *m inv*; **on a large** ~ sur une grande échelle, en grand; ~ **of charges** tableau *m* des tarifs; ~ **down** *vt* réduire

scallop ['skɒləp] *n* coquille *f* Saint-Jacques; *(SEWING)* feston *m*

scalp [skælp] *n* cuir chevelu ♦ *vt* scalper

scampi ['skæmpɪ] *npl* langoustines (frites), scampi *mpl*

scan [skæn] *vt* scruter, examiner; *(glance at quickly)* parcourir; *(TV, RADAR)* balayer ♦ *n (MED)* scanographie *f*

scandal ['skændl] *n* scandale *m*; *(gossip)* ragots *mpl*

Scandinavian [skændɪ'neɪvɪən] *adj* scandinave

scant [skænt] *adj* insuffisant(e); ~**y** *adj* peu abondant(e), insuffisant(e); *(underwear)* minuscule

scapegoat ['skeɪpgəʊt] *n* bouc *m* émissaire

scar [skaː*] *n* cicatrice *f* ♦ *vt* marquer (d'une cicatrice)

scarce ['skeəs] *adj* rare, peu abondant(e); **to make o.s.** ~ *(inf)* se sauver; ~**ly** *adv* à peine; **scarcity** *n* manque *m*, pénurie *f*

scare ['skeə*] *n* peur *f*, panique *f* ♦ *vt* effrayer, faire peur à; **to** ~ **sb stiff** faire une peur bleue à qn; **bomb** ~ alerte *f* à la bombe; ~ **away** *vt* faire fuir; ~ **off** *vt* = **scare away**; ~**crow** *n* épouvantail *m*; ~**d** *adj*: **to be** ~**d** avoir peur

scarf [skaːf] *(pl* ~**s** *or* **scarves**) *n (long)* écharpe *f*; *(square)* foulard *m*

scarlet ['skaːlət] *adj* écarlate; ~ **fever** *n* scarlatine *f*

scary ['skeərɪ] *(inf)* *adj* effrayant(e)

scathing ['skeɪðɪŋ] *adj* cinglant(e), acerbe

scatter ['skætə*] *vt* éparpiller, répandre; *(crowd)* disperser ♦ *vi* se disperser; ~**brained** *adj* écervelé(e), étourdi(e)

scavenger ['skævɪndʒə*] *n (person: in bins etc)* pilleur *m* de poubelles

scene [siːn] *n* scène *f*; *(of crime, accident)* lieu(x) *m(pl)*; *(sight, view)* spectacle *m*, vue

f; ~**ry** ['si:nərı] n (THEATRE) décor(s) m(pl);
(landscape) paysage m; **scenic** ['si:nɪk] adj
(picturesque) offrant de beaux paysages or
panoramas

scent [sent] n parfum m, odeur f; (track)
piste f

sceptical ['skeptıkəl] (US **skeptical**) adj
sceptique

schedule ['ʃedjuːl, (US) 'skedjuːl] n programme m, plan m; (of trains) horaire m;
(of prices etc) barème m, tarif m ♦ vt prévoir; **on** ~ à l'heure (prévue); à la date
prévue; **to be ahead of/behind** ~ avoir de
l'avance/du retard; ~**d flight** n vol régulier

scheme [ski:m] n plan m, projet m; (dishonest plan, plot) complot m, combine f,
(arrangement) arrangement m, classification
f; (pension ~ etc) régime m ♦ vi comploter,
manigancer; **scheming** ['ski:mɪŋ] adj ru-
sé(e), intrigant(e) ♦ n manigances fpl, intri-
gues fpl

scholar ['skɒlə*] n érudit(e); (pupil) bour-
sier(ière); ~**ly** adj érudit(e), savant(e);
~**ship** n (knowledge) érudition f; (grant)
bourse f (d'études)

school [sku:l] n école f; (secondary ~) collège m, lycée m; (US: university) université
f; (in university) faculté f ♦ cpd scolaire;
~**book** n livre m scolaire or de classe;
~**boy** n écolier m; collégien m, lycéen m;
~**children** npl écoliers mpl; collégiens mpl,
lycéens mpl; ~**girl** n écolière f; collégienne f, ly-
céenne f; ~**ing** n instruction f, études fpl;
~**master** n (primary) instituteur m; (secondary) professeur m; ~**mistress** n institutrice f; professeur m; ~**teacher** n institu-
teur(trice); professeur m

sciatica [saɪ'ætɪkə] n sciatique f

science ['saɪəns] n science f; ~ **fiction** n
science-fiction f; **scientific** [saɪən'tɪfɪk] adj
scientifique; **scientist** ['saɪəntɪst] n scientifique m/f; (eminent) savant m

scissors ['sɪzəz] npl ciseaux mpl

scoff [skɒf] vt (BRIT: inf: eat) avaler, bouffer
♦ vi: **to** ~ **(at)** (mock) se moquer (de)

scold [skəʊld] vt gronder

scone [skɒn] n sorte de petit pain rond au
lait

scoop [sku:p] n pelle f (à main); (for ice
cream) boule f à glace; (PRESS) scoop m;
~ **out** vt évider, creuser; ~ **up** vt ramasser

scooter ['sku:tə*] n (also: motor ~) scooter
m; (toy) trottinette f

scope [skəʊp] n (capacity: of plan, undertaking) portée f, envergure f; (: of person)
compétence f, capacités fpl; (opportunity)
possibilités fpl; **within the** ~ **of** dans les limites de

scorch [skɔ:tʃ] vt (clothes) brûler (légèrement), roussir; (earth, grass) dessécher,
brûler

score [skɔ:*] n score m, décompte m des
points; (MUS) partition f; (twenty) vingt ♦
vt (goal, point) marquer; (success) remporter ♦ vi marquer des points; (FOOTBALL)
marquer un but; (keep ~) compter les
points; ~**s of** (very many) beaucoup de, un
tas de (fam); **on that** ~ sur ce chapitre, à
cet égard; **to** ~ **6 out of 10** obtenir 6 sur
10; ~ **out** vt rayer, barrer, biffer; ~**board**
n tableau m

scorn ['skɔ:n] n mépris m, dédain m

Scorpio ['skɔ:pɪəʊ] n le Scorpion

Scot [skɒt] n Écossais(e)

Scotch [skɒtʃ] n whisky m, scotch m

scotch vt (plan) faire échouer; (rumour)
étouffer

scot-free ['skɒt'fri:] adv: **to get off** ~ s'en
tirer sans être puni(e)

Scotland ['skɒtlənd] n Écosse f

Scots [skɒts] adj écossais(e); ~**man** (irreg)
n Écossais; ~**woman** (irreg) n Écossaise f

Scottish ['skɒtıʃ] adj écossais(e)

scoundrel ['skaʊndrəl] n vaurien m

scour ['skaʊə*] vt (search) battre, parcourir

scourge [skɜ:dʒ] n fléau m

scout [skaʊt] n (MIL) éclaireur m; (also: boy
~) scout m; (girl ~ = (US) guide f; ~ **around**
vi explorer, chercher

scowl [skaʊl] vi se renfrogner, avoir l'air
maussade; **to** ~ **at** regarder de travers

scrabble ['skræbl] vi (also: ~ around:
search) chercher à tâtons; (claw): **to** ~ **(at)**
gratter ♦ n: **S**~ ® (R) Scrabble m ®)

scram [skræm] (inf) vi ficher le camp

scramble ['skræmbl] n (rush) bousculade f,
ruée f ♦ vi: **to** ~ **up/down** grimper/
descendre tant bien que mal; **to** ~ **out** sortir or descendre à toute vitesse; **to** ~
through se frayer un passage (à travers); **to**
~ **for** se bousculer or se disputer pour
(avoir); ~**d eggs** npl œufs brouillés

scrap [skræp] n bout m, morceau m; (fight)
bagarre f; (also: ~ iron) ferraille f ♦ vt jeter,
mettre au rebut; (fig) abandonner, laisser
tomber ♦ vi (fight) se bagarrer; ~**s** npl
(waste) déchets mpl; ~**book** n album m; ~
dealer n marchand m de ferraille

scrape [skreɪp] vt, vi gratter, racler ♦ n: **to
get into a** ~ s'attirer des ennuis; **to** ~
through réussir de justesse; **to** ~ **together** vt
(money) racler ses fonds de tiroir pour réunir

scrap: ~ **heap** n: **on the** ~ **heap** (fig) au
rancart or rebut; ~ **merchant** (BRIT) n
marchand m de ferraille; ~ **paper** n papier
m brouillon; ~**py** adj décousu(e)

scratch [skrætʃ] n égratignure f, rayure f;
éraflure f; (from claw) coup m de griffe ♦
cpd: ~ **team** équipe de fortune or improvi-
sée ♦ vt (rub) (se) gratter; (record) rayer;
(paint etc) érafler; (with claw, nail) griffer ♦
vi (se) gratter; **to start from** ~ partir de zé-

ro; **to be up to** ~ être à la hauteur
scrawl [skrɔːl] *vi* gribouiller
scrawny ['skrɔːnɪ] *adj* décharné(e)
scream [skriːm] *n* cri perçant, hurlement *m*
♦ *vi* crier, hurler
screech [skriːtʃ] *vi* hurler; *(tyres)* crisser;
(brakes) grincer
screen [skriːn] *n* écran *m*; *(in room)* paravent *m*; *(fig)* écran, rideau *m* ♦ *vt (conceal)*
masquer, cacher; *(from the wind etc)* abriter, protéger; *(film)* projeter; *(candidates etc)*
filtrer; ~**ing** *n (MED)* test *m (or* tests) de
dépistage; ~**play** *n* scénario *m*
screw [skruː] *n* vis *f* ♦ *vt (also:* ~ *in)* visser;
~ **up** *vt (paper etc)* froisser; **to** ~ **up one's
eyes** plisser les yeux; ~**driver** *n* tournevis
m
scribble ['skrɪbl] *vt, vi* gribouiller, griffonner
script [skrɪpt] *n (CINEMA etc)* scénario *m*,
texte *m*; *(system of writing)* (écriture *f)*
script *m*
Scripture(s) ['skrɪptʃə*(z)] *n(pl) (Christian)*
Écriture sainte; *(other religions)* écritures
saintes
scroll [skrəul] *n* rouleau *m*
scrounge [skraundʒ] *(inf) vt:* **to** ~ **sth off**
or **from sb** taper qn de qch; ~**r** *(inf) n* parasite *m*
scrub [skrʌb] *n (land)* broussailles *fpl* ♦ *vt*
(floor) nettoyer à la brosse; *(pan)* récurer;
(washing) frotter; *(inf: cancel)* annuler
scruff [skrʌf] *n:* **by the** ~ **of the neck** par
la peau du cou
scruffy ['skrʌfɪ] *adj* débraillé(e)
scrum(mage) ['skrʌm(ɪdʒ)] *n (RUGBY)*
mêlée *f*
scruple ['skruːpl] *n* scrupule *m*
scrutiny ['skruːtɪnɪ] *n* examen minutieux
scuff [skʌf] *vt* érafler
scuffle ['skʌfl] *n* échauffourée *f*, rixe *f*
sculptor ['skʌlptə*] *n* sculpteur *m*
sculpture ['skʌlptʃə*] *n* sculpture *f*
scum [skʌm] *n* écume *f*, mousse *f*; *(pej:
people)* rebut *m*, lie *f*
scurrilous ['skʌrɪləs] *adj* calomnieux(euse)
scurry ['skʌrɪ] *vi* filer à toute allure; **to** ~
off détaler, se sauver
scuttle ['skʌtl] *n (also: coal* ~) seau *m* (à
charbon) ♦ *vt (ship)* saborder ♦ *vi (scamper):* **to** ~ **away** *or* **off** détaler
scythe [saɪð] *n* faux *f*
sea [siː] *n* mer *f* ♦ *cpd* marin(e), de (la)
mer; **by** ~ *(travel)* par mer, en bateau; **on
the** ~ *(boat)* en mer; *(town)* au bord de la
mer; **to be all at** ~ *(fig)* nager
complètement; **out to** ~ au large; *(out)* at
~ en mer; ~**board** *n* côte *f*; ~**food** *n*
fruits *mpl* de mer; ~**front** *n* bord *m* de
mer; ~**going** *adj (ship)* de mer; ~**gull** *n*
mouette *f*
seal [siːl] *n (animal)* phoque *m*; *(stamp)*

sceau *m*, cachet *m* ♦ *vt* sceller; *(envelope)*
coller; (: *with seal)* cacheter; ~ **off** *vt (forbid entry to)* interdire l'accès de
sea level *n* niveau *m* de la mer
sea lion *n* otarie *f*
seam [siːm] *n* couture *f*; *(of coal)* veine *f*,
filon *m*
seaman ['siːmən] *(irreg) n* marin *m*
seance ['seɪɑːns] *n* séance *f* de spiritisme
seaplane ['siːpleɪn] *n* hydravion *m*
search [sɜːtʃ] *n (for person, thing, COMPUT)*
recherche(s) *f(pl)*; *(LAW: at sb's home)* perquisition *f* ♦ *vt* fouiller; *(examine)* examiner
minutieusement; scruter ♦ *vi:* **to** ~ **for**
chercher; **in** ~ **of** à la recherche de; ~
through *vt fus* fouiller; ~**ing** *adj* péné-
trant(e); ~**light** *n* projecteur *m*; ~ **party** *n*
expédition *f* de secours; ~ **warrant** *n*
mandat *m* de perquisition
sea: ~**shore** ['siːʃɔː*] *n* rivage *m*, plage *f*,
bord *m* de (la) mer; ~**sick** ['siːsɪk] *adj:* **to
be** ~**sick** avoir le mal de mer; ~**side**
['siːsaɪd] *n* bord *m* de la mer; ~**side resort**
n station *f* balnéaire
season ['siːzn] *n* saison *f* ♦ *vt* assaisonner,
relever; **to be in/out of** ~ être/ne pas être
de saison; ~**al** *adj (work)* saisonnier(ère);
~**ed** *adj (fig)* expérimenté(e); ~ **ticket** *n*
carte *f* d'abonnement
seat [siːt] *n* siège *m*; *(in bus, train: place)*
place *f*; *(buttocks)* postérieur *m*; *(of trousers)* fond *m* ♦ *vt* faire asseoir, placer;
(have room for) avoir des places assises
pour, pouvoir accueillir; ~ **belt** *n* ceinture
f de sécurité
sea: ~ **water** *n* eau *f* de mer; ~**weed**
['siːwiːd] *n* algues *fpl*; ~**worthy** ['siːwɜːðɪ]
adj en état de naviguer
sec. *abbr* = **second(s)**
secluded [sɪ'kluːdɪd] *adj* retiré(e), à l'écart
seclusion [sɪ'kluːʒən] *n* solitude *f*
second[1] [sɪ'kɒnd] *(BRIT) vt (employee)* affecter provisoirement
second[2] ['sekənd] *adj* deuxième, second(e)
♦ *adv (in race etc)* en seconde position ♦ *n
(unit of time)* seconde *f*; *(AUT:* ~ *gear)* seconde; *(COMM: imperfect)* article *m* de second choix; *(BRIT: UNIV)* licence *f* avec
mention ♦ *vt (motion)* appuyer; ~**ary** *adj*
secondaire; ~**ary school** *n* collège *m*, lycée *m*; ~**-class** *adj* de deuxième classe;
(RAIL) de seconde (classe) *(POST)* au tarif
réduit *(pej)* de qualité inférieure ♦ *adv
(RAIL)* en second; *(POST)* au tarif réduit;
~**hand** *adj* d'occasion; de seconde main;
~ **hand** *n (on clock)* trotteuse *f*; ~**ly** *adv*
deuxièmement; ~**ment** [sɪ'kɒndmənt]
(BRIT) *n* détachement *m*; ~**-rate** *adj* de
deuxième ordre, de qualité inférieure; ~
thoughts *npl* doutes *mpl*; **on** ~ **thoughts**
or (US) **thought** à la réflexion
secrecy ['siːkrəsɪ] *n* secret *m*

secret ['si:krət] *adj* secret(ète) ♦ *n* secret *m*; **in ~** en secret, secrètement, en cachette

secretary ['sekrətrɪ] *n* secrétaire *m/f*; (COMM) secrétaire général; **S~ of State (for)** (BRIT. POL) ministre *m* (de)

secretive ['si:krətɪv] *adj* dissimulé

sectarian [sek'teərɪən] *adj* sectaire

section ['sekʃən] *n* section *f*; (of document) section, article *m*, paragraphe *m*; (cut) coupe *f*

sector ['sektə*] *n* secteur *m*

secular ['sekjulə*] *adj* profane; laïque; séculier(ère)

secure [sɪ'kjuə*] *adj* (free from anxiety) sans inquiétude, sécurisé(e); (firmly fixed) solide, bien attaché(e) (or fermé(e) etc); (in safe place) en lieu sûr, en sûreté ♦ *vt* (fix) fixer, attacher; (get) obtenir, se procurer

security [sɪ'kjuərɪtɪ] *n* sécurité *f*, mesures *fpl* de sécurité; (for loan) caution *f*, garantie *f*

sedan [sɪ'dæn] (US) *n* (AUT) berline *f*

sedate [sɪ'deɪt] *adj* calme; posé(e) ♦ *vt* (MED) donner des sédatifs à

sedative ['sedətɪv] *n* calmant *m*, sédatif *m*

seduce [sɪ'dju:s] *vt* séduire; **seduction** [sɪ'dʌkʃən] *n* séduction *f*; **seductive** [sɪ'dʌktɪv] *adj* séduisant(e); (smile) séducteur(trice); (fig: offer) alléchant(e)

see [si:] (*pt* **saw**, *pp* **seen**) *vt* voir; (accompany): **to ~ sb to the door** reconduire *or* raccompagner qn jusqu'à la porte ♦ *vi* voir ♦ *n* évêché *m*; **to ~ that** (ensure) veiller à ce que +*sub*, faire en sorte que +*sub*, s'assurer que; **~ you soon!** à bientôt!; **~ about** *vt fus* s'occuper de; **~ off** *vt* accompagner (à la gare *or* à l'aéroport etc); **~ through** *vt* mener à bonne fin ♦ *vt fus* voir clair dans; **~ to** *vt fus* s'occuper de, se charger de

seed [si:d] *n* graine *f*; (sperm) semence *f*; (fig) germe *m*; (TENNIS) tête *f* de série; **to go to ~** monter en graine; (fig) se laisser aller; **~ling** *n* jeune plant *m*, semis *m*; **~y** *adj* (shabby) minable, miteux(euse)

seeing ['si:ɪŋ] *conj*: **~ (that)** vu que, étant donné que

seek [si:k] (*pt*, *pp* **sought**) *vt* chercher, rechercher

seem [si:m] *vi* sembler, paraître; **there ~s to be ...** il semble qu'il y a ...; on dirait qu'il y a ...; **~ingly** *adv* apparemment

seen [si:n] *pp of* **see**

seep [si:p] *vi* suinter, filtrer

seesaw ['si:sɔ:] *n* (jeu *m* de) bascule *f*

seethe [si:ð] *vi* être en effervescence; **to ~ with anger** bouillir de colère

see-through ['si:θru:] *adj* transparent(e)

segment *n* segment *m*; (of orange) quartier *m*

segregate ['segrɪgeɪt] *vt* séparer, isoler

seize [si:z] *vt* saisir, attraper; (take posses-

sion of) s'emparer de; (opportunity) saisir; **~ up** *vi* (TECH) se gripper; **~ (up)on** *vt fus* saisir, sauter sur

seizure ['si:ʒə*] *n* (MED) crise *f*, attaque *f*; (of power) prise *f*

seldom ['seldəm] *adv* rarement

select [sɪ'lekt] *adj* choisi(e), d'élite ♦ *vt* sélectionner, choisir; **~ion** [sɪ'lekʃən] *n* sélection *f*, choix *m*

self [self] (*pl* **selves**) *n*: **the ~** le moi *inv* ♦ *prefix* auto-; **~-assured** *adj* sûr(e) de soi; **~-catering** (BRIT) *adj* avec cuisine, où l'on peut faire sa cuisine; **~-centred** (US ~-**centered**) *adj* égocentrique; **~-confidence** *n* confiance *f* en soi; **~-conscious** *adj* timide, qui manque d'assurance; **~-contained** (BRIT) *adj* (flat) avec entrée particulière, indépendant(e); **~-control** *n* maîtrise *f* de soi; **~-defence** (US ~-**defense**) *n* autodéfense *f*; (LAW) légitime défense *f*; **~-discipline** *n* discipline personnelle; **~-employed** *adj* qui travaille à son compte; **~-evident** *adj*: **to be ~-evident** être évident(e), aller de soi; **~-governing** *adj* autonome; **~-indulgent** *adj* qui ne se refuse rien; **~-interest** *n* intérêt personnel; **~-ish** *adj* égoïste; **~-ishness** *n* égoïsme *m*; **~-less** *adj* désintéressé(e); **~-pity** *n* apitoiement *m* sur soi-même; **~-possessed** *adj* assuré(e); **~-preservation** *n* instinct *m* de conservation; **~-respect** *n* respect *m* de soi, amour-propre *m*; **~-righteous** *adj* suffisant(e); **~-sacrifice** *n* abnégation *f*; **~-satisfied** *adj* content(e) de soi, suffisant(e); **~-service** *adj* libre-service, self-service; **~-sufficient** *adj* autosuffisant(e); (person: independent) indépendant(e); **~-taught** *adj* (artist, pianist) qui a appris par lui-même

sell [sel] (*pt*, *pp* **sold**) *vt* vendre ♦ *vi* se vendre; **to ~ at** *or* **for 10 F** se vendre 10 F; **~ off** *vt* liquider; **~ out** *vi*: **to ~ out (of sth)** (use up stock) vendre tout son stock (de qch); **the tickets are all sold out** il ne reste plus de billets; **~-by date** *n* date *f* limite de vente; **~er** *n* vendeur(euse), marchand(e); **~ing price** *n* prix *m* de vente

Sellotape ['seləʊteɪp] (®: BRIT) *n* papier collant *m*, scotch *m* (®)

selves [selvz] *npl of* **self**

semblance ['sembləns] *n* semblant *m*

semen ['si:mən] *n* sperme *m*

semester [sɪ'mestə*] *n* (esp US) semestre *m*

semi ['semɪ] *prefix* semi-, demi-; à demi, à moitié; **~circle** *n* demi-cercle *m*; **~colon** *n* point-virgule *m*; **~detached (house)** (BRIT) *n* maison jumelée *f* *or* jumelle; **~final** *n* demi-finale *f*

seminar ['semɪnɑ:*] *n* séminaire *m*

seminary ['semɪnərɪ] *n* (REL: for priests) séminaire *m*

semiskilled ['semi'skıld] *adj*: ~ **worker** ou-vrier(ère) spécialisé(e)

semi-skimmed milk *n* lait demi-écrémé

senate ['senɪt] *n* sénat *m*; **senator** *n* séna-teur *m*

send [send] (*pt, pp* **sent**) *vt* envoyer; ~ **away** *vt* (*letter, goods*) envoyer, expédier; (*unwelcome visitor*) renvoyer; ~ **away for** *vt fus* commander par correspondance, se faire envoyer; ~ **back** *vt* renvoyer; ~ **for** *vt fus* envoyer chercher; faire venir; ~ **off** *vt* (*goods*) envoyer, expédier; (*BRIT: SPORT: player*) expulser *or* renvoyer du terrain; ~ **out** *vt* (*invitation*) envoyer (par la poste); (*light, heat, signal*) émettre; ~ **up** *vt* faire monter; (*BRIT: parody*) mettre en boîte, parodier; ~**er** *n* expéditeur(trice); ~**off** *n*: a good ~**off** des adieux chaleureux

senior ['si:nɪə*] *adj* (*high-ranking*) de haut niveau; (*of higher rank*): **to be ~ to sb** être le supérieur de qn ♦ *n* (*older*): **she is 15 years his ~** elle est son aînée de 15 ans, elle est plus âgée que lui de 15 ans; ~ **citizen** *n* personne âgée; ~**ity** [si:nɪ'ɒrɪtɪ] *n* (*in service*) ancienneté *f*

sensation [sen'seɪʃən] *n* sensation *f*; ~**al** *adj* qui fait sensation; (*marvellous*) sensa-tionnel(le)

sense [sens] *n* sens *m*; (*feeling*) sentiment *m*; (*meaning*) sens *m*, signification *f*; (*wisdom*) bon sens ♦ *vt* sentir, pressentir; **it makes ~** c'est logique; ~**less** *adj* insensé(e), stupide; (*unconscious*) sans connaissance

sensible ['sensəbl] *adj* sensé(e), raisonna-ble; sage

sensitive ['sensɪtɪv] *adj* sensible

sensual ['sensjʊəl] *adj* sensuel(le)

sensuous ['sensjʊəs] *adj* voluptueux(euse), sensuel(le)

sent [sent] *pt, pp of* **send**

sentence ['sentəns] *n* (*LING*) phrase *f*; (*LAW: judgment*) condamnation *f*, sentence *f*; (*: punishment*) peine *f* ♦ *vt*: **to ~ sb to death/to 5 years in prison** condamner qn à mort/à 5 ans de prison

sentiment ['sentɪmənt] *n* sentiment *m*; (*opinion*) opinion *f*, avis *m*; ~**al** [sentɪ'mentl] *adj* sentimental(e)

sentry ['sentrɪ] *n* sentinelle *f*

separate [*adj* 'seprət, *vb* 'sepəreɪt] *adj* sépa-ré(e), indépendant(e), différent(e) ♦ *vt* sépa-rer; (*make a distinction between*) distinguer ♦ *vi* se séparer; ~**ly** *adv* séparément; ~**s** *npl* (*clothes*) coordonnés *mpl*; **separation** [sepə'reɪʃən] *n* séparation *f*

September [sep'tembə*] *n* septembre *m*

septic ['septɪk] *adj* (*wound*) infecté(e); ~ **tank** *n* fosse *f* septique

sequel ['si:kwəl] *n* conséquence *f*; séquelles *fpl*; (*of story*) suite *f*

sequence ['si:kwəns] *n* ordre *m*, suite *f*; (*film* ~) séquence *f*; (*dance* ~) numéro *m*

sequin ['si:kwɪn] *n* paillette *f*

serene [sə'ri:n] *adj* serein(e), calme, paisi-ble

sergeant ['sɑ:dʒənt] *n* sergent *m*; (*POLICE*) brigadier *m*

serial ['sɪərɪəl] *n* feuilleton *m*; ~ **number** *n* numéro *m* de série

series ['sɪərɪz] *n inv* série *f*; (*PUBLISHING*) collection *f*

serious ['sɪərɪəs] *adj* sérieux(euse); (*illness*) grave; ~**ly** *adv* sérieusement; (*hurt*) grave-ment

sermon ['sɜ:mən] *n* sermon *m*

serrated [se'reɪtɪd] *adj* en dents de scie

servant ['sɜ:vənt] *n* domestique *m/f*; (*fig*) serviteur/servante

serve [sɜ:v] *vt* (*employer etc*) servir, être au service de; (*purpose*) servir à; (*customer, food, meal*) servir; (*subj: train*) des-servir; (*apprenticeship*) faire, accomplir; (*prison term*) purger ♦ *vi* servir; (*be useful*): **to ~ as/for/to do** servir de/à/à faire ♦ *n* (*TENNIS*) service *m*; **it ~s him right** c'est bien fait pour lui; ~ **out**, ~ **up** *vt* (*food*) servir

service ['sɜ:vɪs] *n* service *m*; (*AUT: mainte-nance*) révision *f* ♦ *vt* (*car, washing ma-chine*) réviser; **the S~s** les forces armées; **to be of ~ to sb** rendre service à qn; ~**able** *adj* pratique, commode; ~ **charge** (*BRIT*) *n* service *m*; ~**man** (*irreg*) *n* mi-litaire *m*; ~ **station** *n* station-service *f*

serviette [sɜ:vɪ'et] (*BRIT*) *n* serviette *f* (de table)

session ['seʃən] *n* séance *f*

set [set] (*pt, pp* **set**) *n* série *f*, assortiment *m*; (*of tools etc*) jeu *m*; (*RADIO, TV*) poste *m*; (*TENNIS*) set *m*; (*group of people*) cercle *m*, milieu *m*; (*THEATRE: stage*) scène *f*; (*: scenery*) décor *m*; (*MATH*) ensemble *m*; (*HAIRDRESSING*) mise *f* en plis ♦ *adj* (*fixed*) fixe, déterminé(e); (*ready*) prêt(e) ♦ *vt* (*place*) poser, placer; (*fix, establish*) fixer; (*: record*) établir; (*adjust*) régler; (*decide: rules etc*) fixer, choisir; (*task*) donner; (*exam*) composer ♦ *vi* (*sun*) se coucher; (*jam, jelly, concrete*) prendre; (*bone*) se ressouder; **to be ~ on doing** être résolu à faire; **to ~ the table** mettre la table; **to ~ (to music)** mettre en musique; **to ~ on fire** mettre le feu à; **to ~ free** libérer; **to ~ sth going** dé-clencher qch; **to ~ sail** prendre la mer; ~ **about** *vt fus* (*task*) entreprendre, se mettre à; ~ **aside** *vt* mettre de côté; (*time*) garder; ~ **back** *vt* (*in time*): **to ~ back (by)** retar-der (de); (*cost*): **to ~ sb back £5** coûter 5 livres à qn; ~ **off** *vi* se mettre en route, partir ♦ *vt* (*bomb*) faire exploser; (*cause to start*) déclencher; (*show up well*) mettre en valeur, faire valoir; ~ **out** *vi* se mettre en route, partir ♦ *vt* (*arrange*) disposer; (*argu-ments*) présenter, exposer; **to ~ out to do**

entreprendre de faire, avoir pour but *or* intention de faire; ~ **up** *vt* (*organization*) fonder, créer; ~**back** *n* (*hitch*) revers *m*, contretemps *m*; ~ **menu** *n* menu *m*

settee [se'tiː] *n* canapé *m*

setting ['setɪŋ] *n* cadre *m*; (*of jewel*) monture *f*; (*position: of controls*) réglage *m*

settle ['setl] *vt* (*argument, matter, account*) régler; (*problem*) résoudre; (*MED: calm*) calmer ♦ *vi* (*bird, dust etc*) se poser; (*also:* ~ **down**) s'installer, se fixer; (*calm down*) se calmer; **to** ~ **for sth** accepter qch, se contenter de qch; **to** ~ **on sth** opter *or* se décider pour qch; ~ **in** *vi* s'installer; ~ **up** *vi*: **to** ~ **up with sb** régler (ce que l'on doit à) qn; ~**ment** *n* (*payment*) règlement *m*; (*agreement*) accord *m*; (*village etc*) établissement *m*; hameau *m*; ~**r** *n* colon *m*

setup ['setʌp] *n* (*arrangement*) manière *f* dont les choses sont organisées; (*situation*) situation *f*

seven ['sevn] *num* sept; ~**teen** *num* dix-sept; ~**th** *num* septième; ~**ty** *num* soixante-dix

sever ['sevə*] *vt* couper, trancher; (*relations*) rompre

several ['sevrəl] *adj, pron* plusieurs *m/fpl*; ~ **of us** plusieurs d'entre nous

severance ['sevərəns] *n* (*of relations*) rupture *f*; ~ **pay** *n* indemnité *f* de licenciement

severe [sɪ'vɪə*] *adj* (*stern*) sévère, strict(e); (*serious*) grave, sérieux(euse); (*plain*) sévère, austère; **severity** [sɪ'verɪtɪ] *n* sévérité *f*; gravité *f*; rigueur *f*

sew [səʊ] (*pt* **sewed**, *pp* **sewn**) *vt, vi* coudre; ~ **up** *vt* (re)coudre

sewage ['sjuːɪdʒ] *n* vidange(s) *f(pl)*

sewer ['sjʊə*] *n* égout *m*

sewing ['səʊɪŋ] *n* couture *f*; (*item(s)*) ouvrage *m*; ~ **machine** *n* machine *f* à coudre

sewn [səʊn] *pp* of **sew**

sex [seks] *n* sexe *m*; **to have** ~ **with** avoir des rapports (sexuels) avec; ~**ist** *adj* sexiste; ~**ual** ['seksjʊəl] *adj* sexuel(le); ~**y** ['seksɪ] *adj* sexy *inv*

shabby ['ʃæbɪ] *adj* miteux(euse); (*behaviour*) mesquin(e), méprisable

shack [ʃæk] *n* cabane *f*, hutte *f*

shackles ['ʃæklz] *npl* chaînes *fpl*, entraves *fpl*

shade [ʃeɪd] *n* ombre *f*; (*for lamp*) abat-jour *m inv*; (*of colour*) nuance *f*, ton *m* ♦ *vt* abriter du soleil, ombrager; **in the** ~ à l'ombre; **a** ~ **too large/more** un tout petit peu trop grand(e)/plus

shadow ['ʃædəʊ] *n* ombre *f* ♦ *vt* (*follow*) filer; ~ **cabinet** (*BRIT*) *n* (*POL*) cabinet parallèle formé par l'Opposition; ~**y** *adj* ombragé(e); (*dim*) vague, indistinct(e)

shady ['ʃeɪdɪ] *adj* ombragé(e); (*fig: dishonest*) louche, véreux(euse)

shaft [ʃɑːft] *n* (*of arrow, spear*) hampe *f*;

(*AUT, TECH*) arbre *m*; (*of mine*) puits *m*; (*of lift*) cage *f*; (*of light*) rayon *m*, trait *m*

shaggy ['ʃægɪ] *adj* hirsute; en broussaille

shake [ʃeɪk] (*pt* **shook**, *pp* **shaken**) *vt* secouer; (*bottle, cocktail*) agiter; (*house, confidence*) ébranler ♦ *vi* trembler; **to** ~ **one's head** (*in refusal*) dire *or* faire non de la tête; (*in dismay*) secouer la tête; **to** ~ **hands with sb** serrer la main à qn; ~ **off** *vt* secouer; (*pursuer*) se débarrasser de; ~ **up** *vt* secouer; ~**n** ['ʃeɪkn] *pp* of **shake**; **shaky** ['ʃeɪkɪ] *adj* (*hand, voice*) tremblant(e); (*building*) branlant(e), peu solide

shall [ʃæl] *aux vb*: **I** ~ **go** j'irai; ~ **I open the door?** j'ouvre la porte?; **I'll get the coffee,** ~ **I?** je vais chercher le café, d'accord?

shallow ['ʃæləʊ] *adj* peu profond(e); (*fig*) superficiel(le)

sham [ʃæm] *n* frime *f* ♦ *vt* simuler

shambles ['ʃæmblz] *n* (*muddle*) confusion *f*, pagaïe *f*, fouillis *m*

shame [ʃeɪm] *n* honte *f* ♦ *vt* faire honte à; **it is a** ~ **(that/to do)** c'est dommage (que +*sub*/de faire); **what a** ~! quel dommage!; ~**faced** *adj* honteux(euse), penaud(e); ~**ful** *adj* honteux(euse), scandaleux(euse); ~**less** *adj* éhonté(e), effronté(e)

shampoo [ʃæm'puː] *n* shampooing *m* ♦ *vt* faire un shampooing à; ~ **and set** *n* shampooing *m* (et) mise *f* en plis

shamrock ['ʃæmrɒk] *n* trèfle *m* (*emblème de l'Irlande*)

shandy ['ʃændɪ] *n* bière panachée

shan't [ʃɑːnt] = **shall not**

shanty town ['ʃæntɪ-] *n* bidonville *m*

shape [ʃeɪp] *n* forme *f* ♦ *vt* façonner, modeler; (*sb's ideas*) former; (*sb's life*) déterminer ♦ *vi* (*also:* ~ **up**: *events*) prendre tournure; (: *person*) faire des progrès, s'en sortir; **to take** ~ prendre forme *or* tournure; **-shaped** *suffix*: **heart-shaped** en forme de cœur; ~**less** *adj* informe, sans forme; ~**ly** *adj* bien proportionné(e), beau(belle)

share [ʃɛə*] *n* part *f*; (*COMM*) action *f* ♦ *vt* partager; (*have in common*) avoir en commun; ~ **out** *vi* partager; ~**holder** *n* actionnaire *m/f*

shark [ʃɑːk] *n* requin *m*

sharp [ʃɑːp] *adj* (*razor, knife*) tranchant(e), bien aiguisé(e); (*point, voice*) aigu(guë); (*nose, chin*) pointu(e); (*outline, increase*) net(te); (*cold, pain*) vif(vive); (*taste*) piquant(e), âcre; (*MUS*) dièse; (*person: quick-witted*) vif(vive), éveillé(e); (: *unscrupulous*) malhonnête ♦ *n* (*MUS*) dièse *m* ♦ *adv* (*precisely*): **at 2 o'clock** ~ à 2 heures pile *or* précises; ~**en** *vt* aiguiser; (*pencil*) tailler; ~**ener** *n* (*also: pencil* ~**ener**) taille-crayon(s) *m inv*; ~**-eyed** *adj* qui ne rien n'échappe; ~**ly** *adv* (*turn, stop*) brusquement; (*stand out*) nettement; (*criticize, re-*

tort) sèchement, vertement

shatter ['ʃætə*] vt briser; (*fig: upset*) bouleverser; (: *ruin*) briser, ruiner ♦ vi voler en éclats, se briser

shave [ʃeɪv] vt raser ♦ vi se raser ♦ n: **to have a ~** se raser; **~r** n (*also: electric ~r*) rasoir m électrique

shaving ['ʃeɪvɪŋ] n (*action*) rasage m; **~s** npl (*of wood etc*) copeaux mpl; **~ brush** n blaireau m; **~ cream** n crème f à raser; **~ foam** n mousse f à raser

shawl [ʃɔ:l] n châle m

she [ʃi:] pron elle ♦ prefix: **~-cat** chatte f; **~-elephant** éléphant m femelle

sheaf [ʃi:f] (pl **sheaves**) n gerbe f; (*of papers*) liasse f

shear [ʃɪə*] (pt **~ed**, pp **shorn**) vt (*sheep*) tondre; **~ off** vi (*branch*) partir, se détacher; **~s** npl (*for hedge*) cisaille(s) f(pl)

sheath [ʃi:θ] n gaine f, fourreau m, étui m; (*contraceptive*) préservatif m

shed [ʃed] (pt, pp **shed**) n remise f, resserre f ♦ vt perdre; (*tears*) verser, répandre; (*workers*) congédier

she'd [ʃi:d] = **she had**; **she would**

sheen [ʃi:n] n lustre m

sheep [ʃi:p] n inv mouton m; **~dog** n chien m de berger; **~ish** adj penaud(e); **~skin** n peau f de mouton

sheer [ʃɪə*] adj (*utter*) pur(e), pur et simple; (*steep*) à pic, abrupt(e); (*almost transparent*) extrêmement fin(e) ♦ adv à pic, abruptement

sheet [ʃi:t] n (*on bed*) drap m; (*of paper*) feuille f; (*of glass, metal etc*) feuille, plaque f

sheik(h) [ʃeɪk] n cheik m

shelf [ʃelf] (pl **shelves**) n étagère f, rayon m

shell [ʃel] n (*on beach*) coquillage m; (*of egg, nut etc*) coquille f; (*explosive*) obus m; (*of building*) carcasse f ♦ vt (*peas*) écosser; (*MIL*) bombarder (d'obus)

she'll [ʃi:l] = **she will**; **she shall**

shellfish ['ʃelfɪʃ] n inv (*crab etc*) crustacé m; (*scallop etc*) coquillage m ♦ npl (*as food*) fruits mpl de mer

shell suit n survêtement m (*en synthétique froissé*)

shelter ['ʃeltə*] n abri m, refuge m ♦ vt abriter, protéger; (*give lodging to*) donner asile à ♦ vi s'abriter, se mettre à l'abri; **~ed housing** n foyers mpl (*pour personnes âgées ou handicapées*)

shelve [ʃelv] vt (*fig*) mettre en suspens or en sommeil; **~s** npl of **shelf**

shepherd ['ʃepəd] n berger m ♦ vt (*guide*) guider, escorter; **~'s pie** (*BRIT*) n ≈ hachis m Parmentier

sheriff ['ʃerɪf] (*US*) n shérif m

sherry ['ʃerɪ] n xérès m, sherry m

she's [ʃi:z] = **she is**; **she has**

Shetland ['ʃetlənd] n (*also: the ~s, the ~*

Islands) les îles fpl Shetland

shield [ʃi:ld] n bouclier m; (*protection*) écran m de protection ♦ vt: **to ~ (from)** protéger (de or contre)

shift [ʃɪft] n (*change*) changement m; (*work period*) période f de travail; (*of workers*) équipe f, poste m ♦ vt déplacer, changer de place; (*remove*) enlever ♦ vi changer de place, bouger; **~less** adj (*person*) fainéant(e); **~ work** n travail m en équipe or par relais or par roulement; **~y** adj sournois(e); (*eyes*) fuyant(e)

shilly-shally ['ʃɪlɪʃælɪ] vi tergiverser, atermoyer

shimmer ['ʃɪmə*] vi miroiter, chatoyer

shin [ʃɪn] n tibia m

shine [ʃaɪn] n (pt, pp **shone**) n éclat m, brillant m ♦ vi briller ♦ vt (*torch etc*): **to ~ on** braquer sur; (*polish: pt, pp ~d*) faire briller or reluire

shingle ['ʃɪŋgl] n (*on beach*) galets mpl; **~s** n (*MED*) zona m

shiny ['ʃaɪnɪ] adj brillant(e)

ship [ʃɪp] n bateau m; (*large*) navire m ♦ vt transporter (par mer); (*send*) expédier (par mer); **~building** n construction navale; **~ment** n cargaison f; **~per** n affréteur m; **~ping** n (*ships*) navires mpl; (*the industry*) industrie navale; (*transport*) transport m; **~wreck** n (*ship*) épave f; (*event*) naufrage m ♦ vt: **to be ~wrecked** faire naufrage; **~yard** n chantier naval

shire ['ʃaɪə*] (*BRIT*) n comté m

shirk [ʃɜ:k] vt esquiver, se dérober à

shirt [ʃɜ:t] n (*man's*) chemise f; (*woman's*) chemisier m; **in (one's) ~ sleeves** en bras de chemise

shit [ʃɪt] (*infl*) n, excl merde f (!)

shiver ['ʃɪvə*] n frisson m ♦ vi frissonner

shoal [ʃəʊl] n (*of fish*) banc m; (*fig: also: ~s*) masse f, foule f

shock [ʃɒk] n choc m; (*ELEC*) secousse f; (*MED*) commotion f, choc ♦ vt (*offend*) choquer, scandaliser; (*upset*) bouleverser; **~ absorber** n amortisseur m; **~ing** adj (*scandalizing*) choquant(e), scandaleux(euse); (*appalling*) épouvantable

shod [ʃɒd] pt, pp of **shoe**

shoddy ['ʃɒdɪ] adj de mauvaise qualité, mal fait(e)

shoe [ʃu:] n (pt, pp **shod**) n chaussure f, soulier m; (*also: horse~*) fer m à cheval ♦ vt (*horse*) ferrer; **~lace** n lacet m (de soulier); **~ polish** n cirage m; **~ shop** n magasin m de chaussures; **~string** n (*fig*): **on a ~string** avec un budget dérisoire

shone [ʃɒn] pt, pp of **shine**

shoo [ʃu:] excl ouste!

shook [ʃʊk] pt of **shake**

shoot [ʃu:t] n (pt, pp **shot**) n (*on branch, seedling*) pousse f ♦ vt (*game*) chasser; tirer; abattre; (*person*) blesser (or tuer) d'un coup de fusil *(or* de revolver); *(execute)* fusiller; *(arrow)* tirer; *(gun)* tirer un coup de; *(film)* tourner ♦ *vi (with gun, bow)*: **to ~ (at)** tirer (sur); *(FOOTBALL)* shooter, tirer; **~ down** *vt (plane)* abattre; **~ in** *vi* entrer comme une flèche; **~ out** *vi* sortir comme une flèche; **~ up** *vi (fig)* monter en flèche; **~ing** *n (shots)* coups *mpl* de feu, fusillade *f*; *(HUNTING)* chasse *f*; **~ing star** *n* étoile filante

shop [ʃɔp] *n* magasin *m*; *(workshop)* atelier *m* ♦ *vi (also: go ~ping)* faire ses courses *or* ses achats; **~ assistant** *(BRIT)* *n* vendeur(euse); **~ floor** *(BRIT)* *n (INDUSTRY: fig)* ouvriers *mpl*; **~keeper** *n* commerçant(e); **~lifting** *n* vol *m* à l'étalage; **~per** *n* personne *f* qui fait ses courses, acheteur(euse); **~ping** *n (goods)* achats *mpl*, provisions *fpl*; **~ping bag** *n* sac *m* (à provisions); **~ping centre** *(US* **~ping center)** *n* centre commercial; **~-soiled** *adj* défraîchi(e), qui a fait la vitrine; **~ steward** *(BRIT)* *n (INDUSTRY)* délégué(e) syndical(e); **~ window** *n* vitrine *f*

shore [ʃɔː*] *n (of sea, lake)* rivage *m*, rive *f* ♦ *vt*: **to ~ (up)** étayer; **on ~** à terre

shorn [ʃɔːn] *pp of* **shear**

short [ʃɔːt] *adj (not long)* court(e); *(soon finished)* court, bref(brève); *(person, step)* petit(e); *(curt)* brusque, sec(sèche); *(insufficient)* insuffisant(e); **to be/run ~ of sth** être à court de *or* manquer de qch; **in ~** bref; en bref; **~ of doing** ... à moins de faire ...; **everything ~ of** tout sauf; **it is ~ for** c'est l'abréviation *or* le diminutif de; **to cut ~** *(speech, visit)* abréger, écourter; **to fall ~ of** ne pas être à la hauteur de; **to run ~ of** arriver à court de, venir à manquer de; **to stop ~** s'arrêter net; **to stop ~ of** ne pas aller jusqu'à; **~age** *n* manque *m*, pénurie *f*; **~bread** *n* ≈ sablé *m*; **~change** *vt* ne pas rendre assez à; **~circuit** *n* court-circuit *m*; **~coming** *n* défaut *m*; **~(crust) pastry** *(BRIT)* *n* pâte brisée; **~cut** *n* raccourci *m*; **~en** *vt* raccourcir; *(visit)* abréger; **~fall** *n* déficit *m*; **~hand** *(BRIT)* *n* sténo(graphie) *f*; **~hand typist** *(BRIT)* *n* sténodactylo *m/f*; **~list** *(BRIT)* *n (for job)* liste *f* des candidats sélectionnés; **~lived** *adj* de courte durée; **~ly** *adv* bientôt, sous peu; **~s** *npl*: **(a pair of) ~s** un short; **~sighted** *adj (BRIT)* myope; *(fig)* qui manque de clairvoyance; **~-staffed** *adj* à court de personnel; **~ story** *n* nouvelle *f*; **~-tempered** *adj* qui s'emporte facilement; **~-term** *adj (effect)* à court terme; **~ wave** *n (RADIO)* ondes courtes

shot [ʃɔt] *pt, pp of* **shoot** ♦ *n* coup *m* (de feu); *(try)* coup, essai *m*; *(injection)* piqûre *f*; *(PHOT)* photo *f*; **he's a good/poor ~** il tire bien/mal; **like a ~** comme une flèche; *(very readily)* sans hésiter; **~gun** *n* fusil *m*

de chasse

should [ʃʊd] *aux vb*: **I ~ go now** je devrais partir maintenant; **he ~ be there now** il devrait être arrivé maintenant; **I ~ go if I were you** si j'étais vous, j'irais; **I ~ like to** j'aimerais bien, volontiers

shoulder [ˈʃəʊldə*] *n* épaule *f* ♦ *vt (fig)* endosser, se charger de; **~ bag** *n* sac *m* à bandoulière; **~ blade** *n* omoplate *f*; **~ strap** *n* bretelle *f*

shouldn't [ˈʃʊdnt] = **should not**

shout [ʃaʊt] *n* cri *m* ♦ *vt* crier ♦ *vi (also: ~ out)* crier, pousser des cris; **~ down** *vt* huer; **~ing** *n* cris *mpl*

shove [ʃʌv] *vt* pousser; *(inf: put)*: **to ~ sth in** fourrer *or* ficher qch dans; **~ off** *(inf)* *vi* ficher le camp

shovel [ˈʃʌvl] *n* pelle *f*

show [ʃəʊ] *(pt* **~ed**, *pp* **shown)** *n (of emotion)* manifestation *f*, démonstration *f*; *(semblance)* semblant *m*, apparence *f*; *(exhibition)* exposition *f*, salon *m*; *(THEATRE, TV)* spectacle *m* ♦ *vt* montrer; *(film)* donner; *(courage etc)* faire preuve de, manifester; *(exhibit)* exposer ♦ *vi* se voir, être visible; **for ~** pour l'effet; **on ~** *(exhibits etc)* exposé(e); **~ in** *vt (person)* faire entrer; **~ off** *vi (pej)* crâner ♦ *vt (display)* faire valoir; **~ out** *vt (person)* reconduire (jusqu'à la porte); **~ up** *vi (stand out)* ressortir; *(inf: turn up)* se montrer ♦ *vt (flaw)* faire ressortir; **~ business** *n* le monde du spectacle; **~down** *n* épreuve *f* de force

shower [ˈʃaʊə*] *n (rain)* averse *f*; *(of stones etc)* pluie *f*, grêle *f*; *(also: ~bath)* douche *f* ♦ *vi* prendre une douche, se doucher ♦ *vt*: **to ~ sb with** *(gifts etc)* combler qn de; **to have** *or* **take a ~** prendre une douche; **~proof** *adj* imperméabilisé(e)

showing [ˈʃəʊɪŋ] *n (of film)* projection *f*

show jumping *n* concours *m* hippique

shown [ʃəʊn] *pp of* **show**

show: **~-off** [ˈʃəʊɔf] *(inf)* *n (person)* crâneur(euse), m'as-tu-vu(e); **~piece** *n (of exhibition)* trésor *m*; **~room** [ˈʃəʊrʊm] *n* magasin *m or* salle *f* d'exposition

shrank [ʃræŋk] *pt of* **shrink**

shrapnel [ˈʃræpnl] *n* éclats *mpl* d'obus

shred [ʃred] *n (gen pl)* lambeau *m*, petit morceau *m* ♦ *vt* mettre en lambeaux, déchirer; *(CULIN)* râper; couper en lanières; **~der** *n (for vegetables)* râpeur *m*; *(for documents)* déchiqueteuse *f*

shrewd [ʃruːd] *adj* astucieux(euse), perspicace; *(businessman)* habile

shriek [ʃriːk] *vi* hurler, crier

shrill [ʃrɪl] *adj* perçant(e), aigu(guë), strident(e)

shrimp [ʃrɪmp] *n* crevette *f*

shrine [ʃraɪn] *n (place)* lieu *m* de pèlerinage

shrink [ʃrɪŋk] *(pt* **shrank**, *pp* **shrunk**) *vi* rétrécir; *(fig)* se réduire, diminuer; *(move:*

also: ~ *away*) reculer ♦ *vt* (*wool*) (faire) rétrécir ♦ *n* (*inf*: *pej*) psychiatre *m/f*, psy *mf*; **to ~ from (doing)** sth reculer devant (la pensée de faire) qch; ~**age** *n* rétrécissement *m*; ~**wrap** *vt* emballer sous film plastique

shrivel ['ʃrɪvl] *vt* (*also*: ~ *up*) ratatiner, flétrir ♦ *vi* se ratatiner, se flétrir

shroud [ʃraud] *n* linceul *m* ♦ *vt*: ~**ed in mystery** enveloppé(e) de mystère

Shrove Tuesday ['ʃrəuv-] *n* (le) Mardi gras

shrub [ʃrʌb] *n* arbuste *m*; ~**bery** *n* massif *m* d'arbustes

shrug [ʃrʌg] *vt*, *vi*: **to ~ (one's shoulders)** hausser les épaules; ~ **off** *vt* faire fi de

shrunk [ʃrʌŋk] *pp of* **shrink**

shudder ['ʃʌdə*] *vi* frissonner, frémir

shuffle ['ʃʌfl] *vt* (*cards*) battre ♦ *vt*, *vi*: **to ~ (one's feet)** traîner les pieds

shun [ʃʌn] *vt* éviter, fuir

shunt [ʃʌnt] *vt* (RAIL) aiguiller

shut [ʃʌt] (*pt*, *pp* **shut**) *vt* fermer ♦ *vi* (se) fermer; ~ **down** *vt*, *vi* fermer définitivement; ~ **off** *vt* couper, arrêter; ~ **up** *vi* (*inf*: *keep quiet*) se taire ♦ *vt* (*close*) fermer; (*silence*) faire taire; ~**ter** *n* volet *m*; (PHOT) obturateur *m*

shuttle ['ʃʌtl] *n* navette *f*; (*also*: ~ *service*) (service *m* de) navette *f*

shuttlecock ['ʃʌtlkɒk] *n* volant *m* (*de badminton*)

shy [ʃaɪ] *adj* timide

sibling ['sɪblɪŋ] *n*: ~**s** enfants *mpl* de mêmes parents

Sicily ['sɪsɪlɪ] *n* Sicile *f*

sick [sɪk] *adj* (*ill*) malade; (*vomiting*): **to be ~** vomir; (*humour*) noir(e), macabre; **to feel ~** avoir envie de vomir, avoir mal au cœur; **to be ~ of** (*fig*) en avoir assez de; ~**bay** *n* infirmerie *f*; ~**en** *vt* écœurer; ~**ening** *adj* (*fig*) écœurant(e), dégoûtant(e)

sickle ['sɪkl] *n* faucille *f*

sick: ~ **leave** *n* congé *m* de maladie; ~**ly** *adj* maladif(ive), souffreteux(euse); (*causing nausea*) écœurant(e); ~**ness** *n* maladie *f*; (*vomiting*) vomissement(s) *m(pl)*; ~ **pay** *n* indemnité *f* de maladie

side [saɪd] *n* côté *m*; (*of lake, road*) bord *m*; (*team*) camp *m*, équipe *f* ♦ *adj* (*door, entrance*) latéral(e) ♦ *vi*: **to ~ with sb** prendre le parti de qn, se ranger du côté de qn; **by the ~ of** au bord de; ~ **by** ~ côte à côte; **from ~ to** ~ d'un côté à l'autre; **to take ~s (with)** prendre parti (pour); ~**board** *n* buffet *m*; ~**boards** (BRIT), ~**burns** *npl* (*whiskers*) pattes *fpl*; ~ **drum** *n* tambour plat; ~ **effect** *n* effet *m* secondaire; ~**light** *n* (AUT) veilleuse *f*; ~**line** *n* (SPORT) (ligne *f* de) touche *f*; (*fig*) travail *m* secondaire; ~**long** *adj* oblique; ~**saddle** *adv* en amazone; ~**show** *n* attrac-

tion *f*; ~**step** *vt* (*fig*) éluder; éviter; ~ **street** *n* (petite) rue transversale; ~**track** *vt* (*fig*) faire dévier de son sujet; ~**walk** (US) *n* trottoir *m*; ~**ways** *adv* de côté

siding ['saɪdɪŋ] *n* (RAIL) voie *f* de garage

sidle ['saɪdl] *vi*: **to ~ up (to)** s'approcher furtivement (de)

siege [siːdʒ] *n* siège *m*

sieve [sɪv] *n* tamis *m*, passoire *f*

sift [sɪft] *vt* (*fig*: *also*: ~ *through*) passer en revue; (*lit*: *flour etc*) passer au tamis

sigh [saɪ] *n* soupir *m* ♦ *vi* soupirer, pousser un soupir

sight [saɪt] *n* (*faculty*) vue *f*; (*spectacle*) spectacle *m*; (*on gun*) mire *f* ♦ *vt* apercevoir; **in ~** visible; **out of ~** hors de vue; ~**seeing** *n* tourisme *m*; **to go ~seeing** faire du tourisme

sign [saɪn] *n* signe *m*; (*with hand etc*) signe, geste *m*; (*notice*) panneau *m*, écriteau *m* ♦ *vt* signer; ~ **on** *vi* (MIL) s'engager; (*as unemployed*) s'inscrire au chômage; (*for course*) s'inscrire ♦ *vt* (MIL) engager; (*employee*) embaucher; ~ **over** *vt*: **to ~ sth over to sb** céder qch par écrit à qn; ~ **up** *vt* engager ♦ *vi* (MIL) s'engager; (*for course*) s'inscrire

signal ['sɪgnl] *n* signal *m* ♦ *vi* (AUT) mettre son clignotant ♦ *vt* (*person*) faire signe à; (*message*) communiquer par signaux; ~**man** (*irreg*) *n* (RAIL) aiguilleur *m*

signature ['sɪgnətʃə*] *n* signature *f*; ~ **tune** *n* indicatif musical

signet ring ['sɪgnət-] *n* chevalière *f*

significance [sɪg'nɪfɪkəns] *n* signification *f*; importance *f*; **significant** [sɪg'nɪfɪkənt] *adj* significatif(ive); (*important*) important(e), considérable

signpost ['saɪnpəust] *n* poteau indicateur

silence ['saɪləns] *n* silence *m* ♦ *vt* faire taire, réduire au silence; ~**r** *n* (*on gun*, BRIT: AUT) silencieux *m*

silent ['saɪlənt] *adj* silencieux(euse); (*film*) muet(te); **to remain ~** garder le silence, ne rien dire; ~ **partner** *n* (COMM) bailleur *m* de fonds, commanditaire *m*

silhouette [sɪluː'et] *n* silhouette *f*

silicon chip ['sɪlɪkən-] *n* puce *f* électronique

silk [sɪlk] *n* soie *f* ♦ *cpd* de or en soie; ~**y** *adj* soyeux(euse)

silly ['sɪlɪ] *adj* stupide, sot(te), bête

silt [sɪlt] *n* vase *f*; limon *m*

silver ['sɪlvə*] *n* argent *m*; (*money*) monnaie *f* (en pièces d'argent); (*also*: ~*ware*) argenterie *f* ♦ *adj* d'argent, en argent; ~ **paper** (BRIT) *n* papier *m* d'argent *or* d'étain; ~-**plated** *adj* plaqué(e) argent; ~**smith** *n* orfèvre *m/f*; ~**y** *adj* argenté(e)

similar ['sɪmɪlə*] *adj*: ~ **(to)** semblable (à); ~**ly** *adv* de la même façon, de même

simile ['sɪmɪlɪ] *n* comparaison *f*

simmer ['sɪmə*] *vi* cuire à feu doux, mijoter

simple ['sɪmpl] *adj* simple; **simplicity** [sɪm'plɪsɪtɪ] *n* simplicité *f*; **simply** *adv* (*without fuss*) avec simplicité

simultaneous [sɪməl'teɪnɪəs] *adj* simultané(e)

sin [sɪn] *n* péché *m* ♦ *vi* pécher

since [sɪns] *adv, prep* depuis ♦ *conj* (*time*) depuis que; (*because*) puisque, étant donné que, comme; ~ **then, ever** ~ depuis ce moment-là

sincere [sɪn'sɪə*] *adj* sincère; ~**ly** *adv see* **yours; sincerity** [sɪn'serɪtɪ] *n* sincérité *f*

sinew ['sɪnjuː] *n* tendon *m*

sinful ['sɪnful] *adj* coupable; (*person*) pécheur(eresse)

sing [sɪŋ] (*pt* **sang**, *pp* **sung**) *vt, vi* chanter

singe [sɪndʒ] *vt* brûler légèrement; (*clothes*) roussir

singer ['sɪŋə*] *n* chanteur(euse)

singing ['sɪŋɪŋ] *n* chant *m*

single ['sɪŋgl] *adj* seul(e), unique; (*unmarried*) célibataire; (*not double*) simple ♦ *n* (*BRIT: also*: ~ **ticket**) aller *m* (simple); (*record*) 45 tours *m*; ~ **out** *vt* choisir; (*distinguish*) distinguer; ~**-breasted** *adj* droit(e); ~ **file** *n*: **in** ~ **file** en file indienne; ~**handed** *adv* tout(e) seul(e), sans (aucune) aide; ~**-minded** *adj* résolu(e), tenace; ~ **room** *n* chambre *f* à un lit *or* pour une personne; ~**s** *n* (*TENNIS*) simple *m*; **singly** *adv* séparément

singular ['sɪŋgjulə*] *adj* singulier(ère), étrange; (*outstanding*) remarquable; (*LING*) (au) singulier, du singulier ♦ *n* singulier *m*

sinister ['sɪnɪstə*] *adj* sinistre

sink [sɪŋk] (*pt* **sank**, *pp* **sunk**) *n* évier *m* ♦ *vt* (*ship*) (faire) couler, faire sombrer; (*foundations*) creuser ♦ *vi* couler, sombrer; (*ground etc*) s'affaisser; (*also*: ~ **back**, ~ **down**) s'affaisser, se laisser retomber; **to** ~ **sth into** enfoncer qch dans; **my heart sank** j'ai complètement perdu courage; ~ **in** *vi* (*fig*) pénétrer, être compris(e)

sinner ['sɪnə*] *n* pécheur(eresse)

sinus ['saɪnəs] *n* sinus *m inv*

sip [sɪp] *n* gorgée *f* ♦ *vt* boire à petites gorgées

siphon ['saɪfən] *n* siphon *m*; ~ **off** *vt* siphonner; (*money: illegally*) détourner

sir [sɜː*] *n* monsieur *m*; **S**~ **John Smith** sir John Smith; **yes** ~ oui, Monsieur

siren ['saɪərən] *n* sirène *f*

sirloin ['sɜːlɔɪn] *n* (*also*: ~ **steak**) aloyau *m*

sissy ['sɪsɪ] (*inf*) *n* (*coward*) poule mouillée

sister ['sɪstə*] *n* sœur *f*; (*nun*) religieuse *f*, sœur; (*BRIT: nurse*) infirmière *f* en chef; ~**-in-law** *n* belle-sœur *f*

sit [sɪt] (*pt, pp* **sat**) *vi* s'asseoir; (*be sitting*) être assis(e); (*assembly*) être en séance, siéger; (*for painter*) poser ♦ *vt* (*exam*) passer,

se présenter à; ~ **down** *vi* s'asseoir; ~ **in on** *vt fus* assister à; ~ **up** *vi* s'asseoir; (*straight*) se redresser; (*not go to bed*) rester debout, ne pas se coucher

sitcom ['sɪtkɔm] *n abbr* (= *situation comedy*) comédie *f* de situation

site [saɪt] *n* emplacement *m*, site *m*; (*also: building* ~) chantier *m* ♦ *vt* placer

sit-in ['sɪtɪn] *n* (*demonstration*) sit-in *m inv*, occupation *f* (de locaux)

sitting ['sɪtɪŋ] *n* (*of assembly etc*) séance *f*; (*in canteen*) service *m*; ~ **room** *n* salon *m*

situated ['sɪtjueɪtɪd] *adj* situé(e)

situation [sɪtju'eɪʃən] *n* situation *f*; "~**s vacant**" (*BRIT*) "offres d'emploi"

six [sɪks] *num* six; ~**teen** *num* seize; ~**th** *num* sixième; ~**ty** *num* soixante

size [saɪz] *n* taille *f*, dimensions *fpl*; (*of clothing*) taille; (*of shoes*) pointure *f*; (*fig*) ampleur *f*; (*glue*) colle *f*; ~ **up** *vt* juger, jauger; ~**able** *adj* assez grand(e); assez important(e)

sizzle ['sɪzl] *vi* grésiller

skate [skeɪt] *n* patin *m*; (*fish: pl inv*) raie *f* ♦ *vi* patiner; ~**board** *n* skateboard *m*, planche *f* à roulettes; ~**r** *n* patineur(euse); **skating** ['skeɪtɪŋ] *n* patinage *m*; **skating rink** *n* patinoire *f*

skeleton ['skelɪtn] *n* squelette *m*; (*outline*) schéma *m*; ~ **staff** *n* effectifs réduits

skeptical ['skeptɪkl] (*US*) *adj* = **sceptical**

sketch [sketʃ] *n* (*drawing*) croquis *m*, esquisse *f*; (*THEATRE*) sketch *m*, saynète *f* ♦ *vt* esquisser, faire un croquis *or* une esquisse de; ~ **book** *n* carnet *m* à dessin; ~**y** *adj* incomplet(ète), fragmentaire

skewer ['skjuə*] *n* brochette *f*

ski [skiː] *n* ski *m* ♦ *vi* skier, faire du ski; ~ **boot** *n* chaussure *f* de ski

skid [skɪd] *vi* déraper

ski: ~**er** ['skiːə*] *n* skieur(euse); ~**ing** ['skiːɪŋ] *n* ski *m*; ~ **jump** *n* saut *m* à skis

skilful ['skɪlful] (*US* **skillful**) *adj* habile, adroit(e)

ski lift *n* remonte-pente *m inv*

skill [skɪl] *n* habileté *f*, adresse *f*, talent *m*; (*requiring training: gen pl*) compétences *fpl*; ~**ed** *adj* habile, adroit(e); (*worker*) qualifié(e)

skim [skɪm] *vt* (*milk*) écrémer; (*glide over*) raser; ~, effleurer ♦ *vi*: **to** ~ **through** (*fig*) parcourir; ~**med milk** *n* lait écrémé

skimp [skɪmp] *vt* (*also*: ~ **on**: *work*) bâcler, faire à la va-vite; (: *cloth etc*) lésiner sur; ~**y** *adj* maigre; (*skirt*) étriqué(e)

skin [skɪn] *n* peau *f* ♦ *vt* (*fruit etc*) éplucher; (*animal*) écorcher; ~ **cancer** *n* cancer *m* de la peau; ~**-deep** *adj* superficiel(le); ~**diving** *n* plongée sous-marine; ~**ny** *adj* maigre, maigrichon(ne); ~**tight** *adj* (*jeans etc*) collant(e), ajusté(e)

skip [skɪp] *n* petit bond *or* saut *m*; (*BRIT*:

container) benne *f* ♦ *vi* gambader, sautiller; (*with rope*) sauter à la corde ♦ *vt* sauter

ski pants *npl* fuseau *m* (de ski)

ski pole *n* bâton *m* de ski

skipper ['skɪpə*] *n* capitaine *m*; (*in race*) skipper *m*

skipping rope ['skɪpɪŋ-] (*BRIT*) *n* corde *f* à sauter

skirmish ['skɜːmɪʃ] *n* escarmouche *f*, accrochage *m*

skirt [skɜːt] *n* jupe *f* ♦ *vt* longer, contourner; ~**ing board** (*BRIT*) *n* plinthe *f*

ski slope *n* piste *f* de ski

ski suit *n* combinaison *f* (de ski)

skittle ['skɪtl] *n* quille *f*; **skittles** *n* (*game*) (jeu *m* de) quilles *fpl*

skive [skaɪv] (*BRIT*: *inf*) *vi* tirer au flanc

skulk [skʌlk] *vi* rôder furtivement

skull [skʌl] *n* crâne *m*

skunk [skʌŋk] *n* mouffette *f*

sky [skaɪ] *n* ciel *m*; ~**light** *n* lucarne *f*, ~**scraper** *n* gratte-ciel *m inv*

slab [slæb] *n* (*of stone*) dalle *f*; (*of food*) grosse tranche

slack [slæk] *adj* (*loose*) lâche, desserré(e); (*slow*) stagnant(e); (*careless*) négligent(e), peu sérieux(euse) *or* conscientieux(euse); ~**s** *npl* (*trousers*) pantalon *m*; ~**en** *vi* ralentir, diminuer ♦ *vt* (*speed*) réduire; (*grip*) relâcher; (*clothing*) desserrer

slag heap [slæg-] *n* crassier *m*

slag off (*BRIT*: *inf*) *vt* dire du mal de

slain [sleɪn] *pp of* **slay**

slam [slæm] *vt* (*door*) (faire) claquer; (*throw*) jeter violemment, flanquer (*fam*); (*criticize*) démolir ♦ *vi* claquer

slander ['slɑːndə*] *n* calomnie *f*; diffamation *f*

slang [slæŋ] *n* argot *m*

slant [slɑːnt] *n* inclinaison *f*; (*fig*) angle *m*, point *m* de vue; ~**ed** *adj* = **slanting**; ~**ing** *adj* en pente, incliné(e); ~**ing eyes** yeux bridés

slap [slæp] *n* claque *f*, gifle *f*; tape *f* ♦ *vt* donner une claque *or* une gifle *or* une tape à; (*paint*) appliquer rapidement ♦ *adv* (*directly*) tout droit, en plein; ~**dash** *adj* fait(e) sans soin *or* à la va-vite; (*person*) insouciant(e), négligent(e); ~**stick** *n* (*comedy*) grosse farce, style *m* tarte à la crème; ~**up** (*BRIT*) *adj*: **a ~-up meal** un repas extra *or* fameux

slash [slæʃ] *vt* entailler, taillader; (*fig*: *prices*) casser

slat [slæt] *n* latte *f*, lame *f*

slate [sleɪt] *n* ardoise *f* ♦ *vt* (*fig*: *criticize*) éreinter, démolir

slaughter ['slɔːtə*] *n* carnage *m*, massacre *m* ♦ *vt* (*animal*) abattre; (*people*) massacrer; ~**house** *n* abattoir *m*

slave [sleɪv] *n* esclave *m/f* ♦ *vi* (*also*: ~ *away*) trimer, travailler comme un forçat;

~**ry** *n* esclavage *m*; **slavish** *adj* servile

slay [sleɪ] (*pt* **slew**, *pp* **slain**) *vt* tuer

sleazy ['sliːzɪ] *adj* miteux(euse), minable

sledge [sledʒ] *n* luge *f*

sledgehammer *n* marteau *m* de forgeron

sleek [sliːk] *adj* (*hair, fur etc*) brillant(e), lisse; (*car, boat etc*) aux lignes pures *or* élégantes

sleep [sliːp] (*pt, pp* **slept**) *n* sommeil *m* ♦ *vi* dormir; (*spend night*) dormir, coucher; **to go to ~** s'endormir; **~ around** *vi* coucher à droite et à gauche; **~ in** *vi* (*over~*) se réveiller trop tard; ~**er** (*BRIT*) *n* (*RAIL*: *train*) train-couchettes *m*; (: *berth*) couchette *f*, ~**ing bag** *n* sac *m* de couchage; ~**ing car** *n* (*RAIL*) wagon-lit *m*, voiture-lit *f*; ~**ing partner** (*BRIT*) *n* associé *m* commanditaire; ~**ing pill** *n* somnifère *m*; ~**less** *adj*: **a ~less night** une nuit blanche; ~**walker** *n* somnambule *m/f*; ~**y** *adj* qui a sommeil; (*fig*) endormi(e)

sleet [sliːt] *n* neige fondue

sleeve [sliːv] *n* manche *f*; (*of record*) pochette *f*

sleigh [sleɪ] *n* traîneau *m*

sleight [slaɪt] *n*: ~ **of hand** tour *m* de passe-passe

slender ['slendə*] *adj* svelte, mince; (*fig*) faible, ténu(e)

slept [slept] *pt, pp of* **sleep**

slew [sluː] *vi* (*also*: ~ *around*) virer, pivoter ♦ *pt of* **slay**

slice [slaɪs] *n* tranche *f*; (*round*) rondelle *f*; (*utensil*) spatule *f*, truelle *f* ♦ *vt* couper en tranches (*or* en rondelles)

slick [slɪk] *adj* (*skilful*) brillant(e) (en apparence); (*salesman*) qui a du bagout ♦ *n* (*also*: *oil* ~) nappe *f* de pétrole, marée noire

slide [slaɪd] (*pt, pp* **slid**) *n* (*in playground*) toboggan *m*; (*PHOT*) diapositive *f*; (*BRIT*: *also*: *hair* ~) barrette *f*; (*in prices*) chute *f*, baisse *f* ♦ *vt* (*faire*) glisser ♦ *vi* glisser; **sliding** ['slaɪdɪŋ] *adj* (*door*) coulissant(e); **sliding scale** *n* échelle *f* mobile

slight [slaɪt] *adj* (*slim*) mince, menu(e); (*frail*) frêle; (*trivial*) faible, insignifiant(e); (*small*) petit(e), léger(ère) (*before n*) ♦ *n* offense *f*, affront *m*; **not in the ~est** pas le moins du monde, pas du tout; ~**ly** *adv* légèrement, un peu

slim [slɪm] *adj* mince ♦ *vi* maigrir; (*diet*) suivre un régime amaigrissant

slime [slaɪm] *n* (*mud*) vase *f*; (*other substance*) substance visqueuse

slimming ['slɪmɪŋ] *adj* (*diet, pills*) amaigrissant(e); (*foodstuff*) qui ne fait pas grossir

sling [slɪŋ] (*pt, pp* **slung**) *n* (*MED*) écharpe *f*; (*for baby*) porte-bébé *m*; (*weapon*) fronde *f*, lance-pierre *m* ♦ *vt* lancer, jeter

slip [slɪp] *n* faux pas; (*mistake*) erreur *f*; étourderie *f*, bévue *f*; (*underskirt*) combinai-

son f; (of paper) petite feuille, fiche f ♦ vt
(slide) glisser ♦ vi glisser; (decline) baisser;
(move smoothly): to ~ into/out of se glisser or se faufiler dans/hors de; to ~ sth
on/off enfiler/enlever qch; to give sb the
~ fausser compagnie à qn; a ~ of the
tongue un lapsus; ~ away vi s'esquiver;
~ in vt glisser ♦ vi (errors) s'y glisser; ~
out vi sortir; ~ up vi faire une erreur, gaf-
fer; ~ped disc n déplacement m de vertèbre

slipper ['slɪpə*] n pantoufle f

slippery ['slɪpərɪ] adj glissant(e)

slip road (BRIT) n (to motorway) bretelle f
d'accès

slipshod ['slɪpʃɒd] adj négligé(e), peu soi-
gné(e)

slip-up ['slɪpʌp] n bévue f

slipway ['slɪpweɪ] n cale f (de construction
or de lancement)

slit [slɪt] (pt, pp slit) n fente f; (cut) incision
f ♦ vt fendre; couper; inciser

slither ['slɪðə*] vi glisser; (snake) onduler

sliver ['slɪvə*] n (of glass, wood) éclat m;
(of cheese etc) petit morceau, fine tranche

slob [slɒb] (inf) n rustaud(e)

slog [slɒg] (BRIT) n travailler très dur ♦ n
gros effort; tâche fastidieuse

slogan ['sləʊgən] n slogan m

slop [slɒp] vi (also: ~ over) se renverser; déborder ♦ vt répandre; renverser

slope [sləʊp] n pente f, côte f; (side of
mountain) versant m; (slant) inclinaison f ♦
vi: to ~ down être or descendre en pente;
to ~ up monter; **sloping** adj en pente;
(writing) penché(e)

sloppy ['slɒpɪ] adj (work) peu soigné(e),
bâclé(e); (appearance) négligé(e), dé-
braillé(e)

slot [slɒt] n fente f ♦ vt: to ~ sth into encastrer or insérer qch dans

sloth [sləʊθ] n (laziness) paresse f

slot machine n (BRIT: vending machine)
distributeur m (automatique); (for gambling) machine f à sous

slouch [slaʊtʃ] vi avoir le dos rond, être
voûté(e)

slovenly ['slʌvnlɪ] adj sale, débraillé(e);
(work) négligé(e)

slow [sləʊ] adj lent(e); (watch): to be ~ retarder ♦ adv lentement ♦ vt, vi (also: ~
down, ~ up) ralentir; "~~" (road sign) "ralentir"; ~ly adv lentement; ~ motion n:
in ~ motion au ralenti

sludge [slʌdʒ] n boue f

slue [sluː] (US) vi = slew

slug [slʌg] n limace f; (bullet) balle f

sluggish ['slʌgɪʃ] adj (person) mou(molle),
lent(e); (stream, engine, trading) lent

sluice [sluːs] n (also: ~ gate) vanne f

slum [slʌm] n (house) taudis m

slump [slʌmp] n baisse soudaine, effondre-

ment m; (ECON) crise f ♦ vi s'effondrer,
s'affaisser

slung [slʌŋ] pt, pp of sling

slur [slɜː*] n (fig: smear): ~ (on) atteinte f
(à); insinuation f (contre) ♦ vt mal articuler

slush [slʌʃ] n neige fondue; ~ **fund** n caisse noire, fonds secrets

slut [slʌt] (pej) n souillon f

sly [slaɪ] adj (person) rusé(e); (smile, expression, remark) sournois(e)

smack [smæk] n (slap) tape f; (on face) gifle
f ♦ vt donner une tape à; (on face) gifler;
(on bottom) donner la fessée à ♦ vi: to ~
of avoir des relents de, sentir

small [smɔːl] adj petit(e); ~ **ads** (BRIT) npl
petites annonces; ~ **change** n petite or
menue monnaie; ~ **fry** n (fig) menu fretin;
~**holder** (BRIT) n petit cultivateur; ~
hours npl: in the ~ **hours** au petit matin;
~**pox** n variole f; ~ **talk** n menus propos

smart [smɑːt] adj (neat, fashionable) élé-
gant(e), chic inv; (clever) intelligent(e), as-
tucieux(euse), futé(e); (quick) rapide,
vif(vive), prompt(e) ♦ vi faire mal, brûler;
(fig) être piqué(e) au vif; ~**en up** vi devenir plus élégant(e), se faire beau(belle) ♦ vt
rendre plus élégant(e)

smash [smæʃ] n (also: ~-up) collision f, accident m; (: ~ hit) succès foudroyant ♦ vt
casser, briser, fracasser; (opponent) écraser;
(SPORT: record) pulvériser ♦ vi se briser, se
fracasser; s'écraser; ~**ing** (inf) adj formidable

smattering ['smætərɪŋ] n: a ~ of quelques
notions de

smear [smɪə*] n tache f, salissure f; trace f;
(MED) frottis m ♦ vt enduire; (make dirty)
salir; ~ **campaign** n campagne f de diffamation

smell [smel] (pt, pp smelt or smelled) n
odeur f; (sense) odorat m ♦ vt sentir ♦ vi
(food etc): to ~ (of) sentir (de); (pej) sentir
mauvais

smelly ['smelɪ] adj qui sent mauvais, malo-
dorant(e)

smile [smaɪl] n sourire m ♦ vi sourire

smirk [smɜːk] n petit sourire suffisant or af-
fecté

smock [smɒk] n blouse f

smog [smɒg] n brouillard mêlé de fumée,
smog m

smoke [sməʊk] n fumée f ♦ vt, vi fumer;
~**d** adj (bacon, glass) fumé(e); ~**r** n (person) fumeur(euse); (RAIL) wagon m fu-
meurs; ~ **screen** n rideau or écran m
de fumée; (fig) paravent m; **smoking**
['sməʊkɪŋ] n tabagisme m; "**no smoking**"
(sign) "défense de fumer"; to give up
smoking arrêter de fumer; **smoky**
['sməʊkɪ] adj enfumé(e); (taste) fumé(e)

smolder ['sməʊldə*] (US) vi = smoulder

smooth [smuːð] adj lisse; (sauce) onctueux(euse); (*flavour, whisky*) moelleux(euse); (*movement*) régulier(ère), sans à-coups *or* heurts; (*pej: person*) doucereux(euse), mielleux(euse) ♦ *vt* (*also:* ~ *out: skirt, paper*) lisser, défroisser; (: *creases, difficulties*) faire disparaître

smother ['smʌðə*] *vt* étouffer

smoulder ['sməuldə*] (*US* **smolder**) *vi* couver

smudge [smʌdʒ] *n* tache *f*, bavure *f* ♦ *vt* salir, maculer

smug [smʌg] *adj* suffisant(e)

smuggle ['smʌgl] *vt* passer en contrebande *or* en fraude; **~r** *n* contrebandier(ère); **smuggling** ['smʌglɪŋ] *n* contrebande *f*

smutty ['smʌtɪ] *adj* (*fig*) grossier(ère), obscène

snack [snæk] *n* casse-croûte *m inv*; ~ **bar** *n* snack(-bar) *m*

snag [snæg] *n* inconvénient *m*, difficulté *f*

snail [sneɪl] *n* escargot *m*

snake [sneɪk] *n* serpent *m*

snap [snæp] *n* (*sound*) claquement *m*, bruit sec; (*photograph*) photo *f*, instantané *m* ♦ *adj* subit(e); fait(e) sans réfléchir ♦ *vt* (*break*) casser net; (*fingers*) faire claquer ♦ *vi* se casser net *or* avec un bruit sec; (*speak sharply*) parler d'un ton brusque; **to ~ shut** se refermer brusquement; ~ **at** *vt fus* (*subj: dog*) essayer de mordre; ~ **off** *vt* (*break*) casser net; ~ **up** *vt* sauter sur, saisir; **~py** (*inf*) *adj* prompt(e); (*slogan*) qui a du punch; **make it ~py!** grouille-toi!, et que ça saute!; **~shot** *n* photo *f*, instantané *m*

snare [snɛə*] *n* piège *m*

snarl [snɑ:l] *vi* gronder

snatch [snætʃ] *n* (*small amount*): **~es** of des fragments *mpl or* bribes *fpl* de ♦ *vt* saisir (*d'un geste vif*); (*steal*) voler

sneak [sni:k] (*pt* (*US*) *also* **snuck**) *vi*: **to ~ in/out** entrer/sortir furtivement *or* à la dérobée ♦ *n* (*inf, pej: informer*) faux jeton; **to ~ up on sb** s'approcher de qn sans faire de bruit; **~ers** ['sni:kəz] *npl* tennis *mpl or* baskets *mpl*

sneer [snɪə*] *vi* ricaner; **to ~ at** traiter avec mépris

sneeze [sni:z] *vi* éternuer

sniff [snɪf] *vi* renifler ♦ *vt* renifler, flairer; (*glue, drugs*) sniffer, respirer

snigger ['snɪgə*] *vi* ricaner; pouffer de rire

snip [snɪp] *n* (*cut*) petit coup; (*BRIT: inf: bargain*) (bonne) occasion *or* affaire *f* ♦ *vt* couper

sniper ['snaɪpə*] *n* tireur embusqué

snippet ['snɪpɪt] *n* bribe(s) *f(pl)*

snivelling ['snɪvlɪŋ] *adj* larmoyant(e), pleurnicheur(euse)

snob [snɒb] *n* snob *m/f*; **~bish** *adj* snob *inv*

snooker ['snu:kə*] *n* sorte de jeu de billard

snoop [snu:p] *vi*: **to ~ about** fureter

snooty ['snu:tɪ] *adj* snob *inv*

snooze [snu:z] *n* petit somme ♦ *vi* faire un petit somme

snore [snɔ:*] *vi* ronfler

snorkel ['snɔ:kl] *n* tuba *m*

snort [snɔ:t] *vi* grogner; (*horse*) renâcler

snout [snaut] *n* museau *m*

snow [snəu] *n* neige *f* ♦ *vi* neiger; **~ball** *n* boule *f* de neige; **~bound** *adj* enneigé(e), bloqué(e) par la neige; **~drift** *n* congère *f*; **~drop** *n* perce-neige *m or f*; **~fall** *n* chute *f* de neige; **~flake** *n* flocon *m* de neige; **~man** (*irreg*) *n* bonhomme *m* de neige; **~plough** (*US* **~plow**) *n* chasse-neige *m inv*; **~shoe** *n* raquette *f* (*pour la neige*); **~storm** *n* tempête *f* de neige

snub [snʌb] *vt* repousser, snober ♦ *n* rebuffade *f*; **~-nosed** *adj* au nez retroussé

snuff [snʌf] *n* tabac *m* à priser

snug [snʌg] *adj* douillet(te), confortable; (*person*) bien au chaud

snuggle ['snʌgl] *vi*: **to ~ up to sb** se serrer *or* se blottir contre qn

— **KEYWORD**

so [səu] *adv* **1** (*thus, likewise*) ainsi; **if ~** si oui; ~ **do** *or* **have I** moi aussi; **it's 5 o'clock - ~ it is!** il est 5 heures - en effet! *or* c'est vrai!; **I hope/think ~** je l'espère/le crois; ~ **far** jusqu'ici, jusqu'à maintenant; (*in past*) jusque-là

2 (*in comparisons etc: to such a degree*) si, tellement; ~ **big (that)** si *or* tellement grand (que); **she's not ~ clever as her brother** elle n'est pas aussi intelligente que son frère

3: ~ **much** *adj, adv* tant (de); **I've got ~ much work** j'ai tant de travail; **I love you ~ much** je vous aime tant; ~ **many** tant (de)

4 (*phrases*): **10 or ~** à peu près *or* environ 10; ~ **long!** (*inf: goodbye*) au revoir!, à un de ces jours!

♦ *conj* **1** (*expressing purpose*): ~ **as to do** pour faire *or* afin de faire; ~ (**that**) pour que *or* afin que +*sub*

2 (*expressing result*) donc, par conséquent; ~ **that** si bien que, de (telle) sorte que

soak [səuk] *vt* faire tremper; (*drench*) tremper ♦ *vi* tremper; ~ **in** *vi* être absorbé(e); ~ **up** *vt* absorber

soap [səup] *n* savon *m*; **~flakes** *npl* paillettes *fpl* de savon; ~ **opera** *n* feuilleton télévisé; ~ **powder** *n* lessive *f*; **~y** *adj* savonneux(euse)

soar [sɔ:*] *vi* monter (en flèche), s'élancer; (*building*) s'élancer

sob [sɒb] *n* sanglot *m* ♦ *vi* sangloter

sober ['səubə*] *adj* qui n'est pas (*or* plus) ivre; (*serious*) sérieux(euse), sensé(e); (*colour, style*) sobre, discret(ète); ~ **up** *vt* dessoûler (*inf*) ♦ *vi* dessoûler (*inf*)

so-called ['səʊ'kɔːld] *adj* soi-disant *inv*

soccer ['sɒkə*] *n* football *m*

social ['səʊʃəl] *adj* social(e); (*sociable*) sociable ♦ *n* (petite) fête; ~ **club** *n* amicale *f*, foyer *m*; ~**ism** *n* socialisme *m*; ~**ist** *adj* socialiste ♦ *n* socialiste *m/f*; ~**ize** *vi*: **to** ~**ize (wIth)** lier connaissance (avec); parler (avec); ~ **security** (*BRIT*) *n* aide sociale; ~ **work** *n* assistance sociale, travail social; ~ **worker** *n* assistant(e) social(e)

society [sə'saɪətɪ] *n* société *f*; (*club*) société, association *f*; (*also*: high ~) (haute) société, grand monde

sociology [səʊsɪ'ɒlədʒɪ] *n* sociologie *f*

sock [sɒk] *n* chaussette *f*

socket ['sɒkɪt] *n* cavité *f*; (*BRIT: ELEC*: *also*: wall ~) prise *f* de courant

sod [sɒd] *n* (*of earth*) motte *f*, (*BRIT: inf!*) con *m* (*!*); salaud *m* (*!*)

soda ['səʊdə] *n* (*CHEM*) soude *f*; (*also*: ~ water) eau *f* de Seltz; (*US: also*: ~ pop) soda *m*

sodden ['sɒdn] *adj* trempé(e); détrempé(e)

sofa ['səʊfə] *n* sofa *m*, canapé *m*

soft [sɒft] *adj* (*not rough*) doux(douce); (*not hard*) doux; mou(molle); (*not loud*) doux, léger(ère); (*kind*) doux, gentil(le); ~ **drink** *n* boisson non alcoolisée; ~**en** ['sɒfn] *vt* (r)amollir; (*fig*) adoucir; atténuer ♦ *vi* se ramollir; s'adoucir; s'atténuer; ~**ly** *adv* doucement; gentiment; ~**ness** *n* douceur *f*; ~ **spot** *n*: **to have a** ~ **spot for sb** avoir un faible pour qn; ~**ware** ['sɒftwɛə*] *n* (*COMPUT*) logiciel *m*, software *m*

soggy ['sɒgɪ] *adj* trempé(e); détrempé(e)

soil [sɔɪl] *n* (*earth*) sol *m*, terre *f* ♦ *vt* salir; (*fig*) souiller

solace ['sɒləs] *n* consolation *f*

solar ['səʊlə*] *adj* solaire; ~ **panel** *n* panneau *m* solaire; ~ **power** *n* énergie *f* solaire

sold [səʊld] *pt, pp of* **sell**

solder ['səʊldə*] *vt* souder (*au fil à souder*) ♦ *n* soudure *f*

soldier ['səʊldʒə*] *n* soldat *m*, militaire *m*

sole [səʊl] *n* (*of foot*) plante *f*; (*of shoe*) semelle *f*; (*fish: pl inv*) sole *f* ♦ *adj* seul(e), unique

solemn ['sɒləm] *adj* solennel(le); (*person*) sérieux(euse), grave

sole trader *n* (*COMM*) chef *m* d'entreprise individuelle

solicit [sə'lɪsɪt] *vt* (*request*) solliciter ♦ *vi* (*prostitute*) racoler

solicitor [sə'lɪsɪtə*] *n* (*for wills etc*) ≈ notaire *m*; (*in court*) ≈ avocat *m*

solid ['sɒlɪd] *adj* solide; (*not hollow*) plein(e), compact(e), massif(ive); (*entire*): **3** ~ **hours** 3 heures entières ♦ *n* solide *m*

solidarity [sɒlɪ'dærɪtɪ] *n* solidarité *f*

solitary ['sɒlɪtərɪ] *adj* solitaire; ~ **confinement** *n* (*LAW*) isolement *m*

solo ['səʊləʊ] *n* solo *m* ♦ *adv* (*fly*) en solitaire; ~**ist** *n* soliste *m/f*

soluble ['sɒljʊbl] *adj* soluble

solution [sə'luːʃən] *n* solution *f*

solve [sɒlv] *vt* résoudre

solvent ['sɒlvənt] *adj* (*COMM*) solvable ♦ *n* (*CHEM*) (dis)solvant *m*

━━━━━━━━━━━ **KEYWORD**

some [sʌm] *adj* **1** (*a certain amount or number of*): ~ **tea/water/ice cream** du thé/de l'eau/de la glace; ~ **children/apples** des enfants/pommes

2 (*certain: in contrasts*): ~ **people say that** ... il y a des gens qui disent que ...; ~ **films were excellent, but most** ... certains films étaient excellents, mais la plupart ...

3 (*unspecified*): ~ **woman was asking for you** il y avait une dame qui vous demandait; **he was asking for** ~ **book (or other)** il demandait un livre quelconque; ~ **day** un de ces jours; ~ **day next week** un jour la semaine prochaine

♦ *pron* **1** (*a certain number*) quelques-un(e)s, certain(e)s; **I've got** ~ (*books etc*) j'en ai (quelques-uns); ~ (**of them**) **have been sold** certains ont été vendus

2 (*a certain amount*) un peu; **I've got** ~ (*money, milk*) j'en ai un peu

♦ *adv*: ~ **10 people** quelque 10 personnes, 10 personnes environ

some: ~**body** ['sʌmbədɪ] *pron* = **someone**; ~**how** ['sʌmhaʊ] *adv* d'une façon ou d'une autre; (*for some reason*) pour une raison ou une autre; ~**one** ['sʌmwʌn] *pron* quelqu'un; ~**place** ['sʌmpleɪs] (*US*) *adv* = **somewhere**

somersault ['sʌməsɔːlt] *n* culbute *f*, saut *m* périlleux ♦ *vi* faire la culbute *or* un saut périlleux; (*car*) faire un tonneau

something ['sʌmθɪŋ] *pron* quelque chose; ~ **interesting** quelque chose d'intéressant

sometime ['sʌmtaɪm] *adv* (*in future*) un de ces jours, un jour ou après; (*in past*): ~ **last month** au cours du mois dernier

some: ~**times** ['sʌmtaɪmz] *adv* quelquefois, parfois; ~**what** ['sʌmwɒt] *adv* quelque peu, un peu; ~**where** ['sʌmwɛə*] *adv* quelque part

son [sʌn] *n* fils *m*

song [sɒŋ] *n* chanson *f*; (*of bird*) chant *m*

son-in-law ['sʌnɪnlɔː] *n* gendre *m*, beau-fils *m*

sonny ['sʌnɪ] (*inf*) *n* fiston *m*

soon [suːn] *adv* bientôt; (*early*) tôt; ~ **afterwards** peu après; **as** ~ **as possible** dès possible, aussitôt possible; *see also* **as**; ~**er** *adv* (*time*) plus tôt; (*preference*): **I would** ~**er do** j'aimerais autant *or* je préférerais faire; ~**er or later** tôt ou tard

soot [sʊt] *n* suie *f*

soothe [suːð] vt calmer, apaiser

sophisticated [səˈfɪstɪkeɪtɪd] adj raffiné(e); sophistiqué(e); (machinery) hautement perfectionné(e), très complexe

sophomore [ˈsɒfəmɔː*] (US) n étudiant(e) de seconde année

sopping [ˈsɒpɪŋ] adj (also: ~ wet) complètement trempé(e)

soppy [ˈsɒpɪ] (pej) adj sentimental(e)

soprano [səˈprɑːnəʊ] n (singer) soprano m/f

sorcerer [ˈsɔːsərə*] n sorcier m

sore [sɔː*] adj (painful) douloureux(euse), sensible ♦ n plaie f; **~ly** adv (tempted) fortement

sorrow [ˈsɒrəʊ] n peine f, chagrin m

sorry [ˈsɒrɪ] adj désolé(e); (condition, excuse) triste, déplorable; **~!** pardon!, excusez-moi!; **~?** pardon?; **to feel ~ for sb** plaindre qn

sort [sɔːt] n genre m, espèce f, sorte f ♦ vt (also: ~ out) trier; classer; ranger; (: problems) résoudre, régler; **~ing office** n bureau m de tri

SOS n abbr (= save our souls) S.O.S. m

so-so [ˈsəʊˈsəʊ] adv comme ci comme ça

sought [sɔːt] pt, pp of **seek**

soul [səʊl] n âme f; **~-destroying** adj démoralisant(e); **~ful** adj sentimental(e); (eyes) expressif(ive)

sound [saʊnd] adj (healthy) en bonne santé, sain(e); (safe, not damaged) solide, en bon état; (reliable, not superficial) sérieux(euse), solide; (sensible) sensé(e) ♦ adv: **~ asleep** profondément endormi(e) ♦ n son m; bruit m; (GEO) détroit m, bras m de mer ♦ vt (alarm) sonner ♦ vi sonner, retentir; (fig: seem) sembler (être); **to ~ like** ressembler à; **~ out** vt sonder; **~ barrier** n mur m du son; **~ effects** npl bruitage m; **~ly** adv (sleep) profondément; (beat) complètement, à plate couture; **~proof** adj insonorisé(e); **~track** n (of film) bande f sonore

soup [suːp] n soupe f, potage m; **in the ~** (fig) dans le pétrin; **~ plate** n assiette creuse or à soupe; **~spoon** n cuiller f à soupe

sour [ˈsaʊə*] adj aigre; **it's ~ grapes** (fig) c'est du dépit

source [sɔːs] n source f

south [saʊθ] n sud m ♦ adj sud inv, du sud ♦ adv au sud, vers le sud; **S~ Africa** n Afrique f du Sud; **S~ African** adj sudafricain(e) ♦ n Sud-Africain(e); **S~ America** n Amérique f du Sud; **S~ American** adj sud-américain(e) ♦ n Sud-Américain(e); **~-east** n sud-est m; **~erly** [ˈsʌðəlɪ] adj du sud; au sud; **~ern** [ˈsʌðən] adj du sud; méridional(e); **S~ Pole** n Pôle m Sud; **~ward(s)** adv vers le sud; **~-west** n sudouest m

souvenir [suːvəˈnɪə*] n (objet) souvenir m

sovereign [ˈsɒvrɪn] n souverain(e)

soviet [ˈsəʊvɪət] adj soviétique; **the S~ Union** l'Union f soviétique

sow¹ [saʊ] n truie f

sow² [səʊ] (pt ~ed, pp sown) vt semer; **~n** [səʊn] pp of **sow²**

soya [ˈsɔɪə] (US **soy**) n: **~ bean** graine f de soja; **~ sauce** sauce f de soja

spa [spɑː] n (town) station thermale; (US: also: health ~) établissement m de cure de rajeunissement etc

space [speɪs] n espace m; (room) place f, espace; (length of time) laps m de temps ♦ cpd spatial(e) ♦ vt (also: ~ out) espacer; **~craft** n engin spatial; **~man** (irreg) n astronaute m, cosmonaute m; **~ship** n = **spacecraft**; **~woman** (irreg) n astronaute f, cosmonaute f; **spacing** n espacement m

spade [speɪd] n (tool) bêche f, pelle f; (child's) pelle; **~s** npl (CARDS) pique m

Spain [speɪn] n Espagne f

span [spæn] n (of bird, plane) envergure f; (of arch) portée f; (in time) espace m de temps, durée f ♦ vt enjamber, franchir; (fig) couvrir, embrasser

Spaniard [ˈspænjəd] n Espagnol(e)

spaniel [ˈspænjəl] n épagneul m

Spanish [ˈspænɪʃ] adj espagnol(e) ♦ n (LING) espagnol m; **the** ~ npl les Espagnols mpl

spank [spæŋk] vt donner une fessée à

spanner [ˈspænə*] (BRIT) n clé f (de mécanicien)

spar [spɑː*] n espar m ♦ vi (BOXING) s'entraîner

spare [spɛə*] adj de réserve, de rechange; (surplus) de or en trop, de reste ♦ n (part) pièce f de rechange, pièce détachée f ♦ vt (do without) se passer de; (afford to give) donner, accorder; (refrain from hurting) épargner; **to ~** (surplus) en surplus, de trop; **~ part** n pièce f de rechange, pièce détachée; **~ time** n moments mpl de loisir, temps m libre; **~ wheel** n (AUT) roue f de secours; **sparing** [ˈspɛərɪŋ] adj: **to be sparing with** ménager; **sparingly** adv avec modération

spark [spɑːk] n étincelle f; **~(ing) plug** n bougie f

sparkle [ˈspɑːkl] n scintillement m, éclat m ♦ vi étinceler, scintiller; **sparkling** [ˈspɑːklɪŋ] adj (wine) mousseux(euse), pétillant(e); (water) pétillant(e); (fig: conversation, performance) étincelant(e), pétillant(e)

sparrow [ˈspærəʊ] n moineau m

sparse [spɑːs] adj clairsemé(e)

spartan [ˈspɑːtən] adj (fig) spartiate

spasm [ˈspæzəm] n (MED) spasme m; **~odic** [spæzˈmɒdɪk] adj (fig) intermittent(e)

spastic [ˈspæstɪk] n handicapé(e) moteur

spat [spæt] pt, pp of **spit**

spate [speɪt] n (fig): **a ~ of** une avalanche or un torrent de

spatter ['spætə*] vt éclabousser

spawn [spɔ:n] vi frayer ♦ n frai m

speak [spi:k] (pt **spoke**, pp **spoken**) vt parler; (truth) dire ♦ vi parler; (make a speech) prendre la parole; **to ~ to sb/of or about sth** parler à qn/de qch; **~ up!** parle plus fort!; **~er** n (in public) orateur m; (also: loud~er) haut-parleur m; **the S~er** (BRIT POL) le président de la chambre des Communes; (US POL) le président de la chambre des Représentants

spear [spɪə*] n lance f ♦ vt transpercer; **~head** vt (attack etc) mener

spec [spek] (inf) n: **on ~** à tout hasard

special ['speʃəl] adj spécial(e); **~ist** n spécialiste m/f; **~ity** n spécialité f; **~ize** vi: **to ~ize (in)** se spécialiser (dans); **~ly** adv spécialement, particulièrement; **~ty** (esp US) n = **speciality**

species ['spi:ʃi:z] n inv espèce f

specific [spə'sɪfɪk] adj précis(e); particulier(ère); (BOT, CHEM etc) spécifique; **~ally** adv expressément, explicitement; **~ation** n (TECH) spécification f; (requirement) stipulation f

specimen ['spesɪmɪn] n spécimen m, échantillon m; (of blood) prélèvement m

speck [spek] n petite tache, petit point; (particle) grain m; **~led** ['spekld] adj tacheté(e), moucheté(e)

specs [speks] (inf) npl lunettes fpl

spectacle ['spektəkl] n spectacle m; **~s** npl (glasses) lunettes fpl

spectacular [spek'tækjulə*] adj spectaculaire

spectator [spek'teɪtə*] n spectateur(trice)

spectrum ['spektrəm] (pl **spectra**) n spectre m

speculation [spekju'leɪʃən] n spéculation f

speech [spi:tʃ] n (faculty) parole f; (talk) discours m, allocution f; (manner of speaking) façon f de parler, langage m; (enunciation) élocution f; **~less** adj muet(te)

speed [spi:d] n vitesse f; (promptness) rapidité f ♦ vi: **to ~ along/past** etc aller/passer etc à toute vitesse; **at full or top ~** à toute vitesse or allure; **~ up** vi aller plus vite, accélérer ♦ vt accélérer; **~boat** n vedette f, hors-bord m inv; **~ily** adv rapidement, promptement; **~ing** n (AUT) excès m de vitesse; **~ limit** n limitation f de vitesse, vitesse maximale permise; **~ometer** [spɪ'dɒmɪtə*] n compteur m (de vitesse); **~way** n (SPORT: also: **~way racing**) épreuve(s) f(pl) de vitesse de motos; **~y** adj rapide, prompt(e)

spell [spel] (pt, pp **spelt** (BRIT) or **~ed**) n (also: magic ~) sortilège m, charme m; (period of time) (courte) période f ♦ vt (in writing) écrire, orthographier; (aloud) épeler; (fig) signifier; **to cast a ~ on sb** jeter un sort à qn; **he can't ~** il fait des fautes d'or-

thographe; **~bound** adj envoûté(e), subjugué(e); **~ing** n orthographe f

spend [spend] (pt, pp **spent**) vt (money) dépenser; (time, life) passer; consacrer; **~thrift** n dépensier(ère)

sperm [spɜ:m] n sperme m

spew [spju:] vt (also: ~ out) vomir

sphere [sfɪə*] n sphère f

spice [spaɪs] n épice f

spick-and-span ['spɪkən'spæn] adj impeccable

spicy ['spaɪsɪ] adj épicé(e), relevé(e); (fig) piquant(e)

spider ['spaɪdə*] n araignée f

spike [spaɪk] n pointe f; (BOT) épi m

spill [spɪl] (pt, pp **spilt** or **~ed**) vt renverser; répandre ♦ vi se répandre; **~ over** vi déborder

spin [spɪn] (pt **spun** or **span**, pp **spun**) n (revolution of wheel) tour m; (AVIAT) (chute f en) vrille f; (trip in car) petit tour, balade f ♦ vt (wool etc) filer; (wheel) faire tourner ♦ vi filer; (turn) tourner, tournoyer; **~ out** vt faire durer

spinach ['spɪnɪtʃ] n épinard m; (as food) épinards

spinal ['spaɪnl] adj vertébral(e), spinal(e); **~ cord** n moelle épinière

spindly ['spɪndlɪ] adj grêle, filiforme

spin-dryer ['spɪn'draɪə*] (BRIT) n essoreuse f

spine [spaɪn] n colonne vertébrale; (thorn) épine f; **~less** adj (fig) mou(molle)

spinning ['spɪnɪŋ] n (of thread) filature f; **~ top** n toupie f; **~ wheel** n rouet m

spin-off ['spɪnɒf] n avantage inattendu; sous-produit m

spinster ['spɪnstə*] n célibataire f; vieille fille (péj)

spiral ['spaɪərl] n spirale f ♦ vi (fig) monter en flèche; **~ staircase** n escalier m en colimaçon

spire ['spaɪə*] n flèche f, aiguille f

spirit ['spɪrɪt] n esprit m; (mood) état m d'esprit; (courage) courage m, énergie f; **~s** npl (drink) spiritueux mpl, alcool m; **in good ~s** de bonne humeur; **~ed** adj vif(vive), fougueux(euse), plein(e) d'allant; **~ual** ['spɪrɪtjuəl] adj spirituel(le); (religious) religieux(euse)

spit [spɪt] (pt, pp **spat**) n (for roasting) broche f; (saliva) salive f ♦ vi cracher; (sound) crépiter

spite [spaɪt] n rancune f, dépit m ♦ vt contrarier, vexer; **in ~ of** en dépit de, malgré; **~ful** adj méchant(e), malveillant(e)

spittle ['spɪtl] n salive f; (of animal) bave f; (spat out) crachat m

splash [splæʃ] n (sound) plouf m; (of colour) tache f ♦ vt éclabousser ♦ vi (also: ~ about) barboter, patauger

spleen [spli:n] n (ANAT) rate f

splendid ['splendɪd] *adj* splendide, superbe, magnifique

splint [splɪnt] *n* attelle *f*, éclisse *f*

splinter ['splɪntə*] *n* (*wood*) écharde *f*; (*glass*) éclat *m* ♦ *vi* se briser, se fendre

split [splɪt] (*pt, pp* **split**) *n* fente *f*, déchirure *f*; (*fig: POL*) scission *f* ♦ *vt* diviser; (*work, profits*) partager, répartir ♦ *vt* (*divide*) se diviser; ~ **up** *vi* (*couple*) se séparer, rompre; (*meeting*) se disperser

splutter ['splʌtə*] *vi* bafouiller; (*spit*) postillonner

spoil [spɔɪl] (*pt, pp* **spoilt** *or* ~**ed**) *vt* (*damage*) abîmer; (*mar*) gâcher; (*child*) gâter; ~**s** *npl* butin *m*; (*fig: profits*) bénéfices *npl*; ~**sport** *n* trouble-fête *m*, rabat-joie *m*

spoke [spəuk] *pt* **speak** ♦ *n* (*of wheel*) rayon *m*; ~**n** ['spəukn] *pp of* **speak**; ~**sman** ['spəuksmən] (*irreg*) *n* porte-parole *m inv*; ~**swoman** ['spəukswumən] (*irreg*) *n* porte-parole *m inv*

sponge [spʌndʒ] *n* éponge *f*; (*also: ~ cake*) ≈ biscuit *m* de Savoie ♦ *vt* éponger ♦ *vi*: to ~ **off** *or* **on** vivre aux crochets de; ~ **bag** (*BRIT*) *n* trousse *f* de toilette

sponsor ['spɒnsə*] *n* (*RADIO, TV, SPORT*) sponsor *m*; (*for application*) parrain *m*, marraine *f*; (*BRIT: for fund-raising event*) donateur(trice) ♦ *vt* sponsoriser; parrainer; faire un don à; ~**ship** *n* sponsoring *m*; parrainage *m*; dons *mpl*

spontaneous [spɒn'teɪnɪəs] *adj* spontané(e)

spooky ['spuːkɪ] (*inf*) *adj* qui donne la chair de poule

spool [spuːl] *n* bobine *f*

spoon [spuːn] *n* cuiller *f*; ~**-feed** *vt* nourrir à la cuiller; (*fig*) mâcher le travail à; ~**ful** *n* cuillerée *f*

sport [spɔːt] *n* sport *m*; (*person*) chic type(fille) ♦ *vt* arborer; ~**ing** *adj* sportif(ive); to **give sb a** ~**ing chance** donner sa chance à qn; ~ **jacket** (*US*) *n* = **sports jacket**; ~**s car** *n* voiture *f* de sport; ~**s jacket** (*BRIT*) *n* veste *f* de sport; ~**sman** (*irreg*) *n* sportif *m*; ~**smanship** *n* esprit sportif, sportivité *f*; ~**swear** *n* vêtements *mpl* de sport; ~**swoman** (*irreg*) *n* sportive *f*; ~**y** *adj* sportif(ive)

spot [spɒt] *n* tache *f*; (*dot: on pattern*) pois *m*; (*pimple*) bouton *m*; (*place*) endroit *m*, coin *m*; (*RADIO, TV: in programme: for person*) numéro *m*; (: *for activity*) rubrique *f*; (*small amount*): **a ~ of** un peu de ♦ *vt* (*notice*) apercevoir, repérer; **on the ~** sur place, sur les lieux; (*immediately*) sur-le-champ; (*in difficulty*) dans l'embarras; ~ **check** *n* sondage *m*, vérification ponctuelle; ~**less** *adj* immaculé(e); ~**light** *n* projecteur *m*; ~**ted** *adj* (*fabric*) à pois; ~**ty** *adj* (*face, person*) boutonneux(euse)

spouse [spauz] *n* époux(épouse)

spout [spaut] *n* (*of jug*) bec *m*; (*of pipe*) orifice *m* ♦ *vi* jaillir

sprain [spreɪn] *n* entorse *f*, foulure *f* ♦ *vt*: to ~ **one's ankle** *etc* se fouler *or* se tordre la cheville *etc*

sprang [spræŋ] *pt of* **spring**

sprawl [sprɔːl] *vi* s'étaler

spray [spreɪ] *n* jet *m* (en fines gouttelettes); (*from sea*) embruns *mpl*; (*container*) vaporisateur *m*; (*for garden*) pulvérisateur *m*; (*aerosol*) bombe *f*; (*of flowers*) petit bouquet ♦ *vt* vaporiser, pulvériser; (*crops*) traiter

spread [spred] (*pt, pp* **spread**) *n* (*distribution*) répartition *f*; (*CULIN*) pâte *f* à tartiner; (*inf: meal*) festin *m* ♦ *vt* étendre, étaler; répandre; (*wealth, workload*) distribuer ♦ *vi* (*disease, news*) se propager; (*also:* ~ **out:** *stain*) s'étaler; ~ **out** *vi* (*people*) se disperser; ~**-eagled** ['spredɪgld] *adj* étendu(e) bras et jambes écartés; ~**sheet** *n* (*COMPUT*) tableur *m*

spree [spriː] *n*: **to go on a** ~ faire la fête

sprightly ['spraɪtlɪ] *adj* alerte

spring [sprɪŋ] (*pt* **sprang**, *pp* **sprung**) *n* (*leap*) bond *m*, saut *m*; (*coiled metal*) ressort *m*; (*season*) printemps *m*; (*of water*) source *f* ♦ *vi* (*leap*) bondir, sauter; **in** ~ au printemps; to ~ **from** provenir de; ~ **up** *vi* (*problem*) se présenter, surgir; (*plant, buildings*) surgir de terre; ~**board** *n* tremplin *m*; ~**-clean(ing)** *n* grand nettoyage de printemps; ~**time** *n* printemps *m*

sprinkle ['sprɪŋkl] *vt*: to ~ **water** *etc* **on,** ~ **with water** *etc* asperger d'eau *etc*; to ~ **sugar** *etc* **on,** ~ **with sugar** *etc* saupoudrer de sucre *etc*; ~**r** ['sprɪŋklə*] *n* (*for lawn*) arroseur *m*; (*to put out fire*) diffuseur *m* d'extincteur automatique d'incendie

sprint [sprɪnt] *n* sprint *m* ♦ *vi* courir à toute vitesse; (*SPORT*) sprinter

sprout [spraut] *vi* germer, pousser; ~**s** *npl* (*also: Brussels* ~**s**) choux *mpl* de Bruxelles

spruce [spruːs] *n inv* épicéa *m* ♦ *adj* net(te), pimpant(e)

sprung [sprʌŋ] *pp of* **spring**

spry [spraɪ] *adj* alerte, vif(vive)

spun [spʌn] *pt, pp of* **spin**

spur [spɜː*] *n* éperon *m*; (*fig*) aiguillon *m* ♦ *vt* (*also:* ~ **on**) éperonner; aiguillonner; **on the** ~ **of the moment** sous l'impulsion du moment

spurious ['spjuərɪəs] *adj* faux(fausse)

spurn [spɜːn] *vt* repousser avec mépris

spurt [spɜːt] *n* (*of blood*) jaillissement *m*; (*of energy*) regain *m*, sursaut *m* ♦ *vi* jaillir, gicler

spy [spaɪ] *n* espion(ne) ♦ *vi*: to ~ **on** espionner, épier; (*see*) apercevoir; ~**ing** *n* espionnage *m*

sq. *abbr* = **square**

squabble ['skwɒbl] *vi* se chamailler

squad [skwɒd] *n* (*MIL, POLICE*) escouade *f*, groupe *m*; (*FOOTBALL*) contingent *m*

squadron ['skwɒdrən] *n* (*MIL*) escadron *m*; (*AVIAT, NAUT*) escadrille *f*

squalid ['skwɒlɪd] *adj* sordide

squall [skwɔːl] *n* rafale *f*, bourrasque *f*

squalor ['skwɒlə*] *n* conditions *fpl* sordides

squander ['skwɒndə*] *vt* gaspiller, dilapider

square [skwɛə*] *n* carré *m*; (*in town*) place *f* ♦ *adj* carré(e); (*inf: ideas, tastes*) vieux jeu *inv* ♦ *vt* (*arrange*) régler; arranger; (*MATH*) élever au carré ♦ *vi* (*reconcile*) concilier; **all ~** quitte; à égalité; **a ~ meal** un repas convenable; **2 metres ~** 2 mètres sur 2; **2 ~ metres** 2 mètres carrés; **~ly** *adv* carrément

squash [skwɒʃ] *n* (*BRIT: drink*): **lemon/orange ~** citronnade *f*/orangeade *f*; (*US: marrow*) courge *f*; (*SPORT*) squash *m* ♦ *vt* écraser

squat [skwɒt] *adj* petit(e) et épais(se), ramassé(e) ♦ *vi* (*also: ~ down*) s'accroupir; **~ter** *n* squatter *m*

squawk [skwɔːk] *vi* pousser un *or* des gloussement(s)

squeak [skwiːk] *vi* grincer, crier; (*mouse*) pousser un petit cri

squeal [skwiːl] *vi* pousser un *or* des cri(s) aigu(s) *or* perçant(s); (*brakes*) grincer

squeamish ['skwiːmɪʃ] *adj* facilement dégoûté(e)

squeeze [skwiːz] *n* pression *f*, (*ECON*) restrictions *fpl* de crédit ♦ *vt* presser; (*hand, arm*) serrer; **~ out** *vt* exprimer

squelch [skweltʃ] *vi* faire un bruit de succion

squid [skwɪd] *n* calmar *m*

squiggle ['skwɪgl] *n* gribouillis *m*

squint [skwɪnt] *vi* loucher ♦ *n*: **he has a ~** il louche, il souffre de strabisme

squirm [skwɜːm] *vi* se tortiller

squirrel ['skwɪrəl] *n* écureuil *m*

squirt [skwɜːt] *vt* jaillir, gicler

Sr *abbr* = **senior**

St *abbr* = **saint; street**

stab [stæb] *n* (*with knife etc*) coup *m* (de couteau *etc*); (*of pain*) lancée *f*, (*inf: try*): **to have a ~ at (doing) sth** s'essayer à (faire) qch ♦ *vt* poignarder

stable ['steɪbl] *n* écurie *f* ♦ *adj* stable

stack [stæk] *n* tas *m*, pile *f* ♦ *vt* (*also: ~ up*) empiler, entasser

stadium ['steɪdɪəm] (*pl* stadia *or* ~**s**) *n* stade *m*

staff [stɑːf] *n* (*workforce*) personnel *m*; (*BRIT: SCOL*) professeurs *mpl* ♦ *vt* pourvoir en personnel

stag [stæg] *n* cerf *m*

stage [steɪdʒ] *n* scène *f*, (*platform*) estrade *f n*; (*profession*): **the ~** le théâtre; (*point*) étape *f*, stade *m* ♦ *vt* (*play*) monter, mettre en scène; (*demonstration*) organiser; **in ~s**

par étapes, par degrés; **~coach** *n* diligence *f*; **~ manager** *n* régisseur *m*

stagger ['stægə*] *vi* chanceler, tituber ♦ *vt* (*person: amaze*) stupéfier; (*hours, holidays*) étaler, échelonner; **~ing** *adj* (*amazing*) stupéfiant(e), renversant(e)

stagnate [stæg'neɪt] *vi* stagner, croupir

stag party *n* enterrement *m* de vie de garçon

staid [steɪd] *adj* posé(e), rassis(e)

stain [steɪn] *n* tache *f*, (*colouring*) colorant *m* ♦ *vt* tacher; (*wood*) teindre; **~ed glass window** *n* vitrail *m*; **~less steel** *n* acier *m* inoxydable, inox *m*; **~ remover** *n* détachant *m*

stair [stɛə*] *n* (*step*) marche *f*; **~s** *npl* (*flight of steps*) escalier *m*; **~case** *n* escalier *m*; **~way** *n* = **staircase**

stake [steɪk] *n* pieu *m*, poteau *m*; (*BETTING*) enjeu *m*; (*COMM: interest*) intérêts *mpl* ♦ *vt* risquer, jouer; **to be at ~** être en jeu; **to ~ one's claim (to)** revendiquer

stale [steɪl] *adj* (*bread*) rassis(e); (*food*) pas frais(fraîche); (*beer*) éventé(e); (*smell*) de renfermé; (*air*) confiné(e)

stalemate ['steɪlmeɪt] *n* (*CHESS*) pat *m*; (*fig*) impasse *f*

stalk [stɔːk] *n* tige *f* ♦ *vt* traquer ♦ *vi*: **to ~ out/off** sortir/partir d'un air digne

stall [stɔːl] *n* (*BRIT: in street, market etc*) éventaire *m*, étal *m*; (*in stable*) stalle *f* ♦ *vt* (*AUT*) caler; (*delay*) retarder ♦ *vi* (*AUT*) caler; (*fig*) essayer de gagner du temps; **~s** *npl* (*BRIT: in cinema, theatre*) orchestre *m*

stallion ['stælɪən] *n* étalon *m* (*cheval*)

stalwart ['stɔːlwət] *adj* dévoué(e); fidèle

stamina ['stæmɪnə] *n* résistance *f*, endurance *f*

stammer ['stæmə*] *n* bégaiement *m* ♦ *vi* bégayer

stamp [stæmp] *n* timbre *m*; (*rubber ~*) tampon *m*; (*mark, also fig*) empreinte *f* ♦ *vi* (*also: ~ one's foot*) taper du pied ♦ *vt* (*letter*) timbrer; (*with rubber ~*) tamponner; **~ album** *n* album *m* de timbres(-poste); **~ collecting** *n* philatélie *f*

stampede [stæm'piːd] *n* ruée *f*

stance [stæns] *n* position *f*

stand [stænd] (*pt, pp* **stood**) *n* (*position*) position *f*, (*for taxis*) station *f* (de taxis); (*music ~*) pupitre *m* à musique; (*COMM*) étalage *m*, stand *m*; (*SPORT*) tribune *f* ♦ *vi* être *or* se tenir (debout); (*rise*) se lever, se mettre debout; (*be placed*) se trouver; (*remain: offer etc*) rester valable; (*BRIT: in election*) être candidat(e), se présenter ♦ *vt* (*place*) mettre, poser; (*tolerate, withstand*) supporter; (*treat, invite to*) offrir (*treat, invite*), payer; **to make** *or* **take a ~** prendre position; **to ~ at** (*score, value etc*) être de; **to ~ for parliament** (*BRIT*) se présenter aux élections législatives; **~ by** *vi* (*be ready*) se tenir prêt(e) ♦ vt fus (opinion) s'en tenir à; (person) ne pas abandonner, soutenir; ~ **down** vi (withdraw) se retirer; (flag (signify) représenter, signifier; (tolerate) supporter, tolérer; ~ **in for** vt fus remplacer; ~ **out** vi (be prominent) ressortir; ~ **up** vi (rise) se lever, se mettre debout; ~ **up for** vt fus défendre; ~ **up to** vt fus tenir tête à, résister à

standard ['stændəd] n (level) niveau (voulu); (norm) norme f, étalon m; (criterion) critère m; (flag) étendard m ♦ adj (size etc) ordinaire, normal(e); courant(e); (text) de base; ~**s** npl (morals) morale f, principes mpl; ~ **lamp** (BRIT) n lampadaire m; ~ **of living** n niveau m de vie

stand-by ['stændbaɪ] n remplaçant(e); **to be on** ~ se tenir prêt(e) (à intervenir); être de garde; ~ **ticket** n (AVIAT) billet m stand-by

stand-in ['stændɪn] n remplaçant(e)

standing ['stændɪŋ] adj debout inv; (permanent) permanent(e) ♦ n réputation f, rang m, standing m; **of many years'** ~ qui dure or existe depuis longtemps; ~ **joke** n vieux sujet de plaisanterie; ~ **order** (BRIT) n (at bank) virement m automatique, prélèvement m bancaire; ~ **room** n places fpl debout

standoffish [-'ɒfɪʃ] adj distant(e), froid(e)

standpoint ['stændpɔɪnt] n point m de vue

standstill ['stændstɪl] n: **at a** ~ paralysé(e); **to come to a** ~ s'immobiliser, s'arrêter

stank [stæŋk] pt of **stink**

staple ['steɪpl] n (for papers) agrafe f ♦ adj (food etc) de base ♦ vt agrafer; ~**r** n agrafeuse f

star [stɑː*] n étoile f; (celebrity) vedette f ♦ vi: **to** ~ **(in)** être la vedette (de) ♦ vt (CINEMA etc) avoir pour vedette; **the** ~**s** npl l'horoscope m

starboard ['stɑːbəd] n tribord m

starch [stɑːtʃ] n amidon m; (in food) fécule f

stardom ['stɑːdəm] n célébrité f

stare [stɛə*] n regard m fixe ♦ vi: **to** ~ **at** regarder fixement

starfish ['stɑːfɪʃ] n étoile f de mer

stark [stɑːk] adj (bleak) désolé(e), morne ♦ adv: ~ **naked** complètement nu(e)

starling ['stɑːlɪŋ] n étourneau m

starry ['stɑːrɪ] adj étoilé(e); ~-**eyed** adj (innocent) ingénu(e)

start [stɑːt] n commencement m, début m; (of race) départ m; (sudden movement) sursaut m; (advantage) avance f, avantage m ♦ vt commencer; (found) créer; (engine) mettre en marche ♦ vi partir, se mettre en route; (jump) sursauter; **to** ~ **doing** or **to do sth** se mettre à faire qch; ~ **off** vi commencer; (leave) partir; ~ **up** vi commencer; (car) démarrer ♦ vt (business) créer; (car) mettre en marche; ~**er** n (AUT)

démarreur m; (SPORT: official) starter m; (BRIT: CULIN) entrée f; ~**ing point** n point m de départ

startle ['stɑːtl] vt faire sursauter; donner un choc à; **startling** adj (news) surprenant(e)

starvation [stɑː'veɪʃən] n faim f, famine f; **starve** [stɑːv] vi mourir de faim; être affamé(e) ♦ vt affamer

state [steɪt] n état m; (POL) État ♦ vt déclarer, affirmer; **the S**~**s** npl (America) les États-Unis mpl; **to be in a** ~ être dans tous ses états; ~**ly** adj majestueux(euse), imposant(e); ~**ment** n déclaration f; ~**sman** (irreg) n homme m d'État

static ['stætɪk] n (RADIO, TV) parasites mpl ♦ adj statique

station ['steɪʃən] n gare f; (police ~) poste m de police ♦ vt placer, poster

stationary ['steɪʃənərɪ] adj à l'arrêt, immobile

stationer ['steɪʃənə*] n papetier(ère); ~'**s (shop)** n papeterie f; ~**y** n papier m à lettres, petit matériel de bureau

stationmaster ['steɪʃənmɑːstə*] n (RAIL) chef m de gare

station wagon (US) n break m

statistic [stə'tɪstɪk] n statistique f; ~**s** n (science) statistique f

statue ['stætjuː] n statue f

status ['steɪtəs] n position f, situation f; (official) statut m; (prestige) prestige m; ~ **symbol** n signe extérieur de richesse

statute ['stætjuːt] n loi f, statut m; **statutory** adj statutaire, prévu(e) par un article de loi

staunch [stɔːntʃ] adj sûr(e), loyal(e)

stave off [steɪv] vt (attack) parer; (threat) conjurer

stay [steɪ] n (period of time) séjour m ♦ vi rester; (reside) loger; (spend some time) séjourner; **to** ~ **put** ne pas bouger; **to** ~ **with friends** loger chez des amis; **to** ~ **the night** passer la nuit; ~ **behind** vi rester en arrière; ~ **in** vi (at home) rester à la maison; ~ **on** vi rester; ~ **out** vi (of house) ne pas rentrer; ~ **up** vi (at night) ne pas se coucher; ~**ing power** n endurance f

stead [sted] n: **in sb's** ~ à la place de qn; **to stand sb in good** ~ être très utile à qn

steadfast ['stedfəst] adj ferme, résolu(e)

steadily ['stedɪlɪ] adv (regularly) progressivement; (firmly) fermement; (: walk) d'un pas ferme; (fixedly: look) sans détourner les yeux

steady ['stedɪ] adj stable, solide, ferme; (regular) constant(e), régulier(ère); (person) calme, pondéré(e) ♦ vt stabiliser; (nerves) calmer; **a** ~ **boyfriend** un petit ami

steak [steɪk] n (beef) bifteck m, steak m; (fish, pork) tranche f

steal [stiːl] (pt **stole**, pp **stolen**) vt voler ♦ vi voler; (move secretly) se faufiler, se déplacer furtivement

stealth [stelθ] *n*: **by ~** furtivement

steam [sti:m] *n* vapeur *f* ♦ *vt* (*CULIN*) cuire à la vapeur ♦ *vi* fumer; **~ engine** *n* locomotive *f* à vapeur; **~er** *n* (bateau *m* à) vapeur *m*; **~ship** *n* = **steamer**; **~y** *adj* embué(e), humide

steel [sti:l] *n* acier *m* ♦ *adj* d'acier; **~works** *n* aciérie *f*

steep [sti:p] *adj* raide, escarpé(e); (*price*) excessif(ive)

steeple ['sti:pl] *n* clocher *m*

steer [stɪə*] *vt* diriger; (*boat*) gouverner; (*person*) guider, conduire ♦ *vi* tenir le gouvernail; **~ing** *n* (*AUT*) conduite *f*; **~ing wheel** *n* volant *m*

stem [stem] *n* (*of plant*) tige *f*; (*of glass*) pied *m* ♦ *vt* contenir, arrêter, juguler; **~ from** *vt fus* provenir de, découler de

stench [stentʃ] *n* puanteur *f*

stencil ['stensl] *n* stencil *m*; (*pattern used*) pochoir *m* ♦ *vt* polycopier

stenographer [ste'nɒɡrəfə*] (*US*) *n* sténographe *m/f*

step [step] *n* pas *m*; (*stair*) marche *f*; (*action*) mesure *f*, disposition *f* ♦ *vi* tenir le gou- ♦ *vi*: **to ~ forward/back** faire un pas en avant/arrière, avancer/reculer; **~s** *npl* (*BRIT*) = **stepladder**; **to be in/out of ~ (with)** (*fig*) aller dans le sens (de)/être déphasé(e) (par rapport à); **~ down** *vi* (*fig*) se retirer, se désister; **~ up** *vt* augmenter; intensifier; **~brother** *n* demi-frère *m*; **~daughter** *n* belle-fille *f*; **~father** *n* beau-père *m*; **~ladder** (*BRIT*) *n* escabeau *m*; **~mother** *n* belle-mère *f*; **~ping stone** *n* pierre *f* de gué; (*fig*) tremplin *m*; **~sister** *n* demi-sœur *f*; **~son** *n* beau-fils *m*

stereo ['steriəʊ] *n* (*sound*) stéréo *f*; (*hi-fi*) chaîne *f* stéréo *inv* ♦ *adj* (*also*: **~phonic**) stéréo(phonique)

sterile ['sterail] *adj* stérile; **sterilize** ['sterilaiz] *vt* stériliser

sterling ['stɜ:lɪŋ] *adj* (*silver*) de bon aloi, fin(e) ♦ *n* (*ECON*) livres *fpl* sterling *inv*; **a pound ~** une livre sterling

stern [stɜ:n] *adj* sévère ♦ *n* (*NAUT*) arrière *m*, poupe *f*

stew [stju:] *n* ragoût *m* ♦ *vt, vi* cuire (à la casserole)

steward ['stju:əd] *n* (*on ship, plane, train*) steward *m*; **~ess** *n* hôtesse *f* (de l'air)

stick [stɪk] (*pt, pp* **stuck**) *n* bâton *m*; (*walking ~*) canne *f* ♦ *vt* (*glue*) coller; (*inf: put*) mettre, fourrer; (: *tolerate*) supporter; (*thrust*): **to ~ sth into** planter or enfoncer qch dans ♦ *vi* (*become attached*) rester collé(e) or fixé(e); (*be unmoveable: wheels etc*) se bloquer; (*remain*) rester; **~ out** *vi* dépasser, sortir; **~ up** *vi* = **stick out**; **~ up for** *vt fus* défendre; **~er** *n* auto-collant *m*; **~ing plaster** *n* sparadrap *m*, pansement

adhésif

stickler ['stɪklə*] *n*: **to be a ~ for** être pointilleux(euse) sur

stick-up ['stɪkʌp] (*inf*) *n* braquage *m*, hold-up *m inv*

sticky ['stɪkɪ] *adj* poisseux(euse); (*label*) adhésif(ive); (*situation*) délicat(e)

stiff [stɪf] *adj* raide; rigide; dur(e); (*difficult*) difficile, ardu(e); (*cold*) froid(e), distant(e); (*strong, high*) fort(e), élevé(e) ♦ *adv*: **to be bored/scared/frozen ~** s'ennuyer à mort/ être mort(e) de peur/froid; **~en** *vi* se raidir; **~ neck** *n* torticolis *m*

stifle ['staifl] *vt* étouffer, réprimer

stigma ['stɪɡmə] *n* stigmate *m*

stile [stail] *n* échalier *m*

stiletto [stɪ'letəʊ] (*BRIT*) *n* (*also*: **~ heel**) talon *m* aiguille

still [stɪl] *adj* immobile ♦ *adv* (*up to this time*) encore, toujours; (*even*) encore; (*nonetheless*) quand même, tout de même; **~born** *adj* mort-né(e); **~ life** *n* nature morte

stilt [stɪlt] *n* (*for walking on*) échasse *f*; (*pile*) pilotis *m*

stilted ['stɪltɪd] *adj* guindé(e), emprunté(e)

stimulate ['stɪmjuleɪt] *vt* stimuler

stimulus ['stɪmjuləs] (*pl* **stimuli**) *n* stimulant *m*; (*BIOL, PSYCH*) stimulus *m*

sting [stɪŋ] (*pt, pp* **stung**) *n* piqûre *f*; (*organ*) dard *m* ♦ *vt, vi* piquer

stingy ['stɪndʒɪ] *adj* avare, pingre

stink [stɪŋk] (*pt* **stank**, *pp* **stunk**) *n* puanteur *f* ♦ *vi* puer, empester; **~ing** (*inf*) *adj* (*fig*) infect(e), vache; **a ~ing ...** un(e) foutu(e) ...

stint [stɪnt] *n* part *f* de travail ♦ *vi*: **to ~ on** lésiner sur, être chiche de

stir [stɜ:*] *n* agitation *f*, sensation *f* ♦ *vt* remuer ♦ *vi* remuer, bouger; **~ up** *vt* (*trouble*) fomenter, provoquer

stirrup ['stɪrəp] *n* étrier *m*

stitch [stɪtʃ] *n* (*SEWING*) point *m*; (*KNITTING*) maille *f*; (*MED*) point de suture; (*pain*) point de côté ♦ *vt* coudre, piquer; (*MED*) suturer

stoat [stəʊt] *n* hermine *f* (avec son pelage d'été)

stock [stɒk] *n* réserve *f*, provision *f*; (*COMM*) stock *m*; (*AGR*) cheptel *m*, bétail *m*; (*CULIN*) bouillon *m*; (*descent, origin*) souche *f*; (*FINANCE*) valeurs *fpl*, titres *mpl* ♦ *adj* (*fig*: *reply etc*) classique ♦ *vt* (*have in ~*) avoir, vendre; **~s and shares** valeurs (mobilières), titres; **in/out of ~** en stock or en magasin/épuisé(e); **to take ~ of** (*fig*) faire le point de; **~ up** *vi*: **to ~ up (with)** s'approvisionner (en); **~broker** ['stɒkbrəʊkə*] *n* agent *m* de change; **~ cube** *n* bouillon-cube *m*; **~ exchange** *n* Bourse *f*

stocking ['stɒkɪŋ] *n* bas *m*

stock: ~ **market** n Bourse f, marché financier; ~ **phrase** n cliché m; ~**pile** n stock m, réserve f ♦ vt stocker, accumuler; ~**taking** (BRIT) n (COMM) inventaire m

stocky ['stɒkɪ] adj trapu(e), râblé(e)

stodgy ['stɒdʒɪ] adj bourratif(ive), lourd(e)

stoke [stəʊk] vt (fire) garnir, entretenir; (boiler) chauffer

stole [stəʊl] pt of **steal** ♦ n étole f

stolen ['stəʊlən] pp of **steal**

stolid ['stɒlɪd] adj impassible, flegmatique

stomach ['stʌmək] n estomac m; (abdomen) ventre m ♦ vt digérer, supporter; ~**ache** n mal m à l'estomac or au ventre

stone [stəʊn] n pierre f; (pebble) caillou m, galet m; (in fruit) noyau m; (MED) calcul m; (BRIT: weight) = 6,348 kg ♦ adj de or en pierre ♦ vt (person) lancer des pierres sur, lapider; ~**-cold** adj complètement froid(e); ~**-deaf** adj sourd(e) comme un pot; ~**work** n maçonnerie f

stood [stʊd] pt, pp of **stand**

stool [stuːl] n tabouret m

stoop [stuːp] vi (also: have a ~) être voûté(e); (: ~ down: bend) se baisser

stop [stɒp] n arrêt m; halte f; (in punctuation: also: full ~) point m ♦ vt arrêter, bloquer; (break off) interrompre; (also: put a ~ to) mettre fin à ♦ vi s'arrêter; (rain, noise etc) cesser, s'arrêter; to ~ **doing sth** cesser or arrêter de faire qch; to ~ **dead** vi s'arrêter net; ~ **off** vi faire une courte halte; ~ **up** vt (hole) boucher; ~**gap** n (person) bouche-trou m; (measure) mesure f intérimaire; ~**over** n halte f; (AVIAT) escale f; ~**page** ['stɒpɪdʒ] n (strike) arrêt de travail; (blockage) obstruction f; ~**per** ['stɒpə*] n bouchon m; ~ **press** n nouvelles fpl de dernière heure; ~**watch** ['stɒpwɒtʃ] n chronomètre m

storage ['stɔːrɪdʒ] n entreposage m; ~ **heater** n radiateur m électrique par accumulation

store [stɔː*] n (stock) provision f, réserve f; (depot) entrepôt m; (BRIT: large shop) grand magasin m; (US) magasin m ♦ vt emmagasiner; (information) enregistrer; ~s npl (food) provisions; **in** ~ en réserve; ~ **up** vt mettre en réserve; accumuler; ~**room** n réserve f, magasin m

storey ['stɔːrɪ] (US **story**) n étage m

stork [stɔːk] n cigogne f

storm [stɔːm] n tempête f; (thunder~) orage m ♦ vi (fig) fulminer ♦ vt prendre d'assaut; ~**y** adj orageux(euse)

story ['stɔːrɪ] n histoire f; récit m; (US) = **storey**; ~**book** n livre m d'histoires or de contes

stout [staʊt] adj solide; (fat) gros(se), corpulent(e) ♦ n bière brune

stove [stəʊv] n (for cooking) fourneau m; (: small) réchaud m; (for heating) poêle m

stow [stəʊ] vt (also: ~ away) ranger; ~**away** n passager(ère) clandestin(e)

straddle ['strædl] vt enjamber, être à cheval sur

straggle ['strægl] vi être (or marcher) en désordre; (houses) être disséminé(e)

straight [streɪt] adj droit(e); (hair) raide; (frank) honnête, franc(franche); (simple) simple ♦ adv (tout) droit; (drink) sec, sans eau; **to put** or **get** ~ (fig) mettre au clair; ~ **away**, ~ **off** (at once) tout de suite; ~**en** vt (also: bed) arranger; ~**en out** vt (fig) débrouiller; ~**-faced** adj impassible; ~**forward** adj simple; (honest) honnête, direct(e)

strain [streɪn] n tension f; pression f; (physical) effort m; (mental) tension (nerveuse); (breed) race f ♦ vt (stretch: resources etc) mettre à rude épreuve, grever; (hurt: back etc) se faire mal à; (vegetables) égoutter; ~s npl (MUS) accords mpl, accents mpl; ~**ed** adj (muscle) froissé(e), (laugh etc) forcé(e), contraint(e); (relations) tendu(e); ~**er** n passoire f

strait [streɪt] n (GEO) détroit m; ~s npl: **to be in dire** ~s avoir de sérieux ennuis (d'argent); ~**jacket** n camisole f de force; ~**laced** adj collet monté inv

strand [strænd] n (of thread) fil m, brin m; (of rope) toron m; (of hair) mèche f; ~**ed** adj en rade, en plan

strange [streɪndʒ] adj (not known) inconnu(e); (odd) étrange, bizarre; ~**ly** adv étrangement, bizarrement; see also **enough**; ~**r** n inconnu(e); (from another area) étranger(ère)

strangle ['stræŋgl] vt étrangler; ~**hold** n (fig) emprise totale, mainmise f

strap [stræp] n lanière f, courroie f, sangle f; (of slip, dress) bretelle f

strapping ['stræpɪŋ] adj costaud(e)

strategic [strə'tiːdʒɪk] adj stratégique.

strategy ['strætədʒɪ] n stratégie f

straw [strɔː] n paille f; **that's the last** ~! ça, c'est le comble!

strawberry ['strɔːbərɪ] n fraise f

stray [streɪ] adj (animal) perdu(e), errant(e); (scattered) isolé(e) ♦ vi s'égarer; ~ **bullet** n balle perdue

streak ['striːk] n bande f, filet m; (in hair) raie f ♦ vt zébrer, strier ♦ vi: **to** ~ **past** passer à toute allure

stream [striːm] n ruisseau m; courant m, flot m; (of people) défilé ininterrompu, flot ♦ vt (SCOL) répartir par niveau ♦ vi ruisseler; **to** ~ **in/out** entrer/sortir à flots; ~**er** ['striːmə*] n serpentin m; (banner) banderole f; ~**lined** ['striːmlaɪnd] adj aérodynamique; (fig) rationalisé(e)

street [striːt] n rue f; ~**car** (US) n tramway m; ~ **lamp** n réverbère m; ~ **plan** n plan m (des rues); ~**wise** (inf) adj futé(e), réaliste

strength [streŋθ] *n* force *f*; (*of girder, knot etc*) solidité *f*; **~en** *vt* fortifier; renforcer; consolider

strenuous ['strenjʊəs] *adj* vigoureux(euse), énergique

stress [stres] *n* (*force, pressure*) pression *f*; (*mental strain*) tension (nerveuse), stress *m*; (*accent*) accent *m* ♦ *vt* insister sur, souligner

stretch [stretʃ] *n* (*of sand etc*) étendue *f* ♦ *vi* s'étirer; (*extend*): **to ~ to** *or* **as far as** s'étendre jusqu'à ♦ *vt* tendre, étirer; (*fig*) pousser (au maximum); **~ out** *vi* s'étendre ♦ *vt* (*arm etc*) allonger, tendre; (*spread*) étendre

stretcher ['stretʃə*] *n* brancard *m*, civière *f*

strewn [struːn] *adj*: **~ with** jonché(e) de

stricken ['strɪkən] *adj* (*person*) très éprouvé(e); (*city, industry etc*) dévasté(e); **~ with** (*disease etc*) frappé(e) *or* atteint(e) de

strict [strɪkt] *adj* strict(e)

stride [straɪd] (*pt* **strode**, *pp* **stridden**) *n* grand pas, enjambée *f* ♦ *vi* marcher à grands pas

strife [straɪf] *n* conflit *m*, dissensions *fpl*

strike [straɪk] (*pt, pp* **struck**) *n* grève *f*; (*of oil etc*) découverte *f*; (*attack*) raid *m* ♦ *vt* frapper; (*oil etc*) trouver, découvrir; (*deal*) conclure ♦ *vi* faire grève; (*attack*) attaquer; (*clock*) sonner; **on ~** (*workers*) en grève; **to ~ a match** frotter une allumette; **~ down** *vt* terrasser; **~ up** *vt* (*MUS*) se mettre à jouer; **to ~ up a friendship with** se lier d'amitié avec; **to ~ up a conversation (with)** engager une conversation (avec); **~r** *n* gréviste *m/f*; (*SPORT*) buteur *m*; **striking** ['straɪkɪŋ] *adj* frappant(e), saisissant(e); (*attractive*) éblouissant(e)

string [strɪŋ] (*pt, pp* **strung**) *n* ficelle *f*; (*row: of beads*) rang *m*; (: *of onions*) chapelet *m*; (*MUS*) corde *f* ♦ *vt*: **to ~ out** échelonner; **the ~s** *npl* (*MUS*) les instruments *mpl* à cordes; **to ~ together** enchaîner; **to pull ~s** (*fig*) faire jouer le piston; **~ bean** *n* haricot vert; **~(ed) instrument** (*MUS*) instrument *m* à cordes

stringent ['strɪndʒənt] *adj* rigoureux(euse)

strip [strɪp] *n* bande *f* ♦ *vt* (*undress*) déshabiller; (*paint*) décaper; (*also*: **~ down**: *machine*) démonter ♦ *vi* se déshabiller; **~ cartoon** *n* bande dessinée

stripe [straɪp] *n* raie *f*, rayure *f*; (*MIL*) galon *m*; **~d** *adj* rayé(e), à rayures

strip lighting (*BRIT*) *n* éclairage *m* au néon *or* fluorescent

stripper ['strɪpə*] *n* strip-teaseur(euse) *f*

strive [straɪv] (*pt* **strove**, *pp* **striven**) *vi*: **to ~ to do/for sth** s'efforcer de faire/d'obtenir qch

strode [strəʊd] *pt of* **stride**

stroke [strəʊk] *n* coup *m*; (*SWIMMING*) nage *f*; (*MED*) attaque *f* ♦ *vt* caresser; **at a ~** d'un (seul) coup

stroll [strəʊl] *n* petite promenade ♦ *vi* flâner, se promener nonchalamment; **~er** (*US*) *n* (*pushchair*) poussette *f*

strong [strɒŋ] *adj* fort(e); vigoureux(euse); (*heart, nerves*) solide; **they are 50 ~** ils sont au nombre de 50; **~hold** *n* bastion *m*; **~ly** *adv* fortement, avec force; vigoureusement; solidement; **~room** *n* chambre forte

strove [strəʊv] *pt of* **strive**

struck [strʌk] *pt, pp of* **strike**

structural ['strʌktʃərəl] *adj* structural(e); (*CONSTR: defect*) de construction; (*damage*) affectant les parties portantes

structure ['strʌktʃə*] *n* structure *f*; (*building*) construction *f*

struggle ['strʌgl] *n* lutte *f* ♦ *vi* lutter, se battre

strum [strʌm] *vt* (*guitar*) jouer (en sourdine) de

strung [strʌŋ] *pt, pp of* **string**

strut [strʌt] *n* étai *m*, support *m* ♦ *vi* se pavaner

stub [stʌb] *n* (*of cigarette*) bout *m*, mégot *m*; (*of cheque etc*) talon *m* ♦ *vt*: **to ~ one's toe** se cogner le doigt de pied; **~ out** *vt* écraser

stubble ['stʌbl] *n* chaume *m*; (*on chin*) barbe *f* de plusieurs jours

stubborn ['stʌbən] *adj* têtu(e), obstiné(e), opiniâtre

stuck [stʌk] *pt, pp of* **stick** ♦ *adj* (*jammed*) bloqué(e), coincé(e); **~-up** (*inf*) *adj* prétentieux(euse)

stud [stʌd] *n* (*on boots etc*) clou *m*; (*on collar*) bouton *m* de col; (*earring*) petite boucle d'oreille; (*of horses: also*: **~ farm**) écurie *f*, haras *m*; (*also*: **~ horse**) étalon *m* ♦ *vt* (*fig*): **~ded with** parsemé(e) *or* criblé(e) de

student ['stjuːdənt] *n* étudiant(e) ♦ *adj* estudiantin(e); d'étudiant; **~ driver** (*US*) *n* (*conducteur(trice)*) débutant(e)

studio ['stjuːdɪəʊ] *n* studio *m*, atelier *m*; (*TV etc*) studio

studious ['stjuːdɪəs] *adj* studieux(euse), appliqué(e); (*attention*) soutenu(e); **~ly** *adv* (*carefully*) soigneusement

study ['stʌdɪ] *n* étude *f*; (*room*) bureau *m* ♦ *vt* étudier; (*examine*) examiner ♦ *vi* étudier, faire ses études

stuff [stʌf] *n* chose(s) *f(pl)*; affaires *fpl*, trucs *mpl*; (*substance*) substance *f* ♦ *vt* rembourrer; (*CULIN*) farcir; (*inf: push*) fourrer; **~ing** *n* bourre *f*, rembourrage *m*; (*CULIN*) farce *f*; **~y** *adj* (*room*) mal ventilé(e) *or* aéré(e); (*ideas*) vieux jeu *inv*

stumble ['stʌmbl] *vi* trébucher; **to ~ across** *or* **on** (*fig*) tomber sur; **stumbling block** *n* pierre *f* d'achoppement

stump [stʌmp] *n* souche *f*; (*of limb*) moignon *m* ♦ *vt*: **to be ~ed** sécher, ne pas savoir que répondre

stun [stʌn] *vt* étourdir; abasourdir

stung [stʌŋ] *pt, pp of* **sting**

stunk [stʌŋk] *pp of* **stink**

stunning *adj* (*news etc*) stupéfiant(e); (*girl etc*) éblouissant(e)

stunt [stʌnt] *n* (*in film*) cascade *f*, acrobatie *f*; (*publicity ~*) truc *m* publicitaire ♦ *vt* retarder, arrêter(r) **~ed** *adj* rabourgri(e); (*growth*) retardé(e); **~man** (*irreg*) *n* cascadeur *m*

stupendous [stju'pendəs] *adj* prodigieux(euse), fantastique

stupid ['stju:pɪd] *adj* stupide, bête; **~ity** [stju:'pɪdɪtɪ] *n* stupidité *f*, bêtise *f*

sturdy ['stə:dɪ] *adj* robuste; solide

stutter ['stʌtə*] *vi* bégayer

sty [staɪ] *n* (*for pigs*) porcherie *f*

stye [staɪ] *n* (*MED*) orgelet *m*

style [staɪl] *n* style *m*; (*distinction*) allure *f*, cachet *m*, style; **stylish** ['staɪlɪʃ] *adj* élégant(e), chic *inv*

stylus ['staɪləs] (*pl* **styli** *or* **~es**) *n* (*of record player*) pointe *f* de lecture

suave [swɑ:v] *adj* doucereux(euse), onctueux(euse)

sub... [sʌb] *prefix* sub..., sous-; **~conscious** *adj* subconscient(e); **~contract** *vt* sous-traiter

subdue [səb'dju:] *vt* subjuguer, soumettre; **~d** *adj* (*light*) tamisé(e); (*person*) qui a perdu de son entrain

subject [*n* 'sʌbdʒɪkt, *vb* səb'dʒekt] *n* sujet *m*; (*SCOL*) matière *f* ♦ *vt*: **to ~ to** soumettre à; exposer à; **to be ~ to** (*law*) être soumis(e) à; (*disease*) être sujet(te) à; **~ive** [səb'dʒektɪv] *adj* subjectif(ive); **~ matter** *n* (*content*) contenu *m*

sublet ['sʌb'let] *vt* sous-louer

submarine [sʌbmə'ri:n] *n* sous-marin *m*

submerge [səb'mə:dʒ] *vt* submerger ♦ *vi* plonger

submission [səb'mɪʃən] *n* soumission *f*; **submissive** [səb'mɪsɪv] *adj* soumis(e)

submit [səb'mɪt] *vt* soumettre ♦ *vi* se soumettre

subnormal ['sʌb'nɔ:məl] *adj* au-dessous de la normale

subordinate [sə'bɔ:dɪnət] *adj* subalterne ♦ *n* subordonné(e)

subpoena [sə'pi:nə] *n* (*LAW*) citation *f*, assignation *f*

subscribe [səb'skraɪb] *vi* cotiser; **to ~ to** (*opinion, fund*) souscrire à; (*newspaper*) s'abonner à; être abonné(e) à; **~r** *n* (*to periodical, telephone*) abonné(e); **subscription** [səb'skrɪpʃən] *n* (*to magazine etc*) abonnement *m*

subsequent ['sʌbsɪkwənt] *adj* ultérieur(e), suivant(e); conséqutif(ive); **~ly** *adv* par la suite

subside [səb'saɪd] *vi* (*flood*) baisser; (*wind,*

feelings) tomber; **~nce** [sʌb'saɪdəns] *n* affaissement *m*

subsidiary [səb'sɪdɪərɪ] *adj* subsidiaire; accessoire ♦ *n* (*also: ~ company*) filiale *f*

subsidize ['sʌbsɪdaɪz] *vt* subventionner; **subsidy** ['sʌbsɪdɪ] *n* subvention *f*

substance ['sʌbstəns] *n* substance *f*

substantial [səb'stænʃəl] *adj* substantiel(le); (*fig*) important(e); **~ly** *adv* considérablement; (*in essence*) en grande partie

substantiate [səb'stænʃɪeɪt] *vt* étayer, fournir des preuves à l'appui de

substitute ['sʌbstɪtju:t] *n* (*person*) remplaçant(e); (*thing*) suẽcédané *m* ♦ *vt*: **to ~ sth/sb for** substituer qch/qn à, remplacer par qch/qn

subterranean [sʌbtə'reɪnɪən] *adj* souterrain(e)

subtitle ['sʌbtaɪtl] *n* (*CINEMA*) sous-titre *m*

subtle ['sʌtl] *adj* subtil(e)

subtotal [sʌb'təutl] *n* total partiel

subtract [səb'trækt] *vt* soustraire, retrancher; **~ion** *n* soustraction *f*

suburb ['sʌbə:b] *n* faubourg *m*; **the ~s** *npl* la banlieue; **~an** [sə'bə:bən] *adj* de banlieue, suburbain(e); **~ia** [sə'bə:bɪə] *n* la banlieue

subway ['sʌbweɪ] *n* (*US: railway*) métro *m*; (*BRIT: underpass*) passage souterrain

succeed [sək'si:d] *vi* réussir ♦ *vt* succéder à; **to ~ in doing** réussir à faire; **~ing** *adj* (*following*) suivant(e)

success [sək'ses] *n* succès *m*; réussite *f*; **~ful** *adj* (*venture*) couronné(e) de succès; **to be ~ful (in doing)** réussir (à faire); **~fully** *adv* avec succès

succession [sək'seʃən] *n* succession *f*; **3 days in ~** 3 jours de suite

successive [sək'sesɪv] *adj* successif(ive); consécutif(ive)

such [sʌtʃ] *adj* tel(telle); (*of that kind*): **~ a book** un livre de ce genre, un livre pareil, un tel livre; (*so much*): **~ courage** un tel courage ♦ *adv* si; **~ books** des livres de ce genre, des livres pareils, de tels livres; **~ a long trip** un si long voyage; **~ a lot of** tellement *or* tant de; **~ as** (*like*) tel que, comme; **as ~** en tant que tel, à proprement parler; **~-and-such** *adj* tel ou tel

suck [sʌk] *vt* sucer; (*breast, bottle*) téter; **~er** *n* ventouse *f*; (*inf*) poire *f*

suction ['sʌkʃən] *n* succion *f*

sudden ['sʌdn] *adj* soudain(e), subit(e); **all of a ~** soudain, tout à coup; **~ly** *adv* brusquement, tout à coup, soudain

suds [sʌdz] *npl* eau savonneuse

sue [su:] *vt* poursuivre en justice, intenter un procès à

suede [sweɪd] *n* daim *m*

suet [suɪt] *n* graisse *f* de rognon

suffer ['sʌfə*] *vt* souffrir, subir; (*bear*) tolérer, supporter ♦ *vi* souffrir; **~er** *n* (*MED*)

malade *m/f*; **~ing** *n* souffrance(s) *f(pl)*
sufficient [sə'fɪʃənt] *adj* suffisant(e); **~ money** suffisamment d'argent; **~ly** *adv* suffisamment, assez
suffocate ['sʌfəkeɪt] *vi* suffoquer; étouffer
sugar ['ʃʊgə*] *n* sucre ♦ *vt* sucrer; **~ beet** *n* betterave sucrière; **~ cane** *n* canne *f* à sucre
suggest [sə'dʒest] *vt* suggérer, proposer; *(indicate)* dénoter; **~ion** *n* suggestion *f*
suicide ['suɪsaɪd] *n* suicide *m*; *see also* **commit**
suit [suːt] *n* *(man's)* costume *m*, complet *m*; *(woman's)* tailleur *m*, ensemble *m*; *(LAW)* poursuite(s) *fpl*; procès *m*; *(CARDS)* couleur *f* ♦ *vt* aller à; convenir à; *(adapt):* **to ~ sth to** adapter *or* approprier qch à; **well ~ed** *(couple)* faits l'un pour l'autre, très bien assortis; **~able** *adj* qui convient; approprié(e); **~ably** *adv* comme il se doit *(or se devait etc)*, convenablement
suitcase ['suːtkeɪs] *n* valise *f*
suite [swiːt] *n* *(of rooms, also MUS)* suite *f*; *(furniture):* **bedroom/dining room ~** (ensemble *m* de) chambre *f* à coucher/salle *f* à manger
suitor ['suːtə*] *n* soupirant *m*, prétendant *m*
sulfur ['sʌlfə*] *(US)* *n* = **sulphur**
sulk [sʌlk] *vi* bouder; **~y** *adj* boudeur(euse), maussade
sullen ['sʌlən] *adj* renfrogné(e), maussade
sulphur ['sʌlfə*] *(US* **sulfur**) *n* soufre *m*
sultana [sʌl'tɑːnə] *(CULIN)* raisin (sec) de Smyrne
sultry ['sʌltrɪ] *adj* étouffant(e)
sum [sʌm] *n* somme *f*; *(SCOL etc)* calcul *m*; **~ up** *vt, vi* résumer
summarize ['sʌməraɪz] *vt* résumer
summary ['sʌmərɪ] *n* résumé *m*
summer ['sʌmə*] *n* été *m* ♦ *adj* d'été, estival(e); **~house** *n* *(in garden)* pavillon *m*; **~time** *n* été *m*; **~ time** *n* *(by clock)* heure *f* d'été
summit ['sʌmɪt] *n* sommet *m*
summon ['sʌmən] *vt* appeler, convoquer; **~ up** *vt* rassembler, faire appel à; **~s** *n* citation *f*, assignation *f*
sump [sʌmp] *(BRIT)* *n* *(AUT)* carter *m*
sun [sʌn] *n* soleil *m*; **in the ~** au soleil; **~bathe** *vi* prendre un bain de soleil; **~burn** *n* coup *m* de soleil; **~burned** *adj* = **sunburnt**; **~burnt** *adj* *(tanned)* bronzé(e)
Sunday ['sʌndeɪ] *n* dimanche *m*; **~ school** *n* ≈ catéchisme *m*
sundial ['sʌndaɪəl] *n* cadran *m* solaire
sundown ['sʌndaʊn] *n* coucher *m* du *(or* de) soleil
sundries ['sʌndrɪz] *npl* articles divers
sundry ['sʌndrɪ] *adj* divers(e), différent(e) ♦ *n:* **all and ~** tout le monde, n'importe qui
sunflower ['sʌnflaʊə*] *n* tournesol *m*

sung [sʌŋ] *pp of* **sing**
sunglasses ['sʌnglɑːsɪz] *npl* lunettes *fpl* de soleil
sunk [sʌŋk] *pp of* **sink**
sun: **~light** ['sʌnlaɪt] *n* (lumière *f* du) soleil *m*; **~lit** *adj* ensoleillé(e); **~ny** *adj* ensoleillé(e); **~rise** *n* lever *m* du *(or* de) soleil; **~ roof** *n* *(AUT)* toit ouvrant; **~set** *n* coucher *m* du *(or* de) soleil; **~shade** *n* *(over table)* parasol *m*; **~shine** *n* (lumière *f* du) soleil *m*; **~stroke** *n* insolation *f*; **~tan** *n* bronzage *m*; **~tan lotion** *n* lotion *f or* lait *m* solaire; **~tan oil** *n* huile *f* solaire
super ['suːpə*] *(inf)* *adj* formidable
superannuation ['suːpərænjʊ'eɪʃən] *n* *(contribution)* cotisations *fpl* pour la pension
superb [suː'pɜːb] *adj* superbe, magnifique
supercilious [suːpə'sɪlɪəs] *adj* hautain(e), dédaigneux(euse)
superficial [suːpə'fɪʃəl] *adj* superficiel(le)
superimpose [suːpərɪm'pəʊz] *vt* superposer
superintendent [suːpərɪn'tendənt] *n* directeur(trice); *(POLICE)* ≈ commissaire *m*
superior [suː'pɪərɪə*] *adj, n* supérieur(e); **~ity** [suːpɪərɪ'ɒrɪtɪ] *n* supériorité *f*
superlative [suː'pɜːlətɪv] *n* *(LING)* superlatif *m*
superman ['suːpəmæn] *(irreg)* *n* surhomme *m*
supermarket ['suːpəmɑːkɪt] *n* supermarché *m*
supernatural [suːpə'nætʃərəl] *adj* surnaturel(le)
superpower ['suːpəpaʊə*] *n* *(POL)* superpuissance *f*
supersede [suːpə'siːd] *vt* remplacer, supplanter
superstitious [suːpə'stɪʃəs] *adj* superstitieux(euse)
supervise ['suːpəvaɪz] *vt* surveiller; diriger; **supervision** [suːpə'vɪʒən] *n* surveillance *f*; contrôle *m*; **supervisor** ['suːpəvaɪzə*] *n* surveillant(e); *(in shop)* chef *m* de rayon
supine ['suːpaɪn] *adj* couché(e) *or* étendu(e) sur le dos
supper ['sʌpə*] *n* dîner *m*; *(late)* souper *m*
supple ['sʌpl] *adj* souple
supplement [*n* 'sʌplɪmənt, *vb* sʌplɪ'ment] *n* supplément *m* ♦ *vt* compléter; **~ary** *adj* supplémentaire; **~ary benefit** *(BRIT)* *n* allocation *f* (supplémentaire) d'aide sociale
supplier [sə'plaɪə*] *n* fournisseur *m*
supply [sə'plaɪ] *vt* *(provide)* fournir; *(equip):* **to ~ (with)** approvisionner *or* ravitailler (en); fournir (en) provision *f*, réserve *f*; *(~ing)* approvisionnement *m*; **supplies** *npl* *(food)* vivres *mpl*; *(MIL)* subsistances *fpl*; **~ teacher** *(BRIT)* *n* suppléant(e)
support [sə'pɔːt] *n* *(moral, financial etc)*

soutien *m*, appui *m*; (*TECH*) support *m*, soutien ♦ *vt* soutenir, supporter; (*financially*) subvenir aux besoins de; (*uphold*) être pour, être partisan de, appuyer; ~**er** *n* (*POL etc*) partisan(e); (*SPORT*) supporter *m*

suppose [sə'pəʊz] *vt* supposer; imaginer; **to be ~d to do** être censé(e) faire; ~**dly** [sə'pəʊzɪdlɪ] *adv* soi-disant; **supposing** [sə'pəʊzɪŋ] *conj* si, à supposer que +*sub*

suppress [sə'prɛs] *vt* (*revolt*) réprimer; (*information*) supprimer; (*yawn*) étouffer; (*feelings*) refouler

supreme [sʊ'priːm] *adj* suprême

surcharge ['sɜːtʃɑːdʒ] *n* surcharge *f*

sure [ʃʊə*] *adj* sûr(e); (*definite, convinced*) sûr, certain(e); ~**!** (*of course*) bien sûr!; ~ **enough** effectivement; **to make ~ of sth** s'assurer de *or* vérifier qch; **to make ~ that** s'assurer *or* vérifier que; ~**ly** *adv* sûrement; certainement

surety ['ʃʊərətɪ] *n* caution *f*

surf [sɜːf] *n* (*waves*) ressac *m*

surface ['sɜːfɪs] *n* surface *f* ♦ *vt* (*road*) poser un revêtement sur ♦ *vi* remonter à la surface; faire surface; ~ **mail** *n* courrier *m* par voie de terre (*or* maritime)

surfboard ['sɜːfbɔːd] *n* planche *f* de surf

surfeit ['sɜːfɪt] *n*: **a ~ of** un excès de; une indigestion de

surfing ['sɜːfɪŋ] *n* surf *m*

surge [sɜːdʒ] *n* vague *f*, montée *f* ♦ *vi* déferler

surgeon ['sɜːdʒən] *n* chirurgien *m*

surgery ['sɜːdʒərɪ] *n* chirurgie *f*; (*BRIT: room*) cabinet *m* (de consultation); (: *also*: ~ **hours**) heures *fpl* de consultation

surgical ['sɜːdʒɪkəl] *adj* chirurgical(e); ~ **spirit** (*BRIT*) *n* alcool *m* à 90°

surly ['sɜːlɪ] *adj* revêche, maussade

surname ['sɜːneɪm] *n* nom *m* de famille

surplus ['sɜːpləs] *n* surplus *m*, excédent *m* ♦ *adj* en surplus, de trop; (*COMM*) excédentaire

surprise [sə'praɪz] *n* surprise *f*; (*astonishment*) étonnement *m* ♦ *vt* surprendre; (*astonish*) étonner; **surprising** [sə'praɪzɪŋ] *adj* surprenant(e), étonnant(e); **surprisingly** *adv* (*easy, helpful*) étonnamment

surrender [sə'rɛndə*] *n* reddition *f*, capitulation *f* ♦ *vi* se rendre, capituler

surreptitious [sʌrəp'tɪʃəs] *adj* subreptice, furtif(ive)

surrogate ['sʌrəgɪt] *n* substitut *m*; ~ **mother** *n* mère porteuse *or* de substitution

surround [sə'raʊnd] *vt* entourer; (*MIL etc*) encercler; ~**ing** *adj* environnant(e); ~**ings** *npl* environs *mpl*, alentours *mpl*

surveillance [sɜː'veɪləns] *n* surveillance *f*

survey [*n* 'sɜːveɪ, *vb* sɜː'veɪ] *n* enquête *f*, étude *f*; (*in housebuying etc*) inspection *f*, (rapport *m* d')expertise *f*; (*of land*) levé *m* ♦ *vt* enquêter sur; inspecter; (*look at*) embras-

ser du regard; ~**or** [sə'veɪə*] *n* (*of house*) expert *m*; (*of land*) (arpenteur *m*) géomètre *m*

survival [sə'vaɪvəl] *n* survie *f*; (*relic*) vestige *m*

survive [sə'vaɪv] *vi* survivre; (*custom etc*) subsister ♦ *vt* survivre à; **survivor** [sə'vaɪvə*] *n* survivant(e); (*fig*) battant(e)

susceptible [sə'sɛptəbl] *adj*: ~ **(to)** sensible (à); (*disease*) prédisposé(e) (à)

suspect [*n, adj* 'sʌspɛkt, *vb* səs'pɛkt] *adj, n* suspect(e) ♦ *vt* soupçonner, suspecter

suspend [səs'pɛnd] *vt* suspendre; ~**ed sentence** *n* condamnation *f* avec sursis; ~**er belt** *n* porte-jarretelles *m inv*; ~**ers** *npl* (*BRIT*) jarretelles *fpl*; (*US*) bretelles *fpl*

suspense [səs'pɛns] *n* attente *f*, incertitude *f*; (*in film etc*) suspense *m*

suspension [səs'pɛnʃən] *n* suspension *f*; (*of driving licence*) retrait *m* provisoire; ~ **bridge** *n* pont suspendu

suspicion [səs'pɪʃən] *n* soupçon(s) *m(pl)*

suspicious [səs'pɪʃəs] *adj* (*suspecting*) soupçonneux(euse), méfiant(e); (*causing suspicion*) suspect(e)

sustain [səs'teɪn] *vt* soutenir; (*food etc*) nourrir, donner des forces à; (*suffer*) subir; recevoir; ~**able** *adj* (*development, growth etc*) viable; ~**ed** *adj* (*effort*) soutenu(e), prolongé(e)

sustenance ['sʌstɪnəns] *n* nourriture *f*; (*money*) moyens *mpl* de subsistance

swab [swɒb] *n* (*MED*) tampon *m*

swagger ['swægə*] *vi* plastronner

swallow ['swɒləʊ] *n* (*bird*) hirondelle *f* ♦ *vt* avaler; ~ **up** *vt* engloutir

swam [swæm] *pt of* **swim**

swamp [swɒmp] *n* marais *m*, marécage *m* ♦ *vt* submerger

swan [swɒn] *n* cygne *m*

swap [swɒp] *vt*: **to ~ (for)** échanger (contre), troquer (contre)

swarm [swɔːm] *n* essaim *m* ♦ *vi* fourmiller, grouiller

swarthy ['swɔːðɪ] *adj* basané(e), bistré(e)

swastika ['swɒstɪkə] *n* croix gammée

swat [swɒt] *vt* écraser

sway [sweɪ] *vi* se balancer, osciller ♦ *vt* (*influence*) influencer

swear [swɛə*] (*pt* **swore**, *pp* **sworn**) *vt, vi* jurer; ~**word** *n* juron *m*, gros mot

sweat [swɛt] *n* sueur *f*, transpiration *f* ♦ *vi* suer

sweater ['swɛtə*] *n* tricot *m*, pull *m*

sweaty ['swɛtɪ] *adj* en sueur, moite *or* mouillé(e) de sueur

Swede [swiːd] *n* Suédois(e)

swede [swiːd] (*BRIT*) *n* rutabaga *m*

Sweden ['swiːdn] *n* Suède *f*; **Swedish** ['swiːdɪʃ] *adj* suédois(e) ♦ *n* (*LING*) suédois *m*

sweep [swiːp] (*pt, pp* **swept**) *n* coup *m* de

balai; (*also*: *chimney* ~) ramoneur *m* ♦ *vt* balayer; (*subj*: *current*) emporter ♦ *vi* (*hand, arm*) faire un mouvement; (*wind*) souffler; ~ **away** *vt* balayer; entraîner; emporter; ~ **past** *vi* passer majestueusement *or* rapidement; ~ **up** *vi* balayer; ~**ing** *adj* (*gesture*) large; circulaire; **a** ~**ing statement** une généralisation hâtive

sweet [swiːt] *n* (*candy*) bonbon *m*; (*BRIT*: *pudding*) dessert *m* ♦ *adj* doux(douce); (*not savoury*) sucré(e); (*fig*: *kind*) gentil(le); (*baby*) mignon(ne); ~**corn** *n* maïs *m*; ~**en** *vt* adoucir; (*with sugar*) sucrer; ~**heart** *n* amoureux(euse); ~**ness** *n* goût sucré; douceur *f*; ~**pea** *n* pois *m* de senteur

swell [swel] (*pt* ~**ed**, *pp* **swollen** *or* ~**ed**) *n* (*of sea*) houle *f* ♦ *adj* (*US*: *inf*: *excellent*) chouette ♦ *vi* grossir, augmenter; (*sound*) s'enfler; (*MED*) enfler; ~**ing** *n* (*MED*) enflure *f*; (*lump*) grosseur *f*

sweltering ['sweltərɪŋ] *adj* étouffant(e), oppressant(e)

swept [swept] *pt*, *pp* of **sweep**

swerve [swɜːv] *vi* faire une embardée *or* un écart; dévier

swift [swɪft] *n* (*bird*) martinet *m* ♦ *adj* rapide, prompt(e)

swig [swɪɡ] (*inf*) *n* (*drink*) lampée *f*

swill [swɪl] *vt* (*also*: ~ *out*, ~ *down*) laver à grande eau

swim [swɪm] (*pt* **swam**, *pp* **swum**) *n*: **to go for a** ~ aller nager *or* se baigner ♦ *vi* nager; (*SPORT*) faire de la natation; (*head, room*) tourner ♦ *vt* traverser (à la nage); (*a length*) faire (à la nage); ~**mer** *n* nageur(euse); ~**ming** *n* natation *f*; ~**ming cap** *n* bonnet *m* de bain; ~**ming costume** (*BRIT*) *n* maillot *m* (de bain); ~**ming pool** *n* piscine *f*; ~**ming trunks** *npl* caleçon *m or* slip *m* de bain; ~**suit** *n* maillot *m* (de bain)

swindle ['swɪndl] *n* escroquerie *f*

swine [swaɪn] (*inf*!) *n* (*pl inv*) salaud *m* (!)

swing [swɪŋ] (*pt*, *pp* **swung**) *n* balançoire *f*; (*movement*) balancement *m*, oscillations *fpl*; (*MUS*: *also rhythm*) rythme *m*; (*change*: *in opinion etc*) revirement *m* ♦ *vt* balancer, faire osciller; (*also*: ~ *round*) tourner, faire virer ♦ *vi* se balancer, osciller; (*also*: ~ *round*) virer, tourner; **to be in full** ~ battre son plein; ~ **bridge** *n* pont tournant; ~ **door** (*US* ~**ing door**) *n* porte battante

swingeing ['swɪndʒɪŋ] (*BRIT*) *adj* écrasant(e); (*cuts etc*) considérable

swipe [swaɪp] (*inf*) *vt* (*steal*) piquer

swirl [swɜːl] *vi* tourbillonner, tournoyer

swish [swɪʃ] *vi* (*tail*) remuer; (*clothes*) froufrouter

Swiss [swɪs] *adj* suisse ♦ *n inv* Suisse *m/f*

switch [swɪtʃ] *n* (*for light, radio etc*) bouton *m*; (*change*) changement *m*, revirement *m* ♦ *vt* changer; ~ **off** *vt* éteindre; (*engine*) arrêter; ~ **on** *vt* allumer; (*engine, machine*)

mettre en marche; ~**board** *n* (*TEL*) standard *m*

Switzerland ['swɪtsələnd] *n* Suisse *f*

swivel ['swɪvl] *vi* (*also*: ~ *round*) pivoter, tourner

swollen ['swəʊlən] *pp* of **swell**

swoon [swuːn] *vi* se pâmer

swoop [swuːp] *n* (*by police*) descente *f* ♦ *vi* (*also*: ~ *down*) descendre en piqué, piquer

swop [swɒp] *vt* = **swap**

sword [sɔːd] *n* épée *f*; ~**fish** *n* espadon *m*

swore [swɔː*] *pt* of **swear**

sworn [swɔːn] *pp* of **swear** ♦ *adj* (*statement, evidence*) donné(e) sous serment

swot [swɒt] *vi* bûcher, potasser

swum [swʌm] *pp* of **swim**

swung [swʌŋ] *pt*, *pp* of **swing**

syllable ['sɪləbl] *n* syllabe *f*

syllabus ['sɪləbəs] *n* programme *m*

symbol ['sɪmbəl] *n* symbole *m*

symmetry ['sɪmɪtrɪ] *n* symétrie *f*

sympathetic [sɪmpə'θetɪk] *adj* compatissant(e); bienveillant(e), compréhensif(ive); (*likeable*) sympathique; ~ **towards** bien disposé(e) envers

sympathize ['sɪmpəθaɪz] *vi*: **to** ~ **with sb** plaindre qn; (*in grief*) s'associer à la douleur de qn; **to** ~ **with sth** comprendre qch; ~**r** *n* (*POL*) sympathisant(e)

sympathy ['sɪmpəθɪ] *n* (*pity*) compassion *f*; **sympathies** *npl* (*support*) soutien *m*; **left-wing etc sympathies** penchants *mpl* à gauche *etc*; **in** ~ **with** (*strike*) en *or* par solidarité avec; **with our deepest** ~ en vous priant d'accepter nos sincères condoléances

symphony ['sɪmfənɪ] *n* symphonie *f*

symptom ['sɪmptəm] *n* symptôme *m*; indice *m*

syndicate ['sɪndɪkət] *n* syndicat *m*, coopérative *f*

synonym ['sɪnənɪm] *n* synonyme *m*

synopsis [sɪ'nɒpsɪs, *pl* -siːz] (*pl* **synopses**) *n* résumé *m*

syntax ['sɪntæks] *n* syntaxe *f*

synthetic [sɪn'θetɪk] *adj* synthétique

syphon ['saɪfən] *n*, *vb* = **siphon**

Syria ['sɪrɪə] *n* Syrie *f*

syringe [sɪ'rɪndʒ] *n* seringue *f*

syrup ['sɪrəp] *n* sirop *m*; (*also*: *golden* ~) mélasse raffinée

system ['sɪstəm] *n* système *m*; (*ANAT*) organisme *m*; ~**atic** [sɪstə'mætɪk] *adj* systématique; méthodique; ~ **disk** *n* (*COMPUT*) disque *m* système; ~**s analyst** *n* analyste fonctionnel(le)

T t

ta [tɑː] (*BRIT: inf*) *excl* merci!

tab [tæb] *n* (*label*) étiquette *f*; (*on drinks can etc*) languette *f*; **to keep ~s on** (*fig*) surveiller

tabby ['tæbɪ] *n* (*also*: ~ **cat**) chat(te) tigré(e)

table ['teɪbl] *n* table *f* ♦ *vt* (*BRIT: motion etc*) présenter; **to lay** *or* **set the** ~ mettre le couvert *or* la table; **~cloth** ['-klɔθ] *n* nappe *f*; ~ **d'hôte** ['tɑːbl'dəʊt] *adj* (*meal*) à prix fixe; **~lamp** *n* lampe *f* de table; **~mat** ['teɪblmæt] *n* (*for plate*) napperon *m*, set *m*; (*for hot dish*) dessous-de-plat *m inv*; ~ **of contents** *n* table *f* des matières; **~spoon** ['teɪblspuːn] *n* cuiller *f* de service; (*also*: ~spoonful: *as measurement*) cuillerée *f* à soupe

table football *n* baby-foot *m*

tablet ['tæblət] *n* (*MED*) comprimé *m*; (*of stone*) plaque *f*

table tennis *n* ping-pong *m* ®, tennis *m* de table

table wine *n* vin *m* de table

tabloid ['tæblɔɪd] *n* quotidien *m* populaire

tabulate ['tæbjʊleɪt] *vt* (*data, figures*) présenter sous forme de table(s)

tack [tæk] *n* (*nail*) petit clou ♦ *vt* clouer; (*fig*) direction *f*; (*BRIT: stitch*) faufiler ♦ *vi* tirer un *or* des bord(s)

tackle ['tækl] *n* matériel *m*, équipement *m*; (*for lifting*) appareil *m* de levage; (*RUGBY*) plaquage *m* ♦ *vt* (*difficulty, animal, burglar etc*) s'attaquer à; (*person: challenge*) s'expliquer avec; (*RUGBY*) plaquer

tacky ['tækɪ] *adj* collant(e); (*pej: of poor quality*) miteux(euse)

tact [tækt] *n* tact *m*; **~ful** *adj* plein(e) de tact

tactical ['tæktɪkəl] *adj* tactique

tactics ['tæktɪks] *npl* tactique *f*

tactless ['tæktləs] *adj* qui manque de tact

tadpole ['tædpəʊl] *n* têtard *m*

taffy ['tæfɪ] (*US*) *n* (bonbon *m* au) caramel *m*

tag [tæg] *n* étiquette *f*; ~ **along** *vi* suivre

tail [teɪl] *n* queue *f*; (*of shirt*) pan *m* ♦ *vt* (*follow*) suivre, filer; **~s** *npl* habit *m*; ~ **away,** ~ **off** *vi* (*in size, quality etc*) baisser peu à peu; **~back** (*BRIT*) *n* (*AUT*) bouchon *m*; ~ **end** *n* bout *m*, fin *f*; **~gate** *n* (*AUT*) hayon *m* arrière

tailor ['teɪlə*] *n* tailleur *m*; **~ing** *n* (*cut*) coupe *f*; **~-made** *adj* fait(e) sur mesure; (*fig*) conçu(e) spécialement

tailwind ['teɪlwɪnd] *n* vent *m* arrière *inv*

tainted ['teɪntɪd] *adj* (*food*) gâté(e); (*water, air*) infecté(e); (*fig*) souillé(e)

take [teɪk] (*pt* **took**, *pp* **taken**) *vt* prendre; (*gain: prize*) remporter; (*require: effort, courage*) demander; (*tolerate*) accepter, supporter; (*hold: passengers etc*) contenir; (*accompany*) emmener, accompagner; (*bring, carry*) apporter, emporter; (*exam*) passer, se présenter à; **to** ~ **sth from** (*drawer etc*) prendre qch dans; (*person*) prendre qch à; **I** ~ **it that ...** je suppose que ...; ~ **after** *vt fus* ressembler à; ~ **apart** *vt* démonter; ~ **away** *vt* enlever; (*carry off*) emporter; ~ **back** *vt* (*return*) rendre, rapporter; (*one's words*) retirer; ~ **down** *vt* (*building*) démolir; (*letter etc*) prendre, écrire; ~ **in** *vt* (*deceive*) tromper, rouler; (*understand*) comprendre, saisir; (*include*) comprendre, inclure; (*lodger*) prendre; ~ **off** *vi* (*AVIAT*) décoller ♦ *vt* (*go away*) s'en aller; (*remove*) enlever; ~ **on** *vt* (*work*) accepter, se charger de; (*employee*) prendre, embaucher; (*opponent*) accepter de se battre contre; ~ **out** *vt* (*invite*) emmener, sortir; (*remove*) enlever; **to** ~ **sth out of sth** (*drawer, pocket etc*) prendre qch dans qch; ~ **over** *vt* (*business*) reprendre ♦ *vi*: **to** ~ **over from sb** prendre la relève de qn; ~ **to** *vt fus* (*person*) se prendre d'amitié pour; (*thing*) prendre goût à; ~ **up** *vt* (*activity*) se mettre à; (*dress*) raccourcir; (*occupy: time, space*) prendre, occuper; **to** ~ **sb up on an offer** accepter la proposition de qn; **~away** (*BRIT*) *adj* (*food*) à emporter ♦ *n* (*shop, restaurant*) qui vend de plats à emporter; **~off** *n* (*AVIAT*) décollage *m*; **~over** *n* (*COMM*) rachat *m*; **takings** ['teɪkɪŋz] *npl* (*COMM*) recette *f*

talc [tælk] *n* (*also*: ~**um powder**) talc *m*

tale [teɪl] *n* (*story*) conte *m*, histoire *f*; (*account*) récit *m*; **to tell ~s** (*fig*) rapporter

talent ['tælənt] *n* talent *m*, don *m*; **~ed** *adj* doué(e), plein(e) de talent

talk [tɔːk] *n* (*a speech*) causerie *f*, exposé *m*; (*conversation*) discussion *f*, entretien *m*; (*gossip*) racontars *mpl* ♦ *vi* parler; **~s** *npl* (*POL etc*) entretiens *mpl*; **to** ~ **about** parler de; **to** ~ **sb into/out of doing** persuader qn de faire/ne pas faire; **to** ~ **shop** parler métier *or* affaires; ~ **over** *vt* discuter (de); **~ative** ['tɔːkətɪv] *adj* bavard(e); ~ **show** *n* causerie (télévisée *or* radiodiffusée)

tall [tɔːl] *adj* (*person*) grand(e); (*building, tree*) haut(e); **to be 6 feet** ~ ≈ mesurer 1 mètre 80; ~ **story** *n* histoire *f* invraisemblable

tally ['tælɪ] *n* compte *m* ♦ *vi*: **to** ~ **(with)** correspondre (à)

talon ['tælən] *n* griffe *f*; (*of eagle*) serre *f*

tame [teɪm] *adj* apprivoisé(e); *(fig: story, style)* insipide

tamper ['tæmpə*] *vi*: **to ~ with** toucher à

tampon ['tæmpən] *n* tampon *m* (hygiénique *or* périodique)

tan [tæn] *n (also: sun~)* bronzage *m* ♦ *vt, vi* bronzer ♦ *adj (colour)* brun roux *inv*

tang [tæŋ] *n* odeur *(or* saveur) piquante

tangent ['tændʒənt] *n (MATH)* tangente *f*; **to go off at a ~** *(fig)* changer de sujet

tangerine [tændʒə'riːn] *n* mandarine *f*

tangle ['tæŋgl] *n* enchevêtrement *m*; **to get in(to) a ~** s'embrouiller

tank [tæŋk] *n (water ~)* réservoir *m*; *(for fish)* aquarium *m*; *(MIL)* char *m* d'assaut, tank *m*

tanker ['tæŋkə*] *n (ship)* pétrolier *m*, tanker *m*; *(truck)* camion-citerne *m*

tantalizing ['tæntəlaɪzɪŋ] *adj (smell)* extrêmement appétissant(e); *(offer)* terriblement tentant(e)

tantamount ['tæntəmaunt] *adj*: **~ to** qui équivaut à

tantrum ['tæntrəm] *n* accès *m* de colère

tap [tæp] *n (on sink etc)* robinet *m*; *(gentle blow)* petite tape ♦ *vt* frapper *or* taper légèrement; *(resources)* exploiter, utiliser; *(telephone)* mettre sur écoute; **on ~** *(fig: resources)* disponible; **~-dancing** ['tæpdɑːnsɪŋ] *n* claquettes *fpl*

tape [teɪp] *n* ruban *m*; *(also: magnetic ~)* bande *f* (magnétique); *(cassette)* cassette *f*; *(sticky)* scotch *m* ♦ *vt (record)* enregistrer; *(stick with ~)* coller avec du scotch; **~ deck** *n* platine *f* d'enregistrement; **~ measure** *n* mètre *m* à ruban

taper ['teɪpə*] *n* cierge *m* ♦ *vi* s'effiler

tape recorder *n* magnétophone *m*

tapestry ['tæpɪstrɪ] *n* tapisserie *f*

tar [tɑː*] *n* goudron *m*

target ['tɑːgɪt] *n* cible *f*, *(fig)* objectif *m*

tariff ['tærɪf] *n (COMM)* tarif *m*; *(taxes)* tarif douanier

tarmac ['tɑːmæk] *n (BRIT: on road)* macadam *m*; *(AVIAT)* piste *f*

tarnish ['tɑːnɪʃ] *vt* ternir

tarpaulin [tɑː'pɔːlɪn] *n* bâche (goudronnée)

tarragon ['tærəgən] *n* estragon *m*

tart [tɑːt] *n (CULIN)* tarte *f*; *(BRIT: inf: prostitute)* putain *f* ♦ *adj (flavour)* âpre, aigrelet(te); **~ up** *(BRIT: inf) vt (object)* retaper; **to ~ o.s. up** se faire beau(belle), s'attifer *(pej)*

tartan ['tɑːtən] *n* tartan *m* ♦ *adj* écossais(e)

tartar ['tɑːtə*] *n (on teeth)* tartre *m*; **~(e) sauce** *n* sauce *f* tartare

task [tɑːsk] *n* tâche *f*, **to take sb to ~** prendre qn à partie; **~ force** *n (MIL, POLICE)* détachement spécial

tassel ['tæsəl] *n* gland *m*; pompon *m*

taste [teɪst] *n* goût *m*; *(fig: glimpse, idea)* idée *f*, aperçu *m* ♦ *vt* goûter ♦ *vi*: **to ~ of** *or* **like** *(fish etc)* avoir le *or* un goût de; **you can ~ the garlic (in it)** on sent bien l'ail; **can I have a ~ of this wine?** puis-je goûter un peu de ce vin?; **in good/bad ~** de bon/mauvais goût; **~ful** *adj* de bon goût; **~less** *adj (food)* fade; *(remark)* de mauvais goût; **tasty** ['teɪstɪ] *adj* savoureux(euse), délicieux(euse)

tatters ['tætəz] *npl*: **in ~** en lambeaux

tattoo [tə'tuː] *n* tatouage *m*; *(spectacle)* parade *f* militaire ♦ *vt* tatouer

tatty *(BRIT: inf) adj (clothes)* frippé(e); *(shop, area)* délabré(e)

taught [tɔːt] *pt, pp of* **teach**

taunt [tɔːnt] *n* raillerie *f* ♦ *vt* railler

Taurus ['tɔːrəs] *n* le Taureau

taut [tɔːt] *adj* tendu(e)

tax [tæks] *n (on goods etc)* taxe *f*; *(on income)* impôts *mpl*, contributions *fpl* ♦ *vt* taxer; imposer; *(fig: patience etc)* mettre à l'épreuve; **~-able** *adj (income)* imposable; **~ation** [tæk'seɪʃən] *n* taxation *f*; impôts *mpl*, contributions *fpl*; **~ avoidance** *n* dégrèvement fiscal; **~ disc** *(BRIT)* *n (AUT)* vignette *f* (automobile); **~ evasion** *n* fraude fiscale; **~-free** *adj* exempt(e) d'impôts

taxi ['tæksɪ] *n* taxi *m* ♦ *vi (AVIAT)* rouler (lentement) au sol; **~ driver** *n* chauffeur *m* de taxi; **~ rank** *(BRIT)* *n* station *f* de taxis; **~ stand** *n* = **taxi rank**

tax: **~ payer** *n* contribuable *m/f*; **~ relief** *n* dégrèvement fiscal; **~ return** *n* déclaration *f* d'impôts *or* de revenus

TB *n abbr* = **tuberculosis**

tea [tiː] *n* thé *m*; *(BRIT: snack: for children)* goûter *m*; **high ~** *n* collation combinant goûter et dîner; **~ bag** *n* sachet *m* de thé; **~ break** *(BRIT)* *n* pause-thé *f*

teach [tiːtʃ] *(pt, pp taught) vt*: **to ~ sb sth**, **~ sth to sb** apprendre qch à qn; *(in school etc)* enseigner qch à qn enseigner; **~er** *n (in secondary school)* professeur *m*; *(in primary school)* instituteur(trice); **~ing** *n* enseignement *m*

tea cosy *n* cloche *f* à thé

teacup ['tiːkʌp] *n* tasse *f* à thé

teak [tiːk] *n* teck *m*

team [tiːm] *n* équipe *f*; *(of animals)* attelage *m*; **~work** *n* travail *m* d'équipe

teapot ['tiːpɔt] *n* théière *f*

tear¹ [tɛə*] *(pt* **tore**, *pp* **torn)** *n* déchirure *f* ♦ *vt* déchirer ♦ *vi* se déchirer; **~ along** *vi (rush)* aller à toute vitesse; **~ up** *vt (sheet of paper etc)* déchirer, mettre en morceaux *or* pièces

tear² [tɪə*] *n* larme *f*; **in ~s** en larmes; **~ful** *adj* larmoyant(e); **~ gas** *n* gaz *m* lacrymogène

tearoom ['tiːrum] *n* salon *m* de thé

tease [tiːz] *vt* taquiner; *(unkindly)* tourmenter

tea set *n* service *m* à thé

teaspoon ['tiːspuːn] *n* petite cuiller; *(also:* ~ful: *as measurement)* ≈ cuillerée *f* à café

teat [tiːt] *n* tétine *f*

teatime ['tiːtaɪm] *n* l'heure *f* du thé

tea towel *(BRIT) n* torchon *m* (à vaisselle)

technical ['teknɪkəl] *adj* technique; ~**ity** [teknɪ'kælɪtɪ] *n (detail)* détail *m* technique; *(point of law)* vice *m* de forme; ~**ly** *adv* techniquement; *(strictly speaking)* en théorie

technician [tek'nɪʃən] *n* technicien(ne)

technique [tek'niːk] *n* technique *f*

technological [teknə'lɒdʒɪkəl] *adj* technologique; **technology** [tek'nɒlədʒɪ] *n* technologie *f*

teddy (bear) ['tedɪ-] *n* ours *m* en peluche

tedious ['tiːdɪəs] *adj* fastidieux(euse)

tee [tiː] *n (GOLF)* tee *m*

teem [tiːm] *vi:* **to ~ (with)** grouiller (de); **it is ~ing (with rain)** il pleut à torrents

teenage ['tiːneɪdʒ] *adj (fashions etc)* pour jeunes, pour adolescents; *(children)* adolescent(e); ~ *n* adolescent(e)

teens [tiːnz] *npl:* **to be in one's ~** être adolescent(e)

tee-shirt ['tiːʃɜːt] *n* = T-shirt

teeter ['tiːtə*] *vi* chanceler, vaciller

teeth [tiːθ] *npl of* tooth

teethe [tiːð] *vi* percer ses dents

teething ring ['tiːðɪŋ-] *n* anneau pour bébé qui perce ses dents

teething troubles *npl (fig)* difficultés initiales

teetotal ['tiː'təʊtl] *adj (person)* qui ne boit jamais d'alcool

telegram ['telɪgræm] *n* télégramme *m*

telegraph ['telɪgrɑːf] *n* télégraphe *m*; ~ **pole** *n* poteau *m* télégraphique

telephone ['telɪfəʊn] *n* téléphone *m* ♦ *vt (person)* téléphoner à; *(message)* téléphoner; **on the ~** au téléphone; **to be on the ~** *(BRIT: have a ~)* avoir le téléphone; ~ **booth** *(BRIT) n* = **telephone box**; ~ **box** *n* cabine *f* téléphonique; ~ **call** *n* coup *m* de téléphone, appel *m* téléphonique; ~ **directory** *n* annuaire *m* (du téléphone); ~ **number** *n* numéro *m* de téléphone; **telephonist** [tə'lefənɪst] *(BRIT) n* téléphoniste *m/f*

telescope ['telɪskəʊp] *n* télescope *m*

television ['telɪvɪʒən] *n* télévision *f*; **on ~** à la télévision; ~ **set** *n* (poste *f* de) télévision *m*

telex ['teleks] *n* télex *m*

tell [tel] *(pt, pp* told) *vt* dire; *(relate: story)* raconter; *(distinguish):* **to ~ sth from** distinguer qch de ♦ *vi (talk):* **to ~ (of)** parler (de); *(have effect)* se faire sentir, se voir; **to ~ sb to do** dire à qn de faire; ~ **off** *vt* réprimander, gronder; ~**er** *n (in bank)* caissier(ère); ~**ing** *adj (remark, detail)* révélateur(trice); ~**tale** *adj (sign)* éloquent(e), révélateur(trice)

telly ['telɪ] *(BRIT: inf) n abbr (= television)* télé *f*

temp [temp] *n abbr (= temporary)* (secrétaire *f*) intérimaire *f*

temper ['tempə*] *n (nature)* caractère *m*; *(mood)* humeur *f*; *(fit of anger)* colère *f* ♦ *vt (moderate)* tempérer, adoucir; **to be in a ~** être en colère; **to lose one's ~** se mettre en colère

temperament ['temprəmənt] *n (nature)* tempérament *m*; ~**al** [temprə'mentl] *adj* capricieux(euse)

temperate ['tempərət] *adj (climate, country)* tempéré(e)

temperature ['temprɪtʃə*] *n* température *f*; **to have** *or* **run a ~** avoir de la fièvre

temple ['templ] *n (building)* temple *m*; *(ANAT)* tempe *f*

temporary ['tempərərɪ] *adj* temporaire, provisoire; *(job, worker)* temporaire

tempt [tempt] *vt* tenter; **to ~ sb into doing** persuader qn de faire; ~**ation** [temp'teɪʃən] *n* tentation *f*

ten [ten] *num* dix

tenacity [tə'næsɪtɪ] *n* ténacité *f*

tenancy ['tenənsɪ] *n* location *f*; état *m* de locataire

tenant ['tenənt] *n* locataire *m/f*

tend [tend] *vt* s'occuper de ♦ *vi:* **to ~ to do** avoir tendance à faire

tendency ['tendənsɪ] *n* tendance *f*

tender ['tendə*] *adj* tendre; *(delicate)* délicat(e); *(sore)* sensible ♦ *n (COMM: offer)* soumission ♦ *vt* offrir

tenement ['tenəmənt] *n* immeuble *m*

tenet ['tenət] *n* principe *m*

tennis ['tenɪs] *n* tennis *m*; ~ **ball** *n* balle *f* de tennis; ~ **court** *n* (court *m* de) tennis; ~ **player** *n* joueur(euse) de tennis; ~ **racket** *n* raquette *f* de tennis; ~ **shoes** *npl* (chaussures *fpl* de) tennis *mpl*

tenor ['tenə*] *n (MUS)* ténor *m*

tenpin bowling *(BRIT) n* bowling *m* (à dix quilles)

tense [tens] *adj* tendu(e) ♦ *n (LING)* temps *m*

tension ['tenʃən] *n* tension *f*

tent [tent] *n* tente *f*

tentative ['tentətɪv] *adj* timide, hésitant(e); *(conclusion)* provisoire

tenterhooks ['tentəhʊks] *npl:* **on ~** sur des charbons ardents

tenth [tenθ] *num* dixième

tent peg *n* piquet *m* de tente

tent pole *n* montant *m* de tente

tenuous ['tenjuəs] *adj* ténu(e)

tenure ['tenjuə*] *n (of property)* bail *m*; *(of job)* période *f* de jouissance

tepid ['tepɪd] *adj* tiède

term [tɜːm] *n* terme *m*; *(SCOL)* trimestre *m* ♦ *vt* appeler; ~**s** *npl (conditions)* conditions *fpl*; *(COMM)* tarif *m*; **in the short/long ~** à court/long terme; **to come to ~s with** (*problem*) faire face à

terminal ['tɜːmɪnl] *adj* (*disease*) dans sa phase terminale; (*patient*) incurable ♦ *n* (*ELEC*) borne *f*; (*for oil, ore etc, COMPUT*) terminal *m*; (*also: air ~*) aérogare *f*; (*BRIT: also: coach ~*) gare routière

terminate ['tɜːmɪneɪt] *vt* mettre fin à; (*pregnancy*) interrompre

terminus ['tɜːmɪnəs] (*pl* **termini**) *n* terminus *m inv*

terrace ['terəs] *n* terrasse *f*; (*BRIT: row of houses*) rangée *f* de maisons (*attenantes*); **the ~s** *npl* (*: SPORT*) les gradins *mpl*; **~d** *adj* (*garden*) en terrasses

terracotta ['terə'kɒtə] *n* terre cuite

terrain [te'reɪn] *n* terrain *m* (*sol*)

terrible ['terəbl] *adj* terrible, atroce; (*weather, conditions*) affreux(euse), épouvantable; **terribly** ['terəblɪ] *adv* terriblement; (*very badly*) affreusement mal

terrier ['terɪə*] *n* terrier *m* (*chien*)

terrific [tə'rɪfɪk] *adj* fantastique, incroyable, terrible; (*wonderful*) formidable, sensationnel(le)

terrify ['terɪfaɪ] *vt* terrifier

territory ['terɪtərɪ] *n* territoire *m*

terror ['terə*] *n* terreur *f*; **~ism** *n* terrorisme *m*; **~ist** *n* terroriste *m/f*

terse [tɜːs] *adj* (*style*) concis(e); (*reply*) sec(sèche)

Terylene ['terɪliːn] (®) *n* tergal *m* (®)

test [test] *n* (*trial, check*) essai *m*; (*of courage etc*) épreuve *f*; (*MED*) examen *m*; (*CHEM*) analyse *f*; (*SCOL*) interrogation *f*; (*also: driving ~*) (examen du) permis de conduire ♦ *vt* essayer; mettre à l'épreuve; examiner; analyser; faire subir une interrogation à

testament ['testəmənt] *n* testament *m*; **the Old/New T~** l'Ancien/le Nouveau Testament

testicle ['testɪkl] *n* testicule *m*

testify ['testɪfaɪ] *vi* (*LAW*) témoigner, déposer; **to ~ to sth** attester qch

testimony ['testɪmənɪ] *n* témoignage *m*; (*clear proof*): **to be (a) ~ to** être la preuve de

test: **~ match** *n* (*CRICKET, RUGBY*) match international; **~ pilot** *n* teste *m* d'essai; **~ tube** *n* éprouvette *f*

tetanus ['tetənəs] *n* tétanos *m*

tether ['teðə*] *vt* attacher ♦ *n*: **at the end of one's ~** à bout (de patience)

text [tekst] *n* texte *m*; **~book** *n* manuel *m*

textile *n* textile *m*

texture ['tekstʃə*] *n* texture *f*; (*of skin, paper etc*) grain *m*

Thames [temz] *n*: **the ~** la Tamise

than [ðæn, ðən] *conj* que; (*with numerals*): **more ~ 10/once** plus de 10/d'une fois; **I have more/less ~ you** j'en ai plus/moins

que toi; **she has more apples ~ pears** elle a plus de pommes que de poires

thank [θæŋk] *vt* remercier, dire merci à; **~s** *npl* (*gratitude*) remerciements *mpl* ♦ *excl* merci!; **~ you (very much)** merci (beaucoup); **~s to** grâce à; **~ God!** Dieu merci!; **~ful** *adj*: **~ful (for)** reconnaissant(e) (de); **~less** *adj* ingrat(e); **T~sgiving (Day)** *n* jour *m* d'action de grâce (*fête américaine*)

─────────── *KEYWORD*

that [ðæt] *adj* (*demonstrative: pl those*) ce, cet +*vowel or h mute*, *f* cette; **~ man/ woman/book** cet homme/cette femme/ce livre; (*not this*) cet homme-là/cette femme-là/ce livre-là; **~ one** celui-là(celle-là)

♦ *pron* **1** (*demonstrative: pl those*) ce; (*not this one*) cela, ça; **who's ~?** qui est-ce?; **what's ~?** qu'est-ce que c'est?; **is ~ you?** c'est toi?; **I prefer this to ~** je préfère ceci à cela *or* ça; **~'s what he said** c'est *or* voilà ce qu'il a dit; **~ is (to say)** c'est-à-dire, à savoir

2 (*relative: subject*) qui; (*: object*) que; (*: indirect*) lequel(laquelle), lesquels(lesquelles) *pl*; **the book ~ I read** le livre que j'ai lu; **the books ~ are in the library** les livres qui sont dans la bibliothèque; **all ~ I have** tout ce que j'ai; **the box ~ I put it in** la boîte dans laquelle je l'ai mis; **the people ~ I spoke to** les gens auxquels *or* à qui j'ai parlé

3 (*relative: of time*) où; **the day ~ he came** le jour où il est venu

♦ *conj* que; **he thought ~ I was ill** il pensait que j'étais malade

♦ *adv* (*demonstrative*): **I can't work ~ much** je ne peux pas travailler autant que cela; **I didn't know it was ~ bad** je ne savais pas que c'était si *or* aussi mauvais; **it's about ~ high** c'est à peu près de cette hauteur

──────────────────────────

thatched [θætʃt] *adj* (*roof*) de chaume; **~ cottage** chaumière *f*

thaw [θɔː] *n* dégel *m* ♦ *vi* (*ice*) fondre; (*food*) dégeler ♦ *vt* (*: also: ~ out*) (faire) dégeler

─────────── *KEYWORD*

the [ðiː, ðə] *def art* **1** (*gen*) le, la *f*, l' +*vowel or h mute*, les *pl*; **~ boy/girl/ink** le garçon/la fille/l'encre; **~ children** les enfants; **~ history of the world** l'histoire du monde; **give it to ~ postman** donne-le au facteur; **to play ~ piano/flute** jouer du piano/de la flûte; **~ rich and ~ poor** les riches et les pauvres

2 (*in titles*): **Elizabeth ~ First** Elisabeth première; **Peter ~ Great** Pierre le Grand

3 (*in comparisons*): **~ more he works, ~ more he earns** plus il travaille, plus il gagne de l'argent

theatre ['θɪətə*] *n* théâtre *m*; (*also: lecture* ~) amphi(théâtre) *m*; (MED: *also: operating* ~) salle *f* d'opération; ~**-goer** *n* habitué(e) du théâtre; **theatrical** [θɪ'ætrɪkəl] *adj* théâtral(e)

theft [θeft] *n* vol *m* (*larcin*)

their [ðɛə*] *adj* leur; (*pl*) leurs; *see also* **my**; ~**s** *pron* le(la) leur; (*pl*) les leurs; *see also* **mine**¹

them [ðem, ðəm] *pron* (*direct*) les; (*indirect*) leur; (*stressed, after prep*) eux(elles); *see also* **me**

theme [θiːm] *n* thème *m*; ~ **park** *n* parc *m* (d'attraction) à thème; ~ **song** *n* chanson principale

themselves [ðəm'selvz] *pl pron* (*reflexive*) se; (*emphatic, after prep*) eux-mêmes(elles-mêmes); *see also* **oneself**

then [ðen] *adv* (*at that time*) alors, à ce moment-là; (*next*) puis, ensuite; (*and also*) et puis ♦ *conj* (*therefore*) alors ♦ *adj*: **the** ~ **president** le président d'alors *or* de l'époque; **by** ~ (*past*) à ce moment-là; (*future*) d'ici là; **from** ~ **on** dès lors

theology [θɪ'ɒlədʒɪ] *n* théologie *f*

theoretical [θɪə'retɪkəl] *adj* théorique

theorize ['θɪərɑɪz] *vi* faire des théories

theory ['θɪərɪ] *n* théorie *f*

therapy ['θerəpɪ] *n* thérapie *f*

KEYWORD
---

there [ðɛə*] *adv* **1**: ~ **is**, ~ **are** il y a; ~ **are 3 of them** (*people, things*) il y en a 3; ~ **has been an accident** il y a eu un accident

2 (*referring to place*) là, là-bas; **it's** ~ c'est là(-bas); **in/on/up/down** ~ là-dedans/là-dessus/là-haut/en bas; **he went** ~ **on Friday** il y est allé vendredi; **I want that book** ~ je veux ce livre-là; ~ **he is!** le voilà!

3: ~, ~ (*esp to child*) allons, allons!

---

thereabouts [ðɛərə'bauts] *adv* (*place*) par là, près de là; (*amount*) environ, à peu près

thereafter [ðɛər'ɑːftə*] *adv* par la suite

thereby [ðɛə'bɑɪ] *adv* ainsi

therefore ['ðɛəfɔː*] *adv* donc, par conséquent

there's ['ðɛəz] = **there is**; **there has**

thermal ['θɜːml] *adj* (*springs*) thermal(e); (*underwear*) en thermolactyl (®); (COMPUT: *paper*) thermosensible; (: *printer*) thermique

thermometer [θə'mɒmɪtə*] *n* thermomètre *m*

Thermos ['θɜːməs] (®) *n* (*also:* ~ *flask*) thermos *m or f inv* (®)

thermostat ['θɜːməustæt] *n* thermostat *m*

thesaurus [θɪ'sɔːrəs] *n* dictionnaire *m* des synonymes

these [ðiːz] *pl adj* ces; (*not "those"*): ~ **books** ces livres-ci ♦ *pl pron* ceux-ci(celles-ci)

thesis ['θiːsɪs] (*pl* **theses**) *n* thèse *f*

they [ðeɪ] *pl pron* ils(elles); (*stressed*) eux(elles); ~ **say that ...** (*it is said that*) on dit que ...; ~'**d** = ~ **had**; ~ **would**; ~'**ll** = **they shall**; ~ **will**; ~'**re** = ~ **are**; ~'**ve** = **they have**

thick [θɪk] *adj* épais(se); (*stupid*) bête, borné(e) ♦ *n*: **in the** ~ **of** au beau milieu de, en plein cœur de; **it's 20 cm** ~ il/elle a 20 cm d'épaisseur; ~**en** *vi* s'épaissir ♦ *vt* (*sauce etc*) épaissir; ~**ness** *n* épaisseur *f*; ~**set** *adj* trapu(e), costaud(e); ~**skinned** *adj* (*fig*) peu sensible

thief [θiːf] (*pl* **thieves**) *n* voleur(euse)

thigh [θaɪ] *n* cuisse *f*

thimble ['θɪmbl] *n* dé *m* (à coudre)

thin [θɪn] *adj* mince; (*skinny*) maigre; (*soup, sauce*) peu épais(se), clair(e); (*hair, crowd*) clairsemé(e) ♦ *vt*: **to** ~ (**down**) (*sauce, paint*) délayer

thing [θɪŋ] *n* chose *f*; (*object*) objet *m*; (*contraption*) truc *m*; (*mania*): **to have a** ~ **about** être obsédé(e) par; ~**s** *npl* (*belongings*) affaires *fpl*; **poor** ~! le(la) pauvre!; **the best** ~ **would be to** le mieux serait de; **how are** ~**s?** comment ça va?

think [θɪŋk] (*pt, pp* **thought**) *vi* penser, réfléchir; (*believe*) penser ♦ *vt* (*imagine*) imaginer; **what did you** ~ **of them?** qu'avez-vous pensé d'eux?; **to** ~ **about** sth/sb penser à qch/qn; **I'll** ~ **about it** je vais y réfléchir; **to** ~ **of doing** avoir l'idée de faire; **I** ~ **so/not** je crois *or* pense que oui/non; **to** ~ **well of** avoir une haute opinion de; ~ **over** *vt* bien réfléchir à; ~ **up** *vt* inventer, trouver; ~ **tank** *n* groupe *m* de réflexion

thinly *adv* (*cut*) en fines tranches; (*spread*) en une couche mince

third [θɜːd] *num* troisième ♦ *n* (*fraction*) tiers *m*; (AUT: *gear*) troisième (vitesse) *f*; (BRIT: SCOL: *degree*) ≈ licence *f* sans mention; ~**ly** *adv* troisièmement; ~ **party insurance** (BRIT) *n* assurance *f* au tiers; ~**rate** *adj* de qualité médiocre; **the T**~ **World** *n* le tiers monde

thirst [θɜːst] *n* soif *f*; ~**y** *adj* (*person*) qui a soif, assoiffé(e); (*work*) qui donne soif; **to be** ~**y** avoir soif

thirteen [θɜː'tiːn] *num* treize

thirty ['θɜːtɪ] *num* trente

KEYWORD
---

this [ðɪs] *adj* (*demonstrative*: *pl* **these**) ce, cet +*vowel or h mute*, cette *f*; ~ **man/woman/book** cet homme-ci/cette femme/ce livre; (*not that*) cet homme-ci/cette femme-ci/ce livre-ci; ~ **one** celui-ci(celle-ci)

♦ *pron* (*demonstrative*: *pl* **these**) ce; (*not that*

one) celui-ci(celle-ci), ceci; **who's ~?** qui est-ce?; **what's ~?** qu'est-ce que c'est?; **I prefer ~ to that** je préfère ceci à cela; **~ is what he said** voici ce qu'il a dit; **~ is Mr Brown** *(in introductions)* je vous présente Mr Brown; *(in photo)* c'est Mr Brown; *(on telephone)* ici Mr Brown

♦ *adv (demonstrative)*: **it was about ~** big c'était à peu près de cette grandeur *or* grand comme ça; **I didn't know it was ~ bad** je ne savais pas que c'était si *or* aussi mauvais

thistle ['θɪsl] *n* chardon *m*

thorn [θɔːn] *n* épine *f*

thorough ['θʌrə] *adj (search)* minutieux(euse); *(knowledge, research)* approfondi(e); *(work, person)* consciencieux(euse); *(cleaning)* à fond; **~bred** *n (horse)* pur-sang *m inv*; **~fare** *n* route *f*; **"no ~fare"** "passage interdit"; **~ly** *adv* minutieusement; en profondeur; à fond; *(very)* tout à fait

those [ðəʊz] *pl adj* ces; *(not "these")*: **~ books** ces livres-là ♦ *pl pron* ceux-là(celles-là)

though [ðəʊ] *conj* bien que +*sub*, quoique +*sub* ♦ *adv* pourtant

thought [θɔːt] *pt, pp of* think ♦ *n* pensée *f*; *(idea)* idée *f*; *(opinion)* avis *m*; **~ful** *adj (deep in thought)* pensif(ive); *(serious)* réfléchi(e); *(considerate)* prévenant(e); **~less** *adj* étourdi(e); qui manque de considération

thousand ['θaʊzənd] *num* mille; **two ~** deux mille; **~s of** des milliers de; **~th** *num* millième

thrash [θræʃ] *vt* rouer de coups; donner une correction à; *(defeat)* battre à plate couture; **~ about, ~ around** *vi* se débattre; **~ out** *vt* débattre de

thread [θred] *n* fil *m*; *(of screw)* pas *m*, filetage *m* ♦ *vt (needle)* enfiler; **~bare** *adj* râpé(e), élimé(e)

threat [θret] *n* menace *f*; **~en** *vi* menacer ♦ *vt*: **to ~en sb with sth/to do** menacer qn de qch/de faire

three [θriː] *num* trois; **~-dimensional** *adj* à trois dimensions; **~-piece suit** *n* complet *m* (avec gilet); **~-piece suite** *n* salon *m* comprenant un canapé et deux fauteuils assortis; **~-ply** *adj (wool)* trois fils *inv*

thresh [θreʃ] *vt (AGR)* battre

threshold ['θreʃhəʊld] *n* seuil *m*

threw [θruː] *pt of* throw

thrift [θrɪft] *n* économie *f*; **~y** *adj* économe

thrill [θrɪl] *n (excitement)* émotion *f*, sensation forte; *(shudder)* frisson *m* ♦ *vt (audience)* électriser; **to be ~ed** *(with gift etc)* être ravi(e); **~er** *n* film *m* *(or* roman *m or* pièce *f)* à suspense; **~ing** *adj* saisissant(e),

palpitant(e)

thrive [θraɪv] *(pt ~d, throve, pp ~d)* *vi* pousser, se développer; *(business)* prospérer; **he ~s on it** cela lui réussit; **thriving** ['θraɪvɪŋ] *adj (business, community)* prospère

throat [θrəʊt] *n* gorge *f*; **to have a sore ~** avoir mal à la gorge

throb [θrɒb] *vi (heart)* palpiter; *(engine)* vibrer; **my head is ~bing** j'ai des élancements dans la tête

throes [θrəʊz] *npl*: **in the ~ of** au beau milieu de

throne [θrəʊn] *n* trône *m*

throng [θrɒŋ] *n* foule *f* ♦ *vt* se presser dans

throttle ['θrɒtl] *n (AUT)* accélérateur *m* ♦ *vt* étrangler

through [θruː] *prep* à travers; *(time)* pendant, durant; *(by means of)* par, par l'intermédiaire de ♦ *adj (ticket, train, passage)* direct(e) ♦ *adv* à travers; **to put sb ~ to sb** *(BRIT: TEL)* passer qn à qn; **to be ~** avoir la communication; *(esp US: have finished)* avoir fini; **to be ~ with sb** *(relationship)* avoir rompu avec qn; **"no ~ road"** *(BRIT)* "impasse"; **~out** [θruː'aʊt] *prep (place)* partout dans; *(time)* durant tout(e) le(la) ♦ *adv* partout

throve [θrəʊv] *pt of* thrive

throw [θrəʊ] *(pt* threw, *pp* thrown) *n* jet *m*; *(SPORT)* lancer *m* ♦ *vt* lancer, jeter; *(SPORT)* lancer; *(rider)* désarçonner; *(fig)* décontenancer; **to ~ a party** donner une réception; **~ away** *vt* jeter; **~ off** *vt* se débarrasser de; **~ out** *vt* jeter; *(reject)* rejeter; *(person)* mettre à la porte; **~ up** *vi* vomir; **~away** *adj* à jeter; *(remark)* fait(e) en passant; **~-in** *n (SPORT)* remise *f* en jeu

thru [θruː] *(US)* = through

thrush [θrʌʃ] *n (bird)* grive *f*

thrust [θrʌst] *(pt, pp* thrust) *n (TECH)* poussée *f* ♦ *vt* pousser brusquement; *(push in)* enfoncer

thud [θʌd] *n* bruit sourd

thug [θʌg] *n* voyou *m*

thumb [θʌm] *n (ANAT)* pouce *m*, arrêter une voiture; **to ~ a lift** faire de l'auto-stop; **~ through** *vt (book)* feuilleter; **~tack** *(US)* *n* punaise *f (clou)*

thump [θʌmp] *n* grand coup; *(sound)* bruit sourd ♦ *vt* cogner sur ♦ *vi* cogner, battre fort

thunder ['θʌndə*] *n* tonnerre *m* ♦ *vi* tonner; *(train etc)*: **to ~ past** passer dans un grondement *or* un bruit de tonnerre; **~bolt** *n* foudre *f*; **~clap** *n* coup *m* de tonnerre; **~storm** *n* orage *m*; **~y** *adj* orageux(euse)

Thursday ['θɜːzdeɪ] *n* jeudi *m*

thus [ðʌs] *adv* ainsi

thwart [θwɔːt] *vt* contrecarrer

thyme [taɪm] *n* thym *m*

tiara [tɪ'ɑːrə] *n (woman's)* diadème *m*

tick [tɪk] n (sound: of clock) tic-tac m; (mark) coche f; (ZOOL) tique f; (BRIT: inf): **in a ~** dans une seconde ♦ vi faire tic-tac ♦ vt (item on list) cocher; **~ off** vt (item on list) cocher; (person) réprimander, attraper; **~ over** vi (engine) tourner au ralenti; (fig) aller or marcher doucettement

ticket [ˈtɪkɪt] n billet m; (for bus, tube) ticket m; (in shop: on goods) étiquette f; (for library) carte f; (parking ~) papillon m, p.-v. m; (~ collector n contrôleur(euse); **~ office** n guichet m, bureau m de vente des billets

tickle [ˈtɪkl] vt, vi chatouiller; **ticklish** adj (person) chatouilleux(euse); (problem) épineux(euse)

tidal [ˈtaɪdl] adj (force) de la marée; (estuary) à marée; **~ wave** n raz-de-marée m inv

tidbit [ˈtɪdbɪt] (US) n = titbit

tiddlywinks [ˈtɪdlɪwɪŋks] n jeu m de puce

tide [taɪd] n marée f; (fig: of events) cours m ♦ vt: **to ~ sb over** dépanner qn; **high/low ~** marée haute/basse

tidy [ˈtaɪdɪ] adj (room) bien rangé(e); (dress, work) net(te), soigné(e); (person) ordonné(e), qui a de l'ordre ♦ vt (also: ~ up) ranger

tie [taɪ] n (string etc) cordon m; (BRIT: also: neck~) cravate f; (fig: link) lien m; (SPORT: draw) égalité f de points; match nul ♦ vt (parcel) attacher; (ribbon, shoelaces) nouer ♦ vi (SPORT) faire match nul; finir à égalité de points; **to ~ sth in a bow** faire un nœud à or avec qch; **to ~ a knot in sth** faire un nœud à qch; **~ down** vt (fig): **to ~ sb down (to)** contraindre qn (à accepter); **to be ~d down** (by relationship) être fixer; **~ up** vt (parcel) ficeler; (dog, boat) attacher; (prisoner) ligoter; (arrangements) conclure; **to be ~d up** (busy) être pris(e) or occupé(e)

tier [tɪə*] n gradin m; (of cake) étage m

tiger [ˈtaɪɡə*] n tigre m

tight [taɪt] adj (rope) tendu(e), raide; (clothes) étroit(e), très juste; (budget, programme, bend) serré(e); (control) strict(e), sévère; (inf: drunk) ivre, rond(e) ♦ adv (squeeze) très fort; (shut) hermétiquement, bien; **~en** vt (rope) tendre; (screw) resserrer; (control) renforcer ♦ vi se tendre, se resserrer; **~fisted** adj avare; **~ly** adv (grasp) bien, très fort; **~rope** n corde f raide; **~s** (BRIT) npl collant m

tile [taɪl] n (on roof) tuile f; (on wall or floor) carreau m; **~d** adj en tuiles; carrelé(e)

till [tɪl] n caisse (enregistreuse) ♦ vt (land) cultiver ♦ prep, conj = **until**

tiller [ˈtɪlə*] n (NAUT) barre f (du gouvernail)

tilt [tɪlt] vt pencher, incliner ♦ vi pencher, être incliné(e)

timber [ˈtɪmbə*] n (material) bois m (de construction); (trees) arbres mpl

time [taɪm] n temps m; (epoch: often pl) époque f, temps; (by clock) heure f; (moment) moment m; (occasion, also MATH) fois f; (MUS) mesure f ♦ vt (race) chronométrer; (programme) minuter; (visit) fixer; (remark etc) choisir le moment de; **a long ~** un long moment, longtemps; **for the ~ being** pour le moment; **4 at a ~** à la fois; **from ~ to ~** de temps en temps; **at ~s** parfois; **in ~** (soon enough) à temps; (after some ~) avec le temps, à la longue; (MUS) en mesure; **in a week's ~** dans une semaine; **in no ~** en un rien de temps; **any ~** n'importe quand; **on ~** à l'heure; **5 ~s 5** 5 fois 5; **what ~ is it?** quelle heure est-il?; **to have a good ~** bien s'amuser; **~ bomb** n bombe f à retardement; **~ lag** (BRIT) n décalage m; (in travel) décalage horaire; **~less** adj éternel(le); **~ly** adj opportun(e); **~ off** n temps m libre; **~r** n (TECH) minuteur m; (in kitchen) compte-minutes m inv; **~scale** n délais mpl; **~-share** n maison f (or appartement m) en multipropriété; **~ switch** (BRIT) n minuteur m; (for lighting) minuterie f; **~table** n (RAIL) (indicateur m) horaire m; (SCOL) emploi m du temps; **~ zone** n fuseau m horaire

timid [ˈtɪmɪd] adj timide; (easily scared) peureux(euse)

timing [ˈtaɪmɪŋ] n minutage m; chronométrage m; **the ~ of his resignation** le moment choisi pour sa démission

timpani [ˈtɪmpənɪ] npl timbales fpl

tin [tɪn] n étain m; (also: ~ plate) fer-blanc m; (BRIT: can) boîte f (de conserve); (for storage) boîte f; **~foil** n papier m d'étain or aluminium

tinge [tɪndʒ] n nuance f ♦ vt: **~d with** teinté(e) de

tingle [ˈtɪŋgl] vi picoter; (person) avoir des picotements

tinker [ˈtɪŋkə*] n (gipsy) romanichel m; **~ with** vt fus bricoler, rafistoler

tinkle [ˈtɪŋkl] vi tinter

tinned [tɪnd] (BRIT) adj (food) en boîte, en conserve

tin opener [ˈ-əʊpnə*] (BRIT) n ouvre-boîte(s) m

tinsel [ˈtɪnsəl] n guirlandes fpl de Noël (argentées)

tint [tɪnt] n teinte f; (for hair) shampooing colorant; **~ed** adj (hair) teint(e); (spectacles, glass) teinté(e)

tiny [ˈtaɪnɪ] adj minuscule

tip [tɪp] n (end) bout m; (gratuity) pourboire m; (BRIT: for rubbish) décharge f; (advice) tuyau m ♦ vt (waiter) donner un pourboire à; (tilt) incliner; (overturn: also: ~ over) renverser; (empty: also: ~ out) déverser; **~-off** n *(hint)* tuyau *m*; ~**ped** (*BRIT*) *adj* (*cigarette*) (à bout) filtre *inv*

tipsy ['tɪpsɪ] (*inf*) *adj* un peu ivre, éméché(e)

tiptoe ['tɪptəʊ] *n*: **on** ~ sur la pointe des pieds

tiptop ['tɪp'tɒp] *adj*: **in** ~ **condition** en excellent état

tire ['taɪə*] *n* (*US*) = **tyre** ♦ *vt* fatiguer ♦ *vi* se fatiguer; ~**d** *adj* fatigué(e); **to be** ~**d of** en avoir assez de, être las(lasse) de; ~**less** *adj* (*person*) infatigable; (*efforts*) inlassable; ~**some** *adj* ennuyeux(euse); **tiring** ['taɪərɪŋ] *adj* fatigant(e)

tissue ['tɪʃu:] *n* tissu *m*; (*paper handkerchief*) mouchoir *m* en papier, kleenex *m* (®); ~ **paper** *n* papier *m* de soie

tit [tɪt] *n* (*bird*) mésange *f*; **to give** ~ **for tat** rendre la pareille

titbit ['tɪtbɪt] *n* (*food*) friandise *f*; (*news*) potin *m*

title ['taɪtl] *n* titre *m*; ~ **deed** *n* (*LAW*) titre (constitutif) de propriété; ~ **role** *n* rôle principal

titter ['tɪtə*] *vi* rire (bêtement)

TM *abbr* = **trademark**

KEYWORD

to [tu:, tə] *prep* **1** (*direction*) à; ~ **go** ~ **France/Portugal/London/school** aller en France/au Portugal/à Londres/à l'école; ~ **go** ~ **Claude's/the doctor's** aller chez Claude/le docteur; **the road** ~ **Edinburgh** la route d'Édimbourg

2 (*as far as*) (jusqu')à; ~ **count** ~ **10** compter jusqu'à 10; **from 40** ~ **50 people** de 40 à 50 personnes

3 (*with expressions of time*): **a quarter** ~ **5** 5 heures moins le quart; **it's twenty** ~ **3** il est 3 heures moins vingt

4 (*for, of*) de; **the key** ~ **the front door** la clé de la porte d'entrée; **a letter** ~ **his wife** une lettre (adressée) à sa femme

5 (*expressing indirect object*) à; ~ **give sth** ~ **sb** donner qch à qn; ~ **talk** ~ **sb** parler à qn

6 (*in relation to*) à; **3 goals** ~ **2** 3 (buts) à 2; **30 miles** ~ **the gallon** ≈ 9,4 litres aux cent (km)

7 (*purpose, result*): ~ **come** ~ **sb's aid** venir au secours de qn, porter secours à qn; ~ **sentence sb** ~ **death** condamner qn à mort; ~ **my surprise** à ma grande surprise

♦ *with vb* **1** (*simple infinitive*): ~ **go/eat** aller/manger

2 (*following another vb*): ~ **want/try/start** ~ **do** vouloir/essayer de/commencer à faire

3 (*with vb omitted*): **I don't want** ~ je ne veux pas

4 (*purpose, result*) pour; **I did it** ~ **help you** je l'ai fait pour vous aider

5 (*equivalent to relative clause*): **I have**

things ~ **do** j'ai des choses à faire; **the main thing is** ~ **try** l'important est d'essayer

6 (*after adjective etc*): **ready** ~ **go** prêt(e) à partir; **too old/young** ~ **...** trop vieux/jeune pour ...

♦ *adv*: **push/pull the door** ~ tirez/poussez la porte

---

toad [təʊd] *n* crapaud *m*

toadstool *n* champignon (vénéneux)

toast [təʊst] *n* (*CULIN*) pain grillé, toast *m*; (*drink, speech*) toast ♦ *vt* (*CULIN*) faire griller; (*drink to*) porter un toast à; ~**er** *n* grille-pain *m inv*

tobacco [tə'bækəʊ] *n* tabac *m*; ~**nist** [tə'bækənɪst] *n* marchand(e) de tabac; ~**nist's (shop)** *n* (bureau *m* de) tabac *m*

toboggan [tə'bɒgən] *n* toboggan *m*; (*child's*) luge *f*

today [tə'deɪ] *adv* (*also fig*) aujourd'hui ♦ *n* aujourd'hui *m*

toddler ['tɒdlə*] *n* enfant *m/f* qui commence à marcher, bambin *m*

to-do [tə'du:] *n* (*fuss*) histoire *f*, affaire *f*

toe [təʊ] *n* doigt *m* de pied, orteil *m*; (*of shoe*) bout *m* ♦ *vt*: **to** ~ **the line** (*fig*) obéir, se conformer; ~**nail** *n* ongle *m* du pied

toffee ['tɒfɪ] *n* caramel *m*; ~ **apple** (*BRIT*) *n* pomme caramélisée

toga ['təʊgə] *n* toge *f*

together [tə'geðə*] *adv* ensemble; (*at same time*) en même temps; ~ **with** avec

toil [tɔɪl] *n* dur travail, labeur *m* ♦ *vi* peiner

toilet ['tɔɪlət] *n* (*BRIT*: *lavatory*) toilettes *fpl* ♦ *cpd* (*accessories etc*) de toilette; ~ **paper** *n* papier *m* hygiénique; ~**ries** ['tɔɪlətrɪz] *npl* articles *mpl* de toilette; ~ **roll** *n* rouleau *m* de papier hygiénique; ~ **water** *n* eau *f* de toilette

token ['təʊkən] *n* (*sign*) marque *f*, témoignage *m*; (*metal disc*) jeton *m* ♦ *adj* (*strike, payment etc*) symbolique; **book/record** ~ (*BRIT*) chèque-livre/-disque *m*; **gift** ~ bon-cadeau *m*

told [təʊld] *pt, pp of* **tell**

tolerable ['tɒlərəbl] *adj* (*bearable*) tolérable; (*fairly good*) passable

tolerant ['tɒlərnt] *adj*: ~ (**of**) tolérant(e) (à l'égard de)

tolerate ['tɒləreɪt] *vt* supporter, tolérer

toll [təʊl] *n* (*tax, charge*) péage *m* ♦ *vi* (*bell*) sonner; **the accident** ~ **on the roads** le nombre des victimes de la route

tomato [tə'mɑ:təʊ] (*pl* ~**es**) *n* tomate *f*

tomb [tu:m] *n* tombe *f*

tomboy ['tɒmbɔɪ] *n* garçon manqué

tombstone ['tu:mstəʊn] *n* pierre tombale

tomcat ['tɒmkæt] *n* matou *m*

tomorrow [tə'mɒrəʊ] *adv* (*also fig*) demain ♦ *n* demain *m*; **the day after** ~ après-demain; ~ **morning** demain matin

ton [tʌn] *n* tonne *f* (*BRIT* = 1016kg; *US* = 907kg); (*metric*) tonne (= 1000 kg); ~**s** *of* (*inf*) des tas de

tone [təun] *n* ton *m* ♦ *vi* (*also:* ~ *in*) s'harmoniser; ~ **down** *vt* (*colour, criticism*) adoucir; (*sound*) baisser; ~ **up** *vt* (*muscles*) tonifier; ~**-deaf** *adj* qui n'a pas d'oreille

tongs [tɒŋz] *npl* (*for coal*) pincettes *fpl*; (*for hair*) fer *m* à friser

tongue [tʌŋ] *n* langue *f*; ~ **in cheek** ironiquement; ~**-tied** *adj* muet(te); ~ **twister** *n* phrase *f* très difficile à prononcer

tonic ['tɒnɪk] *n* (*MED*) tonique *m*; (*also:* ~ *water*) tonic *m*, Schweppes *m* (®)

tonight [tə'naɪt] *adv, n* cette nuit; (*this evening*) ce soir

tonsil ['tɒnsl] *n* amygdale *f*; ~**litis** *n* angine *f*

too [tuː] *adv* (*excessively*) trop; (*also*) aussi; ~ **much** *adv* trop de ♦ *adj* trop; ~ **many** trop de; ~ **bad!** tant pis!

took [tuk] *pt of* **take**

tool [tuːl] *n* outil *m*; ~ **box** *n* boîte *f* à outils

toot [tuːt] *n* (*of car horn*) coup *m* de klaxon; (*of whistle*) coup de sifflet ♦ *vi* (*with car horn*) klaxonner

tooth [tuːθ] (*pl* **teeth**) *n* (*ANAT, TECH*) dent *f*, ~**ache** *n* mal *m* de dents; ~**brush** *n* brosse *f* à dents; ~**paste** *n* (*pâte f*) dentifrice *m*; ~**pick** *n* cure-dent *m*

top [tɒp] *n* (*of mountain, head*) sommet *m*; (*of page, ladder, garment*) haut *m*; (*of box, cupboard, table*) dessus *m*; (*lid: of box, jar*) couvercle *m*; (: *of bottle*) bouchon *m*; (*toy*) toupie *f* ♦ *adj* du haut; (*in rank*) premier(ère); (*best*) meilleur(e) ♦ *vt* (*exceed*) dépasser; (*be first in*) être en tête de; **on** ~ **of** sur; (*in addition to*) en plus de; **from** ~ **to bottom** de fond en comble; ~ **up** (*US* ~ **off**) *vt* (*bottle*) remplir; (*salary*) compléter; ~ **floor** *n* dernier étage; ~ **hat** *n* haut-de-forme *m*; ~**-heavy** *adj* (*object*) trop lourd(e) du haut

topic ['tɒpɪk] *n* sujet *m*, thème *m*; ~**al** *adj* d'actualité

top: ~**less** ['tɒpləs] *adj* (*bather etc*) aux seins nus; ~**-level** ['tɒp'levl] *adj* (*talks*) au plus haut niveau; ~**most** ['tɒpməust] *adj* le(la) plus haut(e)

topple ['tɒpl] *vt* renverser, faire tomber ♦ *vi* basculer; tomber

top-secret ['tɒp'siːkrət] *adj* top secret(ète)

topsy-turvy ['tɒpsɪ'tɜːvɪ] *adj, adv* sens dessus dessous

torch [tɔːtʃ] *n* torche *f*; (*BRIT: electric*) lampe *f* de poche

tore [tɔː*] *pt of* **tear**[1]

torment [*n* 'tɔːment, *vb* tɔː'ment] *n* tourment *m* ♦ *vt* tourmenter; (*fig: annoy*) harce-

ler

torn [tɔːn] *pp of* **tear**[1]

tornado [tɔː'neɪdəu] (*pl* ~**es**) *n* tornade *f*

torpedo [tɔː'piːdəu] (*pl* ~**es**) *n* torpille *f*

torrent ['tɒrənt] *n* torrent *m*

tortoise ['tɔːtəs] *n* tortue *f*; ~**shell** *adj* en écaille

torture ['tɔːtʃə*] (*BRIT POL*) *n* torture *f* ♦ *vt* torturer

Tory ['tɔːrɪ] (*BRIT POL*) *adj* tory, conservateur(trice) ♦ *n* tory *m/f*, conservateur(trice)

toss [tɒs] *vt* lancer, jeter; (*pancake*) faire sauter; (*head*) rejeter en arrière; **to** ~ **a coin** jouer à pile ou face; **to** ~ **up for sth** jouer qch à pile ou face; **to** ~ **and turn** (*in bed*) se tourner et se retourner

tot [tɒt] *n* (*BRIT: drink*) petit verre; (*child*) bambin *m*

total ['təutl] *adj* total(e) ♦ *n* total *m* ♦ *vt* (*add up*) faire le total de, additionner; (*amount to*) s'élever à; ~**ly** ['təutəlɪ] *adv* totalement

totter ['tɒtə*] *vi* chanceler

touch [tʌtʃ] *n* contact *m*, toucher *m*; (*sense, also skill: of pianist etc*) toucher ♦ *vt* toucher; (*tamper with*) toucher à; **a** ~ **of** (*fig*) un petit peu de; une touche de; **to get in** ~ **with** prendre contact avec, se mettre en contact avec; **to lose** ~ (*friends*) se perdre de vue; ~ **on** *vt fus* (*topic*) effleurer, aborder; ~ **up** *vt* (*paint*) retoucher; ~**-and-go** *adj* incertain(e); ~**down** *n* atterrissage *m*; (*on sea*) amerrissage *m*; (*US: FOOTBALL*) touché-en-but *m*; ~**ed** *adj* (*moved*) touché(e); ~**ing** *adj* touchant(e), attendrissant(e); ~**line** *n* (*SPORT*) (ligne *f* de) touche *f*; ~**y** *adj* (*person*) susceptible

tough [tʌf] *adj* dur(e); (*resistant*) résistant(e), solide; (*meat*) dur, coriace; (*firm*) inflexible; (*task*) dur, pénible; ~**en** *vt* (*character*) endurcir; (*glass etc*) renforcer

toupee ['tuːpeɪ] *n* postiche *m*

tour ['tuə*] *n* voyage *m*; (*also: package* ~) voyage organisé; (*of town, museum*) tour *m*, visite *f*; (*by artist*) tournée *f* ♦ *vt* visiter

tourism ['tuərɪzm] *n* tourisme *m*

tourist ['tuərɪst] *n* touriste *m/f* ♦ *cpd* touristique; ~ **office** *n* syndicat *m* d'initiative

tournament ['tuənəmənt] *n* tournoi *m*

tousled ['tauzld] *adj* (*hair*) ébouriffé(e)

tout [taut] *vi*: **to** ~ **for** essayer de raccrocher, racoler (*also: ticket* ~) revendeur *m* de billets

tow [təu] *vt* remorquer; (*caravan, trailer*) tracter; **"on** (*BRIT*) **or in** (*US*) ~**"** (*AUT*) "véhicule en remorque"

toward(s) [tə'wɔːd(z)] *prep* vers; (*of attitude*) envers, à l'égard de; (*of purpose*) pour

towel ['tauəl] *n* serviette *f* (de toilette); ~**ling** *n* (*fabric*) tissu éponge *m*; ~ **rail** (*US* ~ **rack**) *n* porte-serviettes *m inv*

tower ['tauə*] *n* tour *f*; ~ **block** (*BRIT*) *n* tour *f* (d'habitation); ~**ing** *adj* très haut(e), imposant(e)

town [taʊn] n ville f; **to go to ~** aller en ville; (fig) y mettre le paquet; **~ centre** n centre m de la ville, centre-ville m; **~ council** n conseil municipal; **~ hall** n ≈ mairie f; **~ plan** n plan m de ville; **~ planning** n urbanisme m

towrope ['təʊrəʊp] n (câble m de) remorque f

tow truck (US) n dépanneuse f

toy [tɔɪ] n jouet m; **~ with** vt fus jouer avec; (idea) caresser

trace [treɪs] n trace f ♦ vt (draw) tracer, dessiner; (follow) suivre la trace de; (locate) retrouver; **tracing paper** n papier-calque m

track [træk] n (mark) trace f; (path: gen) chemin m, piste f; (: of bullet etc) trajectoire f; (: of suspect, animal) piste f; (RAIL) voie ferrée, rails mpl; (on tape, SPORT) piste f; (on record) plage f ♦ vt suivre la trace or la piste de; **to keep ~ of** suivre; **~ down** vt (prey) trouver et capturer; (sth lost) finir par retrouver; **~suit** n survêtement m

tract [trækt] n (GEO) étendue f, zone f; (pamphlet) tract m

traction ['trækʃən] n traction f; (MED): **in ~** en extension

tractor ['træktə*] n tracteur m

trade [treɪd] n commerce m; (skill, job) métier m ♦ vi faire du commerce ♦ vt (exchange): **to ~ sth (for sth)** échanger qch (contre qch); **~ in** vt (old car etc) faire reprendre; **~-in price** n prix m à la reprise; **~mark** n marque f de fabrique; **~ name** n nom m de marque; **~r** n commerçant(e), négociant(e); **~sman** (irreg) n (shopkeeper) commerçant; **~ union** n syndicat m; **~ unionist** n syndicaliste m/f

tradition [trə'dɪʃən] n tradition f, **~al** adj traditionnel(le)

traffic ['træfɪk] n trafic m; (cars) circulation f ♦ vi: **to ~ in** (pej: liquor, drugs) faire le trafic de; **~ circle** (US) n rond-point m; **~ jam** n embouteillage m; **~ lights** npl feux mpl (de signalisation); **~ warden** n contractuel(le)

tragedy ['trædʒədɪ] n tragédie f

tragic ['trædʒɪk] adj tragique

trail [treɪl] n (tracks) trace f, piste f; (path) chemin m, piste; (of smoke etc) traînée f ♦ vt traîner, tirer; (follow) suivre ♦ vi traîner; (in game, contest) être en retard; **~ behind** vi traîner, être à la traîne; **~er** n (AUT) remorque f; (US) caravane f; (CINEMA) bande-annonce f; **~er truck** (US) n (camion m) semi-remorque m

train [treɪn] n train m; (in underground) rame f; (of dress) traîne f ♦ vt (apprentice, doctor etc) former; (sportsman) entraîner; (dog) dresser; (memory) exercer; (point: gun etc): **to ~ sth on** braquer qch sur ♦ vi sui-

vre une formation; (SPORT) s'entraîner; **one's ~ of thought** le fil de sa pensée; **~ed** adj qualifié(e), qui a reçu une formation; (animal) dressé(e); **~ee** n stagiaire m/f; (in trade) apprenti(e); **~er** n (SPORT: coach) entraîneur(euse); (: shoe) chaussure f de sport; (of dogs etc) dresseur(euse); **~ing** n formation f; entraînement m; **in ~ing** (SPORT) à l'entraînement; (fit) en forme; **~ing college** n école professionnelle; (for teachers) ≈ école normale; **~ing shoes** npl chaussures fpl de sport

traipse [treɪps] vi: **to ~ in/out** entrer/sortir d'un pas traînant

trait [treɪ(t)] n trait m (de caractère)

traitor ['treɪtə*] n traître m

tram ['træm] (BRIT) n (also: **~car**) tram(way) m

tramp [træmp] n (person) vagabond(e), clochard(e); (inf: pej: woman): **to be a ~** être coureuse ♦ vi marcher d'un pas lourd

trample ['træmpl] vt: **to ~ (underfoot)** piétiner

trampoline ['træmpəliːn] n trampoline m

tranquil ['træŋkwɪl] adj tranquille; **~lizer** (US **~izer**) n (MED) tranquillisant m

transact [træn'zækt] vt (business) traiter; **~ion** n transaction f

transatlantic ['trænzət'læntɪk] adj transatlantique

transfer [n 'trænsfə*, vt træns'fɜː*] n (gen, also SPORT) transfert m; (POL: of power) passation f; (picture, design) décalcomanie f; (: stick-on) autocollant m ♦ vt transférer; passer; **to ~ the charges** (BRIT: TEL) téléphoner en P.C.V.

transform [træns'fɔːm] vt transformer

transfusion [træns'fjuːʒən] n transfusion f

transient ['trænzɪənt] adj transitoire, éphémère

transistor [træn'zɪstə*] n (ELEC, also: **~ radio**) transistor m

transit ['trænzɪt] n: **in ~** en transit

transitive ['trænzɪtɪv] adj (LING) transitif(ive)

transit lounge n salle f de transit

translate [trænz'leɪt] vt traduire; **translation** [trænz'leɪʃən] n traduction f; **translator** [trænz'leɪtə*] n traducteur(trice)

transmission [trænz'mɪʃən] n transmission f

transmit [trænz'mɪt] vt transmettre; (RADIO, TV) émettre

transparency [træns'pærənsɪ] n (of glass etc) transparence f; (BRIT: PHOT) diapositive f; **transparent** [træns'pærənt] adj transparent(e)

transpire [træns'paɪə*] vi (turn out): **it ~d that ...** on a appris que ...; (happen) arriver

transplant [vb træns'plɑːnt, n 'trænsplɑːnt] vt transplanter; (seedlings) repiquer ♦ n (MED) transplantation f

transport [*n* 'trænspɔːt, *vb* træns'pɔːt] *n* transport *m*; (*car*) moyen *m* de transport, voiture *f* ♦ *vt* transporter; **~ation** [trænspɔː'teɪʃən] *n* transport *m*; (*means of* ~) moyen *m* de transport; ~ **café** (*BRIT*) *n* ≈ restaurant *m* de routiers

trap [træp] *n* (*snare, trick*) piège *m*; (*carriage*) cabriolet *m* ♦ *vt* prendre au piège; (*confine*) coincer; ~ **door** *n* trappe *f*

trapeze [trə'piːz] *n* trapèze *m*

trappings ['træpɪŋz] *npl* ornements *mpl*; attributs *mpl*

trash [træʃ] (*pej*) *n* (*goods*) camelote *f*; (*nonsense*) sottises *fpl*; ~ **can** (*US*) *n* poubelle *f*

trauma ['trɔːmə] *n* traumatisme *m*; **~tic** *adj* traumatisant(e)

travel ['trævl] *n* voyage(s) *m(pl)* ♦ *vi* voyager; (*news, sound*) circuler, se propager ♦ *vt* (*distance*) parcourir; ~ **agency** *n* agence *f* de voyages; ~ **agent** *n* agent *m* de voyages; **~ler** (*US* **~er**) *n* voyageur(euse); **~ler's cheque** (*US* **~er's check**) *n* chèque *m* de voyage; **~ling** (*US* **~ing**) *n* voyage(s) *m(pl)*; ~ **sickness** *n* mal *m* de la route (*or* de mer *or* de l'air)

travesty ['trævəstɪ] *n* parodie *f*

trawler ['trɔːlə*] *n* chalutier *m*

tray [treɪ] *n* (*for carrying*) plateau *m*; (*on desk*) corbeille *f*

treacherous *adj* (*person, look*) traître(esse); (*ground, tide*) dont il faut se méfier

treachery ['trɛtʃərɪ] *n* traîtrise *f*

treacle ['triːkl] *n* mélasse *f*

tread [trɛd] (*pt* **trod**, *pp* **trodden**) *n* pas *m*; (*sound*) bruit *m* de pas; (*of tyre*) chape *f*, bande *f* de roulement ♦ *vi* marcher; ~ **on** *vt fus* marcher sur

treason ['triːzn] *n* trahison *f*

treasure ['trɛʒə*] *n* trésor *m* ♦ *vt* (*value*) tenir beaucoup à

treasurer ['trɛʒərə*] *n* trésorier(ère)

treasury ['trɛʒərɪ] *n*: **the T~**, (*US*) **the T~ Department** le ministère des Finances

treat [triːt] *n* petit cadeau, petite surprise ♦ *vt* traiter; **to ~ sb to sth** offrir qch à qn

treatment ['triːtmənt] *n* traitement *m*

treaty ['triːtɪ] *n* traité *m*

treble ['trɛbl] *adj* triple ♦ *vt, vi* tripler; ~ **clef** *n* (*MUS*) clé *f* de sol

tree [triː] *n* arbre *m*

trek [trɛk] *n* (*long*) voyage; (*on foot*) (longue) marche, tirée *f*

tremble ['trɛmbl] *vi* trembler

tremendous [trə'mɛndəs] *adj* (*enormous*) énorme, fantastique; (*excellent*) formidable

tremor ['trɛmə*] *n* tremblement *m*; (*also*: **earth** ~) secousse *f* sismique

trench [trɛntʃ] *n* tranchée *f*

trend [trɛnd] *n* (*tendency*) tendance *f*; (*of events*) cours *m*; (*fashion*) mode *f*; **~y** *adj* (*idea, person*) dans le vent; (*clothes*) dernier cri *inv*

trepidation [trɛpɪ'deɪʃən] *n* vive agitation *or* inquiétude *f*

trespass ['trɛspəs] *vi*: **to ~ on** s'introduire sans permission dans; **"no ~ing"** "propriété privée", "défense d'entrer"

trestle ['trɛsl] *n* tréteau *m*

trial ['traɪəl] *n* (*LAW*) procès *m*, jugement *m*; (*test: of machine etc*) essai *m*; **~s** *npl* (*unpleasant experiences*) épreuves *fpl*; **to be on** ~ (*LAW*) passer en jugement; **by ~ and error** par tâtonnements; ~ **period** *n* période *f* d'essai

triangle ['traɪæŋgl] *n* (*MATH, MUS*) triangle *m*

tribe [traɪb] *n* tribu *f*; **~sman** (*irreg*) *n* membre *m* d'une tribu

tribunal [traɪ'bjuːnl] *n* tribunal *m*

tributary ['trɪbjutərɪ] *n* (*river*) affluent *m*

tribute ['trɪbjuːt] *n* tribut *m*, hommage *m*; **to pay ~ to** rendre hommage à

trice [traɪs] *n*: **in a ~** en un clin d'œil

trick [trɪk] *n* (*magic ~*) tour *m*; (*joke, prank*) tour, farce *f*; (*skill, knack*) astuce *f*, truc *m*; (*CARDS*) levée *f* ♦ *vt* attraper, rouler; **to play a ~ on sb** jouer un tour à qn; **that should do the ~** ça devrait faire l'affaire; **~ery** *n* ruse *f*

trickle ['trɪkl] *n* (*of water etc*) filet *m* ♦ *vi* couler en un filet *or* goutte à goutte

tricky ['trɪkɪ] *adj* difficile, délicat(e)

tricycle ['traɪsɪkl] *n* tricycle *m*

trifle ['traɪfl] *n* bagatelle *f*; (*CULIN*) ≈ diplomate *m* ♦ *adv*: **a ~ long** un peu long

trifling ['traɪflɪŋ] *adj* insignifiant(e)

trigger ['trɪgə*] *n* (*of gun*) gâchette *f*; ~ **off** *vt* déclencher

trim [trɪm] *adj* (*house, garden*) bien tenu(e); (*figure*) svelte ♦ *n* (*haircut etc*) légère coupe; (*on car*) garnitures *fpl* ♦ *vt* (*cut*) couper légèrement; (*NAUT: a sail*) gréer; (*decorate*): **to ~ (with)** décorer (de); **~mings** *npl* (*CULIN*) garniture *f*

trinket ['trɪŋkɪt] *n* bibelot *m*; (*piece of jewellery*) colifichet *m*

trip [trɪp] *n* voyage *m*; (*excursion*) excursion *f*; (*stumble*) faux pas ♦ *vi* faire un faux pas, trébucher; (*go lightly*) marcher d'un pas léger; **on a ~** en voyage; ~ **up** *vi* trébucher ♦ *vt* faire un croc-en-jambe à

tripe [traɪp] *n* (*CULIN*) tripes *fpl*; (*pej: rubbish*) idioties *fpl*

triple ['trɪpl] *adj* triple

triplets ['trɪplɪts] *npl* triplés(ées)

triplicate ['trɪplɪkɪt] *n*: **in ~** en trois exemplaires

tripod ['traɪpɒd] *n* trépied *m*

trite [traɪt] (*pej*) *adj* banal(e)

triumph ['traɪʌmf] *n* triomphe *m* ♦ *vi*: **to ~ (over)** triompher (de)

trivia ['trɪvɪə] (*pej*) *npl* futilités *fpl*

trivial ['trɪvɪəl] *adj* insignifiant(e); (*common-*

place) banal(e)

trod [trɔd] *pt of* **tread**

trodden ['trɔdn] *pp of* **tread**

trolley ['trɔlɪ] *n* chariot *m*

trombone [trɔm'bəʊn] *n* trombone *m*

troop [tru:p] *n* bande *f*, groupe *m* ♦ *vi*: ~ **in/out** entrer/sortir en groupe; ~**s** *npl* (MIL) troupes *fpl*; (: *men*) hommes *mpl*, soldats *mpl*; ~**ing the colour** (BRIT) *n* (*ceremony*) le salut au drapeau

trophy ['trəʊfɪ] *n* trophée *m*

tropic ['trɔpɪk] *n* tropique *m*; ~**al** *adj* tropical(e)

trot [trɔt] *n* trot *m* ♦ *vi* trotter; **on the** ~ (BRIT: *fig*) d'affilée

trouble ['trʌbl] *n* difficulté(s) *f(pl)*, problème(s) *m(pl)*; (*worry*) ennuis *mpl*, soucis *mpl*; (*bother, effort*) peine *f*; (POL) troubles *mpl*; (MED): **stomach** *etc* ~ troubles gastriques *etc* ♦ *vt* (*disturb*) déranger, gêner; (*worry*) inquiéter ♦ *vi*: **to** ~ **to do** prendre la peine de faire; ~**s** *npl* (POL *etc*) troubles *mpl*; (*personal*) ennuis, soucis; **to be in** ~ avoir des ennuis; (*ship, climber etc*) être en difficulté; **what's the** ~? qu'est-ce qui ne va pas?; ~**d** *adj* (*person*) inquiet(ète); (*epoch, life*) agité(e); ~**maker** *n* élément perturbateur, fauteur *m* de troubles; ~**shooter** *n* (*in conflict*) médiateur *m*; ~**some** *adj* (*child*) fatigant(e), difficile; (*cough etc*) gênant(e)

trough [trɔf] *n* (*also*: *drinking* ~) abreuvoir *m*; (: *feeding* ~) auge *f*; (*depression*) creux *m*

trousers ['traʊzəz] *npl* pantalon *m*; **short** ~ culottes courtes

trout [traʊt] *n inv* truite *f*

trowel ['traʊəl] *n* truelle *f*; (*garden tool*) déplantoir *m*

truant ['truənt] (BRIT) *n*: **to play** ~ faire l'école buissonnière

truce [tru:s] *n* trêve *f*

truck [trʌk] *n* camion *m*; (RAIL) wagon *m* à plate-forme; ~ **driver** *n* camionneur *m*; ~ **farm** (US) *n* jardin maraîcher

trudge [trʌdʒ] *vi* marcher lourdement, se traîner

true [tru:] *adj* vrai(e); (*accurate*) exact(e); (*genuine*) vrai, véritable; (*faithful*) fidèle; **to come** ~ se réaliser

truffle ['trʌfl] *n* truffe *f*

truly ['tru:lɪ] *adv* vraiment, réellement; (*truthfully*) sans mentir; *see also* **yours**

trump [trʌmp] *n* (*also*: ~ *card*) atout *m*; ~**ed up** *adj* inventé(e) (de toutes pièces)

trumpet ['trʌmpɪt] *n* trompette *f*

truncheon ['trʌntʃən] (BRIT) *n* bâton *m* (d'agent de police); matraque *f*

trundle ['trʌndl] *vt*, *vi*: **to** ~ **along** rouler lentement et bruyamment

trunk [trʌŋk] *n* (*of tree, person*) tronc *m*; (*of elephant*) trompe *f*; (*case*) malle *f*; (US:

AUT) coffre *m*; ~**s** *npl* (*also*: *swimming* ~**s**) maillot *m or* slip *m* de bain

truss [trʌs] *n* (MED) bandage *m* herniaire ♦ *vt*: **to** ~ (**up**) (CULIN) brider, trousser

trust [trʌst] *n* confiance *f*; (*responsibility*) charge *f*; (LAW) fidéicommis *m* ♦ *vt* (*rely on*) avoir confiance en; (*hope*) espérer; (*entrust*): **to** ~ **sth to sb** confier qch à qn; **to take sth on** ~ accepter qch les yeux fermés; ~**ed** *adj* en qui l'on a confiance; ~**ee** *n* (LAW) fidéicommissaire *m/f*; (*of school etc*) administrateur(trice); ~**ful**, ~**ing** *adj* confiant(e); ~**worthy** *adj* digne de confiance

truth [tru:θ, *pl* tru:ðz] *n* vérité *f*; ~**ful** *adj* (*person*) qui dit la vérité; (*answer*) sincère

try [traɪ] *n* essai *m*, tentative *f*; (RUGBY) essai ♦ *vt* (*attempt*) essayer, tenter; (*test: sth new: also*: ~ *out*) essayer, tester; (LAW: *person*) juger; (*strain*) éprouver ♦ *vi* essayer; **to have a** ~ essayer; **to** ~ **to do** essayer de faire; (*seek*) chercher à faire; ~ **on** *vt* (*clothes*) essayer; ~**ing** *adj* pénible

T-shirt ['ti:ʃɜ:t] *n* tee-shirt *m*

T-square ['ti:skwɛə*] *n* équerre *f* en T, té *m*

tub [tʌb] *n* cuve *f*; (*for washing clothes*) baquet *m*; (*bath*) baignoire *f*

tubby ['tʌbɪ] *adj* rondelet(te)

tube [tju:b] *n* tube *m*; (BRIT: *underground*) métro *m*; (*for tyre*) chambre *f* à air

TUC *n abbr* (BRIT: = *Trades Union Congress*) confédération *f* des syndicats britanniques

tuck [tʌk] *vt* (*put*) mettre; ~ **away** *vt* cacher, ranger; ~ **in** *vt* rentrer; (*child*) border ♦ *vi* (*eat*) manger (de bon appétit); ~ **up** *vt* (*child*) border; ~ **shop** (BRIT) *n* boutique *f* à provisions (*dans une école*)

Tuesday ['tju:zdeɪ] *n* mardi *m*

tuft [tʌft] *n* touffe *f*

tug [tʌg] *n* (*ship*) remorqueur *m* ♦ *vt* tirer (sur); ~**-of-war** *n* lutte *f* à la corde; (*fig*) lutte acharnée

tuition [tju:'ɪʃən] *n* (BRIT) leçons *fpl*; (: *private*) cours particuliers; (US: *school fees*) frais *mpl* de scolarité

tulip ['tju:lɪp] *n* tulipe *f*

tumble ['tʌmbl] *n* (*fall*) chute *f*, culbute *f* ♦ *vi* tomber, dégringoler; **to** ~ **to sth** (*inf*) réaliser qch; ~**down** *adj* délabré(e); ~ **dryer** (BRIT) *n* séchoir *m* à air chaud

tumbler ['tʌmblə*] *n* (*glass*) verre (droit), gobelet *m*

tummy ['tʌmɪ] (*inf*) *n* ventre *m*

tumour ['tju:mə*] (US **tumor**) *n* tumeur *f*

tuna ['tju:nə] *n inv* (*also*: ~ *fish*) thon *m*

tune [tju:n] *n* (*melody*) air *m* ♦ *vt* (MUS) accorder; (RADIO, TV, AUT) régler; **to be in/out of** ~ (*instrument*) être accordé/désaccordé; (*singer*) chanter juste/faux; **to be in/out of** ~ **with** (*fig*) être en accord/

désaccord avec; ~ **in** *vi* (*RADIO, TV*): **to ~ in (to)** se mettre à l'écoute (de); ~ **up** *vi* (*musician*) accorder son instrument; ~**ful** *adj* mélodieux(euse); ~**r** *n*: **piano ~r** accordeur *m* (de pianos)

tunic ['tju:nɪk] *n* tunique *f*

Tunisia [tju:'nɪzɪə] *n* Tunisie *f*

tunnel ['tʌnl] *n* tunnel *m*; (*in mine*) galerie *f* ♦ *vi* percer un tunnel

turbulence ['tɜ:bjʊləns] *n* (*AVIAT*) turbulence *f*

tureen [tju:ri:n] *n* (*for soup*) soupière *f*; (*for vegetables*) légumier *m*

turf [tɜ:f] *n* gazon *m*; (*clod*) motte *f* (de gazon) ♦ *vt* gazonner; ~ **out** (*inf*) *vt* (*person*) jeter dehors

turgid ['tɜ:dʒɪd] *adj* (*speech*) pompeux(euse)

Turk [tɜ:k] *n* Turc(Turque) *m(f)*

Turkey ['tɜ:kɪ] *n* Turquie *f*

turkey ['tɜ:kɪ] *n* dindon *m*, dinde *f*

Turkish ['tɜ:kɪʃ] *adj* turc(turque) ♦ *n* (*LING*) turc *m*

turmoil ['tɜ:mɔɪl] *n* trouble *m*, bouleversement *m*; **in ~** en émoi, en effervescence

turn [tɜ:n] *n* tour *m*; (*in road*) tournant *m*; (*of mind, events*) tournure *f*, (*performance*) numéro *m*; (*MED*) crise *f*, attaque *f* ♦ *vt* tourner; (*collar, steak*) retourner; (*change*): **to ~ sth into** changer qch en ♦ *vi* (*object, wind, milk*) tourner; (*person: look back*) se (re)tourner; (*reverse direction*) faire demi-tour; (*become*) devenir; (*age*) atteindre; **to ~ into** se changer en; **a good ~** un service; **it gave me quite a ~** ça m'a fait un coup; **"no left ~"** (*AUT*) "défense de tourner à gauche"; **it's your ~** c'est (à) votre tour; **in ~** à son tour; à tour de rôle; **to take ~s (at)** se relayer (pour *or* à); ~ **away** *vi* se détourner ♦ *vt* (*applicants*) refuser; ~ **back** *vi* revenir, faire demi-tour ♦ *vt* (*person, vehicle*) faire faire demi-tour à; (*clock*) reculer; ~ **down** *vt* (*refuse*) rejeter, refuser; (*reduce*) baisser; (*fold*) rabattre; ~ **in** *vi* (*inf: go to bed*) aller se coucher ♦ *vt* (*fold*) rentrer; ~ **off** *vi* (*from road*) tourner ♦ *vt* (*light, radio etc*) éteindre; (*tap*) fermer; (*engine*) arrêter; ~ **on** *vt* (*light, radio etc*) allumer; (*tap*) ouvrir; (*engine*) mettre en marche; ~ **out** *vt* (*light, gas*) éteindre; (*produce*) produire ♦ *vi* (*voters, troops etc*) se présenter; **to ~ out to be ...** s'avérer ..., se révéler ...; ~ **over** *vi* (*person*) se retourner ♦ *vt* (*object*) retourner; (*page*) tourner; ~ **round** *vi* faire demi-tour, (*rotate*) tourner; ~ **up** *vi* (*person*) arriver, se pointer (*inf*); (*lost object*) être retrouvé(e) ♦ *vt* (*collar*) remonter; (*radio, heater*) mettre plus fort; ~**ing** *n* (*in road*) tournant *m*; ~**ing point** *n* (*fig*) tournant *m*, moment décisif

turnip ['tɜ:nɪp] *n* navet *m*

turnout ['tɜ:naʊt] *n* (*of voters*) taux *m* de participation

turnover ['tɜ:nəʊvə*] *n* (*COMM: amount of money*) chiffre *m* d'affaires; (: *of goods*) roulement *m*; (*of staff*) renouvellement *m*, changement *m*

turnpike ['tɜ:npaɪk] (*US*) *n* autoroute *f* à péage

turnstile ['tɜ:nstaɪl] *n* tourniquet *m* (*d'entrée*)

turntable ['tɜ:nteɪbl] *n* (*on record player*) platine *f*

turn-up ['tɜ:nʌp] (*BRIT*) *n* (*on trousers*) revers *m*

turpentine ['tɜ:pəntaɪn] *n* (*also: turps*) (*essence f de*) térébenthine *f*

turquoise ['tɜ:kwɔɪz] *n* (*stone*) turquoise *f* ♦ *adj* turquoise *inv*

turret ['tʌrɪt] *n* tourelle *f*

turtle ['tɜ:tl] *n* tortue marine *or* d'eau douce; ~**neck (sweater)** *n* (*BRIT*) pullover *m* à col montant; (*US*) pullover à col roulé

tusk [tʌsk] *n* défense *f*

tussle ['tʌsl] *n* bagarre *f*, mêlée *f*

tutor ['tju:tə*] *n* (*in college*) directeur(trice) d'études; (*private teacher*) précepteur(trice); ~**ial** [tju:'tɔ:rɪəl] *n* (*SCOL*) (séance *f* de) travaux *mpl* pratiques

tuxedo [tʌk'si:dəʊ] (*US*) *n* smoking *m*

TV ['ti:'vi:] *n abbr* (= *television*) télé *f*

twang [twæŋ] *n* (*of instrument*) son vibrant; (*of voice*) ton nasillard

tweed [twi:d] *n* tweed *m*

tweezers ['twi:zəz] *npl* pince *f* à épiler

twelfth [twelfθ] *num* douzième

twelve [twelv] *num* douze; **at ~ (o'clock)** à midi; (*midnight*) à minuit

twentieth ['twentɪθ] *num* vingtième

twenty ['twentɪ] *num* vingt

twice [twaɪs] *adv* deux fois; ~ **as much** deux fois plus

twiddle ['twɪdl] *vt, vi*: **to ~ (with) sth** tripoter qch; **to ~ one's thumbs** (*fig*) se tourner les pouces

twig [twɪg] *n* brindille *f* ♦ *vi* (*inf*) piger

twilight ['twaɪlaɪt] *n* crépuscule *m*

twin [twɪn] *adj, n* jumeau(elle) ♦ *vt* jumeler; ~**(-bedded) room** *n* chambre *f* à deux lits

twine [twaɪn] *n* ficelle *f* ♦ *vi* (*plant*) s'enrouler

twinge [twɪndʒ] *n* (*of pain*) élancement *m*; **a ~ of conscience** un certain remords; **a ~ of regret** un pincement au cœur

twinkle ['twɪŋkl] *vi* scintiller; (*eyes*) pétiller

twirl [twɜ:l] *vt* faire tournoyer ♦ *vi* tournoyer

twist [twɪst] *n* torsion *f*, tour *m*; (*in road*) virage *m*; (*in wire, flex*) tortillon *m*; (*in story*) coup *m* de théâtre ♦ *vt* tordre; (*weave*) entortiller; (*roll around*) enrouler; (*fig*) déformer ♦ *vi* (*road, river*) serpenter

twit [twɪt] (*inf*) *n* crétin(e)

twitch [twɪtʃ] *n* (*pull*) coup sec, saccade *f*;

(*nervous*) tic *m* ♦ *vi* se convulser; avoir un tic

two [tuː] *num* deux; **to put ~ and ~ together** (*fig*) faire le rapprochement; **~-door** *adj* (*AUT*) à deux portes; **~-faced** (*pej*) *adj* (*person*) faux(fausse); '**~fold** *adv*: **to increase ~fold** doubler; **~-piece (suit)** *n* (*man's*) costume *m* (deux-pièces); (*woman's*) (tailleur *m*) deux-pièces *m inv*; **~-piece (swimsuit)** *n* (maillot *m* de bain) deux-pièces *m inv*; **~some** *n* (*people*) couple *m*; **~-way** *adj* (*traffic*) dans les deux sens

tycoon [taɪˈkuːn] *n*: (**business**) **~** gros homme d'affaires

type [taɪp] *n* (*category*) type *m*, genre *m*, espèce *f*; (*model, example*) type *m*, modèle *m*; (*TYP*) type, caractère *m* ♦ *vt* (*letter etc*) taper (à la machine); **~-cast** *adj* (*actor*) condamné(e) à toujours jouer le même rôle; **~face** *n* (*TYP*) œil *m* de caractère; **~script** *n* texte dactylographié; **~writer** *n* machine *f* à écrire; **~written** *adj* dactylographié(e)

typhoid [ˈtaɪfɔɪd] *n* typhoïde *f*

typical [ˈtɪpɪkəl] *adj* typique, caractéristique

typing [ˈtaɪpɪŋ] *n* dactylo(graphie) *f*

typist [ˈtaɪpɪst] *n* dactylo *m/f*

tyrant [ˈtaɪərnt] *n* tyran *m*

tyre [taɪə*] (*US* **tire**) *n* pneu *m*; **~ pressure** *n* pression *f* (de gonflage)

U u

U-bend [ˈjuːˈbend] *n* (*in pipe*) coude *m*

ubiquitous *adj* omniprésent(e)

udder [ˈʌdə*] *n* pis *m*, mamelle *f*

UFO [ˈjuːfəu] *n abbr* (= *unidentified flying object*) ovni *m*

Uganda [juːˈgændə] *n* Ouganda *m*

ugh [ɜːh] *excl* pouah!

ugly [ˈʌglɪ] *adj* laid(e), vilain(e); (*situation*) inquiétant(e)

UK *n abbr* = **United Kingdom**

ulcer [ˈʌlsə*] *n* ulcère *m*; (*also:* mouth ~) aphte *f*

Ulster [ˈʌlstə*] *n* Ulster *m*; (*inf: Northern Ireland*) Irlande *f* du Nord

ulterior [ʌlˈtɪərɪə*] *adj*: **~ motive** arrière-pensée *f*

ultimate [ˈʌltɪmət] *adj* ultime, final(e); (*authority*) suprême; **~ly** *adv* en fin de compte; finalement

ultrasound [ˈʌltrəˈsaund] *n* ultrason *m*

umbilical cord [ʌmˈbɪlɪkl-] *n* cordon ombilical

umbrella [ʌmˈbrelə] *n* parapluie *m*; (*for sun*) parasol *m*

umpire [ˈʌmpaɪə*] *n* arbitre *m*; (*TENNIS*) juge *m* de chaise

umpteen [ˈʌmptiːn] *adj* je ne sais combien de; **~th** *adj*: **for the ~th time** pour la nième fois

UN *n abbr* = **United Nations**

unable [ˈʌnˈeɪbl] *adj*: **to be ~ to** ne pas pouvoir, être dans l'impossibilité de; (*incapable*) être incapable de

unaccompanied [ˈʌnəˈkʌmpənɪd] *adj* (*child, lady*) non accompagné(e); (*song*) sans accompagnement

unaccountably [ˈʌnəˈkauntəblɪ] *adv* inexplicablement

unaccustomed [ˈʌnəˈkʌstəmd] *adj*: **to be ~ to sth** ne pas avoir l'habitude de qch

unanimous [juːˈnænɪməs] *adj* unanime; **~ly** *adv* à l'unanimité

unarmed [ʌnˈɑːmd] *adj* (*without a weapon*) non armé(e); (*combat*) sans armes

unashamed [ʌnəˈʃeɪmd] *adj* effronté(e), impudent(e)

unassuming [ʌnəˈsjuːmɪŋ] *adj* modeste, sans prétentions

unattached [ˈʌnəˈtætʃt] *adj* libre, sans attaches; (*part*) non attaché(e), indépendant(e)

unattended [ˈʌnəˈtendɪd] *adj* (*car, child, luggage*) sans surveillance

unattractive [ʌnəˈtræktɪv] *adj* peu attrayant(e); (*character*) peu sympathique

unauthorized [ˈʌnˈɔːθəraɪzd] *adj* non autorisé(e), sans autorisation

unavoidable [ʌnəˈvɔɪdəbl] *adj* inévitable

unaware [ʌnəˈwɛə*] *adj*: **to be ~ of** ignorer, être inconscient(e) de; **~s** *adv* à l'improviste, au dépourvu

unbalanced [ˈʌnˈbælənst] *adj* déséquilibré(e); (*report*) peu objectif(ive)

unbearable [ʌnˈbɛərəbl] *adj* insupportable

unbeatable [ʌnˈbiːtəbl] *adj* imbattable

unbeknown(st) [ˈʌnbɪˈnəun(st)] *adv*: **~ to me/Peter** à mon insu/l'insu de Peter

unbelievable [ʌnbɪˈliːvəbl] *adj* incroyable

unbend [ˈʌnˈbend] (*irreg*) *vi* se détendre ♦ *vt* (*wire*) redresser, détordre

unbiased [ʌnˈbaɪəst] *adj* impartial(e)

unborn [ʌnˈbɔːn] *adj* à naître, qui n'est pas encore né(e)

unbreakable [ˈʌnˈbreɪkəbl] *adj* incassable

unbroken [ˈʌnˈbrəukən] *adj* intact(e); (*fig*) continu(e), ininterrompu(e)

unbutton [ˈʌnˈbʌtn] *vt* déboutonner

uncalled-for [ʌnˈkɔːldfɔː*] *adj* déplacé(e), injustifié(e)

uncanny [ʌnˈkænɪ] *adj* étrange, troublant(e)

unceasing [ʌnˈsiːsɪŋ] *adj* incessant(e), continu(e)

unceremonious [ˈʌnserɪˈməʊnɪəs] adj (abrupt, rude) brusque

uncertain [ʌnˈsɜːtn] adj incertain(e); (hesitant) hésitant(e); **in no ~ terms** sans équivoque possible; **~ty** n incertitude f, doute(s) m(pl)

unchecked [ˈʌnˈtʃekt] adv sans contrôle or opposition

uncivilized [ˈʌnˈsɪvɪlaɪzd] adj (gen) non civilisé(e); (fig: behaviour etc) barbare; (hour) indu(e)

uncle [ˈʌŋkl] n oncle m

uncomfortable [ʌnˈkʌmfətəbl] adj inconfortable, peu confortable; (uneasy) mal à l'aise, gêné(e); (situation) désagréable

uncommon [ʌnˈkɔmən] adj rare, singulier(ère), peu commun(e)

uncompromising [ʌnˈkɔmprəmaɪzɪŋ] adj intransigeant(e), inflexible

unconcerned [ʌnkənˈsɜːnd] adj: **to be ~ (about)** ne pas s'inquiéter (de)

unconditional [ˈʌnkənˈdɪʃənl] adj sans conditions

unconscious [ʌnˈkɔnʃəs] adj sans connaissance, évanoui(e); (unaware): **~ of** inconscient(e) de ♦ n: **the ~** l'inconscient m; **~ly** adv inconsciemment

uncontrollable [ˈʌnkənˈtrəʊləbl] adj indiscipliné(e); (temper, laughter) irrépressible

unconventional [ʌnkənˈvenʃənl] adj peu conventionnel(le)

uncouth [ʌnˈkuːθ] adj grossier(ère), fruste

uncover [ʌnˈkʌvə*] vt découvrir

undecided [ˈʌndɪˈsaɪdd] adj indécis(e), irrésolu(e)

under [ˈʌndə*] prep sous; (less than) (de) moins de; au-dessous de; (according to) selon, en vertu de ♦ adv au-dessous; en dessous; **~ there** là-dessous; **~ repair** en (cours de) réparation

under: **~age** adj (person) qui n'a pas l'âge réglementaire; **~carriage** n (BRIT: railway) train m d'atterrissage; **~charge** vt ne pas faire payer assez à; **~coat** n (paint) couche f de fond; **~cover** adj secret(ète), clandestin(e); **~current** n courant or sentiment sous-jacent; **~cut** (irreg) vt vendre moins cher que; **~dog** n opprimé m; **~done** adj (CULIN) saignant(e); (pej) pas assez cuit(e); **~estimate** vt sous-estimer; **~fed** adj sous-alimenté(e); **~foot** adv sous les pieds; **~go** (irreg) vt subir; (treatment) suivre; **~graduate** n étudiant(e) (qui prépare la licence); **~ground** n (BRIT: railway) métro m; (POL) clandestinité f ♦ adj souterrain(e); (fig) clandestin(e) ♦ adv dans la clandestinité, clandestinement; **~growth** n broussailles fpl, sous-bois m; **~hand(ed)** adj (fig: behaviour, method etc) en dessous; **~lie** (irreg) vt être à la base de; **~line** vt souligner; **~ling** (pej) n sous-fifre m, subalterne m; **~mine** vt saper, miner; **~neath** [ˈʌndəˈniːθ] adv (en) dessous ♦ prep sous, au-dessous de; **~paid** adj sous-payé(e); **~pants** npl caleçon m, slip m; **~pass** (BRIT) n passage souterrain; (on motorway) passage inférieur; **~privileged** [ˈʌndəˈprɪvɪlɪdʒd] adj défavorisé(e), économiquement faible; **~rate** vt sous-estimer; **~shirt** (US) n tricot m de corps; **~shorts** (US) npl caleçon m, slip m; **~side** n dessous m; **~skirt** (BRIT) n jupon m

understand [ʌndəˈstænd] (irreg: like stand) vt, vi comprendre; **I ~ that ...** je me suis laissé dire que ...; je crois comprendre que ...; **~able** adj compréhensible; **~ing** adj compréhensif(ive) ♦ n compréhension f; (agreement) accord m

understatement [ˈʌndəsteɪtmənt] n: **that's an ~** c'est (bien) peu dire, le terme est faible

understood [ʌndəˈstʊd] pt, pp of **understand** ♦ adj entendu(e); (implied) sous-entendu(e)

understudy [ˈʌndəstʌdɪ] n doublure f

undertake [ʌndəˈteɪk] (irreg) vt entreprendre; se charger de; **to ~ to do sth** s'engager à faire qch

undertaker [ˈʌndəteɪkə*] n entrepreneur m des pompes funèbres, croque-mort m

undertaking [ʌndəˈteɪkɪŋ] n entreprise f; (promise) promesse f

undertone [ˈʌndətəʊn] n: **in an ~** à mi-voix

under: **~water** [ˈʌndəˈwɔːtə*] adv sous l'eau ♦ adj sous-marin(e); **~wear** [ˈʌndəweə*] n sous-vêtements mpl; (women's only) sous-vêtements mpl; **~world** [ˈʌndəwɜːld] n (of crime) milieu m, pègre f; **~writer** [ˈʌndəraɪtə*] n (INSURANCE) assureur m

undies [ˈʌndɪz] (inf) npl dessous mpl, lingerie f

undiplomatic [ʌndɪpləˈmætɪk] adj peu diplomatique

undo [ˈʌnˈduː] (irreg) vt défaire; **~ing** n ruine f, perte f

undoubted [ʌnˈdaʊtɪd] adj indubitable, certain(e); **~ly** adv sans aucun doute

undress [ˈʌnˈdres] vi se déshabiller

undue [ˈʌndjuː] adj indu(e), excessif(ive)

undulating [ˈʌndjʊleɪtɪŋ] adj ondoyant(e), onduleux(euse)

unduly [ʌnˈdjuːlɪ] adv trop, excessivement

unearth [ʌnˈɜːθ] vt déterrer; (fig) dénicher

unearthly [ʌnˈɜːθlɪ] adj (hour) indu(e), impossible

uneasy [ʌnˈiːzɪ] adj mal à l'aise, gêné(e); (worried) inquiet(ète); (feeling) désagréable; (peace, truce) fragile

uneconomic(al) [ʌniːkəˈnɔmɪk(l)] adj peu économique

uneducated [ʌnˈedjukeɪtɪd] adj (person) sans instruction

unemployed [ˈʌnɪmˈplɔɪd] *adj* sans travail, en *or* au chômage ♦ *n*: **the ~** les chômeurs *mpl*; **unemployment** [ˈʌnɪmˈplɔɪmənt] *n* chômage *m*

unending [ʌnˈendɪŋ] *adj* interminable, sans fin

unerring [ˈʌnˈɜːrɪŋ] *adj* infaillible, sûr(e)

uneven [ˈʌnˈiːvən] *adj* inégal(e); irrégulier(ère)

unexpected [ʌnɪkˈspektɪd] *adj* inattendu(e), imprévu(e); **~ly** *adv* (*arrive*) à l'improviste; (*succeed*) contre toute attente

unfailing [ʌnˈfeɪlɪŋ] *adj* inépuisable; infaillible

unfair [ˈʌnˈfɛə*] *adj*: **~ (to)** injuste (envers)

unfaithful [ˈʌnˈfeɪθful] *adj* infidèle

unfamiliar [ʌnfəˈmɪliə*] *adj* étrange, inconnu(e); **to be ~ with** mal connaître

unfashionable [ˈʌnˈfæʃnəbl] *adj* (*clothes*) démodé(e); (*place*) peu chic *inv*

unfasten [ˈʌnˈfɑːsn] *vt* défaire; détacher; (*open*) ouvrir

unfavourable [ˈʌnˈfeɪvərəbl] (*US* **unfavorable**) *adj* défavorable

unfeeling [ʌnˈfiːlɪŋ] *adj* insensible, dur(e)

unfinished [ʌnˈfɪnɪʃt] *adj* inachevé(e)

unfit [ˈʌnˈfɪt] *adj* en mauvaise santé; pas en forme; (*incompetent*): **~ (for)** impropre (à); (*work, service*) inapte (à)

unfold [ʌnˈfəʊld] *vt* déplier ♦ *vi* se dérouler

unforeseen [ˈʌnfɔːˈsiːn] *adj* imprévu(e)

unforgettable [ʌnfəˈgetəbl] *adj* inoubliable

unfortunate [ʌnˈfɔːtʃnət] *adj* malheureux(euse); (*event, remark*) malencontreux(euse); **~ly** *adv* malheureusement

unfounded [ˈʌnˈfaʊndɪd] *adj* sans fondement

unfriendly [ʌnˈfrendlɪ] *adj* inamical(e), peu aimable

ungainly [ʌnˈgeɪnlɪ] *adj* gauche, dégingandé(e)

ungodly [ʌnˈgɒdlɪ] *adj* (*hour*) indu(e)

ungrateful [ʌnˈgreɪtful] *adj* ingrat(e)

unhappiness [ʌnˈhæpɪnəs] *n* tristesse *f*, peine *f*

unhappy [ʌnˈhæpɪ] *adj* triste, malheureux(euse); **~ about** *or* **with** (*arrangements etc*) mécontent(e) de, peu satisfait(e) de

unharmed [ˈʌnˈhɑːmd] *adj* indemne, sain(e) et sauf(sauve)

unhealthy [ʌnˈhelθɪ] *adj* malsain(e); (*person*) maladif(ive)

unheard-of [ʌnˈhɜːdɒv] *adj* inouï(e), sans précédent

unhurt [ʌnˈhɜːt] *adj* indemne

unidentified [ʌnaɪˈdentɪfaɪd] *adj* non identifié(e); *see also* **UFO**

uniform [ˈjuːnɪfɔːm] *n* uniforme *m* ♦ *adj* uniforme

uninhabited [ʌnɪnˈhæbɪtɪd] *adj* inhabité(e)

unintentional [ʌnɪnˈtenʃənəl] *adj* involontaire

union [ˈjuːnjən] *n* union *f*; (*also:* **trade ~**) syndicat *m* ♦ *cpd* du syndicat, syndical(e); **U~ Jack** *n* drapeau du Royaume-Uni

unique [juːˈniːk] *adj* unique

unison [ˈjuːnɪsn] *n*: **in ~** (*sing*) à l'unisson; (*say*) en chœur

unit [ˈjuːnɪt] *n* unité *f*; (*section: of furniture etc*) élément *m*, bloc *m*; **kitchen ~** élément de cuisine

unite [juːˈnaɪt] *vt* unir ♦ *vi* s'unir; **~d** *adj* uni(e); unifié(e); (*effort*) conjugué(e); **U~d Kingdom** *n* Royaume-Uni *m*; **U~d Nations (Organization)** *n* (Organisation *f* des) Nations unies; **U~d States (of America)** *n* États-Unis *mpl*

unit trust (*BRIT*) *n* fonds commun de placement

unity [ˈjuːnɪtɪ] *n* unité *f*

universal [juːnɪˈvɜːsəl] *adj* universel(le)

universe [ˈjuːnɪvɜːs] *n* univers *m*

university [juːnɪˈvɜːsɪtɪ] *n* université *f*

unjust [ˈʌnˈdʒʌst] *adj* injuste

unkempt [ʌnˈkempt] *adj* négligé(e), débraillé(e); (*hair*) mal peigné(e)

unkind [ʌnˈkaɪnd] *adj* peu gentil(le), méchant(e)

unknown [ˈʌnˈnəʊn] *adj* inconnu(e)

unlawful [ʌnˈlɔːful] *adj* illégal(e)

unleaded [ʌnˈledɪd] *adj* (*petrol, fuel*) sans plomb

unleash [ˈʌnˈliːʃ] *vt* (*fig*) déchaîner, déclencher

unless [ənˈles] *conj*: **~ he leaves** à moins qu'il ne parte

unlike [ˈʌnˈlaɪk] *adj* dissemblable, différent(e) ♦ *prep* contrairement à

unlikely [ʌnˈlaɪklɪ] *adj* improbable; invraisemblable

unlimited [ʌnˈlɪmɪtɪd] *adj* illimité(e)

unlisted [ʌnˈlɪstɪd] (*US*) *adj* (*TEL*) sur la liste rouge

unload [ˈʌnˈləʊd] *vt* décharger

unlock [ˈʌnˈlɒk] *vt* ouvrir

unlucky [ʌnˈlʌkɪ] *adj* (*person*) malchanceux(euse); (*object, number*) qui porte malheur; **to be ~** (*person*) ne pas avoir de chance

unmarried [ˈʌnˈmærɪd] *adj* célibataire

unmistak(e)able [ʌnmɪsˈteɪkəbl] *adj* indubitable; qu'on ne peut pas ne pas reconnaître

unmitigated [ʌnˈmɪtɪgeɪtɪd] *adj* non mitigé(e), absolu(e), pur(e)

unnatural [ʌnˈnætʃrəl] *adj* non naturel(le); (*habit*) contre nature

unnecessary [ˈʌnˈnesəsərɪ] *adj* inutile, superflu(e)

unnoticed [ʌnˈnəʊtɪst] *adj*: **(to go** *or* **pass) ~** (passer) inaperçu(e)

UNO [ˈjuːnəʊ] *n abbr* = **United Nations Organization**

unobtainable [ˈʌnəbˈteɪnəbl] *adj* impossible à obtenir

unobtrusive [ʌnəb'truːsɪv] *adj* discret(ète)

unofficial [ʌnə'fɪʃl] *adj* (*news*) officieux(euse); (*strike*) sauvage

unorthodox [ʌn'ɔːθədɔks] *adj* peu orthodoxe; (*REL*) hétérodoxe

unpack ['ʌn'pæk] *vi* défaire sa valise ♦ *vt* (*suitcase*) défaire; (*belongings*) déballer

unpalatable [ʌn'pælətəbl] *adj* (*meal*) mauvais(e); (*truth*) désagréable (à entendre)

unparalleled [ʌn'pærəleld] *adj* incomparable, sans égal

unpleasant [ʌn'pleznt] *adj* déplaisant(e), désagréable

unplug ['ʌn'plʌg] *vt* débrancher

unpopular [ʌn'pɔpjʊlə*] *adj* impopulaire

unprecedented [ʌn'presɪdəntɪd] *adj* sans précédent

unpredictable [ʌnprɪ'dɪktəbl] *adj* imprévisible

unprofessional [ʌnprə'feʃənl] *adj*: ~ **conduct** manquement *m* aux devoirs de la profession

unqualified ['ʌn'kwɒlɪfaɪd] *adj* (*teacher*) non diplômé(e), sans titres; (*success, disaster*) sans réserve, total(e)

unquestionably [ʌn'kwestʃənəblɪ] *adv* incontestablement

unravel [ʌn'rævəl] *vt* démêler

unreal ['ʌn'rɪəl] *adj* irréel(le); (*extraordinary*) incroyable; ~**istic** [ʌnrɪə'lɪstɪk] *adj* irréaliste; peu réaliste

unreasonable [ʌn'riːznəbl] *adj* qui n'est pas raisonnable

unrelated [ʌnrɪ'leɪtɪd] *adj* sans rapport; sans lien de parenté

unrelenting [ʌnrɪ'lentɪŋ] *adj* implacable

unreliable [ʌnrɪ'laɪəbl] *adj* sur qui (*or* quoi) on ne peut pas compter, peu fiable

unremitting [ʌnrɪ'mɪtɪŋ] *adj* inlassable, infatigable, acharné(e)

unreservedly [ʌnrɪ'zɜːvɪdlɪ] *adv* sans réserve

unrest [ʌn'rest] *n* agitation *f*, troubles *mpl*

unroll ['ʌn'rəʊl] *vt* dérouler

unruly [ʌn'ruːlɪ] *adj* indiscipliné(e)

unsafe ['ʌn'seɪf] *adj* (*in danger*) en danger; (*journey, car*) dangereux(euse)

unsaid ['ʌn'sed] *adj*: **to leave sth** ~ passer qch sous silence

unsatisfactory ['ʌnsætɪs'fæktərɪ] *adj* peu satisfaisant(e)

unsavoury ['ʌn'seɪvərɪ] (*US* **unsavory**) *adj* (*fig*) peu recommandable

unscathed [ʌn'skeɪðd] *adj* indemne

unscrew ['ʌn'skruː] *vt* dévisser

unscrupulous [ʌn'skruːpjʊləs] *adj* sans scrupules

unsettled ['ʌn'setld] *adj* perturbé(e); instable

unshaven ['ʌn'ʃeɪvn] *adj* non *or* mal rasé(e)

unsightly [ʌn'saɪtlɪ] *adj* disgracieux(euse), laid(e)

unskilled ['ʌn'skɪld] *adj*: ~ **worker** manœuvre *m*

unspeakable [ʌn'spiːkəbl] *adj* indicible; (*awful*) innommable

unstable [ʌn'steɪbl] *adj* instable

unsteady [ʌn'stedɪ] *adj* mal assuré(e), chancelant(e), instable

unstuck ['ʌn'stʌk] *adj*: **to come** ~ se décoller; (*plan*) tomber à l'eau

unsuccessful ['ʌnsək'sesful] *adj* (*attempt*) infructueux(euse), vain(e); (*writer, proposal*) qui n'a pas de succès; **to be** ~ (*in attempting sth*) ne pas réussir; ne pas avoir de succès; (*application*) ne pas être retenu(e)

unsuitable ['ʌn'suːtəbl] *adj* qui ne convient pas, peu approprié(e); inopportun(e)

unsure [ʌn'ʃʊə*] *adj* pas sûr(e); **to be** ~ **of o.s.** manquer de confiance en soi

unsuspecting [ʌnsə'spektɪŋ] *adj* qui ne se doute de rien

unsympathetic ['ʌnsɪmpə'θetɪk] *adj* (*person*) antipathique; (*attitude*) peu compatissant(e)

untapped ['ʌn'tæpt] *adj* (*resources*) inexploité(e)

unthinkable [ʌn'θɪŋkəbl] *adj* impensable, inconcevable

untidy [ʌn'taɪdɪ] *adj* (*room*) en désordre; (*appearance, person*) débraillé(e); (*person: in character*) sans ordre, désordonné

untie ['ʌn'taɪ] *vt* (*knot, parcel*) défaire; (*prisoner, dog*) détacher

until [ən'tɪl] *prep* jusqu'à; (*after negative*) avant ♦ *conj* jusqu'à ce que +*sub*; (*in past, after negative*) avant que +*sub*; ~ **he comes** jusqu'à ce qu'il vienne, jusqu'à son arrivée; ~ **now** jusqu'à présent, jusqu'ici; ~ **then** jusque-là

untimely [ʌn'taɪmlɪ] *adj* inopportun(e); (*death*) prématuré(e)

untold ['ʌn'təʊld] *adj* (*story*) jamais raconté(e); (*wealth*) incalculable; (*joy, suffering*) indescriptible

untoward [ʌntə'wɔːd] *adj* fâcheux(euse), malencontreux(euse)

unused¹ [ʌn'juːzd] *adj* (*clothes*) neuf(neuve)

unused² [ʌn'juːst] *adj*: **to be unused to sth/to doing sth** ne pas avoir l'habitude de qch/de faire qch

unusual [ʌn'juːʒʊəl] *adj* insolite, exceptionnel(le), rare

unveil [ʌn'veɪl] *vt* dévoiler

unwanted [ʌn'wɔntɪd] *adj* (*child, pregnancy*) non désiré(e); (*clothes etc*) à donner

unwelcome [ʌn'welkəm] *adj* importun(e); (*news*) fâcheux(euse)

unwell ['ʌn'wel] *adj* souffrant(e); **to feel** ~ ne pas se sentir bien

unwieldy [ʌn'wiːldɪ] *adj* (*object*) difficile à

manier; *(system)* lourd(e)

unwilling ['ʌn'wɪlɪŋ] *adj:* **to be ~ to do** ne pas vouloir faire; **~ly** *adv* à contrecœur, contre son gré

unwind ['ʌn'waɪnd] *(irreg)* vt dérouler ♦ vi *(relax)* se détendre

unwise [ʌn'waɪz] *adj* irréfléchi(e), imprudent(e)

unwitting [ʌn'wɪtɪŋ] *adj* involontaire

unworkable [ʌn'wɜːkəbl] *adj (plan)* impraticable

unworthy [ʌn'wɜːðɪ] *adj* indigne

unwrap ['ʌn'ræp] *vt* défaire; ouvrir

unwritten ['ʌn'rɪtn] *adj (agreement)* tacite

──────── *KEYWORD*

up [ʌp] *prep:* **he went ~ the stairs/the hill** il a monté l'escalier/la colline; **the cat was ~ a tree** le chat était dans un arbre; **they live further ~ the street** ils habitent plus haut dans la rue

♦ *adv* **1** *(upwards, higher):* **~ in the sky/ the mountains** (là-haut) dans le ciel/les montagnes; **put it a bit higher ~** mettez-le un peu plus haut; **~ there** là-haut; **~ above** au-dessus

2: to be ~ *(out of bed)* être levé(e); *(prices)* avoir augmenté *or* monté

3: ~ to *(as far as)* jusqu'à; **~ to now** jusqu'à présent

4: to be ~ to *(depending on):* **it's ~ to you** c'est à vous de décider; *(equal to):* **he's not ~ to it** *(job, task etc)* il n'en est pas capable; *(inf: be doing):* **what is he ~ to?** qu'est-ce qu'il peut bien faire?

♦ *n:* **~s and downs** hauts et bas *mpl*

up-and-coming [ʌpənd'kʌmɪŋ] *adj* plein(e) d'avenir *or* de promesses

upbringing ['ʌpbrɪŋɪŋ] *n* éducation *f*

update [ʌp'deɪt] *vt* mettre à jour

upgrade *vt (house)* moderniser; *(job)* revaloriser; *(employee)* promouvoir

upheaval [ʌp'hiːvəl] *n* bouleversement *m*; branle-bas *m*; crise *f*

uphill ['ʌp'hɪl] *adj* qui monte; *(fig: task)* difficile, pénible ♦ *adv (face, look)* en amont; **to go ~** monter

uphold [ʌp'həʊld] *(irreg)* vt *(law, decision)* maintenir

upholstery [ʌp'həʊlstərɪ] *n* rembourrage *m*; *(cover)* tissu *m* d'ameublement; *(of car)* garniture *f*

upkeep ['ʌpkiːp] *n* entretien *m*

upon [ə'pɒn] *prep* sur

upper ['ʌpə*] *adj* supérieur(e); du dessus ♦ *n (of shoe)* empeigne *f*; **~-class** *adj* de la haute société, aristocratique; **~ hand** *n:* **to have the ~ hand** avoir le dessus; **~most** *adj* le(la) plus haut(e); **what was ~most in my mind** ce à quoi je pensais surtout

upright ['ʌpraɪt] *adj* droit(e); vertical(e);

(fig) droit, honnête

uprising ['ʌpraɪzɪŋ] *n* soulèvement *m*, insurrection *f*

uproar ['ʌprɔː*] *n* tumulte *m*; *(protests)* tempête *f* de protestations

uproot [ʌp'ruːt] *vt* déraciner

upset [*n* 'ʌpset, *vb, adj* ʌp'set] *(irreg: like* set) *n* bouleversement *m*; *(stomach ~)* indigestion *f* ♦ *vt (glass etc)* renverser; *(plan)* déranger; *(person: offend)* contrarier; *(: grieve)* faire de la peine à; bouleverser ♦ *adj* contrarié(e); peiné(e); *(stomach)* dérangé(e)

upshot ['ʌpʃɒt] *n* résultat *m*

upside-down ['ʌpsaɪd'daʊn] *adv* à l'envers; **to turn ~** mettre sens dessus dessous

upstairs ['ʌp'steəz] *adv* en haut ♦ *adj (room)* du dessus, d'en haut ♦ *n:* **the ~** l'étage *m*

upstart ['ʌpstaːt] *(pej)* n parvenu(e)

upstream ['ʌp'striːm] *adv* en amont

uptake ['ʌpteɪk] *n:* **to be quick/slow on the ~** comprendre vite/être lent à comprendre

uptight ['ʌp'taɪt] *(inf)* adj très tendu(e), crispé(e)

up-to-date ['ʌptə'deɪt] *adj* moderne; *(information)* très récent(e)

upturn ['ʌptɜːn] *n (in luck)* retournement *m*; *(COMM: in market)* hausse *f*

upward ['ʌpwəd] *adj* ascendant(e); vers le haut; **~(s)** *adv* vers le haut; **~(s) of 200** 200 et plus

urban ['ɜːbən] *adj* urbain(e)

urbane [ɜː'beɪn] *adj* urbain(e), courtois(e)

urchin ['ɜːtʃɪn] *n* polisson *m*

urge [ɜːdʒ] *n* besoin *m*; envie *f*; forte envie, désir *m* ♦ *vt:* **to ~ sb to do** exhorter qn à faire, pousser qn à faire; recommander vivement à qn de faire

urgency ['ɜːdʒənsɪ] *n* urgence *f*; *(of tone)* insistance *f*

urgent ['ɜːdʒənt] *adj* urgent(e); *(tone)* insistant(e), pressant(e)

urinal *n* urinoir *m*; *(vessel)* urinal *m*

urine ['juərɪn] *n* urine *f*

urn [ɜːn] *n* urne *f*; *(also: tea ~)* fontaine *f* à thé

US *n abbr* = **United States**

us [ʌs] *pron* nous; *see also* me

USA *n abbr* = **United States of America**

use [*n* juːs, *vb* juːz] *n* emploi *m*, utilisation *f*; usage *m*; *(usefulness)* utilité *f* ♦ *vt* se servir de, utiliser, employer; **in ~** en usage; **out of ~** hors d'usage; **to be of ~** servir, être utile; **it's no ~** ça ne sert à rien; **she ~d to do it** elle le faisait (autrefois), elle avait coutume de le faire; **~d to:** **to be ~d to** avoir l'habitude de, être habitué(e) à; **~ up** *vt* finir, épuiser; *(car)* d'occasion; **~ful** *adj* utile; **~fulness** *n* utilité *f*; **~less** *adj* inutile; *(person: hope-*

less) nul(le); **~r** *n* utilisateur(trice), usager *m*; **~r-friendly** *adj* (*computer*) convivial(e), facile d'emploi

usher ['ʌʃə*] *n* (*at wedding ceremony*) placeur *m*; **~ette** [ʌʃə'rɛt] *n* (*in cinema*) ouvreuse *f*

usual ['juːʒuəl] *adj* habituel(le); **as ~** comme d'habitude; **~ly** *adv* d'habitude, d'ordinaire

utensil [juːˈtɛnsl] *n* ustensile *m*

uterus ['juːtərəs] *n* utérus *m*

utility [juːˈtɪlɪtɪ] *n* utilité *f*; (*also: public ~*) service public; **~ room** *n* buanderie *f*

utmost ['ʌtməust] *adj* extrême, le(la) plus grand(e) ♦ *n*: **to do one's ~** faire tout son possible

utter ['ʌtə*] *adj* total(e), complet(ète) ♦ *vt* (*words*) prononcer, proférer; (*sounds*) émettre; **~ance** *n* paroles *fpl*; **~ly** *adv* complètement, totalement

U-turn ['juːˈtɜːn] *n* demi-tour *m*

 V v

v. *abbr* = **verse; versus; volt;** (**= vide**) voir

vacancy ['veɪkənsɪ] *n* (*BRIT: job*) poste vacant; (*room*) chambre *f* disponible

vacant ['veɪkənt] *adj* (*seat etc*) libre, disponible; (*expression*) distrait(e); **~ lot** (*US*) *n* terrain inoccupé; (*for sale*) terrain à vendre

vacate [vəˈkeɪt] *vt* quitter

vacation [vəˈkeɪʃən] *n* vacances *fpl*

vaccinate ['væksɪneɪt] *vt* vacciner

vacuum ['vækjʊm] *n* vide *m*; **~ cleaner** *n* aspirateur *m*; **~-packed** *adj* emballé(e) sous vide

vagina [vəˈdʒaɪnə] *n* vagin *m*

vagrant ['veɪgrənt] *n* vagabond(e)

vague [veɪg] *adj* (*useless*) vague, imprécis(e); (*blurred: photo, outline*) flou(e); **~ly** *adv* vaguement

vain [veɪn] *adj* (*useless*) vain(e); (*conceited*) vaniteux(euse); **in ~** en vain

valentine ['væləntaɪn] *n* (*also: ~ card*) carte *f* de la Saint-Valentin; (*person*) bien-aimé(e) (*le jour de la Sainte-Valentin*)

valiant ['væliənt] *adj* vaillant(e)

valid ['vælɪd] *adj* valable; (*document*) valable, valide

valley ['vælɪ] *n* vallée *f*

valour ['vælə*] (*US* **valor**) *n* courage *m*

valuable ['væljʊəbl] *adj* (*jewel*) de valeur; (*time, help*) précieux(euse); **~s** *npl* objets

mpl de valeur

valuation [væljuˈeɪʃən] *n* (*price*) estimation *f*; (*quality*) appréciation *f*

value ['væljuː] *n* valeur *f* ♦ *vt* (*fix price*) évaluer, expertiser; (*appreciate*) apprécier; **~ added tax** (*BRIT*) *n* taxe *f* à la valeur ajoutée; **~d** *adj* (*person*) estimé(e); (*advice*) précieux(euse)

valve [vælv] *n* (*in machine*) soupape *f*, valve *f*; (*MED*) valve, valvule *f*

van [væn] *n* (*AUT*) camionnette *f*

vandal ['vændl] *n* vandale *m/f*; **~ism** *n* vandalisme *m*; **~ize** ['vændəlaɪz] *vt* saccager

vanguard ['vængɑːd] *n* (*fig*): **in the ~ of** à l'avant-garde de

vanilla [vəˈnɪlə] *n* vanille *f*

vanish ['vænɪʃ] *vi* disparaître

vanity ['vænɪtɪ] *n* vanité *f*

vantage point ['vɑːntɪdʒ-] *n* bonne position

vapour ['veɪpə*] (*US* **vapor**) *n* vapeur *f*; (*on window*) buée *f*

variable ['vɛərɪəbl] *adj* variable; (*mood*) changeant(e)

variance ['vɛərɪəns] *n*: **to be at ~ (with)** être en désaccord (avec); (*facts*) être en contradiction (avec)

varicose ['værɪkəus] *adj*: **~ veins** varices *fpl*

varied ['vɛərɪd] *adj* varié(e), divers(e)

variety [vəˈraɪətɪ] *n* variété *f*; (*quantity*) nombre *m*, quantité *f*; **~ show** *n* (*spectacle m de*) variétés *fpl*

various ['vɛərɪəs] *adj* divers(e), différent(e); (*several*) divers, plusieurs

varnish ['vɑːnɪʃ] *n* vernis *m* ♦ *vt* vernir

vary ['vɛərɪ] *vt*, *vi* varier, changer

vase [vɑːz] *n* vase *m*

Vaseline ['væsɪliːn] (*®*) *n* vaseline *f*

vast [vɑːst] *adj* vaste, immense; (*amount, success*) énorme

VAT [væt] *n abbr* (= *value added tax*) TVA *f*

vat [væt] *n* cuve *f*

vault [vɔːlt] *n* (*of roof*) voûte *f*; (*tomb*) caveau *m*; (*in bank*) salle *f* des coffres; chambre forte ♦ *vt* (*also: ~ over*) sauter (d'un bond)

vaunted ['vɔːntɪd] *adj*: **much-vaunted** tant vanté(e)

VCR *n abbr* = **video cassette recorder**

VD *n abbr* = **venereal disease**

VDU *n abbr* = **visual display unit**

veal [viːl] *n* veau *m*

veer [vɪə*] *vi* tourner, virer

vegetable ['vɛdʒtəbl] *n* légume *m* ♦ *adj* végétal(e)

vegetarian [vɛdʒɪˈtɛərɪən] *adj*, *n* végétarien(ne)

vehement ['viːɪmənt] *adj* violent(e), impétueux(euse); (*impassioned*) ardent(e)

vehicle ['viːɪkl] *n* véhicule *m*

veil [veɪl] *n* voile *m*

vein [veɪn] n veine f; (on leaf) nervure f
velocity [vɪˈlɒsɪtɪ] n vitesse f
velvet [ˈvɛlvɪt] n velours m
vending machine [ˈvɛndɪŋ-] n distributeur m automatique
veneer [vəˈnɪə*] n (on furniture) placage m; (fig) vernis m
venereal [vɪˈnɪərɪəl] adj: ~ **disease** maladie vénérienne
Venetian blind [vɪˈniːʃən-] n store vénitien
vengeance [ˈvɛndʒəns] n vengeance f; **with a ~** (fig) vraiment, pour de bon
venison [ˈvɛnɪsn] n venaison f
venom [ˈvɛnəm] n venin m
vent [vɛnt] n conduit m d'aération; (in dress, jacket) fente f ♦ vt (fig: one's feelings) donner libre cours à
ventilator [ˈvɛntɪleɪtə*] n ventilateur m
ventriloquist [vɛnˈtrɪləkwɪst] n ventriloque m/f
venture [ˈvɛntʃə*] n entreprise f ♦ vt risquer, hasarder ♦ vi s'aventurer, se risquer
venue [ˈvɛnjuː] n lieu m
verb [vɜːb] n verbe m; ~**al** adj verbal(e); (translation) littéral(e)
verbatim [vɜːˈbeɪtɪm] adj, adv mot pour mot
verdict [ˈvɜːdɪkt] n verdict m
verge [vɜːdʒ] n (BRIT) bord m, bas-côté m; "**soft ~s**"(: AUT) "accotement non stabilisé"; **on the ~ of doing** sur le point de faire; ~ **on** vt fus approcher de
verify [ˈvɛrɪfaɪ] vt vérifier; (confirm) confirmer
vermin [ˈvɜːmɪn] npl animaux mpl nuisibles; (insects) vermine f
vermouth [ˈvɜːməθ] n vermouth m
versatile [ˈvɜːsətaɪl] adj polyvalent(e)
verse [vɜːs] n (poetry) vers mpl; (stanza) strophe f; (in Bible) verset m
version [ˈvɜːʃən] n version f
versus [ˈvɜːsəs] prep contre
vertical [ˈvɜːtɪkəl] adj vertical(e) ♦ n verticale f
vertigo [ˈvɜːtɪɡəʊ] n vertige m
verve [vɜːv] n brio m; enthousiasme m
very [ˈvɛrɪ] adv très ♦ adj: **the ~ book which** le livre même que; **the ~ last** le tout dernier; **at the ~ least** tout au moins; ~ **much** beaucoup
vessel [ˈvɛsl] n (ANAT, NAUT) vaisseau m; (container) récipient m
vest [vɛst] n (BRIT) tricot m de corps; (US: waistcoat) gilet m
vested interest [ˈvɛstɪd-] n (COMM) droits acquis
vet [vɛt] n abbr (BRIT: = veterinary surgeon) vétérinaire m/f ♦ vt examiner soigneusement
veteran [ˈvɛtərn] n vétéran m; (also: war ~) ancien combattant

veterinarian [vɛtrəˈnɛərɪən] (US) n = **veterinary surgeon**
veterinary surgeon [ˈvɛtrɪnərɪ-] (BRIT) n vétérinaire m/f
veto [ˈviːtəu] (pl ~es) n veto m ♦ vt opposer son veto à
vex [vɛks] vt fâcher, contrarier; ~**ed** adj (question) controversé(e)
via [ˈvaɪə] prep par, via
viable [ˈvaɪəbl] adj viable
vibrate [vaɪˈbreɪt] vi vibrer
vicar [ˈvɪkə*] n pasteur m (de l'Église anglicane); ~**age** n presbytère m
vicarious [vɪˈkɛərɪəs] adj indirect(e)
vice [vaɪs] n (evil) vice m; (TECH) étau m
vice- prefix vice-
vice squad n ≈ brigade mondaine
vice versa [ˈvaɪsɪˈvɜːsə] adv vice versa
vicinity [vɪˈsɪnɪtɪ] n environs mpl, alentours mpl
vicious [ˈvɪʃəs] adj (remark) cruel(le), méchant(e); (blow) brutal(e); (dog) méchant(e), dangereux(euse); (horse) vicieux(euse); ~ **circle** n cercle vicieux
victim [ˈvɪktɪm] n victime f
victor [ˈvɪktə*] n vainqueur m
Victorian [vɪkˈtɔːrɪən] adj victorien(ne)
victory [ˈvɪktərɪ] n victoire f
video [ˈvɪdɪəu] cpd vidéo inv ♦ n (~ film) vidéo f; (also: ~ cassette) vidéocassette f; (: ~ cassette recorder) magnétoscope m; ~ **tape** n bande f vidéo inv; (cassette) vidéocassette f
vie [vaɪ] vi: **to ~ with** rivaliser avec
Vienna [vɪˈɛnə] n Vienne f
Vietnam [vjɛtˈnæm] n Viêt-nam m, Vietnam m; ~**ese** [vjɛtnəˈmiːz] adj vietnamien(ne) ♦ n inv Vietnamien(ne); (LING) vietnamien m
view [vjuː] n vue f; (opinion) avis m, vue ♦ vt voir, regarder; (situation) considérer; (house) visiter; **in full ~ of** sous les yeux de; **in ~ of the weather/the fact that** étant donné le temps/que; **in my ~** à mon avis; ~**er** n (TV) téléspectateur(trice); ~**finder** n viseur m; ~**point** n point m de vue
vigorous [ˈvɪɡərəs] adj vigoureux(euse)
vile [vaɪl] adj (action) vil(e); (smell, food) abominable; (temper) massacrant(e)
villa [ˈvɪlə] n villa f
village [ˈvɪlɪdʒ] n village m; ~**r** n villageois(e)
villain [ˈvɪlən] n (scoundrel) scélérat m; (BRIT: criminal) bandit m; (in novel etc) traître m
vindicate [ˈvɪndɪkeɪt] vt (person) innocenter; (action) justifier
vindictive [vɪnˈdɪktɪv] adj vindicatif(ive), rancunier(ère)
vine [vaɪn] n vigne f; (climbing plant) plante grimpante

vinegar ['vɪnɪgə*] n vinaigre m
vineyard ['vɪnjəd] n vignoble m
vintage ['vɪntɪdʒ] n (year) année f, millésime m; ~ **car** n voiture f d'époque; ~ **wine** n vin m de grand cru
viola [vɪ'əulə] n (MUS) alto m
violate ['vaɪəleɪt] vt violer
violence ['vaɪələns] n violence f
violent ['vaɪələnt] adj violent(e)
violet ['vaɪələt] adj violet(te) ♦ n (colour) violet m; (plant) violette f
violin [vaɪə'lɪn] n violon m; ~**ist** n violoniste m/f
VIP n abbr (= very important person) V.I.P. m
virgin ['vɜ:dʒɪn] n vierge f ♦ adj vierge
Virgo ['vɜ:gəu] n la Vierge
virile ['vɪraɪl] adj viril(e)
virtually ['vɜ:tjuəlɪ] adv (almost) pratiquement
virtual reality n (COMPUT) réalité virtuelle
virtue ['vɜ:tju:] n vertu f; (advantage) mérite m, avantage m; by ~ of en vertu or en raison de; **virtuous** ['vɜ:tjuəs] adj vertueux(euse)
virus ['vaɪərəs] n (also: COMPUT) virus m
visa ['vi:zə] n visa m
visibility [vɪzɪ'bɪlɪtɪ] n visibilité f
visible ['vɪzəbl] adj visible
vision ['vɪʒən] n (sight) vue f, vision f; (foresight, in dream) vision
visit ['vɪzɪt] n visite f; (stay) séjour m ♦ vt (person) rendre visite à; (place) visiter; ~**ing hours** npl (in hospital etc) heures fpl de visite; ~**or** n visiteur(euse); (to one's house) visite f, invité(e)
visor ['vaɪzə*] n visière f
vista ['vɪstə] n vue f
visual ['vɪzjuəl] adj visuel(le); ~ **aid** n support visuel; ~ **display unit** n console f de visualisation, visuel m; ~**ize** ['vɪzjuəlaɪz] vt se représenter, s'imaginer
vital ['vaɪtl] adj vital(e); (person) plein(e) d'entrain; ~**ly** adv (important) absolument; ~ **statistics** npl (fig) mensurations fpl
vitamin ['vɪtəmɪn] n vitamine f
vivacious [vɪ'veɪʃəs] adj animé(e), qui a de la vivacité
vivid ['vɪvɪd] adj (account) vivant(e); (light, imagination) vif(vive); ~**ly** adv (describe) d'une manière vivante; (remember) de façon précise
V-neck ['vi:'nek] n décolleté m en V
vocabulary [vəu'kæbjulərɪ] n vocabulaire m
vocal ['vəukəl] adj vocal(e); (articulate) qui sait s'exprimer; ~ **cords** npl cordes vocales
vocation [vəu'keɪʃən] n vocation f; ~**al** adj professionnel(le)
vociferous [vəu'sɪfərəs] adj bruyant(e)
vodka ['vɒdkə] n vodka f
vogue [vəug] n: in ~ en vogue f

voice [vɔɪs] n voix f ♦ vt (opinion) exprimer, formuler
void [vɔɪd] n vide m ♦ adj nul(le); ~ **of** vide de, dépourvu(e) de
volatile ['vɒlətaɪl] adj volatil(e); (person) versatile; (situation) explosif(ive)
volcano [vɒl'keɪnəu] (pl ~**es**) n volcan m
volition [və'lɪʃən] n: **of one's own** ~ de son propre gré
volley ['vɒlɪ] n (of gunfire) salve f; (of stones etc) grêle f, volée f; (of questions) multitude f, série f; (TENNIS etc) volée f; ~**ball** n volley(-ball) m
volt [vəult] n volt m; ~**age** n tension f, voltage m
volume ['vɒlju:m] n volume m
voluntarily adv volontairement
voluntary ['vɒləntərɪ] adj volontaire; (unpaid) bénévole
volunteer [vɒlən'tɪə*] n volontaire m/f ♦ vt (information) fournir (spontanément) ♦ vi (MIL) s'engager comme volontaire; **to** ~ **to do** se proposer pour faire
vomit ['vɒmɪt] vt, vi vomir
vote [vəut] n vote m, suffrage m; (cast) voix f, vote; (franchise) droit m de vote ♦ vt (elect): **to be** ~**d chairman** etc être élu président etc; (propose): **to** ~ **that** proposer que ♦ vi voter; ~ **of thanks** discours m de remerciement; ~**r** n électeur(trice); **voting** ['vəutɪŋ] n scrutin m, vote m
voucher ['vautʃə*] n (for meal, petrol, gift) bon m
vouch for [vautʃ] vt fus se porter garant de
vow [vau] n vœu m, serment m ♦ vi jurer
vowel ['vauəl] n voyelle f
voyage ['vɔɪdʒ] n voyage m par mer, traversée f; (by spacecraft) voyage
vulgar ['vʌlgə*] adj vulgaire
vulnerable ['vʌlnərəbl] adj vulnérable
vulture ['vʌltʃə*] n vautour m

W w

wad [wɒd] n (of cotton wool, paper) tampon m; (of banknotes etc) liasse f
waddle ['wɒdl] vi se dandiner
wade [weɪd] vi: **to** ~ **through** marcher dans, patauger dans; (fig: book) s'évertuer à lire
wafer ['weɪfə*] n (CULIN) gaufrette f
waffle ['wɒfl] n (CULIN) gaufre f; (inf) verbiage m, remplissage m ♦ vi parler pour ne

rien dire, faire du remplissage

waft [wɑːft] vt porter ♦ vi flotter

wag [wæg] vt agiter, remuer ♦ vi remuer

wage [weɪdʒ] n (also: ~s) salaire m, paye f ♦ vt: **to ~ war** faire la guerre; **~ earner** n salarié(e); **~ packet** n (enveloppe f de) paye f

wager ['weɪdʒə*] n pari m

waggle ['wægl] vt, vi remuer

wag(g)on ['wægən] n (horse-drawn) chariot m; (BRIT: RAIL) wagon m (de marchandises)

wail [weɪl] vi gémir; (siren) hurler

waist [weɪst] n taille f; ~**coat** (BRIT) n gilet m; **~line** n (tour m de) taille f

wait [weɪt] n attente f ♦ vi attendre; **to keep sb ~ing** faire attendre qn; **to ~ for** attendre; **I can't ~ to ...** (fig) je meurs d'envie de ...; ~ **behind** vi rester (à attendre); ~ **on** vt fus servir; **~er** n garçon m (de café), serveur m; **~ing** n: **"no ~ing"** (BRIT: AUT) "stationnement interdit"; **~ing list** n liste f d'attente; **~ing room** n salle f d'attente; **~ress** n serveuse f

waive [weɪv] vt renoncer à, abandonner

wake [weɪk] (pt woke, ~d, pp woken, ~d) vt (also: ~ up) réveiller ♦ vi (also: ~ up) se réveiller ♦ n (for dead person) veillée f mortuaire; (NAUT) sillage m

Wales [weɪlz] n pays m de Galles; **the Prince of ~** le prince de Galles

walk [wɔːk] n promenade f; (short) petit tour; (gait) démarche f; (path) chemin m; (in park etc) allée f ♦ vi marcher; (for pleasure, exercise) se promener ♦ vt (distance) faire à pied; (dog) promener; **10 minutes' ~ from** à 10 minutes à pied de; **from all ~s of life** de toutes conditions sociales; ~ **out** vi (audience) sortir, quitter la salle; (workers) se mettre en grève; ~ **out on** (inf) vt fus quitter, plaquer; **~er** n (person) marcheur(euse); **~ie-talkie** n talkie-walkie m; **~ing** n marche f à pied; **~ing shoes** npl chaussures fpl de marche; **~ing stick** n canne f; **~out** n (of workers) grève-surprise f; **~over** (inf) n victoire f or examen m etc facile; **~way** n promenade f, cheminement m piéton

wall [wɔːl] n mur m; (of tunnel, cave etc) paroi m; **~ed** adj (city) fortifié(e); (garden) entouré(e) d'un mur, clos(e)

wallet ['wɒlɪt] n portefeuille m

wallflower ['wɔːlflaʊə*] n giroflée f; **to be a ~** (fig) faire tapisserie

wallop ['wɒləp] (BRIT: inf) vt donner un grand coup à

wallow ['wɒləʊ] vi se vautrer

wallpaper ['wɔːlpeɪpə*] n papier peint ♦ vt tapisser

walnut ['wɔːlnʌt] n noix f; (tree, wood) noyer m

walrus ['wɔːlrəs] (pl ~ or ~es) n morse m

waltz [wɔːlts] n valse f ♦ vi valser

wan [wɒn] adj pâle; triste

wand [wɒnd] n (also: magic ~) baguette f (magique)

wander ['wɒndə*] vi (person) errer; (thoughts) vagabonder, errer ♦ vt errer dans

wane [weɪn] vi (moon) décroître; (reputation) décliner

wangle ['wæŋgl] (BRIT: inf) vt se débrouiller pour avoir; carotter

want [wɒnt] vt vouloir; (need) avoir besoin de ♦ n: **for ~ of** par manque de, faute de; **~s** npl (needs) besoins mpl; **to ~ to do** vouloir faire; **to ~ sb to do** vouloir que qn fasse; **~ed** adj (criminal) recherché(e) par la police; **"cook ~ed"** "on recherche un cuisinier"; **~ing** adj: **to be found ~ing** ne pas être à la hauteur

wanton ['wɒntən] adj (gratuitous) gratuit(e); (promiscuous) dévergondé(e)

war [wɔː*] n guerre f; **to make ~ (on)** faire la guerre (à)

ward [wɔːd] n (in hospital) salle f; (POL) canton m; (LAW: child) pupille m/f; ~ **off** vt (attack, enemy) repousser, éviter

warden ['wɔːdən] n gardien(ne); (BRIT: of institution) directeur(trice); (: also: traffic ~) contractuel(le); (of youth hostel) père m or mère f aubergiste

warder ['wɔːdə*] (BRIT) n gardien m de prison

wardrobe ['wɔːdrəʊb] n (cupboard) armoire f; (clothes) garde-robe f; (THEATRE) costumes mpl

warehouse ['wɛəhaʊs] n entrepôt m

wares [wɛəz] npl marchandises fpl

warfare ['wɔːfɛə*] n guerre f

warhead ['wɔːhɛd] n (MIL) ogive f

warily ['wɛərɪlɪ] adv avec prudence

warm [wɔːm] adj chaud(e); (thanks, welcome, applause, person) chaleureux(euse); **it's ~** il fait chaud; **I'm ~** j'ai chaud; ~ **up** vi (person, room) se réchauffer; (water) chauffer; (athlete) s'échauffer ♦ vt (food) (faire) réchauffer, (faire) chauffer; (engine) faire chauffer; **~-hearted** adj affectueux(euse); **~ly** adv chaudement; chaleureusement; **~th** n chaleur f

warn [wɔːn] vt avertir, prévenir; **to ~ sb (not) to do** conseiller à qn de (ne pas) faire; **~ing** n avertissement m; (notice) avis m; (signal) avertisseur m; **~ing light** n avertisseur lumineux; **~ing triangle** n (AUT) triangle m de présignalisation

warp [wɔːp] vi (wood) travailler, se déformer ♦ vt (fig: character) pervertir

warrant ['wɒrənt] n (guarantee) garantie f; (LAW: to arrest) mandat m d'arrêt; (: to search) mandat de perquisition

warranty ['wɒrəntɪ] n garantie f

warren ['wɒrən] n (of rabbits) terrier m; (fig: of streets etc) dédale m

warrior ['wɒrɪə*] n guerrier(ère)

Warsaw ['wɔːsɔː] n Varsovie

warship ['wɔːʃɪp] n navire m de guerre

wart [wɔːt] n verrue f

wartime ['wɔːtaɪm] n: **in ~** en temps de guerre

wary ['wɛərɪ] adj prudent(e)

was [wɒz, wəz] pt of **be**

wash [wɒʃ] vt laver ♦ vi se laver; (sea): **to ~ over/against sth** inonder/baigner qch ♦ n (clothes) lessive f; (~ing programme) lavage m; (of ship) sillage m; **to have a ~** se laver, faire sa toilette; **to give sth a ~** laver qch; **~ away** vt (stain) enlever au lavage; (subj: river etc) emporter; **~ off** vi partir au lavage; **~ up** vi (BRIT) faire la vaisselle; (US) se débarbouiller; **~able** adj lavable; **~basin** (US **~bowl**) n lavabo m; **~cloth** (US) n gant m de toilette; **~er** n (TECH) rondelle f, joint m; **~ing** n (dirty) linge m; (clean) lessive f; **~ing machine** n machine f à laver; **~ing powder** (BRIT) n lessive f (en poudre); **~ing-up** n vaisselle f; **~ing-up liquid** n produit m pour la vaisselle; **~-out** (inf) n désastre m; **~room** (US) n toilettes fpl

wasn't ['wɒznt] = **was not**

wasp [wɒsp] n guêpe f

wastage ['weɪstɪdʒ] n gaspillage m; (in manufacturing, transport etc) pertes fpl, déchets mpl; **natural ~** départs naturels

waste [weɪst] n gaspillage m; (of time) perte f; (rubbish) déchets mpl; (also: household ~) ordures fpl ♦ adj (leftover): **~ material** déchets mpl; (land, ground: in city) à l'abandon ♦ vt gaspiller; (time, opportunity) perdre; **~s** npl (area) étendue f désertique; **~ away** vi dépérir; **~ disposal unit** (BRIT) n broyeur m d'ordures; **~ful** adj gaspilleur(euse); (process) peu économique; **~ ground** (BRIT) n terrain m vague; **~paper basket** n corbeille f à papier; **~ pipe** n (tuyau m de) vidange f

watch [wɒtʃ] n montre f; (act of ~ing) surveillance f; guet m; (MIL: guards) garde f; (NAUT: guards, spell of duty) quart m ♦ vt (look at) observer; (: match, programme, TV) regarder; (spy on, guard) surveiller; (be careful of) faire attention à ♦ vi regarder; (keep guard) monter la garde; **~ out** vi faire attention; **~dog** n chien m de garde; (fig) gardien(ne); **~ful** adj attentif(ive), vigilant(e); **~maker** n horloger(ère); **~man** (irreg) n see **night**; **~strap** n bracelet m de montre

water ['wɔːtə*] n eau f ♦ vt (plant, garden) arroser ♦ vi (eyes) larmoyer; (mouth): **it makes my mouth ~** j'en ai l'eau à la bouche; **in British ~s** dans les eaux territoriales britanniques; **~ down** vt (milk) couper d'eau; (fig: story) édulcorer; **~colour** (US **~color**) n aquarelle f; **~cress** n cresson m

(de fontaine); **~fall** n chute f d'eau; **~ heater** n chauffe-eau m; **~ing can** n arrosoir m; **~ lily** n nénuphar m; **~line** n (NAUT) ligne f de flottaison; **~logged** adj (ground) détrempé(e); **~ main** n canalisation f d'eau; **~melon** n pastèque f; **~proof** adj imperméable; **~shed** n (GEO) ligne f de partage des eaux; (fig) moment m critique, point décisif; **~-skiing** n ski m nautique; **~tight** adj étanche; **~way** n cours m d'eau navigable; **~works** n (building) station f hydraulique; (fig) ♦ **~y** adj (coffee, soup) trop faible; (eyes) humide, larmoyant(e)

watt [wɒt] n watt m

wave [weɪv] n vague f; (of hand) geste m, signe m; (RADIO) onde f; (in hair) ondulation f ♦ vi faire signe de la main; (flag) flotter au vent; (grass) ondoyer ♦ vt (handkerchief) agiter; (stick) brandir; **~length** n longueur f d'ondes

waver ['weɪvə*] vi vaciller; (voice) trembler; (person) hésiter

wavy ['weɪvɪ] adj ondulé(e); onduleux(euse)

wax [wæks] n cire f; (for skis) fart m ♦ vt cirer; (car) lustrer; (skis) farter ♦ vi (moon) croître; **~works** npl personnages mpl de cire ♦ n musée m de cire

way [weɪ] n chemin m, voie f; (distance) distance f; (direction) chemin m, direction f; (manner) façon f, manière f; (habit) habitude f, façon; **which ~? - this ~** par où? - par ici; **on the ~** (en route) en route; **to be on one's ~** être en route; **to go out of one's ~ to do** (fig) se donner du mal pour faire; **to be in the ~** bloquer le passage; (fig) gêner; **to lose one's ~** perdre son chemin; **under ~** en cours; **in a ~** dans un sens; **in some ~s** à certains égards; **no ~!** (inf) pas question!; **by the ~ ...** à propos ...; **"~ in"** (BRIT) "entrée"; **"~ out"** (BRIT) "sortie"; **the ~ back** le chemin du retour; **"give ~"** (BRIT: AUT) "cédez le passage"; **~lay** ['weɪleɪ] (irreg) vt attaquer

wayward ['weɪwəd] adj capricieux(euse), entêté(e)

we [wiː] pl pron nous

weak [wiːk] adj faible; (health) fragile; (beam etc) peu solide; **~en** vi faiblir, décliner ♦ vt affaiblir; **~ling** n (physically) gringalet m; (morally etc) faible m/f; **~ness** n faiblesse f; (fault) point m faible; **to have a ~ness for** avoir un faible pour

wealth [welθ] n (money, resources) richesse(s) f(pl); (of details) profusion f; **~y** adj riche

wean [wiːn] vt sevrer

weapon ['wepən] n arme f

wear [wɛə*] (pt **wore**, pp **worn**) n (use) usage m; (deterioration through use) usure f; (clothing): **sports/baby~** vêtements mpl de sport/pour bébés ♦ vt (clothes) porter; (put on) mettre; (*damage: through use*) user ♦ *vi* (*last*) faire de l'usage; (*rub etc through*) s'user; **town/evening** ~ tenue *f* de ville/soirée; ~ **away** *vt* user, ronger ♦ *vi* (*inscription*) s'effacer; ~ **down** *vt* user; (*strength, person*) épuiser; ~ **off** *vi* disparaître; ~ **out** *vt* user; (*person, strength*) épuiser; ~ **and tear** *n* usure *f*

weary ['wɪərɪ] *adj* (*tired*) épuisé(e); (*dispirited*) las(lasse); abattu(e) ♦ *vi*: **to ~ of** se lasser de

weasel ['wiːzl] *n* (ZOOL) belette *f*

weather ['weðə*] *n* temps *m* ♦ *vt* (*tempest, crisis*) essuyer, réchapper à, survivre à; **under the ~** (*fig: ill*) mal fichu(e); ~**-beaten** *adj* (*person*) hâlé(e); (*building*) dégradé(e) par les intempéries; ~**cock** *n* girouette *f*; ~ **forecast** *n* prévisions *fpl* météorologiques, météo *f*; ~ **man** (*irreg: inf*) *n* météorologue *m*; ~ **vane** *n* = ~**cock**

weave [wiːv] (*pt* **wove**, *pp* **woven**) *vt* (*cloth*) tisser; (*basket*) tresser; ~**r** *n* tisserand(e)

web [web] *n* (*of spider*) toile *f*; (*on foot*) palmure *f*; (*fabric, also fig*) tissu *m*

wed [wed] (*pt, pp* **wedded**) *vt* épouser ♦ *vi* se marier

we'd [wiːd] = **we had**; **we would**

wedding ['wedɪŋ] *n* mariage *m*; **silver/golden** ~ (**anniversary**) noces *fpl* d'argent/d'or; ~ **day** *n* jour *m* du mariage; ~ **dress** *n* robe *f* de mariée; ~ **ring** *n* alliance *f*

wedge [wedʒ] *n* (*of wood etc*) coin *m*, cale *f*; (*of cake*) part *f* ♦ *vt* (*fix*) caler; (*pack tightly*) enfoncer

Wednesday ['wenzdeɪ] *n* mercredi *m*

wee [wiː] *adj* (SCOTTISH) petit(e); tout(e) petit(e)

weed [wiːd] *n* mauvaise herbe ♦ *vt* désherber; ~**killer** *n* désherbant *m*; ~**y** *adj* (*man*) gringalet

week [wiːk] *n* semaine *f*; **a ~ today/on Friday** aujourd'hui/vendredi en huit; ~**day** *n* jour *m* de semaine; (COMM) jour ouvrable; ~**end** *n* week-end *m*; ~**ly** *adv* une fois par semaine, chaque semaine ♦ *adj* hebdomadaire ♦ *n* hebdomadaire *m*

weep [wiːp] (*pt, pp* **wept**) *vi* (*person*) pleurer; ~**ing willow** *n* saule pleureur

weigh [weɪ] *vt, vi* peser; **to ~ anchor** lever l'ancre; ~ **down** *vt* (*person, animal*) écraser; (*fig: with worry*) accabler; ~ **up** *vt* examiner

weight [weɪt] *n* poids *m*; **to lose/put on ~** maigrir/grossir; ~**ing** *n* (*allowance*) indemnité *f*, allocation *f*; ~**lifter** *n* haltérophile *m*; ~**y** *adj* lourd(e); (*important*) de poids, important(e)

weir [wɪə*] *n* barrage *m*

weird [wɪəd] *adj* bizarre

welcome ['welkəm] *adj* bienvenu(e) ♦ *n* accueil *m* ♦ *vt* accueillir; (*also:* bid ~) souhaiter la bienvenue à; (*be glad of*) se réjouir de; **thank you - you're** ~! merci - de rien *or* il n'y a pas de quoi!

weld [weld] *vt* souder; ~**er** *n* soudeur(euse)

welfare ['welfɛə*] *n* (*well-being*) bien-être *m*; (*social aid*) assistance sociale; ~ **state** *n* Etat-providence *m*; ~ **work** *n* travail social

well [wel] *n* puits *m* ♦ *adv* bien ♦ *adj*: **to be** ~ aller bien ♦ *excl* eh bien!; bon!; enfin!; **as** ~ aussi, également; **as** ~ **as** (*in addition to*) en plus de; ~ **done!** bravo!; **get** ~ **soon** remets-toi vite!; **to do** ~ bien réussir; (*business*) prospérer; ~ **up** *vi* monter

we'll [wiːl] = **we will**; **we shall**

well: ~**-behaved** ['welbɪ'heɪvd] *adj* sage, obéissant(e); ~**-being** ['welbiːŋ] *n* bien-être *m*; ~**-built** ['wel'bɪlt] *adj* (*person*) bien bâti(e); ~**-deserved** *adj* (bien) mérité(e); ~**-dressed** *adj* bien habillé(e); ~**-heeled** (*inf*) *adj* (*wealthy*) nanti(e)

wellingtons ['welɪŋtənz] *npl* (*also:* wellington boots) bottes *fpl* de caoutchouc

well: ~**-known** ['wel'nəʊn] *adj* (*person*) bien connu(e); ~**-mannered** ['wel'mænəd] *adj* bien élevé(e); ~**-meaning** ['wel'miːnɪŋ] *adj* bien intentionné(e); ~**-off** ['wel'ɒf] *adj* aisé(e), riche; ~**-read** ['wel'red] *adj* cultivé(e); ~**-to-do** ['weltə'duː] *adj* aisé(e); ~**-wishers** ['welwɪʃəz] *npl* amis *mpl* et admirateurs *mpl*; (*friends*) amis *mpl*

Welsh [welʃ] *adj* gallois(e) ♦ *n* (LING) gallois *m*; **the** ~ *npl* (*people*) les Gallois *mpl*; ~**man** (*irreg*) *n* Gallois *m*; ~ **rarebit** *n* toast *m* au fromage; ~**woman** (*irreg*) *n* Galloise *f*

went [went] *pt* of **go**

wept [wept] *pt, pp* of **weep**

were [wɜː*] *pt* of **be**

we're [wɪə*] = **we are**

weren't [wɜːnt] = **were not**

west [west] *n* ouest *m* ♦ *adj* ouest *inv*, de *or* à l'ouest ♦ *adv* à *or* vers l'ouest; **the W~** *n* l'Occident *m*, l'Ouest *m*; **the W~ Country** (BRIT) *n* le sud-ouest de l'Angleterre; ~**erly** *adj* (*wind*) d'ouest; (*point*) à l'ouest; ~**ern** *adj* occidental(e), de *or* à l'ouest ♦ *n* (CINEMA) western *m*; **W~ Indian** *adj* antillais(e) ♦ *n* Antillais(e); **W~ Indies** *npl* Antilles *fpl*; ~**ward(s)** *adv* vers l'ouest

wet [wet] *adj* mouillé(e); (*damp*) humide; (*soaked*) trempé(e); (*rainy*) pluvieux(euse) ♦ *n* (BRIT: POL) modéré *m* du parti conservateur; **to get** ~ se mouiller; "~ **paint**" "attention peinture fraîche"; ~ **blanket** *n* (*fig*) rabat-joie *m inv*; ~ **suit** *n* combinaison *f* de plongée

we've [wiːv] = **we have**

whack [wæk] *vt* donner un grand coup à

whale [weɪl] *n* (ZOOL) baleine *f*

wharf [wɔːf] (*pl* **wharves**) *n* quai *m*

——————— KEYWORD ———————

what [wɒt] *adj* quel(le); ~ **size is he?** quelle taille fait-il?; ~ **colour is it?** de quelle couleur est-ce?; ~ **books do you need?** quels livres vous faut-il?; ~ **a mess!** quel désordre!
♦ *pron* **1** (*interrogative*) que, *prep* +quoi; ~ **are you doing?** que faites-vous?, qu'est-ce que vous faites?; ~ **is happening?** qu'est-ce qui se passe?, que se passe-t-il?; ~ **are you talking about?** de quoi parlez-vous?; ~ **is it called?** comment est-ce que ça s'appelle?; ~ **about me?** et moi?; ~ **about doing ...?** et si on faisait ...?
2 (*relative: subject*) ce qui; (: *direct object*) ce que; (: *indirect object*) ce +*prep* +quoi, ce dont; **I saw** ~ **you did/was on the table** j'ai vu ce que vous avez fait/ce qui était sur la table; **tell me** ~ **you remember** dites-moi ce dont vous vous souvenez
♦ *excl* (*disbelieving*) quoi!, comment!

whatever [wɒt'evə*] *adj*: ~ **book** quel que soit le livre que (*or* qui) +*sub*; n'importe quel livre ♦ *pron*: **do** ~ **is necessary** faites (tout) ce qui est nécessaire; ~ **happens** quoi qu'il arrive; **no reason** ~ pas la moindre raison; **nothing** ~ rien du tout
whatsoever [wɒt'səʊevə*] *adj* = **whatever**
wheat [wiːt] *n* blé *m*, froment *m*
wheedle ['wiːdl] *vt*: **to** ~ **sb into doing sth** cajoler *or* enjôler qn pour qu'il fasse qch; **to** ~ **sth out of sb** obtenir qch de qn par des cajoleries
wheel [wiːl] *n* roue *f*; (*also: steering* ~) volant *m*; (*NAUT*) gouvernail *m* ♦ *vt* (*pram etc*) pousser ♦ *vi* (*birds*) tournoyer; (*also:* ~ *round: person*) virevolter; ~**barrow** *n* brouette *f*; ~**chair** *n* fauteuil roulant; ~ **clamp** *n* (*AUT*) sabot *m* (de Denver)
wheeze [wiːz] *vi* respirer bruyamment

——————— KEYWORD ———————

when [wen] *adv* quand; ~ **did he go?** quand est-ce qu'il est parti?
♦ *conj* **1** (*at, during, after the time that*) quand, lorsque; **she was reading** ~ **I came in** elle lisait quand *or* lorsque je suis entré
2 (*on, at which*): **on the day** ~ **I met him** le jour où je l'ai rencontré
3 (*whereas*) alors que; **I thought I was wrong** ~ **in fact I was right** j'ai cru que j'avais tort alors qu'en fait j'avais raison

whenever [wen'evə*] *adv* quand donc ♦ *conj* quand; (*every time that*) chaque fois que
where [wɛə*] *adv, conj* où; **this is** ~ c'est là que; ~**abouts** ['wɛərə'baʊts] *adv* où donc ♦ *n*: **nobody knows his** ~**abouts** personne ne sait où il se trouve; ~**as**

[wɛər'æz] *conj* alors que; ~**by** *adv* par lequel (*or* laquelle *etc*); ~**upon** *adv* sur quoi
wherever [wɛər'evə*] *adv* où donc ♦ *conj* où que +*sub*
wherewithal ['wɛəwɪðɔːl] *n* moyens *mpl*
whet [wet] *vt* aiguiser
whether ['weðə*] *conj* si; **I don't know** ~ **to accept or not** je ne sais pas si je dois accepter ou non; **it's doubtful** ~ il est peu probable que +*sub*; ~ **you go or not** que vous y alliez ou non

——————— KEYWORD ———————

which [wɪtʃ] *adj* **1** (*interrogative: direct, indirect*) quel(le); ~ **picture do you want?** quel tableau voulez-vous?; ~ **one?** lequel(laquelle)?
2: **in** ~ **case** auquel cas
♦ *pron* **1** (*interrogative*) lequel(laquelle), lesquels(lesquelles) *pl*; **I don't mind** ~ peu importe lequel; ~ (**of these**) **are yours?** lesquels sont à vous?; **tell me** ~ **you want** dites-moi lesquels *or* ceux que vous voulez
2 (*relative: subject*) qui; (: *object*) que, *prep* +lequel(laquelle); **the apple** ~ **you ate/is on the table** la pomme que vous avez mangée/qui est sur la table; **the chair on** ~ **you are sitting** la chaise sur laquelle vous êtes assis; **the book of** ~ **you spoke** le livre dont vous avez parlé; **he knew,** ~ **is true/I feared** il le savait, ce qui est vrai/ce que je craignais; **after** ~ après quoi

whichever [wɪtʃ'evə*] *adj*: **take** ~ **book you prefer** prenez le livre que vous préférez, peu importe lequel; ~ **book you take** quel que soit le livre que vous preniez
whiff [wɪf] *n* bouffée *f*
while [waɪl] *n* moment *m* ♦ *conj* pendant que; (*as long as*) tant que; (*whereas*) alors que; bien que +*sub*; **for a** ~ pendant quelque temps; ~ **away** *vt* (*time*) (faire) passer
whim [wɪm] *n* caprice *m*
whimper ['wɪmpə*] *vi* geindre
whimsical ['wɪmzɪkəl] *adj* (*person*) capricieux(euse); (*look, story*) étrange
whine [waɪn] *vi* gémir, geindre
whip [wɪp] *n* fouet *m*; (*for riding*) cravache *f*; (*POL: person*) chef de file assurant la discipline dans son groupe parlementaire ♦ *vt* fouetter; (*eggs*) battre; (*move quickly*) enlever (*or* sortir) brusquement; ~**ped cream** *n* crème fouettée; ~**-round** (*BRIT*) *n* collecte *f*
whirl [wɜːl] *vt* faire tourbillonner; faire tournoyer ♦ *vi* tourbillonner; (*dancers*) tournoyer; ~**pool** *n* tourbillon *m*; ~**wind** *n* tornade *f*
whirr [wɜː*] *vi* (*motor etc*) ronronner; (: *louder*) vrombir
whisk [wɪsk] *n* (*CULIN*) fouet *m* ♦ *vt* fouetter; (*eggs*) battre; **to** ~ **sb away** *or* **off** em-

mener qn rapidement

whiskers ['wɪskəz] *npl* (*of animal*) moustaches *fpl*; (*of man*) favoris *mpl*

whisky ['wɪskɪ] (*IRELAND, US* **whiskey**) *n* whisky *m*

whisper ['wɪspə*] *vt, vi* chuchoter

whistle ['wɪsl] *n* (*sound*) sifflement *m*; (*object*) sifflet *m* ♦ *vi* siffler

white [waɪt] *adj* blanc(blanche); (*with fear*) blême ♦ *n* blanc *m*; (*person*) blanc(blanche); ~ **coffee** (*BRIT*) *n* café *m* au lait, (café) crème *m*; ~**collar worker** *n* employé(e) de bureau; ~ **elephant** *n* (*fig*) objet dispendieux et superflu; ~ **lie** *n* pieux mensonge; ~ **paper** *n* (*POL*) livre blanc; ~**wash** *vt* blanchir à la chaux; (*fig*) blanchir ♦ *n* (*paint*) blanc *m* de chaux

whiting ['waɪtɪŋ] *n inv* (*fish*) merlan *m*

Whitsun ['wɪtsn] *n* la Pentecôte

whittle ['wɪtl] *vt*: **to ~ away**, ~ **down** (*costs*) réduire

whizz [wɪz] *vi*: **to ~ past** *or* **by** passer à toute vitesse; ~ **kid** (*inf*) *n* petit prodige

who [hu:] *pron* qui; ~**dunit** [hu:'dʌnɪt] (*inf*) *n* roman policier

whoever [hu:'evə*] *pron*: ~ **finds it** celui(celle) qui le trouve(, qui que ce soit), quiconque le trouve; **ask ~ you like** demandez à qui vous voulez; ~ **he marries** quelle que soit la personne qu'il épouse; ~ **told you that?** qui a bien pu vous dire ça?

whole [həʊl] *adj* (*complete*) entier(ère), tout(e); (*not broken*) intact(e), complet(ète) ♦ *n* (*all*): **the ~ of** la totalité de, tout(e) le(la); (*entire unit*) tout *m*; **the ~ of the town** la ville tout entière; **on the ~, as a ~** dans l'ensemble; ~**food(s)** *n(pl)* aliments complets; ~**hearted** *adj* sans réserve(s); ~**meal** (*BRIT*) *adj* (*bread, flour*) complet(ète); ~**sale** *n* (vente *f* en) gros *m* ♦ *adj* (*price*) de gros; (*destruction*) systématique ♦ *adv* en gros; ~**saler** *n* grossiste *m/f*; ~**wheat** *adj* = ~**meal**; **wholly** ['həʊlɪ] *adv* entièrement, tout à fait

--- KEYWORD ---

whom [hu:m] *pron* **1**. (*interrogative*) qui; ~ **did you see?** qui avez-vous vu?; **to ~ did you give it?** à qui l'avez-vous donné?

2 (*relative*) que, *prep* + qui; **the man ~ I saw/to ~ I spoke** l'homme que j'ai vu/à qui j'ai parlé

whooping cough ['hu:pɪŋ-] *n* coqueluche *f*

whore [hɔ:*] (*inf: pej*) *n* putain *f*

--- KEYWORD ---

whose [hu:z] *adj* **1** (*possessive: interrogative*): ~ **book is this?** à qui est ce livre?; ~ **pencil have you taken?** à qui est le crayon que vous avez pris?, c'est le crayon de qui

que vous avez pris?; ~ **daughter are you?** de qui êtes-vous la fille?

2 (*possessive: relative*): **the man ~ son you rescued** l'homme dont *or* de qui vous avez sauvé le fils; **the girl ~ sister you were speaking to** la fille à la sœur de qui *or* de laquelle vous parliez; **the woman ~ car was stolen** la femme dont la voiture a été volée

♦ *pron* à qui; ~ **is this?** à qui est ceci?; **I know ~ it is** je sais à qui c'est

why [waɪ] *adv* pourquoi ♦ *excl* eh bien!, tiens!; **the reason ~** la raison pour laquelle; **tell me ~** dites-moi pourquoi; ~ **not?** pourquoi pas?; ~**ever** *adv* pourquoi donc, mais pourquoi

wicked ['wɪkɪd] *adj* mauvais(e), méchant(e); (*crime*) pervers(e); (*mischievous*) malicieux(euse)

wicket ['wɪkɪt] *n* (*CRICKET*) guichet *m*; terrain *m* (*entre les deux guichets*)

wide [waɪd] *adj* large; (*area, knowledge*) vaste, très étendu(e); (*choice*) grand(e) ♦ *adv*: **to open ~** ouvrir tout grand; **to shoot ~** tirer à côté; ~**angle lens** *n* objectif *m* grand angle; ~**awake** *adj* bien éveillé(e); ~**ly** *adv* (*differing*) radicalement; (*spaced*) sur une grande étendue; (*believed*) généralement; (*travel*) beaucoup; ~**n** *vt* élargir ♦ *vi* s'élargir; ~ **open** *adj* grand(e) ouvert(e); ~**spread** *adj* (*belief etc*) très répandu(e)

widow ['wɪdəʊ] *n* veuve *f*; ~**ed** *adj* veuf(veuve); ~**er** *n* veuf *m*

width [wɪdθ] *n* largeur *f*

wield [wi:ld] *vt* (*sword*) manier; (*power*) exercer

wife [waɪf] (*pl* **wives**) *n* femme *f*, épouse *f*

wig [wɪg] *n* perruque *f*

wiggle ['wɪgl] *vt* agiter, remuer

wild [waɪld] *adj* sauvage; (*sea*) déchaîné(e); (*idea, life*) fou(folle); (*behaviour*) extravagant(e), déchaîné(e); ~**s** *npl* (*remote area*) régions *fpl* sauvages; **to make a ~ guess** émettre une hypothèse à tout hasard; ~**erness** ['wɪldənəs] *n* désert *m*, région *f* sauvage; ~**goose chase** *n* (*fig*) fausse piste; ~**life** *n* (*animals*) faune *f*; ~**ly** *adv* (*behave*) de manière déchaînée; (*applaud*) frénétiquement; (*hit, guess*) au hasard; (*happy*) follement

wilful ['wɪlfʊl] (*US* **willful**) *adj* (*person*) obstiné(e); (*action*) délibéré(e)

--- KEYWORD ---

will [wɪl] (*vt: pt, pp* **willed**) *aux vb* **1** (*forming future tense*): **I ~ finish it tomorrow** je le finirai demain; **I ~ have finished it by tomorrow** je l'aurai fini d'ici demain; ~ **you do it? - yes I ~/no I won't** le ferez-vous? - oui/non

2 (*in conjectures, predictions*): **he ~** *or* **he'll**

be there by now il doit être arrivé à l'heure qu'il est; **that ~ be the postman** ça doit être le facteur
3 (*in commands, requests, offers*): **~ you be quiet!** voulez-vous bien vous taire!; **~ you help me?** est-ce que vous pouvez m'aider?; **~ you have a cup of tea?** voulez-vous une tasse de thé?; **I won't put up with it!** je ne le tolérerai pas!
♦ *vt*: **to ~ sb to do** souhaiter ardemment que qn fasse; **he ~ed himself to go on** par un suprême effort de volonté, il continua
♦ *n* volonté *f*; testament *m*

willing ['wɪlɪŋ] *adj* de bonne volonté, serviable; **he's ~ to do it** il est disposé à le faire, il veut bien le faire; **~ly** *adv* volontiers; **~ness** *n* bonne volonté
willow ['wɪləʊ] *n* saule *m*
willpower ['wɪl'paʊə*] *n* volonté *f*
willy-nilly ['wɪlɪ'nɪlɪ] *adv* bon gré mal gré
wilt [wɪlt] *vi* dépérir; (*flower*) se faner
wily ['waɪlɪ] *adj* rusé(e)
win [wɪn] *n* (*in sports etc*) victoire *f* ♦ *vt* gagner; (*prize*) remporter; (*popularity*) acquérir ♦ *vi* gagner; **~ over** *vt* convaincre; **~ round** (*BRIT*) *vt* = **~ over**
wince [wɪns] *vi* tressaillir
winch [wɪntʃ] *n* treuil *m*
wind¹ [wɪnd] *n* (*also MED*) vent *m*; (*breath*) souffle *m* ♦ *vt* (*take breath*) couper le souffle à
wind² [waɪnd] (*pt, pp* **wound**) *vt* enrouler; (*wrap*) envelopper; (*clock, toy*) remonter ♦ *vi* (*road, river*) serpenter; **~ up** *vt* (*clock*) remonter; (*debate*) terminer, clôturer
windfall ['wɪndfɔːl] *n* coup *m* de chance
winding ['waɪndɪŋ] *adj* (*road*) sinueux(euse); (*staircase*) tournant(e)
wind instrument *n* (*MUS*) instrument *m* à vent
windmill ['wɪndmɪl] *n* moulin *m* à vent
window ['wɪndəʊ] *n* fenêtre *f*; (*in car, train, also:* **~ pane**) vitre *f*; (*in shop etc*) vitrine *f*; **~ box** *n* jardinière *f*; **~ cleaner** *n* (*person*) laveur(euse) de vitres; **~ ledge** *n* rebord *m* de la fenêtre; **~ pane** *n* vitre *f*, carreau *m*; **~-shopping** *n*: **to go ~-shopping** faire du lèche-vitrines; **~sill** *n* (*inside*) appui *m* de la fenêtre; (*outside*) rebord *m* de la fenêtre
windpipe ['wɪndpaɪp] *n* trachée *f*
wind power *n* énergie éolienne
windscreen ['wɪndskriːn] *n* pare-brise *m inv*; **~ washer** *n* lave-glace *m inv*; **~ wiper** *n* essuie-glace *m inv*
windshield ['wɪndʃiːld] (*US*) *n* = **windscreen**
windswept ['wɪndswept] *adj* balayé(e) par le vent; (*person*) ébouriffé(e)
windy ['wɪndɪ] *adj* venteux(euse); **it's ~** il y a du vent
wine [waɪn] *n* vin *m*; **~ bar** *n* bar *m* à vin;

~ cellar *n* cave *f* à vin; **~ glass** *n* verre *m* à vin; **~ list** *n* carte *f* des vins; **~ waiter** *n* sommelier *m*
wing [wɪŋ] *n* aile *f*; **~s** *npl* (*THEATRE*) coulisses *fpl*; **~er** *n* (*SPORT*) ailier *m*
wink [wɪŋk] *n* clin *m* d'œil ♦ *vi* faire un clin d'œil; (*blink*) cligner des yeux
winner ['wɪnə*] *n* gagnant(e)
winning ['wɪnɪŋ] *adj* (*team*) gagnant(e); (*goal*) décisif(ive); **~s** *npl* gains *mpl*
winter ['wɪntə*] *n* hiver *m*; **in ~** en hiver; **~ sports** *npl* sports *mpl* d'hiver; **wintry** ['wɪntrɪ] *adj* hivernal(e)
wipe [waɪp] *n*: **to give sth a ~** donner un coup de torchon (*or* de chiffon *or* d'éponge) à qch ♦ *vt* essuyer; (*erase: tape*) effacer; **~ off** *vt* enlever; **~ out** *vt* (*debt*) éteindre, amortir; (*memory*) effacer; (*destroy*) anéantir; **~ up** *vt* essuyer
wire ['waɪə*] *n* fil *m* (de fer); (*ELEC*) fil électrique; (*TEL*) télégramme *m* ♦ *vt* (*house*) faire l'installation électrique de; (*also:* **~ up**) brancher; (*person: send telegram to*) télégraphier à; **~less** ['waɪəlɪs] (*BRIT*) *n* poste *m* de radio; **wiring** ['waɪərɪŋ] *n* installation *f* électrique
wiry ['waɪərɪ] *adj* noueux(euse), nerveux(euse); (*hair*) dru(e)
wisdom ['wɪzdəm] *n* sagesse *f*; (*of action*) prudence *f*; **~ tooth** *n* dent *f* de sagesse
wise [waɪz] *adj* sage, prudent(e); (*remark*) judicieux(euse) ♦ *suffix*: **...wise: timewise** *etc* en ce qui concerne le temps *etc*; **~crack** *n* remarque *f* ironique
wish [wɪʃ] *n* (*desire*) désir *m*; (*specific desire*) souhait *m*, vœu *m* ♦ *vt* souhaiter, désirer, vouloir; **best ~es** (*on birthday etc*) meilleurs vœux; **with best ~es** (*in letter*) bien amicalement; **to ~ sb goodbye** dire au revoir à qn; **he ~ed me well** il m'a souhaité bonne chance; **to ~ to do/sb to do** désirer *or* vouloir faire/que qn fasse; **to ~ for** souhaiter; **~ful** *adj*: **it's ~ful thinking** c'est prendre ses désirs pour des réalités
wistful ['wɪstful] *adj* mélancolique
wit [wɪt] *n* (*gen pl*) intelligence *f*, esprit *m*; (*presence of mind*) présence *f* d'esprit; (*wittiness*) esprit; (*person*) homme/femme d'esprit
witch [wɪtʃ] *n* sorcière *f*; **~craft** *n* sorcellerie *f*

——— **KEYWORD**

with [wɪð, wɪθ] *prep* **1** (*in the company of*) avec; (*at the home of*) chez; **we stayed ~ friends** nous avons logé chez des amis; **I'll be ~ you in a minute** je suis à vous dans un instant
2 (*descriptive*): **a room ~ a view** une chambre avec vue; **the man ~ the grey hat/blue eyes** l'homme au chapeau gris/

aux yeux bleus
3 (*indicating manner, means, cause*): ~ **tears in her eyes** les larmes aux yeux; **to walk ~ a stick** marcher avec une canne; **red ~ anger** rouge de colère; **to shake ~ fear** trembler de peur; **to fill sth ~ water** remplir qch d'eau
4: **I'm ~ you** (*I understand*) je vous suis; **to be ~ it** (*inf: up-to-date*) être dans le vent

withdraw [wɪθ'drɔː] (*irreg*) *vt* retirer ♦ *vi* se retirer; **~al** *n* retrait *m*; **~al symptoms** *npl* (*MED*): **to have ~al symptoms** être en état de manque; **~n** *adj* (*person*) renfermé(e)
wither ['wɪðə*] *vi* (*plant*) se faner
withhold [wɪθ'həʊld] (*irreg*) *vt* (*money*) retenir; **to ~ (from)** (*information*) cacher (à); (*permission*) refuser (à)
within [wɪð'ɪn] *prep* à l'intérieur de ♦ *adv* à l'intérieur; **~ his reach** à sa portée; **~ sight of** en vue de; **~ a kilometre of** à moins d'un kilomètre de; **~ the week** avant la fin de la semaine
without [wɪð'aʊt] *prep* sans; **~ a coat** sans manteau; **~ speaking** sans parler; **to go ~ sth** se passer de qch
withstand [wɪθ'stænd] (*irreg*) *vt* résister à
witness ['wɪtnəs] *n* (*person*) témoin *m* ♦ *vt* (*event*) être témoin de; (*document*) attester l'authenticité de; **to bear ~ (to)** (*fig*) attester; **~ box** *n* barre *f* des témoins; **~ stand** (*US*) *n* = **box**
witticism ['wɪtɪsɪzəm] *n* mot *m* d'esprit; **witty** ['wɪtɪ] *adj* spirituel(le), plein(e) d'esprit
wives [waɪvz] *npl of* **wife**
wizard ['wɪzəd] *n* magicien *m*
wk *abbr* = **week**
wobble ['wɒbl] *vi* trembler; (*chair*) branler
woe [wəʊ] *n* malheur *m*
woke [wəʊk] *pt of* **wake**
woken ['wəʊkən] *pp of* **wake**
wolf [wʊlf, *pl* wʊlvz] (*pl* **wolves**) *n* loup *m*
woman ['wʊmən] (*pl* **women**) *n* femme *f*; **~ doctor** *n* femme *f* médecin; **~ly** *adj* féminin(e)
womb [wuːm] *n* (*ANAT*) utérus *m*
women ['wɪmɪn] *npl of* **woman**; **~'s lib** (*inf*) *n* MLF *m*; **W~'s (Liberation) Movement** *n* mouvement *m* de libération de la femme
won [wʌn] *pt, pp of* **win**
wonder ['wʌndə*] *n* merveille *f*, miracle *m*; (*feeling*) émerveillement *m* ♦ *vi*: **to ~ whether/why** se demander si/pourquoi; **to ~ at** (*marvel*) s'émerveiller de; **to ~ about** songer à; **it's no ~ (that)** il n'est pas étonnant (que +*sub*); **~ful** *adj* merveilleux(euse)
won't [wəʊnt] = **will not**
woo [wuː] *vt* (*woman*) faire la cour à;

(*audience etc*) chercher à plaire à
wood [wʊd] *n* (*timber, forest*) bois *m*; **~ carving** *n* sculpture *f* en *or* sur bois; **~ed** *adj* boisé(e); **~en** *adj* en bois; (*fig*) raide; inexpressif(ive); **~pecker** *n* pic *m* (*oiseau*); **~wind** *n* (*MUS*): **the ~wind** les bois *mpl*; **~work** *n* menuiserie *f*; **~worm** *n* ver *m* du bois
wool [wʊl] *n* laine *f*; **to pull the ~ over sb's eyes** (*fig*) en faire accroire à qn; **~len** (*US* **~en**) *adj* de *or* en laine; (*industry*) lainier(ère); **~lens** *npl* (*clothes*) lainages *mpl*; **~ly** (*US* **~y**) *adj* laineux(euse); (*fig: ideas*) confus(e)
word [wɜːd] *n* mot *m*; (*promise*) parole *f*; (*news*) nouvelles *fpl* ♦ *vt* rédiger, formuler; **in other ~s** en d'autres termes; **to break/keep one's ~** manquer à sa parole/tenir parole; **~ing** *n* termes *mpl*; libellé *m*; **~ processing** *n* traitement *m* de texte; **~ processor** *n* machine *f* de traitement de texte
wore [wɔː*] *pt of* **wear**
work [wɜːk] *n* travail *m*; (*ART, LITERATURE*) œuvre *f* ♦ *vi* travailler; (*mechanism*) marcher, fonctionner; (*plan etc*) marcher; (*medicine*) agir ♦ *vt* (*clay, wood etc*) travailler; (*mine etc*) exploiter; (*machine*) faire marcher *or* fonctionner; (*miracles, wonders etc*) faire; **to be out of ~** être sans emploi; **to ~ loose** se défaire, se desserrer; **~ on** *vt fus* travailler à; (*principle*) se baser sur; (*person*) (essayer d')influencer; **~ out** *vi* (*plans etc*) marcher ♦ *vt* (*problem*) résoudre; (*plan*) élaborer; **it ~s out at £100** ça fait 100 livres; **~ up** *vt*: **to get ~ed up** se mettre dans tous ses états; **~able** *adj* (*solution*) réalisable; **~aholic** [wɜːkə'hɒlɪk] *n* bourreau *m* de travail; **~er** *n* travailleur(euse), ouvrier(ère); **~force** *n* main-d'œuvre *f*; **~ing class** *n* classe ouvrière; **~ing-class** *adj* ouvrier(ère); **~ing order** *n*: **in ~ing order** en état de marche; **~man** (*irreg*) *n* ouvrier *m*; **~manship** *n* (*skill*) métier *m*, habileté *f*; **~s** *n* (*BRIT: factory*) usine *f* ♦ *npl* (*of clock, machine*) mécanisme *m*; **~ sheet** *n* (*COMPUT*) feuille *f* de programmation; **~shop** *n* atelier *m*; **~ station** *n* poste *m* de travail; **~-to-rule** (*BRIT*) *n* grève *f* du zèle
world [wɜːld] *n* monde *m* ♦ *cpd* (*champion*) du monde; (*power, war*) mondial(e); **to think the ~ of sb** (*fig*) ne jurer que par qn; **~ly** *adj* de ce monde; (*knowledgeable*) qui a l'expérience du monde; **~wide** *adj* universel(le)
worm [wɜːm] *n* ver *m*
worn [wɔːn] *pp of* **wear** ♦ *adj* usé(e); **~-out** *adj* (*object*) complètement usé(e); (*person*) épuisé(e)
worried ['wʌrɪd] *adj* inquiet(ète)
worry ['wʌrɪ] *n* souci *m* ♦ *vt* inquiéter ♦ *vi*

s'inquiéter, se faire du souci

worse [wɜːs] *adj* pire, plus mauvais(e) ♦ *adv* plus mal ♦ *n* pire *m*; **a change for the** ~ une détérioration; **~n** *vt, vi* empirer; ~ **off** *adj* moins à l'aise financièrement; (*fig*): **you'll be ~ off this way** ça ira moins bien de cette façon

worship ['wɜːʃɪp] *n* culte *m* ♦ *vt* (*God*) rendre un culte à; (*person*) adorer; **Your W~** (*BRIT: to mayor*) Monsieur le maire; (: *to judge*) Monsieur le juge

worst [wɜːst] *adj* le(la) pire, le(la) plus mauvais(e) ♦ *adv* le plus mal ♦ *n* pire *m*; **at** ~ au pis aller

worth [wɜːθ] *n* valeur *f* ♦ *adj*: **to be** ~ valoir; **it's** ~ **it** cela en vaut la peine, ça vaut la peine; **it is** ~ **one's while (to do)** on gagne (à faire); **~less** *adj* qui ne vaut rien; **~while** *adj* (*activity, cause*) utile, louable

worthy [wɜːðɪ] *adj* (*person*) digne; (*motive*) louable; ~ **of** digne de

---

KEYWORD

would [wʊd] *aux vb* **1** (*conditional tense*): **if you asked him he** ~ **do it** si vous le lui demandiez, il le ferait; **if you had asked him he** ~ **have done it** si vous le lui aviez demandé, il l'aurait fait

2 (*in offers, invitations, requests*): ~ **you like a biscuit?** voulez-vous *or* voudriez-vous un biscuit?; ~ **you close the door please?** voulez-vous fermer la porte, s'il vous plaît?

3 (*in indirect speech*): **I said I** ~ **do it** j'ai dit que je le ferais

4 (*emphatic*): **it WOULD have to snow today!** naturellement il neige aujourd'hui! *or* il fallait qu'il neige aujourd'hui!

5 (*insistence*): **she ~n't do it** elle n'a pas voulu *or* elle a refusé de le faire

6 (*conjecture*): **it** ~ **have been midnight** il devait être minuit

7 (*indicating habit*): **he** ~ **go there on Mondays** il y allait le lundi

---

would-be ['wʊdbiː] (*pej*) *adj* soi-disant
wouldn't ['wʊdnt] = **would not**
wound¹ [wuːnd] *n* blessure *f* ♦ *vt* blesser
wound² [waʊnd] *pt, pp of* **wind²**
wove [wəʊv] *pt of* **weave**
woven ['wəʊvən] *pp of* **weave**
wrap [ræp] *vt* (*also*: ~ **up**) envelopper, emballer; (*wind*) enrouler; **~per** *n* (*BRIT: of book*) couverture *f*; (*on chocolate*) emballage *m*, papier *m*; **~ping paper** *n* papier *m* d'emballage; (*for gift*) papier cadeau
wrath [rɒθ] *n* courroux *m*
wreak [riːk] *vt*: **to** ~ **havoc (on)** avoir un effet désastreux (sur)
wreath [riːθ, *pl* riːðz] (*pl* ~**s**) *n* couronne *f*
wreck [rek] *n* (*ship*) épave *f*; (*vehicle*) véhicule accidenté; (*pej: person*) loque humaine

♦ *vt* démolir; (*fig*) briser, ruiner; **~age** *n* débris *mpl*; (*of building*) décombres *mpl*; (*of ship*) épave *f*
wren [ren] *n* (*ZOOL*) roitelet *m*
wrench [rentʃ] *n* (*TECH*) clé *f* (à écrous); (*tug*) violent mouvement de torsion; (*fig*) déchirement *m* ♦ *vt* tirer violemment sur, tordre; **to** ~ **sth from** arracher qch à *or* de
wrestle ['resl] *vi*: **to** ~ **(with sb)** lutter (avec qn); **~r** *n* lutteur(euse); **wrestling** *n* lutte *f*; (*also: all-in wrestling*) catch *m*
wretched ['retʃɪd] *adj* misérable; (*inf*) maudit(e)
wriggle ['rɪgl] *vi* (*also*: ~ **about**) se tortiller
wring [rɪŋ] (*pt, pp* **wrung**) *vt* tordre; (*wet clothes*) essorer; (*fig*): **to** ~ **sth out of sb** arracher qch à qn
wrinkle ['rɪŋkl] *n* (*on skin*) ride *f*; (*on paper etc*) pli *m* ♦ *vt* plisser ♦ *vi* se plisser
wrist [rɪst] *n* poignet *m*; **~watch** *n* montre-bracelet *f*
writ [rɪt] *n* acte *m* judiciaire
write [raɪt] (*pt* **wrote**, *pp* **written**) *vt, vi* écrire; (*prescription*) rédiger; ~ **down** *vt* noter; (*put in writing*) mettre par écrit; ~ **off** *vt* (*debt*) passer aux profits et pertes; (*project*) mettre une croix sur; ~ **out** *vt* écrire; ~ **up** *vt* rédiger; **~-off** *n* perte totale; **~r** *n* auteur *m*, écrivain *m*
writhe [raɪð] *vi* se tordre
writing ['raɪtɪŋ] *n* écriture *f*; (*of author*) œuvres *fpl*; **in** ~ par écrit; ~ **paper** *n* papier *m* à lettres
wrong [rɒŋ] *adj* (*incorrect: answer, information*) faux(fausse); (*inappropriate: choice, action etc*) mauvais(e); (*wicked*) mal; (*unfair*) injuste ♦ *adv* mal ♦ *n* tort *m* ♦ *vt* faire du tort à, léser; **you are** ~ **to do it** tu as tort de le faire; **you are** ~ **about that, you've got it** ~ tu te trompes; **what's** ~? qu'est-ce qui ne va pas?; **to go** ~ (*person*) se tromper; (*plan*) mal tourner; (*machine*) tomber en panne; **to be in the** ~ avoir tort; **~ful** *adj* injustifié(e); **~ly** *adv* mal, incorrectement; ~ **side** *n* (*of material*) envers *m*
wrote [rəʊt] *pt of* **write**
wrought [rɔːt] *adj*: ~ **iron** fer forgé
wrung [rʌŋ] *pt, pp of* **wring**
wry [raɪ] *adj* désabusé(e)
wt. *abbr* = **weight**

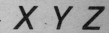

Xmas ['eksməs] *n abbr* = **Christmas**
X-ray ['eksˈreɪ] *n* (*ray*) rayon *m* X; (*photo*)

radio(graphie) f

xylophone ['zaɪləfəʊn] n xylophone m

yacht [jɒt] n yacht m; voilier m; ~**ing** n yachting m, navigation f de plaisance; ~**sman** (irreg) n plaisancier m

Yank(ee) [jæŋk(ɪ)] (pej) n Amerloque m/f

yap [jæp] vi (dog) japper

yard [jɑːd] n (of house etc) cour f; (measure) yard m (= 91,4 cm); ~**stick** n (fig) mesure f, critères mpl

yarn [jɑːn] n fil m; (tale) longue histoire

yawn [jɔːn] n bâillement m ♦ vi bâiller; ~**ing** adj (gap) béant(e)

yd. abbr = **yard(s)**

yeah [jɛə] (inf) adv ouais

year [jɪə*] n an m, année f; **to be 8 ~s old** avoir 8 ans; **an eight-~-old child** un enfant de huit ans; ~**ly** adj annuel(le) ♦ adv annuellement

yearn [jɜːn] vi: **to ~ for sth** aspirer à qch, languir après qch; **to ~ to do** aspirer à faire

yeast [jiːst] n levure f

yell [jɛl] vi hurler

yellow ['jɛləʊ] adj jaune

yelp [jɛlp] vi japper; glapir

yeoman ['jəʊmən] (irreg) n: ~ **of the guard** hallebardier m de la garde royale

yes [jɛs] adv oui; (answering negative question) si ♦ n oui m; **to say/answer ~** dire/répondre oui

yesterday ['jɛstədeɪ] adv hier ♦ n hier m; ~ **morning/evening** hier matin/soir; **all day ~** toute la journée d'hier

yet [jɛt] adv encore; déjà ♦ conj pourtant, néanmoins; **it is not finished** ~ ce n'est pas encore fini or toujours pas fini; **the best** ~ le meilleur jusqu'ici or jusque-là; **as** ~ jusqu'ici, encore

yew [juː] n if m

yield [jiːld] n production f, rendement m; rapport m ♦ vt produire, rendre, rapporter; (surrender) céder ♦ vi céder; (US: AUT) céder la priorité

YMCA n abbr (= Young Men's Christian Association) YMCA m

yoghourt ['jɒɡət] n yaourt m

yog(h)urt ['jɒɡət] n = **yoghourt**

yoke [jəʊk] n joug m

yolk [jəʊk] n jaune m (d'œuf)

──────── *KEYWORD*

you [juː] pron **1** (subject) tu; (polite form) vous; (plural) vous; ~ **French enjoy your food** vous autres Français, vous aimez bien manger; ~ **and I will go** toi et moi or vous et moi, nous irons
2 (object: direct, indirect) te, t' +vowel; vous; **I know** ~ je te or vous connais; **I gave it to** ~, je vous l'ai donné, je te l'ai donné
3 (stressed) toi; vous; **I told YOU to do it**

c'est à toi or vous que j'ai dit de le faire
4 (after prep, in comparisons) toi; vous; **it's for** ~ c'est pour toi or vous; **she's younger than** ~ elle est plus jeune que toi or vous
5 (impersonal: one) on; **fresh air does** ~ **good** l'air frais fait du bien; ~ **never know** on ne sait jamais

you'd [juːd] = you had; you would

you'll [juːl] = you will; you shall

young [jʌŋ] adj jeune ♦ npl (of animal) petits mpl; (people): **the** ~ les jeunes, la jeunesse; ~**er** adj (brother etc) cadet(te); ~**ster** n jeune m (garçon m); (child) enfant m/f

your ['jɔː*] adj ton(ta), tes pl; (polite form, pl) votre, vos pl; see also **my**

you're ['jʊə*] = you are

yours [jɔːz] pron le(la) tien(ne), les tiens(tiennes); (polite form, pl) le(la) vôtre, les vôtres; ~ **sincerely/faithfully/truly** veuillez agréer l'expression de mes sentiments les meilleurs; see also **mine**[1]

yourself [jɔːˈsɛlf] pron (reflexive) te; (: polite form) vous; (after prep) toi; vous; (emphatic) toi-même; vous-même; see also **oneself**; **yourselves** pl pron vous; (emphatic) vous-mêmes

youth [juːθ, pl juːðz] n jeunesse f; (young man: pl youths) jeune homme m; ~ **club** n centre m de jeunes; ~**ful** adj jeune; (enthusiasm) de jeunesse, juvénile; ~ **hostel** n auberge f de jeunesse

you've [juːv] = you have

YTS (BRIT) n abbr (= Youth Training Scheme) ≈ TUC m

Yugoslav adj yougoslave ♦ n Yougoslave m/f; ~**ia** n Yougoslavie f

yuppie ['jʌpɪ] (inf) n yuppie m/f

YWCA n abbr (= Young Women's Christian Association) YWCA m

zany ['zeɪnɪ] adj farfelu(e), loufoque

zap [zæp] vt (COMPUT) effacer

zeal [ziːl] n zèle m, ferveur f; empressement m

zebra ['ziːbrə] n zèbre m; ~ **crossing** (BRIT) n passage clouté or pour piétons

zero ['zɪərəʊ] n zéro m

zest [zɛst] n entrain m, élan m; (of orange) zeste m

Zimbabwe [zɪmˈbɑːbwɪ] n Zimbabwe m

zinc [zɪŋk] n zinc m

zip [zɪp] n (also: ~ **fastener**) fermeture f éclair ® ♦ vt (: ~ **up**) fermer avec une fermeture éclair ®; ~ **code** (US) n code postal; ~**per** (US) n = **zip**

zodiac ['zəʊdɪæk] n zodiaque m

zone [zəʊn] n zone f

zoo [zuː] n zoo m

zoom [zuːm] vi: **to ~ past** passer en trombe; ~ **lens** n zoom m

zucchini [zuːˈkiːnɪ] n(pl) courgette(s) f(pl)